Macromedia® Flash® 8 Bible

Robert Reinhardt and Snow Dowd

WILEY

Wiley Publishing, Inc.

Macromedia® Flash® 8 Bible

Published by
Wiley Publishing, Inc.
111 River Street
Hoboken, NJ 07030-5774
www.wiley.com

Copyright © 2006 by Wiley Publishing, Inc., Indianapolis, Indiana

ISBN-10: 0-471-74676-2
ISBN-13: 978-0-471-74676-8

Manufactured in the United States of America

10 9 8 7 6 5 4 3 2 1

1B/RZ/QR/QW/IN

Published by Wiley Publishing, Inc., Indianapolis, Indiana
Published simultaneously in Canada

For general information on our other products and services or to obtain technical support, please contact our Customer Care Department within the U.S. at 800-762-2974, outside the U.S. at 317-572-3993 or fax 317-572-4002.

Wiley also publishes its books in a variety of electronic formats. Some content that appears in print may not be available in electronic books.

Library of Congress: 2005936651

About the Authors

After discovering Macromedia Flash while working on an art project, Robert soon realized that there was a need for more comprehensive documentation of its capabilities. In 1998, not many people had even heard of Flash and publishers were wary of the limited market, but IDG Books Worldwide, Inc. (now Wiley Publishing, Inc.) committed to doing the *Flash 4 Bible*. The rest, as they say, is history. After studying and working together in Toronto for five years, Robert Reinhardt and Snow Dowd established a multimedia consulting and design company in Los Angeles in 1999, called [*the* MAKERS]. Five years in the Hollywood Hills saw them through the dotcom boom and bust and gave them the chance to work on a wide range of projects — without ever having to wear wool socks. Now based in Portland, Oregon, [*the* MAKERS] continue to do work for entertainment companies, educational institutions, entrepreneurs, independent artists, and nonprofit organizations — and enjoy wearing stylish rain boots.

Robert Reinhardt — With a degree in photographic arts, Robert takes a holistic approach to the creation of compelling multimedia. In addition to development and content creation through [*the* MAKERS], Robert works with Schematic (www.schematic.com) as Vice President of the Multimedia Platforms Group. Robert has led various assignments including multimedia data analysis applications for Nielsen's Media and Entertainment division and creating interactive applications for The Weather Channel's WeatherClassroom.com, DC Comics, and Microsoft Windows XP Media Center Edition spotlights for major cable networks.

When he isn't building or consulting on Flash projects, Robert loves to teach and write about Flash. In addition to this book, he is the coauthor of the *Flash MX 2004 ActionScript Bible* (Wiley, 2004), as well as *Macromedia MX: Building Rich Internet Applications* (Macromedia Press, 2003). He has developed and taught Flash workshops for Lynda.com, Art Center College of Design, Portland State University, and Ed2Go, as well as conducted on-site training and seminars for clients in the United States and Canada such as LodgeNet and Scripps Networks. Robert has been a regular featured speaker at the *FlashForward*, *FlashCan*, *FlashBelt*, and *SIGGRAPH* conferences. Robert and Snow were members of the Web Graphics committee for the *SIGGRAPH 2004* conference. Robert is also a writing partner for CommunityMX.com.

Snow Dowd — Snow initially collaborated with Robert Reinhardt on multimedia, film, and photography-based installation projects while earning a BFA in Image Arts and New Media at Ryerson University. During this time, she was also the production manager for Design Archive, one of Canada's preeminent architectural photography studios. Working with renowned photographers and an exacting international client base of architects and designers helped her gain a deeper appreciation for images, architecture, and industrial design.

Fully immersed in digital production since 1998, Snow is able to synthesize her background in visual arts and communication theory with an ever-evolving software toolkit. Focusing on content architecture and interface design, Snow strives to create print and Web projects that are beautiful, functional, and memorable. Snow was honored to be featured in the June 2005 spotlight on FlashGoddess.com — a great place to go if you've been wondering where all the women are in the Flash world.

About the Technical Editors

Ezra Freedman — Ezra is a Senior Manager of the Multimedia Platforms Group at Schematic, a Los Angeles-based services company that develops interface and technology solutions for the Web, television, and mobile devices. He has served as lead architect and developer on many successful Web and mobile applications and is currently working on projects for the Macromedia Mobile and Devices team.

Zach Zsukula — Zach is a designer and technologist working for Schematic in New York City. He has worked on projects ranging from coding the recently re-launched ABCNews.com to designing and animating the Web site for Warner Bros.' *Ocean's Twelve*. After escaping Los Angeles, Zachary now resides in Williamsburg, Brooklyn, and also works with bands, photographers, and arts organizations through his studio, No Printcode (www.noprintcode.com).

Credits

Senior Acquisitions Editor
Michael Roney

Project Editor
Katharine Dvorak

Technical Editors
Ezra Freedman
Zach Zsukula

Copy Editor
Lauren Kennedy

Editorial Manager
Robyn Siesky

Vice President and Executive Group Publisher
Richard Swadley

Vice President and Publisher
Barry Pruett

Senior Permissions Editor
Laura Moss

Project Coordinator
Michael Kruzil

Graphics and Production Specialists
Beth Brooks
Lauren Goddard
Denny Hager
Joyce Haughey
Barbara Moore
Lynsey Osborn
Melanee Prendergast
Alicia B. Smith
Julie Trippetti

Quality Control Technicians
John Greenough
Jessica Kramer

Media Development Specialist
Shannon Walters

Proofreading and Indexing
TECHBOOKS Production Services

Foreword

The Flash community as a whole is at a crossroads. There is no other application out there that has the power to take down a visitor's computer while looking so spiffy. With the release of Flash 8, we as a community have the ability to change the look and feel — and the performance — of the Web like never before. Flash as a rich media environment is being assaulted from all sides: DHTML, AJAX, Microsoft's Sparkle and Avalon, and so on. No longer is Flash alone in this space. This is a good thing because competition drives innovation and sends the message that web-based multimedia applications are here to stay.

Macromedia has focused the majority of changes in Flash 8 around the design aspect of Flash. Flash 8 has much improved font rendering, graphic effects, and a whole host of other changes. These changes improve the workflow for the designer, but more importantly give the designer many new options for expressing his or her creativity.

There are lots of great Flash sites out there in the world. There are also just as many bad Flash sites that leave a bad impression of Flash in users' minds. One of my rules of thumb is that if a "skip" button is necessary, the application is probably not necessary. The days of intro movies has passed (thankfully) and it is time we begin to create rich applications using Flash 8. In the *Flash 8 Bible*, Robert Reinhardt and Snow Dowd encapsulate all of the changes in the newest version of Flash in such a concise, easy-to-follow manner, that the quality of your Flash design and development will reach this higher level.

Flash enables designers to develop, developers to design, and novices to create professional experiences. No other application available today can rival Flash for its ease of use, powerful development capabilities, multimedia features, and design power.

The book you are holding in your hands can help you avoid all of the common pitfalls that arise when just starting out in Flash, while explaining all the new features. Designers have been given many more tools, such as FlashType, blend modes, and bitmap caching. Mac users will notice increased performance within the Player, which is a welcome update. ActionScript gurus will appreciate the ability to control design elements at run-time, and improved debug and file uploading capabilities. Video performance and quality have been vastly improved over previous versions. Dynamic loading of GIFs and PNGs are a welcome addition as is the alpha channel support for video, stand-alone video encoder, and all the other video improvements. Robert explains how to make the most of these updates in clear and concise language.

This is a very exciting time for Flash developers and designers, new and old, as Flash 8 arrives in all its glory. With the *Flash 8 Bible* in your library, you will be able to leverage the new features and use the power Macromedia has given us in a responsible way. Let's show the world what Flash is capable of and no longer use Flash simply to have Flash on a page. Let's build Flash applications that the users feel they cannot live without; design rich media experiences that go beyond the intro movie, the slide show, and the audio player and instead truly immerse the user in ways never before possible on the Internet.

Tom Crenshaw
Technical Manager
Rich Internet Application Development
AOL

NOTE: Some features discussed in this Foreword are only available in the Professional version of Flash 8. Please check your documentation to verify which capabilities are available within your version of Flash.

Preface

In 1997, Macromedia acquired a small Web graphics program, FutureSplash, from a company named FutureWave. FutureSplash was a quirky little program with the astounding capability to generate compact, vector-based graphics and animations for delivery over the Web. With Macromedia's embrace, Flash blossomed. Now Flash has obtained ubiquity. The Flash Player plug-in ships with most major browsers and operating systems. Flash graphics appear not only all over the Web, but also on television and movie screens, on phones, on kiosks, and even in art galleries.

As the Web-surfing public and the development community have continued to demand more of Flash, Macromedia has delivered. After some MX-sized growing pains, Macromedia went out into the world and sat with people using their programs to see what they used, what they needed, and how Studio 8 could support daily workflow and specialized tasks more effectively. The result is a release that promotes expressiveness and enhances efficiency while encouraging best practices in development — a functional and an inspiring combination that has earned rave reviews from visual designers and code-oriented developers at all levels.

The Flash 8 interface is consistent with other Macromedia Studio 8 products; it has tool options and other editing features contained in streamlined panels and lots of small but important changes to the authoring environment. The Mac interface is finally catching up to the Windows interface, with support for tabbed panels and enhancements to the coding environments in Flash 8 and Dreamweaver 8.

Flash movies can communicate directly with server-side scripts and programs, using standard URL-encoded variables, XML-formatted structures, Web services, or powerhouse data transfers from Flash Remoting -enabled servers. Sounds can be imported and exported as MP3 audio, for high-quality music on the Web at the smallest file sizes. Flash Player 8 now supports nearly every Web file format you'll ever come across. Native JPEG, PNG, GIF, and FLV loading streamlines production and maintenance of dynamic high-volume image sites. The new FLVPlayback component and the addition of custom tools, custom effects, and behaviors offer Flash users of all skill levels some exciting possibilities. Evidence of the dominance of the Flash format can be found in the wide range of third-party developers creating applications that output to the Flash movie format (.swf files). Flash has fulfilled its promise of becoming the central application for generating interactive content for delivery on the Web; the potential only seems to expand as more developers tap into the data-handling power of Flash and its increasingly sophisticated graphics capabilities as it continues to grow beyond the computer screen.

Is there any other Flash book for you?

The *Macromedia Flash 8 Bible* is the most comprehensive and exhaustive reference on Flash. It helps you get started on your first day with the program and will still be a valuable resource when you've attained mastery of the program. When you're looking for clues on how to integrate Flash with other programs so that you can deliver unique and compelling content in the Flash format, you'll know where to turn.

Flash is not just a single tool. You can think of Flash as a multitasking application. It's an illustration program, an image/sound/video editor, an animation machine, and a scripting engine, all rolled into one. In this book, we look at each of these uses of Flash and explain how all the features work together.

To address advanced scripting topics and more server-side development issues, Robert coauthored the *Flash MX 2004 ActionScript Bible* with Joey Lott (Wiley, 2004), which has been updated and expanded in the new *Flash 8 ActionScript Bible* (Wiley, 2006). If you're already adept at creating animation and basic interactive interfaces in Flash and you want to expand your knowledge of more complex coding techniques, you may want to compare the table of contents in this book with that of the *ActionScript Bible* to determine which book covers the topics you're most interested in.

How to Get the Most out of this Book

Here are some things to know so you can get the most out of this book:

First, to indicate that you need to select a command from a menu, the menu and command are separated by an arrow symbol. For example, if we tell you to select the default workspace layout from the Flash application menu, the instructions will say to choose Window ⇨ Workspace Layout ⇨ Default.

Parts I and II of the book are entirely dedicated to project planning and getting familiar with the Flash interface. Parts III and IV explain how to generate animation and integrate other media files into your Flash movies. Parts V through VIII gradually introduce you to the power of ActionScript. Part IX shows you how to take advantage of Flash components to quickly create dynamic applications that support live data. Finally, Part X covers other programs and techniques that will enhance your Flash projects. Although this book was written to take a beginner by the hand, starting from page one, you can also use it as a reference. Use the index and the table of contents to find what you're looking for, and just go there, or jump in anywhere. If you already know Flash and want to get some details on sound, for example, just go to the "Integrating Media Files with Flash" section (Part IV).

This is a real-world production book: We've worked hard to ensure that our lessons, examples, and explanations are based on professional conventions. We've also continued the use of expert tutorials to bring you tips and techniques from talented people in the Flash industry, so that you can benefit from their specialized expertise. Tutorials that do not relate to Flash 8 but still offer some valuable information on specific topics have been archived online: you can find them at www.flashsupport.com/archive.

The CD-ROM that accompanies this book contains many of the source Flash project files (.fla), with original artwork and ActionScript for the examples and lessons in the book. To help you get started, we've also included an installer for the trial version of Flash Professional 8.

In order to create a forum for the delivery of updates, notes, and additional sample files, we have established an integrated Web site specifically for the *Flash Bible* series: www.flashsupport.com. At the Web site, you'll find new material and corrections that may be added after the book goes to print, and moderated forums where readers can share information or ask questions. We invite you to contribute your comments and suggestions for this edition so that we can continue to improve the material.

We have created a chapter-based evaluation system that makes it easy for you to let us know what parts of this book were most (or least) useful to you. Please visit www. flashsupport.com/feedback and let us know what you think of the content as you progress through the book.

Icons: What Do They Mean?

Although the icons are pretty standard and self-explanatory (they have their names written on them!), here's a brief explanation of what they are and what they mean.

Tips offer you extra information that further explains a given topic or technique, often suggesting alternatives or workarounds to a listed procedure.

Notes provide supplementary information to the text, shedding light on background processes or miscellaneous options that aren't crucial to the basic understanding of the material.

When you see the Caution icon, make sure you're following along closely to the tips and techniques being discussed. Some external applications may not work exactly the same with Flash on different operating systems and some workflows have inherent risks or drawbacks.

If you want to find related information to a given topic in another chapter, look for the cross-reference icons.

The New Feature icons point out differences between Flash 8 and previous versions of Flash.

For related information, resources, or software available online, look for the Web resource icons.

This icon indicates that the CD-ROM contains a related file and points you to the folder location.

How This Book Is Organized

This book has been written in a format that gives you access to need-to-know information very easily in every section (or Part) of the book. If you are completely new to Flash, then you'll want to read Parts I through VI. After you have developed a familiarity with the Flash interface and the new drawing and effects tools, you can proceed to Parts VII and VIII. We've included step-by-step descriptions of real Flash projects to help you "leap" from the intro topics to the advanced topics. These sections of the book guide you through the production process, helping you apply ActionScript and production techniques that may be new to you.

If you've already used Flash, then you may want to review the changes to the Flash 8 interface in Part I, and then jump right into other specific parts to learn more about character animation, ActionScript, creating artwork and content in other applications, and integrating Flash with HTML. There are many new features and workflow enhancements for new and experienced users alike in every section of the book, so even if you've done a lot of work in Flash, it's worth scanning each Part for an introduction to new tools and techniques.

Part I: An Introduction to Flash Web Production

The first part of this book explores the Flash file format and how Flash 8 fits into the evolution of the program (Chapter 1), explains the context in which Flash movies interact on the Web (Chapter 2), and gives an overview of multimedia planning and some specific techniques and suggestions that will make your Flash project development less painful and more productive (Chapter 3).

Part II: Mastering the Flash Environment

This part gives you all the information you need to feel comfortable in the Flash 8 authoring environment. Get an introduction to, and some tips for customizing, the Flash UI (Chapter 4). Learn where to find your drawing tools and how to use them efficiently (Chapter 5), and then discover all the ways that Flash helps you to organize and optimize project assets (Chapter 6). Learn key color concepts relevant to multimedia production and find out why Flash has the best color tools yet (Chapter 7). Jump into using text editing tools and see how to get the best looking type and the smallest file sizes in your Flash projects (Chapter 8). Finally, learn how to modify text and graphics to get the most out of your Flash artwork (Chapter 9).

Part III: Creating Animation and Effects

After you've learned how to find your way around the Flash interface and to create static graphics, you can get some perspective on animation strategies (Chapter 10). Learn to make things move and how to work with different symbol types to optimize your animation workflow (Chapter 11). Add polish and pizzazz with Timeline Effects, Advanced Color properties and the new Flash 8 Filters and Blend modes (Chapter 12). Put layers to use for organization and special effects (Chapter 13). Finally, get special production tips for professional character animation and broadcast-quality graphics (Chapter 14).

Part IV: Integrating Media Files with Flash

Now that you're fluent in the Flash workspace, take your projects to the next level by adding sound, special graphics, and video assets. In Chapter 15, you learn the basics of digital sound, and see which file formats can be imported into Flash and how to import, optimize, and export high-quality sound for different types of projects. Chapter 16 gives you an overview of how to bring vector or raster artwork from other programs into Flash and how to protect image quality while optimizing your Flash movies. Chapter 17 introduces the exciting new video features of Flash 8, including the new On2 VP6 codec.

Part V: Adding Basic Interactivity to Flash Movies

Learn how to start using Flash actions to create interactive and responsive presentations. Get oriented in the Flash 8 Actions panel, which brings back Normal mode as Script Assist (Chapter 18). Use ActionScript in Flash movies to control internal elements on multiple time-lines, such as nested Movie Clips (Chapter 19). Use Flash 8 components to create fast, clean interfaces for multipart presentations that also include some of the Accessibility options (Chapter 20).

Part VI: Distributing Flash Movies

You need to learn how to export (or publish) your Flash presentations to the .swf file format for use on a Web page, or within presentations on other formats. Chapter 21 details options in the Flash 8 Publish Settings, and provides tips for optimizing your Flash movies in order to achieve smaller file sizes for faster download performance. If you prefer to hand-code your HTML, then read Chapter 22, which describes how to use the `<embed>` and `<object>` tags, how to load Flash movies into framesets, and how to create plug-in detection systems for your Flash movies. If you want to find out how to create a Flash stand-alone projector, or use the Flash stand-alone player, then check out Chapter 23.

Part VII: Approaching ActionScript

Learn the basic elements of ActionScript syntax (Chapter 24), and how to use ActionScript to control properties and methods of `MovieClip` objects (Chapter 25). Learn about making functions and arrays (Chapter 26), detecting Movie Clip collisions, and using the `ColorTransform`, `Sound`, and `PrintJob` classes for dynamic control of movie elements (Chapter 27).

Part VIII: Applying ActionScript

Get an introduction to runtime MP3, JPEG/PNG/GIF, and FLV loading features as well as how to share and load assets in multiple .swf files (Chapter 28). Start creating Flash movies that send data with the `LoadVars` object and learn to integrate XML data with Flash movies (Chapter 29). Take control of text fields using new HTML tags, the `TextFormat` class, CSS (Cascading Style Sheets) and new anti-aliasing options (Chapter 30). Part VIII includes a detailed chapter dedicated to building a Flash game from the ground up (Chapter 31) and finishes with a chapter of troubleshooting tips and suggested best-practices for project architecture (Chapter 32).

Part IX: Integrating Components and Data-Binding

Find out how to use the many of the User Interface components that ship with Flash 8 to enhance your Flash projects (Chapter 33). Learn how to use the visual data-binding features of the Component Inspector panel and create your own ActionScript code to pass data and events between components (Chapter 34). Finally, build a Gallery component from scratch that works with dynamic PHP scripts to load image thumbnails and display full-size down-loadable JPEG images (Chapter 35).

Part X: Expanding Flash

Every multimedia designer uses Flash with some other graphics, sound, and authoring applications to create a unique workflow that solves the problems of daily interactive project development. The bonus chapters in Part X, included on the CD-ROM as PDF files, show you how to manage raster graphics (Chapter 36) and vector graphics (Chapter 37) and how to create content in popular applications such as Macromedia Fireworks, and Adobe Photoshop. This part also covers topics relevant to Flash production using Dreamweaver 8 (Chapter 38).

Part XI: Appendixes

In the appendixes, you'll find directions for using the CD-ROM (Appendix A) and a listing of contact and bio information for the guest experts is also available (Appendix B). Included on the CD-ROM as PDF files is bonus information on digital sound basics that explains sound sampling rates and bit-depths (Appendix C), and information on digital video basics (Appendix D).

Getting in Touch with Us

You can find additional information, resources, and feedback from the authors and other readers at www.flashsupport.com. We want to know what you think of individual chapters in this book. Visit www.flashsupport.com/feedback to send us your comments.

If you have a great tip or idea that you want to share with us, we'd like to hear from you. You can also send comments about the book to info@theMakers.com.

Also, check Appendix B to learn more about this book's various contributors and guest experts — including URLs of their work and contact information for people who don't mind being contacted directly by our readers.

For quality concerns or issues with the CD-ROM, you can call the Wiley Customer Care phone number: (800) 762-2974. Outside the United States, call 1 (317) 572-3994, or contact Wiley Customer Service by e-mail at techsupdum@wiley.com. Wiley Publishing, Inc. will provide technical support only for CD-ROM installation and other general-quality control items; for technical support on the applications themselves, consult the program's vendor.

Macromedia Wants to Help You

Macromedia has created a Feature Request and Bug Report form to make it easier to process suggestions and requests from Flash users. If you have an idea or feature request for the next version or you find a bug that prevents you from doing your work, let the folks at Macromedia know. You can find the online form at www.macromedia.com/support/email/wishform.

The simple fact is this: If more users request a specific feature or improvement, it's more likely that Macromedia will implement it.

Regardless of your geographic location, you always have access to the global Flash community for support and the latest information through the Macromedia Online Forums at http://webforums.macromedia.com/flash.

For inspiration and motivation check out the Site of the Day, weekly features, and case studies at www.macromedia.com/showcase.

Acknowledgments

This book would not have been possible without the dedication and talent of many people. Although much of the content in this edition has changed to reflect changes in the tools, there is also a good deal of content from dedicated contributors that has been carried over from the previous edition. We are always grateful for the added breadth and depth the tutorials from our guest experts bring to the content. First and foremost, we would like to thank the Flash development community. In our combined experiences in research and multimedia production, we haven't seen another community that has been so open, friendly, and willing to share advanced tips and techniques. It has been gratifying to be involved as the community keeps expanding and to see the innovators in the first wave of Flash development become mentors to a whole new generation. Thank you all for continuing to inspire and challenge audiences and each other with the possibilities for Flash.

We would like to thank everyone at John Wiley & Sons who supported us as we researched and revised, week after week. Katharine Dvorak, our project editor, was clever, kind, and charming enough to get the job done while maintaining a cheerful demeanor. Lauren Kennedy is the best copy editor we've ever had. She polished up rusty sentences that had made it past our editors on earlier editions and caught a few things that slipped by our tech editors, too. As always, our endless gratitude goes to Michael Roney, our acquisitions editor. Steadfast, optimistic, and supportive, Mike was a human shield who kept the faith and ran interference for us even as we pushed deadlines (repeatedly) to overhaul a best-selling book.

Ezra Freedman and Zach Zsukula, our technical editors, were dedicated and creative, as they waded carefully through example files and reams of text in a determined effort to anticipate our readers' perspective. We always prefer to hear "it's broken" *before* the book has gone to print!

A special thanks to all of the Schematic Flash team who tested examples as we created them, especially John Barton and Billy Shin. Jennifer Goodie provided weekend (and nighttime!) support for many PHP questions for the Gallery component in Chapter 35. Peng Lee gave us timely advice for several examples in the book, and Beau DeSilva spent many nights rendering the 3D wasp footage used in Chapter 17.

Many of the scripts provided in this book would not be complete without the "instant messenger" help provided by Joey Lott, Paul Newman, Danny Patterson, Guy Watson and Rob Williams,. We'd also like to thank Richard Blakely and Jerry Chabolla at Influxis.com for providing the Flash Media Server hosting for this book's streaming video examples.

David Fugate, our literary agent at Waterside Productions, has been through every revision of the *Flash Bible* series. The bad news and the good news is that David has left Waterside to launch his own company (LaunchBooks), so this will be his last edition of the *Flash Bible*, but the start of many new endeavors.

Of course, this book about Flash wouldn't even exist without the hard work of the people at Macromedia who make it all possible. Many thanks to the developers, engineers, and support staff at Macromedia, especially Mike Downey, Mike Chambers, Doug Benson, Gary Grossman,

Erica Norton, San Khong, Jeff Kamerer, Mally Gardiner, and Jen deHaan, who stayed up day and night to answer our questions and ease our learning curve during the development of Flash 8. Scott Unterberg worked magic as he oversaw one of the most enjoyable and productive beta programs that we've ever been involved with. We're also indebted, as always, to all our intrepid fellow developers and authors, who helped us to get our bearings in early versions of Flash 8.

Tutorials at a Glance

Contents at a Glance

Contents

Part IV: Integrating Media Files with Flash   459

Chapter 15: Adding Sound 461

Part V: Adding Basic Interactivity to Flash Movies 619

Part IX: Integrating Components and Data-Binding   1105

Chapter 33: Using Components 1107

An Introduction to Flash Web Production

If you're new to Flash or to multimedia production, this section gets you started on the right foot. If you are a veteran Flash user, this section gives you some perspective on the evolution of Flash and the workflow options available in Flash 8.

Chapter 1 provides a comprehensive overview of the strengths and weaknesses of the Flash format and some background on where Flash came from and how it has evolved. Chapter 2 explores the various ways that Flash movies interact with other Web formats and introduces some of the issues that need to be considered when planning for specific audiences. Chapter 3 has expanded coverage of tools and strategies for multimedia project planning, including detailed descriptions of how to create flowcharts, site maps, and functional specification documents.

Understanding the Flash 8 Framework

Since its humble beginnings as FutureSplash in 1997, Macromedia Flash has matured into a powerful tool for deploying a wide range of media content. With every new version released, the possibilities have increased for imaginative and dynamic content creation — for the Web and beyond. Macromedia has responded to the development community's unprecedented embrace of Flash by expanding advanced features and enhancing tools for new users. Never before has Flash incorporated so many new features in a single release.

In this chapter, we introduce Flash 8 and explore the many possibilities that are available for your productions. We also discuss how Flash compares to or enhances other programs that you may be familiar with.

Flash movies are usually viewed in a few different ways. The most common method is from within a Web browser, either as an asset within an HTML page or as a Web site completely comprised of a master Flash movie using several smaller Flash movies as loaded SWF assets. The Flash Player is also available as a stand-alone application (known as a *projector*), which can be used to view movies without needing a Web browser or the plug-in. This method is commonly used for deployment of Flash movies on CD-ROMs, floppy disks, or other offline media formats.

 Cross-Reference You can learn more about projectors and stand-alones in Chapter 23, "Using the Flash Player and Projector."

The Brave New World of Expressiveness

Flash has seen significant development over the years in both capability and design. Consistently with each new release, developers push the technology into new territory. In its current iteration, Flash 8 is perhaps the single largest upgrade to the Flash Player's visual effects engine. While past upgrades to Flash (notably Flash MX and Flash MX 2004) were largely received as "developer-focused" enhancements, Flash 8 raises the bar for what visual designers can expect to achieve with Flash productions. Flash 8, of course, continues to satisfy both designers and programmers — all of the new author-time visual effects in Flash 8 and Flash Player 8 are fully programmable with ActionScript, the programming language of Flash.

Just as Flash MX 2004 was available in two editions, you can produce Flash Player 8 content in either Flash Basic 8 or Flash Professional 8. Both editions share many core updates to Flash MX 2004, including our following favorites:

✦ **FlashType:** Flash Player 8 features a new text-rendering engine dubbed FlashType. Now, you can format text with superior anti-aliasing for small text sizes. In previous versions of the Flash Player, you needed to use specific fonts, such as miniml.com's pixel-based fonts, to display 8-point text in Flash movies. With FlashType, you can set the anti-aliasing to a specific mode for more legible small text with just about any font face.

✦ **Script Assist:** Flash MX 2004 saw the disappearance of Normal mode from the Actions panel. Fortunately, for beginners learning to use ActionScript, Macromedia has re-engineered Normal mode as Script Assist in Flash 8. Now, when you're having difficulty adding actions or remembering their parameters, you can turn on Script Assist in the Actions panel.

✦ **Macintosh document tabs:** Past versions of the Flash authoring environment offered a tabbed interface for documents in the Windows versions. Now, if you're a Mac user, you can enjoy the ease of tabbed documents in the Flash 8 authoring environment.

✦ **Improved search in the Flash 8 Help panel:** The Flash 8 Help panel has been updated with more examples and help pages, but the Help panel also offers better search functionality. Now, search terms appear highlighted in the found pages, which greatly enhances your ability to see just where your desired search terms are located within longer help pages.

✦ **Expanded work area:** In previous versions of Flash, large symbols or graphic elements may have been too large (greater than 1,000 pixels) to see offstage and manipulate. Now, the work area in Flash 8 grows to accommodate the size of your offstage elements.

✦ **Stroke enhancements:** Line strokes in Flash Player 8 movies can now have a variety of line caps and scaling effects. You learn more about these features in Chapter 5, "Drawing in Flash."

✦ **9-slice scaling:** Have you ever had artwork that scaled undesirably when you stretched the symbol instance horizontally or vertically? With the new 9-slice scaling feature, you can prevent corners of artwork scaling in the same fashion as the rest of the symbol content.

✦ **Enhanced gradient creation:** Gradients in Flash Player 8 movies can now feature up to 16 colors, and the Gradient Transform tool enables you to precisely control the location of the gradient focal point.

✦ **Object Drawing model:** If you like drawing multiple shapes on the same layer, the new Object Drawing model enables you to prevent shapes from modifying the other shapes on the layer. In Flash MX 2004 and earlier, if you overlapped primitive shapes, the overlapping segments would be erased from the shape(s). Drawing objects are a hybrid graphic type introduced to Flash 8 to make the drawing environment more flexible and more like other drawing applications such as Adobe Illustrator. Drawing objects combine some of the features of primitive shapes, groups, and symbols. You can learn more about the new Object Drawing model in Chapter 5, "Drawing in Flash."

✦ **Video Import wizard:** Continuing with Flash MX 2004's video encoding capabilities, you have greater control over compression options during the video import process. You can find more information about this feature in Chapter 17, "Displaying Video." (Note that the Video Import wizard in the Professional version includes more options.)

✦ **Flash Player detection update:** Flash 8 improves the Flash Player detection capabilities in the Publish Settings' HTML tab. Flash 8 can now create one HTML page that detects a target version of the Flash Player and displays the appropriate content.

✦ **Script editor:** Now, both the Basic and Professional editions of the Flash authoring environment can create and edit ActionScript files (.as). With Flash MX 2004, only the Professional edition had this capability.

✦ **Improved Library panel:** You can now browse the libraries of multiple active Flash document files (.fla) in the Library panel. A drop-down menu conveniently enables you to switch from one library to another. You can pin the current library to prevent it from changing context when another Flash document is active, and you can spawn a new Library panel if you prefer to have two or more Library panels open.

If you use Flash Professional 8, sometimes referred to as Flash Pro 8, you can take advantage of the following additional features as well:

✦ **Flash Player 8 Filters and Blend modes:** Perhaps the single most important update to Flash Professional 8 is the capability to add filter effects and blend modes to Movie Clip symbol instances. You can apply blur effects, drop shadows, glow effects, and more using the Property inspector's new Filters tab or ActionScript. Blend modes enable you to layer Movie Clip instances with different visual effects, enabling new types of masking. You learn more about filters and blend modes in Chapter 12, "Applying Filters and Effects."

✦ **Custom easing controls:** You now have more control over easing in the Property inspector for Motion and Shape tweens. You can re-create tweens that previously were only easily achieved with ActionScript, such as elastic and bounce effects.

✦ **Advanced components:** Flash Pro 8 ships with more components than the standard version, including data connectors that can tap XML and Web service-based data sources. The basic version of Flash 8 has 14 components, whereas the Professional version has 42 components, including the FLVPlayback component we discuss next. We explore many of the User Interface components in Chapter 33, "Using Components."

✦ **FLVPlayback component:** The new FLVPlayback component is the only new component in Flash Professional 8, but it's a huge powerhouse for video playback. Unlike its MediaPlayback component predecessor, the FLVPlayback component is much smaller in terms of file size for your Flash movie file (.swf). You can use SMIL configuration files with the FLVPlayback component. There are several skins available for the component, and you can create your own custom set of playback controls with the FLV Playback Custom UI components. You learn more about this component in Chapter 17, "Displaying Video."

✦ **Flash 8 Video Encoder:** One of the most amazing aspects of Flash Pro 8 isn't even in the authoring environment! A separate application called the Flash 8 Video Encoder installs with Flash Pro 8 that enables you to export Flash Video files (.flv). The Flash 8 Video Encoder can batch process several files, and enables you to add cue points that are embedded with the .flv file. The FLV QuickTime Export plug-in is also installed with Flash Pro 8. This plug-in enables you to export Flash Video from professional video applications such as Adobe After Effects, Apple Final Cut Pro, and Apple QuickTime Player Pro. This tool actually installs a QuickTime component that can be used by most QuickTime-aware programs. The quality of the video produced by this tool can be far better than the native Video Import wizard. To learn more about the use of this tool, see Chapter 17, "Displaying Video."

✦ **Video alpha channel support:** Flash Player 8's new video codec, On2 VP6, supports an 8-bit alpha channel, which can mask your video clip. This exciting feature enables you to composite video clips more seamlessly on top of other Flash content. You learn more about video alpha channels in Chapter 17, "Displaying Video."

✦ **Data binding:** The Component Inspector panel, available in both editions of Flash 8, has additional Bindings and Schema tabs in the Professional edition. These interfaces enable you to easily attach dynamic data to components. You learn more about data binding in Chapter 34, "Binding Data and Events to Components."

✦ **Project management:** The Project panel, available only in Flash Pro 8, organizes all of the files associated with your Flash projects. You can create and define sites in Flash Pro 8, just as you do in Dreamweaver. The same site definition files are used between the two programs, making it easy to edit files in either application. The Project panel can publish multiple Flash document files (.fla) at once, and it can be integrated with Microsoft SourceSafe to version-track your source code. You can learn more about the Project panel in Chapter 3, "Planning Flash Projects."

✦ **Mobile emulator enhancements:** If you produce Flash content for mobile devices in the FlashLite format, you'll love the new emulator environments in Flash Pro 8. You can emulate playback of your Flash movie in several device skins, including several Nokia and Symbian OS phones.

Many enhancements are not directly seen in the authoring environment, though. While there are two editions of Flash 8, there's still only one Flash Player 8 that's used to view the movies published from either edition. Flash Player 8 adds the following enhancements, among others:

✦ **Improved small font size rendering:** You can enable text fields in Flash documents to optimize the display of small font sizes during playback. Flash Player 8–compatible movies have improved anti-aliasing at small text sizes if you enable the feature on the text field displaying the text.

✦ **Improved video quality:** As we mentioned earlier in this chapter, Flash Player 8 features a brand-new video codec, On2 VP6. This codec provides superior image quality and compression over the older Sorenson Spark codec available in Flash Players 6 and 7. .flv files using this new codec can be loaded directly into a Flash movie file (.swf) at run time, using `NetStream` objects in ActionScript. To learn how to load .flv files in this manner, read Chapter 28, "Sharing and Loading Assets."

Tip   You still need Macromedia Flash Communication Server MX to truly stream Flash Video files (.flv) at run time. The FLV loading feature of Flash Player 7 and higher progressively downloads the video file, while Flash Communication Server can stream any portion of a video file. You must use Flash Player 8 to progressively load an .flv file that uses the new On2 VP6 codec. Note that the new release of Flash Communication Server is now called Flash Media Server.

✦ **File upload/download capability:** You can now use Flash Player 8 to offer file upload and download interfaces to your users. Once the domain of HTML forms, Flash movies can now offer browse dialog boxes that enable the user to select one or more files on the system to upload to your own application server. You learn more about this feature in Chapter 33, "Using Components"

✦ **Tougher security restrictions:** Flash Player 8 implements new security policies for data loaded into Flash Player 6 or higher movies. There are new local and network security policies for .swf files, as we discuss in Chapter 21, "Publishing Flash Movies."

✦ **Better runtime performance:** Macromedia has added a new runtime bitmap caching feature for `MovieClip` objects, which greatly enhances the speed that graphics can animate within the Flash movie. In our own tests, we found that even our most complex Flash movies ran better and faster in Flash Player 8.

Tip This is a relatively simple feature to test. Open one of your most intensive Flash movies created in Flash MX 2004, and publish it as a Flash Player 8 movie from Flash 8. Run the new movie in Flash Player 8 and see if you notice a difference.

✦ **Automatic player updates:** The Windows and Macintosh versions of Flash Player 8 can now be updated automatically. This great enhancement means that you can more reliably use enhancements that Macromedia may make available in minor revisions of Flash Player 8, not to mention future major revisions of Flash Player.

Tip If you're targeting a Flash Player 7 audience, you might want to consider targeting Flash Player 8 as well. Why? Flash Player 7 also features automatic player updates. By default, Flash Player 7 will check Macromedia's site every 30 days for new player updates. This process occurs silently in the background, and doesn't require the user to upgrade his or her player installation manually. Theoretically, then, within 30 days of the release of any new Flash Player, including Flash Player 8, most browsers that had Flash Player 7 will then use Flash Player 8.

For a complete list of features in each edition of Flash 8, see the Help pages in the Help panel's booklet, Getting Started with Flash ⇨ Getting Started ⇨ What's new in Flash.

Web Resource Before you buy or upgrade Flash 8, we highly recommend that you take a look at the detailed feature comparison table on Macromedia's site at:

`www.macromedia.com/software/flash/basic/`

Tip Given that most of the expressiveness improvements, such as filter effects and blend modes, are only available in Flash Professional 8, we strongly suggest that you use Flash Professional 8 for any studio-level production work.

Macromedia also released new versions of Dreamweaver and Fireworks, as part of the Studio 8 software bundle. The user interfaces for Flash, Dreamweaver, and Fireworks are very similar, each touting a Property inspector, dockable panel sets, and specialized tools to integrate the products with one another.

Cross-Reference To learn more about enhancing your Flash production with Dreamweaver and Fireworks, refer to Part X, "Expanding Flash."

Although the broad array of Flash work created by Web designers and developers already speaks for itself, the sleek interface and the powerful additional features of Flash 8 surely inspire more challenging, functional, entertaining, informative, bizarre, humorous, beautiful, and fascinating experiments and innovations.

There are probably more ways to use Flash than there are adjectives to describe them, but here are just a few examples:

✦ Forms for collecting user information and dynamically loading custom content based on this interaction

✦ Real-time interaction with multiple users on a forum or support site, including live audio/video feeds of connected parties

✦ A video portfolio using native Flash 8 video import capabilities and dynamic loading of content

✦ Animated ID spots and loading screens with built-in download detection

✦ A practical Web utility, such as a mortgage calculator or a search tool

✦ Robust chat rooms based on XML and server-socket technology

✦ An audio interface dynamically pulling in requested songs using native Flash 8 support for MP3 loading

✦ Interactive conceptual art experimentations involving several users, 3D, or recording and playback of user interaction

✦ Shopping and e-commerce solutions built entirely using Flash and server-side technology

✦ Alternative content or movie attributes based on system capability testing (if a device or desktop doesn't support audio streaming, then a text equivalent of the audio transcript is presented to the user)

✦ Projectors used for creating slide show presentations in the style of PowerPoint, either on CD-ROM or an alternative storage device

✦ Broadcast quality cartoons, advertising, or titling

✦ Optimized animations for the Web, and for portable devices such as cell phones or Pocket PCs

✦ An interface that addresses accessibility issues by modifying certain elements when a screen reader is active

✦ Flash movies specifically exported for use in digital video projects requiring special effects and compositing

This list is obviously far from complete and is ever-expanding with each new release of the program. As you can probably tell from this list, if you can imagine a use for Flash, it can probably be accomplished.

The topography of Flash 8

Before you attempt to construct interactive projects in Flash, you should be familiar with the structure of the authoring environment. Even if you already know a previous version of Flash, this is advisable. That's because with the release of Flash 8, Macromedia has again added many new features to the interface and has either moved or improved other features and functionalities. So, to get a firm footing in the new interface, we strongly suggest that you work your way through this book — from the beginning.

 Cross-Reference Chapter 4, "Interface Fundamentals," introduces the updated Flash 8 interface and gives you tips for customizing your workspace and optimizing your workflow.

Moreover, you need to proactively plan your interactive projects before you attempt to author them in Flash. An ounce of preplanning goes a long way during the production process. Don't fool yourself—the better your plan looks on paper, the better it performs when it comes to the final execution.

Cross-Reference
We detail the foundation for planning interactive Flash projects in Chapter 3, "Planning Flash Projects," and you will find these concepts reiterated and expanded in chapters that discuss specific project workflows. Chapter 20, "Making Your First Flash 8 Project," is a great place to start applying these planning strategies.

We've consolidated the overview of interactive planning in the early chapters of the book. In later chapters, we've included step-by-step descriptions of real-world projects that allow you to see how all the theory and planning suggestions apply to the development of specific projects.

Cross-Reference
Chapter 31, "Creating a Game in Flash," walks you through the logic required to design and script a functional and engaging game. Chapter 35, "Building an Image Gallery Component," describes the process of creating an entire component from the ground up, utilizing many of the new filter effects in Flash Player 8.

There are two primary files that you create during Flash development: Flash document files (.fla) and Flash movie files (.swf). We discuss both of these formats next.

File types in Flash 8

Flash document files (.fla) are architected to provide an efficient authoring environment for projects of all sizes. Within this environment, content can be organized into scenes, and the ordering of scenes can be rearranged throughout the production cycle. Layers provide easy separation of graphics within each scene, and, as Guide or Mask layers, they can also aid drawing or even provide special effects. The Timeline shows keyframes, motion and shape tweens, labels, and comments. The Library (which can be shared amongst movies at author-time or at run time) stores all the symbols in your project, such as graphics, fonts, animated elements, sounds or video, and components.

Flash documents

Throughout this book, you will see us refer to Flash documents, which are the .fla files created by Flash 8 when you choose File ➪ New and choose Flash Document from the General category tab. Unlike some graphic applications, such as Macromedia FreeHand or Adobe Illustrator, the file extension for Flash documents does not reflect the version of the authoring tool. For example, Flash 5, Flash MX, Flash MX 2004, and Flash 8 save Flash documents as .fla files. You cannot open later version documents in previous versions of the authoring tool. You do not use Flash documents with the Flash Player, nor do you need to upload these files to your Web server. Always keep a version (and a backup!) of your Flash document.

Tip
Flash 8 allows you to resave your Flash 8 document file (.fla) as a Flash MX 2004 document file (.fla). Choose File ➪ Save As and select Flash MX 2004 Document in the Save as type menu. If you save the document in this manner, you can open the Flash document file (.fla) in the Flash MX 2004 authoring application.

Figure 1-1 shows how Flash documents are composed of individual scenes that contain keyframes to describe changes on the Stage. What you can't see in this figure is the efficiency of sharing Flash Libraries among several Flash documents, loading other Flash movies into a parent, or "master," Flash movie using the `loadMovie()` action, or creating interactive elements with scripting methods.

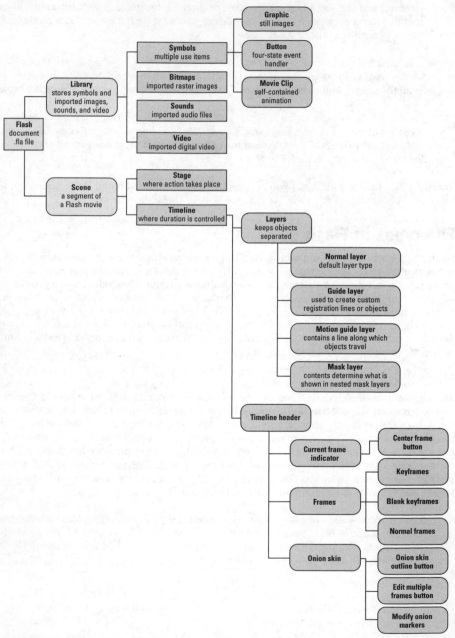

Figure 1-1: Elements of a Flash document (.fla) in the authoring environment

Introducing Flash Player 8

The difference between the naming conventions of the Flash Player plug-in and the Flash authoring software is potentially confusing. Macromedia refers to its latest release of the player as Flash Player 8, tagging the version number at the end of the name instead of following in the naming convention of its predecessors (that is, "Flash 5 Player"). One probable reason the Flash Player is numbered, rather than dubbed "MX" like the authoring software, is because a standard sequential number is required for plug-in detection.

Flash Player 8 continues to integrate MSAA (Microsoft Active Accessibility) technology to support assistive technologies, such as screen readers to make Flash content more accessible to people with disabilities. Playback on the Macintosh has been improved, while the file size of the player download has been kept small (despite the addition of new features).

Flash movies

When you publish or test a Flash document, Flash 8 creates a Flash movie file with the .swf file extension. This file format is an optimized version of the Flash document, retaining only the elements from the project file that are actually used. Flash movies are uploaded to your Web server where they are usually integrated into HTML documents for other Web users to view. You can protect your finished Flash movies from being easily imported or edited in the authoring environment by other users.

Caution   The Protect from import option in the Publish Settings does not prevent third-party utilities from stripping artwork, symbols, sounds, and ActionScript code from your Flash movies. For more information, read Chapter 21, "Publishing Flash Movies."

Much of the information contained originally within a Flash document file (.fla) is discarded in the attempt to make the smallest file possible when exporting a Flash movie file (.swf). When your movie is exported, all original elements remain but layers are essentially flattened and run on one timeline, in the order that was established in the Flash document. Practically all information originally in the file will be optimized somehow, and any unused Library elements are not exported with the Flash movie. Library assets are loaded into and stored in the first frame they are used in. For optimization, reused assets are only saved to the file once and are referenced throughout the movie from this one area. Bitmap images and sounds can be compressed with a variety of quality settings as well.

Tip   Flash Player 6 and higher movies can be optimized with a specialized Compress Movie option that is available in the Flash tab of the Publish Settings dialog box (File ➪ Publish Settings). When you apply this option, you will see drastic file-size savings with movies that use a significant amount of ActionScript code.

Refer to Figure 1-2 for a graphic explanation of the characteristics of the Flash movie file (.swf) format.

Cross-Reference   We discuss Flash Player detection in detail in Chapter 22, "Integrating Flash Content with Web Pages."

Cross-Reference   We introduce guidelines for creating accessible content for the Flash Player 8 in Chapter 20, "Making Your First Flash 8 Project."

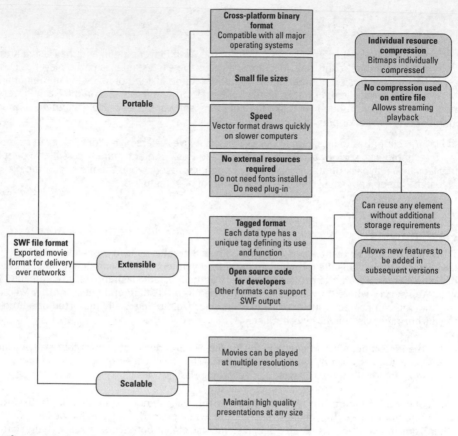

Figure 1-2: Overview of the Flash movie (.swf) format

There are several other ways in which Flash movies, or their parts, can be played back or displayed. Since Flash 4, the Publish feature has offered provisions for the export of movies or sections of movies to either the QuickTime digital video format, the QuickTime Flash layer vector format, or the Animated GIF format. Parts of movies can also be exported as a series of individual bitmaps or as vector files. Single frames can also be exported to these formats.

Flash ActionScript files

ActionScript is the programming language used within Flash 8 to create interactive functionality within the movie. You can store ActionScript code in external text files with the .as file extension. You can open .as files directly in Flash 8 or your preferred code editing application. ActionScript files can be brought into a Flash movie using the #include directive or the import keyword.

Flash Video files

 The Flash Video file format (.flv file extension) is used by the Flash 8 Video Encoder or another video encoding application such as Sorenson Squeeze or On2 Flix to export video. You can not open .flv files in the Flash 8 authoring tool, but you can import them into a Flash document file (.fla) or you can load them at run time into Flash Player 7 or higher movies. .flv files can also be uploaded to a Flash Communication Server application and streamed in real time to Flash Player 6 or higher movies.

Flash Debug files

 A Flash Debug file (.swd file extension) is created whenever you choose the Debug Movie command from the Control menu in the Flash 8 authoring environment. You can not play an .swd file on its own; rather, the .swd file augments the functionality of the .swf file during the debugging process. The .swd file contains information related to trace( ) actions and break-points within your Flash movie.

 You learn more about the debugging process in Chapter 32, "Managing and Troubleshooting Flash Movies."

Flash Component files

 The Flash Component file format (.swc file extension) is used for compiled clips that you purchase from third-party vendors or download from Macromedia Exchange (www.macromedia.com/exchange). You can't directly open an .swc file in the Flash 8 authoring environment, but you can copy .swc files to your local settings for Flash 8 so that the components show up in the Components panel. On Windows, you can copy .swc files to the following location. Note that ; denotes a continuation of the directory path:

```
C:\Documents and Settings\[Your User Name]\Local Settings\Application
Data\Macromedia\Flash 8\en\Configuration\Components
```

On the Macintosh, you can copy to this location:

```
[Startup disk]: Users: [Your User Name]: Library: Application Support: Æ
Macromedia: Flash 8: en: Configuration: Components
```

These locations are only used to store additional components; the default components for Flash 8 are stored in the program folder for Flash 8.

Flash Project files

 If you use Flash Professional 8, you can create Flash Project files (.flp file extension) in the Project panel. A Flash Project file is essentially an XML file that stores the names of files associated with a project.

The Many Faces of Flash 8

Flash is a hybrid application that is like no other application. On the immediate surface, it may seem (to some) to be a simple hybrid between a Web-oriented bitmap handler and a vector-drawing program, such as Macromedia FreeHand or Adobe Illustrator. But while Flash is indeed such a hybrid, it's also capable of much, much more. It's also an interactive multi-media-authoring program and a sophisticated animation program suitable for creating a range of animations — from simple Web ornaments to broadcast-quality cartoons. As if that weren't enough, it's also the host of a powerful and adaptable scripting language.

ActionScript has evolved from a limited drag-and-drop method of enabling animation to a full-fledged object-oriented programming language very similar to JavaScript. Flash ActionScript can work in conjunction with XML (eXtensible Markup Language), HTML, and many other applications and parts of the Web. Flash content can be integrated with many server-side technologies, including Flash Remoting MX and Flash Communication Server MX, and the Flash Player offers built-in support for dynamically loading images, MP3s, movies, and other data. Flash can work seamlessly with ColdFusion, other application servers running PHP, Microsoft .NET services, and XML socket servers to deliver streamlined dynamic interactive experiences.

So, what's this evolving hybrid we call Flash really capable of? That's a question that remains to be answered by developers such as you. In fact, we're hoping that you will master this application and show us a thing or two. That's why we've written this book: to put the tool in your hands and get you started on the road to your own innovations.

Because Flash is a hybrid application capable of just about anything, a good place to start working with this powerhouse is to inquire, what are the components of this hybrid? And if they were separated out, how might their capabilities be described? Those are the questions that we answer in this chapter.

Bitmap handler

In truth, Flash has limited capabilities as an image-editing program. It is more accurate to describe this part of the Flash application as a bitmap *handler*. Bitmap images are composed of dots on a grid of individual pixels. The location (and color) of each dot must be stored in memory, which makes this a memory-intensive format and leads to larger file sizes. Another characteristic of bitmap images is that they cannot be scaled without compromising quality (clarity and sharpness). The adverse effects of scaling an image up are more pronounced than when scaling down. Because of these two drawbacks—file sizes and scaling limitations—bitmap images are not ideal for Web use. However, for photographic-quality images, bitmap formats are indispensable and often produce better image quality and lower file sizes than vector images of equivalent complexity.

Vector-based drawing program

The heart of the Flash application is a vector-based drawing program, with capabilities similar to either Macromedia FreeHand or Adobe Illustrator. A vector-based drawing program doesn't rely upon individual pixels to compose an image. Instead, it draws shapes by defining points that are described by coordinates. Lines that connect these points are called paths, and vectors at each point describe the curvature of the path. Because this scheme is mathematical, there are two distinct advantages: Vector content is significantly more compact, and it's thoroughly scalable without image degradation. These advantages are especially significant for Web use.

Vector-based animator

The vector animation component of the Flash application is unlike any other program that preceded it. Although Flash is capable of handling bitmaps, its native file format is vector-based. So, unlike many other animation and media programs, Flash relies on the slim and trim vector format for transmission of your final work. Instead of storing megabytes of pixel information for each frame, Flash stores compact vector descriptions of each frame. Whereas a bitmap-based animation program (such as Apple's QuickTime) struggles to display each bitmap in rapid succession, Flash quickly renders the vector descriptions as needed and with far less strain on either the bandwidth or the recipient's machine. This is a huge advantage when transmitting animations and other graphic content over the Web.

Video compressor

Flash Player 6 and higher include a built-in video engine — the Sorenson Spark codec — which means that the Flash Player plug-in can be considered one of the world's smallest video plug-ins. Flash Player 8 features an additional video codec, the On2 VP6 codec, which has superior compression and image quality. You can import source video files directly into Flash 8 document files (.fla), or create separate Flash Video files (.flv) that load into your Flash movies. Users do not need to have Apple QuickTime, RealSystems RealOne, or Microsoft Windows Media Player installed in order to view video in a Flash movie. Unlike Director Shockwave, which accommodates video but still requires Apple QuickTime to be installed to play back the video, Flash Player 6 and higher provide a seamless solution.

Cross-Reference To learn more about this exciting aspect of Flash authoring, refer to Chapter 17, "Displaying Video." We also discuss the Flash 8 Video Encoder and Sorenson Squeeze, applications designed to create the highest-quality Flash video content.

Audio player

Since Flash Player 6, Flash movie files (.swf) have had the capability to load MP3 files during run time. You can also import other audio file formats into a Flash document file (.fla) during author-time. Sounds can be attached to keyframes or buttons, for background tracks or sound effects. A sound file's bytes can be distributed evenly across a timeline, so that the .swf file can be progressively downloaded into the Flash Player, enabling a movie to start playing before the entire sound file has been downloaded.

Multimedia authoring program

If the heart of Flash is a vector-based drawing program, then the body of Flash is a multimedia-authoring program (or authoring *environment*). Flash document files (.fla) can contain multiple media assets, including sound, still graphics, animation, and video. Moreover, Flash is a powerful tool for creating truly interactive content because it enables you to add (ActionScript) commands to dynamically control movie file (.swf) playback. Whether you are designing simple menu systems or customized and intuitive experimental interfaces, Flash content can be authored to recognize and respond to user input.

Animation sequencer

Most multimedia-authoring programs have a component for sequencing content as animation, and Flash is no exception. But in Flash, the animation sequencer is the core of the application. The Timeline window controls the display of all content — static or animated — within your Flash project. Within the Timeline window, there are two areas that enable you to organize content in visual space and in linear time.

Layers and layer folders enable you to keep track of content that has been placed into your Flash document. The visibility of each layer can be controlled independently, making it easier to isolate specific elements as you are authoring. Layers are viewed from front to back within each frame of the Timeline—items on upper layers overlay other items on lower layers. Any number of items can be placed on a single layer, but you have less control over the stacking order within a layer. Within the same layer, ungrouped vector lines and shapes will always be on the bottom level, whereas bitmaps, text, grouped items, and symbol instances will be on the upper level.

Tip
Flash 8 documents can use Layer folders. This is invaluable for organizing projects that involve many separate elements.

Cross-Reference
For a detailed "tour" of the Flash 8 environment, refer to Chapter 4, "Interface Fundamentals." We discuss the process of making artwork and managing groups and symbols in Chapter 5, "Drawing in Flash," and in Chapter 6, "Symbols, Instances, and the Library," respectively.

The structure that creates the illusion of movement in a Flash movie is a series of frames. Each frame represents a still moment in time. By controlling how the Playhead moves through these frames, you can control the speed, duration, and order of an animated sequence.

By changing the content in your layers on each frame, you can manually create frame-by-frame animation. However, one of the things that makes Flash such a popular animation machine is its ability to auto-interpolate or *tween* animation. By defining the content on a beginning and an end keyframe and applying a Motion tween or a Shape tween, you can quickly create or modify animated shape transformations and the movement of elements on the Stage.

Cross-Reference
We discuss the many ways of creating Flash animation in Part III: "Creating Animation and Effects."

Within one Flash document, you can also set up a series of separate scenes; each scene is a continuation of the same Main Timeline, but scenes can be named, and reordered at any time. Scenes play through from first to last without interruption unless Flash's interactive commands ("actions") dictate otherwise.

Cross-Reference
We introduce the steps for using ActionScript for simple control of movie playback in Part V: "Adding Basic Interactivity to Flash Movies."

Programming and database front end

The past few versions of Flash brought a vast expansion of the possibilities for integrating Flash interfaces with server-side technology and dynamic loading of content using XML, ColdFusion, and new server technologies such as PHP, ASP, JSP, Flash Remoting MX, and Flash Communication Server MX. These improvements largely came out of the development and maturity of ActionScript as a viable programming language. Flash has developed into an alternative front end for large databases, which means it can serve as an online store, MP3 player, or multiuser game and chat room—an amazing feat for an "animation program"!

With Flash 8, there are even more possibilities at your fingertips. One of the extended functionalities in this version is the incorporation of components supporting advanced data-aware capabilities. You can load JPEGs, GIFs, PNGs, MP3s, and Flash Video files into Flash at run time (or "on the fly"), without having to use a special server technology. You can use a wide range of data formats, from XML to Web Services (SOAP) to Flash Remoting.

There are many other enhancements to the programming environment and functionality of Flash that experienced users will appreciate and new users will come to value. ActionScript 2.0 continues the evolution of Flash's scripting language to a much more mature format, more closely adhering to ECMAScript 4. These changes support ActionScript's move toward acceptance as a standard, object-oriented programming (OOP) language on its own.

Summary

✦ Flash 8 combines many of the key tools for multimedia authoring into one nimble program. The integration it facilitates with other programs and languages promotes better Web content and more advanced applications.

✦ Flash content is not only found on the Web. For example, it is also used for CD/DVD-ROM authoring, broadcast graphics, offline interfaces, and business presentations.

✦ Flash 8 is a multifaceted application that can create a wide range of interactive products for the ever-growing variety of Web-enabled devices that surfers use to access the Internet.

✦ Careful planning of Flash development will undoubtedly save you time and effort in the long run.

✦ ✦ ✦

Exploring Web Technologies

Over the years, many technologies have been developed to work in conjunction with Macromedia Flash. Understanding the process of integrating these technologies will no doubt enable you to create more interactive and complex productions. If you're new to Flash, or you're looking for new ways to enhance or broaden the vision or scope of your Flash productions, you'll benefit from reading this chapter. It explores the placement of Flash within an ever-growing toolset for universal and "standards-based" Web development in use today.

Contextualizing Flash in the Internet Evolution

If you follow the development of "bleeding edge" technology, you may have noticed how often software is created, updated, and made obsolete. At times, this cycle seems to happen almost on a daily basis. But exactly how many practical—and affordable—options exist for Web development? How can production teams develop consistent frameworks with a variety of server technologies to efficiently build Flash presentations and applications? In this section, we discuss how Flash 8 continues to push the direction and limits of the Internet.

High expectations for Web experiences

Despite the devastation to Web production brought about by the "dotbomb" era (that is, the economic recession that occurred after many dotcom companies went out of business), the people visiting your Web sites or using your Web-based applications still want to experience engaging interfaces with amazing graphics and sound. Clients who hire you expect that you can produce this type of material. Clients may also believe that everyone will be able to visit the site and download material instantaneously (regardless of connection speed limitations), and that every visitor will have the same experience. Before you consider whether Flash is the best tool to meet your clients' goals, let's step back for a moment and consider Flash's history.

With every release of a new version of Flash, Web developers have access to bigger and better capabilities. We've seen a vast evolution from the early days in 1997 of mere vector animations, which vastly reduced file sizes of standard GIF animations. In 1998, Flash 3 made a marked improvement by introducing more control over these animations. At that time, Web sites with small games started to arrive on the development scene. That was also the year when Macromedia Generator was introduced, enabling dynamic graphics and data for Flash movies. Many companies were apprehensive about investing in Flash development because Flash was relatively new, although it was gaining ground as an accepted form of Web delivery.

In 1999, when Flash 4 was introduced, this attitude changed a great deal. The new version was much more powerful, and could accomplish many of the tasks that Generator provided in the past. Database interaction and dynamic content were suddenly possible in real time. However, Flash 4 was still a difficult application for developers to use; the programming interface for ActionScript code was limited by drag-and-drop functionality (which was only avoidable by using third-party software). This problem no longer existed in the 2000 release of version 5. Flash 5 incorporated XML data, and ActionScript "grew up" to come closer to an object-oriented programming (OOP) language that strongly resembled JavaScript.

In 2002, Web designers and developers were handed the sixth version of Flash, dubbed "MX." Flash MX marked Macromedia's success at integrating all of their software products into a universal framework, where ColdFusion, Dreamweaver, Fireworks, Director, and FreeHand could all be used together to produce a new breed of Web experiences, including Rich Internet Applications. With the new software and player, XML data was processed remarkably faster, movies were made accessible to those with physical challenges, and Macromedia Generator was no longer necessary to incorporate dynamic graphics. Flash Player 6 could load JPEG and MP3 files at run time. Developers could create reusable components that greatly decreased development time. Also, Flash Player 6 introduced support for video playback. Flash movies also became more browser-friendly with named anchors that enabled specific sections of Flash movies to be bookmarked. ActionScript continued its development into more of a "real" programming language, as more objects and event handling were exposed in application programming interfaces (APIs). Perhaps most important, Flash Player 6 could integrate with new data transfer methods made available by Flash Remoting MX, which enabled serialized data to move more efficiently from application servers (such as ColdFusion MX) to Flash movies. Flash Communication Server MX 1.0 and 1.5, released shortly after Flash MX, enabled Flash movies to synchronize live data among several connected users simultaneously—developers could create live chat rooms, multiplayer games, and shared whiteboards, just to name a few applications. Flash Communication Server also added the capability to stream live or prerecorded audio/video streams to Flash Player 6.

With all of these capabilities, it's hard to imagine that Macromedia could pack anything else into the Flash authoring environment or the Flash Player. But with the release of Flash MX 2004, Macromedia continued its commitment to pushing the Web to a new definition of excellence. Flash Player 7 was overwhelmingly optimized for speed. Everything from video playback to text rendering to ActionScript performance has been vastly improved over Flash Player 6. This feature alone has encouraged business clients and Web surfers alike to adopt the new player version; everyone loves faster performance. Of course, there was a whole lot more to Flash Player 7. It enabled you to customize the contextual menu (that is, the right-click menu) that's displayed by Flash movies running in the player, and, by default, HTML hyperlinks within Flash text support Open in New Window and Copy Link options in the contextual menu. On the Windows platform, mouse wheel scrolling was now supported for internal Flash elements. Small text sizes could be rendered more cleanly (or crisply). JPEG or SWF content could be loaded and displayed inline with Flash text. Style sheets and CSS files added new formatting options to Flash text, enabling you to share styles from DHTML documents with your Flash content. Video lovers were enticed by the capability to load Flash Video files (.flv) directly into Flash movies, without the use of Flash Communication Server MX. Printing control was far superior in Flash Player 7 and ActionScript with the new `PrintJob` API. Flash MX's UI components had been completely revamped and released as V2 components, and Flash MX Pro 2004 Pro could use Data and Streaming Media components.

Introduce Flash Player 8. Flash Player 8 picks up where Flash Player 7 left off. Flash Player 8 further improves text rendering capabilities with the new FlashType engine. Now you can pull off 8-point type without resorting to a limited range of pixel-based fonts. The new filter and blend modes will revolutionize the visual expressiveness of Flash user interfaces and animated content. The truly amazing On2 VP6 video codec will push more and more Windows Media, QuickTime, and RealOne media producers over to Flash Video. The expanded image file support for runtime loading in ActionScript leaves no excuses for building your own image management utilities in Flash — with Flash Player 8 you can load PNG, JPEG, progressive JPEG, and GIF images into the Flash movie.

In the span of eight years, we have seen an incredible evolution of Flash's predecessor FutureSplash to the most widely installed Web-based plug-in technology today: Flash 8. When Flash 5 was released, Flash was undoubtedly the key for Web branding, and it seemed as though every company wanted Flash content on its Web site. Flash has continued to enjoy this popularity, despite opponents calling the technology "unusable." You could almost compare the introduction of Flash to that of the color television. It's difficult to return to largely static HTML pages after seeing the interactivity, animation, eye candy, and innovation that Flash sites offer to Web surfers — even those on slow connections or portable devices. Because of Macromedia's efforts to keep the file size of the Flash Player smaller than most browser plug-ins, and the fact that it has been preinstalled on most systems for some time now, Flash remains a widely accessible and acceptable technology for Web deployment.

To Flash or not to Flash?

One of the crucial tasks of a Web designer or developer's job is to decide if Flash is the most appropriate tool to achieve the goals of a given project. Consider why you want — or need — to employ Flash in your work, because there are occasions when it may *not* be the best choice. It may not be wise to use this technology merely because it is "the thing to do" or is "cool." If you're pitching Flash projects to clients, it's a good idea to be prepared with reasons why Flash is the best tool to use to get the job done. Later in this chapter, we consider the benefits of other technologies, but for now consider what Flash can (and cannot) offer your projects.

An effective use of Flash

With the Flash 8 authoring tool, you can create a wide range of presentation material or develop fully functional applications that run in a Web browser or on handheld devices:

✦ **Flash generates very small file sizes while producing high-quality animation with optimal sound reproduction.** Even companies making world-renowned cartoons, such as Disney, use Flash for some of their work. Because of their small file sizes, Flash movies (such as cards or announcements) can even be sent via e-mail.

✦ **Nearly any multimedia file format can be integrated into Flash.** Vector images (such as EPS, FreeHand, Illustrator, and PDF files), bitmaps (GIF, PCT, TIF, PNG, and JPG), sound files (such as WAV, AIF, or MP3), and video (such as AVI and MOV) are all importable into your movies. Plug-in technology or third-party software is not required (although it does exist) to accomplish these imports. Nor is it required to play back your movies in Flash Player 8. Significant editing advantages sometimes exist when using imported files, such as symbol and layer formatting from FreeHand and Fireworks files. These features can be beneficial if you will be working with a client's raw resources.

✦ **Precise layouts with embedded fonts are possible with Flash.** Formatting is usually inconsistent when you use HTML to describe page layouts, and formatting can easily vary from one browser to the next. You can be confident your movies will be formatted and displayed consistently when viewed with the Flash Player.

New Feature

Flash Player 8 adds support for crisp-looking text at small point sizes. In previous versions of Flash, most embedded fonts did not display legibly at these sizes. You now have more control over how fonts render at small point sizes.

✦ **Text, movies, images, and sound files can be displayed in your movie from a remote data source.** You can incorporate dynamic content into your movie as long as the data source (such as a database or XML file) can be accessed from your host Web server or application server. Flash Player 8 can consume Web Services directly, allowing you to build B2B (business to business) applications that take advantage of public or private data sources, such as weather reports and stock information.

✦ **Just as you can receive information from a database in your movie, you can send data from your movie to the database.** Flash movies can accept user input and send the data to a server. Built-in components make it easier and faster than ever before to build interactive elements that do not require an advanced knowledge of ActionScript. Your forms have the potential to be much more engaging with animation or sound additions. You can also use this technology to track user progression throughout your site and send the information to a database.

✦ **With the proper server-side software, you can produce multiuser interactivity.** Since Flash 5, you have been able to use XML sockets for transmission of data between a socket server and one or more connected Flash movies. XML operates much faster using Flash Player 6 and higher. Also, with the release of Flash Communication Server MX, developers now have a consistent API to create multiuser applications. Remote Shared Objects, one of the mechanisms employed by Flash Communication Server MX, use an efficient and optimized binary protocol, Real-Time Messaging Protocol (RTMP), to broadcast data updates.

✦ **Several Flash movies can be loaded into one large container movie.** You can create a master Flash movie and then load many Flash assets into it for each individual area of the interface or presentation. Using this method of asset management enables you to delegate tasks in a team production environment, where several designers and developers can work simultaneously. This workflow also enables you to create byte-optimized large Web sites and applications, in which assets are downloaded on an "as needed" basis while the user interacts with the Flash movie.

Tip

Flash Pro 8 features a Project panel that can tap versioning system software such as Microsoft SourceSafe. The Project panel has several file check-in and check-out features that Dreamweaver users will find familiar.

✦ **You can dynamically load images and MP3 files using Flash Player 6 or higher.** These versions of the Flash Player can load standard JPEG image files and progressively download and play MP3 files. Flash Player 7 can also progressively download Flash Video (.flv) files over the standard Web protocol, HTTP. Flash Player 8 can also load progressive JPEG, PNG, and GIF image formats.

Note

A *progressive download* is any file type that can be used before the entire file is actually received by the Flash Player. Progressive downloads are usually cached by the Web browser. You can stream MP3 files with the use of Flash Communication Server MX 1.5. This server uses true streaming of all audio and video content, where nothing is cached by the Flash Player or the Web browser.

✦ **Creating components in Flash 8 enables developers to form reusable template interfaces or assets for Flash movies.** The components that ship with Flash 8 greatly reduce the development time of interfaces that require common UI elements such as text input areas and radio buttons. Components can be easily customized in the Property inspector, and many settings can be changed without the use of ActionScript.

Note

Flash 8 uses the .swc file format for components in Flash documents. Components can be precompiled, which means that you cannot edit their internal elements or code unless you have access to the original source .fla file used to create them.

✦ **The Flash Player is available on many different platforms and devices, including Windows, Macintosh, Solaris, Linux, OS/2, SGI IRIX, Pocket PC, and even some mobile telephones.** Refer to www.macromedia.com/shockwave/download/alternates for the latest version available for these and other alternative platforms. Just about any Web surfer will be able to view Flash content by downloading and installing the latest version of the Flash Player.

✦ **Movies can be developed to run presentations of their own, commonly known as Projectors.** Projectors are Flash movies running from an embedded player, so you do not need a browser to view or use them. They can be burned onto DVDs or CD-ROMs, or saved to any other media-storage device.

✦ **Like HTML pages, content from Flash movies can be sent to a printer.** The PrintJob API in Flash Player 7 or higher ActionScript language offers you the capability to precisely control the layout of the printed page. The quality of the printed artwork and text from Flash movies is remarkable. Unlike previous versions of the Flash Player, you can send multiple pages to the printer at once and create content on the fly for the printed output.

These are only some of the things that Flash movies can do. Regardless of the intent of your production, verifying the use of this software is usually a good idea during preproduction. In the following subsection, we consider situations in which you may not want to use Flash to develop your content.

We'd like to hear how you've come to use Flash technology in your projects. Post your comments at www.flashsupport.com/howdoyouflash.

When not to use Flash

If you're enthusiastic about Flash and have used Flash for previous Web projects, you can easily develop a bias in favor of Flash. It may even be hard to consider that other options could be better for development. Knowing which technology is best for each solution will assist you in offering the best quality products to your clients.

✦ **Flash movies play in a Web browser using a plug-in.** Despite the near ubiquity of the Flash Player, there are still some users who may need to download it. If you're using Flash 8 to create Flash Player 8 movies, many Web visitors trying to view your site may need to update their players. It is also important to keep in mind that some workplaces or institutions (such as schools) will not allow their workers or students to install applications that include plug-ins and ActiveX controls on the systems.

✦ **The type and version of a Web browser can affect the functionality of a Flash movie.** While internal ActionScript code should largely remain unaffected by browser brand and version, some scripting and interactivity with HTML documents (using JavaScript or VBScript) may be browser dependent.

Tip   Later releases of Flash Player 6 and all subsequent releases of the Flash Player now support the WMODE (Window Mode) parameter of Flash content across most browsers—previously, this parameter was only supported by Internet Explorer on Windows. If you've ever seen transparent-background Flash ads that whiz across the browser window, then you're already familiar with the use of the WMODE parameter. For more information on this parameter, read Chapter 38, "Working with Dreamweaver 8," which is included as a PDF file on this book's CD-ROM.

✦ **Web browsers will not automatically redirect to alternative content if the Flash Player is not installed.** You, as a developer, are required to create detection mechanisms for the Flash Player.

New Feature   Flash 8 has an updated detect version option in the Publish Settings. You can learn more about this feature in Chapter 21, "Publishing Flash Movies." To learn how to use this detection feature and other custom detection methods for the Flash Player, refer to Chapter 22, "Integrating Flash Content with Web Pages."

✦ **3D file formats cannot be directly imported or displayed in Flash movies.** To achieve 3D-style effects, frame-by-frame animation or ActionScript is required. Macromedia Director, however, has built-in features for importing, creating, and manipulating 3D content.

Tip   In Chapter 17, "Displaying Video," you learn how a video of a 3D model can be used for 3D-like effects in a Flash Video.

✦ **Typical search engines (or spiders) have a difficult time indexing the content of Flash movies.** When you make Flash-based sites, you should create some alternative HTML content that can be indexed by search engines. If you simply place Flash movies in an otherwise empty HTML document, your Web site will not likely be indexed.

New Feature   Flash 8 enables you to add metadata to your Flash movie files (.swf). This metadata is added in the Document Properties (Modify ⇨ Document) of the Flash document, and can be published with all Flash Player versions of the document. This metadata can be indexed by search engines to provide better placement of your Flash content within search results.

✦ **Flash sites were never meant to completely replace text-based HTML sites.** For sites largely based on textual information with basic or simple graphics, there may be little point to using Flash. Selecting and printing text content from Flash movies is not always as intuitive as that of standard HTML sites. At this time, the Accessibility features of Flash Player 6 and higher are supported only by Internet Explorer for Windows when used in conjunction with a select number of screen readers. A greater number of assistive technologies, however, support HTML pages.

Tip You can add right-click menu support to HTML-styled text containing URL links. For example, this feature of Flash Player 7 and higher movies enables a user to open a link in a new browser window.

✦ **In many circumstances, HTML is quicker, easier, and cheaper to develop than Flash content.** There are many established applications supporting HTML development, and clients can tap an ever-increasing designer and developer base for cheaper and competitive pricing.

Of course, there are always exceptions to any rule, and these suggestions should be considered as guidelines or cautions to be examined before you embark on any Flash development. In the following subsection, we examine other tools used to create multimedia content.

Alternative methods of multimedia authoring

Now let's focus on Flash's competition in the multimedia authoring arena. This section is not intended to give you a comprehensive background on these technologies. Rather, we seek simply to give you some context of Flash as it exists in the rest of the multimedia world.

Dynamic HTML

Dynamic HTML (DHTML) is a specialized set of markup tags that tap into an extended document object model (DOM) that version 4 browsers or higher can use. Using <layer> or <div> tags, you can create animations and interactive effects with Web-authoring tools ranging from Notepad or TextEdit to Macromedia Dreamweaver. You can actually combine Flash content with DHTML to create Flash layers on top of other HTML content. One problem with DHTML is that Netscape and Internet Explorer do not use it in the same way. Usually, you need to make sure you have a specialized set of code (or minor modifications) for each browser type.

Tip Flash Player 7 and higher movies support the use of cascading style sheets (CSS) to share formatting specifications from DHTML pages with Flash text fields. Refer to Chapter 30, "Applying HTML and Text Field Formatting," for an introduction to this feature.

XML and XSL

XML stands for eXtensible Markup Language. XML looks like HTML, but it's really a language that can manage structured or related data, such as pricing information, contact information, or anything else that you would store in a database. XSL stands for eXtensible Stylesheet Language. XSL documents apply formatting rules to XML documents. Together, XML and XSL documents can create interactive data-driven Web sites. While most browsers in use today can read and display XML and XSL documents, some older browsers (prior to 4 browser versions) do not support these formats. The Flash Player can be installed on just about every graphical Web browser available, regardless of the browser's version. As such, you can potentially reach more users with Flash content than you can with XML and XSL content. As you see later in this chapter, XML can also be used to supply data to Flash.

Note   The rise of AJAX, or Asynchronous JavaScript and XML, is enabling non-Flash technologies in the Web browser to provide more seamless Rich Internet Application-like functionality. For more information on AJAX, see the AJAX section at www.flashsupport.com/links.

Macromedia Director

Originally, Macromedia's flagship product, Director, was *the* multimedia powerhouse authoring solution. Since its inception in the 1980s, Director has had the benefit of many years to establish its mature interface and development environment. Director can integrate and control many media types, including video, audio, and entire Flash movies. Director also has an Xtras plug-in architecture, which enables third-party developers to expand or enhance Director's capabilities. For example, you can use an Xtra plug-in to tap hardware-specific input and output, such as a motion detector or pressure-sensitive plate connected to the computer's serial port. More recently, Director 8.5, MX, and MX 2004 have added true 3D modeling support. You can create Shockwave games with textured models and lighting effects! However, there are two major drawbacks to Shockwave Director: It requires a larger download for the full player installation, and the player is available only for Windows and Macintosh platforms. Director remains a popular authoring tool for CD-ROM and DVD-ROM development.

Macromedia Authorware

Authorware, like Flash, was originally a technology developed by another company and then bought by Macromedia to add to its software lineup. Since this acquisition, Macromedia has significantly developed the features and capabilities of Authorware. It is an authoring application and a companion plug-in technology, with similar audio/video integration capabilities as Macromedia Director. However, Authorware was developed with e-learning in mind. You can use it to structure training solutions and monitor student learning. We mention Authorware as a potential competitor to Flash because many Flash developers use Flash to create Web-training modules that interact with server-side databases.

Scalable Vector Graphics

The Scalable Vector Graphics (SVG) format is widely supported by some of the largest names in the industry, such as Microsoft and Adobe. This format has even been approved as a graphics standard for the Web by the World Wide Web Consortium (W3C), whose purpose is to form universal protocols regarding Web standards. SVG is much more than a graphics format; it is also an XML-based development language. Adobe Illustrator 11, GoLive 6, and LiveMotion 1 create files based on this technology. Adobe also creates the plug-in for using this file format on the Web, but the W3C is pushing for all browsers to provide built-in support for the format so that a third-party download is unnecessary. This may be necessary if SVG is ever to become a viable content format because Web surfers have been quite slow to adopt the SVG plug-in. For more information on this topic, you can refer to www.w3c.org/Graphics/SVG and www.adobe.com/svg.

Microsoft PowerPoint

PowerPoint is usually considered a tool for making offline presentations to show in business meetings, conferences, and seminars. What is perhaps not as well-known is how PowerPoint is sometimes used online for presenting such content. A PowerPoint viewer plug-in enables your browser to handle these files, and PowerPoint can export HTML versions of slide shows. While PowerPoint enables anyone from a designer to a programmer to easily create slide-show presentations, Flash can be considered a more robust tool for creating dynamic, high-impact presentations.

SMIL, Real Systems RealPlayer, and Apple QuickTime

SMIL (Synchronized Multimedia Integration Language) also looks a lot like HTML markup tags. SMIL enables you to layer several media components in SMIL-compatible players such as the RealOne Player and the QuickTime Player. You probably have seen SMIL at work when you load the RealOne Player and see the snazzy graphics that compose the channels interface. With SMIL, you can layer interactive buttons and dynamic text on top of streaming video or audio content. You may not even think of SMIL as a competing technology, but rather a complementary one—Flash can be one of the multimedia tracks employed by SMIL! You can even use Flash as a track type in QuickTime, without the use of SMIL. When Flash 4 was released, Macromedia and Apple announced QuickTime Flash movies, which enable you to create Flash interfaces that layer on top of audio-video content. The RealOne Player will also play "tuned" Flash files directly, without the use of SMIL. A tuned Flash file is weighted evenly from frame to frame to ensure synchronized playback. Note, however, that tuned files usually need to be strict linear animations without any interactive functionality.

Note   Several multimedia companies are developing proprietary plug-in-based authoring tools for Web multimedia. To participate in a discussion of multimedia formats, check out the forum at `www.flashsupport.com/mediaformats/`.

Exploring Companion Technologies

Now that you have a clear understanding of how Flash fits into the current World Wide Web, we can begin to discuss the technologies that contribute to Flash's well-being. In today's world of the Web developer, you not only need to know how to create your Flash movies, but also how to implement Flash into existing environments, such as a Web browser or your business client's Web-ready (or not-so-Web-ready) application servers and related data sources.

HTML is here to stay

HTML is not going anywhere, regardless of the prolific nature of Flash on the Web. Using HTML to your advantage is very important because it is undeniably the best solution for certain forms of Web deployment. In addition, sites constructed entirely in Flash often require HTML to function properly. Here's how HTML works with Flash:

✦ **Displaying and formatting the movie on a Web page requires HTML.** It isn't always easy to hand-code HTML to work with ActiveX for Internet Explorer and the plug-in for Mozilla-compatible browsers at the same time.

✦ **Placing some content within a Flash movie is not possible, so you will sometimes need to link it from your movie to an HTML page.** For instance, some PDF files cannot be imported into a Flash 8 document and will need to be linked from the Flash movie to be viewed separately with Acrobat Reader. Or, you may need to access video files created for the RealOne Player or Windows Media Player. You can place links to these source files, or link to an HTML document that embeds the source file.

Tip   If you want to integrate PDF documents with Flash movies, you might want to explore Macromedia FlashPaper. FlashPaper is a Flash movie file (.swf) that contains a document viewer and the document itself, enabling you to embed large print-ready documents on the Web or even within your own Flash movies. For more information on FlashPaper, see the FlashPaper section at `www.flashsupport.com/links`.

✦ **If your end-user is not willing or able to view your Flash content, HTML enables you to provide an alternative version of your Web site.** Despite the addition of accessibility options into Flash Players 6 and 7, which enable screen-reader interaction, not all screen readers are currently able to access this feature. An HTML version of your content is sure to reach most of this potential audience.

Many people find learning, and perhaps even using, HTML to be painful and tedious. Accommodating the differences among browsers can sometimes be time-consuming and dry work. However, knowing some HTML is highly recommended and well worth the effort. HTML should be understood by any Web professional. If you are uncomfortable with the code, using Macromedia Dreamweaver will help your transition into the HTML world.

Client-side scripting using JavaScript

ActionScript and JavaScript are similar beasts, especially since Flash 5 and Flash MX. Flash MX 2004 and Flash 8 have increased the similarity between the two languages, so by learning one language, you will be able to translate this knowledge with relative ease. Already knowing some JavaScript when entering the Flash realm definitely puts you at a strong advantage. However, JavaScript itself is frequently used in conjunction with Flash, as follows:

✦ With JavaScript, you can create customized browser pop-up windows that open from Flash movies. By "customized," we mean browser windows that don't have any scroll bars, button bars, or menu items across the top of the browser window.

✦ JavaScript can pass data into the Flash movie when the Web page containing the movie loads. Some browsers enable you to continually pass data back and forth between Flash and JavaScript. Also, you are able to dynamically pass variables from JavaScript right into the Flash movie.

✦ JavaScript can be used to detect the presence or absence of the Flash Player plug-in in the user's Web browser. Likewise, you can use VBScript on Internet Explorer for Windows to detect the Flash Player ActiveX control. JavaScript (or VBScript) can redirect the Web browser to alternative content if the player is not installed.

✦ Flash movie properties such as width and height can be written on the fly using JavaScript. You can also detect various system properties (which is also possible using ActionScript) in JavaScript code, and pass this information into Flash.

New Feature   Flash Player 8 introduces the new `ExternalInterface` API, which enables you to more easily pass parameters between a Flash movie and JavaScript. For more information on this new functionality, read Chapter 22, "Integrating Flash Content with Web Pages."

The world of Web Services

If you are using Flash Pro 8, you can tap an emerging new world of data transfer directly to your Flash movies. If you've stayed in the loop of Web technologies, you've likely heard of *Web Services*, which is a generic term to describe a standardized approach to transfer data from one Web application to another. Web Services use a format known as Web Services Description Language (WSDL), which uses a type of XML formatting called Simple Object Access Protocol (SOAP). It's not really important to know these acronyms as much as it is to understand what they do. WSDLs (pronounced "whiz-duhls") enable you to share complex data structures in a uniform, standardized manner. As long as a technology such as Flash

Player 7 and higher or ColdFusion MX can interpret a Web Service, it can utilize its data. And because all WSDLs use the same formatting, your Flash movie can easily access data from public services offered by various companies on the Web. Some of these services are free, such as those found at www.capescience.com. Others are more restricted, such as Amazon.com's Web Service program, which is only available to registered associates. You can create your own Web Services with application servers such as Macromedia ColdFusion MX as well. Web Services simply provide a gateway from which your Flash movie can access data over the Internet.

Just about anyone can become an Amazon.com associate. See http://associates. amazon.com for more details about enrolling in Amazon's developer program for Web Services. You don't have to use Amazon.com's Web Service, but it's a fun source of information to keep you engaged while you're learning how to use Web Services with your Flash content.

Don't forget Flash Remoting! Flash Player 6 and higher can send and receive data using Flash Remoting gateways, which can be installed on a variety of application servers. Flash Remoting is built into ColdFusion MX and provides a faster and more efficient means of transferring data between a Flash movie and an application server than Web Services can accomplish.

Macromedia server technologies

Nowadays, it's always helpful to have more than just client-side Flash development skills. With the release of Flash Communication Server MX, Flash Remoting MX, and more recently, Macromedia Flex, more and more business clients are looking for experienced Flash designers and developers to add real-time interactivity to their company's Web sites or Internet-aware applications. Applications created for Flash Communication Server MX use server-side ActionScript (ASC files) to describe and control the interactivity between a Flash movie and the server's resources, including real-time streaming audio/video media and synchronized data updates between multiple Flash clients and the application.

Recognizing Project Potential

In this section, we provide an overview of the categories of Flash projects that you can produce. This is just a starting point to prime your creative juices and break through any self-imposed limiting perceptions that you may have about Flash media. The categories we have devised here are by no means industry standard terms — they're broad, generalized groups into which most Flash development will fall.

Linear presentations

In the early days of Internet growth, Flash shorts (cartoons) were the media buzz. These cartoons generally played from start to finish in a very linear fashion. Generally speaking, these movies load and then play — and count on catching the user's attention through the story and animation. These movies sometimes contain advanced ActionScript for animation, including randomized movement or content.

Note Linear Flash presentations do not necessarily have to be displayed within a Web browser—or even online. Several film-production and advertising companies use Flash to create high-quality animation for use in broadcast TV and feature films.

Interactive presentations

Interactive presentations represent the next step up from linear presentations. They provide the user control over the way information is presented, the flow, or the experience altogether. Usually, Web sites of any construct will be considered an interactive presentation. If you have information or content in a section somewhere in a movie or Web site, then you probably have an interactive presentation. An interactive presentation will enable end-users to choose the content they see, by enabling them to navigate throughout a site, bypassing some content while accessing other content. A Flash movie in this category may have all the content viewed stored in a container movie, or across several Flash files linked to a main site.

Data-driven presentations

The data-driven presentations category of Flash development represents any movies that load external data (either dynamic or static) to deliver the presentation to the user. For example, a weather site that uses Flash may download dynamic Flash graphics of precipitation maps to display to the site's visitors. These graphics may be customized for each user of the site, depending on where he or she lives. *Data-driven* may even simply mean that text information within the Flash movie changes from time to time. Simply put, any time information is separated from the actual Flash movie, you can say it is data-driven.

Data-driven applications (or Rich Internet Applications)

The data-driven applications category is somewhat loosely defined as those Flash movies that enable the user to accomplish some sort of task or enable a transaction from the Flash movie to use an external remote data source. For example, an online Flash ATM (that is, bank machine) could allow a bank customer to log in to the bank's secure server, and transfer funds from one account to another or pay a bill. All of these tasks would require a transaction from the Flash movie to the bank's server. Another example could be an online Flash shopping cart, in which visitors add products to their virtual carts, and check out with their final order. Again, these tasks would require data to be sent from and received by the Flash movie. The term Rich Internet Application, or RIA, was coined during the Macromedia MX product line launch, and implies the use of integrated data and rich media within a graphical user interface (GUI), in or out of a Web browser. Typically, RIAs combine Flash movies with one or more server-side technology, such as Flash Remoting MX and Flash Communication Server MX.

Web Resource We'd like to know what you think about this chapter. Visit `www.flashsupport.com/feedback` to send us your comments.

Summary

✦ Expectations of Web sites produced by Flash developers and designers grow with every new version of Flash. With an ever-increasing list of features and capabilities included with each version of the Flash Player, sites not facilitating new technology (such as new forms of interaction or media content) can easily become overlooked or considered uninteresting.

✦ Flash 8 has many features that make it a vital piece of authoring software for Web sites and applications. Some of the main reasons to use it include small movie file sizes and the capability to integrate rich media content.

✦ There are several multimedia file formats available on the Web today. Although most users have many of the popular plug-ins installed, some users have restricted bandwidth and computer system environments. Flash has the capability to produce small movie files that can play identically across several platforms and devices.

✦ In order to develop advanced Flash projects, you should know the necessary HTML, JavaScript, and data-formatting standards (which now include Web Services) that enable Flash to interact with other environments and data sources. These languages broaden the capabilities for interactivity and access to large amounts of data.

✦   ✦   ✦

Planning Flash Projects

Ｏne of the most important steps — if not *the* most important
step — to producing great Flash content is *knowing* what steps
you'll have to take to move from the concept or idea of the Flash
movie to the finished product. This chapter explores the basics
of Flash production and how to use the Project panel in Flash 8 to
organize your files. Whether you're a freelance Web consultant (or
designer) or a member of a large creative or programming department, knowing how to manage the Flash content production will save
you plenty of headaches, time, and money.

Note   The Project panel is available only in Flash Professional 8 (also known
as Flash Pro 8).

Workflow Basics

No matter what the size or scope, every project in which you choose
to participate should follow some type of planned workflow. Whether
it's for print, film, video, or Web delivery (or all four!), you should
establish a process to guide the production of your presentation.

Before we can explore the way in which Flash fits into a Web production workflow, we need to define a holistic approach to Web
production in general. Figure 3-1 shows a typical example of the
Web production process within an Internet production company.

Note   The phases of production have been coined differently by various
project managers and companies. Some interactive agencies refer
to preproduction as an "architecture phase" or a "planning phase."

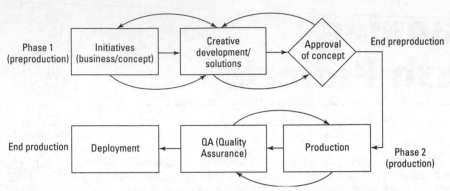

Figure 3-1: Two of the most common phases when generating Web content are preproduction and the actual production phase.

Phase I: Establishing the concept and goals

As a Web developer or member of a creative team, you will be approached by companies (or representatives for other departments) to help solve problems with projects. A problem may or may not be well defined by the parties coming to you. The goal of Phase I is to thoroughly define the problem, offer solutions for the problem, and approve one or more solutions for final production.

Defining the problem

Before you can help someone solve a problem, you need to determine what the problem is and whether there is more than one problem. When we say *problem,* we don't mean something that's necessarily troublesome or irritating. Think of it more as a math problem, where you know what you want — you're just not sure how to get there. When you're attempting to define a client's problem, start by asking them the following questions:

✦ What's the message you want to deliver? Is it a product that you want to feature on an existing Web site?

✦ Who's your current audience?

✦ Who's your ideal audience? (Don't let them say, "Everyone!")

✦ What branding materials (logos, colors, and identity) do you already have in place?

✦ Who are your competitors? What do you know about your competitors?

The next to last question points to a bigger picture, one in which the client may already have several emotive keywords that define their brand. Try to define the emotional heart and feeling of their message — get them to be descriptive. Don't leave the meeting with the words *edgy* or *sexy* as the only descriptive terms for the message.

Tip   Never go into a meeting or a planning session without a white board or a big pad of paper. Documenting everyone's ideas and letting the group see the discussion in a visual format is always a good idea. If all participants are willing, it's often useful to record the meeting with a digital voice recorder or video camera, so that it can be reviewed outside of the meeting. There are also new products on the market that enable you to record every detail of a meeting, such as Macromedia Breeze Live, which enables you to conduct live meetings, as well as record them, over the Internet. Robert often uses his Tablet PC with Microsoft OneNote to record live audio that's synchronized with his notes from the meeting. You can find more information about Macromedia Breeze Live at www.macromedia.com/breeze.

Information Architects

You may have already been bombarded with the idea of *information architecture*. Information architecture is the method by which sought data is represented and structured. Good information architecture is usually equivalent to intuitive user interface design—visitors to a well-organized Web site won't spend much time searching for what they want.

We mention information architecture because the steps in Phase I are similar to the steps that traditional architects take to build a comprehensive design and production strategy *before* they start to build any structure. Although this may seem obvious enough, the sad fact remains that many Internet sites (or projects) are planned as they're constructed. Indeed, we're told that production must move at Internet speed; thus, directives may be given without thorough research into other solutions for a given problem.

You can also start to ask the following technical questions at this point:

✦ What type of browser support do you want to have?

✦ Do you have an idea of a Web technology (Shockwave; Flash; Dynamic HyperText Markup Language, or DHTML; Scalable Vector Graphics, or SVG) that you want to use?

✦ Does the message need to be delivered in a Web browser? Can it be in a downloadable application such as a stand-alone player? A CD-ROM? A DVD?

✦ What type of computer processing speed should be supported? What other types of hardware concerns might exist (for example, hi-fi audio)?

Of course, many clients and company reps look to *you* for the technical answers. If this is the case, the most important questions are

✦ Who's your audience?

✦ Who do you *want* to be your audience?

Your audience determines, in many ways, what type of technology to choose for the presentation. If the client says that Ma and Pa from a country farm should be able to view the Web site with no hassle, then you may need to consider a non-Flash presentation (such as HTML 3.0 or earlier), unless it's packaged as a stand-alone player that's installed with a CD-ROM (provided to Ma and Pa by the client). However, if they say that their ideal audience is someone who has a 56K modem and likes to watch cartoons, then you're getting closer to a Flash-based presentation. If the client has any demographic information for their user base, ask for it up front. Putting on a show for a crowd is difficult if you don't know who's *in* the crowd.

Determining the project's goals

The client or company reps come to you for a reason—they want to walk away with a completed and *successful* project. As you initially discuss the message and audience for the presentation, you also need to get a clear picture of what the client expects to get from you.

✦ Will you be producing just one piece of a larger production?

✦ Do they need you to host the Web site? Or do they already have a Web server and a staff to support it?

✦ Do they need you to maintain the Web site after handoff?

✦ Do they expect you to market the presentation? If not, what resources are in place to advertise the message?

✦ When does the client expect you to deliver proposals, concepts, and the finished piece? These important dates are often referred to as *milestones*. The payment schedule for a project is often linked to production milestones.

✦ Will they expect to receive copies of all the files you produce, including your source .fla files?

✦ What are the costs associated with developing a proposal? Will you do work on speculation of a potential project? Or will you be paid for your time to develop a concept pitch? (You should determine this *before* you walk into your initial meeting with the client.) Of course, if you're working with a production team in a company, you're already being paid a salary to provide a role within the company.

At this point, you'll want to plan the next meeting with your client or company reps. Give them a realistic time frame for coming back to them with your ideas. This amount of time will vary from project to project and will depend on your level of expertise with the materials involved with the presentation.

Creative exploration: Producing a solution

After you leave the meeting, you'll go back to your design studio and start cranking out materials, right? Yes and no. Give yourself plenty of time to work with the client's materials (what you gathered from the initial meeting). If your client sells shoes, read up on the shoe business. See what the client's competitors are doing to promote their message—visit their Web sites, go to stores and compare the products, and read any consumer reports that you can find about your client's products or services. You should have a clear understanding of your client's market and a clear picture of how your client distinguishes their company or their product from their competitors'.

After you (and other members of your creative team) have completed a round of research, sit down and discuss the findings. Start defining the project in terms of mood, response, and time. Is this a serious message? Do you want the viewer to laugh? How quickly should this presentation happen? Sketch out any ideas you and any other member of the team may have. Create a chart that lists the emotional keywords for your presentation.

At a certain point, you need to start developing some visual material that articulates the message to the audience. Of course, your initial audience will be the client. You are preparing materials for them, not the consumer audience. We assume here that you are creating a Flash-based Web site for your client. For any interactive presentation, you need to prepare the following:

✦ An organizational flowchart for the site

✦ A process flowchart for the experience

✦ A functional specification for the interface

✦ A prototype or a series of comps

Tip   You can use tools such as Microsoft Visio (www.microsoft.com/visio) or Omni Group's OmniGraffle for Mac (www.omnigroup.com/applications/omnigraffle). For more information on the *Visio 2003 Bible,* published by Wiley, go to www.flashsupport.com/books/visio.

An *organizational flowchart* is a simple document that describes the scope of a site or presentation. Other names for this type of chart are *site chart, navigation flowchart,* and *layout flowchart.* It includes the major sections of the presentation. For example, if you're creating a Flash movie for a portfolio site, you might have a main menu and four content areas: About, Portfolio, Resumé, and Contact. In an organizational flowchart, this would look like Figure 3-2.

A *process flowchart* constructs the interactive experience of the presentation and shows the decision-making process involved for each area of the site. There are a few types of process charts. A basic process flowchart displays the decisions an end-user will make. For example, what type of options does a user have on any given page of the site? Another type of flowchart shows the programming logic involved for the end-user process chart. For example, will certain conditions need to exist before a user can enter a certain area of the site? Does he have to pass a test, finish a section of a game, or enter a username and password? Refer to Figure 3-3 for a preliminary flowchart for a section of our portfolio Web site. We discuss the actual symbols of the flowchart later in this chapter.

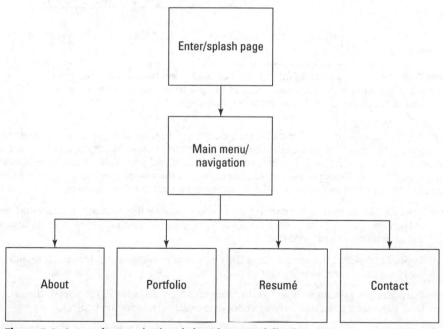

Figure 3-2: A sample organizational chart for a portfolio site

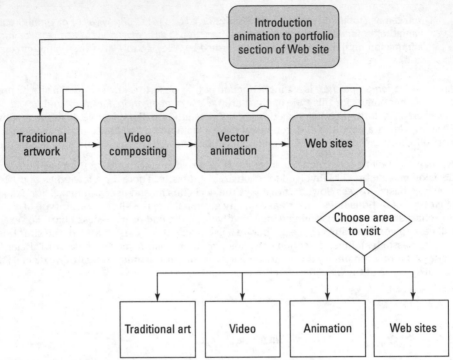

Figure 3-3: The user watches an intro animation and is led through several short subsequent animations detailing each area of the portfolio. The user can then go to an area of his choice after this animation is complete.

A *functional specification* (see Figure 3-4) is a document that breaks down the elements for each step in the organizational and/or process flowchart. This is by far the most important piece of documentation that you can create for yourself and your team. Each page of a functional specification (functional spec, for short) lists all the assets used on a page (or Flash keyframe, Movie Clip) and indicates the following information for each asset:

✦ **Item ID:** This is part of the naming convention for your files and assets. It should be part of the filename, or Flash symbol and instance name. It should also be used in organizational and process flowcharts.

✦ **Type:** This part of the spec defines the name you're assigning to the asset, in more natural language, such as Home Button.

✦ **Purpose:** You should be able to clearly explain why this element is part of the presentation. If you can't, then you should consider omitting it from the project.

✦ **Format:** This column indicates what technology (or what component of the technology) will be utilized to accomplish the needs of the asset. In an all-Flash presentation, list the symbol type or timeline element (frames, scene, nested Movie Clips) necessary to accomplish the goals of the asset.

Project:	Flash interface v2.0		Section:	1 of 5 (Main Menu)
No.	**Type**	**Purpose**	**Content**	**Format**
1.A	Navigation bar	To provide easier access to site content.		A menu bar that is fixed at the top edge of the browser window.
1.A.1	Directory buttons	To provide a means of accessing any of the portfolio sections.	Names each content area. For example: audio, video, graphics, etc.	Horizontal menu list or ComboBox component (skinned).
1.A.2	Home button	Allows user to always get back to the opening page	The text:ì homeî	Button component (skinned).
1.A.3	Search field	To provide a means of entering a specific word or prhase to search site contents.	A white text search field with the word ìsearchî	Flash dynamic text field.
1.A.4	Sign up	Captuers the users email address for a site mailing list.	Text field(s) to enter name and e-mail address.	Button component generating a pop-up. Sign up using ColdFusion.
1.A.5	Back button	Allows the user to see the last page viewed without losing menu items	The textì back.î	Button component (skinned).
1.A.6	Logo or ID	Proives a means of personal branding.	A spider web, with text of the website name in Arial Narrow.	Graphics in Freehand and Flash.

Figure 3-4: This functional spec displays the six components of a Flash-based navigation bar, which will appear on the main menu of our portfolio content site.

Note

Functional specs come in all shapes and sizes. Each company usually has their own template or approach to constructing a functional spec. The client should always approve the functional spec, so that you and your client have an agreement about the scope of the project.

Finally, after you have a plan for your project, you'll want to start creating some graphics to provide an atmosphere for the client presentation. Gather placement graphics (company logos, typefaces, photographs) or appropriate "temporary" resources for purposes of illustration. Construct one composition, or *comp*, that represents each major section or theme of the site. In our portfolio content site example, you might create a comp for the main page and a comp for one of the portfolio work sections, such as "Animation." Don't create a comp for each page of the portfolio section. You simply want to establish the feel for the content you will create for the client. We recommend that you use the tool(s) with which you feel most comfortable creating content. If you're better at using FreeHand or Photoshop to create layouts, then use that application. If you're comfortable with Flash for assembling content, then use it.

Caution   Do not use copyrighted material for final production use, unless you have secured the appropriate rights to use the material. However, while you're exploring creative concepts, use whatever materials you feel best illustrate your ideas. When you get approval for your concept, improve upon the materials that inspired you.

Then you'll want to determine the time and human resources required for the entire project or concept. What role will you play in the production? Will you need to hire outside contractors to work on the presentation (for example, character animators, programmers, and so on)? Make sure you provide ample time to produce and thoroughly test the presentation. When you've determined the time and resources necessary, you'll determine the costs involved. If this is an internal project for your company, then you won't be concerned about cost so much as the time involved — your company reps will want to know what it will cost the company to produce the piece. For large client projects, your client will probably expect a project rate — not an hourly or weekly rate. Outline a time schedule with milestone dates, at which point you'll present the client with updates on the progress of the project.

Exploring the details of the workflow process any further is beyond the scope of this book. However, there are many excellent resources for project planning. One of the best books available for learning the process of planning interactive presentations is Nicholas Iuppa's *Designing Interactive Digital Media* (Butterworth-Heinemann, 1998). We strongly recommend that you consult the *Graphic Artists Guild Handbook of Pricing & Ethical Guidelines* (Graphic Artists Guild, 2003) and the *AIGA Professional Practices in Graphic Design: American Institute of Graphic Arts* (Allworth Press, 1998), edited by Tad Crawford, for information on professional rates for design services.

Approving a final concept and budget

After you have prepared your design documents for the client, it's time to have another meeting with the client or company rep. Display your visual materials (color laser prints, inkjet mockups, and so on), and walk through the charts you've produced. In some situations, you may want to prepare more than one design concept. Always reinforce how the presentation addresses the client's message and audience.

Web Resource   Todd Purgason's tutorial on Flash and FreeHand offers some excellent suggestions for creating high-impact presentation boards in FreeHand and tips on how to reuse graphics in print and Web projects. You can find this archived tutorial online at www.flashsupport.com/archive.

When all is said and done, discuss the options that you've presented with the client. Gather feedback. Hopefully, the client prefers one concept (and its budget) and gives you the approval to proceed. It's important that you leave this meeting knowing one of two things:

✦ The client has signed off on the entire project or presentation.

✦.The client wants to see more exploration before committing to a final piece.

In either case, you shouldn't walk away not knowing how you'll proceed. If the client wants more time or more material before a commitment, negotiate the terms of your fees that are associated with further conceptual development.

Designing for Usability, **by Scott Brown**

As the authors of this book mention earlier in this chapter, the first step in developing a Flash site, or any other type of site, is to define the information architecture. In this tutorial, I'll show you how to define the goals and mission of the site.

Defining the goals and mission of the site

When you define the mission and goals for your project, you lay the foundation upon which to build it. To create a solid project foundation, you must begin by questioning everything, especially the company's business model. Start with these questions:

- ✦ What is the mission or purpose of the organization?

- ✦ Why does this organization want a Web site?

- ✦ Will the Web site support the mission of the organization?

- ✦ What are the short- and long-term goals of the Web site?

- ✦ Who is the intended audience?

- ✦ Why will people come to the site?

- ✦ Is the organization trying to sell a product?

- ✦ What is the product or products?

- ✦ Do we have a unique service?

- ✦ What makes the service different?

- ✦ Why will people come to the site for the first time?

- ✦ Will they ever come back?

- ✦ Why would they come back?

The list of questions can go on forever. After you've gathered a list of questions, you need to get the answers. Ask around the organization, ask your friends, ask strangers, ask anyone. After you've collected the answers, filter through them to create a list of goals based on the responses. From this list of goals, you must further define the answer to the question, "Who is the audience?"

Defining the audience

The audience can be defined as the potential users of the site and their intentions or tasks when they come to your site. Are they kids or adults? Are they Generation X, Y, or Z? Are they into rave music or country music?

So, who is your audience? It's not an easy question because there are so many possibilities. Start with a list of all the possible audiences that the organization would like to reach, and then rearrange the list in a ranking order of most important audience to least important audience. From the audience-ranking list, create a list of the possible goals and needs each audience has.

Creating character scenarios

With the list of possible goals, take the process one step further by creating scenarios for the users. Think of it as writing a screenplay for your Web site. Create multiple characters who represent the majority of the visitors, giving them hobbies, likes, dislikes, and, most important, a task to complete on the site. The object of the scenario game is to get into the characters' heads to learn why and how they would use your site. Approaching the design from their viewpoints makes it easier for you to create a list of the needs and wants of the characters, a wish list if you will.

After you write the scenarios, the next step in the process is to gather the team together and analyze the Web sites of the competition.

Note from the authors: Character scenarios are often referred to as use case scenarios.

Analyzing the competition

Studying the competition gives you the chance to generate a list of the kinds of features they are offering and to determine whether your feature list, the one that you created from the scenarios, is missing anything. If your wish list lacks anything in comparison to your competition, now is a good time to expand the user's functionality requirements, and to return to the scenarios to determine whether the competition's functionality matches your characters' needs. If it does, you should try to elaborate on the competition's functions and create new functions of your own — the classic case of outdoing your competition.

Reaching a consensus on what good design is

At this time in the process, have the team come together to develop a definition of what is "good site design." This step is most beneficial for any contract designer trying to gain an understanding of the client's design viewpoint. To create this ""good design" definition, the team should observe a good number of sites and document everybody's likes and dislikes for each one. This way, everyone on the team will have a better understanding of what to strive for and what to avoid.

Structuring the content

Now you should have several documents to refer to — the project mission statement, the user functionality needs (wish list), and the organization's definition of good design. With these three documents in hand, the next step is to blend them into one master menu of content inventory. Think of each item on this list as a building block. You now have all the blocks needed to construct the site. The only problem is that these blocks are in a big pile and lack organization (structure). Naturally, the next step is to begin creating layouts of the site, providing structure. But before you can begin the page layout process, you need to educate yourself on some Web site usability issues.

Identifying factors of usability

Usability is a much-debated concept, but generally it means creating a site/project/ interface that is functional and that your audience understands. A usable site aims to be a natural extension of a user's expectations and needs. A user-friendly site tries to mirror its structure to that of the user's experience and goals. Just to make the task at hand a little more complex, keep in mind that user expectations learned in other areas of life affect how the user will think your site works. So, how can you design a site to meet your user's expectations? Well, if you did your homework on your audience and wrote the character scenarios, you should have a pretty good idea of the target audience's expectations. Given you know the general background of the user, you could include *metaphors* in the structure of the site. Using metaphors is a great way to help users draw upon knowledge they already have, thereby making the site easier to use. Matching the site structure to the user's experience minimizes the amount of time it takes for the user to learn how to operate or navigate the site. The shorter the learning curve for the site, the better. If you come to a site when you have a specific goal in mind, and it takes you ten minutes to figure out how to achieve your goal, would you call that a positive experience? Most likely not!

Your goal as the designer is to create an attractive site without distracting users from their goals. Forcing users to spend a noticeable amount of time trying to learn how to achieve their goals is very taxing on their patience, and it is a good way to create a negative experience. If you're trying to sell something, chances are you want customers to be happy, not annoyed. One way to make your customers' experience more enjoyable is to make it as easy as possible. So, how do you create a positive experience? Let's start with the most basic of user needs: the ability to navigate.

Users need to know at all times where they are in the site, where they have been, and where they can go. When developing a navigation system, be sure to keep the navigation visually consistent. Inconsistency in the navigation can confuse and frustrate the user. A great concept for a navigational aid is the use of a breadcrumb trail. The breadcrumb system is a visual way to show users the path they took to get to their current position in the site. This navigational convention is used on many resource sites and even in the Flash authoring environment itself — as you click to edit grouped shapes or symbols, the steps you take appear as text labels on the bar above the Stage. Beyond displaying the path of the user, this system gives the user the ability to backtrack to any page displayed in the path. However, remember that navigation is not the goal of the user, only an aid. The user is there to find or buy something; the user is there for the content. So, make the content the first read on all your pages. Navigational elements are there to support the content, not eclipse it.

Of course, navigation isn't the only factor to consider when designing for usability. Other variables, such as the length of text on a page, can affect the usability of a site tremendously. It's a fact that reading text on a monitor is far more taxing on the eyes than reading text on paper. Therefore, people are less inclined to read large amounts of text on the Web. As designers, we must accommodate these changes in reading patterns. Keep these simple guidelines in mind when writing text for the Web. Try to make the text scannable, because readers skim Web content. Bold the important ideas or put key information in bulleted lists. But most of all, keep the text short.

In addition to the treatment of text, there are several other tips to help improve the usability of a site. The concept of redundant links is an excellent method to support users with different backgrounds and goals. With redundant links, a user has more than one way to get to the desired content. The user may have the option to click a text link, a graphic link, or even a text link that is worded differently. Each redundant link should be designed to accommodate a wide range of users. So, where on the page should all these usability elements go?

I can't tell you where you should place your navigation system or your redundant links. However, I can provide you with some information from eye-tracking studies that will help you make an educated decision. Yes, it is true that usability researchers are able to actually monitor and record what you're looking at when you're viewing a Web site. Researchers have found that when a Web page loads, our eyes are looking at the center of the page, then move over to the left, and then sometimes to the right. Of course, these findings are dependent on the user's cultural background. Nevertheless, the scary finding is that the users rarely look to the right! This is most likely because most sites use the right side of the page as a place to add sidebar elements, items of lesser importance. This is also a good example of how a user's experience can affect his future experiences. So, how does Flash fit into Web site usability considerations?

Flash is a great design tool to create amazing interfaces. Flash gives the designer the freedom to create almost anything he desires. But the flexibility Flash gives to the designer is also the tool's greatest weakness from a usability perspective. Flash is great for creating animation; however, inexperienced Web designers can easily go overboard. Just because you can animate an object doesn't mean that you should. The eye is very sensitive to the smallest amount of animation or movement in its peripheral view, pulling the viewers' attention away from the site's main content. On the plus side, animation used as a transitional element is very beneficial for the user. Animated transitions enable the user to follow the navigation process, and gain a better understanding of how the site might work.

Similar to the problem of animation abuse, Flash enables the designers to create their own graphical user interface (GUI) elements. This is great for the designers, but users are often left out in the cold with all this newfound freedom. This design freedom forces the user to learn, almost from scratch, how to operate a scroll bar or a navigation bar. If you recall, I mentioned earlier the importance of a short learning curve for the users. The extreme creative versions of standardized GUI elements might rank high on the "cool" scale, but they really throw a monkey wrench into the user's goal and expectations. GUI standards are developed to help create a consistent experience across all platforms, thereby eliminating any unpleasant surprises. Again, these usability problems can be avoided in Flash if you understand the issues at hand and are able to find solutions based on the set standards.

Other usability issues with Flash arise from the actual plug-in nature of Flash. Unfortunately, because Flash requires a plug-in to work in Web browsers, Flash movies are unable to take advantage of some of the browser's built-in capabilities, such as the Back button and the tool's capability to display history for the links by changing the color of the links that have been clicked. The problem with the browser's Back button is that when a user clicks the button, the browser takes the user back to the previous HTML page, not to the previous state in the Flash movie. It's not a nice surprise for unsuspecting users. One solution to this problem is to pop up the Flash movie in a new browser window (via JavaScript) with all the browser's navigation elements removed (in other words, no toolbar, no location bar, no menus, and so on). No Back button on the browser, no problem right?

Cross-Reference

Fortunately, ActionScript can often smooth out the discrepancies between the default browser behaviors and Flash movie functionality. For an introduction to some ActionScript solutions, refer to Part VI, "Distributing Flash Movies."

Tip Named anchor keyframes, available in Flash Player 6 or higher movies, is a feature that makes it easier for users to navigate a Flash movie. For an example of named anchors in action, refer to Chapter 20, "Making Your First Flash 8 Project."

Building mockups of the site

You are now ready to begin mocking up the site structure using index cards, sticky notes, and other common office supplies. Creating these paper mockups saves the development team a large amount of time. The beauty of the paper mockups is that you can quickly create a navigational system and find the major flaws without spending long hours developing a beautiful rendering of a structure that may be flawed. There is nothing worse than spending months developing a product with a faulty structure only to discover the mistake just before launch!

Testing the site on real users

Testing the site is the most important step in creating a usable site. The key to testing the site is *not* to test it on people in the organization, but to test it on people in the target audience. Test the site on the real users. It's usually easier to test the site by using people who are familiar with the project. The problem with that practice is that the people are familiar with the project. You want to test fresh eyes and minds in order to get optimum feedback. For testing purposes, create a list of several tasks to complete on the site. The tasks should be pulled from the list of possible users' goals defined in the early steps of the project. As the test subjects navigate through your project, pay close attention to how long it takes them. How many times did they have to click to find what they were looking for? How many had to resort to using a search feature (or wished that they could)? What elements seemed to cause confusion or delay? What elements attracted or held the users' attention? After each test subject has completed a task, or tried, give her a post-task questionnaire with questions such as:

"How would you rate the quality of the content on this site?"

Unacceptable −3 −2 −1 0 1 2 3 Excellent

Also, leave some room for the test subject to elaborate on the questions. After the testing is finished, review your findings and determine what needs to be fixed. After the problems are fixed, test the site again, but on new users. Repeat the process until you have a product that meets the defined goals of the organization and the users. Keep asking yourself this question: Is the interface helping the users accomplish their goals? When all else fails, you can always depend on the greatest guideline of the century: keep it simple. Oh, how true.

Tip If this process is new to you, don't waste time "reinventing the wheel" when there are plenty of resources on this topic that can get you started. Jakob Nielsen has achieved near-celebrity status as a result of his strong opinions on this topic and has written several books that some consider definitive. Steve Krug has written another popular book on this topic, with a forward by Roger Black, entitled *Don't Make Me Think: A Common Sense Approach to Web Usability, Second Edition* (New Riders Press, 2005). For more information on this book, see www.flashsupport.com/books/krug.

Phase II: Producing, testing, and staging the presentation

When your client or company executives have signed off on a presentation concept, it's time to rock and roll! You're ready to gather your materials, assemble the crew, and meet an insane production schedule. This section provides a brief overview of the steps you need to take to produce material that's ready to go live on your Web site.

Assembling assets

The first step is to gather (or start production of) the individual assets required for the Flash presentation. Depending on the resources you included in your functional spec and budget, you may need to hire a photographer, illustrator, animator, or music composer (or all four!) to start work on the production. Or, if you perform any of these roles, then you'll start creating rough drafts for the elements within the production. At this stage, you'll also gather high-quality images from the client for their logos, proprietary material, and so on.

Making the Flash architecture

Of course, we're assuming that you're creating a Flash-based production. All the resources that you've gathered (or are working to create) in Phase 1 will be assembled into the Flash movie(s) for the production. For large presentations or sites, you'll likely make one master Flash movie that provides a skeleton architecture for the presentation, and use `loadMovie()` to bring in material for the appropriate sections of the site.

Before you begin Flash movie production, you should determine two important factors: frame size and frame rate. You don't want to change either of these settings midway through your project. Any reductions in frame size will crop elements that weren't located near the top-left portion of the Stage — you'll need to recompose most of the elements on the Stage if you used the entire Stage. Any changes in your frame rate will change the timing of any linear animation and/or sound synchronization that you've already produced.

Staging a local test environment

As soon as you start to author the Flash movies, you'll create a local version of the presentation (or entire site) on your computer, or a networked drive that everyone on your team can access. The file and folder structure (including the naming conventions) will be consistent with the structure of the files and folders on the Web server. As you build each component of the site, you should begin to test the presentation with the target browsers (and Flash Player plug-in versions) for your audience.

HTML page production

Even if you're creating an all-Flash Web site, you need a few basic HTML documents, including:

✦ **A plug-in detection page** that directs visitors without the Flash Player plug-in to the Macromedia site to download the plug-in.

✦ **HTML page(s) to display any non-Flash material** in the site within the browser.

You will want to construct basic HTML documents to hold the main Flash movie as you develop the Flash architecture of the site.

Staging a server test environment

Before you can make your Flash content public, you need to set up a Web server that is publicly accessible (preferably with login and password protection) so that you can test the site functionality over a non-LAN connection. This also enables your client to preview the site remotely. After quality assurance (QA) testing is complete (the next step that follows), you'll move the files from the staging server to the live Web server.

We've noticed problems with larger .swf files that weren't detected until we tested them from a staging server. Why? When you test your files locally, they're loaded instantly into the browser. When you test your files from a server — even over a fast DSL (digital subscriber line) or cable modem connection, you have to wait for the .swf files to load over slower network conditions. Especially with preloaders or loading sequences, timing glitches may be revealed during tests on the staging server that were not apparent when you tested locally.

Tip   You should use the Simulate Download feature of the Bandwidth Profiler in the Test Movie environment of Flash 8 to estimate how your Flash movies will load over a real Internet connection. See Chapter 21, "Publishing Flash Movies," for more discussion of this feature.

Quality assurance testing

In larger corporate environments, you'll find a team of individuals whose sole responsibility is to thoroughly test the quality of a nearly finished production (or product). If you're responsible for QA, then you should have an intimate knowledge of the process chart for the site. That way, you know how the site should function. If a feature or function fails in the production, QA reports it to the creative and/or programming teams. QA teams test the production with the same hardware and conditions as the target audience, accounting for variations in:

✦ Computer type (Windows versus Mac)

✦ Computer speed (top-of-the-line processing speed versus minimal supported speeds, as determined by the target audience)

✦ Internet connection speeds (as determined by the target audience)

✦ Flash Player plug-in versions (and any other plug-ins required by the production)

✦ Browser application and version (as determined by the target audience)

Web Resource   It's worthwhile to use an online reporting tool to post bugs during QA. Many companies use the open source (freeware) tool called Mantis, a PHP/MySQL solution. You can find more information about Mantis at www.mantisbt.org/. Another popular bug reporting tool is Bugzilla (www.bugzilla.org).

After QA has finished rugged testing of the production, pending approval by the client (or company executives), the material is ready to go live on the site.

Maintenance and updates

After you've celebrated the finished production, your job isn't over yet. If you were contracted to build the site or presentation for a third party, you may be expected to maintain and address usability issues provided by follow-ups with the client and any support staff they might have. Be sure to account for periodic maintenance and updates for the project in your initial budget proposal. If you don't want to be responsible for updates, make sure you advise your clients ahead of time to avoid any potential conflicts after the production has finished.

You should have a thorough staging and testing environment for any updates you make to an all-Flash site, especially if you're changing major assets or master architecture files. Repeat the same process of staging and testing with the QA team that you employed during original production.

You can find an online archived PDF version of Eric Jordan's tutorial, "Interface Design," on the book's Web site at www.flashsupport.com/archive. This tutorial was featured in the *Flash MX Bible* (Wiley, 2002).

Using the Project panel in Flash Professional 8

In this final section of the chapter, we'll show you how to use the Project panel in Flash Pro 8 using some sample files we provide on this book's CD-ROM. You'll jump right into the Project panel, so you may want to review some of the content in the Help panel of Flash 8 before proceeding. The Using Flash ➪ Working with Projects section in the Help panel (Help ➪ Flash Help) contains useful information about the Project panel.

Before you start using the Project panel, consider a scenario in which you would *want* to use the feature. The Project panel lets you organize and group all of the files related to a Flash production. You can include any file type you want in the Project panel. All of the asset names and locations are stored in a Flash Project file, which uses an .flp file extension. This file is essentially an .xml file that describes the files you want to manage.

Once you've created a Flash Project file, you can quickly open any document directly in Flash or another application. You can publish one or more Flash documents in the project. But more important, you can use the Project panel to directly upload content to your FTP server or a local network server. The Project panel can check in and check out files, so that other members on your team know that you're working on them.

The Project file is linked to a *site definition* in the Project panel. The site definition is exactly the same site you may have created in Macromedia Dreamweaver. If you've made a site in Dreamweaver, it's automatically available in Flash 8 as well.

One important factor to keep in mind when you use the Project panel is that you should only open a local copy of the project's files on your computer. In this way, everyone working on the project has his or her own copy of the files. One member of the team can be editing, implementing, and testing changes while other members are doing the same with their copies. When a member is done editing a file, she can check the file back into the server.

Unless you're implementing a version control system with your project files, you should *not* edit the same file that another person is using. Currently, Flash Pro 8 only ships with support for Microsoft SourceSafe, a version control product. You can develop your own plug-in, though, for your particular version control product. Version control systems can merge changes to the same document. For example, if two people edit the same ActionScript document (.as file), the version control system merges the changes into one file and even flags potential conflicts during the process. The Project panel cannot perform this type of merge without the assistance of a separate software product such as SourceSafe. Also, it's important to note that version control software cannot merge changes in two Flash documents (.fla files) because such files are binary, not ASCII (or Unicode). Usually, version control systems can only merge text documents.

Here's a quick review of the procedures you follow:

1. Establish a site definition in Flash Pro 8. This definition describes where you'll store your local copy of the project files, and where to upload the master copies of the project.

2. Add the files to the Flash Project file in the Project panel of Flash Pro 8.

3. Open, edit, and test one of the sample files.

4. Create a new blank document to add to the project.

5. Publish an entire project.

The headings that follow elaborate on these five steps, and include the step numbers for easy reference.

1. Establishing a project and a site

Before you can start making or editing documents in Flash Pro 8 for a project, you need to define a site that the Project panel can use. In this section, you learn how to define a site and establish a local mirror copy of your site's files on your machine.

1. On your computer, choose a location that you can use to store all of the files with a project. For example, if you're on Windows, you can create a folder named Sites at the root of your C drive. If you're on a Mac, you can create a folder named Sites at the root of your startup drive, such as Macintosh HD.

2. Inside of the Sites folder, copy the robertreinhardt.com folder from the ch03/ starter_files folder located on this book's CD-ROM. As shown in Figure 3-5, the robertreinhardt.com folder has two subfolders, dev and prod.

   The dev folder, short for *development*, will contain any source files, specifications, planning documents, raw assets (images, video, and sound), and so on. The fla folder inside of the dev folder holds all Flash documents (.fla files) for the project.

   The prod folder, short for *production*, will contain any and all files that will be part of the final application, as a publicly accessible Web site or application. The prod folder has only one nested folder, wwwroot, for this example. The wwwroot folder holds the files that will be uploaded to the public root folder of your Web server. These files are also called *runtime* files, as they will run in the Flash Player and Web browser from the live Web site. All of the Flash movies (.swf files), runtime assets (JPEGs, MP3s, FLVs, and so on), and HTML documents will be kept here. The copy of wwwroot from the CD-ROM includes several subfolders to store external assets necessary for the Flash movie (.swf file) at run time.

Tip   The prod folder can also contain other folders, such as a Flash Communication Server applications folder or a database folder, which holds other assets related to services available on your Web server.

Figure 3-5: The layout of folders for a site named robertreinhardt.com

3. Now you're ready to create a Flash Project file to put into the project folder you created in the last step. Open Flash Professional 8. Choose Window ➪ Project (Shift+F8).

4. Click the Create a new project link in the Project panel (shown in Figure 3-6).

Figure 3-6: The Project panel

5. In the New Project dialog box, browse to the `robertreinhardt.com` folder on your computer. Save a new project file named `reinhardt_site.flp` in this location, as shown in Figure 3-7.

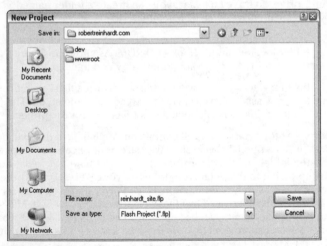

Figure 3-7: The New Project dialog box

6. With a project file created, you're ready to define a site in Flash Pro 8. In the Project panel, click the Version Control button, which features an icon of two arrows pointing in opposite directions. In this menu, choose the Edit Sites option, as shown in Figure 3-8.

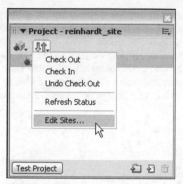

Figure 3-8: The Version Control menu

7. In the Edit Sites dialog box, you may see other sites already defined (as shown in Figure 3-9). If you use Macromedia Dreamweaver, you can use these sites, or create a new site for the project. For this example, create a new site by clicking the New button.

Figure 3-9: The Edit Sites dialog box

8. In the Site Definition dialog box, specify a name for the site such as `robertreinhardt.com`. Most important, specify the path to the `robertreinhardt.com/prod/wwwroot` folder in the Local Root field, as shown in Figure 3-10. For the Email and Check Out Name fields, type your own information. In the Connection parameters, you must decide how you will connect to the testing (or live) server that will host the "master" copy of all project documents. You can use a location that's accessible via FTP, the local network, or a SourceSafe database. This location also stores the lock files (.lck files) necessary for members in your team to check in and check out documents. When you're finished specifying the connection details, you may want to click the Test button to make sure that Flash Pro 8 can connect to the location. Click OK to close the dialog box, and click the Done button in the Edit Sites dialog box.

Note   The Connection parameters shown in Figure 3-10 are for demonstration purposes only. These parameters will not connect to an actual FTP site. If you use an FTP connection, make sure that the FTP Directory field specifies the path to the public HTML or Web folder for the site. The public Web folder of your server will vary depending on your server's operating system and Web server software. Also, with the `dev` and `prod` folder setup for this example, only the files in the `wwwroot` folder can be checked in and out. If you want to be able to check in and out files in the `dev` folder, you need to make sure that your local and remote folders have identical folder hierarchies.

Figure 3-10: The Site Definition dialog box

9. Now, you'll link the newly defined site to your `reinhardt_site.flp` project file. Right-click (or Control+click on Mac) the `reinhardt_site` file in the Project panel, and choose Settings. In the Project Settings dialog box, choose `robertreinhardt.com` in the Site menu. Refer to Figure 3-11. Click OK to close the dialog box.

Figure 3-11: The Project Settings dialog box

2. Adding files to the project

After you've created a Flash Project file and defined a site for the project, you're ready to start adding files to the project.

1. Begin the process of re-creating the folder structure of the local site folders in the `reinhardt_site.flp` project file. In the Project panel, click the Add Folder icon at the lower-right corner of the panel. Name the first folder `dev`. Repeat this process until you have created all the folder names you had in the local `robertreinhardt.com` folder, including the subfolders. When you are finished, you should have the same folder structure shown in Figure 3-12.

Caution   Unlike Macromedia Dreamweaver, the Flash Project panel does not automatically create a folder structure for the defined site. You must create each folder in the Project panel, and add individual files.

Figure 3-12: The folder structure of the site within the project file

2. Select the fla folder you created in the last step, and click the Add File button in the lower-right corner of the Project panel. Browse to the Sites ➪ robertreinhardt.com ➪ dev ➪ fla folder and select the bio_100.fla file located there. Repeat this process for all of the files contained in the robertreinhardt.com folder. Do not add the reinhardt_site.flp file itself. When you are finished, your Project panel should resemble Figure 3-13.

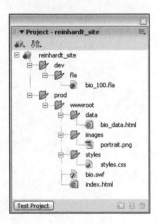

Figure 3-13: The folder and document structure of the site within the project file

3. It's highly likely that you'll have more than one Flash document (.fla file) in a project. As such, you should define the default document for the project. This file should be the master file, the one "most in charge" per se. This could be the Flash document that controls the loading of other runtime assets or the document that contains the most code. In the dev folder of the Project panel, right-click (or Control+click on the Mac) the bio_100.fla document and choose Make Default Document in the contextual menu. The icon of the document should change to a downward-pointing green arrow.

3. Committing and editing files in the project

Once you have added files to your project, you should commit the files to your testing server. In this section, you learn how to commit project files and how to open and edit documents from the Project panel.

1. When you are finished creating folders and adding files to your Flash Project file, you should check in the runtime files to your remote testing server. You can do this procedure only if you have defined a site for the project file. Choose the wwwroot folder in the Project panel. Right-click (or Ctrl+click on the Mac) the folder, and choose Check In. Flash Pro 8 then connects to your remote server and checks in the nested files and folders within the wwwroot folder. When the files and folders have been successfully checked in, a lock appears next to them (see Figure 3-14).

2. When you're ready to edit a specific file in Flash Pro 8, right-click (or Control+click on the Mac) the file in the Project panel and choose Check Out in the contextual menu. Try this step with the bio.swf document. Once you have checked out this file, double-click its corresponding .fla file, bio_100.fla, to edit it in the Flash authoring environment.

Note   When you have checked out a file, you'll see a green check mark next to the file icon. Other members of your team subscribed to the same project will see a lock next to the same file in their Project panels. If you don't check out the .swf file associated with a .fla file, you will not be able to publish or test the Flash movie (.swf file).

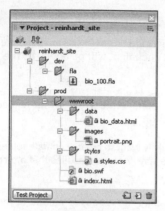

Figure 3-14: A file that is checked in displays a lock icon.

3. With `bio_100.fla` open, take a look at how the `bio.swf` file (located in the `wwwroot` folder) is published. Choose File ➪ Publish Settings. In the Formats tab, notice that relative paths are declared for the `bio.swf` and `index.html` files (see Figure 3-15) in the Flash and HTML fields, respectively. The `../../prod/wwwroot/` prefix tells Flash 8 to publish these files two folders above the `fla` folder, inside of the `prod/wwwroot` folder. Click Cancel to close the dialog box. Leave `bio_100.fla` open for the next series of steps in the following section.

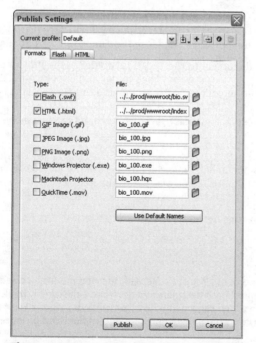

Figure 3-15: You can publish files with relative paths in the Formats tab.

4. Adding new files to the project

In this section, you learn how to create a new ActionScript document (.as) using code extracted from the bio_100.fla document. This ActionScript document will be added to the project file as well.

1. From your desktop, browse to the location of the fla folder (for example, C:\Sites\ robertreinhardt.com\dev\fla). At this location, create a new folder named includes. This folder will be used to store ActionScript files.

Note

If you're writing ActionScript 2.0 class files, you'd likely want to create separate folders in the fla folder to store them. The includes folder is specifically for .as files that are compiled into your Flash movie via the #include directive.

2. In Flash Professional 8, add the same folder name (includes) as a child of the fla folder in the Project panel.

3. From the Flash 8 main menu bar, choose File ➪ New. In the General tab of the New Document dialog box, choose ActionScript File and click OK. When the new document opens, save the empty file as functions.as in the includes folder you created in Step 1. Leave the functions.as document open.

4. Go back to the bio_100.fla document. In the Timeline window, select frame 1 of the actions layer and open the Actions panel (F9, or Option+F9 on Mac). Select lines 1–78 and press Ctrl+X or ⌘+X to cut the code from the frame. Be sure to leave the init(); line of code in the actions list.

5. Switch back to the functions.as document, and choose Edit ➪ Paste (Ctrl+V or ⌘+V) to move the code into the document. Save and close the functions.as document.

6. Now, add the functions.as document to the includes folder of the Project panel. Right-click (Control+click on the Mac) the includes folder and choose Add File. Browse to the includes folder on your local drive, and add the functions.as file.

Caution

Changes to a Flash Project file are automatically saved. As such, be careful whenever you modify the project contents.

7. Go back to the bio_100.fla document, and select frame 1 of the actions layer and open the Actions panel (F9, or Option+F9 on Mac). Add the following line of code at the top of the Script pane (line 1), above the existing init(); line of code:

```
#include "includes/functions.as"
```

This directive tells Flash 8 to insert the contents of the functions.as document at the time of publishing or testing.

Tip

Notice that we don't include the functions.as file with the runtime files located within the wwwroot folder. Many beginner Flash designers and developers mistakenly think that .as files should be uploaded to a live Web server with the other runtime files of a Flash project. Any .as file you use with a Flash document is automatically compiled and included in the .swf file that references it.

8. Save and close the bio_100.fla document.

5. Publishing the entire project

In this final section, you'll learn how to test an entire project, and upload the updated runtime files to your testing server.

1. Before you can publish or test the project, you'll need to unlock the files that will be published by Flash: `bio.swf` and `index.html`. Check out these files in the `wwwroot` folder of the Project panel.

2. Click the Test Project button in the lower-left corner of the Project panel. Flash Pro 8 will publish all of the Flash documents (.fla files) in the project file. In our example, there's only one .fla file, `bio_100.fla`. The newly published `bio.swf` file, located in the `wwwroot` folder, then opens in the Test Movie environment.

3. If everything is working correctly, check in the `bio.swf` and `index.html` documents. If there was an error during testing, double-check the code added in the last section for syntax errors. The Output panel will likely provide clues about any errors associated with improper URLs for runtime assets.

You can find the final site files in the `ch03/final_files` folder of the *Flash 8 Bible* CD-ROM. If you try to open the `reinhardt_site.flp` document from the CD-ROM (or a copy of it), you'll likely need to relink the documents to the locations of the copies on your system.

We'd like to know what you think about this chapter. Visit `www.flashsupport.com/feedback` to send us your comments.

Summary

✦ Your clients rely on you to understand and guide the production process involved with Flash content creation.

✦ Careful planning helps you to create Flash solutions that best meet the goals of your project. The technical issues, such as usability, target audience, and delivery platform, should be balanced with the aesthetic aspects of experience design.

✦ To structure the development of Flash projects, many Web developers use a two-phase production model that involves six milestones: Business Initiative, Creative Solutions, Approval, Production, QA, and Delivery.

✦ During the production period, it is helpful to keep six key concepts in mind: asset assembly, a master Flash architecture, a local test environment, HTML page layout, a server staging environment, and proper QA testing. After production is finished, you also need to devise a strategy for systematic maintenance.

✦ You can use the Project panel in Flash Professional 8 to manage all of the Flash documents for a site or application.

✦   ✦   ✦

Mastering the Flash Environment

When you're ready to jump in and get started on the road to efficient and painless production, this section will give you all the information you need to feel comfortable in the Flash authoring environment. Chapter 4 introduces you to the Flash workspace and gives you tips for customizing the UI. You will learn the difference between a window and a panel and discover some of the time-saving features that have been added to Flash 8. Chapter 5 is where you'll find coverage of all the Flash drawing and selection tools, including an explanation of the new Object Drawing mode. You'll also learn how to control snapping behavior and how to create and edit groups. In Chapter 6, you'll find out what makes Flash so much more powerful than simple vector graphics programs. Symbols and symbol instances are the basis for all optimized Flash projects and the Library gives you all the options you'll need to keep your project assets organized. Chapter 7 includes coverage of color issues specific to Web production and explains how to use the Color Swatches and Color Mixer panels to enhance your projects with custom colors, gradients, bitmap fills, and more. Chapter 8 guides you through the various options for creating and editing text in Flash, including Dynamic and Input text and vertical text and the new anti-alias settings. You will also learn how to control font display and find out how to create and use font symbols. Finally, in Chapter 9, you will be introduced to the more advanced tools for editing graphics and text in Flash, including the Free Transform and Gradient Transform tools.

Interface Fundamentals

This chapter gives you a tour of the Flash workspace and the various methods for organizing and navigating your documents. We define fundamental features of the authoring environment, but in some cases, defer the explanation of more-complex functionality to later chapters. This chapter orients new users to the program and introduces experienced users to some of the new Flash 8 features.

Cross-Reference

As we discussed in the Preface of this book, Flash is available in two versions: Flash Basic 8 and Flash Professional 8. We outline the specific differences between the two versions in Chapter 1, "Understanding the Flash 8 Framework." All of the features available in Flash Basic 8 are also available in Flash Professional 8, but many of the new features that have been added to the latest release are only available in Flash Professional 8.

Note

From the authors' perspective, there is not much incentive to upgrade from Flash MX 2004 unless you can take advantage of the new features in Flash Professional 8. With this in mind, we wrote this version of the book from the perspective of using the Professional, or "full," version of Flash. If you're working with the Basic version and you don't find a feature described in the book or demonstrated in an exercise, you may want to download the trial version of Flash Professional 8 from Macromedia's Web site. In all other cases, assume that the interface feature or functionality we describe in this chapter (or elsewhere in the book), applies in both versions of the program.

Getting Started

When you walk into a studio, the first thing you need to know is where to find your tools. Although you might have an idea of where to start looking based on experience, nothing improves your workflow more than being able to reach for something without hesitation. This kind of familiarity and comfort in a workspace is a prerequisite for the mastery of any craft.

Fortunately, many of the features of the Flash 8 interface will look familiar to you if you've worked in other graphics applications.

However, there are many unique features that you will need to understand before you can tackle your Flash projects with the ease of an expert. We begin by introducing the Flash interface and pointing out the tools available for managing and customizing your Flash "studio." We've done our best to keep new terminology consistent with the interface. Where inconsistencies occur, we've tried to choose terms most consistent with other Macromedia products and documentation.

Note   In an effort to maintain consistent terms and UI names across the various programs in the Studio 8 family, Macromedia has changed some familiar terms and added some new ones. In some cases, changes to a UI term may not be implemented consistently in all menus, dialog boxes, and Help documents—we hope the context of the term will give you enough clues to sort out what it refers to. Rest assured that you're not imagining things: Like most software, Flash just has a few growing pains with each new version.

You'll soon notice that there is often more than one way to access an option. As we describe the steps for carrying out a task, we include shortcut keys or menu paths in parentheses. You should feel comfortable and ready to get to work in no time.

Welcome to Flash Basic 8 and Flash Professional 8

Whether you've been using Flash since the early days of version 2, or you've just opened the program for the first time, you'll quickly see that the Flash interface has finally matured — enough to remain recognizable from one release to another! As Flash has grown and evolved, the interface has been through a number of variations, but Flash 8 continues to build upon the streamlined panel system that was introduced with Flash MX. One of the most obvious UI changes in version 8 is the option to use tabbed panels on the Mac side. Some small but significant modifications have also been made to the look and function of common tools, menus, and panels. We will cover them as we discuss workflows for specific tasks throughout the book.

The core interface is consistent between Basic 8 and Professional 8 — but the feature differences between the Basic version and the Professional version are more significant in Flash 8 than they were in Flash MX 2004. Even if you are new to Flash and you plan to work mainly with the design and graphics side of the program, you will miss the best new features if you go with the Basic version. Macromedia focused on expressiveness as much as on efficiency in this release, and as a result, Flash 8 should help users at all levels be creatively inspired. Some of the most significant changes to Flash 8 are hinted at in the interface, but we'll give you a peek under the hood in this chapter.

Tip   Want to know more about "expressiveness"? Search for it in the Flash Help panel with the menu set to "All books."

Start Page

The Start Page gives you quick access to tutorials and other help features and provides a handy way to choose the file you want to open or create. The Start Page shown in Figure 4-1 is for the Flash Professional 8 version. The Start Page for Flash Basic 8 will show fewer file types in the Create New list, but still functions as a quick access point to recent items, templates, and Macromedia resources.

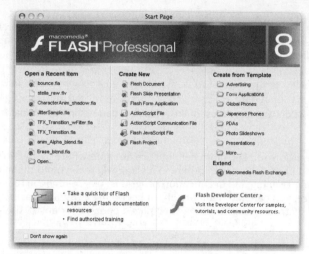

Figure 4-1: The Start Page provides quick access to file lists, templates, and resource links.

Note   The other Macromedia applications in the Flash 8 Studio suite use a similar Start Page.

New Feature   Flash content for mobile phones is increasingly popular, and Macromedia supports developers with a whole suite of new templates designed specifically for phones.

By default, the Start Page should appear when you first launch Flash and any time you close all Document windows while the program is running. After you have opened or created a new file, the Start Page automatically closes to make room on your desktop. If you prefer not to use the Start Page, select the Don't show again check box at the bottom of the panel, or change the settings for On launch in General Flash Preferences (Edit ➪ Preferences or Flash ➪ Preferences). This leaves you with the more limited, but familiar, option of using the application File menu (or shortcut keys) to create and open files.

The links at the bottom of the Start Page connect you to the built-in Help system in Flash as well as to online content available through the Macromedia Web site. These links are worth investigating if you want to get a quick introduction to Flash:

✦ **Take a quick tour of Flash:** This link launches your default Web browser and loads an orientation presentation from Macromedia. The presentation includes audio and images, so make sure you have your speakers or your headphones on when you connect.

Web Resource   You don't need to have Flash installed to view this presentation. If you would like to introduce other friends or co-workers to the new features of Flash 8, you can direct them to the presentation online at `www.macromedia.com/software/flash/flashpro/productinfo/features/`.

✦ **Learn about Flash documentation resources:** This link directs you to the support section of Macromedia's Web site. The documentation for Flash has grown with each release and the support site is a good way to find your way through the online manuals, tutorials, and example files available for Flash users at different levels.

Web Resource

You do need to be connected to the Internet to access Macromedia's support site: `www.macromedia.com/support/documentation/(language)/flash`, but once you get there you have the option of downloading most of the reference manuals in PDF format for future reference.

✦ **Find authorized training:** Do you need more help but are not sure where to start? Do you have skills that you'd like to share with others? This link will take you to the main info site for Macromedia's Training and Certification programs: `www.macromedia.com/support/training`. Here, you can find out more about becoming a training partner, find books and certified instructors, or download self-paced courses for any of the Studio 8 applications.

One of the most useful links in the Start Page is to Macromedia Flash Exchange (under the Extend title). If you are connected to the Internet, you can browse the Flash Exchange for helpful tools and add-ons that Flash developers have made available through Macromedia's site.

Help menu options

The Flash Help menu is your gateway to local versions of the documentation and examples on Macromedia's support site. The tabbed interface introduced in Flash MX 2004 has been dropped in favor of a centralized list. Rather than clicking back and forth between two different Help modes, you can now browse or search a listing of available Help topics and use the new drop-down menu to choose the "books," or categories of Help content, you want to view. An accordion divider separates the main reference content from the table of contents (or book listings) that will expand or collapse to show sublistings as you use the control icons at the top of the panel. You can also navigate books and subcategories using the expand and collapse arrows on the left edge of the book list. To adjust the division of the book list and the content area (shown in Figure 4-2), simply hover over the dividing line until you see a dual arrow cursor; then drag the divider until you're happy with the panel split.

If you don't want to muddle around in the Help panel, the Flash application Help menu offers quick shortcuts to commonly used reference content. Unless you've removed the help files from your Flash installation, you can access a number of offline resources directly from the Help menu. These resource topics will launch the Help panel and load the offline HTML content you have requested. First, have a look at the What's New in Flash 8 link to get an overview of the new features. Next, if you're a new user, you may want to browse the tutorial content for general Flash tasks under Getting Started with Flash.

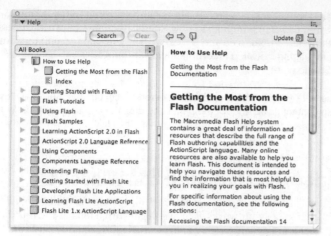

Figure 4-2: The streamlined Flash 8 Help panel includes a drop-down menu to help you sort a list of reference categories or "books," and a search field to find content on specific topics.

Here is a summary list of the reference options available from the main Help menu:

✦ **Help ➪ Flash Help:** Opens the Help panel. Set the drop-down menu to show All books to browse through a comprehensive list of help topics, or use the Search button to find a specific term or task.

✦ **Help ➪ Getting Started with Flash:** Opens the Help panel at the beginning of a comprehensive series of descriptions and examples to help you get started with common Flash tasks.

✦ **Help ➪ LiveDocs:** Loads the online version of the most recently updated Flash help files with comments and notes from other Flash users.

✦ **Help ➪ What's New in Flash 8:** Accesses summary text introducing new features of Flash Basic 8 and Flash Professional 8.

Tip

Although it is not included in the application Help menu, the ActionScript 2.0 Language Reference is listed in the Help panel in the ActionScript 2.0 book. The guide includes a series of documents with detailed information on various aspects of the ActionScript language with notes on syntax changes in the latest version and information you need to know if you want to update old Flash files to work with Flash Player 8.

Macromedia has also included guided entry points to a vast array of online resources. The Flash Exchange is an online resource created to support use and development of Flash extensions. It is a great place to look for new tools, components, and effects that you can download and add to your Flash toolkit. The Flash Support Center is Macromedia's original online resource, sometimes also referred to as the Designer's or Developer's (Des/Dev) Resource Center. This is Macromedia's primary vehicle for the distribution of up-to-date information about Flash and Flash-related topics. It is a searchable area with current (and archived) articles on many Flash topics. You can also find links to downloads, documentation, forums, and many other invaluable Flash-related resources and updates. Use Help ⇨ Manage Extensions to load the control panel for managing installed Macromedia extensions for Flash as well as other applications in the Studio suite.

Tip
The Help panel can be docked with other panels in your workspace, but it is much easier to read or search for help content if you undock the panel and drag the size box horizontally to make it wider. Use the keyboard shortcut (F1) to show or hide the Help panel whenever you need to.

The Flash 8 interface on Macintosh and Windows

Before discussing the various Flash menu items, panels, and miscellaneous dialog boxes that you can use to control and customize your workspace, we begin with a look at the interface with its default array of toolbars and panels as they appear on Macintosh and Windows. Use the application menu to select Window ⇨ Workspace Layout ⇨ Default if you want to load or reload the default setup.

The implementation of panels is consistent across both Mac and Windows. Throughout the book, we discuss each panel in context with the tools and tasks where it is used. As you'll quickly find, there are many ways to arrange these panels for a customized workflow. Your preferred panel layouts for different tasks can be saved as custom Workspace Layouts and recalled from the Workspace Layouts menu.

Tip
In Flash MX 2004, a specific arrangement of panels in the authoring environment was called a Panel Set. In Flash 8, this is now called a Workspace Layout. Flash 8 does not ship with prearranged Developer and Designer layouts but you can still save and load your own custom sets for different tasks.

New Feature
The default Workspace Layout includes two modified panel groups that have been introduced to support new features and reduce clutter in Flash 8: a Property inspector with tabs for Properties, Parameters, and Filters and a Color panel group that puts the Color Mixer panel and the Color swatches panel into a handy tabbed layout. The expanded Library panel also includes a new drop-down menu for loading Library content from different documents without having to manage multiple floating panels.

Figure 4-3 shows how the default layout (Window ⇨ Workspace Layouts ⇨ Default) looks on the Mac. Figure 4-4 shows how the same panel set looks on Windows with the Professional version of Flash 8.

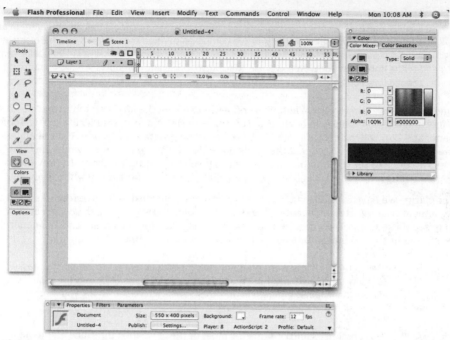

Figure 4-3: The default layout for Flash Professional 8 as it appears on Macintosh OS X

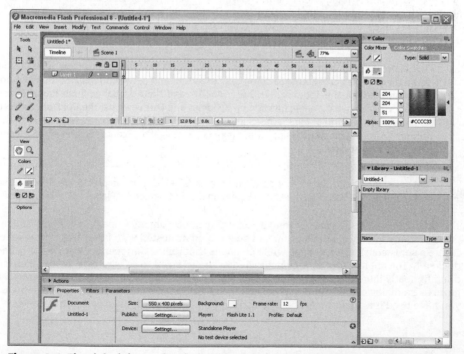

Figure 4-4: The default layout for Flash Professional 8 as it appears on Windows XP

Note   Although there are some visible differences between Macintosh and Windows interfaces for Flash 8, these are largely due to differences in the operating systems that are apparent in any application. For the sake of clarity, we've compared the two overall interfaces here showing a default panel layout for each version of the program before discussing individual UI items. For the most part, however, we use Macintosh OS X and Windows XP illustrations interchangeably, pointing out differences only when they directly affect workflow.

One minor way in which the Windows version differs from the Mac version is that the Tools panel and the Controller can be docked (or undocked) to the program window. The Tools panel and Controller can be dragged to the edge of the program window to dock seamlessly in the Windows interface. Note that the Tools panel docks only to the sides, while the Controller can also dock to the top and bottom, as well as mesh with other toolbars. To prevent docking while moving either the Tools panel or Controller, press the Control key while dragging.

For clarity, we have capitalized terms that refer to specific Flash interface features such as Document window, Stage, Timeline, Workspace Layout, Tools panel, and Options area. You may see these words lowercase in other parts of the text, where they are used as general terms rather than as labels for specific parts of the Flash interface.

Note   In Flash MX 2004, UI items were grouped into subfolders related to production tasks. The Flash 8 Window menu puts all of the main panels and UI items back into the main list with only a few "special" panels grouped in an Other Panels subfolder. Thank you Macromedia — fewer mouse miles are always a good thing!

We describe the actual uses and options for most of these various interface elements in the context of where the elements are applied. To get started with Flash, we will introduce the Property inspector, Tools panel, Document window, Scene panel, Timeline, and Controller, along with the related menu items. We discuss the remainder of the panels and windows, and how they are used, in chapters on drawing, animation, interactivity, and other specific production topics.

Note   The Main toolbar is an optional feature only available on the Windows version of Flash. This toolbar gives you quick access to commonly used tool and panel options and it should not be confused with the Tools panel. The Controller and the Edit bar options found in the Toolbars menu have the same function on Windows and Mac versions. The Controller is used to control the position of the Playhead in the Timeline, and the Edit bar (which docks to the top of the Document window) includes controls for navigating Scenes, editing symbols, and changing View settings.

Cross-Reference   We cover the use of the History panel in Chapter 9, "Modifying Graphics." We describe the Project panel, available only in Flash Professional 8, in Chapter 3, "Planning Flash Projects."

The difference between a *window* and a *panel* may not be obvious right away. For practical purposes, any interface element that can be grouped or nested with other like elements to create a set is considered a panel, while elements that remain independent or can only be docked to the application or Document window are referred to as windows. Some UI elements don't fit neatly into one of these categories. For example, the Start Page actually behaves more like a dialog box: It cannot be docked with other panels and it disappears as soon as you have used it to make a choice. The Tools panel cannot be docked with other panels either and it does not have any of the display controls that "real" panels have. Don't let these minor details slow you down. After working in the Flash environment for a short time, most quirks become so familiar that you won't even notice them—unless you have to write a book about how to use Flash!

What to expect from the Property inspector

The Property inspector is a centralized place to access most common options for various authoring items. You can select or modify many options directly in the Property inspector, but for some items, buttons appear that you can use to launch additional menus or dialog boxes. Generally, you will only need to access separate panels for a few specialized editing tasks. Figure 4-5 shows how the Property inspector changes to display options relevant to the currently selected item.

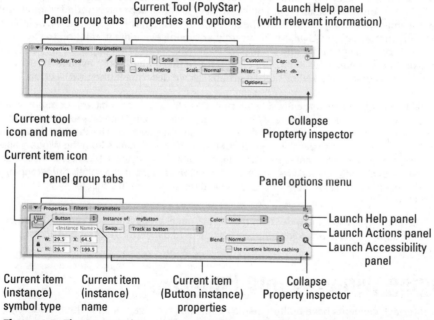

Figure 4-5: The Property inspector, as it appears when the PolyStar tool is active (top), and when a Button symbol instance is selected (bottom)

The top figure shows the Property inspector (collapsed), as it appears when the PolyStar tool is active (selected in the Tools panel)—displaying Stroke and Fill colors and options, buttons for launching Settings dialog boxes for line styles and tool options, and the icon for launching the Help panel. The bottom figure shows the Property inspector (expanded), as it appears when a Button symbol instance is selected on the Stage—displaying instance properties and options. The launcher icon for the Help panel is still available, and icons for launching the Actions panel and the Accessibility panel are also visible when the Property inspector is expanded.

Notice the tabs at the top of the Property inspector for switching between Properties, Filters, and component parameters. We explain the applied uses of these tabs in later chapters where we introduce Filters and components in more detail. For now, all you need to know is that you can use the Filters tab to apply and sort Filter effects and use the Parameters tab to access component parameters in the Property inspector.

Depending on what is currently selected, the Property inspector will display relevant attributes for a document, frame, symbol instance, component instance, shape, or text box. Pop-up menus and editable value fields make it quick and easy to make changes without hunting through panel sets or the application menu. As shown in Figure 4-5, when an element is selected that can have code attached to it, a gray arrow appears on the right edge of the Property inspector. Clicking this icon launches the Actions panel for editing code on individual frames or symbol instances.

Because the Property inspector and the Tools panel provide access to all tool options (with the exception of some drawing and text attributes that are adjusted in the Preferences window), there are only four panels that you might need to open separately for additional options while drawing and editing graphics on the Stage. They are Color Mixer, for adding alpha, gradients, and custom colors; Align, for accurately arranging elements in relation to each other or to the Stage; Transform, for quickly making exact size or rotation adjustments; and History, for tracking or changing your edits. You can optimize this simple setup even further by sorting panels into custom stacked or tabbed groups, as we describe in the next section.

New Feature   Tabbed panel groups make the workspace in Flash 8 much more efficient. Commonly used editing panels are now in two ready-made panel groups: Color (with tabs for the Color Mixer and Color Swatches panels), and Align & Info & Transform (with tabs for the panels as listed). To invoke one of these panel groups, select any of the panel names from the Window application menu and the whole group will appear with the selected tab active. If these panel groups don't suit your workflow, you have the option of isolating the panels or regrouping or stacking them in custom configurations as we describe later in this chapter.

Tip   The Property inspector is wider than most other panel groups, but you can make use of all the horizontal space by adding other commonly-used panels for quick tabbed access.

Managing Windows and Panels

Most interface elements have built-in display controls (see Figure 4-6 for the tabbed panel controls that you will see on both Mac and Windows versions), but you can also manage what appears in your workspace with the main application menu. Rather than go through a laundry list of all the application menu options, we will note the various features that apply to individual windows and panels as we describe their uses.

Tip   To make the interface easier to use, Macromedia kindly made the whole title bar of the panels active so that you can expand or collapse a panel by clicking anywhere in the top gray bar, not only on the Expand/Collapse arrow.

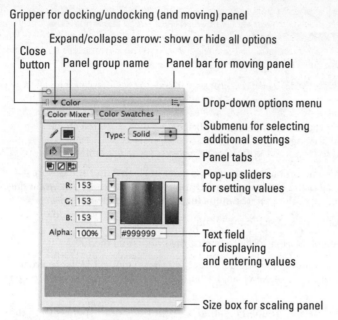

Gripper for docking/undocking (and moving) panel

Expand/collapse arrow: show or hide all options

Close button

Panel group name

Panel bar for moving panel

Drop-down options menu

Submenu for selecting additional settings

Panel tabs

Pop-up sliders for setting values

Text field for displaying and entering values

Size box for scaling panel

Figure 4-6: The controls we note here on the tabbed Mac Color panel group are consistent with the control icons you will see on other panels for both Mac and Windows.

Contextual menus

As in many other programs, you will find Flash contextual menus pop up in response to a right-click on a selected item in the Timeline, Library panel, or on the Stage. (Control+click for the Mac if you don't have a two-button mouse.) Contextual menus duplicate most functions and commands that are accessible either through the application menu or through the various panels and dialog boxes, which we discuss in this chapter. Because contextual menus show you only those options relevant to the element you have selected, they provide a handy authoring shortcut that can also help you get familiar with Flash.

Grouping and stacking panels

Panel groups are a familiar UI convention for Windows users, but this is a brand-new option in Flash for Mac users. Figure 4-7 shows the tabbed panel group that includes the Align panel, Info panel, and Transform panel.

Figure 4-7: Tabbed panel groups are more space efficient than stacked or individual floating panels.

As we mentioned earlier, some prebuilt panel groups exist in Flash 8, but the Group...with command in the contextual menu (or in the panel Options menu) is the key to modifying or making your own panel groups. Here are the steps for managing panel groups:

1. Select any open panel (or a specific tab within a panel group).

2. Click the Options menu or right-click to invoke the contextual menu.

3. Use the Group with... command to select either another panel in the list to create a new tabbed group configuration or New panel group to make the currently selected panel independent.

4. As long as a set of panels is grouped together, selecting any of the panels from the Window menu will invoke the whole panel group.

5. To remove a panel from a group, select it's tab and then use the Options menu or the contextual menu to choose Close (panel name) or Group (panel name) with ⇨ New panel group.

Grouping panels for tabbed access is more space efficient than just docking or stacking panels, but you will probably still want to stack some panels or panel groups to keep your workspace orderly. To stack or dock panels, follow these steps:

1. Grab the panel (or panel group) by clicking on the dotted gripper icon in the top-left corner of the panel.

Caution   Do not release the mouse until the panel is ready to dock!

2. Drag the panel until it overlaps another open panel or panel group.

3. When Flash recognizes the panel overlap, a blue docking highlight will appear at the top or bottom of the panel that you want to dock to — dragging your panel toward the top of another panel will stack it above and dragging your panel toward the bottom of another panel will stack it below.

4. Release the mouse and the panel will dock so it can be moved and opened or closed with other panels in the same stack.

Unstacking or undocking panels is easy: Just click the gripper to pull any panel away from the other panels in a stack and make it free-floating. Figure 4-8 shows a panel stack and a free-floating panel.

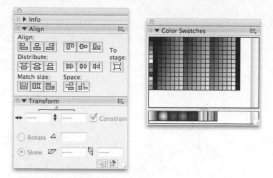

Figure 4-8: Ungrouped panels can be stacked (left) or floated individually (right).

Focus: Making panels or windows active

Prior to Flash 4, only one area of the application required users to pay attention to focus — when they were selecting colors for either the stroke or fill — because it was easy to confuse the two. As the interface has grown to include more panels and windows that can be active at different times within the Flash environment, focus has become an important aspect of the program. What is focus? *Focus* is a term used to describe which part of the application is active, or has priority, at a given time. For example, all panels, such as the Actions panel, do not automatically "have focus" — this means that you have to click within the panel to begin working there. Similarly, to return to the Document window or Stage to edit an element, you must click there to return focus to that aspect of the application. The Property inspector can actually remind you what area or element is active because it displays the attributes of the currently active item. Otherwise, if a panel or dialog box doesn't seem to respond, just remember to *focus* on what you're doing.

Creating custom Workspace Layouts

Whether you have chosen a layout from the Window menu (Window ➪ Workspace Layout) or have just opened Flash with the default display, one of the first things you'll want to learn is how to customize the Flash environment to suit your workflow. Whether you're working on an 800 x 600 laptop screen, a 1024 x 768 dual-monitor setup, or a 1,920 x 1,200 LCD, panels give you the flexibility to create a layout that fits your screen real estate and production needs.

To save your current panel layout as a custom set that can be accessed from the Workspace Layout menu the next time you open Flash, follow these simple steps:

1. Open and arrange (by grouping or stacking) any panels that you want to include in your custom layout.

2. Go to Window ➪ Workspace Layout ➪ Save Current.

3. You will be prompted by a dialog box to name your workspace layout. Enter a name that will help you remember why you made that panel set, such as **animation** or **scripting**.

4. Your custom layout will now appear in the list of available Workspace Layouts (Window ➪ Workspace Layout).

Deleting or renaming Workspace Layouts is easy in Flash 8. Select Window ⇨ Workspace Layout ⇨ Manage to invoke the new dialog box for editing the list of saved layouts. As shown in Figure 4-9, you have the option of renaming or deleting any of the files that appear in the Workspace Layouts menu.

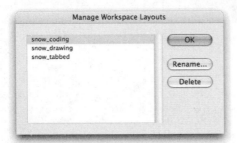

Manage Workspace Layouts

snow_coding
snow_drawing
snow_tabbed

OK

Rename...

Delete

Figure 4-9: The new Flash 8 dialog box for managing saved Workspace Layouts makes it easy to delete or rename your custom layouts.

Do you really love your custom layout? You can save Workspace Layouts just as you would project files in order to share them with other people or take them with you when you upgrade to a newer version of Flash (or move to another machine). When you want to add them to your current version of Flash, just place the files in the Workspace Layouts folder and they'll appear in the menu, ready for you to use. The only limitation is that Workspace Layout files cannot be shared between the Mac and Windows versions of Flash.

Workspace Layouts are stored in a folder on your hard drive. Once you find the Workspace Layout files, you can either add or delete any of these files and the Workspace Layout menu in Flash will update to show only the files that you currently have saved there.

✦ The standard directory path on Windows is:

```
C:\Documents and Settings\(username)\Local Settings\Application Data\
Macromedia\Flash 8\(language)\Configuration\Workspace
```

✦ The standard directory path on Mac is:

```
HD\Users: (username)\Library: Application Support\Macromedia\Flash 8\
(language)\Configuration\Workspace
```

On the CD-ROM

Everyone will have a different way of organizing her workspace, but to get you started, we have included some of the panel layouts that we use regularly for you to try out. In the ch04 folder on the CD-ROM, you'll find a WorkspaceLayouts folder with a Mac set from Snow and a Windows set from Rob. Save these files to your Workspace folder and see if you like them. Keep in mind that you can use a panel set as a starting point for your own custom layout—move, close, or add panels as you like, and then use the Save Workspace Layout command and give the layout a new name. It will be added to your Workspace folder and will be available in the Workspace Layout menu.

Keyboard shortcuts

Keyboard shortcuts allow you to work more quickly because you avoid the hassle of clicking through a menu to activate a feature with your mouse. This is a workflow trick that many people use even when working in text-editing applications. Instead of browsing to the Edit menu to find the Copy command, you can just press the key combination Ctrl+C (or ⌘+C on Mac). We have included the default keyboard shortcuts for most tools and features as they are introduced by listing them in parentheses after the tool or menu item name. When key options are different on Mac and Windows, we list both. Thus the convention for showing the keyboard shortcut for Copy in both Windows and Mac would be Ctrl+C or ⌘+C.

A default set of keyboard shortcuts is available without having to change any settings and these shortcuts are listed after most commands in the various application menus. However, if you would like to use different shortcut keys for certain tasks or add a new shortcut key for a custom Panel group or tool, you can make changes to the default settings in the Keyboard Shortcuts dialog box shown in Figure 4-10.

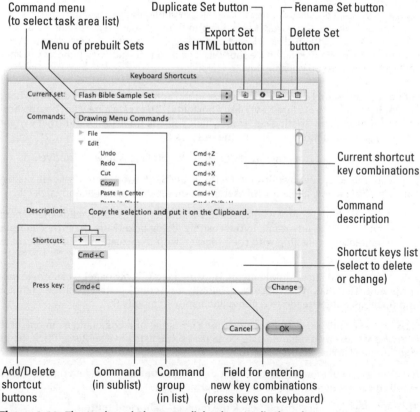

Figure 4-10: The Keyboard Shortcuts dialog box as displayed on Mac OS X. The appearance is slightly different on Windows, but the options available are the same.

Tip   By default, Flash uses the Macromedia Standard set of built-in keyboard shortcuts, which is designed to be consistent on most applications in the Studio 8 family. You can also select a built-in keyboard shortcut set from one of several popular graphics applications, including Adobe Illustrator and Adobe Photoshop. Instead of manually changing a duplicate of the Macromedia Standard set to match your favorite program, simply switch the Current Set using the menu list.

As shown in Figure 4-10, the Keyboard Shortcuts dialog box enables you to customize your Flash keyboard shortcuts to maintain consistency with other applications or to suit a personalized workflow. Not only can you choose keyboard shortcuts developed from other applications, but you can also save your modifications and custom settings. A full explanation of this dialog box follows.

Note   Flash includes a special set of keyboard shortcuts for the Actions panel. This is a boon for coders who may wish to use different shortcuts when editing in the Actions panel than when working in the Document window.

Tip   For the experienced coder, the Actions panel also supports the known keyboard shortcut "accelerators" such as Ctrl+Arrow key to jump to the next space (end/beginning of words/ expressions). You can also click selected blocks and Ctrl+drag (or Option+drag on Mac) to copy them. There are many of these shortcuts, and if you are authoring hundreds of lines of code, they will save you valuable time.

You will find the Keyboard Shortcuts dialog box in the application menu (Edit ⇨ Keyboard Shortcuts, or in OS X go to Flash ⇨ Keyboard Shortcuts). To create a new keyboard shortcut, you must first duplicate an existing set, from which you can then add or subtract existing shortcuts to form your custom set. Here's the process:

1. Select a shortcut set from the Current set submenu. This is now the active set.

2. Duplicate the active set by clicking the Duplicate Set button. The Duplicate dialog box appears. Enter a new name for this set in the Duplicate name field and click OK.

    A similar procedure is employed to rename a shortcut set. Simply click the Rename Set button and enter the new name in the ensuing dialog box. (Note that you can rename all the built-in sets that ship with the program, with the exception of the Macromedia Standard set.)

3. Select a commands list (Mobile menu, Drawing menu, Tools panel, Test Movie menu, Script edit, Timeline, Workspace Accessibility, or Actions panel) from the Commands pop-up menu either to add to a command list or to modify it.

4. Next, in the commands list, choose either a grouping or a command from one of the previously chosen commands lists. Note that some lists have sublists. Click the plus sign (or small arrow on the Mac) to expand a particular category.

5. Now choose a command that you want to add (or subtract)—a description of the selected command appears in the Description area.

6. To delete the existing shortcut, click the minus (–) shortcut button.

7. To add a shortcut for this command, click the plus (+) shortcut button; then enter the shortcut key combination in the Press Key entry box. Simply press keys on the keyboard, rather than type the key names. Click Change and then OK to close the dialog box.

8. Or, to change an existing command, select the command and click the Change button.

9. To delete a shortcut set, click the Delete Set button, and then select the set to be deleted from the Delete Set dialog box and click the Delete button. (Because you cannot delete the built-in sets that ship with the program, they do not appear in the Delete Set dialog box.)

New Feature The Export Set as HTML button in the Keyboard Shortcuts dialog box (shown in Figure 4-10) is a fantastic way to create a formatted table of shortcut keys that you can post near your desk or share with other people. This option enables you to name the file and choose a location to save it. Drag the saved HTML file into a browser window to see a nicely formatted reference table that you can read onscreen or print out.

Note Like Panel set files, Keyboard Shortcut sets are stored on your hard drive. You'll find them in the `Keyboard Shortcuts` folder in the First Run folder that is in the same location as the Configuration folder that we listed in the previous section for Workspace Layouts. You can navigate to this location on your hard drive and copy, back up, restore, delete, or otherwise manipulate any of these files from this folder. Keyboard shortcuts are transferable between machines, although we have had no success transferring them across platforms.

The Tools panel

The vertical bar titled Tools that appears by default on the left side of the interface is referred to as the Tools panel. If you haven't just installed Flash, or if someone else has changed the defaults in Flash, you may not see the Tools panel on your screen. You can find it in the main Window menu (Window ➪ Tools) or invoke it with shortcut keys (Ctrl+F2 or ⌘+F2).

Controlling the Tools panel

The Tools panel cannot be scaled or minimized, but it can be hidden (and unhidden) along with other panels by choosing Window ➪ Hide Panels or by pressing the F4 key, or it can be opened and closed independently by choosing Window ➪ Tools (Ctrl+F2 or ⌘+F2).

Note If you're using a Windows machine, don't confuse Tools with the menu item for Toolbars, which refers to a set of optional menus we described in the section, "The Flash 8 interface on Macintosh and Windows" earlier in this chapter.

On Macintosh, the Tools panel is always a free-floating panel that you can move anywhere on the screen. On Windows, you can deploy the Tools panel as either a floating panel, or as a panel that's docked to either edge of the Flash program window. Docking means you drag a floating panel to the edge of the program window, where it then melds or sticks to the border of the window. It remains "stuck" there until you move it to another position or close it.

Tip On Windows, to drag the Tools panel to the edge of the program window, yet prevent it from docking, press the Ctrl key while dragging.

If you would rather not see the tooltips that display when tool icons are pointed to in the Tools panel, you can turn them off in your General Preferences. (In OS X, go to Flash ➪ Preferences ➪ General; in Windows, go to Edit ➪ Preferences ➪ General, and under Selection options, uncheck Show tooltips.)

Reading the Tools panel

The Tools panel is organized in four main sections (see Figure 4-11 for tool icons and shortcut keys). The top section contains all 17 Flash tools, as follows from left to right and top to bottom: Selection (arrow), Subselection, Free Transform, Gradient Transform, Line, Lasso, Pen, Text, Oval, Rectangle (with PolyStar in submenu), Pencil, Brush, Ink Bottle, Paint Bucket, Eyedropper, and Eraser. The second section contains the Flash View tools: the Hand and Zoom. Beneath the View tools is the Color area, with swatches for assigning Stroke color and Fill color, and buttons for Black and White, No Color, and Swap Color (to reverse stroke and fill colors). The last section of the Tools panel is the Options area, where some of the available tool modifiers appear for any active tool.

New Feature   The Free Transform tool and the Gradient Transform tool (known in Flash MX 2004 as the Fill Transform tool) have been placed closer to the top of the Tools panel to make them easier to find. The Gradient Transform tool has been renamed because gradients can now be applied and modified on strokes as well as fills.

Cross-Reference   We explain the application of individual tools and options in the Tools panel in the chapters related to specific production topics that make up the remainder of Part II, "Mastering the Flash Environment."

Using Tool options

Depending on the tool selected, the Options area may display some of the options, or properties, that control the functionality of that particular tool, while other controls may appear in the Property inspector or in a panel that launches separately. Of the options located in the Options area, some appear as submenus with multiple options, while others are simple buttons that toggle a property on or off. (For example, if the Lasso tool is selected, the Magic Wand option can be turned on or off by clicking a toggle button in the Options area.) If an option has more than two settings, these are generally available in a submenu.

Many of the options that appear within the Options area of the Tools panel can also be accessed from the Property inspector, from the application menu, or with keyboard shortcuts.

Caution   The migration of tool options from the Tools panel to the Property inspector is not entirely consistent in this version. For example, you invoke the Rectangle Settings dialog box for controlling the corner radius of a rectangle by clicking the Round Rectangle radius icon in the Options area of the Tools panel (or by double-clicking the icon for the Rectangle tool), but you can only access the controls for the PolyStar tool by clicking an Options button in the Property inspector. Although we can hope that options will be more fully integrated into the Property inspector with future versions of Flash, for now you sometimes have to look back in the Options area of the Tools panel for modifiers that you might expect to appear in the Property inspector. Conversely, many tool options do not show up in the Tools panel, so even if the Options area appears empty, look in the expanded Property inspector to be sure you haven't missed anything.

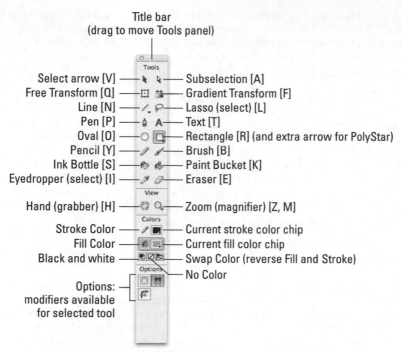

Title bar
(drag to move Tools panel)

Select arrow [V] ——— Subselection [A]
Free Transform [Q] ——— Gradient Transform [F]
Line [N] ——— Lasso (select) [L]
Pen [P] ——— Text [T]
Oval [O] ——— Rectangle [R] (and extra arrow for PolyStar)
Pencil [Y] ——— Brush [B]
Ink Bottle [S] ——— Paint Bucket [K]
Eyedropper (select) [I] ——— Eraser [E]

Hand (grabber) [H] ——— Zoom (magnifier) [Z, M]

Stroke Color ——— Current stroke color chip
Fill Color ——— Current fill color chip
Black and white ——— Swap Color (reverse Fill and Stroke)
——— No Color

Options: ———
modifiers available
for selected tool

Figure 4-11: The Mac Tools panel is shown here with the keyboard shortcuts for each tool. Aside from system display characteristics and docking behavior, the Tools panel is identical on both Mac and Windows.

All the tools accessed from the Tools panel have keyboard equivalents, or shortcuts, that are single keystrokes. For example, to access the Selection tool — which is the tool with the black arrow icon, located in the upper-left corner of the Tools panel — you can simply press the V key when the Stage or Timeline is in focus. Thus, the V key is the keyboard shortcut for the Selection tool on both Mac and Windows. This is faster than moving the mouse up to the Tools panel to click the Selection tool, and it saves mouse miles on repeated tasks. To help you learn and remember shortcuts, throughout this book when we mention a new tool, the keyboard shortcut for that tool follows in parentheses, like this: Selection tool (V).

Customizing the Tools panel

Customize Tools Panel is an option that was added in Flash MX 2004 to support custom tools. There is just one new tool (PolyStar) that was added to the shipping version of Flash MX 2004, but developers have been creating a whole new generation of Flash tools. Because the Tools panel is the most convenient place to store and access drawing tools, Macromedia has provided a user-friendly interface that makes it possible to add, delete, or rearrange the tools (and icons) that appear in the Tools panel. Open the dialog box shown in Figure 4-12 by choosing Edit ➪ Customize Tools Panel (or Flash ➪ Customize Tools Panel on a Mac) from the application menu. A preview of the Tools panel on the left side of the dialog box makes it easy to select any of the squares to add or delete the tools that are stored in each section of the panel.

The interface is very flexible, making it possible to put all your tools in one square if you want to, or even add the same tool to multiple squares—unless you enjoy changing things just for the sake of changing them, the main reason to use this option is really to add new tools.

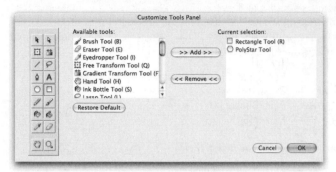

Figure 4-12: Use the Customize Tools Panel dialog box to add or rearrange the tools available in the Tools panel.

The PolyStar tool is a good example of how you can store new tools that you want to use in Flash. The PolyStar tool was added to Flash MX 2004, and unlike the original Flash Oval tool and Rectangle tool, it did not get its own square in the Tools panel. The PolyStar tool had to move in and share a square with the Rectangle tool. The PolyStar icon is only visible in the Tools panel when the tool has been selected from the drop-down menu triggered by clicking and holding the Rectangle tool icon. Any tool square that has more than one tool stored in it will display a small black arrow below the currently active tool to indicate that a drop-down menu is available. By default, the tool icons will appear in the drop-down list in the order that they are added to the Current selection list in the Customize Tools Panel dialog box. The first tool added to the list will show up in its assigned square in the Tools panel unless one of the other tools in the same square is selected from the drop-down menu. The most recently selected tool in any square will be visible until Flash is restarted or another tool is selected from the same square.

All assigned tool shortcut keys remain mapped to individual tools and can be used to activate a specific tool regardless of which square the tool is stored in. If all of the tools are removed from a square, that space on the Tools panel is left blank. Thanks to the Restore Default button in the Customize Tools Panel dialog box, you can have fun moving, grouping, or even deleting tools from different tool squares with the knowledge that you can always go back to the original layout. To illustrate the steps for adding a new Flash tool and storing it in the Tools panel, we have included a brief tutorial on a custom Grid tool developed by Joey Lott.

Adding New Tools to Flash, **by Joey Lott**

Authors' Note: Although it is beyond the scope of this book to describe the steps involved in actually scripting your own custom tools for Flash, we can tell you how to use custom tools that other developers have made. Joey Lott has generously agreed to let us include the code for one of his Flash tools on the CD-ROM. This brief tutorial is adapted from Joey's notes on how to install and use his "Grid" tool. We hope you will be able to follow these same steps to use other custom tools available from Macromedia or from generous developers in the Flash community.

The first step to using a custom tool is to find the files that Flash needs to make the tool work in the authoring environment and the icon that will be visible in the Tools panel. Unless you happen to know some brainy coders, the best place to look for new custom tools is in the Flash Exchange area of Macromedia's site (www.macromedia.com/exhange).

The three files you will want to find and download are as follows:

✦ An XML file that describes the functionality of the tool and controls any "settings" that can be used to modify the final result

✦ A JavaScript–Flash file (.jsfl) that implements required methods for manipulating the Flash authoring tool based on parameters specified by the XML file

✦ A .png file that will appear in the Tools panel as the icon for the custom tool

On the CD-ROM

We have included Grid.xml, Grid.jsfl, **and** Grid.png **on the CD-ROM in the** CustomTool **subfolder of the** ch04 **folder.**

You have to save these files in your Flash 8 Tools folder so that the tool can be applied in the authoring environment.

✦ The standard directory path on Windows is:

C:\Documents and Settings\(username)\Local Settings\Application Data\
Macromedia\Flash MX 8\(language)\Configuration\Tools

✦ The standard directory path on Mac is:

HD\Users: (username)\Library\Application Support\Macromedia\Flash 8\
(language)\Configuration\Tools

After the three files for the Grid tool are saved to the Tools folder, the Grid tool is added to the list of available tools in the Customize Tools Panel dialog box.

The steps for adding the Grid tool icon to a square on the Tools panel are the same as those used to assign any other tool to a specific location in the panel:

1. Open the Customize Tools Panel dialog box (Edit⇨ Customize Tools Panel or Flash⇨ Customize Tools Panel).

2. Select a location square on the Tools panel preview on the left side of the dialog box, select the Grid Tool from the list of Available tools, and click the Add button. (As shown in Figure 4-13, we chose to add the Grid Tool to the Line Tool square.)

3. Click OK to apply your changes and close the dialog box.

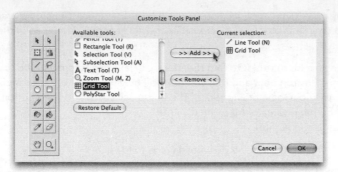

Figure 4-13: Any tool added to the Tools folder—by saving the relevant .xml, .jsfl, and .png files there—will appear in the Available tools list in the Customize Tools Panel dialog box.

Now that the Grid tool icon has been added to the Tools panel, you will be able to select it from the square that you chose to store it in. As with the PolyStar tool, you will notice that when the Grid tool is active, an Options button appears in the Property inspector. Use this button to launch the Tool Settings dialog box (shown in Figure 4-14) where it is possible to control the number of rows and columns that you want to draw with the Grid tool.

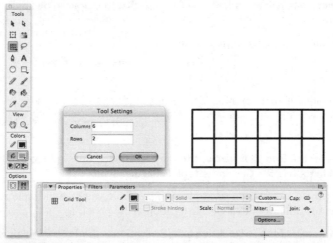

Figure 4-14: After they have been added to the Tools panel, custom tools and options can be used as easily as other standard Flash tools.

After you choose settings for the grid and click OK to close the dialog box, you can draw a grid as easily as you would draw a rectangle with the Rectangle tool: Click the Stage and drag horizontally to create width and vertically to create height—the live preview lets you see how the grid looks before you release the mouse. You can select individual lines in the final vector grid, modify them with other drawing tools, group the lines, or convert them into a reusable symbol. This is a simple tool, but it creates perfect grids every time and saves you time and mouse miles, too!

Let's hope there will be many more useful and creative tools available that will open new possibilities for your Flash designs. You can continue to save other custom tool files to your Tools folder and they will be added to the Available tools list in the Customize Tools Panel dialog box.

Caution

Obviously, it would be a big mistake to save a custom tool file to your Tools folder if it had the same name as an existing tool. Unless you want to overwrite existing Flash tools, make sure you're using unique names for any custom tools that you add. If you'd rather not change the name of a tool, simply add a unique number to the tool name to avoid overwriting other files with the same name.

You can remove tool icons from the Tools panel at any time without actually deleting the files stored in the Tools folder, but if you decide you don't need a tool anymore, or if your available tool list gets too cluttered, simply remove the relevant .xml, .jsfl, and .png files from the Tools folder (save them somewhere else if you liked the tool, trash them if you didn't).

The Document Window

The Document window is the work table of your Flash project. This window tells you what document (.fla) is currently active and shows you where you are working in the project. When you open or create a new Flash file, a new Document window appears on the screen. You can have multiple files open simultaneously — click to move from one Document window to another. You have the option of choosing a document type from the Start Page (discussed earlier in this chapter; shown in Figure 4-1) or from the New Document dialog box invoked by the New File command: File ➪ New (Ctrl+N or ⌘+N).

Tip

If you prefer to bypass the New Document dialog box, you can create and open a basic Flash document in one step, by using the shortcut command Alt+Ctrl+N (or Option+⌘+N on a Mac).

Figure 4-15 shows the New Document dialog box for Flash Professional 8. The dialog box includes a General tab for opening Flash documents and a Templates tab for opening Flash documents with prebuilt elements that you can use as guides for designing specific kinds of presentations.

In addition to the basic Flash document (.fla) file type available in Flash Basic, Flash Professional includes several specialized file types that can be opened from the General tab. These files give developers more options for application development and script editing.

Cross-Reference

For more information on working with slides (a new file type introduced in Flash MX 2004), search Flash Help for the term "slides" or check out the most current documentation on the Macromedia Web site at:

www.macromedia.com/support/documentation/en/flash/index.html#jsapi

Advanced authoring with Flash JavaScript and Flash Form applications is beyond the scope of this book, but if you want to take your Flash development to the next level, the *Flash 8 ActionScript Bible* by Joey Lott (Wiley, 2006) provides more information on these topics.

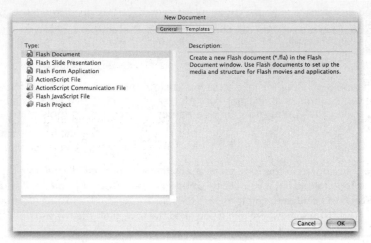

Figure 4-15: Use the New Document dialog box in Flash Professional 8 to create new documents or open template files.

Controlling the Document window

Even when you choose to hide all panels (F4), the Document window remains visible — closing the window will close your Flash project. On Macintosh, the Document window is always free-floating and can be moved anywhere onscreen by grabbing the top of the panel with your mouse, or scaled by dragging the size box in the lower-right corner. By default, on Windows, the Document window is maximized to fill the workspace and it cannot be scaled or moved independently, unless you first click the document Restore Down button (between the Minimize button and the Close button) in the top-right corner of the window (below the larger buttons that control the application). This will "free" the Document window from other panels in the program window so that you can move it around and scale it.

Flash 8 optimizes screen real estate and makes it easier to work with multiple documents by automatically grouping open Document windows into the same tabbed format used for panels. As you create new documents or open existing documents during a session in Flash, they will be added as sequential tabs along the top of the Document window. Click any tab to switch to a specific document, click and drag a tab to move it to a new position in the tab order, and click the small "x" icon to close a Document.

Tip

If you prefer not to work with tabbed Document windows, you can turn off this new Flash 8 default setting by deselecting the first check box in the Preferences panel under the General category.

Tip

If you need to see two tabbed Document windows side by side (to facilitate dragging items from one file to another or to compare two files), use the `Duplicate Window` command (Window ➪ Duplicate Window) to make a clone of an original document. Any changes made in the cloned window will also apply to the original file that will still be available in the tabbed main Document window. Duplicate Document windows are indicated by a colon after the name followed by a number (a duplicate of `myFile` would be labeled `myFile:2` then `myFile:3`, and so on), but these numbers do not affect the saved file name. To make things less confusing, you can close the tabbed version of the document and keep the free-floating clone as your working version. Take note of the shortcut keys for this command if you use it often: Alt+Ctrl+K or Option+⌘+K.

The main reason you may want to alter the default placement of the Document window is to organize your panel layouts to suit a dual-monitor workstation. Although you can drastically change the size and location of the Document window, generally you will want it centered in your workspace and scaled to allow you to comfortably work with objects on the Stage. Figure 4-16 shows the Document window on Macintosh as it appears with default settings and with the Document Properties dialog box open.

New Feature

The Document Properties dialog box includes two helpful new fields for entering metadata for your published Flash files. Title and description information entered in Document Properties will be embedded in the published .swf file as metadata that will help search engines to find and catalog your Flash content. Unfortunately, this information is not automatically carried over to the .html file published from Flash.

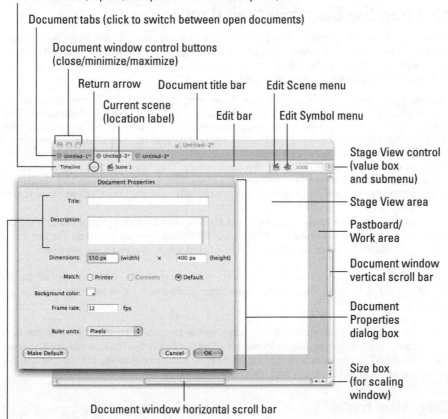

Timeline button (expand/collapse docked Timeline panel)

Document tabs (click to switch between open documents)

Document window control buttons (close/minimize/maximize)

Return arrow   Document title bar   Edit Scene menu

Current scene (location label)   Edit bar   Edit Symbol menu

Stage View control (value box and submenu)

Stage View area

Pastboard/ Work area

Document window vertical scroll bar

Document Properties dialog box

Size box (for scaling window)

Document window horizontal scroll bar

Title and Description fields (enter information to embed as meta-data)

Figure 4-16: The Document window as it appears with the Document Properties dialog box open

The default document settings of Flash will automatically create new documents with a size of 550 x 400 pixels, a white background color, and a frame rate of 12. All of these attributes are displayed in the Property inspector and can be changed at any time. Clicking the Size button in the Property inspector launches the Document Properties dialog box where you can enter a custom size or use the Match options to automatically create a document that fits your current printer page settings (Printer), include all the elements you have placed into your document (Contents), or restore the default size setting (Default).

Tip   If you wish to change the default settings for all new documents, invoke the Document Properties panel by clicking the Size button on the Property inspector or choosing Modify ⇨ Document (Ctrl+J or ⌘+J) from the application menu. After you have chosen the attributes you would like to assign to new documents, click the Make Default button at the bottom of the panel.

Reading the Document window

The white Stage area is the central part of the Document window that becomes the visible area or "screen" of a published Flash movie (.swf). As we noted earlier, you can change the color and size of this "background" at any time, but it is best to establish these settings before you begin creating other elements.

The light gray Work area (also called the *Pasteboard* in Flash 8) that frames the Stage enables you to place elements into your project while keeping them out of the visible area. This is useful if you want to show only part of an element or animate it as it moves onto the Stage. A good example of the utility of the Pasteboard feature can be seen in some cartoons in which very large background artwork hangs off the Stage (or View area) until it's called upon or tweened through to create the effect of a camera pan. The Stage and the Pasteboard are always available in the Document window. The default panel layout also includes the Timeline docked at the top of the Pasteboard, because this is generally the most convenient place to use it.

Tip   You can strip the Timeline panel out of the Document window and leave it free–floating, or you can redock it to the top or bottom of the Pasteboard. On Windows, you can also dock the Timeline to either side of the Pasteboard, but this is usually an awkward view.

The narrow bar located above the Stage and Pasteboard is referred to as the Edit bar (shown in context in Figure 4-16). This bar contains three icons and a value box that help you navigate within a document.

Tip   When the Timeline is docked at the top of the Document window, the Edit bar appears above the Timeline by default. To move the Edit bar below the Timeline (where it appeared in Flash MX), hold down Shift+Ctrl (or Shift+⌘ on Mac) and double-click the Edit bar. Repeat the same steps to move it back above the Timeline at any time.

Stage view control

Although the scale value box is at the end of the bar, we will discuss it first because it can be useful even when you first begin putting artwork on the Stage. This value box, called the Stage View control, shows you the current scale of the Stage area and enables you to type new percentages or select a preset value from a submenu.

Note   The view percentages are based on the pixel dimensions of your project, as defined in Document properties, and your screen resolution. For example, if your project size is 500 x 400 pixels and your screen resolution is 1024 x 768, then the Stage area would occupy almost 50 percent of your screen if view scale was set to 100 percent (Ctrl+1 or ⌘+1).

The first three settings in the View submenu list are Fit in Window, Show Frame (Ctrl+2 or ⌘+2), and Show All (Ctrl+3 or ⌘+3); these settings will automatically scale your Stage view to fit your current Document window size in various ways. Fit in Window scales the Stage view to fill the current Document window without cropping the visible area. Show Frame sets the Stage view to a scale that fits the content of a frame in the Document window; if there is nothing on the current frame, the Stage view is set at a scale that shows the entire Stage area within the current Document window size. Show All sets the Stage view to a scale that includes any elements you have placed on the Pasteboard outside the Stage. You can find these same view options from the application menu (View ⇨ Magnification).

There are two additional tools available in the Tools panel (see Figure 4-11), which will also control your view of the Stage and Work area within the Document window.

The Hand tool (H) allows you to move the Stage area within the Document window by "grabbing" it (clicking and dragging). Double-clicking the Hand icon in the Tools panel quickly gives you the same Stage view as choosing the menu item Show Frame.

Tip   To toggle the Hand tool on while using any other tool, without interrupting your selection, hold down the spacebar.

The Zoom tool, or magnifier (Z, M), does just what the name implies — adjusts the scale of your Stage view. The available magnification range is between 8 percent and 2,000 percent. However, you can apply this handy tool in a few ways. With the Zoom tool active, clicking consecutively on the Stage will pull in closer to artwork with the *Enlarge* option (Ctrl+[+] or ⌘+[+]), or move farther away with the *Reduce* option (Ctrl+[–] or ⌘+[–] key). Each click adjusts the Stage view magnification by half. Pressing the Option or Alt key as you click toggles the Zoom tool between Enlarge and Reduce. Double-clicking the Zoom tool icon in the Tools panel always scales the Stage view to 100 percent (Ctrl+1 or ⌘+1). One last way of applying the Zoom tool while it is active in the Tools panel is to drag a selection box around the area that you want to fill the Document window. Flash will scale the Stage view to the highest magnification (up to 2,000 percent), which fills the Document window with the selected area.

Edit options

Now back to the other icons on the Edit bar. The location label on the top-left edge of the window shows you the current scene and what part of the project you are editing. The sequence of labels that displays in this area are sometimes referred to as *breadcrumbs* because these labels show the steps, or the path, leading back to the Main Timeline from the location you're editing. When in Edit mode, you can use these sequential labels to step your way back to the Main Timeline of the current scene, or click the arrow in front of the labels to return to the Main Timeline of the first scene in your project. To the right is the Edit Scene icon, and at the far right is the Edit Symbols icon. Click these icons to access menus of scenes or symbols in the current document that can be opened and edited within the Document window.

Using scenes

The Scene panel (Shift+F2 or Window ➪ Other panels ➪ Scene) enables you to add, name, and sequence scenes. By default, when your Flash movie (.swf) is published, the scenes play in the order in which they are listed, as shown in Figure 4-17. Scenes can help to organize a Flash project into logical, manageable parts. However, with the increasingly robust power of ActionScript, there's been a trend among many developers to move away from scene-based architecture. Using individual Flash movies instead of scenes to organize sections of a project results in files that download more efficiently and that are easier to edit due to their modular organization. It's like the difference between one huge ball of all-purpose twine that's the size of a house, and a large drawer filled with manageable spools — sorted neatly according to color and weight.

Dividing logical project parts into separate documents also facilitates efficiency in team environments, where developers can be working on different pieces of a project simultaneously. Scenes can still be useful for organizing certain types of projects, such as simple presentations without a lot of graphics, or for animators who prefer to organize a cartoon in one file before handing it off for integration into a larger site structure.

Adding named anchor keyframes is another useful option for linear Flash presentations. These enable Forward and Back buttons in a Web browser to jump from frame to frame or scene to scene to navigate a Flash movie. For more on how to set and publish named anchor keyframes, refer to Chapter 20, "Making Your First Flash 8 Project."

Tip   You turn the option of making the first keyframe in a new Scene a named anchor keyframe on or off in the Timeline section of the General Preferences panel (Ctrl+U or ⌘+U).

Caution   Named anchors work well on Windows browsers but almost always fail on Mac browsers, so this is not a reliable option for Web navigation within a Flash movie if you expect some visitors to your site to be using Mac systems.

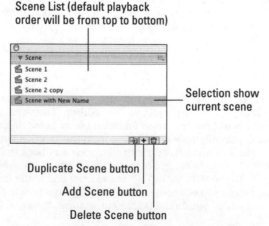

Figure 4-17: The Scene panel showing document scenes in the order they will play back by default

To navigate and modify scenes from within the Document window:

✦ Click the Edit Scene button on the Edit bar and then choose the desired scene from the submenu.

✦ Navigate to a specific scene from the application menu with the View ➪ Go To command.

✦ To add a new scene, either use the Scene panel's Add button — indicated by the plus sign — or, from the Insert menu, use Insert ➪ Scene. New scenes will continue in the same autonumbering sequence started with Scene 1. Thus, even if you delete Scene 2, the next added scene will be named Scene 3.

✦ Use the Duplicate button on the Scene panel to make a copy of a scene, including all content on the scene's Timeline.

✦ To delete a scene, use the Scene panel's Delete button — indicated by the trashcan icon. (To bypass the alert asking if you want to delete the scene, use Ctrl+click or ⌘+click.)

✦ To rename a scene, simply double-click the scene name within the Scene panel and type a new name. Using numbers in scene names will not affect playback order; the scenes will play from the top to the bottom of the list.

✦ To rearrange scene order, simply click and drag a scene to alter its position in the Scene panel list. You can use actions to direct the movie to access scenes outside the default linear order. For more about actions, refer to Chapter 18, "Understanding Actions and Event Handlers."

Caution
Although scenes give you the visual impression of having a whole new timeline to work on, they are really continuations of the Main Timeline that begins in the first scene of your document. If you're using any actions to control your movie playback, it's important to avoid duplicate naming on frame labels or named anchors. Thus, even if it seems logical, it isn't a good idea to label the beginning of each new scene "intro," because you won't be able to differentiate these labels as easily for targeting with ActionScript.

Using Document window menu options

There are several options available from the application menu that control display or editing in the Document window. These can be helpful when you're creating or placing elements on the Stage. All of these can be accessed from View on the application menu (notice the shortcut key combinations listed after most commands). The basic functions of these various commands are as follows:

✦ **Goto:** Leads to a submenu of scenes in the current movie, including four handy shortcuts to the First, Previous, Next, and Last scenes. This menu is also available from the Edit scene icon on the Edit bar in the Document window.

✦ **Zoom In:** Increases the scale of the Stage view by 50 percent.

✦ **Zoom Out:** Decreases the scale of the Stage view by 50 percent.

✦ **Magnification:** Leads to the same view options that are available in the Stage View Control on the top right of the Document window. Note that three of these options also have corresponding keyboard shortcuts.

✦ **Preview Mode:** Leads to a menu of various settings for rendering and displaying content in the authoring environment:

- **Outlines:** Simplifies the view of elements on the Stage by showing all shapes as outlines, and all lines as thin lines. This option is helpful when reshaping graphic elements. It also speeds up the display of complex scenes and can assist in getting the general timing and sense of a movie. It is a global equivalent of the outline options available in the Timeline window for layers and frames.

- **Fast:** Turns off both anti-aliasing and dithering to speed up the display. The default is *off*, to create the most accurate screen image, and it is only recommended that you turn this option *on* if you need to reduce demand on your processor.

- **Antialias:** Dithers the edges of shapes and lines so that they look smoother onscreen. It can also slow the display, but this is only an issue with older video cards. This is actually a toggle in opposition with the Fast command: Turn this On and Fast goes Off.

- **Antialias Text:** As with Antialias, this is also a toggle in opposition to the Fast command. It smoothes the edges of text *only* and is most noticeable on large font sizes. You can only have one Antialias option on at a time, so you can make a choice between smoothing text or smoothing shapes, depending on what content you're working with.

- **Full:** Use this option for the most "finished" or high-definition preview. If you are working on intensive animation, it may slow down rendering of the display in the authoring environment.

✦ **Work area:** Makes the light-gray area that surrounds the Stage available for use — this is now called the Pasteboard, but the command in the Window menu didn't get updated before Flash 8 was released. When the Work area is visible, your Stage area will display centered in the Document window when you apply Show Frame or Show All. If the Work area (Pasteboard) has been turned off in the View menu, then the Stage will align to the top-left of the Document window.

Caution   Items that are selected and offstage when View ➪ Work area is toggled off can still be deleted, even if they are not visible. So it's best if you don't have anything selected when you choose to hide the Work area (Pasteboard).

✦ **Rulers:** Toggles the reference Rulers (which display at the top and left edges of the Work area) on or off — use Modify ➪ Document (Ctrl+J or ⌘+J) to change units of measurement. Rulers are a helpful reference for placing guides to align elements in a layout.

✦ **Grid:** Toggles visibility of the background Stage grid on or off. This grid does not export with the final Flash movie (.swf), but it does serve as an authoring reference. You can control the appearance of the Grid and the precision of grid snapping by adjusting the settings in the dialog box invoked with the Edit Grid command. When the Snap to grid option is active, it works even if the Grid is not visible. Edited Grid settings can be saved as the default by clicking the Save Default button, which enables you to have these setting as presets for all subsequent Flash movies.

Note The default Grid size of 18 pixels is equal to 0.25 inch. Grid units can be changed by entering the appropriate abbreviation for other units of measurement (for example: 25 pt, 0.5", 0.5 in, 2 cm, and so on) in the Grid Spacing entry boxes. Although the specified units *will* be applied to the grid, they will be translated into the current unit of measurement for the Ruler. Thus, if the Ruler is set to pixels, and the Grid units are changed to 0.5 in, then, on reopening the Grid dialog box, the Grid units will be displayed as 36 pix (because pixels are allocated at 72 pix = 1"). Changing Ruler units via Modify ⇨ Document also changes Grid units.

✦ **Guides:** When Rulers are turned on, you can drag horizontal or vertical Guides onto the Stage from respective rulers. These four commands control the parameters of these Guides:

  • **Show Guides:** This is a simple toggle to either show or hide Guides that you have dragged out from the rulers.

  • **Lock Guides:** This is a toggle that either locks or unlocks all current Guides. This is useful to prevent Guides from accidentally being moved after you have placed them.

  • **Edit Guides:** This command invokes the Guides dialog box, where Guide Color and Guide-specific snap accuracy can be adjusted. Also included are check boxes for the other three Guide commands: Show Guides, Snap to Guides, and Lock Guides. This enables you to establish Guide settings and then click the Save Default button to have these settings as presets for all subsequent Flash movies. To delete all Guides from the Stage, press the Clear All button.

  • **Clear All:** The Clear All command gets rid of all visible guides in the current document. It does the same thing as the Clear All button in the Edit Guides dialog box.

✦ **Snapping:** Leads to a menu of various options for controlling snapping behavior in the authoring environment.

Note When Snap to Pixels is turned on, a 1-pixel grid appears when the Stage view is magnified to 400 percent or higher. This grid is independent of the Show Grid command.

✦ **Hide Edges:** Hides selection patterns so that you can edit items without the visual noise of the selection pixel "highlight." This only applies to currently selected items and allows a clean view without having to lose your selection. Most useful for seeing colors or fine lines that may appear visually distorted by the selection pattern.

✦ **Show Shape Hints:** This toggles Shape Hints to make them visible or invisible. It does not disable shape hinting. Shape Hints are used when tweening shapes.

Cross-Reference For more about Shape tweens (or Shape Morphing) refer to Chapter 11, "Timeline Animation."

✦ **Show Tab Order:** This is a toggle to turn on or off numbers that will mark the tab order set in the Accessibility panel for elements in the authoring environment.

Working with Flash templates

The library of predefined Flash documents available in the Templates tab of the New Document dialog box (or in the Create from Template list of the Start Page) is a great starting point for creating many common Flash presentations. The templates shown in Figure 4-18 are listed in both Flash Basic and Flash Professional, but some of the templates can only be used in the pro version of the program.

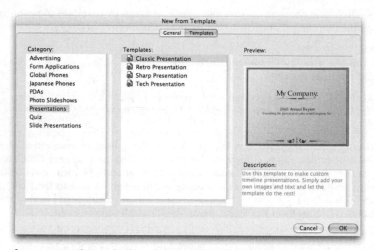

Figure 4-18: The prebuilt templates that ship with Flash provide a good starting point for authoring many common Flash presentations.

To work with a Flash template, open it as you would any other Flash document. You can then add your own content to the Stage or modify the Timeline following the guides in the template and save the finished document with a new name.

Cross-Reference   For descriptions of each of the available templates, do a search for "Using templates" in the Flash Help panel.

You can also create your own reusable template from any Flash document by choosing File ➪ Save As Template. Before the template is saved, you are given options for naming, assigning a category, and description—making it easy to manage a whole library of custom templates. The preview visible for each template is actually just the content on the first frame of the template document. In some cases, this does not provide much visual information for how the template might be used. If you use templates often or if you create your own templates, you may find it helpful to modify the default previews to make them more informative.

Tip   Although each template type has a different file structure and may contain different content, the preview for any template will include only the visible content in the Stage area on the first frame of the template file. Changing the content in the first frame of a template file will also change the preview for that template.

Tip   The standard directory path for the Templates folder on Windows is:

```
C:\Program Files\Macromedia\Flash 8\(language)\
Configuration\Templates
```

The standard directory path on Mac is:

```
HD/Applications/Macromedia Flash 8/Configuration/Templates
```

Web Resource   If you are interested in creating custom template previews, visit www.flashsupport.com/ archive to find Bill Perry's tutorial and example files from the *Flash MX 2004 Bible*.

The Timeline Window

The Timeline is like nothing you will find in your analog studio, unless you have a time machine that enables you to move forward and backward in time and up and down between dimensions. This may seem like a rather far-fetched analogy, but understanding the behavior and purpose of a timeline is often the most foreign new concept to grasp if you have not worked in other time-based applications (such as Macromedia Director). A clear understanding of timelines is critical to production in Flash. Even if you know how to use all your other tools, not knowing the Timeline makes working in Flash like trying to work in a studio with no light.

Note   Flash MX Professional 2004 introduced an alternative to the Timeline authoring structure with form-based templates for application authoring. For more information on this feature, search in the Help panel Features booklet or under Using Flash for "Slide screens and form screens."

The Timeline window is really composed of two parts: the Layer section, where content is "stacked" in depth; and the Timeline/Frames section, where content is planned out in frames along the duration of your movie, like on a strip of motion picture film. In the Layer section, you can label or organize your "stacks" of frame rows. You can also lock or hide individual layers or just convert their display to colored outlines on the Stage while you are editing. In the Timeline section you can control where and for how long content is visible and how it changes over time to animate when the movie plays back. You can also add actions to control how the Playhead moves through the Timeline, making it start and stop or jump to a specific frame.

Cross-Reference   You can find more on controlling the timeline for specific animation techniques in Chapter 11, "Timeline Animation." Actions are introduced in Part V, "Adding Basic Interactivity to Flash Movies."

Controlling the Timeline window

On both Macintosh and Windows, the default position for the Timeline is docked at the top of the Document window, which is often the most logical place to put it. If you don't see the Timeline when you open Flash, go to Window ➪ Timeline (Ctrl+Alt+T or ⌘+Option+T) to bring it up onscreen.

Tip   The Timeline text is actually a small button that serves the same purpose as the minimize/
maximize triangle icon in most other panels. Clicking the Timeline button expands or collapses it faster than using the application menu to open and close it completely. This also
makes it easy to collapse the Timeline window so that it doesn't take up screen space, while
still leaving it available to expand again when you need it. The Timeline button remains in
the Edit bar at the top of the Document window even if the Timeline panel is undocked.

You can always adjust the position, size, and shape of the Timeline to suit your workflow. You
can dock the Timeline to any edge of the Document window, but you cannot group it with other
panels. You can, however, move it anywhere as a floating window, even exile it to a second
monitor — leaving the Document window all for the Stage and Pasteboard.

✦ Move the Timeline by clicking and dragging the title bar at the top of the window. If the
Timeline is docked, click anywhere in the gray area above the layer stack and drag to
undock the Timeline and reposition it.

✦ If it's undocked, resize the Timeline by dragging any edge (Windows), or the gripper/
size box in the lower-right corner (Mac). If it's docked, drag the bar at the bottom of the
Timeline that separates the layers from the Stage area, either up or down.

✦ To resize the layer area for name and icon controls (to accommodate longer layer names
or to apportion more of the view to frames), click and drag the bar that separates the
layer name and icon controls from the Timeline frame area.

Using the Timeline Controller toolbar

The Controller (Window ⇨ Toolbars ⇨ Controller) is a small bar of buttons that provides basic
control of the Playhead. Access to the Controller can be helpful if you need to pan back and
forth along an extended section of the Timeline. You can keep it onscreen as a floating bar, and
on Windows you can also dock it anywhere along the top or bottom of the Document window.
Some developers prefer using the Controller to using shortcut keys for moving the Playhead.
Along with the commands available on the Controller bar, the application Control menu also
lists some more advanced options, which we discuss in following chapters as they relate to
animation and actions.

Caution   Playback speed within the document (.fla) is not as accurate as it is in the movie file (.swf),
so the Controller is not intended as a replacement for the Test Movie command (Control ⇨
Test Movie or Ctrl+Enter or ⌘+Return).

As you can see in Figure 4-19, the buttons on the Controller will be familiar to anyone who has
used a remote control. The only special function to note is that the Play button toggles to start
and stop; you don't have to use the Stop button.

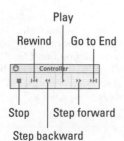

Figure 4-19: The Controller showing callouts for the buttons as
they are used to control movement of the Playhead

Tip Using shortcut keys is often the preferred way to move along the Timeline. On both Windows and Mac, pressing the Enter/Return key will work as a toggle to start and stop the Playhead. If you prefer to move along the Timeline frame by frame, pressing the period key (.) moves forward one frame and pressing the comma (,) moves back one frame. A more intuitive way to remember these keys is to look for the less than (<) and greater than (>) symbols.

Reading the Timeline

The Timeline graphically orders Flash content across two dimensions — time and depth — and provides you with some options for how this content is displayed on the Stage and within frames on the Timeline.

Visual display of time

The order of time is displayed by the sequence of frames arranged horizontally, from left to right, as they appear within the duration of your project. Thus, if your movie is set to 20 frames per second, frame 40 occurs at the 2-second point of your animation.

Note Although they say that time and space are without limits, the Flash authoring environment supports about 32,000 frames, and the .swf format only officially supports around 16,000, which is actually so long that you might never find your way from one end of the Timeline to the other. Organizing your work with scenes and Movie Clips, or even in multiple documents, should save you from ever having to use a Timeline even a tenth of this length.

Web Resource For more details on the limits of Flash, refer to the Macromedia Tech Note Index:

www.macromedia.com/support/flash/ts/documents/bigflash.htm.

You can insert, delete, copy, paste, and reorder frames as well as convert them to various specific frame types that control how elements will animate. Current frame settings display in the Property inspector when a frame is selected, and you can also add/change a frame name or tween type here. The main controls for editing frames are found in the contextual menu (right-click on Windows or Control+click on Mac) or from the Timeline submenus under Edit, Insert, and Modify in the application menu.

Tip As you work with frames, you'll find shortcut keys invaluable. These shortcut keys are listed in the application menu following most commands.

Visual display of depth

The Timeline layers enable you to separate content onto individual "transparent" work surfaces within the Document window. This enables you to animate or edit elements individually even if they occupy the same Timeline (or frame) space as other elements in the document. These layers are arranged vertically, holding content that stacks in the Document window from bottom to top. They enable you to organize content, actions, comments, labels, and sounds so that you will be able to quickly find the parts of the project that you want to edit.

Tip Layer folders are a huge help to organizing multilayered documents. With layers moved inside a folder, they can be opened up for editing or hidden away (collapsed) to reduce the number of layers you have to navigate.

You can insert, delete, move, or rename layers and folders, as well as adjust how content is displayed in the editing environment. Items placed on layers higher in the layer stack can visually obscure other items in layers beneath them, without otherwise affecting each other. With the layer control icons shown at the top of the layer stack, you can set layer visibility (the Eye icon), editability (the Lock icon), and the display mode (the Square icon) to regular or outline only. Note, however, that these settings are visible within the editing environment only and do not affect the appearance of the final movie (.swf).

Timeline window features

Figure 4-20 shows the Timeline window, as it appears when it is undocked or floating. The various controls of the window interface are labeled here, but we defer detailed explanations of some of these controls to the drawing and animation chapters where we show you how they are applied.

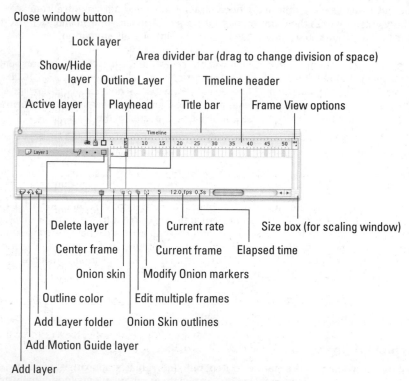

Figure 4-20: The floating Timeline window with callouts showing the principal features and control elements

As shown in Figure 4-20, the principal features and controls of the Timeline are:

Window features

✦ **Title bar:** This identifies the Timeline, but to collapse or expand the Timeline you have to click the Timeline button in the Edit bar of the Document window.

✦ **Timeline header:** The Timeline Header is the ruler that shows frame numbers and measures the time of the Timeline — each tick is one frame.

✦ **Playhead or Current frame indicator:** The red rectangle with a line extending down through all layers is the Playhead. The Playhead indicates the current frame. Drag it left or right along the Timeline to move from one area of the Timeline to another. Push it beyond the visible area to force-scroll the Timeline. You can also drag the Playhead at a consistent rate for a preview of your animation; this is called "scrubbing the Timeline."

Tip

On Windows, if you have a mouse with a scroll wheel, you can scroll up and down through the layers, or by holding down the Shift key while you scroll, you can move the Playhead forward and backward along the Timeline. If all of your layers (or layer folders) are already visible in the Timeline window, then the scroll wheel will just scroll you forward and backward along the Timeline without moving the Playhead.

Layer controls

✦ **Active layer icon:** To make a layer active, either click the layer's name, or select a frame or group of frames. Then the pencil icon appears, indicating that the layer is now active. That's in addition to this more obvious clue: The Layer bar of the active layer is a darker gray than that of inactive Layer bars. Although you can select multiple layers or content on multiple layers, only one layer will be marked as active at a time. For more about frame selection and editing behaviors, please see the section "Editing frames and layers," which follows this one.

✦ **Show/Hide layer toggle:** Click the dot beneath the eye icon to hide the contents of a layer from view on the Stage. When the layer is hidden, a red X appears over the dot. To return the layer to visibility, click the X. To hide or show all layers at once, simply click on the eye icon directly.

Caution

Hidden layers do export, and any content on the Stage within a hidden layer will become visible upon export. Even if the content is offstage and not visible, it may add considerably to the file size when a Flash movie (.swf) is published, so you should save your document (.fla) and then delete these layers or convert them to Guide layers before your final export.

✦ **Lock/Unlock layer toggle:** This toggle locks or unlocks the layer to either prevent or enable further editing. When the layer is locked, a padlock icon appears over the dot. To lock/unlock all layers at once, click directly on the lock icon.

✦ **Outline Layer toggle:** This toggles the colored layer outlines on or off. When on, the filled square icon changes into an outline, and all elements in that layer appear as colored outlines in the Document window. The outline color for the layer can be changed with the Outline Color control of the Layer Properties dialog box, which can be accessed by double-clicking the square Outline color icons in the layer stack or by choosing Modify ⇨ Timeline ⇨ Layer Properties from the application menu.

✦ **Frame View options:** This button, at the far-right end of the Timeline, accesses the Frame View options menu, which affords many options for the manner in which both the Timeline header and the frames are displayed.

✦ **Add layer:** Simply click this button to add a new layer above the currently active layer. By default, layers are given sequential numeric names. Double-click the layer name in the Layer bar to change the name. Click and drag any part of the Layer bar to move it to a new position in the stack, or drag it on top of a folder layer to place it inside the folder.

✦ **Add Motion Guide layer:** Motion guide layers are used to move elements along a path. This button adds a Motion guide layer directly above (and linked to) the currently active layer. To learn about using Motion guide layers, refer to Chapter 13, "Applying Layer Types."

✦ **Add Layer folder:** This button enables you to create folders for storing groups of layers. New folders will automatically be placed above the currently selected layer and labeled in the same number sequence as layers. They can be renamed or moved in the same way as other layers.

✦ **Delete layer:** This button deletes the currently active layer, regardless of whether it is locked. Flash always retains one layer in the Timeline, so if you only have one layer in your document, you can't delete it unless you add another layer to the Timeline.

Tip   Because using the Delete key on your keyboard does not remove an active layer or folder, but rather removes all of the content from those frames, it can be helpful to get in the habit of right-clicking (Windows) or Control+clicking (Mac) a layer that you want to remove, and choosing Delete from the contextual menu. You can always click the trash icon to dump a selected layer or folder, but sometimes the contextual-menu click is a work habit that can be easily applied.

Frame controls

✦ **Center frame:** Click this button to shift the Timeline so that the current frame is centered in the visible area of the Timeline.

✦ **Onion skin:** This enables you to see several frames of animation simultaneously.

✦ **Onion Skin outlines:** This enables you to see the outlines of several frames of animation simultaneously.

✦ **Edit Multiple frames:** In general, Onion skinning permits you to edit the current frame only. Click this button to make each frame between the Onion Skin markers editable.

✦ **Modify Onion markers:** Click this button to evoke the Modify Onion Markers pop-up. In addition to making manual adjustments, you can use the options to control the behavior and range of Onion skinning.

Cross-
Reference   Onion skinning is further described in Chapter 11, "Timeline Animation."

Timeline Status displays

✦ **Current frame:** This indicates the number of the current frame.

✦ **Current rate:** This indicates the frame rate of the movie, measured in frames, or frames per second (fps). The program default of 12 fps is usually a good starting point. Ideally, you should do some testing in the final playback environment before deciding on an optimal frame rate. You can double-click the Frame Rate Indicator to invoke the Document Properties dialog box (Modify ⇨ Document or Ctrl+J or ⌘+J), or set the frame rate directly in the Property inspector.

Note The fps setting is not a constant or absolute — it really means "maximum frame rate." The actual frame rate is dependent upon a number of variables, including download speed, processor speed, and machine resources; these are variables over which you have no control. However, another factor, over which you do have control, is the intensity of the animation: Complex movement with multiple elements or many layers of transparency is more processor intensive than simple movement. Previewing real-world playback speed at different frame rates — on various machines — early on in your development process is *very* important.

✦ **Elapsed time:** This indicates the total movie time, measured in seconds (or tenths of a second), which will elapse from frame 1 to the current frame — provided that the movie is played back at the optimal speed.

Editing frames and layers

After you learn to recognize the visual conventions of the Timeline and how it displays different types of frames, you will be able to learn a lot about what is happening in an animation just by reading the Timeline. Figure 4-21 illustrates the Flash conventions for frame and layer display.

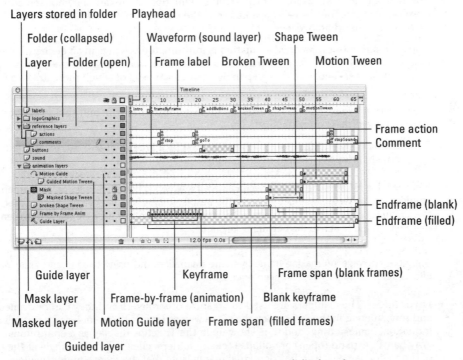

Figure 4-21: Flash Timeline conventions for naming and display of various frame and layer types

The Timeline features noted in Figure 4-21 are defined as follows:

✦ **Keyframe:** A keyframe is any frame in which the contents of the frame may differ from the contents of either the previous or subsequent frames. Filled (black) circles on the Timeline mark keyframes with content.

✦ **Blank keyframe:** A keyframe that does not contain any content has the same behavior as any keyframe, but it is marked by an empty (white) circle on the Timeline.

✦ **Frame span:** Frame spans are the sections from a keyframe to an endframe (up to, but not including, the next keyframe to the right). Note that these spans can be selected by double-clicking, and dragged as a whole to a different location.

  • **Filled frame(s):** The intermediate frames in a span, following to the right of a keyframe (with content), are shaded gray.

  • **Empty frame(s):** The intermediate frames in a span, following to the right of a blank keyframe, are white. A black line also outlines the entire span.

  • **Endframe:** The final frame of a span, marked with a small white rectangle and a vertical line to the right of the rectangle.

✦ **Frame-by-Frame animation:** Frame-by-frame animation is animation composed entirely of keyframes. In a frame-by-frame animation, the content on every frame is changed manually (rather than tweened).

✦ **Tweened animation:** Tweened animation is movement or change in an element interpolated by Flash over a range of frames that extend between two keyframes. An arrow stretching across a colored frame span designates a tween, of which there are two varieties:

  • **Motion tweens:** Motion tweens are indicated by a blue tint and can be applied only to groups or symbols.

  • **Shape tweens:** Shape tweens are indicated by a green tint and can be applied only to primitive (nongrouped) shapes.

Note   A dashed line replaces the normal tween arrow if a tween is broken or missing an element required for the tween to render properly. The best fix for this is to remove the tween, check the contents of the beginning and ending keyframe to ensure that they are ready to tween, then reapply the tween to the beginning keyframe.

Cross-Reference   For more coverage on making frame-by-frame animation and using tweens and Timeline Effects, refer to Chapter 11, "Timeline Animation."

✦ **Layer folder:** These folders are used to organize other layers and they can be named and repositioned in the layer stack the same way as layers. Layer folders do not have individual frame settings and thus show up in the Timeline display as a continuous gray bar. To expand (open) or collapse (close) folders, click the arrow toggle at the left of the folder name or use the contextual menu. Note that dragging a folder inside another folder creates subfolders.

✦ **Motion Guide layer:** A Motion Guide layer is used to guide an animated item along a vector path. For more about Motion Guide layers, refer to Chapter 13, "Applying Layer Types."

✦ **Mask layer:** A Mask layer is a layer that is used to selectively obscure the layers beneath it. For more about Mask layers, refer to Chapter 13, "Applying Layer Types."

✦ **Label:** Labels are used to give frames meaningful names, rather than using frame numbers. The advantage of this is that named keyframes can be moved without breaking ActionScript calls assigned to them. Upon export, labels are included as part of the .swf. Use the field in the Property inspector to add a label to a selected frame. Press Enter/Return after typing a frame label or comment to ensure that the label takes.

✦ **Comment:** Comments are special labels, preceded by a double-slash (//). Comments do not export, so you can be as descriptive as you need to be without adding to the .swf size. However, you won't be able to read long comments unless you leave a lot of space between keyframes. Add comments in the Property inspector the same way as you add labels; just be sure your text is preceded by two forward-slash characters.

Note   The Property inspector includes a menu for selecting a frame text Type. After you type into the Frame text field, you can select from three options in the Type menu: Name, Comment, or Anchor. Note: A frame "name" is generally referred to as a label.

✦ **Waveform:** This squiggly blue line in the sound layer is the waveform of a placed sound. This visual reference for your sound makes it easier to synchronize animated elements to a soundtrack.

✦ **Frame actions:** The small *a*s in frames 10, 20, and 58 of the actions layer designate the presence of frame actions.

On the CD-ROM   If you want to see how the various layer and frame types look in the authoring environment and what happens when you publish the file, open `framesAndLayers.fla` (the Timeline shown in Figure 4-21) from the `ch04` folder on the CD-ROM.

Frame specifics

The Timeline might look a bit chaotic or confusing at first but there are a lot of cues to help you keep track of the content of your file. Empty keyframes are marked with an empty circle (white dot), the last frame of a span is marked with the empty bar icon, and keyframes with content are marked with a filled circle (black dot).

Flash MX 2004 introduced the option of using either Flash 4 or Flash 5 frame-selection behavior. In Flash 4, individual frames could be selected just by clicking them, even if they were part of a *span* (a series of frames following a keyframe). With Flash 5, Span-based selection was introduced as the default behavior — all the frames in a span would be selected just by clicking one frame. Since Flash MX, the default has gone back to Flash 4 selection style, but double-clicking a frame selects a span. For the option of going back to the Flash 5 selection style, go to Edit ⇨ Preferences (or Flash ⇨ Preferences on OS X) and in the General section, under Timeline Options, select the Span-based selection check box.

Tip   Although double-clicking a frame in the default selection style will select a span of frames, if the span is moved, it will automatically extend along the Timeline until it meets another keyframe. This can be helpful or annoying depending on what you are trying to accomplish. With Span-based selection behavior enabled, when you relocate a span, it does not auto-extend and the original span length is preserved.

So that you can better understand the various frame-editing options available, we have listed them here with notes on the ways you can accomplish your intended result. Some of the methods differ depending on whether you have enabled Span-based selection as we described previously. For users of previous versions of Flash, this may take a little getting used to. For new users, deciding on a preference will be a matter of testing out both selection style options. The default methods are listed here first, followed by the methods that differ when Span-based selection is turned on.

The default Flash 8 selection methods are as follows:

✦ **Selecting frames:** The methods for selecting single frames and spans of frames have not changed since Flash MX.

   • **Frame spans:** To select a span of frames extending between two keyframes, double-click anywhere between the keyframes.

   • **Single frames:** To select a single frame within a span, or a keyframe outside of a span, simply click to select it.

   • **Multiple frames or spans:** To select multiple frames along the Timeline (within a span or independent of a span), click and drag in any direction until you have selected all the frames you want to include in the selection. You can also use Shift+click to add to a selection of frames.

Note   The difference between selecting a frame by dragging over it, and moving a frame by selecting it and then dragging can be hard to differentiate. At first, you may find yourself moving frames that you only wanted to select. The trick is to be sure that you don't release the mouse after you click a frame before you drag to select other frames. Conversely, if your intention is to move a frame or a series of frames, you have to click and release the mouse to select them first and then click again and drag to move them.

✦ **Moving frames:** Select the frame(s) that need to be moved and then drag them to the new location.

✦ **Extending the duration of a span:** There are two ways to change the duration of a span, which is the same result as inserting frames (F5) or removing frames (Shift+F5) after a keyframe. To change where a span begins, select the keyframe and then drag the keyframe to the position where you want the span to begin. To change where a span ends, Ctrl+click or ⌘+click the endframe and drag it to where you want the span to end, or select a blank frame beyond the endframe where you want the span to end and insert a frame (F5). This automatically extends the span and moves the endframe to the frame you have selected.

Note   If you click and drag any nonkeyframe (frame or endframe) without pressing the Ctrl key (or the ⌘ key on Mac), the frame is automatically converted into a keyframe as it is dragged to the new location.

✦ **Copying frames:** Select the frame(s) that you want to copy. Choose Edit ➪ Timeline ➪ Copy Frames from the main menu and then Paste Frames into a new location, or press the Alt or Option key while clicking and dragging to copy selected frames to another location in the Timeline.

✦ **Pasting frames:** Select the frame where you want the copied or cut frames to be inserted (Flash automatically adds frames or layers below and to the right of the selected frame to accommodate the pasted content), and choose Edit ➪ Timeline ➪ Paste Frames from the menu.

Caution

Edit ➪ Copy (Ctrl or ⌘+C) is not the same as Edit ➪ Timeline ➪ Copy Frames (Alt+Ctrl+C or Option+⌘+C). Using Copy will only "remember" and copy the content from a single keyframe, while Copy Frames "remembers" and copies content from multiple keyframes and even from multiple layers. To insert this content correctly in a new location, you have to remember to use the corresponding Paste commands: Paste (Ctrl+V or ⌘+V), or Paste Frames (Alt+Ctrl+V or Option+⌘+V). You may notice that the contextual menu offers only the plural options (Copy Frames or Paste Frames). This is because the plural command will safely work to move content from a single frame or from multiple frames. The singular command is just a simpler shortcut key to use if you know that you only want the content from one keyframe.

✦ **Inserting frames:** Select the point at which you would like to insert a new frame, and select Insert Frame (F5) from the contextual menu or from the application menu (Insert ➪ Frame). The visual "clue" that frames have been inserted is that the endframe of a span is moved to the right — this will also push any following keyframes further along the Timeline.

✦ **Inserting keyframes:** Select the point at which you would like to insert a new keyframe, and select Insert Keyframe (F6) from the contextual menu or from the application menu (Insert ➪ Timeline ➪ Keyframe). Note that keyframes can be inserted within a span without extending the span (or pushing the endframe to the right). Thus, inserting a keyframe actually converts an existing frame into a keyframe. So unlike frames, keyframes can be inserted without pushing other frames further down the Timeline.

✦ **Inserting blank keyframes:** Select the point at which you would like to insert a new blank keyframe, and select Insert Blank Keyframe (F7) from the contextual menu or from the application menu (Insert ➪ Timeline ➪ Blank Keyframe). Inserting a blank keyframe within a span clears all content along the Timeline until another keyframe is encountered.

Note

If you already have content in the current layer and you insert a keyframe, a new keyframe will be created that duplicates the content of the endframe immediately prior. But if you insert a blank keyframe, the content of the prior endframe will cease and the blank keyframe will, as its name implies, be void of content.

On the CD-ROM

For a hands-on example of frame-based Timeline editing, refer to the file frames_example. fla in the ch04 folder of the CD-ROM that accompanies this book.

✦ **Removing frames (to shorten a span):** Select the frame(s) that you want to remove, and then choose Remove Frames (Shift+F5) from the contextual menu or from the application menu (Edit ➪ Timeline ➪ Remove Frames). This does not work for removing keyframes; instead, it will remove a frame from the span to the right of the keyframe, causing all the following frames to move back toward frame 1.

✦ **Clearing a keyframe:** To remove a keyframe and its contents, select the keyframe and choose Clear Keyframe (Shift+F6) from the contextual menu or from the application menu (Modify ⇨ Timeline ⇨ Clear Keyframe). When a keyframe is cleared, the span of the previous keyframe is extended to fill all frames until the next keyframe on the Timeline. The same thing happens if you insert a keyframe in a span and then Undo it (Ctrl+Z or ⌘+Z). Apply Undo (Edit ⇨ Undo) twice — the first Undo deselects the keyframe, and the second Undo clears it.

✦ **Cutting frames (leaves blank frames or keyframes):** To replace selected frames in a span with blank frames, while keeping content in the remainder of the span intact, select the frame(s) you want to "blank" and then choose Cut Frames (Alt+Ctrl+X on Windows or Option+⌘+X on Mac) from the contextual menu or from the application menu (Edit ⇨ Timeline ⇨ Cut Frames). This "pulls" the content out of only the selected frames, without interrupting content in surrounding frames or shifting any keyframes on the Timeline. The content that you cut can be pasted into another position on the Timeline (as we described previously).

Caution

Selecting a frame or keyframe and using the Delete key will remove the content from the entire span, but will not remove the keyframe itself, or change the length of the span. You can delete content from multiple layers this way, but it will leave all the empty frames and keyframes on the Timeline.

Tip

Flash MX 2004 introduced a command called Clear Frames (Alt+Delete or Option+Delete). This is a flexible command that will eliminate the content on a selected frame, keyframe, or span of frames without changing the number of frames in a span. If you select a keyframe and apply Clear Frames, the keyframe will be cleared and the content of the keyframe will be removed. If you select a normal frame and apply Clear Frames, the selected frame will be converted into a blank keyframe to eliminate the content in that frame while preserving the content in other frames within the same span. This command is also listed in the contextual menu and in the application menu under Edit ⇨ Timeline ⇨ Clear Frames.

✦ **Editing the contents of a keyframe:** Select the keyframe where you want to edit content. This moves the Playhead to the selected frame so that its content is visible in the Document window, where it can be edited. Note that if you edit content on a keyframe or frame within a span, the changes will apply to the current frame and the span it is part of.

We detail numerous techniques for editing content in later chapters of this book that address specific types of content. For the most relevant information, look for chapters that describe the types of content you are working with — vector art, bitmaps, sound, video, and so on.

The Span-based selection methods are as follows:

✦ **Frame spans:** To select a span of frames extending between two keyframes, simply click anywhere between the keyframes.

✦ **Single frames within a span:** To select a single frame within a span, press the Ctrl key (on Windows) or the ⌘ key (on Mac) and click a frame. Keyframes or endframes can usually be selected with a simple click.

✦ **Single frames not within a span:** To select a single frame that is not implicated with a span, simply click to select it.

✦ **Multiple frames or spans:** To select multiple frames along the Timeline (within a span or independent of a span), use Shift+click to add to a selection of the frames.

Figure 4-22 shows a Timeline that illustrates some editing points. The top layer shows the Original layer, with content starting on a keyframe on frame 1, followed by a span of 19 frames, putting the endframe on frame 20. This layer was copied into all three lower layers, with the result that the initial content of all four layers was the same. When a frame was inserted at frame 10 of the Insert frame layer, the content was extended, pushing the endframe of the span to frame 21. When a keyframe was inserted at frame 10 of the Insert keyframe layer, the content was maintained in the new keyframe, but the span was not extended, as indicated by the gray filled frames in the span from frame 10 to frame 20. When a blank keyframe was inserted at frame 10 of the Insert blank keyframe layer, the content was cleared following the new blank keyframe, as indicated by the white frames extending from frame 10 to frame 20.

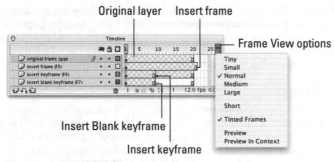

Figure 4-22: Editing on the Timeline

Cross-Reference

For more information about how frames are used to author and control animation, refer to Chapter 11, "Timeline Animation."

Layer specifics

Knowing how to work with layers makes all the difference between a well-ordered project and a chaotic mess of elements that you may never be able to sort out if you have to come back to edit later on. The necessity of a logical folder structure and consistent naming conventions is even more crucial in a team environment, where someone else may have to try to find her way around in your document. Like most good production habits, this may seem like extra work at first, but over time it pays off. As your projects get more complex and your archive of Flash documents grows, the few additional steps you take early on will be invaluable down the road.

Being organized doesn't mean you have to always put every layer into a folder, but rather that you just try to find the most efficient way of keeping track of where you've placed different elements. To make it easier to remember what content is on different layers, it's a good habit to give your layers meaningful names. It can also be helpful to use consistent abbreviations that help you to recognize what type of content is described by the name (such as "MC" for Movie Clip or "Anim" for animation). To edit a layer name, simply double-click the layer's name on the Layer bar and type into the text field.

Tip   With all Flash projects in our studio, we begin the layer structure by creating three layers titled "actions," "labels," and "functions" — these are always kept at the top of the layer stack. On projects that we want to document very carefully, we also add a "comments" layer where the type of action or function added on the other layers can be noted. Although these layers don't hold content that is visible on the Stage, they make it easy to quickly find any actions placed on the Timeline and to see labels and comments that give an indication of how the movie is structured.

Cross-Reference   For detailed methods and suggestions on organizing Flash documents, see Chapter 3, "Planning Flash Projects," Chapter 20, "Making Your First Flash 8 Project," and Chapter 35, "Building an Image Gallery Component."

By default, new layers are stacked on top of the currently active layer. To rearrange layers, click in the area between the layer name and the layer toggle icons, and drag the Layer bar to the desired position in the layer stack and release. To move layers into a folder, click and drag the Layer bar onto any layer with a folder icon. To move a layer back out of a folder, drag it to a position above the folder name bar or below all the other layers contained in the folder.

The Layers contextual menu

Because many of the controls for layer options are built into the Timeline window, layer properties are one of the few attributes that are not displayed in the Property inspector (frame properties are visible when any layer is selected). The contextual menu (right-click on Windows or Control+click on Mac) provides convenient access to most of the commands you will need when editing layers — including commands otherwise found in the Layer Properties dialog box or in the application menu:

✦ **Show All:** Shows all layers. If some layers have had their visibility turned off, this makes them all visible.

✦ **Lock Others:** Unlocks the active layer and locks all other layers.

✦ **Hide Others:** Makes the currently active layer visible if it is not visible, and hides all others.

✦ **Insert Layer:** Inserts a new layer above the currently active layer with an auto-numbered name that continues the number sequence of existing layers and folders.

✦ **Delete Layer:** Deletes the active layer and all content stored on that layer.

✦ **Guide:** Transforms the current layer into a Guide layer — a reference layer that will only be visible in the authoring environment (.fla).

✦ **Add Motion Guide:** Inserts a new Motion guide layer directly above the current layer and automatically converts the current layer into a guided layer.

Note A Guide layer differs from a Motion guide layer. A Motion guide layer is linked to a guided layer, which usually contains a tweened animation that follows a path drawn on the Motion guide layer. A Guide layer is not linked to a guided layer and is most often used for placing a bitmap design composition, or other items used for design reference that should not be visible in the final movie (.swf). Neither Guide layers nor Motion guide layers export with the project when the file is tested or published.

✦ **Mask:** Transforms the current layer into a Mask layer.

✦ **Show Masking:** Use this command on either the Mask or the masked layer to activate the masking effect. Essentially, this command locks both layers simultaneously, which makes the masking effect visible.

✦ **Insert Folder:** Inserts a new folder above the currently active layer or folder with an auto-numbered name that continues the number sequence of existing layers and folders.

✦ **Delete Folder:** Deletes the currently active folder, along with all the layers stored in that folder.

✦ **Expand Folder:** Opens the current folder to make any layers stored inside visible in the layer stack and on the Timeline.

✦ **Collapse Folder:** Closes the current folder to hide any layers stored in the folder. The elements existing on these stored layers will still be visible in the Document window and in the movie (.swf), but the keyframe rows will not show up along the Timeline.

✦ **Expand All Folders:** Opens all folders to show any stored layers visible in the layer stack and on the Timeline.

✦ **Collapse All Folders:** Closes all folders to hide any layers that have been placed in folders. The elements existing on these stored layers will still be visible in the Document window and in the movie (.swf), but the keyframe rows will not show up along the Timeline.

✦ **Properties:** Invokes the Layer Properties dialog box for the currently active layer. The Layer Properties dialog box can also be invoked directly by double-clicking the "page" icon or the colored square icon on any layer, and is always available in the application menu (Modify ➪ Timeline ➪ Layer Properties).

Cross-Reference For in-depth coverage of using layer types, refer to Chapter 13, "Applying Layer Types."

Using Frame View options

The main place to find options for controlling the appearance of the Timeline within the window is in the submenu available from the Frame View options button, shown in Figure 4-22. This could also be called the "train track button" because the icon looks similar to the symbol used on maps to show railroads.

As noted previously, the Frame View options menu is used to customize the size, color, and style of frames displayed within the Timeline. These features can prove very helpful when you're working with cartoon animation and want to see each frame previewed. Or, if you're working on an extremely long project with a huge Timeline, it can be helpful to tweak the size of the individual frames, so that you can see more of the Timeline in the Timeline window.

When you use the Frame View option in conjunction with the Layer Height option of the Layer Properties dialog box, you can customize your Timeline display in several ways to better suit your particular project. Your options include

✦ **Tiny, Small, Normal, Medium, Large:** These options afford a range of sizes for the width of individual frames. When working on extremely long animations, narrower frames facilitate some operations. Wider frames can make it easier to select individual frames and to read frame labels or comments.

✦ **Short:** This option makes the frames shorter in height, permitting more layers to be visible in the same amount of space. When working with many layers or folders, short layers help speed the process of scrolling through the stack.

✦ **Tinted Frames:** This option toggles tinted frames on or off. With Tinted Frames on, the tints are as follows:

- **White:** Empty or unused frames (for any layer). This is the default. The white color of empty or unused frames is unaffected regardless of whether Tinted Frames is on or off.

- **Gray:** There are two kinds of gray frames: (a) The evenly spaced gray stripes in the default (empty) Timeline are a quick visual reference that indicates every fifth frame, like the tick marks on a ruler. These stripes appear regardless of whether Tinted Frames are enabled. (b) The solid gray color with a black outline, which appears when Tinted Frames are enabled, indicates that a frame contains content, even if it isn't visible on the Stage.

- **Blue:** Indicates a Motion tween span.

- **Green:** Indicates a Shape tween span.

Note   Regardless of whether Tinted Frames is enabled, Flash displays tween arrows (and keyframe dots) across a tween. However, with Tinted Frames disabled, tweened spans are indicated by colored arrows, instead of colored fills, that show the type of tween.

- **A red arrow:** Indicates a Motion tween, when Tinted Frames are off.

- **A green arrow:** Indicates a Shape tween, when Tinted Frames are off.

✦ **Preview:** As shown in composite Figure 4-23, the preview option displays tiny thumbnails that maximize the element in each frame. Thus, the scale of elements is not consistent from frame to frame.

✦ **Preview in Context:** As shown in the lower frame preview of composite Figure 4-23, when previewed in context, the same animation is seen with accurate scale from frame to frame (because elements are not maximized for each frame).

Note   The preview in frames option only shows content in keyframes. Thus, if you use this option to view a tweened animation, you will only see images displayed on the Timeline for the first and last frames of the animation.

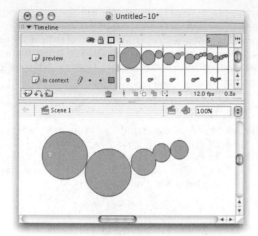

Figure 4-23: In this composite screenshot, the Timeline is displayed with the two preview options—Preview (top) and Preview in Context (middle)—for the same frame-by-frame animation sequence (bottom).

Printing

Although Flash is considered a Web and animation program, it fully supports printed output. The functionality and specific dialog boxes vary slightly from the Mac to the PC—while other variations are subject to which printers and printer drivers are installed on your machine. The File ➪ Page Setup dialog box is the most standard aspect of the program and the choices for paper size, margins, center positioning, and orientation are pretty intuitive.

However, the options available in the Layout area of the Page Setup dialog box on Windows or in the Print Margins dialog box on Mac (File ➪ Print Margins) deserve a little more attention. The options here are:

✦ **Frames:** Use this drop-down menu to choose to print either All Frames of the animation or the ecological default, which is to print the First Frame Only.

✦ **Layout:** There are three basic options:

- **Actual Size:** This prints the frame at full size, subject to the accompanying Scale setting: At what scale do you want to print your frames? You enter a percentage.

- **Fit on One Page:** This automatically reduces or enlarges the frame so that it fills the maximum printable area, without distortion.

- **Storyboard:** This enables you to print several thumbnails per page in the following arrangements: Boxes, Grid, or Blank. There are accompanying settings for Frames Across, Frame Margin, and Label Frames. This is a great tool for circulating comps and promotional materials.

Tip   When printing Storyboard layouts, use File ➪ Print Preview on Windows (or File ➪ Print ➪ Preview on Mac) to ensure optimal results.

✦ **Print Margins** (Mac only): Note the Disable PostScript check box. When you're printing single large areas of color surrounded by complex borders, problems may occur on PostScript printers. If you encounter such problems, try using the Disable PostScript check box in the Mac Print Margins dialog box (Edit ⇨ Print Margins) or in the Windows Preferences dialog box (Edit ⇨ Preferences ⇨ General ⇨ Printing Options). Otherwise, divide the complex area into several simpler areas and use the Modify commands (Modify ⇨ Shape ⇨ Smooth/Straighten/Optimize) to reduce the complexity of these areas (which may, however, drastically alter your artwork — so save first!).

✦ **Print Preview:** On Windows, use the Print Preview command to see an on-screen preview of how the printed output looks, based upon the options you've chosen in the Page Setup dialog box. On Macintosh, the Preview button is found in the Print dialog box (File ⇨ Print) and will generate a PDF to give a preview of how the final page looks, based upon the options you've chosen in the Print Margins dialog box.

✦ **Print:** Just print it! (The Mac option for Preview is found here as well.)

✦ **Send** (PC only): This command invokes the default e-mail client so that you can readily send the Flash file as an attachment.

It is important to note that the Document background color (or Stage color) will not be included on printed output. If you want the background color to appear in your printed output, you must create a filled rectangle of the color that you want in the background and place it on a layer behind the other elements. The printer will then recognize this as artwork and include it in the output.

Summary

✦ Flash 8 retains the familiar interface of Flash MX 2004, while making room for some additional authoring tools and enhanced features.

✦ Although Flash is available in two versions, the interface is consistent between Flash Basic 8 and Flash Professional 8. Flash Basic 8 will support all of the authoring tasks that were possible in Flash MX 2004. Flash Professional 8 offers some additional templates, components, and specialized features that support development of rich Internet applications.

✦ The Start Page and robust Help features get you started quickly, while the options for saving custom Workspace Layouts and custom keyboard shortcut sets make it easy to optimize your workspace for specific production needs.

✦ The Property inspector and the streamlined panel structure make the interface intuitive and consistent with other programs in the Macromedia Studio 8 family.

✦ Tabbed panels make it easier to optimize screen space and customize the editing environment to suit your monitor configuration and work style.

✦ Layer folders and frame-editing options make it easy to organize and navigate your document structure.

✦ Although Flash is mainly used to produce Web content, it fully supports printed output.

✦ If you need a quick reminder on any of the fundamental interface elements, this chapter will be your reference.

✦   ✦   ✦

Drawing in Flash

This chapter introduces the primary tools for creating and manipulating vector graphics in Flash, as well as some features of the
Flash environment that affect how elements behave. The primary
drawing tools have self-explanatory names: the Line, Oval, Rectangle,
PolyStar, Pencil, Brush, and Eraser. However, these tools all have a
variety of options and modifiers that make them more sophisticated
than they may at first appear. In this chapter, you learn to apply the
primary options of these tools to create shapes and line art.

The selection tools — Selection (arrow), Lasso, and Subselection —
are found in the top section of the Tools panel and these work as
your "hands" within the drawing space of Flash, enabling you to
select elements or grab and adjust specific parts of a shape or line.

The Pen is a powerful tool that draws lines by laying down editable
points. You use both the Pen and Subselection tools to manipulate
the points; you can also use them to select and edit all lines and
shapes to manually optimize artwork.

The built-in shape-creation tools of Flash and the adjustable shape-
recognition settings make it easy even for people who "can't draw a
straight line" to create usable elements for Flash interfaces.

In addition to drawing, in this chapter, you also learn to apply some
of the terrific tools Flash provides to help you organize and align elements as you create layouts.

Cross-Reference If you're comfortable using the core Flash drawing tools and design
panels, you can skip to Chapter 9, "Modifying Graphics" for a deeper
look into the options available for editing artwork, including the
Free Transform tool, the Envelope modifier, and the Commands feature that you can use to record and repeat authoring steps.

The primary drawing tools — Line, Oval, Rectangle, PolyStar, Pencil,
Brush, and Eraser — can be divided into two groups: geometric
shapes and freehand lines and strokes. Line, Oval, Rectangle, and
PolyStar fall into the first category; Pencil, Brush, and Eraser fall into
the second. The PolyStar tool was a valuable Flash MX 2004 addition
to the default Tools panel. You can find it in the Rectangle tool submenu and use it to create a variety of shapes, from triangles to fancy
starbursts.

In This Chapter

Using shape and
drawing tools

Working with
Drawing Objects

Setting Brush and
Eraser modes

Creating optimized
lines and curves

Choosing fill and
stroke styles

Using selection tools
and options

Controlling snapping
behavior

Aligning, scaling, and
rotating artwork

Knowing the Edit
menu commands

Note   The default fill and stroke settings that Flash launches with are sufficient to get started with any of the drawing tools, but we introduce many more inspiring choices in the "Using Fill and Stroke Controls" section, later in this chapter.

New Feature   The new Object Drawing option in the Tools panel provides a workaround to the standard overlap and merge behavior of raw graphics. If you prefer shapes or lines on the same layer to behave more like groups and not interfere with each other as you are drawing, you can enable the Object Drawing mode and work with any of the standard drawing and shape tools to create well-behaved, autonomous Drawing Objects.

Using Geometric Shape Tools

The prebuilt geometric shapes available for creating graphics in Flash are easy to access from the Tools panel. The Line, Oval, and Rectangle tools are straightforward but infinitely useful. The PolyStar tool creates a wide variety of geometric shapes defined by the Tool Settings dialog box — available from the Options button in the Property inspector. You can use custom stroke styles and the various fill options (described later in this chapter) with these basic shapes to create nearly any graphic you may need. Geometric shapes are already optimized and you can combine or modify them in multiple ways to create more complex artwork.

Note   In other parts of this book, the term *primitive shape* is used to refer to any shape that is not grouped or converted into a symbol. Creating and using symbols is covered in Chapter 6, "Symbols, Instances, and the Library."

The Line tool

Drawing with the Line tool (N) enables you to create a perfectly straight line that extends from a starting point to an endpoint, simply by clicking a start position and dragging to the end position before releasing the mouse. Just select the Line tool in the Tools panel and start drawing in the Document window. You can select various line styles and stroke heights from the Property inspector, as well as set the color with the pop-up Color Swatches panel accessible from the Stroke color chip on either the Property inspector or the Tools panel. We describe the various options for line styles and colors later in this chapter. Snapping settings and Guides can be used to help control where a line is placed and how precisely it connects to other lines. The Line tool conforms to the snapping settings we describe later in this chapter, in the "Simplifying snapping settings" section.

Tip   To restrict the line to 45-degree-angle increments, hold down the Shift key as you drag out the line.

Figure 5-1 shows how a line previews as you drag, and how it appears when the mouse is released and the current line style and stroke height settings are applied.

Figure 5-1: Line tool preview (top) and the final line (bottom), displayed when the mouse button is released and line style is rendered

Flash 8 includes a long-awaited control for selecting cap styles on lines. In older versions of Flash, all lines had rounded ends or caps. Creating a flat or squared-off end on a line was only possible by converting a line to a fill and then manually modifying the points that defined the fill. With the new Cap option menu in the Properties panel, you can quickly switch a stroke from a rounded end to a square end to a flat or no cap end. Figure 5-2 illustrates how these new cap styles render on a 10 pt line.

Figure 5-2: A 10 pt line rendered with different cap styles. These styles can be applied to any line using the new Cap style menu in the Properties panel: None (top), Round (center), Square (bottom).

The Oval tool

Drawing with the Oval tool (O) creates a perfectly smooth oval. You draw ovals by clicking and then dragging diagonally from one "corner" of the oval to the other — dragging more vertically creates a taller oval, whereas dragging more horizontally creates a wider oval.

Tip To constrain the shape to a perfect circle, hold down the Shift key before releasing the mouse.

The Oval tool has no unique options, but it can be filled with any of the fill colors available in the Color Swatches panel (described in the "Choosing colors" section later in this chapter) as well as "outlined" with any of the stroke styles or colors. Figure 5-3 shows some of the huge variety of shapes you can create using the Oval tool with different stroke and fill settings.

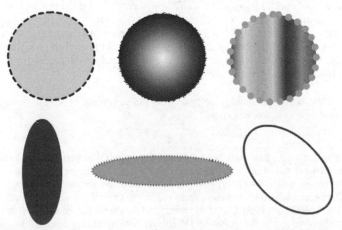

Figure 5-3: Shapes created with the Oval tool, using different stroke and fill settings

New Feature   The Oval tool now has a Settings dialog box that you can use to set the width and height of an oval, and Flash will draw it for you. To access this feature, select the Oval tool in the Tools panel (O), then hold down the Alt (or Option) key as you click in the Document window where you want the shape to be drawn. The dialog box shown in Figure 5-4 will pop up and you can set the width and height (in pixels). By default, the Draw from center check box is selected, if you prefer the shape to be drawn from the top-left corner (originating where you clicked), then deselect the check box.

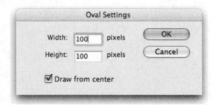

Figure 5-4: The new Oval Tool Settings dialog box can be used to generate shapes with precise width and height settings, rather than estimating size as you draw them manually.

The Rectangle tool

The Rectangle tool (R) creates perfect rectangles, which means that all four sides are parallel, regardless of the length or width of the shape. Draw rectangles by clicking to place a starting corner and then dragging toward the opposite corner of your shape until you have the size and shape that you want.

Tip   To constrain the rectangle to a perfect square, hold down the Shift key before releasing the mouse.

Aside from choosing the stroke and fill to apply to a shape drawn with the Rectangle tool, an option on the Tools panel launches the Rectangle Settings dialog box for choosing the radius for corners on the rectangle. The radius is set to 0 pt by default, to create rectangles with square or 90-degree corners. The maximum radius setting is 999 pt, but anything higher than 35 pt produces almost the same kind of shape as the Oval tool, unless the shape is drawn very large, or elongated to create the classic "pill button" shape.

Tip   A quick way to launch the Rectangle Settings dialog box (for radius settings only) is to double-click the Rectangle tool button in the Tools panel.

New Feature   Like the Oval tool, the Rectangle tool now has a Settings dialog box that you can use to set the width, height, and corner radius of a rectangle, and Flash will draw it for you. To access this feature, select the Rectangle tool in the Tools panel (R), then hold down the Alt (or Option) key as you click in the Document window where you want the shape to be drawn. The dialog box shown in Figure 5-5 will pop up and you can set the width and height (in pixels) and the radius (set in the same way here as it is in the radius-only Rectangle Settings dialog box). By default, the Draw from center check box is selected, if you prefer the shape to be drawn from the top-left corner (originating where you clicked), then deselect the check box.

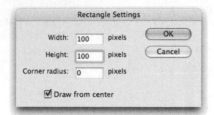

Figure 5-5: The new Rectangle Tool Settings dialog box can be used to generate shapes with precise width and height settings, in addition to specific radius settings — which are also available in the radius-only Rectangle Settings dialog box.

Choosing a more moderate radius setting creates rounded rectangles or squares with softened corners (see Figure 5-6). You'll want to choose this setting before you create a shape with the Rectangle tool because the radius cannot be reapplied or easily modified after the shape is drawn.

Tip
To adjust the corner radius while you're dragging out your rectangle shape, there is a handy shortcut. Before you release the mouse, use the Up arrow key (↑) to decrease the radius setting (making the corners more square), or use the Down arrow key (↓) to increase the radius setting (making the corners more rounded). The relationship between the arrow keys and the radius settings is counter-intuitive, but just think "Up arrow = more square, Down arrow = less square." After you release the mouse, the radius setting will stick and the arrow keys will go back to their usual behavior of moving selected items up or down on the Stage.

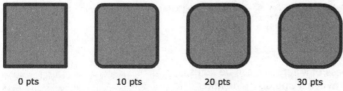

0 pts   10 pts   20 pts   30 pts

Figure 5-6: Rectangles drawn with different radius settings create different degrees of roundness on the corners.

Caution
The Set Corner Radius button is not a toggle, so if you change the radius setting, you have to set it back to 0 in the Rectangle Settings dialog box to return to drawing standard rectangles. Any radius setting entered in the Rectangle Settings dialog box accessed by Alt (or Option) +clicking in the Document window while the Rectangle tool is selected in the Tools panel will also be transferred to the radius-only Rectangle Settings dialog box.

Flash 8 Join and Miter settings

If you are the kind of illustrator or designer who has been looking for more precise control over line intersection or join styles, you will be pleased to find two new options in the Flash 8 Properties panel. As shown in Figure 5-7, the new Join menu includes three settings — Miter,

Round, and Bevel — that you can apply to create three different join styles on any of your drawings or shapes with intersecting lines.

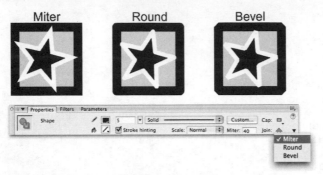

Figure 5-7: The three join styles available in the new Join menu create corners with different types of line intersection.

When you select the Miter join style, you can further adjust the angle of the join by entering a setting between 1 and 60 in the Miter field. As shown in Figure 5-8, the visual difference between these different Miter angles is very subtle and for most graphics you will probably be happy with the default setting of 60, which results in nice sharp corners.

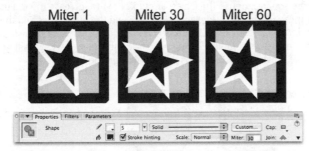

Figure 5-8: The sharpness of Miter joins can be adjusted by entering a setting between 1 and 60 in the Miter field.

The PolyStar tool

We can't count the number of times we had to modify a rectangle manually just to create a simple triangle in old versions of Flash — fortunately, Flash MX 2004 introduced a painless way to create a variety of geometric shapes. The PolyStar tool is so named because it is a multipurpose tool that can make a whole variety of different polygons and stars. If you're using the default Tools set in Flash 8, you'll find the PolyStar as a subset of the Rectangle tool — click and hold your mouse over the Rectangle button on the Tools panel to invoke the drop-down menu with the PolyStar tool, as shown in Figure 5-9.

Figure 5-9: The PolyStar tool is grouped with the Rectangle tool in the Tools panel.

The PolyStar tool does not have a shortcut key assigned to it, but the shortcut key for the Rectangle tool (R) will always activate the Rectangle tool, even if the PolyStar tool is visible in the Tools panel, because it was the last tool used from that Tools panel location.

When the PolyStar tool is active, an Options button appears in the Property inspector to invoke a Tool Settings dialog box that enables you to control the type of shape you want to draw. The composite in Figure 5-8 includes the Property inspector as it appears when the PolyStar tool is active and the Tool Settings dialog box with the two shape styles available: polygon or star. You can set the number of sides for either shape by entering a value between 3 and 32 in the Number of Sides field. As shown at the top of Figure 5-10, a standard five-sided star is as easy to create as a triangle—that is, a polygon with three sides.

If you are a little confused by the inconsistent workflow for accessing Settings dialog boxes for the different drawing tools, don't worry, we were too! Hopefully, these glitches will be smoothed out in future releases of Flash. For now, we just have to live with the fact that there isn't an Options button in the Property inspector for launching the Settings dialog box for the Oval or Rectangle tool and that the Settings dialog box for the PolyStar tool doesn't show up when you Alt (or Option) + click in the Document window.

The fields in the Tool Settings dialog box look the same whether you select polygon or star in the Style menu, but Star point size does not affect polygon shapes. If you are drawing a star, enter any number between 0 and 1 to control the depth of the star points. This might not look like much of a range, but you can enter decimal numbers, so you actually have 99 possible settings! As shown in Figure 5-11, numbers closer to 0 create sharper stars and numbers closer to 1 create blockier shapes.

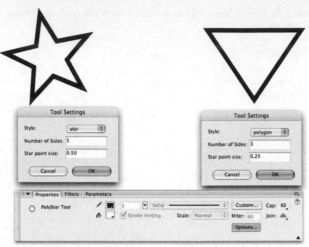

Figure 5-10: A composite figure showing the Options button in the Property inspector (bottom) that launches the Tool Settings dialog box, used to create different shape styles (top)

Star point size: 0.00   Star point size: 0.50   Star point size: 1.00

Figure 5-11: Star point size decimal settings between 0 and 1 create various star shapes.

Using Drawing Tools

The tools for drawing freehand lines and strokes in Flash come with options for applying different combinations of line processing and shape recognition. So, what does that mean exactly? These are general terms for a class of options that you can set to assist accurate drawing and manipulation of basic shapes. These options can be applied dynamically as you draw with the Pencil or Brush tool, or applied cumulatively to an item selected with the Selection tool to clean up a shape or line that you've already drawn. These are some of the Flash assistants that can help even a drafting-challenged designer create sharp-looking graphics with ease.

> **Note**   The biggest challenge when drawing in Flash is finding a happy medium between the degree of line variation and complexity required to get the graphic look you want, and the optimization and file size that you need to keep your artwork Web friendly.

The Pencil tool

You use the Pencil tool to draw lines and shapes. At first glance, it operates much like a real pencil. You can use the Pencil tool with different line styles as you draw a freeform shape. But a deeper examination reveals that, unlike a real pencil, you can set the Flash Pencil tool to straighten lines and smooth curves as you draw. You can also set it to recognize or correct basic geometric shapes. For example, a crude lumpy oval can be automatically recognized and processed into a true, or *perfect*, oval. You can further modify these shapes and lines after you've drawn them using the Selection and Subselect tools.

When the Pencil tool is active, one option besides the Object Drawing toggle appears in the Tools panel. This is actually a button for the Pencil Mode pop-up menu, which sets the Pencil tool's current drawing mode. The three modes, or drawing styles, for the Pencil are Straighten, Smooth, and Ink. These settings control the way that line processing occurs as you draw.

Figure 5-12 shows the same freehand drawing done with the different Pencil modes. The drawing on the left was done with the Straighten mode, the drawing in the middle was done with Smooth mode, and the drawing on the right was done with Ink mode. As you can see, each mode is more effective for certain types of lines and shapes.

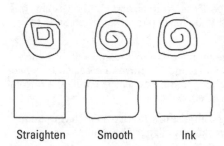

Straighten   Smooth   Ink

Figure 5-12: Similar sketches made using the three different Pencil modes to show how line processing affects various shapes: Straighten (left), Smooth (center), and Ink (right).

To create a pleasing finished result, you'll most likely use different Pencil modes when working on individual elements of your drawing. Here are some notes on the characteristics of the three Pencil drawing modes that you can select in the Tools panel:

✦ **Straighten:** Drawing with the Straighten option processes your drawings while taking into account both line and shape recognition. This means that nearly straight lines are straightened, and wobbly curves are smoothed. Approximate geometric shapes, such as ovals, rectangles, and triangles, are recognized and automatically adjusted.

✦ **Smooth:** Drawing with the Smooth option reduces the zeal with which Flash automatically processes your drawings. With the Smooth option, line straightening and shape recognition are not applied, but curved lines are smoothed. Additionally, a line that ends near another line is joined automatically, if the Connect Lines tolerance is set to Can be Distant.

✦ **Ink:** Drawing with the Ink option turns off all line processing. Lines remain as you've drawn them. Your lines are *not* smoothed, straightened, or joined. There will always be a slight difference between the line preview and the final, rendered line, but this setting is as close to raw sketching as you can get in the Flash drawing environment.

Adjusting Drawing Settings

You may adjust the degree to which shape recognition processes your drawings as you create them with the Pencil with the Drawing Settings found in Edit ➪ Preferences ➪ Drawing (or Flash ➪ Preferences ➪ Drawing). By default, all the Drawing Settings are Normal. You can adjust each option to make it more specific or more general. The optimal setting combinations depend on the style of drawing that you're trying to achieve, but in general, you really only need to adjust the default Normal settings for these controls if you find that you aren't getting the look you want using the Straighten, Smooth, or Ink modes with the Pencil tool.

You can also choose to further simplify lines and shapes that you have drawn with the Pencil in Ink mode by using the Selection tool to select what you've drawn and then using either the Smooth or Straighten modifiers. Or, for maximum control, manually edit extraneous points with either the Pen or the Subselect tool (as we describe in the Pen and Subselect sections later in this chapter). Here are the various Drawing Settings and options available in Preferences:

✦ **Connect Lines:** The Connect Lines setting adjusts how close lines or points have to be to each other before Flash automatically connects them into a continuous line or shape. This setting also controls how close to horizontal or vertical a line has to be for Flash to set it at an exact angle. The options are Must be Close, Normal, and Can be Distant. This setting also controls how close elements need to be to snap together when Snap to Objects is turned on.

✦ **Smooth Curves:** Smooth Curves simplifies the number of points used to draw a curve when the Pencil is in Straighten or Smooth mode. Smoother curves are easier to reshape and are more optimized, whereas rougher curves will more closely resemble the original lines drawn. The options are Off, Rough, Normal, and Smooth.

✦ **Recognize Lines:** The Recognize Lines setting controls how precise a line has to be for Flash to recognize it as a straight line and automatically align it. The options are Off, Strict, Normal, and Tolerant.

✦ **Recognize Shapes:** The Recognize Shapes setting controls how accurately you have to draw basic geometric shapes and 90-degree or 180-degree arcs for them to be recognized and corrected by Flash. The options are Off, Strict, Normal, and Tolerant.

✦ **Click Accuracy:** Click Accuracy determines how close to an element the cursor has to be for Flash to recognize it. The settings are Strict, Normal, and Tolerant.

These drawing settings do not modify the Straighten and Smooth options for the Selection tool, which only reduce point complexity with each application to a shape or line that has already been drawn.

The Brush tool

You use the Brush tool to create smooth or tapered marks and to fill enclosed areas. Unlike the Pencil tool, which creates marks with a single row of anchor points, the Brush tool actually creates marks using filled shapes. The fills can be solid colors, gradients, or fills derived from bitmaps. Because the Brush paints only with a fill, the Stroke color chip does not apply to the marks drawn with the brush. The Brush tool is especially well suited for artwork created using a drawing tablet. A number of settings and options are available when the Brush tool is active, giving you precise control over the type of marks that it makes.

New Feature

In an attempt to better support animators who draw directly in Flash, Macromedia has once again modified the smoothing controls for the Brush tool. If you worked with Flash MX 2004, you may remember that a Smoothing setting in the Property inspector is available when the Brush tool is active. Use the value field or the slider menu to select a Smoothing setting between 0 and 100. The default value is 50, as it was in Flash MX 2005. Values from 0 to 39 use the Flash MX 2004 algorithm to add more points to the shape as you draw, making precise strokes with lots of internal path points to match the original stroke more closely. Values from 40 to 60 apply the new Flash 8 smoothing algorithm to create more efficient paths with a moderate deviation from the original stroke. Values from 61 to 100 use the looser Flash MX 2004 algorithm, adding fewer points to the shape and creating "smoother" strokes that may look very different than your original marks. You can use the Smoothing setting when you are drawing on a tablet or with your mouse.

The Brush mode menu

The Brush tool includes options for controlling exactly where the fill is applied. The Brush mode option menu reveals five painting modes that are amazingly useful for a wide range of effects when applying the Brush tool: Paint Normal, Paint Fills, Paint Behind, Paint Selection, and Paint Inside, as shown in Figure 5-13.

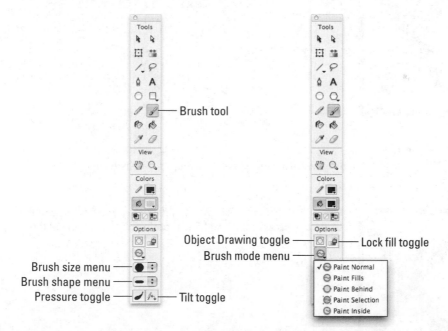

Figure 5-13: The Brush tool and options (left); the Brush mode settings menu (right)

Note

The Pressure toggle and the Tilt toggle will only be visible in the Options area if you have a drawing tablet installed on your system.

To learn more about tablets and read some fun tutorials, visit www.wacom.com.

The following images depict various ways in which the Brush modes interact with drawn and painted elements. The base image is a solid white rectangle drawn with a black outline. The boat outline is drawn with the Pencil tool in dark gray on top of the rectangle.

 Painting with the background color (such as white) is not the same as erasing. Although painting with a background color may appear to accomplish something similar to erasing, you are, in fact, creating a filled item that can be selected, moved, edited, deleted, and erased. Even if you can't see it, it adds to your file size. Only erasing erases!

Paint Normal mode

Paint Normal mode, shown in Figure 5-14, applies brush strokes over the top of any lines or fills.

5-14: In Paint Normal mode, a dark-gray brush mark covers all elements: background, outline, fill, and drawn lines.

Paint Fills mode

Paint Fills mode, shown in Figure 5-15, applies brush strokes to replace any fills, but leaves lines untouched.

Figure 5-15: In Paint Fills mode, a dark-gray brush mark covers the white background and fill without painting over any of the lines.

Paint Behind mode

Paint Behind mode applies brush strokes only to blank areas and leaves all fills, lines, or other items untouched. As shown in Figure 5-16, the only areas the brush mark covers are those in the background, outside the frame of the picture. Effectively, the brush has gone behind the entire shape. If the stroke had originated within the frame, it would have covered the white fill and gone behind the drawn gray lines and the black outline.

Figure 5-16: In Paint Behind mode, the gray brush mark is only visible on the background outside the frame because it has gone behind the white fill and the lines.

Paint Selection mode

Paint Selection mode applies brush strokes only to selected fills. In Figure 5-17, a selection was made by Shift+clicking both the white fill inside the boat and inside the sail. The same gray brush marks drawn on the previous figure are now visible only inside the selected fills.

Figure 5-17: With Paint Selection mode, only the selected white fills have been covered by the brush marks.

Paint Inside mode

Paint Inside mode, shown in Figure 5-18, applies brush strokes only to the singular fill area where the brush stroke was first initiated. As the name implies, Paint Inside never paints over lines. If you initiate painting from an empty area, the brush strokes won't affect any existing fills or lines, which approximates the same effect as the Paint Behind setting.

Figure 5-18: With Paint Inside mode, the brush marks only cover the area where the stroke is first started. Lines separate the white fills inside the sail and the boat shape from the background where the stroke was initiated, so those areas are not painted.

Brush size and shape options

Although similar to Stroke height and style, the Brush size and Brush shape settings are unique to the Brush tool.

Cross-Reference   The Lock Fill option is common to both the Brush tool and the Paint Bucket tool. For coverage of using the Lock Fill option with the Brush tool and the Paint Bucket tool, refer to Chapter 9, "Modifying Graphics."

In Flash, the size of applied brush marks is always related to the Zoom setting. Therefore, using the same brush diameter creates different-sized brush marks depending on what Zoom setting you work with in the Document window (see Figure 5-19). You can paint over your whole stage in one stroke, even with a small brush diameter, if your Zoom is at a low setting such as 8 percent. Or you can use a large brush diameter to make detailed lines if your Zoom is at a high setting such as 1,500 percent.

Figure 5-19: Marks made using the same brush size applied with the Document View at different percentages of Zoom

The Brush Shape option is a drop-down menu with nine possible brush shapes that are based on the circle, ellipse, square, rectangle, and line shapes. (Refer to Figure 5-9.) The oval, rectangle, and line shapes are available in various angles. You can combine these stock brush shapes with the range of brush sizes available in the Brush Size menu to generate a wide variety of brush tips. When using shapes other than circles, note that the diameter sizes chosen in the Brush Size menu apply to the broadest area of any brush shape.

Additional Brush options for drawing tablets

If you use a pressure-sensitive tablet for drawing, two extra options appear in the Tools panel when the Brush tool is active. (The Pressure and Tilt toggles are shown at the bottom of the Tools panel in Figure 5-9.) The Pressure toggle enables you to use pen pressure on a tablet to vary the thickness of brush marks as you draw. Working on a tablet with this option, you can create organic-looking strokes that taper or vary in width as you change the amount of pressure applied to the tablet surface.

Tip   To achieve pressure-sensitive eraser marks, use the eraser on the tablet pen while the Brush tool is active, rather than the Eraser tool in the Tools panel.

Figure 5-20 shows a series of tapered marks created with a pressure-sensitive tablet using a single Brush size and a consistent Zoom setting.

Figure 5-20: Drawing with the Brush tool on a pressure-sensitive tablet (with the Pressure option turned on in the Tools panel) creates tapered, calligraphic marks.

If you're drawing on a tablet that supports this feature, activating the Tilt toggle enables you to control the thickness and direction of strokes with the movement of your wrist. The degree of tilt is determined by the angle between the top of your stylus (or pen) and the top edge of the drawing tablet. This is a very subtle control that you'll most likely notice if you're using a large, tapered (or "flat") brush style — and if you spend hours drawing on a tablet! We didn't include a figure to illustrate this feature because it is hard to tell from finished artwork how it affects your drawings, but experienced artists will appreciate the "feel" that this option adds to the drawing environment.

Note   Support for the Tilt feature varies on different drawing tablets. If you have a Wacom tablet, you can get current drivers and feature documentation from www.wacom.com. It is beyond the scope of this book to describe different types and features of drawing tablets, but the drawing options available in Flash 8 have been tested on a wide range of tablets, so the chances are good that they will work for you.

The Eraser tool

The Eraser tool (E) is used in concert with the shape and drawing tools to obtain final, usable art. As the name implies, the Eraser tool is primarily used for rubbing out mistakes. When the Eraser tool is active, three options appear on the Tools panel, as shown in Figure 5-21. Eraser mode and Eraser Shape are both drop-down menus with multiple options. For Eraser Shape, you can select rectangular or oval erasers in various sizes. Eraser modes are similar to the Brush modes we described previously.

You use the Eraser tool's one unique option, the Faucet toggle, to clear enclosed areas of fill. Using the Faucet is the equivalent of selecting a line or a fill and then deleting it, but the Faucet accomplishes this in one easy step. Select the Eraser tool, choose the Faucet option, and then click on any line or fill to instantly erase it. Clicking on any part of a selection with the Faucet deletes all elements in the selection.

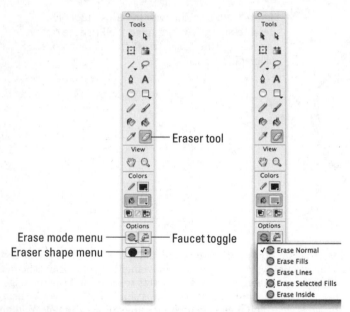

Figure 5-21: The Eraser tool has three basic options: Eraser mode, Eraser Shape, and Faucet.

The interaction of Eraser modes and artwork is consistent with the Brush modes available for the Brush tool. The only difference is that instead of adding a mark to a specified part of a drawing, the Eraser removes marks in a specified part of a drawing. Aside from Erase Normal, Erase Fills, Erase Selected Fills, and Erase Inside, which you will recognize from the previous descriptions of Brush modes, there is also an Erase Lines mode that enables you to remove any lines without disrupting fills.

Note   The Eraser tool erases only lines and fills that are in the current frame of the scene. It won't erase groups, symbols, or text. When you need to erase a part of a group, you have two options: Select the group and choose Edit ➪ Edit Selected from the application menu (or double-click the group), or select the group and choose Modify ➪ Ungroup from the application menu (Ctrl+Shift+G or ⌘+Shift+G).

New Feature Drawing Objects have some of the same characteristics as groups, but they can be treated like raw shapes when you're using the Eraser tool—no need to break them apart.

The only alternative to using the Eraser tool to remove graphic elements or areas of drawings is to select them with the Selection, Subselect, or Lasso tool, and then delete them by pressing the Delete (or Backspace) key.

Tip To quickly erase everything in the current keyframe (even from multiple layers), double-click the Eraser tool in the Tools panel. Don't double-click on the Stage with the Eraser selected; just double-click the Eraser button on the Tools panel. And—poof!—everything in the keyframe is gone.

Creating Precise Lines with the Pen Tool

You use the Pen tool (P) to draw precision paths that define straight lines and smooth curves. These paths define adjustable line segments, which may be straight or curved—the angle and length of straight segments is completely adjustable, as is the slope and length of curved segments. To draw a series of straight-line segments with the Pen tool, simply move the cursor and click successively: Each subsequent click defines the end point of the line. To draw curved line segments with the Pen tool, simply click and drag: The length and direction of the drag determines the depth and shape of the current segment. Both straight and curved line segments can be modified and edited by adjusting their anchor points and tangent handles. In addition, any lines or shapes that have been created by other Flash drawing tools can also be displayed as paths (points on lines) and edited with either the Pen tool or the Subselect tool (described in the section, "Putting Selection Tools to Work").

Creating shapes with the Pen tool takes a little practice, but it will produce the most controlled optimization of artwork. Because no points are auto-created, every line and curve is defined only with the points that you have placed. This saves having to delete points from an overly complex path that may result from drawing with the Pencil or the Brush tool.

Tip If you're working on a background color that is too similar to your Layer Outline Color, the points on your line will be difficult to see and adjust. Remember that you can always change the Layer Outline Color to contrast with the background.

The Preferences for the Pen tool are located in the Pen tool section of the Drawing Preferences dialog box. (Choose Edit ➪ Preferences ➪ Drawing, or on OS X, Flash ➪ Preferences ➪ Drawing.) There are three optional settings to control preview, point display, and cursor style:

✦ **Show pen preview:** When you select this option, Flash displays a preview of the next line segment, as you move the pointer, before you click to make the next endpoint and complete the line.

✦ **Show solid points:** Select this option to display selected anchor points as solid points, and unselected points as hollow points. The default is for selected points to be hollow and for unselected points to be solid.

✦ **Show precise cursors:** This option toggles the Pen tool cursor between the default Pen tool icon and a precision crosshair cursor. This can make selecting points much easier and is recommended if you're doing detailed adjustments on a line.

Tip   You can also use a keyboard shortcut to toggle between the two Pen cursor displays: Caps Lock toggles between the precise crosshair icon and the Pen icon when the Pen tool is active.

As Figure 5-22 shows, the Pen tool displays a number of different icons to the lower right of the cursor. These Pen *states* tell you at any given time what action the Pen can perform on a line. The Pen states are shown in this composite image, which is a detail of a path describing a white line over a light-gray background, shown at a Zoom setting of 400 percent.

Pen Icons
A: Empty state area (x)
B: Complete to End Point (o)
C: Remove Point (-)
D: Add Point (+)
E: Convert Point (^)

Pen/Subselect Icons
F: Adjust Line
G: Adjust Point

Point Icons
H: Selected (Filled)
I: Unselected (Empty)
J: Single tangent handle
K: Double tangent handle

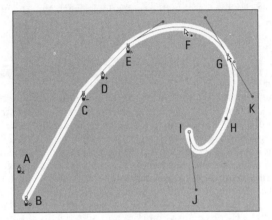

Figure 5-22: In addition to the choice between the cursor icon and crosshair, the Pen tool displays seven Pen states that indicate the Pen's function under various circumstances.

The seven Pen states are as follows:

✦ The Pen displays a small *(x)* when it's simply over the Stage (A).

✦ When the Pen hovers over an endpoint, it displays an *(o)* to indicate that this is an endpoint (B). Click this point to connect a continuation of this path or, when making a closed shape, to close the path.

✦ When the Pen hovers over a corner point, it displays a minus (–) sign to indicate that clicking this corner point deletes it (C).

✦ When the Pen is over a path (a line between two points), it displays a plus (+) sign to indicate that clicking there adds a point to the path (D).

✦ When the Pen hovers over an existing point, it displays a carat (^) to indicate that clicking that point turns it into a corner point (E).

✦ With the Ctrl (or ⌘) key pressed, the Pen behaves like the Subselect arrow, so it switches to the hollow arrow icon with a filled black box (F) over lines, or a hollow white box (G) over points.

✦ When adjusting a path with either the Pen tool or the Subselect arrow, the default for selected points is a filled circle (H), whereas unselected points display as hollow squares (I). Note that the unselected points display a single tangent handle (J), bound toward the selected point, which displays two tangent handles (K).

Now that you've toured the various Pen tool icons and Pen states, it's time to start drawing and see how these actually apply as you work. To draw and adjust a straight-line segment with the Pen tool, follow these steps:

1. With the Pen tool active in the Tools panel, click to place the first point of your line on the Stage (wherever you want the line to start).

2. Then choose the next point and continue to click to create subsequent points and define individual line segments.

3. Each subsequent click creates a corner point on the line that determines the length of individual line segments.

Note

Each click will be a point along a continuous line. To end one line and begin a new line, double-click to place the final point in a line. This "breaks" the line so that the next click will place a starting point for a new line rather than a continuation of the same line. A line should be ended or completed — by double-clicking or by closing your shape — before using the editing keys we describe in Step 4 and Step 5.

4. To adjust straight segments, press the Ctrl (or ⌘) key and click a point to select it. Continue pressing the Ctrl (⌘) key as you drag and move the point to change the angle or length of the segment.

5. Or, with the Ctrl (⌘) key pressed, click and drag on the tangent handles of the point to adjust the line. Remember that corner points occur on a straight segment or at the juncture of a straight segment and a curved segment.

Tip

When you're creating straight lines with the Pen tool, press the Shift key to constrain lines to either 45-degree or 90-degree angles.

To draw and adjust a curved line segment with the Pen tool, follow these steps:

1. Click to create the first anchor point, and without releasing the mouse, drag the Pen tool in the direction you want the curve to go.

2. When the preview of the line matches the curve that you want in the final line, release the mouse and then move to click and place the next point in the segment. Repeat this process to create subsequent curve points for curved segments.

3. Or simply click elsewhere without dragging to place a point and make the subsequent segment a straight line with a corner point.

4. As when adjusting straight segments, press the Ctrl (⌘) key and click a point to select it; continue pressing the Ctrl (⌘) key as you drag and move the point to change the angle or length of the segment.

5. Or, when the Ctrl (⌘) key is pressed, click and drag the tangent handles of the point to adjust the depth and shape of the curve.

Although both corner points and curve points may be adjusted, they behave differently:

✦ Because a corner point defines a corner, adjusting the tangent handle of a corner point only modifies the curve that occurs on the same side as the tangent handle that is being adjusted.

✦ Because a curve point defines a curve, moving the tangent handle of a curve point modifies the curves on both sides of the point.

✦ To convert a corner point into a curve point, simply select the point with the Subselection arrow, and while pressing the Alt (Option) key, drag the point slightly. A curve point with two tangent handles will appear, replacing the original corner point.

✦ To adjust one tangent handle of a curve point independent of the other handle, hold down the Alt (Option) key while dragging the tangent handle that you want to move.

✦ Endpoints cannot be converted into curve points unless the line is continued or joined with another line. To join two endpoints, simply click one endpoint with the Pen tool and then move to the point you want to connect it with and click again. A new line segment will be created that joins the two points.

✦ You can also use the arrow keys, located on your keyboard, to nudge selected corner and curve points into position. Press the Shift key to augment the arrow keys and to make them nudge 10 pixels with each click.

Note   You can also reshape any lines or shapes created with the Pen, Pencil, Brush, Line, Oval, Rectangle, or PolyStar tools as we describe in the section, "Putting Selection Tools to Work," later in this chapter.

Using Fill and Stroke Controls

Now that you know where to find and use the drawing tools, it's time to get more creative with color and line styles. In the following sections, we introduce you to the controls for setting the fill and stroke applied to artwork drawn in Flash.

Choosing colors

The stroke and fill colors that will be applied with any of the drawing tools are determined by the current settings of the color chips located in the Flash Tools panel and in the Property inspector. You can set the fill and stroke colors before you draw something, or select an element on the Stage and adjust it by choosing a new color from the stroke or fill Swatches. The Oval, Rectangle, PolyStar, Brush, and Paint Bucket tools all generate shapes based on the current fill settings — you can select colors before you draw a new shape or select an existing shape and modify it by changing the fill and stroke colors.

The color chips in the Tools panel display the most recently selected colors and are always visible regardless of which tool you're using. The Property inspector shows the color chip of the currently active item, and only displays the chips if they can be applied with the tool you have active or to the item you have selected. Thus, if you select the Line tool, both Stroke and Fill color chips will be visible on the Tools panel, but the Property inspector will display only a Stroke color chip. Although these chips indicate the current color, they're really also buttons: Click any color chip to select a new color from the pop-up Swatches menu. The Swatches menu is shown in Figure 5-23 as it pops up from the Tools panel (top) or from the Property inspector (bottom).

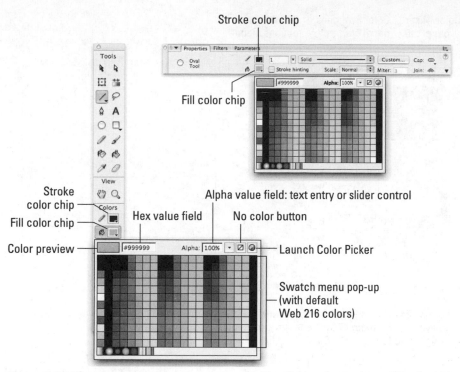

Figure 5-23: The current Swatches pop-up invoked by clicking the Stroke or Fill color chip in the Tools panel (left), or by clicking a color chip on the Property inspector (top right)

The pop-up Color Swatches display the same color options as the main Color Swatches panel shown in Figure 5-24. Use shortcut keys (Ctrl+F9 or ⌘+F9) or select Window ⇨ Color Swatches from the application menu to launch the Color Swatches panel. The Flash 8 Swatches pop-up includes a new Alpha value box as well as a Hexadecimal color value box, another iteration of the No Color button (when it applies), and a button that launches the Color Picker. The Swatches menu evoked with the Fill color chip includes the same solid colors available for Stroke, as well as a range of gradient fill styles along the bottom of the panel.

Cross-Reference We discuss the custom palette options available in the Color Swatches panel in detail, along with the Color Mixer panel and other colorful issues in Chapter 7, "Applying Color."

Color Mixer   Color Swatches   Swatch panel
panel tab   panel tab   options menu

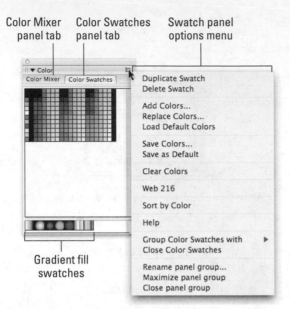

Gradient fill
swatches

Figure 5-24: The default Color Swatches palette as displayed in the main Color panel group — which also enables tabbed access to the Color Mixer panel

Choosing line styles

In Flash, for all tools that draw or display a line or outline, you control the thickness of the line — or stroke — either by dragging the Stroke Height slider or by entering a value in the Stroke Height numeric entry box. Both of these controls are available in the Properties panel, as shown in Figure 5-25. The stroke options are only visible when they can be applied — if a drawing tool that creates lines is active in the Tools panel or if you have selected an element with a stroke.

Note   Generally, in Flash, lines that are independent or not attached to any fill are referred to as *lines,* whereas lines or outlines on a filled shape are referred to as *strokes.* You use the same tools to create and edit lines and strokes.

Changes to stroke color and style apply to lines or curves drawn with the Pen, Line, Pencil, Oval, Rectangle, and PolyStar tools. For shapes, the changes apply only to the outline, not to the fill. As with fill color settings, you can select a stroke color and style before you create any artwork (as long as the tool you're going to use is active in the Tools panel), or you can select a line in the Document window with the Selection tool and change it's appearance with the settings in the Property inspector.

When dragging the Stroke height slider, the numeric entry box updates and displays a height read-out analogous to the current position of the slider. This also functions as a precise numeric entry field. Simply enter a value to create a stroke with a specific height or thickness. Permissible values range from 0.1 to 200, with fractions expressed in decimals.

Stroke style setting   Launch custom
stroke style
dialog box

Stroke height setting

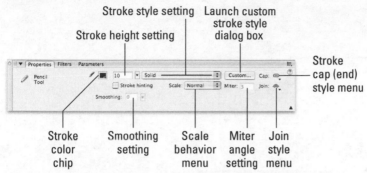

Stroke
cap (end)
style menu

Stroke
color
chip

Smoothing
setting

Scale
behavior
menu

Miter
angle
setting

Join
style
menu

Figure 5-25: The Properties panel gives you all the controls you
need to select the stroke height, color, and style, as well as a new
option to control how strokes will scale in the Flash Player.

**New
Feature**

In older versions of Flash, the largest Stroke height available was 10. In Flash 8, you can now
set stroke heights up to 200. In our experience, any stroke with a height setting of more than
about 25 becomes rather unwieldy. If you need a mark that big, you are probably better off
using one of the shape tools to create a filled area instead of a giant stroke.

Note

Depending upon the level of zoom, the height difference of some lines may not be visible
onscreen — even though zooming in closer enables you to see that the stroke height is correct.
Lines set to a height of 1 pixel or lower appear to be the same thickness unless the Stage view
is zoomed to 200 percent or closer. However, all line heights still print correctly on a high-
resolution printer and will be visible in your final Flash movie (.swf) to anyone who zooms in
close enough.

The Stroke Style drop-down menu (see Figure 5-25) offers the choice of Hairline or six standard,
variable-width strokes. Hairline strokes always have the same 1-pixel thickness, even if the
mark or shape that they outline is scaled larger after the stroke is applied. You can select and
combine the other six line styles with any stroke height. If these styles do not deliver the line
look you need, the Custom button (to the right of the Style menu) invokes a Stroke Style dialog
box (see Figure 5-26), which you can use to generate custom line styles by selecting from a
range of properties for each preset line. Basic properties include Stroke Thickness and Sharp
corners. Other settings vary depending on what style of stroke you choose.

**New
Feature**

The new Scale menu for strokes in the Properties panel enables you to control how lines will
scale when symbols are scaled in the authoring environment or the Flash movie is scaled
in the Flash Player. For those of us who've struggled with keeping lines at a consistent size in
older versions of Flash, this new menu is a welcome addition to Flash 8.

Note

Points are the default unit of measurement for determining the spacing and thickness of line
segments in the Stroke Style dialog box.

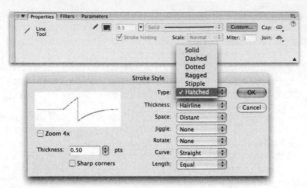

Figure 5-26: The Stroke Style dialog box is invoked with the Custom button on the Property inspector. The properties displayed vary depending on the style of line you select for adjustment.

To closely examine a custom line before you begin drawing with it, select the Zoom 4x check box beneath the preview area of the Line Style dialog box. Note the Sharp corners check box, which toggles this Line Style feature on or off — select the check box to turn Sharp corners on.

Tip   Although there is no way to save custom line styles within the Stroke Style dialog box, you can create a separate document (.fla) and save samples of your favorite lines there. This will ease your workflow if you want to reuse custom line styles extensively. You can apply these styles quite easily to other lines by opening the document and using the Eyedropper tool in conjunction with the Ink Bottle tool. For more information, see the sections on the Eyedropper and the Ink Bottle tools in Chapter 9, "Modifying Graphics."

Of course, the best way to get an idea of the variety of possible strokes is to experiment with settings and sizes for each style, but there are a few things to keep in mind as you work with stroke styles in Flash:

✦ The Hairline line style provides a consistent line thickness that doesn't visually vary at different zoom levels. This is the best line style to choose if you're creating artwork that you want to scale without losing the original line width. Regardless of whether an object with this stroke is enlarged or reduced in size, the hairline stroke always displays as 1-point wide (as shown in Figure 5-27).

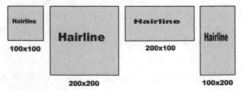

Figure 5-27: Hairline strokes always display at 1-point, even if they are scaled in the authoring environment or in the Player.

✦ The Solid line style draws a smooth, unbroken line. The customization variables for this style are limited to Thickness and Sharp corners. These two variables can also be adjusted on all line styles. The Solid line style is the optimal style for Web viewing because it requires fewer points to describe it and is consequently less file-intensive. The smaller file sizes theoretically translate into faster download times when the art-work is transmitted over the Web. This really only becomes an issue if you're making extensive use of complex line styles.

✦ The Hatched line style thickness settings are different from the point size thickness set-tings that are available for all lines. The default thickness setting (measured in points) defines the thickness or height of the overall hatched line, whereas the hatch thickness setting defines the width of the individual vertical strokes that create the density of the hatched line texture.

Controlling Stroke Scale behavior

The new Scale option is only available for Solid lines, but it is very helpful for ensuring the consistency of scaled UI elements with outlines such as buttons. The various scaling behaviors you can set using the Scale menu will only work if you convert the raw stroke into a symbol. To make this easier to understand, here are the steps for applying the Scale option:

1. Select a Solid line style.

2. Set the stroke height to any height between 0.1 and 200.

3. Select the Scale behavior that will work best for the specific element:

   • **None:** This produces a stroke that does not scale. A Solid stroke with Scale set to None will have the same consistency as a Hairline but you are able to use any stroke height — rather than being restricted to the 1-point height for Hairline strokes. Figure 5-28 shows how a sample graphic with a 3-point stroke and a Scale setting of None will appear when transformed with different amounts of scaling.

   • **Horizontal:** This produces a stroke that scales to match the horizontal transfor-mation of an item. Vertical transformations will have no effect on the scale of the stroke. Figure 5-29 shows how a sample graphic with a 3-point stroke and a Scale setting of Horizontal will appear when transformed with different amounts of scaling.

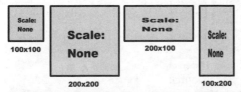

Figure 5-28: Strokes with Scale set to None will always display with the original stroke height.

Figure 5-29: Strokes with Scale set to Horizontal will only scale in proportion to horizontal transformations.

- **Vertical:** This produces a stroke that scales to match the vertical transformation of an item. Horizontal transformations will have no effect on the scale of the stroke. Figure 5-30 shows how a sample graphic with a 3-point stroke and a Scale setting of Vertical will appear when transformed with different amounts of scaling.

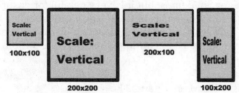

Figure 5-30: Strokes with Scale set to Vertical will only scale in proportion to vertical transformations.

- **Normal:** This produces a stroke that scales proportionally when it is scaled in any direction. This is generally the best setting to use if you want lines to maintain the same relative size as other scaled elements. However, if you want lines to have a fixed size no matter how big or small other elements are scaled, it is best to use the None setting. Figure 5-31 shows how a sample graphic with a 3-point stroke and a Scale setting of Normal will appear when transformed with different amounts of scaling.

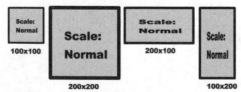

Figure 5-31: Strokes with Scale set to Normal will scale in proportion with the greatest transformation in any direction.

4. Convert the graphic that contains the stroke into a symbol (Movie Clip, Graphic, or Button).

5. Scale instances of the symbol in the authoring environment or in the Player and you will notice how the stroke scaling is constrained based on the Scale setting that you applied to the original stroke (in Step 3).

If you have ever tried to reuse a graphic that needed to be scaled while maintaining a specific size ratio to other elements — either relative or fixed — you will appreciate the new level of control the Scale menu affords. The most common use for this option is constraining the scale behavior of a custom button that has to be adjusted to fit text of varying lengths. Generally, you want the stroke on the button to remain consistent while the button is stretched to accommodate the text. If you apply the Vertical Scale behavior, you will have a button with a stroke that stays the same no matter how long you stretch it horizontally to fit your text. But if you decide the buttons need to be a bit bigger overall, you can apply a vertical transformation and the stroke will grow proportionally. What more could we ask for?

Optimizing Drawings

Aside from making a drawing more geometric, the main advantage of simplifying a shape or line is that it reduces the number of points that Flash has to remember and, thus, reduces the final file size. This is especially important for projects such as cartoons or animations that include a large number of hand-drawn shapes.

The most powerful tool for optimizing artwork precisely is found in the Optimize Curves dialog box invoked by choosing Modify ⇨ Shape ⇨ Optimize. This feature gives you a slider control to set the amount of smoothing applied between None and Maximum. You can also choose to apply optimization repeatedly for greater reduction in points. Selecting the Use multiple passes check box repeats the smoothing process until no further optimization can be achieved. The totals message notifies you how many points have been removed and what percentage reduction has been achieved each time you apply the modification. Figure 5-32 shows a sketch drawn with the Pencil tool in Ink mode before and after multiple passes of Optimize Curves are applied. The reduction in points is displayed in the dialog box. For illustration purposes, we made a drastic adjustment by applying Optimize Curves set at Maximum. For practical purposes, you should find a balance between optimization and drawing complexity by testing a range of settings.

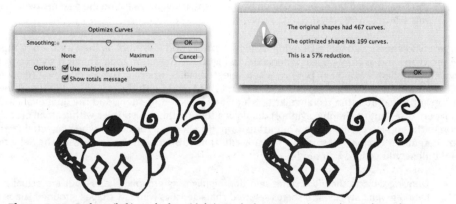

Figure 5-32: Before (left) and after (right) Optimize Curves is used to reduce the complexity of a drawing made with the Brush tool with default smoothing. The reduction in points translates directly into a smaller file size.

Putting Selection Tools to Work

Selection tools enable you to choose items that you want to edit in the Document window, as well as move or reshape specific elements. The three main selection tools — Selection, Subselect, and Lasso — provide different selection styles you can use for different editing tasks. The Subselect arrow is used primarily as a companion to the Pen tool.

Tip   When you are busy with another tool, you can temporarily toggle to the Selection tool by pressing the Ctrl key.

The Selection tool

The Selection (arrow) tool (A) is used most commonly to select and move items — or multiple items — on the Stage. It is also used to reshape lines and shapes, in a way that is familiar to users who have worked in other vector graphics applications. The Selection tool's neighbor, which is differentiated with a white, rather than a black, arrowhead, is the Subselect tool. The Subselect tool is most useful for moving and editing anchor points created with the Pen tool and adjusting tangents on Bezier curves.

You can use the Selection tool to reshape a line or shape by pulling on the line (or shape) itself, or on its endpoints, curves, or corners. You can also use the Selection tool to select, move, and edit other Flash graphic elements, including groups, symbols, buttons, and text. When you click a raw stroke or fill, a mesh pattern appears to indicate that it has been selected. If the item you click is a symbol, a group, or a Drawing Object, a thin colored line (called a *Highlight*) indicates the selection status. You may set the highlight color in the General Preferences dialog box found under Edit ➪ Preferences (or in OS X, under Flash ➪ Preferences).

Tip   To temporarily turn off the selection mesh while editing an element, use View ➪ Hide Edges (Ctrl+H or ⌘+Shift+E). To toggle it back on, enter the same keyboard shortcut again. Even if you have toggled the selection off on one element, it will be visible on the next element that you select.

Figure 5-33 shows a shape, a Drawing Object, a group, and a symbol as they look when unselected (top) and as they appear when selected with the Selection tool. The first oval (a primitive shape), displays a mesh pattern when selected (left), whereas the second oval (drawn with the Object Drawing option turned on) and third oval (with the stroke and fill combined in a group) display a thin rectangular border when selected (center), and the final oval (which was converted into a Graphic symbol) displays a thin rectangular border with a small crosshair icon in the top-left corner and a white transformation point in the center when selected (right). You can move groups and symbols but not edit them directly on the Stage with the Selection tool unless you go into Edit mode.

New Feature   Drawing Objects show the same selection highlight as grouped shapes, but are actually a hybrid graphic style, which shares selected characteristics with raw shapes, grouped shapes, and Graphic symbols. Like raw shapes, you can modify Drawing Objects directly on the Stage with the Selection tool and any of the tools related to fills and strokes. Like grouped shapes, Drawing Objects will not erase or merge with other shapes if they overlap on the same layer (unless special commands are applied). Like symbols, Graphic Objects can be Motion tweened.

Cross-Reference We explain the various ways of using grouped shapes in graphics in Chapter 9, "Modifying Graphics," and we discuss using and editing symbols in Chapter 6, "Symbols, Instances, and the Library."

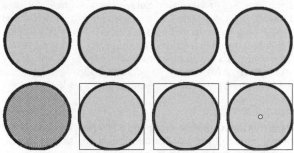

Figure 5-33: Selection tool selection Highlights (L-R) for a shape, a Drawing Object, a group, and a symbol.

In addition to clicking a line to select it, you can select one or more items by dragging a marquee around them when the Selection tool is active. This operation is called *drag-select*. You can add additional items to a current selection by pressing the Shift key and clicking the items in sequence. When you drag-select to make a selection, previously selected items are deselected and excluded from the selection. In order to include previously selected items, press the Shift key as you drag-select. When a group is selected and you drag to move them on the Stage, holding down the Shift key constrains the movement range of the elements to 45 degrees. This is helpful if you need to move an element up or down while keeping it on the same axis or baseline.

Deselect one or more items by using any of the following methods:

✦ Pressing the Escape key

✦ Choosing Edit ➪ Deselect All

✦ Using the keyboard shortcut Ctrl+Shift+A (or ⌘+Shift+A)

✦ Clicking anywhere outside all the selected items

You can also use the Selection tool for duplicating items. Simply select an item (or line segment) with the Selection tool and press the Alt (Option) key while dragging the item to a new location. The original item remains in place, and a new item is deposited at the end of your drag stroke.

Caution Selecting a line with the Selection tool and then holding down the Alt (Option) key while dragging it to a new location will duplicate it. Holding down the Alt (Option) key before dragging a line segment (that has not been selected) with the Selection tool will add a new Corner point.

Moving multiple elements with the Selection tool

Text boxes and groups are selected as single elements and move as a single unit. After you create text in a text box (we discuss text features in Chapter 8, "Working with Text"), Flash treats the text as one block, or group, meaning that all the individual letters move together when the box is selected. Similarly, a group of graphic elements — such as lines, outlines, fills, or shapes — can be grouped and moved or manipulated as a single element. However, when you move an item that is not grouped, only the selected part is moved. This situation can be tricky when you have ungrouped fills and outlines because selecting one without the other could unintentionally break up your shape. To group elements, select them all and apply the Modify ⇨ Group command (Ctrl+G or ⌘+G). If necessary, you can ungroup them later using Modify ⇨ Ungroup (Ctrl+Shift+G or ⌘+Shift+G). We discuss grouping further in Chapter 9, "Modifying Graphics."

Tip   Double-clicking the fill of a shape that has an outline stroke and a fill will select both. You can also use this strategy on lines with multiple sections. Double-clicking one section selects all the connected parts of a line, rather than just the closest segment.

The new Drawing Object mode makes it easier to keep strokes and fills together. Drawing Objects behave like grouped shapes — when you click anywhere on the shape, the stroke and fill will both be selected so they move together. If you have drawn shapes with the Object Drawing toggle turned off, you can use the Modify ⇨ Group command (Ctrl+G or ⌘+G) to group the lines and fills or use the Modify ⇨ Combine Objects ⇨ Union command to convert the raw lines and fills into a Drawing Object.

Modifying Selection preferences

In most cases, the default behavior for selection tools will support your workflow, but there are two preferences that you can modify to adjust selection behavior:

✦ **Turn off Shift select:** Prior to Flash 4, additional elements were added to a selection simply by clicking them. To use this older selection style, go to Edit ⇨ Preferences and under General ⇨ Selection Options, clear the Shift select check box.

✦ **Turn on Contact-sensitive selection:** The standard selection behavior in Flash requires that a lasso or selection marquee completely enclose a group, Drawing Object, or symbol in order to select it. If you prefer to have these items included in a selection when the marquee touches any visible part, go to Edit ⇨ Preferences and under General ⇨ Selection options, select the Contact-sensitive selection and Lasso tools check box. Figure 5-34 illustrates the different selection results that you will get when a marquee partially encloses a group, Drawing Object, or symbol when Contact-sensitive selection is left off (top) and when it is turned on (below).

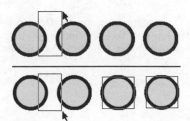

Figure 5-34: To change the default nonselection result of partial selections in Flash (top), you can turn on the new Contact-sensitive selection behavior to select even partially enclosed items (below).

Using Selection-tool arrow states to adjust or move drawings

In addition to the actions accomplished by selecting a line (or line section) and clicking an option, three arrow states — Move Selected Element, Reshape Curve or Line, and Reshape Endpoint or Corner — enable you to reshape and move parts of your drawings. It works like this: As you move the Selection tool over the Flash Stage, the arrow curser changes state to indicate what tasks it can perform in context with various items (the line or fill) closest to the Selection tool's current position.

Tip   When reshaping brush strokes or other filled items with the Selection tool, make sure that you don't select both the stroke and fill before trying to reshape the outline. If you do, you'll be able to move only the entire brush stroke — you won't be able to reshape it.

Figure 5-35 shows a series of (magnified) images that demonstrate the various arrow states as they appear and are applied. On the left, the original shape is shown with the arrow states displayed as the cursor is moved over the center of the shape, over a corner (B), and over a line (C). The center image shows the preview as the Reshape Corner arrow is used to extend the corner of the square and the Reshape Curve arrow is used to stretch the curve. The final image on the right shows the resulting changes to the original square.

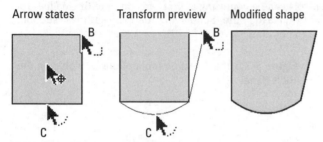

Figure 5-35: Selection tool arrow states used to reshape and reposition an element: Move Selected Item arrow, Reshape Corner arrow (B), and Reshape Curve arrow (C).

Figure 5-36 shows the various Selection tool arrow states used to modify a line. The lower images show the arrow state cursors, the center images show the preview as the mouse is dragged, and the top images show the resulting changes to the line when the mouse is released. You will notice that lines have to be selected in order to be moved without changing their shape with the Selection tool. If the line is not selected, the arrow only displays Reshape Corner or Reshape Curve states. If you want to add an angle to a line rather than add a curve, switch from Reshape Curve to Add Corner Point by holding down the Alt (or Option) key before clicking and dragging a line segment.

Caution   The icon visible next to the Selection tool arrow does not update when you switch from Reshape Curve to Add Corner Point by holding down the Alt (or Option) key, but the behavior will change. After you click and move the line, the icon will update to match the behavior.

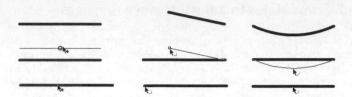

Figure 5-36: Using Selection tool arrow states to reshape and reposition a line. (Left to right) Move Selected Item, Reshape Corner, Reshape Curve, Add Corner Point.

Tip   Some brush strokes are easier to reshape if you view them as Outlines (as we described in Chapter 4, "Interface Fundamentals").

Knowing your Selection tool options

Figure 5-37 shows the three options that appear at the bottom section of the Tools panel when the Selection tool is active: Magnet (or snap to objects), Smooth, and Straighten. Because the various snap controls can be confusing at first, we compare the Magnet tool with the other snap settings available in Flash in the "Simplifying snapping settings" section, later in this chapter.

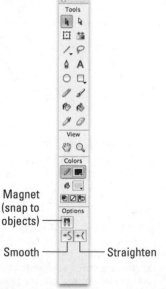

Figure 5-37: The Selection tool options available on the Tools panel

Magnet (snap to objects)

Smooth   Straighten

The Smooth and Straighten options available with the Selection tool (when a raw shape or Drawing Object is selected) are best used to clean up drawings by smoothing irregular curves or straightening crooked lines. Smoothing or Straightening reduces the number of bumps and variations (or points of transition) in a complex shape or line by reducing the number of points. The simplest curve or line will only be described by one point at each end.

To simplify a shape or line, click the Selection tool and select the item you've just sketched. Then click the Straighten or Smooth button in the Tools panel (or use Modify ⇨ Shape ⇨ Straighten or Modify ⇨ Shape ⇨ Smooth) to begin shape recognition. For hard-edged items such as a polygon, click the Straighten button repeatedly until your rough sketch reaches the level of angularity that you like. For smooth-edged items that approximate an oval or an arc, click the Smooth button repeatedly until your rough sketch has the amount of desired roundness. As shown in Figure 5-38, the simplified shape usually needs some further adjustment to get the result that you want after some of the points have been removed. The tools used for adjusting individual curves and points are the Pen tool and the Subselect tool.

Original   Smooth   Straighten

Figure 5-38: A drawing made with the Pencil tool (left), can be selected with the Selection tool and simplified with the Smooth or Straighten options.

You can apply the Smooth and Straighten options with the Selection tool to any selected shape or line to reduce the number of points and simplify the form. The specific effect that these options have on your graphics is dependent on the Drawing Settings that were used to create the original lines. By minimizing complexity in freehand drawings or shapes, Smooth and Straighten gradually reduce an erratic graphic into the most simplified form that can be described with the fewest points possible. You will notice that the Smooth and Straighten options won't have a visible effect on a perfect geometric shape, such as a square, circle, or triangle — this is because Flash uses shape recognition to determine that these forms are already optimized and cannot be simplified any further.

Although these assistants nudge a sketch or line style in the direction that you want, they don't add information; so don't be surprised if it takes a few tries to get the right balance between rough drawing and shape recognition.

The Lasso tool

The Lasso (L) is a flexible tool, somewhat resembling the selection equivalent of the Pen tool crossed with the Pencil tool. You use the Lasso primarily to make freeform selections and to group-select odd or irregular-shaped areas of your drawing. After areas are selected, they can be moved, scaled, rotated, or reshaped as a single unit. You can also use the Lasso tool to split shapes, or select portions of a line or a shape. As shown in Figure 5-39, it has three options in the Tools panel: the Polygon mode button, the Magic Wand, and the Magic Wand properties.

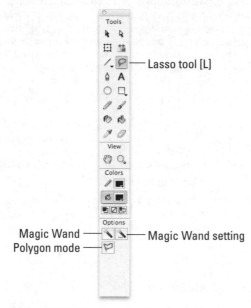

Figure 5-39: The Lasso tool and options

The Lasso tool works best if you drag a loop around the area you want to select. (Hence, the tool name Lasso!) But if you slip or if you don't end the loop near where you started, Flash closes the loop with a straight line between your starting point and the endpoint. Because you can use the Lasso tool to define an area of any shape — limited only by your ability to draw and use the multiple selection capabilities of Flash — the Lasso tool gives you more control over selections than the Selection tool.

Tip   To add to a previously selected area, hold down the Shift key before initiating additional selections.

Polygon mode

Polygon mode affords greater precision when making straight-edged selections, or in mixed mode, selections that combine freeform areas with straight edges. To describe a simple polygon selection, with the Lasso tool active, click the Polygon mode button to toggle on Polygon selection mode. In Polygon mode, you create selection points with a mouse click, causing a straight selection line to extend between mouse clicks. To complete the selection, double-click.

Mixed mode usage, which includes Polygon functionality, is available when the Lasso tool is in Freeform mode. To work in Freeform mode, the Polygon option must be in the off position. While drawing with the Freeform Lasso, press the Alt (Option) key to temporarily invoke Polygon mode. (Polygon mode continues only as long as the Alt (Option) key is pressed.) As long as the Alt (Option) key is pressed, a straight selection line extends between mouse clicks. To return to Freeform mode, simply release the Alt (or Option) key. Release the mouse to close the selection.

Note

> Sometimes aberrant selections—selections that seem inside out, or that have a weird, unwanted straight line bisecting the intended selection—result from Lasso selections. That's usually because the point of origination of a Lasso selection is the point to which the Lasso snaps when the selection is closed. It takes a little practice to learn how to plan the point of origin so that the desired selection is obtained when the selection is closed.

The Magic Wand option and Magic Wand properties

The Magic Wand option of the Lasso tool is used to select ranges of a similar color in a bitmap that has been broken apart. After you select areas of the bitmap, you can change their fill color or delete them. Breaking apart a bitmap means that the bitmap image is subsequently seen by Flash as a collection of individual areas of color. (This is not the same as tracing a bitmap, which reduces the vast number of colors in a continuous-tone bitmap to areas of solid color.) After an image is broken apart, you can select individual areas of the image with any of the selection tools, including the Magic Wand option of the Lasso tool.

The Magic Wand option has two modifiable settings: Threshold and Smoothing. To set them, click the Magic Wand settings button to launch the Magic Wand Settings dialog box (shown in Figure 5-40) while the Lasso tool is active.

Figure 5-40: Use the Magic Wand Settings dialog box to adjust the selection range and level of smoothing

The Threshold setting defines the breadth of adjacent color values that the Magic Wand option includes in a selection. Values for the Threshold setting range from 0 to 200: The higher the setting, the broader the selection of adjacent colors. Conversely, a smaller number results in the Magic Wand making a narrower selection of adjacent colors. A value of zero results in a selection of contiguous pixels that are all the same color as the target pixel.

The Smoothing setting of the Magic Wand option determines to what degree the edge of the selection should be smoothed. This is similar to anti-aliasing. (Anti-aliasing dithers the edges of shapes and lines so that they look smoother onscreen.) The options are Smooth, Pixels, Rough, and Normal.

The Subselection tool

The Subselection (arrow) tool (A) is the companion for the Pen and is found in the Tools panel to the right of the Selection tool. The Subselection tool has two purposes:

✦ To either move or edit individual anchor points and tangents on lines and outlines.

✦ To move individual objects.

When you are moving the Subselection tool over a line or point, the hollow arrow cursor displays one of two states:

✦ When over a line, it displays a small, filled square next to it, indicating that the whole selected shape or line can be moved.

✦ When over a point, it displays a small, hollow square, indicating that the point will be moved to change the shape of the line.

Tip   If you use the Subselection tool to drag a selection rectangle around two items, you'll find that clicking and dragging from any line of an item enables you to move only that item, but clicking on any point on an item enables you to move all items in the selection.

Figure 5-41 shows the use of the Subselection tool to move a path (A), to move a single point (B), to select a tangent handle (C), and to modify a curve by adjusting its tangent handle (D). Note that a preview is shown before releasing the handle.

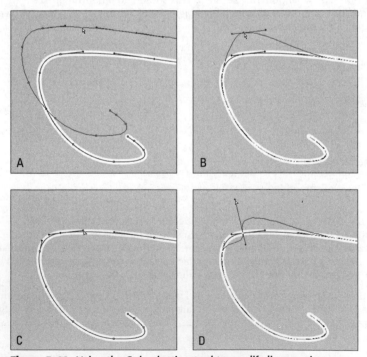

Figure 5-41: Using the Subselection tool to modify lines and curves

The Subselection tool is most useful for modifying and adjusting paths. To display anchor points on a line or shape outline created with the Pencil, Brush, Line, Oval, or Rectangle tools, simply click the line or shape outline with the Subselection tool. This reveals the points that define the line or shape. Click any point to cause its tangent handles to appear. If you have a shape that is all fill, without any stroke, you'll need to position the cursor precisely at the edge of the shape in order to select or move it with the Subselection tool.

To convert a corner point into a curve point, follow these steps:

1. Click to select the point with the Subselection tool.

2. While pressing the Alt (Option) key, click and drag the point.

3. A curve point with tangent handles appears, replacing the original corner point.

Note By holding down the Ctrl (or ⌘) key, the Pen tool can be used to mimic the function of the Subselection tool for moving lines or points but not for converting a curve point into a corner point.

An important use of the Pen tool/Subselection tool combo is editing lines for optimal file size. The simpler your shapes, the smaller your file size and the faster your movie downloads. Most often, this involves deleting extraneous points. There are a few ways to delete points:

✦ Select the line or outline with the Subselection tool, which causes the individual points to appear as hollow circles along the line. Select the point that you wish to remove. Press the Delete key.

✦ Select a line or outline with the Pen tool, and then move the cursor over the point that you want to remove. The cursor updates and displays a small inverted v (^) to the lower right, which is the Corner Point cursor. Click the point with the Corner Point cursor, and continue to hover over the point. After clicking with the Corner Point cursor, the cursor updates and displays a small minus sign (–) to the lower right, which is the Delete Point cursor. Click the point with the Delete Point cursor to delete it.

✦ When deleting more than one point from a closed shape, such as an oval or polygon, use the Subselection tool to drag and select any number of points. Press Delete to eliminate the selected points. The path heals itself, closing the shape with a smooth arc or line.

 Tip If you use the Subselection tool to select a path and then Shift+select several points on it, those points can be moved in unison by dragging or by tapping the arrow keys.

Designing and Aligning Elements

After you've drawn some lines or shapes, you'll want to organize them in your layout. Flash provides some useful tools to help with moving or modifying elements that are familiar if you've worked in other graphics programs. Aside from using the Flash Grid and manually placed Guides with various snap settings to control your layout, you can quickly access the Align panel or the Info panel to dynamically change the placement of elements on the Stage. The Transform panel is the most accurate way to modify the size, aspect ratio, rotation, and even the vertical or horizontal "slant" of an element.

The precise alignment possible with panels and snapping controls is especially helpful if you're working with detailed artwork or multiple shapes that need to be arranged in exact relation to each other.

Simplifying snapping settings

There are five independent snapping settings in Flash. Snapping is a feature that gives you guidance when moving elements on the Stage and helps to align elements accurately in relation to each other, to the drawing grid, to guides, or to whole pixel axis points. The five different snapping controls can be turned on and off in the View ➪ Snapping submenu or in the new Edit Snapping dialog box (shown in Figure 5-42), launched by choosing View ➪ Snapping ➪ Edit Snapping (Ctrl+/ or ⌘+/).

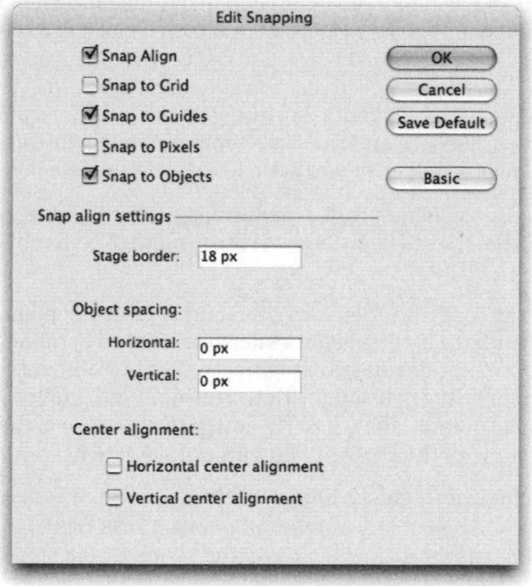

Figure 5-42: You can control Snapping settings in the new Edit Snapping dialog box.

You can tell that an item is snapping by the appearance of dotted guide lines, as shown in the Snap Align example (see Figure 5-43), or by the appearance of a small circle beside the Selection tool arrow cursor, as shown in the Snap to Object and Snap to Grid examples (see Figure 5-44 and Figure 5-45). For best control of snapping position, click and drag from the center point or from an outside edge of an element.

The five main snapping modes are adjusted and applied as follows:

Snap Align

This feature gives you relative visual alignment guides as you move elements on the Stage. You'll either love or hate this option because it's the most "interactive" of all the snapping settings. The controls for Snap Align are in the Advanced settings of the Edit Snapping dialog box (shown in Figure 5-42). By default, Snap Align is set to display visual guides to alert you when an element is within 18 pixels of the Movie border (aka the Stage edge), or within 0 pixels of another element in your layout.

As you move an element around on the Stage you will see dotted lines (see Figure 5-43) that alert you when the edge of the element is exactly 18 pixels from the edge of the Stage, or 0 pixels from the next closest fixed element. The dotted guide lets you know when the edges of the two elements are touching (or perfectly aligned), either vertically or horizontally. Modify the Movie border settings to change the alert or alignment distance between elements and the edge of the Stage. Modify the Horizontal or Vertical Snap tolerance settings to change the alert distance between elements. If you also want to see guides when elements are aligned to the center point of other elements, select the Horizontal or Vertical Center alignment check boxes.

Tip If you change the Horizontal or Vertical Snap Align settings to show a dotted line when an item is a specific distance from another item (such as 10 pixels — this was the default setting in Flash MX 2004), you will still see the dotted line show up when the items are touching or within 0 pixels of each other. The fixed-distance Snap Align cue can be very helpful if you are trying to arrange items but you need them to be more than 0 pixels apart.

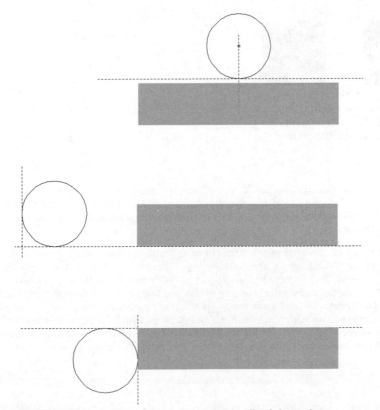

Figure 5-43: Snap Align guides give visual feedback for various alignment settings.

Snap to Objects

The Snap to Objects setting is a toggle that causes items being drawn or moved onscreen to snap to or align with other items on the Stage. Click the magnet icon in the Tools panel to turn snapping on or off (Shift+Ctrl+/ or Shift+⌘+/), or choose View ➪ Snapping ➪ Snap to Objects (a check mark is displayed next to the command if it's on). To control the tolerance of the magnet or the "stickiness" of the snap, use the Connect Lines setting found in Edit ➪ Preferences ➪ Drawing (or in OS X, Flash ➪ Preferences ➪ Drawing). By default, the Connect Lines tolerance is set at Normal. To make the magnet stronger, change the tolerance to Can be distant; to make it less strong, use Must be close. The Connect Lines control will help you to connect lines cleanly when drawing shapes or outlines.

As shown in Figure 5-44, Object snapping is indicated by the "o" icon near the center point as an item is moved from its original position (left). When the item is dragged close enough to another item to snap to it, the "o" icon gets slightly larger, which indicates to you to release the mouse (right). This same visual cue will work if you drag an item by a corner point rather than from a center point. Ovals can be aligned to the center point or to any point along their outer edge.

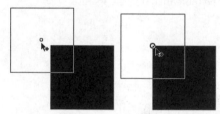

Figure 5-44: Snap to Objects indicated by a change in the size of the center point (or corner point) "o" icon as an item is moved to overlap with another item

Snap to Grid

Snap to Grid (Ctrl+Shift+' [apostrophe] or ⌘+Shift+' [apostrophe]) is an option available under View ➪ Snapping ➪ Snap to Grid, which will help to align elements to guides or to the background grid. If Snap to Grid is turned on, elements show the snap icon by the Arrow cursor when you drag them close to a line in your grid, whether the grid is visible or not.

To control the tolerance of this snapping feature, use the settings found under View ➪ Grid ➪ Edit Grid (Ctrl+Alt+G or ⌘+Option+G). The Grid Settings dialog box also includes check boxes for Snap to Grid and View Grid — these just give you another way to turn these tools on or off. Adjust the default horizontal and vertical spacing of the grid lines by entering new pixel values in the text fields. The first three settings in the Snap Accuracy menu are the same as those for Snap to Object, but there is an additional setting, Always Snap, which constrains elements to the grid no matter where you drag them. Figure 5-45 shows the default 18-pixel gray grid as it displays when it's made visible (View ➪ Grid ➪ Show Grid) with the Stage view zoom at 400 percent.

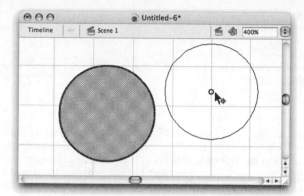

Figure 5-45: The snap icon as it appears when an element is dragged onto a grid line with Snap to Grid turned on (snapping works regardless of whether the grid is visible or not)

Snap to Guides

As we described in the previous chapter, guides are vertical or horizontal visual alignment tools that can be dragged onto the Pasteboard or Stage *when Rulers are visible*: Choose View ➪ Rulers (Ctrl+Alt+Shift+R or ⌘+Option+Shift+R). If Snap to Grid is turned on when you drag guides out, they will be constrained to the grid; otherwise you will be able to place guides anywhere. After guides are set, they will be visible even if you turn Rulers off; to toggle guide visibility use View ➪ Guides ➪ Show Guides (Ctrl+; [semicolon] or ⌘+; [semicolon]). As shown in Figure 5-46, Snap to Guides enables you to align an element to a guide, even if it is not aligned with the grid.

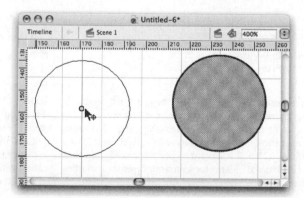

Figure 5-46: The snap icon as it appears when an element is dragged onto a guide with Snap to Guides turned on

Note   Snap to Guides is independent of Snap to Grid, but guides can be placed only outside the grid when Snap to Grid is turned off.

Tip   Rulers have to be visible to drag a guide onto the Stage, but after guides are placed, rulers can be turned off and guides will still be visible.

Snap to Pixels

Snap to Pixels is the only "global" setting that causes all elements to align with a one-pixel grid that is only visible when the View scale is set to 400 percent or greater. This setting does not necessarily help you to align elements with each other, but it does help to keep elements from being placed "between pixels" by constraining movement of elements on the X and Y axes to whole pixels, rather than allowing decimals. There is no shortcut key for turning Snap to Pixels on, but you can always toggle it on and off from the View menu by checking or unchecking View ➪ Snapping ➪ Snap to Pixel. Figure 5-47 shows how the pixel grid displays when the View scale is at 400 percent. Items are constrained to whole pixel axis points if they are dragged from the center or from an outside edge.

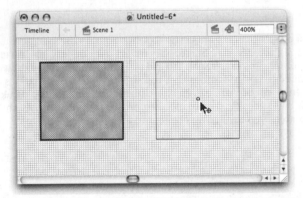

Figure 5-47: The pixel grid visible when View scale is at 400 percent or higher with Snap to Pixels turned on

Caution   If an item is positioned between pixels — for example if the X, Y position is 125.5, 200.5 — the Snap to Pixel feature will not *correct* the position to a whole pixel value. Snap to Pixels only constrains the movement of items to whole pixel values. Thus, the item example given here could only be dragged to a new location by *moving* in whole pixel values; so it might end up at a new location such as 130.5, 225.5. If you want to keep items aligned to whole pixel values, use the input fields in the Property inspector to manually enter a starting location with whole pixel X, Y values — then use the Snap to Pixel option to *keep* items aligned with the one pixel grid.

Tip   When you are working with an oval or other nonsquare polygon, you will notice that the X, Y values in the Property inspector may still show decimal pixel values even when Snap to Pixels is turned on. If you use the Info panel to change the shape's registration point from the default top-left setting to the center (click the center square in the Registration grid), you will have more success positioning and tracking the shape with whole pixel values.

Design panels

When you are drawing in Flash, the design panels — Align, Info, and Transform — can be your best friends. Use the Align panel to align, *regularize* (match the sizes of), or distribute several items on Stage, either relative to each other or to the Stage area. Use the Info panel to modify the coordinates and dimensions of an item. Or use the Transform panel to scale, rotate, and skew an item.

In Flash 8, the Align panel (Ctrl+K or ⌘+K), the Info panel (Ctrl+I or ⌘+I), and the Transform panel (Ctrl+T or ⌘+T) are grouped into a tabbed panel by default that will launch when you select any of the individual panels from the Window menu. It is handy to have these panels in a tabbed group, but if you prefer to work with them as single floating panels, use the Group...with ⇨ New panel group command to separate the panels.

The Align panel

The Align panel (Ctrl+K or ⌘+K), shown in Figure 5-48, is one of many features for which you'll be grateful every time you use it. It enables you, with pixel-perfect precision, to align or distribute items relative to each other or to the Stage.

Figure 5-48: Use the Align panel to both size and arrange items with ease.

The Align panel has five controls. The icons on the buttons show visually how selected items can be arranged:

✦ **To stage:** On the far right, you will notice a To stage button. When this button is selected, all adjustments are made in relation to the full Stage. To stage is actually a toggle you can turn on or off at any time — it will retain the last chosen state even if the panel is closed and reopened.

✦ **Align:** There are six buttons in this first control. The first group of three buttons is for horizontal alignment, and the second group of three is for vertical alignment. These buttons align two or more items (or one or more items with the Stage) horizontally (top, middle, bottom) or vertically (left, middle, right).

✦ **Distribute:** This control also has six buttons: three for horizontal distribution and three for vertical distribution. These buttons are most useful when you have three or more items that you want to space evenly (such as a row of menu items). These buttons distribute items equally, again vertically or horizontally. The different options enable you to distribute from edge to edge, or from item centers.

✦ **Match size:** This control enables you to force two or more items of different sizes to become equal in size, and match items horizontally, vertically, or both.

✦ **Space:** This option enables you to space items evenly, again, vertically or horizontally. You may wonder how this differs from Distribute. Both are similar in concept, and if your items are all the same size, they will have the same effect. The difference becomes more apparent when the items are of different sizes:

- Distribute evenly distributes the items according to a common reference (top, center, or bottom). For example, if one item is larger than the others, it may be separated from the other items by less space, but the distance between its top edge and the next item's top edge will be consistent with all the selected items.

- Space ensures that the spacing between items is the same; for example, each item might have exactly 36 pixels between it and the next.

To align an item to the exact center of the Stage, do the following:

1. Click to select the item that you want to center.

2. Click the To Stage toggle in the Align panel.

3. Click the Align horizontal center button.

4. Click the Align vertical center button.

The Info panel

Use the Info panel (Ctrl+I or ⌘+I), shown in Figure 5-49, to give precise coordinates and dimensions to your items. Type the values in the fields provided, and by default your item will be transformed relative to its top-left corner.

Caution   The registration point set in the Registration grid is actually a global setting that "sticks" even after you close the panel and change tools. Once you change the registration point from top-left to center, any new shapes or symbols that you create will automatically have a center registration point. In most cases, it is best to stick with the default top-left registration point because this is the standard for items that are loaded or positioned with ActionScript. Changing the registration point on one item back to top-left will not have any effect on other items that were created with a center registration point.

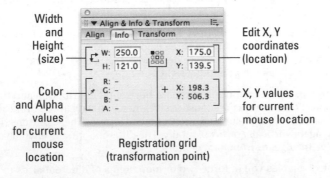

Figure 5-49: Use the Info panel options to change the location and appearance of an item.

The Info panel has these controls:

✦ **Width:** Use this numeric entry field to alter the width of a selected item.

✦ **Height:** Use this numeric entry field to alter the height of a selected item.

Tip

Units for both Width and Height are measured in the units (pixels, inches, points, and so on) set in the Ruler Units option of the Document Properties dialog box found under Modify ⇨ Document (Ctrl+J or ⌘+J). Note, however, that upon changing the unit of measurement, the item must be deselected and then reselected in order for these readouts to refresh and display in the current units.

✦ **Registration grid:** The Registration grid is located just to the left of the numeric entry fields that are used for adjusting the X and Y location of any selected item. This grid consists of nine small squares. Together, these squares represent an invisible bounding box that encloses the selected item. Every shape created in Flash, even circles, resides within an imaginary rectangular bounding box that includes the extremities of the shape. The Registration grid enables you to position the selected item relative to either the upper-left corner or the center of its bounding box. Click either square to define which origin point to use for position or size adjustments.

Note

The X (horizontal) and Y (vertical) coordinates are measured from the upper-left corner of the Flash Stage, which is the origin with coordinates 0,0.

✦ **X:** Use this numeric entry field to either read the X coordinate of the item or to reposition the item numerically, relative to the center point on the X (or horizontal) axis.

✦ **Y:** Use this numeric entry field to either read the Y coordinate of the item or to reposition the item numerically, relative to the center point on the Y (or vertical) axis.

✦ **RGBA:** This sector of the Info panel gives the Red, Green, Blue, and Alpha values for graphic items and groups at the point immediately beneath the cursor. Values for symbols, the background, or interface elements do not register.

✦ **+ X: / + Y:** This sector of the Info panel gives the X and Y coordinates for the point immediately beneath the cursor — including offstage or Pasteboard values. A negative X value is to the left of the Stage, whereas a negative Y is located above the Stage.

To scale or reposition an item, select the item and then open the Info panel with shortcut keys or by choosing Window ⇨ Info:

✦ Choose to scale or reposition the item relative to either the center or the upper-left corner. (The selected square turns black to indicate that it is selected.)

• To work relative to the center, select the center square of the Registration grid.

• To scale relative to the upper-left corner, click the top-left square of the Registration grid.

✦ To scale the item numerically, enter new values in the Width and Height fields, and then click elsewhere or press Enter to apply the change.

✦ To reposition the item numerically, enter new values in the X and Y fields (located in the *upper* half of the panel), then either press Enter or click outside the panel to apply the change.

The Transform panel

The Transform panel (Ctrl+T or ⌘+T) gives you precise control over scaling, rotating, and skewing an item. With this panel, instead of making adjustments "by eye" — that may be imprecise — you enter numeric values in the appropriate fields and apply them directly to the selected item. As shown in Figure 5-50, the value fields in the Transform panel make it easy to modify the size and position of an element. However, once transformations are applied to an ungrouped shape or line, these numbers reset when the shape is deselected.

Tip   If you're using the Property inspector to resize an item by pixel values, you'll appreciate the constrain option. When an item is selected on the Stage, a small lock icon appears beside the Width and Height fields in the Property inspector. Click the lock to preserve the aspect ratio of an element as you enter a new value for width or height.

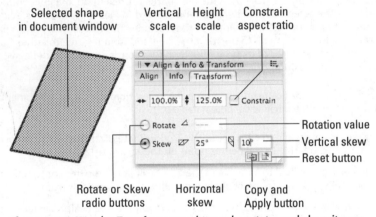

Figure 5-50: Use the Transform panel to scale, rotate, and skew items.

Some other powerful transform options are available from the Tools panel and from the Transform submenu of the Modify menu. We explain these more-complex editing tools in Chapter 9, "Modifying Graphics." However, the best place to start with transform options is the Transform panel, and these options are applied as follows:

✦ **Scale:** Use this to size the selected item by percentage. Enter a new number in the Scale field and press the Enter key. The shape scales to the specified percentage of its original size. To constrain the shape to its current proportions, click the Constrain check box. After a line or shape is deselected, the values in the Transform panel reset. The quickest way to get back to the original settings is to immediately use Edit ➪ Undo (Ctrl+Z or ⌘+Z) until it is reset. You can also get back to the original size mathematically by applying a new percentage that compensates for the changes you made before deselecting the item.

Tip   When you are using the Transform panel with groups and symbol instances, you can reference or reset the original settings, even after the item has been deselected. We explain making and using symbols in Chapter 6, "Symbols, Instances, and the Library."

✦ **Rotate:** Click the radio button and then specify a rotation for the selected item by entering a number in the Rotate field. Press the Return or Enter key to apply the change to the selected item. The item will be rotated clockwise around its center point. To rotate an item counterclockwise, enter a negative number in the Rotate field.

✦ **Skew:** Items can be *skewed* (slanted in the horizontal or vertical direction) by selecting the Skew radio button, and then entering values for the horizontal and vertical angles. Press the Return or Enter key and the item will be skewed to the values entered.

✦ **Copy and Apply transformation:** Press this button and Flash makes a copy of the selected item (including shapes and lines) with all transform settings that have been applied to it. The duplicate is pasted in the same location as the original — select it with the Selection tool and move it to a new position to separate it from the original. Your original is left unchanged.

✦ **Reset:** This button, at the bottom-right corner of the panel, removes all transformation settings for a selected object. You can always use the Reset button for instances, groups, or type blocks to get back to 100-percent scale with no rotation or skew. However, after a shape or line is deselected, this button does not work. For shapes, this is really more like an "Undo All" button than a Reset button.

The Edit menu

We discuss many of the commands in the Edit menu in Chapter 4, "Interface Fundamentals," but some of these commands can be helpful for creating or modifying graphics and are worth mentioning again here:

✦ **Undo:** When you make a mistake, before you do anything else, apply this command to get back to where you started. The default number for combined Undos that Flash remembers is 100; the maximum number is 300. Because Undo "memory" occupies system memory, you can set this level much lower if you find you don't rely on it. This setting is controlled in the General tab of the Flash Preferences dialog box.

New Feature

In Flash 8, it is now possible to switch the Undo behavior from Document-level (Flash MX 2004-style) to Object-level (legacy Flash-style). Document-level Undo stores a combined history stack for all items in the current document, while Object-level Undo stores individual history stacks for each item stored in the Library. The benefit of using Document-level Undo (the default setting for Flash 8) is that more commands or editing steps can be undone. For a complete list of steps that cannot be undone if you opt to use Object-style Undo (including most Create and Delete commands in the Library panel), refer to the section on Using the Undo, Redo, and Repeat menu commands in the Using Flash booklet in the Help panel. The Undo behavior and the number of undo steps that you wish to buffer are controlled in the General section of the Preferences dialog box: File ➪ Preferences or Flash ➪ Preferences.

Note

Undo does not transcend Focus: You cannot Undo work on the Stage from the ActionScript panel — you must first return focus to the Stage to exercise Undo.

✦ **Redo:** The anti-Undo, this redoes what you just undid.

✦ **Repeat:** If you have not just used Undo, you will see this as an option that enables you to "double" whatever edit you may have made, or to apply it to another item.

Cross-Reference   The History panel provides a flexible, nonlinear option for backtracking or repeating steps as you create and edit graphics. You can also use the History panel in conjunction with the Commands menu to track and save authoring steps that you can archive and reuse. We discuss these features in Chapter 9, "Modifying Graphics."

✦ **Cut:** This removes any selected item(s) from the Document window and places it on the Clipboard.

✦ **Copy:** This copies any selected item(s) and places it on the Clipboard, without removing it from the Document window.

✦ **Paste in Center:** Disabled if nothing has been copied or cut, this command pastes items from the Clipboard into the currently active frame on the currently active layer. You can also paste text into panel value fields.

Note   The Paste in Center command places items in the center of the *currently visible* area in the Document window, not in the center of the Stage. Double-click the Hand icon in the Tools panel to center the Stage in the Document window before using Paste in Center if you want the pasted item to be placed in the center of the Stage.

✦ **Paste in Place:** This is like Paste, except that it pastes the object precisely in the same area of the Stage (or Work area) from which it was copied (but it can be on a new Layer or Keyframe).

✦ **Paste Special (PC only):** This is a Windows-only menu that enables some specialized copying of content into Flash. This is not recommended when working in a cross-platform environment because it is platform specific and limits how the document can be edited on other platforms.

✦ **Clear:** This removes a selected item(s) from the Stage *without* copying it to the Clipboard.

✦ **Duplicate:** This command duplicates a selected item or items, without burdening the Clipboard. The duplicated item appears adjacent to the original.

✦ **Select All:** This selects all items in the Document window in the currently active keyframe of the project.

✦ **Deselect All:** This deselects all currently selected items.

✦ **Find and Replace:** This command launches a powerful new option that enables you to specify elements in a current Flash document or Scene and modify them with settings you choose in the Find and Replace dialog box. For more detailed information on using the Find and Replace command, refer to Chapter 9, "Modifying Graphics."

✦ **Find Next:** This is a shortcut that searches through a Flash document or Scene and finds the next item that matches the criteria set in the Find and Replace dialog box.

✦ **Timeline:** This submenu provides access to the most common commands used to modify frames in the Timeline: Cut Frames, Copy Frames, Paste Frames, Clear Frames, Remove Frames, and Select All Frames. These commands are also available in the contextual menu on any frame in the Timeline.

✦ **Edit Symbols:** Select an instance of a symbol and choose this command to modify the content of the symbol in Edit mode, an edit space that is independent from the Stage. For more about symbols and editing symbols, refer to Chapter 6, "Symbols, Instances, and the Library."

✦ **Edit Selected:** This command is only enabled if a group or symbol is selected on the Stage. It makes a selected group or symbol available in Edit mode. This same kind of edit space is invoked for symbols by choosing Edit Symbol.

✦ **Edit in Place:** This command opens a selected group or symbol in a separate tab of the Document window (shown in the location label area of the Document window), and enables you to edit this group or symbol while still seeing the other elements on the Stage, dimmed in the background for reference.

Tip

Double-clicking a group or symbol on the Stage with the Selection tool has the same result as choosing the Edit in Place command.

✦ **Edit All:** From Edit mode, Edit All is used to go back to editing the main Flash scene. You can also do this by clicking on the Scene location label of the Document window.

Summary

✦ Using the geometric shapes available from the Tools panel is a quick, accurate way of creating basic elements that you can customize with various fill and stroke styles.

✦ New Settings dialog boxes for the Oval tool and the Rectangle tool finally make it possible for you to set the width and height of these shapes *before* they are drawn.

✦ The Pencil, Brush, and Pen tools enable you to draw freeform or Bezier lines that you can edit using the Selection tool arrow options and the Subselection tool.

✦ The new Object Drawing option can be turned on while creating graphics with any of the drawing or shape tools. Drawing Objects are hybrid graphics that share selective characteristics with shapes, grouped shapes, and Graphic symbols.

✦ Enhanced Smoothing controls, a Tilt toggle, and a Pressure toggle give artists who use tablets lots of options to customize the Flash drawing environment.

✦ The new Scale control in the Property inspector gives you more precise control over strokes that will be scaled in the authoring environment (as symbol instances) or in the Flash Player (as final published content).

✦ Optimizing artwork manually by editing points with the Subselection tool, or automatically by using the Optimize Curves option, can greatly reduce file size by simplifying lines and curves.

✦ By adjusting and applying the various snapping modifiers, you can control how "auto" alignment behavior affects elements as you work. The new Edit Snapping dialog box enables you to set or modify Snapping behaviors quickly.

✦ Flash 8 gives you the option of using Flash MX 2004-style Undo (Document-level) or going back to the legacy style Undo (Object-level). There are advantages to using Document-level Undo (which is the default in Flash 8), but Macromedia added the legacy option in response to users who wanted to go back to the Undo style that they were familiar with from older versions of Flash.

✦ ✦ ✦

Symbols, Instances, and the Library

Symbols are the key to file-size efficiency and interactive power in Flash. A *symbol* is a reusable element that resides in the current movie's document Library, which you access with Window ⇨ Library (⌘/Ctrl+L). After you convert an item in your Flash movie into a symbol, each time you use that item on your Main Timeline or within a Movie Clip timeline, you're working with an *instance* of the original symbol. Unlike using individual graphic elements, you can use many instances of a symbol, with little or no addition to the file size.

Using symbols helps reduce the file size of your finished movie because Flash needs to save the symbol only once. Each time a given symbol is used in the project, Flash refers to its original profile. To support the variations of an instance, Flash needs to save information about the *differences* only — such as size, position, proportions, and color effects. If a separate graphic was used for each change, Flash would have to store a complete profile of all the information about that graphic — not just the changes, but also all of the points that specify what the original graphic looks like.

Furthermore, symbols can save you a lot of time and trouble, particularly when it comes to editing your movie. That's because changes made to a symbol are reflected in each instance of that symbol throughout the movie. Let's say that your logo changes halfway through production. Without symbols, you would have to find and change each copy of the logo. However, if you've used symbol instances, you need only edit the original symbol — the instances are automatically updated throughout the movie.

In this chapter, you learn to create and edit basic symbol types stored in your document Library. You also learn to use symbol instances, both within the Main Timeline and within other symbols, and to modify individual instances of a symbol. We'll briefly introduce special symbol types associated with Components and Timeline Effects.

Cross-Reference

We discuss applying and editing Timeline Effects in more detail in Chapter 12, "Applying Filters and Effects." We cover using and modifying Components in Chapter 33, "Using Components."

Understanding the Document Library

The Library (⌘/Ctrl+L) is the storehouse for reusable elements, known as *symbols,* which can then be placed as symbol *instances* within a Flash movie. Imported sounds and bitmaps are automatically placed in the Library. Upon creation, Graphic symbols, Button symbols, and Movie Clip symbols are also stored in the Library. It's a good practice to convert main items within a Flash document into symbols, and to then develop your project from instances derived from these original symbols.

The main document Library panel is used to access stored assets for any files that are currently available in the tabbed Document window. Each file has its own unique Library list that will display all symbol assets used in the file as well as any assets that were imported or added to the Library to be saved with the file.

New Feature

The Flash 8 Library panel includes a new drop-down menu that provides quick access to the Library list of any project files (.fla) loaded into the Document window. Changing the view within the main Library panel in Flash 8 is faster and more space efficient than opening and managing multiple Library panels in older versions of Flash.

Note

In Figure 6-1, the document Library is shown in Wide state, whereas the Common Libraries are shown in Narrow state. All Library panels can be toggled between these two view options by clicking the wide or narrow rectangle icons on the right margin of the panel or scaled manually by dragging the lower-left corner of the panel.

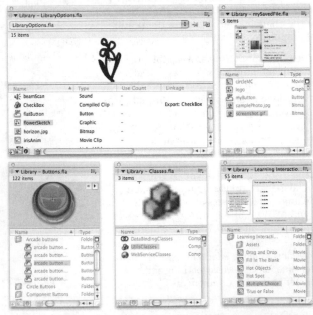

Figure 6-1: The main Library panel provides access to assets for open .fla files (top-left). Common Libraries (bottom) and other saved .fla files (top-right) can be opened as External Libraries and used as asset source files.

Working with Common Libraries and External Libraries

External Libraries are panels that open separately from the main Library panel to provide access to stored assets for files that are not currently open in the Document window. You can open any saved Flash file as an External Library by choosing File ➪ Import ➪ Open External Library and browsing to the file that you want to load. All the stored symbols from your selected file will be visible in a floating External Library panel, but the document will not be visible in the Document window and you cannot edit the symbols in the External Library unless you copy them to the main Library panel or to the Stage of a file that is open in the Document window.

Flash ships with three External Libraries called Common Libraries. These panels hold ready-made elements that you can drag into any document Library (or onto the Stage or Pasteboard in an open Document Window) to use in your own projects. Common Libraries behave exactly like any other External Library. Choose Window ➪ Common Libraries to open the submenu of Common Libraries that ship with Flash. The Buttons and Learning Interactions Libraries contain a selection of prebuilt Flash elements that you can reuse in any Flash project. The Classes Library contains compiled scripts that are used with the components that ship with Flash 8. Macromedia stores these elements in the Classes Library as Compiled Clips to encapsulate the code.

You can open and use the Common Library panels and any other External Library panels as free-floating panels (as shown in Figure 6-1) or you can stack or group them for tabbed access (as shown in Figure 6-2). After you copy assets to one of the document asset lists in the main Library panel (or into any of your project files in the Document window), you can close the External Library and work with the copied symbols without changing the original symbol source.

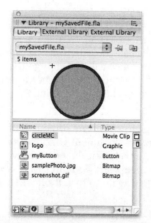

Figure 6-2: You can organize Common Libraries and External Libraries into panel stacks (left) or tabbed groups (right).

If you find it hard to keep track of which Library is your "real" library—or the asset list for the project file that you are currently working on—you will appreciate the visual clue that Macromedia has included with the Library feature. The asset list directly linked to the project file that is currently open in the Document window is rendered in black text (refer to the document Library panel shown on the right in Figure 6-2), while any asset lists for other project files or External Libraries are rendered in gray text (refer to the Buttons Library panel shown on the left in Figure 6-2). This difference is subtle in the authoring environment but it does help your main Library panel list stand out if you are working with multiple libraries.

Tip

To add your own buttons, symbols, or even complete libraries for specific projects, first save them in a Flash document (.fla) with a descriptive name; then place that Flash file in the Libraries folder within the Configuration folder for Flash 8 on your hard drive.

The source files for the External Libraries that show up in the Common Libraries menu are stored in the Libraries folder of the Configuration folder for Flash 8.

✦ The standard directory path on Windows is:

```
C:\Program Files\Macromedia\Flash 8\(language)\Configuration\Libraries
```

✦ The standard directory path to the application config folder on Mac is:

```
HD\Applications\Macromedia Flash 8\Configuration\Libraries
```

Note

The Sounds Library is no longer shipped with Flash, but you can create your own library of sounds if you have a collection of optimized files that you plan to reuse in future projects. Simply load the sounds into one Flash document (.fla) and save the file in the Libraries folder within the Flash 8 Configuration folder on your hard drive. If you have the sounds that were available in the Flash MX Sounds Library, you could also move that folder to the Libraries folder to access them from the Common Libraries menu in Flash 8.

Working with multiple Document Libraries

The new Flash 8 Library panel includes a drop-down menu (shown in Figure 6-3) that lists all currently open files. This is a great space-saver that makes it much easier to switch between different document Libraries without having to manage separate floating panels. By default, the Library panel will switch views as you tab from one document to another in the Document window, but changing the Library view will not change the Document view — in other words, the Library panel is slaved to the Document panel but not the other way around. This makes it easy to access a different Library while maintaining the view of your current file in the Document window.

If you want to keep a Library asset list for one project visible in the Library panel while tab-bing to a different project file in the Document window, you can use the handy new Pin toggle in the Library panel. Click the tack or pushpin icon (shown in Figure 6-3) to pin or "stick" the current asset list so it won't change when you tab to a new project in the Document window. Don't forget to click the Pin toggle again to turn it off when you want to un-stick the Library asset list.

There are times when you may want to see the contents of more than one Library at a time — to compare files or to drag items from one Library to another. Fortunately, Macromedia included a handy button in the Library panel that supports this workflow. Click the New library panel button (shown in Figure 6-3) to create a duplicate floating Library panel at any time. You can then use the drop-down menu to switch the project view in one of the Library panels to compare items or to drag the contents of one Library to another. Like External Libraries or other floating panels, Document Library panels can be grouped (for tabbed access), stacked, or floated as individual panels.

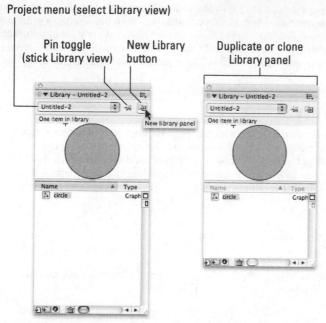

Figure 6-3: The Flash 8 document Library panel includes a new project menu, Pin toggle, and New Library button. As shown, you can use the New library panel button to launch a clone panel (right) for the current project view in the main document Library (left).

You can access elements stored in the Library of any other Flash document (without opening the actual .fla file in the Document window) by choosing File ⇨ Import ⇨ Open External Library from the application menu and browsing to an .fla file. The Library will open next to the Document window of your current project as a floating panel that can be handled exactly like any of the Common Libraries. External Libraries (Library panels for files that are not open in the Document window) do not show up in the drop-down menu of the main Document Library panel, but they can be grouped or stacked with the main Document Library if you need to keep them handy without eating up screen space.

You can copy assets from an External or Common Library to a current Document Library by dragging items from the source Library onto the current document Stage, or directly into the Library panel. This will also work if you have two documents open, and you want to move assets between the two Libraries. It is also then possible to drag or copy and paste elements directly from one document Stage onto another, or drag an item from a source document Stage into a current document's Library.

New Feature

In Flash 8, open documents are loaded into the new tabbed Document window. If you want to view more than one Document Stage at a time, use the Window ⇨ Duplicate Window command to create a clone of one of the tabbed documents. You can then use the tabbed UI in the main Document window to switch views to any other open document while keeping a view of the cloned document in the duplicate Document window.

The shared Library feature, introduced in Flash MX, makes it possible to link assets between project files (.fla) during production using *Authortime* sharing, or to link multiple published movie files (.swf) on the server with *Runtime* sharing. Shared libraries create a more optimized workflow than saving individual copies of assets in multiple documents. You can learn more about linking symbols in your project files in the "Using Authortime Shared Libraries" section later in this chapter.

Reading the Library

Every Flash document has its own Library, which is used to store and organize symbols, sounds, bitmaps, and other assets such as video files. As shown in Figure 6-4, the item highlighted — or selected — in the Sort window is previewed in the Preview window. Each item in the Library has an icon to the left of the name to indicate the asset type. Click any heading to sort the window by Name, Kind (type), Use Count, or Linkage (all headings shown in Figure 6-1).

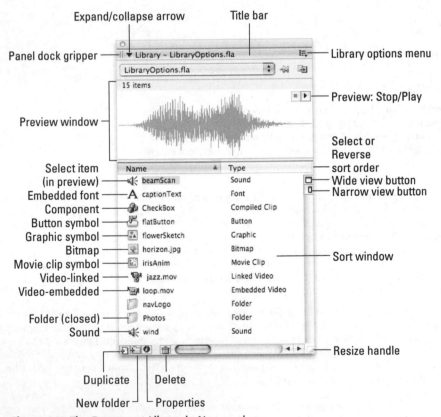

Figure 6-4: The Document Library in Narrow view

If the item selected in the Library is a Button symbol, a Movie Clip, or a sound file with more than one frame on its timeline, a controller appears in the upper-right corner of the Preview window. This Preview Stop/Play controller pops up to facilitate previewing these items. It's equivalent to the Play command in the options menu. As shown in Figure 6-5, the Library options pop-up menu lists a number of features, functions, and controls for organizing and working with items in the Library.

Figure 6-5: The Library panel and the options pop-up menu

The following commands, found in the Library options menu, enable you to add or modify content stored in your document Library.

✦ **New Symbol:** Choose this command to launch the Create New Symbol dialog box where you can name and choose Properties for a symbol. Then click OK to open Edit mode and place or create graphics on the symbol timeline. When a new symbol is created, it is stored at the root of the Library Sort window. You can drag it inside of any existing Library folders.

✦ **New Folder:** Items in the Library can be organized in folders. The New Folder command simply creates a new folder within the Sort window. New folders are "untitled" by default ⌘ double-click the folder text to type a custom folder name. This menu command is equivalent to the New Folder button at the bottom of the Library panel.

✦ **New Font:** Use this command to invoke the Font Symbol Properties dialog box, which is the first step in creating a Font Symbol for use within a Shared Library.

✦ **New Video:** Creates a new empty `Video` object in the Library.

✦ **Rename:** Use the Rename command to rename the currently selected item in the Sort window. Double-click on any item title in the list to achieve the same thing.

✦ **Move to New Folder:** Use the Move to New Folder option to open the New Folder dialog box. Click OK to automatically insert the new folder in the Library Sort window. The currently selected item in the Library is stored in the new folder.

Note   You can also move Library items to folders by dragging them onto any Folder icon.

✦ **Duplicate; Delete:** Select Duplicate to create a copy of an item and Delete to delete an item in the Sort window.

✦ **Edit:** Choose Edit to access the selected symbol in Edit mode.

Tip   Double-clicking a symbol on the Stage takes you into Edit in Place mode, a variant of Edit mode that enables you to see other elements on the Stage dimmed in the background for layout reference as you modify the symbol.

✦ **Edit with:** Provided that you have appropriate external applications installed, most imported assets (such as sounds, bitmaps, and vectors) will have this command available to jump to the external editing environment of your choice.

✦ **Properties:** This command invokes the related Properties dialog box for the particular symbol type—Sound, Bitmap, Symbol, Component, or Video Properties. The Properties dialog box is a central control that enables you to rename an element, access Edit mode, or access the Linkages dialog box from one location. This is also where you can define or edit the Source for any element.

✦ **Linkage:** Use this command to invoke the Linkage options dialog box. Linkage means that you can assign an identifier string to a Movie Clip symbol, a Font symbol, a sound, or a `Video` object so that it can be accessed with ActionScript. This is an aspect of Shared Libraries.

✦ **Component Definition:** This Library option invokes the Define Component dialog box, which you use to assign variables to Movie Clips to create your own Components. (Components are Movie Clips with customizable behavior that can be reused in projects.)

Tip   A library of precompiled components is available in the Components panel. To set parameters for the compiled Components that ship with Flash, you must use the Component Inspector panel or the Parameters tab in the Property inspector.

✦ **Select Unused Items:** Select Unused Items to find any items stored in the Library that have not been used in the current project.

Tip   Unused items will not be included in your published movie file (.swf), but they will add weight to your project file (.fla). The Select Unused Items command is a handy way to find these files so you can delete them to streamline your project file. Use Save and Compact or Save As to save your .fla file minus the extra weight of the unused items that you have deleted from the Library.

✦ **Update:** Use this option if you've edited items subsequent to importing them into Flash. Items will be updated without the bother of re-importing. You can also use this option to swap in a new element of the same kind to replace an item already used in your project.

✦ **Play (or Stop, if currently playing):** If the selected asset has a timeline or is otherwise playable (such as a sound), click this to preview the asset in the Library Preview window. If the asset is currently playing, this option is updated to Stop—in which case, click to stop playing.

✦ **Expand Folder/Collapse Folder:** Use this command to toggle the currently selected folder in the asset window open or closed.

✦ **Expand All Folders/Collapse All Folders:** Use this command to toggle all folders and subfolders in the asset window open or closed.

✦ **Shared Library Properties:** Use this command to invoke the Shared Properties dialog box, which is another aspect of runtime Shared Libraries.

✦ **Keep Use Counts Updated:** Use this command to tell Flash to continuously keep track of the usage of each symbol. If you're working with multiple, complex graphics and symbols, this feature can slow down your processor.

✦ **Update Use Counts Now:** Use this option to tell Flash to update the usage of each symbol. This command is a one-time check and is probably less of a drain on system resources than the previous command, which checks continuously.

Selecting New Symbol, Duplicate, or Properties from the options menu launches the Symbol Properties dialog box, shown in Figure 6-6. Use this dialog box to give the symbol a unique name and assign it a behavior (as a symbol type—Graphic, Button, or Movie Clip). However, if you choose the Properties option for a sound asset, then the Sound Properties dialog box appears.

Assign symbol behavior   Launch Symbol Edit mode

Figure 6-6: The Symbol Properties dialog box. Note the button for Advanced options—this expands the dialog box to include Linkage and Source information for the selected element.

Organizing the Library

When your movies start to become complex, you'll find that the Library gets crowded, and it can be hard to find symbols. When this happens, you'll appreciate the capability to create and name folders for your symbols. You can organize your Library folders however you like, but here are a few suggestions for greater productivity:

✦ Create a separate folder for each Scene.

✦ Create folders for symbol types, such as buttons, sounds, or bitmap imports.

✦ Store all symbols or graphics that relate to a specific element (such as a logo or an animated element) together in one folder.

When you build complex layered structures in your movie — a Movie Clip symbol on the first frame of a Button symbol, with a text symbol on the layer above it, and a sound on the layer above that — the Library doesn't visually track this hierarchy. But you can indicate this — just put all the associated symbols in a folder with a name that describes the final element. You can also nest folders within other folders. Working with folders in the Library is almost exactly the same as working with folders in the Layers area of the Timeline window, as follows:

✦ To create a folder, click the folder icon at the bottom-left corner of the Library.

✦ To move a file or folder into another folder, simply drag it over the target folder icon.

✦ To move a folder that's been nested within another folder back to the top level of the Library, drag the folder until it is just above the Library list and over the word Name and release.

Note   Putting symbols in different folders does not affect the links between them and their instances (as opposed to the way moving a graphic file into a new folder breaks an existing link on a Web page). Flash tracks and updates all references to Library items whenever you rename or move them into separate folders (within the same Library).

The Movie Explorer is a great way of getting a visual overview of the nested relationship of symbols, Movie Clips, and other items within your document. Refer to the end of this chapter for more on the Movie Explorer.

Caution   If you change the Undo behavior in your Flash Preferences from Document-level to Object-level, you'll lose the option to undo some authoring steps. For example, any item that is deleted from the Library is gone forever, including all instances throughout the current document (.fla). If you decide that you shouldn't have deleted an item, the only cure is to close the file without saving any changes. When you reopen the file, the Library should be intact as it was the last time the file was saved.

Resolving conflicts between Library assets

Importing or copying an asset into your current project Library will occasionally invoke a Resolve Library Conflict alert box asking if you want to Replace Existing Items and Instances. This alert box appears when you are trying to add a new asset to your Library with the same name as an asset already present in your current document. If you choose not to replace the existing item, the newly added items will have the word *copy* added to their filenames. For example, if you have an item named *photo* in your current Library and attempt to add another item to the Library with the same name, the new item is given the name *photo copy* in the Library. To rename the added item, simply double-click on the item name in the Library list and type a new name.

If you choose to replace the existing item in your Library, all instances will be replaced with the content of the newly added item. If you choose to cancel the import or copy operation, the selected items will not be added to your current document and the existing items stored in the Library will be preserved.

Tip   Flash offers an option to Import to Library that is especially useful when you want to bring in a series of items. Instead of having all the items dumped onto the Stage in your Document window, you can load them directly into the project Library. Select File ⇨ Import ⇨ Import to Library.

Defining Content Types

Understanding the behavior of various media types and learning to streamline asset management unlocks the true potential of Flash for combining compelling content with small file sizes. The basic structures for storing, reusing, and modifying content within a Flash project are not complicated, but the reason for using various symbol types does deserve explanation.

Raw data

When you create graphics directly in Flash, using the shape tools, text tool, or any of the other drawing tools, you produce raw data or *primitive shapes*. You can copy and paste these elements into any keyframe on the Timeline, but they do not appear in the project Library. Each time the element appears, Flash has to read and render all the points, curves, and color information from scratch because the information is not stored in the Library. Even if the shape looks exactly the same on keyframe 10 as it did on keyframe 1, Flash has to do all the work to re-create the shape every time it appears. This quickly bloats the size of the .swf file. Also, because each element is completely independent, if you decide to make any changes, you have to find and edit each appearance of an element manually. This is a daunting task if your project involves animation or nested symbols.

Tip   The Find and Replace feature (Option/Alt+F), makes it much easier to accomplish mundane editing tasks on multiple items within your Flash project file. We introduce the myriad uses for Find and Replace in Chapter 9, "Modifying Graphics."

Tip   If you want to convert a raw graphic into a Drawing Object after it has been created, select the graphic on the Stage and apply the Modify ⇨ Combine Objects ⇨ Union command from the main menu. The raw graphic will then behave exactly like any other Drawing Object. To revert a Drawing Object to a raw graphic, use the Modify ⇨ Break Apart command.

Drawing Objects

You create Drawing Objects by turning the Object Drawing option toggle on in the Tools panel while using any of the drawing or shape tools. Drawing Objects were introduced in Flash 8 to make it easier to work with raw graphics. Drawing Objects have some of the characteristics of a raw shape, a group, and a Graphic symbol. They can be modified directly on the Stage (without having to click in to Edit mode) but they are self-contained and will not merge with or cut into other graphics on the same layer — unless you apply one of the Combine Objects commands. They can be Motion tweened like a symbol but they are not stored in the Library unless they are converted into one of the true symbols types. The hybrid characteristics of Drawing Objects will suit some workflows very well, but some graphic artists will prefer to work in normal or Non-Object Drawing mode. Drawing Objects can be combined seamlessly with raw graphics and symbols, and turning the Object Drawing option on or off will not have any effect on graphics you have already created.

Caution   Shapes or lines made with the new Drawing Object toggle turned on have some special behaviors in the authoring environment, but like primitive shapes and groups, Drawing objects are not stored in the Library unless they are converted into symbols.

Groups

The first step toward making raw data more manageable is to use groups. By grouping a filled shape with its outline stroke, for example, it becomes easier to select both parts of the shape to move around in your layout. If you added a text element that you also wanted to keep aligned with your artwork, you could add this to the group as well. Groups can be inclusive or cumulative, so that you can select multiple elements and create one group (⌘/Ctrl+G) that can be accessed on the same edit level by double-clicking the whole group once. If you add another element (even another group) to the first group, you will find that you have to click in to a deeper level to edit individual elements. In this way, groups can grow more and more complicated, which is helpful if you're trying to keep multiple elements in order.

The important thing to remember about groups, however, is that they are *not* symbols. Although groups have a similar selection highlight to symbols, you will notice that they don't have a crosshair icon in the center, and that the group information won't appear in your project Library. No matter how careful you are about reusing the same raw data and grouping elements to keep them organized, when it comes to publishing your movie (.swf) or trying to update any single element, you will be no better off than if you had just placed raw elements wildly into your project. Flash still treats each shape and line as a unique element, and the file size grows exponentially each time you add another keyframe containing any of your raw data, even if it is grouped. The best way to use groups in your project is for managing symbols, or to organize elements that you plan to keep together and convert into one symbol.

Caution   Using groups will help organize raw shapes or other elements in your .fla files, but it will not help to optimize the final .swf file. Using a lot of groups in your project file can actually *add* weight to the final published .swf.

Native symbols

Imported sound, video, bitmap, or font symbols are stored automatically in the Library to define *instances* of the asset when it is used in the project. In addition, three basic *container* symbol types can be created in the Flash authoring environment: Movie Clip symbols, Graphic symbols, and Button symbols, which all have timelines that can hold images, sounds, text, or even other symbols. Although it is possible to make the behavior of a symbol instance different from the behavior of the original symbol, it is generally best to decide how you plan to use a certain element and then assign it the symbol type that is appropriate to both its content and expected use in the project.

Tip   Dragging a primitive shape or group into the Library panel from the Stage automatically invokes the Convert to Symbol dialog box so that you can name and assign a symbol type to the element before it is added to your Library.

To make a decision on what type of symbol to use, it helps to have a clear understanding of the benefits and limitations of each of the symbol types available in Flash. Each symbol type has specific features that are suited to particular kinds of content. Each symbol type is marked with a unique icon in the Library, but what all symbols have in common is that they can be reused within a project as symbol instances, all defined by the original symbol. A Flash project Library may contain any or all of the symbol types in the following sections, all created directly in Flash.

Note

If you use Timeline Effects to auto-create animation or visual effects, the symbols added to the Library to contain the animation are usually Graphic symbols by default (rather than Movie Clips), so that you can view the final effects just by scrubbing the Timeline.

Graphic symbols

Graphic symbols are used mainly for static images that are reused in a project. Flash ignores any sounds or actions inside a Graphic symbol. Graphic symbols do not play independently of the Main Timeline and thus require an allocated frame on the Main Timeline for each frame that you want to be visible within the symbol. If you want a Graphic symbol to loop or repeat as the Main Timeline moves along, you have to include another whole series of frames on the Main Timeline to match the length of the Graphic symbol timeline for each loop.

A drop-down menu in the Property inspector enables you to control Graphic symbol playback. Select a Graphic symbol instance in your document and open the Property inspector to access the three settings in the Options for graphics menu:

✦ **Loop:** This is the default setting for Graphic symbols. If the Graphic symbol extends along a timeline beyond its original length, the symbol will restart from the beginning. Graphic symbol looping does not play independently of the Main Timeline like Movie Clip looping — you still have to match the number of frames on the Main Timeline with the number of frames that you want to play in the Graphic symbol timeline.

✦ **Play Once:** This setting eliminates looping by allowing the Graphic symbol timeline to play, then holding on its last frame if it extends along a timeline beyond its original length.

✦ **Single Frame:** This setting will hold the Graphic symbol on one frame so that it will behave like a static graphic. You can select a specific frame within the Graphic symbol timeline to display as the static graphic. The appearance of the Graphic symbol will be the same regardless of how far it extends along a timeline.

Movie Clip symbols

Movie Clips are actually movies within a movie. They're good for animations that run independently of the movie's Main Timeline. They can contain actions, other symbols, and sounds. You can also place Movie Clips inside of other symbols and they are indispensable for creating interactive interface elements such as animated buttons.

Movie Clips can continue to play even if the Main Timeline is stopped. Thus, they need only one frame on the Main Timeline to play back any number of frames on their own timeline. By default, Movie Clips are set to loop. So, as long as there is an instance of the Movie Clip visible on the Main Timeline, it can loop or play back the content on its own timeline as many times as you want it to, without needing a matching number of keyframes on the Main Timeline. Movie Clip playback can be controlled with ActionScript from any timeline or even from an external code (.as) file.

Button symbols

Button symbols are used for creating interactive buttons. Button symbols have a timeline limited to four frames, which are referred to as *states*. These states are related directly to user interaction and are labeled Up, Over, Down, and Hit. Each of these button states can be defined with graphics, symbols, and sounds. After you create a Button symbol, you can assign independent actions to various instances in the main movie or inside other Movie Clips. As with Movie Clips, Button symbols only require one frame on any other timeline to be able to play back the three visible states (frames) of their own timeline.

Components

Components are prebuilt Movie Clips for interactive Flash elements that can be reused and customized. Flash MX-style, or *uncompiled*, components are visible in the root folder of the Library along with a folder that holds the elements used to build the component. Flash MX 2004-style, or *compiled*, V2 Components are represented by a single generic icon in the Library. Each Component has its own unique set of ActionScript methods that enable you to set options at run time.

Imported media elements

A Flash project Library also stores certain types of imported assets to define instances of the asset when instances are used in the movie. You can place these imported assets into native Flash symbol structures by converting a bitmap into a Graphic symbol or placing a Sound inside a Button symbol, for example.

Bitmaps

Bitmaps are handled like symbols: The original image is stored in the Library and any time the image is used in the project it is actually a copy, or an *instance,* of the original. To use a bitmap asset, drag an instance out of the Library and onto the Stage. You manage Export settings for individual bitmaps from within the Library by choosing Properties from either the contextual menu or the Library options menu. However, you will not be able to apply Color or Alpha effects or any Flash 8 Filters to the bitmap instance unless you convert it into a native Flash symbol type (Graphic symbol, Button, or Movie Clip).

New Feature If you worked with bitmaps in older versions of Flash, you will notice how much better images look in Flash 8. The improved rendering engine does a much better job of smoothing scaled and rotated images and keeps the appearance of bitmaps more consistent between the authoring environment and the Player.

Cross-Reference Bitmaps can be targeted with ActionScript to change their appearance dynamically at run time. Although this takes some time to learn, the end result is usually a more optimized file that runs faster and is easier to modify or update. If you feel ready to move on from manual tweens and author-time effects to dynamic code-driven animation and effects, a good place to start is the *Flash 8 ActionScript Bible* by Joey Lott (Wiley, 2006).

Vector graphics

Vector graphics, upon import from other applications, arrive on the Flash Stage as a group, and unlike bitmaps, may be edited or manipulated just like a normal group drawn in Flash. These elements will not be stored in the Library until they have been converted to a native symbol type.

Graphic symbols versus Movie Clip symbols*

Graphic symbols are a quick and tidy way of placing static information into a timeline, whereas Movie Clip symbols animate independently on their own timeline. Graphic symbols should be used to hold single frames of raw data, or multiple frames when it is important to preview your work while designing it, as with linear animation. You must use Movie Clips when ActionScript is involved, or when an animation must run regardless of what is happening around it. However, using one type of symbol instead of the other may not always involve clear-cut choices, because, often, either works. Consequently, to use symbols effectively, it's important to know the pluses, minuses, and absolutes of both Graphic symbols and Movie Clips. Here are some tips to keep in mind:

✦ Instance properties of Graphic symbols (height, color, rotation, and so on) are frozen at design time, whereas Movie Clips can have their instance properties set on the fly with ActionScript. This makes Movie Clips essential for programmed content such as games.

✦ Scrubbing the Main Timeline (previewing while working) is not possible with Movie Clips, although it is possible with Graphic symbols. This makes Graphic symbols essential for animating cartoons. Eyes open, eyes closed — it's that big of a difference.

✦ Movie Clips can't (easily) be exported to video or other linear mediums. This is only significant if you plan to convert your .swf files to another time-based format.

✦ A Graphic symbol's instance properties are controlled (modified) at design time, with the options available in the Property inspector. One advantage is that this is simple and sure because you have an instant preview of what's happening. In addition, this information is embedded right in that particular instance of the Graphic symbol — meaning that, if it is either moved or copied, all of this information comes with it.

✦ You can control a Movie Clip's instance properties at design time or set them with ActionScript. This gives it great flexibility, although it's a little more abstract to work with ActionScript. One advantage is that the actions do not need to be directly linked to the Movie Clip, which has the concurrent disadvantage that you must take care when moving Movie Clips that have visual qualities defined with ActionScript.

✦ Graphic symbols that are animated (have more than one frame), and are nested with other animated Graphic symbols, may have problems with synchronization. For example, if you have a pair of eyes that blink at the end of a ten-frame Graphic symbol, and you put the Graphic symbol containing those eyes within a five-frame Graphic symbol of a head . . . the eyes will never blink. The head Graphic symbol will run from frame 1 to frame 5, and then return to frame 1, only displaying the first five frames of the eyes Graphic symbol. Or, if you nest the eyes Graphic symbol into a 15-frame head Graphic symbol, they will blink on frame 10, and then every 15 frames. That's ten frames, then blink, and then they loop back to frame 1; however, when reaching frame 5 this time, the movie they are in loops back to frame 1 (it's a 15-frame movie), and, thus, resets the eyes to frame 1.

✦ Movie Clips do not have the problem/feature described in the preceding bullet point. They offer consistent, independent timeline playback.

Authors' note: This comparison was contributed by Robin and Sandy Debreuil for the *Flash 5 Bible* and we still like how they articulate the important distinction between Graphic symbols and Movie Clip symbols.

We discuss vectors in greater detail in Chapter 16, "Importing Artwork," and in Chapter 37, "Working with Vector Graphics," which is included as a PDF file on the CD-ROM.

Drawing Objects are a new option in Flash 8 for making vector graphics easier to handle and edit. Drawing Objects have some of the same characteristics as a group but they can also be Motion tweened without being converted into symbols. Although Drawing Objects are a handy option in the authoring environment, they do not get stored in the Library and will have the same impact on file size as other raw vector graphics.

Sounds

The Library also handles Sounds like symbols. However, they can be assigned different play-back behavior after they are placed on a timeline. Flash can import (and export) sounds in a range of sound formats. Upon import, these sound files reside in the Library. To use a sound, drag an instance of the sound out of the Library and onto the Stage. You manage export settings for sound files within the Library by choosing Properties from either the contextual menu or the Library options menu. You can define playback behavior and effects with the Property inspector after placing a sound on a timeline.

Importing and using sounds effectively is a critical topic we cover in Chapter 15, "Adding Sound."

Video assets

Video assets, as with Font symbols, can be embedded or linked. Embedded video assets, like bitmaps, can have Color, Alpha, and Filter effects applied if they are first converted to a native Flash symbol type.

Flash 8 supports alpha channels in video files. This opens up a whole range of exciting new options for integrating video with other Flash content. For comprehensive coverage of working with video in Flash 8, refer to Chapter 17, "Displaying Video."

Font symbols

Font symbols are symbols created from font files to make them available for use in dynamic text fields. Font symbols can also be defined as shared fonts to make them available to multiple movie files (.swf) without the file size burden of embedding the font into each file individually.

Editing Symbols

Because every instance of a symbol is linked to the original, *any* edit applied to that original is applied to every instance. There are several ways to edit a symbol, which we cover in the following sections.

Modifying a symbol in Edit mode

Edit mode opens the Stage and timeline of the selected symbol in the Document window, replacing the view of the current keyframe in the Main Timeline with a view of the first keyframe in the symbol's timeline. To open a symbol in Edit mode, do one of the following:

✦ Select an instance on the Stage and choose Edit ➪ Edit Symbols, or Edit Selected from the application menu.

✦ Select an instance on the Stage and right-click (Command/Ctrl+click). Then choose Edit from the contextual menu.

✦ Select an instance on the Stage and use the shortcut key (⌘/Ctrl+E).

✦ Double-click a symbol in the Document Library. (Double-clicking Bitmaps, Sound, Video, and other nonnative symbol types launches the Properties dialog box instead of opening Edit mode.)

Editing a symbol in a new window

This method is useful if you're working on two monitors and want to quickly open a new window to edit in while keeping a view of the Main Timeline open and available. On Macintosh, these two windows are always separate, but you can click on either window to switch back and forth. On Windows, you can switch between these windows by choosing from the Window menu.

To edit a symbol in a new window, select an instance on the Stage and right-click (Command/Ctrl+click); then select Edit In New Window from the contextual menu.

Editing a symbol in place

The advantage of Edit in Place is that, instead of opening the symbol in a separate edit space, you can edit your symbol in context with the surrounding movie. Other elements present on the current keyframe are visible but dimmed slightly and protected from any edits you make on the selected symbol. To edit a symbol in place, do one of the following:

✦ Select an instance on the Stage and choose Edit ➪ Edit in Place from the application menu.

✦ Select an instance on the Stage and right-click (Command/Ctrl+click). Then select Edit in Place from the contextual menu.

✦ Double-click the instance on the Stage.

Editing symbols from the Library

You might not have an instance of your symbol available to select for editing in the Document window, but you can still edit it. Just edit it from the Library. Open your movie's Library with Window ➪ Library from the application menu (⌘/Ctrl+L). Select the symbol in the Library that you want to edit and do one of the following:

✦ Double-click the symbol's icon (not its name), in the Library list.

✦ Right-click (Command/Ctrl+click) and then select Edit from the contextual pop-up menu.

✦ If you have opened the Symbol Properties dialog box (see Figure 6-6), you can move to Edit mode by clicking the Edit button.

Returning to the Main Timeline or scene

After you've edited your symbol, you'll want to go back to the scene in the Main Timeline to make sure that your changes work properly. Just do one of the following:

✦ Choose Edit ➪ Edit Movie from the application menu or use the shortcut keys — ⌘/Ctrl+E.

✦ Double-click in any empty area of the Edit Stage.

✦ Click the Return arrow at the left edge of the Edit bar to step back through any nested timelines until you reach the Main Timeline.

✦ Select the scene name in the left corner above the Stage view in the Document window, as shown in Figure 6-7.

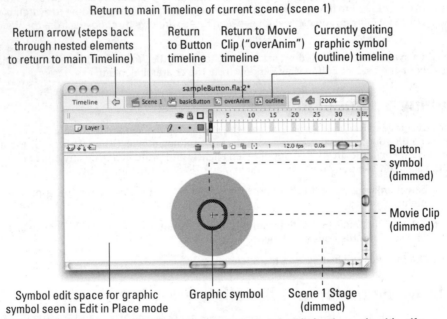

Return to main Timeline of current scene (scene 1)

Return arrow (steps back through nested elements to return to main Timeline)

Return to Button timeline

Return to Movie Clip ("overAnim") timeline

Currently editing graphic symbol (outline) timeline

Button symbol (dimmed)

Movie Clip (dimmed)

Symbol edit space for graphic symbol seen in Edit in Place mode

Graphic symbol

Scene 1 Stage (dimmed)

Figure 6-7: The location label in the Document window Edit bar is used to identify the current edit space and to return to the Main Timeline of the current scene.

Working with Timeline Effect symbols

Timeline Effects were a new addition to Flash MX 2004. They offer some shortcuts to making animation and effects on the Timeline. Although you can still create your own animation and effects by manually altering graphics and creating custom tweens, you may be able to get the result you want faster and more easily with Timeline Effects.

Cross-Reference   We discuss the application of various Timeline Effects and settings in detail in Chapter 9, "Modifying Graphics."

Editing and Developing

Development in Flash occurs in one of two places: in the Main Timeline and on the Stage; or within a symbol, which has its own edit space and timeline. But how do you know when you are on the Scene Stage or when you are in Edit mode? Here's one clue: At the top of the Document window is the Edit bar. If you're working on the Scene Stage, you'll see a single tab with the name of the scene. Unless you name your scenes, this tab should simply say, Scene 1 (or Scene 2). However, in Edit mode, a second tab appears to the right of the scene name: This tab displays the name and icon of the current group or symbol (Movie Clip, Graphic symbol, or Button symbol). If you're editing a nested symbol, more tabs may appear. In this manner, you have convenient access to the hierarchy of your assets, no matter how deeply they are nested.

The Edit bar appears above the (docked) Timeline by default, but you can move it below the Timeline by holding down Shift+⌘ (Mac) or Shift+Alt (Windows) and double-clicking the Edit bar. Use the same command again to move the Edit bar back to the default location.

Edit mode is much like working on the regular Stage. You can draw with any of the drawing tools, add text, place symbols, import graphics and sound, and use ActionScript. When you're done working with a symbol, you have an encapsulated element, whether it is a static Graphic, a Movie Clip, or a Button. You can place this element as many times as needed on your Stage or within other symbols. Each time you place it, the symbol's entire contents and timeline (if it is a Button or a Movie Clip) will be placed as well, identical to the original symbol stored in the Library. Remember that even if you access Edit mode from an instance on the Stage, all changes that you make will propagate to every other instance derived from the original symbol in the Library. The only color changes that you can make to one instance at a time without affecting the other instances of the same symbol are those you apply using the Color menu on the Property inspector, or by applying Filters and blend modes to instances as we explain in the following section, "Modifying Instance Properties."

The Stage (if it is not zoomed to fill the screen) is surrounded by a gray area. This is the Work area or Pasteboard, and it indicates the visible edges of the final movie as defined in the Document properties. The dimensions of any symbol, however, are not limited to the size of the Stage. If you make your symbols too large, when you place them on the Stage, portions that fall outside of the Stage will not be visible in the final movie (.swf), but they will still be exported and will add to the file size. Remember that it is always possible to scale a symbol instance to make it smaller than the original symbol if necessary.

New Feature

Flash 8 filters and blend modes are an improvement over Timeline Effects for modifying graphics because they are rendered dynamically at run time and don't clutter up the Library with extra symbols or break when you try to combine them with other symbols or effects. However, animated effects are easier to create using Timeline Effects, so they still serve a purpose.

In most production workflows in this book, we advise you to use Movie Clip symbols to contain animation. However, you will find that Timeline Effects automatically create a Graphic symbol to hold the visual effect or animation. We refer to these animated Graphic symbols as Timeline Effect symbols.

You can apply Timeline Effects to raw shapes or to any of the native Flash symbol types—Flash auto-generates symbols as needed to render the applied effect. Where possible, Macromedia chose to make Graphic symbols the default symbol type for Timeline Effects because it enables you to view the animation in the authoring environment just by scrubbing the Timeline. Timeline Effects are rendered based on the options chosen in various Timeline Effects dialog boxes, rather than on the basic tween settings available in the Property inspector.

After you apply a Timeline Effect to an item, you have the option of going back and changing the settings to modify and re-render the Effect so long as the Timeline Effect symbol is not opened in Edit mode. If you try to open a Timeline Effect symbol in Edit mode from the Document window, you will get a warning box. As shown in Figure 6-8, directly editing a Timeline Effect symbol will disable the Timeline Effect Settings option.

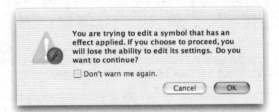

Figure 6-8: The warning box triggered by trying to open a Graphic symbol in Edit mode from the Document window after a Timeline Effect is applied

It *is* possible to change the contents of the nested symbols in an animation or effect created with a Timeline Effect, but the only way to access these symbols, while preserving the settings option, is through the project Library. Rather than selecting the symbol with the visible Timeline Effect applied on the Stage, look in the Library for the folder that contains the nested Graphic symbols and open these static symbols in Edit mode to make changes that will be applied to the instances used in the Timeline Effect. Any changes you make will be visible in the Main Timeline Effect symbol in the root of the Library folder (and on the Main Timeline).

Modifying Instance Properties

Every instance of a symbol has graphic variables that you can modify. These properties only apply to the specific instance—not to the original symbol. Display properties such as brightness, tint, and alpha (transparency) can all be modified without creating a new symbol. An instance can also be scaled, rotated, and skewed. Flash 8 Filters and blend modes enable a whole new range of cool visual effects that you can apply to symbol instances. With the Behavior menu in the Property inspector, you can also change the symbol type behavior of an instance without changing the original symbol. As we previously discussed, any changes you make to the original symbol in Edit mode will be updated in each instance—this still holds true even if some of the instances also have properties that are modified individually.

Note   You can add or modify properties (Color Effects, Transparency, Filters) on Timeline Effect symbol instances without losing the ability to adjust the original Effect settings.

Applying basic color effects to symbol instances

Each instance of a symbol can have a variety of color effects applied to it. The basic effects are changes of brightness, tint, and *alpha* (transparency). Tint and alpha changes can also be combined for special effects. To apply color effects to a symbol instance using the Property inspector:

1. Select the instance in the Document window that you want to modify.

2. Select one of the options from the Color drop-down menu in the Property inspector. Figure 6-9 shows the basic color effect options that can be applied to any symbol type.

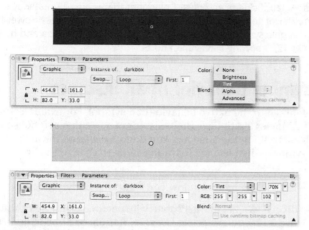

Figure 6-9: The Color menu has basic options to choose from (top). After a color effect is selected, the settings for that effect are available in the Property inspector (bottom).

The options available from the Properties Color menu are as follows:

- **None:** No effect is applied.

- **Brightness:** Adjusts the relative brightness or darkness of the instance. It ranges from 100 percent (white) to –100 percent (black); the default setting is 0 percent (no visible change to instance appearance). Use the slider to change the value or just type a numeric value into the entry field.

- **Tint:** Enables you to shift the color of an instance. Either select a hue with the color picker, or enter the RGB values directly. Then, select the percentage of saturation (Tint Amount) by using the slider or by entering the percentage in the entry field. This number ranges from 0 percent (no saturation) to 100 percent (completely saturated).

- **Alpha:** Enables you to modify the transparency of an instance. Select a percentage by using the slider or by entering a number directly. The Alpha percentage (or visibility setting) ranges from 0 percent (completely transparent) to 100 percent (no transparency).

- **Advanced:** When you select the Advanced option from the Color menu, a Settings button appears to the right of the menu. The Settings button invokes the Advanced Effect dialog box that enables you to adjust both the tint and alpha settings of an instance. The controls on the left reduce the tint and alpha values by a specified percentage, whereas the controls on the right either reduce or increase the tint and alpha values by a constant value. The current values are multiplied by the numbers on the left, and then added to the values on the right.

Cross-Reference The Advanced option includes a range with negative alpha values. Potential uses for this capability, together with more information about using the Color menu and other methods of transforming symbol instances, are detailed in Chapter 9, "Modifying Graphics."

New Feature The new Flash 8 Filters tab includes an Adjust Color filter that is also a great way to change the color and saturation of text, Movie Clip, or Button symbol instances. However, Filters can't be applied to Graphic symbols. For more coverage of the new Filters and how to use them, refer to Chapter 12, "Applying Filters and Effects."

Changing the symbol behavior of an instance

You don't need to limit yourself to the native behavior of a symbol. For example, there may be times when you want a Movie Clip to have the behavior of a Graphic symbol so that you can preview animation by scrubbing the Timeline. You don't have to go through the extra effort of creating a new symbol — just use the following steps to change the behavior of the instance as needed:

1. Select the instance in the Document window you want to modify.

2. From the Behavior drop-down list in the Property inspector, select the desired behavior. As shown in Figure 6-10, you can select Graphic, Button, or Movie Clip behavior.

Figure 6-10: You can change the behavior of any selected symbol instance with the drop-down menu in the Properties tab of the Property inspector.

Cross-Reference The more-complex uses of symbol instances are covered in Parts V, "Adding Basic Interactivity to Flash Movies," and VII, "Approaching ActionScript."

Swapping symbols

There may be times when you need to replace an instance of one symbol with an instance of another symbol stored in your project Library. Luckily, you don't have to go through and re-create your entire animation to do this — just use the Swap Symbol feature, illustrated in Figure 6-11. This feature only switches the instance of the symbol for an instance of another symbol — all other modifications previously applied to the instance will remain the same. Here's how to swap symbols:

1. Select the instance that you want to replace.

2. Click the Swap symbol button in the Properties tab of the Property inspector, choose Modify ➪ Symbol ➪ Swap Symbol from the application menu, or right-click (Command/Ctrl+click) and choose Swap Symbol from the contextual menu.

3. Select the symbol that you want to put into the place of your current instance from the list of available symbols in your project Library.

4. Click OK to swap the symbols.

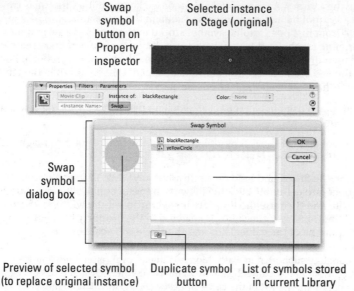

Swap symbol button on Property inspector

Selected instance on Stage (original)

Swap symbol dialog box

Preview of selected symbol (to replace original instance)

Duplicate symbol button

List of symbols stored in current Library

Figure 6-11: Use the Swap Symbol dialog box to choose a replacement for a symbol instance without losing any transformations that have already been applied.

Building Nested Symbol Structures

Understanding the various symbol types individually is the first step, but the next step is integrating these building blocks to create organized, optimized Flash projects that will be extensible, easy to edit, and fast to build. Although we cover the workflow for different types of Flash projects in depth in other parts of this book, we can synthesize the overview of different symbol types by walking through the steps of creating a Button symbol with some nested animation and Graphic symbols.

To demonstrate building an animated Flash movie from various symbol types, we made a Button symbol called basicButton that uses some raw shapes, some Graphic symbols, and some Movie Clips, all nested inside a Button symbol timeline.

On the CD-ROM

The completed source file (sampleButton.fla) for this series of demonstrations is on the CD-ROM that accompanies this book in the ch06 folder.

Converting a raw shape into a Graphic symbol

The best way to begin creating any graphic element is to first consider the final shape that you need and to try to find the most basic primitive shapes that you can use to build that element. Keep in mind that instances can be scaled, skewed, and adjusted with Color effects. Instead of drawing three circles to make a snowman, you would make just one circle and convert that into a symbol so that you could build your snowman from scaled instances of just one symbol stored in the Library. A resourceful animator we know built a Christmas tree by reusing instances of a symbol he had made for a dog's tail in the same animation — a wagging tail and a tree all built from just one Graphic symbol stored in the Library! Raw graphics can be converted into Graphic symbols after they have been drawn, or you can first create a new Graphic symbol and then draw the raw shapes directly inside the Graphic symbol in Edit mode — either way, the end result is a contained visual element that is stored in the Library to define any instances that you need to place in your movie.

To build the simple graphics used in basicButton, you can begin by converting a primitive shape into a Graphic symbol:

1. Select the Oval tool and set the fill color to green and the stroke color to black with a stroke height of 3.

2. Create an oval on the Stage, and hold down the Shift key while dragging out the shape to create a perfect circle. Double-click the fill with the Selection tool to select both the stroke and the fill, and then use the Property inspector to set the width to 75 and the height to 75. (If the Constrain check box is selected in the Property inspector, you only need to enter **75** in one of the value fields and the circle will scale evenly.)

New Feature

An alternative workflow supported in Flash 8 for creating an oval (after completing Step 1), is to Option/Alt+click in the Document window to invoke the new Oval Settings dialog box. Enter **75** for the width and height of the circle and click OK. Flash will render a circle in the Document window, centered on the point you clicked.

Note

If you open the Library panel — Window ➪ Library (⌘/Ctrl+L) — you will notice that the shape you've drawn is not visible in the Sort window because raw data is not stored in the Library.

3. While the stroke and the fill are both still selected, press F8 or choose Modify ➪ Convert to Symbol from the application menu.

4. In the Convert to Symbol dialog box, choose Graphic for the behavior and give the symbol the name **plainCircle.** Then click OK. You should now see the plainCircle symbol with the Graphic symbol icon next to it in the Library panel.

Tip

You always have the choice of creating artwork on the Main Timeline and then converting it into a symbol *or* first inserting a new symbol and then creating artwork on the symbol time-line. Either workflow will achieve the same end result. In the plainCircle example, start by selecting Insert ➪ New Symbol (⌘/Ctrl+F8). Enter the settings noted in Step 4. Then complete Steps 1 and 2 to draw the circle on the Graphic symbol timeline rather than on the Main Timeline. When you go back to the Main Timeline, you won't see an instance of plainCircle on the Stage, but the Graphic symbol should now be in the Library and you can drag an instance into the Document window whenever you need it.

You can now reuse instances of this Graphic symbol in your document in as many places as you need it just by dragging an instance onto the Stage from the Library panel.

Note

For the basicButton example, you will need an instance of plainCircle inside of a new Button symbol rather than on the main Stage, so you can delete any instances of plainCircle from the Main Timeline.

Using Graphic symbols in a Button

Button symbols are similar to Movie Clips that have a special timeline structure linked to mouse states. For a Button to take you to a new point on the Main Timeline or to load any other elements, ActionScript needs to be added to the Button instance.

Cross-Reference   We discuss adding actions to buttons for more advanced interactivity in Chapter 18, "Understanding Actions and Event Handlers."

In this example, the button simply works as a structure for an animation that reacts to the mouse. Begin by inserting a new Button symbol:

1. Click the New Symbol button in the Library panel or choose Insert ➪ New Symbol from the application menu or use the shortcut keys (⌘/Ctrl+F8).

2. In the Create New Symbol dialog box, choose Button as the behavior and for this example, give the symbol the name **basicButton.** Then click OK.

3. This Button symbol is now stored in the Library and automatically opens in Edit mode in the Document window, so you can add some content to the button.

4. You will notice that the button Timeline shows four keyframes with labels that define the button state by mouse behavior: Up, Over, Down, and Hit. These various keyframes can have multiple layers and contain any visual element or sound that you want. The button states function as follows:

   - **Up:** Any elements placed in the Up keyframe will be associated with the button as it appears on the Stage when it is present but not activated by any mouse interaction.

   - **Over:** Any elements placed in the Over keyframe will be associated with the button when the mouse rolls over it on the Stage, but as soon as the mouse rolls off the button it will revert to its Up state.

   - **Down:** Any elements placed in the Down keyframe will be associated with the button only when the mouse is over it and clicked and held down — as soon as the mouse is released, the button will revert to its Over state.

   - **Hit:** The Hit keyframe is actually never visible on Stage, but this instead defines the area of the button that is "sensitive" to the mouse. Whatever shape is present on this frame will be considered part of the button's *hit area*. It is important to note that it is better not to have holes or gaps in the hit area unless it is intended. For example, if you have text as a button, it is best to use a solid rectangle that matches the width and height of the total text area. Using the actual text would result in an irregular button hit area — whenever the mouse rolled into the space between letters, the button would revert to its Up state and could not be clicked.

Tip   If you ever need an "invisible" button in your project, you can create one by adding artwork to the Hit keyframe only of a Button symbol. The button will be visible in the authoring environment as a pale green preview shape (defined by the graphics in the hit state), but when the .swf file is published, the only indication that a button is on the Stage is the change in the mouse cursor when it enters the Hit area. You can add ActionScript to an invisible button to trigger events in your animation or to control the behavior of other elements in your movie. We discuss invisible buttons in more detail in Chapter 18, "Understanding Actions and Event Handlers."

For this example, you will be creating animation to be placed into the various visible states, but the main shape of the button will always be consistent, so you can begin by creating a layer to define the main shape of the button.

5. Rename Layer 1 of the Button symbol Timeline as **buttonOutline** and insert two frames (F5) after the first keyframe to create a span of three frames (visible for Up, Over, and Down).

6. With the Playhead set on the first keyframe, drag an instance of plainCircle onto the Button Stage and make sure that it is now visible in the Up, Over, and Down states of the button, but not on the Hit state.

7. Center the instance on the button Stage by using the Align panel (⌘/Ctrl+K). Select the instance of plainCircle and copy it to the clipboard (⌘/Ctrl+C).

8. Create a new layer and name it **hitArea.** Insert a blank keyframe (F7) on frame 4 (Hit). To paste the copy of plainCircle into the center of the blank Hit keyframe, use Paste in Place (⌘/Ctrl+Shift+V). If you have done a straightforward paste instead, make sure that the instance of plainCircle is centered to the button Stage.

9. The Timeline of your Button symbol should now look like Figure 6-12.

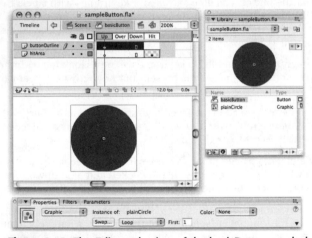

Figure 6-12: The Edit mode view of the basicButton symbol Timeline, with Up, Over, Down, and Hit states defined with instances of the plainCircle Graphic symbol

10. Return to the Main Timeline by clicking the Scene 1 label in the Edit bar or by double-clicking an empty area of the Stage.

11. If you don't see an instance of your basicButton on the Stage of the Main Timeline, drag an instance out of the Library and place it on the first frame of the Main Timeline.

Animating Graphic symbols in a Movie Clip

After you have created some Graphic symbols to define your basicButton, you can now start building some animation to add to it. You can build animation by placing artwork in keyframes on the Main Timeline, but this limits how you can use the animation, and can make it difficult to add more elements to your project without disturbing the keyframe structure of the animation. If you need animated elements that can be reused, and quickly moved to different parts of the Main Timeline or placed into a Button symbol timeline, it is best to begin by creating a Movie Clip.

1. Click the New Symbol button in the Library panel or choose Insert ➪ New Symbol from the application menu or use shortcut keys (⌘/Control+F8).

2. In the Symbol Properties dialog box, choose Movie Clip as the behavior and give this symbol the name **overAnim.**

3. Create a new circle on the first frame of the Movie Clip timeline with a black stroke (with a height of 3) and no fill. Select the outline with the Selection tool and use the Property inspector to set its width and height to 25. Then use the Align panel to center it on the Stage.

4. Convert this raw shape into a Graphic symbol (Modify ➪ Convert to symbol or F8) with the name **outline.**

5. Insert a keyframe (F6) on frame 10 of the Movie Clip timeline so that you have a span of frames from frame 1 to frame 10 with the outline Graphic symbol visible.

6. Select the instance of outline on keyframe 10 and use the Property inspector to scale it up to 50 high and 50 wide.

7. Now select keyframe 1 and use the Property inspector to set a Motion tween. This creates an animation of the outline Graphic symbol scaling up from its original size to the larger size that you gave it in frame 10.

8. The Timeline of your Movie Clip should now look like Figure 6-13.

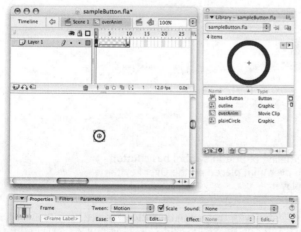

Figure 6-13: The symbol Timeline of the Movie Clip "overAnim" showing a Motion tween of the Graphic symbol "outline," from frame 1 to frame 10

Adding a Movie Clip to a Button symbol

The final step in our example is to add the overAnim Movie Clip to the basicButton symbol. This is the secret to animated Button symbols — by nesting multiframe Movie Clip animations into the single frames assigned to the Up, Over, and Down states of the Button symbol timeline, you can create different animated "reactions" as the mouse rolls over or clicks the button.

1. To go back inside your button and add animation in Edit mode, double-click the instance of basicButton on the Stage or the symbol in the Library.

2. Create a new layer in the Button Timeline and name it **outlineAnim.** Make sure that this new layer is above the original buttonOutline layer.

3. On the outlineAnim layer, insert a new keyframe (F6) on frame 2 (Over).

4. Drag an instance of overAnim from the Library onto the button Stage in the keyframe you just created, and use the Align panel to center it.

5. To ensure that the animation is only visible on the Over state of the button, make sure that the content on the overAnim layer only occupies one frame on the Button symbol Timeline. If the overAnim symbol extends into frame 3, either insert a blank keyframe (F7), or remove a frame (Shift+F5) to keep it contained on frame 2.

6. Your Button symbol Timeline should now look like Figure 6-14.

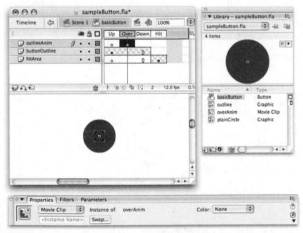

Figure 6-14: The Timeline of Button symbol basicButton with the Movie Clip overAnim placed on the Over keyframe of the outlineAnim layer

You can test your Button symbol with this animation added to see how it is working, by pressing ⌘+Return or Ctrl+Enter on the keyboard to view the movie (.swf) in the Test Movie environment. Now when you roll over the green button with your mouse, you should see the outline circles animate. Remember that you still only have one keyframe on your Main Timeline, so this demonstrates how both a Button symbol and a Movie Clip symbol will play back their own timelines even if they are placed into a single frame on another timeline. You still need to add some animation for the Down state of the basicButton, so close the Test Movie (.swf) window to go back to the Button timeline in the Document window.

Modifying a Movie Clip instance

Instead of creating an entirely new animation to display on the Over state of our basicButton, you can reuse the overAnim Movie Clip and change its appearance by adding a Color effect to the instance.

1. Double-click the basicButton symbol instance to enter Edit mode. Add a new layer to the Button symbol timeline and name it **outlineAnimTint.**

2. Insert a blank keyframe on frame 3 (Down).

3. Drag an instance of the overAnim Movie Clip from the Library, or just copy the Over frame on the outlineAnim layer and paste it into the blank keyframe you just created.

4. Select the instance of the overAnim Movie Clip that you placed on the Down keyframe and, with the Property inspector, select Tint from the Color effect menu. Choose white as the tint color from the Swatches that pop up from the color chip and then enter a tint value of 100 percent by using the slider or by typing into the value box.

5. Your Button symbol Timeline should now look like Figure 6-15.

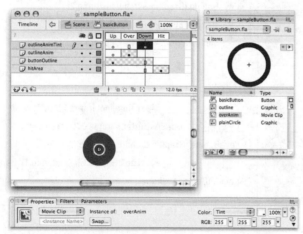

Figure 6-15: The basicButton Timeline with an instance of the overAnim Movie Clip placed on the Down keyframe and modified with a Color Tint

Test your animated button again (⌘+Return or Ctrl+Enter) and you will see that the animation now appears when you click the button. But instead of the original black that appears on the Over state, the animation for the Down (click) state is white. The three visible states of your button should now resemble Figure 6-16.

Up state

Over state

Down state

Figure 6-16: The finished animated button as it appears in the Up, Over, and Down states

You have seen how symbols are created, nested, and modified and you are probably realizing that this basic animated Button symbol is only the beginning.

On the CD-ROM
If you would like to deconstruct another layered symbol structure, we have included a silly, but slightly more complex, animated Button on this book's CD-ROM. You will find the source file, `surpriseButton.fla`, in the `ch06` folder. Figure 6-17 shows the three visible button states and diagrams the basic symbol nesting.

As your symbol structures get more layered and complex, it can be helpful to have some guidance when you are trying to navigate to a specific item in your project, or just trying to remember exactly how you organized things as you were building. Although careful use of layer names, frame labels, and symbol names is indispensable, the Movie Explorer (introduced later in this chapter) is a great assistant for finding your way through the structure of any Flash document.

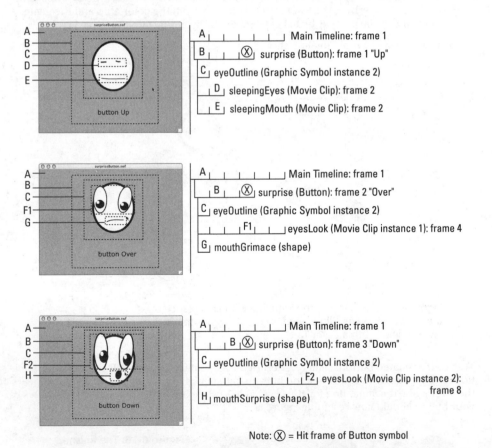

Note: Ⓧ = Hit frame of Button symbol

Figure 6-17: The animation as it appears in the three visible button states, Up, Over, and Down (left), with a diagram of the basic nested elements visible in each state (right)

9-Slice Scaling for MovieClip backgrounds

Have you ever tried to resize the same background graphic to fit different content and found that the aspect ratio or corner angles were no longer consistent? This can be frustrating, and the workarounds in older versions of Flash—creating unique graphics for each use or manually splitting up scalable and nonscalable areas of a background or border—were time-consuming and sometimes ineffective. The good news is that Flash 8 includes a new feature designed to solve this problem. The 9-slice, or Scale 9, option helps you selectively define the scaleable area of a MovieClip to make it easier to transform and reuse.

To truly appreciate this feature you have to try it. Here's how:

1. Create a new symbol in your Flash Document (Insert ➪ New Symbol).

2. Enter a name for your symbol and select Movie Clip as the symbol type.

3. Select the check box in the lower-left corner to Enable guides for 9-slice scaling (shown in Figure 6-18).

Figure 6-18: Enable guides for 9-slice scaling is a new option in Advanced symbol properties.

Tip   Expand the Symbol Properties dialog box by clicking the Advanced button if you don't see the check box for 9-slice scaling.

4. Click OK and enter the edit space for the new symbol; you'll notice a grid of dotted guidelines on the Stage. These four guides are used to split shapes into nine different regions (or slices) to control how the graphic will be interpolated at run time if the MovieClip instance is scaled.

5. Don't worry about the guides just yet. Create your artwork on the Stage with any of the shape or drawing tools.

Note   The most common use for Scale 9 is to preserve the corners on rounded rectangles used as button icons. For our example, we created a rounded rectangle by setting Fill and Stroke in the Property inspector, activating the Rectangle tool in the Tools panel, and then holding down the Option (or Alt) key and clicking on the Stage to invoke the Rectangle Settings dialog box. This makes quick work of creating a button icon — simply enter a width, height, and corner radius and click OK. The rectangle will be drawn on the Stage for you.

6. Make sure your graphic is positioned in the center of the Stage — select all elements and use the center horizontal and center vertical buttons in the Align panel with the align To stage toggle turned on.

7. Once you have your graphic sized and aligned as you would like it, click and drag the guides to position them so that the curved areas of your graphic will not be distorted when the scaled instance is rendered in the .swf. This is difficult to describe with text, but Figure 6-19 shows a centered rectangle with guides positioned to protect the rounded corners of the rectangle while allowing the center area of the graphic to be stretched when the symbol instance is scaled.

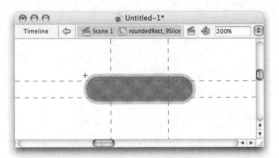

Figure 6-19: You can drag the four slice guides to isolate the outside edges of a graphic that should be protected when the center area is stretched to scale.

8. To test the results of 9-slice scaling on your symbol, return to the Main Timeline and drag an instance of your symbol onto the Stage. Use the Transform tools or the Transform panel to change the size or aspect ratio of the symbol instance. We scaled the rounded rectangle symbol instance in our example horizontally to 125 percent.

Tip   A symbol with 9-slice scaling enabled will display with the dotted grids in the preview pane of the Library panel. The grids are not visible when the symbol is placed on the Stage.

The final effect of 9-slice scaling is only visible in the published .swf. If you scale a symbol instance in the authoring environment, the corners of the shape will look distorted, with or without 9-slice scaling, as shown in Figure 6-20.

Caution   To edit the position of 9-slice guides, open the symbol in Edit mode by double-clicking the symbol in the Library list. Adjusting guides while in Edit in Place mode (invoked by double-clicking a symbol instance on the Stage) can have unpredictable results.

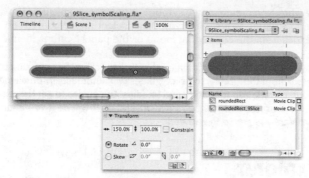

Figure 6-20: In the authoring environment, a symbol instance with 9-slice scaling enabled (right) will show the same distortion on the corners as a symbol instance without 9-slice scaling (left) when the instances are scaled.

The difference between 9-slice scaling and normal scaling is only visible in the published .swf. When you publish or test your movie (as shown in Figure 6-21), you'll see that the symbol without 9-slice scaling (left) is distorted when it's scaled larger while the symbol with 9-slice scaling enabled (right) scales gracefully and preserves the original shape of the rounded corners.

Figure 6-21: The symbol with 9-slice scaling enabled is rendered consistently in the .swf without any distortion. The rounded corners at the original size (top-right) match the rounded corners at the scaled size (lower-right).

On the CD-ROM   The example file shown in this section is also saved on the CD-ROM. Open 9Slice_ symbolScaling.fla or .swf from the ch06 folder.

How does this magic happen? If the final symbol is scaled horizontally, the three center sections (from left to right) will stretch while the corners and the top and bottom edges are constrained. If the final symbol is scaled vertically, the three sections (from top to bottom) will stretch while the corners and the left and right edges are constrained. If the symbol is scaled in both directions, the t-shaped center section will stretch to fit, while the corners remain protected. It might take a few tries to get the hang of using 9-slice scaling, but it will save you a lot of time if you need to design consistent scalable graphics.

You can enable 9-slice scaling when you create a new symbol or you can enable it in the Symbol Properties dialog box for existing Movie Clip symbols — select the symbol in the Library list and choose Properties from the contextual menu or the panel Options menu.

Tip   If you create a Movie Clip with artwork first and then enable 9-slice scaling by accessing the Symbol Properties dialog box from the Library, the slice guides will automatically be aligned to the outside edges of your artwork. You may still need to adjust the guides to get the exact result that you want, but the starting point will be much closer than it will be if you enable the 9-slice scaling guides *before* you create the artwork.

Using the Movie Explorer

The Movie Explorer panel is a powerful tool for deciphering movies and finding items within them. You can open it from the application menu by choosing Window ➪ Movie Explorer (Option/Alt+F3).

Note   The Find and Replace command will be a much more efficient choice if your goal is to dig up specific elements such as fonts or colors that you wish to replace in your project file. We discuss the many uses of the Find and Replace feature in Chapter 9, "Modifying Graphics." We include coverage of the Movie Explorer here because it is still the best tool for discovering the structure of a file.

The Movie Explorer is an especially useful tool for getting an overview and for analyzing the structure of a Flash movie. This means that you can see every element in its relationship to all other elements, and you can see this all in one place. However, it's also useful for troubleshooting a movie, for finding occurrences of a particular font, and for locating places where you refer to a certain variable name in any script throughout a movie. As an editing tool, you can use it as a shortcut to edit any symbol, for changing the properties of an instance, or even for doing multiple selections and then changing the attributes of the selected items. Furthermore, the Find function is an incredible timesaver when working on complex project files.

Figure 6-22 shows the Movie Explorer as well as the Movie Explorer Settings dialog box, which you can open by clicking the Customize Which Items to Show button in the Movie Explorer (Customize is the far right icon in the row of filter buttons.).

Figure 6-22: The Movie Explorer displaying the file structure for the button example we created in the previous section

Filtering buttons

As shown in Figure 6-22, there are several icon buttons across the top of the Movie Explorer panel. These are called filter buttons and they have icons representative of their function. Click any button to toggle the display of those elements in your file. Note, however, that the Movie Explorer's display becomes more crowded as you select more buttons — and that it performs more slowly because it has to sift more data. From left to right, the buttons filter the display of the following kinds of content:

- ✦ Text
- ✦ Button symbols, Movie Clips, and Graphic symbols (placed instances)
- ✦ ActionScript
- ✦ Video, Sounds, and Bitmaps (placed instances)
- ✦ Frames and Layers
- ✦ The Movie Explorer Settings dialog box

Also note the Find field. It enables you to search through all items currently displayed in the Movie Explorer to find specific elements by typing in the name of the symbol, instance, font name, ActionScript string, or frame number.

The Display List

Below the icons is a window with the Display list. Much like Windows Explorer, or the Mac Finder, the Movie Explorer displays items hierarchically, either by individual scene or for all scenes. These listings are expandable, so if you have selected the Text button, an arrow (or on Windows, a plus [+] sign) will appear beside the name of any scene that includes text. Clicking the arrow (or plus sign) displays all the selected items included in that scene. This type of visual data display is also referred to as a "tree structure." Clicking a plus sign (or arrow) expands a "branch" of the tree. At the bottom of the Display list, a status bar displays the full path for the currently selected item.

In Figure 6-23, the Text filter button has been selected. As shown, clicking the arrow sign beside the Text icon in the Display list shows the complete text, including basic font information.

Figure 6-23: The Movie Explorer for the surpriseButton example that is included on the CD-ROM, with the Text filter button chosen to view text and font information inside the file

The Movie Explorer Options menu

The Options menu is accessed by clicking the options triangle in the upper-right corner of the Movie Explorer panel. These commands enable you to control how much detail is shown in the Display list and also to perform edits or revisions after you've found the specific items that you want to modify:

✦ **Goto Location:** For a selected item, this transports you to the relevant layer, scene, or frame.

✦ **Goto Symbol Definition:** This jumps to the symbol definition for the symbol that's selected in the Movie Elements area. (For this to work, both Show Movie Elements and Show Symbol Definitions must be toggled on.)

✦ **Select Symbol Instances:** This jumps to the scene containing instances of the symbol that is selected in the Symbol Definitions area. (For this to work, both Show Movie Elements and Show Symbol Definitions must be toggled on.)

✦ **Find in Library:** If the Library window is not open, this opens the Library and highlights the selected item. Otherwise, it simply highlights the item in the Library.

✦ **Rename:** This enables you to easily rename selected items.

✦ **Edit in Place:** Use this to edit the selected symbol in context on the Stage.

✦ **Edit in New Window:** Use this to edit the selected symbol in Edit mode in a separate window from the main Document window.

✦ **Show Movie Elements:** One of two broad categories for how filtered items are viewed in the Display List, Show Movie Elements displays all elements in the movie, organized by scene.

✦ **Show Symbol Definitions:** This is the other category of the Display List, which shows all the items that are related to each symbol. Both Show Movie Elements and Show Symbol Definitions may be displayed simultaneously.

✦ **Show All Scenes:** This toggles the display of Show Movie Elements between selected scenes and all scenes.

✦ **Copy All Text to Clipboard:** Use this command to copy text to the Clipboard. Text may then be pasted into a word processor or into another editing application.

Cross-Reference

We discuss text-related features in more detail in Chapter 8, "Working with Text."

Caution

Unfortunately, getting text back into Flash is not as easy as copying it to the Clipboard. If you copy a large amount of text to another application, you have to manually update individual text blocks in your Flash document to integrate any changes that were made to the text outside of Flash.

✦ **Cut:** Use this command to cut selected text.

✦ **Copy:** Use this command to copy selected text.

✦ **Paste:** Use this command to paste text that has been copied from Flash or another application.

- ✦ **Clear:** Use this command to clear selected text.

- ✦ **Expand Branch:** This expands the hierarchical tree at the selected location; it's the menu equivalent of clicking the tiny plus (+) sign or right-facing arrow.

- ✦ **Collapse Branch:** This collapses the hierarchical tree at the selected location; it's the menu equivalent of clicking the tiny minus (–) sign or down-facing arrow.

- ✦ **Collapse Others:** This collapses the hierarchical tree everywhere except at the selected location.

- ✦ **Print:** The Movie Explorer prints out, with all the content expanded, displaying all types of content selected.

You can also access the commands found in the Movie Explorer options menu via the contextual menu.

The contextual menu

Select an item in the Movie Explorer and right-click (Command/Ctrl+click) to invoke the contextual menu related to that particular item. Nonapplicable commands are grayed-out.

Figure 6-24 shows the contextual menu of the Movie Explorer. Among the most useful commands is the Goto Location option at the top. When you can't find an item (because it's on a masked layer or is invisible), this command can be a lifesaver.

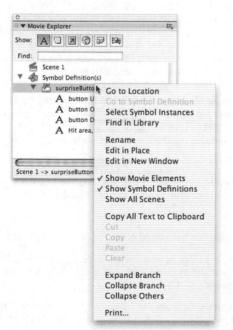

Figure 6-24: The Movie Explorer's contextual menu

When you are planning or looking for ways to improve a project, the Movie Explorer can provide an excellent map to the structure and function of what you've already accomplished.

Whenever it's relevant, print out the Movie Explorer; this can function as project documentation for finished work, providing a reference of all scripting and Movie Clip placement. As such, it can make it much easier to return to a project months later. It can also facilitate collaboration amongst developers, whether they share the same studio or need to communicate long distance. Finally, for all the reasons we listed in this chapter, you can also use the Movie Explorer as a tool for both learning and teaching.

Now that you have a handle on working with symbols in one project file, let's go to the next step and see how you can work with symbols in multiple Flash files.

Using Authortime Shared Libraries

Flash gives you two options for working with shared assets: Authortime and Runtime shared Libraries. Authortime sharing enables a development team to maintain consistency during production on multiple versions of a file or on various project files that use the same symbols by using a centralized internal source .fla file for fonts or other assets. Runtime sharing reduces file sizes and makes it easier to dynamically update content in projects that involve multiple .swfs without having to republish all the files. In Runtime sharing, a Library of assets is created and published as a source movie (.swf) that is uploaded to the server to be shared with multiple linked movies (.swfs). Source assets in shared libraries can include any element that is normally created in a Flash movie, as well as assets such as bitmaps, fonts, sounds, or video that are imported and usually embedded in individual project files (.fla).

Runtime sharing involves URLs and linkage info, but Authortime sharing is relatively simple and can be accomplished without even publishing any .swf files. You can update or replace a symbol in your current project (.fla) with any other symbol accessible on your local network. Any transformations or effects applied to instances of the symbol in your project file will be preserved, but the contents of the symbol stored in the project Library will be replaced with the contents of the new (or modified) source symbol that you choose to link to.

Note   For clarity, we will refer to the currently open .fla file as a *project file*, and the .fla that contains symbols that you want to link to, as the *source file*. In real-world production, you can give the files any name you like. However, adding a special identifier such as "Library" or "Source" to the .fla filenames that you plan to use for sharing can help you (and your team) minimize confusion.

On the CD-ROM   We have included two sample files with some basic symbols that you can use to try out the symbol-linking feature. Both shapeProject.fla and shapeSource.fla are in the ch06 folder on this book's CD-ROM.

To link a symbol from one project Library to another, you need a source file and a project file. Open the project file and follow these steps.

1. In the current project Library panel, select the symbol (Graphic symbol, Button, or Movie Clip), that you want to link to a source symbol.

2. Choose Properties from the contextual menu or from the Library options menu and under Source in the Symbol Properties dialog box, click the Browse button to find the .fla file that contains the symbol you want to use as a source. After you find the .fla that will be your source, select it in the file list and click the Open button (as shown in Figure 6-25).

Figure 6-25: Browsing for a source file in the Symbol Properties dialog box

Tip You can also click the Advanced button in the Create New Symbol dialog box to access Source options and set linkage when you first create a symbol in your project.

3. The Select Source Symbol dialog box (shown in Figure 6-26) will open automatically to enable you to choose the specific symbol in the source Library that you want to link to the symbol in your current project file. Select a symbol in the source Library file list and click OK to close the Select Source Symbol dialog box.

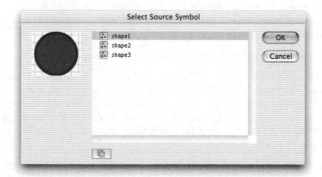

Figure 6-26: The Select Source Symbol dialog box, where you specify a linked symbol

4. Before you close the Symbol Properties dialog box, notice that the path to the source file is now listed and that you can select a check box for Always update before publishing (as shown in Figure 6-27). Select this check box if you want Flash to check for changes in the source file and automatically update all linked symbols each time you publish an .swf from the project file.

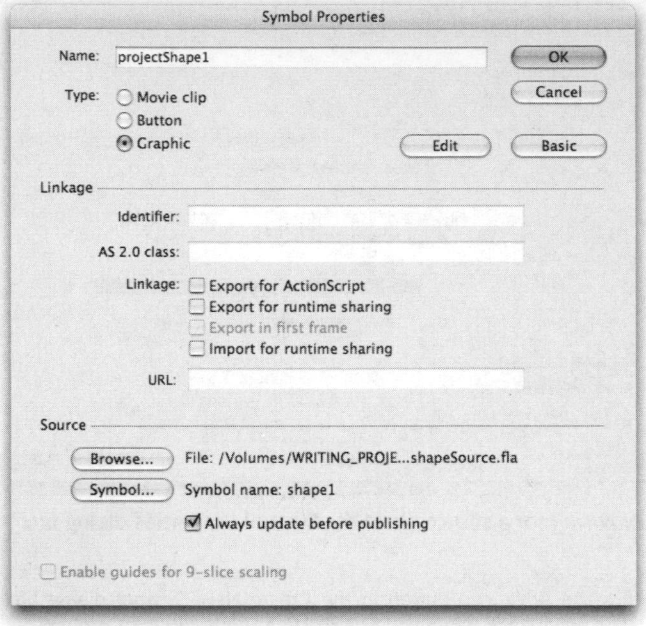

Figure 6-27: The source path shown in the Symbol Properties dialog box with the Always update before publishing check box selected

5. Click OK to close the Symbol Properties dialog box.

6. The symbol name in your project Library will remain the same, but the content of the symbol in all instances used in your project file should now contain the updated content that will match the content of the symbol you chose in the source file.

7. Save your project file to preserve the linkage information for your symbol.

Should any changes be made to the content of the symbol in the source .fla, you can either publish an .swf from the project file to see Flash automatically check for changes and update all linked symbols (with the Always update before publishing check box selected in the Symbol Properties dialog box), or you can use the Update command to manually get the most recent version of the symbol into your project file before you publish an .swf. To see how this works, follow these steps:

1. Open the source .fla and make some changes to the symbol (using Edit mode) that you originally linked to and then save and close the file. You can change the appearance of the symbol, but don't change the symbol name.

2. Open a project file that contains the symbol you wish to update and either ensure that the Always update before publishing check box is selected in Symbol Properties before publishing an .swf to force Flash to check for changes to the source symbol and automatically update your project Library, or go to Step 3.

3. Select the symbol in the Library and use the options menu or the contextual menu to select the Update command.

4. In the Update Library Items dialog box (shown in Figure 6-28), select the symbol that you edited in the source Library and click the Update button.

5. You will now see the content of the symbol in your project Library updated to reflect the changes made in the source file.

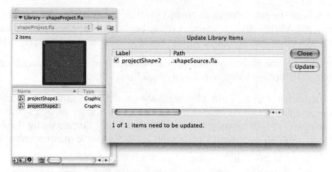

Figure 6-28: Use the Update Library Items dialog box to manually update the content of symbols in your project file.

It probably seems like more hassle than it's worth to keep content current in one or two files, but you will find it very helpful should you need to update symbols in multiple project files consistently.

Summary

✦ You can organize the Library with folders and symbols, and rearrange assets without breaking their linkage to instances deployed within the project.

✦ The new Flash 8 Library panel streamlines the controls for working with multiple documents. Rather than having to manage a separate Library panel for each open document, you can now view different Library lists within a single panel.

✦ Symbols are the building blocks of Flash. They save you time, reduce your file size, and add flexibility to your movies. When you use ActionScript to control symbol behavior or display, symbols are considered as objects within an object-oriented authoring environment.

✦ Flash handles imported sounds, bitmaps, and video assets as symbols. They reside in the Library, and instances of these assets are deployed within a Flash project.

✦ In addition to imported assets, there are three other kinds of symbols that can be created within Flash: Graphic symbols, Movie Clips, and Button symbols.

✦ Movie Clip symbols and Button symbols have timelines that play independently from the Main Timeline. Although Graphic symbols also have their own timelines, they are still tied to the Main Timeline and require a frame for every frame of their own timeline that will be visible.

✦ Timeline Effects auto-create symbols as needed to render an applied effect.

✦ Using symbol instances within a project is as easy as dragging an asset or symbol from the Library and onto the Stage, although it's usually best to have a new layer ready and to have the appropriate keyframe selected.

✦ You can edit symbols a number of ways. Any edits to a symbol in Edit mode are reflected by all instances of that symbol throughout the project.

✦ 9-slice scaling solves the problem of distorted graphics due to inconsistent scaling on multiple symbol instances. Finally, you can reuse and resize a rounded rectangle or pill button without worrying about mismatched stroke widths and stretched corners.

✦ You cannot open Timeline Effect symbols in Edit mode from the Document window without disabling the option to adjust the original Effect Settings.

✦ The Property inspector offers a central control for modifying individual symbol instances. You can modify the color and transparency of instances of a symbol via the Color effect controls. Furthermore, you can reassign symbol types using the Behavior drop-down menu, and can even replace specific instances with other symbol instances by using the Swap symbol button.

✦ The Filter tab in the Flash 8 Property inspector enables some fun new transformations that you can apply to text, Movie Clips, or Button symbol instances only.

✦ The Movie Explorer is a powerful tool for navigating movies and finding specific items within them.

✦ Shared Libraries streamline your workflow if a project involves multiple files that use assets that may need to be updated. Shared libraries are also useful for keeping files current and consistent in a team production environment.

✦   ✦   ✦

Applying Color

Before we get into the specifics of applying color with Flash, we want to discuss some of the fundamental theory behind working with color that's destined for display on the Web. Limited color displays are not as common as they were in the early days of Web graphics, but it is useful to have a basic understanding of the various contexts and limitations of digital color. This chapter introduces some resources that may be helpful to you for Flash work and as references for color issues that may come up in other productions. Whether you're designing corporate graphics or creating a photo album to share online, consistent and accurate color is a key factor in the quality of your projects. An overview of the reasons and methods for using Web-safe color will get you on good footing. We then explore the options available in Flash for choosing and modifying your color palette using the Color Swatches panel and how colors can be accessed from the Tools panel. We also show you how to work with the Property inspector menus, Color Swatches panel, and Color Mixer panel to select, change, mix, and apply solid colors, gradients, and even bitmap fills.

Cross-Reference
Flash symbol instances can be tweened so that they will change color over time. Although this involves color, the selection of colors for the original symbol used in the keyframes of the tween is merely a rudimentary application of fill and line color, as we describe in this chapter. We discuss applying the Color Effect controls available in the Property inspector to symbol instances in Chapter 9, "Modifying Graphics." We cover methods for controlling color with ActionScript and the Flash Color Object in Chapter 25, "Controlling Movie Clips."

New Feature
We cover the new Filters and Blend modes available in Flash Professional 8 in Chapter 12, "Applying Filters and Live Effects." You can use these new features to modify the color and appearance of symbols, but they do not replace the basic color tools (described in this chapter) used to modify text, shapes, and Graphic symbols.

Introducing Color Basics

Computer monitors display color by using a method called *RGB color*. A monitor screen is a tightly packed array of pixels arranged in a grid, where each pixel has an address. For example, a pixel that's located 16 rows down from the top and 70 columns over from the left might

---

In This Chapter

Introducing color basics

Working with Flash color

Organizing the Color Swatches panel

Creating and importing custom color sets

Using the Color Mixer panel to modify colors

Adding transparency to strokes and fills

Making and applying gradient fills

Selecting bitmap fills

have an address of 70,16. The computer uses these addresses to send a specific color to each pixel. Because each pixel is composed of a single red, green, and blue dot, the colors that the monitor displays can be "mixed" at each pixel by varying the individual intensities of the red, green, and blue color dots. Each individual dot can vary in intensity over a range of 256 values, starting with 0 (which is *off*) to a maximum value of 255 (which is *on*). Thus, if red is *half-on* (a value of 127), while green is *off* (a value of 0), and blue is fully *on* (a value of 255), the pixel appears reddish-blue or purple.

The preceding paragraph describes unlimited, full color, which is sometimes referred to as *24-bit color.* Newer computers use 24-bit color to deliver cleanly rendered graphics without a hitch. However, older computer systems are incapable of displaying full color. Limited color displays are either 8-bit or 16-bit displays. Although a full discussion of bit-depth is beyond the scope of this book, it is important to note several points:

✦ 24-bit color is required to accurately reproduce photographic images and smooth color transitions in gradients.

✦ Because 8-bit and 16-bit systems are color challenged, they can display only a limited number of colors, and they must dither-down anything that exceeds their *gamut,* which is their expanse of possible colors. *Dithering* means that, in order to approximate colors that are missing from the palette, the closest colors available are placed in proximity to each other to fool the eye into seeing a blended intermediate color. This can result in unwanted pixel patterns.

✦ Some image formats, such as GIF, use a color palette that limits them to 256 colors. This is called *indexed color.* Indexed color is ideally suited for reproducing vector graphics that have solid fills and strokes, but will often create noticeable *banding* (uneven color) when applied to photographic images.

✦ Bitmap (or photographic) images will not accurately translate an indexed color palette, so matching color between GIF images and JPEG images can be unpredictable because the JPEG will expand the original indexed palette of a GIF file to include colors that may not be within the Web-safe color palette.

✦ Calibration of your monitor is essential for accurate color work. For more information, check out the ColorVision Web site at `www.colorvision.com`.

Discussing Web-safe color issues

Web-safe color is a complex issue, but what it boils down to is this: The Macintosh and Windows platforms handle their color palettes differently, so browsers don't have the same colors available to them across platforms. This leads to inconsistent, unreliable color — unless you're careful to choose colors for Web design from the Web-safe palette. The Web-safe palette is a selection of 216 colors that's consistent on both the Mac and Windows platforms for Netscape, Explorer, and Mosaic browsers. The Web-safe palette contains only 216 of 256 possible indexed colors, because 40 colors vary between Mac and Windows displays. Use the Web-safe palette to avoid color shifting and to ensure greater design (color) control.

By default, the Color Swatches panel (Ctrl+F9 or ⌘+F9) loads with Web 216 colors, and if the swatches are modified, this swatch palette can always be reloaded from the Options menu at the upper right of the panel. Web 216 restricts the color palette to Web-safe colors. However, *intermediate colors* (meaning any process or effect that generates new colors from two Web-safe colors) — such as gradients, color tweens, filters, transparent overlays, and alpha transitions — will not be constrained to Web-safe colors.

When there are more than 16 million possible colors, why settle for a mere 216? Consider your audience. Choose a color strategy that will enable the majority of your viewers to view your designs as you intend them to appear. For example, if you're designing an e-commerce site for a very broad audience on a mix of platforms, then you might seriously consider limiting your work to the Web-safe palette. (If you choose this route, then hybrid swatches may enable you to access colors that are technically unavailable, while remaining within the hardware limitations of your audience.) On the other hand, if you're designing an interface for a stock photography firm whose clients are mainly art directors with high-end Mac machines, then color limitations are probably not an issue. In either case, keep in mind that no one will see the exact same colors that you see. The variables of hardware, calibration, ambient light, and environmental influences are unavoidable. If you do settle for 216 colors, remember that the value of color in Web design (or any design or art for that matter) has to do with color perception and design issues, and numbers have little to do with that.

Using hexadecimal values

Any RGB color can be described in hexadecimal (hex) notation. This notation is called *hexadecimal* because it describes color in base-16 values, rather than in base-10 values like standard RGB color. This color value notation is used because it describes colors in an efficient manner that HTML and scripting languages can digest. Hex notation is limited to defining *flat color,* which is a continuous area of undifferentiated color. In HTML, hexadecimal notation is used to specify colored text, lines, backgrounds, image borders, frame cells, and frame borders.

A hexadecimal color number has six places. It allocates two places for each of the three color channels: R, G, and B. So, in the hexadecimal example 00FFCC, 00 signifies the red channel, FF signifies the green channel, and CC signifies the blue channel. The corresponding values between hexadecimal and customary integer values are as follows:

16 integer values: 0 1 2 3 4 5 6 7 8 9 10 11 12 13 14 15

16 hex values: 0 1 2 3 4 5 6 7 8 9 A   B   C   D   E   F

The Web-safe values in hexadecimal notation are limited to those colors that can be described using combinations of the pairs 00, 33, 66, 99, and FF. White is described by the combination FFFFFF, or all colors *on* 100 percent. At the other end of the spectrum, black is described by the combination 000000, all colors on 0 percent, or *off.* A medium gray would be described by the combination 666666, or all colors on 40 percent.

Using custom Web-safe colors

The basic Web-safe color palette will be broad enough for most project needs, but if you feel too limited by these colors, you can create custom-mixed Web-safe colors. Tools exist to help you to build patterns composed of Web-safe colors that fool the eye into seeing a new color. These are essentially blocks of preplanned dithers, built out of the Web-safe palette, that augment the usable palette while retaining cross-platform, cross-browser color consistency:

✦ **ColorSafe:** An Adobe Photoshop filter plug-in that generates hybrid color swatches with this logic. ColorSafe (Mac and Windows) is available directly from BoxTop Software at www.boxtopsoft.com.

✦ **ColorMix:** An easy online utility that interactively delivers hybrid color swatches, much like ColorSafe. It is free at www.colormix.com. After you mix a custom dithered swatch, you can download it and save it as a GIF for import into Flash.

✦ **More Crayons:** Some designers have proposed an updated approach to Web color, with a suggested palette of 4,096 Web-smart colors rather than the traditional 216 Web-safe colors. For more information on this idea and tools for generating color schemes in an expanded Web palette, visit www.morecrayons.com.

After you've created some custom swatches and saved them to a folder on a local machine, you can use them in your Flash projects by importing the GIF directly to your document Library and using the Color Mixer panel to apply the GIF as a bitmap fill. Figure 7-1 shows two Web-safe colors used to create a custom-dithered GIF swatch and the mixed custom Web-safe color as it displays when it's imported to Flash.

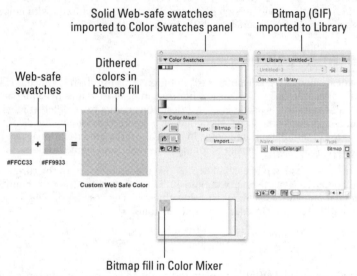

Figure 7-1: Two Web-safe colors mixed to create a custom-dithered color. The dithered GIF file was imported to the Flash Library and the solid Web-safe colors used in the GIF were added to the Color Swatches panel.

Note that the dithered GIF color is displayed only in the Mixer panel under the Bitmap fill option, whereas the solid Web-safe colors can be added directly to the Color Swatches panel. We describe the steps for adding colors from a GIF file to the Color Swatches panel in the "Importing custom palettes" section later in this chapter, and we describe the steps for applying a bitmap fill in the section "Selecting bitmap fills."

Using color effectively

According to some designers, the issue of color on the Web has been seriously confused by the misperception that people can set numbers to give them Web-safe colors, and that, if they do this, they will have *good* color. Have you ever noticed that as soon as someone starts designing onscreen, it's as if he's forgotten anything he may have learned about legibility and design on the printed page? When designers get caught up in the excitement of layered patterns and multicolored text, they have a tendency to overlook the obvious problem, which is that the result is entirely illegible. Although we all want to be creative and unique, certain color rules can actually be more liberating than restricting.

Although unconventional design choices can add an element of surprise, a touch of humor, or just a visual punch that will help your layout stand out from the rest, it is vital that you don't compromise your end goal. When you get noticed, you want to deliver your message successfully—whether that message is "Buy this product" or just "Hey, this is a cool site." If you start to carefully deconstruct the layouts that grab your attention, you will probably find that there are consistencies to the choices that were made in the design, regardless of the content. You'll begin to notice that even the most bizarre or cutting-edge designs share certain features that make them eye-catching and memorable.

Much of the underlying strategy in a design may be transparent, or not *consciously* perceived by the viewer. But don't make the mistake of thinking that individual preference is completely unpredictable. The secret to successful design is leveraging the unconscious visual language that your audience is physically and culturally conditioned to respond to. Individual viewers may have specific preferences for certain colors or styles, but they will all recognize and understand many of the same visual conventions.

Although learning to apply all these conventions and to integrate them into your own design style can take years of study and practice, there are some fundamental "truths" that will serve you well, no matter how long you've been designing:

✦ **Color is relative:** Humans perceive color relative to the context of other colors in which the color is set. Most art schools offer at least one course about color. They often start with color experiments that are conducted with pieces of colored paper. An early assignment is to make three colors look like more than three colors—by placing small scraps of the same color on larger pieces of different colors. Students are always amazed to learn how much a person's perception of a single color is influenced when it's placed on different-colored backgrounds. Figure 7-2 shows how the same shade of gray can appear lighter or darker depending on the background color. The lesson is that color is *not* an absolute—it never was before computers, and it never will be to the human eye.

Figure 7-2: The same gray circle displayed on different background values will appear to be darker or lighter by comparison.

✦ **Contrast is king:** Only one thing is more important than color: contrast. *Contrast* is the relative difference in lightness or darkness of items in a composition. Here's a good test: Take a colorful design that you admire and reduce it to grayscale. Does it still work? Contrast is a major factor in good color composition. Figure 7-3 shows different amounts of contrast created by relative differences in value.

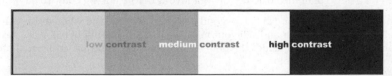

Figure 7-3: Varying levels of color contrast determine legibility and emphasis.

To ensure a strong design, it can be helpful to work on your initial layouts in grayscale. When you have contrast working for you, then you can start to add color with the confidence that the design will not be visually *muddy*—or hard to read—because of poor contrast. Often, the same color scheme can be a disaster or a huge success, all depending on the contrast you create in the design. The concept of contrast also applies to other characteristics of your design—size, texture, even mood. Try to use contrast wherever you want to create emphasis or add drama. But remember: If you make everything huge and flashing red, or extra-small and pale gray, you will no longer have any contrast. The strength of contrast is in variety. Figure 7-4 shows how contrast can be achieved by varying the size and style of your text—even if the font stays the same. Create even more contrast by mixing fonts with different visual character: a sans-serif with thick strokes will contrast nicely with a script font with calligraphy-style strokes.

low contrast   **MEDIUM** contrast   **HIGH** contrast

Figure 7-4: Variety in the size and shape of elements will also add visual contrast.

✦ **Less is more:** Keep in mind that the power of contrast should always be used in moderation. White text on black backgrounds can be great for headlines, but after more than a few paragraphs, it will make the reader feel as though her retina is actually being burned by the text on the screen—one of the best ways to keep someone from actually reading your copy. Also, don't be afraid of empty space; the impact of individual elements is often dependent on having a little room to breathe. One element in a striking color will be much more effective than a whole page filled with competing colors.

✦ **Start at the beginning:** Visual hierarchy is the best secret weapon in any designer's arsenal. Although you may not be sure what the most important element is in your design, if you don't give your reader a place to start, chances are you'll lose his attention. By deciding on the order of importance for elements in your design and then using contrast, size, and color to guide the reader through your layout, you'll create motivation for him to actually stick around long enough to absorb your message. Think of your content as the elements of a good story: In order to make the narrative compelling, you have to have a catchy intro, a juicy middle, and a rewarding ending or payoff. You might argue that you want to let readers make their own choice about where to start (like starting at the back of a novel), but if you don't create a visual structure, the reader won't feel empowered to make any choices. Presented with a big muddle of uncertain order, he will most likely move on to a design where he can find the beginning, middle, and end at a glance, before deciding what he wants to read first. Figure 7-5 shows a layout with poorly defined visual hierarchy compared to an example with stronger contrast and clearer hierarchy. The page with the more clearly defined hierarchy gives the reader more clues about the order of importance of each element on the page. Of course, these examples don't even use color, but as we mentioned earlier, it can be best to plan the structure of your layout before adding color to support it.

Here's the bottom line: Color can help a good design look *great,* and when used with strategy, it can help engage the viewer and sell your message. But no amount of color can save a poorly planned design, so consider the underlying structure, contrast, and visual hierarchy of your layout before adding color.

Weak contrast = muddy visual hierarchy   Strong contrast = clear visual hierarchy

Figure 7-5: Adding contrast to a weak design (left) makes for a stronger visual hierarchy (right) and orients readers in your layout.

Innumerable books on color theory and many different software solutions that can provide inspiration and take the guesswork out of choosing color schemes are out there. These are just two sources that can help you create harmonious color families for your designs:

✦ **Color Schemer:** A handy utility that will generate a palette of harmonious colors for any key color that you want to start with. Although the full version of the software is for Windows only, the online version is helpful regardless of what platform you use. Try it out at www.colorschemer.com/online.html.

You can generate lists of RGB or hexadecimal colors from the Web-safe palette and choose to darken or lighten all colors in the palette until you find the exact color set you like. Color Schemer also offers a basic color tutorial that will help you understand how to generate harmonious palettes. You can find it at www.colorschemer.com/tutorial.html.

✦ *Pantone Guide to Communicating with Color:* A wonderful reference book by color guru Leatrice Eiseman (published by North Light Books in 2000). This colorful book includes a wealth of information about the science and psychology of color, as well as a guide to a whole range of color families, grouped according to mood. Get inspired to add meaningful color to your projects.

Tip

The Pantone system for specifying ink color is the industry standard for communication between designers and printers. Pantone swatch books are indispensable and well worth the investment if you do any print work. Visit www.pantone.com to learn more. Pantone has also developed systems to help designers and retailers who need to specify and display color consistently in a digital environment. Visit www.therightcolor.com to learn more if you are developing online catalogues or other projects that require precise color matching. Pantone also offers swatch books with both CMYK and Hex color values printed on them to make color matching between screen graphics and printed graphics easier. If you are a designer who "thinks in Pantone," you might find it worthwhile to invest in Pantone's Colorist software. Available for Windows and for Mac, Colorist makes Pantone swatches available from programs that do not have built-in Pantone color libraries (including Flash and Fireworks).

Working in the Color Swatches Panel

The Color Swatches panel (Ctrl+F9 or ⌘+F9) is the most commonly used source for selecting colors as you work in Flash. Although the controls for loading or modifying specific palettes are available only on the main Color Swatches panel, both the Tools panel and the Property inspector give you quick pop-up menus to access whatever colors are currently loaded. If the main Color Swatches panel isn't visible, you can always find it in the application menu under Window ➪ Color Swatches. Figure 7-6 shows the Fill Swatches for the default Web 216 colors as they display in the pop-up menu in the Tools panel (A), the Property inspector (B), and on the main Color Swatches panel (C). The Color Swatches panel is shown with the Options menu that is invoked by clicking the top-right corner of the panel.

New Feature   In Flash 8, there is now a handy Alpha field in the Swatches pop-up menu that provides a quick way to change the transparency of a selected color. In older versions of Flash, you adjust Alpha levels on fill colors using the Color Mixer panel — this is still an option.

Tools that create fields of color, or fills, include the Brush, the Paint Bucket, and the various Shape tools. Each of these tools is accompanied by the Fill color button, which appears in the Tools panel and in the Property inspector. Although the Fill Swatches pop-up is similar to the Stroke pop-up, it has one significant difference: It includes another row of swatches at the bottom, which are gradient swatches — click one to fill with a prebuilt gradient style.

Tools that create lines, or strokes, include the Line, Pencil, Ink Bottle, Pen, and — because they create outlines around fills — any of the Shape tools. These tools rely on the Stroke color button, which appears in both the Tools panel and the Property inspector.

For all drawing tools, basic color selection is accomplished by clicking either the Stroke or Fill color buttons, and then choosing a color from the Swatches pop-up. This pop-up displays the same swatch set that is currently loaded in the Color Swatches panel. It also includes a hexadecimal color-entry box — which facilitates keyboard entry, as well as cut-and-paste of hex values. Depending upon the tool you select, the Swatch menu available from the Tools panel may display a No Color button above the solid swatches as well as a button that launches the Color Picker.

New Feature   In Flash 8, you can remove a fill or stroke from a selected shape or Drawing Object by using the None (or No Color) button in any of the Swatches menus. The old method of using Edit ➪ Clear or pressing the Backspace (Delete) key to remove a line or stroke still works if the line or stroke shows the selection grid — shapes can be selected directly; Drawing Objects must be in Edit mode.

Tip   If you decide after you invoke the Swatches pop-up that you don't want to change your selected color after all, hit the Escape key or make sure that your mouse is over the original color swatch when you click to close the pop-up.

The color chips displayed on the Tools panel will always display the most recently selected Stroke and Fill colors, while the Property inspector will display the color chips relevant to the active tool or the currently selected item.

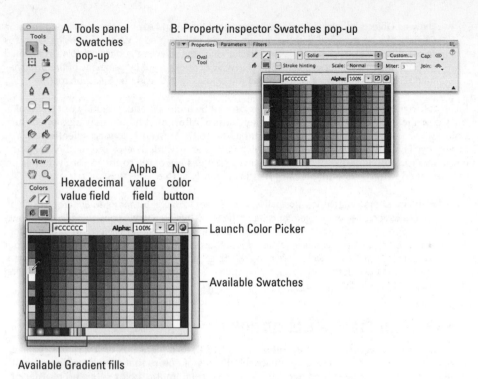

A. Tools panel Swatches pop-up

B. Property inspector Swatches pop-up

Hexadecimal value field

Alpha value field

No color button

Launch Color Picker

Available Swatches

Available Gradient fills

C. Color Swatches panel with options

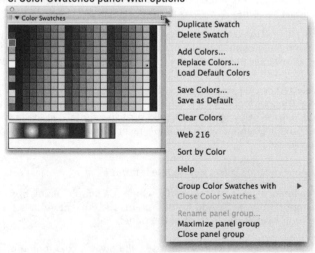

Figure 7-6: The default color palette as it displays in the Tools panel pop-up (A), Property inspector pop-up (B), and on the Color Swatches panel (C)

Note Drawing Objects behave like grouped shapes, but the fill and stroke colors applied to Drawing Objects can be modified without opening them in Edit mode. When a Drawing Object is selected (by single-clicking) with the Selection tool, the selection grid isn't visible (as it would be on a raw shape), but you can apply a new fill or stroke color by using any of the Swatches menus. To open a Drawing Object in Edit mode, double-click with the Selection tool.

If the color you want is not available in the current Swatches menu, you may opt to invoke the Color Picker by clicking the Color Picker button. Alternatively, you may also open the Color Mixer panel to create a new color and add it to the currently loaded selection of swatches. The Color Swatches panel enables you to load, add, delete, and modify various color sets for individual documents. Whatever changes are made to the Color Swatches panel will be saved with the document (.fla) that is currently active.

Tip With any of the Swatch pop-ups active, your cursor icon will turn into an Eyedropper. If you roll the Eyedropper over colors outside of the swatches area while continuing to hold down the mouse, you will notice that you can "sample" colors from anywhere on your desktop. When you find a color you like, release your mouse and the color will load into Flash as your currently selected color. Don't forget to add the color to the Color Swatches panel if you want to save it in the color library of your current file. We describe the steps for adding and saving swatches later in this chapter.

Color Swatches panel options

Think of the Color Swatches panel (refer to Figure 7-6) as a paint box or a way to organize your existing swatches and to manipulate the display of colors that are available in the other panels. Use the Color Swatches panel to save color sets, import color sets, and reorder or change selected colors. The options menu of the Color Swatches panel provides the controls used to sort or modify individual swatches as well as various color sets:

✦ **Duplicate Swatch:** Use this to duplicate a selected swatch. It can be useful when you want to make a range of related color swatches by duplicating and then editing a series of swatches with the Color Mixer panel.

Tip You can duplicate a selected swatch with just two clicks. First, select a swatch with the Selection tool or use the Dropper tool to pick a color from any item on the Stage. As you move the pointer into the space below the current solid swatches set (above the gradient swatches), the pointer icon changes from a dropper into a paint bucket. Just click and a new swatch is added to the color set.

✦ **Delete Swatch:** Botched a swatch? Select and delete it here.

✦ **Add Colors:** Opens the Import Color Swatch menu, which is a simple dialog box used to locate, select, and import color sets. Add Colors retains the current color set and appends the imported color set at the bottom of the panel.

Caution Be careful about creating huge color sets! In some cases, the Swatch color pop-ups may extend beyond the visible screen and you'll have to use the Color Swatches panel to be able to scroll to choose colors that are hidden off-screen. This can happen if you add colors from a complex GIF image to the default Web 216 set.

✦ **Replace Colors:** Also opens the Import Color Swatch menu. However, Replace Colors replaces the current color set when it loads the selected color set. With the exception of the gradient swatches, if the current set has not been saved, it will be lost.

✦ **Load Default Colors:** Clears the current color set and replaces it with the default Web 216 swatch palette. Again, if the current set has not been saved, it will be lost. Flash allows you to change the specification for your default color palette if you prefer not to use Web 216. (See Save as Default.)

✦ **Save Colors:** Opens the Export Color Swatch menu, which is used to name and save color sets to a specific location on your hard drive. Color sets may be saved in either the Flash Color Set (.clr) or Color Table (.act) format, which can be used with Macromedia Fireworks and Adobe Photoshop. Gradients can only be imported and exported from Flash using the .clr format.

✦ **Save as Default:** Saves the current swatch set as the default set to be loaded in the Color Swatches panel for all new Flash documents.

✦ **Clear Colors:** Removes all colors currently loaded in the Color Swatches panel, leaving only the black and white swatches and a grayscale gradient.

✦ **Web 216:** Loads the Web-safe palette. This option makes it safe to mess with the swatches in Flash because no matter what you do, you can always just reload this original default color set.

Tip

You can override the default Web 216 color set by switching the Color Mixer panel to either the RGB or HSB (hue, saturation, brightness) color spaces. You can then mix your own fresh colors, add them to the Color Swatches panel, and save that palette as the default. Another alternative is to locate the Photoshop Color Tables on your hard drive (or download a specialty color table from the Web) and replace the default set with a broader gamut.

✦ **Sort by Color:** This organizes the swatches by hue rather than by mathematical number and can visually be a more logical way to find colors in your current set. Note, however, that once you apply this sort, you have no way to toggle back to your original swatch order (other than reloading the default Web 216 swatch set). So it is best to save any custom palette first before sorting so that you have the option of going back to the other display if you prefer it. Figure 7-7 shows the Web 216 palette as it appears sorted numerically (left) and as it appears sorted by hue (right).

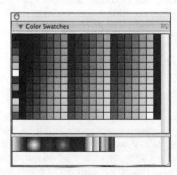
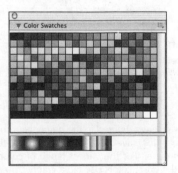

Web 216 swatches in default order   Web 216 swatches sorted by color

Figure 7-7: The default Web 216 palette as it appears sorted by number (left), and how it appears after being sorted by hue with the Sort by Color command (right)

Importing custom palettes

The option of loading custom swatches is helpful if you're developing a Flash project that you want to match with a predefined palette—whether this is out of necessity or just for inspiration. For example, you can match your Flash elements to a corporate logo or to the range of hues in a photo that you love. In addition to loading the colors in a specific GIF file, Flash allows you to load RGB color palettes from other graphics applications, which have been saved as Color Tables (in the .act format).

Loading a custom GIF color palette

To simplify your Flash swatch selection to match the colors in a company logo or other GIF image, follow these steps:

1. Clear the currently loaded color set by choosing Clear Colors in the Color Swatches panel options menu.

2. Choose Add Colors from the Color Swatches panel options menu and, in the Import Color Swatch dialog box, specify the GIF file that you want to define the imported color set.

3. Flash will load the colors from the GIF image into the Color Swatches panel and you can then save the document (.fla) to keep these colors as the loaded set.

4. To organize the loaded color set in the Color Swatches panel by hue, choose the Sort by Color option. You can always add or delete swatches from this new set.

5. If you want to use your custom color set in other files, use the Save Colors command in the Color Swatches panel options menu to save a Color Table (.act) or Flash Color Set (.clr).

A sample source GIF image and the resulting imported Swatches palette are shown in Figure 7-8.

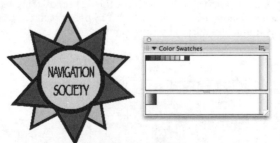

Figure 7-8: The simple logo GIF file that we specified as the source for a custom Swatches palette. The resulting swatches match the colors in the logo.

Tip   The color settings defined in the original authoring environment (such as Adobe Illustrator or Photoshop) for saved GIF files will affect the colors available for loading to the Flash swatches panel. For the widest range of colors, use 256 colors and an adaptive palette. To get only the exact colors used in a graphic, manually restrict the number of colors that can be included by typing in a number that matches the number of colors in the original graphic. For example, if a logo that you plan to use as a source file for your swatches is red, blue, yellow, black, and white, restrict the GIF to five colors when you export it from the original authoring application.

Creating and loading a custom Color Table

If you want to save a color palette that will match the hues in a photograph, you can also generate a Color Table in Adobe Photoshop or Macromedia Fireworks.

To create a Color Table in Adobe Photoshop (or Illustrator), follow these steps:

1. Open a source bitmap image (.jpeg, .tif, or .psd).

2. Use the Save for Web command to access the settings that allow you to choose the file type and color space that you wish to export. To create a Color Table, set the file type to GIF, choose adaptive color, and choose the number of colors you wish to include in the color table. Although you can include anywhere from 2 to 256 colors in your Color Table, you will not likely need more than 16. Preview the swatches with the Color Table tab in the lower left of the interface (next to Image Size).

Note   Although Photoshop includes a menu option for creating a Color Table (Image ➪ Mode ➪ Color Table), this option is available only if the source image is first converted to Indexed color. Also, the Color Table dialog box only offers limited control of the swatches that will be exported, so we prefer to use the Save for Web workflow.

3. When you have a set of swatches that you are happy with, choose Save Color Table from the Color Table options menu. The settings used for the sample file are shown in Figure 7-9.

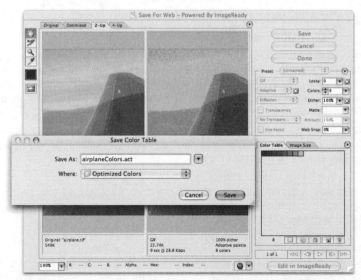

Figure 7-9: Use the Save for Web command and the Color Table settings in Adobe Photoshop to create a custom color set from a photograph.

4. Give the Color Table a name that you will remember (such as airplaneColors) and save the .act file to a folder where you can find it again. Creating a Custom Palettes folder on your system, where you can store and organize any of the Color Tables or source GIFs that you may want to use again, is a good idea.

5. Open a Flash document (.fla), and from the Color Swatches panel options menu choose Add Colors if you want new colors added to the currently loaded set (or Replace Colors if you want to use only your new colors).

6. From the Import Color Swatch dialog box, browse to your Color Table (.act) file and select it. Flash will load the new colors into the Color Swatches panel and you can then sort and save this set with your document.

The sample source bitmap image and the resulting Color Table loaded into the Color Swatches panel are shown in Figure 7-10.

Figure 7-10: A photo used to generate a Color Table (.act), and the resulting color set loaded into the Flash Color Swatches panel

To create a Color Table in Macromedia Fireworks, follow these steps:

1. Open a source bitmap image (.jpeg, .tif, or .psd).

2. Open the Optimize panel (Window ➪ Optimize) to access the settings that allow you to choose the file type and color space that you wish to export. To create a Color Table, set the file type to GIF, choose adaptive color, and choose the number of colors you wish to include in the color table. To preview the swatches, select the Preview (or 2-Up) tab in the main image window.

3. When you have a set of swatches that you are happy with, choose Save Palette from the Optimize panel options menu. The settings used for the sample .act file (on the CD-ROM) are shown in Figure 7-11.

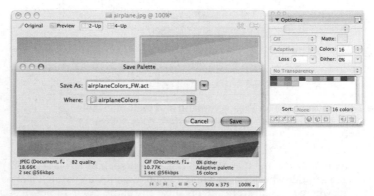

Figure 7-11: Use the Optimize panel in Fireworks to create a custom color set from a photograph.

4. Continue with Steps 4 through 6 in the previous instructions.

On the CD-ROM

In the example, we created a Color Table from an image of an airplane wing. You can find the source bitmap (`airplane.jpg`) and the Photoshop Color Table (`airplaneColors.act`) files, along with a Flash document (`airplaneColors.fla`) that has a JPG imported and the color palette loaded in the `airplaneColors` folder in the `ch07` folder on the CD-ROM.

Using the Color Mixer Panel

Think of the Color Mixer panel as the "boss" of the Color Swatches panel. The Color Swatches panel handles the color inventory and serves up the available colors, but the Color Mixer panel has the power to modify those colors and add the variations to the current set. The Color style menu available on the Color Mixer panel allows you to choose the type of color pattern that you want to work with—including solid colors, linear and radial gradients, and bitmap fills.

New Feature

In Flash 8, gradient styles can be used with strokes as well as with fills. This option has great potential for creating custom line styles for borders and other decorative lines.

As shown in Figure 7-12 and Figure 7-13, the Color Mixer panel enables you to create new colors, with settings in any of three color spaces — RGB, HSB, or hex — using either manually entered values or the "rainbow" color picker field. All colors are handled with four channels, which are RGBA (red, green, blue, alpha); these values can be individually adjusted using the Color value fields and slider controls. The Tint slider control enables you to dynamically shift your current color darker or lighter. A Fill or Stroke color selected in any of the Swatch menus will be displayed in the Mixer panel where it can be modified.

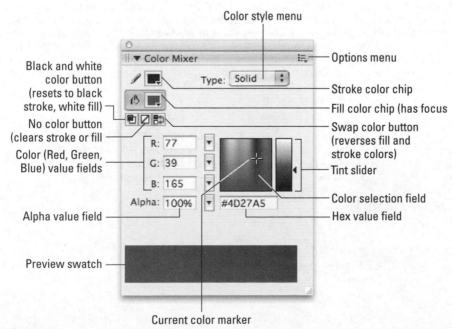

Figure 7-12: The Flash 8 Color Mixer panel

As shown in Figure 7-13, colors modified in the Color Mixer panel can be added to the palette loaded in the Color Swatches panel — just select Add Swatch from the Color Mixer panel options menu and the color will be added below the colors currently loaded in the Color Swatches panel.

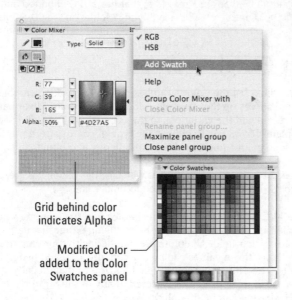

Grid behind color indicates Alpha

Modified color added to the Color Swatches panel

Figure 7-13: Colors modified in the Mixer panel can be added to the Color Swatches panel.

Any color swatch selected in the Color Swatches panel will be loaded into the Mixer panel as a starting point only — modifications made in the Mixer panel will not change the original color in the Color Swatches panel. The new color or gradient that you create using the controls in the Color Mixer panel (shown in Figure 7-14) will be added as a new swatch only when you select Add Swatch from the options menu. You can always edit your custom color by selecting the new (saved) swatch, but the modified version will be treated as a new color and will also have to be added to the Color Swatches panel separately.

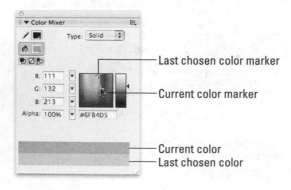

Last chosen color marker

Current color marker

Current color
Last chosen color

Figure 7-14: The Color Mixer panel preview swatch splits to compare colors as you use the color picker or the Tint slider to make adjustments.

Caution   The colors you create and add to the Color Swatches panel will be saved with the document (.fla) as long as you do not reload the default set or overwrite the loaded swatch set. If you want to save your custom mixed colors, remember to save the Flash color set (.clr) to a folder using the Save Colors command in the Color Swatches panel before you reload the default Web 216 color set or Replace Colors with a new palette.

When you select a color from the Swatches pop-up palette, the cursor converts to a Dropper tool that enables you to sample color from anywhere in the interface just by dragging the dropper and clicking the color you want to pick up. You can pluck colors from icons in the Flash application, from any element that you have in the Document window, and even from elements on your desktop or in other application windows that are currently open.

Tip   The same Dropper feature is available from any of the Swatches pop-ups, but the colors you select this way will not be stored in the Color Swatches panel unless you use the Color Mixer panel menu's Add Swatch option.

Caution   To pick up colors with the Dropper tool outside of the Flash application itself, be careful not to release the mouse button while you move the mouse from the Swatches in the Color Mixer panel to the other color that you want to sample. If you release the mouse button before moving it to the color you want to sample, you will be able to pick up colors from inside the Flash application only.

Adjusting fill and stroke transparency

The Alpha control in the Color Mixer panel (and in the Swatches pop-ups) is used to adjust the transparency of stroke and fill colors, either to modify a selected graphic (shape or Drawing Object) or to create a new color that can be added to the Color Swatches panel.

There are two ways to change the Alpha value for a selected color: Either drag the Alpha slider until the preview display looks right, or enter a numeric value directly in the Alpha value box. Numeric entry is useful when you already know what level of transparency is required, while the slider is useful for tweaking the transparency by eye to get it just right — as indicated in either the stroke or fill color chip or the color preview in the Color Mixer panel. In Figure 7-15, a stroke color and a fill color have both been adjusted to 50 percent alpha and then added to the Color Swatches panel. While the Alpha slider is being dragged to a new setting, the preview displays the original 50 percent Alpha value (at the bottom) as well as the current 25 percent Alpha value (at the top). The rectangle below the panels shows the 50 percent alpha stroke and fill applied to a shape. The Flash grid has been turned on (View ⇨ Grid ⇨ Show Grid), so that the alpha is easier to see — on a flat white background, the color just looks lighter rather than transparent.

Caution   Alpha transparency will result in more of a performance hit than a color tint, especially if there are a lot of overlapping animated transparencies. If you can achieve the effect that you want by using a *tint* instead (fading to a solid color), then save the Alpha effect for graphics that you need to layer on top of other elements or textured backgrounds.

New Feature   You can apply blend modes to symbols to create different types of layered effects. We describe this new Flash 8 feature in Chapter 9, "Modifying Graphics."

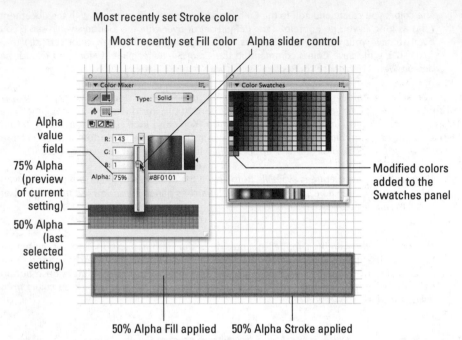

Most recently set Stroke color

Most recently set Fill color   Alpha slider control

Alpha value field

75% Alpha (preview of current setting)

50% Alpha (last selected setting)

Modified colors added to the Swatches panel

50% Alpha Fill applied   50% Alpha Stroke applied

Figure 7-15: New levels of Alpha can be applied to Fills and Strokes and the modified swatches can be added to the Swatches panel for reuse.

Working with gradient fills

Gradients are composed by blending two or more colors together in bands across a plane (*a linear gradient*) or from the center to the edge of an object in concentric circles (*a radial gradient*). You can modify these two basic styles of gradient fill to create virtually unlimited variations.

Figure 7-16 shows the gradient editing controls in the Mixer panel, with the preview display for a linear gradient on the left, and for a radial gradient on the right. When working with linear gradients, the position of the color pointers on the Edit bar will correspond to control points on the blend from left to right. When used in conjunction with radial gradients, the Gradient Edit bar corresponds to the *radius*, or a slice from the center out to the edge, of the circular gradient. Color pointers at the left end of the Gradient Edit bar represent the center — or inside — of the radial gradient, while color pointers at the right end represent the outside border. The active color pointer is identified by a black fill in the pointer, and unselected color pointers have a white fill in the pointer.

The main Color Swatches panel and any of the fill Swatches pop-ups display the prebuilt linear and radial gradients that are included in the default palette. To edit an existing gradient swatch, just select it from the any of the fill Swatches pop-ups or select it from the main Color Swatches panel, and it will be loaded into the Mixer panel where the relevant controls will be displayed automatically. The other option is to start by choosing a gradient style from the central Color style menu on the Mixer panel to load a basic linear or radial gradient. After you create a custom gradient in a document, your settings will appear when you go back to the Mixer panel menu. To start with an unmodified default gradient, just select one from the fill Swatches palette. Figure 7-17 shows the two methods of selecting a gradient style to work with.

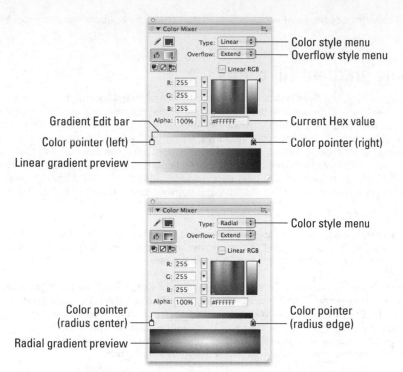

Color style menu
Overflow style menu

Gradient Edit bar
Color pointer (left)
Linear gradient preview

Current Hex value
Color pointer (right)

Color style menu

Color pointer
(radius center)
Radial gradient preview

Color pointer
(radius edge)

Figure 7-16: The Color Mixer panel displaying edit controls and preview for a linear gradient (top) and for a radial gradient (bottom)

Color style menu   Swatches pop-up

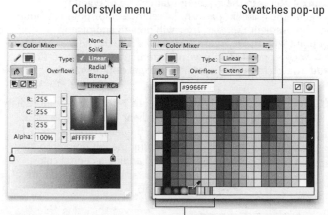

Gradient swatch area: default gradients and saved custom gradients

Figure 7-17: You can select default gradient styles (and saved custom gradients) from any of the fill Swatches pop-ups, or set one of the basic grayscale gradient styles with the Color style menu in the Color Mixer.

Note   The Fill Transform tool has been improved and is now called the Gradient Transform tool in Flash 8.

Controlling gradient fill colors

The colors in a gradient and the distribution of blending are adjusted by sliding the color pointers along the Gradient Edit bar in the Mixer panel. These pointers are the access points to the key colors that define the gradient. After you click on a pointer to make it active, you can assign the color that will be blended in its range, either by double-clicking to invoke the Swatches pop-ups or by picking a color in the color selection field. You can also use the value fields and the color slider controls to modify an assigned color in a gradient the same way as any solid color. Flash 8 provides more robust support for gradient creation. Although you probably won't ever need to exceed the old limit of 8 points, Flash 8 has doubled the limit to 16 points.

New Feature   The Color proxy chips used to assign colors to gradient pointers in Flash MX 2004 have been replaced with handy Swatches pop-ups that are invoked by double-clicking any of the color pointers along the gradient Edit bar in the Color Mixer panel.

Caution   When you are editing a gradient fill, selecting a solid color swatch from the Color Swatches panel does not have the same effect as selecting a solid color swatch from the Swatches pop-up in the Color Mixer panel. Clicking a solid color swatch in the Color Swatches panel will replace your entire gradient in the Color Mixer with a solid fill style. Clicking a swatch from a Swatches pop-up on one of the gradient color pointers will only replace the color on the currently selected pointer — leaving the rest of your gradient intact.

You can adjust the pattern of the blend by clicking and dragging any of the color pointers to slide them to new positions along the Gradient Edit bar. You can add additional color pointers to the gradient range by clicking anywhere along the Gradient Edit bar. These additional pointers will create new control points in the gradient that can be dragged to new positions or assigned new colors to define the gradient pattern. To remove color pointers, simply drag them downward away from the Gradient Edit bar; they will detach and disappear, taking their assigned color and control point with them. Figure 7-18 shows a basic radial gradient modified with the addition of a new color pointer. To save a custom gradient to your Color Swatches panel, choose Add Swatch from the Color Mixer panel options menu.

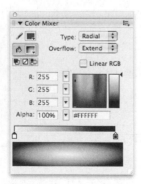

Figure 7-18: A two-point radial gradient from white to black (on the left), modified by setting the left pointer to gray and adding a central color pointer set to white (on the right)

Two-point radial gradient   Three-point radial gradient

By selecting an element on the Stage, you can also apply or modify an existing gradient fill or stroke using the Mixer panel. When an item is selected in the Document window, you will see the current fill and stroke displayed in the Color Mixer panel. Any changes you make in the Color Mixer panel while the item is selected will be updated on the item dynamically. Remember to select Add Swatch from the options menu if you want to store the new gradient in the Color Swatches panel.

New Feature

In Flash MX 2004, fills and strokes on items in the Document window are loaded into the Color Mixer panel by using the swatches pop-up in the Property inspector. In Flash 8, the workflow has been streamlined — the current fill (or stroke) of any selected item is automatically loaded in the Color Mixer panel.

Tip

To make it easier to see how a gradient looks in a selected shape, you can toggle off the display of the selection mesh by using Shift+Ctrl+E (Shift+⌘+E).

If you need some new ideas for gradient styles, Macromedia Fireworks is a great addition to your tool kit. Flash 8 supports the import of Fireworks PNG files, and most filters and gradient styles added in Fireworks will be preserved and editable when the file is imported to Flash. Fireworks ships with a huge library of ready-made gradient styles, including simple but handy Rectangle and Contour styles and fancier ones such as Satin, Starburst, and Ripple. Some of these gradient styles are too complex for the Flash authoring environment to support, but you can import them as bitmaps and jump out to Fireworks to edit them if you need to. You can add Fireworks gradient styles that Flash supports to your Swatches panel and reuse or modify them. Now those same old shaded buttons you have to keep making might just be more fun!

Using Alpha settings with gradients

As we mentioned previously, all the normal Color sliders and value fields will apply to control points on a gradient. You may have noticed already that this means you can add alpha to the blend range of any gradient. To create a soft transition between a bitmap or a patterned background and a solid color, you can create a gradient from a 0 percent alpha to a 100 percent alpha of the same solid color. To demonstrate just one application of this feature, we will walk through the steps of adding the appearance of a vignette (or softened edge) to a photograph imported into Flash:

1. Import a bitmap into Flash and place it on the Stage; then lock the bitmap layer.

2. Create a new layer above the bitmap layer and name it **gradient** (see Figure 7-19).

3. Open the Mixer panel and set the gradient style to radial, or select the default grayscale radial gradient from the fill Color Swatches panel. Set the stroke color to black, with a stroke height of 2. Leave the Overflow menu on the default (Extend) setting.

New Feature

The new Overflow style menu for gradient and bitmap fills in the Flash 8 Color Mixer panel provides more control over fill rendering. Three Overflow settings determine how the edges of a gradient or bitmap image will be rendered if they need to extend beyond the bounding box of the original applied fill. We include more detailed coverage of these settings in Chapter 9, "Modifying Graphics."

4. Select the gradient layer and then use the Rectangle tool to drag out a rectangle on the Stage that is the same size as the photograph on the layer below (see Figure 7-20).

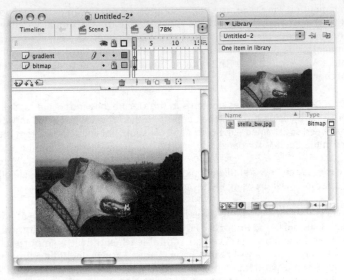

Figure 7-19: An imported bitmap placed on the Stage with a new layer above it for the gradient

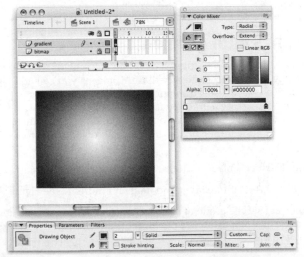

Figure 7-20: Finished rectangle with a radial gradient fill and a black stroke of 2. The rectangle is dragged out to match the size of the photograph on the layer below.

5. Select the fill of the rectangle and then select the left (white) color pointer on the Gradient Edit bar and assign it a color of black (see Figure 7-21). Set the Alpha value on the left color pointer to 0 percent.

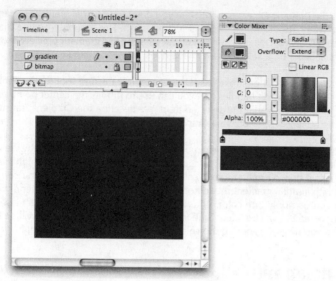

Figure 7-21: Both color pointers assigned a color of black for the selected gradient fill

6. Press Shift+Ctrl+E (Shift+⌘+E) to hide the selection mesh and adjust the position of the color pointers by sliding them along the Gradient Edit bar, until you like the way the blend looks on top of the photo (see Figure 7-22).

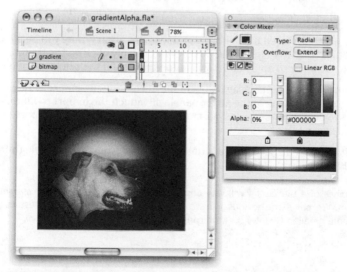

Figure 7-22: The final gradient can be previewed as the color pointer is moved to adjust the edges of the alpha blend.

Tip

If you applied the Drawing Object option when you drew the original gradient rectangle, you won't have to worry about turning off the selection mesh. The thin blue outline that shows up on a selected Drawing Object doesn't interfere with the live gradient preview like the dotted mesh that appears on a selected raw shape does.

New Feature

Select any gradient item (fill or stroke) with the Gradient Transform tool (in the Tools panel) and you will see the new edit handles that you can use to modify the center point, scale, and rotation of your gradient within the selected item. We describe the Gradient Transform tool in more detail in Chapter 9, "Modifying Graphics."

Note

As you read through the steps in this example, you might have wondered why we assigned the same color to both color pointers; since one of the pointers is set to an alpha value of 0 percent, perhaps it doesn't matter which color is used? The answer is that you *can* create a "fade" effect with a radial gradient made from two different colors, but the blend will not be clean unless you use only one color. Although the end point of the gradient assigned an alpha value of 0 percent will be "clear," the interstitial bands of the gradient will be tinted by whatever color you have assigned to the color pointer before changing the alpha value.

Selecting bitmap fills

Another handy feature available in the Color Mixer panel is the Bitmap fill option. This option enables you to choose any bitmap, in the Library or elsewhere on your system, to use as a fill for shapes drawn in Flash. When the image loads into a selected shape, it tiles to fill the shape.

To apply a bitmap fill directly to an existing shape, perform the following steps:

1. Select the fill of a shape (or select a Drawing Object) with the Selection tool.

2. Open the Mixer panel and choose Bitmap from the Color style menu.

3. If you have bitmaps stored in your current document library, they will be available from the Bitmap Preview area of the Mixer panel. Simply click on the thumbnail of the bitmap that you want to apply and it will automatically fill the selected shape.

4. If you do not have any bitmaps available in the current document, selecting Bitmap from the Color style menu in the Mixer panel will launch the Import to Library dialog box, where you can browse your system and specify a bitmap to be imported and applied as a fill.

Figure 7-23 shows a selected shape with a bitmap fill applied from the available thumbnails in the Mixer panel Preview area.

Note

The appearance of a Bitmap fill will vary depending on how it is loaded (or assigned) to a specific item. We cover the various ways of loading Bitmap fills and the results you can expect in more detail in Chapter 9, "Modifying Graphics."

Preview of active Bitmap fill

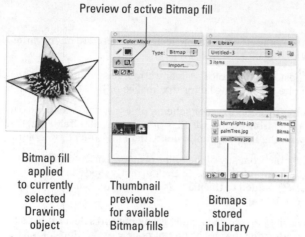

Bitmap fill
applied
to currently
selected
Drawing
object

Thumbnail
previews
for available
Bitmap fills

Bitmaps
stored
in Library

Figure 7-23: A bitmap fill applied to a selected shape. The bitmap is chosen from images stored in the library, which are displayed as thumbnails in the Mixer panel Preview area.

Working with Droppers, Paint Buckets, and Ink Bottles

So far in this chapter, we've introduced the various ways of controlling your palette and setting stroke and fill colors on items selected with the Selection tool. There is one other set of tools used for applying colors and fills that will make modifying existing artwork even easier. You have already seen the Dropper tool in action when you select a color from any of the Swatches pop-ups — the Arrow pointer automatically converts to a dropper and allows you to pick up a color from any visible element to be loaded into the active fill or stroke color chip.

This same tool can be summoned at any time by clicking on the Eyedropper tool (I) icon in the Tools panel. You will notice that when the Eyedropper tool is used to pick up a fill color or bitmap, it immediately converts into the Paint Bucket tool (K) if you roll outside the area of the item you've sampled. The Paint Bucket enables you to dump the selected fill into any other shape just by clicking inside its fill area. If you have a fill or stroke selected when you invoke the Eyedropper tool, any other fill or stroke (color or style) that you pick up with the Dropper tool will be applied instantly to the selected item.

When you sample a stroke with the Eyedropper tool, it converts into an Ink Bottle tool (S), which you can use to apply the stroke to any other item. If the item already has a stroke, it will be modified, and if the item did not previously have a stroke, the Ink Bottle will add one.

Web Resource We'd like to know what you think about this chapter. Visit `www.flashsupport.com/feedback` to fill out an online survey with your comments.

Summary

✦ The science of color on the computer is far from accurate. There are many variables involved in the presentation of color over the Web.

✦ Web-safe color does not ensure "good color" — many strategies go into applying color skillfully, but contrast can be the defining factor that makes or breaks your design.

✦ Although Flash doesn't directly support color scheme plug-ins, colors can be loaded into the Color Swatches panel from source GIF files or custom Color Table (.act) files, or they can be sampled with the Dropper tool to load them into the active color chip.

✦ The Swatches pop-up available from any of the color previews or color pointers in the Color Mixer gives immediate, intuitive access to the currently loaded swatches and all custom colors that have been added to the main Color Swatches panel. It also permits direct insertion of hexadecimal values.

✦ The Color Mixer panel is used to create and modify gradients and select bitmaps to be used as fills, in addition to adjusting the alpha and tint of new or existing colors. Custom colors added to the current swatches will be available in any of the Swatches pop-ups.

✦ Flash 8 supports 16-point gradients — allowing twice the number of control points within a gradient blend than previous versions of Flash.

✦ The Eyedropper, Paint Bucket, and Ink Bottle tools work together to select and apply fill and stroke colors. We discuss the options for these tools, along with the Gradient Transform and Free Transform tools, in Chapter 9, "Modifying Graphics."

✦ Advanced color capabilities of Flash include color tweening, scriptable color, and negative alpha. We discuss these topics in depth in subsequent chapters.

✦   ✦   ✦

Working with Text

For designers who love fonts, Flash is a dream come true. Even if you never plan to animate anything, you may want to use Flash simply to see your fonts displayed how you want them, wherever and whenever you need them on the Web. Of course, there are a few exceptions to this unequivocal freedom, but Flash has options that give you text styles to meet nearly any project criteria.

New Feature
An improved anti-aliasing engine in Flash 8 solves one of the few problems that have troubled designers striving for text perfection in their Flash layouts. You will find a more detailed description of the various anti-alias options later in this chapter.

Because Flash is a vector program, it enables you to integrate most fonts within the movie without any fuss. For standard text content, this means that fonts don't have to be rendered into bitmap elements — the .swf files that Flash publishes (or exports) will include all the necessary information for the font to display properly on every browser as long as the Flash Player is installed.

In this chapter, we introduce the various text types available in Flash and explain how and why they are used. This chapter also covers some basic font management issues and offers strategies for handling fonts in your project files (.fla) as well as in your published movies (.swf).

New Feature
Flash 8 includes a Filters tab in the Property inspector for a new menu of live filters that you can apply to text without first converting the text into graphic shapes. This feature facilitates experimentation by making it easier for you to add or change an effect on the fly while preserving the editability of your text fields.

Flash includes some nifty Static text options for handling vertical and right-to-left-reading text. We will show you these options, along with the other character and paragraph controls and the new live filters available in the Property inspector. In this chapter, we will also touch on some features for optimizing text and working with international character sets in Flash.

Considering Typography

Typography is the formal term for the design and use of text. Although Flash has the capability to deliver finely designed typography to your audience, this is no guarantee that it solves all type design challenges.

Unfortunately, no matter how well Flash renders text, it can't disguise bad design or make up for a designer's lack of knowledge about working with type. As with color, sound, animation, or any other specialized area of production, the amount you can learn about typography is really only limited by your interest.

Although many people can get by without ever studying typography formally, they are missing the chance to leverage one of the most powerful and complex tools of graphic design. Computers have changed the way that final designs are created, but they have not changed the fundamental principles and uses of typography. The best part about studying typography is that your knowledge will be equally useful no matter what medium or digital tool you are working with.

Because type is such an important and long-standing aspect of design, there are innumerable resources available to guide and inspire you. Just wander through the graphic design section of any bookstore or do a search online for *typography,* and you will find something that can introduce you to the basics or help develop the skills you already have.

This chapter includes some common typography terms that are familiar to most people who have designed with text. Although a more detailed explanation of the source and meaning of these terms is beyond the scope of this book, you will be able to follow visually how things like *tracking* and *leading* apply to text in Flash.

If you are unfamiliar with typography, here are some excellent resources to get you started:

✦ *The Non-Designer's Type Book* by **Robin Williams** (Peachpit Press, 1998): This is a classic book that is still helpful to anyone who needs a friendly introduction to the world of type and some ground rules for using text effectively.

✦ *The Elements of Typographic Style* by **Robert Bringhurst** (Hartley and Marks Publishers, 2004): This is a manual of typography and book design that concludes with appendices of typographic characters, currently available digitized fonts, and a glossary of terms.

✦ *Jan Tschichold: A Life in Typography* by **Ruari McLean** (Princeton Architectural Press, 1997): This is an inspiring and informative biography of the life and work of one of the most influential masters of modern typography.

✦ *Type in Use: Effective Typography for Electronic Publishing* by **Alex W. White** (W. W. Norton & Company, 1999): This book offers a concise primer on the history of publication design and includes many useful examples of effective strategies for designing pages with type.

✦ *The End of Print* by **Lewis Blackwell and David Carson** (Chronicle Books, 2002) **and** *David Carson 2ndsight: Grafik Design after the End of Print* by **Lewis Blackwell** (Universe, 1997): These colorful books chart the creative evolution of one of the most legendary mavericks of contemporary graphic design who has become an inspirational teacher and lecturer.

Text Field Types in Flash

Flash allows you to include text in your projects in a variety of ways. Often one Flash project will contain several different text types, each suited to a specific kind of content. We describe the steps for creating text boxes and editing type later in this chapter, but will begin here with an overview of the three main text types used in Flash:

✦ **Static:** Static text boxes are used for display type or text content created at author-time (in the .fla), that won't change at run time (in the .swf).

✦ **Dynamic:** Dynamic text fields are used to hold text content that is generated at run time from a live data source, or text that will be updated dynamically, such as weather information or sports' scores.

✦ **Input:** Input text fields are exactly what they sound like, fields created for text that users enter at run time. You use input text fields whenever you need users to do things such as enter passwords or answer questions.

Note For the purpose of brevity, we often refer to both Dynamic and Input text fields as *editable text fields* because both text-field types can be modified at run time (unlike Static text boxes, which can be modified only at author-time).

On the CD-ROM You will find examples of text field styles in the `textSamples.fla` file in the `ch08` folder on the CD-ROM.

The Text tool is used to create text boxes and to enter and modify type. When you first create a text box in Flash, the default text type is Static, but you can assign it a different text type in the Property inspector at any time. Subsequent text boxes are automatically assigned the type style you have selected most recently. This makes it quicker to create a series of text boxes of the same type, but it means you should double-check the settings if you need text boxes of different types.

Figure 8-1 shows the basic controls that appear in the collapsed Property inspector when the Text tool is selected from the Tools panel.

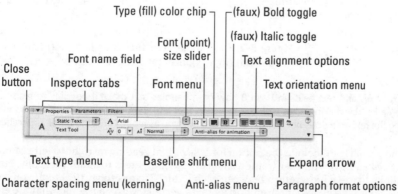

Figure 8-1: The basic text options that appear in the (collapsed) Property inspector when the Text tool is active or a Static text box is selected on the Stage

To make it easy to access the new filters available in Flash 8, the Property inspector has been modified to make room for the Parameters tab and the Filters tab to the right of the Properties tab. To switch views from Properties to either Parameters or Filters, simply click the relevant tab if the Property inspector is open or use the Window ➪ Properties submenu to select the tab view that you want active when the Property inspector appears.

Static text boxes

Although the term *Static text* sounds limiting, this type of text box actually offers the most design options at author-time. Static text boxes can be scaled, rotated, flipped, or skewed, assigned alpha levels, and modified with filters while preserving editable text characters. Static text can also be animated or layered like any other graphic element in Flash. By default, Flash embeds the outlines for any fonts used in Static text for display on other machines, but you may also choose to specify a generic device font to reduce the size of your final movie or to eliminate *anti-aliasing* (or *smoothing*) on small text.

Flash 8 replaces the old Alias text button with a more sophisticated menu of anti-aliasing options. An improved rendering engine built into Flash Player 8, and precise authoring controls in the Property inspector, make it much easier to find a setting that renders smooth, legible text, even at small point sizes. If it turns out that you still prefer aliased text, simply choose the Bitmap text (no anti-alias) setting from the drop-down menu and you will get the same result as you did with the Alias text button in Flash MX 2004.

The Link entry field is another helpful feature in the Property inspector that allows you to select sections of Static or Dynamic (horizontal) text and enter a URL to create a text link to a Web page or to an e-mail address in your Flash movie without any additional coding.

By default, Static text boxes are horizontal, and they can be either *expanding* boxes, which allow you to keep typing along one line as it extends to fit the type, or *fixed-width* boxes, which constrain your text box to a set width and auto-wrap the text to fit. These two types of text fields look the same when you select them by clicking once with the Selection tool, but when you double-click, you can see the text box handle icon that indicates the current behavior of the box. Figure 8-2 shows the respective icons for expanding, or *label,* text and for fixed-width, or *block,* horizontal Static text.

   Figure 8-2: The handle icons for expanding (left) and fixed-width (right) horizontal Static text boxes

All text boxes and text fields in Flash 8 now have handles that make it possible to resize the text area just by clicking once with the selection tool and then dragging one of the handles. Scaling the text area does not change the size of the type as it does in some other applications.

Static text boxes in Flash include the option for left-to-right-reading or right-to-left-reading vertical text boxes. Have you ever wanted a line of text characters to stack vertically, but found it tedious to use a hard return between each letter? Thanks to vertical text, you can easily switch your type alignment from horizontal to vertical, with characters that are either stacked or rotated. This eliminates the headache of trying to read sideways while editing type—with a simple menu choice you can switch from vertical to horizontal and back again with no hard returns or freehand rotations required. Figure 8-3 illustrates how the vertical text and rotate text options change the orientation of Static text.

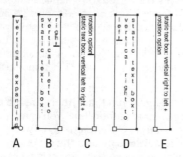

Figure 8-3: Vertical text box orientations: (A) vertical expanding, (B) vertical fixed-height left to right, (C) vertical fixed-height left to right with rotate option, (D) vertical fixed-height right to left, and (E) vertical fixed-height with rotate option

Aside from giving designers authoring in English more options for cool layouts, this feature makes Flash much friendlier for designers authoring in language sets that require vertical or right-to-left character flow. As we describe in the "Vertical text options" section later in this chapter, you can modify the alignment of vertical text to anchor it to the top, center, or bottom of the text box.

Although the default orientation for text in Flash is horizontal and left to right, you can modify the Vertical text settings in the Text category of the Flash Preferences dialog box, as shown in Figure 8-4 (File ➪ Preferences or, in OS X, Flash ➪ Preferences). To make all new Static text boxes automatically orient vertically, select the Default text orientation check box. To change the default text flow, select the Right to left text flow check box. You also have the option of disabling kerning on vertical text by selecting the No kerning check box.

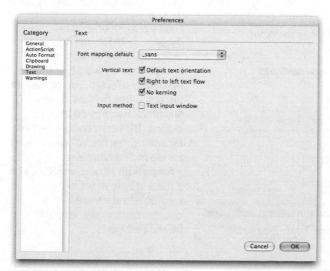

Figure 8-4: Changing the default Vertical text settings in the Preferences dialog box

Editable text fields: Dynamic and Input

Editable text, like Static text, begins as a *block,* but when it's converted to Dynamic or Input behavior, these editable text boxes are referred to as *text fields.* Think of an editable text field as an empty window with a name attached to it. When text or data is sent to the Flash movie (.swf), it is sent to a specific named text instance, which ensures that it will be displayed in the proper window or editable text field. Dynamic text fields can display information supplied from a database, read from a server-side application, or loaded from another Flash movie (or another part of the same Flash movie).

Because Dynamic text fields are generated or edited on the fly (at run time), there are limitations on how much you can control the appearance of the text at author-time. You cannot apply special formatting or shape modifications (such as *skewing* or *kerning*) directly to Dynamic text fields. However, Flash recognizes Dynamic text field instances the same way other Movie Clip instances recognize Dynamic text field instances, so you can assign a name to a Dynamic text field instance and use ActionScript to control its appearance.

Note   All editable text fields are recognized as nameable instances of the `Text Field` object. You should only use variable names to identify editable text fields for backwards compatibility with legacy versions of the Flash Player (Flash Player 5 or older), and the variable name or `var` attribute of a text field should not be the same as its instance name.

You can author Dynamic text horizontally in expanding or fixed-width fields, but you cannot rotate or modify it with the Vertical text option. Figure 8-5 shows how a Dynamic or Input text field will display when it's unselected (A) and how the field type is indicated by the handle icons when the text is double-clicked. If you plan to work with multiline text fields, but you have limited space for the text, you can set the text field behavior to *scrollable* in the Text menu (Text ➪ Scrollable); this enables the text to extend outside the visible area of the text box.

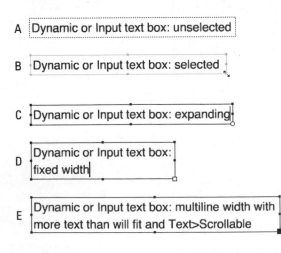

Figure 8-5: An unselected Dynamic or Input text field is indicated in the authoring environment by a dashed outline (A); when selected, you can adjust the size of the field by dragging any of the handles on the blue outline (B); when double-clicked for editing, the field displays either an expanding handle icon (C), or a fixed-width handle icon (D); and if the text field is set to be *scrollable,* the square handle changes from white/empty to black/filled (E).

When the Render text as HTML button in the Property inspector is toggled on, Flash recognizes rich text formatting, such as links and font styles indicated in Dynamic text with HTML tags, and applies them when the text is rendered in the Flash movie (.swf).

Tip If you change the size of an expanding text field by dragging one of the selection handles, the field automatically converts into a fixed-width text field. To change a fixed-width text field into an expanding text field, double-click the square fixed-width handle icon.

The Text Tool and the Property Inspector

Although Flash is neither an illustration program, like Macromedia FreeHand, nor a traditional page-layout program, like Adobe Illustrator or Quark, its text-handling capabilities are robust and easy to use. While you can create nearly any style of text directly in Flash, you can also import text created in other applications as *vector* artwork. With compatible applications such as Illustrator and FreeHand, you can even preserve your type as editable text boxes when it is imported to Flash.

Working with the Text tool

The Text tool, shown in Figure 8-6, delivers a broad range of control for generating, positioning, and modifying text. Although the Text tool is located in the Flash Tools panel, when the tool is active, the controls for working with text are in the Property inspector.

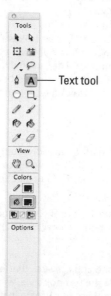

Figure 8-6: The Text tool is used to create text boxes and text fields in Flash.

— Text tool

Creating Static text boxes

To create text in your current Flash document, click the Text tool in the Tools panel (or press T on your keyboard) to activate it. You may choose to create new text in your Document window with either of two methods:

✦ **Label text:** To enter text on one extending line, click on the Document Stage and begin typing. To control the width of a line of label text, you can either enter hard returns with the Enter or Return key as you type, or you can convert the label text into block text by dragging any of the handles to a specific width or height — the round label text icon will change to a square block text icon to indicate that the box is now constrained.

Tip

If your text continues beyond the viewable area of the Document window, you can add some line breaks, click and drag to move the label text box, or choose View ➪ Work Area to make the entire text label visible.

✦ **Block text:** To define the area that will constrain your type by auto-wrapping as you enter more characters, click on the Document Stage and drag the text area to the width that you want. You can change the width of your block text at any time by dragging the handles that appear when the text area is selected or in Edit mode. Refer to Figure 8-2 (right image) for an example of the square box text icon.

Tip

Convert a text block into label text by double-clicking the square corner icon (visible in Edit mode), which will be changed to a round icon to indicate that the box is now extending instead of constrained.

New Feature

Use the new blue handles that appear when you select a text box with the Selection tool in Flash 8 to change the size of your text boxes or text fields without double-clicking or using the Text tool to enter Edit mode. The icons that indicate whether a text box is extending (label text) or constrained (block text) are still only visible in Edit mode.

One characteristic of the Flash text tool that might surprise you is that Static text boxes that do not contain any text are cleared from the Stage. As long as a Static text box contains even one character, it remains on the Stage until you delete or move it manually. Adobe Illustrator has adopted this same behavior because it eliminates the hassle of a project cluttered by empty invisible text boxes. Editable text fields *will* remain visible even if you have not entered any text characters at author-time.

Modifying or deleting text

Flash handles text as a group, which allows you to use the Text tool to edit the individual letters or words inside a text area at any time by clicking on the text box and then typing or drag-selecting specific characters. To select the whole block or group of text, you can click once anywhere on the text with the Selection tool.

To delete individual characters, click and drag to select them with the Text tool or use the Backspace key (the Delete key on a Mac). To delete a whole group of text, select it with the Selection tool and then use the Backspace key (or Delete key).

Tip

Double-clicking a text block with the Selection tool invokes Edit mode and activates the Text tool — this enables you to modify the individual characters or change the text box style, without having to switch to the Text tool first. You can use the shortcuts you use to navigate in the Actions panel in an active text box as well. For example, the Ctrl+arrow key (⌘+arrow key on a Mac) shortcut moves the cursor to the beginning or end of a word, and holding down the Shift key at the same time selects the word.

You can use most common text editing/word processing commands in Flash. Cut, Copy, and Paste move selected text within Flash and also between Flash and other applications that handle type. Flash provides a built-in Check Spelling command and a handy Search and Replace command.

The Check Spelling settings are quite sophisticated and you can customize them using the Spelling Setup dialog box available from the application menu (Text ➪ Spelling Setup), or launched with the Setup button in the Check Spelling dialog box. As shown in Figure 8-7, these options enable you to work with language-specific features and to control what areas of your Flash document to include when Check Spelling is applied.

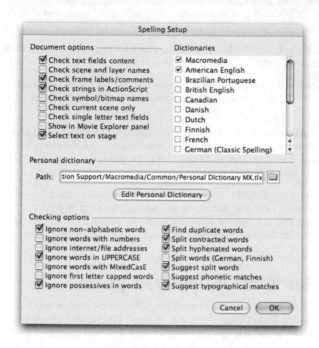

Figure 8-7: The Spelling Setup dialog box gives you a range of settings to control how the Check Spelling command is applied to your documents.

After you choose your settings, you can choose Text ➪ Check Spelling from the application menu, and Flash opens the Check Spelling dialog box (shown in Figure 8-8). You can then go through various text elements in your Flash document and modify or replace errors (with the help of suggestions), as you would in any other program with a spell check feature.

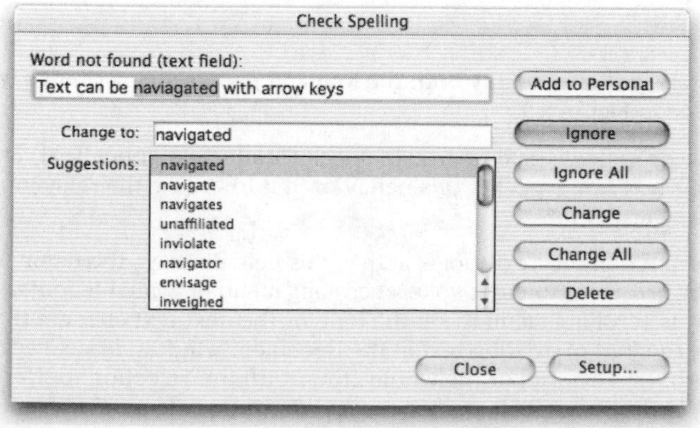

Figure 8-8: Check spelling with ease in Flash

The Movie Explorer panel makes it easy to find and modify text if you are working with a complex document. To access this feature if it is not already open, use the application menu (Window ➪ Movie Explorer) or the Alt+F3 (Option+F3) shortcut keys to invoke the Movie Explorer panel, and modify text in any of the following ways:

✦ **To see all the text used in your current document:** Set the Movie Explorer to Show Text with the option button at the top of the panel. The contents of each text box will be listed along with the font and point size that is used.

✦ **To search for a specific item:** Enter the font name, instance name, frame number, or ActionScript string in the Find field of the Movie Explorer panel.

✦ **To edit the contents of individual text boxes:** Double-click any listing in the Movie Explorer panel, and type in the field as you would if you were editing a filename in any other list.

✦ **To specify a new font or font size:** Select any text item listing that you want to change in the Movie Explorer and then simply change the font settings in the Property inspector. Use Shift+select to select multiple items in the Movie Explorer if you want to apply a change to more than one text box at a time.

✦ **To copy text:** Use the Copy command in the Movie Explorer options menu to copy a currently selected line of text to the Clipboard. Or to copy all the text in your current document to the Clipboard without having to select items individually in the Movie Explorer, use the Copy All Text to the Clipboard command in the Movie Explorer options menu.

Setting text attributes in the Property inspector

The Text tool does not include options in the Tools panel because the extensive text controls are centrally located in the Property inspector. You create all Flash text in text blocks or boxes using the same Text tool, but when you create text, you can assign it specific behavior with the Property inspector.

Although you can always access font style and size menus from the application menu (Text ➪ Font, Text ➪ Size, and Text ➪ Style), the options for controlling text are not visible in the Property inspector unless the Text tool is active or you select a text box with the Selection tool. The options available in the Property inspector vary slightly, depending on the kind of text you select.

Static text options

When working with Static text, you can modify both the font and paragraph attributes with the following options (shown in Figure 8-9):

✦ **Text type menu:** This drop-down enables you to specify Static Text, Input Text, or Dynamic Text for your text box type. Set this behavior first to invoke the relevant options in the Property inspector.

✦ **Font field (and menu):** When the Text tool is active, this field displays the name of the current font. Click the arrow button to invoke a scrolling menu of available fonts. Choose a font from this scrolling menu to set the font for the next text element that you create. Or, to change the font of existing text in the Document window, first select individual characters with the Text tool or the whole group with the Selection tool, and then choose a different font from the scrolling menu. When you select a font from the Property inspector menu, you'll see a preview of the highlighted font in the style or typeface that will display.

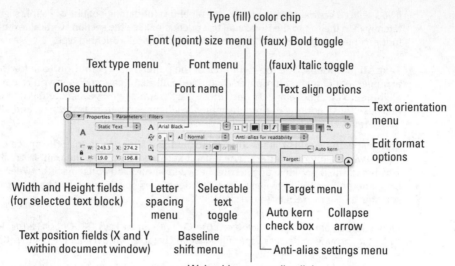

Figure 8-9: The main options available for Static text in the (expanded) Property inspector

✦ **Font size:** You can select the size of your type either with a pop-up slider or in a point size entry field. When the Text tool is active, it displays the current font size in the entry field. You can change the font size by typing a specific point size number in the field. If you click the arrow button to the immediate right of the text entry field, a pop-up slider enables you to select a font size — as you move the slider, the font size number updates in the entry field.

✦ **Type Color chip:** Click this button to invoke the Swatches pop-up menu, which in addition to offering current and temporary swatches, also enables you to acquire a color from anywhere within the interface by sampling with the dropper arrow.

✦ **Bold and Italic:** The Bold option is a radio button that toggles selected text between Normal and faux Bold. The Italic option is another radio button. It toggles selected text between Normal and faux Italic.

Note

Many computer programs (including Flash) that handle type permit you to approximate a bold and/or italic version of a font, even if this style is not available in the original installed font; this has led to some confusion about font styles. If a font was originally designed to include a bold or italic version, it will be appropriately named in the font menu (such as Century Schoolbook Bold), and will be selected as a *separate* typeface. With many fonts, the faux bold or italic style may display very similarly to the designed Bold or Italic style, but with well-designed fonts, the shapes and proportions of individual characters are designed separately for each style. Theoretically, the original designed letter shapes for each style should look better than a normal letter shape thickened with an outline to create a faux Bold style, or slanted to create a faux Italic style.

✦ **Text Orientation menu:** This pop-up menu enables you to select the flow direction for your text. The default is Horizontal, which orients text from Left to Right in rows along a horizontal baseline. The vertical text options are Vertical Left to Right, and Vertical Right to Left — these options automatically orient the text in columns that progress from left to right or from right to left, respectively.

Note   If you select a Vertical text orientation, the other text formatting options will apply slightly differently than they do to the Horizontal text orientation. See the section "Vertical text options" for descriptions of the controls that are relevant to vertically oriented type.

✦ **Text Align options:** The top-right area of the panel displays four buttons for the arrangement of text: Left, Center, Right, and Full Justification. When you're editing, the alignment you choose affects only those paragraph(s) you've selected. When entering text, use these options to predetermine the alignment before text entry, and all subsequent text will be aligned accordingly.

✦ **Letter spacing menu:** You use this value field and slider to change the space or tracking between individual letters. The default setting of 0 applies the built-in tracking and kerning of the font, while any setting between +1 and +60 adds space between characters, and any setting between –1 and –60 decreases space between characters (extreme settings cause the letters to overlap).

Tip   With a section of text selected, you can use Ctrl+Alt+arrow keys (⌘+Option+arrow keys on a Mac) to increase or decrease spacing between characters. The higher the Zoom setting, the smaller the spacing increments will be.

✦ **Baseline shift:** Three options are in this drop-down menu. Normal resets text to the baseline. Superscript shifts Horizontal text above the baseline and Vertical text to the right of the baseline. Subscript sets Horizontal text below the baseline and Vertical text to the left of the baseline.

✦ **Anti-alias option menu:** Use this menu to select the level of anti-aliasing (or smoothing) to apply when the Flash Player renders your type. If you do not want to include font outlines in your file, select Use device fonts and text will be rendered using a font that is available on each user's computer.

Note   The Alias text button and the Use device fonts check box have been replaced in Flash 8 with the new and improved Anti-alias settings menu. Now there are no excuses for jagged or blurry text (unless they serve some stylistic purpose).

✦ **Auto kern check box:** If the font includes built-in kerning information, which evens out the spaces between letterforms, select this to activate automatic kerning.

✦ **Paragraph Format Options:** The Edit format options button (paragraph icon) invokes the paragraph Format Options dialog box shown in Figure 8-10, with additional text controls.

Figure 8-10: The paragraph Format Options dialog box for horizontal text invoked with the Edit format options button in the Property inspector

Note   The default units of measurement (pixels) for both the margin and indentation entries of the paragraph Format Options dialog box are determined by the Ruler units setting on the file. You can change Ruler units in the Document Properties dialog box, which you access from the application menu with Modify ⇨ Document or from the keyboard by pressing Ctrl+J (⌘+J on a Mac).

✦ **Selectable:** Use this toggle button to make selected text, or text that's entered subsequently, selectable when it's displayed on users' machines. This allows users to copy and paste your text into other text-editing applications or browser windows.

✦ **Link entry:** This option is only available for Horizontal Static or Dynamic text fields. By selecting a text box or an individual word in the Document window, and then entering a URL in this Link entry field, you can add a hyperlink to selected text. The text link will be identified in the authoring environment with a dotted underline — the underline will not be visible in the published .swf file, but the mouse pointer will change to indicate a link when it is over the text.

✦ **Target menu:** This menu is accessible after you enter a URL in the Link field, and it allows you to select a destination for the loaded URL. The options will be familiar to anyone who has worked with HTML page structures. For more information, refer to the description of the getURL() action in Chapter 18, "Understanding Actions and Event Handlers."

Application menu commands

Some of the text settings in the Property inspector are also available from the application Text menu:

✦ Under Text ⇨ Font, you can select from the same available fonts listed in the Property inspector Font menu, but the list is slightly larger so it is easier to read.

✦ Under Text ⇨ Size, you can select a specific font point size from a list, instead of using the Font size slider in the Property inspector.

✦ Under Text ⇨ Style, the commands include

　• **Plain:** Ctrl+Shift+P (⌘+Shift+P on a Mac)

　• **Bold:** Ctrl+Shift+B (⌘+Shift+B on a Mac)

　• **Italic:** Ctrl+Shift+I (⌘+Shift+I on a Mac)

　• **Subscript**

　• **Superscript**

✦ Under Text ⇨ Align, the commands include

　• **Align Left:** Ctrl+Shift+L (⌘+Shift+L on a Mac)

　• **Align Center:** Ctrl+Shift+C (⌘+Shift+C on a Mac)

　• **Align Right:** Ctrl+Shift+R (⌘+Shift+R on a Mac)

　• **Justify:** Ctrl+Shift+J (⌘+Shift+J on a Mac)

✦ Under Text ⇨ Letter Spacing, you will find a list of options that offer an alternative way to adjust the space between characters. If you have the Property inspector open as you apply these commands manually, you will see the letter spacing or tracking value field update. Manual tracking has the advantage that you can apply it either to selected (highlighted) text characters or to the pair of text characters on either side of the cursor:

- **Increase:** To increase text character spacing by one half-pixel, press Ctrl+Alt+→ (⌘+Option+→). To increase text character spacing by two pixels, press Shift+Ctrl+Alt+→ (Shift+⌘+Option+→).

- **Decrease:** To decrease text character spacing by one half-pixel, press Ctrl+Alt+← (⌘+Option+←). To decrease text character spacing by two pixels, press Shift+Ctrl+Alt+← (Shift+⌘+Option+←).

- **Reset:** To reset text character spacing to normal, press Ctrl+Alt+↑ (⌘+Option+↑).

✦ **Scrollable:** The final item in the Text menu is an option that is only available when an editable text box is selected. When applied to a Dynamic text field, this option makes it possible to enter and scroll through text that extends beyond the frame of the text box. Apply this option by choosing Text ➪ Scrollable from the application menu or from the contextual menu when a Dynamic text box is selected, or by pressing Shift and double-clicking the handle of a Dynamic text box.

Vertical text options

Some of the options that are visible in the Property inspector change slightly when you choose a Vertical orientation for your text box.

✦ **Text Align options:** These buttons now function to align the arrangement of text in a vertical text box to Top, Middle, Bottom, and Full Justification. When entering text, use these options to predetermine the alignment before text entry, and all subsequent text will be aligned accordingly.

✦ **Auto kern check box:** On Vertical text, this setting can be overridden by the Vertical text settings in the Flash Preferences dialog box (refer to Figure 8-4). When No Kerning is selected in Preferences, then the Auto-Kerning toggle in the Property inspector will only apply to Horizontal text.

✦ **Rotate toggle:** This very handy button (which appears to the right of the Text Orientation menu) flips the characters in your Vertical text box so that the type is turned sideways — or actually resting on the vertical baseline. This is an effective alternative to creating Horizontal text and then using Free Transform to rotate the text box 90 degrees.

✦ **Edit format options:** The Edit format button invokes the paragraph Format Options dialog box (see Figure 8-11) with additional text controls specifically for vertical text.

Figure 8-11: The paragraph Format Options dialog box for Vertical text invoked with the Edit format options button in the Property inspector

Editable text options

The options available for Dynamic and Input text are predominantly the same, but there are a few important options that are unique for these two Editable text types. Figure 8-12 shows the Property inspector as it displays when you specify Dynamic behavior for your text. We label only the additional options not shown in Figure 8-9 here.

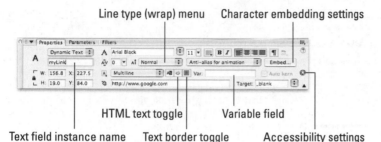

Figure 8-12: The additional options available in the Property inspector when Dynamic text behavior is selected

The following options are common to both Dynamic and Input text:

✦ **Text field instance name:** As we described previously, this identifier allows the Flash Player to put your dynamic data in the correct field.

✦ **Line type:** Use this drop-down menu to choose how your text will be organized in the text field. Choose between Single Line, Multiline (with line breaks), and Multiline with no text wrap.

✦ **HTML text:** When this toggle is turned on, Flash preserves rich text styles when displaying Dynamic text. This includes font, font style, hyperlink, paragraph, and other formatting consistent with permissible HTML tags. You can also enable HTML so that the entry field will accept formatting that has been assigned to it in the Actions panel. For more information on this, refer to Chapter 30, "Applying HTML and Text Field Formatting."

✦ **Text border:** Use this toggle to draw the text field with a border and a white background that will be visible in your published movie (.swf).

✦ **Variable:** This field is now redundant with the Instance name field, but if you use it for backwards compatibility, you should assign it a different name than your instance to avoid confusion.

✦ **Character embedding:** When preparing a file for export, you can control how much font information is included with the .swf. The Embed button invokes the Character Embedding dialog box (see Figure 8-13), in which you can specify that no characters are embedded by clicking the Don't Embed button; or you can pick from a long list of character or *glyph* sets to be embedded. You can also enter a more selective range of characters by typing them directly into the field at the bottom of the dialog box (under "Include these characters:"). The Auto Fill button automatically loads all the unique glyphs or characters in the currently selected text box into the Include field to be embedded with the final .swf. The counter for total number of glyphs (at the bottom of the dialog box) updates based on your settings to show the total number of unique glyphs that will be embedded with the final exported file.

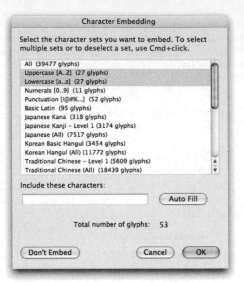

Figure 8-13: The Character Embedding dialog box for specifying embedded font information to be exported with your final .swf

 Note   The Character Embedding options include international language sets and specialized sets such as music symbols. These glyph sets can be very large, but this is a useful feature if you are creating dynamic text fields that will need to display specialized characters.

The Link and Target value fields are not available in the Property inspector when Input text behavior is selected, because you cannot add links to text that users will be entering. The only additional control available in the Property inspector for Input text fields is the Maximum Characters value field. Use the Maximum Characters value field to specify the maximum number of characters that a user can enter in this particular text field. The number of characters can be limited to any number between 0 and 65,535. This feature is generally used for controlled content, such as passwords.

Font Export and Display

By default, Flash embeds all fonts used in Static text boxes in order to deliver WYSIWYG (what-you-see-is-what-you-get) display in the published movie (.swf.). As long as font outlines are available for the text you use in your Flash document (.fla), the published movie (.swf) displays consistently, regardless of which fonts the user has installed on his machine.

In order to edit a Flash project (.fla), you need to have the original fonts available, unless you are willing to view the document with a substitute font in the authoring environment. If you select a text box that is displayed with a substitute font, you should still see the name of the original font listed in the Property inspector, although it will be marked by parentheses. As long as the font formatting is not modified, Flash preserves all the original font information so that when the document (.fla) is opened again on a machine that has the original font, any edits that were made using the default font are rendered correctly. Although you can make text edits while working with a default font, you need to have the original font installed in order to publish the final movie (.swf) with the design intact.

Smoothing text with anti-alias settings

The consistent text display of embedded fonts is what endears Flash to type-obsessed designers, but there is a small price to pay: Every embedded font adds to the final file size, and anti-aliasing (smoothing) can sometimes make fonts too blurry. The good news is that for most projects, the additional weight is not an issue, and the new anti-aliasing controls in Flash 8 make it easy to customize the level of anti-aliasing as needed. If file size is a critical issue, you may choose to use device fonts or a runtime shared library. If you prefer the look of bitmap (aliased) fonts, that setting is still available in the Font rendering menu (see Figure 8-14).

Figure 8-14: The new Flash 8 Font rendering menu makes it easier to choose a setting that will suit your design style and file size requirements.

Figure 8-15 compares aliased with anti-aliased text in two published .swfs: one with Anti-alias for readability applied (left) and one with Anti-alias for animation applied (right).

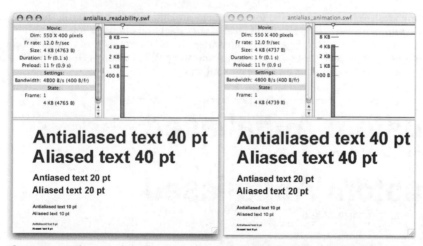

Figure 8-15: The two default settings for anti-aliasing in Flash 8 (readability and animation) render more smoothly than Bitmap text. Anti-alias for animation (right) results in a slightly smaller file size than Anti-alias for readability (left).

The Anti-alias for readability setting does an amazing job of rendering smooth, legible type, even at small sizes. This setting has only two drawbacks: It contributes to larger file sizes and it can only be rendered with Flash Player 8. The Anti-alias for animation setting smoothes text almost as well as the Anti-alias for readability setting but it ignores kerning information in order to create slightly smaller files and to render animated text more quickly. This is the only anti-aliasing option that will render on older versions of the Flash Player.

Caution   Advanced Flash 8 anti-alias settings (Anti-alias for readability and Custom anti-alias) will not render if text is skewed or flipped, but work fine if text is rotated or scaled. The advanced anti-alias settings do not carry over to files that are exported in .png format or printed. If the more advanced anti-alias settings "break," the text will be auto-rendered with the more simplified Anti-alias for animation setting.

If you feel the need to polish your text further, use the Custom anti-alias controls (shown in Figure 8-16) to adjust the thickness and sharpness of the rendered text. With a little trial-and-error, you should find the exact level of anti-aliasing that suits the size and style of the font you are using.

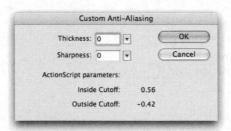

Figure 8-16: Custom anti-alias controls in Flash 8 make it easier to find a setting that smoothes text just how you like it.

The settings ranges for thickness and for sharpness are different, but for both, "normal" is 0. Select a higher number to increase the level of the effect and choose a lower number to decrease or reverse the effect. Figure 8-17 illustrates "high," "normal," and "negative" combined settings, but these settings are really only meaningful if you adjust them individually and observe the results on your own specific font sample.

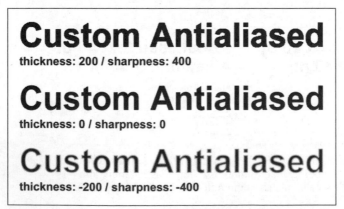

Figure 8-17: The combination of thickness and sharpness set in the Custom Anti-Aliasing dialog box will determine the look of your rendered anti-aliased text.

Caution
Anti-alias for readability and Custom anti-aliasing settings only work on files published for Flash Player 8. To make your files compatible with older versions of the Flash Player, you must use Anti-alias for animation, bitmap (aliased) text, or device fonts. For very large text (larger than 48 point), the more simplified Anti-alias for animation setting is recommended over the advanced Flash 8 settings. It is best to use advanced anti-aliasing options to improve the legibility of very small text or unusual text styles on projects that do not need to be backwards compatible.

Note
If you are working on OS X, you may not notice much difference between aliased and anti-aliased text because the system applies automatic smoothing on any screen text, even on application menu lists. Although this feature cannot be turned off completely, the text smoothing controls in your System preferences panel (in the Appearance category) allow you to specify between the lowest setting (only smoothes text larger than 12 points) and the highest setting (only smoothes text larger than 4 point). The default setting smoothes any text larger than 8 points.

Rendering outlines with the Bitmap text setting

The Bitmap text option in the Flash 8 Text rendering menu replaces the Flash MX 2004 Alias text button. This option still makes it possible to quickly convert any selected text from anti-aliased to a prerendered aliased outline that will be embedded with the final .swf. The aliased outline will add less to your file size than the anti-aliased font information, if the font is at a size below about 24 point. Another advantage of using the Bitmap text button is that you can create a "custom" aliased outline from any font on your machine, which gives you many more creative options than the three basic device fonts. Unlike device fonts, text converted to aliased outlines in Flash can also be rotated or scaled — although it doesn't always look that great, at least it does display in the published .swf.

Despite the benefits of using bitmap text, we can't say it's a *great* option because it doesn't always give you the crisp, clean results you might hope for. In fact, this feature is only really useful when it's applied to fonts in the mid-size range. When it's applied to fonts between 12 and 24 point, the Bitmap text feature will render a fairly crisp outline and will eliminate the "blur" associated with anti-aliased text smoothing. Unfortunately, when it's applied to smaller text (between 6 and 11 point), most fonts completely fall apart and became illegible blocky pixel shapes. On text larger than 24 point, the Bitmap text feature usually makes the text look rough, and can bloat the file size more than including standard font outlines will.

Understanding device fonts

Device fonts are three basic font style designators identified by a preceding underscore in your font menu. These fonts will be familiar to anyone who has worked with HTML text. Although they are not as exciting as some custom fonts, entire design styles are based on these "generic" fonts — think minimal and unpretentious. You will find the three device font designations, _sans, _serif, and _typewriter, in either the Property inspector font menu or in the application menu under Text ➪ Font. These device font labels tell the Flash Player to use any equivalent font available on a viewer's system. The formatting that you have applied to the text in your Flash document (.fla), such as bold or italic style and point size, will be preserved and applied to the font the Flash player selects from the viewer's system to render the text in your movie (.swf).

To give you an idea of how device fonts relate to installed fonts, _sans usually becomes Arial or Helvetica, _serif usually becomes Times or Times New Roman, and _typewriter becomes Courier. Because these settings utilize the default fonts on the user's machine, Flash doesn't have to include their outlines in the exported .swf, and the final movie file size is reduced.

Device fonts are always available and always take little time to render, but they cannot be rotated or skewed and occasionally they will vary slightly in their metrics from player to player and across platforms. Another important difference between standard embedded fonts and device fonts is that embedded fonts will be anti-aliased or smoothed by Flash, while device fonts will be unsmoothed or aliased.

Working with the Use Device Fonts setting

You will notice that even if you have not used one of the device fonts from your font menu, you can still select the Use Device Fonts setting in the Text rendering menu. This is a terrific "compromise" option if you strive for more specific control over the Flash Player's font choices, but still want to take advantage of the file size savings afforded by device fonts. When the Use Device Fonts setting is applied, the font is not embedded — only the Font name, Font family/style (serif/sans serif/monospace), and other information are added to specify the font, which adds no more than 10 or 15 bytes to the final .swf file. This information is used so that the Flash player on the user's system will know if the font is installed or not. If the original font is available, it will display exactly as you designed it. If the original font is not present, then the Flash Player will still know whether the substitute font should be serif or sans serif.

The Use Device Fonts option also works as a toggle to turn off anti-aliasing. This means that even if the user has all the fonts used in your Flash movie installed, Use Device Fonts changes how the type displays:

✦ **When Use Device Fonts is selected:** No anti-aliasing or smoothing is applied to any device font, regardless of its presence on your system.

✦ **When Use Device Fonts is *not* selected:** The font outline is embedded and all characters are smoothed (even if the font is available). Smoothed text can sometimes be too blurry at small point sizes.

To accurately preview the Use Device Fonts setting on your machine, if you have a font manager (as most Web designers do), you need to make sure you're careful about your font activation settings. Make sure Global activation is turned *off* to limit the number of fonts that the Flash player can find for rendering the movie (.swf).

For best results with this specific Use Device Fonts option, we suggest that you limit your font selection to those fonts that most of your audience is likely to have (all those common fonts that come installed with their machines), or those that will translate into one of the default device fonts without wreaking havoc on your design. It is better to be conservative and design your layout using Times, Arial, and Courier than to go wild with custom fonts that will most likely be substituted very differently when the movie is viewed on someone else's machine. Otherwise, for unusual fonts, we suggest that you either embed the full font outline information (and apply one of the anti-alias settings) or, for limited areas of text (such as headlines), that you use the Bitmap text option to generate a custom aliased outline or break the text apart to manually create vector shapes, as we describe later in this chapter.

Troubleshooting font display

Although Flash does an amazing job of displaying fonts consistently and cleanly, even on different platforms, the success of your font export depends entirely on the quality and completeness of the font information available when the Flash document is created (.fla). Because Flash can access font information on your system while you are working in the authoring environment, many of the font display problems that can come up during production will only be visible when the Flash movie (.swf) is published.

To display fonts in the published movie (.swf), the Flash Player relies on the font information embedded in the movie, or on the fonts installed on the user's system. If there are discrepancies between the information available to the Flash Player and the font information that was available to the Flash authoring application when the document was created, you will run into font display problems.

When you encounter problems with fonts (as you almost always do at some point), a good guide to font management is indispensable. We can't describe everything that can go wrong when working with fonts here, and solutions will often vary depending on how you are storing and managing your fonts. Ideally, you should find resources that are specific to the platform and programs you are using.

Tip   A good general guide to some basic font-management techniques for Macintosh users is *How to Boss Your Fonts Around* by Robin Williams (Peachpit Press, 1998). Even if you are a Windows user, this book can give you some basic background on how fonts and font management utilities work.

TrueType, Type 1 PostScript, and bitmap fonts (Mac only) can all be used in Flash. Although Flash exports the system information about the fonts that are used, a damaged or incomplete font may still display correctly in the authoring environment (.fla). However, the exported movie (.swf) will appear incorrectly on other systems if the end-user doesn't have the font installed. This is due to the fact that Flash can display the font within the editor by using the screen font; it does not recognize that particular font's outline and can't export information needed to display the text in the .swf. You can avoid font display problems by using device fonts (_sans, _serif, or _typewriter fonts).

Controlling font substitution

If Flash cannot find font information on your machine to match what is specified in a file (.fla) when you open it in the authoring environment, you will be notified by the Missing Fonts alert box (shown in Figure 8-18), and prompted to select fonts installed on your system to substitute for display.

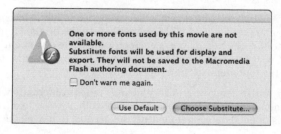

Figure 8-18: The Missing Fonts alert box appears when fonts used in a Flash file (.fla) are not found on the local machine.

Note If you publish or export a document without viewing any of the scenes containing missing fonts, the alert box only appears when Flash attempts to publish or export the .swf.

The first time that a scene with missing font information is displayed in the authoring environment, you will be prompted by the Missing Fonts alert box to choose one of the following options:

✦ **Choose Substitute:** To specify individual substitutions from the fonts available on your system for each missing font, click this button to invoke the Font Mapping dialog box (see Figure 8-19). This dialog box lists all fonts specified in the document that Flash can't find on your system. To choose a substitute font for a missing font, select the font name in the Font Mapping list and then choose a font installed on your machine from the Substitute font pop-up menu. Click OK to apply the settings and close the dialog box.

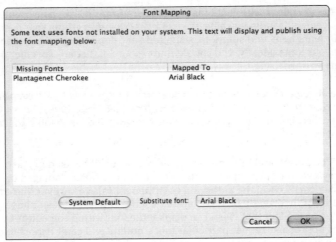

Figure 8-19: The Font Mapping dialog box used to view missing fonts and to modify mapping of substitute fonts

✦ **Use Default:** This button substitutes all missing fonts with the Flash system default font and dismisses the Missing Fonts alert box. If you don't use the button on the first alert box, you have another chance to choose this setting by using the System Default button in the Font Mapping dialog box (see Figure 8-19).

✦ **Turn Alert Off:** To disable the alert box in the current document, select the Don't warn me again check box.

Even though the text is displayed in a substitute font, Flash includes the name of the missing font in the Property inspector font menu (see Figure 8-20). Flash preserves the original font specification when the file is saved so that the text displays correctly when the document (.fla) is opened on a system with the missing fonts installed. You can even apply the missing font to new text by selecting it from the font menu in the Property inspector.

Because appearance attributes such as size, leading, and kerning may render differently with a substitute font, you may have to adjust any modifications you make while viewing text in a substitute font when the document is opened on a machine with the original font available.

Figure 8-20: The missing font name is displayed in the font menu, even when text is displayed in a substitute font in the authoring environment.

Tip

To turn the Missing Fonts alert box off for all documents, clear the Warn on missing fonts check box in the Warnings category of Flash Preferences (Edit ➪ Preferences or Flash ➪ Preferences for OS X). To turn alerts on again, reselect the check box.

To view all the missing fonts in the currently active document or to reselect font mappings, choose Edit ➪ Font Mapping (or in OS X, Flash ➪ Font Mapping) from the application menu and repeat the same steps we described previously to choose new substitute fonts. To view all the font mapping settings saved on your system or to delete font mappings, close all Flash documents before opening the Font Mapping dialog box or making changes to the listed mapping.

Using Miniml Fonts in Flash, by Craig Kroeger

For those of you who are not familiar with Miniml fonts, these are bitmap fonts designed by Craig Kroeger and J. D. Hooge to remain crisp (aliased) in Flash and they can be used as an alternative to generic device fonts. These aliased fonts are particularly useful at small sizes, where anti-aliasing can reduce legibility. This is a real concern when designing Flash applications for devices. (See Figure 8-21.)

ALIASED TEXT
ANTIALIASED TEXT

Figure 8-21: Crisp aliased text (top) compared to blurry anti-aliased text (lower)

There are free versions of the Miniml fonts, included on this book's CD-ROM in the ch8 folder — you may use these to test what you can do with them. Professional versions of these fonts are available at www.miniml.com.

There is also a sample source file (Miniml.fla) on the CD-ROM that shows how the fonts are used in various text field examples. In order for the Miniml fonts to work properly (with no anti-aliasing), consider these guidelines:

✦ **Select font:** When the Miniml fonts have been installed on your system, you can select them from the Font menu in the same way as any other available font.

✦ **Font size:** Miniml fonts must be set to 8 points or any multiple of 8 (16, 24, 32, and so on). The numbers in the font name refer to the font style, not what point size it should be set to.

✦ **Vertical Static text:** Miniml fonts can be used on a vertical axis when they are rotated with the rotate option in Flash (not rotated manually or with Transform settings).

✦ **Spacing Static text:** Only Static text can have adjusted character spacing. When adjusting the character spacing, use whole-pixel values to keep the text aliased. Professional Miniml fonts have versions with increased Letter spacing for use with Dynamic or Input text fields.

✦ **Paragraph alignment:** Do not use Center paragraph alignment — only use Left or Right.

✦ **Embed font:** You must embed the Miniml fonts when using Dynamic or Input text fields. In Character Options, select the Select All Characters check box to embed the complete font. To reduce overall fill size, only embed the characters you need in your text. Static text is automatically embedded.

✦ **Snap to Pixels:** Use the Snap to Pixels feature under View ➪ Snapping in the application menu to keep fonts clear. When the fonts are not on whole _x and _y values, they will appear blurry. If you are not using Snap to Pixels, make sure to check your Info panel to set the text box _x and _y values to whole pixels, using the top-left corner as the registration point. To ensure consistent placement of text after you have converted a text box into a symbol, reposition the registration point of the symbol by dragging it from the center to the top-left corner of the text box. (See Figure 8-22.)

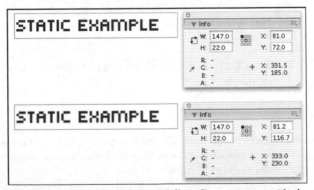

Figure 8-22: To keep text crisp (aliased), use Snap to Pixels or the Info panel to set X,Y values to whole pixels (top). If text boxes are not aligned to whole X,Y values, then the font will be anti-aliased (bottom).

✦ **Using Miniml fonts in motion:** When you are using Miniml fonts in animation, round the _x and _y values to whole values to keep them crisp. Use the following ActionScript to round the numbers down to the closest integer:

```
_x = Math.floor(_x);
_y = Math.floor(_y);
```

✦ **Preview in the Flash Player:** Preview your finished movie in the Flash Player (.swf) to see the aliased text displayed correctly because it may appear anti-aliased in the authoring environment (.fla).

This may seem like a lot of rules, but following them will help you get the most out of Miniml.

Note from the authors: This tutorial was written as a guide for using a specific series of pixel fonts (called Miniml fonts) designed by Craig Kroeger and J. D. Hooge, but much of the advice that Craig offers for using his fonts can be applied to any bitmap or pixel fonts that you use with Flash. There are many sources for bitmap fonts, but hopefully the free versions that Craig and J. D. allowed us to include on the CD-ROM will give you an idea of their benefits and limitations.

Font Symbols and Shared Font Libraries

Using Font symbols and Shared libraries in your Flash authoring workflow offers several benefits that can make it worth the little time it takes to set them up. Although you can nest a Static text box inside any other symbol type if you want to reuse a specific text element in your movie, this does not change how the text is published in the Flash document. Using instances of a symbol to place repeated text elements, such as logos or taglines, offers the same benefits as converting artwork into symbols — you can make changes to the symbol stored in the Library and it will be propagated to every instance in your document, and you can also modify the appearance of individual instances without changing the original symbol.

The difference between text nested in another symbol type and a real Font symbol is that Font symbols can actually be used to store the display information for an entire font. When placed into a runtime Shared library, Font symbols can be used to link text in one movie to the font display information in a source movie; this allows you to use custom fonts without having to embed the font information in every Flash movie (.swf) individually. This workflow is especially effective on projects that involve multiple .swf files using the same custom fonts. The bonus is that if your client suddenly decides that they prefer "Leonardo script" to "Chickenscratch bold" (or whatever font switcheroo they might come up with), you can make the change in your source Font symbol without even opening any of the other files (as long as the new font is given the same name and it still fits in your layouts).

This all sounds great so far, right? Now for the reality check: Because you are storing font information in a separate file from your layouts, there is one more factor that you have to manage. The source font library (.swf) can be in the same directory as your other movie (.swf) files or it can be stored on a completely different server. It is very important to decide on the storage location of your source font files (.fla and .swf) before you begin linking text in your other Flash documents (.fla) to shared Font symbols because the URL that defines the relative or absolute path is stored in each .fla file and your font links will be broken if you later change the source movie's location.

Note   Runtime shared assets do not need to be available on your local network when you are editing .fla documents that rely on linked assets, but the shared asset .swf must be available at your specified URL in order for the published movies (.swf) to display the linked assets at run time.

As you can imagine, having your font links fail is a major disaster, so many developers believe that relying on an external font source isn't worth the risk. On the other hand, there is always an element of uncertainty with Web delivery, so it might not be fair to eliminate what is otherwise an excellent way to optimize font management in your Flash layouts. As with any Web production, just be sure to test early and often as you develop a Flash project that uses shared fonts.

You can use Shared libraries to store other symbol types, but it is best to organize different kinds of assets in separate .fla files. For now, we'll focus on making Font symbols and creating a source file for a Shared font library.

Creating a Font symbol

Font symbols can be integrated in your workflow in two ways. If you plan to use Font symbols within a Flash document (.fla) simply as a way to make edits faster in that one document, and you don't mind exporting the font information with every .swf, you can create a Font symbol directly in the main Library of your current document and rely on author-time sharing to update instances of the font. However, if you want to save file size by linking to the Font symbol information for runtime sharing, you should open a new Flash document before creating your Font symbols. In either case, the initial steps for creating a Flash Font symbol are the same:

1. Open the Library panel where you want to store the Font symbol.

2. From the Library options panel, choose New Font (see Figure 8-23).

3. The Font Symbol Properties dialog box appears so that you can enter a name for your Font symbol and select the font you want to embed in the file (see Figure 8-24). The name that you enter shouldn't be the same as the original font name but rather should indicate how the font is being used in your project. For example, if you are using an Impact font for your titles, instead of naming the Font symbol "Impact," you could name it "titleFont" or some other name that will inform you (and the rest of your team) how the font is being used.

4. If you also want the option to use faux Bold or Italic style on text linked to your Font symbol, select the Style check boxes for Bold and/or Italic to include these characters with the embedded font. Select the Bitmap text check box to create aliased outlines of your font symbol. If you choose to render an aliased outline of a font, you also need to enter the font size that you want to use by typing it in the Size field. This will increase the size of your source movie only — the additional size will not be passed on to other .swf files that link to the Font symbol for runtime sharing.

Caution   If you create a Font symbol without the Bold or Italic options selected in the Font Symbol Properties dialog box and then try to apply the options in the Property inspector to create faux Bold or Italic style on text that is linked to the symbol, you will encounter one of two problems. If the text you are modifying is in a Static text box, then the applied styles will display, but the additional font information for the modified characters will be exported with your published file, thus increasing the size of the .swf. If the text you are modifying is in a

Dynamic or Input text field, the text will not display in the published .swf file because the Flash Player will not find the font information needed to render the Bold or Italic type on-the-fly. These same rules apply to aliased outlines rendered at a specific font size.

Figure 8-23: Choosing to insert a new Font symbol from the Library panel options menu

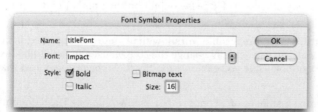

Figure 8-24: Selecting a font to store in the new Font symbol and giving it a reference name

5. Now when you browse the font menu available in the Property inspector or from the application menu (Text ➪ Font) you will see your new font listed with the other fonts installed on your system. Font symbols are also differentiated from regular fonts in the menu with an asterisk (*) following the name it has been given (see Figure 8-25).

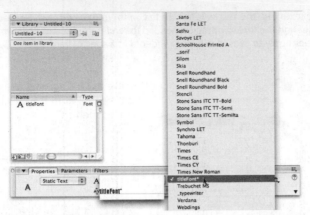

Figure 8-25: Font symbol names are followed by an asterisk in the Property inspector font menu (or in the application Text menu). Font symbols are also added to the Library list.

The next step required to use the Font symbol in your project depends on how you choose to integrate Font symbols into your workflow. As we mentioned earlier in this chapter, using symbols for author-time asset sharing can make it easier to propagate changes throughout a document, but any assets used in your document will still be embedded in each movie (.swf) that you publish. Creating a separate library for storing symbols and linking these as runtime shared assets in multiple movies takes a little more work, but it gives you the benefit of both streamlined updates and smaller file sizes. The most appropriate workflow depends on the scope and content of your particular project and on how willing you are to manage the risks involved with using runtime shared assets.

Updating Font symbols at author-time

If you intend to use a Font symbol as an author-time shared asset only, you can simply leave it in your current Library so that the font is available in the font menu whenever you want to use it in your project. You will be able to modify any of the text boxes that use your Font symbol in the same way as any other text. There is no limit on the number of colors or sizes that you can use or on what you can type into each text box.

The main reason that this is a more flexible workflow than simply nesting text inside other symbols for reuse is that you can actually change the *content* used in individual text boxes that reference a Font symbol, while you can only modify the *appearance* of text that is nested in a symbol instance.

The process for updating instances of a Font symbol used within one Flash document (.fla) is much the same as updating any other symbol type or imported asset stored in the Library:

1. Open the current document Library and select the Font symbol that you want to modify.

2. Choose Properties from the Library options menu or from the contextual menu.

3. In the Font Symbol Properties dialog box, simply select a new font from the font menu, but don't change the font name that you had previously chosen. (Now it makes sense why naming your Font symbol with the same name shown in the font menu isn't a good idea, right?)

You will find that all text that was in your old font will be updated to the new font that you have chosen, while maintaining all other formatting and style attributes.

Tip

If you don't see your text boxes update to the new font immediately after you change it in the Font Symbol Properties dialog box, you may need to click one of the text boxes with the Selection tool — this will usually prompt Flash to refresh the display.

Using Font symbols in runtime Shared libraries

In order to make your Font symbol available for use in other Flash movies without having to embed the font information in each file, you will need to create links from individual *destination* files to your *source* file or Shared library. This workflow optimizes file sizes by eliminating the storage of redundant font information between linked movies. As with HTML files, you have to specify a path in order for the Flash Player to locate font information in one movie (.swf) for text display in another. Because the font information is retrieved from an .swf file by the Flash Player and supplied to another .swf for text display, it is referred to as *runtime* asset sharing.

If you have already followed the steps to create a Font symbol in an otherwise empty Flash document (.fla), the next part of the process is to enter an identifier and a location (path) that will "lead" the Flash Player to your Shared library. As we mentioned previously, you will need to know where the published source movie (.swf) will be stored before you can create font links to other documents. The location (or path) can be relative or absolute.

Tip

To keep your linkage intact while preserving source file version numbers as you develop your project, you might want to use the Publish Settings dialog box to give your published source .swf a generic name (such as titleFontSource.swf) while using a more specific naming convention for your source .fla files (such as titleFontSource101.fla). This eliminates the hassle of going back to your destination movies and changing the linkage information if you decide you need to move to a new version name to keep track of modifications to your source file (.fla).

To help clarify how runtime shared fonts are stored and accessed, we will walk through the three possible scenarios for Font symbol use and show you how each is displayed in the authoring environment (.fla) and in the published movie (.swf).

On the CD-ROM

The Flash files illustrated in this section are included in the ch8 folder on the CD-ROM. You will find both the fontSource files (Shared library file) and the fontLink files (destination document) in the fontSymbols_complete folder with final linkage properties. As long as the files are kept together in the same storage location, the font linkage should remain intact. If you want to use unfinished files to complete the steps in this section, open the files in the fontSymbols_start folder. We have also included a fontEmbed example file with the same text entered on the Stage, but with embedded font information (including uppercase, lowercase, and punctuation for Impact), instead of linked font information to demonstrate the significant difference in file size.

The first file you will be working with is a source document, or the Flash document that contains the Font symbols that you want to use as runtime shared assets.

Caution

If you are using the files from the CD-ROM to follow this example, you may need to modify the Font symbol in fontSource.fla to match a font that you have on your system (instead of "Impact") before you can use Test Movie to publish the .swf file (Step 5).

1. Open your source document and select your Font symbol in the Library. If you are look-ing at the files on the CD-ROM, open `fontSource.fla` from the `fontSymbol_start` folder and select the Font symbol called NewFont in the Library.

2. Open the Linkage Properties dialog box (see Figure 8-26) by choosing Linkage from the Library options menu or from the contextual menu.

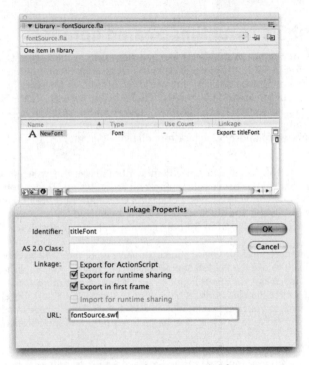

Figure 8-26: Setting up Linkage Properties for a Font symbol in the Flash source document (.fla)

3. Enter an identifier that will help you to remember what this Font symbol is used for in your project (such as `titleFont`). The identifier will be displayed after the Font sym-bol name in the Library. Don't close the Linkage Properties dialog box until you have completed the next step.

4. The URL field is where you enter the path to the storage location for the source movie (.swf) that you will publish after you have finished choosing settings in the source doc-ument (.fla.) The link can be relative or absolute depending on how you will be storing your project .swfs:

   • If you are planning to keep the source movie (.swf) in the same folder as your individual destination movies (.swf), then all you need to enter in the URL field of the Linkage Properties dialog box is the name of your source .swf file — in our example `fontSource.swf`.

- If the source .swf file will be stored in a different folder or even on a separate server than the destination (linked) .swf files, you need to enter an absolute path (Web address) in the URL field to specify the exact storage location of your source .swf file, such as `http://yourserver.com/projectdirectory/sourceName.swf`.

5. Now you can save your source .fla file to the final storage location using File ⇨ Save (Ctrl+S or ⌘+S) and test your source .swf using Control ⇨ Test Movie (Ctrl+Enter or ⌘+Return). Although nothing is displayed in the published .swf, if you turn on the Bandwidth Profiler (from the application menu: View ⇨ Bandwidth Profiler, or with shortcut keys Ctrl+B or ⌘+B), you will see the size of the font information for all of the embedded characters included in your Font symbol. Our sample font symbol source file was 19K (see Figure 8-27).

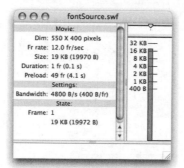

Figure 8-27: The published source movie (.swf) with embedded font information for the Font symbol to be used in other destination movies as a runtime shared asset

You have successfully created and saved a runtime shared asset. Now you can create another Flash document that references the font information stored in `fontSource.swf` so that you can use your custom font without having to embed the font information:

1. Create a new Flash document or open the `fontLink.fla` file from the CD-ROM, and make sure that you have the Library panel for the current document open.

2. There are two ways of linking another document to the font information in your Shared library:

- If you have already created a document that uses Font symbols as described in the section on author-time sharing and decide to link to a runtime shared asset instead, you can enter the identifier and the URL of the Shared library movie (.swf) in the Linkage properties for any Font symbol in your Library. To enter linkage information manually, you need to have a Font symbol in the document Library selected so that you can access the Linkage Properties dialog box from the options menu or from the contextual menu. Enter the identifier and the URL exactly as they appear in your font source file, but Import for runtime sharing is auto-selected instead of Export for runtime sharing (see Figure 8-28). You should now find that all instances of the Font symbol in your current document are updated with the Font information stored in the shared asset movie (.swf) — as long as it is available on your server when you publish the movie for your current document.

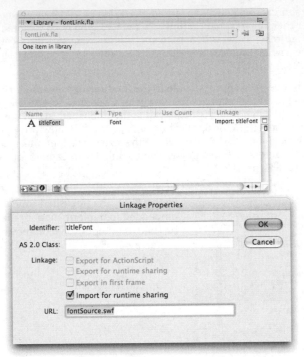

Figure 8-28: Linkage settings for a Font symbol in a destination movie refer to the font information stored in the runtime Shared library

- If you are authoring a document (.fla) that does not yet contain any Font symbols and you want to link to your runtime shared asset, you can simply drag the Font symbol from the source library into the current document Library. With your destination document and Library panel open, choose File ➪ Open or File ➪ Import ➪ Open External Library and navigate to the Flash document (.fla) for your shared asset. You can then drag your source Font symbol from the shared asset library and drop it into your destination document Library. If you access Linkage properties for the Font symbol that you dragged into your Library, you will see that Flash automatically inserts the identifier and URL for the shared asset. You can now use the font in your new document and it will be linked to the font information stored in the runtime shared asset movie (.swf).

3. When a Font symbol in your Library has the identifier and URL entered in its Linkage properties, you can use the linked font in your document by selecting it from your font menu and using the Text tool as you normally would. When you publish your movie (.swf), you will notice that your file size is much smaller than it would be with embedded font information. For an example of this, compare the file size listed in the Bandwidth Profiler shown in Figure 8-29 (linked = 235 B), with Figure 8-30 (embedded = 4644 B).

Figure 8-29: The published .swf file from a document
using linked font information from a runtime shared asset

4. If you decide that you want to disable runtime sharing for a Font symbol in a destination document, you can clear the Import for runtime sharing check box in the Linkage Properties dialog box. The font information for the characters used in your file will now be embedded with the .swf file, so the file size will be larger, but the Flash Player will not require access to the shared asset.

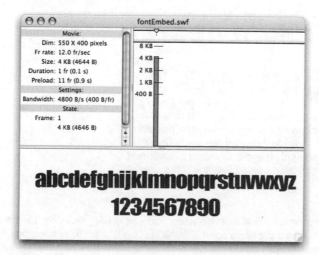

Figure 8-30: The published .swf file from a document using
embedded font information

Caution   Text rendered with advanced anti-alias settings (Anti-alias for readability or Custom anti-aliasing) must be embedded. For text using linked font information, use the Anti-alias for animation setting.

Modifying Text

In addition to all of the text-handling capabilities we discussed earlier in this chapter, there are some fun ways that you can modify the appearance of text to create custom effects. In Flash MX 2004, the effects that could be added to editable text were limited. A static text field could be scaled or skewed or flipped and its color or alpha could be changed. But if you wanted to create a drop shadow or special fill effect, it was necessary to break the text apart to create individual shapes. One of the biggest design features of Flash 8 is the new live Filters that can be applied to text or graphics to create special effects.

On the CD-ROM   We have included the Flash files for the modified text shown in this section on the CD-ROM. If you want to look at these in the Flash authoring environment, you can open the file `modifyText_mx2004.fla` or `modifyText_F8_filters.fla` in the `ch8` folder.

Editing text manually

Figure 8-31 illustrates some of the ways that text can be modified without using filters. Any of these styles of manually modified text are compatible with older versions of the Flash Player.

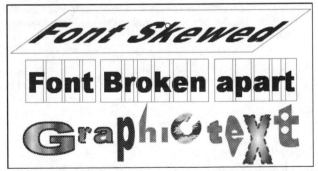

Figure 8-31: Text boxes can be modified with Free Transform options (top). To create individual characters, apply Break apart once (middle), and apply it again to create graphic text (bottom). Graphic text can be modified like any other shape in Flash.

Tip   If you plan to animate individual text characters, you can quickly move each letter onto its own layer by first applying the Break apart command (Ctrl+B or ⌘+B) to a text box and then using the Distribute to Layers command (Shift+Ctrl+D or Shift+⌘+D).

Custom text information adds to your file size, so it is best to reserve these treatments for special text such as titles or graphics. If you are working with longer sections of text (such as an article or a story), it is better to use common fonts or device fonts to help keep your files smaller and to make the text easier to read.

Tip With long sections of text, you may need to add scrolling, and this is much easier to do if you use Dynamic text or live Filters. If you use modified Static text or graphic text, it is still possible to add scrolling behavior by creating animation and controls manually, but this is more time-consuming and requires your final .swf to have more information embedded in it.

Scaling text

By selecting a text box with the Free Transform tool, you can scale your text by dragging the transform handles, but this is not recommended as a way to increase the size of text unless it has been broken into vector shapes. Flash has to interpolate the normal font outlines to scale text this way, so it can result in jagged edges when the movie is published. When sizing text, it is much better to simply choose or enter a larger point size in the font menu to ensure a clean outline when the text is exported.

Sampling and sharing text attributes

If you want to use the same font attributes on a variety of text boxes, it is often best to modify one text box so that it has all the qualities you want—including color, size, font, style, and line or character spacing. You then have two options for transferring these attributes to other text boxes using the Eyedropper tool:

✦ **To modify existing text boxes:** You can select other text boxes with the Selection tool and then activate the Eyedropper tool in the Tools panel and click on your modified text to sample its attributes and transfer them to all the other selected text boxes simultaneously. This is much more efficient and consistent than trying to remember what settings you used and changing them manually on different text boxes.

✦ **To set attributes for new text boxes:** You can load the visual attributes of any manually modified text into the Property inspector by activating the Eyedropper tool and clicking on the text to acquire its appearance. The Text tool is automatically activated after text is sampled, so you can immediately begin creating new text with the settings now loaded in the Property inspector.

Converting text into vector shapes

The Break apart command (Ctrl+B or ⌘+B) is used to reduce symbols to grouped shapes, and it can also be used to modify Static text. Applying Break apart once to a text box breaks a line of text into individual characters; applying the command again converts the characters into *graphic text* (vector lines and fills). Individual text characters can be grouped or changed to symbols. To make it easier to use individual characters in Motion tweened animation, you can apply the Distribute to Layers command (Modify ➪ Timeline ➪ Distribute to Layers) to automatically place each character on its own layer.

Graphic text can be modified using any of the drawing tools, reshaped with the Selection and Subselect tools, or distorted with any of the Free Transform options. You can also select special fills, such as bitmaps or gradients, to create patterned text, or use the Eraser tool to delete pieces of the letter shapes (see Figure 8-32).

Figure 8-32: Using the Eraser tool to delete parts of a graphic letter shape

However, after text characters have been converted to lines and fills, they can no longer be edited as text. Even if you regroup the text characters and/or convert the text into a symbol, you can no longer apply font, tracking, or paragraph options. To streamline your workflow, consider how you can combine graphic text with normal text for some effects — rather than converting all text into graphic shapes.

There are a few tips and guidelines to remember when converting text to shapes in Flash:

✦ To convert text characters to component lines and fills, you must first select or highlight the text characters that you want to convert. Then choose Modify ⇨ Break apart from the application menu. To undo, choose Edit ⇨ Undo (Ctrl+Z or ⌘+Z) from the application menu.

✦ Rotation and Break apart can only be applied to fonts with available outline information, such as TrueType fonts.

✦ On Macs, PostScript fonts can only be broken apart if a type manager is installed that will handle PostScript fonts.

✦ Bitmap fonts disappear from the screen if you attempt to break them apart.

✦ Breaking apart a text field that has Filters applied to it will remove the Filters before the text is converted into shapes.

As you experiment with graphic text, you may want to refer to some of the other chapters that cover working with shapes.

Using Timeline Effects on Static text

Flash MX 2004 introduced a new series of "ready-made" effects that can be applied and modified using the Timeline Effect Settings dialog box. To apply these effects, select a Static text box with the Selection tool and use the contextual menu or the Insert menu to browse to Timeline Effects and choose one of the effects in the drop-down menu. When you select an effect to apply, a dialog box pops up to allow you to tweak the settings to get exactly the look you want before Flash renders the final Graphic symbols that create the effect. Figure 8-33 shows the dialog box with a preview of the animated Blur effect created by default settings. You can modify the scale, direction, and duration of the blur animation and use the Update Preview button to test different settings.

You can go back and adjust the settings for your effect by selecting the text and choosing Modify ⇨ Timeline Effects ⇨ Edit Effect or choosing Timeline Effects ⇨ Edit Effect from the contextual menu.

Caution   If you manually edit a Timeline Effect Graphic symbol in Edit mode (by double-clicking it on the Stage or in the Library), you lose the option to go back and adjust the settings for the effect.

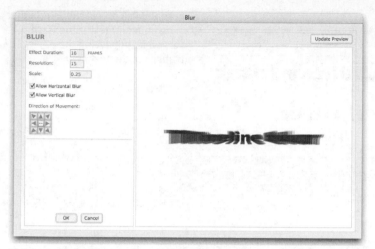

Figure 8-33: Settings and preview window for the Blur Timeline effect

Although Timeline Effects *can* be applied to Dynamic text or Input text, Flash is not sophisticated enough to magically re-render the effect if the text is changed during run time — the Graphic symbol rendered in the authoring environment is just exported with the .swf file and if the text is changed, the effect will no longer match up. Although Filters (described in the next section) offer a much more flexible way to modify the look of text, even if it is changed at run time, Timeline Effects are a great shortcut for making animation. If you need a good-looking drop-shadow or blur, Filters are the best approach, but if you want exploding text or an animated blur, Timeline Effects will do the trick.

Caution

The possibilities for combining Timeline Effects with Filters are interesting but not always reliable. The Expand and Explode animated Timeline Effects are intensive and will generally ignore your Filter effects. Even if they are rendered properly, Filters cannot be added or edited *after* you have applied a Timeline Effect. Fortunately, if a Timeline Effect doesn't work out as you hoped, you can always remove it and your Filters will be restored and editable again.

Moving beyond the box with Filter effects

Flash 8 Filters open up the possibilities of creative text treatments like never before. With one handy little tab added to the Property inspector (Filters), you can now modify your text without breaking it apart. Filters can even be applied to Dynamic text because they are rendered at run time; they're "live." Filters are easy to add and combine and you can edit the content of your text field at any time without breaking the effect. Figure 8-34 shows just a few simple examples of how you can modify text fields using Flash 8 Filters.

Filters can be found in the Property inspector under the Filters tab. If you don't see the Filters tab, try opening it from the application menu: Window ➪ Properties ➪ Filters. To apply Filters to a text field, select the text field, then use the controls in the Filters tab to add or adjust Filters (see Figure 8-35). Filters can be combined and layered to create a wide range of visual effects.

Figure 8-34: A few of the effects that can be added to text using Flash 8 Filters while preserving the editability of the text field

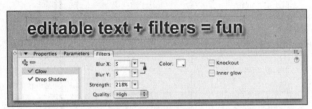

Figure 8-35: Adding and combining Filters on text fields is easy with the Filter tab in the Property inspector.

Summary

✦ Flash offers robust and well-organized text editing controls, but you can make the most of these tools only if you are familiar with, at least, the basic principles of typography.

✦ Studying the history of type in visual communications is one of the most practical and inspiring things you can do to improve your design skills.

✦ The option for converting any font into an aliased outline that can be embedded with the final movie (.swf) introduced with Flash MX 2004 is still available in Flash 8 — this overrides the default smoothing or anti-aliasing that can make some text look slightly blurry.

✦ Complete font information must be available on your system in order for Flash to render and export the text properly to the final movie (.swf). If you need to open a Flash file (.fla) that includes fonts not available on your system, you can choose temporary substitute fonts without damaging the original font information stored in the file.

✦ Creating Font symbols and storing them in Shared libraries for either author-time updates or runtime linkage can help you to manage large projects by centralizing font sources and making updates faster and easier.

✦ You can add visual interest to your text with Timeline Effects and Filters while still keeping options open for editing the content of the text field.

✦ The new Filters in Flash 8 are an easy and amazingly versatile method of adding style to all types of text fields. Because Filters are rendered dynamically, they can be applied to Dynamic text even if the content changes at run time.

✦   ✦   ✦

Modifying Graphics

After becoming familiar with the Flash authoring environment and learning to use the Drawing tools, you are now ready to move on to the fun part: messing with the basic shapes and text elements you have made to achieve custom results.

In this chapter, we revisit some of the core tools to show you new ways to apply them. We also introduce some specialized tools that exist only to transform your artwork. Following a look at how the Eyedropper, Paint Bucket, and Ink Bottle work together to modify strokes and fills, we'll show you how to use the Gradient Transform tool to create custom fills.

The Modify Shape submenu offers some special commands you can apply to alter lines and fills, whereas the Modify Transform submenu includes various options for skewing, stretching, rotating, flipping, and rotating shapes.

Before explaining the Flash stacking order and how to create compound shapes, we introduce the powerful Free Transform tool and the Envelope modifier that enables you to warp and distort multiple shapes simultaneously. Other features worth exploring include the stepped Break apart command on text and the indispensable Distribute to Layers command — these two features combined make animating text infinitely easier than it was in early versions of Flash.

Cross-Reference For coverage of Advanced Color Effects, Timeline Effects, and the new Flash 8 Filters refer to Chapter 12, "Applying Filters and Effects."

Last but not least, we'll cover the Find and Replace command and the History panel. We'll introduce the options for these flexible features and demonstrate some ways you can use them to modify your graphics, without even using any tools!

As we introduce various techniques and tools, we show you how to apply them for modifying artwork and adding the illusion of depth and texture to your 2D graphics.

Sampling and Switching Fills and Strokes

You can always use the Selection tool to select a stroke or fill so that you can delete, move, or modify it using any of the Swatches pop-ups or the Stroke Style menu on the Property inspector. But, what do you

◆ ◆ ◆ ◆

In This Chapter

Sampling and swapping fills and line styles

Applying the Gradient Transform tool to control gradient and bitmap fills

Using Modify Shape options

Working with the Free Transform tool and the Info panel: Skewing and rotating

Stacking, grouping, and arranging item types

Combining Drawing Objects

Creating and managing compound shapes

Using Break apart and Trace bitmap

Autopilot editing with Find and Replace

Using the History panel to create custom commands

◆ ◆ ◆ ◆

do if you want to add a stroke or fill to a shape that was drawn without one or the other? The answer to this dilemma is found in a trio of tools that work nimbly together to provide one of the most unique graphics-editing solutions found in Flash. You use the Eyedropper tool to acquire fill and stroke styles or colors, and use the Paint Bucket and Ink Bottle tools to transfer these characteristics to other shapes.

Note   These tools will only apply changes directly to shapes or Drawing Objects, so to modify an element that has been grouped or converted into a symbol, you must first access the element in Edit mode.

The Eyedropper tool

As we introduced in Chapter 7, "Applying Color," the dropper icon that appears when you use the Selection tool to select colors from any of the pop-up Swatches menus is similar to the Eyedropper tool available in the Tools panel. However, when pulled out of the Tools panel directly, the Eyedropper tool (I) has slightly different behavior. Although you cannot use the Eyedropper tool to sample colors from elements outside the Document window, you can use it to sample line and fill styles or to simultaneously change the stroke and the fill color chips to the same sampled color.

Note   When used to acquire colors, the Color swatches panel Eyedropper tool is limited to acquiring colors from swatches within the panel. However, the droppers that you access from the Swatches pop-ups in the Color Mixer panel, Tools panel, or Property inspector can acquire colors from other visible areas, such as the system background, items on the desktop, or items that are open in other applications. The only "trick" to this is to press and hold the mouse over any of the color chips and only release the mouse when you are hovering over the color that you want to sample. The preview in the Swatches pop-up changes as you roll over different colors, and the color chip changes when you release the mouse to load the color that you have selected.

Cross-Reference   For more information about this feat, refer to Chapter 7, "Applying Color."

The Eyedropper tool doesn't have any options in the Tools panel because they are all built in. As you hover over an item, the Eyedropper tool displays a small icon to indicate whether it is over a line or a fill that can be sampled by clicking. When a line is sampled, the Eyedropper tool automatically converts to the Ink Bottle tool, and when a fill is sampled, the Eyedropper tool converts to the Paint Bucket tool.

The composite image shown in Figure 9-1 shows the icons displayed when you use the Eyedropper tool to sample a fill (A) and apply it to another shape with the Paint Bucket tool (B), and sample a stroke (C) and apply it to another shape with the Ink Bottle tool (D).

Any items already selected when the Eyedropper tool samples a stroke or fill will immediately acquire the applicable stroke or fill style. This is the quickest way to transfer the fill or line styles of one element to a whole group of elements. Figure 9-2 shows the Eyedropper tool used to sample a fill with one (A) or more (B) elements already selected.

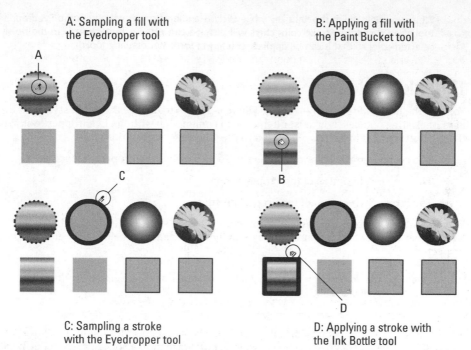

A: Sampling a fill with
the Eyedropper tool

B: Applying a fill with
the Paint Bucket tool

C: Sampling a stroke
with the Eyedropper tool

D: Applying a stroke with
the Ink Bottle tool

Figure 9-1: The Eyedropper tool used to sample a fill and apply it with the Paint Bucket tool (A, B) and to sample a stroke and apply it with the Ink Bottle tool (C, D)

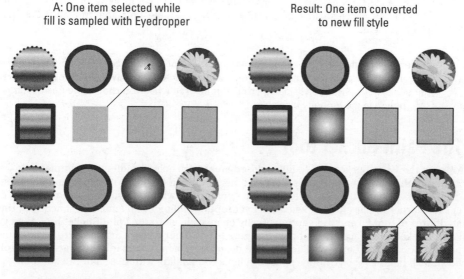

A: One item selected while
fill is sampled with Eyedropper

Result: One item converted
to new fill style

B: Two items selected while
fill is sampled with Eyedropper

Result: Two items converted
to new fill style

Figure 9-2: The Eyedropper tool also instantly converts selected elements to the sampled fill or stroke style.

Note   When you hold down the Shift key while clicking a line or stroke color with the Eyedropper tool, the Fill and the Stroke color chips will both be converted simultaneously to the newly selected color so that it can be applied with any of the other drawing tools.

The Ink Bottle tool

You use the Ink Bottle tool (S) — refer to Figure 9-1 (D) — to change the color, style, and thickness of existing outlines. It is most often used in conjunction with the Eyedropper tool. When the Ink Bottle tool is in use, pay attention to the following three options:

✦ The current Stroke Color option on the Tools panel or the Property inspector

✦ The Line Height option of the Property inspector

✦ The Stroke Style option of the Property inspector

The Ink Bottle will apply the current stroke color and line style, either sampled with the Eyedropper tool or chosen from the pop-up in the Tools panel or the controls in the Property inspector.

 Caution   When you click to sample a line with the Ink Bottle tool, all other currently *selected* lines are changed simultaneously.

The Ink Bottle tool is especially useful for applying custom line styles to multiple lines. You can build a collection of custom line styles either off Stage or in a special custom line palette that is saved as a single-frame Flash movie. You can then acquire these line styles whenever you want to reuse them.

 Tip   You can add Flash files with Graphics libraries that you plan to reuse to the application's Libraries folder so that they will be easily accessible from the Window ➪ Common Libraries menu.

 Caution   Depending on the level of zoom, some lines may not display accurately on the screen — though they will print correctly on a high-resolution printer. You may adjust Stroke Height (or thickness) in the Stroke Style dialog box that is invoked when you choose the Custom stroke style option in the Property inspector.

The Paint Bucket tool

You use the Paint Bucket tool to fill enclosed areas with color, gradients, or bitmap fills. Although the Paint Bucket tool is a more robust tool than the Ink Bottle tool, and it can be used independently, it's most often used in conjunction with the Eyedropper tool. As we discussed earlier in this chapter, when the Eyedropper tool picks up a fill, it first acquires the attributes of that fill and then automatically changes itself to the Paint Bucket tool. When the Paint Bucket tool is active, as shown in Figure 9-3, two options are available from the Tools panel: Lock Fill and Gap size. The Gap size drop-down menu offers four settings to control how Flash handles gaps or open spaces in lines when filling with the Paint Bucket tool.

When you use the Eyedropper tool to acquire a fill that is a broken-apart bitmap, the Eyedropper tool is automatically swapped for the Paint Bucket tool and a thumbnail of the bitmap image appears in place of the fill color chip. This procedure also automatically engages the Paint Bucket Lock Fill option.

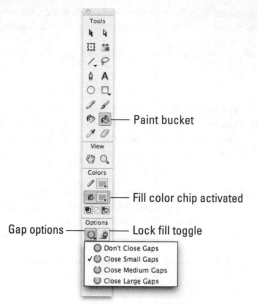

Figure 9-3: The Paint Bucket tool and Gap size options

Paint bucket

Fill color chip activated

Gap options — Lock fill toggle

○ Don't Close Gaps
✓○ Close Small Gaps
○ Close Medium Gaps
○ Close Large Gaps

The final appearance of a bitmap fill can vary greatly depending on how you apply it. Figure 9-4 shows a series of shapes all filled with the same bitmap to illustrate the various results achieved from using different steps to define the fill.

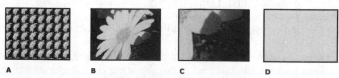

A   B   C   D

Figure 9-4: (A) A shape filled with the Paint Bucket using a bitmap fill sampled with the Eyedropper or selected in the Mixer panel; (B) a shape drawn with the Rectangle tool using a bitmap fill selected in the Mixer panel or applied after the shape was drawn using the Selection tool and Mixer panel fill style menu; (C) a broken apart bitmap sampled with the Eyedropper tool and then applied to the finished shape using the Paint Bucket tool; (D) a shape filled with the Paint Bucket tool, using a color sampled from the bitmap with the Swatches color dropper tool

Caution　Using the Paint Bucket to fill with white (or the background color) is not the same as erasing. Painting with white (or the background color) may appear to accomplish something similar to erasing. However, you are, in fact, creating a filled item that can be selected, moved, deleted, or reshaped. Only erasing erases!

Another behavior of the Paint Bucket tool that can be helpful to recognize is that the exact location where you click to apply the Paint Bucket tool defines the highlight point for the fill. This has no visible effect when filling with solid colors, but when filling with gradients it will affect how the fill is rendered within the boundaries of the shape. Figure 9-5 illustrates how the highlight of a gradient fill varies based on where it was "dumped" with the Paint Bucket.

Tip   You can also adjust the highlight and the center point of the rendered gradient with the Gradient Transform tool after a shape is filled.

Figure 9-5: The highlight location of gradient fills can be defined by the position of the Paint Bucket tool when the fill is applied to a shape.

As with the Ink Bottle tool, the Paint Bucket tool can be especially useful for applying custom fill styles to multiple items. You can build a collection of custom fill styles either off-screen (on the Pasteboard) or in a special, saved, custom-fills-palette, single-frame Flash movie. You can then acquire these fills whenever necessary.

Caution   If you click with the Paint Bucket tool on one of several selected fills, *all* of the selected fills will be simultaneously changed to the new fill.

Using the Paint Bucket Gap size option

As shown in Figure 9-3, the Gap size option drop-down offers four settings that control how the Paint Bucket treats gaps when filling. These settings are Don't Close Gaps, Close Small Gaps, Close Medium Gaps, and Close Large Gaps. These tolerance settings enable Flash to fill an outline if the endpoints of the outline aren't completely joined, leaving an open shape. If the gaps are too large, you may have to close them manually with another drawing tool. Figure 9-6 illustrates how the Gap size option settings affect the Paint Bucket fill behavior.

Tip   The level of zoom changes the apparent size of gaps. Although the actual size of gaps is unaffected by zoom, the Paint Bucket's interpretation of the gap is dependent upon the current Zoom setting. When zoomed in very close, the Paint Bucket tool will find it harder to close gaps; when zoomed out, the Paint Bucket tool will find it easier to close gaps.

Using the Paint Bucket Lock Fill option

The Paint Bucket's Lock Fill option is the same as the Brush Lock Fill option—it controls how Flash handles areas filled with gradient color or bitmaps. When this button is turned on, all areas (or shapes) painted with the same gradient or bitmap appear to be part of a single, continuous, filled shape. The Lock Fill option locks the angle, size, and point of origin of the current fill to remain constant throughout any number of selected shapes. Modifications made to the fill in one of the shapes will be applied to the other shapes filled using the same Lock Fill option.

Cross-Reference   Working with gradient colors is discussed in Chapter 7, "Applying Color."

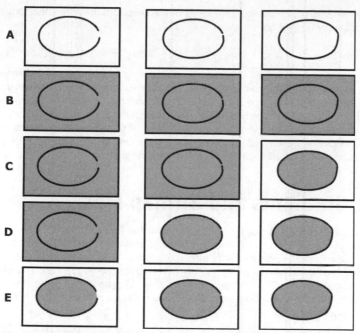

Figure 9-6: Paint Bucket fill applied with various Gap size settings: (A) original oval outline with decreasing gap sizes, left to right, with no fill; (B) gray fill applied with Don't Close Gaps; (C) gray fill applied with Close Small Gaps; (D) gray fill applied with Close Medium Gaps; (E) gray fill applied with Close Large Gaps

To demonstrate the distinction between fills applied with or without the Lock Fill option, we created five shapes and filled them with a bitmap with Lock Fill off. As shown in Figure 9-7, on the left, the image was rendered separately from one shape to the next. On the right, those same shapes were filled with the same bitmap, but with Lock Fill on. Note how the image is now continuous from one shape to the next. Bitmap fills are automatically tiled to fill a shape, so the bitmap fill on the right was also scaled using the Gradient Transform tool to make it easier to see the continuation of the image between the various shapes.

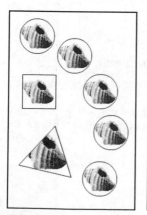 

Figure 9-7: Fill applied with Lock Fill turned off (left), compared with fill applied with Lock Fill turned on and then scaled using the Gradient Transform tool (right)

Note   When you use the Eyedropper tool to pick up a fill or gradient from the scene, the Lock Fill button is automatically toggled on.

Caution   If the shapes you are filling with the Paint Bucket tool were created with the Object Drawing option turned on, you will be able to use the Lock Fill option to get a fill that continues from one shape to the next, but when you try to adjust the fill with the Gradient Transform tool, you will find that the fills are transformed individually instead of as a group. The workaround for this glitch is to use raw shapes when you apply a locked fill that you plan to transform. If you started with Drawing Objects, use the Break Apart command before you try to use the Gradient Transform tool to adjust a continuous fill on multiple shapes.

Transforming Gradients and Bitmap Fills

The Gradient Transform tool (F) was originally an option for the Paint Bucket tool, but in Flash MX 2004, it was given a home on the main Tools panel, right next to the Free Transform tool. Gradient Transform is used only to modify bitmap or gradient fills and will not apply to simple color fills. The Gradient Transform does many of the same things the Free Transform tool does, but it only modifies the *fill* of a shape without changing the stroke or outline appearance at all. This is a lot like shifting, rotating, or scaling a larger piece of material behind a frame so that a different portion is visible.

The Gradient Transform tool has only one option in the Tools panel, but, as with the Eyedropper tool, it does apply differently depending on the type of fill selected. To use the Gradient Transform tool, select it in the Tools panel, and then simply click an existing gradient or bitmap fill. A set of three or four adjustment handles appears, depending on the type of fill. The following three transformations can be performed on a gradient or bitmap fill: adjusting the fill's center point, rotating the fill, and scaling the fill. The extra set of adjustment handles displayed on bitmap fills enables them to be skewed. The Magnet option in the Tools panel toggles on Snapping behavior—making it easier to constrain transformations to even adjustment increments. Figure 9-8 illustrates the various adjustment handles on three types of fills.

The position of these handles may shift if a fill (or bitmap fill) has been variously copied, rotated, or pasted in any number of ways. The fundamental rules are as follows:

✦ The round center handle moves the center point.

✦ The extra center pointer on radial gradients moves the highlight.

✦ The round corner handle with the short arrow rotates.

✦ The square edge handles scale either vertically or horizontally.

✦ The round corner handle with a long arrow scales symmetrically.

✦ The diamond-shaped edge handles on bitmap fills skew either vertically or horizontally.

Tip   To see all the handles when transforming a large element or working with an item close to the edge of the Stage, choose View ➪ Work Area from the application menu or use the shortcut keys Shift+Ctrl+W (Shift+⌘+W).

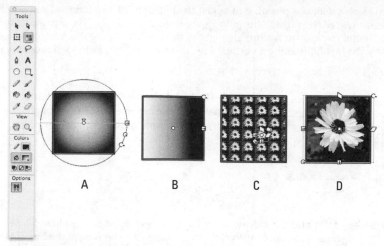

Figure 9-8: The Gradient Transform tool applied to a Radial gradient (A), a Linear gradient (B), a tiled Bitmap fill (C), and a scaled Bitmap fill (D). Each handle type has an icon to indicate its function.

Adjusting the center point with the Gradient Transform tool

If the fill is not aligned in the shape, as you would like it to be, you can easily move the center point to adjust how the fill is framed by the shape outline. To adjust the center point, follow these steps:

1. Deselect the fill if it has been previously selected.

2. Choose the Gradient Transform tool.

3. Click the fill.

4. Bring the cursor to the small circular handle at the center of the fill until it changes to a four-arrow cursor, pointing left and right, up and down, like a compass, indicating that this handle can now be used to move the center point in any direction.

5. Drag the center circular handle in any direction you want to move the center of the fill.

Figure 9-9 shows a radial gradient (left) repositioned with the Gradient Transform tool (right).

Figure 9-9: Adjusting the center point of a gradient fill with the Gradient Transform tool

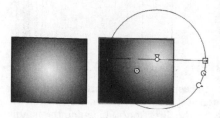

A new feature in Flash 8 makes it possible to adjust the highlight of a radial gradient without moving the center point of the fill. As shown in Figure 9-10, you can drag the extra pointer above the center point circle to move the highlight of the gradient along the horizontal axis. If you want to move the highlight along a vertical axis, use the rotate handle to change the orientation of the fill.

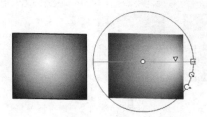

Figure 9-10: A new Flash 8 Gradient Transform handle makes it possible to adjust the highlight of a radial gradient without moving the center point of the fill.

Tip   The Paint Bucket tool is also a handy way to set the highlight point of a gradient fill. Select the gradient that you want to apply, then click in the shape where you want the highlight to be. You can keep clicking in different areas of the shape with the Paint Bucket to move the highlight around until you like it.

Rotating a fill with the Gradient Transform tool

To rotate a gradient or bitmap fill, find the small circular handle that's at the corner of the fill. (In a radial gradient, choose the lower circular handle.) This circular handle is used for rotating a fill around the center point. Simply click the circular handle with the Rotate cursor and drag clockwise or counterclockwise to rotate the fill. Figure 9-11 shows a bitmap fill (left) as it appears when rotated clockwise (right).

Tip   Activate the Snapping toggle in the Tools panel if you want to use Snapping behaviors to help guide rotating or scaling of a fill. (Turn behaviors on or off in the application menu under View ➪ Snapping.)

Figure 9-11: Rotating a bitmap fill with the Gradient Transform tool

Adjusting scale with the Gradient Transform tool

To resize a bitmap fill symmetrically (to maintain the aspect ratio), find the round-corner handle with an arrow icon, which is usually located at the lower-left corner of the fill. On rollover, the diagonal arrow icon appears, indicating the direction(s) in which the handle resizes the fill. Click and drag to scale the fill symmetrically. On radial gradients, you use the round-corner handle with the longer arrow icon to scale with the gradient aspect ratio constrained. Linear gradients only have one handle for scaling, and this handle always scales in the direction of the gradient banding.

To resize a fill asymmetrically, find a small square handle on either a vertical or a horizontal edge, depending on whether you want to affect the width or height of the fill. On rollover, arrows appear perpendicular to the edge of the shape, indicating the direction in which this handle resizes the fill. Click and drag a handle to reshape the fill.

Figure 9-12 shows the three fill types with their respective scale options. Linear gradient fills (left) can only be scaled in the direction of the gradient banding, but they can be rotated to scale vertically (lower) instead of horizontally (upper). Radial gradient fills (center) can be expanded symmetrically (upper) with the circular handle, or asymmetrically (lower) with the square handle. As with Linear gradients, they can be rotated to scale vertically rather than horizontally. Bitmap fills (right) can be scaled by the corner handle to maintain the aspect ratio (upper), or dragged from any side handle to scale asymmetrically (lower).

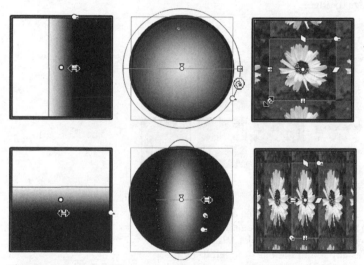

Figure 9-12: Scaling fills symmetrically (top) and asymmetrically (bottom)

Caution

Adjusting bitmap fills with the Gradient Transform tool can be tricky business. On tiled fills, the transform handles are often so small and bunched together that they are difficult to see. On full-size bitmaps, the handles are sometimes outside the Stage and it can be hard to find the handle that you need. It can also be unpredictable where the handles will appear when you select a bitmap fill with the Gradient Transform tool — often they are outside the shape where the fill is visible. Our advice is to use this workflow only when you have no other choice. In general, it is a much better idea to decide on the size for a bitmap and create a Web-ready image that you can use without scaling before you import it to Flash.

Note

The right column of Figure 9-12 is a good example of how changes applied to one tile in a bitmap fill will be passed to all the other tiles within the shape.

Setting gradient fill overflow styles

As you work with scaled gradient fills, you will quickly notice that your shape is always filled from edge to edge but that the fill area may not appear quite how you'd like it to. In previous versions of Flash, you were stuck with the solid color fill around the edges when a gradient was scaled smaller inside of a shape. In Flash 8, this default behavior is now part of the Overflow menu in the Color Mixer panel that gives you some other options for how a gradient renders when it is scaled down. As shown in Figure 9-13, there are three different overflow styles:

Extend: Extends the colors on the outside edge of the gradient to create a solid fill beyond the edge of the rendered gradient

Reflect: Alternates flipped (reflected) versions of the original gradient until the shape is filled from edge to edge

Repeat: Renders the color pattern of the original gradient repeatedly until the shape is filled from edge to edge

Figure 9-13: Different overflow styles applied to a Linear gradient (top right) and a Radial gradient (bottom right) using the Overflow menu in the Color Mixer panel (left). Overflow styles applied to the fills from left to right: Extend, Reflect, Repeat.

Skewing a bitmap fill with the Gradient Transform tool

To skew a bitmap fill horizontally, click the diamond-shaped handle at the top of the image; arrows appear, parallel to the edge of the fill, indicating the directions in which this handle skews the fill. Drag to skew the image in either direction. Figure 9-14 shows a bitmap skewed horizontally (left) and vertically (right). Note that the skew procedure is still active after it has been applied, meaning that the skew may be further modified — this behavior is common to all functions of the Gradient Transform tool.

Note   Gradient fills cannot be skewed; they can only be scaled on the horizontal or vertical axis.

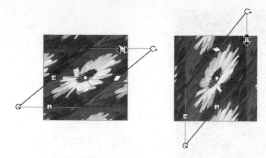

Figure 9-14: Skewing a bitmap fill with the Gradient Transform tool

Tip   If you get carried away with the Gradient Transform tool and you want to get back to the original fill position and size, double-click the center icon of the shape and all transformations will be reset.

Gradient Transform Used for Lighting Effects

You will apply the Gradient Transform tool most often to get a patterned fill or a gradient aligned and sized within its outline shape. A simple way of adding more depth to shapes is to modify gradient fills so that they appear to reflect light from one consistent source. You can choose to emulate a soft light for a more even illumination, or to emulate a hard, focused light that emphasizes dramatic shadows. As you create a composition on the Stage, you can use the Gradient Transform tool to modify individual elements so that they appear to share a common light source. Figure 9-15 illustrates how a default radial gradient (left) can be modified to emulate a soft (center) or hard (right) illumination.

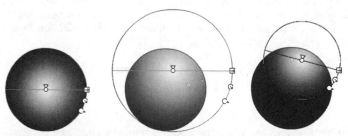

Figure 9-15: Applying Gradient Transform to create different illumination effects

To show how these lighting effects can be applied to create the illusion of 3D, we created a little scene using only radial fills that were modified with the Gradient Transform tool. Figure 9-16 shows the radial gradients as they appeared when we drew them with the default settings (left) and how the scene appeared after we modified the gradients with Gradient Transform and some basic shape scaling as we describe later in this chapter.

On the CD-ROM   If you want to deconstruct this example, we have included the file on the CD-ROM with both the unmodified and the final transformed shapes. You will find the file named SphereLighting.fla in the ch09 folder of the CD-ROM.

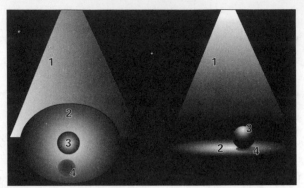

Figure 9-16: The Fill Transform tool used to modify default radial gradient fills (left) to create the illusion of 3D lighting effects (right)

Applying Modify Shape Menu Commands

The three specialized commands found in the application menu (under Modify ➪ Shape) provide modification options that you cannot achieve with any other tools in Flash.

Convert Lines to Fills

Lines to Fills does exactly what its name implies: It converts lines defined by single points into shapes defined by an outline of editable points. To apply the Lines to Fills command, simply select any lines that you wish to convert before choosing Modify ➪ Shape ➪ Convert Lines to Fills. After a line has been converted in this way, you can edit it like any other filled shape, including adding bitmap or gradient fills or applying the Selection or Subselection tools to adjust the corners and curves of the outlined shape.

Cross-Reference   We discuss the Selection tool and the Subselection tool in Chapter 5, "Drawing in Flash."

New Feature   In Flash 8, you can render strokes and lines using gradients without converting them into fills.

Creating scalable artwork

The Lines to Fills command is especially important because it provides the one solution for maintaining line to fill ratios when scaling raw graphics that would require lines to display at smaller than 1 point size. Fills do not have the same display limitation as lines and they will maintain visual consistency as they are scaled larger or smaller. In Figure 9-17, the image on the left was drawn using the pencil tool to make lines around the eyes and on the whiskers of the cat cartoon. When it was scaled, the lines were not visually consistent with the fills. The image on the right was modified using the Lines to Fills command before scaling it down to 25 percent size. In this case, the ratio between the outlines around the eyes and the whiskers was consistent with the other filled shapes in the cartoon.

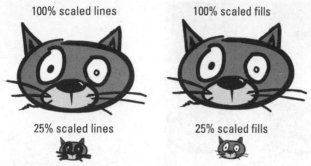

100% scaled lines   100% scaled fills

25% scaled lines   25% scaled fills

Figure 9-17: Use the Lines to Fills command to ensure consistency when scaling raw graphics

Tip   If you convert your raw graphic into a symbol before you scale it, the ratio of lines to fills will also stay consistent.

Note   Remember that in Flash, the smallest line size that can be displayed is 1 point. Lines with a height of less than 1 point will all appear to be the same size onscreen when viewed at 100-percent scale. The difference in size is only visible when the View is scaled larger (zoomed in). However, the lines print correctly on a high-resolution printer and will be visible in the published .swf if the content is zoomed.

Expand Fill

The Expand Fill command has two options you can use to size fills up or down evenly on all sides of a shape. To apply the command, select the fill(s) that you want to modify. Then choose Modify ⇨ Shape ⇨ Expand Fill. The Expand Fills dialog box appears, where you can choose to expand or inset (shrink) the fill by a specific pixel value. Keep in mind that this command applies differently than a normal scale modification. The fill expands or shrinks from all sides evenly, so an extreme modification can cause a shape to bloat to the extent that unfilled areas are obscured, or conversely it can cause a shape to shrink to the point that some of the areas are no longer visible. When applied moderately, the Expand Fill command can be very helpful for adjusting multiple filled shapes consistently, without scaling lines in the same area of the artwork.

Caution   You cannot apply the Expand Fill command to Drawing Objects with strokes unless you first break them apart or open them in Edit mode so that you can select the fill without also selecting the stroke.

Figure 9-18 includes a rectangle, a cartoon cat, and a sketch of some grapes. The original shapes are shown on the left, the expanded fills in the center, and the inset fills on the right. As you can see, expanding fills often obscures the strokes surrounding a shape, whereas choosing to inset a fill leaves space between the fill and any surrounding stroke.

Figure 9-18: Modifying an original shape (left) with the Expand Fill command using the Expand option (center) or the Inset option (right) will respectively bloat or shrink a fill by a specified pixel amount.

Note   Each of the fills in the graphics shown in Figure 9-18 were added by clicking or Shift-clicking (rather than dragging out a selection marquee) to avoid including any strokes in the final selection that was modified with the Expand Fill command.

You can also use the Expand Fill command to create custom text forms. Figure 9-19 shows how the original text shape (left) can be modified using either the Expand or Inset option. To create bloated balloon-like text (center), or shrunken, eroded text (right), you first have to apply the Modify ➪ Break apart command (Ctrl+B or ⌘+B) twice to reduce the text to simple filled shapes. By selecting all of the letter shapes before applying the Expand Fill command, you can modify the whole word at the same time.

Expand **Expand** Expand
A   B   C

Figure 9-19: Text broken apart into letter shapes (A) can be expanded (B) or inset (C) to create custom text effects.

Soften Fill Edges

The Soften Fill Edges command is the closest thing to a static blur that is compatible with older versions of Flash. Fortunately, Flash 8 supports a much more sophisticated Blur Filter that renders smoother softened edges and enables you to change the color of the item even after the Blur is applied. The only advantages that the Soften Fill Edges command has over the Blur filter are that you can use it to modify raw shapes and Drawing Objects and can render it inside or outside the item's original fill boundary. This command, as with the Expand Fill command, can only be applied to fills and gives you the option to expand or inset the shape by a specific number of pixels.

Caution Flash enables you to select a line and choose the Soften Edges command from the Modify ⇨ Shape menu. After you apply the command, however, the line will just disappear from the Stage — surprise! If you make this mistake, you can recover your line by immediately choosing Edit ⇨ Undo (Ctrl+Z or ⌘+Z).

The blurry effect of Soften Fill Edges is created by a series of banded fills around the original fill that decrease in opacity toward the outermost band. You can control the number and width of these bands by entering values in the Soften Fill Edges dialog box (shown in Figure 9-20) to create a variety of effects, from a very subtle blurred effect to a dramatic stepped appearance around the edges of the fill.

Figure 9-20: The Soften Fill Edges dialog box with settings for controlling the edge effect

The Soften Fill Edges dialog box controls the following features of the fill modification:

✦ **Distance:** Defines the number of pixels the original shape will expand or shrink

✦ **Number of steps:** Sets the number of bands that appear around the outside edge of the fill

✦ **Expand or Inset:** Controls whether the bands will be added to the outside edge of the fill (expand) or stacked on the inside edge of the shape (inset)

Figure 9-21 shows how the original fill (left) appears after Soften Fill Edges is applied with the Expand option (center), or with the Inset option (right).

Figure 9-21: Applying Soften Fill Edges with the Expand option and with the Inset option

The width of the individual bands equals the total number of pixels set in Distance divided by the Number of steps. When the edge of the shape is magnified, the individual bands can clearly be seen. Figure 9-22 compares a series of eight bands, each 1-pixel wide, created by using a Distance setting of 8 with a Number of steps setting of 8 compared with the smooth softened edge that results from applying a Blur filter with an X and Y setting of 8.

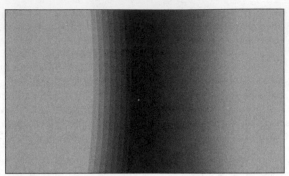

Figure 9-22: A magnified view of the banded edge of a fill created by applying Soften Fill Edges (left) compared to the smooth softened edge created by applying the new Flash 8 Blur filter (right)

As with the Expand Fill command, Soften Fill Edges can create interesting text effects when applied to broken-apart letter shapes. Figure 9-23 shows an effect created by combining the original white text with a "shadow" made by applying the Soften Fill Edges command to a broken apart copy of the text that was filled with dark gray.

Soften Fill Edges

Figure 9-23: A shadow effect created by layering the original text over a copy that was broken apart, filled with dark gray and modified using Soften Fill Edges

New Feature   You can achieve an effect similar to the shadow shown in Figure 9-23 by applying the new Glow filter to an editable text field and selecting the knockout option. We cover the various Flash 8 filters in Chapter 12, "Applying Filters and Effects."

Free Transform Commands and Options

The commands we have looked at so far in this chapter are generally used for localized modification of lines or fills. In this section, we introduce some commands that are applied to create more dramatic change of whole items or even groups of items.

You can apply the basic transform commands to any element in the Flash authoring environment, but it is important to know that any transformations applied to symbols, groups, Drawing Objects, or text blocks are saved in the Info panel even if they are unselected and then reselected later. This enables you to easily revert these items to their original appearance. The transform settings for primitive shapes, on the other hand, are reset to the default values in the Info panel as soon as they are deselected. This means that while a primitive shape is actively being modified, you can revert to the original appearance, but as soon as you apply a change and deselect the shape, its modified appearance will be considered original the next time you select it.

As shown in Figure 9-24, there are various ways to access the transform commands available in Flash.

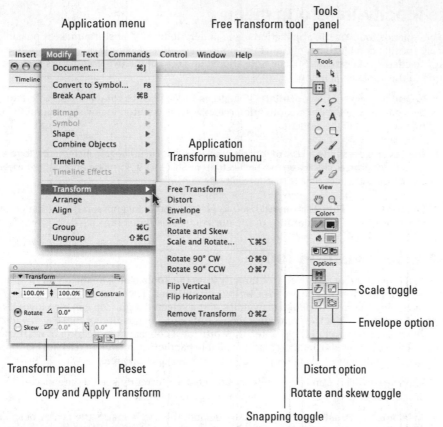

Figure 9-24: The various ways to access transform commands in Flash – the Transform panel (lower-left), the Modify Transform submenu (center), and the Free Transform tool (right).

The Transform panel

The Transform panel (Ctrl+T or ⌘+T) includes value fields for horizontal and vertical scale percentages, degrees of rotation, and degrees of vertical and horizontal skew. You can use these fields for visual reference or as a way to enter precise transform values. The Transform panel also includes two important buttons.

 The **Copy and Apply Transform** button is used to duplicate the selected item with all transformations included. When you select this button, you may not notice that anything has happened to your selected item — this is because Flash places the duplicate exactly on top of the original. To see both the original and the duplicate, drag the duplicate to a new position in the Document window.

 The **Reset** button will revert a transformed symbol, group, or text field to its original appearance and return all values in the Transform panel to the default settings. You can also achieve this by choosing Modify ➪ Transform ➪ Remove Transform. If you only want to remove the most recently applied modification, use Edit ➪ Undo (Ctrl+Z or ⌘+Z).

The Modify Transform menu

The commands found in the application menu under Modify ➪ Transform make it possible to choose specific combinations of transform options as well as a couple of "shortcuts" for commonly needed modifications. Special note should be taken of the two commands that are unique to the application menu:

✦ **Rotate 90 degrees CW or Rotate 90 degrees CCW:** Used to rotate any selected items by a half-turn in the chosen direction (clockwise or counterclockwise) around the central axis point of the selection.

Tip   You can also use shortcut keys to rotate any selected item in 90-degree increments. To rotate an item 90-degrees clockwise, use Shift+Ctrl+9 or Shift+⌘+9. To rotate an item 90-degrees counterclockwise, use Shift+Ctrl+7 or Shift+⌘+7.

✦ **Flip Vertical or Flip Horizontal:** Used to place the item in a mirrored position either on the vertical axis (calendar flip) or the horizontal axis (book flip).

The Free Transform tool

The Free Transform tool (Q), available directly from the Tools panel, enables you to apply transform commands dynamically with various arrow icons. These icons appear as you move the pointer over the control points or handles of the selected item. You can also invoke various transform states from the contextual menu. Although the position of these arrow icons can vary with the position of the pointer, they provide a consistent indication of what transformation will be applied from the closest available handle. To finish any transformation, simply deselect the item by clicking outside of the current selection area.

 ✦ **Move arrow:** This familiar arrow indicates that all currently selected items can be dragged together to a new location in the Document window.

 ✦ **Axis point or transformation point:** By default, this circle marks the center of shapes as the axis for most transformations or animation. On symbols, the axis point is in the top-left corner or at axis 0,0. By dragging the point to a different location, you can define a new axis or transformation point for modifications applied to the item. To return the axis point to its default location, double-click the axis point icon.

Note   In Flash, the axis point of symbols is in the top-left corner by default because it is easier to modify an item mathematically if the origin point is 0,0. However, this means that symbols cannot be scaled towards the top or to the left, unless the axis point is first adjusted. Move the axis point to the center of the symbol to enable transformation in all directions. Shapes can be scaled in any direction, and the scale will always originate from the side opposite the handle that is selected.

 ✦ **Skew arrow:** This arrow is generally available on any side of an item between transformation points. By clicking and dragging the outline, you can skew the shape in either direction indicated by the arrows.

 ✦ **Rotate arrow:** This arrow is generally available near any corner of an item. By clicking and dragging, you can rotate the item clockwise or counterclockwise around the transform axis. Note that if you move the arrow directly over the closest corner handle, the Rotate arrow will usually be replaced with the Scale Corner arrow. To rotate around the opposite corner point without moving the axis point, press the Alt (Option) key while dragging. To constrain rotation to 45-degree increments, press the Shift key while dragging.

✦ **Scale Side arrow:** This arrow is available from any handle on the side of an item. Clicking and dragging will scale the item larger or smaller, in one direction only, relative to the transform axis.

✦ **Scale Corner arrow:** This arrow appears only on the corner handles of an item and is used to evenly scale the item larger or smaller, in all directions from the transform axis. To constrain the aspect ratio of the shape, press the Shift key while dragging.

Transforming shapes, symbols, text, and groups

Figure 9-25 shows how a symbol and a shape display differently after they have been modified, deselected, and then reselected with the Free Transform tool. The symbol (left) displays transform handles that are aligned with the originally modified item and the values of the transformation settings are preserved in the Transform panel. The shape (right), however, displays transform handles aligned to default values unrelated to the original modifications, and the values in the Transform panel are also reset to their defaults.

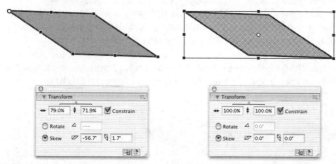

Figure 9-25: The Free Transform handles and Transform panel settings displayed for a symbol (left) and for a shape (right) that have been reselected after an initial modification

Free Transform limit options

The first two options in the Tools panel for the Free Transform tool are toggles to limit the modifications that can be applied to a selected item. It can sometimes be easier to use the Free Transform tool with more specific behavior. When the Rotate and Skew button or the Scale button is toggled on, they will exclude all other modifications.

The Rotate and Skew toggle protects the selected item from being scaled accidentally while you're rotating or skewing it. This Tools panel option is equivalent to choosing Modify ➪ Transform ➪ Rotate and Skew from the application menu.

The Scale toggle protects the selected item from all other transformations while it is being sized larger or smaller. This Tools panel option is equivalent to choosing Modify ➪ Transform ➪ Scale from the application menu.

Free Transform special shape options

The last two options in the Tools panel for the Free Transform tool—Distort and Envelope—are not available for symbols, groups, or text fields. However, when you're transforming primitive shapes or Drawing Objects, you can use these two options to create complex modifications not easily achieved using other Flash tools.

Note　Remember that you can access the primitive shapes in a group or symbol by entering Edit mode. It is also possible to convert text fields into primitive shapes by applying the Break apart command (twice).

Distort works by widening or narrowing the sides of the item, or stretching out the corners. This transform option does not bend or warp the shape; it allows sides of the shape to be scaled individually. To apply Distort, first select a shape with the Free Transform tool in the Tools panel, and turn on the Distort toggle in the Options area of the Tools panel. You will then be able to click and drag handles on the sides or corners of the item to stretch or compress individual sides. This is equivalent to selecting a shape with the Selection tool and choosing Modify ➪ Transform ➪ Distort from the application menu or selecting Distort from the contextual menu.

Tip　You can also apply the Distort option to a shape that has been selected with the Free Transform tool by pressing the Control (⌘) key while dragging a side or corner handle. To taper a shape or move two adjoining corner points an equal distance simultaneously, press the Shift key while dragging any corner handle with the Free Transform tool.

Figure 9-26 shows an original shape being modified with the Distort option (left), and the final shape with distort handles, as they appear when the shape is reselected (right).

Figure 9-26: Free Transform applied to a shape using the Distort option

The Envelope option for the Free Transform tool may be one of the most engaging transform methods available in Flash. Once you try it, you may be stretching, squashing, bending, and warping for hours. On the other hand, as you get used to working with this nifty little option, you will find it faster than ever to create unique shapes.

The Envelope option enables you to work with control points and handles much the same way you would when editing lines or shapes using the Subselection tool. The powerful difference is that the Envelope can wrap around the outside of multiple items so that the control points and handles will curve, scale, stretch, or warp all of the lines and shapes contained within the Envelope selection.

To apply the Envelope, first select a shape or multiple shapes with the Free Transform tool and then toggle on the Envelope option in the Tools panel. The Envelope offers a series of control points and tangent handles. The square points are used to scale and skew the shape(s), whereas the round points are actually handles used to control the curve and warp of the shape(s). You can also access the Envelope option by selecting the shapes you want to transform and choosing Modify ➪ Transform ➪ Envelope from the application menu, or selecting Envelope from the contextual menu.

Figure 9-27 shows an original shape being modified with the Envelope option (left), and the final shape with Envelope handles, as they appear when the shape is reselected (right).

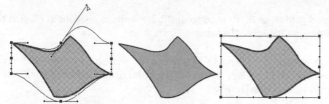

Figure 9-27: Free Transform applied to a shape using the Envelope option

Modifying Item Types

In previous chapters, we have focused on the features of the Timeline and how your Flash projects are ordered in time from left to right. Now we are going to look at the arrangement of items from the front to the back of the Stage, or the stacking order of elements in Flash. In this section, we'll explain how multiple items can be moved together, and how the Union, Break apart, and Trace bitmap commands are applied to change item types.

Stacking order

Within a single layer, Flash stacks items of the same type in the same order they are placed or created, with the most recent item on top, subject to the *kind* of item. The rules that control the stacking order of various kinds of items are simple:

✦ Within a layer, ungrouped primitive shapes or lines are always at the *bottom* level, with the most recently drawn shape or line at the top of that layer's stack. Furthermore, unless you take precautions, drawn items either compound with, or cut into, the drawing beneath them.

✦ Groups, Drawing Objects, and symbols (including bitmaps) stack above lines and shapes in the *overlay* level. To change the stacking order of several items, it's often advisable to group them first, as we describe in the next section of this chapter.

To change the stacking order within a layer, first select the item that you want to move. Then, do one of the following:

✦ **To move the item to the top of the stacking order,** choose Modify ➪ Arrange ➪ Bring to Front (Alt+Shift+↑ or Option+Shift+↑).

✦ **To move an item to the bottom of the stacking order,** choose Modify ➪ Arrange ➪ Send to Back (Alt+Shift+↓ or Option+Shift+↓).

✦ **To move the item up one position in the stacking order,** choose Modify ➪ Arrange ➪ Bring Forward (Ctrl+↑ or ⌘+↑).

✦ **To move the item down one position in the stacking order,** choose Modify ➪ Arrange ➪ Send Backward (Ctrl+↓ or ⌘+↓).

Remember the stacking-order rules: You won't be able to bring an ungrouped drawing above a group or symbol — if you need that drawing on top, group it and then move it, or place it on a separate layer.

Cross-Reference
We detail the Align panel (Ctrl+K or ⌘+K) used to distribute items in a layout in relation to each other or to the Stage in Chapter 5, "Drawing in Flash."

To stack an item in a lower layer above an item in a higher layer, you simply change the order of the layer among the other layers: First, activate the layer, then drag the Layer bar to the desired position in the layer stack of the Timeline.

Tip
Regardless of the number of layers in a Flash project (.fla), neither the file size nor the performance of the final .swf file will be adversely impacted because Flash flattens layers upon export.

Grouping

As we discussed in Chapter 5, "Drawing in Flash," grouping shapes or lines makes them easier to handle. Rather than manipulating a single item, group several items to work with them as a single unit. Grouping also prevents shapes from being merged with or cropped by other shapes. In addition, it's easier to control the stacking order of groups than ungrouped drawings. Here's how to create groups:

1. Use Shift+click to select multiple items or drag a selection box around everything that you want to group. This can include any combination of items: shapes, lines, and symbols — even other groups.

2. Choose Modify ➪ Group (Ctrl+G or ⌘+G). The selected elements are now grouped.

3. To ungroup everything, select the group and then use Modify ➪ Ungroup (Ctrl+Shift+G or ⌘+Shift+G). Ungrouping will only separate grouped items; it will not break apart bitmaps, symbol instances, or text as the Break apart command does.

Caution
Be careful when ungrouping. Your newly ungrouped drawings may alter or eliminate drawings below in the same layer.

To edit a group:

1. Select the group and then choose Edit ➪ Edit Selected, or double-click the group. Everything on Stage — except for items in the group — is dimmed, indicating that only the group is editable.

2. Make changes in the same way you would edit individual primitive shapes or symbols. If there are other groups or symbols included in a larger group, you'll have to click-in deeper to edit those items. You can keep double-clicking on compound groups to gradually move inside to the deepest level or primitive shape available for editing. You can use the location labels to move back out level by level (or double-click an empty area of the Stage), or go to Step 3 to return to the Main Timeline.

3. To stop editing the group, choose Edit ➪ Edit All, or use the location labels to return to the main scene. Other items on Stage return to normal color.

Applying Break apart

The Modify ➪ Break apart command (Ctrl+B or ⌘+B) is rather like an Undo command for groups, Drawing Objects, and symbols as well as a deconstruction tool for text and bitmaps. To use Break apart, simply select an item and then apply the command. Occasionally you will need to apply the Break apart command more than once to reduce a compound group to its core primitive shapes. When applied to a symbol instance, Break apart reduces the instance to primitive shapes that no longer are linked to the original symbol stored in the Library.

Caution   Breaking apart is not entirely reversible; when applied to an animated symbol instance, it will discard all but the current frame of the symbol instance Timeline.

Breaking apart text

When text is reduced to shapes using Break apart, it can be filled with gradients and bitmaps and also modified with the shape Transform options. We show specific examples of using the Break apart command in Chapter 8, "Working with Text," and in Chapter 16, "Importing Artwork." Figure 9-28 illustrates how text is broken apart in two stages, so that the original block (left) is first separated into individual letters (center), and then when broken apart a second time, it is reduced to shapes (right).

Break Break Break

Figure 9-28: A text field (left) broken apart once (center) and then once again (right)

Caution   It is not recommended to break apart symbols or groups that are included in a tweened animation because the results may be unpredictable and not easy to undo. Breaking apart complex symbols or large text blocks can also add to the file size of your final movie.

Creating Metallic Type

To demonstrate how text characters can be modified after they've been converted to shapes, we have applied some gradient fills to create the illusion of shiny metal letters. The file for this effect is titled `metalType.fla` and is included in the `ch09` folder of the CD-ROM. Start with a document that has a dark gray background.

1. First type a word or words on the Stage to create a text block. This effect works best if applied to a bold, sans serif font at a fairly large point size. We used Verdana bold set at 50 pt.

2. Select the text block and apply the Break apart command (Ctrl+B or ⌘+B) once to break the text block into individual letters, and then a second time to convert the letters into shapes.

3. With the letter shapes still selected, load a default grayscale linear gradient into the Color Mixer panel and then adjust it so the gradient is dark at each end with a highlight in the center. Set the left and far right Color pointers to black (#000000) and then add a new Color pointer in the center of the Edit bar and set it to white (#FFFFFF), as shown in Figure 9-29.

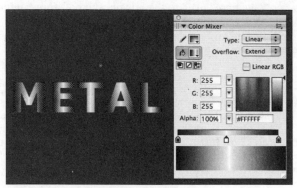

Figure 9-29: Text shapes selected and filled with a custom linear gradient created in the Mixer panel

4. Next use the Fill Transform tool to rotate the gradient fill clockwise to a 45-degree angle in each letter shape. You may also scale each fill slightly or adjust individual center points to align the highlight on each letter, as shown in Figure 9-30.

Figure 9-30: Linear gradients aligned in each letter shape with the Fill Transform tool

5. Now to create a more three-dimensional look, make a copy of all the letter shapes in a new layer below the current layer. Use the Copy (Ctrl+C or ⌘+C) and Paste (Ctrl+V or ⌘+V) commands. Turn the visibility of the original layer off (click the Eye icon) for now, so you can see only the copied letter shapes.

6. Select all the copied letter shapes, and using the Color Mixer panel, reverse the gradient fill colors. Set the center Color pointer to black and both end Color pointers to white, as shown in Figure 9-31.

7. Next, use the Modify ⇨ Shape ⇨ Expand Fill command to expand the fill in all the selected letters by 2 pixels.

8. If you turn the visibility of both layers back on, you should see that you now have two opposing gradient fills and the copied letter shapes are slightly larger than the original letter shapes. Figure 9-32 compares the letters with the original gradient and the letters with the modified gradient.

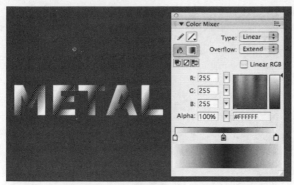

Figure 9-31: Copied letter shapes on a new layer with reversed gradient fill applied

Figure 9-32: Original letter shapes with gradient fill (top) and copied letter shapes with reversed and expanded gradient fill (bottom)

9. Select all the copied letter shapes on the lower layer and drag them behind the original letter shapes so that they're aligned just slightly above and to the right of the original shapes. This creates the illusion of a metallic beveled edge on the original letter shapes, as shown in Figure 9-33.

Figure 9-33: Copied letter shapes aligned behind the original letter shapes to create the illusion of a beveled metallic edge

Breaking apart bitmaps

When applied to bitmaps placed in the Document window, Break apart will make it possible to select the bitmap image with the Eyedropper tool to apply as a fill to other shapes. This is not the same as tracing a bitmap, which reduces the vast number of colors in a bitmap to areas of solid color and converts it to vector format, as we describe in the section that follows. Figure 9-34 shows an imported bitmap placed on the Stage and sampled with the Eyedropper tool to create a colored fill in the rectangle below (left) compared to the same bitmap broken apart and sampled with the Eyedropper tool to create an image fill in the rectangle below (right).

Figure 9-34: A bitmap and the fill that results from sampling it with the Eyedropper tool when it is intact (left) and when it has been broken apart (right)

It isn't necessary to break apart bitmaps to use as fills because they can be specified with the Mixer panel, as we describe in Chapter 7, "Applying Color." But breaking apart bitmaps enables you to selectively edit them and also allows you to modify the visible area of the bitmap with the shape Transform options.

Caution   Although you can apply the Distort and Envelope modifiers of the Free Transform tool to a bitmap after it has been broken apart, they may not give you the result you expect. Instead of distorting or warping the actual bitmap image, you'll find that these modifiers reveal how Flash "sees" bitmap fills. The visible area of the bitmap is not really treated as a shape, but rather as a mask, or shaped window, that enables a certain part of the bitmap to be visible. You can distort or warp the viewable area, but the bitmap itself will not be modified, as it is when you apply the Rotate or Skew modifiers.

Figure 9-35 illustrates a bitmap that has been broken apart (left) so that colored areas in the background of the image can be selected with the Magic Wand option of the Lasso tool (center) and then deleted to leave the flower floating on the white Stage (right). You can clean up any stray areas of unwanted color using the Lasso tool or the Eraser tool.

About the Magic Wand option

You use the Magic Wand option of the Lasso tool (shown at the bottom of the Tools panel in Figure 9-35) to select ranges of a similar color in either a bitmap fill or a bitmap that's been broken apart. After you select areas of the bitmap, you can change their fill color or delete them, without affecting the Bitmap Swatch in the Mixer panel. You can adjust what pixels the Magic wand picks up by modifying the Threshold and Smoothing settings in the dialog box invoked by clicking the Magic wand settings button in the Options area of the Tools panel.

Magic Wand Threshold setting

The Threshold setting defines the breadth of adjacent color values that the Magic Wand includes in a selection. Values for the Threshold setting range from 0 to 200 — the higher the setting, the broader the selection of adjacent colors. Conversely, a smaller number results in the Magic Wand making a narrower selection of adjacent colors.

Figure 9-35: A bitmap broken apart and selectively deleted using the Magic Wand option of the Lasso tool

A value of zero results in a selection of contiguous pixels that are all the same color as the target pixel. With a value of 20, clicking a red target pixel with a value of 55 will select all contiguous pixels in a range of values extending from red 35 to red 75. (If you're familiar with Photoshop, it's important to note that the Flash Threshold is unlike Photoshop, in which a Threshold setting of 20 will select all contiguous pixels in a range of values extending from red 45 to red 65.)

Magic Wand Smoothing setting

The Smoothing setting of the Magic Wand option determines to what degree the edge of the selection should be smoothed. This is similar to anti-aliasing. (Anti-aliasing dithers the edges of shapes and lines so that they look smoother onscreen.) The options are Pixels, Rough, Normal, and Smooth. Assuming that the Threshold setting remains constant, the Smoothing settings will differ as follows:

✦ **Pixels:** Clings to the rectangular edges of each pixel bordering similar colors.

✦ **Rough:** With this setting, the edges of the selection are even more angular than with Pixels.

✦ **Normal:** Results in a selection that's somewhere between Rough and Smooth.

✦ **Smooth:** Delivers a selection with more rounded edges.

Tracing bitmaps

You use the Trace bitmap command to convert an imported image from a bitmap to a native Flash vector graphic with discrete, editable areas of color. This unlinks the image from the original symbol in the Library (and also from the Bitmap Swatch in the Color Mixer panel). It is possible to create interesting bitmap-based art with this command. However, if your intention is to preserve the look of the original bitmap with maximum fidelity, you will have to work with the settings — and you will most likely find that the original bitmap is actually smaller in file size than the traced vector image. Figure 9-36 includes a selected bitmap image on the left, and the final vector image that resulted from the settings shown in the Trace Bitmap dialog box on the right.

Figure 9-36: Select a bitmap (left) and choose settings in the Trace Bitmap dialog box to define the final vector image (right).

To trace a bitmap, follow these steps:

1. Use the Selection tool to select the bitmap that you want to trace—it can be in Edit mode or directly on the Stage.

2. Choose Modify ➪ Bitmap ➪ Trace Bitmap to invoke the Trace Bitmap dialog box and set the options according to your needs:

   - **Color threshold:** This option controls the number of colors in your traced bitmap. It limits the number of colors by averaging the colors based on the criteria chosen in Color threshold and Minimum area. Color threshold compares RGB color values of adjacent pixels to the value entered. If the difference is lower than the value entered, then adjacent pixels are considered the same color. By making this computation for each pixel within the bitmap, Flash averages the colors. A lower Color threshold delivers more colors in the final vector graphic derived from the traced bitmap. The range is between 0 and 500, with a default setting of 100.

   - **Minimum area:** This value is the radius, measured in pixels, which Color threshold uses to describe adjacent pixels when comparing pixels to determine what color to assign to the center pixel. The range is between 1 and 1,000, with the default setting being 8.

   - **Curve fit:** This value determines how smoothly outlines are drawn. Select Very Tight if the shapes in the bitmap are complex and angular. If the curves are smooth, select Very Smooth.

   - **Corner threshold:** This setting determines how sharp edges are handled; choose Many Corners to retain edges and Few Corners to smooth the edges.

3. Click OK. Flash traces the bitmap, and the original pixel information is converted to vector shapes. If the bitmap is complex, this may take a while. Depending on the settings you have chosen, the final look of the traced graphic can vary between being very close to the original or very abstracted.

Tip If your objective is for your traced bitmap to closely resemble the original bitmap, then set a low Color threshold and a low Minimum area. You'll also want to set the Curve fit to Pixels and the Corner threshold to Many Corners. Be aware that using these settings may drastically slow the tracing process for complex bitmaps and result in larger file sizes. If animated, such bitmaps may also retard the frame rate dramatically.

As shown in Figure 9-37, the traced bitmap can vary in how closely it resembles the original bitmap. The image in the center was traced with lower settings to achieve a more detailed image: Color threshold of 25, Minimum area of 2 pixels, Curve fit of Pixels, and Corner threshold of Many Corners. The image on the right was traced with higher settings to create a more abstract graphic image: Color threshold of 300, Minimum area of 25 pixels, Curve fit of Very Smooth, and Corner threshold of Few Corners.

Figure 9-37: Bitmap images can be traced to create different styles of vector graphics by using low settings (center) or high settings (right).

Caution If you drag a bitmap from the Library panel onto the Stage and then attempt to acquire the bitmap fill by first tracing the bitmap and then clicking with the Eyedropper tool, be careful of how selection affects the results. If the traced bitmap is still selected, clicking with the Eyedropper tool acquires the nearest color and replaces the entire traced bitmap with a solid fill of the acquired color. If the traced bitmap is not selected, the Eyedropper tool simply acquires the nearest solid color and loads it into the fill color chip.

Working with Drawing Objects and Combine Object Commands

Drawing Objects are a new hybrid graphic type that is introduced in Flash 8 to make the drawing environment a little more user-friendly. In older versions of Flash, you had to take special care to avoid unexpected results when shapes overlapped on the same layer (as we describe in the section that follows). There are times when compound shapes can be helpful, but most people will find it easier to work with Drawing Objects, and this option is enabled by default when you begin using any of the drawing or shape tools. If you turn the Object Drawing toggle off (in the Options area of the Tools panel) at anytime, it will remain off until you turn it back on. This makes it easy to draw in the mode that suits you best without having to remember to turn the toggle on or off all the time.

Tip   If you draw a shape with the Object Drawing toggle turned off and decide that you would prefer to work with a Drawing Object rather than a raw shape, simply select the shape and use the Modify ⇨ Combine Objects ⇨ Union command to convert the shape into a Drawing Object. Conversely, Drawing Objects can be reverted to raw shapes by using the Modify ⇨ Ungroup or the Modify ⇨ Break Apart command.

In the simplest terms, Drawing Objects are containers for raw shapes. They cannot hold animation (like symbols can) or even other Drawing Objects. If you try to add a Drawing Object to the Stage when you have another Drawing Object open in Edit mode, you will see a warning dialog box when you return to the Main Timeline. As shown in Figure 9-38, Flash will automatically convert the original Drawing Object into a group so that the new Drawing Object can be nested inside it.

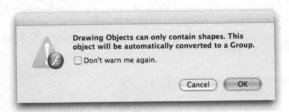

Figure 9-38: Drawing Objects cannot contain animation, symbols, or other Drawing Objects—they are intended as holders for raw shapes only.

If you have worked in Flash before, you may be wondering why you would even bother to use a Drawing Object rather than just using a simple group to manage raw shapes. Like groups, Drawing Objects do not show up in the document Library and they cannot have Filters applied to them. However, unlike groups, you can modify Drawing Objects without having to open them in Edit mode, and they can be Motion tweened. Another key reason to use Drawing Objects is to take advantage of the new Combine Objects commands (as shown in Figure 9-39). These commands will be familiar to anyone who has used the Pathfinder panel in Illustrator:

Union: Merges the selected objects into one combined object

Intersect: Deletes everything except the area of the topmost object where it overlapped the lower objects

Punch: Deletes the topmost object and punches out the area where it overlapped other objects

Crop: Deletes everything except the areas of the lower objects where the upper object overlapped

Figure 9-39: Two Drawing Objects (far left) combined using various Combine Objects commands to get different final results (from left to right): Union, Intersect, Punch, Crop.

There are only a few other things to keep in mind when working with Drawing Objects:

✦ You can modify Drawing Objects with the Selection and Transformation tools in the same way as raw shapes, but you will not be able to select the Fill and Stroke inside a Drawing Object individually unless you open it in Edit mode.

✦ You can change the appearance of the fill and stroke separately just by selecting the object and using any of the swatches menus, but if you try to apply the Expand Fill command to a Drawing Object that contains a stroke, you will see the stroke disappear unless you have ungrouped or broken apart (into raw shapes) the Drawing Object or opened it in Edit mode.

✦ The selection highlight for Drawing Objects and groups selected on the Stage look exactly alike, but you can tell what type of item you are working with by checking the item description in the Property inspector. Groups and Drawing Objects share some characteristics, but they are *not* the same thing.

✦ The Lock Fill option doesn't work with Drawing Objects in the same way that it works with other filled shapes. Although you can use the Lock Fill command to create a fill that visually continues from one object to another, you will find when you try to apply the Gradient Transform tool that you have to adjust the fills individually for each object.

Working with Compound Shapes

If you used older versions of Flash or you have been drawing and modifying artwork in Flash 8 with the Object Drawing option turned off, you've probably noticed that Flash has a unique way of handling lines and fills that reside on the same layer of your document. Items that are the same color merge, whereas items that are a different color replace or cut out other items where they overlap. Flash treats lines or strokes as separate items than fills, so these can be selected and moved or modified independently of each other, even if they are the same color. Figure 9-40 shows how Flash allows lines and fills to be selected individually, even if they are the same color.

Figure 9-40: A gray oval fill with a gray stroke may not appear to have a discrete outline, but Flash allows these two elements to be selected separately.

Tip   By double-clicking an element, you can select all the related segments. This works for selecting the stroke and fill of a shape or for selecting connected sections of a segmented line (such as the four sides of a rectangle).

Both lines and fills are divided into segments at points of intersection. Figure 9-41 shows a fill split into two independent shapes by drawing a line on top of it (top) or modified by merging with a fill of the same color and being cut out by a fill of a different color (bottom).

Figure 9-41: A fill split by an overlapping line drawn on the same layer (top). Two fills of the same color merge into a compound shape when they intersect on the same layer (bottom).

These behaviors can be destructive or helpful to your artwork, depending on how you manage individual elements. The key point to remember is that primitive shapes cannot be overlapped on the same layer while deselected without affecting each other. If items are grouped or converted into Drawing objects or symbols, they remain independent and will not be compounded or deleted by intersection with other items. Items on layers are also autonomous and will not merge with or erase items that exist on other layers.

You can move lines or fills over other primitive shapes without affecting them, as long as they remain selected — as soon as they are deselected, they will intersect or merge with adjacent primitive shapes on the same layer. Figure 9-42 illustrates the process of moving a selected shape over and then off of another shape while keeping the two shapes independent (top), and the result if the shape is deselected while it is overlapping another shape, before being reselected and moved, to create a compound shape (bottom).

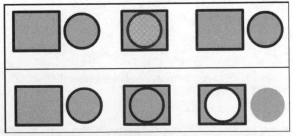

Figure 9-42: A shape moved across another shape while being continuously selected (top) compared to a shape that is deselected while on top of another shape, and then reselected and moved (bottom)

Editing with Find and Replace

Although you can use the Movie Explorer to search for some elements in a project file so that they can be modified, it doesn't automate updates in the same speedy way that the Find and Replace panel, shown in Figure 9-43, does.

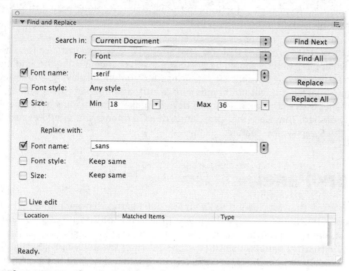

Figure 9-43: The Find and Replace panel makes revisions so easy, they're almost fun.

Note   Although the Find and Replace item in the Edit window does invoke a real panel and not just a dialog box, it is not included with the other panels listed in the Window menu. The logic for this is not exactly clear, but we can guess that Macromedia believed it would be more intuitive to find it in the Edit menu. Although the Find and Replace panel takes up a lot of room on your desktop, you could dock it with other panels for quick access if you prefer that to using the menu or shortcut keys.

If you have used the Find and Replace feature in any other application (even in a basic text-editing program), you will be familiar with the main buttons in the Find and Replace panel (Find Next, Find All, Replace, and Replace All). Open the Find and Replace panel by choosing Edit ➪ Find and Replace in the application menu (Ctrl+F or ⌘+F). The real benefits of this Flash MX 2004 addition to the authoring environment become clearer when you look at the items you can select to search for; these include

- ✦ **Text:** Search for words, partial words, or whole paragraphs in text fields, frames, layers, parameters, strings, or in ActionScript in your current project or current scene.

- ✦ **Font:** Search for fonts by name, style, and even size, within your current project or scene.

- ✦ **Color:** Pick a color from the pop-up swatches (or enter a hexadecimal value in the field) to search for fills, strokes, or text where a specific color is used in the current project or scene.

✦ **Symbol/Sound/Video/Bitmap:** Use the handy drop-down list that lists all symbols (or sounds, or video, or bitmaps) used in your current project to pick a symbol to search for and a symbol to use as a replacement.

As you select each item in the For: drop-down list, options relevant to that item become available in the panel. These options give you very precise control over the type of edits that you want to make. Now that replacing a color or font, or even a specific word in your entire project file, is as easy as making a few quick selections in the Find and Replace panel, those dreaded last-minute revisions might almost seem fun.

Caution

Although any effects or transformations that you have applied to a symbol instance (and any formatting you have applied to text) should be preserved if you change it using the Find and Replace panel, you will have to verify that the newly inserted content displays as you expect it to. If a font is much larger, it might not fit into your layout, or if a replacement bitmap is much larger or smaller than the original, you may have to make some manual adjustments to get everything polished. These are the same kinds of adjustments you would expect to make if you used the Swap symbol feature.

Using the History Panel

Another long-awaited feature that was added to Flash MX 2004 is the History panel (Ctrl+F10 or ⌘+F10), which makes it possible to escape the linear limitations of Undo/Redo. As you work in your project file, the History panel records your editing steps in a sequential list (refer to Figure 9-44). The History panel only stores steps taken in the active project file during the current editing session. It does not store steps from the last time you had a project file open or from other files edited during the same session. You *can* save and move steps from one file or session to another, but it requires you to use some of the special features of the History panel, described later in this section.

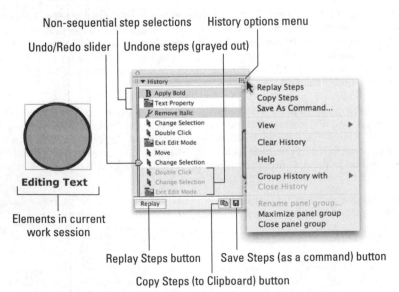

Figure 9-44: The History panel lists steps taken as a file is authored or edited.

New Feature Flash 8 gives you the option of using the Flash MX 2004–style Document-level Undo (which creates one History/Undo stack for all the items in a current session) or the Flash MX and older legacy-style Object-level Undo (which creates a unique History/Undo stack for key editing areas of the Flash authoring environment: Stage, Movie Clip timelines, and the ActionScript panel). The default is set to Document-level Undo, but if you find it helpful to be able to step back through Movie Clip edits individually, you can change this setting in the General section of Flash Preferences. To access the object-level Undo stack, you must open a Movie Clip (not an instance) in Edit mode.

Caution Making changes to your Undo style or number of saved steps in Flash Preferences will clear the History panel — deleting all the Undo steps for your current session.

You can use the History panel as a reminder of the steps taken to create a special graphic effect, or you can use it as a nonlinear authoring control. Should you need to get back to a specific step in your authoring session, you can use Undo (Ctrl+Z or ⌘+Z) over and over and over . . . or you can simply open the History panel and drag the edit pointer on the left side of the panel upwards to go back in time until you reach the point at which you want to jump back into authoring. As long as you don't make any edits at an earlier point in the History list, you can easily scroll forward again if you need to Redo your steps — without wearing out the Ctrl+Y or ⌘+Y keys! However, if you Undo a step (or a series of steps) and then make changes to your project file, you can no longer redo the steps in the History panel. This is where the History panel does behave a little like a time machine — as long as you don't change anything, you can jump backward and forward in time, but as soon as you change something, you lose the option of going "back to the future."

Tip Click to the left of a step in the History panel to jump to that point without scrolling. All steps listed after the point that you click will be undone and grayed out until you scroll forward again (or click to the left of an item closer to the bottom of the list).

The options menu and the buttons along the bottom of the History panel are the keys to the more advanced editing tasks that you can accomplish when you take your steps a step further. (Refer to Figure 9-44 for callouts on the location of History panel controls.)

Replay Steps

The Replay Steps control will repeat or reapply a series of sequential or nonsequential steps in your current History list.

1. Select sequential items by dragging or by Shift+clicking the text labels in the list. Select nonsequential items by Ctrl+clicking (⌘+clicking on Mac).

2. With a step (or series of steps) selected, you can apply the step(s) to a new item — by selecting the item with the Selection tool and clicking the Replay button or choosing Replay Steps from the options menu.

All currently selected steps will be applied (in order) to the item, and a new step labeled "Replay Steps" will be listed in the History panel. You can use the Replay Steps item in the History list to apply the same steps again without having to select the original steps individually.

Copy Steps

This command makes it possible to move steps from one document to another. Here's how it works:

1. Select steps from your History panel list (as we described in the previous section).

2. Choose Copy Steps from the options menu.

3. In the Flash document where you want to reuse the steps, select an item that you want to apply the steps to.

4. Use Edit ⇨ Paste in Center (Ctrl+V or ⌘+V).

The editing steps copied from your original file will be applied to the item in your current file and a new item will be added to the History panel, labeled Paste Steps.

Clear History

This is a helpful command to use if you want to start from a clean slate before performing a series of editing steps that you plan to save. Clear History deletes all the listings in the History panel of your current document. You can't undo this choice, but you will see a Warning dialog box (see Figure 9-45) that gives you the chance to change your mind before it's too late. (Closing a Flash document will also clear the History list.) The number of steps listed in the History panel can be limited by the *Undo levels* set in the General Flash Preferences dialog box. The default setting is 100, but it can be set as high as 300. Every item recorded in the History panel eats up some memory and disk space, so choose the lowest setting that suits your authoring style.

Figure 9-45: The Warning dialog box that appears before the History list is cleared

History View

You want to leave this setting on Default unless you plan to use the History panel as a tool for helping you write new JavaScript commands. This is a very exciting potential use of the History panel, but it is beyond the scope of this book. If you are familiar with JavaScript, you can try different View settings to get more information that helps you to deconstruct the steps in an editing workflow.

Save As Command

If you're not quite ready to start writing your own JavaScript from scratch, this is a terrific shortcut that makes it easy to save and reuse custom editing workflows.

1. Select the step(s) from the History panel that you want to save and reuse.

2. Choose Save As Command from the options menu (or click the small disk icon at the bottom right of the History panel).

3. In the Save as Command dialog box, give the command a meaningful name—you might call the steps used to create a fancy custom type treatment "Headline style."

4. By the magic of Flash, your custom command now appears in the Command menu list.

5. You can apply your specific editing steps in any document by selecting an item and choosing Commands ➪ Headline style (or whatever commands you have created and named).

The options at the top of the application Command menu give you some controls for managing your custom commands and for using commands from other sources. The Get More Commands menu item loads a link to the Macromedia Exchange, where you can find new commands contributed by other Flash developers (look for .jsfl files). If you download a custom command script, you can use the Run Command menu option to browse to the .jsfl file and apply it to an item in your current project. The possibilities are wide open.

We'd like to know what you think about this chapter. Visit `www.flashsupport.com/feedback` to fill out an online form with your comments.

Summary

✦ After you've mastered the basic drawing tools in Flash, there are innumerable methods for modifying artwork to create custom effects.

✦ You can use the Eyedropper, Ink Bottle, and Paint Bucket tools together to select and apply fill and stroke styles to multiple items or to swap styles between items.

✦ You can use the Gradient Transform tool to modify gradient fills and bitmap fills for precise alignment and appearance inside individual shapes.

✦ Flash 8 introduces a new graphic type called a Drawing Object. Drawing Objects share some characteristics with raw shapes, groups, and symbols, but they have a unique role in Flash authoring.

✦ Drawing Objects, like groups or symbols, do not interact when they overlap on the same layer. If you wish to merge or crop Drawing Objects, the new Combine Objects commands provide some options that will be familiar to people who have used pathfinder options in other vector drawing programs.

✦ The Free Transform tool has two powerful options that you can apply to shapes or Drawing Objects only, as well as two options that restrict the Free Transform behavior to make it easier to achieve specific tasks.

✦ Flash organizes artwork with specific parameters, and you can use the Modify ➪ Arrange commands to help define the stacking order when you're working with similar items on the same layer.

✦ You can use the Break apart command to convert bitmaps and text so you can edit them like shapes to create special effects.

✦ You use the Trace bitmap command to convert imported bitmaps into vector graphics with varying degrees of detail.

✦ ✦ ✦

Creating Animation and Effects

Now that you're comfortable with the Flash tools and making static graphic symbols and groups, it's time to move on to creating animated elements and dynamic effects. Chapter 10 introduces some of the fundamental production and planning issues that you need to consider when designing animated elements. Chapter 11 will give you all the information you need to start working with time-based content. Learn to create frame-by-frame and tweened animation and how to use Movie Clips to control display of content on multiple timelines. Chapter 12 is dedicated to introducing the creative possibilities of Timeline Effects, Color Effect properties, and the new filters and blend modes in Flash 8. Chapter 13 introduces the various layer tools that will make your production easier and allow you to add masks and guides. If you are interested in character animation, Chapter 14 provides comprehensive coverage of character animation and the tricks that professional animators use to create engaging and optimized cartoons that can go beyond the Web.

Animation Strategies

Have you ever wondered what makes some animation so compelling and other animation so dull? Regardless of the content of a site, or even the style of the site's graphics, some animation is engaging, whereas other animation is annoying or even pathetic — we've all seen it, limping or flashing across our screens at one time or another.

Of course, your response to animation is partly determined by what you're expecting from an interface (sometimes you want diversion, and other times you want to find information — fast!). Most designers are aware of the issues of usability and relevance they should consider when adding animation to an interface (whether they decide to ignore them or not). But, what happens after you've done all your audience research and content planning and you decide that animation would be appropriate for your project?

The next step should be fun, right? Unfortunately, unless you have the privilege of working with a skilled animator, you're actually entering one of the most complex and challenging areas of visual design. Although most people recognize "good" animation when they see it, the leap from *appreciating* motion to *designing* motion is difficult, even for people who have natural aptitude.

The good news is that you possess an innate understanding of physics, even if you've never taken a science class in your life — you know what to expect when you bounce a ball. But can you interpret the ball's motion and re-create it frame-by-frame in an animation? The challenge of designing motion is translating daily experiences into a time-based, 2D environment. Your eyes and brain will tell you if something isn't right, but how do you know what can be done to correct it? The ability to analyze perceptions that we normally take for granted is the true skill of animation and motion graphics design.

With experience, animators can intuitively finesse the many visual factors that effectively communicate motion — even bending the rules to suit their personal animation styles or to convey specific atmospheres and characters. But, the first step toward making better animation is to become familiar with some of the fundamental concepts and laws that govern matter in the real world.

Establishing Ground Rules

No matter what the style or purpose your animation ultimately has, you'll need to establish guidelines for yourself if you want to create an engaging and convincing experience for the user. This may feel limiting at first, but these self-imposed ground rules make content more meaningful to your audience. The most commonly recognized example of structured, shared expression is music. Even the wildest music is based on an underlying structure of notes and timing (or else it isn't exactly music).

Structure is also one of the key characteristics that shapes great books or even movies. Consider the difference between a private journal and a well-crafted story, or the difference between a home movie and an engrossing film. This doesn't mean that you're stuck repeating the same old narrative over and over again or that you have to follow someone else's rules. But if you have free license to create any experience for your audience, it's even more important to decide on the rules that will guide your designs so that all the elements and animations support your idea.

Artists who prefer not to follow the most commonly used conventions must work even harder to establish their own signature style — or to create content defined by the consistent choices they make. As in music, the possible choices for the basic aspects of animation are practically infinite — a little faster, a little slower, spinning or bouncing or wiggling or jumping or fading or . . . you get the idea. The guidelines that you establish for each project help you make the right decisions. There isn't an exact formula for "good animation" (the variables are too broad), but once you create some rules for yourself, you'll be able to make the choices that best support your goals for a specific animation.

Defining Variables

To establish guidelines that support your design process, you first have to analyze the choices that are relevant to the content. Is the tone of the project peaceful, quiet, fast, slick, funny, scary? Try to be as specific as you can about the approach that best suits your content. Then try to make consistent choices that support that description. Some of the questions that may help you to frame the basic elements of your project include

> What kind of motion suits the style of the project or personality of a character?
>
> How does color communicate your theme or idea?
>
> How does sound support the atmosphere or character?

If you try to make a design that is "all of the above," it will end up being too vague and confusing to keep anyone interested. One of the hardest things to learn as a designer (and to communicate to clients) is that if you try to make a site (or story) that is a little bit of everything, in an attempt to suit all audiences, you'll only weaken your message and your branding, and/or dilute the experience for everyone. The very best designs are consistent enough that they allow anyone to understand them (or at least get what they're about), and specific enough in style that they have a memorable personality and attitude.

Of course, there are some things that do appeal to many people — humor or surprise, well-executed visual complexity, engaging and functional navigation. But even these elements can be too generic; they need to be added to your design with a specific (and hopefully original) style. After you've decided what style is appropriate for the project, you can begin to plan the elements that will create the experience for the audience.

Considering these factors for every project may seem like over-thinking, but try to see how often you can apply at least some of the questions we outline in this section to really focus your design strategy. After a few tries, it should be much easier, and you'll be on your way to establishing a personal style that you can adapt to different projects.

The environment

What planet are you on? As you begin planning and building a virtual environment, even in a 2D space, thinking of it as a real place is helpful. Decide what kind of place you want it to be and what characteristics will help the audience to understand where they are.

Is this a soft, fuzzy world where everything floats gently as it moves, or is this a hard, metallic world where things are heavy and make fast, abrupt movements, or maybe it is even a liquid world where things are very smooth and quiet, with organic movement? These are extreme examples; obviously, the possibilities are endless. Try to include all the factors that define an environment as you experience it visually:

How light or dark is it?

Is everything very distinct or blurred and layered?

How crowded or open is the space?

How quickly can things move?

How much does gravity affect objects?

Is space (depth) limited or endless?

The main thing to keep in mind is that all the elements and movement that you add to the design should help the audience locate themselves in the world you've created. Aside from natural environmental analogies, try to consider historical and cultural context, too. Is the environment meant to have a retro feel or a post-modern feel? Is it influenced by multicultural elements, or defined only by a very specific subculture?

If you find yourself thinking, "Well, all I really want is to make a cool site that the audience will like," then remember the point we made previously: The more specific you can be about the kind of environment you want to create, the better chance you have of making a design that the audience will be interested in. Most of us are pretty jaded viewers by now, and something that looks trendy or resembles a jumble of many other things we've seen before is not likely to hold our attention very long.

The materials

As you consider the overall environment that you want to create, you also have to decide on the smaller details that will be consistent with your idea. Even if you're working purely with Flash strokes and fills, trying to imagine the kinds of materials that would be most appropriate for your graphic elements can be helpful. Do you want elements to be jagged and hard or fuzzy or squishy? How much volume do shapes or graphic elements have? Are any of the items transparent? Considering these questions will help you to make decisions about line styles and perhaps even colors, but most important, these decisions will help you to design motion that will be convincing and appropriate for each item.

If your materials are soft, motion will include a lot of stretching and squashing and maybe even jiggling. If you want materials to seem hard, motion will probably be smoother, with sharper, cleaner transitions. If objects are heavy, they will have a lot more inertia. If objects are very light, they will need to move in a way that conveys weightlessness. Some of these types of motion are hard to describe, but if you can visualize them clearly (or even better, find examples in real life), you'll have an easier time planning and making your animation.

Even if you decide that your "materials" are actually best kept very flat and graphic (such as construction paper or felt cutouts), then you can focus on that kind of look and avoid throwing in gradient fills or shiny highlights. The most important thing is to simply have a clear concept in mind that enables you to make (and explain) the design choices that best support your content.

The motion

Choosing to add animation to an item can be a quick decision, but finding the right kind of motion to add can take a lot more time. If you've made some of the decisions we suggested so far in this chapter, then you'll have a much easier time narrowing down the style of motion that you want to add.

Flash provides some great options for controlling the speed and pattern of motion, but until you have a clear "flight path" mapped out, you won't be able to use these tools effectively. There are few things worse than spending a lot of time creating an animation, only to realize that the motion lacks personality or seems meaningless. Most ineffective animation is the result of poor planning. This is one area of design where endless options can work against you. It can be fun, and helpful for learning, to play with different kinds of movement in Flash, but this isn't the best way to develop a project, unless you're already an experienced animator. "Designing" animation by simply throwing together some random tweens and timeline effects is the visual equivalent of whistling tunelessly or absentmindedly strumming a guitar—entertaining for the person doing it, very annoying for everyone else!

Although experienced animators develop an intuitive sense of timing and rhythm, designers who are just starting to experiment with motion will have a better chance of success if they have a very specific example to refer to. References for animation (or styles of movement) can be found almost anywhere in the real world—you just have to observe carefully, and, if possible, document the motion with video or a sequence of stills. Often, the documentation will surprise you. It wasn't until cameras were used to photograph sequences of horses running that artists realized there were moments during their trot cycles that all four hooves were off the ground.

These are some resources that we have found inspiring as motion references:

✦ **Eadweard Muybridge:** Eadweard Muybridge is a photographer who did some of the first "stop-motion" images ever made. His classic photographic sequences can be found in books published in the Dover Pictorial Archive Series (Dover Publications). The California Museum of Photography provides some background for and examples of Muybridge's work on its Web site: http://photo.ucr.edu/photographers/muybridge/contents.html

✦ **Lawrence Jordan:** Lawrence Jordan created strange and wonderful animated films using cutout graphics and stop-frame animation. In his 40-year career, he produced a body of work that has been influential for many artists working in new media. You can learn more about him in an essay in the *Bright Lights Film Journal* at www.brightlightsfilm.com/30/lawrencejordan.html.

✦ **Bruce Conner:** Bruce Conner is a visionary and groundbreaking artist who works in a variety of mediums. He was honored with an exhibit at the Walker Art Center in 1999–2000, and it has produced the most comprehensive catalogue on his work to date. You can find out more about Bruce Conner on the Walker Art Center Web site at www.walkerart.org/programs/vaexhibconner.html.

If you are interested in seeing work by Bruce Conner and other influential experimental film-makers on DVD, a good source is Canyon Cinema: `http://canyoncinema.com`.

✦ **Erik Natzke:** If you haven't heard of Erik Natzke, then you are in for a treat. This Flash hero has been using Flash to make things move in beautiful ways since way back in Flash 5. He continues to do great work and is generous enough to keep an archive of experiments online at `www.natzke.com/2002.html`. The examples are mainly scripted, dynamic motion rather than timeline-based animation, but they demonstrate the special characteristic of dynamic motion designed in and driven by Flash.

Of course, you probably also have examples in mind of animation that you've seen and admired. Looking at other animators' work can be a great way to analyze "how it's done," but you should always aspire to develop a unique style rather than to copy someone else's directly. The history of animation is rich and full of many examples of diverse styles that have been effective. By looking back at the work done by great animators and filmmakers, you're likely to find something that will inspire you and offer new possibilities for the ways that you can render images and motion on a 2D screen.

Adding Personality

As many great animations have shown, any object can be given its own personality. No medium is really quite as effective as animation for enabling you to give life to the characters that would otherwise stay in your imagination. Even if you don't aspire to be a character animator in the strictest sense, any element that is animated within your Flash projects should have some recognizable personality. You don't have to add eyes and a mouth to an object in order for it to be expressive. In fact, the main expression of any animated element should be conveyed by the way it moves, even more strongly than by the exact composition of the graphic.

You can add personality to a line or a letter as easily as you can add personality to a cartoon character. A common exercise done in art schools to help students realize the expressive power of abstract lines and shapes is to give the students a list of atmospheres or emotions that they have to interpret and communicate with purely abstract lines and forms. The most surprising thing about this exercise is how similar most people's drawings turn out to be. Although the drawings do not include any concrete symbols or signs, students realize how concise their shared visual language really is (even if they aren't always conscious of it).

As an animator, you can draw on the common visual vocabulary to communicate a great deal to your audience without having to spell it out. Most people would probably recognize angry movement or joyous movement if they saw it. Certainly, some personal and cultural variations in interpretation exist, but the basic recognition is usually very consistent. As with some of the other topics we've described so far in this chapter, this is an aspect of motion design that may not seem relevant to every project at first. However, if you take the time to consider how you want to connect with your audience, you'll probably be able to pin down a fairly specific emotional tone or personality that you want your animation to have.

Flash animator Felix Stumpf describes his process for planning and creating atmospheric Flash animation in his tutorial in Chapter 14, "Character Animation Techniques." One of his tools for testing concepts is to create a moodboard with rough animation and sample music that he can then use as a stylistic guide for the final project.

The next step is to observe and experiment to find the kinds of motion that best represent the personality or tone that you want the audience to recognize. Some of the factors that you can consider when designing expressive motion include the following:

✦ **Speed:** How fast or how slowly does an object move? Does it accelerate or decelerate?

✦ **Timing and rhythm:** How does the object's movement loop or change over time? Finding music to help with the timing and pace of an animation is often helpful.

✦ **Consistency or irregularity:** How much variety is there in an object's movement? Does it follow a repeated pattern, or a random path of motion?

✦ **Anticipation or surprise:** Does the object give some visual foreshadowing as it moves, or does it make sudden, unexpected movements?

✦ **Freedom or constraint:** How large or small are the movements that the object can make? Does it move all around your composition or stay in a very restricted area? How much of the object moves at any one time?

The "meaning" of these various kinds of movement can be debated as much as the "meaning" of various colors can. However, it is safe to assume that, overall, enough consistency among viewers exists on the meaning of certain kinds of motion for it to be an effective way of communicating the character of an object. If you're not sure how your audience will read a certain motion, just test it out on a few people — show them what you're working on, and then ask them what emotion or personality *they* think the object has. If enough people recognize the mood that you want your animation to have, you've succeeded! If most people are confused or have very different responses, you probably need to simplify your animation and clarify what you're trying to communicate. It's not likely that most people would be able to read that an object has slightly low self-esteem but is feeling optimistic. However, most people recognize movement consistent with extreme shyness or joy (or any other simple and exaggerated emotion).

Exaggeration is the foundation of the art of animation. Define the kind of movement that may communicate a particular emotion to your audience, and then see how far you can push it. In some cases, you may want very overt movements, and in other cases, you may want more conservative or subtle movements; but by pushing the boundaries, you can assess your options and find the right balance for a particular character or object.

Keeping Ideas Fresh

Some of the greatest modern works of art and music are based on the concept of *permutation* — the process of exploring all the possibilities within a specific, usually limited, group of elements. Permutation of a limited set of options can yield more surprising or unique results than unlimited options because it forces you to work within defined boundaries that enable the content of your work to influence the final result in ways that you may not have previously considered.

For example, if you allow yourself to choose any colors from a full palette, this may seem very liberating. But the truth is, you'll probably choose colors (or at least color combinations) that are familiar or comfortable for you, without even giving some new options a real chance. You can achieve much more inventive uses of color by forcing yourself to work with a truly random selection of colors (or to create an effective design with a more limited palette). You might be surprised by how well pink and brown go together, or by how much you can do with just a few colors. At the very least, experimenting with randomness or intentional limitation in a design can help open up new possibilities and keep your work from getting stale.

Manipulating Perception and Illusion

As you spend time analyzing motion in the real world and motion in more stylized animations, you will become more aware of some of the tricks that your eyes can play on you. Animators, like magicians, know how to take advantage of people's often-unreliable perception to create illusions. By understanding how the audience's eyes and minds put visual information together to "see" things, clever performers and designers are able to convince the audience that they're seeing something that may not actually be happening.

Another interesting phenomenon that makes an animator's job a little easier is referred to as *suspension of disbelief.* This is something you participate in whenever you really *want to believe* you're seeing something—children are often the best at this. When you push doubt aside, your eyes can be very forgiving as your brain works even harder to compensate for any gaps that may spoil the illusion or the spectacle that you want to believe in.

Some visual tricks in animation have been used so consistently that people now expect them as conventions, instead of seeing them as poorly rendered versions of a real-life motion. Most people recognize that a swirling cyclone of lines, with hands and feet or other objects occasionally popping out of it, is usually a fight. The oval blur or circular scribble at the bottom of a character's legs is not a cloud, but, in fact, their feet spinning extra fast. Lines radiating from an object don't mean that it is spiky; instead, they can mean that it is shiny or hot or even smelly. (One old standby cartoon convention is a light bulb appearing over a character's head when she suddenly gets an idea.) Figure 10-1 shows a sequence by animator Richard Bazley that uses the simple but effective technique of blurred lines to simulate motion that is faster than the eye can see. This classic device can be modified to show rockets blasting off or wind rushing by or any object moving so quickly that it becomes a blur.

© 2002 Richard Bazley

Figure 10-1: Blurred lines in an animation effectively communicate the idea of wind or fast-moving elements rushing by.

On the CD-ROM

We have included .swf files for most of the examples we discuss in this chapter on the CD-ROM. Because the figures only show a few frames from an animation, you can get a better idea of how a motion plays by reviewing the files in the ch10 folder of the CD-ROM. We thank animators Richard Bazley, Tom Winkler, and Sandro Corsaro for kindly sharing some of their expert examples with us.

There are innumerable examples of cartoon tricks, but the main thing to keep in mind is that you don't have to draw every detail of a movement to make it convincing. Instead, it's better to find ways that you can exaggerate the motion to make it more *expressive*. A well-executed illusion will save you time drawing and will also make your animation more fun to watch.

Viewpoint, framing, and depth

By thinking of the Flash stage area as a camera viewfinder rather than as a sketch pad, you'll be able to start crafting the various scenes in your animation to have some of the same expressive qualities as shots from a well-edited film. The ability to manipulate the viewpoint is one of the strongest storytelling devices available to filmmakers and animators alike. Audiences have come to accept (and expect) seeing things from new angles and perspectives. Screen images have evolved from the basic wide-angle, theater-audience perspective of early film to the spin-ning, time-defying, 360-degree *Matrix* views of action—don't be afraid to push your "camera" beyond the limits of normal human perception. Choosing how you will frame animation can have as much of an effect on your audience as the actual content in each scene. The traditional bird's-eye or mouse's-eye reconsideration of viewpoint is as effective in a digital design as it is in sketches or drawings. Try to use your content to inspire a framing strategy that adds both interest and meaning to your designs.

Depth is another key element to consider when composing a scene and choosing a viewpoint. Traditional animators are cautious to avoid awkward line intersections caused by overlapping elements. When the lines from two different elements bump into each other unintention-ally, it can make a drawing look flat—this is known as a *tangent*. Tangents interrupt the illusion of depth created by scaling and layering elements in a composition. The main thing to avoid is an overly busy layout that may confuse the viewer's understanding of the picture plane. Try to keep elements that are meant to be behind or in front of other elements from looking as though they are joined or existing uncomfortably in the same space. Add a little more separation between elements to maintain visual clarity.

With careful planning, overlapping elements add depth to your designs. Notice in Figure 10-2 that overlapping the larger figure on the right with the border helps it jump into the fore-ground, whereas overlapping the smaller figure on the left makes it hard to tell which element is supposed to be in front.

Figure 10-2: Overlapping should be planned (as shown in the example on the right) to avoid tangents that may flatten out the depth of the composition (as shown on the left).

Another common device used to add depth to a scene is to choose a viewpoint that enables you to add a natural frame or border around the image. By giving viewers a reference point for where they are located in the plane of the image, you can exaggerate the feeling of depth. In drawing or painting, windows are often used to frame a view in the distance, but in animation, you can find more original frames by choosing unique viewpoints. In a scene from Richard Bazley's animated film *The Journal of Edwin Carp*, he uses the view from the back of a police van to add depth to a simple composition of two characters talking. Imagine how much flatter and less interesting the scene shown in Figure 10-3 would be if the characters were not framed by the outline of the van.

© 2002 Richard Bazley

Figure 10-3: By using a clever but logical framing device, Richard Bazley has added a great deal of depth to this animated scene.

In another scene, Bazley uses the convention of a character running into the camera to enhance the feeling of panic as Edwin Carp's mother runs down a hallway. As shown in Figure 10-4, by using an extreme viewpoint, Bazley makes a simple scene more humorous and dramatic while still being very efficient with his artwork.

© 2002 Richard Bazley

Figure 10-4: By using an extreme viewpoint, an otherwise simple Motion tween can add drama and humor to a scene.

Anticipation

Anticipation is one of the primary techniques used to give animation personality and life. If you haven't spent much time studying animation, it's easy to overlook, but animation without anticipation appears robotic. Anticipation communicates the organic tension that exists in real life motion. Visualize a baseball pitcher winding up before he throws a fastball. If the ball just flew out of his hand without his body first coiling back to gather force, you wouldn't have the visual information to understand that the force was transferred from the pitcher's body to the ball. It would appear that the ball just suddenly had the capability to fly on its own. Figure 10-5 shows a classic example of anticipation as a character gathers force before launching into a run.

Figure 10-5: By winding up before taking off in a run, a character communicates the urgency and force behind his movement.

The principle of anticipation can be used to add extra life to almost any motion. Picture how an element would gather force before jumping into the main movement, and then add a drawing or two to exaggerate that movement in your animation. Generally, anticipation can be communicated by reversing the main motion for a few frames before and after a tween (or frame-by-frame sequence). For example, if an item is going to move to the left, have it back up a little to the right first, and then after it stops moving to the left, have it stagger back a little to the right before reaching its final resting point. If an item is going to suddenly get larger, have it shrink just a little first before popping up to the larger size, and then allow the item to grow just a little beyond the final size so that it can appear to settle into the final size at the end of the animation. These inverted motions at the beginning and ending of an animated sequence are also referred to as *bounces,* because they can be compared to the motion of a ball bouncing. Depending on the effect you're trying to achieve, bounces can be very small and subtle or extremely exaggerated. Figure 10-6 illustrates how a small bounce can be added to give anticipation and follow-through to an animated head turn. This same kind of bounce works equally well on eye blinks and on almost any other small movement that needs a little extra life.

character designs © www.sandrocorsaro.com

Figure 10-6: Subtle bounces add anticipation and follow-through to head turns and other movements.

Although you may not at first be conscious of these extra movements when you watch a cartoon, it is one of the conventions that an audience associates with polished, professional animation. If you start to watch carefully for anticipation and follow-through motions, you'll see them on nearly every movement in well-crafted animations.

Secondary motion

Of course, some items don't need to bounce like a ball, but instead, should flap or float as they move. Though it's helpful to keep the pattern of a bounce in mind, the modified patterns that you apply to items to visually show the forces of acceleration or gravity in motion is called *overlapping action*. A single object or character can have multiple overlapping actions — overlapping action added to smaller details of an item are also called *secondary motion*. After you've planned the basic motion pattern of your main element, consider how you can add life and detail to your animation with overlapping action and secondary motion.

Figure 10-7 shows an example of an animation with overlapping action added to a character's belly as he runs. Secondary motion has been added by also animating the character's hat with overlapping action. The combination of these smaller motion patterns with the pattern of the basic run cycle makes the animation dynamic and gives the character personality.

Web Resource

Expert animator Richard Bazley provided suggestions for efficient and engaging animation in a tutorial he contributed to the *Macromedia Flash MX 2004 Bible* (Wiley, 2004). This tutorial is archived online for readers who wish to learn more about specialized animation techniques. Go to www.flashsupport.com/archive. One of the things you will notice about Bazley's work is that he often adds frame-by-frame secondary motion to make simple tweened animation more dynamic and lifelike.

Figure 10-7: Overlapping action and secondary motion add life and personality to animation.

Understanding the Laws of Nature

Depending on your learning style, you may find it easier to simply observe and copy patterns of movement or to analyze the underlying principles of force that cause these patterns. Either approach can be effective. Even if you're more of a visual person than a theory-oriented person (as many animators are), an overview of some of the basic principles of physics can help to give you a framework for understanding the limitless variations of animated motion. The stylized interpretations of movement found in motion graphics and cartoons often defy the laws of nature — that's what makes them so entertaining. However, if you don't know the basic physics that dictate motion in reality, it can be more difficult to extrapolate convincing motion to fantastic lengths.

Advanced interactive motion can be designed using physics formulas to define the behavior of objects controlled with ActionScript. Although the math may look a little bit intimidating at first, it's often easier to understand when you can get visual feedback on how the numbers directly affect motion patterns. In fact, more than a few top designers claim to be math-impaired, but the beauty of motion controlled by numbers has given them the incentive to learn (or relearn) some of those scary calculus and physics equations. Spending a little time polishing up your math skills can enable you to efficiently script realistic, organic motion that would be insanely time-consuming, or even impossible, to render manually. Even if you never intend to use ActionScript to define the patterns of motion in your animations, a basic understanding of how physics and math can be used to calculate motion makes it much easier to plot movement and plan your drawings. Math and physics, as with color and type, are a powerful part of the vocabulary of motion graphics. Regardless of how you choose to apply them, these principles can be helpful for planning and modifying animation.

Almost all animated motion can be analyzed or designed using Newton's Laws. If you sat through a science class in high school, these scientific descriptions of how objects interact with force will sound familiar. Of course, in animation you aren't required to obey these laws. In fact, you'll probably create more interesting animations by pushing these laws to the limits or even by inverting them to create objects with unexpected behavior.

Law #1: Inertia

Objects that are at rest will stay at rest, and objects in motion will stay in motion unless acted upon by an unbalanced force. In animation terms, objects should show a change in force if they're going to have a change in motion. This is communicated visually with anticipation and with overlapping actions, as we describe earlier in this chapter. Most animation seems much more lifelike with forgiving transitions. Enable objects to ease in and out of motion and to settle into new positions in your composition. Unless you want them to appear robotic, objects don't just change behavior suddenly without showing some anticipation and delayed secondary animation. You can add an element of surprise to an object's movement by intentionally disregarding inertia. For example, if an object stops cold without any visual indication of a change in force, it will appear jarring and hard, or if a very small object takes a long time to accelerate, it will seem hesitant.

Law #2: Acceleration

The acceleration of an object as produced by a net force is directly proportional to the magnitude of the net force, in the same direction as the net force, and inversely proportional to the mass of the object. In animation terms, speed is dependent on a combination of mass and force; increasing force increases speed, whereas increasing mass decreases speed. An important related concept is *terminal velocity*. Although most people have heard this term, not everyone can explain what it means. Basically, once an item is falling fast enough for air resistance to be strong enough to prevent gravity from increasing the speed, then it has reached terminal velocity or the maximum speed of its fall. Objects with greater mass take longer to reach terminal velocity so they accelerate for longer, generally hitting the ground while still accelerating. An object with less mass quickly reaches terminal velocity and appears to float to the ground, because it doesn't gain any more speed. Figure 10-8 shows an animation of the classic acceleration test — two objects dropped from the same height.

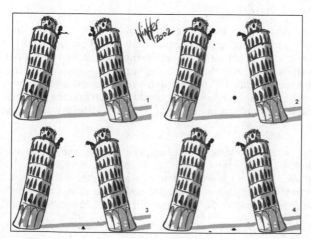

Figure 10-8: Acceleration is determined by mass, and objects with more mass take longer to reach terminal velocity.

By modifying the principles of acceleration, you can create whimsical environments where cannonballs might float and feathers crash to the ground (or any other variation you can think of).

Law #3: Action/reaction force pairs

This is the most commonly quoted of Newton's Laws: "For every action there is an equal and opposite reaction." Although this law is often used as a metaphor for human behavior, it was originally intended to explain how forces interact and affect objects. This is the law that explains how far backwards a character may fall when pulling on a rope that breaks. The force is directed along the rope and acts equally on objects at either end of the rope—the end result is that a character literally pushes himself backwards by pulling on the rope, as shown in Figure 10-9.

Figure 10-9: The force of pulling on a rope causes the character to fly backward when the rope breaks.

This is also the law that explains why a ball bounces back into the air when it strikes the ground. If there weren't any gravity or friction acting on the ball, it would bounce back to the exact height that it originally fell from. The actual result is that the ball reaches only a percentage of its original height with each bounce; this percentage depends on how hard the surface is and how heavy and/or bouncy the ball is. You can plan a realistic series of bounces by using a consistent percentage to calculate the descending height of each bounce. The bounce shown in Figure 10-10 was calculated by using a multiple of 0.5 (or ½) for the distance traveled in each bounce.

On the CD-ROM

This bounce will be much improved by adding some easing to make the acceleration more realistic. To see the final result animated, open the `bounce50percent.swf` file in the `ch10` folder of this book's CD-ROM. Ideally, a convincing bounce also includes some *stretch 'n squash* — one of the most common animation tricks used to make motion look more realistic. We discuss this in more detail in Chapter 14, "Character Animation Techniques."

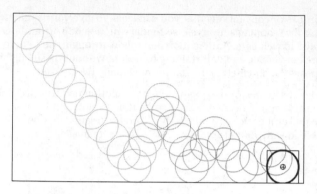

Figure 10-10: A starting pattern for a bounce can be plotted using a consistent multiple to calculate the height of each bounce.

If you're interested in exploring the formulas for more advanced motion patterns, any basic physics textbook will help you get started. Three useful sources that we recommend for motion designers are

✦ *Physics for Game Developers,* by David M. Bourg (O'Reilly & Associates, 2001).

✦ Processing, an open source tool that is being developed to support artists and educators who are interested in learning to work with code structures to create graphics and interactive projects. Although the code is not identical to ActionScript, you will find the examples inspiring and helpful as a beginning step toward using math to describe motion. Visit www.processing.org to learn more. The Learning section of the site includes a growing library of examples with graphics and commented code.

✦ Jack's Page, a Web site created by physics teacher Jack Orb to provide information on basic physics and optics for computer-rendered graphics (with sample JavaScript): www.kw.igs.net/~jackord/j6.html#p1.

We'd like to know what you think about this chapter. Visit www.flashsupport.com/feedback to send us your comments.

Summary

✦ To engage an audience, it's important for motion to have meaning. Meaning is derived when an animation includes visual cues that are part of our common vocabulary.

✦ Motion should support the underlying concept and content of your project. If motion is simply added as decoration without having some connection to the ideas in the content, it distracts, rather than enhances, your design.

✦ Motion can communicate mood, emotion, and personality as effectively as text or color. Although the meaning of certain styles of motion can have a different personal or cultural impact, the way that core emotions are linked to styles of motion is remarkably similar for most people.

✦ Careful observation and documentation of motion in daily life will help you to build a reference library to draw from when creating animation. Exaggeration and interpretation are crucial for developing a personal style. However, your animation will not be convincing unless you can build on a core understanding of motion in the real world.

✦ There are many useful tricks or conventions that you can learn to give your animation a more professional look. Overlapping action and secondary motion add life and personality to basic animated movements. Anticipation and follow-through also help to make an animation more convincing and entertaining to watch. Without these finishing touches, animation appears flat and lifeless, no matter how many tweens you use.

✦ Physics equations can be invaluable for designing advanced motion patterns. Even if you don't have a propensity for numbers, spending some time exploring how basic equations explain force makes it easier to analyze and re-create organic motion. A little math and science combined with your graphics can help to create magic.

✦   ✦   ✦

Timeline Animation

In this chapter, we discuss the basic methods and tools used to create animations in Flash. Animation is the process of creating the illusion of movement or change over time. Animation can be the movement of an item from one place to another, or it can be a change of color over a period of time. The change can also be a morph, or change, from one shape to another. Any change of either position or appearance that occurs over time is animation. In Flash, changing the contents of successive frames (over a period of time) creates animation. This can include any or all of the changes we have mentioned, in any combination.

Note   Animation *is* possible without extending Flash content beyond one frame, but this requires you to apply transformations to graphics using ActionScript commands and/or mathematical equations that are executed by code rather than triggered by the Flash timeline. We suggest you use *The Flash 8 ActionScript Bible* (Wiley, 2006) as a companion to this book when you are ready to go to the next level with your Flash projects.

Basic Methods of Flash Animation

In Flash, there are three basic methods of animation:

✦ **Frame-by-frame animation** is achieved by manually changing the individual contents of each of any number of successive keyframes.

✦ **Tweened animation** is achieved by defining the contents of the start and end points of an animation (with keyframes) and allowing Flash to interpolate the contents of the frames in between. There are two kinds of tweening in Flash:

  • Shape tweening

  • Motion tweening

✦ **Timeline Effects** were introduced in Flash MX 2004. Timeline Effects give you "automated" animation and visual effects that you can apply to shapes or symbols. Timeline Effects are created by prebuilt scripts that you can control by choosing settings in a preview dialog box before the Effect is rendered. After you choose settings and apply an Effect, Flash generates Graphic symbols and adds a new layer to the Timeline to hold the frames needed to display the Effect. You don't even have to make any keyframes!

Advanced Flash developers tend to animate almost exclusively by controlling Movie Clips with ActionScript. Although this might seem intimidating to illustrators or animators who are more comfortable using analog tools, this programmatic approach to creating motion (and even artwork) dynamically makes sense. After all, computer animation is the art of orchestrating items according to various properties over time—and in the digital realm numbers describe all properties, even color. The Timeline Effects feature is a big step toward making this type of authoring more accessible. Coders now have an easy way to distribute or reuse scripted animation and effects, and designers can take advantage of these without having to learn how to write or edit advanced ActionScript.

Cross-Reference   Although the methods for authoring custom Timeline Effects are beyond the scope of this book, we describe the basic process for adding and using a custom Timeline Effect in Chapter 12, "Applying Filters and Effects." In a quick tutorial in the same chapter, we'll show you how to install and use Samuel Wan's "Jitter" Effect. The Timeline Effects that ship with Flash are only the beginning.

Flash components and Timeline Effects make it easier than ever for beginning programmers to integrate ActionScripted elements into Flash projects. But, before you jump into scripted animation, it helps to know how to animate on the Main Timeline with simple groups and graphics.

Frame-by-Frame Animation

The most basic form of animation is frame-by-frame animation. Because frame-by-frame animation employs unique drawings in each frame, it's ideal for complex animations that require subtle changes—for example, facial expressions. However, frame-by-frame animation also has its drawbacks. It can be very tedious and time-consuming to draw unique art for each frame of the animation. Moreover, all those unique drawings contribute to a large file size. In Flash, a frame with unique art is called a *keyframe*. As shown in Figure 11-1, frame-by-frame animation requires a unique drawing for every movement or change, which makes nearly every frame a keyframe.

Figure 11-1: When you use keyframes to gradually add to the artwork, the text appears to be written out letter by letter in the final animation.

The example shown in Figure 11-1 (keyframeText.swf) was created by inserting keyframes (F6) with the same text repeated in every frame and then working backwards to erase the letters in sequential keyframes. In the final effect, the text appears letter by letter until the whole word is written out in keyframe 10. This process of modifying your original artwork to create a sequence is one use of frame-by-frame animation. Another approach is to create completely unique artwork in a series of blank keyframes (F7).

As shown in Figure 11-2, the changes in the lines from frame to frame can add a lot more motion to the final animation. If you are a skilled illustrator, you will be able to keep enough consistency from keyframe to keyframe that it will seem to be the same shape or figure moving to a new position. If you are an aspiring illustrator, you will end up with a lot more variation among your drawings. As long as you are not trying to get a very precise sequence, this variation can actually be a lot of fun to watch—every line will dance and move in your final animation. Keep in mind that you are not restricted to just one series of frames; you can keep adding elements with their own keyframe sequences on separate layers.

The source files for the examples in this section are included on the CD-ROM—they're in the `Keyframe` folder of the `ch11` folder.

The images shown in Figure 11-2 are from the file `faceFramebyFrame.fla`. This sequence of drawings was originally done on top of a short video clip of a real person. If you're learning to draw motion, video can be a good starting point—place it in a guide layer so it won't add to the file size of your final movie. If you work in a loose style, the roughness of the individual traced drawings can add more life to the final animation.

Figure 11-2: A loosely sketched sequence can be paced by adding more "repeater" frames between the unique keyframe images.

Felix Stumpf creates very engaging animation by using video as a reference for lifelike motion. His fluid drawing style adds a unique flair to his finished Flash portfolio presentation at `www.felixstumpf.de`. Learn more about Felix's techniques in his tutorial for Chapter 14, "Character Animation Techniques."

Adding keyframes

To add a keyframe to the Timeline, select the frame that you would like to convert into a keyframe. Then do one of the following:

✦ Convert a frame into a keyframe:

- Right-click (or Control+click on Mac) the frame and select Insert Keyframe from the contextual menu.

- Choose Insert ➪ Timeline ➪ Keyframe from the application menu.

- Press F6 on the keyboard.

✦ Convert a frame into a *blank* keyframe:

- Right-click (or Control+click on Mac) the frame and select Insert Blank Keyframe from the contextual menu.

- Choose Insert ➪ Timeline ➪ Blank Keyframe from the application menu.

- Press F7 on the keyboard.

Note   If you select a frame in a span, the selected frame will be converted to a keyframe without adding to the length of the span. If you insert a keyframe at the end of a span, the keyframe will add to the length of the sequence. If you convert a frame in a span to a blank keyframe, all content will be cleared from the keyframe and the following frames of the span.

Tip   If you need to make a sequence of keyframes, but you would rather not have to press F6 or F7 repeatedly to create individual keyframes, you can select a range of frames and use the Modify ➪ Timeline ➪ Convert to Keyframes (F6) or Modify ➪ Timeline ➪ Convert to Blank Keyframes (F7) command to quickly convert all selected frames to keyframes or blank keyframes.

Creating frame-by-frame animation

The basic steps for creating a frame-by-frame animation are as follows:

1. Start by selecting the frame in which you'd like your frame-by-frame animation to begin.

2. If it's not already a keyframe, use Insert ➪ Timeline ➪ Keyframe (F6) to convert it.

3. Then either draw or import the first image for your sequence into this keyframe. Wherever possible, use symbols and flip, rotate, or otherwise manipulate them for reuse to economize on file size.

4. Select the next frame and either carry the artwork from the previous keyframe forward for modification by adding a keyframe (F6), or, if you want to create a completely new image from scratch or place an imported image, make the next keyframe a blank keyframe (F7).

5. Continue to add keyframes and change the contents of each keyframe until you've completed the animation. Finally, play back your animation by returning to the first keyframe and then selecting Control ➪ Play from the application menu (Enter or Return key), or preview the animation in the test movie environment by choosing Control ➪ Test Movie (Ctrl+Enter or ⌘+Return).

Modifying Multiframe Sequences

To control the pacing of your animation, you can add more frames (F5) between the keyframes (creating a *span*), or add more keyframed (F7) images to the sequence to extend its length. Adding more frames between keyframes will "hold" or pause the animation until the Playhead hits the next keyframe with changed content. In the example shown in Figure 11-2, the face holds on some frames while the butterfly continues to move in keyframed drawings on its own layer. To speed up (or shorten) animation, you can remove frames (Shift+F5) or keyframes (Shift+F6)

Frame Rate and Animation Timing

An underlying factor that will affect the playback of all animation is the project frame rate. The frame rate is displayed in the Document Properties dialog box (Modify ⇨ Document) or in the Property inspector if you click in the Document window of an open file without selecting any items on the Stage. The allowable frame rate range is between 0.01 and 120 fps—the default setting is 12 frames per second (fps). The most commonly used range is somewhere between 12 fps (for most Web sites and for low-bandwidth animation) and 24 fps (for subtle animation and complex effects intended for broadcast).

It might seem like a good idea to push the frame rate higher to get smoother-looking animation, but the reality of Web delivery is that you can't be sure that your audience will have the bandwidth or the processor speed to play back the animation as you intended. There is nothing worse than seeing your gorgeous animation stuttering and dropping frames. In most cases, 12 fps provides all the momentum you need to drive your animation and effects—you can create quick cuts, smooth fades, or anything in between just by adjusting your artwork and pacing your frames appropriately.

Although you can always change the frame rate after you've authored a file, it makes sense to decide on a final frame rate *before* you start designing and testing complex animation sequences. Re-timing animation by inserting or removing frames and changing the duration of tweens is always an option, but it is painful to go back and try to match the original pacing of a file that was created using a different frame rate.

to shorten the sequence. You can make changes in the length of a span by selecting a frame in the span that you want to modify and using the application menu commands (or shortcut keys), or you can simply drag the endframe of the span to change its position on the Timeline.

Tip   If you drag the endframe of a span to a new position, Flash will automatically insert a new keyframe to mark the new position. If you want to change the length of a span without adding more keyframes, hold down the Ctrl or ⌘ key while clicking and dragging the endframe to a new position.

Inserting more frames does work to slow down an animated sequence, but generally if you insert more than two frames between keyframes, the movement will be interrupted and the animation will start to look too choppy. Try adding more keyframes to the sequence with very subtle change to the content in each keyframe if you want to create a slower, smoother animation.

By default, Flash will loop the content on your Timeline, so if you want a sequence to be repeated, you don't need to draw it over and over again. If you notice that your animation disappears before it loops to play again, check to make sure that there are no extra empty frames at the end of the sequence, or that the endframe of one of your sequences is not further down the Timeline than the endframe of the element that disappears. Although you won't see anything on the Stage in these frames, Flash will still play those frames if they exist on the Timeline. Obviously, blank frames can be used in an animation whenever you want to empty the Stage—either as a pause between sequences or to create the illusion that your artwork has disappeared.

To illustrate how blank frames play back in an animation, we've created a silly example with a face and a rectangle that persist in every frame and some text that only exists on some frames (see Figure 11-3).

Figure 11-3: You can insert blank keyframes to clear artwork from the Stage. Remember that the Playhead will continue along the Timeline if there are frames on any one of the layers, even if the artwork on other layers is no longer present.

Onion skinning

Traditional animators worked on layers of transparent cels using a light table. This made it possible for them to create consistent drawings and to plan the pacing of movement in a sequence of cels. As you move from keyframe to keyframe in Flash, you might feel that you are working blind because you can only see the artwork on the current frame. If you are creating artwork for a sequence of related keyframes, it is crucial to have some visual indication or "map" of the changes from frame to frame. Fortunately, Flash has an effective digital version of the traditional light table—this handy feature is called *Onion skinning*. In Flash, Onion skinning enables you to see several frames of your artwork displayed at one time. The Onion markers on the Timeline determine the number of frames that are visible. You can turn Onion skinning on or off whenever you need it using the toggle buttons at the bottom of the Timeline window. As shown in Figure 11-4, there are actually two options for Onion skinning: Onion Skin or Onion Skin Outlines.

Tip

Layers that are locked will not be Onion skinned, even if there is artwork on multiple frames within the Onion Markers—this is helpful if you need to keep the view from getting too cluttered with multiple overlays. Generally, Onion skinning works best if all layers are locked except the layer that you plan to edit.

The current frame (indicated by the position of the Playhead) is displayed at 100 percent opacity, while the other frames in the sequence are displayed at a slightly reduced opacity or as outlines, depending on the Onion Skin button you have selected.

Tip

If you don't like the color of the outlines that display when you turn on Onion Skin Outlines, you can change the setting for Outline color in the Layer Properties dialog box. (Double-click the layer icon or choose Properties from the contextual menu.)

Figure 11-4: Onion Skin will show grayed-out or ghosted artwork on multiple frames, while Onion Skin Outlines will show colored outlines of the artwork on multiple frames. It's hard to see the "color" here, but notice that the lines are thinner with Onion Skin Outlines (right).

The number of frames that are included in the Onion skin display can be controlled either by choosing a setting from the Modify Onion Markers menu (shown in Figure 11-5), or by selecting the round marker handles with the Selection tool and sliding them to a new position on the Timeline. The number of frames that you select from the Modify menu will be shown before and after the current frame — so in our example with Onion 2 selected, the Onion markers actually span five frames (the current frame, plus two frames on each side).

Figure 11-5: You can control the number of frames visible when Onion skinning is turned on with the Modify Onion Markers menu, or by dragging the Onion skin markers to a new position on the Timeline.

Editing multiple frames

One of the drawbacks of manually creating unique artwork on every frame is that changes can be very time-consuming. If you decide to change the color or size of an element or perhaps edit out a feature of your artwork, repeating this edit on every frame of a sequence will be tedious and labor-intensive.

Tip The Find and Replace panel (Edit ⇨ Find and Replace) makes it easy to replace colors and text in a Flash document, but erasing or moving an element that appears in a multiframe sequence can still be time-consuming.

Fortunately, Flash provides a Timeline option that can make repeated edits on multiple frames much more efficient. Edit Multiple Frames enables you to see and select items on multiple frames for simultaneous modification. As shown in Figure 11-6, the Edit Multiple Frames option is turned on with the toggle button at the top of the Document window. When this feature is active, you can use any of the selection methods (Selection tool, Lasso, application menu, or shortcut keys) to select the parts of your artwork that you wish to move, modify, or delete. This feature is especially helpful for edits that need to be consistent from frame to frame, such as moving all of your artwork to a new position in your layout.

Tip Using the Lock feature to protect layers that you don't want to edit makes it much easier to select and edit multiple elements on specific layers. If you use the Lasso tool or the Selection tool to drag-select items on the Stage, only items on unlocked layers will be included in your selection. The Select All command (Edit ⇨ Select All) makes quick work of ensuring that all unlocked elements within the Edit handles will be selected before you apply a change.

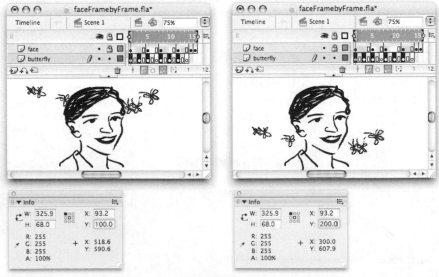

Figure 11-6: With Edit Multiple Frames toggled on, you can select elements on individual keyframes in a sequence (left) to be modified simultaneously (right).

The frames visible and available for selection are marked by a gray span on the Timeline with start and end handles. You can adjust the number of frames included in the span with the Selection tool by clicking and dragging the round handles on the Timeline to a new position.

Using Tweens for Animation

Tweening is one of the most powerful Flash animation features. Whether you are creating character animation or motion graphics, or even the most basic button effect, you will find tweening indispensable. Once you have planned your animation and created the initial artwork, you can use Flash tweening to generate the transitional images between one keyframe and another. This is the tool that makes it possible for artists to quickly generate smooth, precise animation — without spending half their lives manually filling in unique graphics on every frame. Instead, you can establish a beginning point and an end point, and only make drawings, or key art, for each of those points. Then you let Flash interpolate and render, or *tween,* the changes between the keyframes. Tweening can be used to render changes in size, shape, color, position, and rotation. Unlike Timeline Effects, manual tweens are limited only by your imagination — anything is possible with the keyframed artwork that you set up.

Tweening also minimizes file size because you don't have to include unique information on each frame in the animation. Because you define the contents of the frames at the beginning and end point (keyframes), Flash has to save only those graphics, plus the values needed to make the *changes* on the frames in between. Basically, Flash has to store only the difference between the beginning frame and the endframe so that the images on the frames in between can be calculated and rendered.

The other significant benefit of using tweens to generate an animated sequence is that if you want to make a change, you only need to modify the beginning or end point and Flash will instantly update the images in between. Two kinds of tweens can be created in Flash — shape tweens and Motion tweens — each applied for specific purposes. Both tween types are represented on the Timeline by a colored fill with a continuous arrow on the span between the start keyframe and the end keyframe of the animation. Shape tweens are represented by a green fill and Motion tweens by a blue fill. If a tween is incomplete, either because the wrong tween type has been applied or because information on one of the defining keyframes is missing, the continuous arrow will be replaced with a dashed line.

The type of tween that you want to apply is selected from the Tween menu in the Property inspector. As shown in Figure 11-7, the options available for controlling the playback of the final tween depend on the type of tween selected.

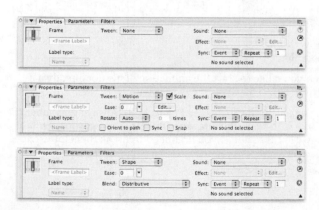

Figure 11-7: When you specify a tween type in the Property inspector, the relevant options for controlling the tween appear.

Shape tweening

Shape tweening is useful for morphing basic shapes — for example, turning a square into a circle, or animating the drawing of a line by tweening from a dot to a finished line. Flash can only shape tween primitive *shapes* or Drawing Objects, so don't even try to shape tween a group, symbol, or editable text — it won't work. You can tween multiple shapes on one layer, but for the sake of organization and animation control, it's best to put each shape on its own layer. This enables you to adjust the speed and length of Shape tweens individually, and also makes it much easier to figure out what's going on if you need to edit the file later.

On the CD-ROM   The smileTween.fla example file is located on the CD-ROM in the shapeTween subfolder of the ch11 folder.

Figure 11-8 shows an animated "smile" created by interpolating the graphics between a dot and a curved stroke with a Shape tween. Flash nimbly handles this simple transition, rendering a gradually extending line on the frames between the dot of the pursed mouth and the final curve of the smile.

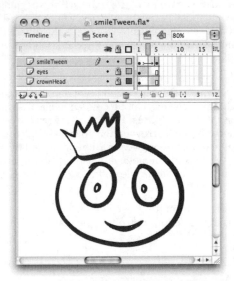

Figure 11-8: After a dot is drawn on keyframe 1 and an arc is drawn on keyframe 5, a Shape tween is applied to render the shapes on the frames in the span between — creating an animation.

Here are the steps for creating a Shape tween:

1. Select the frame in which you'd like to start the animation. If it's not already a keyframe, convert it to one (F6).

2. Then draw your starting image on the Stage (see Figure 11-9). Always remember that Shape tweening only works with *shapes* or Drawing Objects — not groups, symbols, or editable text. To Shape tween these items, you first need to break them into shapes (Modify ➪ Break Apart).

Figure 11-9: The contents of the first keyframe in your span will define the starting point for the Shape tween.

3. Next, insert a keyframe (F6) on the Timeline where you want the animation to end, and modify the artwork to define the end point of the animation (see Figure 11-10). If you want to create the artwork in the final frame from scratch, then insert a blank keyframe (F7) instead of a keyframe that includes the artwork from the first keyframe.

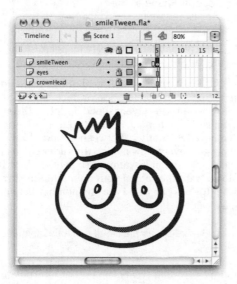

Figure 11-10: The contents of the final keyframe after your span will define the ending point for the Shape tween.

4. Select the keyframe at the beginning of the span that you want to interpolate with a Shape tween. Remember that results will be easiest to control and modify if you tween only one shape per layer.

5. Open the Property inspector if it is not already available by choosing Window ⇨ Properties from the application menu (Ctrl+F3 or ⌘+F3).

6. Choose Shape from the Tween drop-down menu. The span between the start keyframe and the end keyframe of your animation will display with a green fill and an arrow to indicate that a Shape tween has been applied, as shown in Figure 11-11.

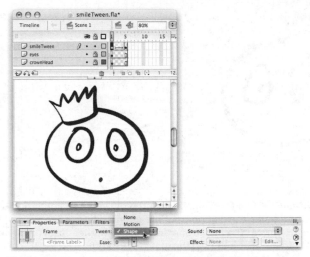

Figure 11-11: On the first keyframe, specify Shape as the tween type with the Property inspector Tween menu.

7. As shown previously in Figure 11-7, the (expanded) Property inspector panel updates to present two options for modifying the Shape tween:

   • Set the Ease slider if you want to vary the rate or speed of the animation. This is useful if you want to create the effect of acceleration or deceleration. If you want your animation to start slowly and progressively speed up, push the slider down to add an Ease In. This will cause In to display adjacent to the slider and will update the value field with a negative number (between –1 and –100). For an animation that starts fast and progressively slows, push the slider up to add an Ease Out. The word Out will appear and a positive number (between 1 and 100) will display in the value field. If you want the rate of your animation to stay constant, leave the slider in the middle (0). You can also type any number between –100 and 100 directly into the Ease value field.

Note   We added an Ease In (–100) to the smileTween sample file to make the animation look a little more realistic.

   • Select a Blend type. Distributive blending creates smoother interpolated shapes, whereas Angular blending creates interpolated shapes that preserve corners and straight lines. If your end points contain shapes with corners and lines, select Angular blending. Otherwise, use the default Distributive blending.

8. Preview the animation by choosing Control ⇨ Play (Enter) from the application menu, or use Control ⇨ Test Movie (Ctrl+Enter or ⌘+Return) to publish an .swf file.

Tip

If the overall speed of the tween seems too fast or too slow, you can extend or reduce the length of the span. The fastest way to increase the span on all visible layers is to move the Playhead to the center of the span, make sure none of the frames are selected on any of the layers and that the layers are all unlocked, then use the F5 key to add more frames. We added five frames to the overall span of the smileTween sample to slow the animation down.

Note

If you accidentally assign the wrong tween type to the start keyframe of your animation or if you delete the artwork on the start or the end keyframes, you will notice that the arrow icon on the Timeline is replaced with a dashed line, and a yellow warning icon appears in the Property inspector. This indicates that the tween is broken or incomplete. To restore the tween, it is usually best to select the first keyframe and choose None from the Tween menu in the Property inspector. Then check your Timeline and your artwork to make sure that you have shapes on both a beginning and an end keyframe for Flash to interpolate. When you think all the elements are in place, select the first keyframe and choose Shape from the Tween menu in the Property inspector to reapply the tween.

Adding Shape Hints

Because Flash calculates the simplest way to interpolate from one shape to another, you occasionally get unexpected results if the shapes are complex or extremely different from one another. Shape tweening becomes less reliable the more points there are to be calculated between the defined keyframes. In our example, we have added a keyframe at the end of the span with the eyes of the character changed from circles to stars. We want the animation to be a smooth transition from the rough circle to the star shape in each eye. As shown in Figure 11-12, a basic Shape tween results in some odd inbetween shapes.

Figure 11-12: When a Shape tween is added to create an animation from one keyframe to another, the transition artwork that Flash generates may not look how you expect it to.

One way of making the inbetween artwork more precise is to insert keyframes in the middle of the Shape tween so that you can manually adjust the shapes that Flash has generated. Another option that enables you to control a tween without modifying any artwork is to add *Shape Hints* for Flash to follow when rendering the inbetween shapes. Shape Hints enable you to specify points on a starting shape that should match with specified points on the final shape. This helps Flash to "understand" how the shapes are related and how the transitional images should be rendered. Compare Figure 11-12 with Figure 11-13 to see the improvement that Shape Hints can make in the precision of inbetween shapes.

On the CD-ROM To compare the difference made by adding Shape Hints to the animation, open eyeTween. fla (or .swf) and eyeTweenHints.fla (or .swf) from the shapeHints subfolder in the ch11 folder on the CD-ROM.

Figure 11-13: Placing shapes on individual layers and adding Shape Hints to control the way that Flash renders inbetween shapes improves the precision of Shape tweens.

Caution When you are copying and pasting a span of frames into a new Timeline—such as from the Main Timeline to a Movie Clip timeline—Flash disconnects the Shape Hints from the shape. When pasting is confined to a single timeline, hints stay as you placed them.

Shape Hints can only be added to artwork on keyframes that define the beginning and ending points of a Shape tween. To add Shape Hints to the artwork in a Shape tween, follow these steps after you have created a basic Shape tween:

1. Begin by selecting a shape on the starting keyframe and choosing Modify ➪ Shape ➪ Add Shape Hint from the application menu (Shift+Ctrl+H or Shift+⌘+H).

2. Flash places a small red circle, labeled with a letter *a*, onto the Stage—this is your first Shape Hint. Additional Hints can be added and they will also be identified alphabetically.

3. To specify a point on your starting shape, use the Selection tool to select and move the first Hint (a)—position it on an area of the shape (for example, a corner or a curve) that you want to match up with an area on the final shape, as shown in Figure 11-14.

4. When you move the Playhead to the final keyframe of your Shape tween, you will see a lettered Hint that matches the one that was placed on the starting keyframe. Position this Hint with the Arrow key so that it marks the area of the final shape that should match up with the area specified on the starting shape. The Hint will only be recognized by Flash if it attaches correctly to the artwork. You will know that your Hints are positioned properly when their fill color changes from red to green on the final keyframe (see Figure 11-15) and from red to yellow on the starting keyframe.

5. Preview the new inbetween shapes by *scrubbing* the Timeline (dragging the Playhead with the Selection tool to review frames in the tweened sequence).

6. Continue to add or reposition Hints until Flash renders the inbetween shapes correctly.

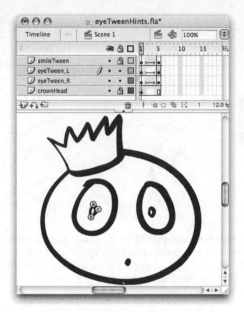

Figure 11-14: Shape Hints positioned on a shape in the starting keyframe for a Shape tween

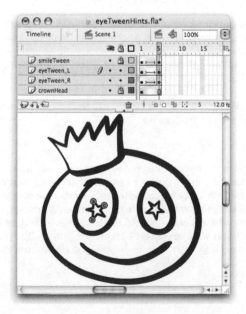

Figure 11-15: Shape Hints aligned to points on a shape in the ending keyframe of the tween

7. To remove an individual Hint, drag it off the Stage with the Selection tool. To remove all Hints from an active keyframe, choose Modify ➪ Shape ➪ Remove All Hints from the application menu. A shortcut is to right-click (Control+click on Mac) any of the Hints to invoke the contextual menu, as shown in Figure 11-16, for these and other options as you are working.

Figure 11-16: The contextual menu offers some options for working with Shape Hints.

Tip

If the Shape Hints are not visible after you have placed them, make sure that the Show All Hints option in the contextual menu is toggled on, or use the application menu to choose View ➪ Show Shape Hints (Alt+Ctrl+H or Option+⌘+H) — this option is only available if the layer and keyframe that contain the Hints are currently active.

Motion tweening

Motion tweening is useful for animating groups, symbols, Drawing Objects, and editable text; however, it cannot be used to animate primitive shapes. As the name suggests, Motion tweening is applied to move an item from one place to another, but it's capable of much more. Motion tweening can also be used to animate the scale, skew, or rotation of items; as well as the color and transparency of a symbol.

Note

Motion tweening can only be applied to one item per layer — use multiple layers to motion tween multiple items in the same span of the Timeline.

New Feature

The little Object Drawing (J) toggle in the options area of the Tools panel will make your production process more streamlined if you are drawing items to animate. Objects can be Shape tweened or Motion tweened without being converted into symbols or broken apart into raw shapes. This new Flash 8 art type is more flexible than standard symbol types or raw shapes. You can make Objects with any of the normal drawing tools as long as you select the Object Drawing toggle. If you want to convert a raw shape into an Object after it is drawn, select the shape, then choose Modify ➪ Combine Objects ➪ Union from the application menu.

The pacing of a Motion tweened sequence can be modified at any point — simply insert a keyframe for each phase of the animation. In addition to the scale and Color effect settings applied directly to the symbol instance, you can adjust the settings in the Property inspector that control Easing (or pace of interpolation for the tween) and rotation on each keyframe of a Motion tween. So, if you use a tween to move a symbol from frame 1 to frame 10 and stop the tween on frame 11, you can have the symbol sit still for 10 frames (no tween), and then start a new tween (of this same symbol on the same layer) with rotation or an alpha fade from frames 20 to 30. The possibilities are almost endless.

New Feature

Flash 8 includes a new Edit button in the Properties panel that invokes a dialog box for controlling Motion tweens with velocity curves. This feature takes the concept of Easing to a new level by enabling you to adjust the speed of an animation along a curved line that covers the entire span of a tween. With velocity curves, you have frame-by-frame control of your animation without adding extra keyframes to a tween. You can also use curves to control the speed of interpolation for individual characteristics of a tween such as color and Filters, as we show later in this chapter.

Like a Shape tween, a Motion tween is more efficient than frame-by-frame animation because it doesn't require unique content for each frame of animation. Yet it is *not* appropriate for all effects — sometimes you'll need to use either frame-by-frame animation or Shape tweening to create the kind of inbetweens you need in a sequence.

On the CD-ROM

Create your own file from scratch, or open `motionTween_start.fla` from the `MotionTween` subfolder of the `ch11` folder on the CD-ROM. To view the final animation, open `motionTween_final.fla` (or .swf) from the same location.

Here's how to create a Motion tween:

1. Select the frame in which you'd like to start your animation. If it's not already a keyframe, make it one by choosing Insert ⇨ Timeline ⇨ Keyframe (F6).

2. Draw or import the image that you want to tween. Just remember that you can only Motion tween groups, symbols (including imported bitmaps — which are, by default, symbols), Objects, and editable text (a text block).

   • If you are using a raw shape, group it, convert it to an Object, or turn it into a symbol.

   • If you already have the element as a symbol in your current Library, you can just drag an instance from the Library onto the Stage. Place each symbol that you want to animate on a separate layer, as shown in Figure 11-17.

   • If you are using editable text or an Object, you don't have to do anything — it's already an element that can be Motion tweened.

Figure 11-17: The artwork on the first keyframe of the span you want to Motion tween should be a text box, a group, an Object, or a symbol on its own layer—anything except a raw shape will work.

3. Select the frame where you want the tween to end and make it a keyframe by choosing Insert ➪ Timeline ➪ Keyframe (F6).

4. Make any modifications to the symbols that you want animated on the beginning and end keyframes, as shown in Figure 11-18. Remember that you can move tweened elements, as well as scale, skew, and rotate them.

Tip   If you're working with symbols, you can also use the Color Effect menu to modify Tint, Alpha, and Brightness. The new Flash 8 Filters are great for adding effects to tweened text or symbols.

Caution   Alpha effects and intensive Filters in Motion tweens will slow most fps (frames per second) settings. The only way to make sure that the fps is honored, no matter how intensive the animation might be, is to use a stream sync sound that loops over the course of any critical fps playback. For more on the relationship between streaming sounds and fps rate, see Chapter 15, "Adding Sound."

Figure 11-18: Modify the features of the symbol on the end keyframe that you want to interpolate with a Motion tween.

5. There are three different ways that you can apply a basic Motion tween to a span between two keyframes:

- Select the beginning keyframe, and then open the Property inspector (Window ➪ Properties) and use the Tween menu to specify a Motion tween.

- Right-click (Control+click on Mac) any frame between the two keyframes and select Create Motion Tween from the contextual menu.

- Select the beginning keyframe or any frame in the span and choose Insert ➪ Timeline ➪ Create Motion Tween from the application menu.

Read This Before Using Create Motion Tween

If you have not converted your artwork into symbols before using the Create Motion Tween command, Flash automatically converts any item in the selected keyframe into a symbol with the generic name of Tween followed by a number (Tween1, Tween2). Although this might seem like a handy shortcut, it actually creates a mess that you will need to clean up later.

Because the symbols are auto-created and named, you will not have the same control over how your Library is organized and how your artwork is optimized. It is much better to analyze the most efficient way to convert your artwork into symbols and to reuse those symbols as much as possible than to allow Flash to make generic symbols that may be redundant. As with all elements in your Flash project, it is also much more useful to assign meaningful names to your symbols that will help you navigate the project when you need to make edits.

Manually creating and naming your own symbols before assigning a tween to specific keyframes helps avoid redundant or confusing items being added to your document (.fla) Library. If you make a habit of using the Property inspector to assign tweens, you will always be reminded if you haven't converted an element into a symbol.

6. Select the first keyframe of your Motion tween and use the options in the Property inspector to add more control to the final tween, as shown in Figure 11-19. We applied an Ease Out value of 100 to the sample `motionTween` file to make the eye motion look more natural.

- **Ease:** Ease settings control the interpolation pattern of a tween. A default setting of 0 will interpolate the changes in the motion tween at a consistent rate from beginning to end. Increasing the Ease value (within a range of 1 to 100) will make the change start more quickly then gradually slow down—creating an *Ease Out*. Decreasing the Ease value (within a range of –1 to –100) will make the change start more slowly and gradually speed up—creating an *Ease In*. Easing in works well to build anticipation, and Easing out works well to make items settle more naturally at the end of a motion.

New Feature

As you try different Ease values, you may realize that you'd like your tween to Ease In *and* Ease Out, but still move quickly in the middle. In older versions of Flash, this was possible in timeline animation, but it required adding additional keyframes and adjusting the Ease values on separate keyframes until the final motion looked right. To create a natural looking tween that Eased in and Eased out required at least six keyframes! Luckily, Flash 8 solves this problem with the Edit panel, providing custom easing control that uses a visual curve to map the rate of interpolation in a tween. Using curves to adjust easing anywhere along a tween rather than applying fixed values only on keyframes opens up a whole range of creative possibilities and makes the process a lot more fun.

- **Rotate:** You can rotate tweened items using this option. Select a rotation type from the drop-down menu and then type the number of rotations in the value field. Automatic rotation rotates your item in the direction that requires the least amount of motion, while Clockwise and Counterclockwise rotate your item in the indicated direction. In both cases, the rotation will be completed as many times as you specify in the value field. If you type 0 in the entry field, or select None from the drop-down menu, no rotation will occur (other than rotation that has been applied to the symbol with the Transform panel).

Figure 11-19: Several options for Motion tweens are available in the Property inspector.

- **Orient to path:** When your item follows a path (or Motion guide), turning this selection on forces the item to orient its movement to that path. We discuss paths in the next chapter.

- **Sync:** When this setting is activated on a tween, you can replace the symbol in the first keyframe and it will automatically be updated in the remaining frames and in any other synchronized keyframes that follow. This setting is also important if your animation is contained within a Graphic symbol. Flash recalculates the number of frames in a tween on a Graphic symbol's Timeline so that it matches the number of frames available on the Main Timeline. Sync ensures that your animation loops properly when the animated symbol is placed in the Main Timeline, even if the frame sequence in the Graphic symbol is not an even multiple of the number of frames assigned to the symbol in the Main Timeline.

Tip　You can tell if a tweened sequence is synchronized by observing that the vertical lines separating the keyframes from the span are not visible when this setting is applied.

- **Snap:** This option snaps your animated item into alignment with a Motion guide. We discuss Motion guides in Chapter 12, "Applying Filters and Effects."

7. Other elements can be Motion tweened on the same span of the Timeline, as long as they are on separate layers (see Figure 11-20). You can interpolate different features on each tween and also apply any control settings that you wish—Flash reads and renders the Motion tween on each layer independently.

Figure 11-20: Multiple items can be animated simultaneously by creating tweens on individual layers.

Note As with Shape tweens, the arrow icon on the Timeline span of your Motion tween will be replaced with a dashed line if the tween is broken or incomplete. A common mistake with Motion tweens is to try to animate multiple elements on the same layer. To restore the tween, it is usually best to select the first keyframe and choose None from the Tween menu in the Property inspector. Then check your Timeline and your artwork to make sure that you have only a single group, Object, or symbol (not a shape) on a layer with both a beginning and an end keyframe for Flash to interpolate. When you think all the elements are in place, select the first keyframe and chose Motion from the Tween menu in the Property inspector to reapply the tween.

Adjusting tweens with Custom Easing

For more precise control over the pacing and appearance of a Motion tween, use the Edit button in the Property inspector to invoke the new Custom Easing controls. (See Figure 11-21.) By default, the Use one setting for all properties check box is selected and the Property menu (shown in Figure 11-21) is grayed out. Using one setting for all properties applies one curve to all the features of your tween—this is consistent with the results you get from standard easing where the color, shape, position, and any other differences between the starting keyframe and the ending keyframe of your tween will be interpolated at the same rate. If you deselect the check box, it is possible to apply individual curves to the various properties of the tweened element—we'll discuss these options in the next section.

When you are first using Custom Easing, you might find it less confusing to experiment with the default setting left on. Even one curve can get pretty complicated as you add control points and adjust the curve handles—it will be easier to see how these changes affect the animation if you work with one combined curve rather than several individual curves.

Tip If you set Easing with the value field or the slider control in the main Property inspector and then click the Edit button, the value of Ease In or Ease Out that you apply will be rendered in the Custom Easing curve. This is a good way to get an idea of how the visual curve control relates to the standard easing values.

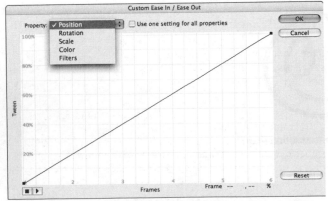

Figure 11-21: Custom Easing enables curve-based control of Motion tweened elements. The default diagonal line creates an even transformation across the span of a tween by mapping the percentage of change consistently to the number of elapsed frames.

Figure 11-22 illustrates an Ease In and an Ease Out translated into individual curves. The vertical axis is marked to track the transformation of the tween as a percentage of the total span, while the horizontal axis is marked to track the progress of the tween on a frame-by-frame basis. If you want an item to Ease In and then Ease Out within the same tween, you'll have to use the Custom Easing controls to combine these two curves into a curve that changes direction.

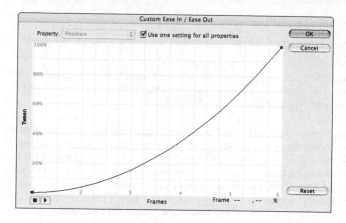

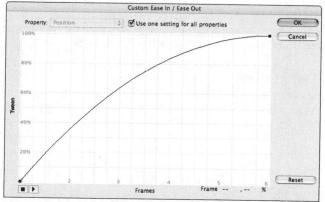

Figure 11-22: An Ease value of −100 (In) set in the Property inspector translates to a gently sloped or concave line in the Custom Easing curve (top). An Ease value of 100 (Out) translates as a gently rounded or convex line (bottom).

Adjusting anchor points along the curved line in the grid created by the intersection of the percent complete axis and the frames elapsed axis enable you to "shift time" — want a transformation to be 75 percent finished by the time a 20-frame tween gets to frame 10? Simply add an anchor point to your curve at the Frame 10 marker and drag the anchor point upward to force the curve to cross the 75% line (instead of the 50% line that it was at by default).

Here are the steps to go from a standard Ease In to a combined Ease In/Ease Out using the Custom Easing Edit option:

On the CD-ROM

Create your own file with a motion tween on the Main Timeline, or open customEasing_start.fla from the MotionTween subfolder of the ch11 folder on the CD-ROM. To view the final animation, open customEasing_final.fla (or .swf) from the same location.

1. Open the sample file and select the first keyframe of the motion tween with the Selection tool.

2. In the Property inspector, set the Ease value to –100 (In) and then click the Edit button to translate the Ease (In) setting to a curve. The line should look like the first curve in Figure 11-22 — a smooth concave line.

Caution

A little bug keeps the easing values set in the Property inspector from being translated to the Custom curve dialog box, unless you bump the values before clicking the Edit button by clicking in the Ease value field and pressing Return (or Enter), or moving the slider to a different value before setting it back to –100. This workaround is only necessary if you want to translate an existing easing value (from a previous edit session) to a custom curve. If during a single edit session, you use the Property inspector to enter a new easing value, and then click the Edit button, Flash will read these values and map them to a custom curve.

3. Click the start anchor point of the line (lower-left) to invoke the edit handle. Drag the edit handle along the bottom of the graph (the 0% tween line) until the handle extends to the frame 10 marker. Your curve should now look like Figure 11-23.

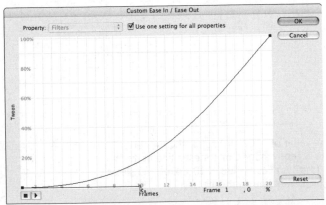

Figure 11-23: An Ease In curve with the start anchor handle extended along the 0% axis

4. Use the play/stop button in the lower-left corner of the Edit window to preview the custom tween settings — you might have to drag the Edit window out of the way so you can see the animation on your artwork in the Document window. At this point, the animation does have an Ease In on the animation, but it isn't anything special yet.

5. Drag the edit handle on the end anchor point (top-right) downward along the right edge (the frame 20 marker) to adjust the curve until it looks similar to the curve in Figure 11-24—a reverse curve. Click the play button again to preview your results. You should now have a gradual Ease In and Ease Out within the span of the original tween.

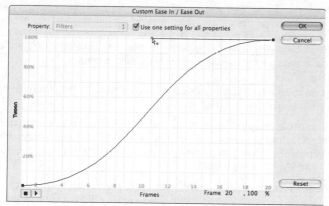

Figure 11-24: You can drag the edit handles on the start and end anchor points of the curve to change the direction and the height of the curve.

It takes some practice to get the feel for using curves to control tweens, but we're sure you can already see how many more options for different styles of motion you'll have if you use Custom Easing:

✦ **Diagonal lines continue in an even motion:** The more closely the percentage of change matches the progression in frames, the more even the transformation will be.

✦ **Gradual curves can add smooth acceleration or deceleration:** A reverse curve that creates gradual slopes at the beginning and end as well as a steeper pitch in the middle will create an EaseIn/Ease Out effect.

✦ **Bumps in a curve can add a stuttering motion:** For example, if an anchor point at the frame 10 marker is set at the 50% change line and you add an anchor point at the frame 15 marker that is set to pull the curve back down to the 25% tween line, you will cause the tween to progress and then reverse and then progress again at a quicker rate to reach 100% transformation by the last frame of the tween.

✦ **Flat (horizontal) lines add pauses:** The frames continue, but the percentage of change is forced to plateau or hold at a specific point of transformation.

✦ **Vertical lines create quick jumps:** The percentage of change has to increase, but it doesn't have any frames to gradually make the change.

Using multiple Custom Easing curves

Now that you've had a chance to try working with a combined Custom Easing curve, you are probably curious about what happens when you deselect the default check box in the Edit panel. The Property menu (shown in Figure 11-21) makes it possible to edit individual tween curves to control the various properties or characteristics of your tweened item.

The default diagonal curve is loaded for each available property so that Flash can do it's best to render the changes at an even rate from the first keyframe to the last keyframe in your tween.

Caution   Deselecting the default Use one setting for all properties check box resets all curves to the standard diagonal line. If you have spent time working on a custom easing curve that is being applied to all the properties of your tween (the default setting) and you decide to deselect the Use one setting for all properties check box, be sure to use the Copy command (Ctrl+C or ⌘+C) to save your curve in the buffer so that you can Paste it (Ctrl+V or ⌘+V) back in to the curve view for the specific property you want to control.

You can modify the curves of any of these properties should you want them to be rendered at a different pace to create a custom tween effect:

✦ **Position:** This controls the pace at which an item moves from one spot to another in your tween. It is possible to reverse an item's movement but it will always end up in the final keyframed position; so it doesn't really work to create true bounce effects but it can be used to add overlapping motion.

✦ **Rotation:** If you have entered any rotation settings in the Property inspector, they can be paced by creating a custom easing curve. This curve will also control the rate of rotation if there is any difference in orientation between an item in the first keyframe and the last keyframe of a tween.

✦ **Scale:** Any differences in size between the item in the first keyframe and the last keyframe of a tween can be interpolated at different rates. You can adjust the curves to create various patterns of scaling. Unfortunately, adjusting the custom easing curve between only two keyframes is not sufficient to create anticipation in an animated motion.

✦ **Color:** You can control any color changes from one keyframe to the next in a tween by shifting the custom easing curve. You can make color changes using the Advanced Color settings in the Property inspector or by using Filters.

✦ **Filters:** If Filters have been applied to create changes in an item's appearance in the span of a tween, the pattern of change can be adjusted with custom easing.

In most cases, you will only need to create custom curves for one or two properties to achieve a very polished final result. The possibilities can be a little overwhelming at first and the flexibility of custom easing curves might work against you — as you modify the curves in myriad ways, it can be difficult to keep track of which curves work best for specific effects. Fortunately, there are a few tricks that can help as you experiment:

✦ Use the Property inspector controls first because these are a little less complicated. The settings you apply with the Property inspector will be translated into curves that you can use as a starting point when you launch the Custom Easing window.

✦ Copy and Paste curves from one property to another if you have created a custom easing setting that you like and you want another property to progress in the same pattern. Simply use the Copy (Ctrl+C or ⌘+C) command while viewing your edited curve, then use the Property menu to change views, and then apply the Paste (Ctrl+V or ⌘+V) command to instantly shift the curve to match your custom settings. This technique also works to copy a custom easing curve from one tween to another.

✦ If a curve gets too complicated or you change your mind, just press the Reset button to get back to the default curve.

As with anything else, it pays to start simple. Experiment with changing the easing curve of one property and if you get something you like, save it before you move on with another modification. If a curve works great to create an interesting effect on one property, try applying it to something else. Before long, you will have a library of files with cool tween patterns that you can copy and paste from rather than having to re-create a curve from scratch each time.

Integrating Multiple Animation Sequences

So far in this chapter, we've looked at creating different types of animation on the Main Timeline. As you can tell, even with the simple examples that we've used, adding multiple tweens to the Main Timeline can soon result in a jumble of colored spans and keyframes that might be hard to navigate when you need to make edits. Authoring all animation sequences on the Main Timeline also puts you at risk of unintentionally displacing multiple sequences as you make edits.

The best solution for keeping your project (.fla) files manageable as you continue to add animation is to move animation sequences off the Main Timeline and organize them instead on individual symbol timelines. This makes it much easier to move or reuse animation and will also ensure that any edits you make to individual animation sequences will not disrupt sequences on other symbol timelines. Graphic symbols and Movie Clip symbols can both be used to hold multiple layers of animation, but they have different uses.

As we discussed in Chapter 6, all symbols have their own timelines, so you could just as easily store an animation in a Graphic symbol as in a Movie Clip. However, there are some important differences to keep in mind:

✦ A Graphic symbol timeline must still be tied to frames on the Main Timeline, while a Movie Clip timeline will play back independently, regardless of how many frames it is assigned on the Main Timeline.

✦ The benefit of using a Graphic symbol to store an animated sequence is that it can be previewed frame by frame directly in the authoring environment, even if it is nested. You *can* preview animation on a Movie Clip timeline in Edit mode, but you will not be able to see how the animation on the Movie Clip timeline syncs with animation on other symbol timelines or with the Main Timeline until you publish the movie or use the Test movie command.

✦ Another significant limitation of Graphic symbols is that they cannot be targeted with ActionScript. Movie Clip symbols can be targeted with ActionScript to control the playback of each symbol instance independently, as opposed to having all animation tied to frame sequences on the same (main) timeline.

The extent to which you separate and nest animated elements will depend on the complexity of the project and also on how you intend to reuse animation. In general, any elements that will always be linked together on playback can be stored in the same symbol. If you want to have the option of altering playback speed or placement of certain elements independently, then these should be stored in discrete symbols. For example, if you have an animated logo that may be used in a project separately from an animated title, then these two elements should be in individual symbols. On the other hand, if the logo always appears in the same way with the title, then these two elements can be stored in a single symbol (on separate layers, if necessary).

Note

Timeline Effects generally render an animated sequence as a multiframe Graphic symbol on the Main Timeline. Although this is not always the recommended symbol type for Flash animation, it does make it possible to view the animation just by scrubbing the Timeline. This was intended to make Timeline Effects more user-friendly for people learning Flash. We cover the uses for and limitations of Timeline Effects in more detail in Chapter 12, "Applying Filters and Effects."

Tip

It is always possible to use the Property inspector to change the behavior (or symbol type) of a symbol instance on the Stage. If you are working with multiple Movie Clips and you need to sync some parts of the animation, it can be helpful to temporarily assign a Movie Clip instance Graphic symbol behavior so that you can see the animation on its timeline in the main authoring environment. Don't forget to switch the instance back to Movie Clip behavior before you publish your movie.

Moving tweens onto symbol timelines

Certainly, it is more efficient to plan your project structure before you begin adding animation so that you can nest animation in symbols as you create it, but Flash is flexible enough to enable you to optimize the organization of your animation sequences even after you have strewn them around on the Main Timeline.

Caution

The only exception to this flexible authoring rule is caused by Timeline Effects. You must create a holder symbol for the Timeline Effect and render the Effect on the symbol timeline rather than on the Main Timeline, to avoid "breaking" the Timeline Effect settings option when you try to re-architect your project file.

To illustrate how tweens are moved from the Main Timeline to symbol timelines, we will modify a file called tweensTimeline.fla, which includes multiple layers with Shape tweens and Motion tweens keyframed on the Main Timeline.

On the CD-ROM

We have included two files in the Integrate subfolder of the ch11 folder on the CD-ROM for you to refer to: the original tweensTimeline.fla with tweens on the Main Timeline and the modified tweensNested.fla, with tweens moved onto symbol timelines.

To reorganize a file (.fla) that has animation built on the Main Timeline, follow these steps:

1. Analyze the Main Timeline carefully to see how the various animated sequences need to relate to each other in the final .swf file. Decide which frame spans and layers you need to keep tied together and which should be independent.

2. Pay close attention to how the transitions between different animated sequences are handled on the Main Timeline. If two different phases of a tween share a common keyframe (for example, if you have scaled an element in one tween and then rotated the same element in another tween that continues from the final keyframe of the first tween), you must keep these tweens together or else insert an additional keyframe before you separate them in order to keep both tweens intact.

Tip

To be certain that linked sequential tweens can be separated without getting messed up, it can be helpful to remove the tween from the end keyframe of the first tweened sequence after inserting another keyframe (F6) to maintain the beginning of the tween that follows. This ensures that there is no interpolation between the end keyframe of the first tween and the start keyframe of the second tween.

3. Double-click the span or Shift-select the beginning and end keyframes of the sequence that you want to move off the Main Timeline.

4. With all frames in the sequence selected, choose Copy Frames from the contextual menu (see Figure 11-25), or Edit ⇨ Timeline ⇨ Copy Frames from the application menu (Alt+Ctrl+C or Option+⌘+C).

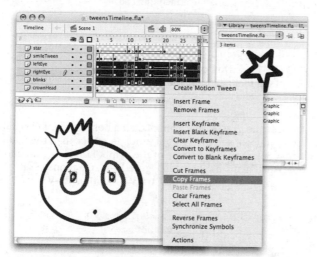

Figure 11-25: You can select frame spans on multiple layers to move at one time. Be sure to use Copy Frames rather than simply Copy to move all the frames to the Clipboard.

5. Create a new symbol by choosing Insert ⇨ New Symbol from the application menu (Ctrl+F8 or ⌘+F8). Assign the symbol Movie Clip or Graphic behavior and give it a name that will be useful for identifying the animation, as shown in Figure 11-26.

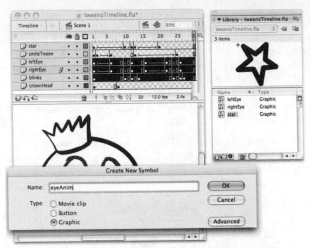

Figure 11-26: In the Create New Symbol dialog box, select a symbol behavior and enter a meaningful name for your new symbol.

6. After you click OK to close the Create New Symbol dialog box, the symbol is automatically opened in Edit mode — you will see the symbol timeline rather than the Main Timeline in the Timeline window. Select the first frame of the symbol timeline and choose Paste Frames from the contextual menu, as shown in Figure 11-27. Or choose Edit ⇨ Timeline ⇨ Paste Frames from the application menu (Alt+Ctrl+V or Option+⌘+V).

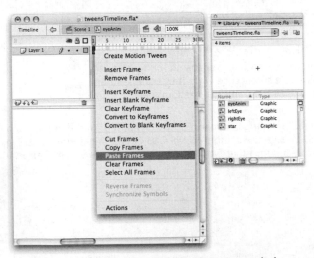

Figure 11-27: Select the first frame in your new symbol timeline and use Paste Frames to insert the frames and layers from the Clipboard.

7. Flash automatically inserts enough layers and frames to accommodate the content you paste into the symbol timeline (see Figure 11-28). Your animation sequence is now stored inside the symbol and you can easily access it from the Library for reuse or editing.

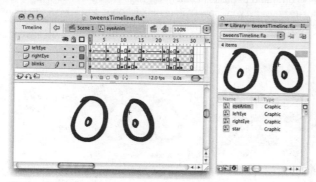

Figure 11-28: When you use Paste Frames to place the content from the Clipboard into your symbol, layers and keyframes are preserved.

Create as many new symbols as you need to hold all of the individual animation sequences that you want to work with in your project. When you are finished, you should have a set of named symbols in your Library that are easy to identify and contain animated elements that will now be efficient to edit or reuse.

Organizing Symbol instances on the Main Timeline

You may have noticed in the last section that we suggested *copying* your animation sequences from the Main Timeline to be pasted into individual symbol timelines — even though this results in redundant content. The rationale for leaving the original sequences on the Main Timeline, rather than cutting them, as you move content into separate symbols, is that they provide a useful reference for where the symbol instances should be placed on the Stage and how they should be arranged on the Main Timeline. The simplest way to "rebuild" your animation, using the nested symbols you have created, is to insert a new layer for each symbol on the Main Timeline directly above the original sequence that was copied. As you drag each symbol instance onto the Stage, you will be able to align the artwork with the original sequence on the Stage and also to determine how many frames the symbol should occupy on the Main Timeline.

Using the example from the previous section, we will show you how to replace the tweened sequences on the Main Timeline with our nested symbol instances.

1. Insert a new layer on the Main Timeline directly above the original tweened sequence by selecting the original layer and using the New Layer button in the Timeline window or choosing Insert ➪ Timeline ➪ Layer from the application menu (or the contextual menu).

Caution

Check the labels above the Timeline to be sure that you are editing the Main Timeline (Scene 1) and not one of the named symbol timelines. If there are any names listed in the crumb menu to the right of Scene 1, click the back arrow or the Scene 1 label to return to the Main Timeline before you start placing symbol instances on the Stage.

2. Drag an instance of your nested animation symbol from the Library onto the Stage in the new layer and align it with the content on the other layers (see Figure 11-29).

Tip Use the Lock Others command to protect content on your original layers while you drag and position the symbol instance on your new layer. Your keyboard arrow keys can be helpful for "nudging" an item into final alignment if dragging is not precise enough.

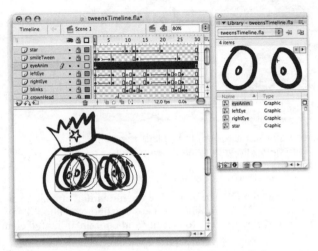

Figure 11-29: The original animation layers can help you to sequence and visually align the new symbol instances as you rebuild your project.

3. After you finish placing the new symbol instance in the Main Timeline, you can delete the layers containing the original tweened sequences (which are now redundant). You will quickly see how much cleaner and easier to modify the Timeline becomes when the tweened and frame-by-frame sequences are replaced with nested symbol instances, as shown in Figure 11-30.

Figure 11-30: The Main Timeline becomes easier to manage as you replace the tweened and frame-by-frame sequences with nested symbol instances.

In the previous example, we moved the timeline animation sequences to Graphic symbol timelines to make it easier to preview the animation on the Main Timeline. However, in most production contexts, it is best to use Movie Clip symbols to hold animation because instances of Movie Clips can be targeted with ActionScript. Also, Movie Clip timelines will loop independently of the Main Timeline, so you can repeat an animation sequence as many times as you like, either by holding on a single frame of the Main Timeline, or by extending the span of the Movie Clip so that it remains visible as the Main Timeline continues to play. In the next section, we will work with Movie Clip symbol instances to demonstrate how to reuse animated symbols and how to add some variation to the instances.

Reusing and Modifying Symbol Instances

Cleaning up the Main Timeline is one good reason to move animation onto symbol timelines. An even better reason is to make it easier to reuse and modify instances of the animated symbols once you have them stored in your Flash Library.

On the CD-ROM

To follow this example, you can start with the `tweensModify_start.fla`, or you can open the `tweensModify_final.fla` file from the `Modify` subfolder in the `ch11` folder on the CD-ROM to see the final result of adding and modifying Movie Clip symbol instances.

In the `tweensModify_start.fla` example file, we have placed multiple instances of a `starSpin` Movie Clip on a new `bkgrndStars` layer in the Main Timeline to create some animated background elements (see Figure 11-31).

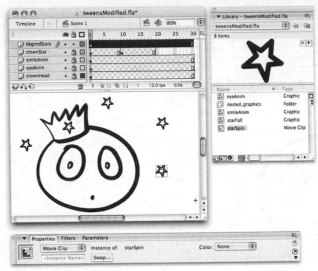

Figure 11-31: Movie Clips make it easy to place multiple instances of an animated element with different effects applied.

Controlling symbol instances with ActionScript

You can use ActionScript to control the playback of each element independently of the Main timeline. For example, rather than stopping everything on the Main Timeline, you can place a stop() action on the starSpin symbol timeline to hold the animation of the stars while the other elements continue to play (as shown in Figure 11-32, top). Any ActionScript placed directly on the symbol timeline will apply to all instances of the symbol. If you are working with Movie Clip symbols, you have the additional option of naming individual symbol instances and *targeting* them with ActionScript placed on a keyframe in the Main Timeline (as shown in Figure 11-32, bottom). This method enables you to stop the animation on some stars, while letting others continue to spin as the animation on the Main Timeline plays.

> **On the CD-ROM** To see the difference between adding ActionScript directly to a symbol timeline to stop all instances and targeting a specific named symbol instance with ActionScript on the Main Timeline, compare stopSymbol.fla (or .swf) with stopInstance.fla (or .swf).

Transforming symbol instances

As we discussed in previous chapters, you can modify the appearance of symbol instances without having to edit the contents of the original symbol. This can be helpful when you are working with static elements, but it really becomes indispensable when you are working with animated elements. Imagine the time it would take to copy and paste a series of tweens or a frame-by-frame sequence on the Main Timeline and then to edit the artwork on each keyframe just to change the scale or the color of your animated element each time you want to use it. Now be very happy that the little extra time spent moving your animated sequences off the Main Timeline and into symbols makes it possible to drag and drop your animated elements and then to scale, rotate, or apply Filters or Color effects to get endless variations without ever having to edit the original keyframe artwork.

Figure 11-32: ActionScript can be added to symbol timelines (top) or used to target symbol instances (bottom) to control the playback of animated elements, independent of the Main Timeline.

On the CD-ROM

We have included the original and the modified version of our example file so that you can see how the symbol instances were changed—compare tweensModify_start.fla and tweensModify_final.fla in the Modify subfolder in the ch11 folder of the CD-ROM.

In our example (see Figure 11-33), we have modified the appearance of some of the animated stars by transforming instances of the original starSpin Movie Clip.

Figure 11-33: By transforming symbol instances, you can add almost endless variation to the appearance of your animated sequences without having to modify any keyframe artwork.

The beauty of symbols is that you always have the option of modifying the appearance of individual symbol instances or making global changes by modifying the artwork in your original symbol. If you decide that an element should be changed every place that it appears, it is much quicker to edit the original symbol than it is to modify all of the symbol instances individually.

Tip

If you decide that you want to keep the static shape, but not the animation or the link to the original symbol in the Library for some of the symbol instances you have placed on the Main Timeline, you can use Modify ➪ Break Apart (Ctrl+B or ⌘+B) to "break" the link to the animated symbol. The original artwork (or static shape) will remain on the Stage, but any changes made to the original symbol in the Library will not be carried over to the now unlinked shape.

Reversing tweens to create smooth loops

The option of reversing a sequence of frames comes in handy when you are creating animation loops. You can reverse a tween or a frame-by-frame sequence as long as there is a keyframe at each end of the sequence that you select. One of the most common ways to achieve this is to copy a sequence of frames for an animation, place it on the Timeline immediately following the original sequence, and then apply the Modify ➪ Timeline ➪ Reverse Frames command to create a seamless loop. When the Timeline is played back, instead of completing one sequence and then jumping directly back to the starting keyframe, you will now have a second sequence that smoothes the transition from the final artwork back to the original artwork on the starting keyframe of the sequence.

On the CD-ROM To see how a straight tween can be modified to make a smoother loop, compare `smile_start.fla` with `smile_loop.fla`. These two files are in the `Modify` subfolder of the `ch11` folder on the CD-ROM.

In our example, we used this technique to animate the mouth from a smile back to a surprised expression.

1. The first step is to copy and paste the frames for the smile animation. (You can place them on the same layer, but for clarity we have placed them on a layer directly under the original smile.)

Note To view the tween frames for the smile animation on the smileAnim timeline, double-click the smileAnim symbol in the Library or an instance of smileAnim on the Stage of the Main Timeline to open the symbol in Edit mode.

You can select all the frames in the sequence and use the Copy Frames command, or hold down the Option (Alt) key while dragging the selected span to a new layer (or position on the Timeline). Make sure that the copied sequence is placed immediately following the original sequence (either on the same layer or on a new layer), as shown in Figure 11-34.

Figure 11-34: Place the copied tween sequence immediately following the final keyframe of the original tween on the symbol Timeline.

2. With all of the frames (and keyframes) of the copied sequence selected, choose Modify ⇨ Timeline ⇨ Reverse Frames from the application menu or from the contextual menu. Flash will automatically rearrange the order of the selected frames so that the animation

is reversed, as shown in Figure 11-35. You can also make adjustments to the length of the sequence or apply different tween settings. For example, you may want to change Easing from In to Out or add some static frames to the end of the timeline to hold the worried expression a bit longer before it loops back to start the smile tween again.

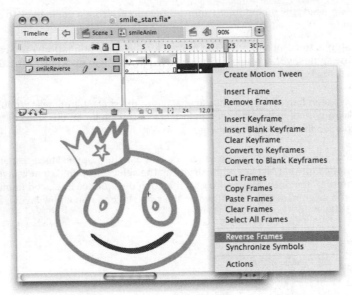

Figure 11-35: After the sequence is reversed, you can make adjustments to polish the loop.

Note   After the animation is reversed, you may find that a broken tween exists on the final keyframe in the reversed sequence. The animation will work fine as is, but to make your tween timeline cleaner, simply select the final keyframe and choose None from the Tween menu in the Property inspector to remove the "broken end" of the tween.

We could fill an entire book with illustrations of the various ways that you can move, edit, and recombine your animated sequences, but the basic principles are always the same. Use symbols to keep your files optimized and your options open. Nest symbols to keep your project organized. Try to keep your Main Timeline uncluttered and easy to modify by putting frame-by-frame animation and tweens on symbol timelines. Use Movie Clip symbols if you plan to target instances of the symbol with ActionScript. Apply Timeline Effects on symbol timelines or as the last step in your editing process if you want to layer different animation techniques. Use Filters rather than Timeline Effects whenever possible because they are more versatile and will not break as easily. Let Flash do as much work for you as possible, but don't be afraid to manually tweak animated sequences by inserting keyframes or modifying artwork. Use layers to keep elements organized and when you need to animate multiple items on the same span of the Timeline. Plan and design your animation in logical sections rather than in complex groups — you can add complexity by nesting multiple symbols. Avoid redundant work and keep your files small and easy to manage by reusing artwork and animation whenever possible.

Summary

✦ The Flash authoring environment includes several features that have been adapted from tools that are used for creating traditional animation. Onion skinning, keyframes, and tweens are the digital equivalents of layered transparent cels, keyart, and manual inbetweens.

✦ There are three basic ways to create animation: frame-by-frame animation; two types of interpolated animation (Shape and Motion tweens); and script-controlled, auto-rendered Timeline Effects. Most projects will require a combination of all three types of animation.

✦ You can use Shape tweens only to interpolate primitive shapes (including broken apart text), and you can use Motion tweens only to interpolate editable text, symbols, bitmaps, or groups. The new Drawing Objects in Flash 8 can be Shape tweened *or* Motion tweened.

✦ You can apply new Flash 8 Filters only to Movie Clips, Button symbols, and text, but they are easier to edit and less likely to break than Timeline Effects.

✦ Tweens add less to file size than frame-by-frame animation because Flash calculates the difference between the keyframes rather than having to store unique artwork for every frame in a sequence. However, tweens can be very processor intensive if complex transitions or alpha layers need to be interpolated and rendered.

✦ You can modify the pace of tweened animation by extending or shortening the span of the tween and also by adjusting the Easing settings to create acceleration or deceleration in a sequence.

✦ The new Custom Easing panel in Flash 8 (invoked by clicking the Edit button in the Property inspector) makes it possible to go beyond the Ease In and Ease Out settings available directly in the Property inspector. This opens a whole range of new possibilities for controlling the interpolation of properties in a tween. Properties can be set to progress along a single curve, or their individual curves can be modified to create more sophisticated tween effects.

✦ You can modify and re-render Timeline Effects from the Settings dialog box that is invoked with the Edit option, unless you have opened them in Edit mode from the Document window or have manually adjusted the rendered frame span in the Timeline. Manually editing a symbol or frame span rendered by a Timeline Effect will "break" the Edit option, but leave you with all the editing options that you can use to modify standard symbols and tweens.

✦   ✦   ✦

Applying Filters and Effects

In this chapter, we'll introduce you to the tools that Macromedia has added to the authoring environment to support *expressiveness* — a key theme that guided feature development for Flash 8. After several Flash product cycles that favored developers with code-oriented updates, Flash 8 tips the scales toward visual designers with some great new effects. Aside from better bitmap smoothing, improved text rendering, and more robust support for imported graphic files, Flash 8 comes loaded with a new Filters panel and a Blend menu built into the Property inspector.

If you've worked with other graphics programs, you'll appreciate the creative potential of these additions to Flash. If you've never used a filter or heard of a blend mode, you'll be relieved to discover how easy it is to apply these features and will be amazed at how much they can do to enhance your projects.

Applying Filters in Flash

Filters offer shortcuts for adding visual polish to your Flash designs. Rather than manually editing shapes to create drop-shadows or adjusting gradient fills to create bevels, you can simply apply a live filter and use the built-in settings to adjust the final effect. Unlike Timeline Effects, filters are rendered on the fly and do not result in any additional symbols being generated and added to the Library. In addition, Filters do not interfere with the "editability" of your content — you can always modify the original text or symbol instance without "breaking" the filter effect. Filters can be layered in any order and you can make modifications to the individual filter settings at any time. You can also add or control filters at run time with ActionScript, but for now we'll focus on applying filters in the authoring environment — which doesn't require any code! Filters are rendered as you add or adjust them so you can always see just what you'll get when the final movie is published.

Adding and adjusting filters

As shown in Figure 12-1, the Filters panel is grouped with the Property inspector in the default Flash Workspace layout. To apply a filter, follow these easy steps:

1. Select an item on the Stage that is compatible with filters — a MovieClip instance, Button symbol instance, or text field.

2. Open the Filters panel (or activate the Filters tab in the Property inspector), then click the plus symbol in the top-right corner to access the drop-down list of available filters.

3. After a filter is selected from the drop-down menu, it will appear in a live list on the left side of the Filters panel and you will see the filter effect (with default settings) applied to your selected item.

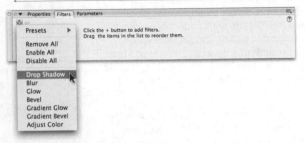

Figure 12-1: The new Flash 8 Filters panel makes it easy to add live effects.

As shown in Figure 12-2, the settings for each filter are loaded into the main part of the panel when an applied filter is selected in the live list. The settings vary for each filter, but once you become familiar with the options, you'll find it easy to adjust individual filters. To remove a filter at any time, simply select the name of the filter in the live list and click the minus (–) symbol at the top of the panel.

Tip   Applied filters can be temporarily toggled off (and back on) to preview different filter combinations by clicking the check mark (or cross icon) that appears to the left of the filter name in the live list.

Figure 12-2: Individual settings for applied filters can be adjusted at any time by selecting a filter in the Filters panel live list.

The default filter settings (shown in Figure 12-3) are a good starting point, and in some cases they might even give you the result you want, though in most cases, you'll need to modify the settings to achieve a satisfactory final effect.

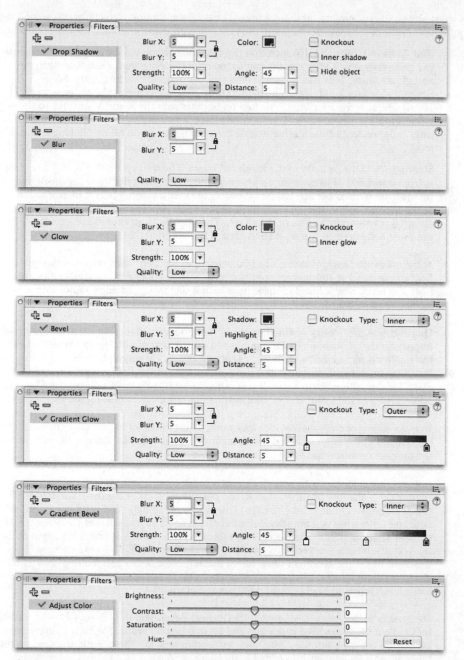

Figure 12-3: Some Flash 8 filter effects have unique controls, but most are created with different combinations of a series of basic settings.

It would be an overwhelming task to document every combination of settings on every filter, but an overview of the main settings will provide you with some guidance for experimentation:

Blur X, Blur Y: Sets the distance that the edge of a shape will be extended horizontally (X) and vertically (Y) to create a graduated or softened edge for shadow, blur, bevel, and glow effects. This has the same effect as the distance setting in the Soften Fill Edges dialog box for shapes. The default blur distance is 5 and the range is from 0 to 100. By default, the lock icon is turned on to constrain the X and Y settings to the same value, creating a symmetrical, graduated effect. If you prefer to make the X and Y settings independent of each other, toggle the constrain option off by clicking the lock icon.

Strength: Sets the opacity of the rendered effect. The default setting is 100. The range is from 0 to 1,000. However, for all practical purposes, the effective range for most filters is from 0 (invisible) to 100 (solid center area with normal fall-off in graduated area). Increasing the strength of a filter beyond 100 percent adds opacity to the stepped (or softened) areas of the shape. The opacity is increased incrementally from the most solid area to the least solid area of the stepped edge.

At the maximum Strength setting of 1,000 percent, all the steps within the Blur distance of a filter are rendered at 100-percent opacity, which usually counteracts the visual impact of the filter. The result is an expanded solid shape with a slightly jagged edge, rather than a nice-looking shadow, blur, or bevel.

Quality: Sets the fidelity or smoothness of the rendered effect. This setting has a major impact on the performance of the published movie. By default, Quality is set to Low. As the quality is increased to Medium or High, gradients are rendered more smoothly and the steps in blurs are softened, but the performance of the final movie is reduced. Your Flash movies will perform better if you can achieve the visual effect you need by making adjustments to the Color and/or Blur settings rather than increasing the Quality setting.

To make a glow or drop-shadow look less harsh, adjust the Color to be a closer match to the background color rather than reduce Strength or increase Quality. Color settings have the least impact on the performance of the final movie.

Color: Click color chips to access currently loaded swatches and set colors used to render Drop shadow or Glow effects. The default solid color for Drop shadow is Black (#000000); the default solid color for Glow is Red (#FF0000). The solid color that is set with the Color chip will automatically fade from solid to transparent to create a soft glow or shadow effect. The Bevel filter requires both a Shadow and a Highlight color — by default, these are set to black (#000000) and white (#FFFFFF), respectively. The Gradient Bevel and Gradient Glow filters make it possible to add multiple colors to rendered gradient effects. Click the color anchors on the gradient strip to access currently loaded swatches and set control points in the gradient.

The opacity of the center color anchor for Gradient Bevels and the left (outer) color anchor for Gradient Glows are fixed in position and set to 0 percent Alpha. The color of these pointers can be changed, but the Alpha level and anchor position can only be changed on the other anchors (or new anchors added to the gradient strip).

Angle: Sets the direction of offset to be applied with the Distance setting. If Distance is set to 0, changing the Angle (or degree of offset) will have no visible effect. The default is a 45-degree angle and the range is 0 to 360 degrees. You can change this setting by manually entering a number (decimals are allowed), or by dragging a small circle icon around a fixed 360-degree arc invoked by clicking the arrow (drop-down menu) icon next to the Angle value field. The higher the Distance setting, the more obvious the off-set direction or Angle will be.

Distance: Sets the pixel value for the distance between the center point of the original item and the center point of the rendered filter (gradient). The default setting is 5 and the range is from –32 to 32 pixels. If the distance setting is 0, the rendered gradient and the original item will be center-aligned.

Caution

If the Distance setting is 0 and the Blur setting is less than 5, it can be hard to see a filter effect if it is rendered outside (or behind) the original item.

In addition to the adjustable settings, there are some check box options that expand the visual possibilities for filters:

Knockout: Converts the original shape into a transparent area, while leaving the rendered effect visible in any area that was not cut out by the original shape.

Filter types: For Blur and Drop shadow filters, this is a check box to switch the rendered gradient from outside to inside the boundary of the original shape. For the multi-color gradient filters (Bevel, Gradient Glow, and Gradient Bevel), the options are listed in a drop-down menu that enables the filter to be set to render inside (Inner), outside (Outer), or inside *and* outside (Full) the boundaries of the original item.

Caution

The Bevel filter works best when left at the default Inside setting. Outside and Full bevels require some adjustment to create a realistic, dimensional result rather than a messy, doubled-up drop-shadow effect.

Tip

Inner Gradient Glow effects are easier to create using a custom gradient fill instead of applying the Gradient Glow filter with the Inner setting. A gradient fill will also be less demanding at run time than a Gradient Glow filter.

Hide object: This option is the secret to creating sophisticated Drop shadows (as we describe later in this chapter). When Hide object is enabled, the original object disappears, but the drop-shadow is preserved.

Note

Although Hide object and Knockout both convert the original shape into a transparent area, they do not have exactly the same result. The Hide object option preserves the entire gradient area rendered by a filter effect, while the Knockout option creates a "cutout" effect when combined with filters that are not set to render inside the boundaries of the original shape. Although Hide object can be selected when the Knockout option is also selected, there is no visible difference to the rendered graphic. If you decide to use the Knockout option, it is best to uncheck the Hide object option to avoid rendering redundant filters at run time.

The filter settings we have described thus far relate to the various gradient-based filters. As you can see from Figure 12-3, the Adjust Color filter settings are unique. The sliders available with the Adjust Color filter settings for adjusting various color qualities will be familiar to anyone who has worked in image editing programs like Photoshop or Fireworks. Flash updates the selected item on the Stage as you make color adjustments, so it is easy to experiment with the filter settings. However, it is important to know when to apply the Adjust Color filter and when to use the color controls available from the Properties panel.

Creating dimensional shadows

One limitation of the new Drop shadow filter is that it does not have a built-in skew setting. The workaround for creating a drop-shadow with more depth illustrates how you can use the Hide object option and the Transform panel to enhance shadows created with the Drop shadow filter. Here are the steps:

1. Place a Text field, Movie Clip, or Button instance on the Stage.

2. Create a new layer below the original content layer: Click the Insert Layer icon in the Timeline (or choose Insert ➪ Timeline ➪ Layer from the application menu). Drag the new layer to reorder it below the original layer in the layer stack.

3. Copy the item from Step 1 to the new layer: Select the keyframe where the item exists and hold the Option key while dragging the keyframe content to the new layer, or select the item and use the copy command (Ctrl+C or ⌘+C on Mac), then activate the new layer and use the Paste in Place command (Shift+Ctrl+V or Shift+⌘+V on Mac).

4. Lock the original content layer.

5. Select the duplicate item on the lower layer and use the Transform panel to apply a Horizontal stretch and skew. As shown in Figure 12-4, we set the horizontal scale to 130 percent and the horizontal skew to –45 degrees.

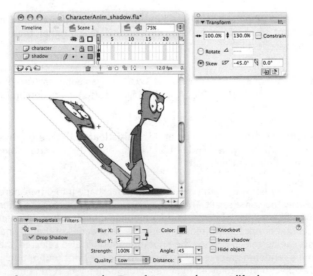

Figure 12-4: Use the Transform panel to modify the duplicate symbol instance so it will create a more realistic offset shadow.

6. Open the Filters panel or activate the Filters tab in the Property inspector.

7. Click the plus symbol and select Drop shadow from the filters list. In the Drop shadow settings, select the Hide object check box. Otherwise, the default settings are a good place to start.

8. As shown in Figure 12-5, the default settings can be modified to create a softer shadow. In our example, the shadow Color was changed to medium gray (#666666), the Strength was set to 50 percent, and the Quality was set to Medium.

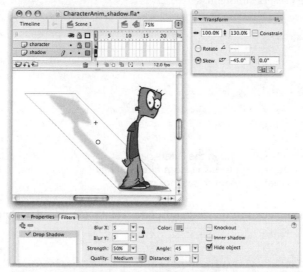

Figure 12-5: A Drop shadow filter applied to the skewed symbol instance with the Hide object option enabled, and a few adjustments to the default settings, result in a realistic, dimensional shadow.

Combining filters and saving custom presets

You can add multiple filters to one item and they will be rendered in the order they appear in the live list, from top to bottom. Changing the order of filters by dragging a filter name up or down in the live list will change the final result of the combined effect, but the settings for each filter will be preserved and editable.

If you have created a special combination of filters or found a custom filter setting that you would like to reuse, the Presets option makes it easy to save and access your own list of filter effects.

To save a filter setting or filter combo to the presets menu, follow these steps:

1. Select the item that has the filters and settings applied that you would like to save.

Note
All filters in the live list for the selected item will be saved with the preset—including any filters that are toggled off. When the custom filter is applied from the Presets menu to another item, the settings will be identical.

2. In the Filters panel, click the plus icon (+) to invoke the filter menu (as shown in Figure 12-6), and from the Presets submenu, select Save As.

Figure 12-6: The Presets submenu in the Filters panel enables you to manage and apply any custom filter settings or filter combinations that you want to save for reuse.

3. Enter a name for your custom filter settings or filter combo (as shown in Figure 12-7) and click OK.

Figure 12-7: You can name and save custom settings for a specific filter or a combination of filters for reuse.

4. The named preset will be added to the bottom of the Presets submenu, along with any other saved Presets (in alphabetical order, as shown in Figure 12-8), and can be applied to other items.

Figure 12-8: Saved filter presets appear alphabetically in the Presets menu — the Presets are saved on an application level for reuse in any active document.

Caution

When a Preset is applied to an item, any other filters that have been applied to that item will be cleared and replaced with the filters (and settings) that were saved with the Preset.

After a Preset is applied to an item, the settings can be modified on that item without corrupting the saved Preset. Unfortunately, the Presets list doesn't have a centralized edit option, but you can select the Rename or Delete option from the Preset submenu to load your list of currently saved presets into dialog boxes that enable you to rename an item or remove an item from the list. If you'd like to share your filter presets with someone else, all you have to do is provide them with the XML file that is saved for each preset in the Flash Configuration folder. The standard file paths for saved filter presets are as follows:

Windows:

```
C:\Documents and Settings\username\Local Settings\Application
Data\Macromedia\Flash 8\language\Configuration\Filters\filtername.xml
```

Macintosh:

```
Macintosh HD/Users/username/Library/Application
Support/Macromedia/Flash 8/language/Configuration/Filters/filtername.xml
```

Once the XML files are copied into the same location on someone else's computer, the presets will appear in her Presets menu when she starts Flash 8. Filter swapping is an easy way to share creative resources and to keep effects consistent for projects that rely on filters for a specific look.

Although you may occasionally find it helpful to combine filters, it is best to try and achieve the result you want by first adjusting the settings of a single filter and/or modifying the symbol instance using the Color Effect settings in the Properties panel or the Transform tools. As with any intensive effect rendered at run time, multiple filters will have a negative impact on the performance of the published Flash movie.

Animating filters with motion tweens

Macromedia has done a great deal of engineering to make it as easy as possible to combine filters with motion tweens for animated effects. The result is a very intuitive system that works behind the scenes to support tweens while preserving editable filter settings.

Note

Filters are not necessarily incompatible with shape tweens, but because filters can only be applied to symbols or text fields and shape tweens can only be applied to primitive shapes, filters and shape tweens never get a chance to work together. The only workaround for this rule is to create a shape tween inside of a Movie Clip and then apply a filter to the Movie Clip. In this case, the final visual result is a combination of a shape tween and a filter, but they remain on separate timelines.

You can apply a filter to an item and then tween it, or you can select an item that has been tweened and add a filter to enhance the motion — in most cases, you'll get exactly the animated effect you were hoping for. The only time you'll need to know what is going on behind the scenes is when you don't get the result you want on the first try.

Here are some notes that should help you troubleshoot if things go wrong when you try to combine filters and Motion tweens:

✦ Filters "stick" to symbol instances, so if you insert a keyframe (with the same content as the initial keyframe), and set up a Motion tween, the settings and the stacking order in the live list will automatically match in the first keyframe and the last keyframe of the tween.

✦ If you add a filter to a symbol in one keyframe of a tween, Flash automatically adds a matching filter with all the settings adjusted to create "no effect" to the symbol in the other keyframe. This is also called a "dummy filter" because it will have no visible effect on the symbol, but it is required to support the tween.

✦ If you remove a filter from a symbol in one keyframe of a tween, Flash automatically clears the matching filter from the other keyframe.

✦ If you apply different filters (or different combinations of filters) on two different keyframes and then apply a tween, Flash will analyze the symbol with the most filters and apply dummy filters to the symbol in the other keyframe to support the tween. The visual difference between the two symbols will be interpolated in the span of the tween.

✦ You can modify filter settings to create a visual change from the first keyframe to the last keyframe in a Motion tween. The differences will be tweened evenly across the span unless you use easing to adjust the interpolation.

✦ The knockout and type of gradient (such as inner, outer, or full) filter settings will not interpolate properly as part of a tween if they are set differently on the beginning and end keyframes. If the filter options in the first keyframe and the end keyframe of a tween are inconsistent and cannot be interpolated properly, Flash will apply the options set in the first keyframe to the frames in the span of the tween.

Using Custom Easing to control filter interpolation

By default, the interpolation of any differences in filter settings from the first keyframe to the last keyframe will match the interpolation of the motion tween — that is, the filters will change at the same rate as any other characteristics of the item that have been modified to create animation in the tween. General Easing settings (adjusted in the Property inspector) will be applied equally to all changes in the characteristics of an item. As we described in the previous chapter, if you need more precise control over the interpolation of different aspects of a tween, you can use Custom Easing to set unique curves for Position, Rotation, Scale, Color, and/or Filters. To access Custom Easing controls, select the first keyframe in the motion tween, then click the Edit button to the right of the Easing controls in the Property inspector. As shown in Figure 12-9, the easing Property menu at the top of the dialog box enables you to load a unique interpolation curve for each of the various properties that can be animated in a tween. You can set a unique curve to apply to all properties, or set unique curves for selected properties, leaving the default curve for others.

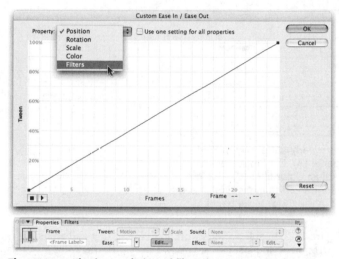

Figure 12-9: The interpolation of filters in a tween can be controlled separately from the interpolation of other characteristics by adjusting a custom easing curve.

Controlling Color: Properties vs. Filters

The Adjust Color filter included in the Flash 8 Filter panel loads a new set of controls for making color adjustment to Movie Clips, Button symbols, and text fields. The best way to explain these new controls is to compare them to standard Flash color settings. Some of these controls are unique and some replicate settings available in the Color Mixer panel (for primitive shapes and Drawing Objects) and/or in the Properties panel Color menu. These three different color control areas are shown in Figure 12-10, with an additional diagram to call out the features of the Color Mixer panel that overlap with slider settings for the Adjust Color filter.

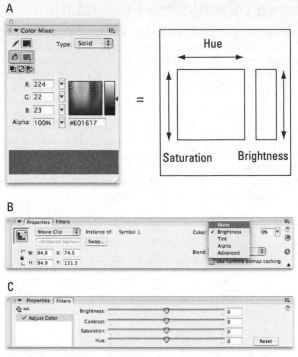

Figure 12-10: The options for adjusting color in Flash 8 include the Color Mixer panel (A), the Properties Color menu (B), and the new Adjust Color filter (C) — which enables instance-level color transformations similar to the raw color edits supported in the Color Mixer panel.

The controls shown in Figure 12-10 enable various workflows for setting and adjusting color in the Flash authoring environment. In most cases, you will start with the Color Mixer panel (or Swatches panel) to choose and/or modify fill and stroke colors for initial primitive shapes or Drawing Objects. After the raw graphics are converted into reusable symbols, the Color controls available in the Property inspector and/or the Adjust Color filter can be applied to modify symbol instances without changing the original fill and stroke colors. The sliders and value fields for adjusting color with either of these options are easy to use and you will most likely achieve the result you want with just a little experimentation. However, there are important differences between the Color Properties settings and the new Adjust Color filter settings, and the interaction of the different settings can become quite complex. To clarify the functions (and the advantages or limitations) of the various settings available with these two options, we have included a brief section for each.

If you'd like to learn more about various color models and the differences between HSV/HSB (hue, saturation, value; or hue, saturation, brightness) and HSL (hue, saturation, lightness) color spaces, a good place to start is Wikipedia: http://en.wikipedia.org/wiki/HSB_color_space.

Adjust Color filter

The most broadly useful tool introduced to Flash 8 with the new filters feature is the Adjust Color filter. Figure 12-11 shows a sample of the range of color transformations that can be achieved with the sliders that load into the Filters panel when you apply the Adjust Color filter to Movie Clip instances, Button instances, or text fields.

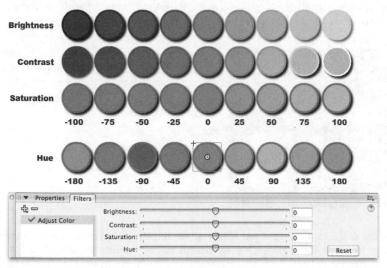

Figure 12-11: The color controls loaded in the Filters panel when the Adjust Color filter is applied enable subtle color transformations of symbol instances and text fields.

The grayscale version of the sample color transformations shown in Figure 12-11 gives you a hint of what is possible with the Adjust Color filter, but the color version of this figure included in the color insert in this book is much more informative.

We have included the source file with the various transformed Movie Clip instances shown in Figure 12-11 on the CD-ROM. Open `AdjustColorFilter.fla` from the `ch12` folder on the CD-ROM to see the samples in the Flash authoring environment. To see these same transformations applied to a sample bitmap, open `AdjustColorFilter_bitmaps.fla` from the same location.

Finally, you can make subtle adjustments (on an instance level) to Movie Clips, Button symbols, and text fields, without having to go back to the Color Mixer panel and change the stroke and fill colors of the original symbol. Unlike the Color control options in the Properties panel, the Adjust Color option in the Filters panel makes it easy to combine different types of color transformation without manually adjusting individual RGB values. By default, all settings are loaded as "neutral" — sliders are set to 0 so that no color transformation is visible on the selected item when the filter is first applied. Color transformations are applied for instant visual feedback as the slider controls or text values are adjusted. Filters apply on an instance level, and settings can be modified at any time by selecting an instance and choosing Adjust Color from the live filter list in the Filters panel. The following values can be applied individually or in combination to Movie Clips, Button symbols, and text fields:

✦ **Brightness:** Alters the RGB values for the original color to make it appear lighter or darker without changing the hue. The range for filter Brightness is –100 to +100. The default or no change value is 0. The numeric value that appears in the Brightness field is added to the RGB values of the original color to create a new shade, within the minimum and maximum values of 0 and 255, respectively. For example, a red fill (255, 0, 0) set to +50 brightness will be transformed into light red (255, 50, 50). The same red fill (255, 0, 0) set to –50 brightness will be transformed into dark red (205, 0, 0). As shown in Figure 12-12, the results of adjusting Brightness in the Filters panel are different than the results of adjusting Brightness in the Properties panel.

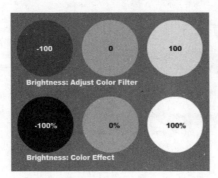

Figure 12-12: Numeric settings applied with the Adjust Color filter Brightness result in less extreme value changes than Percentage settings applied with the Color property Brightness.

Note   Although the range for the Brightness filter and the Brightness option in the Color menu might seem the same at first glance, the significantly different results that these two options achieve are due to one being a relative (or percentage-based) setting and the other being an absolute (or decimal-based) setting. The Brightness filter is applied as an absolute numeric value while the Color property Brightness setting is applied as a relative percentage-based value. Regardless of the original color, setting Color property Brightness to 100% shifts the RGB values to white (255, 255, 255) and –100% Brightness shifts the RGB values to black (0,0,0). Any other Brightness setting is calculated as the percentage between these two extremes, and the RGB values are transformed accordingly.

✦ **Contrast:** At the minimum contrast setting of –100, all RGB values are forced to 64, 64, 64, making everything medium gray. The RGB values at the maximum contrast setting of 100 will vary depending on the original colors, but they will be forced closer to 0 or 255. The default or no change value is 0. The greater the numeric difference between RGB values, the greater the amount of contrast. In visual terms, light colors get lighter and dark colors get darker as contrast is *increased*, whereas all colors are brought closer to medium gray as contrast is *decreased*.

✦ **Saturation:** Saturation can also be thought of as the intensity or purity of color. At the minimum saturation setting of –100, the image will be rendered in grayscale with no color intensity—similar to the hues found closer to the *bottom* of the color selection field in the Color Mixer. At the maximum saturation setting of 100, the colors will be as intense or as close to pure color as possible—similar to the hues found closer to the *top* of the color selection field in the Color Mixer panel.

✦ **Hue:** The Hue slider has a different range than the other Adjust Color filter sliders. To span the full range of the 360-degree color wheel, the slider values are from — 180 to 180. The default or no change value is 0. If you were looking at a real color wheel, reducing the hue value would be equivalent to moving counterclockwise around the wheel, while increasing the hue value would be equivalent to moving clockwise around the wheel. At either extreme (– 180 or 180), the resulting color would be directly opposite the original color on the color wheel. The relationship of colors directly opposite on the color wheel is known as *complementary*.

There are many books and online resources dedicated to color theory and there are many different versions of the color wheel. A good explanation and an illustration of an RBG color wheel can be found at `www.color-wheel-pro.com/color-theory-basics.html`. Color Wheel Pro is one of many software programs available to help designers create successful color schemes using color wheel relationships as a guideline.

The new Flash 8 filters (including the Adjust Color settings) are only compatible with Flash Player 8 (and only available in Flash Professional 8). If you plan to publish content for older versions of the Flash Player (or you are working with Flash Basic 8), you are limited to using the Color controls in the Property inspector to make adjustments to the appearance of symbol instances, or using the Color Mixer panel to modify the original stroke and fill colors in primitive shapes.

Color properties

As we introduced in Chapter 6, "Symbols, Instances, and the Library," the Color menu in the Property inspector provides some options for modifying the appearance of symbol instances without changing the original symbol stored in the Library. After a Color adjustment type is selected from the Color drop-down menu, the controls needed to apply the color adjustment appear in the Property inspector. By default, "neutral" settings (0-percent change) are loaded as a starting point. After the values for a property are modified, they will be stored and loaded as the default when you select another instance. The settings loaded in the Property inspector for the items in the Color menu are simple and intuitive and enable you to make basic color adjustments using familiar controls:

✦ **Brightness:** The Brightness Color property has the same range as the Brightness slider in the Adjust Color filter (–100 to 100); however, as we described previously, the Brightness property creates more drastic color transformations because it is applied as a relative or percentage-based value. At the minimum Brightness setting (–100), all RGB values are forced to black (0,0,0), and at the maximum Brightness setting (100), all RGB values are forced to white (255,255,255).

✦ **Tint:** The color theory definition of a tint is a color produced by adding white to a pure color. The Tint property in Flash enables you to select any color (not just white) to "mix" with the original color. You can also select how much of the new color you want to mix with your original colors — from the lowest setting of 0 percent to the maximum setting of 100 percent. At the minimum setting, the original colors will be unchanged. At the maximum setting, the new tint color will completely replace all of the original colors. At the default setting of 50 percent, the rendered color values will be an even mix of the original colors and the selected tint color.

✦ **Alpha:** This setting controls how opaque the selected instance will be. The values that control alpha are counterintuitive (as they are in the Color Mixer). At the minimum alpha level of 0 percent, the item will be transparent. At the maximum alpha level of 100 percent, the item will be fully opaque or "solid."

Using Advanced Color Effects: Understanding relative and absolute color settings

The Advanced Effect dialog box shown in Figure 12-13 includes two columns of settings for Red, Green, and Blue color channels, plus the setting for Alpha. This dialog box is invoked when a symbol instance is selected on the Stage by selecting Advanced from the Color drop-down menu on the Property inspector, and then clicking the Settings button. Although these columns may seem redundant at first, they actually provide very different options for controlling the appearance of instance color. The important difference between these two types of controls is that the first column creates *relative* changes by applying percentage-based adjustments, while the second column creates *absolute* change by adding or subtracting integer values.

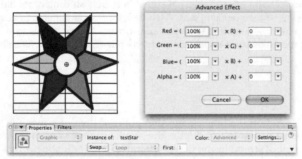

Figure 12-13: The Advanced Effect dialog box shown with the symbol instance `testStar`, with no effect applied

Tip   The most recent transformation that was applied to an item using the simple Color controls will be preserved if you decide to switch to the Advanced option from one of the other options in the Color menu. The equivalent values will be transferred to the RGB or Alpha value fields in the Advanced Color Effects dialog box. This is a helpful way to get started with more complex transformations rather than starting from scratch. For example, you could select a Tint setting and then switch to the Advanced Color option to add an alpha setting that would be combined with the RGB values carried over from the original tint.

Other than playing with these settings, the easiest way to understand what some of the possible combinations produce is to dig out your calculator and find a chart of RGB color swatches (with decimal values rather than Hex values). By taking the RGB values in your original instance, multiplying them by the percentage entered in the relative value field, and adding the value shown in the absolute color field, you will arrive at the new RGB value that will appear in the symbol instance when the effect is applied. If this sounds confusing, read on.

On the CD-ROM   Because color examples are not very helpful illustrated in black and white, we have included the relevant graphics in a Flash file that you can open for reference. Compare the `Advanced Color Effect (relative)` layer with the `Advanced Color Effect (absolute)` layer in `colorEdits.fla` in the `ColorEffectsVsFilters` folder in the `ch12` folder on the CD-ROM.

Relative color control

The first column of values adjusts the color of the instance relative to the percentages of color (or alpha) present in the original with a range of –100 percent to 100 percent. The default, or "no effect," setting is 100 percent. With these controls, 100 percent red does not change everything to pure red or 255 red, but rather it displays 100 percent of the current percentage of red in the existing colors. For example, yellow (255, 255, 0) cannot be made more orange by increasing the amount of red because 255 x 100 percent is still 255 — the maximum amount of red. However, if you reduce the percentage of green to 45 percent of the original value, the ratio of red will be increased, making the visible color shift to orange (255, [255 x 45 percent], 0 or 255, 102, 0).

This process of reducing the amount of the opposite (or complementary) color to alter the ratio of colors is called *subtractive* color adjustment, and it can be helpful to remember some basic color theory to predict how it will alter the appearance of your symbol instance. Because the color value changes that you make are applied to all the colors in your symbol, the overall effect can be more complex than just shifting one color in your palette. You will find, for example, that *reducing* the percentage of red and green to 0 for the testStar symbol instance (see the colorEdits.fla file on the CD-ROM) will cause the gray and white areas to shift to blue, whereas the red and green areas will shift to black, and the originally black areas will remain unaltered.

Because the maximum value for relative Alpha is also 100 percent, this control cannot be used to increase the alpha setting of an instance. For example, a symbol that has an alpha fill of 50 percent cannot be made to appear more solid because 100 percent of 50 percent is still only 50 percent alpha.

Absolute color control

The settings in the right column are referred to as *absolute* color controls because they add or subtract color in concrete amounts regardless of the color values in the symbol instance. The scale of absolute color is from –255 to 255 and the default or "no effect" setting is 0. When absolute color is applied to a symbol instance, it is possible to make more drastic global color changes than you can make with relative color adjustments.

The effect of absolute color value changes made in the Advanced Effect dialog box is similar to the effect of using the Tint option of the Color menu. What makes these controls more advanced is that not only can you add a tint by increasing the value of certain colors, but you can also add an *inverse* tint by using negative values. So, for example, you could add a red tint to all the colors present in the testStar symbol instance, with the exception of white and pure red (which already contain 255 red), by entering a value of 255 Red, or you could add a yellow tint to all colors containing blue by entering a value of –255 Blue; this would make pure blue (0, 0, 255) turn to black (0, 0, 0), and white (255, 255, 255) turn to pure yellow (255, 255, 0).

You can see the original testStar symbol instance and several modified examples, including those described in this section, in the Advanced Color Effect (absolute) layer of colorEdit.fla in the ColorEffectsVsFilters folder in the ch12 folder on the CD-ROM.

Perhaps one of the most unique feats that absolute values can perform is to make a symbol instance that contains alpha fills or strokes appear less transparent. Because the alpha settings are absolute, it is possible to shift an item with an original alpha setting of less than 100 percent to any opacity level between invisible (–255) and completely solid (255).

If you've entered negative values in the relative alpha setting, it is even possible to make an area with an alpha fill visible while solid areas are made invisible. Consider a shape that has an area of solid fill (100 percent or 255 alpha) and an area of transparent color (40 percent or 102 alpha). If this shape is converted into a symbol and then modified using the Advanced Effect options, you could enter a relative alpha value of –100 percent and an absolute alpha value of 255. When these effect settings are applied, the solid fill in the symbol instance would be invisible with 0 percent alpha (255 × –100 percent + 255 = 0), whereas the originally transparent fill would be visible with 60 percent alpha (102 × –100 percent + 255 = 153). Compare the modified `testStar` instance shown in Figure 12-14 with the original instance shown in Figure 12-13.

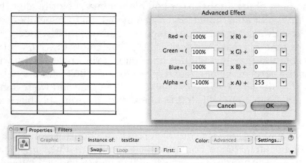

Figure 12-14: Using a combination of relative and absolute Alpha values, the transparency levels in the original `testStar` instance can be inverted.

The confusion that these settings sometimes cause has created debate about whether negative alpha settings can really be applied. As long as you can remember that outside of the absolute settings in the Advanced Effect dialog box, 0 percent alpha is invisible, whereas inside the Advanced Effect dialog box, a 0 alpha setting is equal to no effect, you will be able to prove as we just did, that negative alpha effects can be used to invert alpha values, similar to the way that negative color effects can be used to invert color values.

Layering graphics with blend modes

Flash 8 is the first version of Flash to include blend modes. If you use Photoshop or other image editing applications, you may be familiar with using blend modes, although for many people this remains a somewhat mysterious tool. Blends are rendering tools that analyze the pixel values of overlapping images (the blend image and the underlying base images) to create a rendered image that is a mix of the two. The type of blend applied will determine the formula used to generate the pixel values in the combined image. Blend modes can be applied to Movie Clip and Button symbol instances in the authoring environment using the Blend mode menu in the Properties panel (shown in Figure 12-15). The blend image will interact with any underlying images that it overlaps — even if they are not on the same layer.

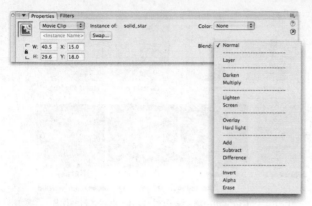

Figure 12-15: The Blend mode menu is available in the Property inspector when you select a Movie Clip or Button instance in Flash 8 Professional.

Tip   The dotted line breaks that separate the blend modes in the Blend menu may seem arbitrary, but they actually differentiate the blend modes into groups based on the type of effect they will have on images. Keep this in mind while you read the descriptions of each blend mode in the next section — you will start to notice similarities in the modes that are grouped.

Understanding blend modes

Predicting the exact outcome of various blend modes is tricky because blends use different formulas on a pixel-by-pixel basis to mix the blended image with underlying images, and the result depends on the pixel values of both the underlying images (or *base color*) and the overlapping image (or *blend color*). The most common advice for working with blends is to experiment until you get a result that you like — we encourage you to do exactly that! However, it is helpful to have some idea of how each blend works and what visual problems they can solve. Compare Figure 12-16, which shows two source bitmaps (left and center), overlapped with blend mode set to Layer or Normal (right), to Figure 12-17, which shows how the images appear with Flash blend modes applied to mix the images in various ways.

Base image   **Blend image**   **Layer (or Normal)**

Figure 12-16: A base image (left) and a blend image (center) overlapped with blend mode set to Normal or Layer create a standard layered graphic with no mixing of pixel values (right).

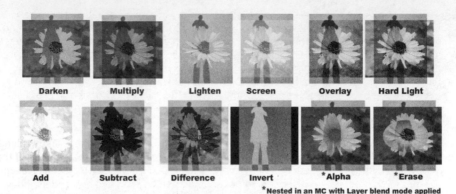

Figure 12-17: The twelve different effects that can be created by applying Flash 8 Blend modes to layered images — the results will vary depending on the images that are combined, but the formula used for each blend type is consistent. Unlike other blend modes, the Alpha and Erase blend modes require a nested structure with a Layer blend applied to the parent symbol instance.

Note   You'll notice that we didn't include an image in Figure 12-17 to illustrate the Layer blend mode applied by itself. That is because the Layer blend mode has no effect, unless it is combined with a nested Erase or Alpha blend mode.

The Blend modes available in Flash 8 Professional include the following:

✦ **Normal:** The default blend mode for new symbol instances. No interpolation is applied and pixel values are left unchanged.

✦ **Layer:** Creates no visual effect on its own, but is required for Alpha and Erase blend modes to work.

✦ **Darken:** Compares the brightness of the pixels in the base image with the pixels in the blend image. Pixels in the base image that are lighter than the blend image are replaced with pixels from the blend image. Pixels in the base image that are darker than the blend image are left unchanged.

✦ **Multiply:** Multiplies the RGB values of the pixels in the base image with the pixels in the blend image. The resulting pixels are a darkened combination of both the base image and the blend image. Multiplying any color with black results in solid black; multiplying any color with white leaves the pixels unchanged.

✦ **Lighten:** Compares the brightness of the pixels in the base image with the pixels in the blend image. Pixels in the base image that are darker than the blend image are replaced with pixels from the blend image. Pixels in the base image that are lighter than the blend image are left unchanged. The blend image always disappears when it's layered over white.

✦ **Screen:** Analyzes the color values and multiples the inverse of the blend and base colors. The resulting pixels are a lightened combination of both the base image and the blend image. Screening with black leaves the base image unchanged. Screening with white produces solid white. The blend image always disappears when it's layered over white.

✦ **Overlay:** Pixels are screened or multiplied depending on the pixel values in the base image. If the base color is lighter than mid-gray, the image is lightened (screened), and if the base color is darker than mid-gray, the image is darkened (multiplied). The blend image overlays the base image while preserving the highlights and shadows of the base image. The resulting image is an even blend of the base image and the blend image, usually with increased contrast in both images. Overlaying black results in a shaded version of the base image. Overlaying white results in a bleached version of the base image. The blend image disappears when it's layered over any pure color (black, white, pure red, pure green, etc.).

✦ **Hard light:** Pixels are screened or multiplied, depending on the pixel values in the blend image. If the blend color is lighter than mid-gray, the image is lightened (screened). If the blend color is darker than mid-gray, the image is darkened (multiplied). The base image is mixed with the blend while preserving the highlights and shadows of the blend image. Overlaying pure black or pure white results in solid black or solid white, respectively.

✦ **Add:** Adds the color values of the blend image to the color values of the base image. The result is a bleached-out combination of the two images. Adding pure white results in a solid white image; adding pure black has no effect on the base image.

✦ **Subtract:** Subtracts the blend color value from the base color value. The result is a darkened combination of the two images. Subtracting pure white from any color results in a solid black image. Subtracting pure black has no effect on the base image.

✦ **Difference:** Analyzes the color values in the base and the blend and subtracts the brighter values from the darker values. The result is a reversal of color values. Black blended with any color has no effect. White blended with any color inverts the color. The resulting image looks like a film negative of the combined images.

✦ **Invert:** Inverts the base image in any areas overlapped by the blend image. The contents of the blend image have no bearing on the transformation of the base color values — the blend image acts merely as an "active area" for the inversion effect.

✦ **Alpha:** Alpha blend mode can be used to apply the contents of a nested Movie Clip with alpha areas as a mask for an image in a parent Movie Clip with Layer blend mode applied.

✦ **Erase:** Erase blend mode can be used to apply the contents of a nested Movie Clip as an eraser to cut out an area of an image in a parent Movie Clip with Layer blend mode applied.

Tip   Using a solid fill with Alpha set to 0% in an Alpha blend will have the same effect as using a solid fill in an Erase blend.

Applying basic blends

That's a lot of visual calculation to try and imagine without actually using blends. The steps for applying the "basic blends" (all but Alpha and Erase) are straightforward:

1. Select a Movie Clip or Button symbol instance that you want to use as a blend image to layer with underlying base images.

Tip

Images on layers above the layer with the blend symbol instance will not be transformed by the blend mode. Don't forget that you can use the Modify ➪ Arrange commands if you need to modify the stacking order of images on the same layer.

2. Click the Properties tab in the Property inspector and from the Blend menu, select a blend type.

That's it! You can see how the blend image interacts with different base images by dragging it to overlap other images in your Flash authoring environment. The Color menu and Filters can be used in combination with blend modes to get different effects. All of these effect tools will interact to transform graphics rendered in the authoring environment, but they will remain editable and each can be adjusted independently on an instance level. You can apply multiple blend modes on the same layer, but only one blend mode to any single symbol instance. The only compound blend modes are Alpha and Erase, which must be applied on a symbol time-line and combined with a Layer blend mode on the parent symbol instance, as we describe in the next section.

Caution

The background color of your Flash movie will interact with blend modes too. This is helpful to remember if the blend image is larger than the base image and you start getting unexpected results in the overhang areas. Applying a Layer mask to the blend image so that it is trimmed to match the base image will remove any unwanted overhang areas that are mixing with the background color.

Applying compound blend modes: Alpha and Erase

Alpha and Erase blends are a great complement to Flash's standard masking tools — which can be counterintuitive at times. If you want to create a cutout in a shape using a traditional mask, you actually have to create a shape on a mask layer that covers all the areas *except* the area you wish to cut out. If you have been working in Flash for a while, this workflow is probably second nature, but when it comes to more subtle mask effects, like gradients or irregular shapes, it can be a headache to have to reverse-engineer a mask graphic. With Alpha blends, what you see is what you get — or rather, what you *don't* see is what you *won't* get! The steps for creating a compound blend are as follows:

1. Create a Movie Clip with content that will function as the base image (or convert an existing graphic that you want to mask into a Movie Clip).

2. Open the Movie Clip in Edit mode to access the Movie Clip timeline: Double-click an instance on the Stage or the symbol name in the Library list.

3. Create a new layer on the Movie Clip timeline above the existing content that will be the base image for the Alpha or Erase blend. To protect the base image(s), you may want to lock all layers but the new layer.

Note

The base image or color can be any graphic type — primitive shape, Drawing Object, bitmap, or symbol instance — as long as it nested inside of a Movie Clip or Button symbol. The blend image has to be a Movie Clip or Button symbol instance.

4. In the new layer, create a graphic that will act as a mask — blend masks are the opposite of normal Flash layer masks in that the content in the Alpha or Erase blend symbol instance will define an area to make *invisible* in the base image rather than define an area to make *visible*.

Caution
Any content in a symbol instance with an Erase blend mode applied will define the area to be punched out of (or erased from) the underlying base image. The content of a symbol instance with an Alpha blend mode applied will have no effect unless it contains areas with transparency—the amount of information erased from the base images will match the level of Alpha transparency in the blend symbol instance. A symbol instance with content set to 0 percent Alpha and applied as an Alpha blend will have the same effect as an Erase blend.

5. Convert the content on the blend layer into a Movie Clip or Button symbol.

6. Select the symbol instance and position it on the Stage (still on the base image Movie Clip timeline) to overlap the base image so that it defines the area you want to Erase or Alpha out, then use the Blend menu in the Properties panel to apply an Alpha or Erase blend mode. The content of the blend image will disappear, but don't panic—continue to the next step to complete the compound blend.

7. Return to the Main Timeline: Double-click an empty area of the Stage or use the Scene button above the Timeline.

8. Select the parent symbol instance (that contains your base image and the currently invisible blend image), and use the Blend menu to apply a Layer blend. (If you opened the base symbol from the Library in Step 2, make sure you have an instance dragged onto the Stage on the Main Timeline so you can apply the Layer blend mode to the instance.)

9. Voila! You should see the content of your blend image punched out (Erase blend) or rubbed out (Alpha blend) of the base image—either the background color of the Flash movie or any underlying images on the Stage will be visible through the empty areas created in the base image.

On the CD-ROM
Open `Erase_blend.fla` from the `Blends` folder in the `ch12` folder on the CD-ROM if you want to analyze an example of the nested symbol structure required to render Erase and Alpha blend modes successfully.

In addition to supporting a more intuitive workflow for creating masks and enabling Alpha-based masks, compound blends can be used to create animated transition effects. Continue to the next section if you would like to try using an Alpha blend to create an animated color fade effect.

Creating an animated Alpha blend

The following example uses an animated Alpha blend to selectively fade out a black and white image to reveal a color image. The trick for this effect is to use two instances of the same color image, with the Adjust Color filter applied to make one instance a grayscale version. There are a lot of steps, but the final file structure is straightforward and the effect is pretty cool, so let's get started:

1. Open a new Flash document.

2. Import a color bitmap and convert it to a Movie Clip (or place an existing Movie Clip instance on the Stage—preferably one with bright colors).

3. Place two instances of the Movie Clip on the Stage so that they are layered and aligned— select both instances and use the Vertical Center and Horizontal Center align commands.

4. Select the topmost Movie Clip instance and use the Adjust Color filter to set the Saturation of the image to –100 — this will drain the color out so that it looks grayscale.

5. With the grayscale Movie Clip instance still selected, use the Blend menu in the Properties panel to apply Layer blend mode. You won't see any visible change yet.

6. Double-click the grayscale Movie Clip instance to access the Movie Clip timeline in Edit mode.

7. Create a new layer at the top of the layer stack in the Movie Clip Timeline. Lock the other layer(s) with the bitmap or graphics you plan to use as a base image.

8. Select the Oval tool (O) in the Tools panel and set the Fill color to use a default radial gradient. Use the Color Mixer panel to apply 0 percent Alpha to the right color anchor. This should create a circular gradient fill that has a transparent center that fades out to black. Set the stroke color to None.

9. Click and drag on the Stage to create a circle that covers only a small area in the center of the original image — in our file, the circle image was 100 x 100 pixels.

10. Select the new circle and convert it into a Movie Clip named `alpha circle`.

11. Use the Blend menu in the Properties panel to apply Alpha blend mode to the `alpha circle` Movie Clip instance. The circle Movie Clip will disappear, but don't panic. As you can see by the filled keyframe on the layer, the content is still there and you can select it to see the selection outline for the invisible instance.

12. Double-click the `alpha circle` instance to access the Movie Clip timeline and insert frames (F5) to extend the span of the circle graphic to frame 20. Convert frame 20 into a keyframe (F6).

13. Select the circle graphic in keyframe 20 and use the Transform panel to increase the size of the circle so that it is larger than the bitmap base image. We scaled the circle up to 400 x 400 pixels.

14. Select keyframe 1 (still in the alpha circle timeline), and apply a Motion tween to animate the small circle scaling up to the size of the larger circle in frame 20.

15. In order to see the Alpha blend applied as a mask, you have to return to the Main Timeline (click the Scene button).

16. The grayscale bitmap image should now have an area in the center that is "erased" in a soft, gradient circle that allows some of the color image to show through.

17. The animated effect will only be visible in the published .swf file or the Test movie environment. Use Ctrl+Return or ⌘+Return to test the file and preview the animation.

On the CD-ROM

To see the final result of our example file, open `anim_Alpha_blend.swf` from the `Blends` folder in the `ch12` folder on the CD-ROM. To analyze the file structure, open `anim_Alpha_blend.fla` from the same location.

You can always go back inside the nested symbols to modify the level of alpha in the blend image or change the style of fill from a radial gradient to a linear gradient or even a solid fill (with alpha set to less than 100 percent). The level of masking will match the level of alpha in the contents of the Alpha blend symbol instance. Alpha blends can be used to mask any type of image — even bitmaps or primitive shapes. The only requirement is that the Alpha blend must be applied to a symbol instance and that symbol instance must be nested inside a Movie Clip with a Layer blend applied. This is just one way of using a blend mode to create an interesting visual effect. There are many other possibilities, and once you understand the workflow for applying basic and compound blends, the rest is just a matter of experimentation!

Using Timeline Effects for Graphics and Animation

Flash MX 2004 introduced a new way of creating animation and visual effects. Rather than manually placing symbol instances on the Stage and inserting tweens on the Timeline, you can simply select an item (shape or symbol) on the Stage and choose a static or animated effect from the Timeline Effect menu. The specific functionality of manual tweens and the differences between Shape tweens and Motion tweens are relatively easy to explain. Timeline effects are a bit more of a muddle. They can be used for effects on static graphics or for adding multiframe animation. Some Timeline effects can only be added to symbols, but most can be added to either shapes or symbols. By default, most Timeline effects render as Graphic symbols on the Timeline, but if they're applied to a Movie Clip symbol, they will inherit that behavior. The only definitive thing we can say about Timeline effects is that they offer some very intriguing possibilities for noncoders to add more sophisticated graphics to their projects. With prebuilt JavaScript-Flash code, Timeline effects make it possible to select an item on the Stage and control its appearance and motion by simply making selections in a Settings dialog box. After you preview and apply your chosen settings, Flash automatically converts the selected item to a Graphic symbol and renders a nested symbol on the Stage and frames on the Timeline to hold the finished Effect or animation. Easy so far, right?

The Timeline effects listed in the application menu under Insert ⇨ Timeline Effects (or in the contextual menu if you have an item selected on the Stage) each invoke their own dialog box. You can tweak settings for these effects and preview the final result before you choose to apply it to a shape or a symbol. With just a few selections in the Settings dialog box, you can add animation or effects that would have taken considerable time to create manually.

The magic of Timeline effects is simply that they can save you a lot of time and make it much less painstaking to change the timing or placement of a rendered animation or visual effect. The mayhem of Timeline effects comes in when you look in your project Library. Macromedia has done a great job of organizing this automated process, but you may still be a little confused by all the symbols and folders that show up in the Library panel after you've applied a few Timeline effects.

If you're planning to just apply some effects, publish an .swf file and move on; you needn't worry about understanding the symbol structures and editing "rules" for Timeline effects. However, if you plan to integrate Timeline effects with other animation that you've created, or if you decide you want to edit an item after an effect has been rendered — which of course you will! — we hope this section makes the process a little less mysterious.

Timeline effect limitations

You *can* do great things with Timeline effects. But before you vow never to use a manual Motion tween again, we'd like to give you a few cautionary notes to consider:

✦ Symbols with Timeline effects added to them cannot be opened in Edit mode without breaking the settings option. You can still edit the nested symbols in a Timeline effect, but you have to open them from the Library list rather than from the instances on the

Stage. Unfortunately, the changes you make to the source symbol may not always be carried over to all instances in the nested effect symbol until you preview it again in the Settings dialog box.

✦ Practically, you are limited to the options available in the Settings dialog box for each Timeline effect. So for example, if you decide you prefer to have a skewed drop-shadow, you will either have to break the settings option to edit the symbols individually, or you'll have to make your own layered symbol instances.

✦ In order to layer multiple Timeline effects (such as adding a fade Transition to an item with a Drop shadow), you have to manually nest the Timeline effect Graphic symbols inside of other symbols.

✦ Timeline effects are generally rendered as nested Graphic symbol structures. The benefit is that you can see animated effects by scrubbing the Timeline. The drawback is that you will end up with redundant symbols in your Library if you apply a Timeline effect to an existing Graphic symbol. Also, your animation will be tied to the Timeline unless you nest it inside a Movie Clip symbol.

✦ Timeline effects add auto-named symbols and layers to your project file, which can make it harder to keep your naming systems consistent and meaningful.

✦ You *can* rename generic symbols and folders in your Library and layers in your Timeline that have been generated by a Timeline effect. However, if you edit the settings on any of your Timeline effects, these items will revert to the generic naming sequence.

✦ You must apply (or reapply) Behaviors *after* you have added Timeline effects. Timeline effects added to an item with an assigned Behavior will nullify the action controlled by the Behavior because it changes the symbol type of the item.

Now, if that wasn't enough to dissuade you from using Timeline effects — and it shouldn't be, unless you are a symbol structure and naming purist — we'll move on to investigate some of the animated Timeline effects that are included with Flash 8.

Timeline effect options

The Timeline effects that ship with Flash 8 are organized into three categories in the Timeline Effects menu (under Insert in the application menu or in the contextual menu for items selected on the Stage):

✦ **Assistants:** These Effects give you a more streamlined way to complete authoring tasks that you could otherwise accomplish using the Transform and Align panels with Color effects or filters.

✦ **Copy to Grid:** This makes it possible to duplicate and distribute multiple copies of an item in rows and/or columns. This effect does not make any change to the appearance of the item, but it gives you the controls you need to create an organized layout of multiples (see Figure 12-18).

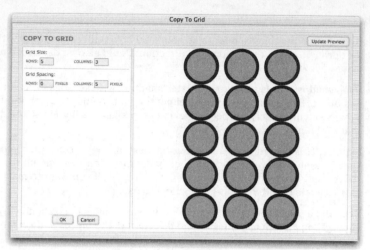

Figure 12-18: Settings and preview for the Copy to Grid Timeline effect

✦ **Distributed Duplicate:** This effect, demonstrated in Figure 12-19, creates a series of copies of an item, distributed along a tangent that can be set by entering the x and y offsets. The copied items can also be shifted in scale, color, and transparency.

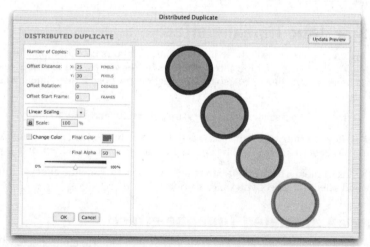

Figure 12-19: Settings and preview for the Distributed Duplicate Timeline effect

✦ **Effects:** These Effects modify the graphic content of your original item:

- **Blur:** Adds something similar to an animated soften fill edges effect with settings for duration, scale, resolution, and direction. Could also be described as an animated "glow" or "drag" effect.

- **Drop shadow:** Adds a static duplicate "shadow" with settings for color, alpha, and offset. This sounds as if it's an effect that you would use a lot, but the truth is, you will most likely get better-looking drop-shadows if you use the new Drop shadow filter or make them manually.

- **Expand:** This is hard to describe, but the best analogy we can give in print is filling a balloon with water. You can specify the direction and amount for an item to stretch and/or squash over a given span of frames. If you want to make an item look as if it is breathing, this is the effect to use.

- **Explode:** If you've been waiting to blow up some logos in Flash, now's your chance! You can specify the size and direction of the pieces and even how far and how fast they fly.

✦ **Transform/Transition:** These Effects are used to add animated changes to the display or position of your original item over a specified range of frames. The most subtle and flexible group of Effects, these are the two that you'll use most often to save production time.

- **Transform:** Change position, scale, rotation, color, and/or alpha.

- **Transition:** Wipe and/or Fade an item in or out.

Applying a static Timeline effect

The static Timeline effects include those listed in the Assistants category, plus the Drop shadow effect. The new Drop shadow filter produces better visual results and is easier to edit than the Drop Shadow Timeline effect, so for all practical purposes, this Timeline effect is deprecated.

The Timeline effects in the Assistants category are still useful and easy to apply:

1. Select an item on the Stage — it can be a shape, Drawing Object, or symbol. As with tweens, it is best to apply Timeline effects to items that exist on their own layer.

2. Use the Insert menu (or the contextual menu) to access Timeline effects. Choose a category and select the effect you want to apply.

Applying an animated Timeline effect

The specific result of frames and symbols rendered by different Timeline effects will vary, but the steps for adding a Timeline effect are consistent.

To add an animated Timeline effect to a shape or symbol, follow these steps:

1. Select an item on the Stage—it can be a shape or a symbol. In our example, we used an imported bitmap. As with Shape or Motion tweens, it is best to apply effects to items that exist on their own layer.

Caution   Although you can select an item in the first keyframe of an existing Motion or Shape tween and apply a Timeline effect to it, in most cases the tween will be broken when the Timeline effect is rendered because the item will be moved to a new layer. As we discuss later in this section, it is best to render the Timeline effect on a separate timeline if you want to combine animation methods.

2. Use the Insert menu (or the contextual menu) to access Timeline effects. Choose a category and select the effect you want to apply. For this example, we'll apply the Transition effect (as shown in Figure 12-20).

Figure 12-20: The various Timeline effects that ship with Flash are organized in categories in the Timeline effects menu.

3. In the Settings dialog box, a preview of the animation will be rendered with the default settings. Modify the settings and use the Update Preview button to test the result until you achieve an effect that you like. (Our Transition example is shown in Figure 12-21.)

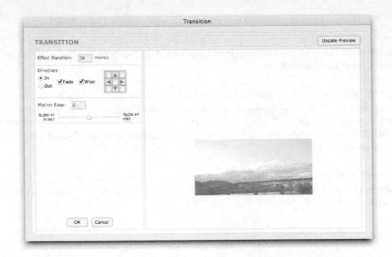

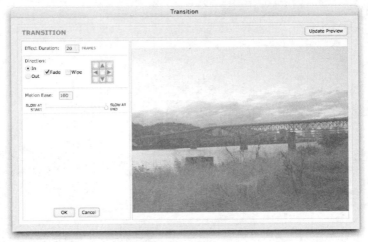

Figure 12-21: The default settings for a Transition Timeline effect (top) can be adjusted and previewed to achieve the final result that you like (bottom).

4. Click OK to close the Settings dialog box and render the effect.

5. If you have applied a complex Timeline effect, it may take a few seconds for Flash to render the symbols and insert the frames on your Timeline to hold the effect.

Note

If there is no other artwork on the layer with the item to which you added a Timeline effect, Flash simply renames the layer when the effect is applied. If there are other symbols or artwork on the layer with the item to which you added the Timeline effect, Flash moves the item to a new layer when the effect is applied. This can lead to duplicate layer names that should be manually changed to keep the structure of your document clear.

6. After the effect is finished, you will see a layer in your Timeline auto-named to indicate the effect that was rendered and the sequence that it was rendered in during your project authoring process. In our example, the layer is named `Transition 1` (see Figure 12-22).

Figure 12-22: After a Timeline effect is rendered, you will see a newly named layer for the animated frame span and you will find symbols in the Library that were generated by Flash to create the effect from your original item.

Tip

If you have created an animation that starts with an alpha setting of 0, you won't see anything on the Stage in the first frame of the new animated frame span. However, if you click the *frame*, you will see the blue selection box on the Stage to indicate the position of your "invisible" artwork.

7. A frame span will extend on the Main Timeline for the duration of the animation if you applied an animated effect to a shape, bitmap, Graphic symbol, or Button symbol. You can preview the animation by scrubbing the Timeline in the authoring environment.

Note

If you apply an animated Timeline effect to a Movie Clip symbol, the animation span is rendered on a Movie Clip timeline, so you will not see frames added to the Main Timeline and you will have to preview the animation in Test Movie mode.

8. As shown in Figure 12-22, you will also find new symbols that Flash rendered to create the Timeline effect added to your Library list. These symbols are given default names that will indicate the type of effect applied and the sequence that it was created in during an edit session.

Caution

This is the only time in this book that we will advise you not to change the default symbol and layer names right away. If you decide to edit the settings for your animated effect, the symbols and layers rendered by Flash will be renamed anyway. The best approach is to rename these items only as a final step in your editing process.

And there you have it—a lovely fade transition that can be adjusted without touching the Timeline or moving any keyframes. If you want to change the pacing or the look of the Timeline effect, use the Edit Effect option in the Timeline effects menu to open the Settings dialog box again. If you decide that the effect is not really what you wanted, use the Remove Effect option in the Timeline effects menu to get rid of it without deleting your original item.

Cross-Reference   Samuel Wan's tutorial, "Using Custom Timeline Effects," explains how to install and use a custom Timeline effect. The script files for Sam's "Jitter" effect are included in the `TFX_custom` folder in the `ch12` folder of the CD-ROM.

Modifying Timeline effect symbols

If you are accustomed to working with tweened animation or compound symbol structures that you have made manually, there are a few differences that will come up when you start working with Timeline effects. Although the symbols added to your Library when you apply a Timeline effect have the same icon as any other Graphic symbol, there are some special rules about how they can (or cannot) be modified.

Flash renders an effect based on the settings you enter in the Timeline Effect dialog box, so once the Graphic symbols for the effect have been rendered, you cannot edit the top-level Graphic symbol directly. Although you can't open the top-level Graphic symbol (with the final rendered effect) in Edit mode without disabling the Edit Effect option, you *can* edit the nested Graphic symbols that are stored in the Effect folder. In most cases, the changes you make to the nested Graphic symbol are passed on to all instances used in the final rendered effect. However, in cases where the effect required incremental mathematical adjustments (such as on a Color Change), you have to use the Edit Effect command to open the Settings dialog box so that the effect can be re-rendered in the Preview window (it will automatically update to include any changes you made to the nested symbols in the Library). You can make additional changes to the effect using the options in the Settings dialog box, or you can simply click OK to close it and go back to the Stage—where you should now see the changes passed on to all of the instances of the effect.

You can also use the instance-editing options available in the Property inspector and the Transform panel to adjust the appearance of a rendered (or top-level) Timeline effect symbol without disabling the Edit Effect option. With the Free Transform tool added to the mix, you should be able to squish, stretch, rotate, tint, and otherwise adjust rendered Timeline effect symbols to suit your fancy. If you are working with a Timeline effect nested in a Movie Clip, you can also use the new Flash 8 filters to increase your creative options.

Using Custom Timeline Effects, by Samuel Wan

Authors' Note: Although it is beyond the scope of this book to describe the steps involved in actually scripting your own Timeline effects, we can tell you how to use custom effects that other developers have made. One of the developers making cool effects is Samuel Wan. He has kindly agreed to let us include the code for one of his very first Flash Timeline effects on the CD-ROM. This brief tutorial is adapted from Sam's notes on how to install and use his "Jitter" effect. We hope you will be able to follow these same steps to use other custom effects available from Macromedia or from generous developers in the Flash community.

The first step to using a custom Timeline Effect is to find the files that Flash needs to make the Effect Settings appear in the authoring environment and to render the final Effect. Unless you happen to know some brainy coders, the best place to look for new Timeline Effects is on the Macromedia Web site.

The two files you will need to install any custom effect are

✦ An XML file that describes the parameters or "properties" of the effect and how the parameters can be customized. These files can be recognized by the .xml file extension.

✦ A JavaScript-Flash file that implements the required methods for manipulating the Flash-authoring tool based on parameters specified by the XML file. These files can be recognized by the .jsfl file extension.

On the CD-ROM We have included `Jitter.xml` and `Jitter.jsfl` on the CD-ROM in the `TFX_custom` subfolder of the `ch12` folder. To see the rendered effect, open `JitterSample.fla` (or .swf) from the same location.

Both of these files have to be saved in your Flash 8 Effects folder so that a custom effect can be applied in the authoring environment:

✦ The standard directory path on Windows is:

```
C:\Documents and Settings\(username)\Local Settings\Application
Data\Macromedia\Flash 8\(language)\Configuration\Effects
```

✦ The standard directory path on Mac is:

```
HD\Users: (username)\Library: Application Support\Macromedia\Flash
8\(language)\Configuration\Effects
```

After you save the XML file and the JSFL file to the Effects folder on your system, you will need to restart Flash to see the custom effect in the Timeline Effect menu.

The steps for applying a custom Timeline effect are the same as the steps for applying a built-in Timeline effect, but the settings available for the effect will be unique. To apply the Jitter effect, follow these steps:

1. Select an item on the Stage (a shape or a symbol).

2. Access the Timeline Effect menu from the Insert menu or from the contextual menu. As shown in Figure 12-23, a new category of effects has been added — Sam's Super Duper Effects are now listed along with the other categories that were described earlier in this chapter. Select Sam's Jitter effect.

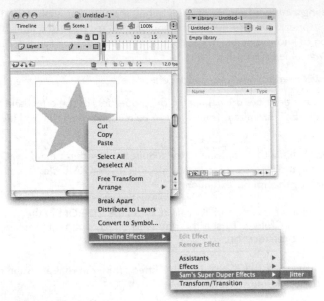

Figure 12-23: After you save the .xml and .jsfl files for a custom Timeline effect in the Effects folder, and you restart Flash, the custom effect is added to the Timeline Effects menu.

3. A Settings dialog box appears on Stage so that you can enter values to control the rendered Jitter effect (refer to Figure 12-24).

Figure 12-24: The Settings dialog box for custom Timeline effects may have a more generic appearance than the Settings dialog box for built-in Timeline effects.

Note   As shown in Figure 12-24, the Settings dialog box for the Jitter effect looks quite different than the Settings dialog box used to apply the Transition Timeline effect we showed you earlier in this chapter (see Figure 12-21). This is one of the quirks of custom Timeline effects. Some developers will include an .swf control for the settings that generates a dynamic preview of the effect, while others will only build the .jsfl and .xml files, which results in a more generic-looking Settings dialog box—similar to the dialog box for drawing tool settings. The purpose and effect of the settings are the same in either interface. The main difference is that you can't preview the effect before you apply it unless you're using an .swf settings dialog box. Fortunately, it is easy to remove an effect at any time, so the generic settings box is not a huge problem—most custom effects will be worth the extra trouble of testing and removing a few different settings before you decide what works best.

4. After you enter values for the frame duration of the effect and the pixel offset, or the amount of jitter, click OK.

5. The animation will be rendered on the Timeline in a layer called "Jitter 1." If you look in the project Library, you will see that the original selected shape has been converted to a Graphic symbol ("Symbol 1") and nested in an animated Graphic symbol ("Jitter 1"), both now stored in the Library (refer to Figure 12-25).

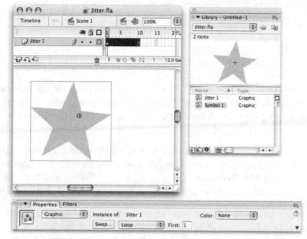

Figure 12-25: The applied Jitter effect adds new symbols to the Library and renders a span of frames on the Timeline to hold the animated Graphic symbol.

To see the final animated Jitter Effect, have a look at the `JitterSample.swf` file in the `TFX_custom` subfolder of the `ch12` folder on the CD-ROM.

That seems like a lot of steps, but it certainly takes less time to install a custom effect than it does to make one from scratch! We hope there will be many more useful and creative effects available that will open new possibilities for your Flash designs. You can continue to save other custom effects files to your Effects folder and they will be added to the Timeline Effects menu.

Obviously, it would be a big mistake to save a custom effect file to your Effects folder if it had the same name as an existing effect. Unless you want to overwrite existing Timeline effects, make sure you're using unique names for any custom effects that you add. If you'd rather not change the name of an effect, simply add a unique number to the effect name to avoid overwriting other files with the same name.

If you decide you don't need an effect anymore, or if your Timeline Effect menu gets too cluttered, simply remove the relevant .xml and .jsfl files from the Effects folder (save them somewhere else if you liked the effect; trash them if you didn't). The next time you restart Flash, the effect will no longer show up in the menu.

Web Resource

We'd like to know what you think about this chapter. Visit www.flashsupport.com/ feedback to fill out an online form with your comments.

Summary

✦ Filters are one of the best new features of Flash 8. They are easy to use and will go a long way toward polishing Flash graphics. The intuitive Filters panel supports a variety of Filter options, including layering filters and saving presets, without any scripting or special timeline structures required.

✦ The built-in filters are a long-overdue addition to the Flash authoring environment, but they are somewhat limited on their own. The good news is that Filters can be combined with Blend modes, Properties, Transform tools, Timeline Effects, and tweens with Custom Easing curves to expand their potential well beyond the default settings.

✦ Custom Easing extends the power of easing beyond linear Ease In and Ease Out — the Custom Easing dialog box launched from the Properties panel enables you to control easing with a curved interpolation path that can have multiple control points for adjusting animated elements. You can apply a single curve to all properties of the tween, or create unique curves to adjust the progression of various properties individually within the same tween.

✦ The new Blend mode menu in the Properties panel brings some of the power of Photoshop into the Flash authoring environment — graphics can be blended in more subtle and interesting ways.

✦ The set of Timeline effects that was introduced with Flash MX 2004 to auto-render layout and animated visual effects has not been modified significantly in Flash 8, but they are a little easier to work with in the new version. There are still limitations on how Timeline effects can be edited or combined with other transformations, but the effects are harder to "break" by accident.

✦ Macromedia has pulled out all the stops to support *expressiveness* in this release. If you can't kick out some cool content with Flash 8, it might be time to pump up your creative fuel or reconsider your career options!

✦   ✦   ✦

Applying Layer Types

In This Chapter

Using Guide layers for reference

Creating Motion guides to control animation

Setting up elements for animation with Distribute to Layers

Applying Mask layers for special effects

Masking animation and creating nested animated masks

Besides storing and organizing the contents of your project (.fla), Flash layers offer some special features that help you create more advanced animation. Standard layers can be locked, hidden, or displayed as outlines, but they can also be converted into Guide layers, Motion guides, or Mask layers. You can use each of these layer types to accomplish specific authoring tasks.

Cross-Reference

You can also use ActionScript to guide or control animation and to apply dynamic masking. For an introduction to these more advanced alternatives to Mask layers and Motion guides, refer to Chapter 27, "Interacting with Movie Clips."

Flash gives you the flexibility to quickly change the behavior of layers at any time in the authoring environment, so that you can take advantage of the special characteristics of each of these layer types as needed.

With the layer buttons at the lower-left corner of the Timeline window, you have the option of creating standard layers, Motion guide layers, and Folder layers. If you have already created a standard layer, you can convert it into any of the special layer types by using the contextual menu (invoked by right-clicking or Ctrl+clicking the layer bar), or by changing settings in the Layer Properties dialog box (invoked by double-clicking the layer icon or by choosing Modify ⇨ Timeline ⇨ Layer Properties from the application menu).

Flash automatically converts layers if you drag them into specific positions in the stacking order with other layer types—although this sounds a bit cryptic, it will make sense as you read about each layer type and how it affects other layers. Each layer type has a unique icon, as shown in Figure 13-1.

Figure 13-1: A unique icon in the layer stack identifies each of the layer types. You can quickly assign or change the behavior of a layer using the contextual menu.

Guide Layers

Guide layers are the only layer types that are not exported with your final Flash movie (.swf). Guide layers are used primarily when you need to use an element as a reference in the authoring environment (.fla), but you don't want it to be part of the finished movie (.swf). To convert an existing layer into a Guide layer, you can use the contextual menu and select Guide. Alternatively, you can invoke the Layer Properties dialog box (shown in Figure 13-2) by double-clicking the layer icon (or choosing Modify ➪ Timeline ➪ Layer Properties from the application menu), and then selecting the Guide check box.

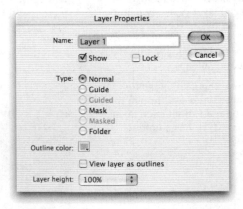

Figure 13-2: Use the Layer Properties dialog box to convert a standard layer into a Guide layer, Mask layer, or even a layer folder.

Tip   As you are developing a project, it can be helpful to "turn off" certain layers while you're testing content on other layers. For example, by temporarily turning a layer that contains a large background graphic into a Guide layer, the movie (.swf) will render more quickly for preview in the test movie environment. Remember to turn all layers that you want exported back into normal layers before publishing your final movie (.swf) — either by unchecking Guide in the contextual menu or by selecting the Normal check box in the Layer Properties dialog box.

You can place bitmaps and video sequences in Guide layers if you want to use them as references for drawings or animated sequences that are drawn in Flash — think of it like working with tracing paper to redraw images. The content on a Guide layer adds to the file size of the Flash document (.fla), but it won't be included with or add to the file size of the exported movie (.swf). Guide layers are also useful when organizing layouts in Flash that require special alignment, such as a circular or diagonal arrangement of multiple elements.

To create a Guide layer that serves as a reference for aligning a custom layout, follow these steps:

1. Add a new layer to your Flash document (.fla) and make it a Guide layer. You have a couple of options for adding a Guide layer:

   - Use the contextual menu or the Layer properties dialog box to convert a standard layer into a Guide layer.

   - Use the Add Motion Guide Layer button to insert a Motion guide layer and then drag the guided layer above the Motion guide layer in the stacking order to revert the Motion guide to a (static) Guide layer.

Note   Guide layers are actually just Motion guide layers that don't have any guided layers nested below them.

2. Drag the Guide layer below your art layers in the stacking order, or add a new layer above the Guide layer if you need a fresh layer for arranging artwork.

3. Place an imported image on the Guide layer for reference, or use the Flash drawing tools to create any guide image needed (such as a circle or a diagonal line).

4. Make sure that Snap to Objects is active by toggling on the Magnet option in the toolbox or choosing View ➪ Snapping ➪ Snap to Objects in the application menu.

Note   The Guide layer workflow is especially helpful if you are trying to match a layout or design comp that might have been given to you in another format. Unfortunately, the Snap to Objects feature only works if the content of your Guide Layer is in a vector format. If you are working with a .pdf or a bitmap in the Guide layer (which is often the case), the Snap to Objects feature won't be any help for aligning items on other layers with the content of the Guide layer.

5. Use the Arrow tool to drag elements on the art layers into alignment with the reference on the Guide layer (see Figure 13-3).

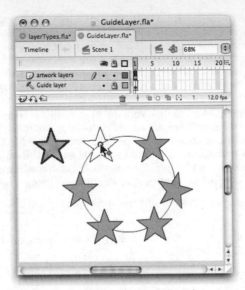

Figure 13-3: Use snapping to align the center point of elements on your art layers with a reference shape or line on your Guide layer (in vector format).

6. When you test your movie (Ctrl+Enter or ⌘+Return), you won't see the content of the Guide layer displayed in the .swf (see Figure 13-4).

Figure 13-4: The content of the Guide layer is not visible when the movie is published or viewed in the test movie environment.

7. Add to or modify the reference content on the original Guide layer or add additional Guide layers if needed.

Motion Guides

The graphics on Motion guide layers, as on Guide layers, are not exported with the .swf file. But it is important to note that Motion guides will actually control the path of movement for an animated element on another layer, rather than simply serving as a visual reference for static content. A Guide layer is automatically converted to a Motion guide layer if another layer is nested below it to become a *guided* layer. To describe it simply, Guide layers can only *suggest* what can be done, whereas Motion guide layers can *control* what something on another layer will do.

The files shown in these Motion guide examples are included on this book's CD-ROM for your reference. You will find the source .fla files in the `motionGuide` subfolder located in the `ch13` folder.

Applying a Motion guide

To define the path for an animated element using a Motion guide, follow these steps:

1. Define a Motion guide layer that contains the guide (or path) and a guided art layer that contains your animated element(s):

   - Select the layer that contains the elements that you want to animate, and then use the Add Motion Guide button to insert a Motion guide layer above your art layer. You can also use the contextual menu or choose Insert ➪ Timeline ➪ Motion Guide from the application menu to add a Motion guide layer.

   - If a Guide layer is already present and you want to convert it into a Motion guide layer, simply drag your art layer below the Guide layer in the stacking order.

   - If you have added a Motion guide layer but your art layer is not nested below it as a guided layer, simply rearrange your layer stack by moving layers until the art layer is indented below the Motion guide layer indicating that it will be guided (see Figure 13-5).

Dragging a Guide layer above a normal layer will not convert it into a Motion guide layer, but dragging a *normal* layer *below* a Guide layer will convert the normal layer into a guided layer and the Guide layer into a Motion guide.

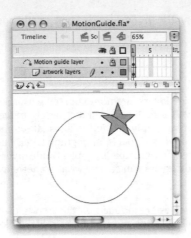

Figure 13-5: One or more art layers can be nested below a Motion guide layer.

2. Create a stroke that will define the path of the animation. You can use the Shape tools or any of the other drawing tools that create raw graphics. Although you can snap your animated elements to the edge of a filled shape, paths are usually defined by a stroke only.

 Caution Although you can snap artwork to align with a grouped shape or an object on your Motion guide layer, the tween will not stick to the path correctly unless the grouped artwork on the Motion guide is ungrouped or the object is broken apart to simplify the elements that define the animation path into raw graphics (strokes and/or fills).

3. Add a Motion tween to the graphics (symbols) on your art layer. Make sure that Snap to Objects is active, and use the Arrow tool to snap the registration point of the animated element to the path on both the beginning and end keyframes of the tween, as shown in Figure 13-6.

 Caution If you apply an animated Timeline Effect directly to a symbol in a guided tween, the tween will be broken and the symbol will no longer animate along the path defined in the Guide layer. Nest your artwork inside of a Movie Clip symbol before applying an animated Timeline Effect if you plan to use Timeline Effect animations in other tweens. For example, before you add a Timeline Effect to spin or fade a graphic that will be tweened along a path defined by a Motion guide, you must place the graphic on its own Movie Clip Timeline. And then apply the Timeline Effect there, rather than on the Timeline where the Motion guide and guided Motion tween is created.

 New Feature You can use the Drop Shadow Timeline Effect without breaking a guided tween, but the new Flash 8 Filters are a much more effective way of modifying the appearance of a symbol instance. You can add multiple Filters without breaking a guided tween, including Drop Shadow, Blur, Glow, and Bevel.

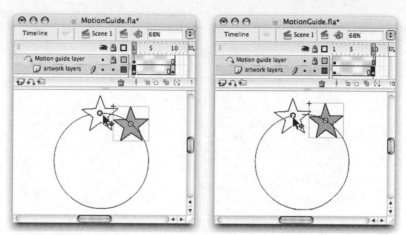

Figure 13-6: Snapping the registration point of the animated item to the Motion guide on the beginning (left) and end (right) keyframes of the tween

Tip

Flash will always choose the most efficient path to animate tweened elements, interpolating the shortest route from the position defined in the starting keyframe to the position defined in the end keyframe. Occasionally, you may want to override this default efficiency. To force Flash to animate an element the "long way around" a closed path, add a gap to the stroke, as shown in Figure 13-6. Although the gap can be very, very small, it should cut the stroke that defines your path, creating a space between the starting point and the ending point of your animation. Flash does not jump gaps in a motion path; instead, it tweens your animated element the long way around the shape.

4. Scrub the Timeline to preview the animated element; it should now follow the path defined in the Motion guide. You can reposition your artwork in the beginning or end keyframes to adjust where the animation starts and stops on the path. You can adjust the path by modifying the stroke on your Motion guide layer. Use the Lock layer toggle to protect other layers as you make adjustments to specific elements. You can also use the settings in the Property inspector to apply easing and rotation to the Motion tween layer, and preview the interpolation by turning on Onion skinning (see Figure 13-7).

5. When the movie (.swf) is published, the stroke on the Motion guide layer will not be exported, but the animation will still be rendered to tween along the path that was defined in the authoring environment (.fla).

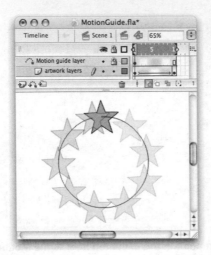

Figure 13-7: Guided tween previewed with Onion skinning turned on

Adding control to animation along a path

Even after you have succeeded in getting your tweened animation to follow the path defined in your Motion guide layer, you may find that the movement of the animated element is not exactly as you would like. Fortunately, there are a few different ways that you can modify how a tweened element follows a Motion guide.

Using Orient to Path

The first control to consider is found in the Property inspector when the first keyframe of your Motion tween is selected — the Orient to path check box (shown in Figure 13-8) forces an item to rotate as it follows a curved path so that it stays aligned or headed along the path. When Orient to path is not active, an animated item maintains the same orientation through- out the tween, with no relation to the curves or loops in its Motion guide.

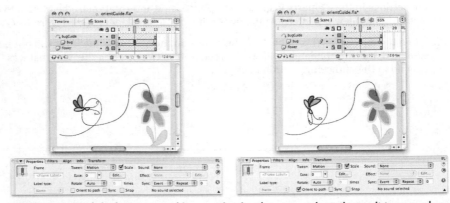

Figure 13-8: By default, a tweened item maintains the same orientation as it tweens along a curved path (as shown on the left). Selecting Orient to path keeps an animated item headed along the curves or loops in a Motion guide (as shown on the right).

Registration and center point alignment

The second important factor that determines how an animated element moves along a Motion guide is where the registration point of the symbol is located. By default, the registration point is generally at the center of the symbol, but this may not be the point of the item that you want to snap to the Motion guide. To modify the alignment of a guided symbol, you can modify the registration point of the symbol (refer to Figure 13-9).

To modify the registration point of a symbol, follow these steps:

1. Click the Arrow tool on the stage to select the symbol on the first keyframe of the tween.

2. Activate the Free Transform tool in the toolbox, and drag the registration point (small white circle icon) to a new location.

3. Use the Arrow tool to snap the newly positioned registration point to the Motion guide.

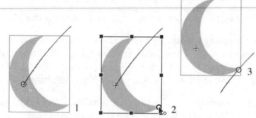

Figure 13-9: When Free Transform is active, you can modify the registration point of a symbol without changing the alignment of the artwork in relation to the center point.

Only one Motion guide can be placed on a layer, but you can use multiple sets of Motion guide and guided layers to create compositions of different guided animations. To see an example using two Motion guides and two guided layers, open multipleGuides.fla (and .swf) from the motionGuides folder in the ch13 folder on the CD-ROM.

Mask Layers

In the real world, a mask is used to selectively obscure items beneath it. In Flash, a Mask layer is used to define the *visible* area of layers nested beneath it. Multiple layers can be nested as *masked* layers beneath a single Mask layer. As with Motion guide layers, the content on Mask layers is not visible in the final .swf because it is intended only to modify how content in nested masked layers is rendered.

The various examples we discussed in this section can be found in the mask subfolder of the ch13 folder. You may find it helpful to examine the structure of these files to understand the many ways that Mask layers can be applied.

Almost any symbol or filled shape (excluding strokes) may be used to create a mask. However, Flash ignores bitmaps, gradients, transparency, colors, and line styles in a Mask layer. Masks may be animated or static. The only other limitations are that you cannot apply a mask to content in another Mask layer, and Mask layers cannot be placed within Button symbol timelines.

Caution   Although groups, text boxes, and Movie Clips or Graphic symbols can all be used to define a mask, only one such item will be recognized on a single Mask layer. You can use multiple primitive shapes to define a mask, but they will override all other items existing on the same Mask layer.

Masking with a filled shape

Here's how to create the simplest form of mask:

1. Make sure that the content that will be visible through the mask is in place on its own layer, with visibility turned on. This will become the masked layer.

2. Create a new layer stacked above the masked layer. This will become the Mask layer.

3. In the Mask layer, create the "aperture" through which the contents of the masked layer will be viewed. This aperture can be any filled item, text, or placed instance of a symbol that includes a filled item. (Of course, lines can be used as masks if they are first converted to fills with the Modify ➪ Shapes ➪ Convert Lines to Fills command.)

4. Now, position your mask content over the content on the masked layer (see Figure 13-10) so that it covers the area that you will want to be visible through the mask.

Figure 13-10: The content on the upper layer defines what is visible in the lower layer(s).

5. Right-click (or Ctrl+click) the layer bar of the Mask layer to invoke the contextual menu (see Figure 13-11), and choose Mask from the menu (or use the Layer Properties dialog box to change the layer behavior from Normal to Mask).

Figure 13-11: Convert the upper layer into a Mask layer by selecting Mask from the contextual menu.

6. The layer icons change to indicate that the masked layer is now subordinate to the Mask layer and both layers are automatically locked to activate the mask. The contents of the masked layer are now visible only through the filled portion(s) of the Mask layer, as shown in Figure 13-12.

Figure 13-12: When the mask is active, the content on the Mask layer is no longer visible, but it will define the visible area of the content on the masked layer underneath.

7. To reposition, or otherwise modify, the Mask layer, temporarily unlock it (see Figure 13-13).

Figure 13-13: With the Mask layer unlocked, the contents are visible and editable.

8. To reactivate masking, lock the Mask layer again (and confirm that the masked layer is also locked). The contextual menu for Mask layers and masked layers includes Show Masking—this handy command locks the Mask layer and all nested masked layers for you.

Caution

When you first start working with Mask layers, it is easy to forget to lock both the Mask layer and the masked layer to make the mask effect visible. If you are ever having trouble editing or viewing your masked effect, just remember that when the layers are unlocked, the mask art is visible and editable, and when the layers are locked, the final masked effect is "turned on."

Masking with a group

Multiple filled shapes can also be grouped and used as a mask, as long as the Mask layer doesn't also contain primitive ungrouped shapes. Grouped shapes on the same layer as ungrouped shapes will be ignored when the Mask is applied. If a mask is composed of multiple items, using a group makes it easier to position the mask, as shown in Figure 13-14.

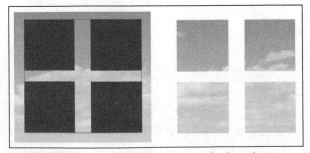

Figure 13-14: Grouped filled shapes make it easier to position complex masks.

Masking with a symbol instance

As you are reminded in nearly every chapter of this book, working with symbols is working smart because doing so helps to reduce file size. Because symbols composed of filled shapes can be used as masks, there's no reason not to use a symbol from your Library to make a mask. (If you've already made a shape on your Mask layer, go ahead and convert it into a symbol so that you can use again without adding to the final file size.) Reusing symbol instances to define masks is especially logical if you are making multiple masks that all have the same basic shape. For example, if you need a rectangular or oval mask, you will often find a symbol in your Library that was created to define the active area of a button or some other basic element. It is smarter to modify an instance of an existing symbol so that it works as a mask than to add redundant elements that increase your file size.

Note   Although in theory you can use a Button symbol instance as mask artwork, note that a Button symbol instance placed into a Mask layer will no longer function as a button. The result of this workflow is similar to selecting a Button symbol instance and assigning it Graphic symbol behavior in the Property inspector.

To illustrate the way that symbols can be reused as both graphic content and as mask elements, we have used instances of a symbol as static content on a masked layer and then Motion tweened another instance of the same symbol on a Mask layer to create an animated oval reveal. Figure 13-15 shows the symbol instance used on the Mask layer (on the left), the symbol instances used on the art layer (in the center), and the final mask effect visible when both layers are locked (on the right).

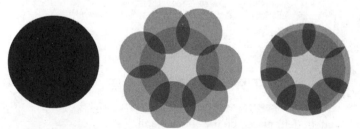

Figure 13-15: Instances of one oval symbol combined to create a graphic and a mask effect

On the CD-ROM   Open the `symbolMask.fla` example from the `mask` folder inside the `ch13` folder on this book's CD-ROM to see the animated effect.

Masking text

Not only can text be masked, but it can also be used to mask other graphics. To mask text, simply set up your Mask and art layers, as we described in the previous section, with the text to be masked on the lower layer, and the filled item that you'll use for your aperture on the Mask layer, as shown in Figure 13-16.

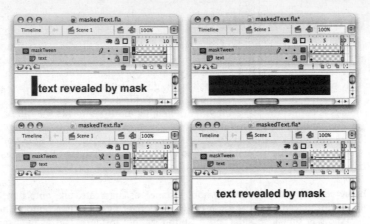

Figure 13-16: Masking a text block with a tweened shape (shown on top) and the final reveal effect (shown on the bottom)

To use text as a mask, the layers should be set up as described previously. In this situation, the text (which goes on the mask layer) will look as though it was filled by whatever is placed on the lower layer. For this to be effective, a larger point size and fuller, bold letterforms are best, as shown in Figure 13-17.

Figure 13-17: A bitmap pattern (left) placed on the art layer and masked with text (right)

Caution   Although you can type as much text as you like in a single text box to apply as a mask, you can have only one text box per Mask layer. To use multiple text boxes as mask elements, add separate Mask layers for each text box.

Because the edges of mask letterforms may be hard to discern if the image underneath is not a solid color, it can be helpful to add a drop-shadow to make the mask letters more legible. However, a drop-shadow or an outline added to the text on the Mask layer would not be visible, so it is necessary to copy the text onto a normal layer stacked above the Mask layer as follows:

1. To keep the text copy aligned with the text mask, use Copy (Ctrl+C or ⌘+C) and Paste in Place (Shift+Ctrl+V or Shift+⌘+V) to place a copy of the text into the normal layer exactly on top of the mask text. After you have copied the text in the Mask layer, lock both the Mask layer and the masked layer to protect them while you are working on the normal layer.

2. The solid copied text completely obscures the masked image below, but using the new Flash 8 Filters, you can apply a Filter and use the Knockout option to drop out the fill of the text characters so that the masked content on the other layers will be visible.

3. Select the copied text, then click the Filters tab in the Property inspector and use the drop-down menu to select the Drop Shadow Filter. The settings that you applied, including the Knockout option, are shown in Figure 13-18. You can adjust the intensity and color of the shadow and the position of the copied (Knocked out) text until you like the end result.

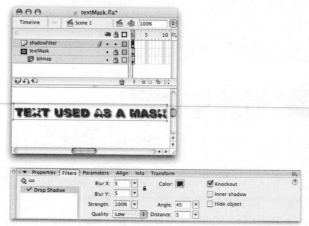

Figure 13-18: Apply a Drop Shadow Filter with the Knockout option to the copy of your text to add more visual definition to the letter shapes.

Tip   The Glow Filter will work to define the text too, as long as you apply the Knockout option.

Cross-Reference   We cover the various Flash 8 Filters in more detail in Chapter 12, "Applying Filters and Effects."

Motion Guides and Movie Clip Masks

As you have seen in the examples so far, you can Shape tween primitive shapes (and Drawing Objects) or Motion tween symbol instances (and Drawing Objects) directly on the Main Timeline in Mask layers to create animated masks. But what if you want to add more control to the movement of a mask? Unfortunately, one of the limitations of Mask layers is that they can't be nested below Motion guide layers to become guided elements. However, by using a Movie Clip symbol instance as the content of your Mask layer, you have the option of adding a Motion guide to the Movie Clip timeline to control the movement of the element that defines your mask.

To create a mask that contains an element controlled by a Motion guide, follow these steps:

1. Set up an art layer and a Mask layer on the Main Timeline as in previous examples. Because the animation of your mask exists on a Movie Clip timeline, you need only one frame on each layer.

2. Unlock the Mask layer and, on the first keyframe of the Main Timeline, insert a new symbol (Ctrl+F8 or ⌘+F8). In the Symbol Properties dialog box, specify Movie Clip behavior and name the symbol (circleAnim in this example), as shown in Figure 13-19.

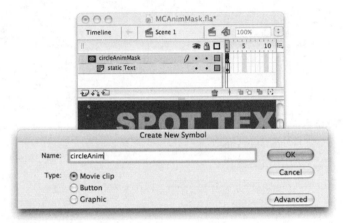

Figure 13-19: Insert a Movie Clip symbol that will contain the Motion guide to control the animated mask content.

3. After you click OK in the Symbol Properties dialog box, Flash automatically opens the symbol timeline in the Document window.

4. Add a Motion guide layer that contains the path for the animation and a guided layer that contains a Motion tween of the symbol that you want to define the final mask, as shown in Figure 13-20.

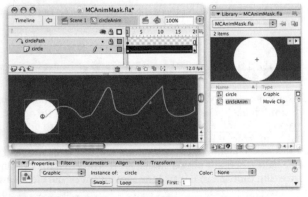

Figure 13-20: A Motion guide and a Motion tween layer added to the Movie Clip timeline

5. When you return to the Main Timeline, you will see only the first frame of the animation that you just created in the Movie Clip (as shown in Figure 13-21). You can select the Movie Clip instance on the Mask layer to alter its position on the Stage.

Figure 13-21: The first frame of the Movie Clip animation visible on the Mask layer in the Main Timeline

6. If you want to see how the whole Motion guide aligns with the content on the masked layer, double-click the Movie Clip symbol instance on the Mask layer to enter Edit-in-place mode (see Figure 13-22). You will now be able to scrub the Movie Clip timeline and see how the animation lines up with (the dimmed out) content on the Main Timeline. You can make adjustments as needed to the Motion guide layer or to the tweened symbol that will define the mask.

Figure 13-22: Use Edit-in-place mode to align the Motion guide on the Movie Clip timeline with the content on the masked layer of the Main Timeline.

7. After you have all the elements aligned and edited, lock both the Mask layer and the masked layer and test the movie (Ctrl+Enter or ⌘+Return) to see how the guided animation in the Movie Clip on the Mask layer reveals the content on the masked layer. Figure 13-23 shows one frame of the Motion tween in the example as it displays in the final .swf.

Figure 13-23: The final .swf previewed in the test movie environment

On the CD-ROM

To see how the finished animated Movie Clip mask example looks, open `MCAnimMask.swf` from the `mask` folder in the `ch13` folder on this book's CD-ROM.

Of course, you can also animate content on masked layers separately from the content on Mask layers. But the endless possibilities for layering masks and masked content starts to get confusing when the additional variable of animation is thrown in. To make the best use of these features, take the extra time to carefully consider the most efficient way to achieve the final effect that you want. First consider what you would like to see on the Stage, and then plan any animation of visible elements. The next step should be adding a mask if needed, and finally adding animation to the mask itself. Try to create your effects with the fewest possible animated elements — you will waste less production time and end up with a more optimized file.

Tip

When working on multiple nested layers, it can be visually confusing to work on animation while all layers are displayed. Use the Eye toggle to hide or show specific layers in the Timeline so that you can concentrate on only the elements that you are currently editing. Also, to avoid changing the wrong items, lock all layers that you are not currently modifying.

Keeping some basic principles in mind as you are working with multiple masks and animated elements will help you to follow the logic of masking in Flash:

✦ The mask always goes above the item that is revealed by it.

✦ Filled items on Mask layers function as windows that reveal content on the masked layers nested beneath them.

✦ The content on Mask layers is only visible in the authoring environment if the Mask layer is unlocked. For the applied mask to preview properly in the authoring environment, both the Mask layer and the masked layer(s) must be locked.

✦ Mask layers will only apply to layers that are nested below them as masked layers. Normal layers or Guide layers that may be lower in the layer stack (but not nested with the Mask layer) won't be affected by the mask.

✦ Multiple layers can be nested below a single Mask layer, but masks cannot be applied to other Mask layers, and each Mask layer can contain only one masking item (with the exception of multiple primitive shapes or Drawing Objects).

✦ Content on Mask layers is not visible in the final movie (.swf).

Using Distribute to Layers

The Distribute to Layers command (Shift+Ctrl+D or Shift+⌘+D) is a great timesaver if you're managing multiple elements that you need to move to animate on individual layers. If you've imported several items to the Document window, or you've created a complex graphic that you decide needs to be split up on different layers, you can use this command to do most of the work for you. Instead of having to manually create new layers and copy and paste items one by one, you can select a number of individual items in the Document window and apply Distribute to Layers to have Flash automatically create a layer for each selected item.

To apply Distribute to Layers, select the items that you want to have moved to discrete layers — these items can be symbols, groups, shapes, text blocks, and even bitmaps or video objects. Choose Modify ⇨ Timeline ⇨ Distribute to Layers from the application menu, or choose Distribute from the contextual menu. Strokes and fills for an individual shape will be kept together on the same layer, as will items in a group or a multipart symbol. The items you select can be on different source layers, but they must all be on the same frame of the Timeline. When items have been distributed to new layers, you can delete any old layers that have been left empty.

The auto-created layers will be stacked from top to bottom below the currently selected layer in the order that the selected items were created. So the most recently created item should be placed on a layer at the bottom of the stack, just above the layer that was formerly below the selected layer, while the item that was created before the others in the selection will be placed at the top of the stack, just below the currently selected layer. If you are completely disoriented by now, have a look at Figure 13-24 to see a file with the layer order before applying Distribute to Layers to the selected items, and look at Figure 13-25 to see how the new layers are stacked and named.

Characters from a broken-apart text block will be stacked in layers in the same order that the text block was created (from left to right, right to left, or top to bottom). Flash names auto-created layers with the following conventions:

✦ A new layer made for any asset stored in the Library (a symbol, bitmap, or video clip) will be given the same name as the asset.

✦ A new layer made for a character from a broken-apart text block will be named with the text character or letter.

Caution When you apply Distribute to Layers to text blocks that have not been broken apart, new layers will be named with the entire text string. It is best to rename these layers because they will usually be difficult to read and may even exceed the 64-character limit for layer names.

✦ A new layer made for a shape (which is not stored in the Library) will be named in the same numeric sequence as other layers in the current document (Layer 1, Layer 2, and so on).

✦ A new layer made for a named symbol instance will be given the instance name instead of the stored symbol name.

Any layer can always be renamed after it has been created.

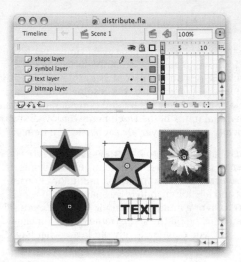

Figure 13-24: A Flash document with the original layer structure for some bitmaps, symbols, shapes, and a broken-apart text block to be distributed to layers

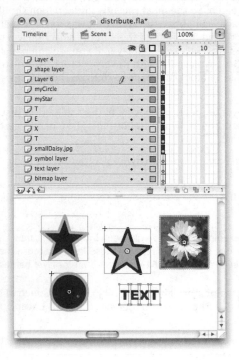

Figure 13-25: The same Flash document after Distribute to Layers has been applied. All selected items have been moved to newly created, auto-named layers, leaving the original layers empty.

Web Resource We'd like to know what you think about this chapter. Visit www.flashsupport.com/ feedback to fill out an online form with your comments.

Summary

✦ The four layer types available in the Flash authoring environment are normal, Mask, Guide, and Motion guide. Mask layers apply to nested masked layers and Motion guide layers apply to nested guided layers. A unique layer icon identifies each layer type.

✦ You can assign or modify layer types in the Layer Properties dialog box, which you invoke by double-clicking any layer icon.

✦ When you select multiple items on the same layer and use the Distribute to Layers command, they can automatically be moved to new, auto-created layers.

✦ You use Guide layers to hold content that is only needed for reference in the authoring environment, or to speed up movie testing as you develop a project — by temporarily keeping the content on specific layers from being exported with the .swf.

✦ To move a tweened element along a specific path, you can add a Motion guide layer to control the animation.

✦ Motion guide layers are actually Guide layers that have another layer nested below them as a guided layer.

✦ Timeline Effects cannot be directly applied to a symbol that is animated along a path with a guided Motion tween — to combine Timeline Effects with Motion guides, you must use nested Movie Clip timelines.

✦ You can mask any content that you create in a Flash document with a static or animated Mask layer.

✦ You can use filled shapes, text, and symbol instances to define the mask area (or window) on a Mask layer, but this content will not be visible in the final movie (.swf).

✦ You can animate the content of a Mask layer by creating a Motion tween or a Shape tween directly on the Main Timeline, but you cannot apply Motion guides to Mask layers. To control the animation of a mask with a Motion guide, use a Movie Clip instance to define the area of the mask. You can then create the Motion tween and the Motion guide layer on the Movie Clip timeline.

✦ You can modify the linkage between various layers at any time by rearranging the order of the layer stack.

✦　　✦　　✦

Character Animation Techniques

Flash is a powerful tool that continues to grow in popularity as a professional production option for creating high-quality cartoons and animated broadcast graphics. The best thing about Flash cartoons is that you don't always *know* they were created in Flash when you see them. Flash allows artists to create characters in nearly any style they can dream up. Although Flash makes it especially easy to produce clean, geometric designs, it can also be used for sketchy hand-drawn styles, or even for collage animation that uses source material from photos or video. This is the result of Flash's unique drawing tools, media-friendly authoring environment, and scalability. By "scalability," we mean that a Flash cartoon can be scaled down for delivery on the Web or scaled up to the size and resolution needed for video or film presentation. Creating broadcast cartoons can be extremely complex — specialized techniques are covered in many books and classes — so we focus on some basics to get you started.

Although Flash includes some special techniques, most of the basic principles of animation apply regardless of the authoring environment or production process you choose. You can often learn more about animation principles by watching classic animated films than by looking at 'toons online — at least at those examples created by "animators" who know how to Motion tween but have not spent any time learning techniques for effective character animation.

A growing number of artists with traditional animation skills are making the transition to working directly in Flash, and there are even a few Flash experts who have taken the time to study animation. Individuals able to combine knowledge of classic animation principles with technical aptitude in Flash have the best chance of finding success in this challenging field.

Working with Large File Sizes

Because Flash output is usually intended for the Web, Flash file size is often a dominant concern. But when creating cartoons for broadcast output, this concern is thrown to the wind. In cartoon land, you create for digital video output via QuickTime or Windows AVI and these file sizes can be huge. It's common for such projects to expand into the gigabytes, so it's important to have the equipment to handle this kind of work. This means the more RAM and hard drive space you have, the happier you will be. If you try to build a full-length animation masterpiece in one Flash file, you'll be setting yourself up for a rocky and inefficient production process. As you continue to add artwork and animation to your Flash file, it takes longer to render an .swf for preview and it takes even longer to render a sequence for raster output. You can use several strategies to make your animation more manageable. As we describe in this section, start with a good storyboard and follow through with a series of separate Flash files organized into scenes.

You'll spend many hours working on your animation, so back it up as often as you can! The project file is precious. Make a habit of keeping incremental backups on various hard drive volumes or archived CDs or DVDs so that you won't lose everything when disaster strikes (it will). A good plan is to make a new copy on a different hard drive volume or disk after each major change, rotating through two or three different storage locations. This way, if Flash eats your project file or a disk or drive fails, you can always go back to the version you saved an hour ago (which should be on a different disk) without losing much time. The same version-ing logic used in other documents can be applied to your Flash animation files: start with myFile_100, go to myFile_101, myFile_102, and so on as you make small adjustments and revisions. When you get to a significant change or a semifinished version of your file, save it as myFile_200, and so on. This makes it easy to find your way back to a specific phase of the project at any time.

Storyboarding scenes and shots

Let's assume that you already have characters and a story and you want to build a cartoon based on that inspired beginning. Although it's okay to experiment and develop characters, never start a serious cartoon project without a storyboard. The storyboard is your roadmap, your plan, your menu of things needed, and your best friend when your project gets compli-cated. The storyboard can be loose and roughly sketched out, but it should help you start to see the flow of your story and to make decisions about how best to communicate it visually.

On the CD-ROM   You'll find a storyboard template on the CD-ROM, in the ch14 folder. It's an .eps (storyboardMAC.eps or storybPC.eps) template form that includes all the essentials of a basic storyboard. Print it out as is, or import it into FreeHand, Illustrator, or Flash, and modify it to suit your needs.

As you sketch the overall story, you can break up the narrative into workable cartoon scenes. Long before Flash, cartoonists used the term "scene" to describe something quite different than a Flash Scene. By cartoon scenes, we mean phases in a narrative, similar to movie or TV scenes. Remember that cartoons are fast-paced adventures — most cartoon scenes last less than 30 seconds. Generally, a cartoon scene can stand alone, but it needs other scenes to complete the story. Fast-paced as it is, 30 seconds of animation still requires between 360 and 720 frames in the Flash Timeline. It becomes unruly if you rely solely upon Flash's Scene fea-ture — you'd do a lot of scrubbing, just trying to cover one scene.

After your cartoon scenes are in order, you can start to establish the camera angles or "shots" for key moments. A *shot* is a break or change in the camera framing or viewpoint. For example, in a soap opera dialogue scene, the camera will cut back and forth between charac-ters to show each person talking — one scene will include many shots. Although the art of cinematography is beyond the scope of this book, the same tricks used to add drama to live action are involved when deciding shots in a cartoon scene. Always try to introduce variety in the viewpoint; think of ways to add interest with close-ups or extreme angles. If you're looking at a series of shots with characters all in the same basic position within the frame, keeping the same distance from the viewer, you're looking at a scene that will turn out to be pretty dull. If you can cut some visual contrast into the scene while still pushing your narrative forward, you'll have a better chance of keeping your viewers hooked in long enough to connect with your characters and to appreciate your story.

Flash Scenes and project files

Never create an entire cartoon in one Flash project file (.fla)! Even trying to load the huge files can cause problems for Flash. Instead, create a separate Flash project file for each storyboard scene and use Flash's Scene function to organize shots within a cartoon scene. (This may seem confusing at first, but the utility of this method will become clear as you work on your masterpiece.) In other words: The Flash project file (.fla) is a storyboard scene, and the shots, or Flash Scenes, are nested within the project file.

Voices, sound effects, and ambient sound

The single most important work you'll do in your cartoon is not the drawing, but the voices of your characters; the voices give the characters heart and depth. In fact, some animators prefer to record the voices first and then use the performance of the voice actors as inspiration for the animated characters' movements and expressions. Obtaining a voice can be as simple as speaking into a microphone in front of your computer or as complex as having a highly paid professional speaking into a microphone in a studio. The key here is not the type of voice, but the emotion put into it. If you capture a unique voice with the right emotion, it can be taken into an editing program, such as Sound Forge or Acid, and tweaked with effects to render the exact cartoon sound that you're looking for. Audio effects, including adjustments to pitch and timing, can always be added digitally; human emotion cannot. Some online voice resources are

- ✦ www.voicecasting.com

- ✦ www.voicetraxwest.com

- ✦ www.world-voices.com

Another important part of cartoons is the use of *sound effects*. Many good sound-effects collections are available on CD-ROM and online. You can even find sound effects CDs in bargain bins at your local music store. A couple of the collections that we keep on hand are *The Ultimate Digital Sound Effects Library* from the Sound Effects Company, and *Crashes, Collisions & Catastrophes* from Madacy Records. We also recommend any of the *Loops for Acid* CDs from Sonic Foundry. The sounds included in these collections can be imported into any sound-editing program to be mixed into your own original soundscapes. If you've never worked with someone who specializes in custom sound creation, you might be amazed at the magic they can add to even simple animation.

 One online source that offers a variety of effects at a broad range of prices, and RealAudio links that allow you to audition them online, is www.radiomall.com. Another popular site that has a subscription-based system for thousands of royalty-free sounds is www.platinumloops.com.

Sometimes, you just can't find the sound you need. Fortunately, it's not difficult to set up your own little *Foley stage* or sound effects recording area. A good shotgun microphone (highly directional for aiming at sound) and DAT recorder are ideal, although you can get by with less.

The capture device (audio tape, DAT, miniDV, MD, and so on) should be portable, not only in order to get it away from the whirring sound of hard drives and fans, but also to enable you to take it on location when needed. Another advantage of a battery-powered portable device is that static from power line voltage won't be a problem. After you get started and begin playing around, you'll be surprised at the sounds that you can create with ordinary objects. Squeeze your dish soap bottle, and you might notice that when amplified, it will make a nice whoosh. Great for the fast limb movement of that character doing a karate chop. Crumpled paper can sound like fire — once you get started, you never know what you might put to use around the house. Be creative — innovate!

The voices and the sound effects in a cartoon grab your attention and punctuate action, but listen more closely when you watch an engaging animated piece (or any film), and you will gain appreciation for the subtle art of *ambient* sounds. These background noises add tone and atmosphere, making a scene rich and believable. Ambient sound should almost be "felt" more than heard so it doesn't distract from your main narrative. Because it is layered behind the more dominant sounds, you can often get away with looping a short sample of ambient sound — think of wind or water sounds or distant city noises, they have some variation but they also tend to have a repetitive rhythm. And of course, don't overdo it. Well-timed silence can be a powerful narrative device, too!

 There are also many great resources available online for further study of sound and sound effects — one tutorial that we found useful was through the webmonkey site at `http://hotwired.lycos.com/webmonkey/98/33/index0a.html`.

Some Cartoon Animation Basics

In the world of film, movies are shot at 24 frames per second (fps); in video and 3D animation, 30 fps is the norm. But for cartoons, 12 to 15 fps is usually all that's needed. The cartoon language of motion that we've all learned since childhood has taught our minds to expect this slightly jumpy quality of motion in a cartoon. As an animator, this is good for you, because 15 fps means half the amount of hand-drawing work that 30 fps requires. It also means that you can get your cartoon done within your lifetime and maybe take a day off here and there. Actually, there are a lot of scenes in which as few as three drawings per second will suffice — depending on how well you can express motion with your art or drawing. The rule of motion here is that things that move quickly require fewer frames (drawings), while things that move slowly require more frames. This is the main reason you'll hardly ever see slow-motion sequences in cartoons. Broadcast cartoons have lots of fast-paced motion. Fewer drawings are produced more quickly, making the production less costly. These are very significant factors when battling tight budgets and scary deadlines.

Expressing motion and emotion

The hardest part of animation is expressing motion and emotion. Learning to do this well saves time and makes your work more effective. One of the best exercises you can do in this respect is to simply watch the world around you. Videotaping cartoons and advancing through them at single-frame speed can give you insight on different ways that the "real world" is translated to cartoon-land. (If you have digitizing capabilities, you can get a more stable frame by capturing a cartoon to your hard drive and then analyzing the results.)

Another good learning trick is to import raster video to your Flash Timeline, so that you can use a live action sequence as your guide and practice drawing on top of it. While this can help you get a feel for the mechanics of motion, it's really just a start. Cartoons are engaging *because* they so often deviate from, or even defy, the predictable motion we see every day.

Exaggerate everything! After all, this is what makes it a cartoon.

We have included a tutorial in this chapter by Felix Stumpf, who uses video as a reference for his simple but wonderfully engaging hand-drawn animations. To see more of his work, visit www.felixstumpf.de.

Tex Avery was a pioneering animator who created cartoons with overblown and hilarious motion, which revolutionized animation. You can read about him at www.brightlights film.com/22/texavery.html.

Anticipation

Anticipation is a technique used to indicate that characters are about to do something, like take off running. Before lunging into the sprint, characters slowly back up, loading all their motion into their feet until their motion reverses and sends them blasting off in the other direction. In a more subtle form, this is shown in Figure 14-1, when Weber the pelican crouches before he takes flight from his perch on the pier.

Figure 14-1: Anticipation is used to accentuate Weber's take-off.

Weight

Keep the weight of objects in mind. This helps to make your cartoon believable. A feather falls more slowly than an anvil. The feather also eases out (slows down) before landing gently on the ground, while the anvil slams into the ground with such force as to make a gashing dent in it. Humor can play a role here by giving extreme weight to things that do not have it (or vice versa), thereby causing a surprise in the viewer's preconceived notion of what should happen — surprise is the seed of humor.

Overlapping actions

Visualize a jogging Santa Claus, his belly bouncing up and down with each step. Because of its weight, his belly is still on a downward motion when the rest of his body is being pushed upward by the thrust of his leg. This opposing motion is known as *overlapping actions*. Overlapping action does not only happen in an up-and-down motion; it can happen in any direction. An example of side-to-side overlapping actions is shown in Figure 14-2. Note that, as the bully thrusts forward, Weber's body reacts in the opposite direction . . . only to catch up just in time for the thrust to reverse and go the other way.

Figure 14-2: Overlapping actions can accentuate movement in any direction.

Blurring to simulate motion

Blurring is a technique or device that animators use to signify a motion that's moving faster than the frame rate can physically show. In film, this manifests itself as a blurred out-of-focus subject (due to the subject moving faster than the camera's shutter can capture). You may have already employed this effect in Photoshop, with the motion blur filter. In cartoon animation, blurring is often (and easily) described with blur lines. Blur lines are an approximation of the moving subject using line or brush strokes that trail off in the direction that the subject is coming from. When used properly, this great device can save hours of tedious drawing. An example of animated motion blur used to indicate a spinning motion is shown in Figure 14-3, which is a sequence in which the *word* "Weber" turns into Weber the pelican.

Figure 14-3: Blur lines simulate the effect of motion that is "faster than the eye can see."

On the CD-ROM
To see animated examples of the blurred line effect, look in the R_Bazley folder inside the ch14 folder on the CD-ROM. Richard Bazley has used blurred lines effectively to create a collapsing ceiling and a rush of wind.

Using Video As a Basis for Fluid, Hand-drawn Animation, by Felix Stumpf

There are as many different styles of hand-drawn animation as there are animators. But, if you want to create vivid animation with a realistic look, using video as a visual reference is a great shortcut. Combining fluid hand-drawn lines with the movement style of live video results in an engaging hybrid that allows room for individual drawing techniques while maintaining lifelike, cinematic scale and motion. Very skilled animators can achieve this type of fluid animation by drawing freehand, but even then, it can be tricky to capture the mannerisms and personality of a real person.

A simple way of capturing these subtle elements, even with very few lines, is to create a series of video stills to use as a template for ink drawings that can be sequenced in Flash and combined with other graphics or sound to complete the scene.

The line animation that I used to introduce myself on my portfolio site (www.felixstumpf .de) was created by importing a still sequence from a video clip shot on a plain background into Photoshop, and then printing the frames out to use under tracing paper as a reference for pen and ink drawings. I find that six drawings per second are usually sufficient to translate the main flow of motion from the video clip to the traced animation.

Note

Shooting on a plain background with lighting that separates the figure from the background makes it much easier to trace the outline of the figure. Most video-editing programs (such as Final Cut or Premiere) will export a series of stills in a format compatible with Photoshop and Flash. I generally use pict files (.pct), but any compatible lossless format will do.

The decision to draw on tracing paper or to import the video stills into Flash or Photoshop and use digital drawing or painting tools to trace over the video image is mostly a stylistic one. With practice, you can create artwork with the same speed and accuracy with analog or digital tools, but you may find that you prefer the look or feel of one over the other for certain projects. I use both methods and the choice is usually dependent on the mood I'm going for in the final piece. Whether I create the line drawings on paper, in Photoshop, or directly in Flash, I use the original video clip (not the still frames) as a guide for positioning and pacing the final image sequence. This is one of the secrets to maintaining lifelike motion in the animated version.

On the CD-ROM

The evolution of the intro to Felix's portfolio site is shown through the clips included in the fstumpf subfolder of the ch14 folder on the CD-ROM. Open video.swf to see the original video footage. Open animation.swf to see how the line drawings are lined up with the video, and open finalversion.swf to see how the polished animation looks with text elements added in Flash.

Figure 14-4, shows a screenshot from the video clip (down-sampled to 8 frames/sec), used as a reference for my drawings. Turning and walking quickly toward the camera while crossing the frame from left to right sets up a dramatic change in scale and position that will give the animated outline more impact.

Figure 14-4: Shooting on a plain background makes it easier to isolate the movement of the figure in the animation.

Figure 14-5 shows my scanned drawings overlaid with the video in Flash to match up with the pacing and position of the original live action. By following the main lines of action but letting some parts of the outline drop out and shift as the figure moves, I am able to add an organic, fluid character to the outline, which makes the interpretation more artistic.

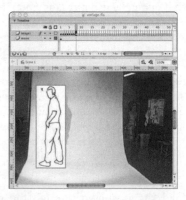

Figure 14-5: Although the pacing and key outlines are sequenced to follow the video template exactly, the sketched lines introduce some looseness.

Figure 14-6 shows a series of stills from the finished animation. The video layer has been removed and the line art translates the original flow nicely.

Frame 8   Frame 21   Frame 36

Figure 14-6: Working with line art gives you the freedom to add other graphic elements or text that interact with the animated figure seamlessly.

Tip   The more images you use, the more fluid your animations will look. I've found that a good rule of thumb is to use 6 images (frames) per second for Web and 25 images (frames) per second for film.

Regardless of which drawing environment you prefer, the key to success is to pay careful attention to the proportions and flow of the still sequence and to be as precise as possible in following the main outlines of the figure. If you choose to draw in Flash, you may find it easier to create one traced outline and then modify that outline in each subsequent frame rather than starting the outline from scratch for each frame. Even small distortions will have a big impact on the final impression of the piece and may throw off the unique characteristics of motion that make the character identifiable. On the other hand, once you get the main action translated smoothly, it can be fun to throw in some variation and take a bit of artistic license to make the visuals more realistic or more fanciful — depending on the final look you're going for. I tend to draw a lot of elements from memory (such as the music player and the rolling paper that the figure interacts with on my portfolio site). This frees me up to invent an environment for the figure and saves a lot of money on props! Combining fluid video-style motion with freehand drawings gives you the benefit of starting with realistic proportions and lifelike movements, but still leaves room for invention and imagination expressed in your own unique drawing style.

Tip   As with any other Flash project, it helps to keep elements organized on individual layers: Keep the video on a Guide layer, import or draw the main image sequence on another layer, and place any additional drawn elements on their own layers.

After I have some traced animation sequences completed, I put them together with sketches of other content and use sample music to rough out my ideas for the flow of the complete site. I call these rough files *moodboards,* and I use them to test my ideas and page designs before I move on to optimizing and integrating final elements in an interactive Flash structure. It takes much less time to prototype a series of screens as a linear animation than it does to build an interactive model, so I can test different versions of my ideas before investing resources on the final project.

One version of my concept for the animation flow with other elements on my portfolio site is illustrated in the `moodboard.swf` file included in the `fstumpf` sub-folder in the `ch14` folder on the CD-ROM. If you compare the moodboard with the final version of my live site, you will notice that the layout is not exactly the same, but the atmosphere is very similar.

Check out the final results of Felix's traced video sketches with other line art elements in his inventive portfolio presentation at `www.felixstumpf.de`.

Animator's Keys and Inbetweening

In Chapter 11, "Timeline Animation," you learned about two Flash animation methods: frame-by-frame and tweening. This section focuses on traditional cartoonist frame-by-frame techniques, together with traditional cartoonist's keys and inbetween methods, to accomplish frame-by-frame animation. Despite the similarity of terminology, this topic heading does not refer to a menu item in Flash. Instead, it should be noted that animation programs such as Flash have derived some program terminology (and methods) from the vintage world of hand-drawn cel animation. Vintage animators used the methods of *keys* and *inbetweening* to determine the action a character will take in a given shot. It's akin to sketching, but with motion in mind. In this sense, keys are the high points, or ultimate positions, in a given sequence of motion. Thus, in vintage animation:

✦ Keys are the pivotal drawings or highlights that determine how the motion will play out.

✦ Inbetweens are the fill-in drawings that smooth out the motion.

In Flash, the usual workflow is to set keyframes for a symbol and then to tween the intervening frames, which harnesses the power of the computer to fill the inbetweens. Although this is fine for many things, it is inadequate for many others. For example, a walk sequence is too subtle and complex to be created simply by shape or motion tweening the same figure — each key pose in the walk requires a unique drawing. So, let's take a look at the traditional use of keys and inbetweens for generating a simple walk sequence that starts and ends according to a natural pace, yet will also generate a walk loop.

Walk cycles (or walk loops)

Humans are incredibly difficult to animate convincingly. Why? Because computers are too rigid — too stiff. Human movement is delightfully sloppy — and we are keenly aware of this quality of human movement, both on a conscious and a subconscious level. (Another term for this is *body language*.) Experienced animators create walk cycles with life not by using perfectly repeating patterns, but rather by using the dynamic quality of hand-drawn lines to add just the right amount of variation to basic movements.

The most difficult aspect of creating a walk cycle is giving the final walk distinctive qualities that support the role that the character plays. This again is something that only gets easier with practice. There is no substitute for drawing skill and time spent studying human movement, but to get started it can be helpful to study a basic walk pattern.

We've included the three walk cycle examples we show in this section on the CD-ROM for you to open and analyze. The frame-by-frame pattern of the different walks can be a good starting point for designing your own walk cycle. You will find the files in the `Walks` folder inside the `ch14` folder of the CD-ROM.

Many 3D programs have prebuilt walk cycles that you can modify. We begin with a basic walk made in Poser (a popular 3D character animation program from e-Frontier) and output it as an image sequence that can be traced in Flash. As you can see in Figure 14-7, this walk cycle was composed of ten different poses, but the final result is fairly generic.

Figure 14-7: A traced sequence from a basic walk cycle that was created in Poser

Notice that the main pivot points of the figure create a balanced pattern that can be used as a basis for many other kinds of figures. Also notice that as the figure moves through the cycle, there is a slight up and down movement that creates a gentle wave pattern along the line of the shoulder. This wave motion is what will keep your figure from looking too mechanical. It is important to remember that the final pose in the cycle is not identical to the first pose in the cycle—this is crucial for creating a smooth loop. Although it might seem logical to create a full cycle of two strides and then loop them, you will get a stutter in the walk if the first and last frames are the same. Whatever pose you *begin* the cycle with should be the next logical "step" after the final pose in your cycle, so that the pattern will loop seamlessly.

Although the figures are shown here with the poses spaced horizontally, you will actually draw your poses on individual frames (best done on a Movie Clip timeline), but align the drawings on top of each other so that the figure "walks in place" as if on a treadmill. Once you have established your walk cycle, you add the horizontal movement by tweening the walk cycle Movie Clip. As shown in Figure 14-8, by using a Motion tween to scale the walk cycle Movie Clip and move it from one corner of the Stage to another, you can create the illusion that the figure is walking toward the viewer.

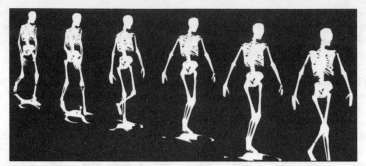

Figure 14-8: A series of angled poses in a walk cycle work well to create the illusion that the figure is walking toward the viewer if the final Movie Clip is scaled as it is Motion tweened from the far corner to the near corner of the Stage.

The speed of the Motion tween has to match the speed of the walk cycle. If the tween is too slow (too little distance or too many frames), the figure will seem to be walking in place. If the tween is too fast (too much distance or too few frames), the figure will seem to be sliding over the ground. Play with the ratio of your Motion tween, and if the figure needs to walk faster or slower, then make adjustments to the walk cycle itself rather than just "pushing" or "dragging" the figure with your Motion tween. Also keep in mind that a figure should seem to walk more quickly as it gets closer to the viewer. In the skeleton walk example, the Motion tween is eased-in so that as the figure gets closer (larger), the walk appears to cover more ground.

Achieving realistic human walk cycles can take hours of work and require very complex walk cycles (often 30 or more poses). Fortunately, many cartoons actually have more personality if they use a simplified or stylized walk cycle that suits the way they are drawn. Figure 14-9 shows a walk cycle that only required three drawings to create a serious but childlike stride for an outlined character.

Figure 14-9: A stylized walk cycle created by flipping and reusing the same three drawings for both legs of an outlined character

Notice that the legs, arms, torso, and head of the character are all animated on separate layers. This allows you to reuse the same drawings for both sides of the body—by simply offsetting the pattern so that the legs swing in opposition to each other, with the leg on the far side layered underneath the leg on the near side. This economy of effort is helpful not only because it is faster, but also because it makes it easier to maintain the symmetry of your character if you are trying to keep the motion simple and stylized.

Repeaters

If you open the source file (`walkToon.fla`), you will notice some spans of nonkeyed frames (repeaters) in the Movie Clip timeline for the cartoon walk. We used these to economize drawing time and to slow the walk of the character. If a speedier walk was called for, we would simply shorten these spans to eliminate repeater frames. A good basic rule about repeaters is to add no more than one repeater frame between keys; adding more causes the smoothness of motion to fall apart. If the motion must proceed more slowly, then you have to draw more inbetweens.

Fortunately, with Flash Onion skinning (the capability to see before and after the current time in a dimmed graphic), which we discuss in Chapter 11, "Timeline Animation," the addition of a few more inbetweens is not an enormous task. In fact, Onion skinning is indispensable for doing inbetweens, and even for setting keys. One pitfall of Onion skinning is the tendency to trace what you're seeing. It takes practice to ignore the onion lines and use them only as a guide. You need to remember that the objective is to draw frames that have slight, but meaningful, differences between them. Although it can mean a lot more drawing, it's well worth it. Because you'll use your walk (and running) cycles over and over during the course of your cartoon, do them well.

Tip

One real timesaver in creating a walk cycle is to isolate the head and animate it separately via layers or grouping. This trick helps to prevent undesirable quivering facial movements that often result from imperfectly traced copies. Similarly, an accessory such as a hat or briefcase can be isolated on a separate layer. Finally, if the character will be talking while walking, make a copy of the symbol and eliminate the mouth. Later, you'll add the mouth back as a separate animation. We describe lip-syncing techniques later in this chapter.

Types of walks

So far, we've covered the mechanics of a walk cycle. But for animators, the great thing about walking—in all its forms—is what it can communicate about the character. We read this body language constantly every day without really thinking about it. We often make judgments about people's moods, missions, and characters based on the way that they carry themselves. Picture the young man, head held high, briskly striding with direction and purpose: He is in control of the situation and will accomplish the task set before him. But if we throw in a little wristwatch checking and awkward arm movements, then that same walk becomes a stressful "I'm late." Or, witness the poor soul—back hunched, arms dangling at his sides. He moves along, dragging his feet as if they each weigh a thousand pounds. That tells the sad story of a person down on his luck. Finally, what about a random pace, feet slipping from side to side, sometimes crisscrossing, other times colliding, while the body moves in a stop-and-start fashion as if it was just going along for the ride? Is that someone who couldn't figure out when to leave the bar? Of course, these are extreme examples. Walks are actually very subtle and there are limitless variations on the basic forms. But if you begin to observe and analyze these details as they occur in everyday life, you'll be able to instill a higher order in your animations. Simply take time to look. It's all there waiting for you to use in your next animation. Then remember that because it's a cartoon, *exaggerate!*

Coloring the Art

In traditional animation, characters were first inked in as outlines and then filled with color and shading. Coloring was the most tedious and time-consuming job of all: endless thousands of cels to be hand painted and dried. Most often, armies of low-paid workers in faraway lands did it. But with Flash it's a snap! That's because of Flash's wonderful (and sometimes mysterious) gap-jumping fill tool, the Paint Bucket. With Flash, you never run out of paint, and it dries instantly—a real timesaver to be sure!

The model sheet

Here's a coloring timesaver that you can use for yourself within Flash: Use a fully colored model of your character at the start of a cycle or scene. This will serve as a color model and will be discarded when the cycle or shot is finished. It's very important to keep a model sheet, which is an archive of color models—finished, fully colored characters—to maintain consistent color across the span of the project. (It's also quite useful at the start of future projects.)

Although Flash has the capability to save color sets, it's still difficult to remember which yellow was used on a certain area of the character, especially when there are ten different yellows in the palette. Making such a color mistake—even a slight shade off—will cause unsightly flicker on playback. The Eyedropper tool makes no mistakes. So, to develop good animation habits, start a model sheet. When you begin a scene, copy the appropriate color model and paste it into the cycle, setting it off to the side of the active art in the first frame (if needed, ungroup it). Acquire the color that you need with the Eyedropper tool and then set about the business of filling.

When filling, we've found that the most efficient method is to go through the entire cycle with one color, filling all objects of that color. Then go back to the beginning and sweep through again, doing the next color. This method saves you the tedium of continually having to change the Paint Bucket's color, and also minimizes the possibility of mistakes. If some places fill while others don't, you'll probably need to adjust the Paint Bucket Gap size modifier.

Tip   The Find and Replace feature in Flash makes it easy to do a global swap if you decide that orange would really be a better color than red (or whatever suits your fancy). With your project file open, choose Edit ⇨ Find and Replace (Ctrl+F or ⌘+F), then use the controls to search the entire document or individual scenes for a color and set the color you want to use instead. Flash does the rest!

Gap problems

There are times when the gaps in a line are not visible but the Paint Bucket tool just won't work. In this case, keep looking because the gaps are there. If it just doesn't work, no matter how much you zoom in and click with the Paint Bucket tool, you may need to zoom in and use the Selection tool to close the gap by adjusting a stroke. In a situation in which it's not aesthetically pleasing to do that, use the Brush tool (set to the same fill color and to paint fills only) to fill the gaps manually. Perhaps this would be the case on a head and neck that you don't want connected to the body (remember we discussed the advantages of animating the head separately earlier). You would use the Brush tool to paint a stroke of fill connecting the inked lines and then fill the larger areas with the Paint Bucket tool.

Speed coloring

A good way to speed up the coloring process is to allocate one of the mouse buttons (if you have a programmable mouse) to perform the keyboard shortcut for step forward advancing (which is the > key). If you have a pressure-sensitive graphics tablet, you can allocate a button on the pen to do the same. With a setup like this, you can leave the cursor in pretty much the same place and click-fill, click-advance, click-fill, click-advance, and so on.

Temporary backgrounds

Another problem that's easily solved is the process of filling areas with white. If you're like most people, you most likely work on the default background color of white, which makes it impossible to distinguish when filling white areas. In this case, it's helpful to create a very light color that you don't plan to use in the final art, something like a light pink. While coloring, temporarily change the background color in the Property inspector or in the Movie Properties dialog box (Modify ➪ Document) to the substitute color for the background of the entire movie. This makes it much easier to see what you're doing when using white as a fill color for objects such as eyeballs, teeth, and clouds. Then, when you're done coloring, you can set the background color back to white.

Flash Character Design Strategies, by Sandro Corsaro

Flash offers a cheaper, faster, and more malleable approach to creating animation than anything in the history of animation. While traditional animation production can be unforgiving, the Flash authoring environment offers animators a variety of starting points in fulfilling their visions. Many creative types who are experienced with Flash can delve into projects with simple thumbnail sketches or even with just concepts in their heads. Purists, and developers working with larger teams, generally prefer the traditional storyboard route. Whether it is intended for Web or broadcast, creating an efficient Flash animation begins and ends with the strategy of your initial design. That design can be on paper, in Flash, or even in your head. What is crucial is that on some level, there is a clear and concise plan in the design. For the purposes of this tutorial, I will show you two simple examples involving design strategy.

By now you should be familiar with the concept of breaking elements into reusable parts or pieces. For Web purposes, this keeps the file small and saves the artist production time. This systemized approach to animation is the evolution of *limited animation* — the cut out system that hasn't changed since it was first applied by Hanna-Barbera for television shows such as *The Flintstones* and *Scooby Doo*. When Fred would talk, his mouth would be on one layer, while his head and body would be on another. If Fred tilted his head during a rant, his mouth and head would tilt during the animation, while his upper body would be held. Why do you think all those great Hanna-Barbera characters always had some sort of accessory (like a tie or necklace) around their necks? This design strategy was effective even with a constrained budget because it allowed for maximum animation with minimal artwork.

Today, Flash has the potential to revolutionize the production process by building on the animation techniques used in the past. Just like the traditional cel method, inactive Flash layers can be "held" while action layers continue with additional frames of movement. The newest feature of this evolution is that symbols, unlike old-school painted cels, can be flipped, stretched, and squashed without having to redraw the artwork. A traditional painted animation cel of a left arm could not be reused for the right arm. On the simplest level, appendages can be flipped, rotated, and scaled to complete character designs. The model sheet I created in Flash of Da Boss (shown in Figure 14-10) is an example of effective reuse of artwork.

Figure 14-10: By designing the character in reusable pieces, you can simplify your workflow while increasing the options for how the character can be animated.

To see the animated Flash version of the model sheet for Da Boss, open `modelSheet.swf` from the `S_Corsaro` subfolder in the `ch14` folder on the CD-ROM.

The script called for this character to be constantly pacing his office. When I designed the character, I broke him into three distinct parts, each with its own animation. The first part was the combed-over hair. I kept it as a separate piece from the head, so it could undulate up and down as he paced. This provides a nice secondary action to his walk. Although the hair is a small detail, without the initial planning, attempting to add it later in the animation process would have proven frustrating and time-consuming. The second animation was the inertia of the heavy upper body. As Da Boss walked, his body needed to convey a sense of weight and power. Utilizing the animation principle of stretch and squash, the symbol of his upper body cycles through various shapes in conjunction with his walk.

The final and most dynamic component of the character's movement is the leg cycle taking place on the layer underneath his upper body. Only one leg has actually been drawn — the other is offset and placed on a lower layer to create a looped walk. As the legs move into each keyframe, the first two elements I described previously are adjusted to create the secondary animation. On the low points of the walk, his weight squashes down, while his hair holds (or pauses) for a momentary beat. A progression of movement follows in the next few keyframes to get to the inverse position of this low point.

Besides the basic model movement, a turnaround was also needed for the animators to work with this character. Obviously, some of the views can be flipped, but what about the front and back? Copy and paste your front view to create your back view. Build on your finished artwork to create the new artwork. Figure 14-11 illustrates how the front view of the Da Boss was modified to create the back view. Unlike the traditional animation process, which travels in distinct and separate stages from point A to B to C, think of Flash animation as a more integrated progression as point A *becomes* B, which *transforms* into C. Always try to build on your work, rather than start from scratch each time you need a new movement or character.

Figure 14-11: With small modifications, the same artwork can be used for the front and back of the character.

Perhaps the most convincing example of the benefits of strategizing your design can be understood by referring to Figure 14-12. These were three different characters intended to be used for broadcast purposes, but the actual animation only had to be created once.

To see how the motion is actually reused in the example shown in Figure 14-12, open `reuseWalk.swf` from the `S_Corsaro` subfolder in the `ch14` folder on the CD-ROM.

Figure 14-12: When a character is designed strategically, you can reuse your animation as well as your artwork to quickly create other characters.

Because of the strategy involved in the original character design, I was able to transform him into the other two characters, reusing both his Graphic symbols and the actual animation. By tweaking the timing of one leg on the run cycle, and obviously making some other artistic changes, the skateboarder character was created from the same artwork as the character running to catch a bus.

Flash is a very sophisticated authoring environment for animation, but, nonetheless, there is no substitute for knowledge of motion. To create truly compelling and intriguing animation in any genre, you must understand the scientific fundamentals of this art. The best place to learn about the principles of animation is in the daily environment around you. Observe the way things move; then strategize how to translate that movement efficiently using the tools available in Flash.

Flash Tweening

You can use Flash tweening to help your cartooning. Now that you've created some symbols, such as the walk cycle, here's where you can save a great deal of time making them slink and prance across the view without drawing every tedious frame. The hard manual drawing work is done; now you'll choreograph the character. Once you've built a library of various walks, runs, turnarounds, and standstills (a piece of walk cycle that ends with the character just standing still), you can use computer power to help you tell a story. Remember that you can always create more symbols of the character as needed — you can even steal from other symbols to create new ones.

Panning

Use the techniques we discussed earlier in this chapter to get your walking symbol looping, stationary in the middle of the view. Then move the background elements to give the illusion of the camera following alongside the walking character, a sort of dolly. We describe the trick for creating extra long pans later in this chapter. It usually requires a little experimentation to get the motion of the background to match the stride of the step. If the timing isn't correct, you'll notice that the feet will seem to skate across the ground. To fix this, adjust the speed of the background by either increasing or decreasing the number of frames in the tween of the background. Another trick is to set the walking symbol to start at one end of the view and to move to the other by tweening the symbol itself. What's really cool is to use a mixture of both. Again, to get it just right, experiment.

Instance swapping

There comes a time when the star of your show must stop walking (or running, or whatever he's doing) and reach into his pocket to pull out a hot rod car and make his getaway. This is where instance swapping comes in. At the end of the tween, create a keyframe on the next frame (the frame immediately following the last keyframe in the tween), and then turn off Motion tweening for that keyframe in the Property inspector. This causes the symbol to stop at whichever frame the cycle ended on in the Timeline. To swap the symbol, follow these steps:

1. Click the symbol to select it on the Stage.

2. Open the Property inspector.

3. Click the Swap Symbol button.

4. In the Swap Symbol dialog box, select the symbol that you want to replace it with (in this case, the one where he reaches into his pocket).

5. Click OK.

If you loop the play of the symbol, you can also choose the frame on which the symbol's cycle will start. Other choices are limiting the symbol to play once and playing just a single frame (still).

 Caution When you swap a symbol instance on a Motion tween, if the Synchronize box is checked, the old symbol instance will not be replaced with the new one, which is Swap Symbol failure. If you turn off tweening on the frame where you swap the symbol, synchronization is not an issue.

Finally, unless you've drawn all your symbols to perfect scale with each other, this new symbol may not fit exactly. No problem! To fix this, simply enable Onion skinning from the Main Timeline, and set it to show the previous frame (the frame the tween ended on). Now you can align and scale the new symbol to match the ghosted image. We can't begin to tell you how much you'll use this simple instance-swapping function when you create your cartoon. This is one of the unique functions that sets Flash apart from all other cel-type animation programs. After you have a modest library of predrawn actions, the possibilities for combining them are endless.

Motion guides

Although not terribly useful for tweening a walking character, the Flash Motion Guide feature is tops for moving inanimate objects. If your character needs to throw a brick, a straight tween between points and some blur lines will do fine. If he needs to lob that brick over a fence to clang a pesky neighbor, then motion guides are the ticket. Here's how:

1. Turn the brick into a Graphic symbol if you haven't already. This makes it easier to make changes to the brick later.

2. Create a Motion Guide layer.

3. Draw an arc from start to destination. This is best done by drawing a line with the Line tool and then retouching it with the Selection tool until you have bent it into the desired arc. This method keeps the motion smooth. (Using the Pencil tool to draw the Motion guide would create too many points and can cause stuttering in the motion.)

Although your brick is flying smoothly, something's wrong. Again, the computer made things too darned smooth. You could insert a few keyframes in the tween and rotate slightly here and there to give it some wobble. But that's still not convincing. You want this brick to mean business! Here's what to do: Because the brick is already a symbol, go back to the brick symbol and edit it, adding a few more frames. Don't add more than three or four frames; doing so will slow it down. At each of these new frames, mess up the brick a little here and there; differ the perspectives a little from one frame to another. Then, when you go back to your main Timeline, the brick should be twitching with vengeance as it sails toward its target.

Lip-syncing

Now here's the part we've all been waiting for . . . a word from our character. If you do it properly, lip-syncing is where a character can really spring to life. You accomplish this by drawing the various mouth positions that are formed for individual *phonemes,* which are the basic units of sound that make up a spoken word. Then these phonemes are melded together into *morphemes,* which are distinct units of a word, like a syllable. Morphemes are then strung together over the course of a sentence to present the illusion of a talking, animated character. Most languages, although populated with thousands of words, are really made up from around 30 to 60 distinct sounds, or phonemes. For cartooning, these phonemes can be reduced to about 10 basic mouth positions. Some of these positions can be repeated for more than one sound because many sounds share roughly the same mouth positions. Although there are more subtleties in the real world, for cartoons, reliance upon transitions between mouth positions is convincing enough.

Earlier, we suggested that the face in an action (walk) cycle should be drawn without a mouth. That's because this method facilitates the use of layers (in the Timeline) for the addition of lip-syncing. To do this, create a layer above the character so that you can freely draw in the mouth positions needed to add lip-syncing. It's also very helpful to put the voice track on another separate layer directly above the Mouth layer. This makes it easy to see the waveform of the sound while you draw, giving important clues to where and when the sound occurs visually.

Since version 4, Flash has had the capability to scrub the Timeline, which means that you can drag the Playhead, or current frame indicator, and hear the sound as you drag. This functionality is limited to streaming sounds, which means that the sounds have their Sync option in the

Property inspector set to Streaming. The capability to hear the sound and see the animation in real time is an important tool for lip-syncing. This real-time feedback is critical for getting the timing just right. There's nothing worse than being plagued with OGMS (Old Godzilla Movie Syndrome), in which the mouth doesn't match the sounds coming from it.

Shape morphing is not for lip-syncing

You may be asking, "What about using shape morphing to save time in lip-syncing?" Well, shape morphing is a wonderful tool, but for lip-syncing, it's more hassle than it's worth. Your mouth drawings will become very complicated because they consist of lips, tongue, teeth, and facial features. Furthermore, because shape morphing only seems to work predictably on the simplest of shapes out of the box, shape hinting is required. Thus, by the time you've set all hinting (and even hinting heavily still leaves you with a mess at times), you might have had an easier time and obtained a better result (with greater control) if you had drawn it by hand.

Expression and lip-syncing

In terms of control and expression, it's important to remember to use the full range of expression when drawing the talking mouths. Happy, sad, or confused—these give life to your character. Furthermore, always emphasize mouth movements on those syllables that correspond with spikes of emotion in the voice track. These sections usually have a spike in the waveform that's easily recognized in the voice track. This device helps to convince the viewer that proper sync is happening.

Lip-sync tricks

There are a few more tricks to help ease the load. When characters talk, they do not always have to be looking you square in the face. Try lip-syncing the first few words to establish that the character is speaking, and then obscure the character's mouth in some natural way. (Refer to Figure 14-13.) The head and body of a character can move with the words being said, but the mouth can be hidden by changing the angle of the head, or with a prop such as a microphone, or even with a moustache—think about this when designing your character's features. A bit of design savvy can save time without detracting from a character's purpose in the story line.

Figure 14-13: Lip-syncing tricks include economy of effort, such as having a character begin to speak and then turn away naturally (left). Appropriate props and even moustaches can also be used to hide mouths (right).

Many animators use a mirror placed nearby and mouth (act out) the words they're trying to draw. This is extremely helpful when learning to do lip-sync. It is also of great help in mastering facial expressions. Just try not to get too wrapped up in drawing every nuance you see.

Sometimes less is more. Another trick that you can use to ease the load is to reuse lip-sync. Do this by copying frames from previous stretches of mouth movements to new locations where the words are the same, and then tweak the copied parts to fit the new dialogue. Still, there is no magic lip-sync button. Even with all these tricks, effective lip-syncing is hard work. It's also one of the more tedious tasks in animation and takes practice to get it right.

Syncing with music and sound effects

Because our brain works to create connections between sound and visual input, it is relatively easy to make movement in your animation match up with audio elements in your soundtrack. If you've already succeeded with lip-syncing work, then this type of syncing is easy. All that's required is a bit of instance swapping set to the beat of the music. If you study your music waveform for visual clues and then scrub it for the sound, you're sure to find the exact section where the change in action (instance swap) needs to go. You don't have to make your sync tight to every note. To keep the shot engaging, sync to the highlights, or hard beats.

Adding sound effects is really the fun part. It's easy and highly effective. Either working from your storyboard, or as you're animating, you'll know where you want to insert a sound effect. For example, when the anvil hits the head, a CLANK is needed there. If the effect you need is on hand, great! Just make sure it has the necessary duration, and then plug it in at the frame where it should start. For broadcast animation, you'll set the sound sync to Streaming for the soundtrack exclusively. In addition to using separate layers for each voice track, it's wise to confine your sound effects to a layer or two. This leads to less confusion; yet using two layers enables more than one sound effect to occur at a time.

On the CD-ROM

For the following Expert Tutorial, we've supplied a short track for your use, `lip_track.wav` or `lip_track.aif`, which you'll find in the `B_Turner` subfolder inside the `ch14` folder of the CD-ROM. These tracks include the major sounds used in the English language.

Lip-Syncing Cartoons, by Bill Turner

For animated characters to really come alive, you need to know how to do lip-sync. To get quality lip-sync effects, you either need to draw them yourself or hire someone else to do it for you. Although this tutorial can't possibly cover every circumstance known to human communication, it can get you started on the road to lip service. There are some prequalifications: First, you must be able to draw in Flash, which usually means drawing with a tablet, preferably a pressure-sensitive graphics tablet (such as a Wacom tablet); and second, you need to have a recorded voice track on its own layer in Flash.

Because lip-sync can't be described in a simple a, b, c routine tutorial, you'll be required to improvise — in your style of drawing. I can't tell you how to do that. Style comes from years of practice and experimentation. But if you do know how to draw and you do have a style, then the intention here is to provide a context in which you might discover the basic trick of lip-sync.

The major sounds, known as phonemes, are less numerous than you might think. It's how these sounds meld together to become words and sentences that add an aura of complexity. Although one might surmise, from the alphabet, that there are 26 sounds, there aren't nearly that many. That's because many letters have the same basic mouth shape, movement, and pronunciation. And because we're now in the land of cartoons, we can simplify even further — the really great cartoons are often the simple ones built of tireless simple reinterpretation.

In this tutorial, to keep it simple, you'll deal with the two dominant views of talking heads: *profile* and *face forward*. A face forward talking head is probably the easiest to animate in Flash because the mouth can be animated on a layer that's situated in the layer stack above a drawing of a mouthless head. A talking head in profile is more difficult because of the need to redraw the portion of the face that extends down from the nose, to and including the chin, for *every* frame. Of course, including nose-to-chin movements can also enhance the animation of a face forward talker, and doing so would make for a more expressive animation. But I want to move quickly here.

In Figure 14-14, you see a mouthless head (provided on the CD-ROM in the B_Turner folder for both demonstration and practice) in both of the basic orientations: face forward and profile.

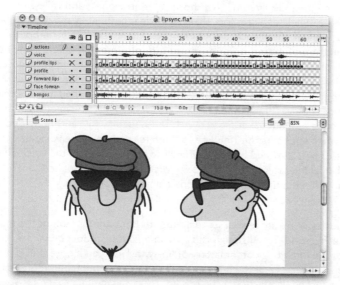

Figure 14-14: A mouthless head in both of the basic orientations: face forward and profile with sound and animation layers for adding lip-sync

The spoken test line reads, "Zinkle Meyers is very talented on the bongo drums. Flip Flap beats his hands on the smooooth skins. Dig the rhythm. Excellent!" Creating lip-sync for this line requires a number of mouth positions. To demonstrate the concepts, the first sentence of this test line is supplied, already drawn to lip-sync. Your task is to draw the mouth positions for the remainder of the spoken text.

On the CD-ROM

To help get you started, Bill Turner supplied a fully functional .fla file for you to work on, with the base character already drawn (`lipsync.fla`). You can find the file in the `ch14/B_Turner` folder on the CD-ROM.

The Sync option

If you were setting this file up from scratch, you'd want to start by placing the voice soundtrack on its own layer in the Timeline. You'd rename this layer with a meaningful name, such as "voice," and then, in the Property inspector, you'd set the Sync option to Stream.

Never use Event as the Sync option for any sound that must sync to the Flash Timeline. Otherwise, the timing of the voice will not be locked to the frame rate, meaning that the mouth drawings may not appear simultaneously with their appropriate sounds, thus losing sync.

Getting into sync

The best way to understand lip-sync is to have the sample file open. Note that there is a visible waveform (the little squiggly stuff) that shows where the peaks and valleys of the sound occur across the Timeline. Note, too, that the voice is brought in as a separate asset. It's on its own layer, separate from background sounds or music. It would be impossible to see the voice within the waveform if it was premixed with other sounds before bringing it into Flash. If you're producing a cartoon show, it's best to have each character recorded separately, particularly in cases in which they may talk over each other simultaneously. This separation gives you more control when animating. In fact, the entire animation is broken into layers for ease of editing. There's at least one layer for each major element. You might also note that the bongo soundtrack is set to event. This is useful while authoring because it mutes the track when scrubbing the Timeline to listen for timings in the voice track. If both were set to streaming, it would be more difficult to concentrate on the voice alone. (You must remember to reset this option to Stream when syncing is completed, or you could just delete that layer until after you are done animating the mouth.)

The phonemes

Now for the phonemes, there are several standard mouth positions for most of the major sounds, as shown in Figure 14-15. Although this is not a rigid rule, it does provide a good basis from which to expand into greater mastery of lip-sync. First, you'll note that the word *Meyers* begins on frame 12 of the animation. The mmmm sound is best represented with the bottom lip tucked slightly under the top lip. Try saying mmmm to see for yourself. In the word *Meyers*, this mmmm sound lasts two frames and is then followed by the long *I* sound. Notice that we didn't sync the word as it is spelled, e-y-e, because that's more complicated than it needs to be. The word Meyers is usually pronounced M-I-ER-Z, with the *ER* being just an *ease-out* (mouth holds shape but gets slightly smaller as phoneme trails off) of the long *I* sound. The word ends with the Z phoneme, which is simply drawn with the mouth slightly open, and the tongue at the top of the mouth.

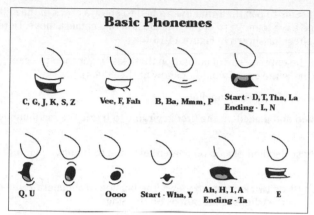

Figure 14-15: You can combine a few basic phonemes to create lip-synced speech.

In the next section of speech, the "very talented" part is a fast-moving set of syllables, so every available frame is needed to represent it. Here, you'll notice that most of the movement occurs when the tongue engages the roof of the mouth for both the *T* and *L* phoneme. Now, because the *T* and *L* are nearly the same mouth position, you can use the luxury of duplicating frames. Similarly, the *V* sound requires the same basic mouth formation as the *M* sound, so you could copy this one as well from the Meyers word. Although the *B* sound, in *bongos*, uses nearly the same mouth as *M* and *V*, we don't copy that one. Here, we draw a new mouth to add a bit of chaos because we don't want the mouth to look like a machine. The logic behind deciding which part to copy and which part to make new drawings for is a large part of the art of lip-sync. In short, it's all about balancing how much new artwork you really want to do, while avoiding obvious repetition.

Now that I've given you an insight into how this is done, I've left the rest of the phrase for you to complete. To accomplish this, you'll probably want to reuse many of the supplied mouth positions to sync the remaining voice. Remember that timing is the most crucial part. You can determine where a new mouth position is needed, or where the mouth needs work, by slowly scrubbing the Timeline. Then, if you need new mouths, simply draw them in. I highly recommend doing this drawing yourself because this practice will start you on your way to becoming a master of lip-sync.

Backgrounds and Scenery

As you have learned in previous chapters, in Flash you work in an area that is called the Stage area. For broadcast animation (or any other kind, for that matter), it is better to think of it as the viewfinder of a camera. The main difference between this camera and the traditional kind, or even those used in 3D animation, is this: *You can't move it.* So, to give the illusion of camera movement, everything within the view must move. This is not as hard as it might seem with Flash's capability to use animated graphic symbols. A good example is in Richard Bazley's animated short, *The Journal of Edwin Carp.*

In a scene where the view seems to pan up from Edwin's bed to show a crack in the ceiling, all of the elements on the Stage have to move to create the illusion of a camera move. Here are the steps for creating this effect, as shown in Figure 14-16:

1. A Graphic symbol of the entire scene of animation that was larger than the camera's view was made (so that white space wouldn't show at the edges).

2. The symbol was placed in the Main Timeline.

3. The symbol was scaled and placed on the first keyframe to frame the medium view of Edwin in his bed.

4. The symbol was then scaled and placed on a later keyframe to frame the view of the cracked ceiling.

5. By tweening between these two keyframed views, the illusion of a camera zoom out and pan up is created as the whole scene moves on the Stage.

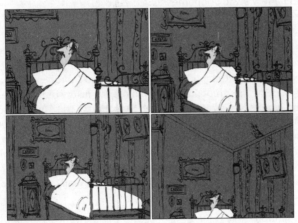

Figure 14-16: A few shots from the bedroom scene in *The Journal of Edwin Carp*

On the CD-ROM

We include this scene and several others from *The Journal of Edwin Carp*, an animated feature film that was done entirely in Flash, on the CD-ROM in the R_Bazley folder inside the ch14 folder.

Web Resource

Richard Bazley describes some of his other clever animation techniques in his tutorial for the *Flash MX Bible* (Wiley) on "2D Character Animation." This tutorial is archived online for readers who wish to learn more about specialized animation techniques. Go to www.flashsupport.com/archive.

Runtime bitmap caching

We're all waiting for the day when intensive animation will play as smoothly on the Web as it does when output for offline viewing. You will be pleased to discover that Flash 8 has brought that day a little bit closer. A new feature enables the Flash Player to optimize playback of complex vector graphics in MovieClip or Button symbols by caching them as bitmaps, or *surfaces*, at run time. The benefit of caching complex vectors as bitmaps is that the Flash Player does not have to tie up the CPU by constantly redrawing these background vectors as other elements are animating in front of them. Your animation will play back faster and smoother. You can apply this option with ActionScript or by selecting a MovieClip (or Button) instance in the Document window and selecting the check box in the Property inspector to Use runtime bitmap caching.

Runtime bitmap caching only optimizes Web playback for Flash movies with complex background images that are static or panned vertically or horizontally. The position, but not the content, of the cached symbol can change without requiring the Flash Player to redraw the vector information. Bitmap caching will fail if the MovieClip (or Button symbol) is larger than 2880 pixels in any direction or if the MovieClip is rotated. You will not notice a significant improvement with bitmap caching on simple vector graphics. Before you publish your final Flash movie, it is always best to test with bitmap caching turned on and turned off to see which delivers the best performance for the specific graphics and animation in your file.

Bitmaps

As we mentioned previously, when you're designing with Flash for the Web, use raster (bitmap) images with a careful eye on their file size. But for broadcast output, there's no limit. Not only can you use as many images as you'd like (within system constraints), but also doing so will make a richer, far more attractive finished product. And, unlike the .swf format, when they're output as raster video, even animations built with a lot of bitmaps will play at the proper frame rate. So move, animate, scale, and rotate them — even play sequences of them. The sky and RAM are the only limits.

QuickTime limitations

Beginning with Flash 4, Flash expanded its import capabilities to include raster video — QuickTime and AVI. When using video output for broadcast, you can export to these formats, too, and video that has been embedded in a Flash project file (.fla) will show up when output to .swf format. In the past, Flash did not recognize alpha channels embedded in the QuickTime 32-bit animation codec (which supports traveling mattes, or alphas). The workaround was to use Mask layers on the video in Flash. One of the most impressive new features of Flash 8 (Professional edition only) is that it *is* now possible to import video with an alpha channel! This is exciting news for anyone who wants to integrate video with her Flash artwork or interface designs in more seamless and creative ways. If you can set up a basic blue or green screen and create some nice alpha channels on your video, you can take advantage of all that work when you bring the video into Flash and start layering your video with other elements.

Remember that you also have the option to link the video file rather than save it within the Flash project file (thank goodness) — Flash makes a pointer to it instead. This keeps your file sizes much more manageable. The only drawback to linking video instead of embedding it is that it won't show up when output to the .swf format.

The option of combining video with vector animation has brought tremendous functionality to Flash because animations can be keyed, or composited, over (or behind) live video without having to recomposite in After Effects. To take advantage of this, keep your live video at the same frame rate as the Flash project. Note, however, that Flash will export only the audio from the video clip in some formats, so you may need to reapply sound in a video-editing application. An alternate solution is to bring the video and audio tracks into Flash separately and to synchronize them there before exporting to your chosen format.

You can find an archived version of the "Exporting Animation" chapter from the *Macromedia Flash MX 2004 Bible* (Wiley, 2004) at www.flashsupport.com/archive. The chapter includes more detailed information about the various options for exporting animation and audio.

Building layered backgrounds in Photoshop

The drawing and effect tools in Flash have become more robust with each release. Flash 8 Professional finally brings the addition of blend modes and more sophisticated gradient controls that make it easier for artists to get the effects that were previously only possible in raster applications. Our suggestion is to try working directly in Flash first, but if you need to go back to Photoshop, you'll be happy to know that the two applications work well together. By using layers in Photoshop to create artwork, multiplane shots are easily accomplished in Flash. Using layers is very important to the organization of the animation. It is not uncommon for a single shot to require more than 20 layers to keep things where they need to be in the visual stacking order. When designing backgrounds (or *scenery,* to be more precise), remember that, at some point, background elements may need to be foreground elements. For instance, the sky will always be in the background, so it is on a layer furthest down in the stack. Other background elements, however, may sometimes need to be in the foreground to facilitate movement of the character, either in front of or behind him. To allow flexibility in how your various elements interact, you should keep them on separate layers.

When creating layered backgrounds, using Photoshop and alpha channels delivers the most versatility. When using Photoshop for scenery elements, it's mandatory to work in layers and to save a master file with all layers intact. Elements can then be exported to individual files (with alpha channels) as needed. (Retaining the master layered Photoshop file gives you maximum options later, if edits or changes occur. It can also be used as a resource for subsequent animations, so don't flatten or discard your master layered Photoshop file. Instead, number and archive it!) Why the alpha channels? When translating the Photoshop elements into Flash vector scenery, they automatically mask themselves — so a little preplanning in Photoshop can save lots of time later.

Flash Mask layers

Whoops! You got to a point where you didn't use layers and now you need a mask. Some situations may be either too complicated or else unforeseeable in the original design. Flash Mask layers can come to the rescue. Here's the good news: You can mask (and animate the mask) interactively with the other elements while in Flash. The bad news is that it might be more difficult to create a precise mask in Flash than to export an alpha channel from the original Photoshop file. A classic example of masking used in character animation is the black circle that closes in on a scene at the end of an animated episode — this simple animated shape mask is easy to add in Flash.

Long pans

Long pans are a standard device of animated cartoons; an example is when Fred Flintstone runs through the house and furniture keeps zipping past (that must be one looooong living room). This can be done a couple of ways in Flash. For landscape backgrounds, it's usually best to first create a very wide graphic (bitmap or vector) of the landscape and then to Motion tween it horizontally, with keyframes for stopping and starting as needed within the tween. If something is either falling or ascending, use a tall graphic and Motion tween vertically. Another solid technique is to create art of the objects that will pan (such as clouds) and then loop them as the background layer, across the view. To get smooth results when using looping, don't use easing in or out with the tween setup. Also, to maintain constant speed, maintain the exact number of frames between the keyframes. Then, copy the tween by Alt (Option) dragging the selected tween frames to the desired area in the Timeline. Repeat copying until you've covered the time needed.

 Caution For Web animation, it is best to use Movie Clips for looping animation, but if you are planning to output your animation to video, you have to lay out all animation in keyframes on the main Timeline (or in Graphic symbols). When it's exported to video, only the first frame of any Movie Clips will display, unless you use After Effects or Macromedia Director to translate the .swf file before final output.

 Web Resource You can find an archived version of the "Exporting Animation" chapter from the *Macromedia Flash MX 2004 Bible* (Wiley, 2004) at www.flashsupport.com/archive. The chapter includes more detailed information about the various options for exporting animation.

In the Weber cartoon scene of a chase along the beach, a camera pan was created by tweening a symbol of the whole beach scene horizontally. As shown in Figure 14-17, the "camera view" reveals only a small area of the larger background scene.

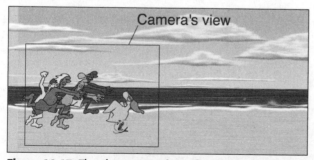

Figure 14-17: The chase scene from the Weber cartoon is created with a looping pan.

 New Feature The Work area in Flash is now called the "Pasteboard," and it has been expanded in Flash 8 to better support workflows that require extra-long graphics that will be tweened across the Stage. This feature is also handy for developers who like to store extra elements off the Stage where they won't be visible in the final .swf. Think of it as the theatre wings of your Flash stage.

Multiplane pans

To provide 3D-motion depth during the pan, keep this rule in mind: An object that is farther away appears to move more slowly (than a nearer object) as it moves across the view. This takes some experimenting to get it right, but once mastered, this will add a professional touch to your animations. For example, in a 100-frame pan of a beach scene looking toward the water:

✦ The sky moves very slowly at 100 pixels total.

✦ The water moves more quickly at 125 pixels total.

✦ The character on the beach moves more quickly than the water at 150 pixels total.

✦ A parked car in the immediate foreground moves most rapidly at 250 pixels total.

Blurring to simulate depth

The multiplane camera was used in early Disney films to give a feeling of depth in the animation of flat artwork. There was physical space between the individual cels when photographed. By using a short depth of field lens, the artwork that was further away from the lens lost focus slightly. (You may have noticed this in still photography yourself.) A good example of this is the pier scene from the Weber cartoon, which is shown in Figure 14-18. Even if you set up your scenery using bitmaps, you can re-create this effect.

In Photoshop, it's a simple case of using incrementally higher doses of Gaussian blur on the layers of your scenery that are farther way. The farther the object is, the more blur that is applied—just be sure that the blur is applied to the alpha channel that Flash will use in compositing. In Flash 8 Professional, gradually apply more intensive levels of blur using the Blur filter. Photographers use this technique to bring attention to the element in the shot that is in focus. Using it in animation enhances the illusion of depth. However, using it in the foreground can also portray various elements, such as fog.

Figure 14-18: The opening pier scene from the Weber cartoon has a feeling of depth created by using increasing levels of blur on the background layers.

Finishing Up

When you have a shot done, it's often helpful to see it play at full speed. Unfortunately, Flash is unable keep up with all of the sounds, bitmaps, and complicated vectors that go into broadcast-quality animation. Plus, it's impossible — even with the most macho of processors — to play the shot at full speed without hiding a bunch of elements. But, hey, you're the director of this masterpiece — it's time for dailies, and you need to see it all.

The best way to do this and to cut down on file size is to export a raster video at 320 x 240 pixels, using the standard QuickTime Video codec (Mac) or the Microsoft Video 1 codec. These codecs are for draft purposes only, so it may have banding and artifacts from compression, but the point is to generate something that even a machine that's ill-equipped for high-end video output can display easily at full frame-rate speed. This method will be of great help in revealing those areas of the animation that still need further tweaking and work before going out to the final published version. The general movement and pace of the shot will make itself known. Look for errors such as unintended jumpiness in frames, and color shifts or inconsistencies between views. Furthermore, your lip-syncing efforts will either be a glory to behold or a disaster in need of medical attention. Other things, such as sound clipping (pops in high volume sound) also become apparent here. To put it bluntly, if the preview makes you cringe, then it needs work — if not, you're on your way to final output.

Final output

Now, after checking endlessly, you're ready for the final video file of the shot to be rendered. Back it up one more time. Then, when you've safely archived your final project file, it's time to choose the codec that your playback equipment can use and render one out for the tube. Then, when you have rendered all your shots at full screen, you can take them into Premiere or After Effects or Macromedia Director for more detailed editing and tweaking, using all the power that these applications offer. For example, you might want music to play gently in the background across all of your scenes. Although this would be a headache to piece together with separate Flash project files, it's a snap in Premiere. Again, the possibilities are endless.

 We describe some suggested workflows for output of character animation in detail in an archived version of the "Exporting Animation" chapter from the *Macromedia Flash MX 2004 Bible* (Wiley, 2004) at `www.flashsupport.com/archive`. We put this chapter online because the workflow has not changed significantly since the last edition and we had to make room for coverage of new features.

CineLook Filters for "Classic" Broadcast Animation, by Evan and Gregg Spiridellis

If you've made it to this section of the book, you are by now well aware that Flash is an amazing tool not only for online animation, but also for broadcast animation.

There is one pitfall with using Flash animation for broadcast purposes: Time and time again, we hear that Flash looks too "Flashy" — meaning that it is too "digital" or "perfect" when transferred. The perfectly flat colors that you get from Flash work great in some circumstances, but when they're transferred for broadcast, they come across as a bit cold and lifeless. Looking at big, even blocks of color on a computer monitor is one thing, but traditional animation needs to look more organic.

We've found the solution in the DigiEffects CineLook 1.5 plug-in for Adobe After Effects. The software is a bit expensive, but if you do a lot of this kind of work, it is worth every penny! It takes your perfect digital files and adds enough imperfection to give your Flash animation a more organic look and feel. In this tutorial, we will explain our process for adding filter effects to a Flash animation file in preparation for broadcast delivery. Although many of the filter effects are very subtle, you can see some of the differences between the original Flash artwork and the final filtered animation in Figure 14-19.

Figure 14-19: Flash artwork that looks too "clean" for broadcast (top) can be modified with filters in AfterEffects to look more organic (below).

For more information and demo versions of the CineLook plug-in, go to www.digieffects.com

Setting up the file

After installing the CineLook plug-in, you're ready to begin. Start by exporting your Flash movie as a QuickTime or AVI file. Open After Effects and set up a new Composition. The dimensions and duration should match your Flash file. Import your QuickTime or AVI file and drag your movie to the Timeline. Select the movie in the Timeline by clicking its layer, and now you can begin to add filters.

Softening with Gaussian Blur

The first thing that we recommend is adding an ever-so-slight Gaussian blur to take the hard "edge" off of the lines in your Flash movie. Go to Effect ➪ Blur & Sharpen. Apply a 0.1 or 0.25 Gaussian blur depending on the style you are trying to achieve.

It is very easy to get carried away with these filters! It is important to find the filter effect that best complements your movie and not go overboard with the effects. After all, you want people to congratulate you on your movie, not your filters!

After the initial Gaussian softening, we can proceed with our "film look" filters.

Adding DE CineLook filters

Make sure that your movie is still selected in the Timeline, go to Effects ➪ DigiEffects CineLook, and select DE CineLook.

The CineLook plug-in allows you to add and control film grain, adjust color temperatures, and view whether your colors are NTSC safe. There is nothing worse then spending hours perfecting your animation only to find that when it's transferred to television, your colors bleed all over the screen.

The first thing you do is run the NTSC Gamut Warning. This will block out any colors that are not NTSC safe and allow you to make the appropriate adjustments. You can adjust your saturation and color levels until nonsafe colors enter the NTSC spectrum. CineLook gives you seven layers of adjustment for your Red, Green, Blue, and White channels or you can transform your entire file to Black and White.

Next you tackle the film grain. This is by far the biggest advantage of the CineLook plug-in. Color film is processed in three layers: red, green, and blue. CineLook enables you to control the amount of grain and the softness of the grain in each color field. Adding a slight grain effect will help activate the big, flat shapes that Flash is notorious for. If done well, this adjustment may not be overtly noticeable to the average viewer, but it will add a more organic feel to your movie. Of course, if it fits the style of your movie, you can go overboard!

Once you find the right grain level for your current animation, you have the option of saving your settings. This makes it possible to get a uniform look throughout an entire project or apply the same effects to multiple projects.

Adding DE FileDamage filters

After polishing your Flash movie with a "film look," you might want to take it one step further and "damage" the film a bit. The FileDamage plug-in is a great tool for making a perfect digital file look more weathered. The descriptively named main categories for adjustment are Flicker, Vertical Scratches, Hair, Dust, and Dirt.

In the old days, shooting film was by no means a precise art form, and it seems that no two consecutive frames ever received the same amount of light. Flicker makes it possible to control the difference in exposure between frames. Select the movie in the timeline, then go to Effects ⇨ DigiEffects CineLook and select DE FileDamage.

The first effect you add is Flicker. FileDamage enables you to control the Amount, Speed, and Variation of exposure differences. This might be difficult to see in side-by-side illustrations, but when the movie plays in real time, Flicker is a very natural effect.

Another disadvantage of traditional film developing (in the early days) was that the celluloid was exposed to the elements at almost every stage of the process. FileDamage allows you to control the amount of hair, dust, and dirt that has mucked up the film along the way.

The Vertical Scratches effect is the perfect "Old Time" filter, and FileDamage allows you to control the Number, Speed, Opacity, and Thickness of the scratches.

Finishing up

Once you've gotten the desired look for your movie, save your settings in the Presets section for future use. If you're all set with your filters, save your After Effects file and go to Composition ⇨ Make Movie to test your movie.

On the CD-ROM

To see a "live" comparison of the before and after files described in this tutorial, open `JibJab_Willy.swf` (original file) and `JibJab_Willy.mov` (filtered file) from the `JibJab` folder in the `ch14` folder on the CD-ROM.

Film filters such as DigiEffects CineLook give you a range of options to take the digital edge off your Flash animation, and when they're done properly, they'll give the impression that you've been scribbling cels in your basement for years!

Note from the authors: We kept this tutorial from the *Macromedia Flash MX 2004 Bible* (Wiley, 2004) because it provides some great guidelines for the kind of adjustments that you might want to make to your pure Flash animation to get it ready for broadcast. The only thing that has changed since Flash MX 2004 is that there are now more options in the Flash authoring environment for modifying the look of your graphics. You might want to try some of the new Flash 8 Filters or Blend modes to soften up your artwork. Ultimately, it is hard to replace expert ready-made filters for adding things like film grain, but keep an eye on the Flash Exchange on Macromedia's site for custom Filters that may soon fill this gap.

We'd like to know what you think about this chapter. Visit www.flashsupport.com/ feedback to fill out an online form with your comments.

Summary

✦ Flash can be a powerful tool for creating broadcast-quality cartoons. In such cases, many of the usual file-size concerns related to Flash development are set aside because the final output will not have to be Web-friendly.

✦ The task of a cartoon animator is to express motion and emotion. Anticipation and overlapping actions are basic tools used by cartoon animators to add drama to a character's movement.

✦ Flash tweening, including instance swapping and Motion guides, is one of the most useful Flash cartooning tools.

✦ Lip-syncing, which is critical to fine cartoon animation, is not a push-button task — even with Flash, an animator must understand the relationship between expression and lip-sync, and have a working knowledge of phonemes, as well as syncing with music and sound effects.

✦ The new Filters and Blend modes in Flash 8 are strong additions to the authoring environment that will make it much easier to achieve sophisticated-looking animation without having to use other applications for special effects.

✦ After a cartoon is created in Flash, final output may include using either Premiere or After Effects for the final polish that makes it look more like "real film."

✦ The key point of this entire chapter is this: Computers can save time, but artists animate!

✦   ✦   ✦

Integrating Media Files with Flash

You can create a wide range of graphic elements directly in Flash, but most projects also require imported assets. This section covers the three main media types that you can use to enhance your Flash projects. Chapter 15 introduces the process for importing and controlling sound in Flash. This chapter also covers various compression options and how to edit and export sound from Flash. Learn techniques that help you to get the most bang per byte in your final Flash movies. Chapter 16 addresses the specific workflow and optimization issues related to importing vector and bitmap artwork (and text) from other programs to the Flash authoring environment. Find out how to maintain color consistency and how to preserve layers and vector outlines when moving graphics from other programs, including Adobe Illustrator, Macromedia FreeHand, Fireworks, and Adobe Photoshop. Flash 8 offers a whole range of possibilities for video content. Chapter 17 focuses on the process for optimizing and integrating video, including coverage of the new On2 VP6 codec and the FLVPlayback component.

Adding Sound

One of the more neglected — or perhaps understated — aspects of multimedia development is sound. Because the majority of people who use Flash or create multimedia come from graphic-arts backgrounds, it's no surprise that sound is often applied as the last effect to an otherwise visually stunning presentation — there may be little or no consideration for the soundtrack in early stages of development. Moreover, it's the one element that is usually taken from a stock source, rather than being original work by the Flash designer. (Exceptions exist, of course, as Flash designers have demonstrated time and time again.)

> **Note** It goes without saying that as Web projects or applications grow in scope, production teams tend to include specific members responsible for unique tasks, from graphic design to user interface design to sound design.

You can use sound in Flash movies to enhance interactive design with navigation elements, such as buttons, to layer the visitor's experience with a background soundtrack, to add narration, or for more experimental uses. In this chapter, we focus on the fundamentals of importing and integrating sound files into your Flash project. We also discuss the intricacies of controlling audio output, with particular attention to MP3 bit rates. You'll learn how to use the Publish Settings dialog box and compare it with the enhanced control that is available for customizing compression from within the Sound Properties dialog box of the Library. This chapter guides you through using audio within a Flash document and suggests tips for getting the most bang per byte in the final Flash movie file (.swf).

> **Cross-Reference** You can read more about sound in Appendix C, "Digital Audio Basics," which is included as a PDF file on this book's CD-ROM. To learn how to load external MP3 files into a Flash movie at run time, read Chapter 28, "Sharing and Loading Assets."

Identifying Sound File Import and Export Formats

Flash 8 can work with a wide variety of sound file formats. In this section, you learn which sound file types you can bring into a Flash document file (.fla) and how Flash can compress audio in a variety of formats in the final Flash movie file (.swf).

Import formats

You can import most sound file formats in either the Windows or Macintosh version of Flash. All major sound file types, such as MP3 and WAV, are compatible on both versions. Once you import a sound file into a Flash document, you can edit the resulting .fla file on either platform.

Flash 8 can import the following sound file formats:

✦ **MP3 (MPEG-1 Audio Layer 3):** Among the many advantages of MP3 sound files for Flash users, the most obvious is that they are cross-platform. Flash 8 can import MP3 files with either Windows or Mac versions of the tool. This single advantage improves Flash workflow in cross-platform environments. Other advantages are the efficiency of MP3 compression, the increasing availability of MP3 files, as well as the ease of creating MP3 files with common players such as Windows Media Player or Apple iTunes. For more information about MP3s, see the "MP3s Demystified" sidebar at the end of the section.

✦ **WAV (Windows Wave):** Until the relatively recent support for MP3, WAV files reigned for nearly a decade as the standard for digital audio on Windows PCs. Still, the WAV format remains the primary acquisition sound format, the format in which you record sound from a microphone or other sound source on your computer. Flash can import WAV files created in sound applications and editors such as SoundForge or ACID. The imported WAV files can be either stereo or mono and can support varying bit depths and frequency rates. You can import WAV files directly into Flash 8 on a Mac.

✦ **AIFF or AIF (Audio Interchange File format):** Much like WAV on the PC, the AIF format is the most commonly used digital audio format for sound acquisition on the Mac. Flash can import AIFF sounds created in sound applications and editors such as Peak, Deck II, or SoundEdit. Like WAV, AIFF supports stereo and mono, in addition to variable bit depths and frequency rates. Unassisted, the Windows version of Flash 8 cannot import this file format. But when QuickTime 4 or later is installed, you can import AIFF files into Flash 8 on Windows. The Windows version of Flash 8 recognizes, properly opens, and can edit Flash documents created on the Mac that contain AIFF sounds.

✦ **Sun AU:** This sound format file (.au) was developed by Sun Microsystems and Next, and it is the native sound format on many Solaris and UNIX systems, just as WAV and AIF are native to Windows and Macintosh, respectively. The Sun AU format is frequently used with sound-enabled Java applets on Web pages.

✦ **QuickTime:** You can import QuickTime audio files (.qta or .mov) directly into Flash 8, provided that you have QuickTime 4 or later installed. Once you import a QuickTime audio file into a Flash document, the sound file appears in the Library just as any other sound would.

✦ **Sound Designer II:** This proprietary audio file format created by Digidesign is used with its signature professional audio suite, Pro Tools. You can import sounds that you save in this file format into the Macintosh version of Flash 8. If you need to use a Sound Designer II file (.sd2 file extension) with the Windows version of Flash 8, you can import the file directly if you have QuickTime 4 or later installed.

Note   With Flash 8, you can link proxy sound files to Musical Instrument Digital Interface (MIDI) and Melody For i-mode (MFI) files that can be played back on mobile devices with Flash Lite. You'll learn more about this feature later in this section.

Tip

Don't rely upon the imported sound that's embedded in the Flash document file (.fla) as your master or backup sound file. Always retain your original master sound file as a backup or for reuse in other multimedia projects.

These sound file types are structural or "architecture" based, meaning that they simply indicate the wrapper used to encode digital audio. Each of them can use a variety of compression techniques or a variety of audio *codecs*. A codec is a compression and *de*compression module for digital media. Sound and video is encoded (compressed) with a specific technique by an application or device. After it is encoded, it can be played back (decompressed) by a media player that has access to the codec module. In order for a sound file to play on your computer, you must have the audio codec used in that file installed on your system. MP3 files, for example, can be compressed in a variety of bit rates and frequencies, as can WAV and AIF files. Once Flash imports a sound file, the wrapper type (AIF, WAV, AU, and so on) is stripped. Flash simply stores the sound file as generic PCM (Pulse Code Modulation) digital audio. Moreover, Flash converts any imported 8-bit sound file into a 16-bit sound file. For this reason, it's best not to use any precompression or low bit depths on your sound files before you bring them into Flash 8.

Note

You can adjust individual MP3 sound files in the Flash document's Library to retain their original compression. This is the sole exception to the rule we just mentioned in the preceding paragraph. As you'll see later in this chapter, however, Flash 8 may need to recompress all sound files in a Flash movie, depending on their use in the movie's timeline.

MP3s Demystified

MP3 is an amazing compression technology as well as a file format. It excels at the compression of a sound sequence — MP3-compressed files can be reduced to nearly a twelfth of their original size without destroying sound quality. MP3 was developed under the sponsorship of the Motion Picture Experts Group (MPEG) using the following logic: CD-quality sound is typically sampled at a bit depth of 16 (16-bit) at sample rate 44.1 kHz, which generates approximately 1.4 million bits of data for each second of sound — but that second of sound includes a lot of data for sounds that most humans cannot hear! By devising a compression algorithm that reduces the data linked to imperceptible sounds, MP3 developers made it possible to deliver high-quality audio over the Internet without excessive *latency* (the delay between loading a sound and playing it). Another way of describing this is to say that MP3 uses perceptual encoding techniques that reduce the amount of overlapping and redundant information that describes sound. As you'll learn later in this chapter, the Flash Player can actually buffer Stream sounds (which you can create from any sound file imported into Flash); this means that the sound begins to play in the Flash movie before the sound file has been downloaded in its entirety. Shockwave Audio, the default audio compression scheme for Macromedia Director–based Shockwave movies, is actually MP3 in disguise.

Export formats

You can decide which sound encoding to use for audio when publishing Flash document files to Flash movie files (.swf). Although the default Publish Settings in Flash 8 is to export all audio with the MP3 format, you can export sound in several other audio formats. We note the benefits and drawbacks of each format in the list that follows.

Note   Flash Professional 8 enables you to export device sounds in a Flash movie, for playback on mobile devices that use file formats such as MIDI and MFI. We provide an overview of this feature in this section.

Regardless of the format that you choose in your document's Publish Settings for exporting your sounds, you can individually specify a compression scheme for each sound in the Flash document's library. Furthermore, each format has specific options and settings that we'll examine later in this chapter.

✦ **ADPCM (Adaptive Differential Pulse-Code Modulation):** ADPCM is an audio compression scheme that converts sound into binary information. It is primarily used for voice technologies, such as fiber-optic telephone lines, because the audio signal is compressed, enabling it to carry textual information as well. ADPCM works well because it records only the difference between samples and adjusts the encoding accordingly, keeping file size low. ADPCM was the default setting for older versions of Flash, such as Flash 2 and 3. It isn't as efficient as MP3 encoding but is the best choice for situations in which compatibility is required with *all* older Flash Players.

✦ **MP3 (MPEG-1 Audio Layer 3):** Over the last three years, MP3 has become the standard for digital audio distributed on the Internet. Although MP3 compression delivers excellent audio quality with small files, it's much more processor-intensive than other compressors. This means that slower computers — and we mean slow, as in Pentium I or pre-PowerMac G3 processors — may gasp when they encounter a high bit-rate MP3 audio while simultaneously processing complex animations. As always, it's wise to know your audience. When in doubt, test your Flash movie with MP3 audio on slower computers. Flash Players 4 and higher support MP3 playback.

Note   Flash Player 4 for the Pocket PC does not support MP3 sound. With Flash Player 6 and higher, you can use ActionScript's `System.capabilities.hasMP3` property to determine if the hosting player device supports MP3 audio. You can learn more about this use of ActionScript in the *Flash MX 2004 ActionScript Bible* (Wiley, 2004) or later editions.

✦ **Raw (Raw PCM):** Flash can export sound to .swf files in a raw audio format. If you use this setting, Flash won't compress any audio. However, uncompressed sound makes very large files that would be useless for Internet-based distribution. As uncompressed sound, audio in the imported sound file retains its original fidelity. We recommend that you use the Raw format only for Flash movies that you intend to distribute on fixed media, like CD-ROM or DVD-ROM, or for Flash movies that you intend to export as linear animation for video-editing purposes.

✦ **Speech (Nellymoser):** This audio codec in Flash MX (Flash Player 6) is specifically designed for audio sources that contain mostly human speech, such as narration or instructional content. Macromedia licensed audio technology from Nellymoser, Inc., which specializes in the development of voice-only audio codecs. All sounds that use the Speech codec are converted to mono sounds. You can see the real power of this codec in live streaming audio delivered by Flash Communication Server MX, as this codec is incredibly efficient and a fast encoder with a low server and client processor overhead. For example, if you want to use a `NetStream` object in ActionScript to stream live audio from a microphone, the Speech codec will optimize the audio information very efficiently. You must use Flash Player 6 or higher to play sounds encoded with this format.

✦ **Device sound:** If you use Flash Professional 8, you can link device sound files to imported sounds in your Flash movie. You use device sounds specifically for playback of Flash movies on mobile devices enabled with Flash Lite, a version of the Flash Player. Because the desktop Flash Player cannot play device sound file formats, you import regular sound files such as MP3s into your Flash document. These sounds are then used in a proxy fashion—you add the sound to event handlers (keyframes, buttons, and so on) just as you would any other sounds. Before you publish the Flash movie file (.swf), however, you change the settings of the sound file in the Library panel to point to a device sound. When the Flash movie is published, the device sound is embedded and used within the Flash movie, not the original imported sound.

We'll examine the specific export options for each audio format later in this chapter. This section will help you determine which format you should use for your specific needs.

Table 15-1 shows the compatibility of Flash's audio export formats with various platforms.

Table 15-1: Audio Export Formats for Flash Players

Export format	Flash 3 or earlier	Flash 4 and 5	Flash 6 or higher	Comments
ADPCM	Yes	Yes	Yes	Good encoding scheme; compatible with all Flash players; works well for short sound effects such as button clicks
MP3	No	Yes	Yes	Best general use encoding scheme; ideal for music tracks *Not compatible with Flash Player 4 for the Pocket PC.
Raw	Yes	Yes	Yes	No compression; lossless; large file sizes
Speech	No	No	Yes	Excellent compression for human speech; avoids "tinny" sounds for voices; ideally suited for real-time compression with Flash server-side applications
Device sound	No	No	No	Sound export feature available in Flash Pro 8; for use with MIDI and MFI files for playback on mobile devices with Flash Lite

Importing Sounds into Flash

In the preceding section, we discussed the various sound formats that Flash 8 can import and export. In addition to covering the merits of the MP3 and Speech codecs, we also explained the uses of platform-specific AIF (Mac) and WAV (Windows) audio files. But we didn't delve into the process of importing sound into Flash 8. So, let's get started.

Note   When working with sound, you may encounter some interchangeable terminology. Generally, these terms — *sound file, sound clip,* and *audio file* — all refer to the same thing, a single digital file in one of several formats, which contains a digitally encoded sound.

Unlike other imported assets, such as bitmaps or vector art, Flash won't automatically insert an imported sound file into the frames of the active layer on the timeline. In fact, you don't have to select a specific layer or frame before you import a sound file. That's because all sounds are sent directly to the Library immediately upon import, regardless of whether you use File ⇨ Import ⇨ Import to Stage or Import to Library. After import, the sound becomes part of the Flash document file (.fla), which may make the file size balloon significantly if the sound file is large. The sound does not become part of the Flash movie file (.swf), nor will it add to the size of the Flash movie *unless* it is assigned to a keyframe, as an instance of that sound, or it is set to export for use in ActionScript.

Tip   Flash Players 6 and higher allow a Flash movie to load MP3 files directly. Earlier versions of the Flash Player required Macromedia Generator (or an equivalent server-side application) to transform sound files into Flash movie files (.swf) on the fly. We'll show you how to load and attach sounds with ActionScript in Chapter 28, "Sharing and Loading Assets."

To import a sound file into the Flash 8 authoring environment, follow these steps:

1. Choose File ⇨ Import ⇨ Import to Library or Import to Stage (Ctrl+R or ⌘+R). For sound assets, these commands work identically.

2. From the Files of type list (Windows) or Show list (Mac) in the Import dialog box, select All Sound Formats.

Caution   On the Mac OS X version of Flash 8, you may need to choose All Files in the Show menu in order to select an appropriate sound file.

3. Browse to the sound file that you want to import.

On the CD-ROM   If you're looking for a sample audio file, you can import the `atmospheres_1.mp3` file found in the `ch15` folder of this book's CD-ROM.

4. Click Open.

The sound file you select is imported into your Flash document file (.fla) and arrives in the document's library with its filename intact. If the Library panel is closed, you can open it by choosing Window ⇨ Library, or by using the keyboard shortcut

(Ctrl+L or ⌘+L). With the Library panel open, locate the sound, and click it to highlight the name of the sound file where it appears in the Library list. The waveform appears in the Library preview pane, as shown in Figure 15-1. Click the Play button above the waveform to audition the sound.

Figure 15-1: This is a stereo sound in the Flash document's library.

Refer to the "Fine-Tuning Sound Settings in the Library" section, later in this chapter, for an explanation of how you can specify unique compression settings for each sound in a document's library.

You may also load sounds from a shared library. Refer to Chapter 28, "Sharing and Loading Assets," to learn more about shared libraries. Chapter 28 also shows you how to preload an MP3 file into a Flash movie file (.swf). To learn how to assign a linkage identifier string to an asset, such as a sound file, refer to Chapter 27, "Interacting with Movie Clips."

You can also import sound files into a Flash document by dragging the sound file from the desktop to the Library panel. On the Macintosh, you can drag the sound file to the Stage as well. This method can be especially useful when you have searched for a sound file using the operating system's search tool (Start ➪ Search in Windows, or Sherlock in the Mac OS), and want to quickly bring the sound file into Flash 8.

How Sound Is Stored in a Flash Movie

Earlier in this chapter, we mentioned that when you import a sound file into a Flash document file (.fla), an entire copy of the sound file is stored within the document. However, when you place a sound on a timeline, a reference is made to the sound in the library. Just as symbol instances refer to a master or parent symbol in the Library, sound "instances" refer to the master sound resource in the Library.

Throughout this chapter, we use the term "instance" for sound assets with this understanding in mind. When the Flash document is published as a Flash movie, the master sound in the Library is compressed and stored *once* in the final movie file (.swf), even though there may be several instances of that sound used through the movie (for example, in multiple frames on multiple timelines).

Continued

Continued

This type of efficient storage, however, applies to Event sounds only. Whenever you use Stream sounds, the sound file is stored in the Flash movie each time you refer to the sound in a Timeline. For example, if you compressed a sound to export from Flash as a 3K sound asset in the final movie file (.swf), you could reuse that sound as an Event sound several times without adding significant bytes to the file size. However, that same compressed sound (at 3K) would occupy 12K in the final movie if it was placed four times as a Stream sound on keyframes within the movie. We'll discuss Event and Stream sounds later in this chapter, so you may want to refer to this sidebar at a later point.

It is also worth mentioning that Flash 8 must have enough available RAM on the computer system to accommodate imported sound files. For example, if you import a 30MB WAV file into a Flash document, then you must have an additional 30MB of RAM available to the application. On 32-bit Windows operating systems and Mac OS X, you will not likely experience problems with memory usage, where virtual memory exists alongside the physical RAM within the computer.

Assigning a Sound to a Button

The interactive experience can be enhanced by the addition of subtle effects. The addition of sounds to correspond with the various states of a button is perhaps the most obvious example. Although this effect can be abused, it's hard to overuse an effect that delivers such meaningful user feedback. Here, we show how different sounds can be added to both the Over (rollOver) and the Down (press) states of a button.

Cross-Reference
For more general information about creating the buttons themselves, see Chapter 6, "Symbols, Instances, and the Library," and see Chapter 18, "Understanding Actions and Event Handlers," to learn how to add code to buttons.

Because buttons are stored in the Library, and because only instances of a Button symbol are deployed within the Flash movie, sounds that are assigned to a button work for all instances of that Button symbol. However, if different sounds are required for different buttons, a new Button symbol must be created (see the following Tip note for an exception to this "rule"). You can create a new Button symbol from the same Graphic symbols as the previous button (provided it was built out of symbols) or duplicate it in the Library panel using the Duplicate command in the Library's options menu.

Tip
With the Behaviors panel, you can quickly assign different sounds to the various instances of the same Button (or Movie Clip) symbol. You'll learn about behaviors related to sound use later in this chapter.

To add a sound to the Down state of a Button symbol, follow these steps:

1. Create a new Button symbol (Insert ➪ New Symbol) or choose a symbol from the Buttons Library (Window ➪ Common Libraries ➪ Buttons).

2. Drag an instance of the button from the Library (or the document's Library) to the Stage.

3. Edit the Button symbol by double-clicking it on the Stage, or by choosing Edit from the Library options menu.

Both methods transfer the working environment into Edit mode.

4. Add a new layer to the button's timeline, label the new layer **sound**, and then add keyframes to this layer in the Over and Down columns.

Your timeline should look similar to Figure 15-2.

Figure 15-2: The timeline for your button should resemble this one.

5. Select the frame of the button state where you want to add a sound for interactive feedback (such as a clicking sound for the Down state), and then access the Property inspector by choosing Window ⇨ Properties ⇨ Properties (Ctrl+F3 or ⌘+F3).

An alternative method (with the frame selected) is to simply drag the sound from the Library panel onto the Stage.

You should now have the Property inspector open, as shown in Figure 15-3. Click the arrow in the lower-right corner of the Property inspector to see all of the options.

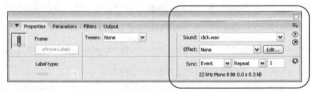

Sound attributes

Figure 15-3: The Property inspector controls the options for sound usage on a given frame.

6. Choose the sound clip that you want to use from the Sound menu.

This menu lists all of the sounds that have been imported and that are available in the library of the current movie. In this example, we used the click.wav sound found in the ch15 folder of the book's CD-ROM.

7. Use the Sync menu to choose *how* you want the sound to play.

For this lesson, simply use the default, which is the Event option. We'll defer our exploration of the other options in the Sync menu to a later section.

You have now added a sound to your button state. Remember that you're still in Edit mode, so to test the button, return to the Scene 1 timeline (that is, the Main Timeline) either by clicking the Scene 1 location label at the upper-left corner of the Document window, or by pressing Ctrl+E (⌘+E). Then choose Control ⇨ Enable Simple Buttons, or Control ⇨ Test Movie.

To add a sound to the Over state of a Button symbol, simply retrace the preceding steps, referencing the Over state of the button wherever appropriate. Remember that different sounds can be assigned to the Up, Over, and Down states of a Button symbol. A sound that is added to the Up state will play whenever the mouse rolls out of a button's hit area.

On the CD-ROM   For a completed example of this button, refer to the Flash movie button_sound_100.fla located in the ch15 folder of the *Macromedia Flash 8 Bible* CD-ROM. This movie has a button with sounds attached and was made with the same technique we describe in this section.

Adding Sound to the Timeline

In addition to the use of sounds to enhance the interactivity of buttons, another popular use for sound in Flash is to provide a background score. The simplest way to achieve this is to place the sound within its own layer in the Main Timeline (Scene 1), at the precise frame in which you want the sound to begin. To do this, you must first import the sound (as we described earlier in this chapter) and create a new layer for it.

On the CD-ROM   If you don't have access to sounds, you can use the sample sound atmospheres_1 to practice. This sound is in the ch15 folder of the *Macromedia Flash 8 Bible* CD-ROM. It is available in both WAV and AIF formats.

Adding sound files to the timeline is similar to assigning sound to a button. To add sounds to a timeline, follow these steps:

1. Add a new layer in the Timeline window and label the layer with the name of the sound.

    You can use a name such as "sound" or "background track."

2. Create a keyframe on the sound layer at the frame where you want the sound to begin.

3. With that keyframe selected, open the Property inspector.

    Make sure you have expanded the view to show all of the sound attributes.

4. If you remembered to import the sound that you want to use, you can now choose that sound clip from the Sound drop-down menu.

    If you find yourself stuck at this point, review the preceding steps and/or retrace your steps through the methodology for adding sound to a button.

5. From the Effect menu, choose how the sound should be handled by Flash.

    The Effect menu offers several preset fading and panning treatments, plus Custom, which invokes the Edit Envelope dialog box. For no special effect, choose None. For more about the Effect presets and the Edit Envelope dialog box, refer to the subsequent section, "Editing Audio in Flash."

6. From the Sync menu, choose one of four options—Event, Start, Stop, or Stream—to control how you want the sound to be synchronized.

    See the next section, "Organizing Sounds on the Timeline," for a detailed explanation of Sync options.

7. Specify how many times you want the sound to loop.

To loop the sound indefinitely (for example, as a background track), choose Loop in the second drop-down menu in the Sync parameters. If you want the sound to loop only for a specific number of times, choose Repeat in the menu and enter a number in the text field to the right of the menu. For specific information about looping Stream sounds, refer to the next section.

8. Perform any last-minute editing or finessing of the sound file (see "Editing Audio in Flash" later in this chapter).

Your sound is now part of the timeline. Its waveform is visible on the layer to which it was added. Test your sound by pressing the Enter key on your keyboard, which plays the timeline. Or, for sound with a Sync setting of Stream, manually "scrub" the sound by dragging the Playhead across the timeline. To perform the most accurate test of the sound, use either Control ⇨ Test Scene or Control ⇨ Test Movie to see and hear it as a Flash movie file (.swf).

Tip   If you sync a sound to the timeline using the Stream feature, you should test your Flash movie file (.swf) on various platforms and machines with different processor speeds, especially if the timeline is always playing animation. What looks and sounds good on a fast Pentium IV might be less impressive on an underpowered legacy machine, like a first- or second-generation Pentium machine.

Organizing Sounds on the Timeline

The Flash Player can play several sound layers at once within a Flash movie; each layer functions like a separate sound channel, and Flash mixes them on playback. This capability of Flash might be considered a built-in economy sound mixer. There is, however, a practical limit because each sound layer potentially increases the movie's file size, while the mix of multiple sounds may burden the computer it's being run on.

New Feature   Flash Player 8 and Flash 8 movies can play up to 32 simultaneous sound channels. In older versions of the Flash Player, you are limited to 8 simultaneous sound channels.

Enhanced viewing of sound layers

Because sound is different from other types of Flash content, some users find that increasing the layer height of the sound layers eases working with multiple sounds in the timeline. That's because a taller layer height provides a better visual cue due to the unique waveforms of each sound. To increase the layer height for individual layers, follow these steps:

1. Right-click (or Control+click on the Mac) the layer in the Timeline window, and then choose Properties from the contextual menu.

2. At the bottom of the Layer Properties dialog box, change the layer height from the default 100 percent to either 200 or 300 percent.

   Note that these percentages are relative to the settings chosen in the options menu (located at the top-right corner) of the Timeline window.

Cross-Reference For more information on the Timeline window, see Chapter 4, "Interface Fundamentals." For an actual example of this enhanced viewing, open the file `enhanced_view.fla`, located in the `ch15` folder on the CD-ROM.

Tip Your movie's frame rate, as specified in the Document Properties dialog box (Modify ⇨ Document), affects the number of frames that a sound occupies on the timeline. For example, at Flash's default setting of 12 frames per seconds (fps), a 30-second sound clip extends across 360 frames of the timeline. At 18 fps, the same 30-second clip expands to 540 frames — but in either case, the time length of the sound is unchanged.

Organizing sound layers with a layer folder

Flash MX introduced a new organization tool for layers in any timeline: layer folders. To nest sound layers in a layer folder, create a new layer folder and then drag each of the sound layers to the folder. As you drop each layer on the folder, it will nest within the folder.

Synchronizing Audio to Animations

In film editors' lingo, to *synchronize*, or *sync*, means to precisely match picture to sound. In Flash, sound can be synchronized to the visual content of the timeline. Flash sync affords several options for the manner in which the audio clip is related to graphics or animation on the timeline. Each of these sync options is appropriate for particular uses, which the following sections discuss.

The Sync options in the sound area of the Property inspector control the behavior of sound in Flash movies, relative to the timeline in which the sound is placed. The Sync option you choose depends on whether your sound is intended to add dimension to a complex multimedia presentation or to add interactivity in the form of button-triggered sound, or whether it is intended to be the closely timed soundtrack of an animated cartoon.

Event

Event is the default Sync option for all sounds in Flash, so unless you change this default to one of the other options, the sound automatically behaves as an Event sound. Event sounds begin with the keyframe in which they occur and then play independently of the timeline. If an Event sound's duration is longer than the remaining frames of its timeline, it continues to play even though playback on the timeline has stopped. If an Event sound requires considerable time to load, the movie pauses at that keyframe until the sound has loaded completely. Event sounds are the easiest to implement and are useful for background sound scapes and other sounds that don't need to be synced. Again, Event is the default Sync setting in the Sound menu of the Property inspector.

Caution Event sounds can degrade into a disturbing inharmonious round of out-of-tune sound loops. If the timeline holding the Event sound loops before the sound has completed, the sound begins again — over the top of the initial sound that has not finished playing. After several loops, the resulting effect can become intolerable. To avoid this effect, use the Start Sync option.

Start

The Start Sync option is similar to an Event option, but with one crucial difference: If any instance of that sound is already playing, then no other instance of that sound can play. In other words, the Start Sync option tells the sound to begin playing only if other instances have finished playing or if it's the first instance of that sound to play. This option is useful if you want to avoid the layering problem we discussed in the previous caution note for Event sounds.

Note Start sounds are actually a type of Event sound. Later in this chapter, when we refer to Audio Stream and Audio Event settings in the Publish Settings dialog box, realize that Start sounds belong to the Audio Event category.

Stop

The Stop Sync option is similar to the Start Sync option, except that any and all instances of the selected sound stop playing when the frame containing the Stop Sync option is played. This option comes in handy when you want to mute a specific sound in a crowd of others. For example, if you created a sound mixer with an arrangement of Button instances, you could assign the Stop Sync option to a mute button for each of the sounds in the mixer.

Stream

Stream sounds are similar to a traditional soundtrack in a video-editing application. A Stream sound locks to the timeline and has priority over visual content. When you choose a Stream sound, the Flash Player attempts to pace the animation in sync with the sound. However, when animations either get too complex or are run on slower machines, the Flash Player skips — or drops — the frames as needed to stay in sync with the Stream sound. A Stream sound stops when the Playhead reaches the last frame that includes the waveform of the Stream sound; likewise, a Stream sound pauses if the timeline containing the Stream sound is stopped. A Stream sound can be *scrubbed*; by dragging the Playhead along the layer's frames in the Timeline window, the Stream sound plays in direct relationship to the content as it appears, frame by frame. This is especially useful for lip-sync and coordinating the perfect timing of sound effects with visual events.

To use sound effectively, it's important to understand how Stream sounds work. When a Flash document is published as a Flash movie file (.swf) and the Sync option for a sound is set to Stream, Flash breaks the sound into chunks that are tied to the timeline. The bytes within the movie are arranged according to the linear order of the Main Timeline (that is, Scene 1). As such, if you have a Stream sound that stretches from frames 1 to 100 of the Main Timeline and the movie contains a total of 200 frames, the Stream sound's bytes will be evenly distributed over the first 50 percent of the file's bytes.

Tip When adding sounds to the timeline, no matter how many times you tell a Stream sound to loop, a Stream sound will stop playing wherever the visual waveform in the Timeline window ends. To extend a Stream sound's duration, add as many frames as necessary to a Stream sound's layer.

Stopping Sounds

The default behavior of Event sounds is for them to play through to the end, regardless of the length of the timeline on which they exist. However, you can stop any sound, including Event sounds. Place another instance of the same sound at the keyframe where the sound should stop and assign this instance as a Stop sync option. This Stop setting can be on any layer, and it will stop all instances of the specific sound. Let's give this a try.

Stopping an Event sound

In this section, we'll show you how to stop an Event sound using two different methods. The first method uses a Stop sound on a keyframe in the Main Timeline (Scene 1). The second method uses a Button instance with a Stop sound on its Down state.

1. Create a Flash document that has an Event sound placed on the first keyframe and has enough frames on the timeline to display the entire waveform of the sound.

On the CD-ROM You can use the enhanced_view.fla file from the book's CD-ROM as a practice file. If you use this file, change the sync setting of the sound to Event in the Property inspector.

2. Create a new layer in the Timeline window, and name this layer stop sound.

3. On the stop sound layer, pick a frame that's about five seconds into the sound displayed on the original layer.

4. Create a keyframe on this frame in the stop sound layer.

5. With this keyframe selected, open the Property inspector.

6. In the Sound menu, choose the same sound file that was used in the original sound layer.

7. In the Sync menu of the Property inspector, choose Stop.

   As a Stop sound, this setting will tell the Flash Player to stop any and all instances of the sound that is specified in the Sound menu.

8. Save your Flash document, and test it (Control ➪ Test Movie).

   When the Playhead reaches the keyframe with the Stop sound, you should no longer hear the Event sound.

Now, we'll show you how to play and mute an Event sound by clicking buttons. You'll place an Event sound on one Button symbol instance, and then a Stop sound on another Button symbol instance.

1. In a new Flash document, create a copy of the Play and Stop buttons from the Circle Buttons folder in the Buttons Library (Window ➪ Common Libraries ➪ Buttons).

   To do this, drag each of the buttons from the Buttons Library panel to your document's Stage. Close the Buttons Library when you are done. Rename Layer 1 to **buttons**. Your document's Stage should resemble Figure 15-4.

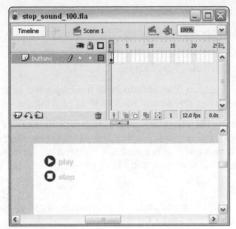

Figure 15-4: The Play and Stop buttons on the Stage

2. Import a sound file to use as your Event sound.

   You can use the `atmospheres_1.mp3` sound file from the book's CD-ROM.

3. In the document's Library panel, double-click the Play button to edit the symbol.

4. In the Timeline window, create a new layer and name it **sound**.

5. Insert a keyframe on the Down state of the sound layer.

6. Select the keyframe made in Step 4, and open the Property inspector.

7. Select the imported sound's name in the Sound menu, and leave the Sync menu at the default Event setting.

   When you are finished, your document should resemble Figure 15-5.

Figure 15-5: This sound will play when the Play button is clicked.

8. Double-click the Stop button in the Library panel.

9. Repeat Steps 3 through 7. This time, however, choose Stop in the Sync menu for the atmospheres_1 sound.

10. Save your document and test it (Control ➪ Test Movie).

   In Test Movie mode, click the Play button. You should hear the imported sound begin to play. When you click the Stop button, the sound should stop playing.

You may have noticed that, if you click the Play button repeatedly, new instances of the sound will begin to play, overlapping with the original playing sound instance. Regardless, the Stop Sync option will stop all of them. If you want to prevent the Play button from enabling this type of overlap, go back to the sound keyframe on the Play button and change its Sync option to Start.

On the CD-ROM
You can find a completed example of the Play and Stop buttons exercise as stop_sound _100.fla, located in the ch15 folder of the book's CD-ROM.

Stopping a single instance of a Stream sound

You can also stop a single instance of a Stream sound. To do this, simply place an empty keyframe in the sound layer at the point where the sound should stop.

1. Open the enhanced_view.fla file, located in the ch15 folder of the book's CD-ROM.

2. Switch the layer view of the atmospheres_1 layer back to 100% in the Layer Properties dialog box.

3. Select the first frame of the atmospheres_1 layer.

4. In the Property inspector, switch the Sync option to Stream.

5. Select frame 60 of the atmospheres_1 layer, and insert a blank keyframe (F7).

   This is the point where the Stream sound will stop playing.

6. Save your Flash document, and test it (Control ➪ Test Movie).

   Notice that the sound stops playing at frame 60. You can open your Bandwidth Profiler (View ➪ Bandwidth Profiler) in the Test Movie mode to see the Playhead move as the movie plays.

The Bandwidth Profiler also reveals something we touched upon earlier: Stream sounds export only the actual portion of the sound that's used in the timeline. In our example, 60 frames' worth of the atmospheres_1 sound was about 12K (at default MP3 compression, 16 kilobits per second, or Kbps).

Stopping all sounds

You can stop the sounds that are playing in all timelines (including Movie Clips) at any point by doing the following:

1. If there isn't already an actions layer on your timeline, add a layer, label it **actions**, and select the frame that occurs at the point where you want all sounds to stop. Make this frame into a keyframe.

2. With the keyframe selected, open the Actions panel by pressing the F9 key, or by navigating to Window ➪ Actions.

The title bar of the Actions panel should read Actions — Frame.

3. Click the Global Functions booklet in the left pane of the panel, and then click the Timeline Control booklet.

4. Double-click the stopAllSounds action.

The ActionScript code,

```
stopAllSounds();
```

appears in the Script pane of the Actions panel, as shown in Figure 15-6.

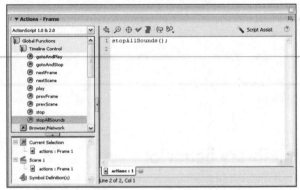

Figure 15-6: Any sound that's currently playing stops when the movie reaches a keyframe with a stopAllSounds() action.

5. Save your Flash document, and then test it with Control ➪ Test Movie.

When the movie's Playhead reaches the frame with the stopAllSounds() action, every sound that is currently playing stops.

The stopAllSounds() action stops only sounds that are playing at the time the action is executed. It will not permanently mute the sound for the duration of the movie. You can proceed to re-initialize any sounds any time after the stopAllSounds() action has executed. If you want to stop playback again, you will have to enable another stopAllSounds() action or use a Stop sound.

Applying Behaviors That Control Sound

One of the features of Flash 8 is the Behaviors panel, introduced in Flash MX 2004. This panel enables you to quickly add interactive functionality to elements of your Flash movie. There are five behaviors in the Sound category of the Behaviors panel. In this section, you learn how each of these behaviors works.

Note Behaviors are essentially prewritten ActionScript code blocks that appear on event handlers, such as keyframes, Button instances, and Movie Clip instances. Just as Dreamweaver behaviors add JavaScript code to HTML documents, Flash behaviors add ActionScript code to your Flash documents.

You can see all of the Sound behaviors by clicking the Add Behavior (+) button in the top-left corner of the Behaviors panel, and choosing the Sound menu item (see Figure 15-7).

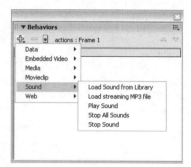

Figure 15-7: The Sound behaviors in the Behaviors panel

Load Sound from Library behavior

This behavior locates a sound item in the Flash movie's library and establishes a reference to that sound, so that the sound can be played later. This behavior can also be used to play the sound.

Caution You must use this behavior before you can use the Play Sound behavior we discuss later in this section.

In practice, you will use this behavior to set up references to any sounds that you wish to use the Play Sound behavior. For example, if you have three sounds in your Library and you want to prepare all three for later use in your Flash movie, you would add three Load Sound from Library behaviors to the first frame of a layer in your Flash document. In the following steps, you learn how to add this behavior to a Flash document.

On the CD-ROM In the following exercise, you can use the `atmospheres_1.wav` or `atmospheres_1.aif` sound file from the `ch15` folder of this book's CD-ROM.

1. Create a new Flash document by choosing File ➪ New.

2. In the New Document dialog box, select Flash Document and click OK.

3. Import a sound file into the Flash document. Choose File ➪ Import to Library and browse to a sound file on your local computer.

You can import one of the sound files from the book's CD-ROM. For this example, we refer to the `atmospheres_1.wav` file.

4. Once the sound is imported into the document's library, open the Library panel (Ctrl+L or ⌘+L).

   You need to create a linkage identifier for the newly imported sound in order for the Load Sound from Library behavior to locate the sound in the library.

5. Select the sound file in the panel, and right-click (or Control+click on the Mac) the sound file.

6. Choose the Linkage option in the contextual menu.

7. In the Linkage Properties dialog box, select the Export for ActionScript check box.

   The sound filename automatically populates the Identifier field. You can leave the name as is, or rename the identifier term. For this example, use the term "song," as shown in Figure 15-8. Click OK to close the dialog box.

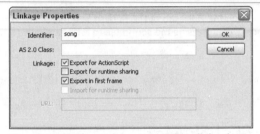

Figure 15-8: The Linkage Properties dialog box

Now, you are ready to access the linked sound in a behavior.

8. In the Timeline window, rename Layer 1 **behaviors**.

9. Select frame 1 of this layer, and open the Behaviors panel (Shift+F3).

10. In the top-left corner of this panel, click the Add Behavior (+) button, and choose Sound ➪ Load Sound from Library.

    A dialog box opens, in which you can enter the parameters for the behavior.

11. In the Linkage ID field, type the identifier you specified in Step 7.

    In the sample, we used the term "song." In the Identifier field, type a unique instance name for this sound. For this example, use **sndSong**. Refer to Figure 15-9. The Play this sound when loaded check box is checked by default. As such, the `atmospheres_1.wav` sound will play as soon as frame 1 is loaded. When you are finished, click OK to close the dialog box.

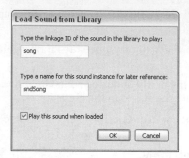

Figure 15-9: The Load Sound from Library parameters

12. Save your Flash document (File ⇨ Save) as `loadsound_behavior.fla`.

13. Choose Control ⇨ Test Movie (Ctrl+Enter or ⌘+Enter).

    As soon as the Flash movie starts, you will hear the `atmospheres_1.wav` sound begin to play.

Note The audio options for Audio event in the Flash tab of the Publish Settings dialog box (File ⇨ Publish Settings) are automatically compressing the sound file to MP3 audio at 16 Kbps.

On the CD-ROM You can find the completed file, `loadsound_behavior.fla`, in the ch15 folder of this book's CD-ROM.

Load streaming MP3 file behavior

This behavior, as the name implies, loads an MP3 file at run time directly from the Flash Player environment. Instead of attaching a sound from the movie's library, this behavior can access an external MP3 file residing on a publicly accessible Web server. Note that "streaming" here means that the MP3 file will begin playback as soon as enough of the file has buffered into the Flash Player.

Note Technically, this type of loading is called a progressive download — it's not true streaming like audio or video from a Macromedia Flash Communication Server application.

In the following exercise, you learn how to use this behavior to play an MP3 file from a remote Web server.

1. Create a new Flash document by choosing File ⇨ New.

2. In the New Document dialog box, select Flash Document and click OK.

3. Rename Layer 1 to **behaviors**.

4. Select this layer's first frame, and open the Behaviors panel (Shift+F3).

5. In the top-left corner of this panel, click the Add Behavior (+) button, and choose Sound ⇨ Load streaming MP3 file.

   When this behavior's dialog box opens, there are two options: Sound Location and Identifier.

6. In the top field, type the URL to an MP3 file that has been copied to a publicly accessible folder on your Web server.

   You can use the following URL to test this example:
   http://www.flashsupport.com/mp3/atmospheres_1_short.mp3

7. In the Identifier field, type **sndBg**.

   This identifier allows you to target the sound with another behavior or in your own ActionScript code.

8. Click OK to close the dialog box.

   See Figure 15-10 for more details.

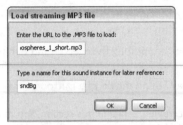

Figure 15-10: The Load streaming MP3 file behavior parameters

9. Save your Flash document as **loadmp3_behavior.fla**.

10. Test your movie by choosing Control ➪ Test Movie (Ctrl+Enter or ⌘+Enter).

    As soon as the movie loads, the MP3 begins to stream into the Flash Player. When enough of the sound has buffered, the MP3 file automatically plays.

Note   You need to have a connection to the Internet in order for this example to work. If you would like to test this example with a local MP3 file, make a copy of the MP3 file directly to the same location as your Flash document. Then, change the URL in the behavior's parameters to atmospheres_1_short.mp3, omitting the http://www.flashsupport.com/mp3/ portion.

On the CD-ROM   You can find the completed file, loadmp3_behavior.fla, in the ch15 folder of this book's CD-ROM.

As indicated by the previous note, you can specify relative URLs (or file locations) in the Sound Location field for this behavior's parameters. For example, if you save your Flash movie file (.swf) in the same location or folder as your MP3 file, you can simply specify the MP3 filename in the Sound Location field. You can also use relative path notation. For example, /myfile.mp3 would load the myfile.mp3 file located one directory above (that is, the parent folder) the Flash movie's location.

Note   With the Load streaming MP3 file behavior, the sound does not loop. If you want to replay the sound, you need to use the Play Sound behavior or target the sound with further ActionScript code.

Play Sound

The Play Sound behavior plays a sound that has been set up with the Load Sound from Library or Load streaming MP3 file behavior. Remember that the Load streaming MP3 file behavior automatically begins playback of the MP3 file, and the Load Sound from Library behavior has an optional parameter that automatically begins playback as well. You can use the Play Sound behavior to

✦ Play a sound that was only set up by the Load Sound from Library behavior, where the Play this sound when loaded checkbox was not selected.

✦ Replay a sound that finished playing or was stopped by the Stop Sound behavior (discussed later in this section).

In the following steps, you learn how to add a Play Sound movie to a Button instance.

On the CD-ROM   Use the `loadsound_behavior.fla` file you created earlier in this section. You can find this file in the `ch15` folder of the book's CD-ROM as well.

1. Open the `loadsound_behavior.fla` document.

2. Select frame 1 of the behaviors layer in the Timeline window, and open the Behaviors panel. Double-click the Load Sound from Library behavior in the Action column of the panel. In the Load Sound from Library dialog box, clear the Play this sound when loaded check box. You do not want the sound to automatically play when the sound loads because you will assign a Play Sound behavior to a button in a later step. Click OK to accept the new setting.

3. Create a new layer named **buttons**, and place this layer below the existing behaviors layer.

4. Save your Flash document as `playsound_behavior.fla`.

   It's always good practice to resave an older document with a new name whenever you are changing the scope of your document.

5. Open the Buttons library by choosing Windows ➪ Common Libraries ➪ Buttons.

6. In this Library, navigate to the Circle Buttons folder, and drag an instance of the Play symbol to the Stage.

   Make sure you have selected the first frame of the buttons layer before you drag the symbol.

7. Select the new Play instance on the Stage, and open the Behaviors panel (Shift+F3).

8. In the top-left corner of this panel, click the Add Behavior (+) button, and choose Sound ➪ Play Sound.

9. In the Play Sound dialog box, type **sndSong** in the Identifier field.

   Remember that the sound loaded in the `loadsound_behavior.fla` file had this same identifier. See Figure 15-11.

Figure 15-11: The Play Sound behavior parameters

10. Save your Flash document, and test the movie (Control ➪ Test Movie).

   When you click the Play button, you hear the `sndSong` instance play.

You can find the completed file, `playsound_behavior.fla`, in the `ch15` folder of this book's CD-ROM.

The Play Sound behavior is the first Sound behavior discussed in this section that has different events from which you can choose in the Behaviors panel, as shown in Figure 15-12.

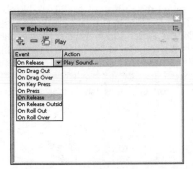

Figure 15-12: The event options available for behaviors attached to buttons

If you prefer the Play Sound behavior to activate with a different mouse event, you can choose another option in the Event combo box.

Stop All Sounds

This behavior inserts the `stopAllSounds()` function into the code of the selected event handler (that is, a keyframe, a Button instance, or a Movie Clip instance). As we discussed earlier in this chapter, the `stopAllSounds()` function halts the playback of any and all playing sounds.

In the next exercise, you'll learn how to stop the playback of multiple sounds with the Stop All Sounds behavior.

On the CD-ROM

Use the `loadmp3_behavior.fla` document as a starting point for this exercise. You can find this document in the `ch15` folder of this book's CD-ROM. This exercise also requires the `robert_video.flv` file located in the same folder of the CD-ROM. Make a copy of this file to your local hard drive.

1. Open the `loadmp3_behavior.fla` document, and create a new layer named **video**.

2. Place this layer below the existing behaviors layer.

3. Save your Flash document as `stopallsounds_behavior.fla`.

   The video file that you import in the next step has a frame rate of 24 fps. As such, you need to change the frame rate of this Flash document to match.

4. Click anywhere on the Stage of your document, and press the Esc key to deselect any selected objects.

5. In the Property inspector, change the frame rate from 12 fps to 24 fps.

   Remember that this document already plays the streaming MP3 file located on the `flashsupport.com` Web server. Now, you will add a video to the Flash movie, to act as a second sound source.

6. Select the first frame of the video layer, and import the `robert_video.flv` video file by choosing File ➪ Import ➪ Import to Stage (Ctrl+R or ⌘+R).

   On the first stage of the import process, titled Select Video, accept the defaults and click the Next button. In the Deployment stage, select the radio button labeled Embed video in SWF and play in timeline and click the Next button. In the Embedding phase, accept the defaults and click the Next button. On the Finish Video Import phase, click the Finish button. After the video file has been imported, the video layer frames will expand to include all of the frames in the `robert_video.flv` clip.

Note

On the Macintosh, the Next button in the Video Import wizard is labeled as Continue.

7. Create a new layer, and rename it **buttons**.

8. Place this layer at the bottom of the layer stack.

9. On frame 1 of the buttons layer, drag an instance of the Stop button from the Circle Buttons folder of the Buttons Library (Window ➪ Common Libraries ➪ Buttons) to the Stage.

10. Place the instance below the video object.

11. Select the new Stop instance, and open the Behaviors panel.

12. Click the Add Behavior (+) button in the panel, and choose Sounds ➪ Stop All Sounds.

    When you choose this behavior, you see a dialog box describing this behavior (see Figure 15-13).

Figure 15-13: The Stop All Sounds behavior dialog box

13. Click OK.

14. Save your Flash document, and test the movie (Control ⇨ Test Movie).

    As the movie plays, you hear the streaming MP3 file and the video's audio track play. If you click the Stop button, all of the sounds stop playing.

On the CD-ROM

You can find the completed file, `stopallsounds_behavior.fla`, in the `ch15` folder of this book's CD-ROM.

You may have noticed that if you allow the movie to continue to play, the movie eventually loops back to the first frame and repeats. You can add a `stop()` action to the last frame of the timeline to prevent the Flash movie from looping.

Cross-Reference

You learn how to apply basic actions to Flash timelines in Chapter 18, "Understanding Actions and Event Handlers."

Tip

To decrease publishing (or testing) time, change the Audio stream compression option to Speech in the Flash tab of the Publish Settings dialog box (File ⇨ Publish Settings). The Speech codec is particularly suited to the audio track of the sample video clip, but it does add more weight, in bytes, to the final .swf file.

Editing Audio in Flash

Although Flash was never intended to perform as a full-featured sound editor, it does a remarkable job with basic sound editing. If you plan to make extensive use of sound in Flash, we recommend that you consider investing in a more robust sound editor. You'll have fewer limitations and greater control over your work.

Web Resource

You can find an archived version of the "Working with Audio Applications" chapter from the *Macromedia Flash MX Bible* (Wiley, 2002) at `www.flashsupport.com/archive`. That chapter discusses several popular sound editors that are commonly used in concert with Flash.

Sound-editing controls

Flash 8 has basic sound-editing controls in the Edit Envelope dialog box, which is accessed by clicking the Edit button in the Property inspector. (As you may recall from previous sections, you must first select the keyframe containing the sound, and then open the Property inspector.) The Time In control and the Time Out control, or Control Bars, in Edit Envelope enable you to change the In (start) and Out (end) points of a sound. You use the envelope handles to create custom Fade-in and Fade-out effects. The Edit Envelope dialog box also enables you to edit each sound channel separately if you are working with a stereo (two-channel) sound.

Note   The edits you apply to a sound file in the Edit Envelope dialog box affect only the specific instance you have assigned to a keyframe. The original file that resides in the Flash document's Library panel is neither changed nor resaved.

A sound's In point is where the sound starts playing, and a sound's Out point is where the sound finishes. The Time In control and the Time Out control are used for setting or changing a sound's In and Out points. Here's how to do this:

1. Start by selecting the keyframe of the sound you want to edit; then access the Property inspector.

2. Click the Edit button in the sound attributes area of the Property inspector to open the Edit Envelope dialog box, shown in Figure 15-14.

Caution   You can not edit the In and Out points if your sound is set to Loop in the Property inspector. Make sure you have it set to Repeat. Oddly, you can go back and set it to Loop after you have set In and Out points in Repeat mode.

3. Drag the Time In control and Time Out control (located in the horizontal strip between the two channels) onto the Timeline of the sound's waveform to define or restrict which section will play.

4. Use the envelope handles to edit the sound volume by adding handles and dragging them up or down to modulate the volume.

5. Click the Play button to hear the sound as edited before returning to the authoring environment.

6. Rework the sound if necessary.

7. When you've finessed the points and are satisfied with the sound, click OK to return to the Property inspector.

8. Save your Flash document.

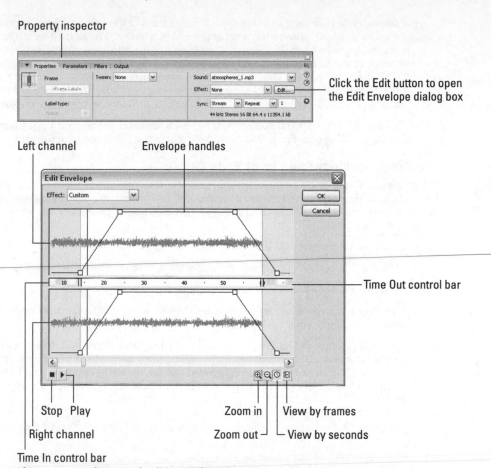

Figure 15-14: The sound-editing tools and options of the Edit Envelope dialog box, which is accessed from the Property inspector

Applying effects from the Effect menu of the Property inspector

You can apply a handful of preset fades and other effects to a sound by selecting the effect from the Effect menu located in the sound attributes area of the Property inspector. For many uses, the Flash presets will be more than sufficient, but if you find yourself feeling limited, remember that more subtle effects can be created in an external sound editor. We describe Flash's preset effects in detail here:

✦ **None:** No effect is applied to either of the sound channels.

✦ **Left Channel/Right Channel:** Plays only the right or left channel of a stereo sound.

✦ **Fade Left to Right/Fade Right to Left:** This effect lowers the sound level of one channel while raising the level of the other, creating a panning effect. The effect occurs over the entire length of the sound.

✦ **Fade In/Fade Out:** Fade In gradually raises the level of the beginning of a sound clip. Fade Out gradually lowers the level at the end of a sound. The default length for either effect is approximately 25 percent of the length of the clip. We've noticed that even if the size of the selection is edited with the control bars, the duration of the Fade In/Fade Out remains the same. (Thus, a 35-second sound clip with an original default Fade In time of 9 seconds, still has a 9-second Fade In time even when the selection's length is reduced to, say, 12 seconds.) You can resolve this problem by creating a custom fade.

✦ **Custom:** Any time you manually alter the levels or audio handles within the Edit Envelope dialog box, Flash 8 automatically resets the Effect menu to Custom.

Creating a custom Fade In or Fade Out

For maximum sound-editing control within Flash, use the envelope handles to create a custom fade or to lower the audio levels (or amplitude) of a sound. In addition to creating custom fades, you can lower the levels creatively to create subtle, low-volume background sounds. Here's how:

1. Select the keyframe of the sound you want to edit.

2. Click the Edit button of the Property inspector to open the Edit Envelope dialog box.

3. Click the envelope lines at any point to create new envelope handles.

4. After handles have been created, you can drag them around to create your desired volume and fading effects.

   The lines indicate the relative volume level of the sound. When you drag an envelope handle downward, the line slopes down, indicating a decrease in the volume level, while dragging an envelope handle upward has the opposite effect. The Edit Envelope control is limited to eight envelope handles per channel (eight for left and eight for right).

Tip   You can remove envelope handles by dragging them outside the Edit Envelope dialog box.

Other controls in the Edit Envelope control

Other useful tools in the Edit Envelope dialog box warrant mention. Refer to Figure 15-14 for their locations.

✦ **Zoom In/Zoom Out:** These tools either enlarge or shrink the view of the waveform, and they are particularly helpful when you're altering the In or Out points or envelope handles.

✦ **Seconds/Frames:** The default for viewing sound files is to represent time in seconds. But viewing time in frames is advantageous for syncing Stream sound. Toggle between viewing modes by clicking either the Seconds or Frames button at the lower right of the Edit Envelope dialog box.

The Repeat/Loop option

This option appears in the Property inspector, yet a measure of its functionality occurs in conjunction with the Edit Envelope dialog box. The Repeat/Loop drop-down menu and field is used to set the number of times that a sound file will repeat (or loop indefinitely). You can use a small looping selection, such as a break beat or jazz riff, for a background soundtrack.

Or loop a short ambient noise for an interesting effect. To test the quality of a looping selection, click the Edit button, which takes you to the Edit Envelope dialog box, where you can click the Play button for a preview of your loop. If the loop isn't perfect or has hiccups, use the In and Out control bars and envelope handles to trim or taper off a blank or adversely repeating section.

Tip   Flash links looped sounds and handles them as one long sound file (although it's really one little sound file played repeatedly). Because this linkage is maintained within the editing environment, the entire expanse of a looped sound can be given a custom effect in the Edit Envelope dialog box. For example, a simple repeating two-measure loop can be diminished over 30 loops. This is a subtle effect that performs well, yet is economical in terms of file size. Note, however, that this applies only to Event sounds.

Sound Optimization Overview

You need to be aware of several considerations when preparing Flash sound for export. For Web-based delivery, the primary concern is to find an acceptable middle ground between file size and audio quality. But the concept of acceptability is not absolute; it is always relative to the application. Consider, for example, a Flash Web site for a record company. In this example, sound quality is likely to be more important than file size because the audience for a record company will expect quality sound. In any case, consideration of both your audience and your method of delivery will help you to determine the export settings you choose. Luckily, Flash 8 has capabilities that enhance the user's experience both by optimizing sounds more efficiently and by providing improved programming features to make download delays less problematic.

There are two ways to optimize your sound for export. The quickest, simplest way is to use the Publish Settings dialog box and apply a one-setting-optimizes-all approach. This can work well if all of your sound files are from the same source. For example, if all of your sound material is speech-based, then you may be able to use global settings to encode all of your Flash sound. However, if you have a variety of sound sources in your movie, such as a combination of musical scores along with narrative tracks, then the Publish Setting dialog box may not deliver the highest possible level of optimization.

If you demand that your Flash movie has the smallest possible file size, or if your Flash project includes audio from disparate sources, or uses a combination of audio types — such as button sounds, background music, speech — it's better to fine-tune the audio settings for each sound in the Library. This method gives you much better control over output.

Cross-Reference   This chapter discusses only the audio-centric Publish features of Flash 8. We explain general Publish Settings features in greater detail in Chapter 21, "Publishing Flash Movies."

Publish Settings for Audio

To take a global approach to the control of audio output quality, choose File ➪ Publish Settings (Ctrl+Shift+F12 or Shift+Option+F12) to access the Publish Settings dialog box. Then choose the Flash tab of the Publish Settings dialog box, shown in Figure 15-15. This tab has three areas where the audio quality of an entire Flash movie can be controlled *globally*.

Tip   You can also access the Flash tab of Publish Settings using the Property inspector. Click the document's Stage or Work Area, and in the Property inspector, click the Settings button to the right of the Publish label.

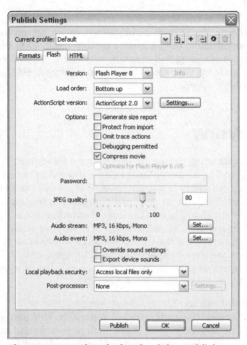

Figure 15-15: The Flash tab of the Publish Settings dialog box has several options to control audio quality.

The Flash tab of the Publish Settings dialog box has three options for controlling audio quality:

✦ **Audio Stream:** Controls the export quality of Stream sounds. To customize, click Set. This gives you a number of options, which we describe in the section that follows. Flash MX supports MP3, which is the optimal streaming format, as well as a new Speech codec.

✦ **Audio Event:** Controls the export quality of Event sounds. To customize, click Set. This gives you the same number of options as the Set button for Audio Stream. We describe these options in the section that follows.

✦ **Override Sound Settings:** If this box is checked, Flash uses the Publish Settings rather than the individual audio settings that are fine-tuned in the Library panel for the current document. For more information, see the section "Fine-Tuning Sound Settings in the Library," later in this chapter.

The Set options

Audio stream and Audio event have individual compression settings, which can be specified by their respective Set button options. If you click either Set button on the Flash tab, the same Sound Settings dialog box appears — it is identical for both Audio Stream and Audio Event, which means that the same options are offered for both types of sound. The Sound Settings dialog box, shown in various permutations in Figure 15-16, displays numerous settings related to the control of audio quality and audio file size. The type of compression you select governs the specific group of settings that appear.

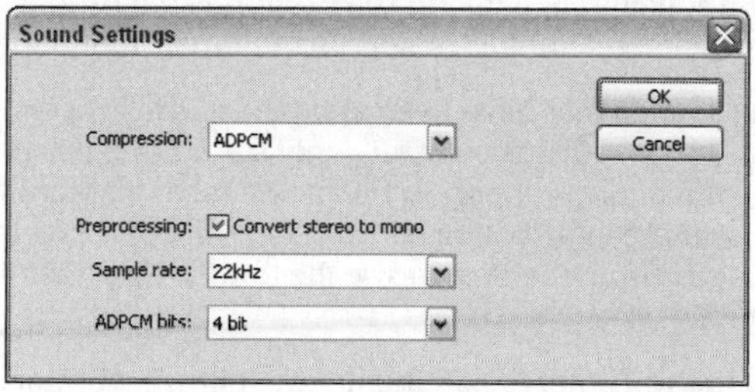

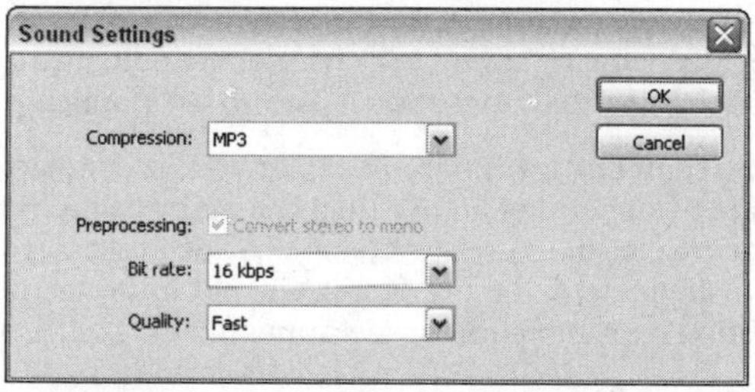

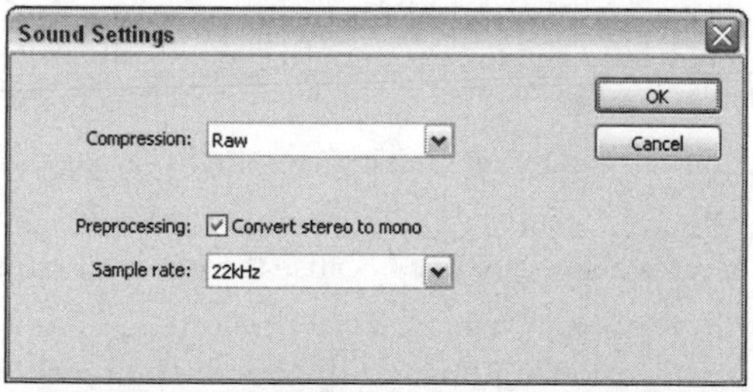

Figure 15-16: The various options in the Sound Settings dialog box

Note   The impact of individual sound settings may be overridden by another setting. For example, a Bit Rate setting of 160 Kbps may not result in good sound if the Quality is set to Fast. Optimal results require attention to *all* of the settings. It's like a set of interlinked teeter-tot-ters: A little experimentation will reveal the cumulative or acquired impact of each setting on the others. However, the need to experiment here is hobbled by the lack of a preview mech-anism. By contrast, tuning a sound in the Library is much more serviceable because there's a sound preview button adjacent to the settings controls. For more about this workflow, refer to the following section of this chapter, "Fine-Tuning Sound Settings in the Library."

The specific options that are available in the Sound Settings dialog boxes are always related to the compression, or audio-encoding scheme, selected in the Compression drop-down menu. That's because different compression technologies support different functionalities:

✦ **Disable:** This option turns off all sounds that have been assigned in the Property inspec-tor to keyframes in any timeline. If this option is selected, only sound that has been linked and attached for use in ActionScript will play in the movie (see Chapter 27, "Interacting with Movie Clips," for more information on this use). All other sound sources assigned in the movie will be omitted from the final movie file (.swf). No additional options accompany this setting.

✦ **ADPCM:** With ADPCM selected in the Compression menu, the following options are available:

• **Convert Stereo to Mono:** Mixes the right and left channel of audio into one (mono) channel. In sound-engineer parlance, this is known as "bouncing down."

• **Sample Rate:** Choose from sampling rates of 5, 11, 22, or 44 kHz. Increasing the sample rate of an audio file to something higher than the native sample rate of the imported file simply increases file size, not quality. For example, if you import 22 kHz sounds into the Flash movie, selecting 44 kHz will not improve the sound quality. For more information on sample rates, see Appendix C, "Digital Audio Basics," on the CD-ROM.

• **ADPCM Bits:** Set the number of bits that ADPCM uses for encoding. You can choose a rate between 2 and 5 bits. The higher the ADPCM bits, the better the audio quality. Flash's default setting is 4 bits.

✦ **MP3:** If you select MP3 in the Compression menu, you can set the following options:

• **Convert Stereo to Mono:** Mixes the right and left channel of audio into one (mono) channel. This is disabled at rates below 20 Kbps because the lower bit rates don't allow stereo sound.

• **Bit Rate:** MP3 measures compression in Kbps. The higher the bit rate, the better the audio quality. Because the MP3 audio compression scheme is very efficient, a high bit rate still results in a relatively small file size. Refer to Table 15-2 for a breakdown of specific bit rates and the resulting sound quality.

• **Quality:** Choose Fast, Medium, or Best quality. These settings determine how well Flash 8 will analyze the sound file during compression. Fast will optimize the audio file in the shortest amount of time, but usually with less quality. Medium will analyze the sound waveform better than the Fast setting, but takes longer to compress. Best is the highest quality setting, but it takes the longest time to compress the sound file. Note that the file size of the final compressed sound will not be affected by any Quality setting—it simply instructs Flash how well it should analyze the sound dur-ing compression. The longer Flash takes to analyze a sound, the more likely the final compressed sound will capture the high highs and the low lows. If you have a fast computer processor, then we recommend you use the Best setting during your final Flash movie publish. During development and testing, you may want to use Fast to avoid long waits.

✦ **Raw:** When Raw (also known as Raw PCM audio) is selected in the Compression menu, there are two options:

- **Convert Stereo to Mono:** Mixes the right and left channels of audio into one (mono) channel.

- **Sample Rate:** This option specifies the sampling rate for the Audio Stream or Audio Events sounds. For more information on sample rate, please refer to Appendix C, "Digital Audio Basics," on this book's CD-ROM.

✦ **Speech:** When the Speech codec is selected in the Compression menu, there is only one option available: Sample Rate. Any sound compressed with the Speech codec will be converted to mono (one-channel) sound. Even though the Speech codec licensed from Nellymoser was designed for 8 kHz, Flash 8 "upsamples" this codec to those frequencies supported by the Flash Player. See Table 15-3 for an overview of these sampling rates and how they affect sound quality.

Table 15-2: MP3 Bit Rate Quality

Bit rate	Sound quality	Good for
8 Kbps	Very bad	Best for simulated moonwalk transmissions. Don't use this unless you want horribly unrecognizable sound.
16 Kbps	Barely acceptable	Extended audio files where quality isn't important, or simple button sounds
20, 24, 32 Kbps	Acceptable	Speech or voice
48, 56 Kbps	Acceptable	Large music files; complex button sounds
64 Kbps	Good	Large music files where good audio quality is required
112–128 Kbps	Excellent	Near-CD quality
160 Kbps	Best	Near-CD quality

Table 15-3: Speech Sampling Quality

Sample rate	Sound quality	Good for
5 kHz	Acceptable	Sound playback over extremely limited data connections, such as 19.2 Kbps wireless Internet modems used by mobile devices
11 kHz	Good	Standard telephone-quality voice audio
22 kHz	Excellent	Not recommended for general Internet use. While this setting produces higher fidelity to the original sound, it consumes too much bandwidth. For comparable sound, we recommend using a midrange MP3 bit rate.
44 kHz	Best	See description for 22 kHz

Tip   As a general rule, if you use the Publish Settings to control audio export globally, we recommend choosing MP3 at 20 or 24 Kbps. This will result in moderate to good sound quality (suitable for most Flash projects), and the ratio of file size to quality will give reasonable performance. 20 to 24 Kbps is an acceptable data rate for speech and short sound effects, while 96 to 128 Kbps is a better data rate for longer sounds and music.

Supporting audio and MP3 playback

Although this is becoming less of an issue with the desktop versions of the Flash Players, it may still be important to consider that MP3 or audio playback may not be supported by all Flash Players, especially device-based players. You can use Flash Player 6 and higher features in the ActionScript language to check the capabilities of the Flash Player installed on a user's system. Using the `System.capabilities` object, you can check to see whether an MP3 decoder is installed. The specific property is

```
System.capabilities.hasMP3
```

Tip   In FlashLite 1.1 or higher, you can use the `_capMP3` global property at run time to determine if MP3 playback is supported on a particular device.

More importantly, though, you can script your movies to check whether the Flash Player has access to general audio output. Some devices with the Flash Player may not have any audio output. This property is

```
System.capabilities.hasAudio
```

Caution   These new additions to the ActionScript language are only available in Flash Player 6 or higher. Earlier versions of the Flash Player will not recognize these objects or properties.

Fine-Tuning Sound Settings in the Library

The Publish Settings dialog box is convenient because it permits you to tweak a minimal set of sound adjustments, whereupon Flash exports all of your "noncustomized" Stream sounds or Event sounds at the same rate and compression. However, if you have many sounds and you are seriously concerned about obtaining the ideal balance of both optimal sound quality and minimum file size, you will need to export them at different rates and compressions. Consequently, for the fullest level of control over the way in which Flash compresses sound for delivery, we recommend you optimize each sound, individually, in the Library panel. In fact, it would be impossible for us to overemphasize this bit of sound advice: *We recommend you optimize each sound, individually, in the Library.*

Tip   As you become more advanced with Flash 8, particularly with ActionScript, you will likely want to load MP3 files directly into Flash Player 6 or higher movies, as they play in the Web browser. We'll discuss these features in Chapter 28, "Sharing and Loading Assets."

Settings for audio in the Library

Audio settings in the Library panel are similar to those we discussed previously for the Publish Settings dialog box. These settings appear in the Sound Properties dialog box, shown in Figure 15-17. To access these settings, either (a) double-click the icon of the sound in the Library; or (b) select the sound as it appears in the Library and (i) click the Properties button, or (ii) choose Properties from the Library panel's options menu; or (c) Right-click the sound symbol in the Library and choose Properties.

Tip   Flash 8 also enables you to access the compression settings alone for a sound file by right-clicking (or Control+clicking on the Mac) the sound file in the Library panel and choosing Export Settings from the contextual menu. The options in the Sound Settings dialog box are the same compression settings that we'll discuss in this section.

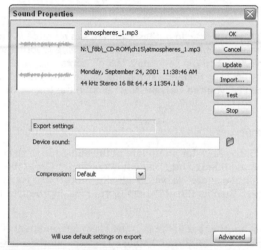

Figure 15-17: The Sound Properties dialog box enables you to control the compression settings and to precisely balance all other related settings for each individual sound in the Library.

The top half of the Sound Properties dialog box displays status information about the sound file: To the far left is a window with the waveform of the selected audio; to the right of the waveform is an area that displays the name of the file together with its location, date, sample rate, channels, bit depth, duration, and file size.

Note   The file location indicates the full absolute path to the sound file (for example, C:\Inetpub\wwwroot\mysound.mp3) if you save your Flash document file (.fla) in a volume or hard drive that is different than the location of the sound file.

The lower half of the dialog box is titled Export Settings. The first setting is a menu used to select the Compression scheme. The Compression options, and the subsequent compression-related options that appear in the other settings, are exactly the same as the sound options of the Publish Settings dialog box we discussed earlier in this chapter.

Note   If you imported an MP3 file, the Sound Properties dialog box automatically displays and enables the Use imported MP3 quality check box. The data rate of the imported MP3 file is then used for any Event sound compression. However, if you use the MP3 file for Stream sounds, the MP3 file is recompressed according to the Stream sound settings in the Publish Settings dialog box.

Estimated results are displayed beneath the Export Settings. Here, the estimated final file size (after compression) of the clip is displayed, together with the compression percentage. This is an extremely important tool that is easily overlooked.

Caution   The estimated final file size is just that, an estimate. In our tests, the file size reported in the Sound Properties dialog box was consistently different from the actual file size reported by the size report generated during publishing. You can generate a text file containing detailed information about your final movie by enabling Generate size report in the Flash tab of the Publish Settings dialog box. Once enabled, you can view the size report in the Output window in Test Movie mode.

The buttons to the right of the Sound Properties dialog box offer the following options:

✦ **Update:** Click this button to have Flash check for an update of the audio file (if the original MP3, WAV, or AIFF file has been modified), and update it accordingly. Generally, this works only on the machine on which the audio file was originally imported. If you stored your files on a network server, then all the members of your Flash production should be able to use this feature.

✦ **Import:** This enables you to import another audio file into the Flash environment. The imported audio file will overwrite the existing sound displayed in the Sound Properties dialog box, but will retain the original sound's name. This feature is useful if you originally imported a placeholder or low-quality sound and need to specify a new file to be used in its place.

✦ **Test:** This excellent feature enables you to audition the export quality of the sound based on the options that you've selected from the Compression menu (and supporting options in the Export Settings).

✦ **Stop:** Click this button to stop (silence) the sound that has been auditioned using the Test button.

Fine-tuning your audio in the Sound Properties dialog box of the Library panel has three benefits. Foremost of these benefits is the ability to set specific compressions and optimizations for each individual sound. Another benefit is the Test button. This is an excellent way to audition your audio file and to know what it will sound like when it is exported with different compression schemes and bit rates — hearing is believing. Finally, the estimated results, which display how each setting will affect the compressed file size, is a powerful tool that helps you obtain the desired balance of quality and file size. In contrast, optimizing sounds with the Publish Settings is more of a blind process — it is not only more global, it's also more of a painful trial-and-error method.

Combining methods for controlling sounds

One of the coolest things about Flash audio is that you can combine the two methods of controlling sounds, using both the Publish Settings and the Library panel's Sound Properties dialog box to streamline your work flow while still maintaining a relatively high degree of control over sound quality. (This method works best if you already have some experience with sound behavior in Flash.)

For example, let's assume that you have three different Event sounds in your Flash project. Two of these are simple button sounds. You decide that you won't require specialized compression for the sound used with the buttons. So, based on your prior experience of sound behavior in Flash, you go directly to the Publish Settings and set Event sounds to publish as MP3 at 48 Kbps with Best quality.

Note   We assume that you have left the sounds used for the buttons untouched in the Library panel, leaving the Compression setting in the Sound Settings dialog box at Default. The Default option tells Flash to handle the compression for these sounds with the Publish Settings.

But the third sound is a loop of background jazz music that you want to be heard at near-CD quality. For this sound, you access the Sound Properties dialog box and try a number of combinations — and test each one — until you find a balance between file size and audio quality that pleases your ears. For example, you may decide to assign this sound to export as an MP3, stereo at 64 Kbps, with Quality set to Best.

Final Sound Advice and Pointers

Here are a few final notes about sound and some pointers to more complex sound-related topics that may help you work with sound files in Flash 8.

VBR (Variable Bit Rate) MP3

Macromedia has licensed the Fraunhofer MP3 codec, which supports streaming MP3 with a constant bit rate. However, neither Flash 8 nor any Flash Player supports Variable Bit Rate (VBR), or VBR MP3, encoding for Stream sounds. VBR MP3 is a variant of MP3 that uses specialized algorithms to vary the bit rate according to the kind of sound that is being compressed. For example, a soprano solo would be accorded a higher bit rate than a crashing drum sequence, resulting in a superior ratio of quality to file size. There are a number of sound applications, such as Apple iTunes, Musicmatch Jukebox, and the MP3 creation packs available for Windows XP Media Player, that export VBR MP3. If you have access to a sound application that exports VBR MP3, you'll be happy to know that you can import your VBR MP3 sound files, which are (theoretically) optimized for file size and quality beyond the compression capabilities of Flash 8, and that you can maintain the compression of such files by doing the following:

✦ In the Flash tab of the Publish Settings dialog box, leave the option to Override Sound Settings unchecked.

✦ In the Sound Properties (or Export Settings) dialog box for each sound in the Library panel, choose Default for the Compression option in Export Settings.

✦ The Sync option (located in the Property inspector) for the sound *cannot* be set to Stream.

If you choose to use VBR MP3 files in your Flash documents, you may need to test the following options of VBR compression in your MP3 creation software:

✦ **Bit rate:** Test the minimum bit rate that VBR will use for the MP3 file. Regular MP3 files use CBR, or Constant Bit Rate, which keeps the sound's bit rate steady through the entire sound file. With VBR, the bit rate can vary in ranges that you specify. Some higher bit rates, such as 320 Kbps, may not import well into the Flash 8 authoring tool.

✦ **Quality:** Most VBR-enabled MP3 software enables you to also pick an arbitrary quality setting for VBR MP3 files. Using terminology like Lowest, Medium Low, and High (and several in between), or percentages (1–100%), you can alter the quality of the bit rate. Note that this "quality" is not necessarily used in the same manner that Flash 8 refers to quality for MP3 compression.

You may find that Flash 8 will give you an import error for some VBR- (and CBR-) encoded MP3 files. If a particular setting creates an MP3 file that can't be imported into Flash 8, then try another bit rate and/or quality combination. However, we have found that Flash 8 has strange inconsistent behavior when it comes to importing MP3 files. For example, you may find that one VBR setting/combination does not work for a particular sound file, but that it works fine for others. Even more strangely, MP3 files that won't import into the Flash 8 authoring environment will load just fine into Flash Player 6 or higher at run time via ActionScript.

Cross-Reference   You can find more information about VBR encoding at the following URL:

    www.fezguys.com/columns/057.shtml

We also recommend reading the "null sound" Flash tutorial at

    www.bluegelmedia.com/tutorials/av/null_sound_technique.htm

This tutorial shows you how to use a Stream sound to kick other Event sounds into streaming mode. Robert Reinhardt contributed a chapter to August de los Reye et al's *Flash Design for Mobile Devices* (Wiley, 2002) covering this technique.

Optimizing sounds for bandwidth usage

It goes without saying that every Internet content creator strives to make every file and data transaction as small and efficient as possible to accommodate the majority of slow network connections in use today. As a Flash designer or developer incorporating sound into your projects, you'll want to properly plan sound usage in an effort to avoid 1MB .swf file downloads.

Table 15-4 explores many of the available network bandwidths that are in use on the Internet. However, as you've likely experienced, it's highly unusual to actually get the full download (or upload) speed out of your network connection. Variables such as network congestion, server load, and phone line conditions affect the quality of your network speed. Using the same "formula" that Macromedia uses to determine approximate download speeds in the Bandwidth Profiler (within Test Movie mode), we calculated estimated bandwidth speeds for the connection speeds shown in Table 15-4. Because Flash 8 displays compressed sound information in Kbps units, we converted these connection speeds into Kbps bit rates. More important, though, we also provided a 50-percent portion of this bit rate, as you'll likely need to save room for other Flash material, such as vector artwork, bitmap graphics, and animations.

Table 15-4: Bit Rates for Flash Movies

Hardware support	Theoretical bandwidth	Estimated bandwidth	Percent of theoretical	100% bit rate	50% bit rate
14.4 Kbps	1.8 KB/s	1.2 KB/s	67	9.6 Kbps	4.8 Kbps
19.2 Kbps	2.4 KB/s	1.6 KB/s	67	12.8 Kbps	6.4 Kbps
28.8 Kbps	3.6 KB/s	2.3 KB/s	64	18.4 Kbps	9.2 Kbps
33.6 Kbps	4.2 KB/s	2.8 KB/s	67	22.5 Kbps	11.2 Kbps
56 Kbps	7 KB/s	4.7 KB/s	67	37.6 Kbps	18.8 Kbps
64 Kbps	8 KB/s	5.4 KB/s	67	43.2 Kbps	21.6 Kbps
128 Kbps	16 KB/s	10.7 KB/s	67	85.6 Kbps	42.8 Kbps
256 Kbps	32 KB/s	21 KB/s	67	168 Kbps	84 Kbps
384 Kbps	48 KB/s	32 KB/s	67	256 Kbps	128 Kbps
768 Kbps	96 KB/s	64 KB/s	67	512 Kbps	256 Kbps
1.5 Mbps	192 KB/s	129 KB/s	67	1,032 Kbps	516 Kbps
11 Mbps	1,408 KB/s	943 KB/s	67	7,544 Kbps	3,772 Kbps

Using Table 15-4 as a guide, try to plan your Flash project for your target audience. Actually, you may have more than one target audience. As such, you may need to develop several versions of your sound assets, with each version targeted to a specific connection speed.

Once you've decided your target audience(s), you can determine the maximum Kbps that your sound files should use. Table 15-5 shows you the bit rates of Raw, Speech, and ADPCM mono sounds. We don't include MP3 bit rates here because they're already calculated (and available) in the Compression menu of the Sound Properties dialog box: 8, 16, 20, 24, 32, 48, 56, 64, 80, 112, 128, and 160 Kbps. In Table 15-5, we show bit rates that are suitable for analog modem connections (14.4, 28.8, 33.6, and 56 Kbps) in bold.

Note

If you'd like to see the actual sample rate used by Flash 8's MP3 compression options, see Table 15-7.

Table 15-5: Mono Bit Rates for Streaming Sound

Sampling rate	Raw	Speech	ADPCM 2-bit	ADPCM 3-bit	ADPCM 4-bit	ADPCM 5-bit
5 kHz	80 Kbps	**10 Kbps**	**10 Kbps**	**15 Kbps**	**20 Kbps**	**25 Kbps**
11 kHz	176 Kbps	**22 Kbps**	**22 Kbps**	**33 Kbps**	44 Kbps	55 Kbps
22 kHz	352 Kbps	44 Kbps	44 Kbps	66 Kbps	88 Kbps	110 Kbps
44 kHz	704 Kbps	88 Kbps	88 Kbps	132 Kbps	176 Kbps	220 Kbps

In Tables 15-6 and 15-7, we calculate the file sizes that one second of mono (one-channel) sound occupies in a Flash movie file (.swf). Use the values in these tables as multipliers for your sound file's actual length. For example, if you know that you have a 30-second soundtrack file, the final Flash movie file size (containing just the audio) would be about 60K with ADPCM 3-bit, 5 kHz compression. Regardless of the actual content of the digital audio, these encodings will produce consistent file sizes based on length and resolution.

Table 15-6: File Sizes in Bytes (KB) for One Second of Mono Audio

Sample rate	Raw	Speech	ADPCM 2-bit	ADPCM 3-bit	ADPCM 4-bit	ADPCM 5-bit
5 kHz	11,037 (10.8)	1,421 (1.4)	1,397 (1.4)	2,085 (2.0)	2,774 (2.7)	3,463 (3.4)
11 kHz	22,061 (21.5)	2,829 (2.8)	2,777 (2.7)	4,115 (4.0)	5,532 (5.4)	6,910 (6.8)
22 kHz	44,109 (43.1)	5,581 (5.5)	5,541 (5.5)	8,296 (8.1)	11,051 (10.8)	13,806 (13.5)
44 kHz	88,205 (86.1)	11,085 (10.8)	11,065 (10.8)	16,576 (16.2)	22,086 (21.6)	27,597 (27.0)

Table 15-7: File Sizes in Bytes (KB) for One Second of Mono MP3 Audio

Bit rate	Size	Output sample rate	Bit rate	Size	Output sample rate
8 Kbps	1,263 (1.2)	11 kHz	56 Kbps	5,605 (5.5)	22 kHz
16 Kbps	2,511 (2.5)	11 kHz	64 Kbps	8,543 (8.3)	44 kHz
20 Kbps	3,135 (3.1)	11 kHz	80 Kbps	10,716 (10.5)	44 kHz
24 Kbps	3,369 (3.3)	22 kHz	112 Kbps	14,980 (14.6)	44 kHz
32 Kbps	4,487 (4.4)	22 kHz	128 Kbps	17,112 (16.7)	44 kHz
48 Kbps	5,605 (5.5)	22 kHz	160 Kbps	17,112 (16.7)	44 kHz

Note   You may notice that some bit rate settings in Table 15-7 create the same file size for the MP3 compression. This is a known bug of Macromedia Flash 8. You may also find that the Convert Stereo to Mono option for MP3 compression does not affect the outcome of some settings.

Extracting a sound from a Flash document

Sometime you may be handed a Flash document file (.fla) that has sound embedded within it and be told that the original sounds have either been lost or are no longer available. Here's how to extract a sound from such a file:

1. Back up the file.

   If the original file is named `sound.fla`, you might resave it as `sound_extraction.fla`. If you want to start with an exercise file, save a copy of the `enhanced_view.fla` file, located on the book's CD-ROM. You can skip Steps 2 through 7 if you are using this file.

2. Add a new layer in the Timeline window, at the top of the layer stack.

3. Label this layer **sound extraction**.

4. With the first frame of this layer selected, open the Property inspector.

5. In the Sound menu, specify the sound file from the Library that you wish to export.

6. Add enough frames to the sound extraction layer so that you can see the entire waveform of the sound file.

7. Delete all other layers.

8. Open the Library panel and locate the sound that needs to be extracted from the file.

   In the example file, the sound is named `atmospheres_1.wav`. Note that any other assets within this file are irrelevant to this process. That's because Flash will use only Library items that have actually been used within the movie.

9. Double-click the sound icon for `atmospheres_1.wav` in the Library panel to invoke the Sound Properties dialog box.

10. Set the Compression to Raw.

    This ensures that the sound will be exported as uncompressed audio.

11. Select a sample rate that matches the one listed to the right of the waveform display, near the top of the Sound Properties dialog box.

    If the sound is specified as a Stereo sound, make sure the Convert Stereo to Mono option is unchecked.

12. Access the Flash tab of the Publish Settings dialog box, and make sure that the Override Sound Settings check box is *not* checked.

    Now you're ready to extract the sound file from the Flash document file (.fla). You've created a movie that will ignore all other assets in the library except this sound, and you've told Flash to export the sound with the original sample rate of the sound, as uncompressed (Raw) audio.

13. Choose File ➪ Export Movie, and specify a file location, name, and file type.

    If you're using the Windows version of Flash 8, choose WAV Audio as the file type. If you're on a Mac, choose QuickTime Video.

14. For Windows users, the Export Windows WAV dialog box appears with those sound specifications. In the Sound Format menu, make sure the audio specifications match those of your audio source in the Library panel; then click OK. For Mac users, the

Export QuickTime Video dialog box appears. Ignore all of the options except Sound Format. In this menu, select the sound setting that matches the specifications of the sound file. For this example, this setting should be 44 kHz 16 Bit Stereo. Click OK.

15. For Windows users, the process is complete. You now have a WAV copy of your Flash movie sound asset. For Mac users, you still have a couple of steps to complete:

1. Open the exported QuickTime movie in the QuickTime Pro Player. You must have the Pro version installed.

2. Choose File ➪ Export.

3. Select Sound to AIFF in the Export menu.

4. Click the Options button, and in the Sound Settings dialog box, set the Compressor to None and choose a sample rate, bit depth, and channel type that match the sound from the Flash document. For this example sound, this should be 44.1 kHz, 16 bit, and Stereo. Click OK.

Note   If you're using Apple QuickTime Pro 7 or higher, choose Linear PCM in the Format menu and the sampling settings that match your source audio in the Flash movie.

5. Finally, specify a filename and location for the exported file, and click Save.

Cross-Reference   We defer several sound-related topics until after our discussion of Flash 8's ActionScripting capabilities. Work your way to Chapter 27, "Interacting with Movie Clips," and Chapter 28, "Sharing and Loading Assets."

Web Resource   We'd like to know what you think about this chapter. Visit www.flashsupport.com/ feedback to send us your comments.

Summary

✦ Flash movie files (.swf) can use four types of audio compression: ADPCM, MP3, Raw, and Speech. ADPCM is compatible with all versions of the Flash Player. MP3 is compatible with most versions of Flash Player 4 and higher. The Speech codec is compatible only with Flash Player 6 and higher.

✦ When sound is imported to a Flash document, it's added and displayed in the Library panel. You can assign sounds from the Library panel to a keyframe on a timeline. You can also use sounds with ActionScript.

✦ Sounds can be assigned to the Up, Over, and Down states of a Button symbol.

✦ The Sync options control how a sound will play in relation to the rest of the timeline.

✦ Use the Loop setting in the Property inspector to multiply the length of the original sound.

✦ Stream sounds force the Flash Player to keep playback of the timeline in pace with the sound.

✦ Use a `stopAllSounds()` action to stop all sounds that are currently playing in the movie.

✦ The Effect menu in the Property inspector contains useful presets for sound channel playback. You can perform custom edits with the Edit Envelope dialog box.

✦ Global audio compression is controlled in the Flash tab of the Publish Settings dialog box.

✦ Use the Sound Properties dialog box in the Library panel to customize the audio compression schemes of individual sounds.

✦ The Sound Properties dialog box enables you to test different compression settings and to hear the results. The Export Settings section of this dialog box also provides useful file size information.

✦ You can bring and export Variable Bit Rate (VBR) MP3 sound files into Flash without degrading the encoding; however, Flash itself cannot encode using VBR.

✦ ✦ ✦

Importing Artwork

Although Flash gives you powerful options for creating and modifying a variety of graphics, you don't have to limit yourself to the Flash authoring environment. That's because Flash also has the capability of importing artwork from a wide range of sources. You can import both vector and raster graphics, and you can use both formats in a variety of ways.

In this chapter, we discuss the differences between vector graphics and raster or bitmap images. We also show you how to import external artwork so that you can use it in a Flash movie, as well as tell you about the Flash features that you can use to handle imported bitmap images and vector graphics.

New Feature

Although the import and edit options have not changed significantly since Flash MX 2004, overall, bitmaps in Flash 8 look better than they ever have. Superior bitmap smoothing results in cleaner-looking images, even if they are scaled in the authoring environment. Another little change that has big creative potential is Flash 8's support for Fireworks filter effects. If you have modified an image in Fireworks, most of the filters will now be preserved as editable when you import a .png to the Flash authoring environment.

We define all the formats that Flash supports and go over some of the issues to consider when preparing artwork for import from various programs. We also introduce some Flash 8 features that are helpful for managing imported assets and give some insight into optimizing your final file size.

Defining Vectors and Bitmaps

In addition to various sound and video formats, Flash supports two types of image formats: vector and bitmap. *Vector* graphic files consist of an equation that describes the placement of points and the qualities of the lines between those points. Using this basic logic, vector graphics tell the computer how to display the lines and shapes, as well as what colors to use, where to put them on the Stage, and at what scale.

Flash is a vector program. Thus, anything that you create with the Flash drawing tools will be described in vector format. Vector graphics have some important benefits: They're small in file size and they scale accurately without distortion. However, they also have a couple of drawbacks: Highly complex vector graphics may result in very large file sizes, and vectors aren't really suitable for creating continuous tones, photographs, or artistic brushwork.

Bitmap (also referred to as *raster*) files are described by an arrangement of individual pixels, which are mapped in a grid — like a piece of graph paper with tiny squares. Each square represents a single pixel, and each of these pixels has specific color values assigned to it. So, as the name implies, a bitmap image maps out the placement and color of each pixel on the screen. A line is "drawn" by filling each unique pixel, rather than simply using a mathematical formula to connect two points as is done with vectors.

Note   Do not be confused by the name *bitmap.* You might already be familiar with the bitmap format used by Windows, which has the file extension .bmp. Although *bitmap* may refer to that particular image format, it's frequently applied to raster images in general, such as GIF, JPEG, PICT, and TIFF files, as well as many others.

Although bitmap images aren't created in Flash, they can be used within Flash projects. To do this, you need to use an external bitmap-editing application and then import the bitmaps into Flash. Figure 16-1 shows a vector image and a bitmap image of the same logo, scaled at 100 percent.

Figure 16-1: A vector image drawn in Flash (left) and the same image imported as a bitmapped GIF graphic (right)

Although these vector and bitmap images are of similar quality at their original size, their differences become more apparent when the same images are scaled to a larger size. Unlike vector graphics, bitmap images become more pixilated as they are scaled larger because there is a finite amount of information in the image and Flash has to spread this information over more pixels. As we explain later in this chapter, Flash is able to interpolate the pixel information by using Smoothing to reduce the jagged appearance of the scaled pixel pattern, but this can also cause the image to look blurred. Figure 16-2 shows the difference between vector and bitmap graphics when scaled in Flash with Smoothing turned off.

Figure 16-2: The same vector (left) and bitmap (right) image scaled to 200 percent in Flash to illustrate the difference in image quality

Simple bitmap images are often larger in file size than simple vector graphics, but very complex bitmap images (for example, a photograph) can be smaller and display better quality than vector graphics of equal complexity. Figure 16-3 shows a bitmap image compared to a vector image of equal complexity (created by tracing the bitmap). The original bitmap is a smaller file and better suited for reproducing the photographic image.

Original bitmap 16 KB   Traced vector image 198 KB

Figure 16-3: File size comparison of an imported bitmap image (left), and a traced vector image of equivalent complexity (right)

The rule of thumb is to use scalable, bandwidth-efficient vector graphics as much as possible within Flash projects, except for situations in which photographs — or photographic-quality, continuous-tone images — are necessary for special content.

> **Tip** Most 8-bit raster images are GIFs, and they are most frequently used for images with large areas of solid color, such as logos and text. Rather than use this image type in Flash, consider re-creating or tracing this artwork with Flash drawing tools. The final Flash movie (.swf) will not only be smaller; it will also look cleaner and be scalable.

Knowing the File Formats for Import to Flash

You can import a variety of assets (in compatible formats) directly into your Flash project Library, or you can import or copy and paste from another application into the Flash Document window. Assets can also be dragged from one Flash Document window or library to another. Files must be a minimum size of 2 pixels by 2 pixels for import into Flash.

> **Caution** Copying and pasting bitmap images into Flash from other applications does not always transfer transparency settings, so it may not be the best workflow for some assets. Using the Import dialog box and specifying that the artwork be imported as an editable object will preserve transparency settings from Macromedia Fireworks .png files.

The import menu (Ctrl+R or ⌘+R) gives you the option to limit imports to a specific format or to choose broad media categories. Unless you find it helpful to have some files grayed out when you dig through lists to find items to import, you will most likely be happy just using the most inclusive menu setting: All Files.

New Feature

One setting that may not be self-explanatory on the Mac is the All PostScript setting that was added to Flash MX 2004 to include .pdf (as well as .ai and .eps) files created in Adobe Illustrator 9 or higher. We describe the specific options available for integrating PDF files into your Flash documents later in this chapter.

Cross-Reference

For a full discussion of importing and handling sound assets, refer to Chapter 15, "Adding Sound." Flash-compatible video formats are documented in Appendix D, "Digital Video Basics," which is included as a PDF file on this book's CD-ROM. For coverage of other bitmap and vector applications, refer to Chapter 36, "Working with Raster Graphics," and Chapter 37, "Working with Vector Graphics," also included as PDF files on the CD-ROM.

For now, let's focus on a brief summary of the image formats for Flash import, as shown in Table 16-1.

Note

The QuickTime warning dialog box that would pop up when bitmap images requiring QuickTime support were imported to older versions of Flash no longer appears. Although QuickTime support is still needed for some file types, the warning has been retired to make the process more seamless.

Table 16-1: Image Formats for Flash Import

File type	Extension	Description	Platform
Adobe Illustrator (v. 9 or 10 files are most compatible)	.ai, .eps	Adobe Illustrator files are imported into Flash as vector graphics (unless they contain bitmap images). The importer plug-in is required to import files from Adobe Illustrator 8 and earlier. The importer for Flash MX 2004 and Flash 8 does not preserve layers in EPS files. To preserve layers, import in AI, PDF, or SWF format.	Windows Macintosh
AutoCAD DXF	.dxf	Drawing eXchange format is the original inter-program format for AutoCAD drafting software. Because this format does not support fills, it is mainly used for drafting plans or schematic drawings. This format is used by most CAD, 3D, and modeling programs for transferring drawings to other programs.	Windows Macintosh

File type	Extension	Description	Platform
(Windows) Bitmap	.bmp, .dib	Although Bitmap is a Windows format for bitmap images, don't be confused by the format name—not all bitmap images are Windows Bitmaps. Bitmap can be used with all Win and some Mac applications. It allows variable bit depths and compression settings with support of alpha channels, and supports lossless compression. It is ideal for high-quality graphics work.	Windows Macintosh
Enhanced Metafile	.emf	Enhanced Metafile is a proprietary Windows format that supports vectors and bitmaps internally. This format is occasionally used to import vector graphics, but for most professional graphics work, this is not a recommended format.	Windows
Flash Movie	.swf, .spl	Flash Player files are exported Flash movies. The movie is flattened into a single layer and scene, and all animation is converted to frame-by-frame animation.	Windows Macintosh
FreeHand	.fh	This is the vector-based format of Macromedia FreeHand (v.7 or later).	Windows Macintosh
GIF image or animated GIF	.gif	Graphic Interchange Format (GIF) was developed by CompuServe as a bitmap image type that uses lossless compression. It is limited to a 256-color (or less) palette, and is not recommended as a high-quality Flash export format, even for Web use.	Windows Macintosh
JPEG image	.jpg	Joint Photographic Experts Group (JPEG) images are a bitmap type that uses lossy compression. Supports 24-bit RGB color. Recommended for Web-friendly compression of photographic images. Because of small file size, JPEG is often the native format for digital still cameras. No support for alpha channels.	Windows Macintosh
MacPaint image	.pntg	This is a legacy format for the old MacPaint program.	Windows Macintosh

Continued

Table 16-1 *(continued)*

File type	Extension	Description	Platform
PDF file (included in the All PostScript import menu option)	.pdf	Portable Document Format is a multipurpose, cross-platform format that preserves fonts, formatting, vector graphics, and bitmap images. Compression is variable and can be chosen when the file is created. PDF files are generally created or edited with Adobe Acrobat and read with the free Adobe Acrobat Reader. Adobe Illustrator and Adobe Photoshop also support PDF import and export. The importer plug-in for Flash 8 uses the GhostScript technology to support PDF files from Adobe Illustrator, with options for handling layers and multipage documents. Photoshop PDF files can also be imported, but text is converted into masked shapes.	Windows Macintosh
PICT image	.pct, .pict	PICT image is compatible with many Win and all Mac applications. It enables variable bit depths and compression settings with support of alpha channels (when saved with no compression at 32 bits), supports lossless compression, and can contain vector or raster graphics. PICT image is ideal for high-quality graphics work.	Windows Macintosh
PNG image	.png	The Portable Network Graphic (PNG) format is another type of bitmap image that supports variable bit depth (PNG-8 and PNG-24) and compression settings with alpha channels. PNG files imported to Flash from Macromedia Fireworks as editable objects (unflattened) will preserve artwork in vector format. Lossless compression schemes make it ideal for high-quality graphics work. It is the recommended media type for imported images with alpha channels or filter effects	Windows Macintosh
Photoshop image (2.5 or higher)	.psd	This is the layered format for most versions of Photoshop—from version 2.5 through version 6. Although Flash 8 supports PSD files, in our experience, PNG files gave more consistent results for imported files with transparency.	Windows Macintosh
QuickTime image	.qtif	This is the static raster image format created by QuickTime. It is not commonly used.	Windows Macintosh
Silicon Graphics image	.sgi	This is an image format specific to SGI machines.	Windows Macintosh

File type	Extension	Description	Platform
TGA image	.tga	The TGA, or Targa, format is a 32-bit format that includes an 8-bit alpha channel. It was developed to overlay computer graphics and live video.	Windows (with QT4) Macintosh
TIFF image	.tif or .tiff	TIFF is a lossless, cross-platform image type used widely for high-resolution photography and printing.	Windows Macintosh
Windows Metafile	.wmf	Windows Metafile is a proprietary Windows format that supports vectors and bitmaps internally. This format is generally used to import vector graphics.	Windows
Toon Boom Studio file	.tbp	This is the vector format for files created with Toon Boom Technologies proprietary animation software. It preserves layers, scenes, sound, and so on, and is imported with support from the Toon Boom Studio Importer plug-in (TBSi) shipped with Flash MX 2004.	Macintosh (with TBSi) Windows (with TBSi)

Tip   Although you can export to the GIF format from Flash, this should be considered an option for raw-information transfer only, not as a means for creating final GIF art. For optimal quality and control, GIFs exported from Flash should be brought into Fireworks for fine-tuning and optimization. A preferable workflow is to export a PNG sequence from Flash that can be brought into Fireworks for fine-tuning and final GIF output.

Preparing Bitmaps

Flash is a vector-based application, but that shouldn't stop you from using bitmaps when you *need* them. There are many situations in which either the designs or the nature of the content require that photographic images be included in a Flash project. You can import a wide variety of bitmap image types, including JPEG, GIF, BMP, and PICT using the methods we describe in the next section.

Considering that it's a vector-based program, Flash supports bitmap graphics extraordinarily well. However, because the most common use of Flash movies is for Web presentations, you always need to keep file size in mind. Here's what you can do to limit the impact of bitmap images on Flash playback performance:

✦ Limit the number of bitmaps used in any one frame of a Flash movie.

✦ Remember that, regardless of how many times the bitmap is placed on the Stage, the actual bitmap (or its compressed version in the .swf file) is downloaded before the first occurrence of the bitmap (or its symbol instance).

✦ Try spreading out bitmap usage, or hide a symbol instance of the bitmap in an earlier frame before it is actually visible, so that it will be loaded when you need it.

Tip   If you need to include several high-resolution bitmap images in your Flash movie, consider using an ActionScript preloader or try breaking up the project into several linked Flash movies.

When you want to bring raster images into Flash documents, you should know what portion of the Flash Stage the image will occupy. Let's assume that you're working with the default Flash document size of 550 x 400 pixels. If you want to use a bitmap as a background image, it won't need to be any larger than 550 x 400 (as long as your movie will not be scalable). So, assuming that you're starting with a high-resolution image, you would downscale the image to the largest size at which it will appear in the Flash movie *before* you import it into Flash; for our example, that would be 550 x 400.

Tip   Use an image-editing program such as Macromedia Fireworks or Adobe Photoshop to downsize the pixel width and height of your source image if necessary.

If you mask bitmaps with a Mask layer in the Flash Timeline, the entire bitmap is still exported. Consequently, before import you should closely crop all images that will be masked in Flash. For example, if all you need to show is a face, crop the image so that it shows the face with as little extraneous background information as possible.

Be aware that Flash doesn't resize (or resample) an image to its viewed or placed size when the Flash movie (.swf) is created. To illustrate how the size of an imported bitmap can impact the size of a final Flash movie (.swf), we compared two different image resolutions used in identical layouts. Using the same source image, we sized the JPEG at two different pixel dimensions, and then placed it in two identical Flash documents (.fla). The first source version of the image had a 400 x 600 pixel dimension, while the second source version had a 200 x 300 pixel dimension — exactly half the size of the first. In both Flash documents, the final image was displayed at 200 x 300 pixels.

In the first Flash document (we'll call it Movie A), we imported the larger JPEG and resized it by 50 percent (using the Info panel) to match the smaller image. In the second Flash document (Movie B), we imported the smaller JPEG and placed it at its original size, occupying the same portion of the Flash Stage as the image in Movie A. Although both Flash movies exported a bitmap of the same display size on the Flash Stage, the resulting .swf files (using the same level of JPEG compression on export) had drastically different file sizes. Movie A was 44.1KB, whereas Movie B was 14.8 KB! Movie A is nearly three times larger than Movie B. The difference in image resolution could be seen when a view magnification greater than 100 percent was used within the Flash Player; the larger JPEG in Movie A was much less pixilated than the smaller JPEG in Movie B.

Raster Images: Resolution, Dimensions, and Bit Depth

Resolution refers to the amount of information within a given unit of measurement. Greater resolutions mean better quality (or more image information). With respect to raster images, resolution is usually measured in pixels per inch (when viewed on a monitor) or dots per inch (when output on film or paper).

What is resolution?

The resolution of an original image changes whenever the scale of the image is changed, while the pixel dimensions remain fixed. Thus, if an original photograph is scanned at 300 pixels per inch (ppi) with dimensions of 2" x 2", subsequently changing the dimensions to 4" x 4" will result in a resolution of 150 ppi. Although a 4" x 4" image at 300 ppi could be interpolated from the original image, true resolution will be *lost* as an image is scaled larger. When an image is digitally enlarged, the graphics application simply doubles existing pixel information, which can create a softened or blurred image. Reducing the scale of an image has few undesirable side effects — although a much smaller version of an original may lose some fine details.

Because all raster images consist of pixels, and because resolution simply describes how many pixels will be arranged in a given area, the most accurate way of referencing raster images is by using the absolute pixel width and height of an image. For example, a 4,000 x 5,000-pixel image could be printed or displayed at any size with variable resolutions. This image could be 4" x 5" at 1,000 ppi, or it could be 8" x 10" at 500 ppi — without any loss of information. Remember that resolution simply describes how much information is shown per unit. When you reduce the pixel width and height of an image, the resolution is lowered accordingly, and after any pixels are thrown out, discarded, or interpolated, they're gone for good.

Raster images: Bit depth

Bit depth is an important factor that influences image quality and file size. *Bit depth* refers to the amount of information stored for each pixel of an image. The most common bit depths for images are 8-bit and 24-bit, although many others exist. An 8-bit image contains up to 256 colors, while a 24-bit image may contain 16.7 million color values. Depending on their file format, some images can also use an 8-bit alpha channel, which is a multilevel transparency layer. Each addition to an image's bit-depth is reflected in a considerable file size increase: A 24-bit image contains three times the information per pixel as an 8-bit image. Mathematically, you can calculate the file size (in bytes) of an image with the following formula (all measurements are in pixels):

```
width × height × (bit depth ÷ 8) = file size
```

Note: You divide bit depth by 8 because there are 8 bits per byte.

When importing 8-bit images in formats such as GIF, BMP, and PICT, it is preferable to use the default Lossless (PNG/GIF) compression setting in Bitmap Properties to avoid adding Flash's default Publish Settings Quality 24-bit JPEG compression. Eight-bit images that use Web-safe color palettes will ensure greater display predictability for people viewing your Flash artwork on older systems with 8-bit video cards.

Preserving Bitmap Quality

When you choose to use bitmap images, remember that they won't scale as well as vector drawings in the authoring environment. Furthermore, bitmaps will become degraded if the viewer scales your final movie so that the bitmap is displayed larger than its original size. Here are a few points to consider that will help you maintain the quality of your presentation when using bitmaps:

✦ Know your audience, and design for the largest screen (at the highest resolution) that your audience may have. Or, if you deviate from this, remember that audience members with optimal equipment will see a low-quality version of your work. If you're using ActionScript to load image assets, consider having low-res and high-res versions of the images available.

✦ Measure your largest hypothetical image dimensions in pixels. One way to determine these dimensions is to use the Flash Info panel to read the size of a placed image or a placeholder shape. Another way is to take a screen capture of your mock-up, and then measure the intended image area in Photoshop.

✦ Create or resize your bitmap image to the maximum hypothetical dimensions. If there are any rotations or skews required, you may have to do a test to see if the final result is cleaner when the transformation is done in your image-editing program or in the Flash authoring environment. The improved bitmap smoothing in Flash 8 delivers better results with modified bitmaps than any previous version of Flash.

✦ Import images into Flash at the maximum required size, and then scale them down to fit into your layout.

The advantage of using this approach is that the movie can be scaled for larger monitors without causing the bitmap image to degrade. The disadvantage is that it requires sending the same large bitmap to all users. A more sophisticated solution is to use JavaScript to detect browser dimensions and then send the appropriately scaled bitmaps to each user. Other workaround solutions that may help preserve the quality of your final presentation without adding file size include the following:

✦ Restrict scaling capability of your published movie. You can do this by using HTML options in the Publish Settings or using ActionScript.

✦ Set the bitmap's compression to Lossless (GIF/PNG) if it is already optimized in GIF format or if you want to preserve an alpha channel or editable filter effects in a .png or a .psd file.

✦ Trace the bitmap to convert it to a vector graphic (covered later in this chapter).

✦ Never apply double JPEG compression to your images. If you have compressed and saved images in JPEG format outside of Flash, be certain to select the Use imported JPEG data check box when importing the images to Flash.

Before sizing and importing bitmaps, you need to consider how you will set the dimensions for the Flash movie (.swf) in the HTML tab of the Publish Settings dialog box. You also need to know whether the bitmap is to be scaled in a Motion tween. If the Flash movie scales beyond its original pixel width and height (or if the bitmap is scaled larger in a tween), then bitmap images will appear at a lower resolution with a consequent degradation of image quality.

If you're uncertain of the final size that you need for a bitmap in Flash, it may be best to import a temporary low-resolution version of the image — being careful to store your original high-resolution version where you can find it later. Whenever you need to place the bitmap, drag an instance of the symbol onto the Flash Stage. Then, during final production and testing, after you've determined the required pixel size for the maximum scale of the final bitmap, create and swap-in a higher-resolution image, as follows:

1. Double-click the icon of the original low-resolution bitmap in the Flash Library to access the bitmap's properties.

2. In the Bitmap Properties dialog box, click the Import button and select the new, higher-resolution version of the bitmap.

   After import of the high-res image, all instances of the bitmap will update automatically, with the scaling, animation, and placement of the image maintained.

Importing and Copying Bitmaps

Flash has the option to import bitmaps directly to the document Library, in addition to the standard option of importing to the document Stage. When a bitmap file is imported to the Stage, it will be added to the Library as well. To import a bitmap into Flash, follow these steps:

1. If you want to import an item to the Stage, make sure that there's an active, unlocked layer.

   If no layer is available for placement of the imported item, the Import to Stage command is dimmed and you will only be able to use the Import to Library option.

2. Choose File ➪ Import to Stage (Ctrl+R or ⌘+R) or File ➪ Import to Library.

   The Import (or the Import to Library) dialog box opens (shown in Figure 16-4).

3. Navigate to the file that you'd like to import, select it, and click the Import or Import to Library button.

The important difference between Import and Import to Library is that the latter option places the asset directly into the document Library without placing an instance on the Stage.

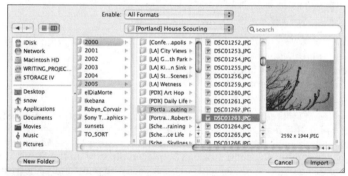

Figure 16-4: The Import dialog box as it appears on Mac OS X. You can import multiple files in the same batch by selecting them from the file list before clicking Import.

Because Flash offers full support for the PNG image format (including lossless compression and multilevel transparency and some Fireworks filters), PNG is an ideal format for images that you intend to import into Flash. The PNG format has two types: PNG-8 and PNG-24. Generally, only PNG-24 images support 24-bit color and an alpha channel, but the file sizes can often be prohibitive. Macromedia Fireworks makes it possible to create PNG-8 files with transparency for import to Flash.

Cross-Reference　　We discuss the PNG format in depth in Chapter 36, "Working with Raster Graphics," which is included as a PDF file on the CD-ROM.

Caution When you are using bitmap images with transparent areas, display problems can occasionally occur with certain color settings and file types. For troubleshooting assistance, refer to the Macromedia TechNote on "Transparency support in Flash" at: www.macromedia.com/support/flash/ts/documents/transparent_bitmaps.htm.

Importing sequences

When using the Import to Stage option, if you select an image from a series of images in the same storage location that include sequential numbers at the end of their filenames, Flash prompts you to import the files as a sequence. If that's what you want to do, click Yes in the dialog box (shown in Figure 16-5) to have Flash import all the files and place them in numeric sequence on successive keyframes of the current Timeline. Otherwise, click No, and only the single file that you've selected will be placed on the Stage.

Figure 16-5: You can import images in a numbered sequence and place them on successive keyframes automatically using the Import to Stage option.

If you are importing a series of stills to be used sequentially to create animation (stills from a video sequence, for example), this feature can save a lot of the time you would spend placing and ordering images manually. The most efficient workflow is to create a Movie Clip symbol before importing the images, so that the sequence can be placed directly on the Movie Clip timeline. This method creates an animated element that can easily be placed anywhere in your Flash project. If you have already imported a sequence to the Main Timeline and decide that it would be more easily managed as a symbol, simply create a Movie Clip, and then cut the images from the Main Timeline and paste them into the Movie Clip timeline.

 Web Resource For more coverage on how to create bitmap sequences from QuickTime video, go to the archived *Flash MX Bible* (Wiley, 2002) Chapter 41, "Working with QuickTime," available online at www.flashsupport.com/archive.

Although sequential import is not an option when using Import to Library, it is possible to manually select multiple images for import while using either of the Import dialog boxes. In order to bring more than one file into Flash in the same batch, Shift+click to select multiple items in sequence or use Ctrl+click (or ⌘+click) to select multiple nonsequential items in the file list of the Import dialog box.

Copying and pasting a bitmap into Flash

Here's how to use the Clipboard to import a bitmap into Flash:

1. Copy the bitmap from your image-editing application to your Clipboard.

   Most programs support the Ctrl+C or ⌘+C shortcut key.

2. Return to Flash and make sure that you have an active, unlocked layer that you can paste the bitmap into; this can be on the Main Timeline or on any symbol timeline.

3. Paste the bitmap onto the Stage by choosing Edit ➪ Paste in Center from the menu (Ctrl+V or ⌘+V).

Caution

When you are pasting a selected area from Photoshop, any transparency (alpha channel) is ignored or will render with unpredictable patterns that you'll have to mask out in Flash. The bitmap name will also be replaced with a default numbered asset name. In most cases, results will be much more consistent if you import the image file rather than copying and pasting it into Flash.

Setting Bitmap Properties

The Bitmap Properties dialog box, shown in Figure 16-6, has several options that are used to control the quality of your imported bitmaps. Settings in the Bitmap Properties dialog box will override the default JPEG compression setting for the document that is controlled in the Flash tab of the Publish Settings dialog box (File ➪ Publish Settings).

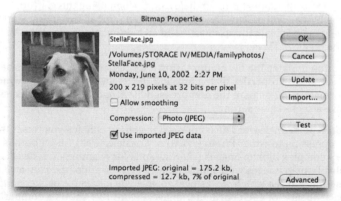

Figure 16-6: The Bitmap Properties dialog box controls the compression settings applied to bitmaps imported into Flash.

New Feature

The Advanced button expands the Bitmap Properties dialog box to show Linkage properties. In addition to importing or exporting for runtime sharing, bitmaps can now be set to export for ActionScript in Flash 8. If you decide to enter or modify Linkage properties for a bitmap after it has been imported, you can access these same options by selecting the symbol in the Library and choosing Linkage from the contextual menu or from the Options menu.

Follow these steps to use the Bitmap Properties dialog box:

1. Open the Library panel by choosing Window ⇨ Library (Ctrl+L or ⌘+L) to access bitmaps in your current project (.fla).

2. Double-click one of the bitmap's icons, or use the contextual menu to open the Bitmap Properties dialog box.

   You can also select Properties from the Library Options menu, or, with the bitmap highlighted, click the Properties button at the bottom of the Library panel.

3. Now, set the properties of your bitmap as needed:

   • **Preview window:** This displays the bitmap according to the current settings.

Tip

Although the preview window in the Bitmap Properties dialog box may show only a small portion of your image, you can move the picture around within the preview window by clicking and dragging the image to view different areas.

   • **Name:** This is the name of the bitmap, as indicated in the Library. To rename the bitmap, highlight the name and enter a new one.

   • **Image Path, Date, Dimensions:** Beneath the filename, Flash lists the local path, dimensions, and date information for the source of the imported image (not available if you pasted the image from the Clipboard).

   • **Update:** This feature enables you to re-import a bitmap if it's been altered outside of Flash. Flash tracks the original location of the imported bitmap and will look for the original file in that location when the Update button is clicked.

   • **Import:** This opens the Import Bitmap dialog box. When using this button, the new imported bitmap will replace the current bitmap (and all instances, if any), while retaining the original bitmap's name and all modifications that have been applied to the image in Flash.

   • **Test:** This button updates the file compression information, which appears at the bottom of the Bitmap Properties dialog box and the image in the Preview window. Use this information to compare the compressed file size to the original file size after you have selected new settings.

   • **Compression type drop-down:** The compression setting enables you to set the bitmap's compression to either Photo (JPEG) or Lossless (PNG/GIF). Photo is good for very complex bitmap images (photographs for example); Lossless is better for graphic bitmap images with simple shapes and fewer colors. Play around with these settings to see which works best to give you a balance between file size and image fidelity for each particular image. Figure 16-7 shows a comparison of these two settings applied to an imported GIF image (top) and applied to an imported JPEG image (bottom). The GIF with default lossless compression is only 4.7 KB. Applying a reduced JPEG Quality compression of 50 results in a larger file size (7 KB) for a poorer-looking image. Conversely, the JPEG with a Quality of 50 is only 9 KB, while the JPEG forced to lossless compression is 145.6 KB, without a huge difference in display quality.

Figure 16-7: Top: A GIF image imported to Flash using PNG/GIF (Lossless) compression (left) and imported with forced JPEG (Lossy) compression (right). Bottom: A JPEG image imported to Flash using JPEG (Lossy) compression (left) and imported with forced PNG/GIF (Lossless) compression (right).

- **Use imported JPEG data/Use Document default quality:** If the imported image is a JPEG, the first option will appear — select this check box to avoid double JPEG compression. If the image is not a JPEG, the second option will appear — select this check box to apply the global JPEG Quality setting defined in the Publish Settings dialog box for your current document. To select a new compression setting for an image, clear the check box beside Use imported JPEG data or Use Document default quality, and enter a new setting between 1 and 100 in the Quality value field. This is not recommended for imported JPEGs because it will result in double JPEG compression. On uncompressed source files, higher Quality settings produce better quality images but also larger file sizes. Figure 16-8 includes a JPEG published with imported data and a JPEG published with a reduced Quality setting (double JPEG compression).

Note

The Quality settings applied in the Bitmap Properties dialog box will not be visible in the authoring environment. The quality for images displayed on the Stage will appear the same regardless of the Flash JPEG settings. You will see a difference in the image (and the file size) only when you publish the movie (.swf). You *can* see smoothing in the authoring environment, making it easier to decide which images look better with smoothing applied.

Figure 16-8: The same bitmap image as it displays in the published Flash movie (.swf) using imported JPEG data (left) and using a reduced Quality setting of 10 (right)

- **Allow Smoothing (anti-aliasing):** Select this check box to enable Flash to anti-alias, or smooth, the edges of an image. Results may vary according to the image. Generally, this is not recommended for non-scaled graphics because it can soften the image. However, smoothing can be beneficial for reducing jagged edges on low-res images scaled in an animation. Smoothing in Flash 8 is greatly improved over older versions of Flash, so it can be applied with less caution. Figure 16-9 shows the effect of smoothing applied to a GIF image (top), and smoothing applied to a JPEG image (bottom).

4. Click OK.

All copies of this bitmap used in Flash are updated to the new settings.

For specific bitmap compression recommendations for different types of source files, please refer to the "Making Sense of Bitmap Compression" section, later in this chapter.

Figure 16-9: Compare the images with Flash smoothing (right) to the images with no smoothing (left).

Being Prepared for Common Problems

Flash retains existing JPEG compression levels on any imported JPEG image, but, if specified in the Bitmap Properties dialog box, it applies additional JPEG compression (set in the Quality field) when the movie is published or exported. Recompressing an image that has already been compressed usually leads to serious image degradation, due to the introduction of further compression artifacts. When importing JPEGs, you'll note that the Use imported JPEG data check box is selected by default in the Bitmap Properties dialog box. This is the preferred setting because recompressing a JPEG is generally detrimental to image quality.

Tip   If you import JPEG images, make sure that you either test the results of further JPEG compression or select the Use imported JPEG data check box in the Bitmap Properties dialog box, which is accessible from the Flash Library.

You can apply compression settings to each individual bitmap in the Library with the Flash Bitmap Properties dialog box to determine the quality that you need before you use the general JPEG settings in the Export Movie or Publish Settings dialog box. Any Quality defined in the Bitmap Properties dialog box will override the JPEG Quality in Publish Settings. To apply the Publish Settings compression to an image, you must select the Use document default check box in the Bitmap Properties dialog box.

Cross-Reference   We discuss JPEG export settings for Flash movies (.swf) in greater detail in Chapter 21, "Publishing Flash Movies."

Note   There was a known problem in Flash MX, referred to as *bitmap shift,* in which the position (and even colors) occasionally shifted from one instance to another of the same image. Flash MX 2004 resolved this small but important workflow issue.

Cross-browser consistency

We've received more than a few queries about image formats and Flash's capability to transcend issues of browser inconsistency, so here's the answer. Many image formats, such as PNG, are not supported across all browsers. When you import such an image format into Flash and publish or export to the SWF format, you have accomplished browser independence — because the Flash movie (.swf) is browser independent and the image has been encapsulated within the SWF format. (The image is not being sent to the browser in the imported format and then magically empowered to display.) Conversely, if you export any Flash document (.fla) to PNG or to any other format that's subject to cross-browser inconsistency, browser independence is lost.

JPEG rotation

This is a tricky problem to analyze. When animation that includes a bitmap is rendered and the image is displayed at an angle, it can be distorted. The manner of distortion changes depending on whether it was rotated in Photoshop and imported with the angle, or if it was imported into Flash on the square and subsequently rotated.

✦ When rotated in Flash, hard edges, such as text or high-contrast areas of an image, may appear choppy—as if they had been cut out with pinking shears. Yet, when zoomed, this effect is less problematic.

✦ When rotated in Photoshop, prior to import into Flash, some hard edges are less choppy. However, the file size will increase (to accommodate the larger overall shape), and the background will become a fixed color unless it is imported in lossless PNG format. A flutter or pixel-stepping pattern may occur along the edges of the transition between the background and the image. Straight lines and text will appear smoother and more acceptable at 100-percent scale, but at 200-percent zoom, text looks worse than the same image rotated in Flash.

Before rotating a bitmap in Flash, you should perform a few tests to see how your specific bitmap will be affected by the combination of compression, zoom, smoothing, and rotation (either in or out of Flash). Your choices and your decision will vary, subject to the content of the bitmap and the manner in which it will be used within Flash.

New Feature

Overall, bitmap smoothing is greatly improved in Flash 8. Even rotated images look much cleaner and are less likely to be jagged than in older versions of Flash. In most of our tests, the results were actually best when images were rotated in Flash rather than rotated in an image-editing program before import.

Applying Alpha, Color Effects, and Filters to bitmaps

A bitmap has some of the same advantages as the native Flash symbol types: It is automatically added to the Library when you import it, and instances can be dragged onto the Stage and even used in Motion tweens. However, Filters can't be applied to raw bitmaps and the Color (and Alpha) Effects are not available in the Property inspector when you select a bitmap instance. If you wish to change the alpha settings or color tint of an imported image or apply any of the new Flash 8 Filters, you have two easy options:

✦ Convert the bitmap into a Flash symbol type (F8)—use Movie Clip or Button symbol behavior if you want to use Flash Filters. You can use the same name for the symbol instance as the original bitmap image. Filters will be available in the Filters tab, and Color Effect settings will be available in the Properties tab of the Property inspector when you select the new (converted) symbol instance. Unfortunately, if you have placed other instances of the raw bitmap in your Flash file before nesting the bitmap in a symbol, not all of the instances of the bitmap will be automatically linked to the symbol you create, and you cannot use the Swap button to insert a Flash symbol instance in place of a bitmap instance.

Tip

Library folders are very helpful for managing large sequences of images that need to be converted into symbols. We usually create a "Bitmap source" folder and an "Image symbol" folder to make it easy to keep track of where all the assets are. Keep in mind that edits to the bitmap will be visible in the Flash symbol, but changes to the Flash symbol will not change the original bitmap.

✦ You *can* use Timeline Effects to add alpha or color changes to a bitmap instance. Flash still converts the image into a Graphic symbol before the Effect is applied, but you don't have to worry about doing it as a separate step.

Of course, using an external image-editing program is always an option, too. The features we describe in the next section can assist you if you plan to edit images outside of Flash.

Using the Bitmap Buttons in the Property Inspector

When a bitmap is selected in the Document window, the Property inspector displays the bitmap's name, symbol type, current size, and X, Y location. In addition to these basic bitmap properties, the Property inspector offers two useful options—the Swap button and the Edit button.

Swap

The Swap button invokes the Swap Bitmap dialog box (shown in Figure 16-10), allowing you to specify a different bitmap from the current project Library to replace the bitmap selected in the Document window. This can be considered a localized equivalent of the Import option of the Bitmap Properties dialog box. Rather than replacing the original bitmap symbol in the Library and all instances of the image, the Swap button will simply replace the currently selected bitmap instance without altering the symbols in the Library or any of the other instances of the bitmap that may occur in your project. (This feature is also available from the application menu under Modify ⇨ Bitmap ⇨ Swap bitmap.)

Figure 16-10: The Swap Bitmap dialog box lists all the bitmap symbols available in your current project Library.

Edit

The Edit button of the Property inspector will open the selected bitmap for editing outside of Flash, either in your default image editing application or the application that was used to save the bitmap file, if it is installed on your system. After you edit the image and choose Save, it will automatically be updated in the Flash document. If you prefer to select a specific application for editing a bitmap, select the bitmap in the Library before choosing Edit With from the options menu or the contextual menu. The Edit With menu item launches the Select External Editor dialog box that enables you to browse or search for a specific application installed on your system (or network). When you have selected the application of your choice, it will be launched and the bitmap is opened for editing.

Note Bitmaps imported from Fireworks as .png files specified as editable objects cannot be edited with an external image editor, so the Edit button will not be visible in the Property inspector when these items are selected in the Flash authoring environment.

Making Sense of Bitmap Compression

Although we did some sample testing to try to show you all the possible image-compression combinations and the final results, the truth is that the optimal settings are entirely dependent on the quality of the original image and the final appearance needed in the context of your design. The main goal when testing various compression strategies should always be to find a balance between image quality and file size. The ideal balance will vary depending on the purpose the image serves in your presentation. For example, when using bitmap images in animation sequences, you may find that you can get away with using higher compression settings because the detail in the image may not be as important as it would be if you used the image in a catalogue or some other presentation where the detail and color would be more critical.

The following compression workflows are intended to serve only as general guidelines. You will have to experiment with the specific value settings in each case to find the best results for your particular content and project needs.

24-bit or 32-bit lossless source files

If you have 24-bit (or 32-bit including an alpha channel), high-resolution source images saved without compression in PNG-24, PICT, or TIFF format, you have two workflow options:

✦ **Set JPEG compression in Bitmap Properties dialog box:** If you want to control the compression applied to each imported image individually, clear the Use document default quality check box in the Bitmap Properties dialog box and choose a JPEG compression (Quality) setting that achieves the best balance of image quality and file size for each imported image in your Library. This approach gives you the option of applying more compression to some images than to others.

✦ **Set JPEG compression in Publish Settings dialog box:** If your source images have similar color and content, as well as consistent resolution, you may find it more efficient to use the compression settings in the Publish Settings dialog box to apply the same JPEG compression to all of your images. This makes it faster to test different compression settings on all the images in your project at once. If this is the workflow that you choose, make sure that the Use document default quality check box is selected in the Bitmap Properties dialog box for each imported image—this ensures that the Quality settings in the Publish Settings dialog box will be applied when the Flash movie (.swf) is published.

The main benefit to importing uncompressed source files is that you will not be tied to a specific resolution and thus will maintain the option of changing compression settings at any time in the development process. The main drawback is that your project files (.fla) will be much larger, and each time you test your movie (.swf), you will have to wait for Flash to apply JPEG compression on the images. This might not seem important at first, but the cumulative time loss over the course of developing a project does add up.

Tip

As we mentioned previously, it can be helpful to work with lower resolution place-holder images as you develop a project. You can use the Import option in the Bitmap Properties dialog box to load your high-resolution images in the final stages of the project.

The image formats PNG-24, PICT, and TIFF also support alpha channels when they're saved with 32-bit color. Alpha channels enable the import of complex masks that might otherwise be difficult to create in Flash. You may be surprised to see that even after you apply Flash JPEG compression to an imported PNG, PICT, or TIFF image, the transparency is maintained. You might say that Flash lets you have your alpha and eats the file size, too.

Cross-Reference

The process for creating alpha channels in PICT and TIFF files is slightly different from that used for PNG files. For more information on creating alpha channels in source bitmaps, refer to Chapter 36, "Working with Raster Graphics," on the CD-ROM.

Caution

Although Macromedia Fireworks files are saved with the .png file extension, the options for importing Fireworks PNG files are different from those for importing PNG files saved from Photoshop or other image-editing programs. For more information about importing Fireworks PNG files, refer to the section "Importing Vector Artwork" later in this chapter.

8-bit lossless source files

Source files in 8-bit formats are restricted to 256 (or fewer) colors and are optimized to a file size that is Web-friendly. These files are usually saved in GIF or PNG-8 format and are best suited for graphics that have simple shapes and limited colors, such as logos or line drawings. PNG-8 and GIF files can still support an alpha channel, but unlike 24-bit images, you will not want to apply any JPEG compression to these files when they're brought into Flash.

Caution

To avoid display problems, when exporting GIF files with transparency for use in Flash, the index color and the transparency color should be set to the same RGB values. If these settings are not correct, transparent areas in the imported GIF may display as solid colors in Flash. For more information on this issue, refer to the Macromedia TechNote on Transparency support in Flash at www.macromedia.com/support/flash/ts/documents/transparent_bitmaps.htm.

Applying JPEG compression to 8-bit files generally results in larger files and degraded image quality (refer to Figure 16-7). To preserve the clean graphic quality of 8-bit images, follow these steps:

1. In the Bitmap Properties dialog box, make sure that Lossless (PNG/GIF) compression is selected.

   This is the default for imported 8-bit images, but it never hurts to double-check to ensure that it hasn't been changed by mistake.

2. Decide whether to leave the default setting for Allow smoothing in Bitmap Properties.

   The image will have sharper edges if this option is unchecked, so it is best to make a decision on this setting depending on whether you prefer smoothed edges when the image is scaled larger.

Remember that the JPEG Quality specified in Publish Settings will not apply to imported images that have been set to Lossless compression in the Bitmap Properties dialog box.

Source files with lossy compression

Although JPEG is the native bitmap compression format in Flash, you may want to use an alternative application for optimal JPEG compression on images. In our experience, JPEG compression from Macromedia Fireworks often produces smaller file sizes and more consistent image quality than JPEG compression applied in Flash. If you have created an optimized Web-ready JPEG using your preferred lossy compression method or a client has delivered source files in JPEG format, you will want to avoid adding additional compression to these images when importing to Flash.

Note   JPEG images saved with the option for progressive download selected could not use imported JPEG data when brought into Flash prior to Flash MX 2004. Flash MX 2004 and Flash 8 give you the option to use imported JPEG data for JPEG images saved with or without the progressive download option.

If you find that a JPEG file size is not reduced enough to fit the parameters of a particular project, it is better to go back to the uncompressed source file to redo the JPEG compression than it is to apply additional compression in Flash. As in all media production, double JPEGing images in Flash produces diminishing returns — by the time you get the file down to a size that you want, it has so many compression artifacts that it is generally unusable. By going back to the uncompressed source file and adjusting your compression settings to produce a new JPEG file, you end up with a cleaner image and a smaller file size than you would by compounding the JPEG compression in Flash.

For optimal results when importing JPEG images to Flash projects, the main settings to consider are the Use imported JPEG data and the Allow Smoothing check boxes in the Bitmap Properties dialog box.

✦ To maintain the original JPEG compression of your imported image, simply select the check box to Use imported JPEG data from the Bitmap Properties dialog box. When this check box is selected, the original compression will be preserved and the JPEG Quality specified in Publish Settings will not be added to your imported JPEG image.

✦ Smoothing is only advised if you will be scaling the JPEG image in Flash and you want to minimize the jagged edges with anti-aliasing. The compromise of Smoothing is that the image will also appear slightly blurred — this may or may not be desirable depending on the detail in the original image.

Although you can clear the Use imported JPEG data check box and choose a setting in the Quality field, remember that this compression will be added to the compression on the original image and will cause inferior results.

Converting Rasters to Vectors

Have you ever wanted to take a scan of a "real" pen-and-ink drawing that you made and turn it into a vector graphic? It's not incredibly hard to do, and the results are usually pretty close to the original (see Figure 16-11). You can also turn continuous tone or photographic images into vector art, but the converted version will not likely bear much resemblance to the original. However, this can be useful for aesthetic effects.

Figure 16-11: Compare the raster version (left) of the sketch to its traced vector version (right).

As we described in Chapter 9, "Modifying Graphics," bitmap images can be traced in Flash to convert them to vector shapes. Figure 16-3 illustrated why this is not recommended for complex photographic images — the file size will be huge and the image quality will not be as satisfactory as the original bitmap. However, converting rasters to vectors allows you to create some unique visual effects in Flash. After an image has been traced, you can use any of the Flash tools available for shapes, including the Distort and Envelop options of the Free Transform tool. You can also select parts of the image individually to modify colors, or even add custom gradient or bitmap fills.

The Trace bitmap command is different from using the Break apart command on a bitmap. When an image is broken apart, it is perceived by Flash as areas of color that can be modified or sampled for use as a fill in other shapes. Break apart actually duplicates the automatic conversion handled by the Mixer panel to show bitmaps from the Library in the bitmap fill menu. Although you can modify images that are broken apart with the drawing and painting tools, you cannot select individual parts of the image with the Selection tool or apply the Optimization command, Smooth/Straighten options, or Distort and Envelop modifiers as you can with a traced vector image.

To apply Trace bitmap, select a bitmap image that has been imported to Flash (ideally with lossless compression and no Smoothing) and placed on the Stage; then choose Modify ➪ Bitmap ➪ Trace Bitmap from the application menu to invoke the Trace Bitmap dialog box, as shown in Figure 16-12.

Figure 16-12: Use the Trace Bitmap dialog box to select settings for converting a raster image into vector shapes.

We detail the settings for the Trace bitmap command in Chapter 9, but the default settings can be a good place to start. Higher Color Threshold and Minimum Area values reduce the complexity of the resulting Flash artwork, which means smaller file sizes. This process is most effective when applied to simple images with strong contrast. In these cases, tracing a bitmap graphic can actually reduce the file size and improve the appearance of the scaled image. The settings shown in Figure 16-12 were used to trace the GIF image shown in Figure 16-13. When viewed at a scale of 200 percent, the difference in image quality can clearly be seen, and this difference will be exaggerated the more the images are scaled — the vector image will remain smooth, while the bitmap image will break apart and look increasingly jagged.

Tip   The traced vector lines and fills created from an imported bitmap are not always exact, but you can use the Smooth and Straighten modifiers or any of the other drawing tools to "touch up" the artwork.

Figure 16-13: Images with simple shapes and limited colors will be more scalable when converted from bitmap (left) to vector art (right) using the Trace bitmap command.

In order to get the best results from using Trace bitmap, we advise reducing the number of colors in the original image before importing it to Flash. Figure 16-14 shows an imported image that was converted to indexed color and reduced to ten colors in Photoshop before saving as a GIF image for import to Flash. After the image is traced, you can simplify the shapes further by applying the Optimize command (Modify ⇨ Shape ⇨ Optimize), which simplifies the image and reduces the final file size. You can also use any of the drawing tools to further modify the image.

Figure 16-14: A reduced-color GIF image (left) can be traced and then simplified using the Optimize command and Eraser tool in Flash (right).

Using External Vector Graphics

All artwork drawn in Flash is vector-based; however, not all vector graphics are created the same. As shown in Table 16-1, Flash offers robust support for external vector formats, including Macromedia FreeHand and Adobe Illustrator. Some vector graphics may be simple objects and fills, whereas others may include complex blending or paths that add significant weight to a Flash movie. Although most vector graphics are by nature much smaller than raster graphic equivalents, don't assume that they're optimized for Flash use.

Importing vector graphics from other applications is fairly simple and straightforward. However, because most vector graphics applications are geared for print production (for example, publishing documents intended for press), you need to keep some principles in mind when creating artwork for Flash in external graphics applications:

✦ **Limit or reduce the number of points describing complex paths.**

✦ **Limit the number of embedded typefaces (or fonts).** Multiple fonts add to the final movie's (.swf) file size. As we describe later in this chapter, converting fonts to outlines is one way to avoid adding extra fonts to your Flash file.

✦ **To ensure color consistency between applications, use only RGB colors (and color pickers) for artwork.** Flash can only use RGB color values, and automatically converts any CMYK colors to RGB colors when artwork is imported. Color conversions can produce unwanted color shifts.

Note

When Flash imports a vector file with any placed grayscale images, the images will be converted to RGB color, which will also increase the file size.

✦ **Unless you're using Macromedia FreeHand or Fireworks, you may need to replace externally created gradients with Flash gradients, or accept the file size addition to the Flash movie.** Gradients created in other drawing applications are not converted to editable Flash gradients when the file is imported; instead they will be rendered as complex banded graphics with clipping paths or as rasterized, bitmap images.

✦ **Preserve layers where possible to help keep imported artwork organized.** Some vector formats use layers, and Flash can recognize these layers if the graphic file format is correctly specified. Layers keep graphic elements separate from one another and can make it easier to organize items for use in animation.

✦ **If the artwork you are importing includes large areas of solid color, such as a plain background, consider excluding those parts of the graphic from import.** They can easily be replaced in Flash after the more complex parts of the artwork are brought in.

Importing Vector Artwork

Vector graphics from other applications can be imported into Flash with relative ease using the Import to Stage or Import to Library command. Browse for files using the All Files or All PostScript setting to make most vector file formats selectable. Vector files in most formats, including EPS, PDF, and AI, will invoke the standard Import Options dialog box (shown in Figure 16-15). Use the settings to control how your file will be handled in the Flash authoring environment. As long as you do *not* choose Rasterize everything, vector graphics are generally imported as groups, and can be edited just like a normal group drawn in Flash.

Note   Flash MX 2004 and Flash 8 support import of PDF and EPS files created with Adobe Illustrator. With PDF files, you have the option to preserve layers and to convert multipage documents into Flash scenes or keyframes. Both the PDF and EPS formats are included in the All PostScript file import option.

Figure 16-15: The Import Options dialog box used for setting conversion options for most imported graphics files

Vector artwork will only be saved in the Library on import if it includes clipping paths or gradients that cannot be converted to editable Flash fills. In these cases, Flash automatically adds a folder of nested Graphic symbols with masks or bitmap symbols to the Library to preserve the appearance of elements that cannot be converted to Drawing Objects or simple grouped shapes.

Caution   Adobe Illustrator 6.0 is the only version that can be imported to Flash in AI format with placed bitmap images. If you are importing Adobe Illustrator layouts with placed bitmap images and you also need to preserve editable text and vector graphics, the best option is to save the layout as an Adobe PDF file before importing it to Flash. Although EPS files will import to Flash with placed bitmaps and editable text, you will not be able to preserve layers, and placed bitmaps will be converted to nested PNG files with layer masks.

You can also copy and paste or even drag and drop artwork from external applications, but this gives you less control over how the vector information will be translated in Flash — for example, transparency or special fill types may be lost and any layers will be flattened into the currently selected Flash layer.

Because generic numbered layer names, such as Layer 1, may be redundant with layers already present in your Flash document, it is helpful to give layers meaningful names in the original file before importing to Flash. To avoid unexpected color shifts, it is recommended that you convert your color space to RGB in any external application before saving files that will be imported to Flash.

Caution   You must specify Illustrator 7 or higher in the Adobe Illustrator document options when saving AI files to ensure color consistency for artwork imported to Flash. If you choose Illustrator 6 or lower format, then RGB values will not be saved and color shifts may result. When saving EPS files from Illustrator for import to Flash, be sure to *deselect* the CMYK PostScript option to avoid color shifts when the file is converted to RGB on import to Flash.

To import a vector file to Flash, simply follow these steps:

1. To import a file to the Stage of your Flash document, make sure that you have an empty, unlocked layer selected, and choose File ➪ Import ➪ Import to Stage.

2. In the Import dialog box, choose a file format to browse using the Files of Type (Win) or Show (Mac) menu.

Note   EPS files saved from FreeHand will not be selectable in the file list with Show: FreeHand. Use Show: All PostScript or Show: All Files to import EPS files from most applications.

3. Find the vector file that you wish to import and select it from the file list. Then choose Import.

4. If the application you are importing from includes options for how the artwork will be placed in Flash, you will be prompted to make choices from the Import Options dialog box.

   Depending on your options, the artwork will be imported to a single layer or to multiple layers or keyframes in your Flash document after you click OK.

Note   If you choose to rasterize the vector artwork into a bitmap image when importing to Flash, remember to apply JPEG compression using the Quality setting in the Bitmap Properties dialog box, or if the Use document default quality check box is selected, set JPEG Quality in the Publish Settings dialog box before exporting your Flash movie (.swf).

5. To edit the imported graphic with Flash shape tools, ungroup the elements (Shift+Ctrl+G or Shift+⌘+G) or double-click parts of the group or Drawing Object until you are able to select strokes and fills in Edit in place mode.

Tip   Double-clicking a grouped item or Drawing Object takes you into Edit in place mode, but if the item is in a compound group, you may have to continue double-clicking through the nested elements until you are able to isolate the stroke and fill of one part of the group for modification.

6. To store elements in the Library so they are reusable, convert them to Graphic symbols or Movie Clip symbols.

Tip   If you have imported a layered sequence into multiple Flash keyframes, consider cutting and pasting the frames into a new Movie Clip symbol to keep the Main Timeline uncluttered.

Although you can scale, move, or rotate the grouped elements, to modify individual parts of the graphic you must either ungroup the elements or go into Edit mode until you are able to select the strokes and fills of a particular element.

New Feature   Where possible, imported graphics are interpolated as Flash 8 Drawing Objects. This makes it easier to edit stroke and fill properties without having to ungroup or click into Edit mode.

Any small inconsistencies in fill style are easy to fix once the elements are ungrouped in Flash. Remember that you can delete fills, add strokes, scale, or otherwise modify the imported artwork with any of the Flash tools.

To make the artwork efficient to reuse and update, it is best to convert the whole graphic into a symbol. If you intend to animate parts of the graphic individually, then convert these into discrete symbols and place them on separate layers.

Cross-Reference   For more information on working with Drawing Objects and grouped artwork in Flash, refer to Chapter 9, "Modifying Graphics." For more information on using symbols, refer to Chapter 6, "Symbols, Instances, and the Library."

Tip   If you use a program such as Macromedia FreeHand that enables you to define Flash-compatible symbols and layers in your graphic files, you can save some time when the file is imported to Flash.

Here's how to use the Clipboard to import a vector image into Flash:

1. Select all vector elements that you wish to include.

2. Copy the selected items from your vector drawing application to the Clipboard.

   Most programs support Ctrl+C or ⌘+C.

3. Return to Flash and make sure that you have an active, unlocked layer that you can paste the vectors into. This can be on the Main Timeline or on any symbol Timeline.

4. Paste the graphics onto the Stage by choosing Edit ➪ Paste in Center from the menu (Ctrl+V or ⌘+V).

5. You may want to group or move parts of the pasted graphic onto new layers in your Flash document for better organization and for animation.

Importing Macromedia Fireworks files

Macromedia Fireworks offers one of the most flexible file formats for import into Flash. Fireworks PNG files can contain bitmap and vector artwork, as well as text, layers, guides, and even frames. Fireworks PNG files can be imported into Flash as either flattened images or as editable objects, with various options for handling the contents of the file. When importing images exported from Fireworks into Flash, you will be prompted by the Fireworks PNG Import Settings dialog box (shown in Figure 16-16) to make selections for the following import options:

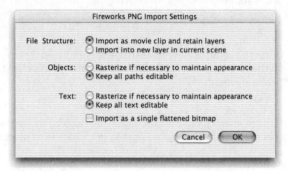

Figure 16-16: Use this special import dialog box to choose conversion settings for Fireworks PNG files.

New Feature   Flash 8 can now support many Fireworks effects and blends. If an effect is supported in Flash, it will be preserved as an editable Flash filter. If an effect is too complex for Flash to preserve, the image can be rasterized to preserve the appearance of the image, but the effect will not be editable in the Flash authoring environment.

✦ To import the PNG as one rasterized image to the current layer or to the Library, select Import as single flattened bitmap. When this option is selected, all other options will be unavailable. If you choose this option, you may want to apply Flash JPEG compression to the bitmap image either in Bitmap Properties or in Publish Settings. To edit a flattened image, you can launch Fireworks from inside Flash and edit the original PNG file (including any vector data or text).

✦ To import more complex files, select one of the following File Structures:

   • Import as movie clip and retain layers to import the PNG file to a new Movie Clip timeline with all frames and layers intact inside a Movie Clip symbol.

   • Import into new layer in current scene to import the PNG file into a single new layer in the current Flash document at the top of the stacking order. All Fireworks layers will be flattened, but not rasterized unless specified, and any frames in the Fireworks file will be included on the new layer.

✦ For Objects, select either Rasterize if necessary to maintain appearance to rasterize Fireworks fills, strokes, and effects in Flash as part of a bitmap image, or select Keep all paths editable to preserve vector paths in Flash. Some Fireworks fills, strokes, and effects may be lost on import.

✦ For Text, you can select the same options as those listed for Objects.

As with most files created in external applications, you will find that rasterized and flattened Fireworks vector artwork and text will import more consistently to Flash, but you also lose all the benefits of having editable vector art and text. Although the option for launching Fireworks at any time to edit the original PNG file does make rasterized Fireworks images less limiting than other bitmaps, it is usually worth the little extra time you might need to spend simplifying your artwork to get it to import to Flash with vectors and editable text intact. Any special fills or textures that have been applied to your text in Fireworks will be lost if you choose to preserve editable text on import to Flash.

Note While gradients imported from FreeHand are converted to raw Flash shapes with gradient fills, gradients imported from Fireworks are converted to Movie Clip symbols that will appear in the Library in a folder labeled `Fireworks Objects`—it is still possible to edit the gradient fill just by opening the symbol in Edit mode (or double-clicking the symbol instance).

Caution If you import a Fireworks PNG file by cutting and pasting into Flash, all vector elements will be rasterized into a flattened bitmap image.

Importing Macromedia FreeHand files

FreeHand is one of the most compatible applications for transferring vector artwork into Flash. When importing FreeHand files, you can preserve library symbols and pages in addition to layers and text blocks. You may also choose a specific page range to import. Figure 16-17 shows the options available from the FreeHand Import dialog box, which is invoked when importing files with the FreeHand extension (.fh) into Flash. Although FreeHand can export a variety of file formats, including SWF and EPS, the native FH format will give you the most editing options for files imported to Flash.

Cross-Reference For more information on working with FreeHand files, refer to Chapter 37, "Working with Vector Graphics," on this book's CD-ROM. You will also find some sample FreeHand files in the `ch37` folder on the CD-ROM.

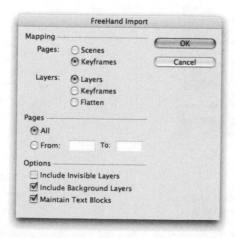

Figure 16-17: The FreeHand Import dialog box is used to specify how the vector file will be handled when placed into Flash.

Remember to convert your FreeHand file to RGB color mode. If the file is in CMYK, it will be converted automatically on import to Flash and this may cause unexpected color shifts. There are some other special considerations when importing FreeHand artwork. To ensure seamless translation of FreeHand elements imported into Flash, observe the following guidelines:

✦ Any placed grayscale elements in FreeHand will be converted to RBG color when imported to Flash, which may increase file size.

✦ EPS files placed in FreeHand will not be viewable when imported to Flash, unless you select the Convert Editable EPS when Imported option in FreeHand Import Preferences before you place an EPS into FreeHand. Regardless of the settings used, Flash will not display information for any placed EPS imported from FreeHand.

✦ Strokes with square caps will be converted into rounded caps in Flash—you can convert them back into square caps using the new Flash 8 Cap style menu in the Property inspector.

✦ Be cautious with compound shapes: When importing overlapping elements that you want to keep intact in Flash, place them on separate layers in FreeHand and import the layers into Flash. If items on a single layer are overlapping when imported, they will be divided or merged at intersection points in the same way as primitive shapes created in Flash.

✦ Flash now supports up to 16 colors in an imported gradient fill. If a gradient created in FreeHand contains more than 16 colors or special styles (such as contour), Flash uses clipping paths to interpret the gradient. Clipping paths increase file size. To work around this issue, use gradients that contain 16 or fewer colors and use standard gradient styles in FreeHand or replace the imported gradient with a Flash gradient fill as described later in this chapter.

✦ Imported FreeHand blends also increase Flash file size because Flash interprets each step in a blend as a separate path.

As shown in Figure 16-18, Flash recognizes text and gradient fills imported from FreeHand and Fireworks, making it easy to edit these elements directly in Flash.

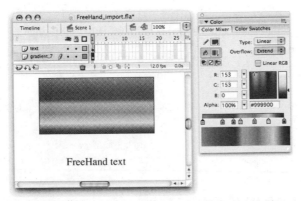

Figure 16-18: You can edit FreeHand and Fireworks files directly in Flash, but you still need to convert shapes and text elements into symbols to store in the Library for reuse.

Tip

Remember that gradients created in Macromedia FreeHand or Adobe Illustrator can be directly exported to SWF format as Flash gradients. However, if the gradient contains more than 16 colors or uses special alignment (such as contour gradients), Flash adds clipping paths when it is imported. Also, remember that FreeHand blends will always be interpreted by Flash as a series of paths, which can increase file size and sometimes add banding to the blend.

Animating Imported Vector Graphics

A handy feature of many popular illustration programs is support for layers. Just like layers in a Flash document (.fla), layers in illustration programs enable you to keep individual groups of graphics separate from one another. A simple technique with animating vector graphic files is to animate or tween each layer separately in the Flash authoring environment.

An example of an easily converted illustration movie is a logo. If you have created artwork in FreeHand or Illustrator and have kept the elements separated by layers, then you can quickly create an interactive Flash graphic.

On the CD-ROM

For this exercise, you can use the sample logo, `daisyLogo.ai` or `daisyLogo.pdf`, in the `ch16` folder of the CD-ROM. If you use the example file, start at Step 4.

1. Create a layered graphic in FreeHand or Illustrator.

   Before each part of the element is created, make a new named layer for it.

2. If you use extensive text controls (such as kerning, leading, tracking, and so on), then convert the text to outlines (or paths).

3. Save the layout. Flash MX 2004 and Flash 8 support direct import of Adobe PDF files, in addition to Illustrator or FreeHand files.

Caution

CMYK colors shift when imported into the RGB color space of Flash. Moreover, some masking and cropping information (for bleeds) may not be interpreted correctly by Flash. To see the color difference between CMYK import and RGB import for the logo used in this example, refer to the color insert.

4. Import the file into Flash, being certain to select the option to preserve your artwork in layers and vector format.

   You may want to create a new scene or symbol to contain the imported graphic(s). Otherwise, the layers from the imported file will be stacked with your current layers (as shown in Figure 16-19).

On the CD-ROM

The roughly grouped artwork and preserved layers of the original logo file imported to Flash (shown in Figure 16-19) can be viewed by opening `daisy_AI_import.fla`, located in the `ch16` folder of the CD-ROM.

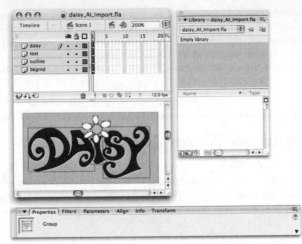

Figure 16-19: Layered vector graphic imported as grouped artwork in Flash layers on the Main Timeline

5. You may convert the layered elements into symbols for reuse or easier modification later.

    You will need to make button symbols for any element that you want to use interactively (such as the flower animation triggered by the mouse). Repeat this step for every layer.

6. Now add any Flash tweens or actions to the groups or symbols in each layer.

    At this point, you could continue creating a full Flash project with other components, or export a Flash movie (.swf). The project Timeline for the finished animated example on the CD-ROM is shown in Figure 16-20.

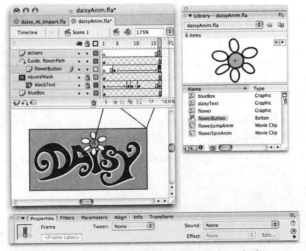

Figure 16-20: Imported artwork converted to Flash symbols and tweened to create an animated logo

As you can see, in just a few straightforward steps, you can create an animated logo and turn many other translations of vector graphics into interactive presentations that can be included in other projects or in e-mail. Whenever you're developing complicated layered work in an illustration application such as FreeHand or Illustrator, you can take advantage of those layers in Flash.

On the CD-ROM

Check out the completed interactive logo, `daisyAnim.fla or daisyAnim.swf`, located in the `ch16` folder of the CD-ROM.

Optimizing Vectors

All vector graphics are made up of paths in one shape or another. A path can be as simple as a straight line with two points, a curved line with two points, or 500 or more points along an irregular shape or fill. For this reason, vector graphics are best suited for graphic images such as logos, architectural drawings, and clip art that do not include continuous tones. Fonts are also made up of paths. As you've seen with Flash-drawn graphics, you can scale them to any size without any loss of resolution, unlike raster (bitmap) artwork, which cannot scale larger than its original size without loss of resolution.

Note

Vector graphics are eventually *rasterized,* so to speak. The vector formatting for drawn shapes and text is more of a simplified storage structure that contains a mathematical description (that is, smaller than a bit-for-bit description) of an object or set of objects. When the vector graphic is displayed, especially with anti-aliasing, the video card needs to render the edges in pixels. Likewise, the PostScript RIP (Raster Image Processor) of a laser printer needs to convert the vector information, or an EPS (Encapsulated PostScript) file, into printer "dots."

When you use imported vector graphics in Flash movies, you should minimize the number of points describing curved lines or intricate outlined graphics (for example, "traced" raster images). The problem with creating cool graphics in vector-based applications such as Illustrator, FreeHand, and 3D Studio Max is the large number of points used to describe lines. When these graphics are imported into Flash, animations are slower and harder to redraw (or refresh) on the computer screen. In addition, the file size of the Flash movie grows considerably. Most vector applications include features that will enable you to optimize or simplify artwork before importing it to Flash.

Cross-Reference

For tips on optimizing vector artwork in other applications, including Adobe Illustrator, Streamline, and Macromedia FreeHand, as well as coverage of export options, refer to Chapter 37, "Working with Vector Graphics," on this book's CD-ROM.

There are also a number of ways that you can simplify artwork after it has been imported to Flash. We have discussed many of these Flash features in previous chapters, but we will briefly summarize them here.

Tracing complex vector artwork

Many graphics programs, such as Discreet 3D Studio Max and Adobe Dimensions, can create some astonishing vector-based graphics. However, when you import vector versions of those graphics into Flash, they either fall apart (display horribly) or add unrealistic byte chunks to your Flash movie. But this doesn't mean that you can't use these intricate graphics in your Flash movies. You can try several different procedures with intricate vector artwork, including smoothing, as described previously, to make complex graphics more Flash-friendly.

Depending on the specific use of the artwork, you may also be able to output small raster equivalents that won't consume nearly as much space as highly detailed vector graphics. However, in some instances, the best solution is a bit more labor-intensive. To get just the right "translation" of a complex vector graphic in your Flash movie, you may need to try redrawing the artwork in Flash. Sound crazy and time-consuming? Well, it's a bit of both, but some Flash designers spend hour after hour getting incredibly small file sizes from "hand-tracing" vector designs in Flash.

For example, if you made a highly detailed technical drawing of a light bulb, and wanted to bring it into Flash, you could import the original version of the drawing into Flash, place it on a locked Guide layer, and use Flash drawing tools to re-create a stylized sketch version of the object (see Figure 16-21).

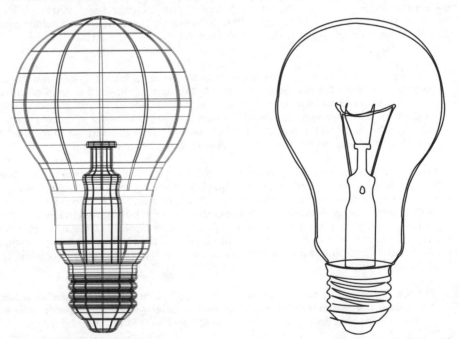

Figure 16-21: Compare the original imported vector artwork of the light bulb (left) with the stylized version drawn in Flash (right).

Tip   Many other Flash SWF tools can help to speed up the work of optimizing vector artwork—for example, Electric Rain's Swift 3D can simplify 3D models and output .swf files. The art and science of creating 3D Flash graphics is a complex topic that is beyond the scope of this book. If this is an area that you would like to learn more about, we suggest you refer to *The Flash MX 3D Graphics Bible* by Matthew David (Wiley, 2003).

Converting text to outlines

Another aspect of vector graphics that you need to keep in mind—especially when working with other designers—is font linking and embedding. With most vector file formats, such as Illustrator, FreeHand, or EPS, you can link to fonts that are located on your system. However, if you give those files to someone who doesn't have those fonts installed, then he won't be able to see or use the fonts. Some formats enable you to embed fonts into the document file, which circumvents this problem. However, whether the fonts are linked or embedded, you may be unnecessarily bloating the size of the vector graphic.

You can break apart imported text in Flash by using the Modify ➪ Break apart command (Ctrl+B or ⌘+B). You have to first break the text into letters and then break them apart a second time to get basic shapes.

You can also convert any text into outlines (or *paths*) in most drawing or illustration programs (see Figure 16-22). In Macromedia FreeHand, select the text as a text block (with the Selection tool, not the Text tool) and choose Text ➪ Convert to Paths. In Adobe Illustrator, select the text as an object and choose Type ➪ Create Outlines.

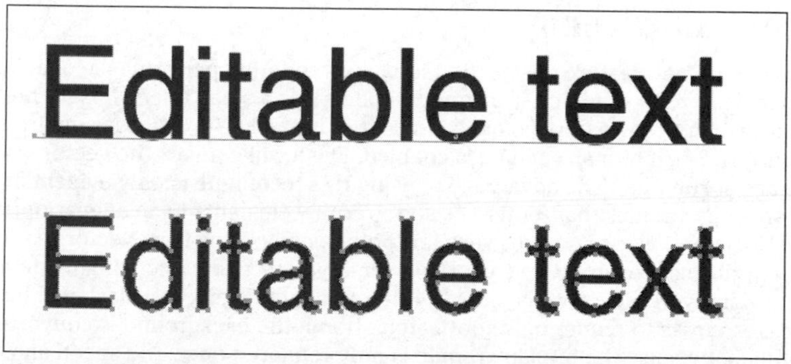

Editable text

Editable text

Figure 16-22: Make sure that you have finished editing your text before converting it into outlines. The text at the top can be edited, whereas the text at the bottom can only be modified as individual shapes.

If you have a lot of body text in the graphic, you may want to copy the text directly into a Flash text box and use a _sans, _serif, or other device font. These fonts do not require additional file information (as embedded fonts do) when used in a Flash movie.

Optimizing curves

You can also reduce the complexity of paths within Flash by using the Modify ➪ Shape ➪ Optimize command. This has the same effect as the Simplify command in FreeHand, with a couple of extra options. When working with bitmaps or symbols, be sure to use the Modify ➪ Break apart command, and if you are working with a group, ungroup it (Modify ➪ Ungroup) before you use the Optimize command (Alt+Shift+Ctrl+C or Option+Shift+⌘+C) — you can't optimize groups or symbols. The Optimize Curves dialog box enables you to specify multiple passes, which means that Flash will optimize the graphic at a given setting as much as it possibly can. Figure 16-23 shows the effect of maximum smoothing on a complex seashell graphic.

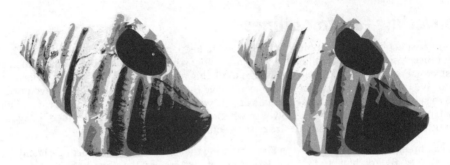

Figure 16-23: A complex vector graphic simplified with maximum smoothing

Cross-Reference   For a more detailed description of the Optimize curves options, refer to Chapter 5, "Drawing in Flash."

Runtime Bitmap caching

Flash 8 includes a brand-new feature designed to improve rendering performance of animation that uses complex vector graphics. This option appears as a small check box in the Property inspector when a Movie Clip instance is selected in the Flash authoring environment (as shown in Figure 16-24). If bitmap caching is enabled, Flash will convert the vector graphic into a bitmap image at run time. The advantage of using this technique is only evident as you start to build more complex files that require Flash to redraw elements in an animation. If your vector artwork is optimized and uses very few points, converting from vector to bitmap will not offer any performance improvements. However, if you have created a highly detailed vector background that you will use to layer with other animated elements, Flash will be able to dedicate more resources to rendering smooth animation if the background is converted into a cached bitmap. Because the bitmap graphic is only rendered once, the speed and smoothness of your animation will not be hindered by Flash having to constantly redraw the points and lines that make up your vector background. These same principles apply if you are using a very complex vector graphic that is motionless but modified with Filter effects. Bitmap caching makes it possible for Flash to convert the complex vectors into a simpler pixel surface while it dedicates resources to rendering the Filter transformations.

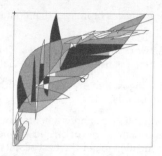

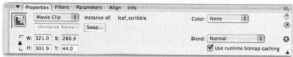

Figure 16-24: Bitmap caching can be enabled in the Property inspector when a Movie Clip or Button symbol is selected in the authoring environment.

There are a few limitations to bitmap caching that you should keep in mind:

✦ Bitmap caching uses significantly more memory than rendering vectors. Use bitmap caching only when it will noticeably improve the performance (smoothness) of your animation.

✦ If your animation requires a tight zoom on vector content, it will look pixilated if the cache as bitmap option is enabled for that item.

✦ Bitmap caching will fail if it is applied to a symbol that is larger than 2,880 pixels tall or wide.

✦ If the graphic with bitmap caching enabled is nested inside of another symbol that is rotated or scrolled, bitmap caching will be ignored for the nested graphic.

✦ If the Flash Player runs out of memory (producing an error), bitmap caching will be canceled.

Cross-Reference   Bitmap caching can also improve performance on applications with scrolling text fields or overlapping windows. For an example of using bitmap caching with a scrollable text field, refer to Chapter 30, "Applying HTML and Text Field Formatting."

Web Resource   We'd like to know what you think about this chapter. Visit www.flashsupport.com/ feedback to fill out an online form with your comments.

Summary

✦ Flash can use a variety of external media, which enables you to select the most effective format for various types of content.

✦ Bitmap smoothing has been greatly improved in Flash 8. Even rotated or scaled bitmaps will look smoother and less jagged on the edges than they would in previous versions of Flash.

✦ Bitmaps are best suited for photographic images or images that contain detailed shading and/or complex color blends.

✦ Bitmaps can be converted to vector artwork in a variety of ways. This process works best on simplified bitmap images or when it is used to create special image effects.

✦ Vector graphics are most often used for logos, line drawings, and other artwork that does not include complex patterns and blends.

✦ Flash supports the import of layers, editable text, and gradients from some graphics applications, including Macromedia FreeHand, Fireworks, and Adobe Illustrator. You will need to put some care into preparing files to get the best results, but being able to reuse your file structure and editable elements created in other applications can save you a lot of time.

✦ Flash 8 has more robust support for imported gradients and will preserve many Fireworks effects as editable filters in the Flash authoring environment.

✦ The new bitmap caching feature in Flash 8 can greatly improve playback performance in movies that use complex vector graphics as background elements or scrolling content.

✦ Most graphics applications include their own options for reducing the complexity of vector art. However, using Flash's various tools for optimizing vector artwork can also be an effective way to reduce your final file size.

✦   ✦   ✦

Displaying Video

One of the most exciting features introduced with Macromedia Flash Player 6 was the power to add digital video footage to a Flash movie file (.swf)! Designers and developers alike had long awaited this feature. With Flash Player 6 or higher, video can be played without relying upon additional browser or system plug-ins such as Apple QuickTime or Real Systems RealOne player. Flash Player 7 improved the capabilities and performance of video playback, enabling you to load .flv files directly into Flash movies at run time from a standard Web server, without the aid of Flash Communication Server. With Flash Player 8, you can take advantage of a new video codec, the On2 VP6 codec, which yields better compression (that is, smaller file size) with superior image quality to the Sorenson Spark codec used in Flash Player 6 and 7.

> **Note** You learn more about the new capabilities of the VP6 codec later in this chapter.

Macromedia has added more tools to make it easier for you to integrate video into your Flash movies. In this chapter, we show you how to perform a wide range of video procedures, from importing a source clip to playing the video clip within the FLVPlayback component.

> **Note** This chapter explores the Flash 8 Video Encoder, which is only available with Flash Professional 8. If you are using the trial version of Flash Basic 8, make sure you have switched it to Flash Pro 8 in the Help menu.

Integrating Video: The Solutions

In Flash 8, there are four ways in which you can deploy video content. In the following sections, we provide a high-level overview of these methods.

Loading a Flash Video file at run time

Starting with Flash Player 7-compatible movies, you can load Flash Video files (.flv) at run time. When we say "run time," we mean that you can create a separate Flash Video file (.flv), upload it to your Web server, and use ActionScript code or a component to load the video directly into your Flash movie (.swf) as it plays in the Web browser. You can create Flash Video files by:

✦ Importing a video file into a Flash document, and then exporting the Embedded Video symbol from the document's Library panel as a Flash Video file (.flv).

✦ Encoding a Flash Video file with the new Flash 8 Video Encoder application, which is enabled with Flash Professional 8.

✦ Exporting a Flash Video file (.flv) from a QuickTime-compatible application and the FLV QuickTime plug-in that is enabled with Flash Pro 8.

✦ Using a third-party video compression tool designed to export Flash Video files (.flv) such as Sorenson Squeeze or On2 Flix.

Real-time streaming a Flash Video file at run time

In the previous section, you learned that it's possible to load a Flash Video file directly into a Flash movie file (.swf) as it plays in a Web browser. However, when you use this type of loading, the Flash Video file is loaded and cached as any other asset accessed at run time. As such, if you have a large video file but only want to watch the last portion of the video, you'll have to wait until most of the video file has been downloaded.

One way you can offer your users the fastest access to Flash Video files (.flv) is to stream the video in real time with Macromedia Flash Communication Server or a Flash Video Streaming Service provider. With this server technology, a Flash Video file is only temporarily cached in the Flash Player's memory. You can more easily protect copyrighted material, and users can seek to any point in the video with minimal wait times.

Note   Macromedia Flash Communication Server is a specialty server product that works separately from a standard Web server. You can set up and install your own Flash Communication Server, or you can purchase hosting from companies such as MediaTemple or Influxis. The latest version of Flash Communication Server is now called Flash Media Server 2.

Web Resource   For a list of Flash Video Streaming Service providers, see the Flash Video Hosting Providers section at www.flashsupport.com/links.

Embedding video into a Flash movie

The third method that you can use to view video is to embed the video file in the Flash document file (.fla), where it is then published directly inside the Flash movie file (.swf). This method is compatible with Flash Player 6 or higher movies. Flash 8, in either the Basic or Pro edition, can encode your video with the Sorenson Spark or On2 VP6 codec (discussed later in this chapter). It's important to understand that these codecs don't require additional plug-ins for playback — the Web user needs only to have Flash Player 6 or higher (for Sorenson Spark) or Flash Player 8 (for On2 VP6) installed with his browser. Neither Spark nor VP6 use any system-level video codecs; the codecs are built into the Flash Player plug-in.

When you import a video clip as an Embedded Video object, the video is stored in the Library as a Flash Video file (.flv).

Tip

You can also use a third-party application to create a Flash movie file (.swf) with embedded video. These utilities can produce better quality video than the native encoder used by Flash 8.

Linking video with QuickTime Flash

When Flash 4 was released, QuickTime movies could be imported into the Flash authoring environment. There, you could animate and develop Flash content that interacted with the QuickTime movie. However, in Flash 4 and 5, you could only export QuickTime Flash movies (.mov) that required the Apple QuickTime 4 (or higher) Player to view. The QuickTime video files were linked to the Flash document (.fla file), which meant that the Flash document didn't store the actual video content. You can still use linked video files in Flash 8 to create QuickTime Flash movies.

Cross-Reference

You can learn more about QuickTime Flash movies by reading our online PDF archived version of Chapter 41, "Working with QuickTime," from the *Flash MX Bible* by Robert Reinhardt and Snow Dowd (Wiley, 2002). This chapter can be found online at www.flashsupport.com/archive.

Importing the Video

Digital video, as with other external media assets that Flash can import, is something that you need to create before working with it in a Flash document. In today's economic climate, you might not only be a Web designer or developer; you might also wear the part-time hat of a videographer. Be sure to read our coverage of video in Appendix D, "Digital Video Basics" (included as a PDF file on this book's CD-ROM), for a primer on shooting and producing better-looking video. The appendix also discusses the various video formats that you can import into Flash 8.

After you have created a video file in the desired import format, you're ready to prepare the video for use in a Flash movie. This section introduces you to the Sorenson Spark and On2 VP6 codec options available in Flash 8. In the latter half of this section, we walk you through the process of importing one of the sample files on this book's CD-ROM.

An overview of codec options

Flash Player 8 movies have the capability to use a new video codec, On2 VP6. This codec, created by On2 (www.on2.com) has been licensed by Macromedia to be used with Flash Player 8 distribution. This new codec features superior compression and image quality compared to the Sorenson Spark codec used in Flash Player 6 and 7.

Web Resource

You can view side-by-side comparisons of equivalent data rate Flash Video by visiting the Flash Video Comparison link at www.flashsupport.com/links. Compare the quality of a VP6-encoded video clip next to a Spark-encoded one.

The VP6 codec, however, doesn't come without a price. Playback of VP6-encoded files, first of all, requires Flash Player 8. This fact alone means that not everyone will be able to view content encoded with the codec. Flash Player 6 has been out for almost four years, while Flash Player 7 has been out for just over two years. Furthermore, VP6-encoded Flash Video files require twice as much CPU power and twice as much RAM (memory) to play compared to

Spark-encoded clips. Slower machines, such as Apple Power Macintosh G3 computers and Pentium II computers, may have trouble playing back VP6-encoded files.

Tip Make sure you test your Flash Video file's playback on a variety of machines, so that you accurately gauge your expectations for the target audience(s) of your Flash content.

If you're willing to sacrifice visual quality of your Flash Video content and want the security of appealing to a larger audience (that is, people who have either Flash Player 6 or 7 installed, but not Flash Player 8), you may want to encode your video content with the Sorenson Spark codec. The quality of Sorenson Spark encoding is not necessarily poor compared to other Web video codecs; however, the built-in encoder that ships with Macromedia Flash 8 tools can only encode video in the Basic edition of the codec; you'll need to use Sorenson Squeeze or another third-party utility to encode video with the higher quality Pro edition of the Sorenson Spark codec.

Note Flash Player 8 can only decode VP6 video content. If you're broadcasting live camera output from a Flash movie to a Flash Communication Server (or Flash Media Server) application, Flash Player 8 uses the Sorenson Spark codec for all live streams.

Video codecs can compress image data in two different ways — temporally and spatially. A temporal compression algorithm, or *interframe compressor*, compares the data between each frame and stores only the differences between the two. A spatial compression algorithm, also known as *intraframe compression*, compresses the data in each frame, just as the JPEG format compresses data in a still image. Most video codecs designed for Web playback, including Sorenson Spark and On2 VP6, do not use a lossless compression technique. Rather, some color and detail information is thrown out in an effort to minimize the amount of data saved with each frame. For example, if the original video source recorded a sunset with 80 shades of orange, the compressed version of the sunset may only include 50 or fewer shades of orange. You may have noticed the extremes of lossy compression in Web videos where a person's face is hardly distinguishable, looking more blocky than human.

Note Historically speaking, most new codecs developed in the last few years rely upon the ever-increasing computer processor speeds to efficiently decompress each frame of video on playback. For this reason, you may want to test video playback on a number of machines and devices that support your targeted Flash Player version and video decoding.

Sorenson Spark and On2 VP6 use interframe (temporal) compression, but they also use intraframe compression when making keyframes. (You will see how tricky keyframes can be in just a moment.) A keyframe in video footage is similar to a keyframe in a Flash timeline. A keyframe defines a moment in time where a significant change occurs. For example, if a section of video has three hard cuts from one scene to another to another, the compressed version of that video should have a keyframe at the start of each scene. A keyframe then becomes the reference for subsequent frames in the video. When the following frame(s) are compared to the keyframe, only the differences are remembered (or stored) in the video file. As soon as the scene changes beyond a certain percentage, a new keyframe is made in the video. If you use the Video Import wizard, video keyframes are created while the movie is being compressed (or imported) into a Flash 8 document.

Caution

Video keyframes are the reason you should be careful with special effects or video filter usage in transitions from scene to scene in your video production software. The more frequently your video changes from frame to frame, the more keyframes your video file needs. Keyframes take up more file size than interframes between the keyframes.

We also can't overstate the importance of understanding that the new On2 VP6 codec is very processor intensive and RAM hungry. Remember, a Flash Video clip using the On2 VP6 codec requires twice as much processing and memory as an equivalent Flash Video clip using the Sorenson Spark codec. In fact, Macromedia engineers have recommended not using the On2 VP6 codec for any video content with dimensions larger than 640 x 480. Specifically, the On2 VP6 codec uses an arithmetic entropy compression that retains more quality than Sorenson Spark but at the cost of complexity — Sorenson Spark uses a much simpler compression formula (called H.263), which is easier for computer processors to perform. Keeping video data rates below 1 Mbps is critical for any Flash Video clip using the VP6 codec. If you attempt to use larger data rates, the decompressing tasks for VP6-encoded clips will quickly overwhelm the computer processor. If you need to use video data rates higher than 1 Mbps, we recommend that you use Sorenson Spark for your Flash Video encoding. At such high data rates, the quality differences between Spark and VP6 are minimal.

Web Resource

You can learn more about arithmetic entropy compression at `http://en.wikipedia.org/wiki/Arithmetic_coding`.

Compressing video with Flash Basic 8

If you're using Flash Basic or Pro 8, you can import video source files by using the File ➪ Import ➪ Import Video command. However, the options available in the Import Video dialog box (also known as the Video Import wizard) are limited in Flash Basic 8. We discuss the extended options of Flash Pro 8 later in this chapter. First, we'll review the stages of video import. Later in this section, you can follow a step-by-step exercise that shows you how to compress a sample clip on this book's CD-ROM. You can follow along here to familiarize yourself with the process.

Note

If you want to use Flash Video in your Flash document, you must be using Flash Player 6 or higher as the targeted version in the Publish Settings (File ➪ Publish Settings). If you want to use the new On2 VP6 codec, you must target Flash Player 8.

Choosing a source clip: The Select Video screen

When you first select the Import Video option from the File ➪ Import menu in Flash Basic 8, you see the Select Video screen of the Import Video dialog box, as shown in Figure 17-1. On the Select Video screen, you can browse to a video source clip. To proceed to the next stage of import, click the Next button.

Note

On the Mac, all Next buttons within the Video Import wizard process are labeled as Continue buttons.

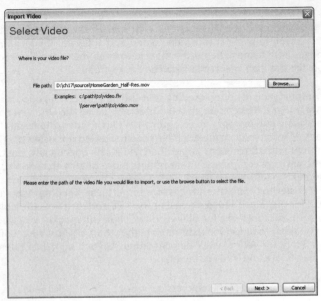

Figure 17-1: The Select Video screen

On the
CD-ROM   You can find several source clips in the ch17/source folder of this book's CD-ROM.

Picking a distribution method: The Deployment screen

After you have selected a source clip, you can choose how you want to include the video clip in your Flash movie. If you're using Flash Basic 8, you have at most two options (as shown in Figure 17-2):

✦ **Embed video in SWF and play in timeline:** This option is selected by default, and adds the encoded video clip to the current Flash document's Library panel. As the note on the right of the Deployment screen indicates, this option can substantially increase your final Flash movie (.swf) file size. Also, because the audio track of the compressed video clip will be within the Flash movie, you should make sure you match the encoder's frame rate to that of your Flash movie.

✦ **Linked QuickTime video for publishing to QuickTime:** This option enables you to import the video clip as a placeholder for a video track in a QuickTime Flash movie published by Flash 8. The final file deployed is still a QuickTime file, but you can use Flash 8 to create content on top of the QuickTime video. You must be importing a QuickTime .mov file into Flash 8 in order to select this option. Also, the Publish Settings of the current Flash document must be set to Flash Player 3, 4, or 5.

Cross-
Reference   You can learn more about QuickTime Flash movies by reading our online PDF archived version of Chapter 41, "Working with QuickTime," from the *Flash MX Bible* by Robert Reinhardt and Snow Dowd (Wiley, 2002). This chapter can be found online at www.flashsupport.com/archive.

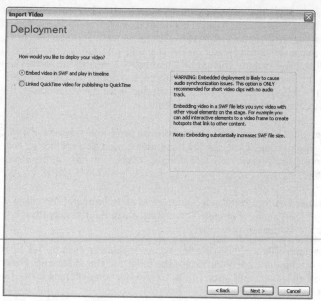

Figure 17-2: The Deployment screen

We discuss the extended deployment options of Flash Pro 8 later in this chapter. If you choose the Embed video in SWF and play in timeline option, the next screen in the process is the Embedding screen. If you choose the QuickTime option, the selected QuickTime video file is placed on the current timeline and the import session is over. Let's proceed to the Embedding screen. Click the Next button to proceed to the next stage of the import process.

Formatting the video content: The Embedding screen

At this stage of the import process, you determine how you want Flash 8 to place the encoded Flash Video content into the current document. On the Embedding screen (shown in Figure 17-3), you can choose from the following options:

✦ **Symbol type:** This menu lets you choose how you want the video content to be nested within the Flash document.

- **Embedded video:** This option simply places the Flash Video clip as an Embedded Video symbol in the Library panel.

- **Movie clip:** This option places the Flash Video clip inside of a Movie Clip symbol in the Library. Note that you still have a separate Embedded Video symbol of the Flash Video clip; this option saves you the step of creating a new Movie Clip symbol and placing the Embedded Video symbol onto its timeline.

- **Graphic symbol:** This option behaves identically to the Movie clip option, except that the video content is nested within a Graphic symbol in the Library panel.

✦ **Audio track:** This menu controls how the audio track (if it exists) of the video asset is handled. The default value, Integrated, keeps the audio track bound inside of the embedded video symbol after import. When you use this option, you control the compression of the audio track via the audio stream settings in the Flash tab of the Publish Settings dialog box (File ➪ Publish Settings). The Separate option tells Flash 8 to store the audio track as a separate Sound asset in the Library panel. If you use this option, you must physically place this Sound asset on the starting keyframe of the video layer in the Timeline window. (You can put the sound on another layer on the same timeline as well.) Be sure to set this sound to use a Stream sync, to ensure proper playback. If you choose None in the menu, the audio track is stripped from the video asset; the audio, then, is not imported into the Flash document.

Tip

If you use the Separate option for the Audio track, you can scrub the video track *and* the audio track in the Timeline window. If you use the Integrated option, you will not be able to scrub the audio track in the Timeline window. Not all video source formats have the Separate or None option available.

✦ **Place instance on stage:** This option, if selected, places an instance of the video clip on the current timeline of the Flash document. The instance will be of the symbol type selected in the menu we discussed previously.

✦ **Expand timeline if needed:** This option, if selected, adds more frames to the current timeline of the Flash document to accommodate the length of the video clip. For example, if the timeline had 10 frames and your clip is 100 frames long, 90 new frames would be added to the timeline.

✦ **Embed the entire video** or **Edit the video first:** These radio buttons determine the next stage of the import process. If you choose Embed the entire video, the next screen is the Encoding screen. If the Edit the video first option is selected, the Split Video screen is next.

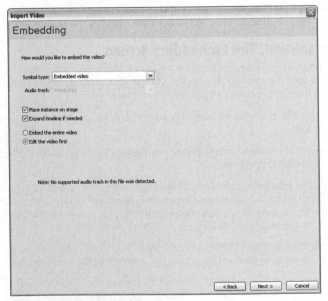

Figure 17-3: The Embedding screen

To show you all of the options of the video import process, let's choose the Edit the video first option and click the Next button.

Editing the video: The Split Video screen

You can specify multiple in and out points for a video file in the Split Video screen, shown in Figure 17-4.

Figure 17-4: The Editing screen of the video import process

Here, you can drag the in and out markers to specific sections of your video file. Click the plus (+) button to add a new segment to the editing list (on the left side of the wizard). You can click the text area of segment names in the editing list to rename the clips — these names translate to the names of the imported video symbols in the document's Library panel.

You can change the in and out points of a segment in the editing list by choosing the segment in the list, altering the in and/or out markers, and clicking the Update clip button.

Note   You cannot apply different compression profiles to individual clips. You can choose only one profile, which is applied to all clips.

When you're done making the edits, you can click the Next button to proceed to the Encoding screen.

Compressing the video: The Encoding screen

This stage is where you determine how you want to compress the original source clip into the Flash Video clip. In Flash 8's Encoding screen (shown in Figure 17-5), you can choose from seven presets as a starting point for your preferred compression options. If you're using Flash Basic 8, you can only modify the advanced settings for Flash 7 presets.

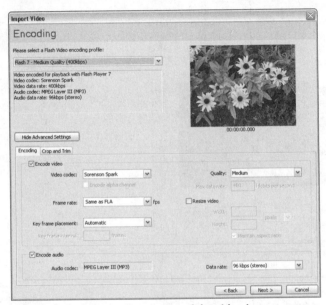

Figure 17-5: The Encoding screen of the video import process

The encoding profiles are listed in two groups, Flash (Player) 7 and Flash (Player) 8. The first four presets create Flash Video encoded with the Sorenson Spark codec and are compatible with Flash Player 6 and higher. The last three presets create Flash Video encoded with the new On2 VP6 codec and are only compatible with Flash Player 8. The presets for each group are ranked according to data rate, from lowest to highest.

If you're using Flash Basic 8, you can only use the advanced settings for the Flash 7 presets; the Flash 8 presets can not be changed. The advanced settings for the Sorenson Spark codec are shown in Figure 17-5. The Encoding tab has two areas:

✦ **Encode video:** This area displays all of the compression options related to the video channel of the video clip.

• **Video codec:** This menu selects the codec used for compression. Sorenson Spark is the only option available in the advanced settings if you're using Flash Basic 8. Note that you can still encode video with the On2 VP6 codec in Flash Basic 8 — simply select one of the Flash 8 presets in the profile menu.

Note   The Encode alpha channel option is only available in Flash Pro 8 when the On2 VP6 codec is selected. We discuss the alpha channel encoding capability of the On2 VP6 codec later in this chapter.

- **Frame rate:** This menu controls the encoded frame rate of the Flash Video clip. If you want the video to synchronize well with the other content in your Flash document, use the Same as FLA option, which encodes the Flash Video clip to the same frame rate as that shown in the Document Properties dialog box for the current Flash document. The Same as source option encodes the Flash Video clip with the same rate as your original video clip. You can also choose fixed frame rates, from 10 frames per second (very choppy) to 30 frames per second (very smooth).

- **Key frame placement:** This option determines how often keyframes within the Flash Video content are created. As we discussed earlier in the chapter, keyframes are needed to store differences between frames in the video clip. If you use the default value, Automatic, Flash 8 determines how often a keyframe should be generated. If you choose Custom, you can specify your own keyframe interval, in the text field below the menu. The lower the value you specify, the more frequently Flash 8 creates keyframes within the Flash Video clip. The higher the value, the less frequently Flash 8 creates keyframes. Be very careful with custom settings here — if your data rate isn't high enough to support the keyframe interval you specify, the overall image quality is sacrificed to maintain the keyframe interval.

- **Quality:** This menu controls the data rate used by the Flash Video clip. This setting, more than any other, influences the file size and image quality of the encoded clip. The Low preset uses a data rate of 150 Kbps, which is more bandwidth than a 56K dial-up modem can support. On the other end of the spectrum, the High preset uses a data rate of 700 Kbps, requiring a broadband Internet connection but yielding superior image quality for the video clip.

- **Resize video:** This option resizes the original dimensions of the source video clip. If selected, you can enter a new width and height for the encoded Flash Video clip. If you've captured high-resolution video footage from your DV camcorder (that is, source video with dimensions of 640 x 480 or larger), you may want to reduce the frame size to a more Web-friendly size, such as 320 x 240. You can create smaller Flash Video file sizes with a combination of smaller video dimensions and reduced data rates.

✦ **Encode audio:** This section of the Encoding tab controls the compression of the audio channel (if one exists) of the Flash Video clip. Regardless of which Flash 8 version you use (Basic or Pro), the Audio codec option can not be modified; all audio channels of video content encoded with Flash 8 will use MP3 compression. However, you can change the data rate of the audio channel, choosing a value between 16 Kbps to 256 Kbps. Unless you're encoding high-quality musical scores, an audio data rate between 32 and 64 Kbps is usually adequate.

Note

The audio data rate is separate from the video data rate. As such, you should mentally add both rates to get a clear picture of the total data rate required for the Flash Video clip. For example, the Flash 7 – Medium preset uses a video data rate of 400 Kbps and an audio data rate of 96 Kbps. The total data rate for the clip, therefore, is 496 Kbps.

The Crop and Trim tab of the Encoding screen, shown in Figure 17-6, enables you to change the borders of your original source clip before it is encoded as Flash Video. You can use the numeric fields to crop the left, top, right, and bottom borders of the source clip. If you crop the content area, a marquee is displayed in the video preview area.

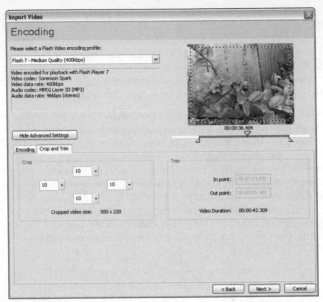

Figure 17-6: The Crop and Trim tab of the Encoding screen

Tip Cropping video clips might be necessary if your original footage is letterboxed (that is, black bands are above and below the actual picture area of the clip), or if you captured video with an analog video capture card that retains black borders on the video clip.

The Trim area of the tab does not contain any editable fields. Rather, you can drag the in and out markers on the controller below the video preview area. If you want to nudge either marker more precisely, click the marker and then use the left or right arrow key to move the marker.

Caution You can not trim your clip if you have opted to use the Split Video screen to divide your original source clip into multiple Flash Video clips.

Tip Even though the Crop and Trim tab isn't displayed for the Flash 8 presets, you can still drag the in and out markers to trim your clip.

When you have finished specifying the encoding parameters for the clip, you're ready to move on to the summary screen. Click the Next button.

Reviewing your settings: The Finish Video Import screen

After you have taken the care to specify the encoding options you want for your Flash Video clip, you can quickly review some of the presets on the final screen, shown in Figure 17-7. Click the Finish button to proceed with video encoding.

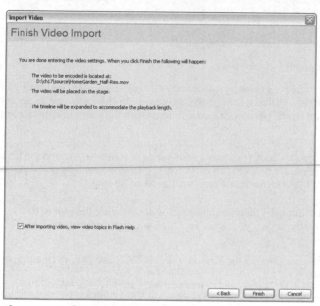

Figure 17-7: The Finish Video Import screen

Tip   You might want to clear the check box at the bottom of this screen, to avoid seeing the Flash Help topics on Flash Video. If you leave this option selected, you can review various help documents related to Flash Video usage within Flash documents.

After you click the Finish button, the Flash Video Encoding Progress dialog box appears, indicating the progress of the video encoding session (see Figure 17-8).

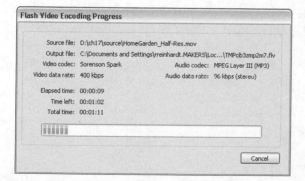

Figure 17-8: The Flash Video Encoding Progress dialog box

Walking through the video import procedure

In this section, we show you how to go through the process of selecting a video file and embedding it in a Flash 8 document.

On the CD-ROM For this example, make a copy of the `HomeGarden_Full-Res.mpg` file from the `ch17/source` folder on this book's CD-ROM to a local folder or your desktop.

1. Open a new Flash document (File ⇨ New).

2. Open the Document Properties (Modify ⇨ Document), and make sure the frame rate is set to 15 fps. Alternatively, you can change the frame rate in the Property inspector. Click any empty area of the Stage or Work area to show the document properties in the Property inspector.

Note Because our sample video clip doesn't display a wide range of movement within the frame, we can elect to use a slower frame rate such as 15 fps. If your video content contains more action, you may want to use a higher frame rate, such as 24 or 30 fps.

3. Choose File ⇨ Import ⇨ Import Video. In the Select Video screen, browse to the QuickTime file that you copied to your system. Once you have selected the file, click the Next button.

4. On the Deployment screen, choose the Embed video in SWF and play in timeline option and click the Next button.

5. On the Embedding screen, choose Embedded video in the Symbol type menu. Match the other options shown in Figure 17-9, and click the Next button.

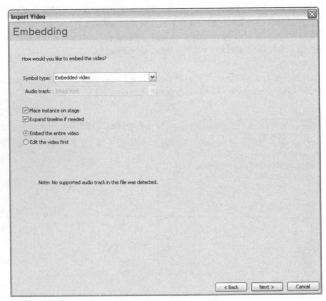

Figure 17-9: The Embedding screen options

6. On the Encoding screen, choose the Flash 8 – Medium Quality preset. This preset uses the new On2 VP6 codec available in Flash Player 8, and uses a video data rate of 400 Kbps, yielding a better-than-average image quality for the video clip (see Figure 17-10). Click the Next button to proceed to the next screen.

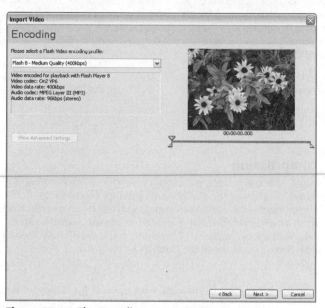

Figure 17-10: The Encoding screen options

7. On the Finish Video Import screen, review your settings and click the Finish button. Flash 8 begins the encoding process.

8. The video clip appears on the Main Timeline of the current Flash document. Flash 8 automatically centers the video clip and adds the necessary frames to the layer as well. Rename Layer 1 to **sample video**.

9. Save your Flash document as sampleVideo_100.fla, and test it (Ctrl+Enter or ⌘+Enter). If you open the Bandwidth Profiler (Ctrl+B or ⌘+B), you can see that the Flash movie (.swf) is 3833 KB, or 3.74 MB. Considering the content is just over one minute long, that is a data rate close to 500 Kbps. If this file size is too large, repeat this exercise selecting a lower data rate in the Encoding screen of the Import Video dialog box.

10. You can further modify the quality of the video clip's audio track by adjusting the Audio Stream settings in the Publish Settings. Our sample clip has a silent audio track, but chances are that your own video content (or the other samples on the book's CD-ROM) will have audio channels. By default, Flash 8 uses MP3 compression at 16 Kbps, mono, with Fast quality. Open the Publish Settings dialog box (File ➪ Publish Settings), and click the Flash tab. Click the Set button for the Audio Stream option, and choose a new codec and/or bitrate. For example, you can choose MP3 compression at 20 Kbps, mono, with Best quality. This will produce a slightly larger file size with better audio quality than the default. Close the Publish Settings dialog box, and retest your movie.

You may want to repeat this exercise, experimenting with a different compression profile or even creating a custom profile of your own. Try other sample video files on the book's CD-ROM as well.

To learn more about using Embedded Video symbol types in Flash movies, read our archived coverage of Embedded Video from the *Flash MX 2004 Bible* at www.flashsupport.com/archive. The workflow for using Embedded Video has not changed in Flash 8, and if you're publishing Flash Player 7 or higher content, we strongly recommend you use external .flv files instead of Flash .swf files with Embedded Video content.

You can find the completed file, sampleVideo_100.fla, in the ch17 folder of this book's CD-ROM.

Adjusting audio compression

As strange as it may sound, the audio track of a digital video file is imported and retained in its original source format. Flash 8 uses the global audio settings found in the Publish Settings dialog box to control the compression applied to your imported video's audio track. Most important, audio linked to an embedded video is treated as Stream sound so that it will be properly synched to the playback of the video. Therefore, you must specify the video's audio compression in the Audio Stream options of the Publish Settings dialog box.

You can use the new Separate option in the Audio track menu of the Advanced settings area of the Video Import wizard to extract the audio of a video file to its own Sound asset in the Library. See our prior coverage of this feature in this chapter.

Extracting .flv files from Embedded Video symbols

Regardless of which version of Flash 8 you are using, you can export an existing Embedded Video symbol as a separate .flv file from the Flash document file (.fla). To follow along with this exercise, open the sampleVideo_100.fla document from the ch17 folder of this book's CD-ROM.

1. With the sample document open in Flash 8, open the Library panel (Ctrl+L or ⌘+L).

2. Right-click the Embedded Video symbol in the Library panel, and from the contextual menu, choose Properties.

3. In the Video Properties dialog box, click the Export button. In the Export FLV dialog box, browse to a location to save the Embedded Video content as an .flv file.

If you change the Type option to Video (ActionScript-controlled) in the Video Properties dialog box, the Export button becomes disabled. The only way to re-enable the Export button is to switch the Type option back to Embedded, click the Cancel button, and re-open the Video Properties dialog box.

Once you've saved an .flv file, you can use the .flv file with your own custom NetStream objects in ActionScript code, or you can load the file into the FLVPlayback component (available in Flash Pro 8 only).

On the CD-ROM

You can find the extracted .flv file, HomeGarden_Half-Res.flv, in the ch17/source folder of this book's CD-ROM.

Deploying existing .flv files with Flash Pro 8

If you use Flash Professional 8, you have several more options for deploying and encoding Flash Video content. In this section, you learn about how to deploy an existing .flv file that you have uploaded to your Web server. The Flash Pro 8 Video Import wizard automatically sets up the parameters for a new FLVPlayback component in your Flash document.

Create a new Flash document and choose File ➪ Import ➪ Import Video in Flash Pro 8. The Select Video screen of the Import Video dialog box (see Figure 17-11) presents you with two options:

✦ **On your computer:** This field and Browse button enable you to select a digital video source clip on your local computer or computer network.

✦ **Already deployed to a web server, Flash Video Streaming Service, or Flash Communication Server:** This option, only available in Flash Pro 8, enables you to enter a fully-qualified domain name pointing to an existing .flv file on a server.

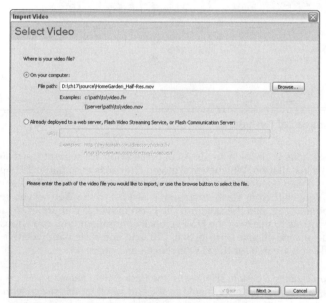

Figure 17-11: The Select Video screen in Flash Pro 8

Choose the second radio button option in this screen, and enter the following URL:

```
http://www.flashsupport.com/video/lizard_112k_vp6.flv
```

Click the Next button to proceed to the Skinning screen.

If you enter a URL to a Flash Video file (.flv) in the Select Video screen, the Flash Pro 8 version of the Video Import wizard takes you directly to the Skinning screen (see Figure 17-12). Here, you choose the playback control skin for your video clip. This skin is used by the FLVPlayback component instance that the Video Import wizard places on to the current document's stage at the end of the importing process.

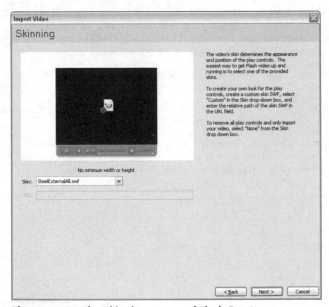

Figure 17-12: The Skinning screen of Flash Pro 8

You can select one of several skins in the Skin menu. All of these skins are separate .swf files included with the Flash Pro 8 installation. Whichever skin you choose is automatically copied to the location of the current Flash document you're importing the video file into. This .swf skin file must be uploaded along with your Flash document's .swf file to the Web server, so that the FLVPlayback component can load the skin into the Flash movie. If you prefer to make your own video playback controls to use with the FLVPlayback component, you can choose None in the Skin menu. You can also choose Custom Skin URL and enter the path (relative or absolute) to the skin .swf file you created for the FLVPlayback component.

Cross-Reference   For more information on creating a custom skin, search the Flash 8 Help panel for "SkinFLA." The "Creating a new skin" help file should be the only result for this search term.

After you have picked a skin, click the Next button. As shown in Figure 17-13, you are taken to the Finish Video Import screen (as described in the Flash Basic 8 coverage of the Video Import wizard). The Finish Video Import screen describes the steps you will need to take once you have finished the import process.

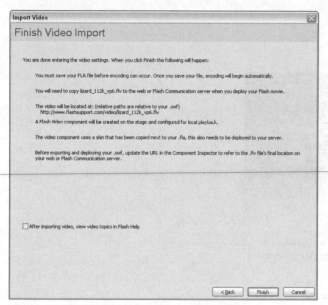

Figure 17-13: The Finish Video Import screen

Click the Finish button. You are prompted to save your Flash document (.fla). Save the document as `deploy_existing.fla` anywhere on your computer. After you have saved the file, Flash Pro 8 loads the metadata from the .flv file you specified during the Import Video process. The width and height data from the .flv file are used to size the instance of the FLVPlayback component that Flash Pro 8 places in the center of your Stage area, as shown in Figure 17-14. Rename Layer 1 to **cfp**, short for component *FLVP*layback. In the Property inspector, name the instance **cfp** as well.

Resave the Flash document, and test the movie (Ctrl+Enter or ⌘+Enter). When the movie loads, the lizard video clip plays in the FLVPlayback component instance (see Figure 17-15). The skin you selected earlier in this exercise is also displayed, enabling you to control the playback of the video clip.

You can find the completed file, `deploy_existing.fla`, in the ch17 folder of this book's CD-ROM.

If you want to try loading another .flv file into the FLVPlayback instance, you don't have to repeat the Import Video procedure. Instead, select the `cfp` instance on the Stage, and open the Property inspector. Select the Parameters tab, and change the `contentPath` value to the new .flv file name (or location). You can also change the skin file in the Parameters tab.

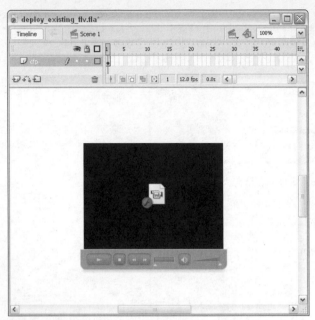

Figure 17-14: The FLVPlayback component

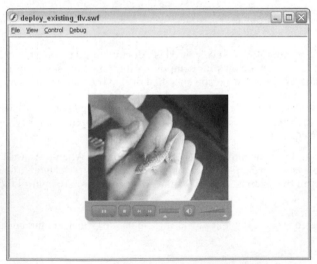

Figure 17-15: The remote video clip playing in the
FLVPlayback component

Compressing and deploying new .flv files with Flash Pro 8's Video Import wizard

Flash Pro 8's Video Import wizard can create stand-alone .flv files. You also have more settings available in the Video Import wizard during the Encoding stage of the importing process. In this section, you learn how to create a Flash Video file (.flv) with Flash Pro 8's Video Import wizard.

You can find sample video source files in the `ch17/source` folder of this book's CD-ROM. You can also find online video archive links in the Public Domain Media Sources heading at `www.flashsupport.com/links`.

1. Create a new Flash document in Flash Pro 8. Save the document as `deploy_new_flv.fla`.

2. Choose File ➪ Import ➪ Import Video. On the Select Video screen, click the Browse button for the On my computer option. Browse to the `stella_raw.mpg` file in the `ch17/source` folder on this book's CD-ROM. Once you've selected the file, click the Next button to proceed to the next screen.

If you select an existing .flv file, the Video Import wizard jumps straight into the Skinning screen, as we described in the last section.

3. On the Deployment screen (shown in Figure 17-16), Flash Pro 8 offers a few more options than the Flash Basic 8 edition. The top three options effectively produce the same result, creating a new .flv file that is used with an FLVPlayback component instance. The only difference between these top three options is that the Finish Video Import summary screen has specific instructions for what needs to be done with the new .flv file after you have finished the encoding process. Select the Progressive download from a web server option, and click the Next button.

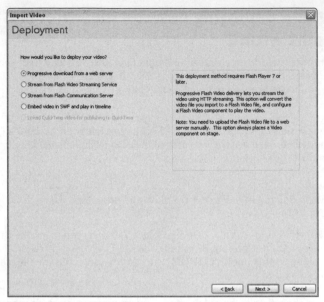

Figure 17-16: The Deployment screen options in Flash Pro 8

4. The Encoding screen, shown in Figure 17-17, has expanded functionality in Flash Pro 8 as well. Not only can you specify advanced options for the Flash 7 presets using Sorenson Spark, but you can also modify the advanced options for the new On2 VP6 codec! For this example, choose the Flash 8 – Medium preset in the profile menu and click the Show Advanced Settings button. Also, we intentionally used the stella_raw.mpg clip because the first three-quarters of the clip should be cut from the clip. Drag the in marker about 22 seconds into the clip, as shown in Figure 17-17. In the Quality menu, choose Custom and type **300** in the Data rate field. Also, check the Resize video option, and enter **320** for the width and **240** for height. Change the audio data rate to 64 kbps, as the audio track for this clip is not high-fidelity — it's just our dog Stella barking. Click the Next button to proceed to the next stage of the import process.

Note   Whenever you change any of the preset values of a profile, the profile name changes to Custom at the top-left corner of the Encoding screen.

Cross-Reference   We explore the new Cue Points tab of the Encoding screen in Flash Pro 8 in the "Creating .flv files with Embedded cue points" section later in this chapter.

5. On the Skinning screen, you can pick a skin for the FLVPlayback component used to play the Flash Video file. For this example, choose the ClearExternalAll.swf skin, as shown in Figure 17-18. Click the Next button to proceed to the summary screen.

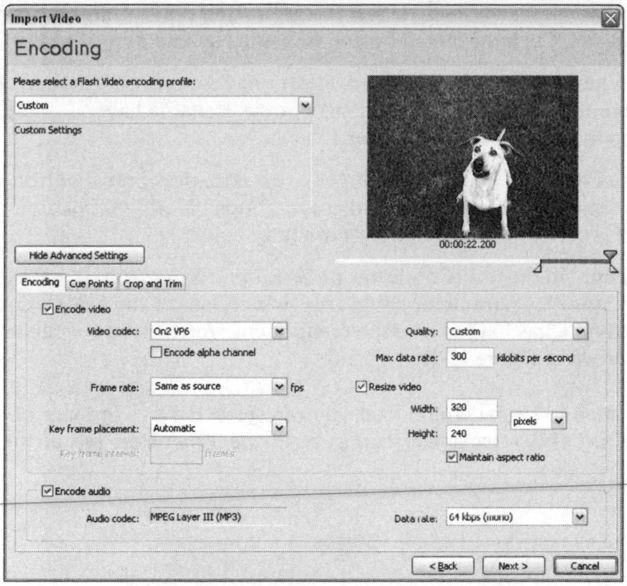

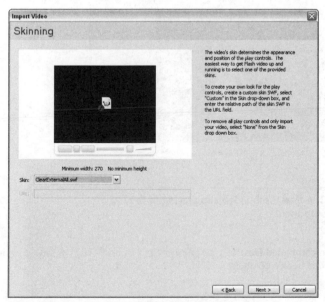

Figure 17-17: The Encoding screen options in Flash Pro 8

Figure 17-18: The Skinning screen options

6. On the Finish Video Import screen, review the importing options and the directives that Flash Pro 8 provides. Click the Finish button to begin the encoding process.

7. After the Flash Video file has been created, Flash Pro 8 inserts an instance of the FLVPlayback component on to the document's Stage. Rename Layer 1 to **cfp**, and name the instance `cfp` in the Property inspector.

8. Because you selected the `ClearExternalAll.swf` skin, the control button graphics are not easily seen on a white background color. Choose Modify ⇨ Document and change the background color to a light or dark gray color.

9. Save the document, and test it (Ctrl+Enter or ⌘+Enter). By default, the FLVPlayback instance has an autoPlay parameter set to true, which means the video starts playing as soon as the .flv file has loaded into the component. You should see Stella jumping up and down, as shown in Figure 17-19.

Note　If you want the video to be paused on load, you can select the `cfp` instance on the Stage and change the `autoPlay` parameter to `false` in the Parameters tab of the Property inspector.

Figure 17-19: The final Flash Video clip playing in the FLVPlayback component

On the CD-ROM　You can find the completed files, `deploy_new_flv.fla` and `stella_raw.flv`, in the `ch17` folder of this book's CD-ROM.

When you're done creating a Flash document using the FLVPlayback component, remember to upload all supporting files to your Web server for deployment, including the skin .swf file, the .flv file, and the main movie .swf file.

Using the FLVPlayback Component

In the last couple of sections, you've seen the FLVPlayback component at work in Flash Pro 8, as inserted into your Flash document with the Video Import wizard. In this segment of the chapter, you learn more "under the hood" usage of the FLVPlayback component. Remember, you can only access the FLVPlayback component in the Flash Pro 8 edition.

Cross-Reference

This part of the chapter explores many ActionScript-based features of the FLVPlayback component and its event model. For an introduction to components, read Chapter 33, "Using Components." We also utilize more advanced ActionScript in many of these examples. To learn more about ActionScript, be sure to read Parts V, VII, VIII, and IX of this book.

Working with the Component Parameters

You don't have to use the Video Import wizard to add an FLVPlayback component instance to your movie. In fact, you can just drag and drop the component from the Components panel (Window ⇨ Components) to the Stage of your Flash document. You can access the following parameters of an FLVPlayback component instance from the Property inspector's Parameters tab.

Note

All of these parameters can also be used in ActionScript, with the same spelling. For example, if you have an instance of the FLVPlayback component named `cfp`, you can set the `autoPlay` parameter to false with code: `cfp.autoPlay = false;`.

✦ `autoPlay`: This parameter determines if the video loaded into the component automatically plays (`true`) or loads in a paused state (`false`).

✦ `autoRewind`: This parameter controls how the video clip behaves when the clip has finished playing. If this parameter is set to `true`, the clip rewinds to the starting frame. If the parameter is `false`, the video freezes on the last frame when reached.

✦ `autoSize`: This parameter determines if the instance should resize to accommodate the width and height of the video content. If this property is set to `true`, then the FLVPlayback component's video display area is the actual pixel width and height of the .flv file. If the parameter is set to `false`, the FLV content is scaled to fit within the display area of the component.

✦ `contentPath`: This property determines which .flv file is loaded into the component. You can use a relative path (for example, `myVideo.flv`), an absolute path (for example, `/videos/myVideo.flv`), or a fully-qualified domain (for example, `http://www.flashsupport.com/video/lizard_112k_vp6.flv`).

✦ `cuePoints`: This property specifies the cue points that are linked to the playback of the FLV file. If you create embedded cue points (see our coverage later in this chapter), this property auto-fills within the Property inspector after you select a new .flv file with the `contentPath` property. If you double-click the `cuePoints` field, the Flash Video Cue Points dialog box opens (see Figure 17-20), where you can create new ActionScript-based cue points or view embedded cue points. Embedded cue points can not be changed. We discuss cue points later in this chapter.

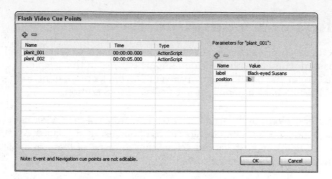

Figure 17-20: The Flash Video Cue Points dialog box

✦ `isLive`: This property determines if the video content is a live stream being published from a Flash Communication Server (or Flash Media Server). The default value is `false`. If set to `true`, the duration of the stream (which is nonexistent for a live stream) is not displayed in the component's UI and the scrub bar is disabled.

✦ `maintainAspectRatio`: This parameter controls how video content fits within the display area of the component. If the display area uses an aspect ratio different than that of the video content and this property is set to `false`, the video will be stretched vertically and/or horizontally to fit the display area. If the property is set to `true`, the video content maintains its aspect ratio regardless of the display area's aspect ratio.

✦ `skin`: This property, when accessed in the Property inspector, opens a dialog box from which you can choose a skin .swf file for the component. The values in this menu match the skins available in the Skinning screen of the Video Import wizard.

✦ `skinAutoHide`: This property controls if the skin .swf used for the component hides itself if the user's mouse cursor is not over the video display area. If set to `false`, the skin is always visible. If set to `true`, the skin disappears when the user's mouse cursor rolls off the component.

✦ `totalTime`: This property determines the duration of the video clip. Generally, you do not need to set this value, as the property is automatically read from the metadata of an .flv file or from the server-side API of a Flash Communication Server. If you do set this value in the Property inspector or with ActionScript, the new value overrides any value specified in metadata of the .flv file.

Caution   In order for the `totalTime` property to be set with a streaming .flv file from Flash Communication Server, you must include the custom code in your Flash Communication Server application script. You can find this code within the `main.asc` file located in the Flash 8 application folder, `Samples and Tutorials\Samples\Components\FLVPlayback`. If you're using a Flash Video Streaming Service provider, this code should already be enabled on the provider end.

✦ `volume`: This property controls the loudness of the .flv file's audio channel, if one exists. You can use a value in the range of 0 to 100, with 0 being absolute silence and 100 being the maximum loudness of the audio channel.

Using FLV Playback Custom UI components

If you have Flash Pro 8, you can also add custom UI components specifically designed to be used with the FLVPlayback component. In ActionScript, you can tell an FLVPlayback instance to use other components for playback control. The following properties represent component references used with the FLVPlayback component:

✦ backButton: This property can specify a custom UI component to seek to previous cue points in the video.

✦ bufferingBar: This property controls which component displays the buffering status of the video clip.

✦ forwardButton: This property specifies the component to seek to cue points past the current playhead time.

✦ muteButton: This property specifies the component that can toggle the muting of the video's audio track.

✦ pauseButton: This property controls which component can pause the video playback.

✦ playButton: This property controls which component can initiate playback of the video file.

✦ playPauseButton: This property specifies which component can toggle between play and stop states of the video stream.

✦ seekBar: This property specifies the component that displays the scrubbing area and Playhead control for the video.

✦ stopButton: This property controls which component stops and resets the stream back to its starting position.

✦ volumeBar: This property specifies the component that controls the volume setting of the video clip.

We'll show you how to practice using a few custom UI components with an FLVPlayback instance.

1. In Flash Pro 8, create a new document and save it as flvplayback_custom.fla.

2. Rename Layer 1 to **cfp**. On frame 1 of this layer, drag an instance of the FLVPlayback component from the FLV Playback – Player 8 nesting to the Stage.

3. In the Property inspector, name the instance **cfp**. Click the Parameters tab, and double-click the value for the skin parameter. In the Select Skin dialog box, set the Skin type to None, as shown in Figure 17-21.

4. Create a new layer named **custom UI**, and place this layer above the cfp layer.

5. Open the Components panel, and expand the FLV Playback Custom UI group. With frame 1 of the custom UI layer selected, drag an instance of the PlayPauseButton component to the Stage. Place the new instance below the cfp instance, near the left corner.

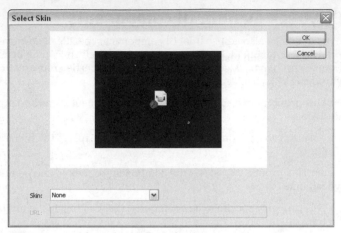

Figure 17-21: The Select Skin dialog box

6. In the Property inspector, name the new instance **cppb**, as shown in Figure 17-22.

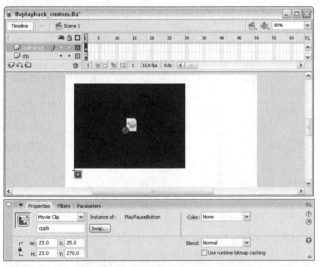

Figure 17-22: The PlayPauseButton component

7. Now, you need to link the cppb instance to the cfp instance in ActionScript. Create a new layer named **actions**, and place it at the top of the layer stack.

8. Select frame 1 of the actions layers, and open the Actions panel (F9, or Option+F9 on Mac). In the Script pane, add the following actions:

```
var cfp:mx.video.FLVPlayback;
var cppb:MovieClip;
cfp.playPauseButton = cppb;
cfp.contentPath = "stella_raw.flv";
```

Note　For this example, make sure you have copied the `stella_raw.flv` file from the `ch17` folder to the same location on your computer where you saved the .fla document in Step 1.

9. Save the Flash document, and test it (Ctrl+Enter or ⌘+Enter). The `stella_raw.flv` file automatically plays in the `cfp` instance. You can click the `cppb` instance to pause the video, and click it again to resume playback.

10. Go back to the Flash document. Let's add another custom UI component. Select frame 1 of the custom UI layer. From the Components panel, drag an instance of the SeekBar component to the Stage, to the right of the PlayPauseButton instance.

11. Name the SeekBar instance **csb** in the Property inspector. Optionally, use the Free Transform tool to stretch the width of the SeekBar instance to span the remaining width of the FLVPlayback instance.

12. Select frame 1 of the actions layer, and open the Actions panel. Add the following bold code to the existing script:

```
var cfp:mx.video.FLVPlayback;
var cppb:MovieClip;
var csb:MovieClip;
cfp.playPauseButton = cppb;
cfp.seekBar = csb;
cfp.contentPath = "stella_raw.flv";
```

13. Save the Flash document, and test it (Ctrl+Enter or ⌘+Enter). You should see the playhead of the SeekBar instance move to the right as the video plays (see Figure 17-23).

Figure 17-23: The SeekBar component displaying the current position of the video

You can continue adding other custom UI components from the Components panel and specifying the new instance names to the corresponding property of the `cfp` instance in the frame 1 script of the actions layer.

Tip   You can also modify the graphics used by the custom UI components. Open the Library panel to view the skin symbols in the `FLV Playback Skins` folder.

On the CD-ROM   You can find the completed file, `flvplayback_custom.fla`, in the `ch17` folder of this book's CD-ROM.

Working with Cue Points

In general terms, a *cue point* is a specific time within a video clip where something of significance occurs. For example, you might want a cue point at the start of each cut or scene within a video, or when something noteworthy is said within the audio track of a video clip. With Flash Video, you can build systems that work with two types of cue points:

✦ **Embedded cue points:** Using the new Flash 8 Video Encoder, which is enabled with Flash Pro 8, you can insert cue points within a video clip before the encoder compresses the clip. The resulting .flv file embeds each cue point on a keyframe in the video track. There are two types of embedded cue points:

- `navigation`: This type of cue point marks the video frame as a point that the user can seek to, using the forward and back buttons of the FLVPlayback component, or with ActionScript code.

- `event`: This type of cue point marks the video frame as a point that can be detected with an event handler in ActionScript code. You can not seek to event cue points unless you modify the functionality of the FLVPlayback component code.

✦ **ActionScript cue points:** This type of cue point is one that is not embedded with the .flv file. An ActionScript cue point is added, as its name implies, via ActionScript code. For example, if your .flv file doesn't have cue points, you can create cue points with an XML file specifying the times and names of the cue points. You can load the XML file at run time, and pass each cue point value to the FLVPlayback component. You can specify ActionScript cue points in the Parameters tab of the Component Inspector panel (or the Property inspector) for an FLVPlayback instance, or using the `FLVPlayback.addASCuePoint()` method.

Caution   By default, ActionScript cue points can not be used as navigation cue points. You need to modify methods of the FLVPlayback instance in order for ActionScript cue points to work with seek buttons. Later in this chapter, you learn how to accomplish this task.

In ActionScript code, you can detect which type of cue point is fired during playback. A cue point object in ActionScript has a `type` property, which is set to a String value of `"navigation"`, `"event"`, or `"actionscript"`.

Creating .flv files with embedded cue points

In this section, you learn how to use the Flash 8 Video Encoder to create cue points for video footage of garden plants. Each plant featured in the video will have a cue point, specifying its name and the location of the name on the screen. The cue points will be used to dynamically create text fields (with drop shadows!) on top of the video. You add both navigation and event cue point types to this footage. The navigation cue points will work with the forward/back seek buttons of the FLVPlayback component, and they will create the text labels for each plant type. The event cue points will remove the text label before the next label fades and blurs on to the stage.

Tip

You can use the Video Import wizard of Flash Pro 8 to create cue points as well, but the Flash 8 Video Encoder saves the settings for each clip. So, if you need to edit the cue points later and recompress the footage, you should use the Flash 8 Video Encoder instead of the Video Import wizard.

On the CD-ROM

Make a copy of the `HomeGarden_Full-Res.mpg` file from the `ch17/source` folder of this book's CD-ROM. Do not try to add the file directly from the CD-ROM from this exercise — one of the drawbacks to the Flash 8 Video Encoder tool is that you can not specify a different output folder for the compressed .flv file.

1. Open the Flash 8 Video Encoder application. On Windows, you can find this application shortcut at Start ➪ Programs ➪ Macromedia ➪ Macromedia Flash 8 Video Encoder. On the Mac, you can find this application here: `Applications: Macromedia Flash 8 Video Encoder: Flash 8 Video Encoder`.

2. Click the Add button on the right-hand side of the application, and browse to your copy of the `HomeGarden_Full-Res.mpg` file. Add this file to the queue.

3. Double-click the new entry in the queue to access the Flash Video Encoding Settings dialog box, as shown in Figure 17-24. Click the Show Advanced Settings button to reveal the Cue Points tab.

Figure 17-24: The Flash Video Encoding Settings dialog box

4. In the Cue Points tab, click the Add (+) button to add a cue point at the start of the video clip. Change the name of the cue point to **plant_001**. Change the Type menu to Navigation. Under the parameters area of the dialog box, click the Add (+) button to add a new parameter named **label**. For the value, type **Black-eyed susans**. Add another

parameter named **position** with a value of **rb**. This position value stands for "right bottom" and it will be used to properly position the `label` text for the cue point. Refer to Figure 17-25 for these settings.

Caution   Watch your spelling for parameter names and values. You must consistently name your parameters in order for your custom ActionScript code to work.

Figure 17-25: The new plant_001 cue point

5. Now, scrub the video playhead below the preview area to the next scene. The next cue point should be added around 4.6 seconds, as shown in Figure 17-26. Add a cue point by clicking the Add (+) button on the left, and name the cue point **exit_001**. Change the Type to Event. For this exercise, you won't need any parameters for event cue points.

Tip   You can click the playhead and nudge it with the left and right arrow keys to finesse the playhead time.

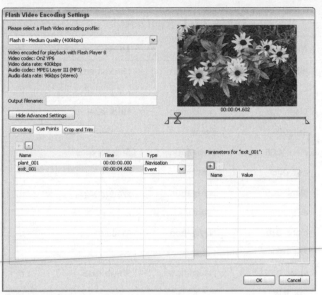

Figure 17-26: The exit_001 cue point

6. Now that you're familiar with the cue point addition process, add the following cue points at the approximate times shown in Table 17-1. (Feel free to choose your preferred values.) When you are finished, your cue point list should resemble Figure 17-27.

Tip   Double-check the label and position parameters for each cue point before you start the encoding process.

Table 17-1: Cue Points for the HomeGarden_Full-Res.mpg File

Time	Name	Type	Label	Position
00:00:00.0	plant_001	Navigation	Black-eyed susans	rb
00:00:04.602	exit_001	Event	-	-
00:00:05.040	plant_002	Navigation	Echinacea	rb
00:00:09.833	exit_002	Event	-	-
00:00:10.251	plant_003	Navigation	Dinnerplate dahlia	rt
00:00:14.854	exit_003	Event	-	-
00:00:15.273	plant_004	Navigation	Pumpkin patch	rt
00:00:23.223	exit_004	Event	-	-
00:00:23.433	plant_005	Navigation	Giant pumpkin	lb
00:00:28.245	exit_005	Event	-	-

Continued

Table 17-1 (continued)

Time	Name	Type	Label	Position
00:00:28.663	plant_006	Navigation	Huckleberry bush	lt
00:00:33.266	exit_006	Event	-	-
00:00:33.475	plant_007	Navigation	Huckleberries	rt
00:00:38.287	exit_007	Event	-	-
00:00:39.333	plant_008	Navigation	Strawberries	rb
00:00:43.309	exit_008	Event	-	-
00:00:44.146	plant_009	Navigation	White roses	lb
00:00:48.749	exit_009	Event	-	-
00:00:49.167	plant_010	Navigation	Mallow	rb
00:00:56.071	exit_010	Event	-	-
00:00:56.490	plant_011	Navigation	Shrub rose	rt
00:01:01.093	exit_011	Event	-	-
00:01:01.511	plant_012	Navigation	Chocolate mint bush	rb
00:01:05.696	exit_012	Event	-	-

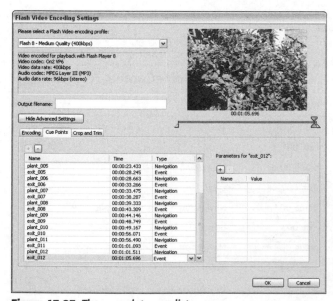

Figure 17-27: The complete cue list

7. Click the Encoding tab. In the encoding profile menu (near the top of the dialog box), choose Flash 8 – Medium Quality (400 kbps). Change the Audio data rate to 16 kbps. This particular video clip has an audio track that is silent (meaning, there is an audio track, but it just recorded silence). Also, check the Resize video option, and clear the Maintain aspect ratio option. Because this video clip is DV footage, the clip uses non-square pixels, and must be squeezed into a square pixel ratio. Type **320** for the width, and **240** for the height (see Figure 17-28).

Tip

Even if you don't need an audio track, we advise you to include a silent audio track for the clip in your video-editing program. We have found that video playback for larger files is significantly closer to the clip's frame rate if there is an audio track to sync to.

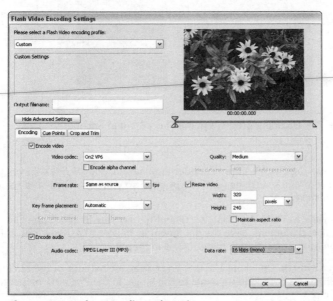

Figure 17-28: The Encoding tab options

8. Click OK to accept all of the new encoding settings. Back in the main application window, click the Start Queue button to begin the encoding process. The lower area of the application window displays the encoding progress, as shown in Figure 17-29.

Figure 17-29: The encoding progress in the Flash 8 Video Encoder application

9. Before you close the Flash 8 Video Encoder application, choose File ➪ Save Queue. This option saves your clip's settings (and cue points!) so you can re-edit and re-encode if you made a mistake.

10. Now, you're ready to build the Flash document to play the .flv file. Open Flash Pro 8, and create a new document. Save the document as cuepoints_embedded.fla, in the same location as the new .flv file compressed in Step 8.

11. Rename Layer 1 to **cfp**. On frame 1 of this layer, drag an instance of the FLVPlayback component from the Components panel to the Stage. In the Property inspector, name the instance **cfp**.

12. In the Parameters tab of the Property inspector, select a skin for the FLVPlayback instance. For our example, we used the SteelExternalAll.swf skin. For the contentPath parameter, browse to the HomeGarden_Full-Res.flv file created in Step 8. The FLVPlayback instance should resize to the dimensions of the .flv file.

13. Create a new layer named **tEmbed**. This layer will be used to hold an embedded font for the video labels. On frame 1 of the tEmbed layer, use the Text tool to create a Dynamic text field off stage, above the Stage area. Type the text **Arial** in the field. In the Property inspector, make sure the type is set to Dynamic, and name the instance **tEmbed**. In the font menu, choose the font face Arial. Click the Embed button, and in the Character Embedding dialog box, select the Uppercase, Lowercase, and Punctuation ranges as shown in Figure 17-30.

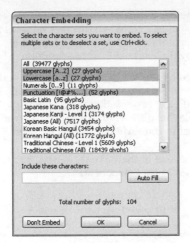

Figure 17-30: The Character Embedding dialog box

14. Create a new layer named **actions**, and place it at the top of the layer stack. Select frame 1 of the actions layer, and open the Actions panel (F9, or Option+F9). Add the code shown in Listing 17-1. This script has the following functions:

- `onVideoMarker`: This function is used as the listener for the `"cuePoint"` event broadcasted by the FLVPlayback instance, `cfp`. The event object (`oEvent`) passed to this listener contains an `info` property, which represents the data of the embedded cue point (`oCue`). The `label` and `position` values that you assigned to each cue point in the Flash 8 Video Encoder are available in the `parameters` property of the cue point object (`oCue`). If the cue point's `type` property is `"navigation"`, then the `showLabel()` function is invoked with the `label` and `position` values. If the cue point's `type` property is `"event"`, the `removeLabel()` function is invoked.

- `showLabel`: This function creates a `TextField` object named `tLabel`, which is positioned on the movie's Stage according to the `position` value passed by the cue point. A `DropShadow` filter is also created and passed to the `filters` property of the `tLabel` instance. The `TextFormat` object, `tf`, specifies the Arial font that was embedded in Step 13.

Cross-Reference

For more information on `TextFormat` objects, read Chapter 30, "Applying HTML and Text Field Formatting."

- `removeLabel`: This function removes the `tLabel` instance from the Stage. Whenever a cue point with a `type` of `"event"` fires, this function is invoked to remove the label from the movie.

- `onScrubStart`: This function is used as a listener of the `"scrubStart"` event broadcasted by the FLVPlayback instance, `cfp`. When the video clip is scrubbed with the seek bar, the `onScrubStart()` function is invoked. Here, the `setInterval()` function is used to continuously invoke the `updateLabel()` function, discussed later in this list.

- **onScrubFinish:** This function is used as a listener of the "scrubFinish" event broadcasted by the FLVPlayback instance, cfp. When the user releases the mouse button from the seek bar, this function is invoked, clearing the setInterval() function initiated by the onScrubStart() function.

- **updateLabel:** This function, invoked by the setInterval() action in the onScrubStart() function, calls the showLabel() function, using label and position data retrieved by the FLVPlayback.findNearestCuePoint() method. This method can use the playhead's current time (cfp.playheadTime) to return the cue point that is closest to the scrubbing arrow of the seek bar.

Cross-Reference

The event-listener model for this script makes use of the Delegate class. You can learn more about the Delegate class in Chapter 33, "Using Components."

Listing 17-1: **The Frame 1 Script**

```
import mx.video.FLVPlayback;
import mx.utils.Delegate;
import flash.filters.DropShadowFilter;

var cfp:FLVPlayback;
var tLabel:TextField;
var bScrubbing:Boolean = false;
var nUpdateID:Number;

function onVideoMarker(oEvent:Object):Void {
   var oCue:Object = oEvent.info;
   var sLabel:String = oCue.parameters.label;
   var sPos:String = oCue.parameters.position;
   if(oCue.type == "navigation" && sLabel != undefined ){
      showLabel(sLabel, sPos);
   } else if(oCue.type == "event" && !bScrubbing){
      removeLabel();
   }
}

function showLabel(sLabel:String, sPos:String):Void {
   var tf:TextFormat = new TextFormat();
   tf.font = "Arial";
   tf.size = 14;
   tf.color = 0xFFFFFF;

   var ds:DropShadowFilter = new DropShadowFilter();
   ds.blurX = 0;
   ds.blurY = 0;
   ds.distance = 1;

   tLabel = createTextField("tLabel", 1, 10, 10, 300, 30);
   tLabel.autoSize = "left";
```

```
      tLabel.embedFonts = true;
      tLabel.antiAliasType = "advanced";
      tLabel.text = sLabel;
      tLabel.setTextFormat(tf);
      tLabel.filters = [ds];

      var sHoriz:String = sPos.toLowerCase().substr(0,1);
      var sVert:String = sPos.toLowerCase().substr(1,1);
      var nX:Number;
      var nY:Number;
      if(sHoriz == "l"){
         nX = cfp._x + 20;
      } else if(sHoriz == "r"){
         nX = cfp._x + cfp.width - 20 - tLabel._width;
      }
      tLabel._x = nX;

      if(sVert == "t"){
         nY = cfp._y + 10;
      } else if(sVert == "b"){
         nY = cfp._y + cfp._height - 80;
      }
      tLabel._y = nY;
   }

   function removeLabel():Void {
      tLabel.removeTextField();
   }

   function onScrubStart():Void {
      bScrubbing = true;
      nUpdateID = setInterval(this, "updateLabel", 30);
   }

   function onScrubFinish():Void {
      bScrubbing = false;
      clearInterval(nUpdateID);
   }

   function updateLabel():Void {
      var oCue:Object = cfp.findNearestCuePoint(cfp.playheadTime);
      if(oCue.type == "navigation"){
         showLabel(oCue.parameters.label, oCue.parameters.position);
      }
   }

cfp.addEventListener("cuePoint", Delegate.create(this, onVideoMarker));
cfp.addEventListener("scrubStart", Delegate.create(this, onScrubStart));
cfp.addEventListener("scrubFinish", Delegate.create(this, onScrubFinish));
```

15. Save the Flash document, and test it (Ctrl+Enter or ⌘+Enter). The video clip should automatically play, displaying the plant names on top of the video display area (Figure 17-31). If you drag the playhead of the seek bar, you should still see the names of the plants appear on top of the video.

Figure 17-31: A dynamic text label on top of the video area

 You can find the completed file, `cuepoints_embedded.fla`, in the `ch17` folder of this book's CD-ROM. This file has an additional blur and fade effect applied to the text, using the BlurFader component we discuss in Chapter 20, "Making Your First Flash 8 Project."

Generating ActionScript cue points with XML

Unless you're planning to encode all of your Flash Video content with the new Flash 8 Video Encoder or the Video Import wizard in Flash Pro 8, you may find yourself looking for another solution to add cue points to Flash presentations that use the FLVPlayback component. You can create cue points at run time using the `FLVPlayback.addASCuePoint()` method, which enables you to specify the time and name of the cue point you want to add, such as:

```
var cfp:FLVPlayback;
var oCue:Object = {
    type: "actionscript",
    time: 5.2,
    name: "plant_002"
};
cfp.addASCuePoint(oCue);
```

 You can only add cue points of type `"actionscript"` or `FLVPlayback.ACTIONSCRIPT` (a constant that returns the String value `"actionscript"`). Event and navigation cue points can only be specified with embedded cue points.

Tip

With the Property inspector's Parameters tab, you can also add ActionScript cue points to an instance of the FLVPlayback component. Select the component instance on the Stage, open the Property inspector, select the Parameters tab, and double-click the `cuePoints` parameter to access the Flash Video Cue Points dialog box. There, you can enter new ActionScript cue points for that component instance.

One of the problems of using ActionScript cue points is that they are not recognized as navigation cue points — you can not use the seek buttons on the FLVPlayback component's skin interface to navigate between cue points you add in Actionscript.

How you define the cue point data to use with the `addASCuePoint()` method is entirely up to you. You can hardcode cue point data in your ActionScript code, as the previous code example illustrates, or you can define your cue points in an external data source, such as an XML file. In this section, you learn how to build an XML file that defines cue points for the garden video clip you used in the previous section.

Creating the cue points in XML

In this section, you build the XML file that defines the cue points for the `HomeGarden_nocue` `.flv` file we provide in the `ch17/cuepoints` folder of this book's CD-ROM. This .flv file has the same video content as the `HomeGarden_Full-Res.flv` file you created in the last section. However, the `HomeGarden_nocue.flv` file does not have any embedded cue points. So, you're going to define those same cue points in an XML file. The basic schema for the XML file for our example is:

```
<points>
  <cue id="value" time="value" label="value" position="value" />
</points>
```

where `cue` is a child node created for each cue point applicable to the video content, with the following attributes:

✦ `id`: The name of the cue point, such as plant_001. You should use unique names with your cue points.

✦ `time`: The point, in seconds, where the cue point should fire during playback or scrubbing of the video content.

✦ `label`: The text label, or caption, to use for a `TextField` instance on top of the FLVPlayback component.

✦ `position`: The location of the label text, relative to the frame of the video content. Acceptable values are `lt` (left top), `rt` (right top), `lb` (left bottom), and `rb` (right bottom).

For this exercise, you generate the same cue points you built in the previous section. As such, the parameters label and position have exact mappings in the XML schema. For more information about XML schemas, read the sidebar "XML Schemas for Cue Points" following this section.

1. Open your preferred text editor such as Macromedia Dreamweaver 8, and create a new XML document (or text file).

2. Save the document as `cuepoints.xml`. If your text editor has the capability to specify a character encoding in the Save As dialog box, choose Unicode UTF-8. If you're using Macromedia Dreamweaver, choose Modify ➪ Page Properties and choose Unicode (UTF-8).

Tip   The default character encoding for Flash Player 6 and higher movies is UTF-8. Whenever possible, make sure you encode any text data loaded into Flash movies as UTF-8.

3. Add the XML code shown in Listing 17-2. This data specifies the same cue points you used in the previous exercise. Note that the time values have been finessed to be more accurate with the cut points in the `HomeGarden_nocue.flv` file.

Tip   One of the benefits of using external cue points is that you can more easily change time values associated with cue points. As you know, once cue points are embedded in an .flv file, you can't edit them. You must re-encode the original source file to change or add cue points to a new .flv file. With ActionScript cue points, you can easily modify the cue point data without building a new .flv file. However, ActionScript cue points are not frame accurate like embedded cue points. For this reason, some values have been changed in the XML version of the cue points.

Listing 17-2: **The XML Cue Point data**

```
<?xml version="1.0" encoding="utf-8"?>
<points>
    <cue id="plant_001" time="0.3" label="Black-eyed susans" position="rb" />
    <cue id="plant_002" time="5.3" label="Echinacea" position="rb" />
    <cue id="plant_003" time="10.5" label="Dinnerplate dahlia" position="rt" />
    <cue id="plant_004" time="15.3" label="Pumpkin patch" position="rt" />
    <cue id="plant_005" time="23.4" label="Giant pumpkin" position="lb" />
    <cue id="plant_006" time="28.4" label="Huckleberry bush" position="lt" />
    <cue id="plant_007" time="33.5" label="Huckleberries" position="rt" />
    <cue id="plant_008" time="39.3" label="Strawberries" position="rb" />
    <cue id="plant_009" time="44.4" label="White roses" position="lb" />
    <cue id="plant_010" time="49.4" label="Mallow" position="rb" />
    <cue id="plant_011" time="56.7" label="Shrub rose" position="rt" />
    <cue id="plant_012" time="61.9" label="Chocolate mint bush" position="rb" />
</points>
```

---

4. Save the document.

On the CD-ROM   You can find the completed file, `cuepoints.xml`, in the `ch17/cuepoints` folder of this book's CD-ROM. The `Listing17-2.as` file in the `ch17` folder also contains this XML data.

In the section, you load the `cuepoints.xml` into an XML object created in ActionScript code.

XML Schemas for Cue Points

An XML schema is the specific hierarchy of node names, values, and attributes that you use with your XML data. The XML schema we created for this section's example is just one way you can establish a structure to arrange cue point information. You can establish your own custom schema, or use one designed by another system. For example, you could break down your cue point data with the following schema:

```
<cuepoints>
   <cuepoint time="49.4">
      <name>plant_001</name>
      <type>actionscript</type>
      <parameters>
         <label>Mallow</label>
         <position>rb</position>
      </parameters>
   </cuepoint>
</cuepoints>
```

This schema is used by Burak's Captionate utility for FLV captions, available at www.buraks.com/captionate. Of course, whenever you create a schema for XML data, you need to be able to parse the schema in your ActionScript code. The schema we created is simpler, assigning values as attributes instead of nested nodes, making it easier to parse the data in ActionScript. In the next section, you learn how to parse the cuepoints.xml file in a Flash movie.

Loading the cue points into the FLVPlayback component

Once you've created the XML file describing the cue point data, you're ready to build the Flash movie that loads the XML file and adds the cue points to an instance of the FLVPlayback component.

On the CD-ROM

Make a copy of the HomeGarden_nocue.flv file from the ch17/cuepoints folder on this book's CD-ROM. You use these files as a starting point for the following exercise.

1. In Flash Pro 8, create a new Flash document and save it as cuepoints_xml.fla.

2. Rename Layer 1 to **cfp**. On frame 1 of this layer, add an instance of the FLVPlayback component from the Components panel. Name this instance **cfp** in the Property inspector.

3. In the Property inspector, select the Parameters tab. For the contentPath parameter, double-click the value to select the HomeGarden_nocue.flv file you copied to your computer from the book's CD-ROM. This .flv file has the same video and audio track as the HomeGarden_Full-Res.flv file you created in the previous section. However, the new .flv file does not have any embedded cue points. Also, change the autoPlay parameter to false. Playback should only begin after the XML data has been loaded and parsed by the Flash movie.

4. Repeat Step 13 from the "Creating .flv files with embedded cue points" exercise earlier in this chapter. The Arial font face needs to be embedded in the Flash movie so that it can be used with dynamic text fields created in ActionScript.

5. Create a new layer named **actions**. Select frame 1 of this layer, and open the Actions panel (F9, or Option+F9). Add the code shown in Listing 17-3. This code is nearly identical to that shown in Listing 17-1, with the exception of the bold code. Here's a breakdown of the new modifications:

- xmlCue **instance:** A new XML object named xmlCue is created, and its onLoad() handler is delegated to a new function, onCueLoad. This function cycles through all of the <cue> nodes and extracts the time, id, label, and position attributes to create oCue objects that are passed to the cfp instance of the FLVPlayback component, using the addASCuePoint() method. When all of the cue points are added, the cfp instance initiates playback with the cfp.play(); action.

- onVideoMarker() **function update:** This function has been modified from the previous version to set up references to the internal cue points array within the FLVPlayback component. Whenever a cue point is fired, the cue point's name is looked up in the component's cue points table, using the FLVPlayback.findCuePoint() method. nIdx variable is set to that cue point's position within the array of cues stored in the cfp instance. A reference to the cue point table (or array) is also stored with the aCues variable. Both nIdx and aCues are used by the onBackClick() and onNextClick() functions we describe next.

- onBackClick() **and** onNextClick() **functions:** Because the cue points that have been added are ActionScript based, the seek buttons do not navigate between the cue points. In order to enable the back and next seek buttons of the FLVPlayback's user interface for ActionScript cue points, the cfp instance's seekToPrevNavCuePoint() and seekToNextNavCuePoint() methods need to replaced. When the FLVPlayback component has initialized, the "ready" event is broadcasted and intercepted by the onReady() function, where the seek methods are overwritten with the onBackClick() and onNextClick() functions. These functions navigate to the next cue point, passed on the value of nIdx. The FLVPlayback.findNearestCuePoint() method is used to return a reference to the cue point object, which contains the time property indicating where within the video clip to seek to next.

Listing 17-3: **The XML Parsing Routine**

```
import mx.video.FLVPlayback;
import mx.utils.Delegate;
import flash.filters.DropShadowFilter;
import com.themakers.effects.BlurFader;

var cfp:FLVPlayback;
var tLabel:TextField;
var bScrubbing:Boolean = false;
var nUpdateID:Number;
var aCues:Array;
var nIdx:Number;

var xmlCue:XML = new XML();
xmlCue.ignoreWhite = true;
xmlCue.onLoad = Delegate.create(this, onCueLoad);
xmlCue.load("cuepoints.xml");

function onCueLoad(bSuccess:Boolean):Void {
    if(bSuccess){
```

```
            var aNodes:Array = xmlCue.firstChild.childNodes;
            for(var i:Number = 0; i < aNodes.length; i++){
                var xn:XMLNode = aNodes[i];
                var oAttribs:Object = xn.attributes;
                var oCue:Object = {
                    type: "actionscript",
                    time: Number(oAttribs.time),
                    name: oAttribs.id,
                    parameters: { label: oAttribs.label, position: oAttribs.position}
                };
                cfp.addASCuePoint(oCue);
            }
            cfp.play();
        }
    }

function onVideoMarker(oEvent:Object):Void {
        var oCue:Object = oEvent.info;
        var sLabel:String = oCue.parameters.label;
        var sPos:String = oCue.parameters.position;
        showLabel(sLabel, sPos);
        var foundCue:Object = cfp.findCuePoint(oCue.name, FLVPlayback.ACTIONSCRIPT);
        nIdx = foundCue.index;
        aCues = foundCue.array;
}

function showLabel(sLabel:String, sPos:String):Void {
        var tf:TextFormat = new TextFormat();
        tf.font = "Arial";
        tf.size = 14;
        tf.color = 0xFFFFFF;

        var ds:DropShadowFilter = new DropShadowFilter();
        ds.blurX = 0;
        ds.blurY = 0;
        ds.distance = 1;

        tLabel = createTextField("tLabel", 1, 10, 10, 300, 30);
        tLabel.autoSize = "left";
        tLabel.embedFonts = true;
        tLabel.selectable = false;
        tLabel.antiAliasType = "advanced";
        tLabel.text = sLabel;
        tLabel.setTextFormat(tf);
        tLabel.filters = [ds];

        var sHoriz:String = sPos.toLowerCase().substr(0,1);
        var sVert:String = sPos.toLowerCase().substr(1,1);
        var nX:Number;
        var nY:Number;
        if(sHoriz == "l"){
```

Continued

Listing 17-3 *(continued)*

```
      nX = cfp._x + 20;
   } else if(sHoriz == "r"){
      nX = cfp._x + cfp.width - 20 - tLabel._width;
   }
   tLabel._x = nX;

   if(sVert == "t"){
      nY = cfp._y + 10;
   } else if(sVert == "b"){
      nY = cfp._y + cfp._height - 80;
   }
   tLabel._y = nY;

   if(!bScrubbing){
      var cfb:BlurFader = createClassObject(BlurFader, "cfb", 2, {dir: "in",
duration: 2, target: tLabel});
   } else if(cfb != null){
      cfb.removeMovieClip();
   }
}
function removeLabel():Void {
   tLabel.removeTextField();
}

function onScrubStart():Void {
   bScrubbing = true;
   nUpdateID = setInterval(this, "updateLabel", 30);
}

function onScrubFinish():Void {
   bScrubbing = false;
   clearInterval(nUpdateID);
}

function updateLabel():Void {
   var oCue:Object = cfp.findNearestCuePoint(cfp.playheadTime);
   showLabel(oCue.parameters.label, oCue.parameters.position);
}

function onBackClick(oEvent:Object):Void {
   var oCue:Object = aCues[nIdx > 0 ? nIdx - 1 : 0];
   var nTime:Number = oCue.time;
   cfp.seek(nTime);
   onVideoMarker({info: oCue});
}

function onNextClick(oEvent:Object):Void {
   var oCue:Object = aCues[nIdx < aCues.length - 1 ? nIdx + 1 : 0];
   var nTime:Number = oCue.time;
```

```
    cfp.seek(nTime);
    onVideoMarker({info: oCue});
}

function onReady(oEvent:Object):Void {
    cfp.seekToPrevNavCuePoint  = Delegate.create(this, onBackClick);
    cfp.seekToNextNavCuePoint = Delegate.create(this, onNextClick);
}

function onFinish(oEvent:Object):Void {
    removeLabel();
}

cfp.addEventListener("cuePoint", Delegate.create(this, onVideoMarker));
cfp.addEventListener("scrubStart", Delegate.create(this, onScrubStart));
cfp.addEventListener("scrubFinish", Delegate.create(this, onScrubFinish));
cfp.addEventListener("ready", Delegate.create(this, onReady));
cfp.addEventListener("complete", Delegate.create(this, onFinish));
```

6. Save the Flash document, and test it (Ctrl+Enter or ⌘+Enter). Once the cue points load into the Flash movie, the text labels should fade and blur onto the Stage, just as they had done with the embedded cue points example.

On the CD-ROM

You can find the completed file, `cuepoints_xml.fla`, in the `ch17/cuepoints` folder of this book's CD-ROM.

Using SMIL Files with the FLVPlayback Component

One of the less touted features of the FLVPlayback component is its capability to load SMIL files. SMIL stands for Synchronized Multimedia Integration Language, which can describe an interactive presentation layer in a multimedia playback environment, such as Real One Player. Real was one of the first companies to actively push SMIL for the creation of interactive Web content involving video and audio playback. SMIL is just a collection of markup tags like HTML or XML. For Flash Video playback, though, SMIL can be used to describe a collection of .flv files encoded with different data rates. In this section, you learn how to create SMIL files that work with either progressive .flv files on a Web server or streaming .flv files on a Flash Communication Server (or Flash Video Streaming Service provider account). The FLVPlayback component picks the appropriate .flv file to play based on the data rate available to the user. Let's look at streaming .flv files first.

Caution

The FLVPlayback component that shipped with Flash Pro 8 had an ActionScript code error that caused inaccurate .flv filenames to be selected from the SMIL file used with the component. We've fixed this error, and recompiled the FLVPlayback component. To avoid this error, you must use the FLVPlayback component stored in the library of the `smil_starter.fla` document located in the `ch17/smil` folder of this book's CD-ROM.

For streaming .flv files

In this section, you learn how to stream .flv files from a Flash Communication Server application (or a Flash Media Server application). All Flash Video Streaming Service providers use Flash Communication Server to stream video and audio content as well. One of the benefits of using a Flash Communication Server is that the bandwidth available to the Flash movie can be determined automatically with a server-side script. As you learn later in this chapter, you have to go through a more manually intense process with nonstreaming .flv files to determine bandwidth.

Note   Even if you don't have a Flash Communication Server, you can still complete this exercise. You access a remote FlashCom account—you only need to have an Internet connection to see this exercise fly!

Setting up the Flash Communication Server Application

In order to use real-time streaming video content with SMIL files and the FLVPlayback component, you need to prepare your Flash Communication Server application with the server-side script that communicates information back to the FLVPlayback component. Macromedia has provided the server-side script in the following folders. Note that the   indicates a continuation of the pathname.

On Windows:

```
C:\Program Files\Macromedia\Flash 8\Samples and Tutorials\Samples\
Components\FLVPlayback
```

On Macintosh:

```
[Applications folder]: Macromedia Flash 8: Samples and Tutorials: Samples:
Components: FLVPlayback
```

In this location, you can find the main.asc file to put in the application folder of your Flash Communication Server. For this example, we use an application named f8b on a Flash Communication Server account provided by Influxis (www.influxis.com). For this exercise, the main.asc is already uploaded to the FlashCom account. If you're using a Flash Video Streaming Service provider account, the necessary server-side code is already in place for you.

Note   Many thanks to Richard Blakely at Influxis for providing hosting to us for sample video files used in this section.

Creating the SMIL file

The schema used by SMIL files to be used with the FLVPlayback component is easy to learn. Here's an overview of the supported tags:

  ✦ head: This section of tags describes the base URL of the video files, and the width and height to be used for all streams.

✦ `meta`: This tag specifies the base URL of the video files, as a `base` attribute. This location can be relative to the .swf file, or an absolute location. Examples include `<meta base="video/" />` and `<meta base="http://www.flashsupport.com/video/" />`. For streaming .flv files, you should specify an RTMP location, such as `<meta base="rtmp://your_streaming_server/appName" />`. You should only specify one `<meta>` tag.

✦ `layout`: This tag specifies the width and height of the FLVPlayback component, within a nested node named `<root-layout>` (see the example in Listing 17-4).

✦ `body`: The body section of tags enumerates the .flv files that are available for playback. These .flv files are not a playlist. Rather, each .flv file has the same content. The content is simply encoded at varying data rates so that there's a wide range of .flv files to choose from.

✦ `switch`: This tag begins the list of .flv files to be chosen from by the FLVPlayback component.

✦ `video` **or** `ref`: Either or these tags can be used to list an .flv file. You must specify a `src` value, indicating the file's name. The `system-bitrate` attribute should be specified for every entry, except for the last. The last entry is the default video file that will be played if the data rate can't be determined or if the user's connection speed is slower than the last specified `system-bitrate` value.

Cross-Reference

The tags listed here are those necessary for our exercises in this chapter. You can find more information in the Flash 8 Help panel if you search for the term "smil."

To create the SMIL file for this exercise:

1. Create a new text document in your preferred text editor, such as Macromedia Dreamweaver 8, Notepad on Windows, or TextEdit on Macintosh.

2. Save the file as `lizard_vp6.smil`.

Caution

You must name your file with an .smil extension in order for the FLVPlayback component to recognize the content as SMIL data.

3. Add the code shown in Listing 17-4 to the text document. This SMIL data lists different data rates for an .flv file.

Listing 17-4: **The SMIL Data**

```
<smil>
    <head>
        <meta base="rtmp://flashbible.rtmphost.com/f8b" />
        <layout>
            <root-layout width="320" height="240" />
        </layout>
    </head>
```

Continued

Listing 17-4 *(continued)*

```
<body>
    <switch>
        <video src="lizardVP6_1Mbps_Stream.flv" system-bitrate="1000000" />
        <video src="lizardVP6_768K_Stream.flv" system-bitrate="768000" />
        <video src="lizardVP6_512K_Stream.flv" system-bitrate="512000" />
        <video src="lizardVP6_384K_Stream.flv" system-bitrate="384000" />
        <video src="lizardVP6_256K_Stream.flv" system-bitrate="256000" />
        <video src="lizardVP6_112K_Stream.flv" system-bitrate="112000" />
        <ref src="lizardVP6_56K_Dial_Up_Stream.flv"  />
    </switch>
</body>
</smil>
```

4. Save the text file. You load this text file into the Flash movie we describe in the next section.

This SMIL file describes the .flv files that you can find in the ch17/smil/progressive /videos folder. These files have already been uploaded to the publicly accessible Flash Communication Server account on www.Influxis.com. The Influxis account URL is specified in the base attribute of the <meta> tag.

You can find the completed SMIL file for streaming content, lizard_vp6.smil, in the ch17/smil/streaming folder of this book's CD-ROM.

Building the Flash movie

Now, you learn how to use our fixed version of the FLVPlayback component to use the SMIL file you created in the last section.

1. Open the smil_starter.fla file located in the ch17/smil folder of this book's CD-ROM. Resave this document as detect_streaming.fla, at the same location as the SMIL file you created in the last section.

2. Rename Layer 1 to **cfp**. On frame 1 of this layer, drag an instance of the FLVPlayback component from the Library panel to the top left area of the Stage.

Do not drag an instance of the FLVPlayback component from the Components panel. The shipped version of the component contains a bug with the SMIL and data rate detection code.

3. Select the instance on the Stage, and in the Property inspector, name the instance **cfp**.

4. Create a new layer named **text**. Place this layer at the top of the layer stack. Below the cfp instance, use the Text tool to add the static text **Detected bandwidth:**. To the right of that text, create a Dynamic text field named **tBitrate**, as shown in Figure 17-32. Optionally, you can set this text field to use the new Anti-alias for readability setting. You must embed the font you use in this Dynamic text field in order for this new feature to work.

Figure 17-32: The text below the FLVPlayback component

5. Create a new layer named **actions**, and place the layer above the text layer. Select frame 1 of the actions layer, and open the Actions panel (F9, or Option+F9 on Mac). Add the code shown in Listing 17-5. Two functions are defined to initiate loading of the SMIL file and indicate the download speed:

   - `init`: This function is invoked as soon as the Flash movie loads. The `onReady()` function is used as a listener for the `"ready"` event broadcasted by the `cfp` instance. The `contentPath` property is set to the name of the SMIL file you created in the last section.

   - `onReady`: This function is invoked when the `"ready"` event fires from the `cfp` instance. Here, the `bitrate` value from the `cfp` instance is retrieved, converted from bits per second to kilobits per second, and used as the value of the `text` value for the `tBitrate` field.

Listing 17-5: **Initiating SMIL Data for Streaming Video**

```
import mx.utils.Delegate;

var cfp:mx.video.FLVPlayback;
var tBitrate:TextField;

init();

function init():Void {
```

Continued

Listing 17-5 *(continued)*

```
    cfp.addEventListener("ready", Delegate.create(this, onReady));
    cfp.contentPath = "lizard_vp6.smil";
}

function onReady(oEvent:Object):Void {
    tBitrate.text = Math.floor((cfp.bitrate/1024)).toString() + " Kbps";
}
```

6. Save the Flash document, and test it (Ctrl+Enter or ⌘+Enter). Depending on the speed of your Internet connection, the appropriate .flv file streams into the FLVPlayback component (see Figure 17-33).

Detected bandwidth: 602 Kbps

Figure 17-33: The .flv file streaming from the Influxis server

On the CD-ROM

You can find the completed file, `detect_streaming.fla`, in the `ch17/smil/streaming` folder of this book's CD-ROM. This document features additional code in the `onReady()` function to display the stream name picked from the SMIL file to the Output panel.

For progressive .flv files

If you're not keen on using a Flash Communication Server to stream files, you can use a good old-fashioned Web server to serve the .flv files listed in a SMIL file. In this section, you learn how to modify the files you created in the last section to work with a Web server.

Modifying the SMIL data

For this exercise, you use the same .flv files used in the streaming example. You can find these video files in the `ch17/smil/progressive/video` folder on this book's CD-ROM. Make a copy of the `video` folder to your computer. The only modification necessary to the SMIL file is the base attribute of the `<meta>` tag. Open the `lizard_vp6.smil` file you created in the last section (as shown in Listing 17-4), and change the `<meta>` tag to:

```
    <meta base="video/" />
```

The `video/` path is relative to the Flash movie you create in the next section. Save the SMIL as `lizard_vp6_http.smil`.

You can find the modified file, `lizard_vp6_http.smil`, in the `ch17/smil/progressive` folder of this book's CD-ROM.

Modifying the Flash movie

As we mentioned earlier in our SMIL coverage, one of the benefits of using a Flash Communication Server to stream video content is that the FlashCom application can determine the download speed of the Flash client movie. If you progressively load .flv files from a Web server, you need to establish some other means to determine bandwidth. In this section, you learn how to load a poster frame of the video (as a JPEG file) into the Flash movie before loading the Flash Video content. Based on the speed of downloading the JPEG file, you can make a fairly accurate determination of the bandwidth.

1. Open the Flash document you created in the previous section, or open the `detect_streaming.fla` file from the `ch17/smil/streaming` folder on this book's CD-ROM. Resave this document as `detect_progressive.fla`, at the same location as the `lizard_vp6_http.smil` file. Both of these files should be in the same parent folder to the video folder. Make a copy of the `lizard.jpg` file from the `ch17/smil/progressive` folder to this location as well.

2. Select frame 1 of the actions layer, and open the Actions panel (F9, Option+F9). Add the bold code shown in Listing 17-6. Instead of directly loading the SMIL file in the `init()` handler, you need to initiate the download of the movie's poster frame image (`lizard.jpg`) to get a decent estimation of the user's available bandwidth. Here's a breakdown of how the functions work:

   - `downloadImage`: This function creates a `MovieClipLoader` instance to track the load progress of the `lizard.jpg` image into the `mcHolder` instance. The `mcHolder` instance is placed at the top-left corner of the `cfp` instance. As such, the poster frame appears on top of the display area of the FLVPlayback component.

   - `onLoadStart`: This function is used as a listener for the `MovieClipLoader` instance. When the poster image begins to load, this function is invoked, marking the time with `getTimer()` that the load was started.

   - `onLoadComplete`: This function is also automatically invoked from the `MovieClipLoader` instance. Here, `getTimer()` is used again to mark the time when the image has finished downloading.

   - `onLoadInit`: This handler is invoked after the JPEG image has fully loaded and initialized within the movie. The `calculateBW()` and `loadContent()` functions are then invoked.

   - `calculateBW`: This function retrieves the total bytes of the JPEG image, and divides that number by the amount of time (in seconds) used to load the image. (Note that the bytes are converted to bits by multiplying by 8.) The data rate is then used to set the `bitrate` property of the `cfp` instance. Once the `bitrate` property is set, the appropriate .flv file from the SMIL file can be selected once the data is loaded. The data rate is also displayed in the `tBitrate` field.

   - `loadContent`: This function loads the `lizard_vp6_http.smil` file you created in the last section.

- onReady: This function has been modified from the last exercise to account for the poster frame image on top of the cfp instance. The mcHolder instance is hidden, and the MovieClipLoader instance is deleted. The other lines of code in this function drill into the private properties of the FLVPlayback component to reveal the name of the .flv file that was selected from the SMIL file.

Listing 17-6: Creating a Bandwidth Detection Script

```
import mx.utils.Delegate;

var cfp:mx.video.FLVPlayback;
var tBitrate:TextField;
var streamName:String;
var nFirstCheck:Number;
var nSecondCheck:Number;
var mcHolder:MovieClip;
var mcl:MovieClipLoader;

init();

function init():Void {
   downloadImage();
   cfp.addEventListener("ready", Delegate.create(this, onReady));
}

function downloadImage():Void {
   mcl = new MovieClipLoader();
   mcHolder = createEmptyMovieClip("mcHolder", 10);
   mcHolder._x = cfp._x;
   mcHolder._y = cfp._y;
   mcl.addListener(this);
   mcl.loadClip("lizard.jpg", mcHolder);
}

function onLoadStart(mc:MovieClip):Void {
   nFirstCheck = getTimer();
}

function onLoadComplete(mc:MovieClip):Void {
   nSecondCheck = getTimer();
}

function onLoadInit(mc:MovieClip):Void {
   calculateBW();
   loadContent();
}

function calculateBW():Void {
   var nTB:Number = mcHolder.getBytesTotal();
   var nTime:Number = nSecondCheck - nFirstCheck;
   var nDataRate:Number = (nTB*8)/(nTime/1000);
   tBitrate.text = Math.floor((nDataRate/1024)).toString() + " Kbps";
```

```
      cfp.bitrate = nDataRate;
}

function loadContent():Void {
   cfp.contentPath = "lizard_vp6_http.smil";
}

function onReady(oEvent:Object):Void {
   var cfp:Object = oEvent.target;
   var oHack:Object = cfp.getVideoPlayer(cfp.activeVideoPlayerIndex);
   streamName = oHack._ncMgr._streamName;
   trace("\tstreamName: " + streamName);
   mcHolder._visible = false;
   delete mcl;
}
```

3. Save the Flash document, and test it (Ctrl+Enter, or ⌘+Enter). Because all of the files
   are local (that is, on your computer), you'll likely see incredibly high data rates
   reported in the text field below the component. However, you can use the download
   simulation feature available in Test Movie to test other connection speeds. As you test
   the movie, choose View ➪ Download Settings ➪ 56K, as shown in Figure 17-34. Open the
   Bandwidth Profiler in order to watch the download simulation (View ➪ Bandwidth
   Profiler). Then, choose View ➪ Simulate Download. The stage of the movie remains
   white while the Flash movie loads. Once the file loads, the poster frame download initiates, and the bitrate of the Flash movie is determined. Then, the appropriate .flv file is
   loaded, as specified by the SMIL file. For the 56K simulation setting, you should see the
   lizardVP6_56K_Dial_Up_Stream.flv play. Feel free to try other download speeds
   with the Simulate Download feature.

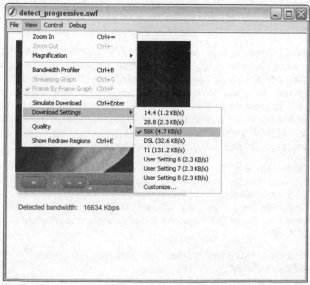

Figure 17-34: Choosing a connection speed

Note   You might be wondering why we didn't simply use the load progress of the actual Flash movie file (.swf) to determine the data rate. Unfortunately, `getBytesLoaded()` and `getBytesTotal()` return the uncompressed bytes of the Flash movie, not the actual file size. As such, accurate bandwidth detection can not be conducted on the .swf file download.

On the CD-ROM   You can find the completed files in the `ch17/smil/progressive` folder of this book's CD-ROM.

Using Appropriate Data Rates with Your Target Audience

You might be wondering why it's worth going through so much hassle to use SMIL files with multiple encodings of video content. To be blunt, serving video over the Web is entirely subjective. You can make anyone wait for a high-quality video file, regardless of the connection speed. In fact, some Web sites only want to offer high-quality video, because their audience has high expectations for online content — if you have a slow connection, you can tough it out and wait for the video to download. There are a few issues you should consider, though, when devising your video deployment strategy for a Web site:

✦ **Streaming or not?** If you decide to use real-time streaming video with Flash Communication Server, you can't make your visitors wait for streaming content. By definition, streaming content is served piece-meal to the Flash movie. Only so much video is stored in the buffer of the Flash Player for streaming content. So, if you push a high data rate stream to a user with a slow connection, the stream buffers as much as it can before playback starts. When playback begins, the buffer is exhausted more quickly than it can be replenished. The video, therefore, will pause. The user continues to experience this start and stop playback of the video. With streaming video, it's critical to offer multiple versions of the same content — unless you know that your target audience can support higher quality content.

✦ **Qualitative experience?** There are cases where you simply can not offer low data rates for video content. For example, a training video that shows a desktop screen capture can not be reduced to 320 x 240 nor can it be drastically compressed — the details of the computer screen captured just won't be decipherable. Another example may be promotional material such as a theatrical film trailer. A movie studio may not want to distribute low-quality video over the Internet; who would be encouraged to see a movie if everything in the promo was blurry? Who wants to watch an action segment at six frames a second? Such experiences could negatively affect the promotion.

✦ **Frame rate versus frame quality?** As you adjust data rates for multiple .flv files of the same content, you may find yourself in a dilemma. Do you reduce the frame rate to preserve image quality of the overall clip, or do you reduce the image quality and use a higher frame rate? Ultimately, the content should direct this decision. If you have a video clip of a dance performance, preserving smooth motion is more important than maintaining a high level of detail.

Whatever you use Flash Video for, be sure to consider these factors as you plan the architecture of your video files and server deployment.

Working with the Flash 8 Video Encoder

Flash Professional 8 ships with an exciting new stand-alone application called the Flash 8 Video Encoder. On Windows, you can find this application at Start Menu ➪ Programs ➪ Macromedia ➪ Macromedia Flash 8 Video Encoder. On Macintosh, on your start-up disk, look for the Flash 8 Video Encoder application in the Applications: Macromedia Flash 8 Video Encoder folder.

When you run the Flash 8 Video Encoder application, you see the interface shown in Figure 17-35.

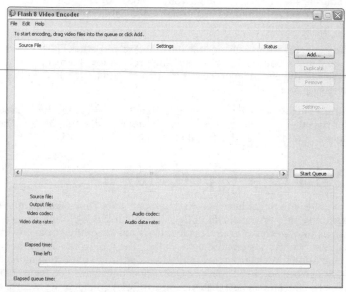

Figure 17-35: The Flash Video 8 Encoder application

The Flash Video 8 Encoder works as a batch processor for the same encoding engine that is used in the Video Import wizard of Flash Pro 8. You can specify all of the same settings in the Flash 8 Video Encoder application. Some benefits to using the Flash 8 Video Encoder application include

✦ **Adding multiple source video files:** You can drag and drop (or browse to) one or more video source files on your computer or network into the application's queue.

✦ **Duplicating settings:** Once you've specified the settings on one source clip, you can click the Duplicate button to add another entry in the queue with the same clip and its settings. You can then adjust the new duplicate's settings to a different data rate.

Caution | You can not save settings from one clip and apply them to a different source clip.

✦ **Saving the queue:** You can save the list of video clips in the queue to resume work in another session. However, you can't save the queue list as an external project file.

Cross-Reference

For a review of the settings you can apply to clips, read our coverage of the Video Import wizard for Flash Pro 8. The same encoding settings are available in the Flash 8 Video Encoder.

The Flash 8 Video Encoder does have some drawbacks that you should keep in mind before starting the encoding process:

✦ **Lack of de-interlacing capability:** If you have a source clip that is captured from an interlaced video source, such as NTSC footage from a miniDV or DVCAM camcorder, then you need to de-interlace the footage in another video-editing application prior to importing the clip into the Flash 8 Video Encoder tool.

✦ **No 2-pass encoding specification:** Unlike Sorenson Squeeze and other Flash Video encoding tools, you can not specify a 2-pass encoding process for video clips. By adding a second pass to the encoding process, the encoder can better analyze the footage for compression and optimization.

✦ **No contrast or filter control:** Some Flash Video encoding tools offer you the capability to adjust the color balance, contrast, and other image tonality adjustments. The Flash 8 Video Encoder does not offer these adjustment controls.

Using the FLV QuickTime Export Plug-in

If you used Flash MX Pro 2004, you might have known that most QuickTime-enabled applications could use an export plug-in to create .flv files direct from your video-editing applications. Flash Pro 8 continues to offer this plug-in. This feature is not accessible from any menu or command in the Flash Pro 8 authoring environment. Rather, the tool works with other video applications such as Adobe After Effects or Apple Final Cut Pro to export high-quality Flash Video files (.flv) that use the Sorenson Spark or On2 VP6 codec. Once you have created an .flv file, you can import the file into a Flash 8 document with the Video Import wizard.

New Feature

The interface for the plug-in is identical to the Flash Video Encoding Settings dialog box featured in the Flash 8 Video Encoder application and the Video Import wizard of Flash Pro 8.

You should be running Apple QuickTime 6.1.1 or higher on your system in order to use the FLV QuickTime Export plug-in. You can download QuickTime 6 at www.apple.com/quicktime. You do not need the Pro version of QuickTime Player to use the plug-in in most video applications. In the next section, though, we demonstrate the use of the plug-in from QuickTime Player Pro. You can't export video (of any type) in the basic version of QuickTime Player.

Most applications that support QuickTime output can utilize the plug-in. In this section, you learn how to export a high-quality Flash Video file (.flv) from Apple QuickTime Player Pro. You must be using the Pro edition of QuickTime Player to complete this exercise. If you don't have QuickTime Player Pro, we suggest that you read through these steps and see if you can apply the same procedure in your preferred video application. Usually, you will find the .flv file option in the settings available in the dialog box opened by the File ➪ Export menu (or some variation thereof) in your video-editing application.

You'll need a source video file to use in QuickTime Player Pro. You can use one of the video files found in the ch17/source folder of this book's CD-ROM.

1. Open QuickTime Player Pro on your Windows or Mac computer.

2. Choose File ➪ Open Movie in New Player, and browse to the location of the video file you want to compress in Flash Video format. For this example, we use the lizard.mpg file from this book's CD-ROM.

3. Once the file has opened in the player, choose File ➪ Export. In the Save exported file as dialog box, choose Movie to Macromedia Flash Video in the Export menu, as shown in Figure 17-36. Do not click any other options at this time.

Figure 17-36: The Export menu option in QuickTime Player Pro, shown in the Windows version

4. Now click the Options button. As you can see in Figure 17-37, the options you see in this dialog box are the same as those available in the Encoding stage of the Video Import wizard of Flash Pro 8. To quickly show you the power of the Flash Video Exporter tool, choose the options shown in Figure 17-37 and click OK.

Note Regardless of the video application you use, the dialog box shown in Figure 17-37 is exactly the same. You always have access to these options from any compatible video-editing program.

5. In the export dialog box of QuickTime Player, click the Save button. (If you want to specify a new location and/or filename, do so before clicking the Save button.) QuickTime then exports the .flv file from the source video file.

After you have created an .flv file, you can import it into a Flash document.

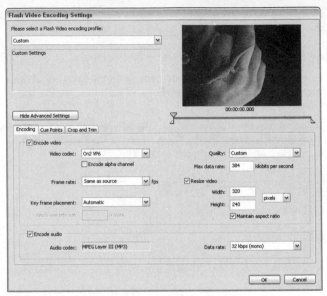

Figure 17-37: The encoding settings

Using Sorenson Squeeze for Flash Video

Needless to say, the plain fact that Macromedia Flash 8 can import and embed video files playable by Flash Player 6 or higher is truly remarkable. Just when you thought you've seen everything, we need to tell you that your journey with Flash video doesn't end with the Flash 8 authoring tool or the Flash 8 Video Encoder. The native video compressor in Flash 8's Video Import wizard is Sorenson Spark Basic edition. What you can't see in the Video Import wizard is that the Basic edition of Sorenson Spark encodes only in CBR, or Constant Bit Rate. CBR encoding means each frame of the video is uniformly compressed, consuming the same (or constant) data rate throughout the entirety of the clip. If you're familiar with MP3 sound, you may already be aware of CBR encoding with music. The same principle applies to video compression as well.

We all know, however, that each frame of video may not require the same amount of data to describe. For example, a solid field of blue (such as a big blue sky) may not need as much data as a field of multicolored flowers, where several pixels in the frame have a different color. If your video footage contains a mixture of compositions and subject matter, it could benefit from another type of encoding known as VBR, or Variable Bit Rate. VBR encoding enables the compressor to change the rate of compression applied to each frame of video. Therefore, one frame may need only 200 bytes, whereas another may need as many as 400 bytes. In practice, just about all video footage can benefit from VBR encoding. One of the drawbacks to encoding with VBR is that it takes longer to compress a video clip than it does with CBR encoding.

Unfortunately, Flash 8's Video Import wizard does not allow you to apply VBR encoding to imported files. Luckily, Sorenson Media offers an application that does: Sorenson Squeeze 4. This application, which is sold separately from Flash 8, comes in two editions:

✦ **Flash only:** This version of Squeeze creates Flash .flv and .swf files using the Sorenson Spark Pro and On2 VP6 codecs, which we describe later in this section.

✦ **Compression Suite:** This version can output several multimedia audio/video formats, including DVD MPEG2, VCD MPEG1, QuickTime video movie files (.mov), Windows Media files, RealPlayer files, Flash Video files (.flv), and Flash movie files (.swf). For the purposes of our coverage, we discuss this version in the remainder of the chapter, but we only use features that are available in both the Flash MX and Compression Suite editions.

Note

At the time of this writing, Sorenson Squeeze was in release version 4.2 for Windows and 4.1 for Macintosh. The 4.2 edition features the new On2 VP6 codec.

Sorenson Squeeze enables you to compress video files with Sorenson Spark Pro, which can use 2-pass CBR or VBR encoding, which means that Squeeze carefully examines each frame of video—twice. On the first pass, Squeeze analyzes the content of each frame. On the second pass, Squeeze performs the actual encoding, using the information it gathered from the first pass. The following list describes the added functionality Sorenson Squeeze offers beyond the native capabilities of Flash 8's Video Import wizard:

✦ **Superior encoding control:** Sorenson Squeeze can use either 1-pass or 2-pass compression with CBR or VBR encoding with your digital video. You can adjust audio and video data rates independently, and specify other codec options not available in Flash 8. We discuss these options in a later section.

✦ **Batch processing:** You can create several output versions of your digital video files with Sorenson Squeeze. Using the compression presets (discussed later), you can make a variety of low- and high-bandwidth movies all in one go.

✦ **Watch folder:** You can have Squeeze automatically compress new files that you save into a specific folder that is watched by Squeeze. As soon as a new file is added to the watch folder, Squeeze begins compressing the file with the presets you've chosen.

✦ **DV capture:** Sorenson Squeeze can capture video directly from a DV source, over an IEEE 1394 (also known as FireWire or iLink) connection. Just connect your DV camcorder or deck to the computer and capture a live feed from the camera.

✦ **Multiple output formats:** Sorenson Squeeze can open several file formats and output several popular audio/video formats, including QuickTime Sorenson Video 3.0, Flash movie file (.swf), or Flash video file (.flv) formats. As such, you can make different movie formats for all of your Web video needs. You can use the Flash movie or Flash video formats with your Flash-based Web material and use other formats for non-Flash Web pages.

✦ **Filter settings:** You can adjust the contrast, brightness, gamma, white restore, and black restore of the video image. Squeeze can also de-interlace your video footage, reduce video noise, crop the video frame, and fade the footage in and/or out. You can even normalize the audio track of the video file.

✦ **Compression presets:** Perhaps the most useful feature of Sorenson Squeeze is the ability to use bandwidth presets for your video compression. Squeeze has predefined compression options for the following connection speeds: Modem, ISDN, Broadband Low, Broadband, Broadband High, LAN CD, and CD High Quality. You can adjust the compression settings of each preset, but you cannot add your own custom presets.

You can download a trial version of Sorenson Squeeze at www.sorensonmedia.com.

Choosing a Flash output file type

After you install the trial version of Sorenson Squeeze 4.2 (or 4.1 on Mac), go ahead and launch the application. The Sorenson Squeeze interface is shown in Figure 17-38. The output formats are represented as three file icons in the application's toolbar.

Figure 17-38: You can choose from several output formats in Sorenson Squeeze 4.2 Compression Suite.

For any given video file, you can enable one or more of these formats to be exported in a batch.

Flash Video

As you learned throughout this chapter, a Flash Video file (.flv) is a video file that has been compressed with the Sorenson Spark or On2 VP6 codec. As such, you can quickly import it into a Flash 8 document—no further video encoding is necessary. Just like regular video files (such as .avi or .mov files), Flash Video files have a frame rate, frame size (dimensions), and an optional audio track. Once you import the Flash Video file into your Flash document, you can add further interactivity to it with ActionScript. You can also dynamically load Flash Video files into a Flash Player 7 or higher movie.

Flash movie

Squeeze can also create fully functional Flash movies (.swf) from your digital video files. If you don't need to add anything to your video in Flash 8, you can simply choose your digital file and specify a compression setting for the Flash movie file (.swf) to be output from Squeeze. Voila! You have an instant Flash movie that can be loaded into an existing Flash movie with the `loadMovie()` action, or viewed independently in a separate HTML document.

Tip   You can create Flash movies (.swf) containing video with frame rates different from Flash movies that load them. This means that you can create a 15 fps Flash movie from Sorenson Squeeze and load it into a slower playing 12 fps Flash movie. As soon as the Flash movie with video starts to play, both movies will play at the speed of the Flash movie with video. Video content is treated just like Stream sound in the Flash Player — it will govern the player's frame rate.

Compressing video with Sorenson Spark Pro and On2 VP6 codecs

In this section of the chapter, we walk you through the process of encoding video with Sorenson Spark Pro and On2 VP6 codecs in Flash .flv files. Flash Video files can be imported into existing Flash 8 documents or loaded at run time into Flash Player 7 or higher movies. .flv files using the On2 VP6 codec can only be loaded into Flash Player 8 or higher.

On the CD-ROM   Make a copy of the `lizard.mpg` file, located in the `ch17/source` folder of this book's CD-ROM.

1. Open Sorenson Squeeze 4.2 (or 4.1 on Mac), and choose File ➪ Open. Browse to the `lizard.mpg` file that you copied from the book's CD-ROM.

2. Expand the Macromedia Flash Video group in the Format & Compression Settings pane, on the left side of the Squeeze interface. Ctrl+select the 256K_Stream preset and the VP6_256K_Stream preset, and click the Apply button. The two presets should now be visible below the lizard.mpg entry in the job list, as shown in Figure 17-39. These presets compress the video clip for 256 Kbps data rates (video and audio combined). The 256K_Stream preset encodes in the Sorenson Spark Pro codec, while the VP6_256K_Stream preset encodes in the new On2 VP6 codec.

Tip   If you want to finesse the codec settings, expand the preset by clicking the plus (+) button. The video and audio codec settings are listed separately. Double-click the codec name to open the Audio/Video Compression Settings dialog box.

3. Now press the plus (+) button in the Filters pane. In the Filter Settings dialog box, assign a name of **Deinterlace Normalize** to the filter, as shown in Figure 17-40. Select the Deinterlace check box and Auto Remove Interlacing in the combo box. Check the Normalize Audio option as well. Click OK.

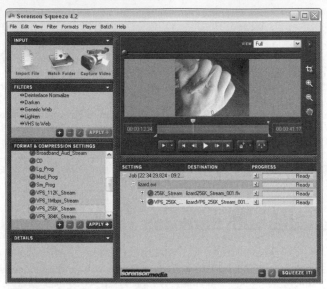

Figure 17-39: The two presets added to the lizard.mpg clip

Figure 17-40: The new Filter Settings dialog box

4. After you've created the new filter, select its name (Deinterlace Normalize) in the Filters pane and click the Apply button. The filter is now applied to the lizard.mpg clip. Notice that the filter is displayed in the Source Settings and each preset for the clip. If you ever want to adjust the filter for both presets, double-click the filter name in the Source Settings nesting. If you want to adjust a filter just for one preset, double-click the filter name in the appropriate preset nesting.

5. Squeeze is ready to encode the Flash Video files from the original source video. Press the Squeeze It! button in the lower right corner of the application window. Squeeze starts the encoding process for the output files. When the compression is finished, click the Close button and quit the Squeeze application.

Working with Video Alpha Channels

One of the most exciting features of the new On2 VP6 codec is its capability to utilize alpha channels within video content. Flash 8 on its own can not create a true alpha channel for a video clip — you need to use a dedicated video effects application such as Adobe After Effects 6.5 or Adobe Premiere Pro 1.5 to create a matte for the video track. The process of selecting areas of the video to mask for transparency is known as *keying*. Essentially, you use the video application to select a key color, which will be used to create a mask for the video. The accuracy and sharpness of a mask depend on the quality of the keying plug-in. Adobe After Effects offers several keying plug-ins to help you professionally matte your video content.

For the purpose of our coverage in the *Macromedia Flash 8 Bible*, we'll provide you with the QuickTime .mov files that already have masks created by Adobe After Effects Pro 6.5. The general process for keying involves a series of steps:

1. **Acquire video footage.** To successfully mask a subject in the video, you should shoot the subject against an evenly lit green screen or blue screen. You may have seen special effects footage shot on such screens, for action thrillers such as *The Matrix*.

2. **Import the footage into a video effects application.** Using a program such as Adobe After Effects, you can add the footage to a composition. Within the composition, you can add key filters to select the green or blue areas of the content.

3. **Render the footage with an alpha channel.** Once you have key filters in place, you can render the footage with an alpha channel. You need to use a video codec that supports alpha channels, such as the Animation codec. In After Effects, make sure you choose RGB + Alpha in the Channels menu of the Video Output settings.

4. **Encode the footage with the On2 VP6 codec.** After you have the rendered QuickTime file, you can process the file with the Flash 8 Video Encoder or Sorenson Squeeze. In the Flash 8 Video Encoder settings, make sure you choose the Encode alpha channel check box.

In the next two sections, we demonstrate how to encode alpha video footage in both Flash 8 Video Encoder and Sorenson Squeeze 4.2.

Live action footage

In this section, you learn how to compress footage of our dog Stella that was shot against a green screen. The footage already has an alpha channel that was created in Adobe After Effects. You superimpose the footage of Stella on a static .png image imported into a Flash document.

On the CD-ROM
Make a copy of the `stella_alpha.mov` file found in the `ch17/source` folder of this book's CD-ROM.

1. Open Sorenson Squeeze 4.2, and import your copy of the `stella_alpha.mov` file.

2. From the Format & Compression Settings pane, expand the Macromedia Flash Video grouping and drag the VP6_256K_Stream preset to the job list.

3. Once the preset is added to the clip, expand the preset below the source clip. Double-click the VP6 Pro codec listing to open the Audio/Video Compression Settings dialog box. Within the Video area of the settings, choose 2-pass VBR in the Method menu. For Frame Rate, choose 1:1. Select the Compress Alpha Data check box. Select the Auto Key Frames Enabled check box. Review the settings shown in Figure 17-41. Click OK to accept the new settings.

Figure 17-41: The Audio/Video Compression Settings dialog box

4. Click the Squeeze It! button to begin the encoding process. When Squeeze finishes, rename the new .flv file to stella_alpha.flv.

Tip

You can modify the output destination and filename from Squeeze by right-clicking the preset's name in the job list and choosing Modify Output File Name.

5. In Flash 8, open the live_action_starter.fla from the ch17/alpha_live_action folder of this book's CD-ROM. Save the document as live_action.fla, in the same location as the .flv file created in Step 4. This document already has a background .png image on the Stage, as well as a masked image of a branch near the trail.

6. Create a layer named **vWin**, and place it between the bg_mask and bg layers.

7. Open the Library panel (Ctrl+L or ⌘+L). Click the options menu of the panel (in the top-right corner) and choose New Video. In the Video Properties dialog box, choose Video as the Type option (see Figure 17-42). Click OK.

Figure 17-42: The Video Properties dialog box

8. Drag an instance of the new Video symbol from the Library panel on the Stage, at frame 1 of the vWin layer.

9. Select the new Video instance, and in the Property inspector, name the instance vWin. Set the width to **152** and the height to **180**. Position the X value at **154** and the Y value at **180**. See Figure 17-43.

Note

The dimension 152 x 180 uses the same aspect ratio as that of the source clip.

Figure 17-43: The vWin instance

10. Create a new layer named **actions**, and place this layer at the top of the layer stack. Select frame 1 of the actions layer, and open the Actions panel (F9, or Option+F9). Add the following code. The code creates a new NetStream instance to play the stella_alpha.flv file, and attaches the stream to the vWin instance.

```
var vWin:Video;
var nc:NetConnection = new NetConnection();
nc.connect(null);
var ns:NetStream = new NetStream(nc);
ns.play("stella_alpha.flv");
vWin.attachVideo(ns);
```

11. Save the Flash document, and test it (Ctrl+Enter or ⌘+Enter). The footage of Stella should be superimposed between the graphic of the branch and the forest background, as shown in Figure 17-44.

Figure 17-44: The alpha video footage playing on top of the forest background

You can find the completed files in the ch17/alpha_live_action folder of this book's CD-ROM.

3D modeling footage

You can also export 3D modeling video from your preferred 3D application. Most 3D applications can export video footage rendered with an alpha channel. In this section, you take a 3D model of a wasp and render it as an animating video mouse cursor in the Flash movie. If the cursor is near the top of the movie, the wasp video scales smaller. As the cursor moves to the bottom of the movie's Stage, the video scales larger.

Make a copy of the wasp_alpha.mov file from the ch17/source folder of this book's CD-ROM.

Many thanks to Beau DeSilva at Schematic for creating the awesome video footage of the wasp.

1. Open the Flash 8 Video Encoder application. Add the wasp_alpha.mov file to the queue.

2. With the clip selected, click the Settings button. In the Flash Video Encoding Settings dialog box, choose the Flash 8 – Medium Quality encoding profile. In the Encoding tab, select the Encode video alpha check box.

3. Choose the Crop and Trim tab, and enter **140** for the left and right trim values. Enter **40** for the bottom trim value (refer to Figure 17-45).

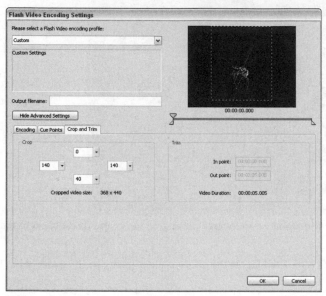

Figure 17-45: The Crop and Trim tab settings

4. Go back to the Encoding tab, and check the Resize video box. Type **185** for the width, and **221** for the height. Click OK to accept the new settings.

5. Click the Start Queue button to begin the encoding process.

6. When the `wasp_alpha.flv` file is finished rendering, go to Flash 8 and open the `3D_model_starter.fla` document in the `ch17/alpha_3D_model` folder. Save this document as `3D_model.fla`, in the same location as the `wasp_alpha.flv` file.

7. Create a new layer named **vWin**, and place the layer above the bg layer. Repeat Steps 7 and 8 from the previous exercise, creating a new `Video` object on frame 1 of this layer.

8. Name the instance `vWin` in the Property inspector. Even though the `wasp_alpha.flv` has different dimensions than those of the `vWin` instance, you do not need to change the width and height in the Property inspector. You add ActionScript code that dynamically resizes the instance in the next step.

9. Create a new layer named **actions**, and place it at the top of the layer stack. Select frame 1 of the actions layer, and open the Actions panel. Add the code shown in Listing 17-7. The core features of the script are outlined in the following list:

- `ns.onStatus`: This handler detects status changes with the video playback. When the video reaches the end of the clip, the `NetStream.Play.Stop` event occurs. At that point, the video should rewind and automatically repeat. The `seek()` method can go to a new point in the clip and resume playback.

- ns.onMetaData: This handler is invoked when the .flv file's metadata is loaded. Here, the vWin instance's width and height are set to the true width and height of the .flv file. Because onMetaData() fires whenever the video repeats, the bInited variable makes sure that the vWin instance is only resized once. After the instance is sized, the onMouseMove() handler is invoked to set the initial scale of the vWin instance.

- onMouseMove: This handler fires whenever the user moves the mouse cursor. Here, the scale of the vWin instance is set to a factor of the mouse's Y position (_ymouse/4). The vWin instance is also snapped to the mouse cursor's position.

Listing 17-7: Using Alpha Video as a Mouse Cursor

```
var vWin:Video;
var bInited:Boolean;

var nc:NetConnection = new NetConnection();
nc.connect(null);

var ns:NetStream = new NetStream(nc);

ns.onStatus = function(oInfo:Object):Void {
    if(oInfo.code == "NetStream.Play.Stop"){
        this.seek(0);
    }
};

ns.onMetaData = function(oData:Object):Void {
    if(!bInited){
        vWin._width = oData.width;
        vWin._height = oData.height;
        bInited = true;
        onMouseMove();
    }
};

onMouseMove = function(){
    vWin._xscale = vWin._yscale = _ymouse/4;
    vWin._x = _xmouse - (vWin._width/2);
    vWin._y = _ymouse - (vWin._height/2);
    updateAfterEvent();
};

vWin.attachVideo(ns);
ns.play("wasp_alpha.flv");
Mouse.hide();
```

10. Save the Flash document, and test it (Ctrl+Enter or ⌘+Enter). The video loads into the vWin instance, and as you move the mouse cursor, the wasp video scales based on the cursor's location, as shown in Figure 17-46.

Figure 17-46: The finished Flash movie

You can find the completed files in the `ch17/alpha_3D_model` folder of this book's CD-ROM.

We'd like to know what you think about this chapter. Visit `www.flashsupport.com/feedback` to send us your comments.

Summary

✦ Flash Video can be deployed as .swf files or .flv files. You can load .flv files from a Web server or stream them from a Flash Communication Server or Flash Video Streaming Service provider.

✦ You can compress source video files in Flash Basic 8 or Flash Pro 8. Flash Pro 8 offers expanded controls for the new On2 VP6 codec.

✦ Flash Player 8 is required for .flv files using the On2 VP6 codec. You can use the Sorenson Spark codec with Flash Video content in Flash Player 6 or higher.

✦ The On2 VP6 codec offers superior compression and image quality compared to Sorenson Spark. However, VP6 requires more computer processing power and memory.

✦ Flash Pro 8's Video Import wizard and the Flash 8 Video Encoder application can add embedded cue points to an .flv file. These cue points can be detected in ActionScript.

✦ The new FLVPlayback component offers you a wide range of control skins and takes the guesswork out of implementing video content with your Flash movies.

✦ You can use SMIL files to control which .flv file is played by the FLVPlayback component.

✦ The Flash 8 Video Encoder can batch process your video clips to the .flv file format.

✦ Sorenson Squeeze 4.2 can create high-quality .flv files in the Sorenson Spark Pro or On2 VP6 codec. Squeeze offers more detailed options for compression presets than the Flash 8 Video Encoder or Video Import wizard.

✦ The On2 VP6 codec supports alpha channels within video content. You can create alpha channels in video applications such as Adobe After Effects.

✦   ✦   ✦

Adding Basic Interactivity to Flash Movies

So far you've been learning how to make *things* — drawing shapes, creating symbols, and working with frames and adding special assets. In the next three chapters you learn how to integrate these various elements and how to make things *happen*. Chapter 18 introduces the concepts you need to understand when adding interactivity to presentations. Chapter 18 also gives you an orientation in the Flash 8 Actions panel, where you will find some changes from Flash MX 2004. Chapter 19 gives you the skills needed to control playback of multiple timelines. Find out how easy it is to use ActionScript to control display of internal elements in your Flash movies, including nested Movie Clips. See how Flash behaviors can be applied to control sound playback. If you want to apply these concepts and techniques to real Flash production, Chapter 20 has just what you need — a step-by-step explanation of how to build a basic Flash presentation with a non-linear interface. The project implements other important features such as components, named anchors, and accessibility options.

Understanding Actions and Event Handlers

Interactivity in a Flash movie can broadly be thought of as the elements that react and respond to a user's activity or input. A user has many ways to give input to a Flash movie, and Flash has even more ways to react. But how does interactivity actually work? It all starts with actions and event handlers.

Actions and Event Handlers

Even the most complex interactivity in Flash is fundamentally composed of two basic parts: the *behavior* (what happens), and the *cause* of the behavior (what makes it happen). Here's a simple example: Suppose you have a looping soundtrack in a movie and a button that, when clicked, turns the soundtrack off. The *behavior* is the sound turning off, and the *cause* of the behavior is the mouse clicking the button. Another example is stopping an animation when it reaches a certain frame on its timeline. When the last keyframe of the animation is played (the *cause*), an action on that keyframe stops the animation (the *behavior*). In Flash, the building blocks of behaviors are referred to as *actions*.

Note   Flash 8 features an interactive authoring tool called the Behaviors panel. Our usage of the term **behaviors** in the preceding description should not be confused with this feature. The Behaviors panel, which you'll learn about later in this chapter, enables you to quickly add an action or a series of actions to a Flash object or keyframe.

The first step in learning how to make interactive movies is becoming familiar with the list of possible actions. However, actions can't act without being told to act *by* something. That something is often the mouse pointer coming in contact with a button, but it can also be a keystroke, or simply a command issued from a keyframe. We refer to any occurrence that can cause an action to happen (such as the button click in the preceding example) as an *event*. The mechanism you use to tell Flash what action to perform when an event occurs is known as an *event handler*. This cause-and-effect relationship seems obvious, but it is an extremely important concept. For the purposes of creating basic interactivity, the difference between an action and the cause of an action is merely a practical detail. As the set of Flash actions, collectively know as *ActionScript*, continues to grow with each release of the Flash authoring tool (and, therefore, the interactive capabilities that they provide), understanding the relationship between actions and the things that cause them can be the key to adding more sophisticated behavior to your movies with traditional programming techniques. Every interactive framework, whether it is Macromedia Flash or Macromedia Director or Apple DVD Studio Pro, has unique handlers for specific events. Table 18-1 relates interactive events with Flash handlers.

Table 18-1: Events and Flash Handlers

Event	Type	Event handler	Example
Playback	Time-based	Keyframes `MovieClip` object `NetStream` object	Timeline plays until it reaches a certain frame; a Movie Clip instance monitors the amount of time that has passed in a movie; when a video stream stops playing, another stream begins playback.
Mouse	User input	`Button` object `MovieClip` object `Mouse` object	A visitor clicks a button; mouse movement detected over a Movie Clip instance.
Key press	User input	`Button` object `MovieClip` object `Key` object	A user presses the Enter key to submit a form; an alert appears if the Caps Lock key is enabled.
Window resize	User input	`Stage` object	A user clicks the maximize button on a Flash projector or Web browser window and Flash elements respond accordingly.
Microphone or Webcam activity	Audio/video input	`Microphone` object `Camera` object	When a user stops talking into a microphone, a graphic turns red; a stream starts to record audio and video when the movement is detected in front of a Webcam.
Data	System-based	`MovieClip` object data objects	Search results display in the Flash movie when the results have fully loaded.

While the breadth and depth of ActionScript involved with the interactions described in Table 18-1 may seem overwhelming, don't worry—we're taking it one step at a time. First, you'll learn about what the new Behaviors panel can do. Then you'll learn how to set up the Actions panel, whose look and feel has changed from previous versions of Flash. Later, we'll look at actions that control movie playback. Later, you'll also learn how to call these actions in various ways with three kinds of event handlers: button manipulation, keyframes, and keystrokes.

What are behaviors?

Flash 8 includes a Behaviors panel, which was introduced in Flash MX 2004. This panel is designed to help a novice who is just starting to use Flash for design and development. You can open the Behaviors panel, shown in Figure 18-1, by choosing Window ➪ Behaviors (Shift+F3).

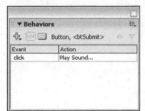

Figure 18-1: The Behaviors panel showing a Button component with a behavior applied

If you create a new Flash document and select the first frame of Layer 1, you can click the Add Behavior (+) button at the top-left corner of the Behaviors panel to see a list of categories (see Figure 18-2).

Figure 18-2: The categories in the Add Behavior menu

These categories represent a variety of objects you can control with one or more behaviors. So what do behaviors do? In the simplest sense, a behavior is automated scripting. When you add a behavior to an event handler, Flash 8 generates the necessary ActionScript code to make that behavior happen. Let's take a quick look at a Web behavior.

1. Create a new Flash document by choosing File ➪ New. In the New Document dialog box, double-click the Flash document item. Save the new document as **button_behavior.fla**.

2. Rename Layer 1 to **button**.

3. Open the Components panel (Ctrl+F7 or ⌘+F7). Expand the User Interface set, and drag an instance of the Button component to the Stage.

Tip   Whenever you place a new element on the Stage, make sure you set its X and Y positions to an integer value in the Property inspector. An integer is a whole number, without any decimals. By placing your elements at integer values, embedded fonts display much more crisply.

4. Select the Button component instance on the Stage, and open the Property inspector. In the <Instance Name> field, type **cbtWeb**. Click the Parameters tab, and in the label field, type **web site** (see Figure 18-3).

Tip   Throughout this book, we use naming conventions for our symbol instances, especially Movie Clip and component instances. The convention for this example uses a three-letter prefix for component names, such cbt. This abbreviation stands for **c**omponent **but**ton. Naming conventions enable you to more quickly review and understand your ActionScript code.

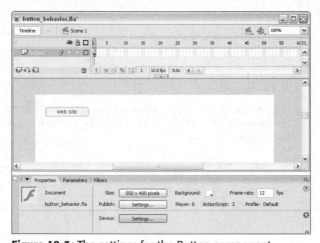

Figure 18-3: The settings for the Button component

5. With the Button instance selected on the Stage, open the Behaviors panel. Click the Add Behavior (+) button, and choose Web ➪ Go to Web Page. In the Go to URL dialog box, type **http://www.flashsupport.com** in the URL field. Choose "_blank" in the Open in menu. Refer to Figure 18-4. Click OK when you are done entering the parameters.

Figure 18-4: The Go to URL settings

6. Now look at the code that Flash 8 created for the behavior. Select the cbtWeb instance, and choose Window ➪ Actions (F9). You'll see the following code:

```
on (click) {

    //Goto Webpage Behavior
    getURL("http://www.flashsupport.com","_blank");
    //End Behavior

}
```

The heart of this code is the event handler, on( ), and the getURL( ) action. When the user clicks the Button component instance, the on( ) handler detects the click and executes (or *invokes*) the getURL( ) action. You'll learn more about these actions later in this chapter.

The click event is available in Flash Player 7 and higher, and is specific to the UI components. This event is not used for standard mouse events on Button symbol instances.

7. Save your Flash document (File➪Save) and choose Control➪Test Movie. When the Flash movie loads, click the button. Your Web browser should open to the www.flashsupport.com Web site, the official support site for this book.

You can find the completed file, button_behavior.fla, in the ch18 folder of this book's CD-ROM.

We won't discuss any other behaviors in this chapter, as you can find specific categories of behaviors explained in other parts of the book:

MovieClip behaviors, Chapter 19, "Building Timelines and Interactions"

Projector behavior, Chapter 23, "Using the Flash Player and Projector"

Sound behaviors, Chapter 15, "Adding Sound"

Behaviors enable you to learn by example — you can add a behavior to an object and look at the code used to describe the interaction.

Experienced Flash developers and programmers will be the first to tell you that it's not a good idea to put a lot of code on objects that are on the Stage. Most scripts are placed on one or more keyframes, or the code is stored in a separate .as file. You learn more about programming practices in Part VII, "Approaching ActionScript."

What is ActionScript?

Every interactive authoring system uses a language (or code) that enables elements within the system to communicate. Just as there are several languages that people use to speak to one another around the globe, there are hundreds of programming languages in use today. In an effort to make Flash more usable to computer programmers, Flash's scripting language, called ActionScript, changed much of its formatting in Flash 5 to mirror JavaScript, a fundamental element for Dynamic HyperText Markup Language (DHTML) and HTML Web pages. Right now, we focus on using the most basic Flash ActionScript.

In Flash MX 2004, ActionScript matured to a whole new version, dubbed ActionScript 2.0, or AS2. ActionScript 2.0 is a different — and more complex — style of coding than what was used in Flash MX and earlier. The ActionScript style used in Flash MX and earlier is now known as ActionScript 1.0, or AS1. It's still perfectly valid to code in either style. ActionScript 2.0 will feel more familiar to developers who have used other object-oriented programming languages such as C++ or Java.

Cross-Reference

If you're interested in learning the fundamental building blocks of ActionScript programming, check out our advanced coverage of ActionScript in Chapters 24 through 35. The three chapters of Part V are intended to provide a starting point for Flash designers and developers who are new to Flash actions and interactive concepts. Exhaustive coverage of the ActionScript language can be found in the *Flash ActionScript Bible* series by Joey Lott and Robert Reinhardt (Wiley).

Navigating the Actions panel

Flash 8 has a specific interface element that enables you to add interactive commands to Flash movies — the Actions panel. Unlike behaviors and the Behaviors panel, you don't use menus to add interactive functionality — you type the ActionScript code describing the interactivity in (or out of) of the Actions panel. You can open the Actions panel in a number of ways:

✦ Go to Windows ➪ Actions

✦ Press the F9 key (or Option+F9 on Mac)

✦ Alt+double-click (or Option+double-click) a keyframe in the Timeline window

If you have a keyframe selected in the Timeline window, the Actions panel will be titled Actions - Frame (see Figure 18-5). If you have a Movie Clip symbol instance selected on the Stage, you'll see the name Actions - Movie Clip. If you have a Button symbol instance selected on the Stage, the Actions panel will be titled Actions - Button. If you have a component selected, the Actions panel will simply read Actions. Don't be confused — there is only one Actions panel. Flash 8 simply lets you know the object to which you are assigning actions.

New Feature

The Actions panel in Flash 8 features a new Script Assist mode. Script Assist enables you to code ActionScript by selecting actions and filling in parameters, instead of writing out all the code by hand. If you used Normal mode in Flash MX or earlier, you'll be happy to know that Normal mode is essentially re-integrated as Script Assist in Flash 8.

As shown in Figure 18-5, the Actions panel in Flash 8 has three distinct areas (counter-clockwise from the left): the Actions toolbox, the Script navigator, and the Script pane. The new Script Assist area is available within the Script pane. There are two auto-snap dividers, one dividing the Actions toolbox and Script navigator from the Script pane, and another subdividing the Actions toolbox and Script navigator. You may want to practice opening and closing these dividers, as well as dragging each to your preferred width and height, respectively. Figures 18-5 and 18-6 show a breakdown of the new Actions panel in Flash 8.

✦ The Actions toolbox contains several nested booklets of ActionScript commands. You can select actions to add to the Script pane.

New Feature

The Actions toolbox now has a booklet selection drop-down menu. The default set of booklets displayed in the toolbox pertain to ActionScript 1.0 and 2.0, but you can switch to other sets of booklets, including Flash Lite 1.0 and Flash Lite 1.1. These booklets only display actions compatible with the Flash Lite 1.0/1.1 players that ship on some mobile phones.

✦ The Script navigator can jump to any script within your Flash document. When you select a keyframe or object in this pane, any code attached to the item is displayed in the Script pane.

Tip The Script navigator shows the actions for the entire document, not just for the current time-line.

✦ The Script pane displays the current code for an item selected on the Stage, a keyframe selected in the Timeline window, or an item selected in the Script navigator. You can type, copy, cut, and paste code into the Script pane, as long as you are not working in Script Assist mode. An options bar is located at the top of the Script pane as well. The options bar contains several buttons to modify, search, debug, or format your code in the Script pane. You can also find most of these options in the panel's options menu, located in the top-right corner of the panel.

Tip You can click the pin icon at the bottom tab of the script in the Script pane. You can pin multiple scripts in the Script pane, and quickly tab between them.

✦ The Script Assist area within the Script pane enables you to visualize your code with contextual parameters, as fill-in text fields or drop-down menus, as shown in Figure 18-6. The Script Assist mode is most useful for beginners learning ActionScript for the first time. To enter Script Assist mode, click the Script Assist button on the options bar of the Script pane. Not all actions have the same ease of use within Script Assist; more complex ActionScript code is not well-suited for Script Assist mode. When Script Assist mode is enabled, you cannot edit code manually within the Script pane, and you cannot switch the active booklet set.

Tip When the Actions panel is in focus, a highlighted bar shows up on the left side of the Script pane. This highlighted color enables you to know if you can start typing in the Script pane.

For this chapter, you'll work primarily within the Timeline Control booklet, located within the Global Functions booklet in the Actions toolbox.

You can add actions to the Script pane in one of three ways:

✦ Drag an action from the Actions toolbox to the Script pane.

✦ Select an action from the Actions menu, accessed by clicking the plus (+) icon.

✦ Double-click an action in the Actions pane.

To delete actions, select the action line(s) in the Script pane, and press the Delete or Backspace key on the keyboard.

Once you have added an action to the Script pane, you can specify parameters (or arguments) for the action. Depending on the action, you may or may not need to type such parameters. By default, Flash 8 provides code hints as you type actions into the Script pane. The Show Code Hint button enables you to see the parameters for an action, as shown in the `gotoAndPlay` action in Figure 18-5.

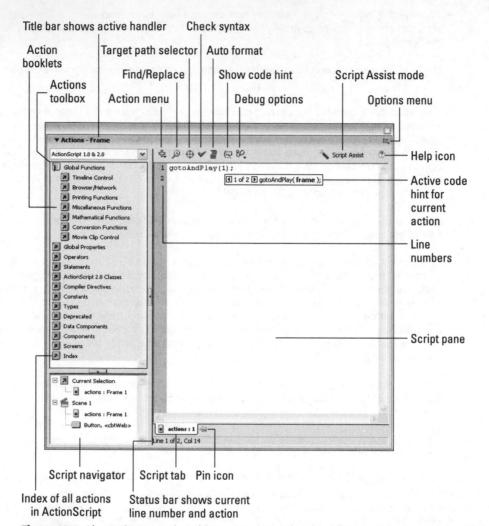

Figure 18-5: The Actions panel enables you to instantly add, delete, or change Flash movie commands.

More importantly, the Script Assist mode makes it much easier for you to add and adjust settings for basic actions, especially those you find in the Timeline Control booklet. You use the Script Assist mode throughout this chapter to learn the basic control actions.

You should get in the habit of clicking the Check Syntax button (the blue check mark) to make sure you didn't mistype an action. If you have an error, the Output panel displays some information related to the error, indicating the line number where the syntax error occurs.

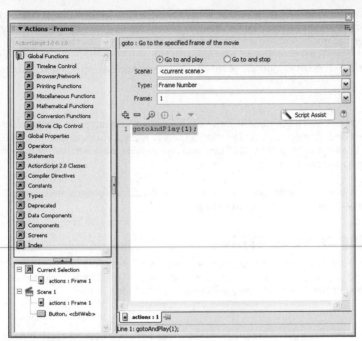

Figure 18-6: The Script Assist mode displays a more user-friendly interface for controlling action parameters.

Cross-Reference

In Chapter 24, "Knowing the Nuts and Bolts of Code," you can also learn about referencing actions in the Help panel of Flash 8.

For now, let's look at two booklets in the Actions toolbox's Global Functions booklet: Timeline Control and Browser/Network. The Timeline Control actions are listed in alphabetical order. The first eight actions in this booklet, including gotoAndPlay, gotoAndStop, play, and stop, control the playback of the movie. The last action, stopAllSounds, is a global command to handle sound playback.

Note

If you're in Script Assist mode, the actions listed in the action booklets may change. The actions in the Timeline Control booklet are reduced to goto, play, stop, and stopAllSounds. The Script Assist mode enables the missing actions in one of the other actions. For example, the gotoAndPlay and gotoAndStop actions are both available in the parameters of the goto action in Script Assist mode. The Browser/Network actions are also truncated in a similar fashion.

The Browser/Network actions—`fscommand`, `getURL`, `loadMovie/loadMovieNum`, `loadVariables/loadVariablesNum`, and `unloadMovie/unloadMovieNum`—enable movies to load external files and communicate with the browser, a Web server, or the stand-alone player. In this chapter, we'll get you up and running with the `getURL` action, which enables you to link to other Web resources outside of the Flash movie (such as Web pages and file downloads).

Note   Throughout this book, you'll see most actions specified with ( ) characters at the end of the action's name. For example, the `gotoAndPlay` action is really a method, and in code, it appears as `gotoAndPlay()`. In Part VII of this book, we provide more detailed information about code terms and practices.

The remaining Action booklets primarily offer extended ActionScript programming capabilities. We discuss many of these actions in later chapters.

A brief primer on code syntax

Some of the most difficult concepts for beginners to understand with code writing are white space, parentheses (( )), semicolons (;), and curly braces ({ }). In the following paragraphs, you learn how each of these affects your ActionScript code.

White space

White space is a collective term referring to any blank areas between lines of code. It includes spaces inserted by the spacebar, indentations inserted with the Tab key, and line returns inserted with the Enter or Return key. When Flash 8 compiles your ActionScript code into the Flash movie, the white space between your lines of code usually will not generate any errors. For example, the following code works exactly the same:

```
on(release){ getURL("mypage.html"); }
```

or

```
on(release){
    getURL("mypage.html");
}
```

or

```
on      (              release ){
getURL("mypage.html");
}
```

However, white space is an issue when it separates the key terms in the action, such as:

```
get URL("mypage.html");
```

The space between `get` and `URL` will cause an error when Flash 8 tries to create the Flash movie.

Tip   To check if your syntax is correct, click the Check Syntax button in the Actions panel. If you do have any white space errors, the Output panel will display information related to the error. Also, if you code has errors, you are prevented from entering the Script Assist mode.

The new Flash 8 interface for Mac OS X

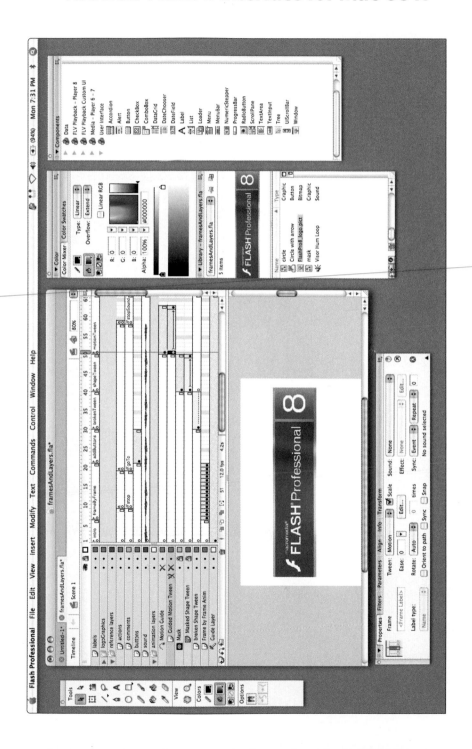

Learn to customize your Flash workspace in Chapter 4

The new Flash 8 interface for Windows XP

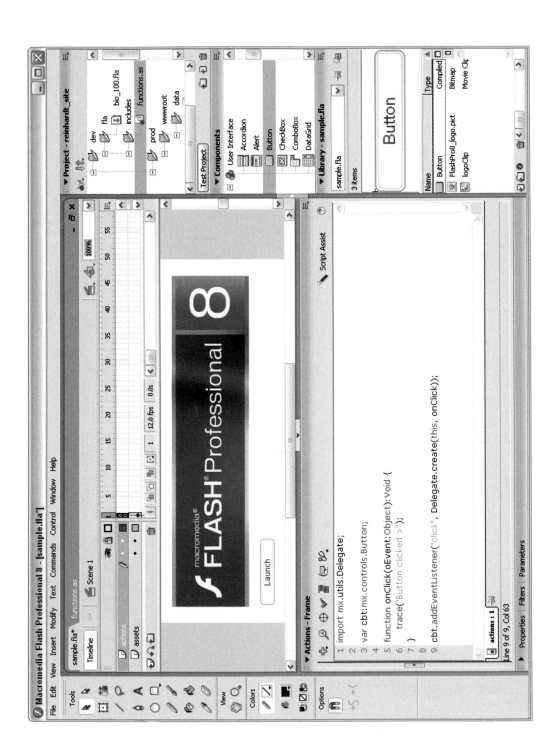

Learn to customize your Flash workspace in Chapter 4

Working with Color

Default Web 216 swatches

Web 216 Sort by Color

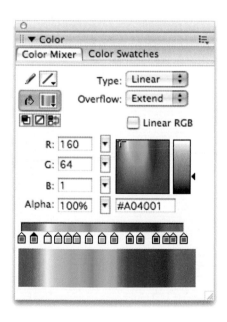

Enhanced gradient controls

Source GIF image and loaded
custom color swatches

Get to know the improved Flash 8 Color panels in Chapter 7

Use the new Adjust Color filter to quickly modify bitmaps or vector graphics

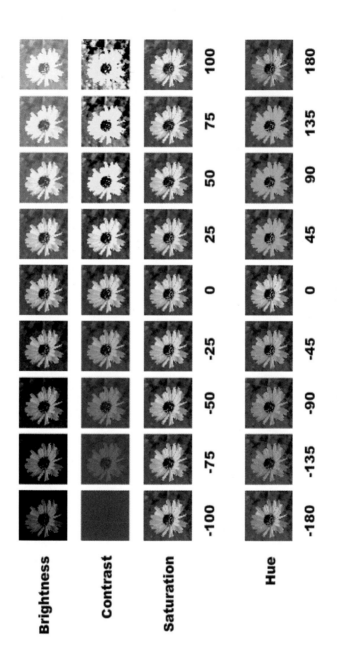

Learn to use Flash 8 Filters and Timeline effects in Chapter 12

Control color with greater ease and accuracy

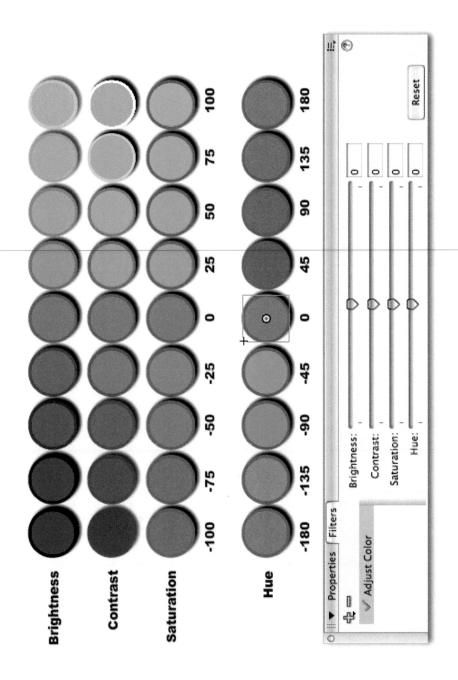

Learn the difference between Color filters and Color properties in Chapter 12

Use the new blend modes for static and animated effects

Learn to apply blend modes and combine them with filters in Chapter 12

Make better drop shadows and other dynamic effects

Learn to apply the new Flash 8 filters, including Drop Shadow, in Chapter 12

Create artwork with Flash drawing and effects tools

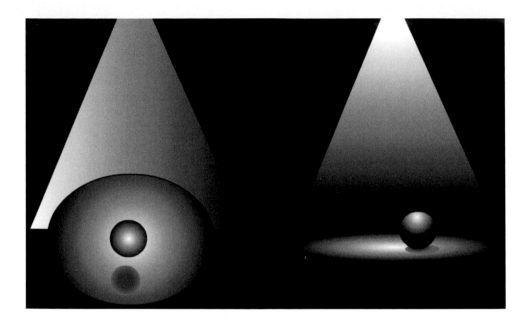

Create and modify custom gradients for lighting effects in Chapter 9

Import and optimize vector artwork in Flash 8

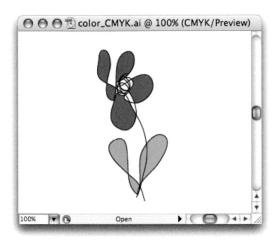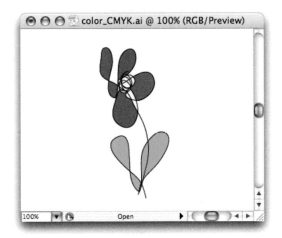

Original vector artwork in Illustrator's CMYK and RGB color spaces

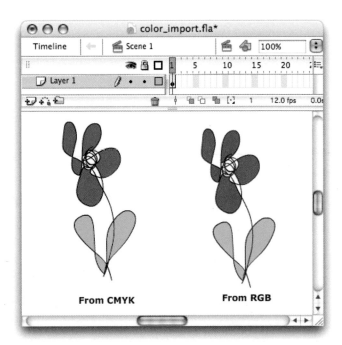

Imported EPS files as displayed in Flash's RGB environment

For guidelines on importing artwork refer to Chapter 16

Animation fundamentals and character animation techniques

Anticipation

Overlapping action

©doodie.com

character designs © **www.sandrocorsaro.com**

Bounces for head turns

Learn from examples by expert animators in Part III

Advanced animation strategies and special effects

Richard Bazley's illustrative animation drawn directly in Flash

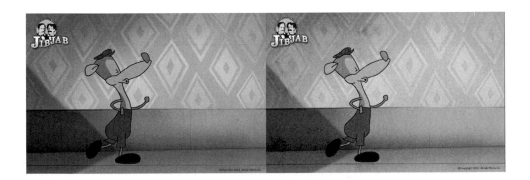

JibJab.com's filter techniques for broadcast animation

Learn from examples by expert animators in Part III

Work with digital video source files

Low-quality sample:
from a digital still camera

Mid-quality sample:
from a DV camcorder

High-quality sample:
from a DVCAM camcorder

Review digital source comparisons in Appendix D on the CD-ROM

Use video as a basis for fluid hand-drawn animation

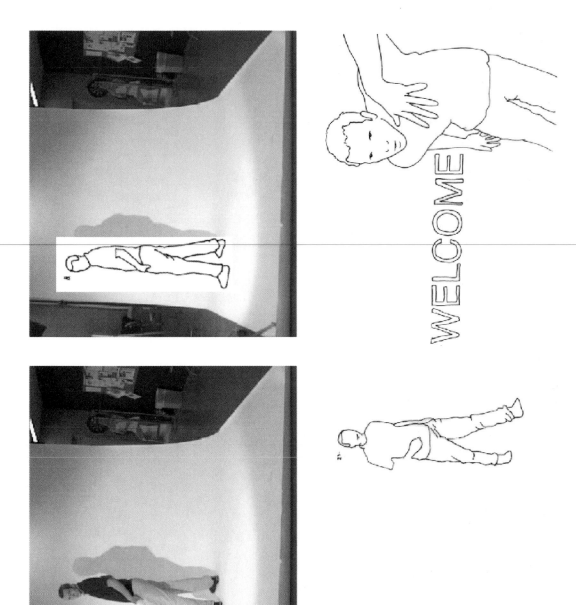

Animator Felix Stumpf explains his technique in Chapter 14

Build complete Flash 8 projects

"Making Your First Flash 8 Project" in Chapter 20

"Creating a Game in Flash" in Chapter 31

Flash 8 project examples relate to real-world workflow

Integrate Flash 8 components with your workflow

"Using the FLVPlayback Component" in Chapter 17

"Building an Image Gallery Component" in Chapter 35

Utilize video and image assets within your Flash movies

Unleash the power of data binding with Flash 8 components

Build a video clip selector with the XMLConnector component

Make a list of cue points for a video clip with ActionScript

Learn a variety of data binding techniques in Chapter 34

Parentheses

Many, but not all, actions require parentheses after the action term, such as on(), getURL(), or even play(). A general rule to remember is that if the action requires a parameter, such as on (release), then parentheses are required as well.

Note   Parameters are also referred to as arguments.

However, many actions, such as play() and stop(), still require parentheses, even though they do not use any arguments. Another rule for parentheses is that any open parenthesis (( ) must eventually be followed by a closing parenthesis ( )). A habit we like to encourage is counting the number of opening parentheses in a script and then counting the number of closing parentheses. If the numbers don't match, you need to review your code to find the place where you forgot to include a parenthesis.

Semicolons and curly braces

You've probably already noticed that most actions include a semicolon (;) at the end of the code line. In practice, many coders forget to include semicolons. Usually, Flash is very forgiving if you omit semicolons, but by no means should you be encouraged to omit them. The general rule for semicolons and curly braces is mutually inclusive: If your action doesn't end with an opening curly brace ({), it should end with a semicolon. As with parentheses, all opening curly braces must eventually be followed by a closing curly brace (}). Curly braces are commonly used with actions beginning with on, such as on() and onClipEvent(), as well as if and function declarations.

Cross-Reference   You'll learn more about if statements and functions in Part VII, "Approaching ActionScript."

Deprecated and Incompatible Actions: What Are They?

As the ActionScript language of Flash continues to expand and encompass new functionality, older actions coexist with newer and better actions (or methods, properties, event handlers, and functions, which we'll discuss later). While Flash Player 8 will continue to support ActionScript 1.0 and earlier actions, it's better not to use older actions if the newest version of the Flash Player has a new way of accomplishing the same task. Older actions that have been replaced with a new action (or new way to perform the same task) are called *deprecated actions*. The Actions panel in Flash 8 houses all deprecated actions in the Deprecated booklet of the Actions pane. Why shouldn't you use these actions? As you'll see in more advanced scripting, Flash 8 has specific syntax to target Movie Clips and determine whether certain frames have loaded, among other features of the ActionScript "dot syntax" language. The following figure shows the actions within the Deprecated ⇨ Actions booklet. Note that there are other groups of deprecated actions inside the Deprecated booklet as well.

Continued

continued

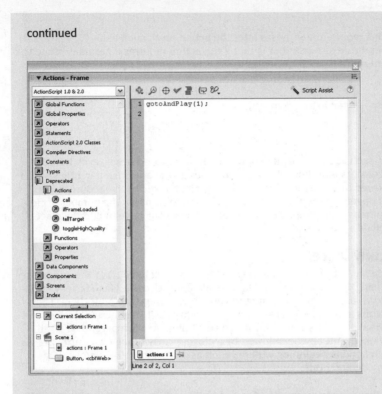

Although you should avoid actions that are highlighted in the Deprecated booklet if possible, Flash Player 8 continues to support them.

Flash 8 will also let you know if certain actions are not supported with the Player version that is selected in the Flash format tab of the Publish Settings (File ➪ Publish Settings). Note that you can also find the Player version setting in the Property inspector when you click an empty area of the Stage or the Work area. If an action is not supported by the version you have selected, the action is highlighted in yellow. The following figure shows this type of highlighting in the Actions panel. You will notice that the tooltip (or rollover description) indicates which version of the Flash Player supports the action.

Flash Player 4 (or earlier) and Flash Lite 1.0/1.1 will not support the `onClipEvent` or `updateAfterEvent` actions (among others), as these actions were introduced in Flash Player 5.

Your First Five Actions

Now that you have a general picture of what actions do, let's look at five common actions in detail. At this point, we're describing only the functionality of each action, not how to add an action to your movie. We provide information on adding an action in the next section, "Making Actions Happen with Event Handlers."

Cross-Reference

You will find coverage of further actions (and full-blown ActionScript) in later chapters.

Actions in the Flash interface appear alphabetically sorted from top to bottom. In the following sections, complementary actions are grouped together.

gotoAndPlay and gotoAndStop

These "go to" actions change the current frame of the movie to the target frame specified as the action's parameter. There are two variations:

✦ `gotoAndPlay`: Changes the current frame to the frame specified, and then executes a `play` action. `gotoAndPlay` provides the capability to show animated sequences as preludes to individual content areas. `gotoAndPlay` also gets frequent use in choose-your-own-adventure style animations, in which the user guides an animated character through different paths in a narrative.

Note

If you use a `gotoAndPlay()` action to go to a frame that has a `stop()` action, the timeline will stop at the new frame.

✦ `gotoAndStop`: Changes the current frame to the frame specified and then halts playback on that frame. `gotoAndStop` is often used to produce toolbar-style interfaces where the user clicks buttons to view different areas of content in a movie.

Both actions enable you to jump to certain areas of the Flash movie. The parameters of these actions start with the largest time unit, the scene, and end with the smallest one, the frame.

You can specify frames in other scenes as the target of `goto` actions with the scene parameter. As shown in the following code, you type the name of the scene first, with double quotes around the name, and then the frame number (without quotes) or frame label. In this example, `"Scene 2"` is the name of the scene and `"animate_in"` is the frame label in that scene to jump to.

```
gotoAndPlay("Scene 2", "animate_in");
```

However, if you only specify one parameter in a `gotoAndPlay` or `gotoAndStop` action, the parameter is interpreted as a frame label. For example, the following code tells the current timeline to jump to its `"menu"` frame label:

```
gotoAndStop("menu");
```

Caution   While we haven't looked at actions specifically for use in Movie Clip instances, make a note that you can't use a `goto` action specifying a scene within a Movie Clip instance. In this case, you should target the Main Timeline to go to and stop (or play) the keyframe label in the desired scene, omitting the Scene's name. For example, `_root.gotoAndStop("prod-ucts");` executed from a Movie Clip Timeline would tell the Main Timeline to go to and stop on the frame label `products`, which would be located in a different scene.

There are three methods of specifying the frame to which the movie should go when it receives a `goto` action. The methods for specifying the frame are

✦ **number:** Specifies the target frame as a number. Frame 1 is the beginning of the movie or scene. Frame numbers span scenes, so if you have a movie with two scenes, each containing 25 frames, and you add a `goto` action with Frame Number set to 50, your action advances the movie to the 25th frame of the second scene. Frame numbers should not use surrounding quotes, as frame labels do. The following action tells the current timeline to jump to frame 10 and start playing:

```
gotoAndPlay(10);
```

Caution   Using frame numbers to specify the targets of `goto` actions can lead to serious scalability problems in Flash movies. Adding frames at the beginning or in the middle of a movie's Timeline causes the subsequent frames to be renumbered. When those frames are renumbered, all `goto` actions that use frame numbers must be revised to point to the correct new number of their target frames.

In the vast majority of cases, `goto` actions that use a frame label to specify target frames are preferable to `goto` actions that use a frame number to specify target frames. Unlike numbered frame targets, `goto` actions with labeled frame targets continue to function properly, even if the targeted frame changes position on the timeline.

✦ **label:** Individual keyframes can be given names via the Label field in the Property inspector. Once a frame is labeled, a `goto` action can target it by name. To specify a label as the target of a `goto` action, type the name of the frame as the action's parameter. The following example tells the Flash movie to go to the frame labeled `"products"` and stop at that frame.

```
gotoAndStop("products");
```

✦ **ActionScript expression:** Specifies the target frame as an interpreted ActionScript code segment. You use expressions to dynamically assign targets of `goto` actions. Here's a quick example of a string variable being used as a frame label in ActionScript 1.0 style:

```
var targetLabel = "products";
gotoAndPlay(targetLabel);
```

Notice that the term `targetLabel` does not use quotes, because it is not the actual frame label name. When the Flash Player interprets this action, it looks up the value of targetLabel, which is `"products"`, and inserts that value into the `gotoAndPlay` action. In ActionScript 2.0, the same action looks like this:

```
var targetLabel:String = "products";
gotoAndPlay(targetLabel);
```

Cross-Reference   Expressions are covered in Chapter 24, "Knowing the Nuts and Bolts of Code."

nextFrame and prevFrame

The `nextFrame` and `prevFrame` actions act like a `gotoAndStop` action, in that they both transport the timeline to a new position and stop.

✦ `nextFrame`: This action tells the current timeline to move forward one frame and stop playback. `nextFrame` can be used in conjunction with `prevFrame` to quickly set up a slide-show-style walkthrough of content, where each of a series of contiguous keyframes contains the content of one "slide." This action does not use any parameters. The following code moves the timeline to the next frame:

```
nextFrame();
```

✦ `prevFrame`: This action moves the current timeline backward one frame and stops playback. For example, if the timeline is on frame 20, and the movie runs a `prevFrame()` action, the timeline moves to frame 19. As with the `nextFrame` action, `prevFrame` does not use any parameters:

```
prevFrame();
```

nextScene and prevScene

These actions advance the Flash movie to a new scene. Here's how they work:

✦ `nextScene`: This action tells the current timeline to move to the first frame of the next scene. You can use `nextScene` for more elaborate slide shows or demonstration movies, where each scene contains animated content with a stop action on the last frame. The last frame of the scene then contains a button using the `nextScene` action. This action does not use any parameters. The following code tells the movie to jump to the next scene:

```
nextScene();
```

✦ `prevScene`: This action jumps the movie to the previous scene. For example, if the playhead is in Scene 2, the timeline moves to the first frame of Scene 1. As with the `nextScene()` action, `prevScene()` does not use any parameters:

```
prevFrame();
```

Note

The `nextScene` and `prevScene` actions do not automatically recycle the scenes when the last or first scene is reached, respectively. For example, if you have three scenes and use a `nextScene` action while the movie is on the last scene, the movie will not jump back to the first scene.

Tip

While you may find it simpler to segment your Flash content across several scenes as you begin to learn Flash, most seasoned Flash designers and developers only use one scene, and separate content across several Movie Clip symbols placed on one or more frames of Scene 1. Scenes are not compatible with standard targeting syntax, as you'll learn in the next chapter.

On the CD-ROM

You can find an example of `nextScene` and `prevScene` usage in the document named `nextScene.fla` in the `ch18` folder of this book's CD-ROM.

play and stop

These simple actions are the true foundations of Flash timeline control. play sets a movie or a Movie Clip instance in motion. When a play action is executed, Flash starts the sequential display of each frame's contents along the current timeline.

The rate at which the frames are displayed is measured as frames per second, or fps. The fps rate can be set from 0.01 to 120 (meaning that the play action can cause the display of as little as 1 frame every 100 seconds to as many as 120 frames in 1 second, subject to the limitations of the computer's processing speed). The default fps is 12.

Once play has started, frames continue to be displayed one after the other, until another action interrupts the flow, or the end of the movie or Movie Clip's timeline is reached. If the end of a movie's timeline is reached, the movie either loops (begins playing again at frame 1, Scene 1), or stops on the last frame.

Once the end of the Movie Clip's timeline is reached, playback loops back to the beginning of the clip, and the clip continues playing. To prevent looping, add a stop action to the last frame of your Movie Clip.

Note   A single play action affects only a single timeline, whether that timeline is the main movie timeline or the timeline of a Movie Clip instance. For example, a play action executed inside a Movie Clip does not cause the Main Timeline to begin playing. Likewise, any goto action on the Main Timeline doesn't migrate to the Movie Clips that reside there. A timeline must be specifically targeted to control playback along that timeline. If there is no specified target, the action is referring to its own timeline. However, this is not the case for animations within Graphic symbol instances. An animation in a Graphic symbol is controlled by actions on the timeline in which the symbol instance is present — Flash ignores actions on a Graphic symbol's timeline.

stop, as you may have guessed, halts the progression of a movie or Movie Clip that is in a play state. stop is often used with buttons for user-controlled playback of a movie, or on frames to end an animated sequence.

Tip   Movie Clip instances placed on any timeline begin to play automatically. Remember to add a stop action on the first frame of a Movie Clip if you don't want it to play right away.

stopAllSounds

A simple but powerful action that mutes any sounds playing in the movie at the time the action is executed, stopAllSounds does not disable sounds permanently — it simply cancels any sounds that happen to be currently playing. It is sometimes used as a quick-and-dirty method for making buttons that shut off background looping soundtracks. stopAllSounds is not appropriate for controlling whether individual (or specific) sounds are played or muted.

getURL

Want to link to a Web page from a Flash movie? No problem. That's what getURL is for. You can find the getURL action in the Global Functions ⇨ Browser/Network booklet of the Actions panel. getURL is simply Flash's method of making a conventional hypertext link. It's nearly the equivalent of an anchor tag in HTML (<a href="...">), except that Flash's getURL can also send variables for form submission. getURL can be used to link to a standard Web page, an FTP site, another Flash movie, an executable, a server-side script, or anything that exists on the Internet or on an accessible local file system.

getURL has three parameters that are familiar to Web builders (the first one, url, is required for this action to work):

✦ **url:** This is the network address of the page, file, script, or resource to which you are linking. Any value is permitted (including ActionScript expressions), but the linked item can be displayed only if the reference to it is correct. url is directly analogous to the HREF attribute of an HTML anchor tag. You can use a relative or absolute URL as well. Examples:

```
http://www.yoursite.com/
ftp://ftp.yoursite.com/pub/documents.zip
menu.html
/cgi-bin/processform.cgi
/script/form.cfm
```

Since Flash 4, getURL can be used to link to documents on the Web from the standalone Flash player. Execution of a getURL action in the stand-alone player causes the default Web browser to launch and load the requested URL.

Tip

You can specify secure domain URLs by using the https protocol for SSL (Secure Socket Layer) connections.

✦ **window:** This is the name of the frame or window in which you wish to load the resource specified in the url setting. The window parameter is directly analogous to the target attribute of an HTML anchor tag. In addition to enabling the entry of custom frame and window names, the window parameter can use the following browser-standard target names:

• "_self": Loads the URL into the same frame or window as the current movie. If you do not specify a window parameter in the getURL action, this behavior will be the default.

• "_blank": Creates a new browser window and loads the URL into it.

• "_parent": Removes the current frameset and loads the URL in its place. Use this option if you have multiple nested framesets, and you want your linked URL to replace only the frameset in which your movie resides.

• "_top": Loads the URL into the current browser and removes all framesets in the process. Use this option if your movie is in a frame, but you want your linked URL to be loaded normally into the browser, outside the confines of any frames.

Note

Frame windows and/or JavaScript windows can be assigned names. You can target these names by manually typing the name in the Window field. For example, if you had a frame defined as <frame name="main". . .>, you could load specific URLs into a frame named main from a Flash movie.

✦ **method:** This parameter enables getURL to function similarly to an HTML form submission. For normal links, the method parameter should be omitted. But in order to submit values to a server-side script, one of the submission methods, "GET" or "POST", should be specified. For a complete discussion on submitting data to a server from a Flash movie (using the new `LoadVars` object), see Chapter 29, "Sending Data In and Out of Flash."

 Tip

`getURL` functions in the Test Movie environment. Both the Flash stand-alone player and the Test Movie command give you access to external and/or local URLs.

Let's look at some quick examples of how you can write a `getURL` action. The following code tells the browser to load the URL, `www.wiley.com`, into the current browser window:

```
getURL("http://www.wiley.com");
```

Alternatively, you can specify a unique target for the loaded URL. The following example loads an HTML document named `menu.html` into a frame named `menu_frame`:

```
getURL("menu.html", "menu_frame");
```

A more advanced usage of the `getURL` action sends variables from the Flash movie to a Web server's script, which is set up to receive the variables. The following code looks up the version of the Flash Player playing the movie and sends to a script that logs the information:

```
var playerVersion = getVersion();
getURL("http://www.mysite.com/scripts/log.cfm", "_self", "GET");
```

As we mentioned with the `goto` actions, you can also use expressions with `getURL` actions. Expressions can be used as parameters of any ActionScript action. The following example uses a string variable to specify the URL used by a `getURL` action:

```
var siteURL = "http://www.flashsupport.com";
getURL(siteURL);
```

You should start familiarizing yourself with the ActionScript notation that Flash uses for each action (see Table 18-2). As you use Flash for more advanced interactivity, you'll need to have a firm grasp of code notation. Part VII, "Approaching ActionScript," teaches you how to start building more advanced code.

Table 18-2: Common Actions and ActionScript Notation

Action	ActionScript notation	Arguments
gotoAndStop	gotoAndStop(arguments);	Scene Name (Frame Label, Number, or Expression)
gotoAndPlay	gotoAndPlay(arguments);	Scene Name (Frame Label, Number, or Expression)
nextFrame	nextFrame();	None
prevFrame	prevFrame();	None
nextScene	nextScene();	None
prevScene	prevScene();	None
play	play();	None

stop	stop();	None
stopAllSounds	stopAllSounds();	None
getURL	getURL(arguments);	url, target frame or window, method for form submission

Making Actions Happen with Event Handlers

The ten common actions we discussed in the previous sections provide many of the behaviors that you need to make an interesting interactive Flash movie. But those actions can't make your movies interactive on their own. They need to be told when to happen. To tell a Flash movie when an action should occur, you need event handlers. Event handlers specify the condition(s) under which an action can be made to happen. For instance, you might want to mouse-click a button to initiate a play() action, or you might want a movie to stop when a certain keyframe in the timeline is reached. Creating interactivity in your movies is simply a matter of deciding what event you want to detect (mouse click, keystroke, and so on), adding the appropriate event handler to detect it, and specifying the action(s) that should be performed when it happens.

Before we describe each event handler in detail, we'll show you an example of exactly how an event handler merges with an action to form a functioning interactive button.

Combining an action with an event handler to make a functioning button

Imagine that you have a short, endlessly looping movie in which a wire-frame cube rotates. Now imagine that you want to add a button to your movie that, when clicked, stops the cube from rotating by stopping the playback of the looping movie. Here's what you need to do:

On the CD-ROM

For this exercise, you can use the rotatingCube.fla file located in the ch18 folder on this book's CD-ROM. The finished file is named rotatingCube_complete.fla.

1. Open the starter Flash document, rotatingCube.fla. Save this document as **rotatingCube_complete.fla** on your local hard drive.

2. Make a new layer called **button.**

3. Place a button on the button layer. You can use Flash 8's sample Stop button found in the class buttons ⇨ Circle Buttons folder of the Buttons library (Window ⇨ Common Libraries ⇨ Buttons). See Figure 18-7 to see this button's placement on the Stage.

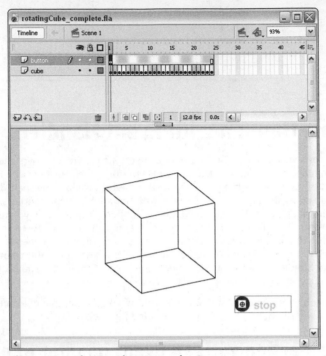

Figure 18-7: The Stop button on the Stage

Tip   Selecting buttons and editing button properties sometimes can be tricky if buttons are enabled in the Flash authoring environment. For easier button manipulation, disable buttons by unchecking Enable Simple Buttons under the Control menu.

4. With the Stop Button instance selected, open the Actions panel (F9). Click the Script Assist button, and open the Global Functions ➪ Movie Clip Control booklet in the Actions toolbox.

5. Double-click the on event handler in the Movie Clip Control booklet, or drag it to the Script pane. A list of mouse events for on appears in the Script Assist area of the Script pane (shown in Figure 18-8). Notice that the release event is automatically checked for you. The release event is one of several mouse-click events (another frequently-used event is press; we describe both later in this chapter in the section titled "The Flash event handlers"). Notice that the event is specified between the parentheses of the on handler in the Script pane. You've now told Flash that you want something to happen when the mouse clicks the button. All that's left is to tell it what should happen. In other words, you need to nest another action within the on (release){} code.

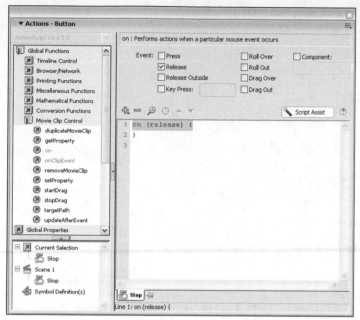

Figure 18-8: Adding a release event to the on handler

6. Now you'll try another method for adding an action to the Script pane. While in Script Assist mode, make sure line 1 in the Script pane is highlighted. Then click the plus (+) button in the toolbar of the Actions panel. From the menu, choose Global Functions ⇨ Timeline Control ⇨ stop, as shown in Figure 18-9.

A `stop` action will be placed between the curly braces ({ }) of the `on` handler. The Script Assist mode automatically formats the code cleanly. The Script pane should now read as follows:

```
on (release){
  stop();
}
```

The `stop` action, represented by the code `stop();`, is contained by the curly braces { and } that mark the beginning and end of the list of actions that are executed when the `release` event occurs (there could be any number of actions in this list). Each action line (handlers excluded) must end with the semicolon (;) character.

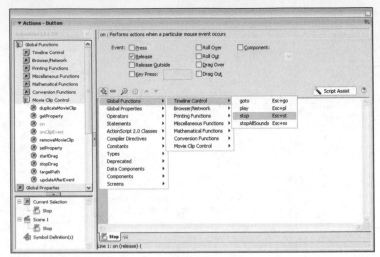

Figure 18-9: Adding a stop action to the on handler.

7. You now have a button in your Flash movie that stops the movie's playback when it is clicked. Save your Flash document (.fla), and test the movie by choosing Control ⇨ Test Movie. When you click the button, the rotating cube animation should stop.

To make any interactivity in your movies, you simply have to apply the basic principles you used to make the stop button: Decide which action (or actions) you want to happen, and indicate when you want that action to happen with an event handler. Let's look now at more event handlers you can use to make those actions happen.

The Flash event handlers

Three primary event handlers exist in Flash: those that detect mouse activity on Button instances (button manipulation), those that recognize when a key is pressed on the keyboard (key presses), and those that respond to the progression of the timeline (keyframes).

Working with mouse events and buttons

Event handlers that occur based on the user's interaction with a button rely entirely on the location and movement of the mouse pointer. If the mouse pointer comes in contact with a Button symbol's Hit area, it changes from an arrow icon to a finger pointer icon. At that time the mouse is described as "over" the button. If the mouse pointer is not over a button, it is said to be *out* or *outside* of the button. General movement of the mouse *without* the mouse button depressed is referred to as *rolling*. General movement of the mouse *with* the mouse button pressed is referred to as *dragging*.

Cross-Reference   If you don't know how to make a Button symbol and its various states, read Chapter 6, "Symbols, Instances, and the Library."

Caution   Event handlers and actions for buttons must be placed only on Button *instances*, not on the four frames in the timeline of the original Button symbol. One of the features in Flash 8 is that it will not enable you to place *any* actions in a Button symbol timeline.

It's worth mentioning that you can assign one or more mouse events to a Button instance's on handler. For example, the following code will be invoked when the user releases the mouse button over or outside of the Hit area of the Flash button:

```
on (release, releaseOutside){
    stop();
}
```

As this code demonstrates, multiple events are separated by a comma (,). You can specify as many events as you need within the parentheses of the on handler.

Here are the mouse-based events for Flash buttons:

press

A single mouse click can actually be divided into two separate components: the downstroke (the *press*) and the upstroke (the *release*). A press event occurs when the mouse pointer is over the Hit area of a button *and* the downstroke of a mouse click is detected. Press is best used for control panel–style buttons, especially toggle switches.

Caution   Typically, developers should program reversible decisions for primary navigation so that users can abort their clicks by rolling the cursor away from the Hit area before releasing the mouse. For example, a user might click a button for more information and decide she would rather not get that information. We do not recommend using the press event for important user moves such as these because it does not give users an opportunity to abort their moves.

release

A release event occurs when the mouse pointer is over the Hit area of a button *and* both the downstroke and the upstroke of a mouse click are detected. The release event is the standard button click event.

Tip   If you use the Track as Menu Item behavior for a Button instance in the Property inspector, a button will respond to a release event over its Hit state even if the mouse was pressed outside of the button's Hit area.

releaseOutside

A releaseOutside event occurs in response to the following series of mouse movements:

1. The mouse pointer moves over a button's Hit area.

2. The mouse button is pressed.

3. The mouse pointer is moved off the button's Hit area.

4. The mouse button is released.

The releaseOutside event can be used to react to an aborted button click.

rollOver

A `rollOver` event occurs when the mouse pointer moves onto the Hit area of a button without the mouse button depressed.

> **Note** To perform standard rollover button effects, such as graphic art changes or sound events, you can insert graphics and sound on to the Over state of the Button symbol timeline. It's common practice, however, to create Movie Clip instances that use mouse event handlers for specialized rollover effects. You learn more about this advanced usage of Movie Clips in Chapter 25, "Controlling Movie Clips." You can also find a bonus file demonstrating Movie Clip–based rollovers at `www.flashsupport.com/bonus/button_transition/button_anim.html`.

rollOut

A `rollOut` event occurs when the mouse pointer moves off of the Hit area of a button without the mouse button depressed. This event is commonly used for switching an advanced button's graphic state back to its original state when the user rolls off the button.

dragOver

A `dragOver` event occurs in response to the following series of mouse movements:

1. The mouse button is pressed when the mouse pointer is outside the Hit area of a Flash button.

2. The mouse pointer moves over the Hit area while the mouse button is still depressed.

The `dragOver` event is rather obscure, but you could use it for special cases of interactivity such as revealing a hidden item in a game. For example, when the mouse button is held down and mouse movement occurs over a specific area, ActionScript can detect the coordinates of the mouse movement and reveal a Movie Clip instance that is otherwise invisible on the Stage.

dragOut

A `dragOut` event occurs in response to the following series of mouse movements:

1. The mouse button is pressed when the mouse pointer is over the Hit area of a Flash button.

2. The mouse pointer moves outside the Hit area of the Flash button, and the mouse button is still depressed.

As with `dragOver`, you'll likely encounter very few situations where the `dragOut` event is necessary. Most of the more complicated mouse events are only useful for Flash games and experimental user interfaces.

Capturing keyboard input

You can also use event handlers to detect events that occur on the user's keyboard. You can enable your Flash movies to "capture" a key press (also known as a *keystroke*) initiated by the user. One way in which ActionScript can detect a keystroke is by using the `keyPress` event. This event lets you execute an action (or series of actions) when the user presses a key on the keyboard. The implementation method for a `keyPress` event handler may be confusing, but it's the least code-intensive (and most designer-friendly) route: To add a `keyPress` event handler, you must first place a button onstage at the frame where you want the keyboard to be active. You then assign the `keyPress` event to the Button instance's `on` handler. Keep in mind, though, that the button's Hit area has no effect on the `keyPress` event detection. As such, even though the `keyPress` event is defined on a button, any key press that occurs in the Flash movie can be captured by the button, regardless of the user's mouse position.

Tip If you are using the button only as a container for your keystroke event handler and you do not want the button to appear on Stage, you should make sure that (in Edit mode for the symbol) all the frames of the Button symbol timeline are blank.

For example, if you have a Button instance on the Stage of your Flash document, you can select the Button instance, open the Actions panel, and add the following code to capture an Enter keystroke:

```
on (keyPress "<Enter>"){
    trace("The Enter key was pressed.");
}
```

Note A trace action sends a message to the Output panel in the Test Movie environment. You'll learn more about trace actions in Part VII, "Approaching ActionScript."

As you can see in this example, you specify the key's name between a set of double quotes, after the keyPress term. Some keys, such as Enter and Escape, require less than (<) and greater than (>) characters as well. You can use the keyPress event in conjunction with other mouse events. The following example detects when the user clicks the mouse button over the Hit state of the Flash button or presses the spacebar anywhere within the Flash movie:

```
on (release, keyPress "<Space>"){
    stop();
}
```

The keyPress event, which was introduced with Flash Player 4, and the newer Key object, introduced with Flash Player 6, open up many possibilities for Flash. Movies can have keyboard-based navigation, buttons can have keyboard shortcuts for convenience and accessibility, and games can have keyboard-controlled objects (such as ships and animated characters). But watch out for some potential "gotchas" to keyboard usage, *specifically with* on *handlers and* keyPress *events*. If you're planning ambitious keyboard-based projects, you may want to check the following list of potential issues first:

✦ Multiple key combinations are not supported. This scenario rules out diagonals as two-key combinations in the classic four-key game control setup. It also means shortcuts such as Ctrl+S are not available. You can, however, use the Shift key in combination with another key to specify an uppercase letter or symbol. (See the case-sensitive note later in this list.)

✦ If presented in a browser, the Flash movie must have "focus" before keystrokes can be recognized. To "focus" the movie, the user must click anywhere in the space it occupies within the browser window. Keyboard-based movies should include instructions that prompt the user to perform this initial mouse click.

Tip You can use the JavaScript focus() method in HTML documents to automatically draw attention to a Flash movie contained within the page. You can use the onLoad event to initiate a JavaScript function that includes the focus() method to enable this behavior as soon as the page loads into the browser.

✦ Because the Escape (Esc), Enter, less than (<), and greater than (>) keys are used as authoring shortcuts in the Test Movie environment, you may want to avoid using them as control keys in your movies. If you need to use those keys in your movies, make sure that you test the movies in a browser, or use the Control ➪ Disable Keyboard Shortcuts option in the Test Movie environment.

✦ keyPress events are case-sensitive. For example, an uppercase letter "S" and a lower-case letter "s" can trigger two different actions. No case-insensitive keystroke event (that is, one that would enable both cases of a letter to trigger the same action) exists for Button instances and the on handler. Achieving case-insensitivity would require two separate on handlers (and their contained actions), one for each case of the letter, on the same Button instance. For example, the following code would stop the current time-line when either the s key or Shift+s key (or the s key with Caps Lock enabled) is pressed:

```
on (keyPress "s"){
     stop();
}
on (keyPress "S"){
     stop();
}
```

Capturing time events with keyframes

The keyframe event handler depends on the playback of the movie itself, not on the user. Just about any action (except the on() and onClipEvent() handlers) can be attached to any keyframe on the timeline. An action attached to a keyframe is executed when the Playhead enters the keyframe, whether it enters naturally during the linear playback of the movie or as the result of a goto action. So, for instance, you may place a stop action on a keyframe to pause the movie at the end of an animation sequence.

In some multimedia applications, keyframe event handlers can differentiate between the Playhead *entering* a keyframe and *exiting* a keyframe. Flash has only one kind of keyframe event handler (essentially, on enter). Hence, as a developer, you do not need to add keyframe event handlers explicitly — they are a presumed element of any action placed on a keyframe. As we mentioned in an earlier note, ActionScript 1.0 and 2.0 can employ a more advanced event model. You learn about different event models in Chapter 25, "Controlling Movie Clips."

Tip

Complex movies can have dozens, or hundreds (or even thousands!), of actions attached to keyframes. To prevent conflicts between uses of keyframes for animation and uses of keyframes as action containers, it is highly advisable to create an entire layer solely for action keyframes. Name the layer **actions** and keep it on top of all your layers for easy access. Remember not to place any symbol instances, text, or artwork on your actions layer. You can also create a labels layer to hold — you guessed it — frame labels.

The process for adding an action to a keyframe is as follows:

1. Create a keyframe on a timeline. This keyframe can exist in the Main Timeline (that is, Scene 1) or a Movie Clip symbol timeline.

2. Select the keyframe in the Timeline window, and open the Actions panel. The Actions panel title should read Actions - Frame.

3. Type your desired actions in the Script pane.

In the next section, you'll get a little more hands-on experience adding actions to both buttons and keyframes.

Creating Invisible Buttons and Using getURL

In this section, you learn how to create an "invisible button" and practice the use of getURL actions. An invisible button is essentially a Button symbol that has only a Hit state defined, with empty Up, Over, and Down states. Once you have created an invisible button, you can use it to convert any type of Flash element into a button. By dragging an instance of the invisible button on top of another piece of artwork or symbol instance on the Stage, you can add interactivity to that element.

On the CD-ROM Make a copy of the themakers_ad_starter.fla file, located in the ch18 folder of the book's CD-ROM. This file contains a sample layout of graphics and text for a mock Flash ad, sized for display on a Pocket PC screen. This document uses a Flash Player 6 version setting in the Publish Settings, which is why some actions in the Actions toolbox's booklets are highlighted in yellow.

With the starter Flash document (.fla) open in Flash 8, quickly familiarize yourself with the existing content. There are four layers on the Main Timeline (Scene 1). The comments layer indicates what the Flash document is, the border layer contains a black outlined box with no fill, the graphics layer contains a Graphic symbol of branding artwork, and the animText layer contains a Movie Clip instance featuring a tweened animation. Go ahead and test this movie (Control ➪ Test Movie) to see how these elements currently play. When the animation finishes, you should see the artwork displayed in Figure 18-10.

Figure 18-10: The artwork of the Flash movie designed for a Pocket PC screen

In this exercise, you're going to add two invisible buttons to this movie. One is an oval-shaped button that fits over the thumbprint graphic, and another is a rectangular-shaped button that fits over the company's name. The thumbprint button, when clicked, opens the e-mail client to send an e-mail to the company. When the user clicks the name button, a new browser window opens displaying the company's Web page.

1. In the starter Flash document, create a new layer named **actions**. Place this layer just underneath the comments layer.

2. Save the starter document as **makers_ad.fla**.

3. Select the first frame of this layer and open the Actions panel (F9). In the plus (+) menu, choose Global Functions ➪ Timeline Control ➪ stop. This will add a stop(); action to the keyframe. Currently, there is more than one frame on the Main Timeline, and if you were to develop this Flash movie further, you wouldn't want the Playhead going past the first frame without some input from the user.

4. With this first frame of the actions layer still selected, open the Property inspector and in the <Frame Label> field, type **//stop.** This will add a frame comment of //stop to the layer in the Timeline window. This comment provides a quick visual cue about the behavior of this keyframe.

5. Now you're going to make your first invisible button. Choose Insert ➪ New Symbol (Ctrl+F8 or ⌘+F8) and make a new Button symbol named **invisibleButton_rect.** This button will be the rectangular button that is placed over the company's name. Flash will take you right inside the symbol's workspace as soon as you press the OK button in the Create New Symbol dialog box.

6. Rename Layer 1 to **hit area graphic.** On this layer of the Button symbol's Timeline, create a keyframe for the Hit state. Move the Playhead in the Timeline window to this new keyframe.

7. Select the Rectangle tool, and draw a uniform square on the symbol's Stage. The square can be any color, although we prefer red for invisible buttons. If you drew the shape with a stroke, delete the stroke. Select the square, and in the Property inspector, give the square a width and height of **50** pixels. Then, using the Align panel, center the square on the Stage. Your Button symbol and Timeline should now resemble Figure 18-11.

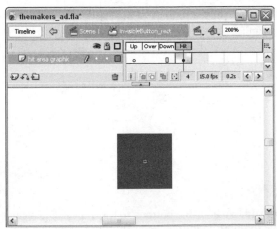

Figure 18-11: The square will act as the active area of the Button symbol.

8. Now, go back to Scene 1 (the Main Timeline), and create a new layer. Rename this layer **btLink**, and place it above the graphics layer.

9. Open the Library panel (Ctrl+L or ⌘+L), and drag an instance of the `invisibleButton_rect` symbol to the Stage. Place this instance over the company's name. In the Property inspector, name this instance **btLink**.

10. Using the Free Transform tool, size the instance to fit the size of the text, without overlapping other elements on the Stage. You'll notice that your Button instance has a transparent aqua blue tint that overlays the underlying elements (as shown in Figure 18-12). This is Flash's way of enabling you to select and manipulate an invisible button. You will not see this color effect for the button when the document is published or tested as a Flash movie file (.swf).

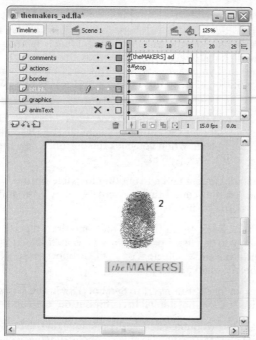

Figure 18-12: The aqua blue tint of the Button instance indicates the presence of a button that has only a Hit state.

11. With the Selection tool, select the Button instance on the Stage, and open the Actions panel (F9, or Option+F9 on Mac). Your Action panel title bar should read Actions - Button. Using the booklets in the Actions toolbox, add an on handler from the Global Functions ➪ Movie Clip Control booklet. Inside the on handler, specify a release event. Your Script pane should show the following code:

```
on (release){
}
```

Tip

Try coding these actions without using the Script Assist mode. At any point, you can click the Script Assist button in the Actions panel to help you write your code.

12. In the Script pane, click the mouse pointer just before the closing curly brace (}) on line 2. Now add a `getURL` action from the Global Functions ➪ Browser/Network booklet. Specify a URL for the first parameter of the action, and a blank browser window target for the second parameter, as shown in the following code:

```
on (release){
    getURL("http://www.theMakers.com", "_blank");
}
```

For this example, we used the URL `http://www.theMakers.com`. When you're linking to domain names, make sure you specify the transfer protocol (such as `http://`, `ftp://`, and so on). If you are linking to relative URLs, specify the name of the HTML document (or other resource) that you want to access. This `on()` handler with the `getURL()` action will direct a button click on this instance to [theMAKERS] Web site, in a new browser window.

13. Save your Flash document, and test it using Publish Preview ➪ HTML (Ctrl+F12 or ⌘+F12). In the browser window, roll over the company's name in the Flash movie. You'll notice that this area is an active button. When you click the button, a new browser window will open, displaying the company's Web page.

14. Now, let's go back to the Flash document and add another invisible button. You'll use a different procedure this time. On the Scene 1 timeline, create a new layer and name it **btEmail.** Place this layer above the btLink layer.

15. On the first frame of the btEmail layer, select the Oval tool, and draw a perfect circle anywhere on the Stage. Again, you can use any fill color you wish. If the circle has a stroke, delete the stroke. With this circle selected, open the Property inspector and give the circle a width and height of **50** pixels.

16. With the circle selected, choose Insert ➪ Convert to Symbol (F8). In the Convert to Symbol dialog box, make a Button symbol named **invisibleButton_oval** and click OK.

17. Now, edit the new symbol, either by double-clicking the instance on the Stage, or by double-clicking its listing in the Library panel. On this symbol's timeline, rename Layer 1 to **hit area graphic**. Now, select the keyframe for the Up state, and drag it to the Hit state. Note that you may need to click, then click and drag the keyframe for this method to work properly. When you are finished, your circle shape should be on only the Hit area of the button's timeline.

18. Go back to the Scene 1 timeline, and you'll notice that your circle button is now an invisible button, just as our rectangular one is. Move the circular invisible button over the thumbprint graphic, and use the Free Transform tool to shape the circle as an oval that closely matches the shape of the thumbprint, as shown in Figure 18-13. Also, name the instance **btEmail** in the Property inspector.

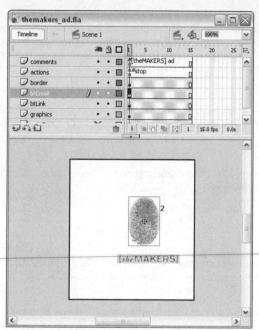

Figure 18-13: The thumbprint graphic now has an invisible button on top of it.

19. With the oval invisible button selected, open the Actions panel. Repeat Steps 11 and 12 of this exercise. This time, however, we'll use a `mailto:` URL, as in `"mailto:info@theMakers.com"`. Type this value as the first parameter of a `getURL` action for this Button instance. For this `getURL` action, however, you do not need to specify a window parameter.

Tip   You can specify subject lines and body text in `mailto:` URLs as well, just as you can with HTML documents. For example, the following code will open a new e-mail message window addressed to `info@theMakers.com`, with a subject line of "Web Feedback" and body text of "Here are my comments." The following code should be typed as one line of code:

```
getURL("mailto:info@theMakers.com?subject=Web%20Feedback&body=H
ere%20are%20my%20comments%3A");
```

20. Save your Flash document once again, and preview it in a browser. When you click the active area over the thumbprint graphic, the default e-mail client on your system should open, displaying a new message window with the To: field predefined to the URL you typed in Step 19.

New Feature   You can also change the title and description metadata published with the .swf file by choosing Modify ⇨ Document. Even though these features are new to Flash 8, the metadata can be included with older .swf formats, including Flash Player 6! If your Flash movie is on a publicly accessible Web page and crawled by a search engine, the metadata can be read by the engine and indexed.

Now you know how to make invisible buttons and add getURL actions to them. In your own work, you may come to realize the true benefit of invisible buttons: You can quickly drag several instances of either invisible button shape (oval or rectangle) to the Stage to create active areas. This offers two benefits: First, you don't have to make Button symbols from regular graphics that don't need four button states, and second, you can make "hidden" areas in interactive puzzles or games.

Tip   As you become more agile with ActionScript, you can start to use Movie Clip instances as button handlers. You learn more about this usage of Movie Clips in Chapter 25, "Controlling Movie Clips."

Web Resource   We'd like to know what you think about this chapter. Visit www.flashsupport.com/feedback to send us your comments.

Summary

✦ ActionScript is Flash's interactive language. It is a set of actions that enables Flash to communicate with internal elements (timelines, symbols, sounds, and so on) and external Web pages and scripts.

✦ The Behaviors panel enables the novice user to quickly add interactive commands to Flash movie elements.

✦ Flash 8 introduces a new scripting mode called Script Assist, which enables you to see your code in a more user-friendly layout.

✦ Flash interactivity is based on a relatively simple structure: An event handler waits for something to happen (a playback point being reached or the user providing input), and when that something does happen, it executes one or more actions (which alter the movie's playback, behavior, or properties; load a file; or execute a script).

✦ The Timeline Control booklet contains the fundamental actions for navigating Flash playback through multiple scenes and keyframes, as well as controlling soundtracks. The Browser/Network booklet contains the getURL action, which can direct the browser window to external Web resources such as HTML pages and FTP downloads.

✦ All actions need an event handler to activate them. Event handlers include keyframes on a timeline, button clicks, mouse movements, and key presses. More advanced event handlers are discussed in later chapters.

✦ Invisible buttons enable you to create interactive areas on top of other Flash artwork or symbols.

✦   ✦   ✦

Building Timelines and Interactions

Unlike most multimedia authoring applications, Flash has the capability to use multiple simultaneous timelines in its movies. So far, most of the examples in this book have only one timeline or have used only one scene. You've seen how to add basic actions to your movies to make them interactive. Now you begin exploring the world of multiple movie timelines using the Movie Clip symbol.

Movie Clips: The Key to Self-Contained Playback

A powerful addition to the Flash format was the Movie Clip symbol, introduced in Flash Player 3. Movie Clips enabled Flash developers to create complex behaviors by nesting self-contained sequences of animation or interactivity inside each other. These sequences could then be placed as discrete, self-playing modules on the Main Timeline (that is, Scene 1). Initially, the key to the power of Movie Clips was their capability to communicate with and control each other via the `tellTarget` action.

In Flash 4, the role of Movie Clips was expanded — they could be used with ActionScript. That capability put Movie Clips at the foundation of advanced interactivity in Flash. In Flash 5, when ActionScript matured into a full-blown scripting language that mirrored JavaScript, Movie Clips became the central object of programming. In Flash MX, Movie Clips could utilize more compiler directives, which enabled them to become full-blown user-interface components. In Flash MX 2004, Movie Clips and components continued to evolve and play a vital role in the organization of a Flash movie's content and interactivity. In Flash 8, Movie Clips gain new filter effects, blend modes, and bitmap-caching optimizations. In this chapter, you'll look at several key features of the Movie Clip symbol.

How Movie Clips interact within a Flash movie

Previous chapters dealt with Flash movies as a single sequence of frames arranged along a single timeline. Whether the playback along that timeline was linear (traditional animation) or nonlinear (where the Playhead jumps arbitrarily to any frame), our example movies have normally comprised only the frames of a single timeline. Ostensibly, a single timeline may seem to provide everything you'd need to create any Flash behavior, but as you get more inventive or ambitious, you'll soon find yourself conceiving ideas for animated and interactive segments that are thwarted by the limits of a single timeline.

Suppose you want to create a looping animation of a dog with its tail wagging. You decide that the tail should wag every 5 seconds and the dog should bark every 15 seconds. On a single timeline, you'd need a loop of 180 frames to accommodate the timing of the bark (assuming a frame rate of 12 frames per second), and repeating keyframes for the wagging tail artwork every 60 frames. Although animating a dog in that manner would be a bit cumbersome, it wouldn't be impossible — until your dog had to move around the screen as an integrated whole. Making the bark and the wagging tail loop while the whole dog moved around complex paths for extended periods of time would quickly become impractical, especially if the dog was only one part of a larger environment.

Now imagine that you could make the dog by creating two whole separate movies, one for the tail and one for the barking mouth and sound. Could you then place those movies as self-contained, animated objects on the Main Timeline, just like a graphic or a button? Well, you can — that's what Movie Clips are all about. Movie Clips are independent sequences of frames (timelines) that can be defined outside the context of the Main Timeline and then placed onto it as objects on a single frame. You create Movie Clips the same way you create a Graphic symbol in Edit mode. Unlike a Graphic symbol, a Movie Clip (as the name somewhat implies) acts in most cases just like a fully functional movie or .swf file, meaning, for instance, that frame actions in Movie Clip timelines are functional. After you have created a Movie Clip as a symbol, you drop instances of it into any keyframe of the Main Timeline or any other Movie Clip timeline. The following are some general Movie Clip principles:

✦ During playback as a Flash .swf file, a Movie Clip instance placed on a timeline begins to play as soon as the frame on which it occurs is reached, whether or not the Main Timeline (or the clip's parent timeline) is playing.

✦ A Movie Clip plays back autonomously, meaning that as long as it is present on the Stage it is not governed by the playing or stopping of the Main Timeline.

✦ Movie Clips can play when the Main Timeline is stopped, or stay halted when the Main Timeline plays.

✦ Like a Graphic or a Button symbol, Movie Clips can be manipulated on the Stage — you can size them, skew them, rotate them, place effects such as alpha blending on them, or tween them, all while the frames within them continue to play.

New Feature Movie Clip instances can now use filter effects and blend modes. You create these effects in real time and set them in the Property inspector or with ActionScript code.

✦ All timelines play at the frame rate specified by the Document Properties dialog box (Modify ➪ Document) or the Property inspector (when the Document window is focused, and all items on the Stage are deselected). However, it is possible to modify playback behavior of a timeline with ActionScript routines.

In our dog wagging and barking example, the tail and head of the dog could be looping Movie Clips, and then those Movie Clips could be nested inside another Movie Clip symbol (representing the entire dog). This "whole" dog clip could then be tweened around the Stage on the Main Timeline to make the dog move. You could use the same principle to move a Movie Clip of a butterfly with flapping wings along a motion path.

One movie, several timelines

Because a Flash movie can have more than one timeline existing in the same space and time, there must be a way to organize Movie Clips within the Main Timeline (Scene 1) of your Flash document. Just as artwork can be placed inside any symbol, symbol instances can be nested within other symbols. If you change the contents of the nested symbol, the parent symbol (the symbol containing the other symbol) will be updated as well. Although this may not seem special, it's of extreme importance to Movie Clips and Flash interactivity. Because the playback of each Movie Clip timeline is independent from any other timeline, you need to know how to tell Flash which Movie Clip you want to control.

The Flash movie diagram in Figure 19-1 illustrates multiple timelines. This Flash movie has two layers on the Main Timeline: Layer 1 and Layer 2. Layer 1 has a Movie Clip (instance "A") that exists for 19 frames on the Main Timeline. Layer 2 has a Movie Clip (instance "B") that exists for 10 frames on the Main Timeline, but it also contains a nested Movie Clip (instance "C").

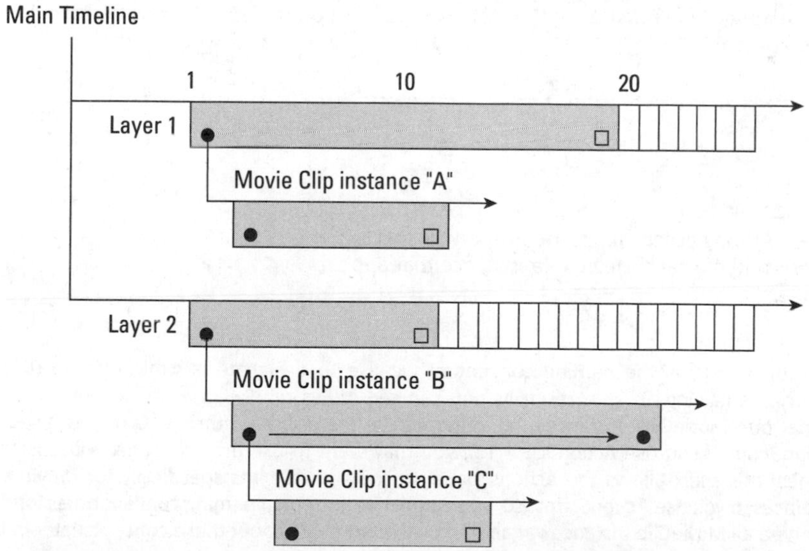

Figure 19-1: This figure shows one method of diagramming Flash timelines.

In Figure 19-1, if the Main Timeline has a `stop` action on the first frame, all three Movie Clips will continue to play unless there are `stop` actions on their first frames or they are told to stop by actions targeted to them. If the Main Timeline plays to frame 20, instance "A" will no longer be on the Stage, regardless of how many frames it may have on its timeline. Figure 19-2 shows a more practical diagram of a timeline hierarchy.

Main Timeline

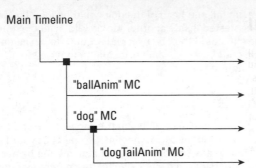

"ballAnim" MC

"dog" MC

"dogTailAnim" MC

Figure 19-2: Flash movies can be flow-charted in this fashion. This diagram is similar to the Movie Explorer's method of displaying Flash movie information.

In Figure 19-2, you can see three Movie Clips. Two of them, `ballAnim` and `dog`, occupy space on the Main Timeline. The other one, `dogTailAnim`, is nested within the `dog` Movie Clip. Each Movie Clip instance on any given timeline *must* have a unique name — you can't have two or more Movie Clip instances on the same timeline using the same instance name. The instance name is specified in the Property inspector, shown in Figure 19-3. To see the settings for a particular instance, you must have the instance selected on the Stage before referencing the Property inspector.

Figure 19-3: Among other things, the Property inspector enables you to name each Movie Clip instance that appears on the Stage.

Tip

The suffix `Anim` is the naming convention we use to designate a symbol name (in the Library) containing an animation. As you can see in Figure 19-3, we use the prefix `mc` to name our MovieClip instances, to differentiate them from other data types used in ActionScript. If you use ActionScript 1.0, you may want to use the `_mc` suffix with instance names; this suffix allows the Actions panel to show code hints specifically for Movie Clip instances. If you use ActionScript 2.0, you can derive your own naming convention as long as you type all MovieClip instance variables. You'll learn more about these concepts later in the chapter.

Now that you understand how multiple timelines can exist within a Flash movie, let's see how you can make Movie Clips communicate with one another.

Targets and Paths Explained

If you already studied Movie Clips in Chapter 6, "Symbols, Instances, and the Library," you probably know that they provide the solution to our animated dog problem. However, you might not have guessed that Movie Clips can also add logic to animation and Flash interfaces. Let's take our animated dog example a little further: When dogs bark, their tails may stop wagging. Our hypothetical dog may look strange if it is barking and wagging at the same time. Suppose we wanted to stop the tail wagging during every bark. We'd have to have some way for the barking head Movie Clip to control the tail Movie Clip so that we could tell the tail to stop wagging when the dog barks, and then tell the tail to return to its wagging loop again when the bark is over.

Well, you have a few ways to control the tail Movie Clip from the barking head Movie Clip. In Flash 3 and 4, the `tellTarget` action was used to let actions on any timeline (including Movie Clip timelines and the Main Timeline) control what happens on any other timeline. How? `tellTarget` simply provided a mechanism for extending basic actions such as `play` and `stop`, enabling them to specify (or *target*) the timeline upon which they should be executed. Targets are any Movie Clip instances that are available at the current "state" of a Flash movie—you can't target a Movie Clip that isn't displayed (or existing) on the Stage. For example, suppose you had two Movie Clips, one on frame 1 and another on frame 10 of the Main Timeline. If the Main Timeline was stopped on frame 1, you couldn't target the Movie Clip on frame 10 because the instance is not on the current frame.

Since Flash 5, developers have been able to direct actions to specific timelines by attaching the same actions as *methods* to a `MovieClip` object (we define methods in the following sidebar). As such, the `tellTarget` action is a deprecated action; it's still supported in current Flash Players, but it's been replaced with more versatile actions and syntax that makes its use outdated. For an overview of deprecated actions, see the sidebar on deprecated actions in the preceding chapter. In this chapter, you work exclusively with the preferred ActionScript dot syntax to control Movie Clip instances. First, however, you need to understand how targeting works in Flash movies.

Note   If you're new to scripting, please read the "What Is Dot Syntax?" sidebar.

Tip   If you're building Flash movies for Flash Lite 1.0/1.1, you need to use the `tellTarget` action to control Movie Clip instances. Flash Lite 1.0/1.1 is based on the Flash Player 4 specification.

What Is Dot Syntax?

Flash 5 introduced a new method of writing all ActionScript called *dot syntax*. Earlier versions of Flash used a natural-language scripting environment that was menu-based, in which actions could be read and understood easily and accessed via pop-up menus and dialog boxes. While most people prefer easy-to-use scripting environments, the production demands of complex interactive projects are often compromised by such menu-driven scripting environments. Computer programmers prefer to create, edit, and debug scripting with a language they can access and modify easily. Consequently, we see the best of both worlds with Flash 8.

ActionScript adheres closely to the ECMA-262 specification, the same specification upon which JavaScript is based. JavaScript is the universal scripting language used by most browsers for Dynamic HTML (DHTML) documents. Therefore, Flash ActionScript uses a dot syntax, also known as *dot notation*. What does that mean? It means that all actions are written within a standard formula that is common with object-oriented programming (OOP) languages:

```
Object.property = value;
```

or

```
Object.method();
```

The examples beg four things to be defined: objects, properties, methods, and values. An *object* is any element in a program (in this case, the Flash movie) that has changeable and accessible characteristics. Objects can be user-defined (in other words, you create and name them) or predefined by the programming language. Flash has several predefined objects, also called *classes*, meaning that they're already built into the ActionScript language. We look at object types in more detail in later chapters. An important object (and perhaps the easiest to conceptualize) is the MovieClip object. Any Movie Clip instance on the Stage is a MovieClip object, such as ballAnim_mc or dogTailAnim_mc. An object has characteristics, or *properties*, that can be updated or changed throughout the movie. An example of a MovieClip property is scale, which is referred to as _xscale and _yscale. We look at MovieClip properties in Chapter 25, "Controlling Movie Clips." Properties always have some data accompanying them. This data is called the property's *value*. Using the previous example, at full size, a MovieClip object's _xscale is 100 (the scale property uses percent as the unit of measure). For a MovieClip object named mcBallAnim, this would be represented in ActionScript syntax as:

```
mcBallAnim._xscale = 100;
```

Finally, objects can be enacted upon by procedures that do something to or with the object. These procedures are called *methods*. One method for the MovieClip object is the gotoAndPlay() method, which you used as a basic action in the previous chapter. In Flash Player 5 or higher movies, methods can be created for your own objects or predefined for existing Flash objects. Any goto action can be used as a method of any MovieClip object, as in:

```
mcBallAnim.gotoAndPlay("start");
```

The preceding example tells the mcBallAnim instance to direct its playback head to the frame label start on its timeline. This chapter helps you understand how to use the gotoAndPlay() method for Movie Clips.

Paths: Absolute and relative modes

Earlier in this chapter, you learned how multiple Movie Clip timelines appear on the Stage. It's entirely possible to nest several Movie Clips within another Movie Clip. To understand how Movie Clips communicate with one other by using actions, you need to have a firm grasp on Movie Clip paths. A path is simply that—the route to a destination, an address *per se*. If you have a Movie Clip instance named mcTailAnim inside a mcDog Movie Clip instance, how is Flash supposed to know? What if there was more than one mcTailAnim in the entire movie, with others nested in other Movie Clips besides the mcDog instance? You can specify a Movie Clip's path in an absolute or a relative mode.

An *absolute path* is the full location information, or target, for a given Movie Clip instance from any other location (or target). Just like your postal address has a street name and number and a ZIP code so that people can find you on a map, all Movie Clips have a point of origin: the Main Timeline (that is, Scene 1). Flash 8 only displays dot notation with absolute and relative paths.

Tip Since Flash MX 2004, the Insert Target Path dialog box no longer shows you dot and slash notations. See the sidebar "Paths in Flash 4 or Earlier Movies" for an explanation of slash notation.

Note Dot notation and dot syntax are synonymous terms, and are used interchangeably throughout this book.

Dot notation follows the ActionScript language conventions. With dot notation, the Main Timeline becomes

    _root

A Movie Clip instance named mcDog on the Main Timeline (or _root) would have an absolute path of

    _root.mcDog

Notice that a period, or dot, separates the term _root from mcDog. The dot denotes a parent-child relationship; the mcDog instance is a "child" of its parent, _root. And, following suit, a Movie Clip instance named mcTailAnim that is nested within the mcDog Movie Clip would have the absolute path of

    _root.mcDog.mcTailAnim

A *relative path* is a contextual path to one timeline from another. From a conceptual point of view, think of a relative path as the relationship between the location of your pillow and the rest of your bed. Unless you have an odd sleeping habit, the pillow is located at the head of the bed. You may change the location of the bed within your room or the rooms of a house, but the relationship between the pillow and the bed remains the same. Another example that can illustrate the difference between absolute and relative references is the postal address example we used earlier. An absolute reference to your residence would use your full street address, city, state, and ZIP code. However, if you're giving directions to a friend of yours who lives nearby, you're more likely to tell your friend, "From your house, walk two blocks down A street, and turn right on B street. I'm five houses down on the left side of the street."

With Flash, relative Movie Clip paths are useful within Movie Clips that contain several nested Movie Clips. That way, you can move the container (or parent) Movie Clip from one timeline to another and expect the inner targeting of the nested Movie Clips to work. To refer to a timeline that is above the current timeline in dot notation, use

```
this._parent
```

Here, the term `this` refers to the current timeline from where the action is being called, and `_parent` refers to the current timeline's parent timeline. You can use relative dot notation to refer up and down the hierarchy at the same time. For example, if you have two nested Movie Clips, such as `mcTailAnim` and `mcBarkingAnim`, within a larger Movie Clip named `mcDog`, you may want to target `mcTailAnim` from `mcBarkingAnim`. The relative dot path for this task is

```
this._parent.mcTailAnim
```

This path tells Flash to go up one timeline from the current timeline, `mcBarkingAnim`, to its parent timeline (the `mcDog` timeline), and then look for the instance named `mcTailAnim` from there.

You can also use successive `_parent` references to travel up in the timeline hierarchy multiple times, such as

```
this._parent._parent
```

Using the `mcDog` instance example again, if you wanted to control the Main Timeline (which is the parent timeline of the `mcDog` instance) from the `mcTailAnim` instance, you could use `_parent._parent` in the target path of an action executed from the `mcTailAnim` timeline.

Note   You can directly control the Main Timeline using the reference `_root`. However, as you'll see later in Chapter 28, "Sharing and Loading Assets," you may load an entire .swf file into a Movie Clip instance, thereby changing the reference to `_root`. Flash Player 7 and higher supports a property of `MovieClip` objects named `_lockroot`, which can help you avoid path problems when loading external .swf files.

Web Resource   Flash designers and developers learning to use ActionScript often encounter scope problems with their code. Scope refers to the code objects that can be "seen" within a given code block, such as a function. You can use the `Delegate` class to help you deal with issues of scope. Robert wrote a free tutorial on CommunityMX.com titled, "Better Practices for Flash Designers - Part 1: Coding Buttons." You can find a link to this article at `www.flashsupport.com/cmx`. This tutorial walks you through the use of the `Delegate` class with Flash buttons. The `Delegate` class can help you avoid using long chains of `_parent` references in your code. We also discuss the `Delegate` class in Chapter 33, "Using Components."

As with absolute paths, we recommend that you become familiar with using the dot notation for relative paths.

Okay, that's enough theory. Now, you're going to practice nesting Movie Clips inside of other Movie Clips, as well as target actions at specific instances using dot notation.

Paths in Flash 4 or Earlier Movies

Before Flash 5, the Main Timeline was represented in a Movie Clip path as a starting forward slash (/) character. The absolute path of a Movie Clip instance named `mcDog` on the Main Timeline is

```
/mcDog
```

Any nested Movie Clips inside of the `mcDog` instance would be referenced after that starting path. For example, the absolute path to `mcTailAnim`, an instance inside the `mcDog` Movie Clip instance, would be

```
/mcDog/mcTailAnim
```

Another / character was put between the two instance names. Think of the / as a substitute for the period or dot (.) in ActionScript target paths. Use of the / character in Movie Clip paths is known as the *slash* notation.

The equivalent to `_parent` in slash notation is a double-dot, as in

```
../
```

The two dots here work just like directory references for files on Web servers; use a pair of dots (`..`) for each timeline in the hierarchy.

Just as `tellTarget` is considered a deprecated action in Flash 8, the slash notation is deprecated syntax. It will still work with current Flash Players, but subsequent versions of the Flash authoring program will continue to be built upon dot notation.

Targeting Movie Clips in Flash 8

In this section, you'll see how to make Movie Clips interact with one another by using dot notation and ActionScript. Specifically, you're going to create the barking and wagging dog example we discuss at the beginning of this chapter. You begin this exercise with a starter Flash document file (.fla) located on the book's CD-ROM.

On the CD-ROM

Open the `stella_starter.fla` file found in the `ch19/stella` folder of this book's CD-ROM.

With the starter file open in Flash 8, test the movie using Control ➪ Test Movie. You'll see that our dog, Stella, is wagging her tail. At timed intervals, she will bark. Right now, her tail keeps wagging as she barks. In this exercise, we'll show you how to stop her tail from wagging while she is barking. Close the Test Movie window and take a look at the Library panel. You'll find the following assets listed:

✦ `bark.wav`: This is the sound file used for Stella's bark. You will find this sound on the bark layer of the barkAnimClip Timeline.

✦ **barkAnimClip:** This Movie Clip symbol contains the animation for Stella's barking head. If you double-click this symbol in the Library panel, you'll see that the timeline has two layers, one for the sound and another for the head animation. This symbol is used in the stellaClip Movie Clip symbol.

✦ **bodyGraphic:** This Graphic symbol is artwork of Stella's body and legs. There is no animation on its timeline. The bodyGraphic symbol is used in the stellaClip Movie Clip symbol.

✦ **headGraphic:** This Graphic symbol is artwork of Stella's head. You'll find a couple of instances of this symbol in the barkAnimClip symbol.

✦ **stellaClip:** This Movie Clip timeline contains instances of the barkAnimClip, bodyGraphic, and tailAnimClip symbols.

✦ **tailAnimClip:** This Movie Clip symbol contains two instances of the tailGraphic symbol. Each instance is rotated differently to create the wagging effect.

✦ **tailGraphic:** This Graphic symbol contains the artwork for Stella's tail.

Tip   As you can see by the names of the symbols, you can adopt naming conventions for your symbol types in the Library panel. All Movie Clip symbols use a "Clip" suffix, and Graphic symbols use a "Graphic" suffix. A naming convention can help you quickly identify the type of asset just by looking at its name.

Now, you're going to add some behaviors to the movie. First, you'll need to name the instances in the movie. ActionScript can find a Movie Clip instance only by its instance name. Using the Property inspector, you'll add instance names to all of the Movie Clip instances.

Once the instances are named, you can then target the instances with ActionScript. In this example, you'll target the mcTailAnim instance from the mcBarkAnim instance. When the keyframe containing the barking mouth inside of mcBarkAnim is reached, the movie will tell mcTailAnim to go to and stop on a specific frame. When the barking is over, mcTailAnim will be told to continue playing.

1. With stella_starter.fla open in Flash 8, resave the document as stella_abso-lute.fla. In this tutorial, you use absolute paths with your targets.

2. Select the instance of the stellaClip symbol on the Stage, on the Main Timeline. Open the Property inspector, and name the instance mcStella in the <Instance Name> field, as shown in Figure 19-4. Rename the stella layer to **mcStella** as well.

3. Double-click the mcStella instance on the Stage to edit the stellaClip symbol in the Library. Select the barkAnimClip symbol instance, and again, using the Property inspector, name this instance mcBarkAnim in the <Instance Name> field. Rename the barkAnim layer to **mcBarkAnim**.

4. Select the tailAnimClip symbol instance located on the tailAnim layer. Name the instance in the Property inspector, using the name mcTailAnim. Rename the tailAnim layer to **mcTailAnim**.

5. With all of the Movie Clip instances named, you can now target actions to specific timelines. Your first goal is to stop the wagging tail while Stella barks. Double-click the mcBarkAnim instance to edit the barkAnimClip symbol's timeline.

6. On the barkAnimClip timeline, create a new layer and rename it **actions**. Place this layer at the top of the layer stack. On frame 14 of this new layer, insert an empty keyframe (F7). Frame 14 is the frame just before the Stream sound on the bark layer begins. On frame 14, you want to tell the mcTailAnim instance to stop playing. So, let's give this keyframe a frame comment that indicates this behavior. With the keyframe selected, open the Property inspector and, in the <Frame Label> field, type **//stop wagging**, as shown in Figure 19-5.

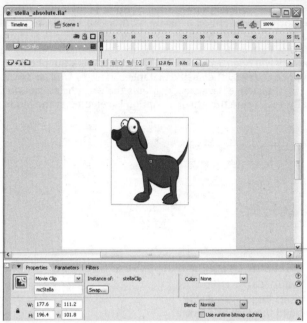

Figure 19-4: You can name Movie Clip instances in the Property inspector.

Figure 19-5: You can use frame comments to describe the actions on a keyframe.

7. After you have assigned a comment on the frame, you're ready to write the ActionScript to perform the described behavior. With frame 14 selected on the actions layer, open the Actions panel (F9). Make sure you are not working in Script Assist mode. Click the Target Path selector icon (see Figure 19-5 for its location). The Insert Target Path dialog box will open, as shown in Figure 19-6. Click the plus icon (+) next to the mcStella instance to reveal the nested instances, mcBarkAnim and mcTailAnim. Select the mcTailAnim instance because it contains the wagging animation that you want to stop. Finally, make sure the Absolute option is selected in the Mode setting. Click OK.

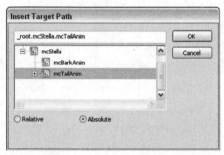

Figure 19-6: The Insert Target Path dialog box can help you build the path to a Movie Clip instance.

8. In the Script pane of the Actions panel, you now see the path to the instance _root.stella_mc.tailAnim_mc. After this name, type .stop();. As you learned in the last chapter, the stop() action will halt a playing timeline. When you are finished, the Script pane should contain the following code:

```
_root.mcStella.mcTailAnim.stop();
```

Tip

If you use the _mc suffix naming convention with your Movie Clip instances, the Actions panel displays a code hint menu when you type the period (.) after the _mc suffix. You can also see these same code hints if you use ActionScript 2.0 strong data-typing with a variable name, which we discuss in Chapter 24, "Knowing the Nuts and Bolts of Code." To try this technique, delete the line of code from Step 8, and type the following code:

```
var mc:MovieClip = _root.mcStella.mcTailAnim;
```

Once you've declared a variable and its data type, the Actions panel can display code hints for that data type. On line 2, type:

```
mc.
```

As soon as you type the period (.) after the variable name mc, the Actions panel displays all of the properties and methods of the MovieClip class. You can click the entry you want to use, and the Actions panel adds it to the existing line of code. If there are other parameters for the new code, the Actions panel display code hints for those parameters as well.

9. Use this same technique to tell the `mcTailAnim` instance to start playing again once the bark has ended. In the barkAnimClip symbol timeline, create yet another actions layer. You can make more than one to prevent overlap of your frame comments. Place this new actions layer beneath the original actions layer. On frame 20 of this second actions layer, insert an empty keyframe (F7). Assign a frame comment of **//start wagging** in the <Frame Label> field of the Property inspector for this keyframe.

10. Repeat Steps 7 and 8 for the action on this keyframe. This time, however, type a `.play();` action from the code hints menu in the Actions panel. When you are finished, the following code should be on frame 20 of the actions layer:

    ```
    _root.mcStella.mcTailAnim.play();
    ```

11. Now you're ready to test your movie. Save the Flash document, and use Control⇨ Test Movie to view your movie. When Stella barks, her tail should stop wagging. When the bark is over, the tail should resume wagging.

On the CD-ROM

This example has shown you how to target Movie Clip instances using absolute paths built with the Insert Target Path dialog box in the Actions panel. However, you can also try using relative paths to target the instances. In the `ch19/stella` folder of the book's CD-ROM, open the `stella_relative.fla` file to see an example of relative path addressing. Note that this example also uses a `gotoAndStop(2)` action on the `//stop wagging` keyframe to make sure Stella's tail is pointed down during the bark. You can also find a completed example file for the exercise you just completed, `stella_absolute.fla`.

Targeting Movie Clips with Behaviors

In this section, you learn how to include the same interactivity of the previous exercise using Flash 8's behaviors feature. Behaviors, as we discussed in the last chapter, are self-contained blocks of ActionScript code that you can easily apply to elements in your Flash movie. In the following steps, you use behaviors instead of hand-coded actions to stop Stella's tail from wagging during the bark cycle.

On the CD-ROM

As the starter file for this exercise, use the `stella_absolute.fla` document in the `ch19/stella` folder of this book's CD-ROM.

1. Open the `stella_absolute.fla` document, and double-click the `mcStella` instance on the Stage.

2. On the stellaClip timeline, double-click the `mcBarkAnim` instance (that is, Stella's head).

3. On the barkAnimClip timeline, select frame 14 on the topmost actions layer. Open the Actions panel (F9), select the existing ActionScript code in the Script pane, and press the Delete or Backspace key to erase the code. Close the Actions panel when you're finished.

4. Rename the topmost actions layer to **behaviors**. Re-select frame 14 of this layer, and open the Behaviors panel (Shift+F3). Click the Add Behavior (+) button and choose Movieclip⇨ Goto and Stop at frame or label. In the dialog box for this behavior, you'll notice a similar interface to that of the Insert Target Path dialog box. Expand the `mcStella` node, and choose the `mcTailAnim` instance. In the frame field, type the number **2**. See Figure 19-7 for a review of the settings. Click OK to accept the settings.

Figure 19-7: The Goto and Stop at frame or label behavior settings

5. Select frame 20 of the lower actions layer, and erase the existing ActionScript code on this keyframe, as you did in Step 3.

6. Rename the lower actions layer **behaviors**. With frame 20 of the lower behaviors layer selected, click the Add Behavior (+) button in the Behaviors panel, and choose Movieclip ➪ Goto and Play at frame or label. In this behavior's dialog box, expand the mcStella node, and choose the mcTailAnim instance. In the frame field, type the number **2**. See Figure 19-8. Click OK to accept the settings.

Figure 19-8: The Goto and Play at frame or label behavior settings

Tip   You can review the ActionScript code that the behavior uses by selecting its keyframe in the Timeline window and opening the Actions panel. Do not edit this code, however, or the behavior will not likely function properly.

7. Save your document as stella_behaviors.fla, and choose Control ➪ Test Movie. The Flash movie should operate the same as the movie you created in the last section. When Stella barks, the tail stops wagging. When the bark is finished, the tail resumes wagging.

You can find the completed example, stella_behaviors.fla, in the ch19/stella folder of this book's CD-ROM.

Integrating Behaviors with Movie Clips

Chapter 15, "Adding Sound," discussed the ins and outs of sound import and use in Flash documents. In this chapter, we show you how to create a sound library using Flash MX 2004's new Behaviors panel. Once the set of sounds is created, you learn how to stop the sounds from keyframes in another Movie Clip timeline.

You'll find sound files (WAV and AIF formats) in the ch19/pianoKeys/sounds folder of this book's CD-ROM. Make a copy of the pianoKeys_starter.fla file for this exercise. This file is located in the ch19/pianoKeys folder.

Overview of the pianoKeys Movie Clip

Open the pianoKeys_starter.fla file. A mcKeys Movie Clip instance is already on the Stage of the Main Timeline. Double-click the mcKeys instance to enter Edit mode, as shown in Figure 19-9. Note that the Timeline window is docked to the left side of the Document window.

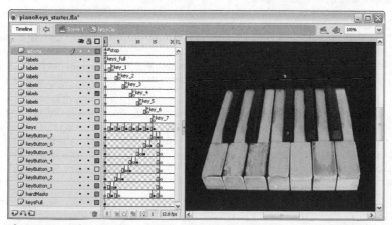

Figure 19-9: The Timeline window showing the frames of the keysClip Movie Clip symbol

The timeline for the keysClip symbol has several layers for individual Button instances and labels. If you test this movie using Control ⇨ Test Movie (Ctrl+Enter or ⌘+Enter), you'll see that the Button instances over each piano key will tell the Playhead of the keysClip timeline to go to that key's frame label. For the first key on the left, the button on layer keyButton_1 has the following action list:

```
on (press, keyPress "a") {
    gotoAndStop ("key_1");
}
on (rollOver) {
    gotoAndStop ("keys_full");
}
```

These actions don't use any dot notation — they are simple navigation actions that you learned in the last chapter. When the keyButton_1 instance is clicked with the mouse, the Playhead moves to the key_1 label on the current timeline, which is the keysClip timeline.

When the timeline goes to the key_1 frame label, a new PNG bitmap of a "pressed" piano key (key_01.png on the keys layer) appears on top of the keys_full.png bitmap that is placed on the bottom keysFull layer. Note that the keys_full.png bitmap is present throughout the entire keysClip timeline. Each Button instance in the keysClip Movie Clip sends the Playhead to the appropriate piano key frame label.

Now that you have an understanding of what's happening in this Movie Clip, let's create some sounds with the Behaviors panel. These sounds will be targeted within the mcKeys instance later in this chapter.

Create sound instances with a behavior

Before you start making sound instances, you need to establish a *naming convention* for your sounds. A naming convention is simply a way of consistently identifying components in any project, in or out of Flash. To a member of a Web production team, the importance of naming conventions cannot be overemphasized — everyone involved with the project should know how to give names to images, sounds, symbol names, instance names, and so on. Even if you work by yourself, a naming convention provides a system of integrating elements from project to project and enables you to identify elements much more easily when you open old files.

1. For each key on the piano, you'll make a unique sound. Each sound will be on its own timeline where it can be targeted to play. Because there are seven keys on this odd piano, you need to import seven sounds into the Flash document. Using File ⇨ Import ⇨ Import to Library, locate the ch19/pianoKeys/sounds folder on the CD-ROM in the back of this book. Import each of the key sounds (AIF or WAV files) into your Flash document. You can import all of the sounds at once if you Shift-select all of the sound files in the Import dialog box.

2. Link each sound in the library, so that the sounds can be referenced by ActionScript (and behaviors). Open the Library panel (Ctrl+L or ⌘+L) and right-click, or Control+click on Mac, the key_1.wav (or key_1.aif) file. Choose Linkage in the contextual menu. When the Linkage Properties dialog box opens, select the Export for ActionScript check box. Change the auto-filled text in the Identifier field to key_1. Refer to Figure 19-10. When you are finished, click OK to accept the settings.

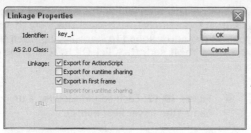

Figure 19-10: The Linkage Properties settings for the key_1.wav (or key_1.aif) file in the Library panel

3. Repeat Step 2 for each sound file in the Library panel, matching the number of the linkage identifier name to the number used in the filename. For example, you should link the `key_2.wav` (or `key_2.aif`) file to `key_2`. When you are finished, expand the width of your Library panel to reveal the Linkage column. Your sound files should have identifiers displayed, as shown in Figure 19-11.

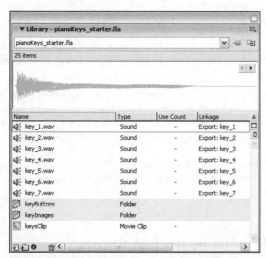

Figure 19-11: The Library panel's Linkage column displays the identifier values for all linked assets.

4. Now you're ready to use behaviors to create ActionScript-ready references to the sounds in the Library. Make sure you are on the Main Timeline (Scene 1) of the `pianoKeys_starter.fla` document. On this timeline, you should see a `mcKeys` layer. Create another layer and rename it **behaviors**.

5. Select the first frame of this new layer, and open the Behaviors panel (Shift+F3). Click the Add Behavior (+) button in the top-left corner of the panel, and choose Sound ⇨ Load Sound from Library from the menu. In the Load Sound from Library dialog box, type **key_1** in the top field, which specifies the linkage ID for the asset you want to

load. In the lower field, type sndKey_1. This term will be the ActionScript object to target with behaviors you'll use later in this exercise. Also, clear the "Play this sound when loaded" check box — you *don't* want the sound to start playing when the movie starts. See Figure 19-12 for a review of these settings. Click OK to accept the parameters of the behavior.

Figure 19-12: Each sound requires a unique instance name (the lower field name).

6. Repeat Step 5 for each sound in the Library, matching the instance name's number to the number used in the linkage identifier. For example, the Load Sound from Library behavior for the key_2.wav (or key_2.aif) file should specify key_2 for the top field and sndKey_2 for the lower field. When you are finished completing this task for every sound in the Library, you should have seven behaviors listed in the Behaviors panel. You can double-click the Action name of each behavior to review that behavior's settings.

7. Save your Flash document as pianoKeys_sounds.fla. Test the movie (Ctrl+Enter or ⌘+Enter). If you hear any sounds play when the movie loads, you forgot to clear the Play this sound when loaded check box on one of the behaviors. Go back and double-click each behavior in the Behaviors panel until you find the one you missed.

You can refer to the pianoKeys_sounds.fla file located in the ch19/pianoKeys folder of this book's CD-ROM. This file has the seven sound files in the Library panel, sorted in the keySounds folder.

Targeting the sounds with more behaviors

Now that you have behaviors set up for the sounds, you're ready to begin controlling the sounds with additional behaviors attached to keyframes in the keysClip timeline. This section of the exercise shows you how to add behaviors to the keysClip timeline that will target the sound instances.

There will be more than one actions layer in this timeline. The actions layer in Step 1 is a new layer in addition to the existing actions layer (with the //stop comment).

1. Enter Edit mode by double-clicking the mcKeys instance on the Main Timeline (Scene 1). On the keysClip Timeline, add a new layer and name it **behaviors**. Move this new actions layer underneath the layer that contains the key_1 frame label, as shown in Figure 19-13.

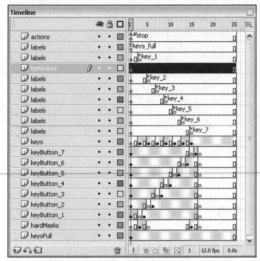

Figure 19-13: Don't be afraid to keep information separated on actions, labels, and behaviors layers. Separating the information will make it much easier for you to access the appropriate sections of your timelines.

2. On frame 3 of the new behaviors layer, you need to add a behavior that will play the first Sound instance, sndKey_1. Remember that the Button instances on the keysClip timeline already move the Playhead to each key's label. Insert a blank keyframe (F7) on frame 3.

3. With the new keyframe selected, open the Behaviors panel (Shift+F3). Click the Add Behavior (+) button, and choose Sound ⇨ Play Sound. In the Play Sound dialog box, type **sndKey_1**, as shown in Figure 19-14. Click OK to close the dialog box.

Figure 19-14: The Play Sound behavior can play a sound set up by the Load Sound from Library behavior.

4. Now, open the Property inspector. With frame 3 of the second actions layer selected, type //**play sound** into the <Frame Label> field. Your Timeline window should resemble Figure 19-15.

Figure 19-15: The //play sound comment lets you know what the behavior on this keyframe does.

At this point, you will want to test your movie to see if the behavior is finding the target and playing the sound. Save your document as `pianoKeys_behaviors.fla`, and use Control ➪ Test Movie to create a Flash movie file (.swf). Make sure that the behavior on the keyframe works by clicking the first key on the piano keyboard (from the left), and that you hear a sound.

5. Now, you need to enable all the other sound instances created by your earlier Load Sound from Library behaviors. Create a new layer and name it **behaviors**. Place the new layer underneath the label layer that contains the `key_2` frame label. Copy the `//play sound` keyframe from the previous actions layer, by selecting the keyframe and choosing Edit ➪ Timeline ➪ Copy Frames. Then, paste the copied keyframe to frame 5 of the new behaviors layer. Select frame 5 and choose Edit ➪ Timeline ➪ Paste Frames.

Tip   You can also copy and paste frames by selecting the frame(s), right-clicking (or Ctrl-clicking on Mac) the frame(s), and choosing Copy Frames or Paste Frames from the contextual menu. Frames are copied to a separate Clipboard than other elements in a Flash document that you use with the standard Edit ➪ Copy and Edit ➪ Paste commands. As such, you can have two types of elements in Clipboard storage simultaneously.

6. Select the new `//play sound` keyframe in the behaviors layer underneath the key_2 frame label layer. Open the Behaviors panel (Shift+F3). You need to change the copied Play Sound behavior to point to the `sndKey_2` instance. Double-click the Play Sound item in the Action column of the panel. In the Play Sound dialog box, change the target to `sndKey_2`, as shown in Figure 19-16.

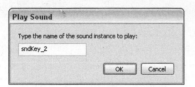

Figure 19-16: This Play Sound behavior targets the sndKey_2 instance.

7. Repeat Steps 5 and 6 for each key and sound. Each `key_` frame label should have its own behaviors layer with a `//play sound` keyframe. Test your movie each time you add a new keyframe with ActionScript. If a particular key doesn't work, check the target's name in the Play Sound settings.

8. When you've finished adding a behavior for every key, save the document and test it. After all's been said and done, you should have a functional Flash piano (well, at least seven keys' worth!) that plays a sound whenever you click a piano key. If you want to change the sounds, you can either update the sound file in the Library or import new ones.

You can refer to the complete exercise file, `pianoKeys_behaviors.fla`, located in the `ch19/pianoKeys` folder of the book's CD-ROM.

We'd like to know what you think about this chapter. Visit `www.flashsupport.com/feedback` to send us your comments.

Summary

✦ Movie Clips are the key to Flash interactivity. Each Movie Clip has its own independent timeline and playback.

✦ Each Movie Clip instance needs a unique name on any given timeline. You cannot reuse the same name on other Movie Clips on a timeline. You can, however, use the same instance name on different timelines.

✦ There are two types of target paths for Movie Clips: absolute and relative. Absolute paths start from the Main Timeline and end with the targeted instance name. Relative paths start from the timeline that's issuing the action(s) and end with the targeted instance name.

✦ The slash and dot notations are formats for writing either absolute or relative paths. The Slash notation is considered deprecated, and should be avoided unless you are authoring for Flash Player 4 or earlier. The dot notation was introduced in Flash 5 and has a more complete syntax for programming in ActionScript.

✦ The Insert Target Path dialog box can help you build the path to a Movie Clip instance, to use with another action.

✦ Behaviors can be used across timelines. For example, an instance of a sound created by a behavior on the Main Timeline can be accessed by another behavior located within another Movie Clip instance.

✦   ✦   ✦

Making Your First Flash 8 Project

◆ ◆ ◆ ◆

In This Chapter

Creating a Main Timeline layout

Making an image slide show

Adding navigation elements to a presentation

Using the TextArea component

Creating an effect with a custom BlurFader component

Inserting named anchors into your Flash movie

Adding accessibility information to movie elements

◆ ◆ ◆ ◆

Now that you've learned the basic principles behind Flash actions, you probably want to start creating a presentation to put on a Web site. This chapter integrates several basic production principles and teaches you how to make a simple interactive Flash movie that has basic navigation and text functionality. After you have completed this chapter's lessons, you'll be more prepared for the nitty gritty of ActionScript in Part VII of the book.

The Main Timeline as the Site Layout

Before you can start creating a Flash project, you need to know what you're communicating — what is the basic concept of the experience? Is this an all-Flash Web site? Is this a Flash animation that introduces some other type of content (HTML, Shockwave Director movies, and so on)? For the purposes of this chapter, you create a Flash movie for a basic all-Flash presentation. In a sense, this project will be the Flash equivalent of a Microsoft PowerPoint presentation. Let's look at the completed project (shown in Figure 20-1) that you will create in this chapter.

On the CD-ROM

In a Web browser, open the `main.html` document, located in the `ch20` folder of this book's CD-ROM. This movie contains two completed sections of the presentation.

When you load the `main.html` file into a Web browser with the Flash Player 8 installed, you see the presentation's title, "Digital Video Production," along with four navigation buttons that take you to each section of the presentation. The opening section, Introduction, has scrolling text featuring the new TextArea UI component. When you click the Video Equipment button in the navigation bar, a Movie Clip featuring five video items is displayed along with another instance of the TextArea component. The Next and Previous buttons enable you to browse the video items. Each video item uses a custom component that blurs and fades the item onto the Stage.

You will also notice that when you click each navigation button, the browser history updates. You can click the Back button of the Web browser to go directly to the previous section of the presentation. In this chapter, we show you how to create named anchors in the Flash document.

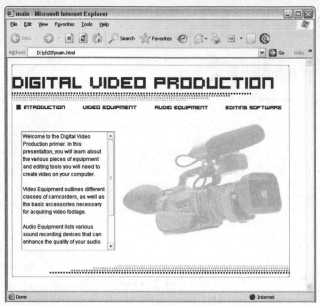

Figure 20-1: The completed presentation

If you have a screen reader installed and are using the Windows operating system, you will hear the screen reader describe each item in the Introduction section. A screen reader is an application that assists visually impaired computer users by speaking text aloud. The Flash Player 8 ActiveX control will only work with screen readers that adhere to the MSAA (Microsoft Active Accessibility) specification built into Windows operating systems. As of this writing, only the Window-Eyes screen reader by GW Micro and JAWS from Freedom Scientific adhere to MSAA. In this chapter, you learn how to add accessibility information to elements in your Flash document.

Creating a plan

Once you know what goals you want to achieve with your Flash content, you should map the ideas on paper (or with your preferred project planning or flowchart software). We create a basic presentation for digital video production that has four areas: introduction, video equipment, audio equipment, and editing software. Our organizational chart for this site has four discrete areas, as shown in Figure 20-2.

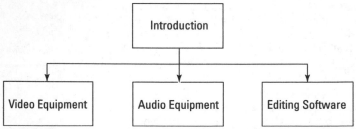

Figure 20-2: Our organizational chart will help us plan our Flash movie architecture.

In this chapter, you create the first two sections: introduction and video equipment. If you prefer, you can continue to develop the presentation with graphics we provide on the CD-ROM.

Determining Flash movie properties

After you've made your organizational chart, you'll want to determine the frame rate, size, and color of the Flash document. We've skipped much of the "real-life" planning involved with Flash Web sites, which we discussed in Chapter 3, "Planning Flash Projects." For this example, we have made a starter Flash document for you to use that contains all of the elements necessary to complete the chapter. This document contains some of the basic graphic elements already positioned on the Stage.

On the CD-ROM
Make a copy of the `main_starter.fla` document, located in the `ch20` folder of this book's CD-ROM. Before you open this file, you should install the Miniml font files from the `ch08` folder.

Open the starter document in Flash 8. This document uses a frame size of 640 x 480 (to maintain the aspect ratio of a computer monitor), a standard frame rate of 12 fps (frames per second), and a white background color. These are set in the Document Properties dialog box, shown in Figure 20-3, which is accessed by choosing Modify ➪ Document (Ctrl+J or ⌘+J).

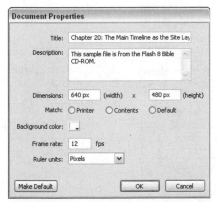

Figure 20-3: The Flash document properties

Mapping presentation areas to keyframes

Once the Flash document properties have been determined, you can create a Main Timeline structure for the presentation. Because there are four areas in the project (introduction, video equipment, audio equipment, and editing software), you'll have keyframes on the timeline that indicate those sections.

1. Create a new layer, and name it **labels**. Place this layer at the top of the layer stack in the Timeline window.

2. With the Selection tool, select frame 10 of the labels layer, and press F7. This creates a keyframe on frame 10.

> **Tip** It's usually a good idea to leave some empty frame space in front of your "real" Flash content. You can later use these empty frames to add a preloader, as discussed in Chapter 28, "Sharing and Loading Assets."

3. With the keyframe selected, open the Property inspector. In the <Frame Label> field, type **intro**. After you have typed the text, press the Tab (or Enter) key to make the name "stick."

4. Repeat Steps 2 and 3 with frames 20, 30, and 40, with the frame labels **video**, **audio**, and **software**, respectively.

5. Select frame 50 of the labels layer, and press F5. This will enable you to read the very last label, software. Your Timeline window should resemble Figure 20-4.

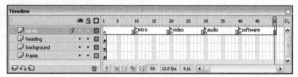

Figure 20-4: You use frame labels to differentiate each section of the site.

6. Select frame 50 on all other layers in the Timeline window, and press F5 to extend the content on these layers across the entire timeline, as shown in Figure 20-5.

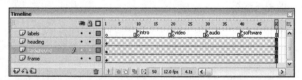

Figure 20-5: The content in the heading, background, and frame layers will be present throughout the entire movie.

7. Save your Flash document as **main_100.fla**.

8. Make a new layer, and rename it **actions**. Place this layer below the labels layer. Add a keyframe on frame 10 of the actions layer, and open the Actions panel (F9). Type the following code into the Script pane:

```
stop();
```

9. Close the Actions panel, and open the Property inspector. Make sure frame 10 of the actions layer is selected. In the <Frame Label> field, type **//stop**. The / / characters assign a frame comment instead of a frame label. Although this step isn't necessary for

the functionality of the movie, frame comments can provide quick and easy access to the designer's or programmer's notes. Your Timeline window should now look like Figure 20-6.

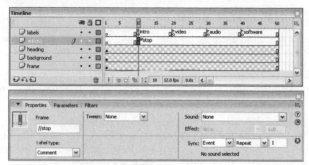

Figure 20-6: Unlike labels, you cannot use frame comments in ActionScript. Comments can provide quick visual references for ActionScript code.

10. Save the Flash document again.

At this point, the Flash document has a skeleton architecture (a blueprint) for your interactive functionality. Now you'll add some content to each section of the movie.

You can find the `main_100.fla` document in the `ch20` folder of this book's CD-ROM.

Main Timeline versus Scene Structure

Arguably, you might be wondering why you are using keyframes to delineate each section, instead of new scenes. There are a few reasons to use one scene (in other words, one Main Timeline):

✦ You can see the entire layout of the site very easily on one timeline.

✦ You can blend interstitials (transitions between each area of the site) over two sections more easily. It's much easier to have one Movie Clip instance span the area between two section keyframes on the Main Timeline.

✦ Scenes are not scriptable objects like Movie Clip instances are. You have greater flexibility with Movie Clips than you do with scenes.

Ultimately, the decision is yours. Make sure that you determine your Flash architecture well before you start production within the Flash 8 authoring environment. It's not a simple task to re-architect the layout once production has begun.

Creating content for each area

In this section, you create navigation artwork for each area of the presentation. You also build some content for the video section.

1. In the Flash document you created in the last section, create a new layer named **menu**. Place this layer beneath the actions layer. Insert a keyframe on frame 10 of the menu layer.

2. On frame 10 of the menu layer, use the Text tool to add a Static text block with the text **Introduction**. For this example, we use the Miniml font hooge 05_53 at 12 points with bold formatting. Use the Property inspector to set these options. Place the text near the left edge of the Stage below the heading, as shown in Figure 20-7.

If you don't have this font installed, copy the Miniml font files from the ch08 folder of the book's CD-ROM.

Figure 20-7: Use the Text tool to add the Introduction text to the Stage.

3. Repeat Step 2 for the text **Video Equipment**, **Audio Equipment**, and **Editing Software**. Space these text blocks across the Stage beneath the heading, as shown in Figure 20-8. Again, all of these text blocks should be on frame 10 of the menu layer. Later, you will convert each of these text blocks to a Button symbol.

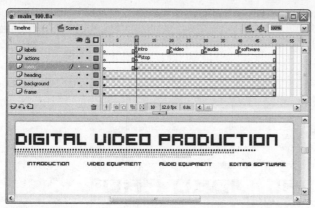

Figure 20-8: Add text that describes each section of the presentation.

Now, you create a graphic that lets the user know which section is currently active. To do this, you add a black square that will appear next to the appropriate text block. When the presentation starts, the black square will be next to the Introduction text. When the user navigates to the Video Equipment section, the black square will appear next to the Video Equipment section. Open the Library panel, and expand the graphics folder. There, you will find a Graphic symbol named marker. You will use this symbol in a moment.

4. Create a new layer on your Main Timeline (that is, Scene 1), and name it **marker**. Place this layer underneath the menu layer.

5. On frame 10 of the marker layer, insert a keyframe. Drag the marker symbol from the Library panel to the Stage. Position the instance of the marker to the left of the Introduction text, as shown in Figure 20-9.

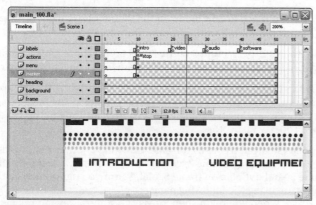

Figure 20-9: This marker designates the active section.

6. Insert another keyframe (F6) on frame 20 of the marker layer — make sure you do not insert empty keyframes. Move the instance of the marker at frame 20 to the left of the Video Equipment text, as shown in Figure 20-10.

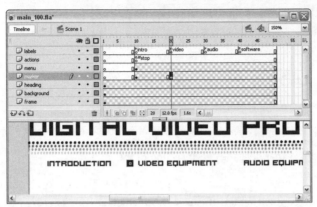

Figure 20-10: When the user goes to the Video Equipment section, the marker will appear next to the Video Equipment text.

7. Repeat Step 6 from frames 30 and 40 of the marker layer, moving the marker instance to the left of the Audio Equipment and Editing Software text, respectively. You now have the marker changing its position for all sections of the timeline.

Now you'll add a slide show of the video equipment that can be used for digital video production. This slide show will appear in the Video Equipment section of the presentation. For this, you create a Movie Clip symbol that has each product graphic on a separate keyframe.

1. Create a new symbol using Insert ➪ New Symbol (Ctrl+F8 or ⌘+F8). Make sure the Type option is set to Movie clip, and give it a name of **videoEquip**.

2. Flash 8 automatically switches to Edit mode on the videoEquip timeline. Rename Layer 1 to **items**.

3. Add keyframes to frames 2, 3, 4, 5, and 6 of the items layer. There are six items in the videoItems folder of the Library panel, and each item is put on its own keyframe.

4. Move the Playhead to frame 1 of the videoEquip timeline, and drag the dvTape Movie Clip symbol from the videoItems folder of the Library panel to the Stage. Once an instance of the symbol is on the Stage, name the instance **mcTape** in the <Instance Name> field of the Property inspector.

5. Continue moving the Playhead to the next frame, dragging another item to the Stage for each frame. Place cameraLow on frame 2, cameraMid on frame 3, cameraHigh on frame 4, dvDeck on frame 5, and dvCable on frame 6. Make sure you name each instance in the Property inspector, using the following names: mcCamLow, mcCamMid, mcCamHigh, mcDeck, and mcCable. When you're finished, press the < and > keys to review your frames. Check Figure 20-11 to compare your work. You may want to center each graphic

on the Stage using the Align panel (Ctrl+K or ⌘+K). As you progress with this exercise, you can adjust the exact placement of each item. Before you proceed to the next step, check that each instance is named in the Property inspector.

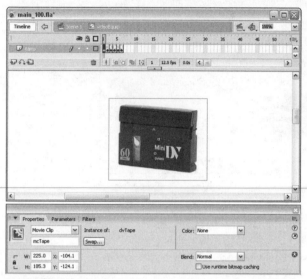

Figure 20-11: You should have six filled keyframes on the item layers of the videoEquip timeline.

6. Now you need to insert an actions layer for this Movie Clip symbol. Create a new layer, and rename it **actions**. Select frame 1 of the actions layer, and open the Actions panel. Add a stop action to make sure the items don't automatically loop when the movie loads:

```
stop();
```

7. Return to the Main Timeline (Scene 1) by clicking the Scene 1 tab in the upper-left corner of the document window.

8. Create a new layer, and rename it **content**. Place this layer underneath the marker layer. Insert a new keyframe on frame 20 of the content layer.

9. Open the Library panel, and drag the **videoEquip** symbol from the Library to the Stage. Place it just left of the center of the Stage, as shown in Figure 20-12. In the Property inspector, name this instance mcEquip.

10. Select frame 30 of the content layer, and press F7. This inserts a blank keyframe. Now, the mcEquip instance will show only in the Video Equipment area of the timeline.

11. Save your Flash document as **main_200.fla**.

Now you have some content in the Flash document. In the next section, you add navigation controls to the presentation.

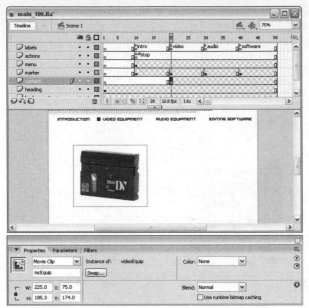

Figure 20-12: The mcEquip instance will only be present in the video section of the timeline.

On the CD-ROM

You can find the `main_200.fla` document in the `ch20` folder of this book's CD-ROM.

Adding Navigation Elements to the Main Timeline

In the last section, you created a timeline for a digital video production presentation. You inserted content placeholders for the intro, video, audio, and software sections of the timeline, and you made a Movie Clip with video item graphics to place in the video section. However, the user has no way of actually getting to any section except the intro frame. In this section, you convert the text blocks in the menu to Button instances, whose actions will control the position of the Playhead on the Main Timeline.

Creating text buttons for a menu

In this part of the exercise, you make menu buttons that will enable the user to navigate to the different areas of the Flash movie.

1. On the Main Timeline of your `main_200.fla` document, select frame 10 of the menu layer.

2. With the Selection tool, select the Introduction text block. Press F8 to convert this text into a symbol. In the Convert to Symbol dialog box, name the symbol **introButton**. Assign it a Button type. Click the top-left corner of the Registration box, as shown in Figure 20-13.

Figure 20-13: The introButton symbol settings

3. Select the Button instance on the Stage, and in the Property inspector, type **btIntro** in the <Instance Name> field. You will not target the button in any ActionScript for this project, but naming your instances is a good habit to get into.

4. Now you need to add a Hit state to the introButton timeline. By default, Flash 8 uses the last frame of a Button symbol timeline for the Hit state, unless content is added to the Hit state keyframe. Double-click the btIntro instance on the Stage to switch to Edit mode.

5. On the timeline of the introButton symbol, select the Hit frame of Layer 1. Press F7 to insert an empty keyframe.

6. Click the Onion Skin Outlines button in the Timeline window toolbar. This enables you to view the previous frames of the introButton timeline, as shown in Figure 20-14.

Figure 20-14: Onion skinning enables you to align the contents of several keyframes accurately.

7. Select the Rectangle tool, and draw a filled rectangle that covers the same area of the Introduction text block. You can use any fill color because the user never sees the Hit state. Make sure you turn off the stroke, or delete the stroke after the shape is drawn. Your button's timeline should resemble the one shown in Figure 20-15.

Figure 20-15: The Hit state defines the "active" area of the Button instance in the movie. When the user's mouse pointer enters this area, the Over frame of the button is displayed.

8. Select the shape you drew in Step 7, and press F8 to convert it to a Graphic symbol named **hitArea**. As with the introButton symbol, make sure the Registration icon is active in the top-left corner. You will reuse this shape for the other buttons in this section.

9. Next you add an Over state to the introButton, so that the user has a visual indication that it's an active button. Select the Over frame of Layer 1, and press F6. This copies the contents of the previous keyframe into the new one. Select the Introduction text block with the Selection tool, and change the fill color to a shade of blue such as #0099CC in the Tools panel or the Property inspector. You can also turn off Onion Skin Outlines at this point.

10. Return to the Main Timeline (that is, Scene 1) of your document, and save your Flash document as **main_300.fla**. Choose Control ⇨ Test Movie to test the states of the introButton.

    You can also use Control ⇨ Enable Simple Buttons to preview the graphical states of a Button instance directly on the Stage.

11. Now you put an action on the btIntro instance. Select the btIntro instance on the Stage, and open the Actions panel (F9). In the Script pane, type the following ActionScript code:

```
on (release) {
    this.gotoAndStop("intro");
}
```

With these actions, the btIntro instance will move the Main Timeline Playhead to the intro frame label when the user clicks the button.

12. If you test your movie at this point, your btIntro instance won't do anything—the Playhead already stops on the intro frame label when the movie starts. Add a button for each section on the site. Repeat Steps 2 to 9 for each section name in your movie. Note that you should reuse the hitArea Graphic symbol from Step 8 for the remaining buttons—use the Free Transform tool to size each new instance of hitArea to match the size of the text block in the Button symbol. You should end up with four Button instances on the Stage: btIntro, btVideo, btAudio, and btSoftware.

Tip   When you're finished making all the buttons, make a folder in the Library panel named **buttons**, and move the Button symbols and the hitArea graphic into the new folder.

13. Repeat Step 11 for each new Button instance. For each Button instance, change the frame label parameter in the gotoAndStop() action to match the name of the button's area (for example, this.gotoAndStop("video"); on the btVideo instance).

Tip   To quickly add the on() handler, type Esc+O+N in succession—not simultaneously. To add the gotoAndStop() action, type Esc+G+S.

14. Save your Flash document as **main_300.fla**, and test it (Ctrl+Enter or ⌘+Enter).

On the
CD-ROM   You can find the main_300.fla document in the ch20 folder of this book's CD-ROM.

When you test your Flash movie, you should be able to click each button to go to each area of the movie—you should see the square marker move to each category name when you click the name. If a button isn't functioning, double-check the code on the instance. Make sure that each Button instance has a Button behavior in the Property inspector. In the next section, you add buttons to the videoEquip Movie Clip symbol, so that the user can browse the pictures of the video items.

Browsing the video items

In this section, you go inside the videoEquip symbol and add some navigation buttons for the video items.

1. From the Main Timeline of your main_300.fla document, double-click the mcEquip instance on frame 20 of the content layer. Flash 8 switches to Edit mode.

2. Make a new layer on the videoEquip timeline, and rename the layer **buttons**. Place this layer below the actions layer.

3. Open the Buttons Library (Window ➪ Common Libraries ➪ Buttons). In the Buttons Library panel, double-click the Circle Buttons folder. Drag the circle button—next instance symbol to the Stage. Place the Button instance below and to the right of the mcTape instance. Name the new Button instance **btNext** in the Property inspector.

4. With the `btNext` instance selected, open the Actions panel. In the Script pane, try using keyboard shortcuts to type the following code. Press Esc+O+N, in succession — not simultaneously. That is, press the Esc key, release the key, press the O key, release, and then press the N key, and release. This sequence adds an `on(){}` handler to the Script pane. Type the keyword **release** between the ( ) of the on handler, and between the { }, type Esc+N+F. This sequence adds a `nextFrame()` action. Finally, press the Auto Format button in the toolbar of the Actions panel. When you are finished, the Script pane should show the following code:

```
on (release){
    nextFrame();
}
```

5. With the circle button — next instance selected, press Ctrl+D (⌘+D) to duplicate the instance on the Stage. Name the duplicate instance **btPrev** in the Property inspector. Move the duplicate instance to the left of the original arrow button. With the Free Transform tool selected, enable the Rotate modifier in the Tools panel. Rotate the duplicated button 180 degrees. Press the Shift key while rotating, to lock in 45-degree steps.

6. Select both arrow buttons, and align them horizontally to each other by using the Align panel. Insert some descriptive text next to the instances, as shown in Figure 20-16.

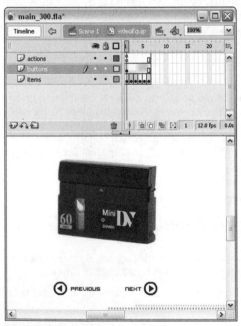

Figure 20-16: Add text to the buttons to describe their functionality.

7. Select the `btPrev` instance, and open the Actions panel. Change the `nextFrame` action to a `prevFrame` action. The Script pane should show the following code:

```
on (release){
    prevFrame();
}
```

8. Save your Flash document as **main_400.fla**, and test it. Click the Video Equipment button, and try the new navigation arrows for your video items catalog.

You can enhance your presentation by adding information in the videoEquip Movie Clip symbol. In the next section, you add a scrolling text window that displays descriptions of the video items.

On the CD-ROM You can find the `main_400.fla` document in the `ch20` folder of this book's CD-ROM.

The topic of Flash usability has received a lot of press, particularly because many Flash interfaces are considered experimental or nonintuitive to the average Web user. Since December 2000, Macromedia has maintained a special section in its Web site: Macromedia Flash Usability. You can read usability tips and view examples of interface design at www.macromedia.com/software/flash/productinfo/usability.

Closely related to usability is accessibility: How easily can someone with a disability access the content within your Flash movie? We show you Flash movie accessibility options in the final section of this chapter.

Text Scrolling with the TextArea Component

Continuing from the previous Flash movie example with the digital video production presentation, you learn how to create basic scrolling text using the TextArea component in Flash 8. You can scroll text in Flash 8 with either the UIScrollBar or the TextArea component. We will demonstrate the use of the TextArea component for one item in the videoEquip symbol to get you started.

1. In the Flash document you created from the previous section, double-click the `mcEquip` instance on the Stage, at frame 10 of the content layer. Flash 8 switches to Edit mode.

2. Add a new layer, and rename it **ctaDesc**. (We use the prefix `cta` to designate a TextArea component, and the `Desc` is short for description.) Move this layer beneath the buttons layer, and select frame 1 of the ctaDescription layer. Now, open the Components panel (Ctrl+F7 or ⌘+F7). In the UI Components nesting, drag an instance of the TextArea component to the Stage, to the right of the `mcTape` instance.

3. Use the Free Transform tool to stretch the component instance. This instance should accommodate several lines of text, as shown in Figure 20-17. The size of the instance should match the size of the text area you wish to display in the scrolling text window. In the Property inspector, name the TextArea instance **ctaDesc**. In the Parameters tab of the inspector, change the `html` setting from `false` to `true`. The `html` setting controls whether or not the instance should interpret HTML tags. Also, change the `editable` setting to `false`; the user should not be able to change the contents of the text field at run time.

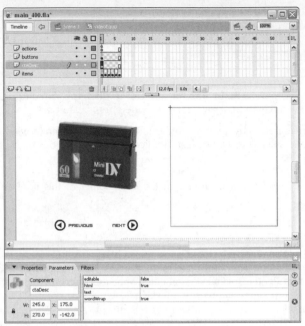

Figure 20-17: This text field will display the text associated with the first video item.

Now, you'll need to supply some text to the `ctaDesc` instance. You can specify text directly in the `text` parameter of the instance in the Property inspector, but for this project, you'll learn how to format HTML text that is assigned in ActionScript to the TextArea component. Open the `item_1.rtf` document in a text editor such as WordPad or TextEdit. This file is located in the `ch20/text` folder of this book's CD-ROM. Now, open the `item_1_formatted.txt` document on the CD-ROM, and compare it to the `item_1.rtf` version. (You may want to enable word wrapping in your text editor so that you can see all of the text in the TXT file.) You'll notice that all of the text in the TXT file is specified in one continuous nonbreaking line. Moreover, any carriage returns in the `item_1.rtf` have been replaced with `<br/>` tags in the TXT version. Some characters, such as the double quotes around the word "data," have been escaped in the TXT file — that is, the character is preceded by a backslash (\ ). These special formatting characters ensure that ActionScript will correctly display the text.

4. Select all of the text in the `item_1_formatted.txt` file, and copy it. Later in this exercise, you'll paste the text into your own ActionScript code.

5. On the videoEquip timeline, create a new layer and rename it **actions - text**. Place this layer at the top of the layer stack. Select frame 1 of the new layer, and open the Actions panel (F9, Option+F9 on Mac). In the Script pane, type the following code:

```
ctaDesc.text = "";
```

6. Between the pair of double quotes you typed in Step 5, paste (Ctrl+V or ⌘+V) the copied text into the Script pane. Initially, the text should be displayed on one line, but you can choose Word Wrap in the options menu of the Actions panel to see all of the text, as shown in Figure 20-18.

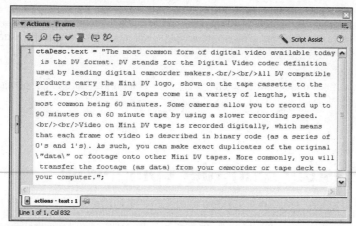

Figure 20-18: The Actions panel displaying the code to assign text to the TextArea component

7. Save the Flash document as **main_500.fla**, and test it (Ctrl+Enter or ⌘+Enter). Click the Video Equipment navigation button, and try the TextArea component. If the text is not displaying or scrolling, go back to the authoring environment and double-check the ActionScript code on frame 1 of the actions - text layer. Do not proceed with any steps until the TextArea component is functioning properly.

8. Now, you're ready to set up the text for the second item on the videoEquip timeline. Select frame 2 of the actions - text layer, and press F7 to insert an empty keyframe. Add the same actions and text as shown in Steps 5 and 6, but this time, copy and paste the text from the `item_2_formatted.txt` file (located in the `ch20/text` folder of this book's CD-ROM).

9. Save your Flash document again, and test it (Ctrl+Enter or ⌘+Enter). When you navigate to the Video Equipment section, you should be able to click the Next button to see the text for item 2.

10. Repeat Step 8 for frames 3, 4, 5, and 6 of the actions - text layer. When you are finished, you should have six separate action keyframes, one per item on the timeline.

11. Save your Flash document again, and test it (Ctrl+Enter or ⌘+Enter). When you go to the Video Equipment section, you should be able to click the Next button to reach each video item's description field, and the field should be scrollable.

The next step in real production would be to finesse the artwork and to add transitional effects between each video item. In the next section, we show you how to add a custom Fade component that we created for your use in this exercise.

Tip

If you want the scroll bar's position to reset for each new item, add the following ActionScript code after you set the text property on each frame:

```
ctaDesc.vPosition = 0;
```

The `vPosition` property controls the vertical position of the scroller. Setting it to zero resets the position to the top. So, if the user scrolls to the bottom of one description and presses the Next button, the next item's description will read from the top. This extra line of code was added to the `main_500.fla` file found on the book's CD-ROM.

On the CD-ROM

You can find the completed document, `main_500.fla`, in the `ch20` folder of this book's CD-ROM.

Using the Custom BlurFader Component

So far, much of the material and artwork used in this presentation could have been accomplished with a traditional HTML page layout in Macromedia Dreamweaver with GIF or JPEG graphics. In this section, you will add a fade effect to each of the video items in the videoEquip symbol. We created a custom component that can be applied to any Movie Clip instance on the Stage. This component will fade in or out a Movie Clip instance, based on settings in the Property inspector. To see this fade effect in action, open the `main.swf` file from the `ch20` folder in Flash Player 8. When you go to the Video Equipment section, each item will fade in. In other words, the alpha of the each Movie Clip instance animates from 0 to 100 percent.

New Feature

In this edition of the *Flash Bible*, we've fully updated the fade component used in previous editions. This new version is built with ActionScript 2.0 and uses the new blur filter effect available in Flash Player 8.

The BlurFader component snaps to Movie Clip instances. Because we built the component for you, you won't find the BlurFader component in the Component panel along with the Flash 8 components. The BlurFader component is located in the starter document's Library and has been saved in each version of the `main_` document that you've created in previous sections. Here's how to add the BlurFader component to the video items in the videoEquip symbol:

1. Open your saved Flash document from the previous section. On frame 20 of the content layer, double-click the videoEquip instance on the Stage to edit the symbol.

2. Select frame 1 of the items layer, and open the Library panel. Drag the BlurFader component to the `mcTape` instance on the Stage. When you release the mouse button, the BlurFader component should snap to the top-left corner of the `mcTape` instance, as shown in Figure 20-19. We made a custom icon for this BlurFader component: a little gradient box with the text BF. This icon will not show up in the actual Flash .swf file — it is displayed only in the authoring environment.

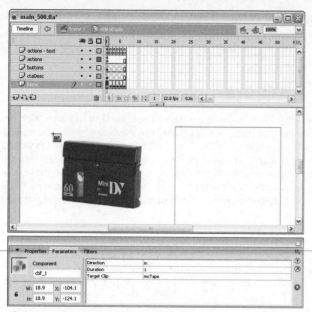

Figure 20-19: The BlurFader component snaps to the top-left corner of the Movie Clip instance.

3. You can view the default settings for the BlurFader component instance in the Property inspector. Select the component instance at the top-left corner of the mcTape instance, open the Property inspector, and click the Parameters tab. This component has three options, as shown in Figure 20-19: Direction (*in* to fade in the targeted instance, *out* to fade out the targeted instance), Duration (how long the transition should last, in seconds), and Target Clip (the Movie Clip instance that the BlurFader component instance has snapped to).

4. Save the Flash document as **main_600.fla**, and test it (Ctrl+Enter or ⌘+Enter). When you click the Video Equipment button, the first video item will fade into the Stage.

5. Repeat Step 2 for the other Movie Clip instances on frames 2, 3, 4, 5, and 6 of the items layer.

6. Save the Flash document again, and test it. After you click the Video Equipment button, click the Next button. Each video item will fade into the Stage.

If you want to use the BlurFader component in other Flash documents, simply drag the BlurFader component from one Library to another document's Library. Alternatively, you can copy and paste the BlurFader component instance from one document to another. Try different Duration values for the BlurFader component (in the Property inspector) to see how the fade animation is affected in the Flash movie.

Note The BlurFader component adds about 2 KB to the file size of your Flash movie file (.swf).

On the CD-ROM You can find the completed document, `main_600.fla`, in the `ch20` folder of this book's CD-ROM.

Adding Named Anchors

Flash Player 6 and higher give Flash movies extended functionality in some Web browsers, allowing the Back and Forward buttons of the browser to navigate to areas *within* the Flash movie. In earlier versions of the Flash Player, the Web browser's Back button would reset the position of the Flash movie to the first frame every time the movie reloaded into the browser. Now, you can add named anchors to Flash movies. Named anchors, when played, alert the browser's history to the location of the current anchor within the Flash movie. When another anchor is played, you can click the browser's Back button to go back to the previous named anchor.

Caution Named anchors are only supported in Web browsers that support `fscommand` and JavaScript interactivity. Currently, Internet Explorer 4 (or higher) on Windows or Netscape 3.*x* to 4.*x* on Windows or Macintosh supports the named anchor feature of Flash Player 6 and 7. Netscape 6 (on any platform) or Internet Explorer on Mac (any version) does not support named anchors.

You can add named anchors to Flash movies in two ways:

✦ Enable the Named Anchor on Scene option in the Preferences dialog box. On Windows, you can access the preferences by choosing Edit ⇨ Preferences. On Mac OS X, choose Flash ⇨ Preferences. You will find the Named Anchor on Scene option in the General category of the Preferences dialog box.

✦ Choose the Anchor option in the Label type menu of the Property inspector. Select a frame in the Timeline window, assign a frame label, and choose the Anchor option in the Property inspector.

In the presentation you're building in this chapter, you do not use any scenes. Therefore, you will add named anchors to all of the frame labels you created in previous sections.

1. Open the last Flash document you created from the previous section. Select frame 10 of the labels layer, and open the Property inspector. Select the Anchor option in the Label type menu, underneath the Frame Label field.

2. Repeat Step 1 for frames 20, 30, and 40 of the labels layer.

3. Open the Publish Settings (File ⇨ Publish Settings). Click the HTML tab, and choose the Flash with Named Anchors option in the Template menu. Click OK to close the Publish Settings dialog box.

4. Save the Flash document as **main_700.fla**, and preview the presentation by choosing File ⇨ Publish Preview ⇨ HTML. Flash 8 creates the Flash .swf file and .html file, and opens the default Web browser. If you have a supported Web browser, you can click each navigation button (that is, Introduction, Video Equipment, and so on) and see the browser's history update. After you have clicked in one section, you can visit the previous section by clicking the browser's Back button.

You can find the `main_700.fla` document in the `ch20` folder of this book's CD-ROM.

To read more about an advanced method of using the Back button with Flash movies and browsers, peruse the Flash and Browser Interactivity category links at `www.flashsupport.com/links`.

Making the Movie Accessible

In the final section of this chapter, we show you how to add accessibility information to your Flash presentation. As we mentioned earlier in this chapter, screen readers on the Windows operating system, working in concert with the Flash Player 6 or higher ActiveX control, can read aloud the content inside of Flash movies. Window-Eyes from GW Micro was engineered to work with Flash Player 6 or higher through the use of MSAA (Microsoft Active Accessibility) technology. As of this writing, Window-Eyes is one of two screen readers capable of accessing Flash content.

You can download a demo version of Window-Eyes for the Windows operating system at `www.gwmicro.com`. This version will only work for 30-minute durations—you will need to restart your computer to initiate a new session.

We recommend that you review the Accessibility information in the new Help panel that ships with Flash 8. Choose the Help ⇨ Flash Help command in the Flash 8 application. We provide a quick overview of the Accessibility features of Flash 8 in this section.

Starting with Flash MX 2004, Macromedia has added accessibility support to the authoring environment as well. This feature enables designers and developers with disabilities to more easily use Flash to author Flash movies. To find out more information about this feature, search with the term "accessibility" in the Help panel.

Screen readers will access information within the Flash movie differently, depending on the features of the specific screen reader. Here we discuss Accessibility options as they relate to Window-Eyes. You will add some content to the Introduction section of the presentation that Window-Eyes can read aloud.

1. In the last Flash document you created in the previous section, insert an empty keyframe at frame 10 of the content layer on the Main Timeline (that is, Scene 1).

2. On frame 10 of the content layer, drag an instance of the TextArea component to the left side of the Stage. In the Property inspector, name this instance **ctaIntro**. Change the `html` setting from `false` to `true`, and set the `editable` setting to `false`.

3. Open the `introduction_formatted.txt` document in the `ch20/text` folder of this book's CD-ROM. Copy the text in this document. Select the `ctaIntro` instance in your Flash document, and paste the copied text into the `text` setting of the Property inspector. Click any area of the Stage, and you should see an automatic preview of the copied text, as shown in Figure 20-20.

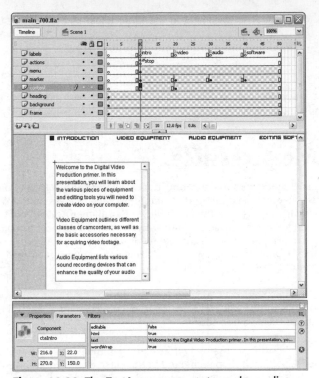

Figure 20-20: The TextArea component can show a live preview of formatted text in the authoring environment. The screen reader can read aloud this text field's contents.

4. With frame 10 of the content layer active, drag an instance of the cameraHigh Movie Clip symbol (located in the `videoItems` folder) from the Library panel to the Stage. In the Property inspector, change the alpha of this instance to 30 percent. Name the instance `mcCamHigh` as well.

Now you will use the Accessibility panel to add information to specific elements in the Introduction section of the presentation. You can open the Accessibility panel in two ways: Select the Movie Clip, Button, Component, or text field instance and click the Accessibility icon in the Property inspector; or choose Window ➪ Other Panels ➪ Accessibility.

You can add general information about your Flash movie by deselecting all elements on the Stage (you can press the Esc key to do this quickly) and opening the Accessibility panel.

The Make Movie Accessible option enables the screen reader to see elements inside the Flash movie. If this option is cleared, the screen reader will not be able to read any elements of the Flash movie.

The Make Child Objects Accessible option enables elements other than the current Name and Description in the Accessibility panel to be accessed by the screen reader.

Clear the Auto Label option. Auto Labeling will tell Flash Player 6 or higher to describe buttons and other elements by associating the closest text object to the element. For example, if you had some text underneath a Button instance, Auto Label would assign this text to the Button instance for the screen reader.

The Name field enables you to assign a title to the Flash movie, while the Description field enables you to add a quick summary about the Flash movie. Window-Eyes will read the Name contents, but not the Description contents. Let's add some general information to the current Flash document.

5. Deselect all of the elements on the Stage, and open the Accessibility panel. Select the Make movie accessible and Make child objects accessible options, and clear the Auto label option. In the Name field, type the presentation's title: **Digital Video Presentation**. In the Description field, type the following text: **A primer for digital video equipment and accessories.** Refer to Figure 20-21.

Figure 20-21: The Accessibility panel controls options for the Flash movie and its elements.

6. Now select the Introduction button on frame 10 of the menu layer. In the Accessibility option, enter the options shown in Figure 20-22. Note that you will not assign a keyboard shortcut description for this example. The Name and Description for this button will be read after the general information you added in the previous step. Window-Eyes will say the word "button" before it reads the name. For this example, Window-Eyes will say, "Button. Introduction. Access the introduction section of the presentation."

Note

If you do want to have a keyboard shortcut read by the screen reader, then you should type the text for any modifier key or combination including the + character, such as Ctrl+E. You will also need to add ActionScript to the Button (or Movie Clip) instance to make the movie respond to the key press that you described in the Accessibility panel.

Figure 20-22: Window-Eyes can read the Name and Description contents for buttons.

7. Repeat Step 6 for each Button instance in the menu layer.

8. Select the `ctaIntro` instance on frame 10 of the content layer, and make sure the Make movie accessible and Make child objects accessible check boxes are selected in the Accessibility panel. It is not necessary to add a description to this text field — the text inside of the field will be read automatically by the screen reader.

9. Select the `mcCamHigh` instance on frame 10 of the content layer, and clear the Make movie accessible option in the Accessibility panel. Not all elements need to be read by the screen reader, and this graphic does not need to be revealed to visually impaired users.

10. Save your Flash document as **main_800.fla**, and preview it in Internet Explorer for Windows. Make sure the Window-Eyes application is active. As soon as the movie loads into the browser, Window-Eyes reads the information for the movie and then reads the name and descriptions of the buttons. Then it will read the text inside of the description text field. After Window-Eyes reads the last Flash element, it speaks the word "bottom," indicating the end of the Web page has been reached. If you add body text to the HTML document, Window-Eyes will read that text as well.

On the CD-ROM You can find the completed Flash presentation, `main_800.fla`, in the `ch20` folder of this book's CD-ROM. This document contains the first two sections of the presentations — on your own, try adding your content to the remaining sections using techniques you learned in this chapter.

You can continue to add more accessibility information to other elements in the Flash document. You can even add information to elements within Movie Clip symbols. Try adding descriptions to the buttons inside of the videoEquip symbol.

Note Screen reader technology can only interface with Flash movies played by the Flash Player 6 or higher ActiveX control. Screen readers cannot access Flash movies played by the standalone Flash Player 6 or higher.

Web Resource We'd like to know what you think about this chapter. Visit `www.flashsupport.com/feedback` to send us your comments.

Summary

✦ Before you can start to create an interface in Flash, you need to have a plan for your Flash movie timeline. Create an organizational chart outlining the sections of the presentation.

✦ Determine your Flash movie properties (frame size, frame rate, and background color) before you undergo production in Flash.

✦ If you don't have final art for a Flash production, you can still create a functional proto-type of the presentation using placeholder graphics. When the final artwork is ready, replace the placeholder graphics with the final artwork.

✦ You can create simple slide shows or product catalogs using sequential keyframes and buttons with `nextFrame()` and `prevFrame()` actions.

✦ The Hit area of a text-based Button symbol should always be defined with a solid shape.

✦ You can achieve basic text scrolling by adding the TextArea component to your Flash movie.

✦ You can apply time-based alpha and blur effects to artwork with the custom BlurFader component.

✦ You can add accessibility information to Flash movies. Windows-based screen readers designed to work with Flash Player 6 or higher, such as GW Micro's Window-Eyes, can read this information.

✦   ✦   ✦

Distributing
Flash Movies

◆ ◆ ◆ ◆

◆ ◆ ◆ ◆

When you finally have your project assembled in the Flash authoring environment and you're ready to prepare it for final presentation, this section explains all the options available for delivering Flash content to your audience. Chapter 21 details just about every option and setting in the Publish Settings of Flash 8 that control your final file size and format. This chapter includes tips for optimizing your file sizes for faster downloads and better performance. Chapter 22 covers several HTML techniques relevant to integrating Flash content on Web pages. Learn how to create plug-in and version detection systems for your Flash movies. This chapter also introduces the new ExternalInterface API for sending commands to JavaScript. If you are planning to distribute Flash content offline or you want to avoid plug-in problems, Chapter 23 walks you through the various methods for creating Flash standalone projectors and using the Flash standalone player.

Publishing Flash Movies

If you have read Parts I through V of the book, you're probably more than ready to get your Flash movies uploaded to your Web server to share with your visitors. This chapter shows you how to create Flash movies (.swf files) from Flash 8 so that your Flash movies can be played with the Flash Player plug-in or ActiveX Control for Web browsers. We'll show you how to test your Flash movies, prepare Flash movie options, and adjust other output formats from Flash 8, such as HTML documents and image formats.

 New Feature In this chapter, you also learn how to take advantage of Flash 8's new Flash Player detection option. If you were familiar with Flash MX 2004's detection feature, you find that Macromedia has reduced the complexity of the feature, without sparing efficiency.

Testing Flash Movies

You have four ways to test your Flash movies: in the authoring environment using the Control ⇨ Play command, in the authoring environment using the Test Movie and Test Scene commands, in a browser using the Publish Preview command, or in the stand-alone Flash Player using Flash movie files (.swf) made with the Publish or Export Movie commands. There are several reasons why you should test your Flash movie file (.swf) before you transfer Flash movies to your Web server or to the intended delivery medium:

✦ Flash documents files (.fla) have much larger file sizes than their Flash movie file (.swf) counterparts. To accurately foretell the network bandwidth that a Flash movie requires, you need to know how large the final Flash movie will be. If the download demand is too overwhelming for your desired Internet connection speed (for example, a 56K modem), you can go back and optimize your Flash document.

✦ The Control ⇨ Play command in the Flash authoring environment does not provide any streaming information. When you use the Test Movie or Scene command, you can view the byte size of each frame and how long it will take to download the .swf file from the Web server.

✦ Movie Clip animations and actions targeting Movie Clip instances cannot be previewed using the standard Control ⇨ Play command (or the Play button on the Controller) in the Flash authoring environment.

Tip   You can temporarily preview Movie Clip symbol instances within the Flash authoring environment (for example, the Timeline window) by changing the Symbol instance behavior to Graphic instead of Movie Clip. Do this by selecting the instance, opening the Property inspector, choosing Graphic in the Behavior drop-down menu, and setting the playback menu to Play Once or Loop. However, if you switch the behavior back to Movie Clip, you will have lost the original instance name of the Movie Clip.

✦ Most scripting done with Flash actions, such as `loadMovie()`, `loadVariables()`, and `startDrag()`, cannot be previewed with the Play command. Enabling Simple Frame Actions or Simple Buttons in the Control menu has no effect with newer scripting actions. You need to use Test Movie to try out most interactive functions in a Flash movie.

Tip   Any actions that require the use of remote server-side scripts, Flash Remoting, or Flash Communication Server MX connections to load variables, movies, or XML data, will work in the Test Movie environment. You do not need to view your .swf files in a browser to test these actions, unless your server-side functionality has IP address restrictions that would prohibit playback from your local machine.

✦ Accurate frame rates cannot be previewed with the Play command (Control ⇨ Play) in the authoring environment. Most complex animations appear jerky, pausing or skipping frames when the Play command is used.

Using the Test Scene or Test Movie command

You can test your Flash movies directly within the Flash 8 interface by using the Control ⇨ Test Movie or Test Scene command. When you choose one of these commands, Flash 8 opens your Flash document in a new window as a Flash movie file (.swf). Even though you are only "testing" a Flash movie, a new .swf file is actually created and stored in the same location as the Flash document file (.fla). For this reason, it is a good idea to always save your Flash document before you begin testing it.

Caution   If your movie is currently titled Untitled-1, Untitled-2, and so on in the application title bar, it usually indicates that the document has not yet been saved. Make sure you save your Flash movie with a distinct name before testing it.

New Feature   Flash 8 now opens all tested movies in a separate nontabbed window. On the Windows version of Flash 8, the Test Movie window now hosts the playback and debugging commands. On the Mac version of Flash 8, the application menu bar changes depending on which type of tab or window was focused (authoring document versus movie file).

Before you use the Test Scene or Test Movie command, you can specify the settings of the resulting Flash .swf file. The Test Scene or Movie command uses the specifications outlined in the Publish Settings dialog box to generate .swf files. We discuss the Publish Settings dialog box later in this chapter. For the time being, you can use the Flash 8 default settings to explore the Test Scene and Movie commands.

Test Movie

When you choose Control ➪ Test Movie (Ctrl+Enter or ⌘+Enter), Flash generates an .swf file of the entire Flash document that is currently open. If you have more than one Flash movie open, Flash 8 creates an .swf file for the one that is currently in the foreground and that has "focus."

Tip   If you use Flash Professional 8, you can publish multiple .fla files at the same time by using the Project panel. To learn more about this feature, read Chapter 3, "Planning Flash Projects."

Test Scene

If you are working on a lengthy Flash document with multiple scenes, you may want to test your scenes individually. You can do this by using Control ➪ Test Scene (Ctrl+Alt+Enter or ⌘+Option+Enter). The process of exporting large movies via Test Movie may require many minutes to complete, whereas exporting one scene will require a significantly smaller amount of time. Movies that require compression for several bitmaps and MP3 sounds usually take the most amount of time to test. As you'll see in the next section, you can analyze each tested scene (or movie) with the Bandwidth Profiler.

Tip   You can use the Test Scene command while in Edit mode to export an .swf file that contains the current symbol timeline. The movie won't contain anything else from your Flash document. Note that the symbol's center point will become the top-left corner of the playback stage.

One Reason to Use Imported MP3 Files

If you have imported raw audio files such as .wav or .aif files into your Flash document, you may notice lengthy wait times for the Test Movie or Publish commands to complete. Why? The default MP3 encoding process consumes much of the computer processor's power and time.

Flash 8 has three MP3 compression qualities: Fast, Medium, or Best. Fast is the default MP3 quality setting—this is by far the fastest method of encoding MP3 sound. Because MP3 uses perceptual encoding, it compares a range of samples to determine how best to compress the sound. Fast compares a smaller range of samples than either Medium or Best. As you increase quality, the sampling range increases.

This process is similar to building 256-color palettes for video files; it's best to look at all the frames of the video (instead of just the first frame) when you're trying to build a palette that's representative of all the colors used in the video. While MP3 doesn't quite work in this fashion, the analogy is appropriate. So, at Best quality, the MP3 encoding scans more of the waveform to look for similarities and differences. However, it's also more time intensive.

Continued

Continued

As strange as it may seem, the quality does not affect the final size of the Flash movie file (.swf). The bit rate of the MP3 sound is the same regardless of the quality setting. Again, we'll use an analogy—consider the file sizes generated by three different digital cameras that have the same number of pixels in the pictures. The best camera, which will have the highest quality lens and

recording mechanism, produces better-looking pictures that capture detail *and* produces the same file size as the others. This is one of the few times where it's not about the amount of information stored in the compressed file—it's a matter of the accuracy and quality of the information within that quantity.

If you want to avoid the wait for Flash 8 to publish Flash movies that use MP3 compression, we recommend that you compress your source audio files to the MP3 format (including support for VBR—Variable Bit Rate—compression) and import those MP3 files into Flash 8. Unless the MP3 sound file is used for Stream Sync audio, Flash 8 will export the audio in its original MP3 compressed format.

For more information on sound in Flash movies, read Chapter 15, "Adding Sound."

Using the Bandwidth Profiler

Do you want to know how long it will take for a 28.8 kilobits per second (Kbps) modem to download your Flash movie or scene? How about a 36.6 Kbps modem? Or a 56 Kbps modem? Or a cable modem? The Bandwidth Profiler enables you to simulate any download speed.

On the CD-ROM

See the `ch21` folder of this book's CD-ROM for a Flash document named `bandwidth.fla`. We use that Flash document for this section.

To use the Bandwidth Profiler, you first need to create a movie or scene to test. When you create a Flash movie with the Control ➪ Test Movie or Scene commands, Flash opens the .swf file in its own window.

View menu

The Test Movie or Test Scene viewing environment opens your Flash movie in a dedicated window with its own View and Control menus.

Note

On the Mac, the View and Control menus appear in the application menu bar, not in the Test Movie window.

The first three commands in the View menu are the same as those of the Flash Player plug-in viewing controls, while the others are specific to the testing environment:

✦ **Zoom In:** Selecting this option enlarges the Flash movie. The shortcut key for this command is Ctrl+= or ⌘+=.

✦ **Zoom Out:** Selecting this option shrinks the Flash movie. The shortcut key for this command is Ctrl+-or ⌘+-.

✦ **Magnification:** This submenu enables you to change the zoom factor of the movie. The Flash movie is displayed at the original pixel size specified in the Modify ⇨ Document dialog box when 100 percent (Ctrl+1 or ⌘+1) is the setting. For example, if the movie size is 500 x 300 pixels, it takes up 500 x 300 pixels on your monitor. If you change the size of the viewing window, the movie may be cropped. The lower section of this submenu enables you to change the viewable area of the Flash movie.

Note

In the Test Movie environment, only the 100% and Show All options are enabled in the View menu. The other magnification options are enabled in the authoring environment.

✦ **Bandwidth Profiler:** To view the Bandwidth Profiler in this new window, use View ⇨ Bandwidth Profiler (Ctrl+B or ⌘+B). The viewing window will expand to accommodate the Bandwidth Profiler. Here's a breakdown of each section of the profiler:

• The left side of the profiler displays three sections: Movie, Settings, and State. Movie indicates the dimensions, frame rate, size (in KB and bytes), duration, and preload (in number of frames and seconds). The Settings area displays the current selected connection speed (which is set in the View ⇨ Download Settings menu). State shows you the current frame playing and its byte requirements. If you're using the Simulate Download feature (discussed later in this section), the State section displays the percent of the movie that has loaded.

• The larger right section of the profiler shows the timeline header and graph. The lower red line beneath the timeline header indicates whether a given frame streams in real time with the current modem speed specified in the Control menu. For a 28.8 Kbps modem, any frame above 200 bytes may cause delays in streaming for a 12 frames per second (fps) movie. Note that the byte limit for each frame is dependent on frame rate. For example, a 24 fps movie has a limit of 120 bytes per frame for a 28.8 Kbps modem connection.

• When the Bandwidth Profiler is enabled, two other commands are available in the View menu: Streaming Graph (Ctrl+G or ⌘+G) and Frame By Frame Graph (Ctrl+F or ⌘+F).

✦ **Streaming Graph:** By default, Flash opens the Bandwidth Profiler in Streaming Graph mode. This mode indicates how the Flash movie streams into a browser (see Figure 21-1). Alternating light and dark gray blocks represent each frame. The size of each block indicates its relative byte size. For our bandwidth.swf example, all the frames will have loaded by the time our Playhead reaches frame 13 when the movie is played over a 56 Kbps connection. The shortcut key for Streaming Graph is Ctrl+G or ⌘+G.

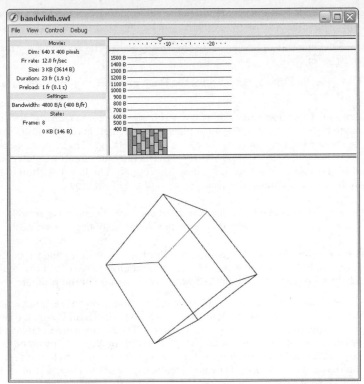

Figure 21-1: The Streaming Graph indicates how a movie will download over a given modem connection. Shown here is our bandwidth.swf as it would download over a 56 Kbps modem.

✦ **Frame By Frame Graph:** This second mode available to the Bandwidth Profiler lays each frame side by side under the timeline header (see Figure 21-2). Although the Streaming Graph enables you to see the real-time performance of a Flash movie, the Frame By Frame Graph enables you to more easily detect which frames are contributing to streaming delays. If any frame block goes beyond the red line of the graph (for a given connection speed), then the Flash Player halts playback until the entire frame downloads. In the bandwidth.swf example, frame 1, weighing in at 420 bytes, is the only frame that may cause a very slight delay in streaming when the movie is played over a 28.8 Kbps connection. The remaining frames are right around 200 bytes each — right at the threshold of 200 bytes per frame for a 28.8 Kbps modem connection playing a 12 fps Flash movie. The shortcut key for Frame By Frame Graph is Ctrl+F or ⌘+F.

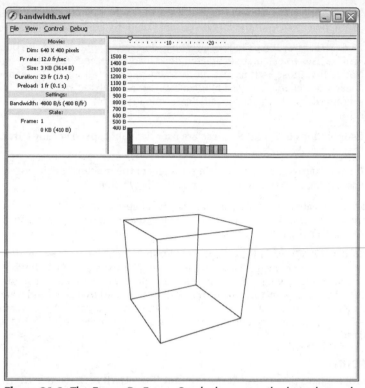

Figure 21-2: The Frame By Frame Graph shows you the byte demand of each frame in the Flash movie.

Note If you use Flash 8's new document title and description fields in the Document Properties dialog box (Modify ➪ Document), you add bytes to the first frame of your Flash movie. Depending on the number of characters you type into the title and description, you shouldn't see much more than a few hundred bytes added to your overall .swf file size.

✦ **Simulate Download:** When the Simulate Download option is enabled, the Bandwidth Profiler emulates the chosen modem speed (in the View ➪ Download Settings menu) when playing the Flash movie. The Bandwidth Profiler counts the bytes downloaded (displayed in the Loaded subsection of the State heading), and shows the download/play progress via a green bar in the timeline header.

Note In versions of Flash prior to Flash MX 2004, the Simulate Download feature was called Show Streaming.

Tip The Simulate Download command also applies to loaded runtime assets, such as SWF, JPEG and MP3 files. For example, when a `loadMovie()` action begins to load another file, the left side of the Bandwidth Profiler shows the progressive download at the simulated download speed.

✦ **Download Settings:** The View menu also features a submenu of connection speeds, which work in tandem with the Streaming and Frame By Frame Graphs:

- **14.4, 28.8, 56K, DSL, T1:** These settings determine what speed the Bandwidth Profiler uses to calculate estimated download times and frame byte limitations. Notice that these settings use more practical expectations of these modem speeds. For example, a 28.8 modem can theoretically download 3.5 kilobytes per second (KB/s), but a more realistic download rate for this modem speed is 2.3 KB/s.

- **User Settings 6, 7, and 8:** These are user-definable speed settings. By default, they are all 2.3 KB/s.

- **Customize:** To change the settings for any of the modem speeds listed previously, use the Customize command to input the new value(s).

✦ **Quality:** The Quality submenu controls the visual appearance of graphics within the Flash movie. By default, all graphics are displayed at High quality. You can choose from Low, Medium, or High quality in this menu.

✦ **Show Redraw Regions:** This new option in Flash 8 enables you to see which areas of the Flash movie are being updated on the screen. For example, if you have a Graphic symbol animation playing in the movie, a red outline frame appears around that portion of the Stage. Any and all redraw regions are bounded by such a red frame. You can use this feature to determine how much work the Flash Player is doing to redraw the Stage — many performance and playback issues are the direct result of too much screen redrawing.

Control menu

Use the Control menu to play (Enter key) or rewind (Ctrl+Alt+R or ⌘+Option+R) the test movie. Rewinding pauses the `bandwidth.swf` movie on the first frame. Use the Step Forward (. or > key) and Step Backward (, or < key) commands to view the Flash movie frame by frame. If a Flash movie doesn't have a `stop()` action on the last frame, the Loop command forces the player to infinitely repeat the Flash movie.

You can use the Disable Keyboard Shortcuts command to turn off the shortcut keys for all of the commands available in Test Movie mode. This is especially useful if you have enabled interactive key presses within ActionScript for your movie. For example, if you enable the Return or Enter key for a button, it will conflict with the Play command (Control ➪ Play). As such, when you press the Enter key while you test your movie, the movie will play to the next frame and the button actions will be ignored.

Debug menu

The Debug menu contains List Objects and List Variables commands. List Objects can be used to show the names of Movie Clip instances or ActionScript Objects in the Output window, while the List Variables command displays the names and values of any currently loaded variables, ActionScript objects, and XML data.

We'll discuss how these features can be used in Chapter 32, "Managing and Troubleshooting Flash Movies."

Using the size report

Flash also lets you view a text file summary of movie elements, frames, and fonts called a size report. In addition to viewing Frame By Frame Graphs of a Flash movie with the Bandwidth Profiler, you can inspect this size report for other "hidden" byte additions such as font character outlines. You can enable the size report to be created by accessing the Publish Settings dialog box (File ⇨ Publish Settings), clicking the Flash tab, and checking the Generate size report option. Once enabled, you can view the size report in two ways:

✦ After you publish, publish preview, or export a Flash movie, go to the folder where the .swf file was created. In that folder, you'll find a text file accompanying the Flash movie. This file is named after your Flash movie's name, followed by "Report" and the .txt file extension, as in `bandwidth Report.txt`.

✦ When you test your Flash movie using the Control ⇨ Test Movie command, the Output panel opens automatically in front of the Test Movie window. The report automatically loads into the Output panel.

On the CD-ROM

A sample size report, called `bandwidth Report.txt`, is included in the `ch21` folder of this book's CD-ROM.

Publishing Your Flash Movies

After you've made a dazzling Flash movie complete with Motion tweens, 3D simulations, and ActionScripted interactivity, you need to make the Flash movie usable for the intended delivery medium — the Web, a CD- or DVD-ROM, or a QuickTime Flash movie, to name a few. As we mentioned in the introduction to this book, you need the Flash 8 application to open .fla files. Because the Flash Player plug-in uses .swf files, you need to export or publish your .fla file in a format that your audience can use. More importantly, Flash documents are authoring documents, while Flash movies are optimized for the shortest delivery times and maximum playback performance.

A Word about the Export Movie Command

Even though Flash streamlines the process of creating Flash movies with the Publish commands (discussed in the next section), it is worth mentioning that the File ⇨ Export Movie command provides another route to creating an .swf file. Although the Publish command is the quickest way to create HTML-ready Flash movies, the Export Movie command can be used to create updated .swf files that have already been placed in HTML documents, or Flash movies that you intend to import into Macromedia Director movies. You can find the "Working with Director" chapter from the *Macromedia Flash MX 2004 Bible* by Robert Reinhardt and Snow Dowd (Wiley, 2003) archived at this book's Web site, `www.flashsupport.com/archives`. In practice, we find that we rarely use the Export Movie command. If you don't need HTML documents published with your Flash movie, simply clear the HTML option in the Formats tab of the Publish Settings dialog box.

You can convert your Flash document files (.fla) to Flash movies files (.swf) by using either the File ⇨ Export Movie, Control ⇨ Test Movie, or File ⇨ Publish/Publish Settings command. You can specify just about all file format properties in one step using the File ⇨ Publish Settings command. After you've entered the settings, the File ⇨ Publish command exports any and all file formats with your specified parameters in one step—all from the Flash 8 application.

The Export Movie and Export Image commands are discussed throughout the book. For more information on exporting still images in raster/bitmap formats, see Chapter 36, "Working with Raster Graphics," included as a PDF fie on this book's CD-ROM. To export vector formats, see Chapter 37, "Working with Vector Graphics," which is also included on the CD-ROM. To export QuickTime or AVI files, see "Exporting Animation" from the *Macromedia Flash MX 2004 Bible* by Robert Reinhardt and Snow Dowd (Wiley, 2003) in the online archive at www.flashsupport.com/archive.

Three commands are available with the Publish feature: Publish Settings, Publish Preview, and Publish. We discuss each of these commands in the following sections.

Publish Settings

The Publish Settings command (File ⇨ Publish Settings) is used to determine which file formats are exported when the File ⇨ Publish command is invoked. By default, new Flash documents created with Flash 8 use Publish Settings that will export a Flash movie file (.swf) and an HTML file with the proper markup tags to utilize the Flash Player 8 plug-in or ActiveX Control. If you want to customize the settings of the exported file types, you should familiarize yourself with the Publish Settings before you attempt to use the Publish command.

The Publish Settings dialog box has many new features that were introduced in Flash MX 2004, with some updates in Flash 8. You should be aware that the default ActionScript language version is AS2.0 for new Flash documents. You learn more about ActionScript and the implications of ActionScript 2.0 in Part VII, "Approaching ActionScript."

Selecting formats

Choose File ⇨ Publish Settings to access the Publish Settings dialog box, which is nearly identical for both the Windows and Macintosh versions of Flash 8. The dialog box opens to the Formats tab, which has check boxes to select the formats in which your Flash document will be published (see Figure 21-3). For each Type that is checked, a tab appears in the Publish Settings dialog box (with the exception of the Windows and Mac projector options). Click each type's tab to specify settings to control the particulars of the movie or file that will be generated in that format.

If you click the Use Default Names button, all of the File fields fill in with the name of your Flash document, followed by the file format's suffix. For example, if your movie is named sample.fla and you click the Use Default Names button, this is the base from which the names are generated in publishing. Thus, sample.swf, sample.html, sample.gif, and so on would result.

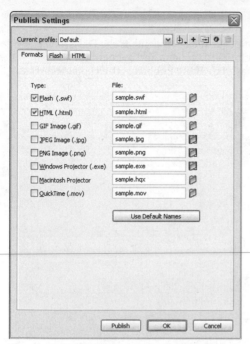

Figure 21-3: The Formats tab of the Publish Settings dialog box enables you to select the published file formats and use default or custom names for these published files.

Tip You can enter nonversion–specific filenames for Flash documents that you incrementally save as you work. For example, if you have a Flash document named main_100.fla, set the Flash movie filename to main.swf, and then every new Flash document version you save (for example, main_101.fla, main 102.fla, and so on) will still produce a main.swf file. This way, you can consistently refer to one Flash movie file (.swf) in your HTML code and incrementally save your Flash documents. However, if you work on large Flash projects with a team of Flash designers and developers, you should consider using version control software, such as CSV or Microsoft SourceSafe. With version control software, you don't need to resave files with new names; rather, you check in your changes to the version control system, which keeps track of each file version. We briefly discuss version control in Chapter 3, "Planning Flash Projects."

Tip You can specify which folder a publish document is created and stored in. All of the file formats have a folder icon to the right of the File field. If you click the folder icon, you can browse to a specific location where your published file will be created. You can use relative or absolute paths with the filenames in the Formats tab.

Using the Flash settings

The primary and default publishing format of Flash 8 documents is the Flash movie .swf format. Only Flash movies retain full support for Flash actions and animations. To control the settings for the Flash movie, choose the Flash tab of the Publish Settings dialog box, as shown in Figure 21-4.

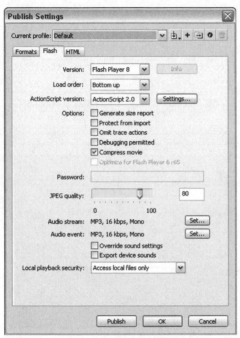

Figure 21-4: The Flash tab of the Publish Settings dialog box controls the settings for a movie published in the Flash format.

Here are your options in the Flash tab:

✦ **Version:** This drop-down menu provides the option to publish movies in any of the Flash movie formats. To ensure complete compatibility with all of the new Flash 8 features, select Flash Player 8. If you haven't used any Flash 5, MX, MX 2004, or 8-specific ActionScript commands, you can use Flash 4. Flash 1 and 2 support only basic animation and interactive functions. Flash 3 supports just about all animation and artwork created in Flash 8, but it doesn't recognize any actions introduced with either Flash 4 or 5, editable text fields (such as form elements), or MP3 audio. If in doubt, you should test your choice of version in that version's Flash Player.

Tip

Flash Professional 8 has a Flash Lite 1.0 and Flash Lite 1.1 option in the Version menu. Flash Lite 1.0/1.1 is a new Flash Player shipping with some mobile phones, such as DoCoMo phones in Japan. If this option is selected, make sure you are using a Stage size that is compatible with the screen size of the mobile handset on which the movie will be deployed. There are several templates available for devices in the Global Phones, Japanese Phones, and PDA categories of the Template tab of the File ➪ New dialog box.

✦ **Load order:** This option determines how the Flash Player will draw the first frame of the Flash movie as it is downloaded to the plug-in or player. When Bottom up (the default) is chosen, the layers load in ascending order: The lowest layer displays first, then the second lowest, and so on, until all of the layers for the first frame have been displayed. When Top down is selected, the layers load in descending order: The topmost layer displays first, then the layer underneath it, and so on. Again, this option affects the display of only the first frame of a Flash movie. If the content of the first frame is downloaded or streamed quickly, you probably won't notice the Load Order's effect.

Note

Load Order does *not* affect the order of actions spread across layers for the same frame. ActionScript will always execute in a top-down fashion; the actions on the topmost layers will execute before actions on lower layers.

✦ **ActionScript version:** This option introduced in Flash MX 2004 controls how ActionScript is compiled in a Flash movie file (.swf). You can choose ActionScript 1.0 or ActionScript 2.0. By default, ActionScript 2.0 is selected. Only use ActionScript 2.0 if you use the new ActionScript 2.0 coding features introduced with Flash MX 2004, or if you use components that ship with Flash 8, such as the FLVPlayback component or the UI components. If you code ActionScript the same way that you did in Flash MX or Flash 5, then choose ActionScript 1.0.

Tip

Flash 8 can compile ActionScript 2.0 code so that it is compatible with Flash Player 6. If you choose ActionScript 2.0 and set the Version menu to Flash Player 6, Flash 8 automatically compiles ActionScript 2.0 in a format that Flash Player 6 understands.

Also, keep in mind that ActionScript 1.0 or 2.0 code is case-sensitive *if* it is published for Flash Player 7 or higher. In Flash Player 7 or higher movies, variables, instance names, and other terms in ActionScript are case-sensitive. For example, if you accidentally refer to a variable named myName as myname, Flash Player 7–compiled movies will not be as forgiving as Flash Player 6–compiled movies.

✦ **Generate size report:** As we discussed earlier in this chapter, the size report for a Flash movie can be very useful in pinpointing problematic bandwidth-intensive elements, such as font characters. When this option is checked, the Publish command exports a text (.txt) file. You can view this document separately in a text-editor application such as Notepad or BBEdit.

✦ **Protect from import:** This option safeguards your Flash movies on the Internet. When enabled, the .swf file cannot be imported into the Flash 8 authoring environment or altered.

Caution

The Protect from import option will *not* prevent a Web browser from caching your .swf files. Also, Macromedia Director can import and use protected Flash movies. Flash utilities such as .swf Decompiler from www.sothink.com can break into any .swf file and extract artwork, symbols, video clips, and sounds. There's even an application called ActionScript Viewer from www.buraks.com/asv that can extract ActionScript from your .swf files! For this reason, you should always use server-side scripts to verify sensitive data such as password entries in Flash movies, rather than internal ActionScripted password checking with if/else conditions. Don't store sensitive information such as passwords in your source files!

✦ **Omit trace actions:** If this option is selected, Flash 8 removes any trace() actions used in your Flash document's ActionScript code. trace() actions will open the Output panel in Test Movie mode for debugging purposes. In general, if you used trace() actions, you will want to omit them from the final Flash movie — they can't be viewed from the standard version of the Flash Player anyway. trace() actions add to the final Flash movie (.swf) file size. For final production and live deployment, you should enable the Omit trace actions option to reduce the overall file size.

✦ **Debugging permitted:** If this option is selected, you can access the Debugger panel from within the Debug Movie environment, or from a Web browser that is using the Flash Debug Player plug-in or ActiveX control. To install the Flash Debug Player plug-in or ActiveX control, go to the Players folder in your Macromedia Flash 8 application folder. There, you will find a Debug folder. With your browser applications closed, run one (or more) of the following files:

- **Install Flash Player 8.msi** to install the ActiveX control for Internet Explorer on Windows 98/ME/2000/XP.

- **Install Flash Player 8 Plugin.msi** to install the plug-in for Mozilla-compatible browsers such as Firefox or Netscape on Windows 95/98/ME/NT/2000/XP.

- **Install Flash Player 8 OSX** to install the plug-in for Mozilla-compatible browsers such as Apple Safari or Mozilla Firefox on Macs running OS X 10.1 or greater.

✦ **Compress movie:** This option compresses Flash Player 6 or higher movies only. When enabled, this compression feature will greatly reduce the size of text or ActionScript-heavy Flash movies. However, you may see little or no size difference on other Flash elements, such as artwork and sounds. Compression cannot be used on Flash Player 5 or earlier movies.

✦ **Optimize for Flash Player 6 r65:** If you decide to publish your Flash movie for Flash Player 6, you can select this check box to further optimize the .swf file. The r65 release of Flash Player 6 introduced enhancements for Flash movie playback that were not available in prior releases of Flash Player 6.

Note

If you select the Optimize for Flash Player 6 r65 option, Flash 8 prompts you with a warning dialog box when you publish the Flash movie. If you use this option, you should use the updated version detection features in the Publish Settings' HTML tab to ensure that visitors trying to view the movie will be redirected to the proper plug-in download page if they are using an earlier version of the player. Specifically, you should enter 6.0.65 in the Version fields of the Publish Settings' HTML tab.

✦ **Password:** If you selected the Debugging permitted option, you can enter a password to access the Debugger panel. Because you can debug movies over a live Internet connection, you should always enter a password here if you intend to debug a remote Flash movie. If you leave this field empty and check the Debugging permitted option, Flash 8 will still prompt you for a password when you attempt to access the Debugger panel remotely. Simply press the Enter key when this prompt appears if you left this field blank.

✦ **JPEG quality:** This slider and text-field option specifies the level of Joint Photographic Experts Group (JPEG) compression applied to bitmapped artwork in the Flash movie. The value can be any value between (and including) 0 to 100. Higher values apply less compression and preserve more information of the original bitmap, whereas lower values apply more compression and keep less information. The value entered here applies to all bitmaps that enable the Use document default quality option, found in the Bitmap Properties dialog box for each bitmap in the document's Library panel. Unlike the audio settings discussed in a moment, no "override" option exists to disregard settings in the Library.

✦ **Audio stream:** This option displays the current audio compression scheme for Stream audio. By clicking the Set button (see Figure 21-4), you can control the compression applied to any sounds that use the Stream Sync setting in the Sound area of the Property inspector (when a sound keyframe has focus). Like the JPEG quality option discussed previously, this compression value is applied to any Stream sounds that use the Default compression in the Export Settings section of each audio file's Sound Properties dialog box in the document's Library. See Chapter 15, "Adding Sound," for more information on using Stream sounds and audio compression schemes.

✦ **Audio event:** This setting behaves exactly the same as the Audio Stream option, except that this compression setting applies to Default compression-enabled Event sounds. See Chapter 15, "Adding Sound," for more information on Event sounds.

Tip

Flash 8 supports imported MP3 audio that uses Variable Bit Rate (VBR) compression. However, Flash cannot compress native sounds in VBR. If you use any imported MP3 audio for Stream Sync audio, Flash will recompress the MP3 audio on export.

✦ **Override sound settings:** If you want the settings for Audio stream and Audio event to apply to all Stream and Event sounds, respectively, and to disregard any unique compression schemes specified in the document's Library, check this option. This is useful for creating multiple .swf file versions of the Flash movie (hi-fi, lo-fi, and so on) and enabling the Web visitor to decide which one to download.

✦ **Export device sounds:** If you are using Flash Professional 8, you have the option of exporting device sounds with your Flash movie. You use this option only if you are using the Flash Lite 1.0 or Flash Lite 1.1 option in the Version menu. To learn more about the use of this feature, use the search phrase "device sound" in the Help panel (Help ➪ Help) in Flash Pro 8.

✦ **Local playback security:** The new feature in Flash 8 enables you to control the access to local or networked assets from the published Flash movie. In prior releases of the Flash Player, a Flash movie file (.swf) could potentially access local files, representing a security hole. A Flash movie, for example, had the capability to load text files on the local computer and transmit the contents of that file to a remote server. Now, local Flash files are able to accept data from both local and network sources. However, if you choose to send data to a network source, you are only able to receive from a network source, with no data available locally. For more information on this feature, search the Help panel in Flash 8 with the term "local playback security." Note that a Flash projector can potentially read local files and transmit information to other networks.

When you are finished entering the settings for the Flash movie, you can proceed to other file type settings in the Publish Settings dialog box. Or you can click OK to return to the authoring environment of Flash 8 so that you can use the newly entered settings in the Test Movie or Scene environment. You can also export a Flash movie (and other file formats currently selected in Publish Settings) by clicking the Publish button in the Publish Settings dialog box.

New Flash Lite Authoring Features in Flash Professional 8, by Ezra Freedman

Macromedia's determination to make Flash Lite a dominant technology for mobile interfaces, applications, and content delivery is clear. In 2005, Macromedia and Nokia (the world's largest handset manufacturer) announced a licensing agreement that will integrate Flash Lite technology into Nokia products. Also in 2005, Macromedia announced the next release of Flash Lite, code named Deuce, which will (among other improvements) be based on the Flash 7 scripting engine and will support ActionScript 2.0. (The current version of Flash Lite, Flash Lite 1.1, is based on the Flash 4 scripting engine and thus requires developers to program using the now antiquated Flash 4 syntax and control structures.)

Flash Lite authoring is only supported in Flash Professional 8. In this version, Macromedia has addressed some of the most significant shortcomings of Flash Lite authoring in Flash MX 2004. In this tutorial, we will introduce the new device document templates and the new Flash Lite Emulator.

Device document templates

In Flash Professional 8, Macromedia has revamped the implementation of Flash Lite document templates. Instead of being tied to a single device, templates are now specific to a class of devices that share key features. The selection of a device template not only loads the appropriate settings for the class of devices, but preselects the appropriate devices for the Test Device menu in the Flash Lite Emulator, which we will discuss in detail later in this section.

To create a new document based on one of the device document templates, choose File ➪ New (or command+N) to bring up the New Document dialog box. Select the Templates tab. At the time of Flash 8's release, there are three template categories specific to Flash for devices: Global Phones, Japanese Phones, and PDAs. Browse the templates available in each category, and select the appropriate template for your project. If you are unsure of which template to select, the Global Phones ➪ Flash Lite 1-1 – Symbian Series 60 template is a good place to begin, as this class of device is readily available for purchase and has been a focus of Macromedia's Flash Lite development efforts.

Flash Lite Emulator

When authoring Flash Lite content for Flash MX 2004 Professional, the Test Movie command launched the same test movie screen as for other types of Flash content. This meant (among other things) that you were not able to view the content as it would appear on the device (for example you could not see its relation to the UI design and color scheme of the device). Additionally, you had to utilize the keyboard to simulate button presses, which was not always intuitive. Enter the new Flash Lite Emulator.

Using the Flash Lite Emulator

To launch the Flash Lite Emulator, open an existing Flash Lite document or create a new document based on one of the device document templates and choose Control ➪ Test Movie (or Command+Enter). The left side of the emulator window is used to select the device you'd like to use for testing. The right side of the emulator window is used to display the movie in the selected device, and enables you to interact with the movie as it would appear and function on the device.

Selecting a Test Device

If you created your Flash Lite movie from one of the new device document templates, the Test Device menu will be prepopulated with the appropriate list of supported devices, as shown in Figure 21-5.

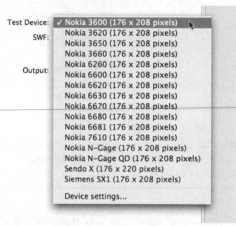

Figure 21-5: The Test Device menu, prepopulated with supported devices for the Flash Lite 1.1 Symbian Series 60 device template.

If you have not yet set a default list of devices and you opened a Flash Lite movie that was created with Flash MX 2004 Professional, or you created the Flash Lite movie by modifying your document's Publish Settings manually to specify Flash Lite 1.0 or Flash Lite 1.1 as the version, the Test Device menu will display "`<None Selected>`".

Tip   When authoring Flash Lite content with Flash Professional 8, always create new movies by selecting a device document template—this eliminates the guesswork involved in selecting appropriate target devices.

Testing the movie

Each time you select a new device in the Test Device menu, the Flash Lite movie will load into the right-hand side of the emulator. You can interact with the movie either by using the corresponding keys on your keyboard, or by clicking on the keys themselves in the device skin pictured around the movie.

SWF information

As shown in Figure 21-6, the SWF information area displays the dimensions and file size of your movie. This area is also used to inform you when the dimensions of the movie you have loaded are not consistent with the dimensions of the target device's screen.

Test Device: Sendo X (176 x 220 pixels) ⬍
SWF: 176 x 208 pixels, 0.65 KB
⚠ SWF will scale to fit device

Output: ☑ Trace
☐ Information
☑ Warnings

Figure 21-6: The SWF information area when the dimensions of the movie loaded are inconsistent with the selected device's screen.

Output options

The Flash Lite Emulator offers three options for output. These options control which types of messages appear in the Output pane while you are testing your Flash Lite movie. Note that these options do not in any way affect the published file.

Trace

The trace check box (enabled by default) specifies whether or not the text specified in `trace()` actions is displayed in the Output pane. This option is especially useful if you have used `trace()` messages extensively for debugging your project. Turning the option on and off can serve as a method of enabling or disabling your debug messages.

Tip   The Flash Lite Emulator does not offer the debug options that are often utilized in the standard test movie window. For this reason, consider using `trace()` options more frequently in your Flash Lite movie to keep track of variable assignments and function calls.

Tip   When you are ready to publish your Flash Lite movies for delivery to a device, ensure that the "Omit trace actions" check box in the Flash tab of the Publish Settings dialog is disabled. This will help to optimize the file size of your movie.

Information

Although the Information check box is disabled by default, it is useful to keep this check box enabled. When enabled, key information regarding the selected device's capabilities is printed to the output pane immediately after the movie loads. This will help you determine, for example, whether or not the targeted device supports input text fields.

Warnings

The Warnings check box (enabled by default) specifies whether or not Flash Lite warnings are displayed in the Output pane. For a comprehensive list of warning messages and their meanings, view Appendix C (titled "Warning and Error Messages") of the Macromedia

Flash Lite 1.1 Authoring Guidelines document. This document is available as part of the free Flash Lite 1.1 CDK (Content Development Kit), which is available for download at www.macromedia.com/devnet/devices/development_kits.html.

Device Settings dialog box

You can modify the list of devices in the Test Device menu through the Device Settings dialog box (another new feature for Flash Professional 8), shown in Figure 21-7. To launch the Device Settings dialog from the Flash Lite emulator, select the Device Settings option in the Test Devices menu.

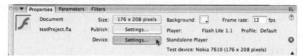

Figure 21-7: The Device Settings dialog box can be launched from the main document editing window's document pane.

Once you have launched the Device Settings dialog box, the first step in determining the appropriate devices for your project is ensuring that the appropriate content type is selected. Flash Professional 8 ships with information for 22 Flash Lite content types. Each content type (also referred to as an application mode) refers to a manner in which a device can play Flash content. For example, some devices can support Flash content as a screensaver — for this reason, Screensaver is listed as a content type. If you are uncertain which content type is appropriate for your project, you should select Standalone Player. The Standalone Player mode supports the widest range of Flash Lite features, and is the standard method used to deploy Flash Lite content.

Note

As you modify your selection for content type, you will see that certain folders on the Available devices list become highlighted (tinted blue) while others are grayed out. The Device Settings dialog box highlights only those folders that contain devices applicable to your selected content type. As you drill down into the top-level folders, you will see that sub-folders (and even the devices themselves) also adhere to this convention.

Once you have selected your target Content Type, you are ready to add devices to the Test Devices list. You can add the devices one at a time (by drilling down to and selecting the device in the available devices list and clicking Add >>) or in groups (selecting a folder in the available devices list and clicking Add >> will add all devices in that folder and its subfolders).

Note that Flash 8 allows you to add devices to the Test Devices list even if they do not support the selected Content Type. You can identify those devices in your Test Devices list that are not supported given the current content type by the absence of a width and height value in the available devices list. Additionally, selecting an unsupported device will cause the Available Stage information area to read "Not supported for the selected content type."

When you are satisfied with your selections, click OK to close the dialog box. You can also click Make Default before clicking OK. If you do, the currently selected content type and Test Devices list will be used as a default when you create new Flash Lite movies that are not already associated with a content type and Test Devices list.

Tip   You should periodically check the Macromedia Web site for new supported devices, as the list of supported devices is expected to grow rapidly. You can access the device profile updates page by clicking on the Check for new devices link located in the lower-left corner of the Device Settings dialog box.

Using the HTML settings

HTML is the language in which most Web pages are written. The HTML tab of the Publish Settings dialog box (see Figure 21-8) has a number of settings that control the way in which Flash 8 publishes a movie into a complete Web page with HTML tags specifying the Flash Player.

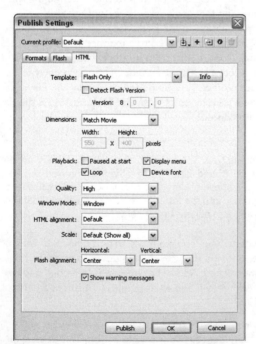

Figure 21-8: The HTML tab controls flexible Flash movie options — you can change these options without permanently affecting the Flash movie.

The settings available in the HTML tab include

✦ **Template:** Perhaps the most important (and versatile) feature of all Publish Settings, the Template setting enables you to select a predefined set of HTML tags to display your Flash movies. To view the description of each template, click the Info button to the right of the drop-down list (shown in Figure 21-8). All templates use the same options listed in the HTML tab — the template simply places the values of those settings into HTML tags scripted in the template. You can also create your own custom templates for your own unique implementation of Flash movies.

You can view the "source" of each template in the HTML folder found inside the `en/FirstRun/HTML` folder (Windows) or the `First Run/HTML` folder (Mac) of the Flash 8 application folder. These template files have .html extensions, and you can use Macromedia Dreamweaver, Notepad (Windows), or TextEdit (Mac) to view and edit the files. All of the preinstalled templates include HTML tags to create an entire Web page, complete with `<head>`, `<title>`, and `<body>` tags. The following templates are available in the HTML tab:

• **Flash For Pocket PC 2003:** With this template, Flash creates an HTML document that can display the Flash movie within the Pocket IE application running on a Pocket PC. This template also creates the necessary tags to display the same Flash movie in the regular desktop versions of Internet Explorer and Netscape. At the time of this writing, Flash Player 6 was the latest public release available for the Pocket PC.

Note

If you are designing Flash movies for the Pocket PC, be sure to check out the PDA document templates. Choose File ➪ New, click the Templates tab, and choose the PDA category. The Windows Mobile templates work with the screen dimensions of most Pocket PCs.

• **Flash HTTPS:** This template looks nearly identical to the Flash Only template (discussed next). The only difference with this template is that the download locations for the ActiveX control and plug-in page use `https://` instead of `http://`. If you are loading your Flash movie file (.swf) from a secure URL and page, it's recommended that any and all URLs used within that document use secure URLs as well. A secure URL always starts with `https://`.

• **Flash Only:** This default template simply inserts the `<object>` and `<embed>` tags for a Flash movie. It does not perform any browser or plug-in detection. If the user does not have the Flash Player plug-in or ActiveX control, the browser may produce an error message, a missing plug-in icon, or a prompt to download the latest plug-in or ActiveX control, depending on the browser configuration. The HTML produced by this template may allow an earlier Flash Player (such as Flash Player 4) to attempt playback of your newer Flash movie. Keep in mind that any version of the Flash Player will try to render any Flash movie file. However, you may get unpredictable results when a newer-version Flash movie loads into an older player.

• **Flash with AICC Tracking:** Use this template if you are creating Flash movies that incorporate components from the Learning Interactions Library (Window ➪ Other Panels ➪ Common Libraries ➪ Learning Interactions). Use it also if you want the components in the Flash movie to comply with the Aviation Industry CBT Committee (AICC) training guidelines. The template will create

JavaScript/VBScript functions that can work with the ActionScript of the learning components. For more information on AICC guidelines, see www.aicc.org. Note that this template will function only in Web browsers that support the fscommand() action from Flash movies.

- **Flash with FSCommand:** Use this template if you are using the fscommand() action in your Flash movies to communicate with JavaScript in the HTML page. The fscommand() is discussed in Chapter 22, "Integrating Flash Content with Web Pages." The necessary <object> and <embed> tags from the Flash Only (Default) template are also included.

- **Flash with Named Anchors:** If you are using named anchors in the Main Timeline of your Flash document, you will want to use this template for your published HTML document. This template creates the necessary JavaScript to enable the Back button on your Web browser with named anchors within your Flash movie. Named anchors allow you to designate specific keyframes (and scenes) that register in the browser's history when played.

- **Flash with SCORM 1.2 Tracking:** This template will create the HTML and JavaScript/VBScript functions to enable communication between Flash movies that use the components from the Learning Interactions Library and the HTML page. SCORM, which stands for Shareable Content Object Reference Model, is a set of guidelines for learning systems created by the U.S. Department of Defense Advanced Distributed Learning (ADL) Initiative. Both SCORM and AICC guidelines aim to promote interoperability among learning and training systems. Note that this template will only function in Web browsers that support the fscommand() from Flash movies.

- * **Flash with SCORM 2004 Tracking:** This template has the same functionality as the last template, except that the codebase has been updated to support SCORM 2004 features.

- **Image Map:** This template does not use or display any Flash movie. Instead, it uses a GIF, JPEG, or PNG image (as specified in the Publish Settings' Format tab) as a client-side image map, via an <img> tag with a USEMAP attribute. Use a frame label of #map in the Flash document file (.fla) to designate which frame is used as the map image. See the section "Using the GIF settings" later in this chapter for more details.

- **QuickTime:** This template creates both the <object> and <embed> tags to display QuickTime Flash movies. You need to enable the QuickTime file type in the Publish Settings' Format tab. A QuickTime Flash movie is a special type of QuickTime movie, playable with QuickTime 4 or higher. QuickTime 4 can recognize Flash 3 features only, QuickTime 5 can play Flash 4, and QuickTime 6 can play Flash 5 movies. Be careful to only use ActionScript features that are compatible with each respective version. You must choose Flash Player 3, Flash Player 4, or Flash Player 5 as the Version option in the Flash tab. Depending on the options selected in the QuickTime tab of Publish Settings, the Flash movie may or may not be stored within the QuickTime movie file — it's possible to create a reference .mov file that links to an .swf file, or you can create a .mov file that embeds the .swf file.

Web Resource

The "Working with QuickTime" chapter, found in previous editions of the *Flash Bible*, has been moved to an online-only location. You can download the .pdf file at www.flashsupport.com/archive.

✦ **Detect Flash Version:** This updated feature of Flash 8 enables you to add version detection to your Flash content. For the most basic use, simply select this check box and leave the default versions. The version displayed in the HTML tab reflects the version of the Flash Player you selected in the Flash tab of the Publish Settings. For more advanced use, you can specify major and minor versions of the currently selected Flash Player version. The Detect Flash Version feature creates all of the necessary JavaScript to detect the Flash Player on modern browsers. The options for this feature include two fields:

- **Minor Revision:** This text field controls the minor version revision number you want to require. Note that, to date, there have been no minor revisions to any publicly released Flash Players — Macromedia has only released incremental revisions.

- **Incremental Revision:** This text field displays the incremental revision number of the Flash Player you want to require. You can edit this value directly in the dialog box. For example, if you chose the Optimize for Flash Player 6 r65 option in the Flash tab, you could enter the number **65** in this field. The detection script would then check for r65 or higher.

New Feature

The Detect Flash Version feature no longer creates an alternate content page, as it did in Flash MX 2004. With Flash 8, the alternate content HTML is specified in the JavaScript. To include your own custom alternate content, you can edit the JavaScript in Macromedia Dreamweaver or your preferred text editor.

✦ **Dimensions:** This setting controls the width and height values of the <object> and <embed> tags. The dimension settings here do not change the original Flash movie; they simply create the area through which your Flash movie is viewed on the Web page. The way that the Flash movie "fits" into this viewing area is determined with the Scale option (discussed later). Three input areas exist: a drop-down menu and two text fields for width and height. The options here are

- **Match Movie:** If you want to keep the same width and height that you specified in the Document Properties dialog box (Modify ⇨ Document), then use this option in the drop-down menu.

- **Pixels:** You can change the viewing size (in pixel units) of the Flash movie window by selecting this option and entering new values in the Width and Height text fields.

- **Percent:** This option scales the movie to the size of the browser window — or a portion of it. Using a value of 100 on both Width and Height expands the Flash movie to fit the entire browser window. If Percent is used with the proper Scale setting (see the description of the Scale setting later in this chapter), the aspect ratio of your Flash movie will not be distorted.

Tip

The ActionScript Stage class and its supporting methods enable you to disable or override automatic scaling of the Flash movie. For example, the following action added to frame 1 of your Flash movie will disable scaling: Stage.scaleMode = "noScale";. If you want to center your Flash movie's stage in a browser window, you can set the size to Percent in the HTML tab, and the Scale setting to No scale.

- **Width and Height:** Enter the values for the Flash movie width and height here. If Match Movie is selected, you shouldn't be able to enter any values. The unit of measurement is determined by selecting either Pixels or Percent from the drop-down menu.

✦ **Playback:** These options control how the Flash movie plays when it is downloaded to the browser. Each of these options has `<object>` and `<embed>` attributes if you want to control them outside of Publish Settings. Note that these attributes are not viewable within the Publish Settings dialog box—you need to load the published HTML document into a text editor to see the attributes.

- **Paused at start:** This is equivalent to adding a `stop()` action on the first frame of the first scene in the Flash movie. By default, this option is off—movies play as soon as they stream into the player. A button with a `play()` action can start the movie, or the Play command can be executed from the Flash Player shortcut menu (by right-clicking or Control+clicking the movie). Attribute: `play="true"` or `"false"`. If `play="true"`, the movie will play as soon as it is loaded.

- **Loop:** This option causes the Flash movie to repeat an infinite number of times. By default, this option is on. If it is not checked, the Flash movie stops on the last frame unless some other ActionScripted event is initiated on the last frame. Attribute: `loop="true"` or `"false"`.

- **Display menu:** This option controls whether the person viewing the Flash movie in the Flash Player environment can access the shortcut menu via a right-click (Windows) or Control+click (Mac) anywhere within the movie area. If this option is selected, the visitor can select Zoom In/Out, 100 percent, Show All, High Quality, Play, Loop, Rewind, Forward, and Back from the menu. If this option is not selected, the visitor can only select About Flash Player from the menu. Attribute: `menu="true"` or `"false"`.

- **Device font:** This option applies to Flash movies played only in the Windows version of the Flash Player. When enabled, this option replaces fonts that are not installed on the Player's system with anti-aliased system fonts. Attribute: `devicefont="true"` or `"false"`.

✦ **Quality:** This menu determines how the Flash artwork in a movie will render. While it would be ideal to play all Flash movies at high quality, slower processors may not be able to redraw anti-aliased artwork and keep up with the frame rate. The options for this setting include the following:

- **Low:** This setting forces the Flash Player to turn off anti-aliasing (smooth edges) completely. On slower processors, this may improve playback performance. Attribute: `quality="low"`.

- **Auto Low:** This setting starts in Low quality mode (no anti-aliasing) but will switch to High quality if the computer's processor can handle the playback speed. Attribute: `quality="autolow"`.

- **Auto High:** This setting is the opposite of Auto Low. The Flash Player starts playing the movie in High quality mode, but if the processor cannot handle the playback demands, it switches to Low quality mode. For most Web sites, this is the optimal setting to use because it favors higher quality first. Attribute: `quality="autohigh"`.

- **Medium:** This quality produces anti-aliased vector graphics on a 2 x 2 grid (in other words, it will smooth edges over a 4-pixel square area), but it does not smooth bitmap images. Artwork will appear slightly better than the Low quality, but not as smooth as the High setting. Attribute: `quality="medium"`. This quality setting will only work with the Flash Player 5 or higher.

- **High:** When this setting is used, the Flash Player dedicates more of the computer's processor to rendering graphics (instead of playback). All vector artwork is anti-aliased on a 4 x 4 grid (16-pixel square area). Bitmaps are smoothed unless they are contained within an animation sequence such as a Motion tween. By default, this setting is selected in the HTML tab of the Publish Settings dialog box. Attribute: `quality="high"`.

- **Best:** This mode does everything that High quality does, with the addition of smoothing all bitmaps — regardless of whether they are in Motion tweens. This mode is the most processor-intensive. Attribute: `quality="best"`.

✦ **Window Mode:** The Window Mode setting works only with any version of the Flash ActiveX control on Internet Explorer for Windows 95/98/ME/NT/2000/XP or with Flash Player 6 r65 and higher for Mozilla-compatible browsers on Windows or Mac OS X. If you intend to deliver to one of these browsers and/or this version of the Flash Player, you can animate Flash content on top of DHTML content. One of the following values can be selected from this menu:

- **Window:** This is the "standard" player interface, in which the Flash movie plays as it would normally, in its own rectangular window on a Web page. Attribute: `wmode="window"`.

- **Opaque Windowless:** Use this option if you want the Flash movie to have an opaque (that is, nontransparent) background and have DHTML or HTML elements behind the Flash movie. Attribute: `wmode="opaque"`.

- **Transparent Windowless:** This option "knocks out" the Flash background color so that other HTML and DHTML elements can show through. You have likely seen this type of Flash movie and effect used on several commercial Web sites, where Flash ads animate across the screen on top of the HTML document. Note that the Flash movie's frame rate and performance may suffer on slower machines when this mode is used because the Flash movie needs to composite itself over other non-Flash material. Attribute: `wmode="transparent"`.

✦ **HTML alignment:** This setting works much like the `ALIGN` attribute of `<img>` tags in HTML documents, but it's used with the `ALIGN` attribute of the `<OBJECT>` and `<embed>` tags for the Flash movie. Note that these settings may not have any effect when used within a table cell (`<td>` tag) or a DHTML layer (`<div>` or `<layer>` tag). The options for this setting include the following:

- **Default:** This option left-justifies the Flash movie in the browser window. If the browser window is smaller than a Flash movie that uses a Pixel or Match Movie dimensions setting (see the Dimensions setting earlier in this section), the Flash movie will be cropped.

- **Left, Right, Top, and Bottom:** These options align the Flash movie along the left, right, top, or bottom edge of the browser window, respectively.

✦ **Scale:** This setting works in tandem with the Dimensions setting discussed earlier in this section, and it determines how the Flash movie displays on the HTML page. Just as big-screen movies must be cropped to fit the aspect ratio of a TV screen, Flash movies may need to be modified to fit the area prescribed by the Dimensions setting. The settings for the Scale option include the following:

- **Default (Show all):** This option fits the entire Flash movie into the area defined by the Dimensions setting without distorting the original aspect ratio of the Flash movie. However, borders may appear on two sides of the Flash movie. For example, if a 300-x-300-pixel window is specified in Dimensions and the Flash movie has an aspect ratio of 1.33:1 (for example, 400 x 300 pixels), then a border fills the remaining areas on top of and below the Flash movie. This is similar to the "letterbox" effect on widescreen video rentals. Attribute: `scale="showall"`.

- **No border:** This option forces the Flash movie to fill the area defined by the Dimensions setting without leaving borders. The Flash movie's aspect ratio is not distorted or stretched. However, this may crop two sides of the Flash movie. Using the same example from Show All, the left and right sides of the Flash movie are cropped when No Border is selected. Attribute: `scale="noborder"`.

- **Exact fit:** This option stretches a Flash movie to fill the entire area defined by the Dimensions setting. Using the same example from Show All, the 400 x 300 Flash movie is scrunched to fit a 300 x 300 window. If the original movie showed a perfect circle, it now appears as an oval. Attribute: `scale="exactfit"`.

- **No scale:** This option prevents the Flash movie from scaling beyond its original size as defined in the Document Properties dialog box (Modify ➪ Document). The Flash Player window size (or the Web browser window size) has no effect on the size of the Flash movie. Attribute: `scale="noscale"`.

✦ **Flash alignment:** This setting adjusts the `salign` attribute of the `<object>` and `<embed>` tags for the Flash movie. In contrast to the HTML Alignment setting, Flash alignment works in conjunction with the Scale and Dimensions settings, and determines how a Flash movie is aligned within the Player window. This setting has the following options:

- **Horizontal:** These options — Left, Center, and Right — determine whether the Flash movie is horizontally aligned to the left, center, or right of the Dimensions area, respectively. Using the same example from the Scale setting, a 400-x-300-pixel Flash movie (fit into a 300 x 300 Dimension window with `scale="noborder"`) with a Flash Horizontal Alignment setting of Left crops only the right side of the Flash movie.

- **Vertical:** These options — Top, Center, and Bottom — determine whether the Flash movie is vertically aligned to the top, center, or bottom of the Dimensions area, respectively. If the preceding example used a Show All Scale setting and had a Flash Vertical Alignment setting of Top, the border would occur only below the bottom edge of the Flash movie.

✦ **Show warning messages:** This useful feature alerts you to errors during the actual Publish process. For example, if you selected the Image Map template and didn't specify a static GIF, JPEG, or PNG file in the Formats tab, Flash returns an error. By default, this option is enabled. If it is disabled, Flash suppresses any warnings during the Publish process.

Using the GIF settings

The Graphics Interchange File (GIF) format, developed by CompuServe, defined the first generation of Web graphics and is still quite popular today, despite its 256-color limitation. In the context of the Publish Settings of Flash 8, the GIF format is used to export a static or animated image that can be used in place of the Flash movie if the Flash Player or plug-in is not installed. Although the Flash and HTML tabs are specific to Flash movie display and playback, the settings of the GIF tab (see Figure 21-9) control the characteristics of a GIF animation (or still image) that Flash 8 will publish.

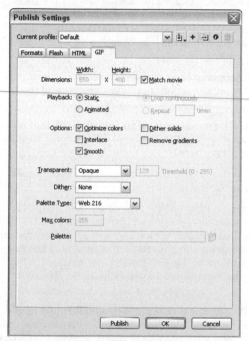

Figure 21-9: You can finesse every subtle aspect of a GIF animation or still image with these settings of the GIF tab of the Publish Settings dialog box.

The settings in the GIF tab include the following:

✦ **Dimensions:** This setting has three options: Width, Height, and Match movie. As you might have guessed, Width and Height control the dimensions of the GIF image. These fields are enabled only when the Match movie check box is unchecked. With Match movie checked, the dimensions of the GIF match those of the Flash Movie that is being published.

✦ **Playback:** These radio buttons control what type of GIF image is created and how it plays (if Animated is chosen):

- **Static:** If this button is selected, then Flash exports the first frame of the Flash movie as a single still image in the GIF format. If you want to use a frame other than the first frame, use a frame label of #Static on the desired frame. Alternatively, you could use the File ➪ Export Image command to export a GIF image from whatever frame the Current Frame Indicator is positioned over.

- **Animated:** If this button is selected, Flash exports the entire Flash movie as an animated GIF file (in the GIF89a format). If you don't want to export the entire movie as an animated GIF (indeed, a GIF file for a Flash movie with more than 100 frames would most likely be too large to download easily over the Web), you can designate a range of frames to export. Use a frame label of #First on the beginning frame of a given range of frames. Next, add a frame label of #Last to the ending frame of the desired sequence of frames. Flash actually is pretty good at optimizing animated GIFs by saving only areas that change over time in each frame — instead of the entire frame.

- **Loop continuously:** When the Animated radio button is selected, you can specify that the animated GIF repeats an infinite number of times by selecting the Loop continuously radio button.

- **Repeat __ times:** This option can be used to set up an animated GIF that repeats a given number of times. If you don't want the animated GIF to repeat continuously, enter the number of repetitions here.

✦ **Options:** The options in the Options settings control the creation of the GIF's color table and how the browser displays the GIF:

  - **Optimize colors:** When you are using any palette type other than Adaptive, this option removes any colors pre-existing in the Web 216 or custom palettes that are not used by the GIF image. Enabling this option can only save you precious bytes used in file overhead — it has no effect on the actual quality of the image. Most images do not use all 216 colors of the Web palette. For example, a black-and-white picture can use only between 3 and 10 colors from the 216-color palette.

  - **Interlace:** This option makes the GIF image download in incrementing resolutions. As the image downloads, the image becomes sharper with each successive "scan." Using this option is typically a personal preference. Some people like to use it for image maps that can provide basic navigation information before the entire image downloads.

  - **Smooth:** This option anti-aliases the Flash artwork as it exports to the GIF image. Text may look better when it is anti-aliased, but you may want to test this option for your particular use. If you need to make a transparent GIF, smoothing may produce unsightly edges.

  - **Dither solids:** This option determines whether solid areas of color (such as fills) are dithered. In this context, this type of dithering would create a two-color pattern to mimic a solid color that doesn't occur in the GIF's color palette. See the discussion of dithering later in this section.

  - **Remove gradients:** Flash gradients do not translate or display very well in 256 or fewer colors. Use this option to convert all Flash gradients to solid colors. The solid color is determined by the first color prescribed in the gradient. Unless you developed your gradients with this effect in mind, this option may produce undesirable results.

✦ **Transparent:** This setting controls the appearance of the Flash movie background, as well as any Flash artwork that uses alpha settings. Because GIF images support only one level of transparency (that is, the transparent area cannot be anti-aliased), exercise caution when using this setting. The Threshold option is available only if Alpha is selected. The options for this setting include the following:

- **Opaque:** This option produces a GIF image with a solid background. The image has a rectangular shape.

- **Transparent:** This option makes the Flash movie background appear transparent. If the Smooth option in the Options setting is enabled, Flash artwork may display halos over the background HTML color.

- **Alpha and Threshold:** When the Alpha option is selected in the drop-down menu, you can control at what alpha-level Flash artwork becomes transparent by entering a value in the Threshold text field. For example, if you enter 128, all alphas at 50 percent become completely transparent. If you are considering an animated GIF that has Flash artwork fading in or out, you probably want to use the Opaque transparent option. If Alpha and Threshold were used, the fade effect would be lost.

✦ **Dither:** *Dithering* is the process of emulating a color by juxtaposing two colors in a pattern arrangement. Because GIF images are limited to 256 colors (or fewer), dithering can often produce better-looking images for continuous tone artwork such as gradients. However, Flash's dithering seems to work best with the Web 216 palette. Dithering can increase the file size of a GIF image.

- **None:** This option does not apply any dithering to the GIF image.

- **Ordered:** This option applies an intermediate level of dithering with minimal file size overhead.

- **Diffusion:** This option applies the best level of dithering to the GIF image, but with larger file size overhead. Diffusion dithering only has a noticeable effect when the Web 216 palette is chosen in Palette Type.

✦ **Palette Type:** As we mentioned earlier in this section, GIF images are limited to 256 or fewer colors. However, this grouping of 256 is arbitrary: Any set of 256 (or fewer) colors can be used for a given GIF image. This setting enables you to select predefined sets of colors to use on the GIF image. See Chapter 7, "Applying Color," for more information on the Web color palette. The options for this setting include

- **Web 216:** When this option is selected, the GIF image uses colors only from the limited 216 Web color palette. For most Flash artwork, this should produce acceptable results. However, it may not render Flash gradients or photographic bitmaps very well.

- **Adaptive:** With this option selected, Flash creates a unique set of 256 colors (or fewer, if specified in the Max colors setting) for the GIF image. However, these adapted colors fall outside of the Web safe color palette. File sizes for adaptive GIFs are larger than Web 216 GIFs, unless few colors are chosen in the Max colors setting. Adaptive GIFs look much better than Web 216 GIFs, but they may not display very well with 8-bit video cards and monitors.

- **Web Snap Adaptive:** This option tries to give the GIF image the best of both worlds. Flash converts any colors close to the 216 Web palette to Web safe colors and uses adaptive colors for the rest. This palette produces better results than the Adaptive palette for older display systems that use 8-bit video cards.

- **Custom:** When this option is selected, you can specify a palette that uses the ACT file format to be used as the GIF image's palette. Macromedia Fireworks and Adobe Photoshop can export color palettes (or color look-up tables) as ACT files.

✦ **Max colors:** With this setting, you can specify exactly how many colors are in the GIF's color table. This numeric entry field is enabled only when Adaptive or Web Snap Adaptive is selected in the Palette Type drop-down menu.

✦ **Palette:** This text field and the folder browse button are enabled only when Custom is selected in the Palette Type drop-down menu. When enabled, this dialog box is used to locate and load a palette file from the hard drive.

Using the JPEG settings

The Joint Photographic Experts Group (JPEG) format is just as popular as the GIF format on the Web. Unlike GIF images, however, JPEG images can use much more than 256 colors. In fact, JPEG files must be 24-bit color (or full-color RGB) images. Although GIF files use lossless compression (within the actual file itself), JPEG images use lossy compression, which means that color information is discarded in order to save file space. However, JPEG compression is very good. Even at its lowest quality settings, JPEG images can preserve quite a bit of detail in photographic images.

Another significant difference between GIF and JPEG is that GIF images do not require nearly as much memory (for equivalent image dimensions) as JPEG images do. You need to remember that JPEG images "uncompress" when they are downloaded to your computer. While the file sizes may be small initially, they still open as full-color images in the computer's memory. For example, even though you may get the file size of a 400-x-300-pixel JPEG image down to 10 KB, it still requires nearly 352 KB in memory when it is opened or displayed.

Flash publishes the first frame of the Flash movie as the JPEG image, unless a `#Static` frame label is given to another frame in the Flash movie. The limited settings of the JPEG tab of the Publish Settings dialog box (see Figure 21-10) control the few variables of this still photo-quality image format:

✦ **Dimensions:** This setting behaves the same as the GIF Dimensions setting. Width and Height control the dimensions of the movie. But these fields are enabled only when the Match movie check box is unchecked. With Match movie checked, the dimensions of the JPEG match those of the Flash Movie.

✦ **Quality:** This slider and text field work exactly the same way as the JPEG Quality setting in the Flash tab of Publish Settings. Higher values apply less compression and result in better quality, but they create images with larger file sizes.

✦ **Progressive:** This option is similar to the Interlaced option for GIF images. When enabled, the JPEG image loads in successive scans, becoming sharper with each pass.

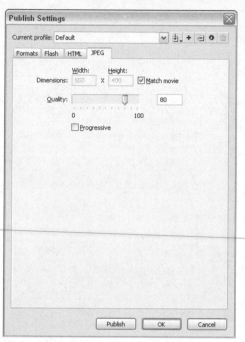

Figure 21-10: The settings of the JPEG tab are limited because JPEGs are still images with relatively few variables to address.

Using the PNG settings

The Portable Network Graphic (PNG) format is another still-image format. The PNG specification was developed in 1996 by the W3C (World Wide Web Consortium), and the format is an improvement over both the GIF and JPEG formats in several ways. Much like JPEG, it is excellent for transmission of photographic quality images. The primary advantages of PNG are variable bit-depths (images can be 256 colors or millions of colors), multilevel transparency, and lossless compression. However, some browsers do not offer full support for all PNG options without some kind of additional plug-in. When in doubt, test your PNG images in your preferred browser.

The settings of the PNG tab (see Figure 21-11) control the characteristics of the PNG image that Flash will publish.

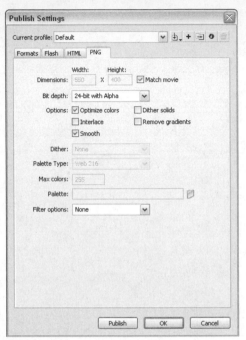

Figure 21-11: The settings found on the PNG tab closely resemble those on the GIF tab. The PNG was engineered to have many of the advantages of both the GIF and JPEG formats.

The PNG tab options are

- ✦ **Dimensions:** This setting works just like the GIF and JPEG equivalents. When Match movie is checked, you cannot alter the Width and Height of the PNG image.

- ✦ **Bit depth:** This setting controls how many colors are created in the PNG image:

  - • **8-bit:** In this mode, the PNG image has a maximum color palette of 256 colors, similar to the palette function of GIF images. When this option is selected, the Options, Dither, Palette Type, Max Colors, and Palette settings can be altered.

  - • **24-bit:** When this option is selected, the PNG image can display any of the 16.7 million RGB colors. This option produces larger files than 8-bit PNG images, but it renders the Flash artwork most faithfully.

  - • **24-bit with Alpha:** This option adds another 8-bit channel to the 24-bit PNG image for multilevel transparency support. This means that Flash will treat the Flash movie background as a transparent area, so that information behind the PNG image (such as HTML background colors) shows through. Note that, with proper browser support, PNG can render anti-aliased edges on top of other elements, such as HTML background images!

Flash 8's PNG export or publish settings do not reflect the full range of PNG options available. PNG can support transparency in both 8-bit and 24-bit flavors, but Flash enables transparency only in 24-bit with Alpha images.

✦ **Options:** These options behave the same as the equivalent GIF Publish Settings.

✦ **Dither, Palette Type, Max colors,** and **Palette:** These settings work the same as the equivalent GIF Publish Settings. Because PNG images can be either 8- or 24-bit, these options apply only to 8-bit PNG images. If anything other than 8-bit is selected in the Bit depth setting, these options are disabled. Please refer to the previous section for more information.

✦ **Filter options:** This drop-down menu controls what type of compression sampling or algorithm the PNG image uses. Note that this does not apply an art or graphic "filter effect" as the filters in Adobe Photoshop do, nor does it throw away any image information—all filters are lossless. It simply enables you to be the judge of what kind of compression to use on the image. You need to experiment with each of these filters on your Flash movie image to find the best filter-to-file-size combination. Technically, the filters do not actually look at the pixel data. Rather, they look at the byte data of each pixel. Results vary depending on the image content, but here are some guidelines to keep in mind:

- **None:** When this option is selected, no filtering is applied to the image. When no filter is applied, you usually have unnecessarily large file sizes.

- **Sub:** This filter works best on images that have repeated information along the horizontal axis. For example, the stripes of a horizontal American flag filter nicely with the sub filter.

- **Up:** The opposite of the sub filter, this filter works by looking for repeated information along the vertical axis. The stripes of a vertical American flag filter well with the up filter.

- **Average:** Use this option when a mixture of vertical and horizontal information exists. When in doubt, try this filter first.

- **Path:** This filter works like an advanced average filter. When in doubt, try this filter after you have experimented with the average filter.

- **Adaptive:** This filter provides the most thorough analysis of the image's color and creates the most accurate color palette for the image. However, it usually provides the largest file sizes for the PNG format.

Creating Windows and Macintosh projectors

To export a Mac stand-alone projector, check the Macintosh Projector option in the Formats tab. To publish a Windows stand-alone projector, check the Windows Projector option in the Formats tab.

The Mac Projector published by Flash 8 is designed for playback on Mac OS X (10.1) and higher. If you want to publish a projector compatible with Mac OS 9.x or earlier, you'll need to use Flash MX 2004 or earlier.

Using the QuickTime settings

Apple QuickTime 4 or higher includes built-in support for Flash tracks and .swf files. As such, you may want to publish QuickTime movie files (.mov) in addition to your Flash movies. If you want to enable QuickTime movie output via the Publish command, make sure that it is selected in the Formats tab of the Publish Settings dialog box.

Web Resource

The QuickTime Publish Settings are discussed at length in an online PDF, "Working with QuickTime." This content, found in previous editions of the *Flash Bible,* has been moved to an online-only location. You can download the PDF file at www.flashsupport.com/ archive.

Publish Preview and Publish Commands

After you have entered the file format types and specifications for each in the Publish Settings dialog box, you can proceed to preview and publish the file types you selected.

Using Publish Preview

The Publish Preview submenu (accessible from File ➪ Publish Preview) lists all of the file types currently enabled in the Publish Settings dialog box. By default, HTML is the first file type available for preview. In general, the first item enabled in the Formats tab of the Publish Settings dialog box is the first item in the submenu and can be executed by pressing Ctrl+F12 or ⌘+F12. Selecting a file type in the Publish Preview menu launches your default browser and inserts the selected file type(s) into the browser window.

Using Publish

When you want Flash to export the file type(s) selected in the Publish Settings dialog box, choose File ➪ Publish (Shift+F12). Flash creates the new files wherever the Flash movie was last saved. If you have selected an HTML template in the HTML tab of the Publish Settings dialog box, you may receive a warning or error message if any other necessary files were not specified. That's it! After you've tested the files for the delivery browser and/or platforms of your choice, you can upload the files to your Web server.

Using Publish Profiles

Flash 8 includes a profiling feature to the Publish Settings. You can save the settings from all of the enabled format tabs in Publish Settings to a custom profile. You can create as many profiles as you need. The profiles that you create are document-specific. They are saved with the Flash document file (.fla), and by design, you cannot access the profiles of one document directly from another. However, you can export a profile from a Flash document and import it into another.

To choose, create, modify, or delete profiles, open the Publish Settings dialog box (File ➪ Publish Settings). At the top of the dialog box, you will find the Profile features available in Flash 8. Refer to Figure 21-12 and the following description list.

Create New Profile Duplicate Profile

Import/Export Profile   Profile Properties

Profile Names   Delete Profile

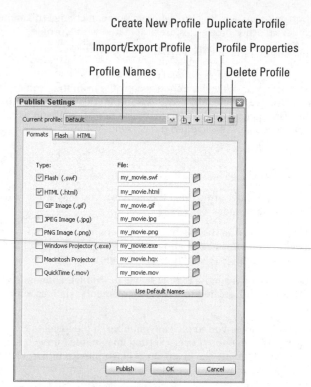

Figure 21-12: The Profile features in the Publish Settings dialog box

✦ **Profile Name:** This drop-down menu displays the currently active profile. Every new Flash 8 document has a Default profile. If you open a Flash document from an earlier version of Flash (that is, Flash MX or Flash MX 2004) in Flash 8 and resave it as a Flash 8 document, the original document Publish Settings are stored in a Flash MX or Flash MX 2004 Settings profile.

✦ **Import/Export Profile:** If you click this button, you can choose Import or Export from this option's menu. If you want to use one document's Publish Settings in another document, you need to first export the current profile. Profiles are exported as XML documents. In the other document, you can then import the XML profile document.

✦ **Create New Profile:** This button adds a new profile name to the Profile Name menu, using the current profile's settings as a starting point. If you click this button, the Create New Profile dialog box appears, prompting you to enter a new profile name.

✦ **Duplicate Profile:** This button makes a copy of the currently active profile. If you click this button, the Duplicate Profile dialog box appears, prompting you to enter a new profile name for the copy.

✦ **Profile Properties:** This button opens a dialog box wherein you can change the name of the currently active profile. No other properties are associated with a profile.

✦ **Delete Profile:** Clicking this button removes the currently active profile from the document.

Changes to profiles do not need to be saved. When you choose a profile from the Profile Name menu, any settings that you change, enable, and so on are automatically saved to the current profile as long as you click OK to close the Publish Settings dialog box. If you click the Cancel button, any changes you make will not be saved to the current profile.

Summary

✦ To minimize your wait during publishing or testing Flash movies, you may want to use MP3 files for all of your Event Sync sounds.

✦ Test your Flash movies and scenes within the Flash authoring environment. The Bandwidth Profiler can provide vital information about frame byte requirements and can help you find problematic streaming areas of the Flash movie.

✦ The size report that can be generated from the Export Movie or Publish commands for Flash movies lists detailed information related to individual elements, such as audio, fonts, and frame byte size.

✦ The Publish Settings dialog box enables you to pick any number of file formats to export at one time. You can control just about every setting imaginable for each file type and use HTML templates to automate the insertion of Flash movies into your Web pages.

✦ Flash movies published from Flash 8 can now have specific local playback security options, preventing unscrupulous Flash content creators from accessing private information on another person's computer.

✦ Flash 8 offers an updated Flash Player version detection feature in the Publish Settings dialog box. With this feature, you can create an HTML page that detects which version of the Flash Player a user has and direct her to appropriate content on your site.

✦ The profiles feature in Flash 8 enables you to quickly load publish presets that you can apply to one or more Flash documents.

✦   ✦   ✦

Integrating Flash Content with Web Pages

In This Chapter

✦ ✦ ✦ ✦

Defining HTML tags and attributes for the Flash Player

Detecting the Flash Player plug-in or ActiveX control

Sending commands with the new `ExternalInterface` API to JavaScript

✦ ✦ ✦ ✦

If you're not one for automated HTML production using templates, this chapter is for you. In this chapter, we teach you the ins and outs of the `<object>` and `<embed>` tags, as well as some tips on how to check for the Flash Player with Flash 8's updated detection features. At the end of this chapter, we examine how Flash movies can interact with JavaScript and DHTML (Dynamic HTML) by using the new `ExternalInterface` actions from Flash.

Writing Markup for Flash Movies

In Chapter 21, you learned how to use the Publish feature, which included automated HTML templates. These templates created the necessary HTML tags to display Flash movies on Web pages. In this section, we discuss the use of Flash movies in your handwritten HTML documents. You can also use this information to alter HTML documents created by the Publish feature.

Note   In the following code examples, we use an asterisk (*) when displaying optional parameters that are not in the default options that are enabled in the Flash Only HTML template. We also use the term *plug-in* to mean both the Netscape/Mozilla-compatible plug-in and the ActiveX control for Flash Player 8.

You can use two tags to place Flash movies on a Web page (such as an HTML document): `<object>` and `<embed>`. You need to include both of these plug-in tags in HTML documents, as each tag is specific to a browser: `<object>` for Internet Explorer (IE) on Windows, and `<embed>` for Mozilla-compatible browsers on Windows and Mac. Each tag works similarly to the other, with some slight differences in attribute names and organization. Remember that if both sets of tags are included with the HTML, only one set of tags is actually read by the browser, depending on which browser is used to view the Web page. Without these tags, the browser cannot display Flash movies with other HTML elements such as images and text.

You can, however, directly link to Flash movie files (.swf) as an alternative method for displaying Flash content. That method, however, precludes the use of parameters to control the look and playback of the Flash movie—it would be the same as loading the Flash movie straight into the stand-alone Flash Player. For more information on direct linking, see Colin Moock's tutorial, "Filling the Browser Windows Using the `<frameset>` Tag," found at the book's Web site, `www.flashsupport.com/archive`.

Using the `<object>` tag

Microsoft Internet Explorer for Windows uses this tag exclusively to enable the Flash Player ActiveX control. When the Flash Only HTML template is used in Publish Settings, the HTML document that is published uses the `<object>` tag in the following way. Some of these options (marked with an asterisk) are created only if you enable/disable specific options in the HTML tab of the Publish Settings dialog box.

Note Flash MX/Flash Player 6 ActionScript introduced a `Stage` object that enables you to control or override many of the same properties that the Player HTML tags specify. For more details on the `Stage` object, refer to the *Flash ActionScript Bible* series by Robert Reinhardt and Joey Lott (Wiley).

```
A.  <object
B.      classid="clsid: clsid:d27cdb6e-ae6d-11cf-96b8-
        444553540000"
C.      codebase="http://fpdownload.macromedia.com/pub/
        shockwave/cabs/flash/swflash.cab#version=8,0,0,0"
D.      width="550" height="400"
E.      id="home"
F.      align="middle">
G.      <param name="allowScriptAccess" value="sameDomain" />
H.      <param name="movie" value="home.swf" />
I.*     <param name="play" value="false" />
J.*     <param name="loop" value="false" />
K.*     <param name="menu" value="false" />
L.      <param name="quality" value="high" />
M.*     <param name="scale" value="noborder" />
N.*     <param name="salign" value="LT" />
O.*     <param name="wmode" value="transparent" />
P.*     <param name="devicefont value="true" />
Q.      <param name="bgcolor" value="#FFFFFF" />
R.*     <param name="flashvars" value="title=My%20Movie" />
S.*     <param name="base" value="." />
T.  </object>
```

Note Flash 8's HTML templates use XHTML-compliant code. Notice that all the tags use lowercase, and that all `<param>` tags end with a `/>`.

A. `<object`: This is the opening tag containing the ID code and locations of the ActiveX control for the Flash Player. Note that this opening tag includes the attributes lettered B through F.

B. `classid`: This lengthy string is the unique ActiveX identification code. If you are inserting the `<object>` tag by hand in a text editor, make sure that you copy this ID string exactly.

C. `codebase`: Like the `codebase` attribute of a Java `<applet>` tag, this attribute of the `<object>` tag specifies the location of the ActiveX control installer file (.cab) as a URL. Notice that the `#version=8,0,0,0` portion of the URL indicates that the Flash Player version 8 should be used. You can also specify specific minor releases, such as `#version=6,0,65,0`, which would require Flash Player 6.0 r65 ActiveX control or higher. If the visitor doesn't have the ActiveX control already installed, Internet Explorer automatically downloads the control from this URL.

Tip   If you want to make a secure Web page with Flash content, make sure the `codebase` URL uses `https://` instead of `http://`.

D. `width` **and** `height`: These attributes control the actual width and height, respectively, of the Flash movie as it appears on the Web page. If no unit of measurement is specified, these values are in pixels. If the % character is added to the end of each value, the attribute adjusts the Flash movie to the corresponding percent of the browser window. For example, if 100 percent was the value for both `width` and `height`, the Flash movie fills the entire browser, except for the browser gutter. See Colin Moock's tutorial at the Web archive for this book to learn how to minimize this gutter thickness.

E. `id`: This attribute of the `<object>` tag assigns a JavaScript/VBScript identifier to the Flash movie, so that it can be controlled by DHTML JavaScript/VBScript functions. By default, this attribute's value is the name of the actual .swf file, without the .swf extension. Each element on a DHTML page should have a unique `id` or `name` attribute. We discuss the `name` attribute in the next section.

F. `align`: This attribute of the `<object>` tag determines how the Flash movie will align on the HTML document. The acceptable values for this attribute are `left`, `right`, `top`, `bottom`, or `middle`. As with `<img>` tags in HTML, the `align` attribute gives very loose layout control. It's likely that you'll want to rely on other HTML tags and Cascading Style Sheets (CSS) to position a Flash movie with other HTML elements.

G. `<param name="allowScriptAccess" value="sameDomain" />`: This is the first set of `<param>` subtags within the `<object></object>` tags. Each parameter tag has a unique `name=` setting, not to be confused with JavaScript `names` or `ids`. `allowScriptAccess` controls how the Flash movie can access JavaScript or VBScript functions contained within the HTML document. A Flash movie can try to invoke a JavaScript or VBScript function by using an ActionScript `fscommand()` or `getURL()` line of code. There are three values supported: `always`, `never`, and `sameDomain`. The value `always` enables the Flash movie to access scripts on the page, while `never` prohibits the Flash movie from accessing scripts. The value `sameDomain`, which is the default value, enables a Flash movie to access scripts on the page *only* if the Flash movie resides on the same domain as the HTML page containing the movie. The `allowScriptAccess` attribute is supported by Flash Player 6 r40 and higher.

H. `<param name="movie" value="home.swf" />`: This parameter determines which Flash movie file (.swf) is loaded into the document. The `value` attribute specifies the filename of the Flash movie, as a relative or absolute URL. Note that you can pass Flash variables to the movie directly by specifying them after the filename. For example, `home.swf?firstName=Joey` will pass a variable named `firstName` with a string value of `Joey` to the `_root` timeline (that is, `_level0`). You can use the newer `flashvars` (item R) HTML attribute to do this type of data transfer as well.

I. `<param name="play" value="false" />`: This optional parameter tells the Flash Player whether it should start playing the Flash movie as it downloads. If `value` equals `false`, the Flash movie loads in a "paused" state, just as if a `stop()` action was placed on the first frame. If the `value` equals `true`, the Flash Player starts playing the movie as soon as it starts to stream into the browser. If this tag is omitted, the Flash Player behaves as if `play` equals `true`.

Note If you do have a `stop()` action on the first frame of your movie, setting play to true will not override the `stop()` action.

J. `<param name="loop" value="false" />`: This optional setting tells the Flash Player whether the Main Timeline should repeat when the Playhead reaches the last frame. If `value` equals `false`, the Playhead will not loop. If `value` equals `true`, the Playhead will loop. If this parameter tag is omitted, the Flash Player by default will loop playback of the Main Timeline.

Note If you have a `stop()` action on the last frame of the Main Timeline, the Flash movie will not loop, regardless of the HTML loop value.

K. `<param name="menu" value="false" />`: This setting controls the display of the Flash Player contextual menu that can be invoked by right-clicking (Windows) or Control+clicking (Mac) the Flash movie in the Web browser. If you set this option to `false`, the menu displays the options shown in Figure 22-1. If you set this option to `true`, all of the options are available to the end-user, as shown in Figure 22-2. Also, the player's Settings option is available in both modes of the menu.

Note The Play, Stop, and Rewind options that were available in Flash Player 6 and earlier are no longer available in Flash Player 7 or higher.

Note If you have installed the Debugger version of Flash Player 8, the contextual menu displays a Debugger option in both modes of the `menu` attribute (`true` and `false`). Figure 22-2 shows the Debugger option. Refer to Chapter 32, "Managing and Troubleshooting Flash Movies" for more information on debugging Flash movies.

Figure 22-1: The Flash Player menu with control options disabled

Figure 22-2: The Flash Player menu with control options enabled

Note

Flash Player 7 and higher supports additional items that you can script into the contextual menu, using the new `ContextMenu` class. You learn how to use this class in Chapter 35, "Building an Image Gallery Component." For more detailed information on the usage of this class, refer to the *Flash ActionScript Bible* series by Robert Reinhardt and Joey Lott (Wiley).

L. `<param name="quality" value="high" />`: This parameter controls how the Flash movie's artwork renders within the browser window. `value` can be `low`, `autolow`, `autohigh`, `high`, or `best`. Most Flash movies on the Web use the `high` value, as this forces the Flash Player to render the movie elements anti-aliased. For a full description of each of the `quality` settings, please refer to the section "Using the HTML settings" in Chapter 21, "Publishing Flash Movies."

M. `<param name="scale" value="noborder" />`: This optional parameter controls how the Flash movie scales in the window defined by the `width` and `height` attributes of the opening `<object>` tag. Its value can be `showall`, `noborder`, `exactfit`, or `noscale`. If this entire subtag is omitted, the Flash Player treats the movie as if the `showall` default setting was specified. The `showall` setting fits the Flash movie within the boundaries of the `width` and `height` dimensions without any distortion to the original aspect ratio of the Flash movie. Again, refer to the "Using the HTML settings" section in Chapter 21 for a complete description of the `scale` settings and how they work within the dimensions of a Flash movie.

N. `<param name="salign" value="lt" />`: This parameter controls the alignment of the Flash movie within the space allocated to the viewing area of the movie in the browser window. For example, if you size your Flash movie to use 100 percent of the width and height of the browser window, a `value` of `lt` aligns the Flash movie to the left and top of the browser window. The acceptable values for this parameter are shown in the following list. For more information, refer to our coverage in Chapter 21, "Publishing Flash Movies."

- `l` : left edge, centered vertically
- `r` : right edge, centered vertically
- `t` : top edge, centered horizontally
- `b` : bottom edge, centered horizontally
- `lt` : left and top edges
- `rt` : right and top edges
- `lb` : left and bottom edges
- `rb` : right and bottom edges

O. `<param name="wmode" value="transparent" />`: This Player option works with all versions of the Flash Player if you are using Internet Explorer (version 3 or higher) for Windows, or with Flash Player 6 r65 or higher on Internet Explorer, Netscape, and most Mac OS X browsers. If you are only targeting an audience that uses these browsers, you can control how the Flash movie's background color appears on top of the HTML or DHTML elements on the Web page. There are three acceptable values:

- `window`: This value is the default appearance of movies playing in the Flash Player on Web pages. With this value, movies play within the area specified by the `width` and `height` attributes (discussed in item D), and the background color of the Flash movie's stage (as defined by Document Properties, or item Q, later in this section) displays.

- `opaque`: This value provides the same visual appearance of the movie's stage as `window` does. However, if you want to animate other DHTML objects in front of or behind a layer containing the Flash movie, it is recommended that you use the `opaque` value.

- `transparent`: This value enables the stage of the Flash movie to act like an alpha channel. When enabled, the Flash movie appears to float on the HTML page, without any background color to reveal the corners of the Flash movie's stage. Again, while this feature is somewhat extraordinary, it will function only with specific browsers and later versions of the Flash Player plug-in. Also, because the browser must anti-alias the Flash artwork on top of other HTML elements, playback of Flash animations may suffer.

P. `<param name="devicefont" value="true" />`: This feature controls how Flash text appears in the browser window and works only on the Windows operating system. Like the device fonts with the Flash authoring environment (_sans, _serif, and _typewriter), this option can display any and all embedded text to system fonts such as Times and Arial. To do this, set `value` to `true`. To disable device font rendering in this fashion, set `value` to `false`. If this tag is omitted from the HTML, the `value` defaults to `false`. Finally, the rules of Flash device fonts apply to system device fonts as well. For example, device or system fonts cannot be masked, rotated, or manipulated with the Transform panel or the Property inspector.

Note   This seldom-used setting does not work predictably from use to use. In our tests, we could not get `devicefont` to work consistently from movie to movie, nor could we propose any reasonable use for it. It's likely that this is a legacy setting, meaning that it was made available for machines that had slow video or computing performance when the Flash Player was first introduced to the market.

Q. `<param name="bgcolor" value="#FFFFFF" />`: This parameter name, `bgcolor`, controls the background color of the Flash movie. If you published an HTML document via the Publish command, the `value` is automatically set to the background color specified by the Modify ⇨ Document command in Flash. However, you can override the Movie setting by entering a different value in this parameter tag. Note that this parameter, like all HTML tags and attributes concerning color, uses hexadecimal code to describe the color. For more information on color, see Chapter 7, "Applying Color."

R. `<param name="flashvars" value="title=My%20Flash%Movie" />`: This Flash Player 6 and higher attribute enables you to declare variables within the Flash movie when it loads into the Web browser. `flashvars` stands for "Flash Variables." This feature enables you to circumvent the browser URL length limitation for declaring variables in the Flash movie's filename, as we discussed in item H of this list. For example, you can use client-side (for example, JavaScript) or server-side (for example, ColdFusion, ASP, PHP) scripting to dynamically write the `value` for this tag in your HTML, passing information from databases into the Flash movie at load time.

Tip

If you use Flash Remoting services with your Flash movie, be sure to declare the `gatewayUrl` variable in `flashvars`. The `gatewayUrl` variable specifies the location of the Flash Remoting gateway, such as `<param name="flashvars" value= "gatewayUrl=http://mydomain.com/flashservices/gateway" />`.

S. `<param name="base" value="." />`: This attribute tells the Flash movie how to interpret any relative paths used with ActionScript. The default value is `"."`, which means that Flash will resolve any relative paths within ActionScript to the same directory that the Flash movie resides in. For example, if `base` is set to `"."`, the following action will look for an HTML document named `form.html` in the same directory as the Flash movie file (.swf):

```
getURL("form.html");
```

You can use dot notation with the `base` attribute, such as `"../"`, or specify a fully-qualified domain name, such as `"http://www.myserver.com/section_1"`, to let the Flash movie know that all relative paths should be resolved from that starting point.

Web Resource

You can read Macromedia's tech notes about the `base` attribute by perusing the links in the "Flash and HTML Tags" category at `www.flashsupport.com/links`.

Caution

In our tests, we only saw the `base` attribute recognized by `getURL()` actions. Other actions that use URLs, such as `loadMovie()`, `LoadVars`, `XML`, and `NetStream`, did not use the `base` attribute to resolve relative URLs. If you keep your Flash movie files (.swf) in a separate folder from assets that need to be loaded into the Flash movies, you should pass the starting path into the Flash movie with `flashvars` (see Item R in this list) and append that value to all of your relative paths in ActionScript.

Also, if you use dot notation with the `base` attribute, such as `"../"`, the path is oddly interpreted relative to the *HTML* document, not the Flash movie.

T. `</object>`: This is the closing tag for the starting `<object>` tag. As we show you later in this chapter, you can put other HTML tags between the last `<param>` tag and the closing `</object>` tag for non-ActiveX–enabled browsers, such as Netscape or Apple Safari. Because Internet Explorer for Windows is the primary browser that currently recognizes `<object>` tags, most browsers simply skip the `<object>` tag (as well as its `<param>` tags) and only read the tags between the last `<param>` and `</object>` tags.

Tip

We recommend that you consistently apply quotes around names and values, such as `<param name="bgcolor" value="#FFFFFF" />`. This syntax is especially important for the `flashvars` attribute.

Using the <embed> tag

Netscape, Mozilla-based browsers, and browsers on a Macintosh (including Internet Explorer for Mac) use the <embed> tag to display nonbrowser native file formats that require a plug-in, such as Macromedia Flash and Shockwave Director or Apple QuickTime. Following is a sample listing of attributes and values for the <embed> tag. Again, attributes with an asterisk are generally optional for most Flash movie playback.

```
A.  <embed
B.      src="home.swf"
C.*     play="false"
D.*     loop="false"
E.      quality="high"
F.*     scale="noborder"
G.*     salign="lt"
H.*     wmode="transparent"
I.*     devicefont="true"
J.      bgcolor="#FFFFFF"
K.      width="550" height="400"
L.*     swLiveConnect="false"
M.      name="home"
N.*     id="home"
O.      align="middle"
P.      allowScriptAccess="sameDomain"
Q.*     flashvars="name=Lucian"
R.      type="application/x-shockwave-flash"
S.*     base="."
T.      pluginspage="http://www.macromedia.com/go/
        getflashplayer">
U.  </embed>
```

A. <embed: This is the opening <embed> tag. Note that lines B through T are attributes of the opening <embed> tag, which is why you don't see the > character at the end of line A.

B. src: This stands for *source,* and it indicates the filename of the Flash movie. This attribute of <embed> works exactly like the movie parameter of the <object> tag.

C. play: This attribute behaves in the same manner as the play parameter of the <object> tag. If you omit this attribute in your HTML, the Flash Player assumes that it should automatically play the Flash movie.

D. loop: This attribute controls the same behavior as the loop parameter of the <object> tag. If you omit this attribute in your HTML, the Flash Player automatically loops playback of the movie's Main Timeline.

E. quality: This attribute controls how the Flash movie's artwork will display in the browser window. Like the equivalent quality parameter of the <object> tag, its value can be low, autolow, autohigh, high, or best.

F. scale: This attribute of <embed> controls how the Flash movie fits within the browser window and/or the dimensions specified by width and height (item K). Its value can be showall (default if attribute is omitted), noborder, exactfit, or noscale.

G. `salign`: This attribute controls the internal alignment of the Flash movie within the viewing area of the movie's dimensions. See the description for the `salign` parameter of the `<object>` tag for more information.

H. `wmode`: This attribute controls the opacity of the Flash movie's background color and works only with specific browser and Flash Player version combinations. See the `wmode` parameter description in the `<object>` tag for more details.

I. `devicefont`: This attribute controls the appearance of any text within a Flash movie and functions correctly only on the Windows operating system. See the description for `devicefont` in the `<object>` tag section.

J. `bgcolor`: This setting controls the Flash movie's background color. Again, this attribute behaves identically to the equivalent `<param>` subtag of the `<object>` tag. See that tag's description in the preceding section.

K. `width` and `height`: These attributes control the dimensions of the Flash movie as it appears on the Web page. Refer to the `width` and `height` descriptions of the `<object>` tag for more information.

L. `swLiveConnect`: This is one attribute that you won't find in the `<object>` tag. This unique tag enables Netscape's LiveConnect feature, which enables plug-ins and Java applets to communicate with JavaScript. By default, this attribute is set to `false`. If it is enabled (the attribute is set to `true`), the Web page may experience a short delay during loading. The latest versions of Netscape don't start the Java engine during a browsing session until a Web page containing a Java applet (or a Java-enabled plug-in such as the Flash Player) is loaded. Unless you use `fscommand()` actions in your Flash movies, it's best to omit this attribute or set its value to `false`.

M. `name`: This attribute works in tandem with the `swLiveConnect` attribute, enabling the Flash movie to be identified in JavaScript. The value given to the `name` attribute will be the Flash movie object name that can be used within your JavaScript programming.

N. `id`: This attribute is also used for JavaScript functionality. It's uncertain whether this value is necessary if the name attribute exists, but Flash MX 2004's Flash with FSCommand HTML template (in the Publish Settings) includes both the `name` and `id` attributes. The `id` attribute should use the same value as the `name` attribute.

O. `align`: This attribute behaves exactly the same as the `align` parameter for the `<object>`. See its description in the preceding section for more information.

P. `allowScriptAccess`: This attribute controls how the Flash movie can access JavaScript from `getURL()` and `fscommand()` actions. See the description of `allowScriptAccess` in the `<object>` tag coverage earlier in this chapter.

Q. `flashvars`: This attribute assigns variables to the Main Timeline of the Flash movie at run time. See the description of `flashvars` in the `<object>` tag coverage earlier in this chapter.

R. `type="application/x-shockwave-flash"`: This attribute tells the browser what MIME (Multipurpose Internet Mail Extension) content-type the embedded file is. Each file type (TIF, JPEG, GIF, PDF, and so on) has a unique MIME content-type header, describing what its content is. For Flash movies, the content-type is `application/x-shockwave-flash`. Any program (or operating system) that uses files over the Internet handles MIME content-types according to a reference chart that links each MIME content-type to its appropriate parent application or plug-in. Without this attribute, the browser may not understand what type of file the Flash movie is. As a result, it may display the broken plug-in icon when the Flash movie downloads to the browser.

S. `base=".":` This attribute tells the Flash movie how to resolve relative paths used in the movie's ActionScript code. See the description of `base` in the `<object>` tag coverage earlier in this chapter.

T. `pluginspage:` Literally "plug-in's page," this attribute tells the browser where to go to find the appropriate plug-in installer if it doesn't have the Flash plug-in already installed. This is not equivalent to a JavaScript-enabled auto installer or detection page. It simply redirects the browser to the URL of the Web page where the appropriate software can be downloaded.

U. `</embed>:` This is the closing tag for the original `<embed>` tag in line A. Some older or text-based browsers such as Lynx are incapable of displaying `<embed>` tags. You can insert alternate HTML (such as a static or animated GIF image with the `<img>` tag) between the `<embed> </embed>` tags for these browsers. Some browsers may require that you insert these alternate tags between a `<noembed></noembed>` set of tags within or after the `<embed></embed>` tags.

Caution   You may be surprised to learn that all versions of Internet Explorer (IE) for the Macintosh cannot read `<object>` tags. Rather, IE for Mac uses a Netscape plug-in emulator to read `<embed>` tags. However, this emulator does not interpret all `<embed>` tags with the same level of support as Netscape. As a result, the `swLiveConnect` attribute does not function on IE for Mac browsers. This means that the `fscommand()` action is not supported on these browsers.

Detecting the Flash Player

What good is an awesome Flash experience if no one can see your Flash movies? Because most Flash content is viewed with a Web browser, it's extremely important to make sure that your HTML pages check for the existence of the Flash Player plug-in before you start pushing Flash content to the browser. There are a variety of ways to check for the Flash Player, and this section provides an overview of the available methods.

New Feature   As we mentioned in the previous chapter, Flash 8 includes an updated Flash Player detection feature within the Publish Settings. You learn how to create a set of detection pages with this new feature later in this chapter.

Plug-in versus ActiveX: Forcing content without a check

The Flash Player is available for Web browsers in two forms: the Flash Player plug-in (as a Netscape-compatible, or Mozilla-compatible, plug-in) and the Flash Player ActiveX control (for use only with Microsoft Internet Explorer on Windows 98/ME/2000/XP).

If you directly insert a Flash movie into a Web page with the `<embed>` tag (for Netscape browsers), one of two scenarios will happen:

✦ The browser has the Flash Player plug-in and will load the Flash movie.

✦ The browser does not have the Flash Player plug-in and displays a broken plug-in icon.

If the second scenario occurs and the `pluginspage` attribute of the `<embed>` tag is defined, the user can click the broken plug-in icon and go to the Macromedia site to download the Flash Player plug-in. If the `pluginspage` attribute is not specified, clicking the broken plug-in icon will take you to a generic Netscape plug-in page.

If you insert a Flash movie into an HTML document with the `<object>` tag (for Internet Explorer on Windows only), one of two scenarios will happen:

✦ The browser has the Flash Player ActiveX control and will load the Flash movie.

✦ The browser does not have the Flash Player ActiveX control and will autodownload and install the ActiveX control file from the Macromedia site.

Note

Newer versions of Windows XP (that is, with Service Pack 2 or SP2 installed) will likely get an additional warning represented as a strip across the top of the Web page attempting to initiate the installation of a new ActiveX control. The user must also click this strip and accept the download of the ActiveX control.

The ActiveX control will autodownload and install only if the `classid` and `codebase` attributes of the Flash movie's `<object>` tag are correctly specified. Depending on the user's security settings, the user needs to grant permission to a Security Warning dialog box to commence the download and install process.

Although using the `<object>` and `<embed>` tags by themselves is by far the simplest method for integrating Flash content into a Web page, it's not the most user-friendly method of ensuring that the majority of your Web visitors can view the Flash content. Flash 8 uses a new JavaScript detection mechanism, updating the Flash sniffer approach used in Flash MX 2004.

Note

Since Flash Player 4 was released, many seasoned Flash developers have used small Flash movies known as *sniffers* to detect the presence of the Flash Player in a user's Web browser. Sniffers are virtually hidden from the visitor to a Web site, and they direct an entry HTML page to a new location (using a `getURL()` action) where the real Flash content (or site) exists. If the Player is not installed, the sniffer movie won't be able to play and direct the HTML page to a new location. If this happens, a special `<meta>` tag in the `<head>` of the HTML document directs the browser location to a screen that informs the visitor to download the plug-in or ActiveX control.

Detecting the Flash Player with Flash 8

In Flash 8, Macromedia has made the process of using a sniffer methodology incredibly simple. In the following steps, you learn how to use the new Detect Flash Version feature to properly direct a user to Flash Player 6 r65 content.

Note   You can check for Flash Player 4 or higher with the Detect Flash Version feature. For demonstration purposes, we chose Flash Player 6 r65 because Flash MX 2004 introduced a new optimization feature for .swf files generated for this version (or higher) of Flash Player 6.

Caution   If you use the Detect Flash Version in Flash MX 2004, be sure to review this section. The feature no longer uses three HTML pages for the detection process. Everything from the detection to the content display to the alternate content display occurs on one HTML page.

1. Create a new Flash document by choosing File ➪ New. In the New Document dialog box, choose Flash Document and click OK. Alternatively, open an existing .fla file that you have created and skip to Step 4.

2. Save the new Flash document as `detection_test.fla`.

3. Add some placeholder text to the stage using the Text tool. As this example is checking for Flash Player 6 r65, you can type **This is Flash Player 6 r65 content.**

4. Choose File ➪ Publish Settings. By default, both the Flash and HTML formats are selected in the Formats tab of the Publish Settings dialog box. The filenames for these formats should reflect the current .fla filename, such as `detection_test.swf` and `detection_test.html`, respectively.

5. To keep the new version settings in a separate profile, click the Create New Profile (+) button at the top of the Publish Settings dialog box. Name the profile **FP6 r65 Detection**, as shown in Figure 22-3. Click OK to close the dialog box, but leave the Publish Settings dialog box open.

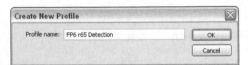

Figure 22-3: The Create New Profile dialog box, showing the new profile name

6. Click the Flash tab. In the Version menu, choose Flash Player 6. In the ActionScript version menu, choose ActionScript 1.0. Select the Optimize for Flash Player 6 r65 check box. Refer to Figure 22-4 for a review of these settings.

7. Click the HTML tab of the Publish Settings dialog box. Select the Detect Flash Version check box. The two editable text fields to the right of the Version label should now be enabled. The major version of the Flash Player is fixed to the Player version you chose in the Flash tab. The first of the two editable fields represents a Minor Revision value; to date, Macromedia hasn't released any minor revisions of the Flash Player, but this feature is enabled just in case Macromedia does release any minor revision during the life cycle of the Flash 8 authoring tool. The second field represents the Incremental Revision value. Since Flash Player 4, Macromedia has released several incremental revisions of the Flash Player for each player cycle.

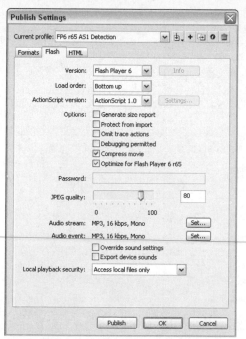

Figure 22-4: The Flash Player 6 r65 settings in the Flash tab

To get a sense of how many incremental revisions of Flash Player 7 were released, see the "Flash Player Release Notes" category at www.flashsupport.com/links.

In Flash MX 2004, Macromedia referred to these two editable values as Major Revision and Minor Revision. With a little revisionist history in Flash 8, Macromedia now refers to Major Revision as Minor Revision and Minor Revision as Incremental Revision.

Type **65** in the second field, as shown in Figure 22-5. If you wanted to check for a different incremental version of Flash Player 6, you could enter that value instead. Click OK to close the dialog box, and go back to the HTML tab of the Publish Settings dialog box.

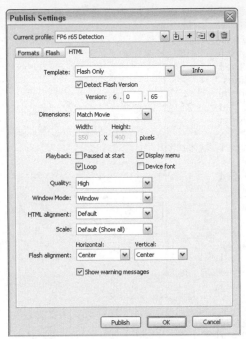

Figure 22-5: The Publish Settings dialog box

8. In the Publish Settings dialog box, click the Publish button. You may see an alert box, as shown in Figure 22-6, letting you know that the Flash movie file (.swf) you are about to publish is only compatible with Flash Player 6 r65 or higher. Click OK in this alert box. Flash 8 generates all of the necessary JavaScript within the published HTML document to properly detect the Flash Player version. Click OK to close the Publish Settings dialog box.

Figure 22-6: The Optimize for Flash Player 6 r65 alert box

9. On your desktop, navigate to the folder where you saved your original .fla file. If you created the sample document in Step 1, you want to find the location of `detection_test.fla`. In this location, you will see the HTML file used for the detection process, the Flash content, and the alternate content.

10. In your own Web browser, load the `detection_test.html` page. If your browser has Flash Player 6 r65 or higher, the browser should display your `detection_test.swf` movie. This process works because the `detection_test.html` page uses JavaScript (or VBScript on Internet Explorer for Windows) to check the installed Flash Player version, if one exists. If you open the HTML document in a text editor such as Macromedia Dreamweaver, you'll see that lines 10–15 declare the version numbers you entered in the HTML tab of the Publish Settings. The JavaScript code compares these values to the version of the Flash Player that loaded the movie. If the Flash Player matches (or exceeds) the version requirements, the Flash content tags (`<object>` and `<embed>`) are written to the HTML page with JavaScript. Otherwise, the alternate content specified on line 147 in the JavaScript code is loaded into the browser window.

Note   Macromedia provides generic alternate content that you should replace with your own preferred HTML tags indicating what you want to the user to do if the version of the Flash Player required is not installed.

11. To accurately test your pages over an Internet connection, upload all of the files (except the .fla file) to your Web server and load the `detection_test.html` document from the Web server URL to redo the test.

On the CD-ROM   You can find all of these files created for this detection example in the `ch22/flash8_detection` folder of this book's CD-ROM. The JavaScript in the `detection_test_f8b.html` version of the document contains additional alternate content that is specified in an `alternate.js` file, also included on the CD-ROM. If you'd like to find the latest "Get Flash Player" graphics to use in your Web pages, go to `www.macromedia.com/macromedia/style_guide/buttons`.

If you want to test the detection mechanism with an older version of the Flash Player, we recommend that you use an older Flash Player installer with Netscape or a Mozilla-compatible browser. The process of uninstalling an ActiveX control used by Internet Explorer is much more difficult to do.

Web Resource   You can find just about every past version of the Flash Player at `www.macromedia.com/cfusion/knowledgebase/index.cfm?id=tn_14266` for testing purposes. As mentioned previously, we recommend that you install the older versions with a Netscape or Mozilla-compatible browser. If you are using Mac OS X, the first Flash Player released for Mac OS X was version 5.

You can set up your Netscape or Mozilla-compatible browser's plug-ins folder to accommodate multiple versions of the Flash Player plug-in. When you installed Flash 8, the first release of Flash Player 8 should have automatically been installed to your Netscape (or Mozilla) browser's `Plugins` (or `plugins`) folder. The plug-in file, named `NPSWF32.dll`, can be moved outside of the `Plugins` folder, into a new parent folder that you create. For the following example, we'll use Mozilla FireFox as our test browser.

Web Resource   Mozilla FireFox is a free Web browser that you can download at `www.mozilla.org/products/firefox/`. FireFox has quickly become the preferred cross-platform browser of many Web developers.

We prefer to create a `_Flash Players` folder in the `C:\Program Files\Mozilla FireFox` folder, and put each Flash Player version plug-in file into its own folder, as shown in Figure 22-7.

Caution Regardless of the Flash Player version you install, all Flash Player plug-in files for Netscape or Mozilla-compatible browsers have the same name on Windows: `NPSWF32.dll`. For this reason, you must isolate multiple installations of the Flash Player into their own folder.

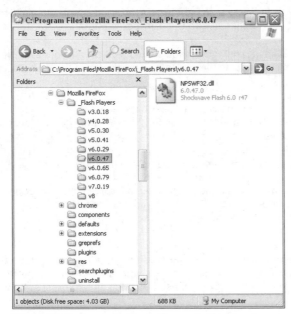

Figure 22-7: A sample Flash Players folder structure for use with Mozilla FireFox on Windows

You can do the same procedure on Mac OS X, where all browsers share the same plug-in folders. That's right! Mozilla, FireFox, Internet Explorer, and Apple Safari all refer to the same plug-ins folder. On your boot disk, such as Macintosh HD, browse to the `Library\Internet Plug-Ins\` folder. In this location, you will find the `Shockwave Flash NP-PPC` plug-in file. As Figure 22-8 shows, you can create a `Library\Internet Plug-Ins (DISABLED)` folder to store other versions of this plug-in file.

Caution On Mac OS X, you may need to re-create the same plug-in structure with the `Users\[Your User Name]\Library\Internet Plug-Ins\` folder. Or, you may just want to remove any Flash Player plug-in files within this folder. Mac OS X should then default to the main `Library\Internet Plug-Ins\` folder.

Figure 22-8: A sample Flash Players folder structure for use with Mozilla FireFox or Apple Safari on Mac OS X

This process takes some time, as you have to download and run each installer from the URL we mentioned in the earlier Web Resource note, and move the NPSWF32.dll file from the Plugins folder to its own folder in the Flash Players folder. When you're done, however, you'll have an efficient system for checking your content against older versions of the Flash Player. Simply move the current NPSWF32.dll file into its appropriate _Flash Players folder, and move the desired test version from its Flash Players folder into the Plugins folder.

Building your own Flash sniffer movie

While the Macromedia Flash 8 detection features work wonderfully, you may want to know how to build your own custom Flash detection sniffer. In this section, you learn how to build a Flash movie that uses client-side ActionScript to direct the browser window to the appropriate content. This sniffer directs each version of the Flash Player to its own unique HTML page. Meaning, Flash Player 3 (or earlier) is directed to a flash3.html page, Flash Player 4 is directed to a flash4.html page, Flash Player 5 jumps to a flash5.html page, and so on.

Making the Sniffer movie

The sniffer movie is a small Flash movie that has the same background color as the HTML document. You do not need any artwork or symbols in this movie.

1. Open Flash 8, and in a new Flash document file (.fla), rename Layer 1 to **actions**.

2. Add a keyframe on frame 2 of the actions layer. With this keyframe selected, open the Actions panel (F9 or Option+F9 on Mac).

3. In the Actions panel, add some ActionScript that checks for Flash Player 3 (or earlier). If Flash Player 3 is detected, then the movie will stop here and launch a URL for Flash 3 movies. If a later version of the player is detected, a separate keyframe labeled `checkPlayer` is called. You can direct each version of the Player to a unique URL. The basic principle of this ActionScript is to use Flash version-specific actions to determine which Player is displaying the movie. Refer to Listing 22-1.

Listing 22-1: **The Detection Script on Frame 2 of the actions Layer**

```
// create a Flash variable, whose value is equal to the
// $version environment variable in Flash Player 4, 5,
// or 6. This action line will not be read by Flash
// Player 3(or earlier).

player = eval("$version");

// The $version value will be in the format:
//
// abc 1,2,3,4
//
// where abc is the operating system (e.g. WIN, MAC)
// and 1 and 2 are the major version designations
// (e.g. 4.0, 5.0, etc.) and 3 and 4 are the minor and
// sub-minor version designations (e.g. r20, r27, etc.)
//
// By default, Flash MX 2004 ships with a Player version equal
// to WIN 7,0,0,0 or MAC 7,0,0,0. However, the Flash
// Player is available on other platforms like UNIX and
// POCKETPC as well.
//
// We just need the major version designation at
// placeholder 1. Using a while loop and substring(), we
// can extract this number, searching for the space (" ")
// between the platform text and the version numbers. The
// major version starts just after the space (" "). The
// Flash Player 3 will disregard this section of code.

playerLength = length(player);

i=1;

while (i<=playerLength) {
    currentChar = substring(player, i, 1);
    if (currentChar eq " ") {
        platform = substring(player, 1, i-1);
        majorVersion = substring(player, i+1, 1);
        break;
    }
```

```
        i = i+1;
    }

    // This code will check the value of majorVersion.
    // Flash Player 3 will not be able to execute the
    // call() action, but Flash Player 4 or higher will.

    if (majorVersion == " ") {
        // Flash Player 3 will execute this code
        // automatically, because it will not interpret
        // the if action.
        getURL("flash3.html");
    } else {
        call("checkPlayer");
    }

    // We will prevent the movie from accidentally looping.

    stop ();
```

4. Now you need to create a keyframe with actions that will be executed by Flash Player 4, 5, or 6. Add a keyframe on frame 5, and in the Property inspector assign a label of **checkPlayer** in the ⟨Frame Label⟩ field. Press the F5 key on frame 20 to add more empty frames to the layer so that you can read the frame label.

5. Select frame 5, and open the Actions panel (F9, or Option+F9). Type the following code into the Script pane. The code in Listing 22-2 checks to see if the Flash Player is version 4, 5, or 6 (or higher).

Listing 22-2: **The Script on the checkPlayer Frame of the actions Layer**

```
// majorVersion will be equal to either 4, 5, 6, 7, or 8 in
// Flash Player 4, 5, 6, 7, or 8 (or higher) respectively.

if (Number(majorVersion) == 4) {
    // Flash Player 4 will execute this code.
    getURL("flash4.html");
} else if (Number(majorVersion) == 5) {
    // Flash Player 5 will execute this code.
    getURL("flash5.html");
} else if (Number(majorVersion) == 6) {
    // Flash Player 6 will execute this code.
    getURL("flash6.html");
} else if (Number(majorVersion) == 7) {
    // Flash Player 7 or higher will execute this code.
    getURL("flash7.html");
} else if (Number(majorVersion) >= 8) {
    // Flash Player 8 or higher will execute this code.
    getURL("flash8.html");
}
```

6. Change the size of the movie frame to 18 px × 18 px, in the Document Properties dialog box (Modify ⇨ Document). Change the background color of the movie to match the background color of the HTML document. Click OK.

New Feature

In Flash 8, you can now specify movie dimensions as small as 1 px × 1 px. While 18 px × 18 px is small enough to remain unnoticeable on a Web page, you can opt to make your Flash movie even smaller.

7. Save the Flash movie as `sniffer.fla`.

8. Open the Publish Settings dialog box (File ⇨ Publish Settings). Make sure the Flash and HTML options are selected in the Formats tab. Rename the HTML file `sniffer_start.html`.

9. In the Flash tab, select Flash Player 4 in the Version drop-down menu.

Note

You are using the Flash Player 4 format because Flash Player 3 ignores all Flash 4 or higher actions, and Flash Player 4 or higher recognizes the formatting of the variable and ActionScript structures. Flash Player 5 .swf files restructure variables and ActionScript (even Flash 4-compatible code) in a manner that doesn't work consistently in Flash Player 4.

10. In the HTML tab, select the Flash Only template. Click the Publish button located at the bottom of the Publish Settings dialog box.

11. When the files have been published, click OK to close the Publish Settings dialog box. Save your document again.

You now have `sniffer_start.html` and `sniffer.swf` files in the same folder as your `sniffer.fla` file. In the next section, you add some additional HTML tags to the `sniffer.html` document.

Integrating the sniffer movie into an HTML document

After you have made the `sniffer.swf` and the `sniffer.html` files, you can modify the HTML document to guide the browser to a unique URL where plug-in information and a download screen are shown. Remember that the ↵ indicates a continuation of the same line of code. Do not insert this character into your HTML document.

1. Open the `sniffer_start.html` file in your preferred HTML document editor. Macromedia Dreamweaver, Notepad (Windows), TextEdit (Mac), or BBEdit (Mac) will do just fine.

2. Somewhere between the `<head>` `</head>` tags, insert the following HTML `<meta>` tag as one line of code:

```
<meta http-equiv="Refresh" content="3;
url=download.html" />
```

This `<meta>` tag has two attributes, `http-equiv` and `content`. The `http-equiv` attribute instructs the hosting Web server to add the value of `http-equiv` as a discrete name in the MIME header of the HTML document. The value of the `content` attribute becomes the value of the MIME entry. Here, the Web browser will interpret the META tag as

```
Refresh: 3; URL=download.html
```

in the MIME header. This name/value pair tells the browser to reload the browser window in three seconds with the file `download.html`. After testing, you may decide to increase the time the browser waits before reloading a new URL. On slower connections (or during peak Internet hours), you may find that three seconds is not long enough for the initial HTML and Flash movie to load into the browser.

Caution Some older browsers may require an absolute URL in the content attribute. This means that you may need to insert a full path to your HTML document, such as `http://www.yourserver.com/download.html`, as the URL in the content attribute.

3. You may want to create some text on this HTML document that indicates its purpose. If the user does not have the plug-in installed, he or she will be staring at a blank white page until the refresh is activated. For the purposes of this example, create an HTML table that centers the text "Checking for Flash Player . . ." on the page.

4. Save the HTML file as `sniffer.html`. If you want this to be the default page for your Web site, you may need to rename this file to `index.html`, `idex.htm`, `index.cfm`, or to whatever filename your Web server is configured to use as a default page. At this point, you need to create a `download.html` file. You also need to create `flash3.html`, `flash4.html`, `flash5.html`, `flash6.html`, and `flash7.html` files for the `getURL()` actions in the `sniffer.swf` movie.

On the CD-ROM We have included sample `sniffer.html`, `download.html`, `flash3.html`, `flash4.html`, `flash5.html`, `flash6.html`, `flash7.html`, and `flash8.html` files in the `ch22/custom_sniffer` folder on this book's CD-ROM. The Flash movie placeholder documents (for example, `flash3.html`, `flash4.html`, and so on) do not contain any Flash content. Note that the `download.html` sample file uses the JavaScript and VBScript player detection discussed in the next section.

When you have your HTML documents ready, you can load the `sniffer.html` document into a browser. If the Flash Player is not installed, then the `meta` tag should transport the browser location to the `download.html` URL. If the Flash Player is installed, then the Flash ActionScript directs the browser to the appropriate page.

Detecting the Flash Player with JavaScript and VBScript

The use of scripts written into an HTML document is also popular for Flash Player detection. If you're getting familiar with ActionScript syntax, you'll find that JavaScript detection code isn't all that complex. JavaScript is a universal scripting language that most 3.0 or higher Web browsers can employ to some capacity. Microsoft's implementation of JavaScript, called JScript, isn't exactly the same as JavaScript found in other browsers. For this reason, you can translate some JavaScript functionality into Microsoft's proprietary Web-scripting language, VBScript.

On the CD-ROM You'll find the HTML, Flash documents, movies, and GIF files for this section in the `ch22/javascript_detection` folder of this book's CD-ROM.

In this section, we look at how to create an HTML document that checks for the presence of the Flash Player plug-in with JavaScript, and the Flash ActiveX control with VBScript. We use two images of a traffic light — one Flash movie with a green light animating on and off, and one GIF image with a red light on — to display the results of our plug-in and ActiveX detection. Many Web sites employ a similar mechanism: Before an HTML page with Flash content can be accessed, visitors are presented with a splash screen telling them whether they have the Flash Player installed. If they don't have it, they can click a link to get the plug-in or ActiveX control. As a backup, many splash pages also include a link to bypass the detection in case the detection fails. This link would take the visitor straight to the HTML document that contains the Flash content.

Caution   The Flash Player can be detected with most JavaScript-enabled Web browsers by using the JavaScript array `navigator.mimeTypes`. The value for this array is always empty for Internet Explorer browsers, including IE 4.5 on Macintosh. IE 5.0 (or higher) for Macintosh provides support for this array. While you can use VBScript to detect for IE on Windows, there is no script plug-in detection available for IE 4.5 on Macintosh. You can however, use the Flash sniffer method, discussed in the previous sections, to detect Flash on IE 4.5 on Macintosh.

Detecting the plug-in with JavaScript

By using JavaScript code, you can set up a testing mechanism that delivers one of two graphics to the visitor's Web browser.

Copy the `script_detection.html` document located in the `ch22/javascript_detection` folder of this book's CD-ROM and open it in your preferred text editor (TextEdit, Notepad, BBEdit, and so on), or, even better, in Macromedia Dreamweaver. Look at lines 22 through 27 in the following listing.

Note   The   indicates a continuation of the same line of code. It should not be written in the actual JavaScript code in the HTML document.

```
22. var plugin = 0;
23. var activeX = 0;
24. var plugin = (navigator.mimeTypes &&
    navigator.mimeTypes["application/x-shockwave-flash"])⤴
    ? navigator.mimeTypes["application/x-shockwave-⤴
    flash"].enabledPlugin : 0
25. if ( plugin ) {
26.    plugin = parseInt(plugin.description.substring⤴
    (plugin.description.indexOf(".")-1)) >= 8
27. }
```

Line 22 initializes a variable `plugin` to save a value that indicates the presence of the Flash Player 8 plug-in on Netscape (or Mozilla, FireFox, IE 5.0 Mac, or Apple Safari). Line 23 initializes a variable called `activeX` to save a value that indicates the presence of the Flash Player 8 ActiveX control. At this point, you assign a value of 0 to these variables, meaning that the plug-in and ActiveX Control are not installed. This is used for worst-case scenarios in which the user may be using a version of JavaScript that doesn't interpret the detection code correctly.

Line 24 is borrowed from the Detect Flash 6 HTML template output from Flash MX (not Flash MX 2004 or Flash 8). It uses the `mimeTypes` array of the `navigator` JavaScript object to determine whether the Flash Player (in any version) is installed. If the Flash Player plug-in is installed, the variable `plugin` is now equal to the value [object Plugin]. If this is `true`, lines 25 and 26 will execute. Using the `description` property of the `Plugin` object, you can determine whether the Flash Player is the correct version. In this example, you check whether it's greater than or equal to 8. Notice that you can use a comparison as the value of the `plugin` variable. If Flash Player 8 (or higher) is installed, `plugin` will equal `true` (or 1); if a lower version is installed, `plugin` will equal `false` (or 0).

Creating a test object in VBScript

At this point, if the visitor is using Netscape (or a Mozilla-based browser, on any operating system) or Internet Explorer on the Macintosh, the variable `plugin` will have a value of either 0 or 1. However, you still need to check for the ActiveX control if the visitor is using Internet Explorer for Windows. Line 13 already initialized a variable called `activeX`. Lines 28 through 33 check to see if VBScript can create a Flash object in the document:

Note   The ⊃ indicates a continuation of the same line of code. It should not be written in the actual JavaScript code in the HTML document.

```
28. else if (navigator.userAgent &&⊃
       navigator.userAgent.indexOf("MSIE")>=0 &&⊃
       navigator.userAgent.indexOf("Windows")>=0){
29.    document.write('<SCRIPT LANGUAGE=VBScript\> \n');
30.    document.write('on error resume next \n');
31.    document.write('activeX = ( IsObject(CreateObject⊃
       ("ShockwaveFlash.ShockwaveFlash.8")))\n');
32.    document.write('<' + '/SCRIPT>');
33. }
```

Line 28 determines whether the visitor is using Internet Explorer on Windows. If that's the browser the visitor is using, lines 29 to 33 will execute. These lines of code create the VBScript that is necessary to check for the existence of the Flash Player 8 ActiveX control. Using the `IsObject()` and `CreateObject()` methods, VBScript can determine whether the ActiveX Control is installed. If it is installed, the variable `activeX` equals `true` (or 1). Note that this variable is available to both JavaScript and VBScript.

Inserting the graphics

After the variables `plugin` and `activeX` have been set appropriately, you can use these variables to either display a Flash movie file (.swf) or a GIF image graphic. In the body of the HTML document, you can reuse the `plugin` and `activeX` variables to insert either the Flash or GIF graphics. Lines 43 through 48 of the HTML document will write the tags to display the Flash movie or the GIF image for Netscape/Mozilla browsers (on any platform) or IE on the Mac.

Note   The ⊃ indicates a continuation of the same line of code. It should not be written in the actual JavaScript code in the HTML document.

```
43. if ( plugin ) {
44.    document.write('<embed src="trafficlightgreen.swf"⤸
       width="105" height="185" swliveconnect="false"  ⤸
       quality="high"></embed><br/>Flash Player 8<br/>plug-in ⤸
       detected.');
45.  } else if (!(navigator.appName &&⤸
       navigator.appName.indexOf("Netscape")>=0 &&⤸
       navigator.appVersion.indexOf("2.")>=0)){
46.      document.write('<a href="http://www.macromedia.com⤸
         /go/getflashplayer/">');
47.      document.write('<img src="trafficLightRed.gif"⤸
         width="105" height="185" border="0" /></a><br/>⤸
         Flash Player 8<br/>plug-in not installed.');
48.  }
```

If the `plugin` variable is not equal to `false` (line 31), line 43 executes. Line 43 uses the `<embed>` tag to insert a Flash movie file (.swf), depicting a green light that animates to a full green color, and the HTML text "Flash Player 8 Plug-in detected." If the `plugin` variable is equal to `false` and the browser is Netscape 2.0 (or Mozilla-compatible) or higher (line 43), then lines 44 and 45 create `<a href>` and `<img>` tags, depicting a static GIF image of a red traffic light that links to the Macromedia download area. Then, JavaScript creates the HTML text "Flash Player 8 plug-in not installed."

Note   The following discussion refers to lines not shown in the code listings for this section. Please refer to these lines (and line numbers) within the `script_detection.html` document in your preferred text editor.

Lines 55 through 64 perform the same functionality for Internet Explorer for Windows. If the `activeX` variable is `true`, then an `<object>` tag is written and a green traffic light animates on. If it's not installed, then a static GIF image of a red traffic light is displayed. Finally, you should do two more things:

✦ Tell IE 4.5 (or earlier) Mac users that you can't detect the Flash Player 8 plug-in.

✦ Tell other users that they can either proceed to the main Flash site, or click the appropriate traffic light to download the plug-in or ActiveX control.

Lines 72 to 75 tell IE 4.5 (or earlier) Mac users that you can't detect their plug-in settings. You can either leave it to them to decide whether they should download the plug-in, or you can direct them to a sniffer movie (discussed in the previous section) to determine whether the plug-in is installed.

Lines 76 to 78 check whether either the plug-in or the ActiveX control is installed. If it is, you tell the visitor to proceed to the main Flash site. Note that you'll want to insert more JavaScript code here that includes a link to your Flash content.

Lines 79 to 87 check whether the plug-in and the ActiveX control are both absent. If neither is installed, you tell them which traffic light (lines 80 to 87) to click.

Although you'll most likely want to spruce up the look and feel of this page to suit your particular site, you can use this scripting layout to inform your visitors about their plug-in or ActiveX control installations.

Using Flash Movies with JavaScript and DHTML

The ActionScripting features of Flash 8 have once again increased the range of interactive and dynamic possibilities for Flash movies on the Web. Prior to Flash Player 4, Flash movies could interact with external HTML or scripts only through the fscommand() action. This meant mapping commands and variables to JavaScript, which, in turn, passed information to the document object model of DHTML, Java applets, or CGI (Common Gateway Interface) scripts. Now that Flash movies can directly send and receive data to server-side CGI scripts, just about anything can be done within the Flash movie. If you want to directly communicate with the Web browser or the HTML document, you need to use JavaScript with either fscommand() actions or the new ExternalInterface API (Application Programming Interface) introduced with Flash Player 8.

 New Feature The ExternalInterface API is part of the flash.external class, and is available in Flash Player 8 or higher. This new set of actions (collectively known as an API) enables you to communicate directly with the Flash movie's hosting environment. Unlike the older fscommand() action, the ExternalInterface API enables you to receive data from the hosting environment immediately, without setting up callback handlers.

A word of caution to Web developers

This section covers the new ExternalInterface API actions, which, when used in Flash movies on Web pages, are supported by the following browsers:

- ✦ Internet Explorer 4.0 and higher for Windows 98/ME/2000/XP
- ✦ Mozilla 1.7.5 and higher
- ✦ Mozilla FireFox 1.0 and higher
- ✦ Apple Safari 1.3 and higher

 Caution At the time of this writing, ExternalInterface API actions are not available yet in Opera.

Our coverage of the ExternalInterface API assumes that you have a working knowledge of JavaScript and Flash ActionScript. If you don't know how to add actions to frames or buttons, please read Chapter 18, "Understanding Actions and Event Handlers." If you don't know JavaScript, you can still follow the steps to the tutorials and create a fully functional Flash-JavaScript movie. However, because this isn't a book on JavaScript, we don't explain how JavaScript syntax or functions work.

Understanding how Flash movies work with JavaScript

As we mentioned earlier, Flash Player has a new class called ExternalInterface. This class has methods that can invoke commands (passing optional arguments, or parameters) from a Flash movie to its hosting environment, such as JavaScript in a Web browser. What does this mean for interactivity? The ExternalInterface API offers the capability to have any Flash event handler (Button instance, onClipEvent(), frame actions, and so on) initiate an event handler in JavaScript. Although this may not sound too exciting, you can use ExternalInterface actions to trigger anything that you would have used JavaScript alone to do in the past, such as updating HTML-form text fields, changing the visibility of HTML elements, or switching HTML background colors on the fly. We look at these effects in the next section.

Flash movie communication with JavaScript is not a one-way street. You can also monitor and control Flash movies with JavaScript. Just as JavaScript treats an HTML document as an object and its elements as properties of that object, JavaScript treats a Flash movie as it would any other element on a Web page. Therefore, you can use JavaScript functions and HTML hyperlinks (<a href> tags) to control Flash movie playback.

Note For JavaScript to receive Flash events, you need to make sure that the attribute allowScriptAccess for the <object> and <embed> tags is set to "sameDomain" or "always". By default, most Flash 8 HTML templates have this set to "sameDomain". If you're testing your Flash movies and HTML documents locally, you should temporarily switch the value to "always"; otherwise, JavaScript will not receive the events from the Flash movie.

Web Resource This edition of the *Flash Bible* features coverage of the new ExternalInterface API available in Flash Player 8. If you'd like to read more about the older fscommand() method of sending data to and from the Flash Player and JavaScript, refer to the archived document at www.flashsupport.com/archive.

Changing HTML attributes

In this section, we show you how to dynamically change the bgcolor attribute of the <body> tag with an ExternalInterface action from a Flash movie while it is playing in the browser window. In fact, the background color will change a few times. Then, after that has been accomplished, you learn how to update the text field of a <form> tag to display what percent of the Flash movie has been loaded.

On the CD-ROM Before you start this section, make a copy of the Flash document countdown _starter.fla located in the ch22/ExternalInterface folder of this book's CD-ROM. This is a starter document to which you will add ActionScript code.

Adding ExternalInterface actions to a Flash movie

Open the countdown_starter.fla Flash document from this book's CD-ROM, and use Control ⇨ Test Movie to play the Flash .swf file. You should notice that the filmstrip countdown fades to white, and then to near-black, and then back to its original gray color. This countdown continues to loop until the entire first scene has loaded into the Flash Player. When the first scene has loaded, playback skips to a video clip of Robert swinging around and around. There's more to the Flash movie, but for now, that's all you need to deal with.

Our goal for this section of the tutorial is to add function calls to specific keyframes in the `countdown_starter.fla` document. When the Flash Player plays the frame with a function call, the Player sends a command and argument string to JavaScript. JavaScript then calls a function that changes the background color to the value specified in the argument string of the function. To be more exact, you'll create a function named `changeBgColor` in ActionScript. This function, when invoked (or "called"), will invoke a corresponding function named `changeBgColor` in the JavaScript code created later in this section. You'll add code to invoke the `changeBgColor()` function to the frames where the color fades to white, black, and gray. When the Flash movie changes to these colors, JavaScript will change the HTML background colors.

Here's the process:

1. Select frame 1 of the actions layer, and open the Actions panel (F9, or Option+F9 on Mac). In the Script pane, add the following code. Make sure you are not in Script Assist mode. This code, written in ActionScript 2.0 syntax, imports the `ExternalInterface` class and creates a `changeBgColor()` function that accepts one argument named `sColor`. This argument is passed to the `call()` method of the `ExternalInterface` class. The `call()` method takes one or more parameters. The first argument is always the name of the method (or function) to call in the hosting environment, and subsequent arguments are passed to the called method. In this example, you only need to pass one argument, `sColor`, to the JavaScript host environment.

```
import flash.external.ExternalInterface;

function changeBgColor(sColor:String):Void {
    ExternalInterface.call("changeBgColor", sColor);
}
```

2. On frame 16 of the Main Timeline, add a keyframe on the actions layer. With the keyframe selected, open the Actions panel (F9, or Option+F9 on Mac). Type the following action into the Script pane:

```
changeBgColor("#FFFFFF");
```

This action invokes the `changeBgColor()` function you defined on frame 1 in the previous step. The argument string #FFFFFF is passed to that function. The Flash function named `changeBgColor()` will pass that argument to the hosting environment's `changeBgColor()` function as well, changing the HTML background color to white.

3. On frame 20, add another action to the corresponding keyframe on the actions layer. With frame 20 selected, open the Actions panel and type the following code:

```
changeBgColor("#333333");
```

The argument "#333333" will be used to change the HTML background color to a dark gray.

4. On frame 21 of the actions layer, follow the same instructions as you did for Step 3, except use "#9E9E9E" for the argument string. This changes the HTML background color to the same color as the Flash movie countdown graphic.

5. On frame 66 of the actions layer, add another action invoking the `changeBgColor()` function. (Add this action after the existing action on this frame.) This time, use an argument string of "#000000", which changes the HTML background color to black.

6. Now that you've added several actions, try them out in the browser. Save the document as `countdown_100.fla`, and open the Publish Settings dialog box (for more information on Publish Settings, refer to Chapter 21, "Publishing Flash Movies"). In the Formats tab, make sure both the Flash and HTML format check boxes are selected. Change the Flash filename to `countdown.swf`, and leave the HTML filename as `countdown_100.html`. Click OK to close the Publish Settings dialog box. Choose the File ⇨ Publish command to export the Flash movie and HTML document.

Next, you'll build the JavaScript code that will be added to the HTML file published by Flash.

Enabling JavaScript for Flash movies

In this section, you add the necessary JavaScript to make the `ExternalInterface.call()` action work in the browser. Remember, you added this action to the `changeBgColor()` function on frame 1 of the Flash movie. What follows in Listing 22-3 is the JavaScript code that defines the custom function `changeBgColor` that we have created for you. Add this code to the `countdown_100.html` file you published in the last section.

Note   The line numbers reflect the actual line numbers in the HTML document.

Listing 22-3: The JavaScript Code to Enable the ExternalInterface Actions

```
5.    <script type="text/javascript" language="javascript">
6.    <!--
7.    function changeBgColor(hexColor){
8.       document.bgColor = hexColor;
9.    }
10.   //-->
11.   </script>
```

The following is a line-by-line explanation of the code:

5. This HTML tag initializes the JavaScript code.

6. This string of characters is standard HTML comment code. By adding this after the opening `<script>` tag, non-JavaScript browsers ignore the code. If this string wasn't included, text-based browsers such as Lynx might display JavaScript code as HTML text.

7. This is where the function `changeBgColor()` is defined. Remember that the `changeBgColor()` function in the Flash ActionScript specifies `"changeBgColor"` in the `ExternalInterface.call()` method. There is one argument defined for the function: `hexColor`, representing the hexadecimal color value passed from the Flash movie.

8. This line of code passes the argument `hexColor` to the `document.bgColor` property, which controls the HTML background color.

9. This line of code ends the function defined in line 7.

10. This end comment in line 10 closes the comment started in line 6.

11. The closing `</script>` tag ends this portion of JavaScript code.

That's it! We also added `<center>` tags around the `<object>` and `<embed>` tags to center the Flash movie on the HTML page, and we changed the `allowScriptAccess` parameter and attribute in the `<object>` and `<embed>` tags, respectively, to `"always"`. Once you've manually added the custom lines of JavaScript code, you can load the HTML document into either Internet Explorer or a Mozilla-compatible browser (see the caveats mentioned at the beginning of this section). When the Flash Player comes to the frames with `changeBgColor()` actions, the HTML background should change along with the Flash movie. Next, you add a `<form>` element that displays the percentage of the Flash movie that has loaded into the browser window.

On the CD-ROM You can find this version of the `countdown_100.fla` document in the `ch22/ExternalInterface` folder on this book's CD-ROM. You will also find `countdown.swf` and a fully JavaScripted HTML document called `countdown_100.html`.

Adding a percentLoaded() method

With Flash Player 8 and the `ExternalInterface` API, JavaScript can also communicate back to the Flash movie. In the Flash movie, you need to define callback handlers using the `ExternalInterface.addCallback()` method. This method lets you set up custom functions that are exposed to the hosting environment.

In this section, you create a JavaScript `percentLoaded()` method to display the Flash movie's loading progress update as a text field of a `<form>` element. First, you add the necessary `ExternalInterface` action and custom function to the Flash movie, next you add HTML `<form>` elements, and then you add the appropriate JavaScript.

1. Open the `countdown_100.fla` file that you modified in the previous section. Select frame 1 of the actions layer, and open the Actions panel (F9, or Option+F9 on Mac). Add the following code after the existing code in the Script pane. Do not type the ⏎ character as it denotes a continuation of the same line of code.

```
function getPercentLoaded():Number {
    var lb:Number = this.getBytesLoaded();
    var tb:Number = this.getBytesTotal();
    return Math.floor((lb/tb)*100);
}
ExternalInterface.addCallback("getPercentLoaded", this,⏎
getPercentLoaded);
```

This function, `getPercentLoaded()`, does not use any arguments. The purpose of the `getPercentLoaded()` function is to return the percent loaded of the Flash movie file (.swf). After the function is declared, it is exposed to JavaScript with the `ExternalInterface.addCallback()` method. This method takes three arguments: the name you want to use in JavaScript to call the Flash function (`"getPercentLoaded"`, although you could specify a different name here to use in JavaScript if you preferred), the scope of the Flash function (`this`, which is the Main Timeline of the Flash movie), and the Flash function name that will be invoked when JavaScript calls the function named as the first argument (`getPercentLoaded`).

2. Save your Flash document as `countdown_complete.fla`, and open the Publish Settings dialog box. In the Formats tab, uncheck the HTML file format, and leave the Flash movie filename to `countdown.swf`. Then publish your Flash movie.

3. In a text editor such as Macromedia Dreamweaver, Notepad, or TextEdit, open the `countdown_100.html` document from the previous section. Immediately resave this document as `countdown_complete.html` to overwrite the one published from Flash 8.

4. Add the following HTML after the `<object>` and `<embed>` tags:

```
<form method="post" action="" name="flashPercent"
style="display:show">
  <input type="text" name="tPercent" size="5"
  style="display:show" />
</form>
```

The code in Step 4 uses two `name` attributes so that JavaScript can recognize them. Also, the DHTML `style` attribute assigns a `display:show` value to both the `<form>` and `<input>` tags.

5. Add the JavaScript code shown in Listing 22-4 to your HTML document after the `changeBgColor()` function. The following `percentLoaded` function tells the browser to update the `<form>` text field with the percent of the Flash movie currently loaded. When the value is greater than or equal to 100, then the text field reads 100 percent and disappears after two seconds. This code also declares a `thisMovie()` function, which returns a reference to the Flash object in the `<object>` or `<embed>` tag. The `thisMovie()` function is used in the `percentLoaded()` function to call the Flash movie's `getPercentLoaded()` function you wrote in Step 1 of this section, to retrieve the loaded percent of the Flash movie. After the `percentLoaded()` function is declared in JavaScript, you use the `setInterval()` function in JavaScript to continuously invoke the `percentLoaded()` function, every 100 milliseconds. This interval is cleared when the Flash movie is fully loaded. (The indicates a continuation to the same line of code. Do not type this character in your code.)

Note   The `thisMovie()` function code is taken directly from Macromedia's `ExternalInterface` API example code shown in the documentation that is accessed through the Help panel. Also, you might notice that JavaScript has some of the same function names as Flash ActionScript does. Both JavaScript and ActionScript have a `setInterval()` function to enable you to call a function continuously at a specific interval.

Listing 22-4: The JavaScript Code for the percentLoaded() Function

```
function thisMovie(movieName) {
    var isIE = navigator.appName.indexOf("Microsoft") != -1;
    return (isIE) ? window[movieName] : document[movieName];
}

function percentLoaded(){
    var nPercent =  thisMovie("countdown").getPercentLoaded();
    if(nPercent >= 100 ){
            document.flashPercent.tPercent.value= "100 %";
```

```
                    setTimeout("document.flashPercent.tPercent.style.display =⤵
                        'none'", 2000);
                    setTimeout("document.flashPercent.style.display = 'none'", 2000);
                    clearInterval(nCheckID);
            } else {
                    document.flashPercent.tPercent.value = nPercent + " %" ;
            }
    }
}

var nCheckID = setInterval(percentLoaded, 100);
```

6. Save the HTML document and load it into a browser. If you run into errors, check your JavaScript syntax carefully. A misplaced ; or } can set off the entire script. Also, the function names specified in the Flash ActionScript code and the JavaScript code are case-sensitive and must be exactly the same. If you continue to run into errors, compare your document to the countdown_complete.html document on this book's CD-ROM. We also recommend that you test the preloading functionality from a remote Web server. If you test the file locally, the Flash movie loads 100 percent instantaneously.

Caution   Remember that this type of interactivity won't work on all browsers, and it requires the use of Flash Player 8.

Okay, that wasn't the easiest task in the world, and, admittedly, the effects might not have been as spectacular as you may have thought. Now that you know the basics of Flash and JavaScript interactivity, however, you can take your Flash movie interactivity one step further.

Web Resource   We'd like to know what you think about this chapter. Visit www.flashsupport.com/ feedback to send us your comments.

Summary

✦ You can customize many Flash movie attributes by adjusting the attributes of the `<object>` and `<embed>` tags in an HTML document. Scaling, size, quality, and background color are just a few of the Flash movie properties that can be changed within HTML without altering the original .swf file.

✦ You can detect the Flash Player plug-in or ActiveX control in a variety of ways: by using the `<object>` and `<embed>` tags alone, by using JavaScript and VBScript to check for the presence of the plug-in or the ActiveX Control, or by inserting a Flash sniffer movie into an HTML document with a special `<meta>` tag.

✦ Flash 8 includes an updated Detect Flash Version feature in the Publish Settings. This feature automatically creates an HTML document with the appropriate JavaScript and HTML tags to check for a version of the Flash Player that you specify.

✦ Flash movies can interact with JavaScript and DHTML elements on a Web page. This type of interactivity, however, is limited to the 4.0 or higher versions of Internet Explorer (on 32-bit Windows versions) and more current versions of Mozilla-compatible browsers.

✦ The Flash Player 8 plug-in can receive events and data from JavaScript. For example, JavaScript can query a Flash movie to determine how much of it has downloaded to the browser.

✦   ✦   ✦

Using the Flash Player and Projector

This chapter, the last in Part VI, explores alternative means of distributing your Flash movies as self-contained executable applications for CD-ROMs or other removable storage devices. We also look at the broad support available for the Flash Player plug-in for Web browsers.

The Stand-Alone Flash Player and Projector

The stand-alone Flash Player and projector enable you to take your Flash right off the Web and onto the desktop without having to worry whether users have the plug-in. In fact, you don't even need to worry about them having browsers! Stand-alone players and projectors have similar properties and limitations, although they're slightly different.

✦ **Stand-alone player:** This is an executable player that comes with Flash 8. You can open any .swf file in this player. The stand-alone player can be found in the Macromedia/Flash 8/ Players/Release folder (Windows) or the Macromedia Flash 8:Players:Release folder (Mac) on the volume where you installed Flash MX 2004.

✦ **Projector:** A projector is an executable copy of your movie that doesn't need an additional player or plug-in to be viewed. It's essentially a movie contained within the stand-alone player. The projector is ideal for distribution of Flash applications on CD-ROMs or DVD-ROMs. Figure 23-1 shows a Flash movie played as a Projector.

For the sake of simplicity, we refer to both projectors and movies played in the stand-alone Flash Player as *stand-alones* in this discussion. Because both the projector and stand-alone player have similar properties and limitations, you can apply everything discussed here to either one you choose to use.

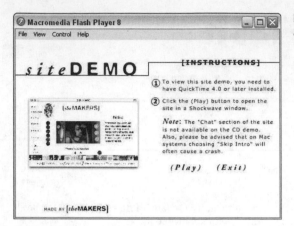

Figure 23-1: A movie playing as a projector

Note   Due to the differences in operating systems, Flash stand-alones on the Mac have the application menu listed in the system bar at the top of the Macintosh desktop area. On Windows, the application menu bar is part of the stand-alone window, as shown in Figure 23-1.

Creating a projector

When you have finished producing a Flash movie, it's fairly simple to turn it into a projector. You have two ways to create a stand-alone projector. Turning your Flash movies into Flash Player 8 stand-alone projectors typically adds 1.47 MB (Windows projectors) or 2 MB (Mac projectors) to the final file size. If you create a Mac projector from the Windows version of Flash MX 2004, the projector will add about 2.9 MB to the size of the .hqx file.

Note   As each new version of Flash is released, the projector size will likely increase. Flash 4 projectors added 280 KB (316 KB Mac) to a movie's file size, Flash 5 added 368 KB (500 KB Mac) to the file size, Flash MX added 800K (1 MB Mac) to a Flash movie's file size, and Flash MX 2004 added 973 KB (1.3 MB Mac) to the movie's size. As the Flash Player's features are expanded, we'll likely see the size of the player continue to increase with each release of Flash.

Method 1: Using the Publish command

The simplest way to make a Flash projector file is to use the Publish feature of Flash 8. In three short steps, you can have a stand-alone Flash movie presentation.

1. Choose File ➪ Publish Settings from the application menu.

2. When the Publish Settings dialog box opens, select the Formats tab and check the projector formats. Publish both Windows and Macintosh projectors using this method. Figure 23-2 shows the Publish Settings dialog box with the appropriate formats selected.

3. Click the Publish button in the Publish Settings dialog box, and your Flash movie will be published in all of the formats (for example, .swf, .gif, .jpg, and projector formats) specified with Publish Settings.

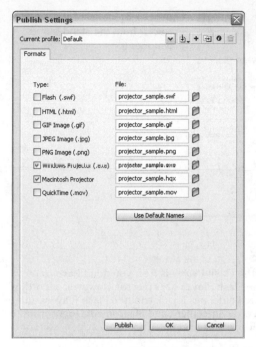

Figure 23-2: Select the projector formats in the Publish Settings dialog box.

Method 2: Using the Stand-alone Flash Player

You can also create a Flash projector file using the stand-alone Flash Player executable file that ships with Flash 8. You can find the stand-alone Flash Player in the Players/Release folder of the Flash 8 application folder.

Note   If you use this method to create a projector, you can make a projector for the current platform only. Thus, if you are using the Windows version of the stand-alone Flash Player, you can create a Windows projector only.

1. Export your Flash movie as an .swf file using File ⇨ Export Movie. Alternatively, you can use the Publish feature to create the .swf file.

2. Open the exported Flash movie file (.swf) in the stand-alone Flash Player.

3. Choose File ⇨ Create Projector from the stand-alone player's application menu, as shown in Figure 23-3.

4. When the Save As dialog box opens, name the Projector and save it.

Tip   If your movie is set to play at full screen (see fscommand coverage later in this chapter), press the Esc key to make the stand-alone player menu bar appear. If the Flash movie is set to play without the application menu, you should use the Publish method to create a projector.

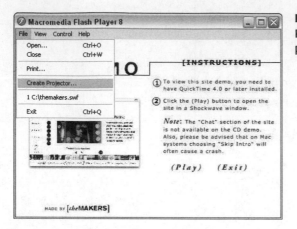

Figure 23-3: Choose File ➪ Create Projector from the stand-alone player menu.

Distribution and licensing

Distribution of stand-alone projectors or the Flash Player is free; you don't have to buy a license to distribute either the stand-alone Flash Player or projector. However, according to Macromedia, you need to follow specific guidelines for distributed Flash Players and projectors. You can download the runtime license agreement and Macromedia logos from the Macromedia Web site. For more information, check out www.macromedia.com/support/shockwave/info/licensing/.

Distribution on CD-ROM or DVD-ROM

The Flash platform has become increasingly popular for use on multimedia CD-ROMs or DVD-ROMs, especially as embedded .swf files in larger Macromedia Director projectors. Stand-alones can be used as front-ends for installations, splash screens for other programs, or even as complete applications. When you combine the good looks of a Flash interface with a few fscommand actions (see the next section for more information) and put them together on a CD-ROM (or DVD-ROM) that's programmed to start automatically on insertion, you have a first-class product.

Caution   As a general rule, don't try to send projector files (.exe files) as attachments to e-mail messages. Most current e-mail clients, such as Microsoft Outlook, will not allow you to open an e-mail containing an executable file, protecting you against computer-virus infections.

fscommand actions

The fscommand actions can be used to provide greater functionality to your stand-alones. These actions can turn a simple Flash movie into something spectacular! When they're combined with additional scripting and executables, you can make fully functional applications. Table 23-1 lists fscommand actions for stand-alones.

Table 23-1: fscommand Actions for Stand-Alones

FSCommand	Arguments	Function
`"fullscreen"`	`"true"` or `"false"`	Expands or contracts the view of the projector. The argument `"true"` sets the stand-alone to full-screen mode, without a title bar. The argument `"false"` sets it to the size specified by the Movie Properties.
`"allowscale"`	`"true"` or `"false"`	Allows for scaling of the movie. The argument `"false"` sets the movie to the size specified by the Document Properties dialog box (Modify ⇨ Document). This doesn't actually keep the stand-alone from being resized; it only keeps the movie inside of it from being scaled.
`"showmenu"`	`"true"` or `"false"`	Toggles the menu bar and the right-click/Control+click menu. The argument `"true"` enables them; `"false"` turns them both off.
`"trapallkeys"`	`"true"` or `"false"`	Captures all key presses, including those that would normally control the player. If you have turned off the menu with the `"showmenu"` command, you will need to manually create a `"quit"` command to exit the player or projector.
`"exec"`	Path to executable (BAT, COM, EXE, and so on)	Opens an executable from within the stand-alone player. The application opens in front of the projector.
`"quit"`	No argument	Closes the stand-alone.

When an `fscommand` action is added in the Actions panel, you can access stand-alone-specific commands from Script Assist mode, as shown in Figure 23-4. Refer to Chapter 18, "Understanding Actions and Event Handlers," for more information on adding actions to Flash frames or buttons.

Note

Flash 5 offered an undocumented save command for use in `fscommand` actions. This command enabled a Windows projector to save variables from the Flash movie to a text (.txt) file on the end-user's system. Although Flash MX, Flash MX 2004, and Flash 8 no longer offer this feature, you can combine Flash movies with Director projectors and the FileIO Xtra to write text files on either Mac or Windows systems. Even better, Flash ActionScript has a `SharedObject` class that enables local storage of information from Flash movies. We demonstrate the use of the `SharedObject` class in Chapter 31, "Creating a Game in Flash."

Caution

Make sure you list the commands and arguments for `fscommand` actions as strings, not as expressions (unless you purposely want to refer to an ActionScript variable). If you do not encapsulate the command and argument in quotes, as in `fscommand("allowscale", "true");`, it may not be interpreted by the stand-alone. Also, in order to use Script Assist with an `fscommand()` action, you must provide two arguments with the function, such as `fscommand("allowscale", "true");`. Otherwise, Script Assist mode returns an error.

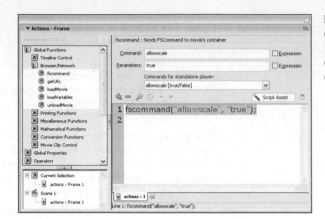

Figure 23-4: If you turn on Script Assist for an `fscommand()` action, you can choose from a list of commands.

You can also open HTML documents (even ones stored on a distributed CD-ROM) in the system's default Web browser by using the `getURL()` action. The following `getURL()` action opens a file named `start.html` that's in the same location as the stand-alone movie:

```
getURL("start.html");
```

Or, alternatively, you can display remote content in the Web browser by specifying absolute URLs, such as:

```
getURL("http://www.theMakers.com/index.html");
```

Although `fscommand` actions are relatively simple to use, Flash ActionScript has a `Stage` object that enables you to control many of the same features of the Flash Player. Refer to the coverage of the `Stage` object in the *Flash ActionScript Bible* series by Robert Reinhardt and Joey Lott (Wiley).

Using a behavior to toggle the screen mode

One of the behaviors included with Flash 8 is the Toggle Full Screen mode behavior, to be used for Flash stand-alone projectors. When you run a Flash projector, you can have the projector take over the user's desktop, getting rid of the application window and menus. This mode is similar to a presentation mode for a PowerPoint file or a QuickTime or Windows Media movie. In the following steps, you learn how to quickly apply this behavior to a Button component.

1. In Flash 8, create a new document.

2. Rename Layer 1 to **button**.

3. Open the Buttons library by choosing Window ➪ Common Libraries ➪ Buttons. In this library, open the Component Buttons folder. With frame 1 of the button layer selected, drag an instance of the pill button component from the library to the Stage. Place the instance in the upper-left corner of the Stage.

4. Select the new instance on the Stage. In the Property inspector, name the instance **cpbToggle**. In the Parameters tab of the inspector, type **Toggle Screen** in the Label field and select the auto-width check box above the field, as shown in Figure 23-5.

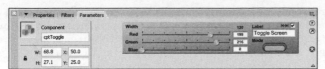

Figure 23-5: The settings for the pill button instance

5. With the instance selected on the Stage, open the Behaviors panel (Shift+F3). Click the Add Behavior (+) button in the panel, and choose Projector ➪ Toggle Full Screen mode. Flash 8 presents a confirmation dialog box, telling you what the behavior does (see Figure 23-6). Click OK.

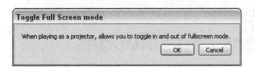

Figure 23-6: The Toggle Full Screen mode behavior dialog box

6. Save your Flash document as `projector_behavior.fla`.

7. Choose File ➪ Publish Settings to open the Publish Settings dialog box. In the Formats tab, choose Windows Projector and Macintosh Projector, as shown in Figure 23-7. Click the Publish button to create the projector files; then click OK to close the dialog box.

Figure 23-7: The Publish Settings dialog box

8. On your desktop, browse to the location where you saved the Flash document in Step 6. Double-click the projector file that corresponds to the operating system you are using. For example, if you're using Windows, double-click the `projector_behavior.exe` file. If you're on a Mac, double-click the `projector_behavior` application file.

9. When the projector starts, the Flash movie should be running in a normal application window. Click the Toggle Screen button to make the movie run in full-screen mode. When you click the button again, the movie should revert to the application window mode.

On the CD-ROM   You can find the completed Flash document, `projector_behavior.fla`, in the `ch23` folder of this book's CD-ROM.

Stand-Alone Limitations and Solutions

When you create a stand-alone, the task may not be as simple as taking your Flash document and exporting it as a projector. In this section, we briefly discuss issues that may affect the performance of your projector.

File sizes

When you distribute your Flash movies as stand-alones, you may think that you won't have to worry about streaming and download. As a consequence, stand-alones are often made considerably larger than a typical Flash movie — which can be a mistake! Very large movies (5 MB or more) may not play well on slower computers with Pentium II (or PowerMac G3) or older processors. Remember that Flash movies require the computer processor to compute all of those vector calculations, especially for rich animation. When you try to give a slower computer a large Flash movie to load, it may not be able to handle it.

Tip   One way to get around this limitation is to break your movies into several smaller movies. You can use the `loadMovie`/`unloadMovie` actions to open and close other movies within the original movie. You should use these actions in your stand-alones.

You should also test your movies on a variety of computers, especially if you plan to put a lot of development time and money into distributing them on CD-ROM. Some processors handle the movies better than others, and you often have to decide which processor you want to target as the lowest common denominator.

File locations

If you use the `"exec"` parameter with an `fscommand()` action to run an application from the projector, you need to make sure that the application file that Flash is targeting is located within a folder named `fscommand`. This folder should be contained in the same folder as the stand-alone projector file. In the sample included on this book's CD-ROM, the stand-alone projector named `start.exe` is allowed to open any application in the `fscommand` folder.

On the CD-ROM   You can find a sample projector structure and file setup in the `ch23/exec` folder of this book's CD-ROM.

Macromedia implemented this security feature with Flash Player 6 stand-alones, and continues to implement the policy with Flash Player 8 stand-alones. By restricting access to executables (that is, application files), users can trust that a Flash movie or projector won't be able to run system-level applications that could potentially corrupt their computer or install a virus.

 Caution As a Web user, you should always be careful of running any type of application file, especially if you receive it in an e-mail or download it from an unknown company's Web site. A malicious user could easily disguise a virus within any executable. Make sure you run applications only, including projectors, from trusted sources.

Using the Flash Player Plug-in for Web Browsers

Flash movies can be played only in Web browsers that have the Flash Player plug-in or ActiveX control installed. Macromedia has made huge strides in making the plug-in prepackaged with newer Web browsers and operating system installation programs, eliminating the need for users to manually download and install the plug-in themselves. Unfortunately, the Flash Player 8 version of the plug-in will likely only be included in future releases of Web browsers and operating systems. Remember that earlier versions of the plug-in can *try* to play Flash movies published for Flash Player 8; however, new features in Flash Player 8-based movies (such as GIF/PNG image support in text fields and loading Flash 8 Video, or .flv files, over HTTP) will not be available.

The Flash Player on Mobile Devices

The development for the Flash Player is so demanding that Macromedia dedicates an entire department's worth of resources to the job. The Flash Player has been made available for Pocket PC devices using the Pocket PC 2002 and 2003 operating systems from Microsoft. Computer hardware manufacturers such as Hewlett-Packard/Compaq and Casio currently manufacture a wide range of PDAs (personal data assistants) that can use the Flash Player via the Pocket Internet Explorer Web browser or a stand-alone player. At the time of this writing, Flash Player 6 was available for most Pocket PCs. As the computer processing power of Palm, Handspring, and Sony devices (that implement the Palm OS) increases, we see Flash Player support being extended to these devices.

Nokia and DoCoMo have released phones in Japan that can play full-color Flash animations as well! These phones use a version of the Flash Player called Flash Lite. With this player, you can create Flash movies that use Flash 5 objects and Flash 4 ActionScript. For more information on Flash Lite and DoCoMo, visit the following page on Macromedia's site:

www.macromedia.com/devnet/devices/i-mode.html

It's no surprise that the Flash Player is being adopted so widely by computer and device manufacturers. The .swf format allows rich media such as animation, sound, and video to be transmitted over incredibly slow (or congested) networks. Until high-speed wireless access becomes more available, we'll likely need to keep wireless connection speeds such as 19.2 Kbps (CDPD-based networks) or 25 to 60 Kbps (GPRS-based networks) in mind while developing Flash movies that can be accessed by a universal audience.

Note For up-to-date information on the Flash Player plug-in, see Macromedia's download page at www.macromedia.com/shockwave/download/alternates.

Supported operating systems

Since Flash 3, Macromedia has greatly expanded its platform support for the Flash Player plug-in. At the time of this writing, you can download Flash Players for Windows 95/98/ME/NT/2000/XP and for Mac Power PCs. By the time this book is published, version 8 players should be available for Linux x86. At conferences worldwide, Macromedia has demonstrated that Flash graphics can be ported to a variety of GUIs (graphical user interfaces) and operating systems. We've also seen Flash graphics showing up in add-on applications for entertainment consoles such as the Sony PlayStation and set-top boxes from Motorola.

Supported browsers

The Flash Player plug-in works best with Mozilla-compatible and Internet Explorer browsers. Any browser compliant with Netscape Navigator 2.0's plug-in specification or Internet Explorer's ActiveX technology can support the Flash Player plug-in or ActiveX control, respectively. Note that Mac versions of Internet Explorer or Apple Safari use a Netscape plug-in emulator to use the Flash Player plug-in rather than an ActiveX control.

For AOL subscribers, any version of AOL's 3.0 through 9.0 browsers (except for the earliest 3.0 release that used a non-Microsoft Internet Explorer shell) will support Macromedia plug-ins.

Caution The Flash action fscommand, when used to communicate with JavaScript, works only with certain browser versions. Currently, no versions of Internet Explorer on the Macintosh (up to version 5.1) or Apple Safari support the fscommand action. Netscape 3.01 through 4.x (on both Macintosh and Windows) or Internet Explorer 3.0 or greater for Windows 95/98/NT/2000/XP is necessary for fscommand implementation. Netscape 6.0 and 6.1 do not support fscommand interactivity with JavaScript. If you're developing Flash movies targeted to Flash Player 8, you should use the new ExternalInterface API introduced with Flash 8. We discuss this new feature set in Chapter 22, "Integrating Flash Content with Web Pages."

For a comprehensive list of supported browsers (and Flash compatibility), please see the Macromedia tech note at www.macromedia.com/support/flash/ts/documents/browser_support_matrix.htm.

Plug-in and Flash movie distribution on the Web

Anyone can download the Flash Player plug-in for free from the Macromedia Web site. You can direct visitors at your Web sites to Macromedia's Flash Player download page, www.macromedia.com/go/getflashplayer. In fact, according to Macromedia's licensing agreement, if you're publishing Flash movies on your Web site, you need to display the "Get Shockwave Player" logo or "Get Flash Player" logo on your Web site. This logo should link to Macromedia's download page, which we just listed. However, you can't distribute the plug-in installer yourself—you need to license the right to distribute any plug-in installer from Macromedia. For more details on licensing, see www.macromedia.com/support/shockwave/info/licensing/.

You can find the official Macromedia button graphics at www.macromedia.com/support/programs/mwm/swb.html.

Plug-in installation

In Chapter 21, "Publishing Flash Movies," we discuss the Publish feature of Flash MX 2004 and the use of preformatted HTML templates to deliver your Flash movies to your Web site. The template and/or handwritten HTML that you use for your Flash-enabled Web pages will determine the degree of difficulty your visitors will have upon loading a Flash movie.

Macromedia has also officially named the auto-update experience of the Flash Player plug-in as Express Install. This feature refers to the nearly pain-free process of upgrading from Flash Player 7 to Flash Player 8. Flash Player 7 was released with an auto-update feature, enabling new versions of the plug-in to download without the hassle of installing an updated ActiveX control or downloading a plug-in installer application.

Web Resource

You can change the auto-update preferences of your Flash Player installation by visiting the following Macromedia Web page:

`www.macromedia.com/support/documentation/en/flashplayer/help/settings_manager05.html`

By default, the Flash Player will check for an updated version of the plug-in every 30 days. You can change the time interval to as little as seven days.

Using the Settings in Flash Player 6 and higher

Flash Player 6 introduced the Settings option from the Flash Player's contextual menu, which can be accessed by right-clicking (or Control+clicking on the Mac) a Flash movie. When you choose the Settings option, the Macromedia Flash Player Settings dialog box opens. This dialog box has four tabs, which we discuss in the following sections.

Privacy

This tab, shown in Figure 23-8, controls the access of the current Flash movie to your Webcam and microphone. Whenever a Flash movie tries to access your Webcam or microphone, the Flash Player opens this tab to ask you for permission. You can choose Allow, which gives the Flash movie access to your camera and microphone, or Deny, which stops the Flash movie from gaining access to these devices. You can also select the Remember check box so that the Flash Player remembers the choice you made, preventing the dialog box from opening during subsequent visits to the same Flash movie (or Web site hosting the Flash movie). If you click the Advanced button in the Privacy tab, a new Web browser opens and loads the help page for the Settings options on Macromedia's site.

Note

Flash movies can stream live audio and video to Flash Communication Server applications by using the `Camera`, `Microphone`, and `NetStream` objects.

Figure 23-8: The Privacy tab

The Privacy option applies to any and all Flash movies hosted on the domain listed in the Privacy tab.

For the most up-to-date information on the Privacy tab, refer to the following page on Macromedia's site:

    www.macromedia.com/support/flashplayer/help/privacy/

You can also access the Global Settings manager on Macromedia's site, which enables you to control the privacy settings for all sites you have visited. Go to the following URL:

www.macromedia.com/support/flashplayer/help/settings/global_
privacy.html

Local Storage

As shown in Figure 23-9, the Local Storage tab controls how much information can be stored on your computer from the Flash Player. Since Flash Player 6, Flash movies can be engineered to store data on the user's machine, with the use of local Shared Objects. The `SharedObject` class in ActionScript enables you to store customized information on a user's machine, just like cookies can store information from a Web application.

Figure 23-9: The Local Storage tab

By default, a Web site and Flash movies hosted on that site can allocate as much as 100 KB of data on a user's machine. If a Flash movie hosted from a Web site requests more than this amount, the Flash Player automatically opens this tab asking for the user's permission to store more data. You can click the Never Ask Again option to prevent the Flash Player from automatically opening this tab when a site requests to store more data than its allotted amount.

You can find the latest information about the Local Storage tab at

www.macromedia.com/support/flashplayer/help/localinfo/.

To learn more about using the `SharedObject` class, refer to Chapter 31, "Creating a Game in Flash." For more extended coverage, read the *Flash ActionScript Bible* series by Robert Reinhardt and Joey Lott (Wiley).

Microphone

The Microphone tab, shown in Figure 23-10, controls the source of audio input to a Flash movie. Depending on your computer system, you may have several audio capture devices listed in this tab's menu. If you don't have an audio capture device on your system, then you may not see any options available in this panel. You can use this tab to control the sensitivity of the microphone (or capture device) by adjusting the slider position. The tab provides real-time audio monitoring with a bar graph. You can click the Reduce Echo check box to minimize the echo or feedback from a speaker that is located near your microphone.

Figure 23-10: The Microphone tab

For more information on Microphone settings, see www.macromedia.com/support/flashplayer/help/microphone.

Camera

The Camera tab, shown in Figures 23-11 and 23-12, controls the camera source used by the Flash Player. If your computer does not have a camera (or digital video capture card, which includes FireWire, or IEEE 1394, cards), then you may not see a camera source listed in this tab. If you have multiple video capture sources, you can use this tab to control which source is used for live streams going out of the Flash movie into a Flash Communication Server application.

Figure 23-11: The default view of the Camera tab

You can click the camera icon in the Camera tab to see live video from your chosen capture source, as shown in Figure 23-12. If you do not see any picture in this area after you click the camera icon, you may have a problem with your capture driver or the Flash Player may be incompatible with the driver.

Figure 23-12: An active preview of a camera's output in the Camera tab

For more information on the Camera tab and its settings, see the following page on Macromedia's site: www.macromedia.com/support/flashplayer/help/camera.

Alternative Flash-Content Players

Macromedia has teamed up with RealSystems and Apple to enable Flash content in the RealOne Player and the QuickTime Player, respectively. By enabling Flash content in other players, Macromedia is promoting the acceptance of Flash as the de facto vector standard for Web graphics. Moreover, with so many alternatives for Flash playback, it is more likely that your Web visitors can see your Flash content.

RealOne Player with Flash playback

With a little effort, you can repackage your Flash movies as RealFlash presentations over the Web. Web visitors can use the RealPlayer G2, RealPlayer 8, or the new RealOne Player to play Flash, RealAudio, or RealVideo (among a long list of RealMedia types) content. RealMedia movies stream from a RealServer (special server software running concurrently with Web server software) into the RealPlayer plug-in (Netscape) or ActiveX control (Internet Explorer).

Note   Since Flash MX, you can no longer publish Flash movies tuned for RealPlayer. You can find more information about Flash and RealPlayer at `service.real.com/help/library/guides/realone/ProductionGuide/HTML/realpgd.htm?page=htmfiles/flash.htm`.

QuickTime Player

Apple introduced playback support for Flash movies with QuickTime 4. Better yet, Macromedia has included QuickTime Flash export options with Flash 4, 5, MX, MX 2004, and 8. A QuickTime Flash movie file (.mov) is essentially a Flash movie file (.swf) packaged as a QuickTime media type.

Web Resource   The QuickTime architecture and QuickTime Flash format are discussed at length in the archived chapter, "Working with QuickTime," available on the book's support site at `www.flashsupport.com/archive`.

You can use the QuickTime HTML template in Publish Settings to create an instant Web page that uses the QuickTime Player plug-in. It uses the `<object>` and `<embed>` tags to prescribe the name, width, height, and plug-in download location.

QuickTime 4 can support only Flash 3 graphics and actions; QuickTime 5 can support Flash 4 SWF format features, including `loadVariables` actions; and QuickTime 6 can support Flash Player 5-based features and ActionScript. Flash movies can act as a timeline navigator for other QuickTime media, such as video or audio. For interactive Flash content, you should limit yourself to Flash 4- or 5-compatible actions.

Note   At the time of this writing, there was not an upgrade to the QuickTime Player that supported Flash Player 6 or higher .swf features.

Shockwave Player

Since Director 6.5, you can include Flash movie files (.swf) in your Director movies, either as stand-alone Director projectors or as part of Shockwave movie files (.dcr) on the Web. The

Flash Asset Xtra is automatically included as part of the default Shockwave plug-in installation process. Among other benefits, Shockwave movies enable you to integrate Flash movies with dynamic 3D models and graphics and use Flash assets with third-party Xtra capabilities.

Cross-Reference For more information on Director and Flash interactivity, please read our archived chapter, "Working with Director," at www.flashsupport.com/archive.

Player Utilities

You can also reformat and modify stand-alones for both Windows and Macintosh. A few software companies create applications specifically designed to modify Flash movies and stand-alones. Here is a list of Web site URLs for those companies:

- ✦ www.flashjester.com
- ✦ www.multidmedia.com
- ✦ www.northcode.com
- ✦ www.screentime.com
- ✦ www.alienzone.com/screensaver_features.htm
- ✦ www.goldshell.com

Some of these companies offer more than just one utility for Flash movie development, such as the JTools of FlashJester. For updates to this list, check out this book's Web site, listed in the Preface of this book.

Tip You can find directories of Flash utilities at www.flashmagazine.com and graphicssoft.about.com/cs/flashtools.

One of our favorite utilities is Versiown, created by Goldshell Digital Media. This handy utility allows you to modify the properties of a Flash (or Director) projector file, specifically .exe versions for Windows. With Versiown, you can

- ✦ Add or modify the version information that shows up in the Properties dialog box, accessible by right-clicking the .exe file and choosing Properties.

- ✦ Add a custom icon for the .exe file of the projector. Together with an icon utility such as IconBuilder from Iconfactory (which is a filter plug-in for Adobe Photoshop), you can make custom .ico files to be used as icons for your Flash projectors.

You can download trial versions of Versiown at www.goldshell.com/versiown. A trial of IconBuilder is available at www.iconfactory.com/ib_home.asp.

Note You can use the Get Info dialog box (Mac OS X) on Mac files to easily replace the icon image for Flash projector files on the Mac. Open the .ico file made from IconBuilder in an image editor such as Adobe Photoshop, use Edit ➪ Select All to select the entire image, copy it to the Clipboard (Edit ➪ Copy), and paste it into the picture area of the Get Info dialog box.

Web Resource We'd like to know what you think about this chapter. Visit www.flashsupport.com/feedback to send us your comments.

Summary

✦ Flash movies can be viewed in Web pages with the Flash Player plug-in or ActiveX control. You can also play Flash movie files (.swf) with the stand-alone Flash Player included with the Flash 8 application, or you can publish a Macintosh or Windows projector that packages the stand-alone Flash Player and .swf file into one executable file.

✦ You can freely distribute a Flash movie projector or stand-alone Flash Player as long as you adhere to the guidelines outlined at Macromedia's Web site.

✦ Flash movies can be distributed with other multimedia presentations such as Macromedia Director projectors. Your Flash movies can be distributed on a CD-ROM or DVD-ROM.

✦ The fscommand() action enables you to control the stand-alone player environment, including its viewing area.

✦ Flash movies can be viewed best with the Macromedia Flash Player plug-in or ActiveX control. However, you can also view Flash movies with third-party products, such as the RealOne Player or the Apple QuickTime Player.

✦ You can enhance your Flash movies with third-party tools such as FlashJester's JTools for Flash.

✦   ✦   ✦

Approaching ActionScript

◆ ◆ ◆ ◆

Now that you're comfortable in the Flash authoring environment, it's time to see what you can do when you move beyond basic timelines and start architecting and controlling content with ActionScript. Chapter 24 introduces the basic syntax of ActionScript code so that you understand why all those brackets, dots, and quote marks are used. In Chapter 25 you learn how to control methods and properties of `MovieClip` objects. If you thought animating Movie Clips was fun, wait until you start to apply more sophisticated control to multiple elements with ActionScript! Chapter 26 covers using functions and arrays, two of the most crucial techniques for organizing and controlling dynamic data. Chapter 27 takes you to the next level of Movie Clip control with an overview of how to detect collisions, and how to use the `ColorTransform`, `Sound`, and `PrintJob` classes to control dynamic movie elements.

◆ ◆ ◆ ◆

Knowing the Nuts and Bolts of Code

For many serious Web developers, Flash's enhanced programming capabilities are the most important new feature of each product release. Just when you think they've added it all, the Macromedia Flash team manages to pull more rabbits out of the hat. Now, more than ever, elements inside Flash movies can be dynamic, have properties calculated on the fly, and respond to user input. Movies can communicate with server-side applications and scripts by sending and receiving processed and raw data. What does this mean for your movies? It means you have the capability to produce truly advanced movies (such as online secure banking applications, product configurators, hotel reservation systems, Flash asteroids, a multiplayer role-playing adventure game, or a navigational interface with a memory of the user's moves, just to name a few). It also means that Flash can be used to produce complex Web applications, such as database-driven e-commerce product catalogs, without the need for proprietary server-side applications.

While many of the individual actions have not changed in Flash 8, the structure of ActionScript programming continues to evolve around the ActionScript 2.0 version specification. ActionScript 2.0 is also known as *AS2*, and we use this abbreviation throughout the book. AS2 programming, introduced in Flash MX 2004, jumped Flash coding to a whole new level — one that adheres more closely to ECMAScript Edition 4-compliant standards. The Actions panel, now in its fourth version, only becomes more efficient at helping you code. Components continue to use the ActionScript 2.0 model, using complex event handling, and make it simpler for you to add interface elements and integrate data into your Flash projects. Flash 8 continues to push the advancement of Rich Internet Applications, or RIAs, which bring a new world of real-time data and ease of use to the Web. These topics, however, are far beyond the scope of motion tweens and animations. In this chapter, we'll introduce you to the programming structure of ActionScript and explain how to start using code within your Flash movies.

Cross-Reference   If you are new to scripting, we highly recommend that you review Part V, "Adding Basic Interactivity to Flash Movies," before you begin this chapter.

Web Resource   For more information about ECMAScript Edition 4, see the original proposal at `www.mozilla.org/js/language/es4/`.

Breaking Down the Interactive Process

Before you can become an ActionScript code warrior, realize that this isn't just a weekend activity—if you want to excel at Flash ActionScripting, you'll need to commit the time and energy necessary for the proper revelations to occur. It's not likely that you'll understand programming simply by reading this chapter (or the whole book). You need to create some trials for yourself, testing your textbook knowledge and applying problem-solving techniques.

You might be thinking, "Oh no, you mean I have to revisit that torture of grade school math?" Not exactly, but programming, like math, requires strong reasoning and justification skills. You need to be able to understand how values (for example, the height of a Movie Clip instance) are determined, what type of changes you can perform on those values, and how changes to one value might affect another value. If you're feeling overwhelmed, don't worry. We take this one step at a time.

Define your problems

Regardless of what interactive authoring tool you use (Macromedia Dreamweaver, Macromedia Flash, Macromedia Director, and so on), you can't begin any production work until you have a clear idea of the product. What is it that you are setting out to do? At this point in the process, you should use natural language to describe your problems; that is, define your objective (or problem) in a way that you understand it. For example, let's say that you want to make a quiz. You'll have to run through a list of goals for that interactive product:

✦ Is it a true/false test?

✦ Or will it be multiple choice?

✦ Or how about fill-in-the-blank?

✦ Is it an essay test?

✦ How many questions will be on the quiz?

✦ Will there be a time limit for each question?

✦ Will you notify the person of wrong answers?

✦ How many chances does the person get to answer correctly?

Other questions, of course, could help define what your product will encompass. Don't try to start Flash production without setting some project parameters for yourself.

Clarify the solution

After you have defined the boundaries for the project, you can start to map the process with which your product will operate. This step involves the procedure of the experience (in other words, how the person will use the product you are creating). With the quiz example, you might clarify the solution as:

1. The user starts the movie and types his or her name.

2. After submitting the name, the user will be told that he or she has 10 minutes to complete a 25-question quiz that's a combination of true/false and multiple-choice questions.

3. Upon acknowledging the instructions (by pressing a key or clicking a button), the timer starts and the user is presented with the first question.

4. The timer is visible to the user.

5. The first question is a true/false question, and the correct answer is False.

6. If the user enters a True response, a red light graphic appears and the sound of a buzzer plays. The user is asked to continue with the next question.

7. If the user enters a false response, a green light graphic appears and the sound of applause plays. The user is asked to continue with the next question.

8. This process repeats until the last question is answered, at which point the score is tallied and presented to the user.

The preceding eight steps are similar to a process flowchart, as we discussed in Chapter 3, "Planning Flash Projects." In real-life production, you would want to clarify Step 8 for each question in the same amount of detail as Steps 5 through 7 did. As you can see, once you start to map the interactive experience, you'll have a much better starting point for your scripting work. Notice that we're already using logic, with our `if` statements in Steps 6 and 7. We're also determining object properties such as `_visible` in Step 4. While you may not know all the ActionScript involved with starting a timer, you know that you have to learn how time can be measured in a Flash movie.

Note   We use the terms *scripting, programming,* and *coding* interchangeably through this chapter and other parts of the book.

Translate the solution into the interactive language

After you have created a process for the movie to follow, you can start to convert each step into a format that Flash can use. This step will consume much of your time as you look up concepts and keywords in this book, the *Flash ActionScript Bible* series by Robert Reinhardt and Joey Lott (Wiley), or Macromedia's updated Help panel that ships with Flash 8. It's likely that you won't be able to find a prebuilt Flash movie example to use as a guide, or if you do, that you'll need to customize it to suit the particular needs of your project. For the quiz example, we could start to translate the solution as:

1. Frame 1: Movie stops. User types name into a text field.

2a. Frame 1: User clicks a submit Button symbol instance to initiate the quiz. The instructions are located on frame 2. Therefore, the Button action uses a gotoAndStop(2) action to move the Playhead to the next frame.

2b. Frame 2: Static text will be shown, indicating the guidelines for the quiz.

3. Frame 2: User clicks a start quiz Button symbol instance. An action on the Button instance starts a timer and moves the Playhead to frame 3.

4. Frame 3: The current time of the timer is displayed in a text field, in the upper-right corner of the Stage.

5. Frame 3: The first question is presented in the center of the Stage. A button with the text True and a button with the text False are located just beneath the question. The correct answer for the question is hidden in a variable name/value. The variable's name is answer, and its value is false. This variable declaration appears as a frame action on frame 3. A variable, called score, will also be declared to keep track of the correct answer count. Its starting value will be 0.

6a. Frame 3: If the user clicks the True button, an if/else action checks whether answer's value is equal to true. If it is, an action sets the _visible of a greenLight_mc Movie Clip instance to true, and initiates and plays a new Sound object for the applause.wav file in your Library. Also, the value of score increases by 1. If the value of answer is not true, then an action sets the _visible of a redLight_mc Movie Clip instance to true, and initiates and plays a new Sound object for the error.wav file in your Library. The value of score will be left as is.

6b. Frame 3: A Button instance appears, and when it's clicked, it takes the user to frame 4.

7a. Frame 3: If the user clicks the False button, an if/else action checks whether answer's value is equal to true. If it is, an action sets the _visible of a greenLight_mc Movie Clip instance to true, and initiates and plays a new Sound object for the applause.wav file in your Library. Also, the value of score increases by 1. If the value of answer is not true, an action sets the _visible of a redLight_mc Movie Clip instance to true and initiates and plays a new Sound object for the error.wav file in your Library. The value of score is left as is.

7b. Frame 3: A Button instance appears, and when it's clicked, it takes the user to frame 4.

Although there is more than one way we could have translated this into ActionScript-like syntax, you'll notice that a few key concepts are presented in the translation: where events occur (frames or buttons), and which elements (for example, Button symbols or Movie Clip instances) are involved.

Most important, you'll notice that we used the same procedure for both the True and the False buttons. Even though we could hardwire the answer directly in the Button actions, we would have to change our Button actions for each question. By placing the same logic within each Button instance, we have only to change the value of the answer variable from frame to frame (or from question to question).

Granted, this example was already translated for you, and 90 percent of your scripting woes will be in the translation process — before you even have a testable Flash movie. You need to learn the basic terminology and syntax of the ActionScript language before you can start to write the scripting necessary for Steps 1 to 7. And that's exactly what the rest of this chapter (and the rest of Part VII) teaches you.

 Cross-Reference Because the vocabulary of the ActionScript language has become so immense, Robert Reinhardt and Joey Lott have created a separate *Bible* series, on Flash ActionScript, to thoroughly address the syntax of ActionScript. However, if you are new to scripting and programming, we recommend that you start with our coverage of ActionScript here before reading the *Flash ActionScript Bible* by Robert Reinhardt and Joey Lott (Wiley).

The Basic Context for Programming in Flash

With the enhanced Actions panel (also known as the ActionScript editor) in Flash 8, you can program interactivity by writing interactive commands directly into the Script pane of the Actions panel.

New Feature

Flash 8's Actions panel can now show you hidden characters, such as character spaces and line breaks, in your code. Choose Hidden Characters from the options menu of the Actions panel to see these characters. Due to the reactions of many Flash designers and beginner developers, the Actions panel also has a new Script Assist feature, which replaces the sorely missed "Normal mode" of Flash MX. For more information on Script Assist, see Chapter 18.

In the Actions panel, you can type your code from scratch, as well as insert your code with the help of Action booklets or the new Script Assist feature. Syntactically, ActionScript looks and feels very much like JavaScript. Macromedia has gone to great lengths to make ActionScript compatible with ECMAScript 4 (the standard programming guidelines derived from JavaScript). And like other object-oriented languages, ActionScript is composed of many familiar building blocks: variables, operators, conditionals, loops, expressions, built-in properties, subroutines, and native functions.

Accessing ActionScript commands

All of the ActionScript commands are found in the Flash interface in the Action booklets or plus (+) button menu of the Actions panel. However, assembling actions with one another is not something Flash 8 automatically performs unless you use the Behaviors panel to add interactive functionality to your movie elements. Although it is beyond the scope of this chapter to fully explain fundamental programming principles, we can give you a sense of the whole of ActionScript by providing an organized reference to each of its parts.

Actions list organization in the Actions panel

In the Actions panel, you can cut, copy, and paste code within the Script pane from one area of your movie to another using Ctrl+X (⌘+X), Ctrl+C (⌘+C), and Ctrl+V (⌘+V), respectively. You are free to select partial or entire lines of code, and modify the code in any way you want. With Flash 8, you can even edit your code in your preferred text editor! If you want to create your own programming macros in other programming applications, you can write your scripts outside of the Flash authoring environment and copy the final code into the Actions panel when you're done.

Tip

To make sure that you don't have any syntax errors after reorganizing code, click the Check Syntax button in the Actions panel toolbar. Flash alerts you if there are scripting errors by placing messages in the Output panel.

Also, use the new Script Navigator in the lower-left corner of the Actions panel to quickly switch back and forth between keyframe or object code. For example, you can choose one frame in the Script Navigator, copy its code, and then switch to another frame to paste the code.

If you decide to write ActionScript with another editor, you can use the #include directive to load the contents of the external code file (.as) into the Flash movie at publish or export time. For more information on the #include directive, read Chapter 32, "Managing and Troubleshooting Flash Movies".

Using Esc Shortcut Keys for Actions

In Flash 8, you can choose to show or hide shortcut keys in the Actions panel. In the options menu of the Actions panel, choose Esc Shortcut Keys (if it's not already checked). Now, click the plus (+) menu of the Actions panel to access ActionScript commands. You'll notice that shortcut keys are defined after the name of the command. For example, loadMovie(), in the Global Functions ⇨ Browser/Network menu, has a keyboard shortcut of Esc+L+M. If you give the Actions panel focus and press the Esc key, then the L key, then the M key, the loadMovie action appears in the actions list of the Script pane, complete with placeholders for arguments. The shortcut will not work if you try to press the keys simultaneously — you must press the keys in sequence, as described in the previous example. Each key must be pressed and released before you type the following key(s) in the shortcut.

The Help panel

Don't know what the methods of the Sound object are? Need to see if the getVersion() function will work in a Flash Player 4–compatible movie? Flash 8 has conveniently nested everything related to help documentation in the Help panel. Among other items, the new Help panel contains all the syntax of the ActionScript language. You can access the Help panel in a few ways:

✦ Choose Help ⇨ Flash Help, or press F1.

✦ Click the Reference icon in the Actions panel.

✦ Right-click (or Control+click on Mac) an action in the left-hand Script pane of the Actions panel and choose View Help in the contextual menu.

We'll quickly show you how to use the new Help panel in an actual Flash document:

1. Open a new document (File ⇨ New).

2. Select frame 1 of Layer 1, and open the Actions panel by pressing F9.

3. Open the Global Functions booklet and click the Browser/Network booklet. Double-click the loadMovie action. The action will appear in the Script pane, as shown in Figure 24-1.

4. Select the text loadMovie in the Script pane, making sure *not* to select the (); portion of the action. Click the Help icon (that is, the circle with the question mark) at the top right of the Actions panel. The Help panel will open, displaying the definition for the loadMovie() action, as shown in Figure 24-2.

You can select other actions from the left pane of the Help panel and view their descriptions.

Tip   You can also print descriptions from the Help panel by choosing Print from the options menu at the top-right corner of the panel, or clicking the Printer icon in the Help panel toolbar.

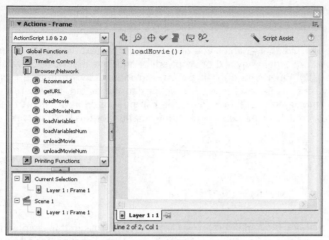

Figure 24-1: The Actions panel with a `loadMovie()` action in the Script pane

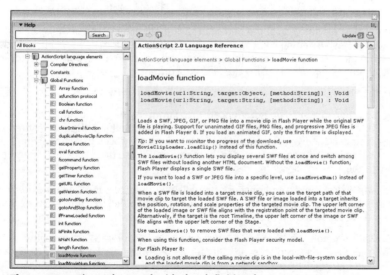

Figure 24-2: The Help panel with the definition for `loadMovie`

ActionScript 1.0 and 2.0

So why all the fuss about ActionScript now? Let's make one thing clear right away: For most Flash designers and developers, or rather for most of the work that's done in Flash, the graduation of ActionScript 1.0 to 2.0 may mean next to nothing at all. This isn't to say that ActionScript 2.0 should be ignored or is not a monumental leap forward for Flash programming — we simply want to calm or allay any fears you might have after reading about ActionScript 2.0 from other sources. If you've used ActionScript in Flash versions prior to MX 2004, then ActionScript 1.0 refers to the coding styles that those versions of the application used.

Using the #include Action

ActionScript has a processing directive that enables you to insert external text files (with an .as file extension). You can write ActionScript in any text or script editor and save that text separately from the Flash document file (.fla). When you publish a Flash movie file (.swf) from the Flash document, Flash 8 will retrieve the .as file and insert the actions to the action list where the `#include` action was issued. For example, the following code can be written in a `contact.as` file, which, as the name implies, contains a person's contact information for the Flash movie:

```
var contactName:String = "Joseph Farnsworth";
var contactStreet:String = "675 Locust Street";
var contactCity:String = "Chicago";
var contactState:String = "IL";
var contactPhone:String = "312-555-1342";
var contactEmail:String = "jfarnsworth@mycompany.com";
```

Note that this code is written in the ActionScript 2.0 format, which we discuss in this chapter. In a Flash document, you could insert this code into a keyframe of the Main Timeline (or a Movie Clip timeline) by using the `#include` action. You can use the `#include` action within any Flash event handler including keyframe, Button instance, `onClipEvent`, and so on:

```
#include "contact.as"
```

Make sure you do *not* insert a semicolon at the end of the `#include` line. Think of the `#include` action as a special tag for Flash 8, letting it know that it should replace the `#include` line of code with all the code within the referred file. The following code will result in a "malformed" error in the Output window, upon testing or publishing the Flash document:

```
#include "contact.as";
```

Why is the `#include` action useful? For experienced programmers, the `#include` command gives you the freedom to write ActionScript in any text editor. You can define entire code libraries of custom functions. You can then reuse the .as files from movie to movie. In ActionScript 2.0, custom classes *must* be defined in a separate .as file, but they do not use the `#include` directive; rather, AS2 classes use the `import` keyword.

Note that the `#include` action is executed only upon publishing or testing the Flash movie. You cannot upload .as files to your Web server for "live" insertion of Flash ActionScript. Anytime you change the .as file, you will need to republish your Flash movie file (.swf).

You can find more information on the `#include` action in Chapter 32, "Managing and Troubleshooting Flash Movies." As we discuss in Chapter 3, "Planning Flash Projects," you can track all of the .as files in the Project panel of Flash Professional 8 as well.

ActionScript 2.0 introduces a couple of major structural changes to the way in which you can code Flash ActionScript. To begin with, it uses strong data typing. You'll learn more about data typing in Chapter 26, "Using Functions and Arrays," but for now, know that ActionScript 2.0 imposes some rules on how you can assign values to variables, functions, and other objects in your code. Unless you're creating code that uses custom classes and object-oriented programming concepts such as inheritance and prototypes, you won't really need to worry about whether your code will work as ActionScript 2.0 code. Another big change with ActionScript

2.0 is case-sensitivity. Prior to Flash Player 7, most ActionScript terms were case-insensitive, meaning you could refer to object references or variables with varying cases, such as:

```
var firstName = "Robert";
var lastName = "Reinhardt";
var fullName = firstName + " " + lastName;
```

In ActionScript 1.0, you could have used the following code as the last line, without receiving an error:

```
var fullName = firstname + " " + lastname;
```

However, in ActionScript 2.0, that same line of code would be incorrect because `firstname` and `lastname` are not using the same case as the original variables.

Why should the distinction between ActionScript 1.0 and 2.0 even be an issue? For starters, when you publish a Flash movie for Flash Player 6, 7, or 8, you need to decide how Flash 8 will compile the ActionScript code in your document. In the Publish Settings dialog box, you can choose which ActionScript version to publish in the Flash tab. Unless directed otherwise, you'll publish most of the Flash movies for Part VII of this book as ActionScript 2.0, even though it pretty much looks and feels like ActionScript 1.0.

One Part of the Sum: ActionScript Variables

In any scripting or programming language, you will need some type of "memory" device — something that can remember the values and properties of objects or significant data. This type of memory device is referred to as a *variable*.

Variables are named storage places for changeable pieces of data (numbers and letters, for starters). One of the first obstacles for designers learning a scripting language is the concept that variable names in and of themselves have no meaning or value to the computer. Remember that the computer can't perform anything unless you tell it to. Even though any given scripting language has a certain set of built-in properties and functions, variables can simplify your scripting workload by creating shortcuts or aliases to other elements of the ActionScript language. One prime example of a "shortcut" variable is the pathname to a deeply nested Movie Clip instance, such as:

```
_root.birdAnim.birdHouse.birdNest.birdEgg
```

truncated to a variable named `mcEgg` as:

```
var mcEgg = _root.birdAnim.birdHouse.birdNest.birdEgg;
```

If you wanted to declare `mcEgg` in ActionScript 2.0 code, you would use the following syntax, which types the `mcEgg` variable as a `MovieClip` object:

```
var mcEgg:MovieClip = _root.birdAnim.birdHouse.birdNest.birdEgg;
```

Once `mcEgg` is declared and given a value, you can reuse it without referring to the lengthy path name, as in:

```
with(mcEgg){
    gotoAndPlay("start");
}
```

The important concept here is that you could just as easily have given mcEgg a different name, such as myPath, or robPath, or whatever word(s) you'd like to use. As long as the syntax and formatting of the expression is correct, you have nothing to worry about.

Another example of a variable that stores path information is the URL to a Web resource, such as a server-side script. Oftentimes, you may have different server URLs for testing and deployment. Instead of changing the URL in every action of the Flash document, you can use a variable name. That way, you only need to change your variable's value once. In the following sample code, a variable named serverURL is set to the actual URL you want to access. You then refer to that serverURL name in other actions, such as getURL().

```
var serverURL = "http://www.flashsupport.com/";
getURL(serverURL);
```

Note   Variables in ActionScript are "typed," meaning that their value is explicitly set to be either a string, number, Boolean, or object. When working with variables, you must therefore know what data type the value is. We discuss data typing in Chapter 26, "Using Functions and Arrays."

Variables in ActionScript are attached to the timeline of the movie or Movie Clip instance on which they are created. If you create a variable x on the Main Timeline, that variable is available for other scripting actions on that timeline. However, from other Movie Clip timelines, the variable is not directly accessible. To access the value of a variable on another timeline (such as a Movie Clip instance), enter the target path to the clip instance in which the variable resides, a dot (.); then enter the variable name. For instance, this statement sets the variable foo to be equal to the value of the variable hitCount in the Movie Clip instance named mcBall:

```
var foo = mcBall.hitCount;
```

This statement, on the other hand, sets the variable foo to be equal to the value of a variable named hitCount on the Main Timeline:

```
var foo = _root.hitCount;
```

Tip   Variables in ActionScript 1.0 are not case-sensitive and cannot start with a number. Variables in ActionScript 2.0 are case-sensitive.

Flash Player 6 introduced a new location to store variables, independent of any timeline: _global. You can access global variables from any object or timeline in the Flash movie — hence the name global. You only need to specify the _global path to assign a value to the global variable. To read a global variable, you simply specify the name. For example, on frame 1 of the Main Timeline, you can specify the following ActionScript in the Actions panel:

```
_global.firstName = "George";
```

Then, if you wanted to use the firstName variable within a Movie Clip instance's timeline, you simply refer to the variable firstName. The following code will insert the firstName variable into a TextField object named user. This code would be placed inside of a Movie Clip symbol containing the TextField object:

```
user.text = firstName;
```

Even though the _global path is not specified, Flash Player 6 or 7 looks for a variable named firstName on the current timeline. If a variable by that name does not exist on the current timeline, Flash Player 6 looks in _global for the variable and returns any value for that variable.

Caution You need to publish your Flash documents as Flash Player 6 or higher movies to use the _global path. The global namespace can be used in ActionScript 1.0 or 2.0. Also, many experienced Flash developers frown upon the use of _global within a Flash document; overuse or overreliance on global variables can result in code that is difficult to debug. Why? Because the variable is global, you don't necessary know which element is setting a new value to the global variable, because the variable is available everywhere. By localizing your variables to custom objects and classes in proper object-oriented programming, you can manage the storage of information within your Flash movies more easily.

String literals

In programmer speak, a string is any combination of alphanumeric characters. By themselves, they have no meaning. It is up to you to assign something meaningful to them. For example, giving a variable the name firstName doesn't mean much. You need to assign a value to the variable firstName to make it meaningful, and you can do something with it. For example, if firstName = "Susan", you could make something specific to "Susan" happen.

You can also use much simpler name/value pairs, such as i = 0, to keep track of counts. If you want a specific Movie Clip animation to loop only three times, you can increment the value of i by 1 (for example, i = i + 1, i += 1, and i ++ all do the same thing) each time the animation loops back to the start. Then, you can stop the animation when it reaches the value of 3.

Expressions

Flash uses the term *expression* to refer to two separate kinds of code fragments in ActionScript. An expression is either a phrase of code used to compare values in a Conditional or a Loop (these are known as *conditional expressions*), or a snippet of code that is interpreted at run time (these are known as *numeric expressions* and *string expressions*). We discuss conditional expressions later in this chapter.

Numeric and string expressions are essentially just segments of ActionScript code that are dynamically converted to their calculated values when a movie runs. For instance, suppose you have a variable, y, set to a value of 3. In the statement $x = y + 1$, the $y + 1$ on the right side of the equal sign is an expression. Hence, when the movie runs, the statement $x = y + 1$ actually becomes $x = 4$, because the value of y (which is 3) is retrieved (or "interpreted") and the calculation $3 + 1$ is performed. Numeric and string expressions are an extremely potent part of ActionScript because they permit most of the parameters used in actions to be based on mathematical calculations and external variables rather than requiring fixed information. Consider these two examples:

✦ The parameter of a gotoAndPlay() action could be set as an expression that returns a random number in a certain range, sending the movie to a random frame:

```
this.gotoAndPlay(Math.round(Math.random()*100));
```

✦ The URL option in a getURL() action could be made up of a variable that indicates a server name and a literal string, which is the file path:

```
var serverName = "http://localhost/";
var filePath = "resources/showRecent.cfm";
getURL(serverName + filePath);
```

As we mentioned in an earlier section, to change all the URLs in your movie from a staging server to a live server, you'd just have to change the value of the server variable. So, to change the latter example's code for a live Web server, you'd simply change the serverName variable, as the following code demonstrates:

```
var serverName = "http://www.flashsupport.com/";
```

All of the other lines of code would stay the same, because you only need to change the server location for the live Web site.

Anywhere that you see the word "expression" in any action options, you can use an interpreted ActionScript expression to specify the value of the option.

To use a string inside an expression, simply add quotation marks around it. Anything surrounded by quotation marks is taken as a literal string. For example, the conditional if (status == ready) wrongly checks whether the value of the variable status is the same as the value of the nonexistent variable ready. The correct conditional would check whether the value of status is the same as the string "ready" by quoting it, as in if (status == "ready").

You can even have expressions that indirectly refer to previously established variables. In ActionScript, you can use the dot syntax (and array access operators) to indirectly refer to variables, or you can use Flash 4's eval() function (to maintain backward compatibility).

We like to use the phrase "setting and getting" to help beginners understand how equations and expressions work in ActionScript code. An equation is any line of code that sets an object or variable to a new value. The order of syntax terms can be confusing to designers and developers new to code writing. Do you specify a value first? How do you know where to insert the equal sign (=)? If you remember the phrase "setting and getting," you'll know how to write basic equations. The variable you want to set (or assign a new value) is always on the left side of the equation, while the new value is always on the right:

```
what you want to set = the value you want to get
```

For example, if you wanted to set a variable named currentTime to the amount of time that has elapsed since the Flash movie started playing in the Flash Player, you would place currentTime on the left side of the equation and place the actual value of the time on the right side:

```
current time in the movie = the number of milliseconds that have elapsed
```

Translated into actual code, this would be:

```
var currentTime = getTimer();
```

Again, another important aspect of variables to remember is that the name of a variable is quite arbitrary. What we called currentTime could just as well be named myTime, movieTime, elapsedTime — or whatever you want to call it. As long as you consistently refer to your variable's name in subsequent ActionScript code, everything will work as expected.

Array access operators

If you have a variable called name_1 declared on the Main Timeline, you can write the expression _root["name_" + "1"] to refer to the value of name_1. How is this useful? If you have more than one variable, but their prefixes are the same (for example, name_1, name_2, name_3, and so on), you can write an expression with two variables as a generic statement to refer to any one of the previously established variables: _root["name_" + i], where i can be any predefined number. This type of expression is most commonly found in a code loop; you learn more about loops later in this chapter.

eval() function and Flash 4's Set Variable

If you want to use old-fashioned ActionScript to indirectly refer to variable names and values, you have two ways to go about it:

✦ Use the Set Variable action, specifying the variable name as a Slash-notated expression:

```
set("/name_" add i, "Robert Reinhardt");
```

✦ Use the eval() function, specifying the variable as an expression:

```
eval("_root.name_" add i) = "Robert Reinhardt";
```

Note   This usage is specific to Flash Player 4 and FlashLite 1.0/1.1 compatibility. Unless you are authoring movies to be compatible for these players, you should use the most current syntax.

Variables as declarations

In most scripting languages, you usually don't have to declare a variable without its value; that is, you don't need to say variable firstName and then address it again with a value. In Flash ActionScript, you don't need to pre-establish a variable in order to invoke it.

Note   As you start to code more complex scripts in ActionScript 2.0, such as creating custom classes, you do need to pre-declare variable names. As you're starting out with more basic scripts, you do not need to be so thorough with your code.

If you want to create a variable on the fly from a Movie Clip to the Main Timeline, you can. Most variables that you use in Flash will be declared in a timeline's keyframes. We'll show you how to create a couple of simple variables in a Flash document:

1. Open a new Flash document (File ➪ New). In the New Document dialog box, choose Flash Document and click OK.

2. Rename Layer 1 to **actions**.

3. Select frame 1 of the actions layer in the Timeline window, and open the Actions panel by pressing the F9 key. Type the following action in the Script pane (see Figure 24-3):

```
var firstName = "Franklin";
```

4. Save your Flash document as variable_frame.fla, and test it (Ctrl+Enter or ⌘+Enter). Choose Debug ➪ List Variables (Ctrl+Alt+V or Option+⌘+V). In the Output panel, you will see the following line of text:

```
Variable _level0.firstName = "Franklin"
```

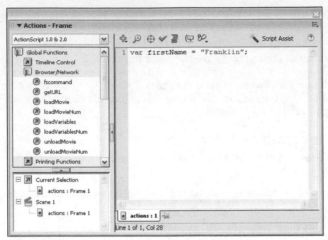

Figure 24-3: A variable declaration in the Actions panel

Tip

By default, the Output panel is grouped with the Property inspector, and you may find it awkward to look for ActionScript messages in this small area. You can undock the Output panel into its own window by clicking the options menu of the Property inspector (with the Output panel tab selected) and choosing Group Output with ⇨ New panel group.

As you can see in this example, the firstName variable is shown at _level0, which is the _root of the current Flash movie. All variables belong to a specific timeline or object.

On the CD-ROM

You can find the sample file, variable_frame.fla, in the ch24 folder of this book's CD-ROM.

Variables as text fields

Since Flash 4, text can be specified as *text fields*. A text field can be used as a dynamic text container whose content can be updated via ActionScript and/or the intervention of a server-side script (known in Flash 8 as *Dynamic text*), or it can accept input from the user (known in Flash 8 as *Input text*).

You can access a text field's properties by selecting the text field and opening the Property inspector. In the inspector, you can define the parameters of the text object, including its Var (for Variable) name and instance name.

Note

Text fields in Flash 8 are TextField objects. The instance name of a TextField object should be different from the Var name. In fact, we recommend that, as a general rule of thumb, you do not specify a Var name for text fields in Flash Player 6 or higher movies.

An Input text field is editable when the Flash movie is played in the Flash Player; the user can type text into the text field. This newly typed text becomes the value of the text field's Var name, or the text property of the text field. On a login screen, you can create an Input text field with an instance name `tLogin`, where the user enters his or her name, such as Joe. In ActionScript, this would be received as `tLogin.text = "Joe"`. Any text that you type into a text field during the authoring process will be that property's initial value.

To review this process of text fields and variable names, let's create a simple example:

1. Create a new Flash document (File ➪ New). In the New Document dialog box, choose Flash Document and click OK.

2. Rename Layer 1 to **textfield**.

3. In the Tools panel, choose the Text tool, and click once on the Stage. Extend the text field to accommodate at least five characters. In the Property inspector (Window ➪ Properties), choose Input Text in the drop-down menu located at the top-left corner of the inspector. Click the Show border button in the inspector. In the `<Instance Name>` field, assign the instance name **tFirstName**. In the Var field, assign the name **firstName_var**. Refer to Figure 24-4.

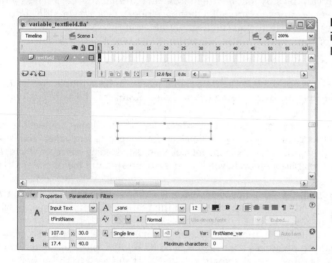

Figure 24-4: The Property inspector settings for the Input Text field

4. Save your Flash document as `variable_textfield.fla`, and test it (Ctrl+Enter or ⌘+Enter). In the Test Movie window, type your name into the `tFirstName` text field. Then, choose Debug ➪ List Variables. Among other information, you will see the following lines of text:

```
Variable _level0.firstName_var = "Holly"
Edit Text: Target="_level0.tFirstName"
    text = "Holly",
    variable = "firstName_var",
```

Note that this sample assumes that the name Holly was typed into the text field.

This simple exercise demonstrates how the Var assignment of a `TextField` object differs from the instance name assignment. The actual text displayed in the `TextField` object can be accessed in two ways: as a variable called `firstName_var`, or as a property of the `TextField` object, `tFirstName.text`. Dynamic text fields behave in the same manner as well.

Declaring Variables in ActionScript

There are several ways to establish, or declare, variables in a Flash movie. You can create them directly with ActionScript (or with `TextField` objects, as shown in the last section), load them from a text file or server-side script, or include them in HTML tags.

Using actions to define variables

The most common way to create a variable is to type the variable's name and value in the Script pane of the Actions panel, on a specific timeline's keyframe. Most basic variables will have values that are string literals.

Loading variables from a predefined source

You can also establish variables by loading them from an external source, such as a text file located on your Web server or even through a database query or a server-side script. By using the `loadVariables()` action, you can load variables in this fashion. There are three primary parameters for the `loadVariables()` action: URL, target, and variables:

```
loadVariables(url, target, [,variables]);
```

The *variables* parameter is optional. In the Help panel pages in the ActionScript Dictionary, any parameters displayed with surrounding left and right brackets ([ ]) are optional.

Note   There's more than one way to load data into Flash Player 5 and higher compatible movies. While you're learning the basics of ActionScript, we recommend that you use the `loadVariables()` function to familiarize yourself with data-loading concepts. If you're publishing Flash Player 6 or higher movies, you should learn the syntax of the `LoadVars` class.

URL specifies the source of the variables to be loaded. This can be a relative link to the variable source (you don't need to enter the full path of the resource). You can specify whether this URL value is a literal value (`"http://www.theMakers.com/cgi-bin/search.cfm"`) or an expression that uses a variable or a combination of variables (`serverURL + scriptPath + scriptApp`). If you want to point to a specific file, type its relative path and name here. If you want to access a database that returns dynamic data, insert the path to the script, such as `"http://www.domain.com/cgi-bin/search.pl"`.

The *target* parameter determines where the variables are to be loaded. You can send the name/value pairs to a level or a timeline target. If you want the variables to be available on the Main Timeline, use `_root` or `_level0`. You can also specify a Movie Clip target using a relative or absolute address. To load to the current Movie Clip (the one initiating the `loadVariables` action), use the target `this`.

The last option is *variables*, and this parameter specifies whether you are sending and loading (in other words, receiving) variables. If you want to load variables from a static source, such as a text file, you should omit this parameter. If you are sending a query to a database-driven engine, then you may need to specify either `"GET"` or `"POST"`. Note that the use of `loadVariables()` in the `GET` or `POST` method means that you are sending variables declared on the active timeline to the specified URL, which, in turn, will send name/value pairs back to the Flash movie.

The formatting of name/value pairs is standard URL-encoded text. If you want to encode name/values in a text file (or a database), you need to use the following format:

```
variable=value&variable=value...
```

Basically, in URL-encoded text, name/value pairs are joined by an ampersand (&). To join multiple terms in a value, use the plus (+) symbol to add a single whitespace character between the terms, as in:

```
name1=Joe+Smith&name2=Susan+Deboury
```

There are several ways to load data into a Flash movie. Flash Player 5 introduced the XML object, and Flash Player 6 introduced the LoadVars object, both of which give you more control over dynamic data. The LoadVars object is discussed in Chapter 29, "Sending Data In and Out of Flash." You also learn more about URL-encoded text in that chapter.

Sending variables to URLs

You can also send variables to a URL by using the getURL() action. Any name/value pairs that are declared on the active timeline will be sent along with the getURL() action if a variable send method is defined (GET or POST). Note that getURL() is only used to send variables out of a Flash movie — it will not retrieve or load any subsequent name/value pairs. If you use a getURL() action on a Movie Clip timeline as follows:

```
var firstName = "Robert";
getURL("/cgi-bin/form.cgi", "_blank", "GET");
```

the Flash movie will send the following request to your server:

```
http://www.server.com/cgi-bin/form.cgi?firstName=Robert;
```

The output of the form.cgi script would be opened in a new browser window ("_blank").

Any terms that follow a question mark (?) in a URL are called a *query string*. The name/value pairs in a query string are usually provided as an input or a filter to a server-side script.

Establishing variables with HTML

You can also send variables to Flash movies in the <embed> and <object> tags that call the Flash movie. In the SRC attribute of <embed> or the param name="movie" subtag of the <object> tag, attach the name/value pairs to the end of the Flash movie filename, separated by a question mark (?).

```
<object ... >
<param name="movie" value="flash.swf?name=Rob" />
<embed src="flash.swf?name=Rob" ... />
```

This method works with Flash Player 4 or later movies. However, Flash Player 6 and higher can recognize the HTML attribute flashvars. Now, you can specify longer strings of name/value pairs that will be declared in the Flash movie as soon as it loads into the Flash Player. The previous method that we showed is limited to strings that are about 1,024 characters long (depending on the Web browser), which include the movie's full URL. With the newer flashvars attribute, you don't need to rely on the URL of the movie. Here's an example of declaring a few variables with the flashvars attribute:

```
<object ...>
<param name="movie" name="flash.swf" />
<param name="flashvars"
name="firstName=Gregory&lastName=Smith&address=1234+Hollywood+Way" />
<embed src="flash.swf"
flashvars="firstName=Greg&lastName=Smith&street=1234+Broadway" ... />
```

In practical use, you would not likely hard code the name/value pairs directly into the HTML document. You can use client-side JavaScript or server-side scripting (such as PHP, ASP.NET, or ColdFusion) to dynamically "write" the name/value pairs into the HTML document before it is served to the user's Web browser.

Creating Expressions in ActionScript

You can write expressions either by manually typing in the primary option fields of ActionScript commands, or by dragging and dropping actions from action booklets in the Actions panel. There are no scripting wizards in Flash; Flash 8 does not automatically script anything for you (not counting components, which already include many lines of code to perform specific tasks for you). However, Flash provides you with booklets of operators, objects, and functions available in the ActionScript language.

Operators

Operators perform combinations, mathematical equations, and value comparisons. See Table 24-1 for a list of common operators in the ActionScript language.

General and numeric operators

These operators are used for common mathematical operations of adding, subtracting, multiplying, and dividing. You can also use these operators to compare numeric values, such as > or <.

```
if (results > 1)
name = "Robert";
_root["name_" + i] = "Ezra";
```

String operators

To join two String values to another in Flash Player 5 or higher movies, use the + string operator, such as:

```
var fullName = firstName + " " + lastName;
```

The Flash Player 4-specific operator add joins one value with another value or expression. If you want to concatenate two variables to create a new variable, use the add string operator. Again, this syntax should be used only for Flash Player 4 or FlashLite 1.0/1.1 movies.

```
set ("fullName", firstName add " " add lastName);
```

Logical operators

These operators join several expressions to create conditions. We discuss these further in the "Checking conditions: if . . . else actions" section of this chapter.

```
// Flash Player 5 and later syntax below

if (results > 1 && newResults < 10){
    // do something...
}

// Flash Player 4 syntax below

if (results > 1 and newResults < 10){
    // do something...
}
```

Table 24-1 describes the ActionScript operators available in Flash 4 and higher syntax.

Table 24-1: ActionScript Operators

Flash 5+	Flash 4	Description
+	+	Adds number values (all player versions) and joins, or *concatenates*, strings in Flash Player 5 and later.
-	-	Subtracts number values.
*	*	Multiplies number values.
/	/	Divides number values.
=	=	Equals; used for assignment of variables, properties, methods, and so on in Flash Player 4 or later.
==	=	Numeric operator: Is equal to; used for comparison in if/else . . . else if conditions.
!=	<>	Numeric operator: Does not equal.
<	<	Less than.
>	>	Greater than.
<=	<=	Less than or equal to.
>=	>=	Greater than or equal to.
( )	( )	Groups operations together, as in x = (x+y) * 3;.
" "	" "	Indicates that the enclosed value should be interpreted as a string, not as an expression.
==	eq	String operator: Is equal to; for example, if (name == "derek") or if (name eq "derek").

Continued

Table 24-1 *(continued)*

Flash 5+	Flash 4	Description
=== (F6+)	N/A	Strict equality operator; both of the compared values must be the same data type and value. This operator is compatible only with Flash Player 6 or higher.
!=	ne	String operator: Is not equal to.
!== (F6+)	N/A	Strict inequality operator; both of the compared values must have different values and data types. This operator is compatible only with Flash Player 6 or higher.
<	lt	Alphabetically before; if the strings compared have multiple characters, the first character determines the alphabetical position.
>	gt	Alphabetically after.
<=	le	Alphabetically before or the same as.
>=	ge	Alphabetically after or the same as.
+	add	Joins two strings together or adds a string to a variable.
&&	and	Logical comparison; requires that two or more conditions be met in a single comparison.
||	or	Logical comparison; requires that one of two or more conditions be met in a single comparison.
!	not	Logical comparison; requires that the opposite of a condition be met in a single comparison.

Checking conditions: if . . . else actions

Conditions lie at the heart of logic. To create an intelligent machine (or application), you need to create a testing mechanism. This mechanism (called a *conditional*) needs to operate on rather simple terms as well. Remember the true/false tests you took in grade school? if/else statements work on a similar principle: If the condition is true, execute a set of actions. If the condition is false, disregard the enclosed actions and continue to the next condition or action.

You can simply create isolated if statements that do not employ else (or else if) statements. Solitary if statements are simply ignored if the condition is false. else statements are used as a default measure in case the tested condition proves false. else if statements continue to test conditions if the previous if (or else if) was false. Refer to the following examples for more insight.

✦ **Basic** if **statement.** The code between the curly braces is ignored if the condition is false.

```
if (condition is true){
     then execute this code
}
```

✦ **Extended** `if...else if...else` **statement.** If the first condition is true, the code immediately after the first condition is executed and the remaining `else if` and `else` statements are disregarded. However, if the first condition is not true, the second condition is tested. If the second condition is true, its code executes and all other statements in the `if` group are ignored. If all conditions prove false, the code between the curly braces of the final `else` is executed:

```
if ( first condition is true){
    then execute this code
} else if (second condition is true){
    then execute this code
} else {
    otherwise, execute this code
}
```

In production, you could have an `if/else` structure that assigned the value of one variable based on the value of another, such as:

```
if (x == 1){
    name = "Margaret";
} else if (x == 2){
    name = "Michael";
} else {
    name = "none";
}
```

Caution   Do not use a single = sign in a condition, as this actually sets the variable's value. For example, if you wrote `if (x = 1){}`, ActionScript actually sets x = 1, and does not check whether x's value is equal to 1. Moreover, the condition always evaluates to `true`. In our experience, many beginners make this common mistake in their ActionScript code. We can't emphasize enough the importance of making sure you use an == operator in `if` and `else if` expressions for "is equal to" comparisons.

You can add an `if` statement in ActionScript by choosing the `if` action from the plus (+) button in the toolbar of the Actions panel, or by selecting it from the Statements ⇨ Conditions/Loops booklet. Between the parentheses of the `if()` statement, shown as the term *condition* in the code hint, enter the expression that identifies what circumstance must exist for the actions in your conditional to be executed. Remember that, in your expression, literal strings must be quoted, and the == operator must be used for string or numeric comparisons. To add an `else` clause, position the text cursor after the closing curly brace (}) of the `if()` statement, and then double-click the `else` or `else if` action in the Statements ⇨ Conditions/Loops booklet.

Note   There's nothing stopping you from just typing the actions directly in the Script pane as well. Use the booklets as a guide at first, to learn about the choices you have available.

Tip   If you find it confusing when to use parentheses or curly braces ({ }) with your code, use the shortcut keys to create code blocks such as `if` statements. With your cursor active in the Script pane, type Esc+I+F in sequence to create the `if` statement with the proper set of parentheses and curly braces.

You can join two conditions using logical compound operators such as and (&&), or (||), or not (!), as in:

```
if (results >1 && newResults < 10){
    gotoAndPlay ("end");
} else if (results > 1 ! newResults < 10) {
    gotoAndPlay ("try_again");
}
```

In this sample code, the first if statement has two expressions — both need to be true in order for the gotoAndPlay("end"); code to execute. If both are not true, the else if condition executes. If the first condition is true *and* the second condition is not true, the gotoAndPlay("try_again"); code executes. If neither the if nor the else if condition is true, then no code is executed.

We'll take a look at a step-by-step example of if statements in the exercise at the end of this chapter.

Branching conditions with switch() and case

In ActionScript, you can also use switch() and case statements. switch() and case can replace extended if and else if actions. Instead of declaring a true/false expression (as with if statements), switch() uses an expression that can return any value — you are not limited to true and false conditions with switch(). In pseudo-code, a switch() code structure looks like this:

```
test a value
    if the value equals this expression
        then execute this code
    if the value equals this expression
        then execute this code
    if none of the expressions match the value
        then execute this code
end test
```

In the previous code example, one or more if statements (called case clauses) can execute. Meaning, the tested value can execute more than one segment of code nested within the clauses. You could translate the previous pseudo-code into the following ActionScript code:

```
var currentFrame = _root._currentframe;
switch(currentFrame){
    case 10:
        helpBox.gotoAndStop("products");
    case 20:
        helpBox.gotoAndStop("services");
    case 30:
        helpBox.gotoAndStop("contact");
    default:
        helpBox.gotoAndStop("error");
}
```

In the previous code example, although it's only possible for currentFrame to equal one value, the default clause will also execute — regardless of the value of currentFrame. However, you may not want to execute the default clause (or multiple case clauses). In this situation, you need to use the break action to "escape" the switch() action. The break action prevents subsequent clauses from being evaluated.

In the following code, only one clause can execute:

```
var currentFrame = _root._currentframe;
switch(currentFrame){
    case 10:
        helpBox.gotoAndStop("products");
        break;
    case 20:
        helpBox.gotoAndStop("services");
        break;
    case 30:
        helpBox.gotoAndStop("contact");
        break;
    default:
        helpBox.gotoAndStop("error");
}
```

You can use switch() actions for many other situations. If you wanted to make a card game in Flash, you could use a switch() expression to pick a card suit based on a random number:

```
1.  var suitNum = Math.round(Math.random()*3);
2.  switch(suitNum){
3.      case 0:
4.          suit = "diamonds";
5.          break;
6.      case 1:
7.          suit = "spades";
8.          break;
9.      case 2:
10.         suit = "hearts";
11.         break;
12.     case 3:
13.         suit = "clubs";
14.         break;
15. }
16. cardFace.gotoAndStop(suit);
```

In this code, a random number is picked (line 1) and used as an expression in the switch() action (line 2). The random number (represented as a variable named suitNum) will then be matched to a case clause. The matching clause will set a variable named suit to equal a specific card suit and exit the switch() action (lines 3 through 15). A Movie Clip instance named cardFace will go to and stop on a frame named after one of the card suits (line 16).

Tip   In a working example of a card game, the switch() code for the suit matching would occur within a function. We discuss functions in Chapter 26, "Using Functions and Arrays."

Note   The switch(), case, and default actions can be used in Flash Player 4 or higher movies. Even though the switch() syntax was only introduced in Flash MX/Flash Player 6, the ActionScript will be compiled to be compatible with Flash Player 4 or 5 if you choose these versions in the Version menu of the Publish Settings' Flash tab.

Loops

A *loop* is a container for a statement or series of statements repeated as long as a specified condition exists. A basic loop has three parts: the condition, the list of statements to be repeated, and a counter update. There are four types of loops in ActionScript:

✦ while

✦ do...while

✦ for

✦ for...in

Each of these loop types has a specific use. Depending on the repetitive actions you wish to loop, you need to decide how best to accommodate your code with loop actions.

Caution   These types of code-based loops do not update the contents of the stage with each pass of a loop execution. If you want to automate changes over time on the stage through code, you'll need to use an onEnterFrame() event handler or a setInterval() function. You learn more about these types of actions in Chapter 25, "Controlling Movie Clips," and Chapter 31, "Creating a Game in Flash."

while (*condition*) { *actions* }

In this loop type, the condition of the loop is evaluated first, and, if it is true, the actions within the curly braces are executed. The actions will loop indefinitely (causing a script error) unless there is a way out of the loop — a counter update. A counter update will increment (or decrement) the variable used in the while condition. Here you see a breakdown of a typical while loop. Note that a variable used in the condition is usually set just before the while action is executed.

```
var count = 1;  // Initial variable
while (count <= 10){  // Condition
  _root["clip_" + count]._xscale = 100/count; // Statements to be repeated
  count = count + 1; // Counter update
}   // Termination of loop
```

In this example, a variable named count starts with a value of 1. The first time the while action executes, count's value is less than (or equal to) 10. Therefore, the actions within the curly braces are executed. The first action in the loop uses the count value to form the name of a Movie Clip instance, clip_1, and alter its X Scale property by a value of 100/1 (which is equal to 100). Then the count variable is incremented by 1, giving it a new value of 2. The while condition is then reevaluated.

The second time the while action is executed, count's value, 2, is still less than (or equal to) 10. Therefore, the actions within the curly braces are executed again. This time, however, the first action in the loop will address the clip_2 instance's X Scale property, and make that property's value 50 (100/2 = 50). Then, count will be incremented by 1, giving it a new value of 3. Again, the while condition is reevaluated.

The while condition will continue to execute its nested actions until count exceeds a value of 10. Therefore, clip_1 through clip_10 will show a decrease in X Scale.

do { *actions* } while (*condition*);

This type of loop is very similar to the while loop we discussed previously, with one important exception: The actions in the do{} nesting are always executed at least once. In a do . . . while loop, the condition is evaluated after the actions in the loop are executed. If the while condition is true, the actions in the do{} nesting will be executed again. If the while condition is false, the loop will no longer execute.

```
count = 1;  // Initial variable
do{  // do loop
  _root["clip_" + count]._xscale = 100/count; // Statements to be repeated
  count = count + 1; // Counter update
} while (count <= 1); // Condition
```

In this example, the actions within the do{} nesting will execute automatically without checking any condition. Therefore, the X Scale of clip_1 will be set to 100, and the count value will increase by 1, giving it a new value of 2. After the actions execute once, the condition is checked. Because the value of count is not less than (or equal to) 1, the loop does not continue to execute.

for (*initialize; condition; next*) { *actions* }

The for loop is a supercondensed while loop. Instead of assigning, checking, and reassigning a variable action in three different actions, a for loop enables you to define, check, and reassign the value of a counter variable.

```
for(i = 1; i <= 10; i++){ // Initial variable value, condition, and update
  _root["clip_" + i]._xscale = 100/i; // Statements to be repeated
}  // Termination of loop
```

This for loop does exactly the same thing as the while loop example we used earlier. When the loop is started, the variable i is given a starting value of 1. A condition for the loop is specified next, i <= 10. In this case, we want the loop to repeat the nested actions until the value of i exceeds 10. The third parameter of the for loop, i++, indicates that i's value should be increased by 1 with each pass of the loop. Note that this parameter can use ++ (to increase by 1) or -- (to decrease by 1) operators. You can also use expressions such as i = i*2 for the update.

for (*variableIterant* in *object*) { *actions* }

The final type of loop, for . . . in, is the most complex looping mechanism. A for . . . in loop does not need a condition statement. Rather, this loop works with a find-and-replace keyword mechanism. Basically, a *variableIterant* is declared, which is simply a placeholder for a property or position index within an object or array, respectively. For every occurrence of the variableIterant, the actions within the for . . . in {} nesting will be executed. The for . . . in loop can only be used with objects and arrays, and even then, not all properties of this element can be enumerated.

```
for(name in _root){  // Placeholder and object
  if(_root[name] instanceof MovieClip){ // Check the data type of the object
    _root[name]._xscale = 50; // Statements to be repeated
  } // end if statement
} // Termination of loop
```

In the preceding code example, the term name is used to designate a property of the _root timeline. In this case, we want to change all Movie Clip instances on the Main Timeline to a 50 percent X Scale value. We don't need to specify the actual target paths of each individual instance—the for . . . in loop will search for all instances on the Main Timeline, apply the change, and exit the loop.

Although this might look a bit confusing, it can be more helpful than you can imagine. Have you ever had a bunch of nested Movie Clip instances that all needed to play at the same time? In Flash 4, you would have had to use several tellTarget(){} actions, each one specifying the target path. You could use a while loop to shorten the lengthy code, but, even still, you would need to list the specific parts of the each Movie Clip path, as in:

```
count = 1;
while(count <= 10){
    path = eval("_root.clip_" + count);
    tellTarget(path){
        play();
    }
    count++;
}
```

In Flash 4, the preceding code block would tell clip_1 through clip_10 to start playing. But what if you didn't know (or care to remember) all the paths to several differently named Movie Clip instances? For example, if you had a Movie Clip instance named nestAnim with several nested Movie Clip instances with different names (for example, squareAnim, triangleAnim, and circleAnim), you would have to specifically name these instances as targets. In Flash Player 5 or higher, the for . . . in loop lets you control any and all nested Movie Clip instances simultaneously:

```
for(name in nestAnim){
    nestAnim[name].play();
}
```

With just three lines of code, all Movie Clip instances in the nestAnim Movie Clip instance will start to play. How? Remember that the variableIterant name is simply a placeholder for a property of the nestAnim Movie Clip object. The for . . . in loop will find every occurrence of an instance inside of nestAnim. And the word name has no significance. You could use a variableIterant myName, and everything would still work fine. Think of the variableIterant as a wildcard in file searches or directory listings in MS-DOS or UNIX:

```
nestAnim[*].play();
```

Although this syntax won't work with ActionScript, it does illustrate the processing of a for . . . in loop. Everything and anything that is playable on the nestAnim timeline will play.

On the CD-ROM   Check out the mcPlay.fla and forInLoop.fla files, located in the ch24 folder of the CD-ROM that accompanies this book.

break

The break action is not a type of loop—it is an action that enables you to quickly exit a loop if a subordinate condition exists. Suppose you wanted to loop an action that hides, at most, clip_1 through clip_10 (out of a possible 20 Movie Clip instances), but you want to have a variable control the overall limit of the loop, as upperLimit does in the following code block.

upperLimit's value could change at different parts of the presentation, but at no point do you want to hide more than clip_1 through clip_10. You could use a break action in a nested if action to catch this:

```
var count = 1;
while(count <= upperLimit){
    if(count > 10){
        break;
    }
    _root["clip_" + count]._visible = false;
    count++;
}
```

Tip You can use break statements to catch errors in your loops (such as during a debug process). However, you may want to check out Flash's breakpoint feature in the Actions and Debugger panels. For more information on this feature, read Chapter 32, "Managing and Troubleshooting Flash Movies."

continue

Like the break action, continue enables you to exit the execution of actions within a loop. However, a continue action won't exit the loop action. It simply restarts the loop (and continues evaluating the current condition). Usually, you will place a continue action with an if nest — otherwise, it will always interrupt the actions within the loop action. For example, if you wanted to omit a particular value from going through the loop actions, you could use the continue action to bypass that value. In the following code block, we hide clip_1 through clip_10, except for clip_5:

```
count = 1;
while(count <= 10){
    if(count == 5){
        count++;
        continue;
    }
    _root["clip_" + count]._visible = false;
    count++;
}
```

Adding a loop to your actions list

To create a loop, add one of the loop-type actions in the Actions panel, using the plus (+) button in the toolbar of the panel (or selecting it from the Statements ➪ Conditions/Loops booklet). With code hints enabled, replace the *condition* code hint term with an expression that describes the conditions under which the loop should continue repeating. Before the end of the loop, be sure to update whatever the loop relies on in order to continue, usually a counter. If you forget to update a counter, you will be stuck forever in the loop, and Flash will imperiously stop the script from continuing.

Loops in ActionScript are not appropriate for running background processes that listen for conditions to become true elsewhere in the movie. While a loop is in progress, the screen is not updated and no mouse events are captured, so most Flash actions are effectively not executable from within a loop. Loop actions are best suited to abstract operations such as string handling (for example, to check each letter of a word to see whether it contains an @ symbol) and dynamic variable assignment.

You should create loops to execute repetitive actions over time, which affect tangible objects in the movie, as repeating frames in Movie Clips. To create a permanently running process, make a Movie Clip with two keyframes. On the first frame, call the subroutine or add the statements that you want to execute; on the second frame use a `gotoAndPlay(1);` action to return to the first frame. Alternatively, you can use the `onClipEvent(enterFrame)`, `onEnterFrame()` handler, or `setInterval()` function to execute repetitive actions.

Properties

Properties are characteristics (such as width and height) of movies and Movie Clips that can be retrieved and set. You can use variables to store the current value of a given property, such as:

```
var xPos = _root._xmouse;
```

which stores the current X position of the mouse pointer (relative to the Stage coordinates of the Main Timeline) in the variable `xPos`.

Built-in functions

ActionScript contains a number of native programming commands known as *functions*. Among others, these functions include `getTimer()`, `getVersion()`, `parseFloat()`, `parseInt()`, `escape()`, and `unescape()`. It's beyond the scope of this chapter (and this book) to discuss the practical use of every new function and ActionScript element in Flash 8. We do, however, discuss many built-in functions throughout this part of the book.

Cross-Reference

Because ActionScript has expanded so much over recent versions of the Flash authoring tool, Robert Reinhardt and Joey Lott created a companion book series on Flash ActionScript to specifically address all the terms of the ActionScript language.

Creating and calling subroutines

Whether they're called functions, subroutines, or methods, most programming languages provide a mechanism for programmers to create self-contained code modules that can be executed from anywhere in a program. ActionScript supports subroutines by using the ActionScript `function` constructor. You can create functions on any timeline, and, just like Movie Clip instances, functions have absolute or relative paths that must be used to invoke them. For example, if you have the following function on a Movie Clip named `functions_mc`, located on the Main Timeline:

```
function makeDuplicate(target, limit){
    for(var i=1; i<=limit; i++){
        _root[target].duplicateMovieClip(target + "_" + i, i);
    }
}
```

then to invoke it from another timeline, you would execute it as follows:

```
_root.functions_mc.makeDuplicate("clip",5);
```

Executing it creates five duplicates of the Movie Clip instance named `clip`, naming the duplicates `clip_1`, `clip_2`, `clip_3`, `clip_4`, and `clip_5`.

Subroutines in Flash Player 4 or Flash Lite 1.0/1.1 Movies

To create a subroutine in Flash Player 4 or Flash Lite 1.0/1.1 movies, first attach an action or series of actions to a keyframe, preferably a keyframe that is never played on the timeline. Next, give that keyframe a label. That's it: you have a subroutine. To call your subroutine from any other keyframe or button, simply add a `call()` action, and then enter the name of the frame containing the subroutine as the parameter of the action. Use the following syntax: Start with the target path to the timeline on which the subroutine keyframe resides, enter a colon (`:`), and then enter the subroutine name (for example, `call ("/bouncingball:getRandom")`). When you call a subroutine, all the actions on the specified keyframe are executed. The subroutine must be present on the movie timeline (either as a keyframe or an embedded Movie Clip instance) for it to work.

Subroutines in Flash Player 4 movies do not accept passed parameters, nor do they return any values. To simulate passing and receiving variable values, set the necessary variable values in the action list that calls the subroutine before the frame is called, and then have the subroutine set other variables that can be retrieved afterward by any other actions.

Creating a Login Sequence with Variables

In this section, we show you how to use variables to create an interactive form in Flash that accepts or rejects user input. You will create two input text fields into which Web visitors will type a username and password. Using ActionScript, you will check the values of the entered data with predefined name/value pairs.

Caution Do not use the following example for secure information over the Web. You could use a logon sequence like this in a Flash adventure game, or modify it to work in a Flash quiz. The logon information is not secure within the confines of a Flash movie file (.swf). This example is intended to demonstrate using conditional statements in a Flash movie.

1. Open a new Flash document.

2. Create two text fields on one layer called **text fields**. Make each text field long enough to accommodate a single first name and/or password. For demonstration purposes, make the text in the text fields large—around 24 points. Make sure that you use a non-white fill color for the text.

3. Access the properties for each text field by selecting the text field (with the Selection tool) and opening the Property inspector, shown in Figure 24-5. In the Text Type drop-down menu, select the Input Text option for both fields. For the top text field, assign the instance name `tUserEnter`. For the other text field, assign the instance name `tPasswordEnter`, enable the Password option, and restrict the text length to eight characters. Do *not* assign a Var name to either text field.

4. Create a new layer and name it **static text**. Create text blocks that describe the two text fields, as shown in Figure 24-6. For example, make a text block with the word **Login:** and another one with the word **Password:**. Align these text blocks to the left of the text fields. Note that these text blocks do not need the Input text behavior; they should be Static text blocks.

Figure 24-5: The `tPasswordEnter` instance will be an input text field with the password option enabled and a restricted character length of eight characters.

Login: _____

Password: _____

Figure 24-6: Here you have four text areas: two Static text blocks on the left, and two Input text fields on the right. The Static text cannot be altered and/or "read" by ActionScript.

5. Create a new Movie Clip symbol (Ctrl+F8 or ⌘+F8), called **errorMessageClip**, that displays an error message, such as INVALID or LOGIN ERROR. Rename Layer 1 of its timeline to **actions**. On that layer, the first frame of the Movie Clip should be blank with a `stop();` frame action.

6. Create another layer called **labels**. On frame 2 of this layer, make a keyframe and assign it the label **start** in the <Frame Label> field of the Property inspector.

7. Then, create a new layer called **anim** and move it underneath the actions layer. On this layer, create a tweening animation of your message fading in and out (or scaling up and down, and so on). Start the Motion tween on frame 2 of the anim layer, underneath the `start` label of the actions layer. You'll need to make the message a Graphic symbol of its own in order to tween the alpha state. Add enough frames and keyframes to cycle this message animation twice. The very last frame of the animation should have a frame action (on the actions layer) `gotoAndStop(1);`. When you are finished with this step, your Movie Clip timeline should resemble the one shown in Figure 24-7.

8. In the main movie timeline (Scene 1), create a new layer called **mcError**. Drag the errorMessageClip symbol from the Library on to the Stage. Position it underneath the user and password text fields. Select the Movie Clip instance on the Stage and access its settings in the Property inspector. Assign the instance name of `mcError`.

Tip   In the Property inspector, you can temporarily change the symbol type of the `mcError` instance to a Graphic instance, and specify frame number 5 in the first field. This technique enables you to more accurately place a symbol that has an empty first frame. When you are finished positioning the instance, make sure you switch the instance behavior back to Movie Clip and rename the instance. Do not change the behavior of the symbol in the Library panel; this method only applies to the symbol behavior on an instance level.

9. Create another layer named **labels**. Assign a frame label of `start` to frame 1 of the labels layer. Add a keyframe to frame 10 of the labels layer, and label it **success**. Make sure all other layers on frame 10 have empty keyframes.

Figure 24-7: The errorMessageClip symbol contains an empty first frame and an animation that begins on the start label. This animation will play only if the user enters an incorrect login.

10. Extend all the layers to frame 20 by selecting frame 20 across all of the layers and pressing F5.

11. Make a new layer called **success** and place a text block and/or other graphics suitable for a successful login entry. It should only appear on frame 10, so if necessary, move its initial keyframe to that frame. When you're finished with the step, your Stage and Main Timeline should resemble Figure 24-8.

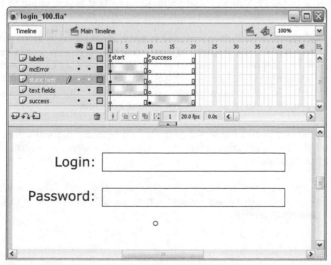

Figure 24-8: Your Main Timeline should have three key elements: a login frame, an error message Movie Clip, and a success frame.

12. Create a new layer on the Main Timeline called **button**, and make a Button symbol on it. You can make one of your own, or use one from Flash's Button library (Window ➪ Common Libraries ➪ Buttons). Place it to the right of or underneath the user and password fields. Select the Button symbol instance, and open the Actions panel. Add the following ActionScript code in the Script pane (note that the ⊃ character indicates a continuation of the same line of code; do not type or insert this character into your actual code):

```
on (release){
  if (tUserEnter.text == "Sandra" && ⊃
    tPasswordEnter.text == "zebra24"){
      this.gotoAndStop("success");
  } else {
      this.mcError.gotoAndPlay("start");
  }
}
```

You can change the compared values for the `tUserEnter.text` and `tPasswordEnter.text` values to whatever string value you desire.

13. Add an empty keyframe (F7) on frame 10 of the button layer.

14. On the Main Timeline, create an **actions** layer, and place it at the top of the layer order. On the first frame, add a `stop();` frame action.

15. Save the Flash document as `login_100.fla`. Test the movie's functionality with the Test Movie command (Control ➪ Test Movie).

Most login forms like this work with the Return or Enter key active to submit the information. However, this key press also has functionality in the Test Movie environment, so assign a key press to the Button symbol instance only *after* you have tested the initial ActionScript code. You can also choose Control ➪ Disable Keyboard Shortcuts in Test Movie mode to avoid any key press conflicts.

As you'll learn later in Chapter 26, a Button instance is not a great place to store a lot of code — it's usually better to place the majority of your code in a keyframe, contained within a function, or better yet, in a separate .as file that is specified in an `#include` directive. For now, however, as you're learning the basics of the ActionScript programming, don't feel pressured to take on too much too fast; make sure you understand the core principles of logic and conditions before you move on to additional programming topics.

See Chapter 32, "Managing and Troubleshooting Flash Movies" for more coverage of code debugging. You'll also find more information about using the Debugger panel and other useful features, such as breakpoints.

You can find the completed example, `login_100.fla`, in the `ch24` folder of this book's CD-ROM. You will also find other logon examples that use different methods to make the user name and password comparisons.

We'd like to know what you think about this chapter. Visit `www.flashsupport.com/feedback` to send us your comments.

Summary

✦ Before you begin to add complex interactivity to your Flash document, you need to break down the steps in the interactive process in a natural language that you can understand.

✦ After you know what you want your presentation to do, you can start to clarify the interactive steps and translate those steps into Flash-compatible actions.

✦ You can add ActionScript to your Flash document with the Actions panel. The Actions panel's Script pane is where you type or insert the actions that are invoked from elements in a Flash movie.

✦ ActionScript 2.0 can declare data types for each variable you use in a Flash movie. This practice, known as *strong typing*, enables you to catch errors within your ActionScript code more easily.

✦ Variables, a programming device, enable you to store property values, strings, paths, or expressions in order to reduce the redundancy of code and to simplify the process of computing information.

✦ Variables can be declared with actions, input, or dynamic text fields, or by loading them from an external data source, such as a server-side script, text document, or HTML-specified `flashvars` values.

✦ Expressions are equations that refer to a mathematical operation, a string concatenation, or an existing code object (another variable or object value).

✦ You can use `if...else if...else` actions to add intelligence to your interactive actions. These actions test a condition and execute a certain set of actions if the condition is true.

✦ Loop actions execute a given set of actions repeatedly until a loop condition is no longer true.

✦ ✦ ✦

Controlling Movie Clips

In Chapter 19, "Building Timelines and Interactions," we established the key role that Movie Clips have within the Flash movie structure. By having a timeline that plays separately from other timelines, Movie Clips enable multiple events to occur—independently or as part of an interaction with other Movie Clips. In this chapter, we explore how to manipulate Movie Clips beyond navigation actions such as `gotoAndPlay()` or `stop()`.

Movie Clips: The Object Overview

Since Flash 5, the implementation of ActionScript has resembled that of true object-oriented programming languages. Much like JavaScript, each element in a Flash movie has a data type. A data type is simply a category to which an element belongs. In the current version of ActionScript (including ActionScript 2.0), there are several data types available— `boolean`, `number`, `string`, `object`, `function`, and `movieclip`, among others.

Tip If you want to see a list of all data types in ActionScript, open the Actions panel (make sure code hints are turned on), and type `var a:`. After you type the colon (:), you'll see a list of supported data types.

For our purposes, a Movie Clip instance *is* an object, and we'll refer to it as such throughout Part VII of this book. An object is any element in Flash that has changeable and accessible characteristics *through ActionScript*. Objects can be user-defined (you create and name them) or predefined by the programming language. The `MovieClip` object is a predefined object, meaning that all of its characteristics are already described in the ActionScript language.

A `MovieClip` object is the same Movie Clip instance you've seen in previous chapters. Any instance of a Movie Clip is a unique object in ActionScript. However, you haven't treated it like an object in your scripting. Before we can proceed with a discussion of Movie Clips as Flash movie assets, you need to understand what predefined characteristics are available in the `MovieClip` object. See Figure 25-1 for more information.

In This Chapter

Understanding the `MovieClip` object

Working with properties of the `MovieClip` object

Creating Mouse Drag behaviors

Event models explained

Making sliders that dynamically change properties

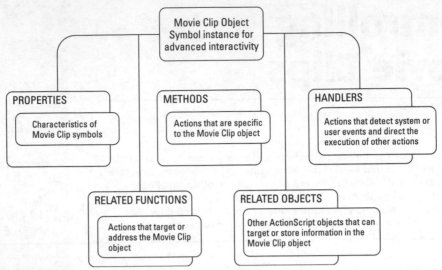

Figure 25-1: An overview of the `MovieClip` object

Movie Clip properties

Each Movie Clip instance has definable properties, or attributes, that control its appearance, size, and position. For example, you can move a Movie Clip instance to a new position on the stage by changing the value of its X or Y coordinate. This property in ActionScript is denoted as _x or _y, respectively. Some properties have read-only values, meaning these values can't be altered. One read-only property is _url, the value of which indicates the download location of the Movie Clip (or .swf file) such as `http://www.yourserver.com/swf/background.swf`. Figure 25-2 is a summary of the properties of the `MovieClip` object. For more information on each property, please refer to Table 25-1, "Flash Movie and Movie Clip Properties."

All properties are preceded by the underscore (_) character. In Table 25-1, each property has an "R" (as in "read") and/or "W" (as in "write") designation. All properties can be read, which means that you can retrieve that property's current value. The values of some properties can also be changed through ActionScript. The table represents these properties with the "W" designation.

Note In Flash Player 4 ActionScript, these properties were retrieved using the `getProperty()` action. Properties are altered using the `setProperty()` action. For Flash Player 5 or higher movies, you should avoid using these actions. Many free online Flash tutorials or samples at sites such as `FlashKit.com` will often be riddled with these deprecated actions.

Cross-Reference We don't review the more advanced properties of the `MovieClip` object in this chapter. For the most comprehensive coverage, refer to the `MovieClip` class coverage in the *Flash ActionScript Bible* series by Robert Reinhardt and Joey Lott (Wiley).

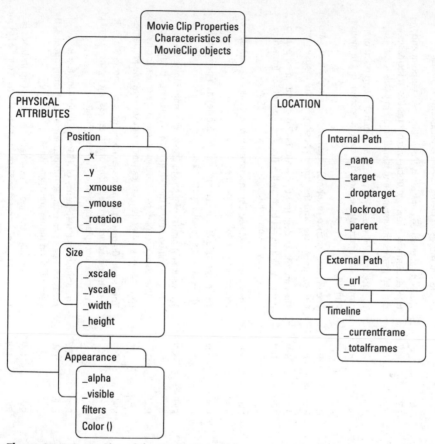

Figure 25-2: Properties of the `MovieClip` object

On the CD-ROM

Use the propInspector Movie Clip in the Library of the `property_inspector.fla` file, located in the `ch25` folder of this book's CD-ROM, to see the values of Movie Clip or Movie properties.

Movie Clip methods

Although the name might sound intimidating, don't be scared. Methods are simply actions that are attached to objects. As you now know, Movie Clips qualify as objects in ActionScript. A method looks like a regular action, except it doesn't (and, in most cases, can't) operate without a dot syntax reference to a target or an object:

Action: `gotoAndPlay("start");`

becomes

Method: `myMovieClip.gotoAndPlay("start");`

Table 25-1: Flash Movie and Movie Clip Properties

Category	Property	Timeline	Flash 4	Flash 5+	Flash 8	Definition
Position	_x	MC	RW	RW	RW	The horizontal distance between a Movie Clip's center point and the top-left corner of the stage upon which it resides. It increases as the clip moves to the right, and is measured in pixels.
		Movie	RW	RW	RW	
	_y	MC	RW	RW	RW	The vertical distance between a Movie Clip's center point and the top-left corner of the stage upon which it resides. It increases as the clip moves downward, and is measured in pixels.
		Movie	RW	RW	RW	
	_xmouse	MC	N/A	R	R	The horizontal distance (in pixels) between the zero point of a Movie Clip (or the Movie) and the current position of the mouse pointer.
		Movie	N/A	R	R	
	_ymouse	MC	N/A	R	R	The vertical distance (in pixels) between the zero point of a Movie Clip (or the Movie) and the current position of the mouse pointer.
		Movie	N/A	R	R	
	_rotation	MC	RW	RW	RW	The amount (in degrees) that a Movie Clip is rotated off plumb. It returns values set both by the Transform panel (or Transform tool) and by ActionScript.
		Movie	RW	RW	RW	
	_xscale	MC	RW	RW	RW	The width of a Movie Clip instance (or Movie) as a percentage of the parent symbol's actual size.
		Movie	RW	RW	RW	
Size	_yscale	MC	RW	RW	RW	The height of a Movie Clip instance (or Movie) as a percentage of the parent symbol's actual size.
		Movie	RW	RW	RW	
	_width	MC	R	RW	RW	The width (in pixels) of a Movie Clip or the main Movie Stage. It is determined not by the width of the canvas but by the width of the space occupied by elements on the Stage (meaning it can be less than or greater than the canvas width set in Movie Properties).
		Movie	R	R	R	
	_height	MC	R	RW	RW	The height (in pixels) of a movie clip or the main movie Stage. It is determined not by the height of the canvas but by the height of the space occupied by elements on the Stage.
		Movie	R	R	R	
Appearance	_alpha	MC	RW	RW	RW	The amount of transparency of a Movie Clip or Movie. It is measured as a percentage: 100 percent is completely opaque; 0 percent is completely transparent.
		Movie	RW	RW	RW	
	_visible	MC	RW	RW	RW	A Boolean value that indicates whether a Movie Clip instance is shown or hidden. It is set to 1 (or true) to show; 0 (or false) to hide. Buttons in "hidden" movies are not active.
		Movie	RW	RW	RW	

Category	Property	Timeline	Flash 4	Flash 5+	Flash 8	Definition
	filters	MC Movie	N/A N/A	N/A N/A	RW RW	This new property in Flash Player 8 enables you to add visual effects to MovieClip objects. The filters property uses an array to describe which filters have been applied to the clip.
	transform	MC Movie	N/A N/A	RW N/A	RW RW	This new property in Flash Player 8 enables you to control physical characteristics of a MovieClip object via transformation object. In Chapter 27, "Interacting with Movie Clips," we discuss the ColorTransform class, which can control the color properties of a MovieClip object.
Internal Path	_name	MC Movie	RW R	RW R	RW R	This property returns or reassigns the Movie Clip instance's name (as listed in the Property inspector).
	_target	MC Movie	R R	R R	R R	This property returns the exact string in Slash notation that you'd use to refer to the Movie Clip instance. To retrieve the dot syntax path, use eval(_target).
	_droptarget	MC Movie	R R	R R	R R	This property returns the name (in Slash notation) of the last Movie Clip upon which a draggable Movie Clip was dropped. To retrieve the dots syntax path, use eval(_droptarget). For usage, see "Creating Draggable Movie Clips" in this chapter.
	_lockroot	MC Movie	RW RW	RW RW	RW RW	This property, only available to Flash Player 7 or higher-compatible movies, enables you to control how a _root reference is interpreted. If the _lockroot property of a MovieClip object is set to true, then any child assets (nested MovieClip objects) will see the parent MovieClip object as _root. For example, if you load an .swf file into a MovieClip object, any _root target in the loaded .swf will point to the MovieClip object.
	_parent	MC Movie	N/A N/A	R R	R R	This property returns a reference to the parent timeline of the current MovieClip object. For example, if an instance named bird_1 exists within another instance named flock_mc, then bird_1._parent refers to the flock_mc instance. * _parent will return only a valid reference from the Main Timeline if the Flash movie is loaded into a MovieClip instance of another Flash movie.

Continued

Table 25-1 *(continued)*

Category	Property	Timeline	Flash 4	Flash 5+	Flash 8	Definition
External Path	_url	MC	R	R	R	This property returns the complete path to the Flash movie (.swf) in which the action is executed, including the name of the Flash movie file (.swf) itself. It can be used to prevent a movie from being viewed if it is not on a particular server.
		Movie	R	R	R	
Timeline	_currentframe	MC	R	R	R	This property returns the number of the current frame (for example, the frame on which the Playhead currently resides) of the Movie or a Movie Clip instance.
		Movie	R	R	R	
	_totalframes	MC	R	R	R	This property returns the number of total frames in a Movie or Movie Clip instance's timeline.
		Movie	R	R	R	
	_framesloaded	MC	R	R	R	This property returns the number of frames that have downloaded over the network.
		Movie	R	R	R	
Global	_quality	Movie	N/A	RW	RW	The visual quality of the Movie. The value is a string equal to: "LOW" (no anti-aliasing, no bitmap smoothing), "MEDIUM" (anti-aliasing on a 2 x 2 grid, no bitmap smoothing), "HIGH" (anti-aliasing on a 4 x 4 grid, bitmap smoothing on static frames), "BEST" (anti-aliasing on a 4 x 4 grid, bitmap smoothing on all frames).
	_focusrect	Movie	RW	RW	RW	A Boolean value that indicates whether a yellow rectangle is shown around buttons when accessed via the Tab key. The default is to show. When set to 0, the Up state of the button is shown instead of the yellow rectangle.
	_soundbuftime	Movie	RW	RW	RW	The number of seconds a sound should preload before it begins playing. The default is five seconds.

MC = Movie Clip; R = Read property (cannot be modified); W = Write property (can be modified)

As actions, interactive commands are executed from the timeline on which they are written. As methods, interactive commands are tied to specific (or dynamic) targets. Figure 25-3 lists many of the methods and Table 25-2 reviews them in more detail. Some methods can be used with Movie Clip instances and with the entire Flash movie (_root, _level0, and so on), while others can only be used with Movie Clip instances. The "Flash 4" column in Table 25-2 indicates if the method (when used as an action) is compatible in Flash Player 4. Some commands need to be written in dot syntax, as a method (designated as "M" in the table) of a timeline or `MovieClip` object. Other commands can be used as actions (designated as "A" in the table), meaning that the `MovieClip` object name need not precede the command.

Cross-Reference

Figure 25-3 and Table 25-2 do not contain all methods of the `MovieClip` class. For comprehensive descriptions and usage of the methods, refer to the *Flash ActionScript Bible* series by Robert Reinhardt and Joey Lott (Wiley).

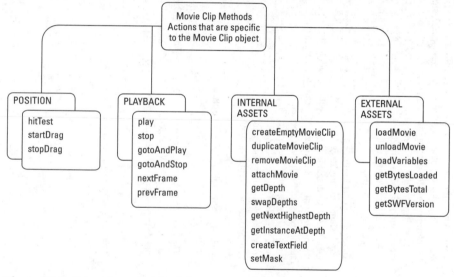

Figure 25-3: Common methods of the `MovieClip` object

Table 25-2: Common Movie and Movie Clip Methods

Category	Method	Flash 4	Definition	Usage

Position	hitTest
	M
		No	Determines if a MovieClip object overlaps with the boundaries of another MovieClip object, or if an X-Y coordinate intersects with a MovieClip instance. For more information on this method, see Chapter 27, "Interacting with Movie Clips."	*timeline.hitTest(MovieClip object);*
				OR
				timeline.hitTest(x coordinate, y coordinate, shapeFlag);
				
				`myMC.hitTest(myOther_mc);`
				`myMC.hitTest(_root._xmouse,`
				`_root._ymouse, true);`

	startDrag M, A	Yes	Enables the user to move a Movie Clip instance on the Stage. The Movie Clip moves (or drags) in tandem with the movements of the mouse. You can specify whether the mouse pointer locks to the center of the Movie Clip instance and if the drag area is constrained to a range of X and Y coordinates (in the parent symbol or timeline space). Constraining the drag area is useful for slider controls.	*timeline.startDrag(lock, min X, min Y, max X, max Y);* `myMC.startDrag(false, 200,0,200,200);`
	stopDrag M, A	Yes	Stops any startDrag action currently in progress. No target needs to be specified with this action.	*timeline.stopDrag();* `myMC.stopDrag();`

Category	Method	Flash 4	Definition	Usage

Playback	play
	M, A
		Yes	Starts playback from the current position of the Playhead on a specified timeline.	*timeline.play();*
				
				`_root.play(); // plays the Main Timeline`
				`_root.myMC.play(); // plays myMC`

	stop
	M, A
		Yes	Stops playback on a specified timeline.	*timeline.stop();*
				
				`_root.stop(); // stops the Main Timeline`
				`_root.myMC.stop(); // stops myMC`

	gotoAndPlay
	M, A
		Yes	Jumps the Playhead of a specified timeline to a label, frame number, or expression, and starts playing from there.	*timeline.gotoAndPlay(position);*
				
				`_root.myMC.gotoAndPlay("start");`
				`// plays from the "start" label of the myMC`
				`timeline`

	gotoAndStop
	M, A
		Yes	Jumps the Playhead of a specified timeline to a label, frame number, or expression, and stops playback.	*timeline.gotoAndStop(position);*
				
				`_root.myMC.gotoAndStop("mute");`
				`// stops playback on the "mute" label of myMC`

	nextFrame M, A	Yes	Moves the Playhead of the specified timeline to the next frame.	*timeline.nextFrame();* `_root.myMC.nextFrame();`
	prevFrame M, A	Yes	Moves the Playhead of the specified timeline to the previous frame.	*timeline.prevFrame();* `_root.myMC.prevFrame();`

Continued

Table 25-2 *(continued)*

Category	Method	Flash 4	Definition	Usage

Internal Assets	`createEmptyMovieClip` M	No	Makes a blank (empty) Movie Clip instance on the Stage (or nested in another Movie Clip instance). The new instance is placed directly above the parent instance, at a specified depth. Higher depth numbers appear above lower depth numbers (for example, a Movie Clip at depth 2 is stacked above a Movie Clip at depth 1).
			
			This method works only in Flash 6 or higher movies played in Flash Player 6 or higher.
				timeline.createEmptyMovieClip(new name, depth);*
				
				`_root.createEmptyMovieClip("myMC", 1);`
				`myMC._x = 50;`
				
				*You should only specify an instance name for the new `MovieClip` object — not a new path. You can only create new instances relative to the instance invoking the method.

	`duplicateMovieClip` M, A	Yes	Makes a copy of an existing Movie Clip instance on the Stage (or nested in another Movie Clip). The new copy is placed directly above the parent instance, at a specified depth. Higher depth numbers appear above lower depth numbers (for example, a Movie Clip at depth 2 is stacked above a Movie Clip at depth 1).	*timeline.duplicateMovieClip(new name*, depth);*
				
				`myMC.duplicateMovieClip("myMC_2", 20);`
				`myMC_2._x = 200;`
				*See note for the `createEmptyMovieClip()` method.

Category	Method	Flash 4	Definition	Usage
	remove MovieClip M, A	Yes	Deletes a previously duplicated Movie Clipinstance. When used as a method, you do not need to specify a target. You cannot remove a Movie Clip instance that is manually inserted on any timeline frame from the Library.	*timeline.removeMovieClip();* `myMC_2.removeMovieClip();`
	attachMovie M	No	Places an instance of from the Library into the specified timeline. Each attached instance requires a unique name and depth. Attached Movie Clip instances can be deleted with `removeMovieClip`.	*timeline.attachMovie(ID*, new name, depth);* `_root.attachMovie("eye", "eye_1", 1);` *You need to specify a unique identifier to linked Movie Clip symbols in the Library, using the Linkage Properties.

	getDepth
	M
		No	Returns the current depth of a duplicated (or attached) `MovieClip` object.
			
			This method only works in Flash 6 movies played in Flash Player 6.
				timeline.getDepth();
				
				`_root.attachMovie("eye", "eye_1", 1);`
				`trace(eye_1.getDepth());`
				
				*If you attempt to retrieve the depth of a Movie Clip instance that you manually placed on the Stage, then ActionScript will return −16383 as the value of `getDepth()`.

	swapDepths
	M
		No	Switches the depth placement of two duplicated or attached Movie Clips. This method is useful for placing one Movie Clip instance in front of (or behind) another instance.	*timeline.swapDepths(target);*
				
				`eye_1.swapDepths(10); // depth`
				`eye_1.swapDepths(eye_2); // target`

Continued

Table 25-2 *(continued)*

Category	Method	Flash 4	Definition	Usage

	`getNextHighestDepth` M	No	Determines if any objects currently exist within depth slots of the current `MovieClip` object, and returns a depth number one higher than an occupied slot. For example, if you duplicated a `MovieClip` object to a depth count of 2, this method would return 3. You can use this method in conjunction with any of the Movie Clip methods that require a depth parameter.
			
			This method works only when issued from a Flash Player 7 or higher movie.
				timeline.getNextHighestDepth0;
				
				`var nextSlot =`
				`myMC.getNextHighestDepth();`

	`getInstanceAtDepth` M	No	Returns the name of an object occupying the specified depth slot. If no object exists at the slot, `undefined` is returned. This method works only when issued from a Flash Player 7 or higher movie.	*timeline.getInstanceAtDepth(depthSlot);* `var isOccupied = myMC.getInstanceAtDepth(1);`

	`createTextField` M	No	Adds a new `TextField` object (that is, a dynamic or input text field) to the `MovieClip` object. This method enables you to add new text fields to your movie at run time.
			
			This method works only when issued from a Flash Player 6 or higher movie.
				timeline.createTextField
				(name, depth, x position, y position, width, height);
				
				`myMC.createTextField("display_txt",`
				`1, 10, 10, 300, 50);`

Category	Method	Flash 4	Definition	Usage
	setMask M	No	Assigns a MovieClip object to be used as the mask for another MovieClip object. This method works only when issued from a Flash Player 6 or higher movie.	*timeline.setMask(instanceName);* `myMC.setMask(clip_mc);`

External Assets	loadMovie
	M, A
		Yes	Loads an external movie file (.swf) or image file into the main movie. As one of the most powerful features of Flash, this method enables you to break up your Flash movie into several smaller components, and load them as needed. This method can load movie files (.swf) or standard JPEG image files (.jpg) into Flash Player 6 or higher movies. Flash Player 8 movies can also load GIF, PNG, and progressive JPEG images into Movie Clip targets.	*timeline.loadMovie(path, send variables*);*
				`myMC.loadMovie("menu.swf");`
				
				OR
				
				`myMC.loadMovie("image.jpg");`
				
				*You can also send Flash variables to the newly loaded .swf file with an optional "GET" or "POST" parameter. We discuss this in Chapter 24, "Knowing the Nuts and Bolts of Code."

	unloadMovie M, A	Yes	Removes an externally loaded movie file (.swf) or image file from the main movie. This method enables you to dump movieassets when they are no longer needed. Use this method for assets loaded into Movie Clip targets.	*timeline.unloadMovie();* `myMC.unloadMovie();`

Continued

Table 25-2 *(continued)*

Category / Method	Flash 4	Definition	Usage
`loadVariables` M, A	Yes	Loads external text-based data into the movie. This method enables you to access data (in the form of variable name/value pairs) from server-side scripts or text files, and place it in a Movie Clip target.	*timeline.loadVariables(path, send variables*)*; `myMC.loadVariables("info.txt");` *See note in loadMovie. We discuss `load Variables()` and the `LoadVars` object in Chapter 29, "Sending Data In and Out of Flash."*
`getBytesLoaded` M	No	Returns the number of bytes that have streamed into the Flash Player for a specified Movie Clip (or movie).	*timeline.getBytesLoaded();* `loadBytes = myMC.getBytesLoaded();`
`getBytesTotal` M	No	Returns the total file size (in bytes) for a loading movie or Movie Clip. Combined with `getBytesLoaded()`, you can use this method to calculate the movie's loaded percentage.	*timeline.getBytesTotal();* `totalBytes = myMC.getBytesTotal();` `loadBytes = myMC.getBytesLoaded();` `newPercent = (loadBytes/totalBytes)*100;`
`getSWFVersion` M	No	Returns the version of the Flash movie as a number. For example, if you create a Flash movie (.swf) to be Flash Player 4-compatible, you can check the version number of that .swf from a Flash Player 7-compatible movie file (.swf).	*timeline.getSWFVersion();* This method can only be invoked from Flash movies created for Flash Player 7 or higher. `myMC.getSWFVersion();`

M = Method; A = Action

Here's how you create a simple example of onClipEvent() in action:

1. Open a new Flash document (File ➪ New).

2. Draw any artwork you wish, and make the artwork a Movie Clip symbol.

3. Select the Movie Clip instance on the Stage. In the Property inspector, name the instance mcTracker.

4. With the mcTracker instance selected on the Stage, open the Actions panel (F9). Type the following code into the Script pane:

```
onClipEvent (mouseMove){
  this._x = _root._xmouse;
  this._y = _root._ymouse;
  updateAfterEvent();
}
```

This code uses onClipEvent() to track the position of the user's mouse, and apply that position to the MovieClip object — effectively moving the MovieClip object with the mouse pointer. The code is executed every time the user's mouse moves. The updateAfterEvent() action will tell the Flash Player to refresh the video display each time a mouse move is detected, resulting in a smoother movement of the object.

5. Save your Flash document as tracker_oce.fla, and test it (Ctrl+Enter or ⌘+Enter). As you move the mouse, the artwork will follow the mouse.

You can find a completed version of the file tracker_oce.fla in the ch25 folder of this book's CD-ROM.

Event methods: The more flexible Movie Clip handler

In Flash Player 6 and higher, event handlers for MovieClip objects can be written and executed from any other event handler. This means that you can code the same event handlers used for onClipEvent() in keyframe or Button instance actions. While this may not seem like a monumental leap forward, this new event model enables you to create event handlers that are not directly attached to physical instances of a Movie Clip on the Stage. For a summary of common event methods, see Table 25-3.

It is beyond the scope of this book to discuss all of the event methods available in ActionScript 1.0 and 2.0. Please refer to the *Flash ActionScript Bible* series by Robert Reinhardt and Joey Lott (Wiley) for more information.

To get a better idea of how this event model works, create this simple example:

1. Create a new Flash document.

2. Draw some artwork, and make it a Movie Clip symbol.

3. Select the new instance on the Stage. Name the instance mcTracker in the Property inspector.

4. Create a new layer on the Main Timeline (that is, Scene 1). Name the layer **actions**.

5. Select frame 1 of the actions layer, and open the Actions panel (F9). Type the following code into the Script pane:

```
var mcTracker:MovieClip;
mcTracker.onMouseMove = function (){
    this._x = _root._xmouse;
    this._y = _root._ymouse;
    updateAfterEvent();
};
```

This code adds an onMouseMove() method to the tracker instance. Each time the user's mouse moves, the function written for the method will execute. We discuss functions in the next chapter.

6. Save your Flash document as tracker_eventmodel.fla, and test it (Ctrl+Enter or ⌘+Enter). The artwork will follow your mouse pointer as you move it on the Stage.

You can find the completed document, tracker_eventmodel.fla, in the ch25 folder of this book's CD-ROM. You will also find another document, tracker_eventmodel_adv.fla, which uses multiple event handlers.

You can continue to add more event methods to the tracker instance, in order for the instance to respond to mouse clicks, time elapsing, and so on.

The new event model for Flash movies only works in Flash Player 6 or higher. If you need to use events with Movie Clips that are compatible with Flash Player 5, then use onClipEvent() handlers.

Table 25-3: Common Flash Player 5 and Higher Event Handlers

Category	onClipEvent (FP5+)	Event Handler (FP6+)	Definition	Usage

Playback	load	onLoad	This event is triggered when (A) a Movie Clip instance first appears on the Stage; (B) a new instance is added with `attachMovie` or `duplicateMovieClip`; or (C) an external Flash movie file (.swf) is loaded into a Movie Clip target.
			
			Note: The `onLoad` method does not function properly on individual instances. When a Flash movie file (.swf) loads into a level or a Movie Clip target, any existing methods will be overwritten, including `onLoad`. See the Usage example to see how `onLoad` can be used. The `onLoad` method, however, is useful for setting parameters for components that are added via ActionScript.
				`onClipEvent(load){`
				　`trace(_name + " has loaded.");`
				`}`
				
				OR
				
				`MovieClip.prototype.onLoad = function(){`
				　`trace("A movie or Movie Clip has loaded.");`
				`};`

	unload	onUnload	This event occurs when (A) a Movie Clip instance exits the Stage (just after the last frame has played on the Main Timeline), or (B) an external Flash movie file (.swf) is unloaded from a Movie Clip target. Actions within this handler type will be executed *before* any actions in the keyframe immediately after the Movie Clip's departure keyframe.	`onClipEvent(unload){`
				　`trace(_name + " has unloaded.");`
				`}`
				
				OR
				
				`mcHolder.onUnload = function(){`
				　`trace(this._name + " has unloaded.");`
				`};`

Continued

Table 25-3 *(continued)*

Category	onClipEvent (FP5+)	Event Handler (FP6+)	Definition	Usage

	enterFrame	onEnterFrame	This event executes when each frame on a Movie Clip instance's timeline is played. The actions within this event handler will be processed *after* any actions that exist on the keyframes of the Movie Clip Timeline. Note that enterFrame events will execute repeatedly (at the same rate as the movie's frame rate), regardless of whether any timelines within the movie are actually playing frames.	```onClipEvent(enterFrame){```
				``` trace(_name + " is playing.");```
				```}```
				
				OR
				
				```mcHolder.onEnterFrame = function(){```
				``` trace(_name + " is playing.");```
				```};```

User Input	mouseMove	onMouseMove	This event is triggered each time the mouse moves anywhere on the Stage. All Movie Clip instances with this event handler defined receive this event. Combined with the hitTest() method, this event can be used to detect mouse movements over Movie Clip instances.	```onClipEvent(mouseMove){```
				``` var myX = _root._xmouse;```
				``` var myY = _root._ymouse;```
				``` if(this.hitTest(myX, myY, true) == true){```
				``` trace("Mouse move over MC.");```
				``` }```
				```}```
				
				OR
				
				```mcHolder.onMouseMove = function(){```
				``` var myX:Number = _root._xmouse;```
				``` var myY:Number = _root._ymouse;```
				``` if(this.hitTest(myX, myY, true)){```
				``` trace("Mouse move over " + this._name);```
				``` }```
				``` updateAfterEvent();```
				```};```

Category	onClipEvent (FP5+)	Event Handler (FP6+)	Definition	Usage

	mouseDown	onMouseDown	This event occurs each time the left mouse button is pressed (or down) anywhere on the Stage. All Movie Clip instances with this event handler receive this event.	`onClipEvent(mouseDown){`
				`  myX = _root._xmouse;`
				`  myY = _root._ymouse;`
				`  if(this.hitTest(myX, myY, true)){`
				`    trace("Mouse press on MC.");`
				`  }`
				`}`
				
				OR
				
				`mcHolder.onMouseDown = function(){`
				`  var myX:Number = _root._xmouse;`
				`  var myY:Number = _root._ymouse;`
				`  if(this.hitTest(myX, myY, true)){`
				`    trace("Mouse press on " + this._name);`
				`  }`
				`};`

	mouseUp	onMouseUp	This event is triggered each time the left mouse button is released (when the user lets up on the mouse button). All Movie Clip instances with this handler receive this event.	`onClipEvent(mouseUp){`
				`  myX = _root._xmouse;`
				`  myY = _root._ymouse;`
				`  if(this.hitTest(myX, myY, true)){`
				`    trace("Mouse release on MC.");`
				`  }`
				`}`
				
				OR
				
				`mcHolder.onMouseUp = function(){`
				`  var myX:Number = _root._xmouse;`
				`  var myY:Number = _root._ymouse;`
				`  if(this.hitTest(myX, myY, true)){`
				`    trace("Mouse release on " + this._name);`
				`  }`
				`};`

Continued

Table 25-3 *(continued)*

Category	onClipEvent (FP5+)	Event Handler (FP6+)	Definition	Usage

	keyDown	onKeyDown	This event occurs when the user presses a key. Combined with the Key.getCode method, you can use this event handler to detect unique key presses.
			
			Note: It's better to use Key.addListener() with a listener object to detect key down events.
				`onClipEvent(keyDown){`
				`  newKey = Key.getCode();`
				`  myKey = Key.UP;`
				`  if(newKey == myKey){`
				`    trace("UP arrow is pressed.");`
				`  }`
				`}`

	keyUp	onKeyUp	This event happens when the user releases a key (when the finger leaves the key). It provides the same functionality as the keyDown event.
			
			Note: It's preferable to use Key.addListener() with a listener object to detect key down events. We discuss this advanced use of the Key class in the *Flash ActionScript Bible* series by Robert Reinhardt and Joey Lott (Wiley).
				`onClipEvent(keyUp){`
				`  newKey = Key.getCode();`
				`  myKey = Key.LEFT;`
				`  if(newKey == myKey){`
				`    trace("LEFT arrow released.");`
				`  }`
				`}`

External Input	data	onData	This event is triggered when (A) the loadMovie action retrieves an external Flash movie file (.swf) and puts it in a Movie Clip target, or (B) the data from a file or script with the loadVariables action (targeted at a Movie Clip instance) is finished loading.
			
			Note: If you're building Flash Player 6 or higher movies, use the LoadVars class to load URL-encoded variables into a Flash movie. Learn more about the LoadVars class in Chapter 29, "Sending Data In and Out of Flash."
				`onClipEvent(data){`
				`  trace("New data received.");`
				`}`
				
				OR
				
				`mcHolder.onData = function(){`
				`  trace("New data received.");`
				`}`

Other classes and functions that use the MovieClip object

You can use Movie Clips with other ActionScript classes to control appearances and sounds, and to manipulate data.

ColorTransform class

This class can control the color effects of the targeted Movie Clip.

 New Feature Flash Player 8 introduces a new `MovieClip` class property, `transform`. The `transform` property controls color transformations applied to a `MovieClip` instance. For more information about this new feature, read Chapter 27, "Interacting with Movie Clips."

Sound class

With this class, you can create virtual sound instances on a Movie Clip Timeline and target them for later use.

Mouse class

This class controls the appearance of the mouse pointer within the Flash movie. After the `Mouse` object is hidden, you can attach a `MovieClip` object to the X and Y coordinates of the mouse pointer.

PrintJob API

Flash MX 2004 and Flash Player 7 introduced the ActionScript class, `PrintJob`. `PrintJob` objects enable you to send MovieClip instances — as pages to a user's printer. The `PrintJob` class offers you more control over printing than previous versions of the Flash Player. You learn more about the `PrintJob` API in Chapter 27, "Interacting with Movie Clips."

 Note You can still use the `print()` function for Flash Player 6 or earlier movies. This function prints a frame (or series of frames) in the targeted timeline. Each frame prints to one piece of paper. Use this function to print high-quality artwork. Note that alpha and color effects applied to `MovieClip` objects do not print reliably with this method — use the `printAsBitmap()` function instead.

with() action

This action enables you to avoid needless replication of object references and paths. By specifying a target for the `with()` action, you can omit the path from nested actions. We demonstrate the `with()` action in the next section.

tellTarget() action

This Flash Player 4-compatible action can direct actions to a specific Movie Clip Timeline. To be compatible with Flash Player 4, you need to use slash syntax for the target path. We strongly discourage you from using `tellTarget()` actions if you are designing Flash Player 5 or higher movies.

Working with Movie Clip Properties

Now that you have a sense of what a Movie Clip can do (or be told to do), it's time for you to get some practical experience with the Movie Clip properties. In this section, we show you how to access Movie Clip appearance properties that control position, scale, and rotation.

Note   The following exercises use Button symbols from the prebuilt Common Libraries that ship with Flash 8. To access buttons from the Common Libraries, use Window ➪ Common Libraries ➪ Buttons to open the Flash library file, and drag an instance of any button into your Flash document. Our examples use Button symbols from the classic buttons folder of the Buttons library.

Positioning Movie Clips

You can change the location of Movie Clip instances on the fly with position properties such as _x and _y. How is this useful? If you want to create multiple Movie Clip instances that move randomly (or predictably) across the Stage, you can save yourself the trouble of manually tweening them by writing a few lines of ActionScript code on the object instance. Here are the steps to take:

1. Create a new Flash document (Ctrl+N or ⌘+N).

2. Rename Layer 1 to **mcCircle**.

3. On frame 1 of the mcCircle layer, draw a simple shape such as a circle. Select the shape and press F8 to convert it into a symbol. Choose the Movie Clip behavior in the Symbol Properties dialog box, and give the new Movie Clip symbol a unique name such as **circleClip**.

4. Select the instance on the stage of the Main Timeline, and in the Property inspector, name the instance mcCircle.

5. Create a new layer on the Main Timeline (that is, Scene 1), and name the layer **actions**.

6. Select frame 1 of the actions layer, and open the Actions panel (F9, or Option+F9 on Mac). Type the following code into the Script pane:

```
mcCircle.onEnterFrame = function(){
     this._x += 5;
};
```

7. Save your document as movieclip_x.fla, and test the movie (Ctrl+Enter or ⌘+Enter). The Movie Clip instance moves across the Stage.

On the CD-ROM   You can find the movieclip_x.fla in the ch25 folder of this book's CD-ROM.

How does this code work? In Step 4, you specified that the onEnterFrame() event method should be assigned to the Movie Clip instance mcCircle. Regardless of the number of frames on any playing timeline, the enterFrame event is triggered continuously. Therefore, any actions nested within the handler will be executed repeatedly.

Your nest contains one action: `this._x += 5`. On the left side of the action, `this` refers to the object instance to which this handler and code has been applied. In your case, `this` refers to your `circle_mc` Movie Clip instance. Immediately after this is the property for the X position, `_x`. By adding the property `_x` to the object `this`, Flash knows that you want to change the value of this property.

On the right side of the action are the operators `+=` and the value 5. By combining the `+` and `=` operators, you've created a shortcut to adding the value of 5 to the current X position of the `circle_mc` Movie Clip instance. Each time the `enterFrame` event occurs, the `circle_mc` object moves 5 pixels to the right.

To show how quickly you can replicate this action on multiple Movie Clips, select the `mcCircle` instance on the Stage, and duplicate it (Ctrl+D or ⌘+D) as many times as you wish. Name each new instance with a different name in the Property inspector, such as `mcCircle_2`, `mcCircle_3`, and so on. For each instance you create, you can duplicate the code on frame 1, specifying the same actions. For example, for the two objects `mcCircle_2` and `mcCircle_3`, you could write the following code on frame 1:

```
mcCircle_2.onEnterFrame = function():Void{
    this._x += 10;
};
mcCircle_3.onEnterFrame = mcCircle_2.onEnterFrame;
```

When you test your movie, each instance moves independently across the Stage. Notice that the `onEnterFrame()` handler for the `mcCircle_3` instance borrows the `onEnterFrame()` handler from `mcCircle_2`. Once a method has been defined for one object, you can reuse it with other objects' methods.

Tip
To move the instance diagonally across the Stage, add the action `this._y += 5` to the `onEnterFrame()` handler. This moves the instance down 5 pixels each time the handler is processed. Also, we'll show you how to consolidate duplicated actions in Chapter 26, "Using Functions and Arrays."

Scaling Movie Clips

In the last example, you learned how to access the `_x` and `_y` properties of the `MovieClip` object. The next example shows you how to use a Button symbol to enlarge or reduce the size of a Movie Clip on the Stage:

1. Create a new Flash document (Ctrl+N or ⌘+N).

2. Draw a shape (or multiple shapes), select the shape(s), and press F8 to convert the artwork into a symbol. Give the Movie Clip symbol a distinct name to identify it in the Library.

3. Select the instance of the Movie Clip on the Stage, and open the Property inspector. Give the Movie Clip a unique name. In this example, we've named the instance `mcCircle`.

4. From the Button library, drag an instance of a button onto the Stage. Name the instance **btnIncr** (short for button increase) in the Property inspector.

5. Now create the ActionScript code that will enlarge the mcCircle Movie Clip instance. Create a new layer named **actions**. Select frame 1 on this layer, and open the Actions panel. Type the following code into the Script pane:

```
btIncr.onRelease = function():Void{
  with (mcCircle){
    _xscale += 10;
    _yscale += 10;
  }
};
```

This code uses the with() action to target the mcCircle instance with a nested group of actions. In this case, you've increased the values of the _xscale and _yscale properties by 10 percent. With each release event on the Button symbol instance, the scale properties of the mcCircle instance will be changed.

6. Save your document as movieclip_scale.fla, and test the movie (Ctrl+Enter or ⌘+Enter). Each time you click the Button instance, your mcCircle instance enlarges by 10 percent.

7. Duplicate the Button instance (Ctrl+D or ⌘+D). With the new copy of the Button instance selected, rename the instance to **btDecr** (short for button decrease) in the Property inspector. Select frame 1 of the actions layer, and add the following code to the existing code in the Actions panel:

```
btDecr.onRelease = function():Void {
  with (mcCircle){
    _xscale -= 10;
    _yscale -= 10;
  }
};
```

By changing the += operator to -=, each click on this Button instance reduces (shrinks) the mcCircle instance by 10 percent.

8. Resave your Flash file and test the movie again. Make sure that each Button instance behaves appropriately. If one doesn't work (or works in an unexpected manner), go back to the Flash document and check the code on both Button instances.

On the CD-ROM You can find the movieclip_scale.fla document in the ch25 folder of this book's CD-ROM.

Caution In this simple exercise, we haven't placed any limits on the how much the Movie Clip can be reduced or enlarged. If you click the reduce button enough times, the Movie Clip instance will actually flip vertically and start enlarging again. We look at creating conditions and logic for Movie Clips in Chapter 27, "Interacting with Movie Clips."

Rotating Movie Clips

Let's move along to the rotation property, `_rotation`, which is used to control the angle at which your Movie Clip is shown. In this sample, you'll use the same Flash document that you created in the previous section.

Note   If you drew a perfect circle in past exercises for the `MovieClip` object, then you will want to edit your Movie Clip symbol to include some additional artwork that provides an indication of orientation and rotation. If you try to rotate a perfect circle, you won't see any visual difference on the Stage. Because the value of the `_rotation` property is determined from the center point of the Movie Clip, you can also move the contents of the Movie Clip (in Edit mode) off-center to see updates in the `_rotation` value.

1. Select the `btIncr` instance you used to enlarge the `mcCircle` Movie Clip instance. Change the button's ActionScript in the Actions panel to:

```
btIncr.onRelease = function():Void {
   mcCircle._rotation += 10;
};
```

2. Now, select the `btDecr` instance you used to shrink the `mcCircle` Movie Clip instance. Change the button's ActionScript in the Actions panel to:

```
btDecr.onRelease = function():Void {
   mcCircle._rotation -= 10;
};
```

3. Save your document as `movieclip_rotation.fla`, and test the movie. Each button should rotate the `circle_mc` Movie Clip instance accordingly.

On the CD-ROM   You can find the `movieclip_rotation.fla` document in the `ch25` folder of this book's CD-ROM.

At this point, you should have a general knowledge of how to access a Movie Clip's properties. Repeat these examples using other properties that can be modified, such as `_width` and `_height`. Try combining all the properties into one Button instance handler, or one event method or `onClipEvent()` handler.

Creating Draggable Movie Clips

Flash Player 4 introduced the drag-and-drop feature, which enables the user to pick up objects with the mouse pointer and move them around the movie Stage. Flash Player 5 added some other ways to use drag-and-drop with the `onClipEvent()` Movie Clip handler. As we briefly discussed, Flash Player 6 and higher ActionScript can use a different event model for `MovieClip` objects. Drag-and-drop in Flash is based entirely on Movie Clips. The only objects that can be moved with the mouse are Movie Clip instances. So, if you want a drawing of a triangle to be moveable by the user, you have to first put that triangle into a Movie Clip, and then place a named instance of that clip onto the Stage. Flash's drag-and-drop support is fairly broad, but more-complex drag-and-drop behaviors require some ActionScript knowledge.

Drag-and-drop basics

In mouse-based computer interfaces, the most common form of drag-and-drop goes like this: A user points to an element with the mouse pointer, clicks the element to begin moving it, and then releases the mouse button to stop moving it. One method of adding drag-and-drop functionality is the use of a button handler with a `MovieClip` instance. A `startDrag()` action is added to an `onPress()` handler for that `MovieClip` instance. Let's try out this technique.

1. Start a new Flash document. Rename Layer 1 to **mcDrag**.

2. Create a circle with the Oval tool. Select the artwork and press F8. In the Convert to Symbol dialog box, select the MovieClip type. Name the symbol **dragClip**. Make sure the registration point is set to the center of the clip.

3. With the new Movie Clip instance selected, open the Property inspector. Give the instance the name `mcDrag`.

4. On the Main Timeline (that is, Scene 1), create a new layer named actions and place this layer at the top of the layer stack. Select the first frame of the actions layer, and open the Actions panel (F9, or Option+F9 on Mac). Type the following code into the Script pane:

```
var mcDrag:MovieClip;
mcDrag.onPress = function():Void {
  this.startDrag();
};
```

Even though this `startDrag()` method will be applied to the same Movie Clip (`this`), a `startDrag()` method can target any Movie Clip from any button, or from any keyframe.

5. At this point, your `MovieClip` instance button, when clicked, causes the instance to start following the mouse pointer. Now you have to tell the Movie Clip to stop following the pointer when the mouse button is released. After the last curly brace (}) highlighted in the actions list of the Script pane, type the following code:

```
mcDrag.onRelease = mcDrag.onReleaseOutside = function():Void{
  this.stopDrag();
};
```

Tip   You should add an `onReleaseOutside()` handler to capture all `release`-based events, just in case the mouse is outside of the hit area of the button when the mouse button is released.

6. Save your Flash document as `movieclip_button_drag.fla`. Test your movie with Control ⇨ Test Movie (Ctrl+Enter or ⌘+Enter). Click the circle and drag it around the Stage. To stop dragging, release the mouse button.

On the CD-ROM   You can find the `movieclip_button_drag.fla` document in the `ch25` folder of this book's CD-ROM.

Did it work? Great! Now we can tell you about the other basic settings for the `startDrag()` action. Next, you'll look at additional features of the `startDrag()` action. You may want to select an existing `startDrag()` action in the Script pane of the Actions panel and click the Reference icon in the panel's toolbar to more clearly see these options.

Lock mouse to center

This setting, which is the first option specified in the parentheses of the `startDrag()` method, controls how the Movie Clip instance will position itself relative to the position of the mouse pointer. There are two values for this option: `true` or `false`. When set to `true`, this option makes the dragged Movie Clip instance center itself under the mouse pointer for the duration of the drag movement. If the dragged Movie Clip instance is not already under the mouse pointer when the `startDrag()` action occurs, the instance will automatically be moved under the pointer, providing that the pointer is not outside the region defined by Constrain to Rectangle (discussed in the next section). The following code will "snap" the center of the Movie Clip instance `mcDrag` to the mouse pointer:

```
mcDrag.startDrag(true);
```

When this option is set to `false`, the Movie Clip instance moves with the mouse pointer from the point at which it was clicked. For example, if you click the draggable object on its left edge, then that's where the object will "snap" the mouse pointer:

```
mcDrag.startDrag(false);
```

Constrain to rectangle

In order to specify the limits of the rectangular region within which a draggable Movie Clip instance can be dragged, you can add parameters to the `startDrag()` method. First, determine the pixel locations of the four corners of the rectangle. The pixel coordinates are set relative to the top-left corner of the Stage upon which the draggable Movie Clip instance resides. For example, the following code would constrain the draggable Movie Clip instance named `mcDrag` to a 300-pixel square region in the top-left corner of the Main Timeline's Stage:

```
drag_mc.startDrag(false, 0, 0, 300, 300);
```

Note   If the draggable Movie Clip instance is located outside of the defined drag region when the `startDrag()` action occurs, the instance is automatically moved into the closest portion of the drag region.

Detecting the drop position: Using _droptarget

In the "Drag-and-drop basics" section, we showed you how to make Movie Clip instances that the user can move around. But what if you want to force the user to move a Movie Clip object into a certain location before you let her drop it? For instance, consider a child's shape-matching game in which a small circle, square, and triangle should be dragged onto corresponding larger shapes. If the child drops the small circle onto the large square or large triangle, the circle returns to its original location. If, on the other hand, the child drops the small circle onto the large circle, the small circle should stay where it is dropped, and the child should receive a "Correct!" message. That kind of game is quite possible in Flash, but it requires some understanding of Movie Clip properties. Here's how it works—you'll use the circle as an example.

1. Open a new Flash document (File ➪ New), and save it as **movieclip_droptarget.fla**.

2. Rename Layer 1 to **mcCircle**.

3. On frame 1 of the mcCircle layer, use the Oval tool to draw a circle that is 100 x 100 pixels. Convert the artwork to a Movie Clip symbol named **circleClip**, and name the instance mcCircle. Scale the artwork to 25 percent in the Transform panel. Position this instance along the bottom left of the Stage, as shown in Figure 25-4.

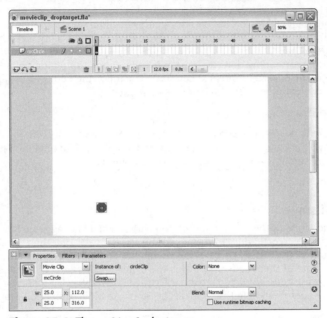

Figure 25-4: The mcCircle instance

4. Copy the mcCircle instance by selecting it on the Stage and choosing Edit ➪ Copy (Ctrl+C or ⌘+C).

5. Create a new layer, and name the layer **mcCircleBig**. Place the layer below the mcCircle layer.

6. On frame 1 of the mcCircleBig layer, choose Edit ➪ Paste (Ctrl+V or ⌘+V). Place the new copy above the original instance, as shown in Figure 25-5. Scale the artwork to 125 percent in the Transform panel, and name the instance mcCircleBig in the Property inspector.

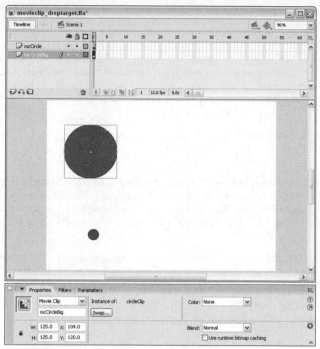

Figure 25-5: The `mcCircleBig` instance

7. Create a new Movie Clip symbol from scratch by choosing Insert ➪ New Symbol (Ctrl+F8 or ⌘+F8). Name the symbol **statusClip**. Inside of this symbol, create a short animation displaying the text "Correct!" Leave the first frame of the symbol empty, and create the text (and supporting tweens, if desired) on frame 2 and higher. Create a frame label named `correct` on frame 2 of a new layer named **labels**, as shown in Figure 25-6. Also, place a `stop();` action on frame 1 of an actions layer in the timeline.

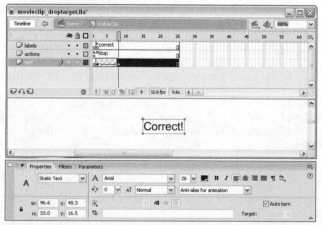

Figure 25-6: The statusClip symbol timeline with a Blur filter tween

8. Go back to the Main Timeline (that is, Scene 1), and place an instance of statusClip along the bottom of the Stage, centered. With the instance selected, open the Property inspector and name the instance `mcStatus`.

9. Now, you will make the `mcCircle` instance draggable by adding some frame actions. On the Main Timeline, create a new layer named **actions** and place this layer above the other layers. Select frame 1 of the actions layer, and in the Actions panel type the following code into the Script pane:

```
var mcCircle:MovieClip;
mcCircle.onPress = function(){
  this.startDrag();
};
```

Here, the `onPress()` method of the `MovieClip` object is used to assign a button press behavior to the instance. In this code, you tell the `mcCircle` instance to start dragging when it is clicked on the Stage. Note that as soon as a Movie Clip instance has a button event assigned to it, the mouse pointer will switch to a finger icon when it rolls over the area of the `MovieClip` object.

10. Next, you need to tell the `mcCircle` instance to stop dragging when the mouse button releases. Underneath the last line of the code from Step 4, type the following code:

```
mcCircle.onRelease = mcCircle.onReleaseOutside = function(){
  this.stopDrag();
  if ( eval(this._droptarget) == mcCircleBig ) {
    mcStatus.gotoAndPlay ("correct");
  } else {
    this._x = 112;
    this._y = 316;
  }
};
```

This code uses the `onRelease()` method. The code for this method will be executed when the mouse button is released after a mouse click on the `mcCircle` instance. The instance is told to stop dragging, and then ActionScript evaluates if the current instance (`this`) is dropped on top of `mcCircleBig`. When the user drops any Movie Clip instance, the instance's `_droptarget` property is updated. The `_droptarget` property specifies the name of the Movie Clip instance upon which the dragged Movie Clip instance was last dropped. If no instance is underneath the dragged instance, `_droptarget` returns nothing (that is, an empty string). If the `_droptarget` is the large circle, then the dragged instance stays where it was dropped and the `mcStatus` Movie Clip instance plays its "Correct!" animation. Otherwise, the dragged instance (`mcCircle`) returns to the X and Y coordinates of its starting point (112, 316).

Note   The `eval()` function is used to convert the slash syntax returned by `_droptarget` into a "real" object reference. On its own, `_droptarget` returns Flash Player 4-compatible syntax. In order to use it with current ActionScript routines, use the `eval()` function to return a proper object reference.

11. Save your Flash document as `movieclip_droptarget.fla`, and test it (Ctrl+Enter or ⌘+Enter). Click and drag the `mcCircle` instance on top of the `mcCircleBig` instance. The dragged instance will stay put on top of the larger circle, and the "Correct!" mes-

sage will animate. Click and drag the mcCircle instance off the mcCircleBig instance, and release the drag outside of the larger circle. The smaller circle will snap back to its original starting point.

You can continue this example with other shapes, using the same methodology. Create a separate onPress() and onRelease() method for each new drag interaction.

For further study, we've included this basic drag-and-drop game as a sample document called movieclip_droptarget.fla in the ch25 folder of this book's CD-ROM. A more advanced example named movieclip_droptarget_adv.fla uses three different shapes, and assigns the handlers to each draggable clip with a for() loop and an array.

Making alpha, scale, and blur sliders

A compelling use of a draggable Movie Clip is a slider that can alter the properties of another object. By checking the position of a Movie Clip, you can use the position's X or Y coordinate value to alter the value of another Movie Clip. In this section, we show you how to create two sliders (one for alpha and another for scale) that will dynamically change the transparency and size of a Movie Clip instance on the Stage. Many thanks to Sandro Corsaro (http://sandrocorsaro.com) for supplying the artwork of our dog Stella and the park sign.

You need to copy the slider_basic_starter.fla file from the ch25 folder of this book's CD-ROM. You'll use premade artwork to understand the functionality of startDrag, stopDrag, and duplicateMovieClip.

Assembling the parts

In this section, you set up the basic composition of the Stage, using elements from the slider_basic_starter.fla Library. You will add artwork of a dog and a park sign to the movie. The dog artwork will be duplicated using the duplicateMovieClip() method, and the duplicate instance will be manipulated by the sliders that you create in the next section. The park sign will be used to remove the duplicate instance using the _droptarget property and the removeMovieClip() method.

1. Open your copy of the slider_basic_starter.fla. Resave this document as slider_basic_100.fla.

2. Rename Layer 1 to **mcDog_1**.

3. Access the document's Library by pressing Ctrl+L or ⌘+L. Open the dogElements folder, and drag the dogClip symbol onto the Stage. Place the instance in the upper-left corner of the Stage.

4. With the dogClip instance selected, open the Property inspector. In the <Instance Name> field, type mcDog_1, as shown in Figure 25-7.

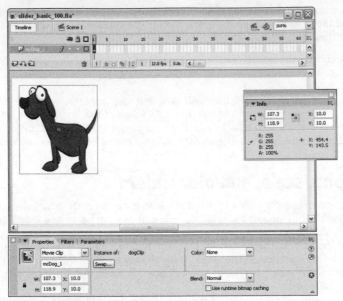

Figure 25-7: The `mcDog_1` instance will be used as your reference `MovieClip` object. The scale and transparency of this dog instance will not be changed.

5. Using the Text tool, add the words **Original Dog** under the `mcDog_1` instance. You don't need to make a new layer for this artwork.

6. Create a new layer and name it **mcSign**. Move this layer below the `mcDog_1` layer. Drag the parkSignClip symbol, located in the `parkSignElements` folder in the Library, to the lower-left corner of the Stage. In the Property inspector, assign the instance the name `mcSign`. In the Transform panel, reduce the size of the `mcSign` instance to **50%**, as shown in Figure 25-8.

7. Create a new layer called **actions**, and place it above all the other layers. Select the first keyframe of this layer. In the Actions panel, add the following actions:

```
var mcDog_1:MovieClip;
mcDog_1.duplicateMovieClip("mcDog_2", 1, {_x: 350,_y: 175});
```

This line of code duplicates the instance `mcDog_1`, names the new instance `mcDog_2`, and places it on the first depth layer of the current timeline (`_root`). However, Flash Player 6 (or higher) ActionScript enables you to do a little more with the `duplicateMovieClip()` method. You can assign an `initObject` parameter that is passed to the duplicated instance. In this example, you create an object with `_x` and `_y` properties that are passed to the `mcDog_2` instance. This argument positions the `mcDog_2` instance at the X coordinate of 350 (350 pixels from the left corner of the Main Timeline Stage) and the Y coordinate of 175 (175 pixels down from the left corner).

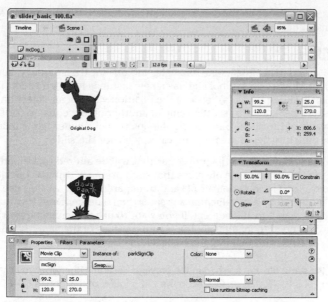

Figure 25-8: The `mcSign` instance will be used to remove duplicates of the `mcDog_1` Movie Clip instance.

8. Save the Flash document, and test the movie (Ctrl+Enter or ⌘+Enter). You should see a new instance of the `mcDog_1` Movie Clip appear on the right side of the Stage (see Figure 25-9).

Figure 25-9: The `duplicateMovieClip()` method creates a new instance of a `MovieClip` object. Unless you alter the new instance's X and Y positions, it will appear directly above the parent instance.

Now that you have some artwork on the Stage, you can manipulate the duplicated Movie Clip with a pair of dynamic sliders.

Building the sliders

In this section, you'll create two sliders: one for scale, and one for transparency. You'll need to make only one slider Movie Clip symbol and use a new instance for each slider. The basic "problems" of a dynamic slider are to (a) retrieve the position value of an object on the slider (you'll call this the slider bar), and (b) set the value of another object equal to (or some factor of) the position value of the slider bar. Finding the position of a slider bar is relatively straightforward. The difficulty lies in creating the value scale for the slider.

Because you have already determined the properties that will be altered (scale and transparency), you need to establish a range of values that each property can use. Luckily, both scale (as _xscale and _yscale in ActionScript) and transparency (as _alpha) use percentage units. However, scale can be any value that's greater than 0 percent and less than 3,200 percent. Alpha has a range of 0 to 100 percent. If you want to use the same parent slider for each property slider, you need to manipulate the position values of the slider bar differently for each property. Let's start with building the basic slider.

Resume using the same file you finished in the previous section. Otherwise, you can open a copy of slider_basic_100.fla, located in the ch25 folder of this book's CD-ROM.

1. Resave the slider_basic_100.fla file as slider_basic_101.fla.

2. Create a new Movie Clip symbol (Ctrl+F8 or ⌘+F8) and name it **sliderClip**. In Edit mode, rename the first layer **sliderRule**. On this layer, drag an instance of the sliderRule Graphic symbol (located in the sliderBarElements folder of the Library) onto the Movie Clip Stage.

3. With the sliderRule graphic selected, open the Info panel. On the right side of the Info panel (on the diagram of the square bounding box), make sure that the registration point is set to the top-left corner of the selection's bounding box. Then enter the values **–28** for the X coordinate and **–12** for the Y coordinate, as shown in Figure 25-10.

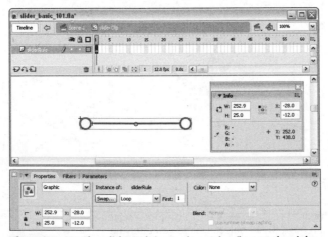

Figure 25-10: The sliderRule's starting point (just to the right of the first left-hand circle) needs to be at the slider Movie Clip's zero X coordinate.

4. Create another layer for the sliderClip symbol and name it **mcPos**. Drag an instance of the sliderBar Movie Clip (located in the `sliderBarElements` folder of the Library) to the sliderClip Movie Clip Stage.

5. With the sliderBar instance selected, open the Transform panel. Type **90** in the Rotate field, and press Enter. In the Info panel, click the center registration point in the bounding box diagram, and enter **100** for the X coordinate and **0** for the Y coordinate.

6. To control the position of the sliderBar instance with ActionScript, you need to assign a unique instance name. Select the sliderBar instance and type `mcPos` in the <Instance Name> field of the Property inspector, as shown in Figure 25-11.

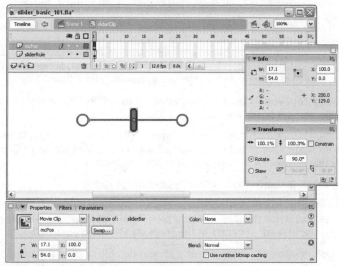

Figure 25-11: The starting X coordinate for the `mcPos` Movie Clip instance is set to 100. When the Flash movie starts, this value will be applied to the scale and alpha properties of the `mcDog_2` instance on the Main Timeline.

7. Now you need to make the `mcPos` Movie Clip instance draggable. In this example, you're going to make a button-free draggable Movie Clip instance, using the newer `onPress()` and `onRelease()` methods for `MovieClip` objects — just as you did in the earlier exercise. Create a new layer in the slider symbol, name it **actions**, and move it above the mcPos layer. Open the Actions panel (F9). Type the following code in the Script pane:

```
var mcPos:MovieClip;
mcPos.onPress = function():Void{
  this.startDrag(true, 0, 0, 200, 0);
};
```

To make the position instance draggable, you need to detect a mouse press event on the `mcPos` instance. When a mouse click occurs on the instance, the actions nested within the `onPress()` function are executed.

The second line of code enables the dragging behavior of the mcPos instance by using the startDrag() method on this. Because it's used as a method and not as an action, you don't need to specify a target instance in the arguments. The arguments prescribed here lock the mouse to the center of the object and constrain the draggable region to a bounding box defined by 0, 0 and 200, 0. This effectively keeps the mcPos instance confined to the line of the sliderRule graphic.

8. Next, you need to be able to stop dragging the mcPos object when the mouse button is released. You'll use the onRelease() handler to define your actions. Open the Actions panel for frame 1 of the actions layer. Type the following code after the last curly brace of the onPress() function:

```
mcPos.onRelease = mcPos.onReleaseOutside = function():Void {
  this.stopDrag();
};
```

This block of code performs in the same manner that your code in Step 7 did. Once a mouse release event (the act of releasing the left mouse button) is detected (line 1), you stop the dragging of the mcPos instance initiated in Step 7 (line 3).

In the following step, you'll create two instances of the sliderClip symbol on the Main Timeline Stage: one for scale, and one for alpha.

9. Exit Edit mode, and return to the Scene 1 Timeline (the Main Timeline). Create a new layer called **mcScale**. Open the Library and drag an instance of the sliderClip to the Stage. Name this instance mcScale in the Property inspector.

10. Move the mcScale instance to the lower right of the Stage.

11. Create another layer called **mcAlpha**. Drag another instance of the sliderClip symbol onto the Stage, and name the instance mcAlpha. Rotate this instance **–90 degrees**. Place the instance just left of center of the Stage, as shown in Figure 25-12.

12. Save your Flash document, and test it. You should be able to drag the position bars on both sliders.

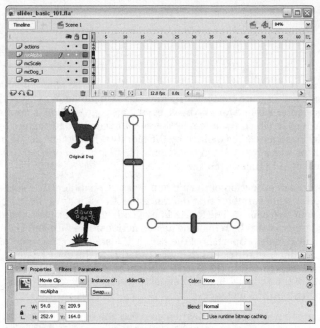

Figure 25-12: At this point, your Flash document's Stage should contain the dogClip and parkSignClip artwork, as well as two instances of the sliderClip symbol.

Checking the positions of the sliders

Once you have a slider bar that is draggable, you need to access the new values of the mcPos instance and apply the values to the properties of the mcDog_2 instance. To do this, you need to have an event handler whose sole job is to check the X coordinate of the mcPos instance. In this section, you'll learn how to make an onEnterFrame() handler on the Main Timeline.

On the CD-ROM

Resume using the Flash document that you created in the last section. If you didn't complete that section, make a copy of the slider_basic_101.fla file located in the ch25 folder of this book's CD-ROM.

1. Save the slider_basic_101.fla file as slider_basic_102.fla.

2. Select frame 1 of the actions layer in the Main Timeline (that is, Scene 1). Open the Actions panel. In the Script pane, after the duplicateMovieClip() action, type the following code:

```
this.onEnterFrame = function():Void {
    var nScale:Number = mcScale.mcPos._x;
    var nAlpha:Number = mcAlpha.mcPos._x;
    with (mcDog_2) {
```

```
        _xscale = nScale;
        _yscale = nScale;
        _alpha = nAlpha;
    }
};
```

Because the event method onEnterFrame() is specified for the Main Timeline (this), this block of code will execute continuously in your Flash movie. Why? Any timeline will continuously enter a frame for playback, even if a stop() action is applied to all timelines. The speed at which the enterFrame event occurs is determined by the frame rate of the Flash movie (as defined by the Modify ➪ Document dialog box). The frame rate of 12 fps was already set in the sample file before you opened it. Therefore, this block will execute 12 times each second.

What happens on each execution of the onEnterFrame() handler? The second and third lines of code create variables that reference the X positions of the mcPos instances with your two sliders. The fourth line of code uses the with() action to target the mcDog_2 object with the remaining nested actions. The fifth and sixth lines of code set the X and Y scale properties of the mcDog_2 instance to the value returned by the current X coordinate of the mcPos instance (relative to the coordinates within the sliderClip symbol) nested within the mcScale instance. The seventh line sets the _alpha property of the mcDog_2 instance equal to the X coordinate of the mcPos instance within the mcAlpha instance.

3. Save your Flash document, and test it. When you drag the bar on the bottom scale slider, notice how the *size* of the mcDog_2 instance increases as you drag it to the right. When you drag the bar down on the left alpha slider, you'll see that the *opacity* of the mcDog_2 instance decreases.

Note   You may be wondering why the X coordinate of the mcPos instance is used for the mcAlpha instance, instead of the Y coordinate. Indeed, you do drag the bar on a vertical axis instead of a horizontal one. However, the mcPos instance exists within the space of the sliderClip symbol, which has a horizontal orientation in the Edit mode. The X coordinate is derived from the Stage of the Edit mode, regardless of the instance's orientation.

Okay, you have the sliders changing the size and opacity of the mcDog_2 instance. However, nothing happens as you drag the bar on the mcAlpha instance toward its upper limit. Because the X coordinate of the mcPos instance starts at 100, you won't see any visual effect to the _alpha property as it increases beyond 100 percent. Therefore, it would be better to have the mcAlpha slider convert the X coordinate of the mcPos instance to a true 0 to 100 range of values.

To do this, you need to develop an equation that will do the work of automatically remapping values to a 0–100 scale. We know that the lowest X coordinate of the position_mc instance is 10, and that the highest X coordinate is 200. If you want the highest position of the bar to provide 100 percent opacity, then you need to divide 200 by a number that will give you 100. Dividing 200 by 2 returns 100. How does that work for the low end? If the X coordinate returns the lowest value of 10, then your lowest opacity value will be 5.

4. With frame 1 of the actions layer of the Main Timeline selected, open the Actions panel (F9, or Option+F9), and modify the seventh line of the onEnterFrame() handler function to read:

```
_alpha = nAlpha/2;
```

5. Save your Flash document and test it. Now, as you drag up with the bar for the `mcAlpha` instance, the opacity increases. As you drag down, it decreases.

So far, so good. However, it would be useful if the `mcAlpha`'s `mcPos` instance started with an X coordinate of 200. This would initialize the `mcDog_2` instance with an opacity of 100 percent. You could physically move the `mcPos` instance within the sliderClip symbol to an X coordinate of 200, but that would increase the scale of the `mcDog_2` instance to 200 percent at the start. To change only the `mcPos` instance of `mcAlpha` at the start of the movie, you'll add another line of code to frame 1 of the actions layer on the Main Timeline.

6. Select frame 1 of the actions layer, and open the Actions panel. Add the following code to the Script pane, after all of the existing code:

```
mcAlpha.mcPos._x = 200;
```

This block of code will execute once, when the `mcPos` instance (a Movie Clip object) first appears (or loads) on the Stage.

7. Save the Flash document and test it. This time, the `mcAlpha`'s bar (its `mcPos` instance) will immediately start at the upper limit.

8. Now, let's take advantage of the new filter effects available in Flash Player 8. Create a new layer on your Main Timeline (that is, Scene 1), and name it **mcBlur**. Make a copy of the `mcScale` instance and paste it on frame 1 of the mcBlur layer.

9. Name the new copied instance **mcBlur** in the Property inspector, and position the instance near the top of the `mcAlpha` slider, parallel to the `mcScale` slider.

10. To enable a blur effect with this slider, you need to modify the code in the `onEnterFrame()` handler on frame 1 of the actions layer. Select this frame, and open the Actions panel. Modify the `onEnterFrame()` handler with the bold code shown below. Do not type the character, as this indicates a continuation of the same line of code.

```
this.onEnterFrame = function():Void {
    var nScale:Number = mcScale.mcPos._x;
    var nAlpha:Number = mcAlpha.mcPos._x;
    var nBlur:Number = mcBlur.mcPos._x;
    var bf:flash.filters.BlurFilter = new
        flash.filters.BlurFilter();
    bf.blurX = nBlur/2;
    bf.blurY = nBlur/2;
    bf.quality = 3;
    with (mcDog_2) {
        _xscale = nScale;
        _yscale = nScale;
        _alpha = nAlpha/2;
        filters = [bf];
    }
};
```

This code creates a new `BlurFilter` instance named `bf`. The same calculation used for the alpha value is used for the blur quantities, `blurX` and `blurY`. The `bf` filter is applied to the `mcDog_2` instance's `filter` property at the end of the `with()` statement.

11. Save the Flash document, and test the movie. The mcDog_2 instance should now initialize with a blurred look, as shown in Figure 25-13.

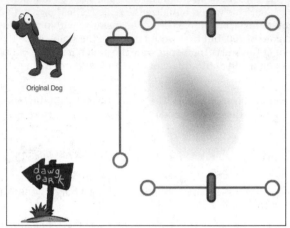

Figure 25-13: The new BlurFilter effect applied to the mcDog_2 instance.

12. In order to keep a clear visual of the mcDog_2 instance when the movie first loads, add this line of code to the end of the script on frame 1 of the actions layer:

```
mcBlur.mcPos._x = 0;
```

13. Save the Flash document, and test it. Now, the mcBlur slider starts at a blurX and blurY value of 0.

Removing Movie Clips

At this point in the chapter, you have three sliders that dynamically control the scale and alpha of the mcDog_2 Movie Clip instance on the Stage. What if you wanted to get rid of the mcDog_2 instance? How would you delete it? The only way to remove a duplicated Movie Clip instance is to use the removeMovieClip() method or action. In this section, we show you how to use the _droptarget property and the removeMovieClip() method of the MovieClip object.

On the CD-ROM Resume using the same document, slider_basic_102.fla, that you created in the last section. Alternatively, you can open the slider_basic_102.fla file located in the ch25 folder of this book's CD-ROM.

1. Select frame 1 of the actions layer on the Main Timeline, and open the Actions panel. Type the following code after the last line of ActionScript currently in the Script pane:

```
mcDog_2.onPress = function():Void{
  this.startDrag (true, 0, 0, 550, 400);
};
mcDog_2.onRelease = mcDog_2.onReleaseOutside = function():Void{
```

```
      this.stopDrag ();
      if(eval(this._droptarget) == mcSign){
        this._parent.onEnterFrame = null;
        this.removeMovieClip();
      }
    };
```

Most of this code is already familiar to you. Here you want to make only your duplicate dog instance (mcDog_2) draggable.

When a mouse press event is detected on the mcDog_2 instance, the function declared within the onPress() method for mcDog_2 will execute. The startDrag() method of the current dog instance (this) will be enabled and constrained to the dimensions of the Flash movie Stage.

When a mouse release event is detected over the mcDog_2 instance, then the stopDrag() method will be executed. The last if statement checks whether the _droptarget property of the current dog instance is equal to the target path of the mcSign instance. If the mcDog_2 instance is over the mcSign instance on the Stage when the dragging stops, then the current dog instance is removed.

Finally, if the mcDog_2 instance is removed, you must reset the onEnterFrame() method assigned to the Main Timeline, the parent of the mcDog_2 instance — otherwise, the onEnterFrame() method will generate errors in the Output window. By assigning a value of null to the Main Timeline's onEnterFrame() handler, the function established earlier will be deleted.

Note We use the eval() action on the _droptarget property because _droptarget returns the path of the target in Slash notation (for Flash Player 4 compatibility). If we use eval() on the _droptarget property, Flash returns the target path in dot syntax, as a true object reference.

2. Save your Flash document as slider_basic_103.fla, and test it. When you drag the mcDog_2 instance over the mcSign instance, the mcDog_2 instance disappears.

On the CD-ROM You can find a completed version of slider_basic_103.fla in the ch25 folder of this book's CD-ROM. Another version, slider_basic_104.fla, has a button handler to re-duplicate the mcDog_2 instance and re-organize the actions within a function.

In the next chapter, you expand your knowledge of ActionScript code by using functions and arrays. These code devices enable you to organize code and data much more efficiently with ActionScript.

Web Resource We'd like to know what you think about this chapter. Visit www.flashsupport.com/feedback to send us your comments.

Summary

✦ The MovieClip object has unique properties, methods, and handlers. Using dot syntax, you can access these characteristics of the MovieClip object.

✦ You can change a Movie Clip instance's position, scale, and rotation using ActionScript. Most physical attributes are accessed by specifying the Movie Clip's path followed by the property name, as in mcInstance._rotation.

✦ You can create draggable Movie Clips in ActionScript without using any Button instances, by using the onPress() and onRelease() methods of the MovieClip object.

✦ The _droptarget property of Movie Clip instance (instance A) indicates the path of the Movie Clip instance (instance B) upon which a Movie Clip instance (instance A) is dropped.

✦ As the sliders example demonstrated, you can use the values of one Movie Clip instance's properties to change the property values of another Movie Clip instance.

✦   ✦   ✦

Using Functions and Arrays

Now that you've had some practice applying ActionScript to
`MovieClip` objects, you can start to explore the programming
concepts behind subroutines and arrays. In this chapter, we introduce you to data types, subroutines, arrays, and complex uses of
functions.

In previous chapters, you may have found yourself repeating the
same actions (or type of actions) in several event handlers within a
movie. Functions enable you to group actions into code blocks,
referred to by custom names. Arrays are a different kind of grouping
mechanism—instead of grouping actions, an array is used to group
multiple items of data. Before we can discuss functions and arrays,
however, you need to understand the types of data that are available
in ActionScript.

What Are Data Types?

Simply put, ActionScript has several types of data that can be
declared (or loaded) into the Flash movie. So far, you have worked
primarily with three types of data in previous chapters: strings, numbers, and `MovieClip` objects. In this section, we define more data
types available in ActionScript.

Understanding data types is rather straightforward. The most difficult aspect of working with data types is knowing which data types
work correctly with the operation you want to perform in
ActionScript. We will show you examples throughout this chapter to
help you understand how data types are used.

String

You've seen `String` data types throughout this book already.
Anytime you have a value in quotes, it is typed as a `String`. If you
have an expression that refers to `String` data types, then its data
type will be a string as well. All of the following examples have a
`String` data type:

```
var firstName = "Frank";
var lastName = "Houston";
var fullName = firstName + lastName;
var pathSuffix = "1";
```

Tip

All text contained with Input and Dynamic text fields have a data type of String. If you need to perform numeric operations with text field values, make sure you convert the string data to number data by using the Number() or parseInt() function. We discuss the number data type in the next section.

Note

Feel free to try out the following code examples in new Flash document files. Create a new file, and rename Layer 1 to actions. Using the Actions panel, add the code examples to frame 1 of the actions layer. After you type each code block, test the movie to see the output from the trace() actions appear in the Output panel.

If a variable has a String data type, then any of the String object methods can be used with that data. For example, if you want to convert the case of all characters in the value of firstName to uppercase (turn "Frank" into "FRANK"), you could do the following operation:

```
var firstName = "Frank";
var firstName = firstName.toUpperCase();
trace("firstName = " + firstName);
```

Here, the String object method toUpperCase() converts any lowercase characters in a string value to uppercase characters. Likewise, you can extract specific information from a string. For example, if you wanted to find where a space occurs within a string, and return the value of the string from the point in the value to the end of the value, you could use the following code:

```
var myVersion = "Netscape 7.2";
var startChar = myVersion.indexOf(" ") + 1;
myVersion = myVersion.substr(startChar);
trace("myVersion = " + myVersion);
```

In the preceding code, the indexOf() method searches for the first occurrence of a space (" ") within the string value for myVersion. indexOf(" ") for myVersion will return the position (as a number, counting from left to right) of the space character. For this example, indexOf(" ") will return 8. Then, 1 is added to this value to determine the character position after the space. In this example, the tenth position of myVersion's value is a "7". Then, by using the slice() method, you can extract the rest of the string from the startChar value of 9. Note that in this example, the final value of myVersion is a string value of "7.2".

Number

A Number data type is any value (or expression value) that refers to a discrete numeric value in ActionScript. A value must be typed as a number in order for it to work properly in mathematical operations.

```
var myAge = "31";
var futureYears = "5";
myAge = myAge + futureYears;
trace("I will be " + myAge + " years old in " + futureYears + " years.");
```

If this code was added to frame 1 of your Flash document and tested, the following `trace()` information would appear in the Output panel:

```
I will be 315 years old in 5 years.
```

Obviously, this isn't the answer you were looking for. Because `myAge` and `futureYears` were specified as string values (with quotes), ActionScript simply concatenated (joined) the two string values as `"31" + "5"`, which is `"315"`. To see these values as numbers, you need to change the code to the following:

```
var myAge = 31;
var futureYears = 5;
myAge = myAge + futureYears;
trace("I will be " + myAge + " years old in " + futureYears + " years.");
```

Now, the values of `myAge` and `futureYears` appear as real numbers to ActionScript, and the mathematical operation will add the values of `myAge` and `futureYears` correctly. The `trace()` output will now read:

```
I will be 36 years old in 5 years.
```

You can convert `string` data values to `number` data values by using the `Number()` function. In the string example from the last section, you could convert the `myVersion` string value to a number value by adding this line of code:

```
myVersion = Number(myVersion);
```

So, you can now perform mathematical operations on the `"7.2"` value of `myVersion`, which is now simply 7.2.

Note   The process of converting one data type to another is sometimes referred to as casting.

Boolean

There will be times when you will designate a variable's value as either `true` or `false`. Variables that use `true` or `false` are said to have a Boolean value. Boolean values are useful for either/or situations, or when you need a toggle switch — just like a light switch, which is on or off. In the code that follows, a variable named `isLoading` is initialized with a `true` value, but later switched to a `false` value when loading is complete:

```
onClipEvent(load){
    var isLoading = true;
    trace("isLoading's type = " + typeof(isLoading));
}
onClipEvent(enterFrame){
    if(this._framesloaded >= this._totalframes){
        isLoading = false;
    }
}
```

This code could be placed on a Movie Clip instance. When the Movie Clip instance appears on the Stage, the `load` event occurs, and the Output panel displays the following:

```
isLoading's type = boolean
```

You can check the data types of declared variables and objects with the `typeof` operator.

MovieClip

As the data type name implies, Movie Clip instances on the Stage have a data type of `MovieClip`. ActionScript distinguishes `MovieClip` objects from other code-based objects so that you can more easily detect `MovieClip` objects in your code. The following variable value will be typed as `movieclip`:

```
var mc = this.ballAnim;
```

As long as a Movie Clip instance named `ballAnim` exists on the current timeline (`this`), then `mc`'s data type will be `movieclip`. If `ballAnim` did not exist, then `mc`'s data type would be `undefined`. Because `mc` is classified as a `movieclip`, methods of the `MovieClip` class can then be applied to it. In the following code, the `gotoAndStop(1)` method will be passed along to `ballAnim`:

```
mc.gotoAndStop(1);
```

Object

This data type refers to most code-based objects you create with ActionScript. The following variables would be typed as `Object`:

```
var myObject = new Object();
```

If you used this code in your Flash movie, you would see `object` types in the Output panel when Debug ⇨ List Variables is used in the Test Movie environment:

```
Variable _level0.myObject = [object #1, class 'Object'] {}
```

Several ActionScript classes will return a data type of `object` if tested with the `typeof` operator. We discuss the `typeof` operator later in this chapter.

Function

In ActionScript, you can define your own subroutines of ActionScript code. We discuss subroutines and constructor functions later in this chapter. The `function` data type will be assigned to any ActionScript code that begins with the `function` action, such as:

```
function myGoto(label){
gotoAndStop(label);
}
```

You can also use the following syntax:

```
var myGoto = function(label){
    gotoAndStop(label);
};
```

Caution There is a difference between declaring a function with the first technique versus the second technique. If you declare a function with the former method, then you can place the function anywhere within your code block, on any layer for a given frame — the function will be available to any other actions declared on that frame. If you use the latter method, the function will be available only to actions that occur below the function declaration and/or layers beneath the layer on which it was declared.

undefined

If you check for the data type of a nonexistent code element, ActionScript will return a data type of undefined. For example, if you tried to create a variable that stored a reference to a MovieClip object that was not currently present on the Stage, a data type of undefined would be returned. Create a new Flash document with no elements on the Stage, in any frame. With the first frame of the document selected, type the following code into the Script pane of the Actions panel:

```
var myMovieClip = mcBallAnim;
trace("the data type of myMovieClip is " + typeof(myMovieClip));
```

Test your Flash movie (Ctrl+Enter or ⌘+Enter). The Output panel will report:

```
the data type of myMovieClip is undefined
```

Strict Typing in ActionScript 2.0

In ActionScript 2.0, introduced with Flash MX 2004, you can declare variables with a strict data type. The format for such declarations is:

```
var variableName:datatype;
```

or

```
var variableName:datatype = value;
```

For example, if you type the following code into the Actions panel, you will declare a strictly typed string variable:

```
var myName:String = "Robert";
```

In this example, the variable myName can only use values that have a data type of String. If a different data type is assigned to the variable, the ActionScript compiler will report an error when you publish or test your Flash movie. Try the following code in a new Flash document, on the first frame:

```
var myName:String;
myName = 7.2;
```

Once you have entered this code, choose Control ➪ Test Movie. The Output panel will report the following error:

```
**Error** Scene=Scene 1, layer=Layer 1, frame=1:Line 2: Type mismatch in
assignment statement: found Number where String is required.
```

Continued

Continued

```
    myName = 7.2;
```

Interesting, eh? That's a pretty specific error message, letting you know that you declared a number where a string value was expected. If you change the second line of code to

```
myName = "Robert";
```

and retest the movie, you will no longer see the error message in the Output panel. So, why is strict typing important, after all is said and done? For the most part, strict typing forces you to carefully plan and map out the goals of your Flash movie, and discourages you from "free-form" coding, or coding haphazardly. By using strict typing with your ActionScript code, you can more easily debug problems in your Flash movies. Throughout this book and for the remainder of this chapter, we'll put strict typing to use. For the most comprehensive coverage of ActionScript 2.0, refer to the *Flash 8 ActionScript Bible* by Joey Lott and Robert Reinhardt (Wiley, 2006).

Checking data types with typeof

Now that you know the various data types in ActionScript, you'll want to know how to check the data type of a given piece of information. Using the typeof operator, you can determine the data type of an ActionScript element. The typeof operator accepts only one option: the name of the ActionScript element that you wish to test. For example, you can trace a variable (or object) type in the Output panel:

```
var firstName:String = "Robert";
trace("firstName has a data type of " + typeof(firstName));
```

When this movie is tested, the Output panel will display:

```
firstName has a data type of string
```

You can use typeof in for . . . in loops, so that actions will be executed with specific data types. The following ActionScript code will take any string variables on the Main Timeline and move them to the _global namespace:

```
for(name in _root){
  if(typeof(_root[name])=="string" && _root[name] != _root["$version"]){
    _global[name] = _root[name];
    delete _root[name];
  }
}
```

This code block will move all variables except the native $version variable to the new _global namespace.

On the CD-ROM   You can see the returned values of the typeof operator in the typeof_simple_AS1.fla, typeof_simple_AS2.fla, typeof_advanced_AS1.fla, typeof_advanced _AS2.fla, and moveVariables.fla files, located in the ch26 folder of this book's CD-ROM.

Checking class type with instanceof

Flash Player 6 introduced the `instanceof` operator to ActionScript. With this operator, you can check the class type of a specific object in ActionScript. A class is similar to a data type, but a little more detailed. As we mentioned in the `Object` data type discussion, some different objects returned `object` as their data type. However, these objects belong to different classes. In fact, you probably noticed the class type showing up in the Output window when you chose Debug ➪ List Variables.

We'll show you an example that compares `typeof` to `instanceof`. Create a new Flash document, and select frame 1 of the default layer. In the Actions panel, type the following code into the Script pane:

```
var dCurrent:Date = new Date();
trace("the data type of dCurrent is " + typeof(dCurrent));
```

After you've written this code, test the Flash movie (Ctrl+Enter or ⌘+Enter). The Output panel will display the following text:

```
the data type of dCurrent is object
```

Now, use the `typeof` operator in an `if` statement. After the last line of code that you typed, enter the following code:

```
if(typeof(dCurrent) == "object"){
  trace("dCurrent has a data type of object");
}
```

When you save and test this movie, the last line of the Output panel will be:

```
dCurrent has a data type of object
```

However, if you wanted to check what kind of object `dCurrent` was, the `typeof` operator would not be able to help you out. Enter the `instanceof` operator. Add the following code to the actions list for frame 1:

```
if(dCurrent instanceof Date){
  trace("currentDate is a Date object");
}
```

When you test the movie, you will see the following text display in the Output panel:

```
dCurrent is a Date object
```

Now, try an `if/else` statement that compares `currentDate` to a different class, such as Sound. Add the following code into the Actions panel for frame 1:

```
if(dCurrent instanceof Sound){
  trace("dCurrent is a Sound object");
} else {
  trace("dCurrent is not a Sound object");
}
```

When you test your movie, you will see the following text displayed in the Output panel:

```
dCurrent is not a Sound object
```

While these are simple tests, you can start to see how `instanceof` allows you to check the class types of your data.

Note   When you use the `instanceof` operator, you do not wrap the compared value in quotes, as you do with `typeof`. For example, do not use `if(dCurrent instanceof "Date")`. Simply refer to the class by name, without the quotes: `if(dCurrent instanceof Date)`.

Overview of Functions as Procedures

A primary building block of any scripting or programming language is a procedure. A procedure is any set of code that you wish to reserve for a specific task. A procedure is useful for code that you wish to reuse in multiple event handlers (for example, Button instances and keyframes). In Flash ActionScript, procedures are called functions, and are created with the `function` action.

What functions do

A function (or procedure) sets aside a block of code that can be executed with just one line of code. Functions can execute several actions, and pass options (called *arguments* or *parameters*) to those actions. All functions must have a unique name, so that you know what to reference in later lines of code. In a way, functions are equivalent to your own custom additions to the Flash ActionScript language. In ActionScript, you can define a function on a specific timeline, and refer to its path and name to execute it.

Note   For Flash Player 4–compatible movies, use the `call()` action to execute code blocks located on other keyframes in the Flash movie.

When to create a function

For people new to scripting, perhaps the most confusing aspect of functions is knowing when to create them in a Flash movie. Use the following guidelines to help you determine when a function should be created:

✦ If you find yourself reusing the same lines of code on several Button instances, `MovieClip` objects, or keyframes, then you should consider moving the actions to a function. In general, you should not pile up ActionScript on any single Button or Movie Clip instance.

✦ If you need to perform the same operation throughout a Flash movie, such as hiding specific Movie Clip instances on the Stage, you should consider defining a function to take care of the work for you.

✦ When you need to perform operations to determine a value (such as determining the current day of the week or calculating values in a mathematical formula), you should move the operations to a function.

How to define a function

When you add a function to a keyframe on the Main Timeline or a Movie Clip timeline, you are defining the function. All functions have a target path, just like other objects in ActionScript. All functions need a name followed by opening and closing parentheses, but arguments (options to pass to the function) inside the parentheses are optional.

Tip

Functions are usually defined at the very beginning of a Flash movie. We recommend only defining functions on timeline keyframes—you can, however, execute functions from any event handler in a Flash movie.

As a simple example, let's say you want to create a function that has one `gotoAndStop()` action. This function will have a shorter name than `gotoAndStop()`, and will be faster to type and use in your ActionScript code. Place this code on the first keyframe of the Main Timeline.

```
function gts():Void {
    this.gotoAndStop("start");
}
```

This function, when evoked, will send the current timeline Playhead to the `start` label You could further expand the functionality of `gts()` by adding an argument, which we'll call `frameLabel`:

```
function gts(frameLabel:String):Void {
    this.gotoAndStop(frameLabel);
}
```

Tip

You can specify ActionScript 2.0 data typing on function arguments as well. Note that the `Void` data type is used to indicate that no value is returned from this function. We talk about return values from functions next.

In this version of the `gts()` function, instead of hard-coding a frame label such as `start` into the actual `gotoAndStop()` action, you specify an argument with the name `frameLabel`. Just like variable names, the names of your function and its arguments are entirely up to you—the name `frameLabel` has no significance. ActionScript simply knows that if you pass an argument to the `gts()` function, that it should place that argument where the `frameLabel` term occurs in your actions. An argument acts as a placeholder for information that will be supplied to the function on a per-use basis; that is, you can specify a different value for `frameLabel` each time you evoke the `gts()` function. You can also use as many (or as few) arguments as you need. Insert a comma between each argument in the function declaration:

```
function calculateRange (min:Number, max:Number):Number{
    var diff:Number = Math.abs(max - min);
    return diff;
}
```

Caution

Beware of naming your functions (and arguments) after already existing ActionScript terms. If in doubt, you should probably choose a word that does not resemble any JavaScript syntax (with later upgrades to ActionScript in mind). You'll see many examples in tutorials or books in which programmers always prefix names with `my`, as in `myColor` or `myLabel`, to avoid any potential naming conflicts.

How to execute a function

After you have defined a function on a timeline's keyframe, you can create actions that refer to the function's actions. The standard method for executing a function is:

```
path_to_function.functionName(arguments);
```

At the end of the previous section, you defined a function named gts() on the Main Timeline. If you added a Button instance to your movie, you could then execute the function from the Button instance with the following code:

```
on(release){
    this.gts("start");
}
```

When this Button instance is clicked, the function gts() on the current timeline (this) is executed, and passed the argument "start". In your function gts(), you defined frameLabel as an argument that occurs in the gotoAndStop() action. Therefore, the Main Timeline will go to and stop on the "start" frame label.

Caution A function cannot be executed unless it was previously defined in the movie and recognized by the Flash Player. The keyframe containing the function declaration needs to be "played" before the function is available for use. For example, if you define a function on frame 10 of a Movie Clip instance that has stopped on frame 1 (and never played to frame 10), the Flash Player will not have registered the function in memory. For this reason, it's usually a good idea to place your functions on the first frame of the Flash movie, or at a location where they will be initialized before you need to use them.

Managing Related Data: The Array Class

Have you ever had a bunch of variables that have a lot in common? For example, do you have variables such as name_1, name_2, name_3, name_4, and so on? These variables look like lists of common information, such as:

```
var name_1:String = "Peng";
var name_2:String = "Django";
var name_3:String = "Jenn";
var name_4:String = "Frank";
```

In programming languages, an array is a list of values that can be addressed by their position in the list. An array is created by using the Array constructor:

```
var visitors:Array = new Array();
```

The preceding code object simply creates the array container for data. You create an array with information already specified, such as:

```
var visitors:Array = new Array("Peng","Django","Jenn","Frank");
```

or

```
var visitors:Array = ["Peng", "Django", "Jenn", "Frank"];
```

To access an item in visitors, you would use the array access operators with an array index number. To access the first position's data, you would use the following code:

```
var message:String = "Hello " + visitors[0] + ", and welcome.";
```

Here, visitors[0] will return the value "Peng". If you traced the message variable, it would read:

```
Hello Peng, and welcome.
```

In most programming languages, the first index value (the starting position) is 0, not 1. In the following table, you'll see how the index number increases with the sample `visitors` array.

Index Position	0	1	2	3
Index Value	Peng	Django	Jenn	Frank

You can set and get the values within an array using the array access operators. You can replace existing array values by setting the index position to a new value, and you can add values to the array by increasing the index number, as in:

```
var visitors:Array = new Array("Peng","Django","Jenn","Frank");
visitors[3] = "Nicole";
visitors[4] = "Candice";
```

In the example, `"Nicole"` replaces `"Frank"`, and `"Candice"` is added to the end of the array. You can also add elements to the array using the `push()` method of the `Array` class, as in:

```
var visitors:Array = new Array("Peng","Django","Jenn","Frank");
var nLength:Number = visitors.push("Nicole","Candice");
```

This code will add `"Nicole"` and `"Candice"` after `"Frank"`, and set the variable `nLength` equal to the `length` of the `visitors` array. `length` is an `Array` property that returns the number of elements in the array. In the preceding example, `nLength` is equal to 6 because there are now six names in the array.

Emulating Arrays in Flash Player 4 or Flash Lite 1.0/1.1 Movies

In Flash Player 4 or Flash Lite 1.0/1.1, you can only emulate arrays, using expressions for variable names. In the earlier array examples, you could create an array-like structure for a Flash Player 4 movie by using the following code:

```
var name_1 = "John";
var name_2 = "Vanessa";
var name_3 = "Jennifer";
var name_4 = "Frank";
```

Then you could use another variable, `i`, to refer indirectly to different `name_` variables, as in:

```
var i = 2;
var currentName = eval("name_" add i);
message = "Hello " add currentName add ", and welcome!";
```

For Flash Player 4 compatibility, the `add` operator (instead of the + operator) and the `eval()` function are used to return the current value of the `name_` variable you want to insert. If you traced the `message` variable, the Output window would display:

```
Hello Vanessa, and welcome!
```

We only mention array emulation in this section because many Flash developers may encounter clients who wish to have Flash movies (or sites) that will work with the Flash Player 4 plug-in, especially for Flash banner ads, or with newer mobile phones that feature Flash Lite 1.0 or 1.1.

Creating a Dynamic Reusable Flash Menu

In this section, you use arrays to create a dynamic code-built menu that you can adjust for any Flash movie. You create a Main Timeline with six sections for a mock photographer's site, and a menu that navigates to those six sections. While that sounds simple enough, you create the menu entirely from ActionScript code. Figure 26-1 displays the menu and its items, as it appears during run time.

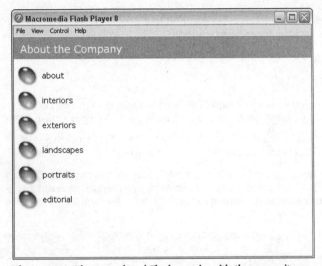

Figure 26-1: The completed Flash movie with the menu items

In the following steps, you build a Flash movie that uses this menu system.

1. Create a new Flash document (Ctrl+N or ⌘+N).

2. Rename Layer 1 **labels**. Create new keyframes (press the F6 key) on frames 2, 10, 20, 30, 40, and 50. Select frame 60 and press F5.

3. Starting on frame 2 of the labels layer, assign the following label names to the keyframes you created in Step 2: **about**, **interiors**, **exteriors**, **landscapes**, **portraits**, and **editorial**.

4. Add a new layer, and name it **actions**. Add a keyframe on frame 2 of the actions layer. With that keyframe selected, open the Actions panel and add a stop(); action. In the Property inspector, type **//stop** in the <Frame Label> field. This creates a frame comment of stop. The stop(); action on frame 2 prevents the Main Timeline from playing past the about section when the movie first loads.

5. Create another layer called **heading**. Add keyframes on this layer, matching the keyframes in the labels layer. Insert some graphics in each keyframe for each section. As a starting point, you can simply add text headings to each section (for example, About the Company, Interior Photography, and so on). You need this heading layer so that you have some indication that the Playhead on the Main Timeline actually moves when an item in the menu is clicked.

6. Create another layer called **background**. Place this layer at the bottom of the layer stack. Draw a filled rectangle that spans the top of the document, as shown in Figure 26-2.

7. Now you create an array that contains the names of each of your frame labels. Add a new layer to the Main Timeline, and name it **menu actions**. Select the first keyframe on the menu actions layer. Open the Actions panel (F9), and add the following code (note that the ⊃ indicates a continuation of the same line of code; do not insert this character into your actual code):

```
var sectionNames:Array = new Array("about", "interiors", ⊃
  "exteriors", "landscapes", "portraits", "editorial")
```

This line of ActionScript creates an `Array` object named `sectionNames`. You can now refer to each section of your timeline using array syntax, such as `sectionNames[0]`, `sectionNames[1]`, and so on. You use this array to build the actual button text in our menu.

8. In the same block of code, add the following line to the Script pane for frame 1 of the menu actions layer, after the existing code:

```
var sectionCount:Number = sectionNames.length;
```

This code creates a new variable named `sectionCount`. The `length` property of an array will return the current number of elements inside of the array. Therefore, because you put six elements into the array (in Step 7), `sectionCount` will be equal to 6. You may be wondering why you just didn't manually insert the value 6 here. The reason for using an array is that you can change the elements of the array at any point, and the rest of your code will update automatically to reflect the changes. In this way, you are building a dynamic menu system.

9. Save your Flash document as `menuArray_100.fla`. At this point, your Flash document should resemble Figure 26-2.

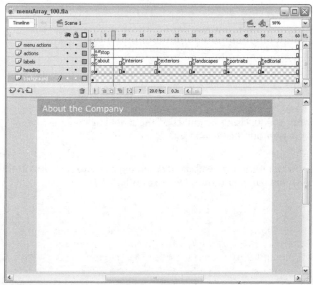

Figure 26-2: The Main Timeline has frame labels and artwork for each section of the presentation.

10. Now you need to create the menu element that you can use to build a dynamic menu from ActionScript. Create a new Movie Clip symbol by pressing Ctrl+F8 (⌘+F8). Name this symbol **itemClip**, and choose the Movie Clip behavior.

11. Within the timeline of the itemClip symbol, rename Layer 1 to **button**. On this layer, create or add a Button symbol. In our example, we used the Oval buttons — the blue button from the `Ovals` folder of the Buttons library (Window ➪ Other Panels ➪ Common Libraries ➪ Buttons). This will be the actual button that appears in the menu. Center your Button instance on the Stage, using the Align panel. In the Property inspector, name the Button instance `btClick`.

12. Add a new layer to the itemClip symbol, and name it **tLabel**. On this layer, create a Dynamic text field that can accommodate the longest name you specified in the `sectionNames` array. In the Property inspector, give this Dynamic text field the instance name `tLabel`. Use whatever font face you prefer. Place the text field to the right of the button, as shown in Figure 26-3.

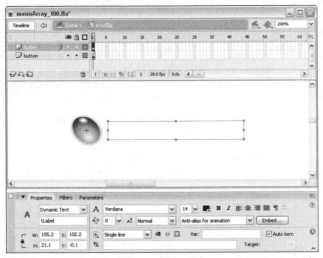

Figure 26-3: The itemClip symbol will be used to create each button in the dynamic menu. Using ActionScript, the tLabel field will be filled with the appropriate section name.

13. Add another layer to the itemClip symbol, and rename it **actions**. Select frame 1 of this layer, and in the Actions panel add the following code:

```
var tLabel:TextField;
var btClick:Button;
tLabel.text = labelName;
btClick.onRelease = function():Void {
    this._parent.targetClip.gotoAndStop(labelName);
};
stop();
```

This code will put the value of a variable named `labelName` into the `tLabel` text field. You will see how `labelName` is declared in Step 18.

The `onRelease()` handler for the `btClick` instance will use the value of a `labelName` variable as the frame label for the `gotoAndStop()` action. Notice that you will control the Playhead of a dynamically-assigned timeline, indicated by `this._parent.targetClip`. This value will be assigned to each menu item with ActionScript in a later step. You will use the itemClip symbol as a prototype for the real buttons in the menu. In the remaining steps of this exercise, you'll create a `MovieClip` object in ActionScript to hold several instances of the itemClip symbol.

14. Save your Flash document.

15. Go back to the Main Timeline (that is, Scene 1). Open the Actions panel for frame 1 of the menu actions layer. Add the following ActionScript to the Script pane, after the existing code:

```
var mcMenu:MovieClip = this.createEmptyMovieClip("mcMenu", 1);
mcMenu._x = 25;
mcMenu._y = 70;
```

This code makes an empty MovieClip instance, named `mcMenu`, at the first depth slot of the Main Timeline (`this`). The variable menu returns a reference to the `mcMenu` instance. In the second and third lines, the X and Y coordinates of the `mcMenu` instance are set to a position just below the heading artwork on the left side of the Stage.

16. Once you have created a `MovieClip` object to contain instances of the itemClip symbol, you're ready to prepare the itemClip symbol for use in ActionScript. In the Library panel (Ctrl+L or ⌘+L), right-click (Control+click on Mac) the itemClip symbol and choose Linkage in the contextual menu. In the Linkage Properties dialog box, select the Export for ActionScript check box, as shown in Figure 26-4. The Identifier field will auto-fill with the symbol's name, itemClip. You can now refer to this identifier in ActionScript to dynamically include the symbol in the Flash movie at run time. Click OK to accept the new linkage parameters.

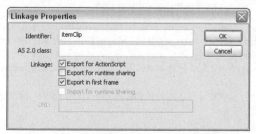

Figure 26-4: The Linkage Properties dialog box

17. Select frame 1 of the menu actions layer, and open the Actions panel. Now, you're ready to add the ActionScript code that will dynamically attach several instances of the itemClip symbol to the `mcMenu` instance created in Step 15. Note that the ⊃ indicates a continuation of the same line of code; do not insert this character into your actual code.

```
for(var i:Number=0; i < sectionCount; i++){
  var depthCount:Number = mcMenu.getNextHighestDepth();
  var item:MovieClip = mcMenu.attachMovie("itemClip", ⤸
    "item_" + i, depthCount);
  item.labelName = sectionNames[i];
  item.targetClip = this;
  item._y = i*45;
}
```

Tip

This code uses the `MovieClip` object method `getNextHighestDepth()`, which takes the guesswork out of determining which depth slots are unoccupied with existing elements.

This code inserts a `for` loop that will attach the itemClip symbol for each element in the `sectionNames` array. It will also set the value of `labelName` in each attached instance (`item`) to the name of the appropriate section name. Notice that you specify `i` for the index number of the `sectionNames` array because the position index of every array starts at 0 — your menu item numbering will also start at 0.

After an instance is attached for the section name, the `targetClip` variable (mentioned in Step 13) is set to the current timeline, `this`. All of your frame labels exist on the Main Timeline, where this code is being invoked.

You then position the `item` instance at multiples of 45. The first `item` is positioned at a Y coordinate of 0 (0 × 45 = 0), the second `item` is positioned at 45 (1 × 45 = 45), the third `item` is positioned at 90 (2 × 45 = 90), and so on.

Tip

Be sure to click the Check Syntax icon in the toolbar of the Actions panel to make sure you didn't make a typo in the code. As an alternative, you can press Ctrl+T or ⌘+T while focus is in the Actions panel.

18. Save your Flash document again, and test it (Ctrl+Enter or ⌘+Enter). Unless you had a syntax error in your ActionScript, you will see a dynamic menu, built by ActionScript (as shown in Figure 26-1). Each menu item has a unique `labelName` value, which is used in the `gotoAndStop()` action by each Button instance.

You can enhance this dynamic menu by adding animation to the itemClip symbol timeline. You can also restructure the ActionScript to work with separate Movie Clips for each `sectionName`, instead of frame labels. If you use this properly, you may never need to script a menu again! Simply change the Button instance artwork and text styles for unique menu interfaces.

On the CD-ROM

You will find the completed `menuArray_100.fla` file in the `ch26` folder of this book's CD-ROM.

Functions as Methods of Objects

We've already discussed functions as procedure mechanisms in Flash movies. You can use functions to define a set of actions that are later executed when the function is invoked. In ActionScript, you can also use functions as methods of other objects. *Methods* are actions mapped to other objects. Unlike properties and values, methods carry out a task with that object. In this section, we deconstruct a Flash document file (.fla) that uses a function to create a menu completely from ActionScript.

On the CD-ROM

Make a copy of the `createMenu_100.fla` file, located in the `ch26` folder of this book's CD-ROM.

Open a local copy of the `createMenu_100.fla` file in Flash 8. You'll notice that the Main Timeline has a setup similar to the `menuArray_100.fla` file that we discussed in the last section. There are a series of labels, indicating sections of the Flash movie. Test this Flash movie, and you'll see a dynamic menu display. Clicking each button takes you to the corresponding section of the Flash movie.

Unlike our previous `menuArray_100.fla` example, however, notice that we have different text on the menu buttons than the text used in the frame labels. For example, the Our Products menu button takes you to the `products` label on the Main Timeline. For this Flash movie, a function with multiple arguments enables you to specify the text of the menu buttons separately from the targeted labels (and timelines).

Select the first frame of the functions layer. In the Actions panel, you'll see this function appear in the Script pane:

```
function createMenu(aSections:Array):Void {
    var sectionCount = aSections.length;
    for(var i=0:Number; i < sectionCount; i++){
        var section:Object = aSections[i];
        var nDepth:Number = this.getNextHighestDepth();
        var item:MovieClip = this.attachMovie("itemClip", "item_"+i, nDepth);
        item.tLabel.text = section.btext;
        item.targetClip = section.clip;
        item.labelName = section.flabel;
        item._y = i*45;
    }
}
```

The `createMenu()` function has one argument: `aSections`. The value of this argument will be supplied via a method of a Movie Clip instance when the function is executed. Similar to our previous `menuArray_100.fla` example, an array is used to store the values of frame labels, button text, and target clips. In this way, you can create ActionScript that correctly uses frame labels in other `goto` actions, without worrying about the text that is actually used as a button item.

Select frame 1 of the actions layer, and view the code in the Actions panel. Some of the same actions from the previous section's example are re-used here. An empty `MovieClip` object named `mcMenu` is created, positioned, and assigned the `createMenu()` function as a method, just as `duplicateMovieClip()` or `attachMovie()` is a method of the `MovieClip` object:

```
mcMenu.createMenu = createMenu;
```

This line of code creates a new method called `createMenu`, specifically for the `mcMenu` instance on the Stage. It also sets this method to use the function `createMenu` as its value. Therefore, whenever you evoke the `createMenu` method of the `menu` object, the actions within the `createMenu` function will run.

Caution   The act of creating and assigning a method name for an object does not actually execute the method or the function. We're simply defining a method for the object, so that it can be evoked later. Do not use parentheses for method (and function) assignment — doing so will execute the function upon assignment.

Note that you can use any method name you prefer — it need not match the name of the function as our example does. So, you could write:

```
mcMenu.customMenu = createMenu;
```

The function `createMenu` also uses the `this` syntax to make the function work in relation to the object that is executing it. `this` will correspond to `mcMenu` for the method assignment `mcMenu.createMenu = createMenu`. However, if we had another menu instance, such as `mcMenu_2`, that used the `createMenu` function as a method, `this` would refer to its path for its method. Herein lies the power of a function as a method of an object — you can assign the same function (and arguments) to several unique objects (or Movie Clip instances) on the Stage.

To execute the method `createMenu` for the `menu` instance, specify the method and any arguments you will supply to the method. In our example, the following line executes the `createMenu()` method for the `mcMenu` instance:

```
mcMenu.createMenu(sectionNames);
```

In this line of code, the `sectionNames` variable is passed as the argument to the `createMenu` function. The `sectionNames` variable is an array of `Object` objects. Each object contains three properties:

✦ `flabel`: This property defines the frame label to be used in the menu item's `gotoAndStop()` action.

✦ `btext`: This property defines the text to appear to the right of the button.

✦ `clip`: This property declares which timeline should invoke the `gotoAndStop()` action.

In our example, three section objects are defined in the `sectionNames` array:

```
var sectionNames:Array = [
                {flabel: "main", btext: "Home", clip: this},
                {flabel: "products", btext: "Our Products", clip: this},
                {flabel: "services", btext: "Our Services", clip: this}
                ];
```

When the `createMenu()` method is evoked, the `createMenu()` function parses the `sectionNames` array into the actions contained with the function. While you do not see the code structure of an array specified in the function, a local variable named `section` represents each object in the `sectionNames` array:

```
var section:Object = aSections[i];
```

where `aSections` as the argument of the `createMenu()` function represents the passed value, `sectionNames`. In this more advanced usage of an array, each index of the array represents the section object with the three named properties. For example, when `aSection[0]` is evaluated in the `for` loop, the following object is returned:

```
{flabel: "main", btext: "Home", clip: this}
```

The section variable is used to take each object and apply its properties to dynamically created instances of the itemClip symbol:

```
item.labelName = section.btext;
item.targetClip = section.clip;
item.targetFrame = section.flabel;
```

The section.clip property is used to let each item instance know which timeline target it should address with its gotoAndStop() action (contained on the Button instance within the itemClip symbol in the Library). The section.flabel property assigns the proper frame label for the gotoAndStop() action for the Button instance, and the section.btext property assigns the text to the tLabel field within the item instance.

This movie also uses a clearMenu() function (and method) to delete the item instances.

Functions as Constructors for Objects

Functions can also be used with the new constructor to create objects with properties and methods assigned by the function. This means that you can use a function to create unique objects, based on parameters that you pass as arguments to the function upon invocation. In this section, we deconstruct another function example that creates an entire sound library with ActionScript, without using any Movie Clip instances.

On the CD-ROM

Make a local copy of the soundObjects.fla file, located in the ch26 folder of this book's CD-ROM.

Open your copy of the soundObjects.fla file in Flash 8. You'll notice that there aren't any Movie Clips and/or physical elements on the Stage. Select the first (and only) frame on the actions layer. Open the Actions panel, and you'll see the following code:

```
function SoundLibrary(begin:Number, end:Number) {
    var snd:Array = this.snd = new Array();
    if(_root.soundLib == undefined){
        var mcLib:MovieClip = _root.createEmptyMovieClip(
            "soundLib", _root.getNextHighestDepth());
    } else {
        var mcLib:MovieClip = _root.soundLib;
    }
    for (var i:Number = begin; i <= end; i++) {
        var nDepth:Number = mcLib.getNextHighestDepth();
        var target:MovieClip = mcLib.createEmptyMovieClip("snd_" +nDepth,
            nDepth);
        snd[i] = new Sound(target);
        snd[i].attachSound("sound_" + i);
    }
}
var soundLib = new SoundLibrary(1, 7);
soundLib.snd[1].start();
soundLib.snd[2].start();
```

There are three sections to this code: the function definition; the object creation and assignment; and the method execution of the Sound objects.

Function definition

The SoundLibrary() function has two arguments: begin and end. Again, these are user-defined function names and arguments. You could rename the function and arguments to your own preferred terms. The for loop in the SoundLibrary() function will create a snd array object within the calling object (this). This array will contain Sound objects that use the sound files in the Library. Note that each of the sounds in the Library have been set to export with the Flash .swf file, as defined by the Linkage Properties for each sound.

Object creation and assignment

After the SoundLibrary() function is defined, you can use it for new objects. In this example, a new object named soundLib is created after the function definition:

```
var soundLib = new SoundLibrary(1,7);
```

First, the object is declared as being on the current timeline (this or _root). By not specifying _root directly, you can load this Flash movie into MovieClip objects in other Flash movies and retain proper targeting paths for the createLib() function. If you test this movie on its own, soundLib will be declared on _root or _level0. Using the new constructor, we create the snd array and Sound objects relative to the soundLib object. We are creating a unique object with specific properties and values. This enables you to make as many objects as you desire, all from one function:

```
var soundLib_1 = new SoundLibrary(1,3);
var soundLib_2 = new SoundLibrary(4,7);
```

These actions (not used in our example) would create two separate soundLib objects, each using a specific range of Sound objects that play linked sound files from the Library.

The numbers specified in the parentheses indicate the sounds to use from the Library. Remember that in our function SoundLibrary(), the begin and end arguments are used to form the linkage identifiers:

```
"sound_" + i
```

where i is defined by the begin argument, and incremented until the end argument value is reached.

Sound object method execution

Finally, after the Sound objects are created within the soundLib object, you can play the sounds with the built-in ActionScript start() method for Sound objects:

```
this.soundLib.snd[1].start();
this.soundLib.snd[2].start();
```

These lines of code tell the Sound objects located in the 1 and 2 index positions of the snd array (in this example, sound_1 and sound_2 from the Library) to play.

This is just one way of using functions to create new objects. You can use functions to create other types of data-based objects for record storage and retrieval.

Caution   The `setVolume()` method of the `Sound` object controls all `Sound` objects linked to the same target timeline. This means that each `Sound` object must target a unique `MovieClip` object, in the `new Sound()` constructor. For example, if you wanted to separately control the volume of five individual sounds, make sure you use a different target `MovieClip` instance for each of those `Sound` objects. To safeguard for this condition, we used the `createEmptyMovieClip()` method in our example to allocate sound resources to a separate timeline, designated by the local variable `target` in the `SoundLibrary()` function.

Converting the function definition to a class definition

You're actually only a few steps away from creating your first ActionScript 2.0 class. Now that you understand how you can use a function as a constructor for a new object type (in this case, `SoundLibrary`), you can easily convert your `SoundLibrary` function into a `SoundLibrary` class.

Note   You need to be using Flash Professional 8 to complete the following steps.

1. Create a new ActionScript document in Flash Pro 8 by choosing File ➪ New, selecting ActionScript File in the General tab of the New Document dialog box (see Figure 26-5), and clicking OK.

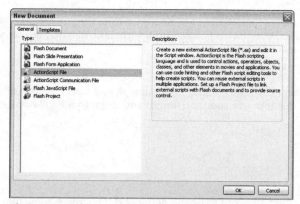

Figure 26-5: The New Document dialog box

2. Save the new document as `SoundLibrary.as`, in the same folder as the `soundObjects.fla` file you copied from the CD-ROM.

Caution   It's necessary to name the .as file the same name as the class you are going to define within the file. The filename is case-sensitive, and the .as file needs to be in the same folder as the .fla file in order for this example to work.

3. Go back to the `soundObjects.fla` file, and resave it as `soundObjects_AS2.fla`.

4. Select frame 1 of the actions layer in the `soundObjects_AS2.fla` document. Cut the entire `SoundLibrary` function by selecting the function code and pressing Ctrl+X or ⌘+X. You should only have three lines of ActionScript code left in your Actions panel.

5. Switch to the `SoundLibrary.as` file, and paste the code into the document (Ctrl+V or ⌘+V).

6. Add the following code around the function code you just pasted. Where you see the `[existing function code]`, you should have the original code from the `soundObjects.fla` document:

```
class SoundLibrary {
    [existing function code]
}
```

7. In order for the `SoundLibrary` class to work, you need to expose the `snd` array. Modify the code with the bold lines shown below:

```
class SoundLibrary {

        public var snd:Array;

        function SoundLibrary(begin:Number, end:Number) {

                snd = new Array();
                if(_root.soundLib == undefined){ ...
```

This modification simply removes the `this` reference from the `snd` array created within the constructor and removes its declaration from within the function because `snd` is declared below the class definition.

8. Save the `SoundLibrary.as` file.

9. Switch back to the `soundObjects_AS2.fla` document, and select frame 1 of the actions layer. Open the Actions panel, and modify the script to the following code:

```
import SoundLibrary;

var soundLib:SoundLibrary = new SoundLibrary(1, 7);
soundLib.snd[1].start();
soundLib.snd[2].start();
```

Here, you use the `import` keyword to let the ActionScript compiler know that you want to use the `SoundLibrary.as` class file. You don't specify the .as file extension when you use the `import` keyword.

10. Save your document, and test it (Ctrl+Enter or ⌘+Enter). You should hear the two sounds play, just as you did with the original example.

On the CD-ROM
You can find the completed files, `soundObject_AS2.fla` and `SoundLibrary.as`, in the ch26 folder of this book's CD-ROM.

We'd like to know what you think about this chapter. Visit www.flashsupport.com/ feedback to send us your comments.

Summary

✦ ActionScript has several data types, including Boolean, Function, MovieClip, Number, Object, and String.

✦ You should create a procedure when the same actions are repeated within a Flash movie, or when you want to avoid storing long action lists within Button instances.

✦ A function is defined with the function action, in the format function name (arguments){actions}.

✦ Arrays can manage related information, such as lists. An array is initiated with the Array constructor, as in myArray = new Array();.

✦ Array elements have an index number, indicating their position in the array. Array index numbers start with 0 and increment by 1 with each new element.

✦ Functions can be used as methods of ActionScript objects. You assign a method by creating a unique method name after the object and setting the method's value equal to a function name (for example, mcMenu.createMenu = createMenu;). Parentheses and arguments are omitted from the method assignment.

✦ You create objects with the function constructor. Functions intended for this use describe properties and methods for objects using the this target path. You create a new object by specifying an object name and setting its value equal to a new instance of the function name, as in myObject = new SoundLibrary(1,7);.

✦   ✦   ✦

Interacting with Movie Clips

This chapter continues your exploration of the MovieClip object in ActionScript. You explore the ins and outs of collision detection for MovieClip objects and learn how to control the visibility of the mouse pointer or to attach a custom cursor to the mouse pointer. You look at other ActionScript elements such as ColorTransform and Sound objects that work with MovieClip objects to create visual and audio effects, respectively.

New Feature Flash Player 8 introduces the ColorTransform class, which enables you to more easily apply color effects to your MovieClip objects.

Tip You will also learn how to print Flash content with the PrintJob class, introduced with Flash Player 7. The Flash Player creates high-quality output for hard copy artwork.

Movie Clip Collision Detection

Have you ever wanted to detect the intersection of two elements in a Flash movie? If two Movie Clip instances overlap on the Stage, how would you know? How would you tell ActionScript to look for an overlap? In ActionScript, there are two primary types of intersections (or collisions):

✦ **User-initiated collisions:** This type of intersection occurs when you click and drag an object (a MovieClip object) and overlap another MovieClip object as you drag or release. You can also consider the mouse pointer an "object" that can intersect with another object. For example, if you move the mouse pointer over a MovieClip object, you can detect when the mouse pointer enters the space of the MovieClip object.

✦ **Script- or time-based collisions:** This type of intersection between objects happens when randomly moving objects collide with one another, such as balls bouncing around the Stage, detecting the edges of the frame, and responding to other boundaries or objects.

In this section, you look at examples in each of these categories. Let's begin with a quick review of the _droptarget property of the MovieClip object.

Using _droptarget

A collision between two MovieClip objects can occur if the user drags one Movie Clip instance to the location of another Movie Clip instance. We first examined the startDrag() action and method in Chapter 25, "Controlling Movie Clips." In the dog movie, you used the _droptarget property of a MovieClip object to detect whether the area of one MovieClip object occupied the area of another MovieClip object. To recap, you can test the intersection of two Movie Clips with the following code:

```
var mc_1:MovieClip;
var mc_2:MovieClip;
mc_1.onPress = function():Void {
  this.startDrag();
};
mc_1.onRelease = mc_1.onReleaseOutside = function():Void {
  trace(eval (this._droptarget));
  if(eval(this._droptarget) == mc_2){
    trace("this MC overlaps mc_2");
  } else {
    trace("this MC does NOT overlap mc_2");
  }
  stopDrag ();
}
```

This code could occur on a MovieClip object named mc_1. When the user clicks the MovieClip instance, the MovieClip.startDrag() method is invoked, and the user can drag the Movie Clip instance on the Stage. When the user releases the mouse, the _droptarget property (which returns target paths in slash syntax) is evaluated to convert the target path to dot syntax. If the _droptarget property returns the path to another instance, the if condition sees whether the path matches mc_2. If the paths match, the trace() action indicating an overlap is executed. Otherwise, a separate trace() action notifies you that the instance is not on top of mc_2.

Collision detection with hitTest()

You can also perform more advanced collision detection using the hitTest() method of the MovieClip object. hitTest() does exactly what it says — it tests to see whether a "hit" occurred between two elements. hitTest() has the following two formats:

```
mc.hitTest(anotherInstance);
```

or

```
mc.hitTest(x coordinate, y coordinate, shapeFlag);
```

With this method, you can determine whether the X and Y coordinates are within the space occupied by the Movie Clip instance. You can use onClipEvents such as mouseMove or newer event handlers such as onMouseMove() to check constantly for a hit occurrence:

```
onClipEvent(mouseMove){
 if(this.hitTest(_root._xmouse, _root._ymouse, true)){
  trace("A hit has occurred");
 }
}
```

or

```
mc.onMouseMove = function(){
 if(this.hitTest(_root._xmouse, _root._ymouse, true)){
  trace("A hit has occurred");
 }
};
```

This code reports a `trace()` action anytime the mouse pointer is moved within the artwork of the Movie Clip instance to which the `onClipEvent` or `onMouseMove()` handler is attached. The shape flag attribute of `hitTest()` defines the actual test area for the hit. If the shape flag is set to `true`, a hit occurs only if the X and Y coordinates occur within the actual artwork of the Movie Clip instance. If the shape flag is set to `false`, a hit occurs whenever the X and Y coordinates occur within the bounding box of the Movie Clip instance. In Figure 27-1, if the left circle uses a shape flag of `true`, a hit is reported whenever the X and Y coordinates occur within the shape of the circle (not within the bounding box). If the right circle uses a shape of `false`, a hit is reported when the X and Y coordinates occur within the bounding box.

Figure 27-1: The shape flag determines the boundary of the Movie Clip instance for the `hitTest()` method.

On the CD-ROM

You can see a working example of shape flags and the `hitTest()` method in the `hitTest_xy.fla` file, located in the `ch27` folder of this book's CD-ROM. Open this Flash document, and test the movie. As you move your mouse within the space of each object, you will notice that the hit area is different for each object. You create your own Flash movie that uses `hitTest()` in our coverage of the `Mouse` object in this chapter.

The other format for the `hitTest()` method is to simply specify a target path to compare for a hit occurrence. With this syntax, you cannot use a shape flag option; if any area of the bounding box for a Movie Clip instance touches the bounding box of the tested instance, a hit occurs. For example, you can modify the ActionScript used earlier to indicate a hit between instances, instead of X and Y coordinates:

```
onClipEvent(mouseMove){
 if(this.hitTest(mc_2)){
  trace("A hit has occurred.");
 }
}
```

or

```
mc_1.onMouseMove = function(){
 if(this.hitTest(mc_2)){
  trace("A hit has occurred.");
 }
};
```

This code assumes that other actions are actually initiating a startDrag() action. Also, we have omitted the other half of the if condition in both this example and the previous example. If you omit a condition operator and test condition, ActionScript assumes that you are testing for a true result (as a Boolean value). The following if conditions are exactly the same:

```
var myMouseClick:Boolean = true;
if(myMouseClick){
 trace("myMouseClick is true.");
}
if(myMouseClick == true){
 trace("myMouseClick is true.");
}
```

Therefore, to test for a true value with any if statement, specify the variable (or method) that has a Boolean value. The hitTest() method yields either a true (a hit has occurred) or a false (no hit has occurred) result. Note that, with scripting languages, it is more common to use the former example for testing true conditions.

On the CD-ROM

You can see a working example of targets and the hitTest() method in the hitTest_target.fla file, located in the ch27 folder of this book's CD-ROM. You will create a Flash movie that uses this type of hitTest() method in our coverage of the Sound class later in this chapter.

Using the Mouse Class

With ActionScript, you can emulate custom mouse pointers (that is, the graphic shown for the mouse pointer) by using the startDrag() behavior (with lock to center true) on Movie Clips containing icon graphics. However, this technique does not hide the original mouse pointer—it appears directly above the dragged Movie Clip instance. ActionScript features a static Mouse class, which has the following two simple methods:

✦ show(): This method reveals the mouse pointer. By default, the mouse pointer appears at the start of a movie.

✦ hide(): This method turns off the mouse pointer's visibility. To reveal the mouse pointer again, execute the show() method.

Once the `Mouse` object (that is, the mouse pointer) is hidden, you can lock a `MovieClip` object containing a new icon graphic to the position of the mouse pointer. In this section, you create a Flash movie with a large circle `MovieClip` object. When the mouse pointer moves into the area of this object, you attach a smaller circle to the mouse pointer's position. The `hitTest()` method will be used to determine when the mouse pointer moves into the area of the large circle, and the `attachMovie()` method of the `MovieClip` object will affix the small circle to the mouse pointer's position.

1. Create a new Flash document (Ctrl+N or ⌘+N). Rename Layer 1 to **mcCircle_big**.

2. Select the Oval tool, and draw a circle. In the Property inspector, set the circle's size to 25 x 25.

3. With the circle artwork selected, press the F8 key to convert the artwork into a Movie Clip symbol. Name the symbol **circleClip**.

4. Name the instance on the Stage **mcCircle_big** in the <Instance Name> field of the Property inspector. Increase the size of this particular instance to 200 x 200, and apply a Tint effect to fill the instance with a different solid color. Center the instance on the Stage using the Align panel.

5. Now you have to link the circleClip symbol in the Library panel to the exported Flash movie file (.swf). Right-click (Control+click on the Mac) the circle symbol, and choose Linkage. Select the Export for ActionScript check box, and the Identifier field auto-fills with the text circleClip, as shown in Figure 27-2. Click OK to accept these settings.

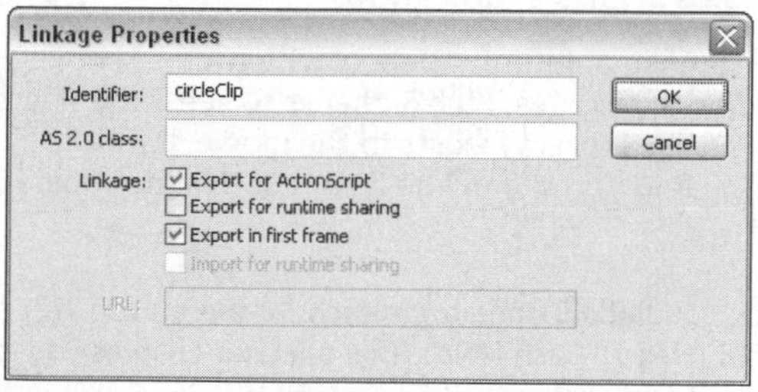

Figure 27-2: The circle symbol is now linked to the Flash movie.

Once the circle symbol is linked, you can dynamically insert the symbol into the Flash movie with ActionScript. Remember that you want to attach the circle to the mouse pointer when it enters the space of the `mcCircle_big` instance.

6. On the Main Timeline (that is, Scene 1), create a new layer and name it **actions**. Select frame 1 of this layer, and open the Actions panel. Type the code shown in Listing 27-1 into the Script pane as follows. Do not type the ⤸ character, which indicates a continuation of the same line of code.

Listing 27-1: The onMouseMove() Handler for the circleLarge_mc Instance

```
1.  var mcCircle_big:MovieClip;
2.
3.  mcCircle_big.onMouseMove = function():Void {
4.      if (this.hitTest(_root._xmouse, _root._ymouse, true)) {
5.          var mc:MovieClip = !(mcCircle_sm instanceof MovieClip) ?
6.              _root.attachMovie("circleClip", "mcCircle_sm", 1) : mcCircle_sm;
7.          mc._x = _root._xmouse;
8.          mc._y = _root._ymouse;
9.          Mouse.hide();
10.         updateAfterEvent();
11.     } else {
12.         if(mcCircle_sm instanceof MovieClip)   mcCircle_sm.removeMovieClip();
13.         Mouse.show();
14.     }
15. };
```

Here, you use the event handler onMouseMove() for MovieClip objects. This handler is assigned to the mcCircle_big in line 3. When the mouse moves in the Flash movie, the function(){} code executes in lines 4 through 15.

If the X and Y positions of the mouse pointer intersects with the mcCircle_big instance, the if condition in line 4 executes. Line 5 checks to see if the new graphic (that is, the circleClip symbol in the Library) exists in the movie. If it doesn't, the symbol is attached to the Main Timeline (_root) in line 5 as well. The new instance is named mcCircle_sm.

Note For more information on the ?: conditional operator, search for the phrase "?: conditional operator" in the Flash Help panel (Help ➪ Flash Help). This operator enables you to check a condition before assigning a value to a variable.

Lines 7 and 8 position the X and Y coordinates of the mcCircle_sm instance by referencing the current position of the mouse pointer (_root._xmouse and _root._ymouse). Line 9 hides the mouse pointer icon, while line 10 uses the updateAfterEvent() function to force a video refresh of the Flash movie. This enables the mcCircle_sm to move very smoothly across the Stage.

Lines 11–14 execute if the mouse pointer is not within the space of the mcCircle_big instance. Line 12 checks to see if mcCircle_sm exists in the movie—if it does, it is removed. The mouse pointer will also reappear when the mouse moves outside of the mcCircle_big instance (line 13).

7. Save your Flash document as mouse_hitTest.fla, and test it (Ctrl+Enter or ⌘+Enter). In the Test Movie window, move the mouse pointer into the space of the large circle. When the mouse enters this area, the small circle from the Library attaches itself to the position of the mouse cursor and hides the original pointer. When you move the mouse out of the large circle, the small circle disappears and the original mouse pointer returns. See Figure 27-3 for these comparisons.

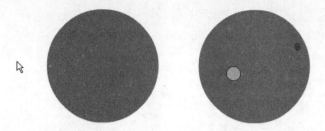

Figure 27-3: The left image shows the mouse outside the large circle, whereas the right image shows the mouse inside the large circle with the small circle attached.

That might seem like a lot of work to hide a mouse pointer, but in the process, you have learned how to attach your own icons to the mouse pointer. You can use this same methodology to add any custom graphic to the mouse pointer. Simply add a different linked symbol to the Library, and change the linkage ID in the attachMovie() method.

On the CD-ROM You can find the completed example, mouse_hitTest.fla, in the ch27 folder of this book's CD-ROM.

Manipulating Color Attributes

The ColorTransform class in ActionScript gives you unprecedented control of the appearance of your MovieClip objects. By controlling the color (and transparency) of your artwork with ActionScript's ColorTransform class, you can:

✦ Create on-the-fly color schemes or "skins" for Flash interfaces.

✦ Enable users to select and view color preferences for showcased products on an e-commerce site.

✦ Instantly change the color attributes of a Flash design-in-progress for a client.

Because color is controlled through the ColorTransform class, we'll quickly review the unique properties within this class. Refer to Table 27-1 for more information. Note that this table is organized by order of practical use.

Caution The ColorTransform class requires Flash Player 8. The older Color class for Flash Player 5 and higher is officially deprecated in Flash Player 8. If you need to control the color of MovieClip instances in Flash Player 7 or earlier movies, use the Color class instead. You can read our archived coverage of the Color class from the *Macromedia Flash MX 2004 Bible* (Wiley, 2004) at www.flashsupport.com/archive.

Table 27-1: Properties for the ColorTransform Class

Property	Definition	Options
`rgb`	Retrieves or sets the RGB offset for the targeted Movie Clip. This property changes all colors in the targeted instance to one	*ct.rgb = 0xRRGGBB;* where: *ct* is the name of the `ColorTransform` object. We'll discuss the creation of `ColorTransform` objects in this section. *RR, GG,* and *BB* are the offset values (in hexadecimal) for the Red, Green, and Blue channels, respectively. solid RGB color.
`[Channel]Multiplier`	Retrieves or sets the multiplier used by a specific color channel in the targeted Movie Clip. Acceptable values are between (and including) −1 and 1. You can preview a channel's multiplier effect by using the left-hand column of values in the Advanced Effect dialog box of the Color mode, as accessed in the Property inspector settings for a Movie Clip instance.	*ct.redMultiplier = 0.2;* *ct.greenMultiplier = 0.65;* *ct.blueMultiplier = −1;* *ct.alphaMultiplier = 0.1;* where: *ct* is the name of a `ColorTransform` object. We'll discuss the intricacies of these properties in the following sections.
`[Channel]Offset`	Retrieves or sets the offset used by a specific color channel in the targeted Movie Clip. Acceptable values are between (and including) −255 and 255. You can preview a channel's offset effect by using the left-hand column of values in the Advanced Effect dialog box of the Color mode, as accessed in the Property inspector settings for a Movie Clip instance.	*ct.redOffset = 100;* *ct.greenOffset = 50;* *ct.blueOffset = 25;* *ct.alphaOffset = 0;* where: *ct* is the name of a `ColorTransform` object. You'll practice the use of offsets in an exercise within this section.

Creating a ColorTransform object

To manipulate the color attributes of a Movie Clip instance, you need to create a new `ColorTransform` object that references the Movie Clip instance. In the following steps, you learn to use the constructor for the `ColorTransform` object. Let's work out the steps required to take control of color properties.

On the CD-ROM For the exercises with the `Color` object, make a copy of the `dogColor_starter.fla` document from the `ch27` folder of this book's CD-ROM. Thank you, Sandro Corsaro, of `www.sandrocorsaro.com`, for supplying the dog artwork!

1. Save the starter file as `dogColor_100.fla`.

2. Select the instance of the dog graphic on the Stage. Open the Property inspector and name this Movie Clip instance `mcDog_1`.

3. Create a new layer on the Main Timeline, and name the layer **buttons**.

4. Open the Components panel and drag an instance of the `Button` component onto the Stage. Place the instance near the left corner of the Stage. We discuss components in more detail in Chapter 33, "Using Components." For now, we'll guide you through the use of this component for the purposes of this exercise.

5. Select the `Button` component instance on the Stage, and open the Property inspector. Make sure the Parameters tab is selected in the inspector. Name this instance `cbtRed`. Type the text **Red** in the label field. Refer to the settings shown in Figure 27-4.

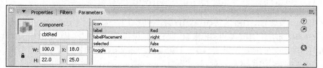

Figure 27-4: The parameters for this instance of the Button component

6. Now you need to create a `changeColor()` function in the movie. This function is executed by the `cbtRed` instance when the button is clicked. Create a new layer on the Main Timeline and name it **actions**. Select frame 1 of the actions layer, and open the Actions panel (F9). Type the following code into the Script pane:

```
1.   import flash.geom.ColorTransform;
2.
3.   var mcDog_1:MovieClip;
4.   var cbtRed:mx.controls.Button;
5.
6.   function changeColor(oEvent:Object):Void {
7.     var sLabel:String = oEvent.target.label.toLowerCase();
8.     if (sLabel == "red") {
9.       var ct:ColorTransform = new ColorTransform();
10.      ct.rgb = 0xFF0000;
```

```
11.       mcDog_1.transform.colorTransform = ct;
12.     }
13. }
14.
15. cbtRed.addEventListener("click", this.changeColor);
```

Line 1 imports the `ColorTransform` class so that the ActionScript compiler can correctly create the Flash movie on publish. Lines 3 and 4 declare the data types of the `mcDog_1` and `cbtRed` instances, respectively.

The `changeColor()` function is defined on lines 6 through 13. In this function, the `oEvent` argument represents an event object that the `Button` instance passes to the function. When the `cbtRed` instance is clicked, `oEvent.target` will equal `cbtRed`. (You'll be adding another instance in short order.) Line 7 of this function establishes a variable named `sLabel` that returns the label text inside of the `target` instance and converts the label text to lowercase. If `sLabel` equals `"red"` in line 8, lines 9 through 11 will execute. Line 9 creates a new `ColorTransform` object called `ct`. Once the `ct` object is initiated, you can access properties of the `ColorTransform` object, such as `rgb`. In line 10, you set the color to pure red, designated by `0xFF0000` in hexadecimal. In line 11, you apply the `ct` instance to the new `colorTransform` property of the `MovieClip.transform` property.

The last line of code (line 15), after the function declaration, tells the `cbtRed` instance to register the `changeColor()` function as a listener for click events. Whenever the `cbtRed` instance is clicked, the `changeColor()` function is invoked.

7. Save the Flash document, and test the movie. Click the `cbtRed` instance on the Stage. The color of the `mcDog_1` Movie Clip should change to bright red. Close the Flash movie, and return to the Flash 8 authoring environment.

8. To see that `rgb` is both a property you can write and read, let's create some `trace()` messages for the Output panel. Go back to the `changeColor()` function on frame 1. Add the following line of code just before the closing curly brace (}) of the `if()` action. Type this as one line of code:

```
trace("ct's RGB numeric value = " + ct.rgb);
```

9. Save the document and test the movie. When you click the `cbtRed` instance, the Output panel opens and displays the following text:

```
ct's RGB numeric value = 16711680
```

10. To change this value back to the hexadecimal value you entered in the `rgb` property, you need to convert the value to base 16. Add the following action after the last `trace()` action from Step 8:

```
trace("ct's RGB hex value = " + ct.rgb.toString(16));
```

11. Save the document and test the movie. When you click the `cbtRed` instance, the Output panel should open and display the new value:

```
ct's RGB numeric value = 16711680
ct's RGB hex value = ff0000
```

However, you won't need to convert `rgb`'s native return value to set another `ColorTransform` object equal to a previous `rgb` value. In the following steps, you will create another dog and `ColorTransform` object team.

12. Duplicate the mcDog_1 Movie Clip instance on the Stage (Edit ➪ Duplicate), and name the new instance mcDog_2 in the Property inspector. Position the mcDog_2 instance to the right of mcDog_1.

13. Duplicate the Button component instance on the Stage, and position the new instance below the original one. In the Property inspector, change its instance name to cbtPassRed. Change its label value to **Pass Red**.

14. Select frame 1 of the actions layer, and open the Actions panel. On the closing curly brace line of the existing if() code in the changeColor() function, add the code shown in bold in Listing 27-2. Also, add the new variables shown in bold formatting at the top of the listing.

Listing 27-2: **Checking for the Pass Red Label**

```
import flash.geom.ColorTransform;

var mcDog_1:MovieClip;
var mcDog_2:MovieClip;
var cbtRed:mx.controls.Button;
var cbtPassRed:mx.controls.Button;

function changeColor(oEvent:Object):Void {
    var sLabel:String = oEvent.target.label.toLowerCase();
    if (sLabel == "red") {
        var ct:ColorTransform = new ColorTransform();
        ct.rgb = 0xFF0000;
        mcDog_1.transform.colorTransform = ct;
        trace("ct's RGB numeric value = " + ct.rgb);
        trace("ct's RGB hex value = " + ct.rgb.toString(16));
    } else if (sLabel == "pass red") {
        var ct:ColorTransform = new ColorTransform();
        ct.rgb = mcDog_1.transform.colorTransform.rgb;
        mcDog_2.transform.colorTransform = ct;
    }
}

cbtRed.addEventListener("click", this.changeColor);
cbtPassRed.addEventListener("click", this.changeColor);
```

Tip

For this example, we wanted to demonstrate the reading and writing of the rgb property. You can also simply pass the transform property, which includes the MovieClip instance's alpha value, to another MovieClip object:

```
mcDog_2.transform.colorTransform =
mcDog_1.transform.colorTransform;
```

15. Save the Flash document and test the movie. When you click the `cbtRed` instance, the `mcDog_1` Movie Clip instance turns red. When you click the `cbtPassRed` instance, the `mcDog_2` Movie Clip instance turns red.

Note   If you click the second `Button` instance first, the `mcDog_2` Movie Clip instance will turn black. Why? Because the first button's actions were not executed, and there was no previous `rgb` property value for the new `rgb` property. Consequently, ActionScript returns a zero value. In hexadecimal color, zero is equivalent to black.

Now that you've had some experience with the `ColorTransform` object's `rgb` property, let's move on to a more complex use of `ColorTransform`. You'll use the Flash document from this exercise, so keep the dogs on the Stage!

On the CD-ROM   You can find the completed Flash document, `dogColor_100.fla`, in the `ch27` folder of this book's CD-ROM.

Setting Multiplier and Offset Values

The `ColorTransform` class also features multiplier and offset properties, which require a more thorough understanding of RGB color space.

The multiplier and offset properties of the `ColorTransform` class are

✦ `redMultiplier` — The Red channel percentage

✦ `redOffset` — The Red channel offset

✦ `greenMultiplier` — The Green channel percentage

✦ `greenOffset` — The Green channel offset

✦ `blueMultiplier` — The Blue channel percentage

✦ `blueOffset` — The Blue channel offset

✦ `alphaMultiplier` — The Alpha channel percentage

✦ `alphaOffset` — The Alpha channel offset

The *multiplier* properties are decimal values, ranging in value from –1 to 1. The *offset* properties are integer-based from –255 to 255 (derived from 24-bit RGB color space, in which each 8-bit color channel can have a range of 256 values).

These properties and values may seem complex, so refer to the Advanced options of the Color menu for symbol instances in the Property inspector for guidance. With the Advanced option chosen in the Color menu, click the Settings button. In the Advanced Effect dialog box, the left-hand color controls are percentage-based (or multipliers), whereas the right-hand controls are offset-based. Admittedly, color is difficult to visualize from numbers. To accurately predict the color changes with `ColorTransform`, we use the Advanced Effect dialog box to help us out.

On the CD-ROM   Make a copy of the `dogColor_100.fla` file if you didn't complete the previous section's exercise. This document is located in the `ch27` folder of this book's CD-ROM.

1. Resave the Flash document from the previous section as `dogColor_200.fla`.

2. Select the original `mcDog_1` Movie Clip instance on the Stage. Open the Property inspector, and choose the Advanced option in the Color menu. Press the Settings button to the right of the menu. In the Advanced Effect dialog box, enter the following value on the left-hand side: **–100%** Blue. On the right-hand side, enter these values: **37** G and **255** B. Refer to Figure 27-5. Click OK to close the dialog box. With these values, the `mcDog_1` instance should be a monochrome blue with yellow eyes. Normally, you would want to write these values down so that you had them to use later. Because you have them printed here in this book, erase them by choosing None from the Color menu in the Property inspector. The `mcDog_1` instance should now appear in its original state.

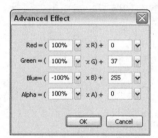

Figure 27-5: These settings will change the color of the `mcDog_1` instance.

3. Duplicate one of the existing `Button` component instances on the Stage. Place the duplicated instance underneath the last `Button` component instance. Name the instance `cbtRabid`. Change the `label` value to **Rabid**.

   With this new instance, you will create some code that will initiate a new `ColorTransform` object. The new object will be given properties that have the same values as those determined in Step 2.

4. Select frame 1 of the actions layer and open the Actions panel (F9, or Option+F9 on Mac). Add the bold code shown in Listing 27-3.

Listing 27-3: **Checking for the rabid Label**

```
import flash.geom.ColorTransform;

var mcDog_1:MovieClip;
var mcDog_2:MovieClip;
var cbtRed:mx.controls.Button;
var cbtPassRed:mx.controls.Button;
```

Continued

Listing 27-3 *(continued)*

```
var cbtRabid:mx.controls.Button;

function changeColor(oEvent:Object):Void {
    var sLabel:String = oEvent.target.label.toLowerCase();
    if (sLabel == "red") {
        var ct:ColorTransform = new ColorTransform();
        ct.rgb = 0xFF0000;
        mcDog_1.transform.colorTransform = ct;
        trace("ct's RGB numeric value = " + ct.rgb);
        trace("ct's RGB hex value = " + ct.rgb.toString(16));
    } else if (sLabel == "pass red") {
        var ct:ColorTransform = new ColorTransform();
        ct.rgb = mcDog_1.transform.colorTransform.rgb;
        mcDog_2.transform.colorTransform = ct;
    } else if (sLabel == "rabid"){
        var ct:ColorTransform = new ColorTransform();
        ct.blueOffset = 255;
        ct.blueMultiplier = -1;
        ct.greenOffset = 37;
        mcDog_1.transform.colorTransform = ct;
    }
}

cbtRed.addEventListener("click", this.changeColor);
cbtPassRed.addEventListener("click", this.changeColor);
cbtRabid.addEventListener("click", this.changeColor);
```

In the preceding code, you created a new ColorTransform instance named ct. In addition to rgb, ColorTransform instances can have offset and multiplier values for each color (and alpha) channel. In Listing 27-3, you assigned the values you determined in Step 2. Offset values have a one-to-one relationship with the offset values displayed in the Advanced Effect dialog box, but multiplier values are divided by 100. So, if you have a multiplier value of –100 in the Advanced Effect dialog box, the equivalent ColorTransform multiplier value would be –1. After you have set the appropriate offset and/or multiplier values, you apply the ct instance to the colorTransform property of the transform property of the mcDog_1 instance.

Note   The ColorTransform class is one of two types of alterations to Movie Clips that can be made with the Transform class. The transform property of the MovieClip class uses the Transform class, which is new to Flash Player 8 and encompasses a wide range of characteristics that can be applied to the MovieClip class. For more detailed information of the Transform class, refer to the *Macromedia Flash 8 ActionScript Bible* (Wiley, 2006).

5. Save the Flash document, and test the movie. Click the new Button instance that you added in Step 3. The colors of the mcDog_1 Movie Clip instance should change to match those you saw in Step 2. Close the Test Movie window, and return to the Flash 8 authoring environment.

Now you will create a button that restores the original look of the mcDog_1 Movie Clip instance.

6. Duplicate one of the Button instances, and place the new instance underneath the last Button instance. In the Property inspector, name this component instance cbtRestore. Change the label value to **Restore**.

7. Select frame 1 of the actions layer, and open the Actions panel (F9). Add the bold code shown in Listing 27-4 to the Script pane.

Listing 27-4: **Checking for the Restore Label**

```
import flash.geom.ColorTransform;

var mcDog_1:MovieClip;
var mcDog_2:MovieClip;
var cbtRed:mx.controls.Button;
var cbtPassRed:mx.controls.Button;
var cbtRabid:mx.controls.Button;
var cbtRestore:mx.controls.Button;

function changeColor(oEvent:Object):Void {
   var sLabel:String = oEvent.target.label.toLowerCase();
   if (sLabel == "red") {
          var ct:ColorTransform = new ColorTransform();
          ct.rgb = 0xFF0000;
          mcDog_1.transform.colorTransform = ct;
          trace("ct's RGB numeric value = " + ct.rgb);
          trace("ct's RGB hex value = " + ct.rgb.toString(16));
   } else if (sLabel == "pass red") {
          var ct:ColorTransform = new ColorTransform();
          ct.rgb = mcDog_1.transform.colorTransform.rgb;
          mcDog_2.transform.colorTransform = ct;
   } else if (sLabel == "rabid"){
          var ct:ColorTransform = new ColorTransform();
          ct.blueOffset = 255;
          ct.blueMultiplier = -1;
          ct.greenOffset = 37;
          mcDog_1.transform.colorTransform = ct;
   } else if (sLabel == "restore"){
          var ct:ColorTransform = new ColorTransform();
          mcDog_1.transform.colorTransform = ct;
   }
}

cbtRed.addEventListener("click", this.changeColor);
cbtPassRed.addEventListener("click", this.changeColor);
cbtRabid.addEventListener("click", this.changeColor);
cbtRestore.addEventListener("click", this.changeColor);
```

In Listing 27-4, you simply need to create a new `ColorTransform` instance (ct) and pass it to the `colorTransform` property of the `MovieClip` instance, `mcDog_1`. A new `ColorTransform` instance has default multiplier and offset values. So, when it's passed to a `MovieClip` object, the color properties are set back to the original values.

8. Save the Flash document again, and test the movie. Click the `cbtRabid` instance you created in Step 3. After the `mcDog_1` Movie Clip instance changes color, click the `cbtRestore` instance you created in Step 6. Voila! The `mcDog_1` Movie Clip instance reverts to its original color. Click the `cbtRed` instance that you created in the previous section. This button changes the appearance of the `mcDog_1` Movie Clip instance to a solid red color. Now click the `cbtRestore` instance—the `mcDog_1` Movie Clip instance reverts to its original look!

On the CD-ROM You can find the completed document, `dogColor_200.fla`, in the `ch27` folder of this book's CD-ROM.

While the `ColorTransform.rgb` property can alter basic color properties of `MovieClip` objects, the offset and multiplier properties are the color-control powerhouse. Any look that you can accomplish with the Advanced Effect dialog box, you can reproduce with the `ColorTransform` class.

Enabling Sound with ActionScript

ActionScript offers many classes, and one of the most exciting classes to use is the `Sound` class. As with most classes, the `Sound` class has predefined methods that you can use to control each new `Sound` class. Table 27-2 provides an overview of the `Sound` class and its common methods.

New Feature Flash Player 8 can support up to 32 channels of audio (or 16 channels of stereo audio) simultaneously.

Table 27-2: Common Methods for the Sound Class

Method	Definition	Options
attachSound	Creates a new instance of a sound file (.aif or .wav) available in the Library. The new instance becomes a part of the Sound instance and can be targeted with Sound instance methods. Unlike attached Movie Clips, attached sounds do not require a depth number.	*soundObject.attachSound(libraryID);* where: *soundObject* refers to the Sound instance's name. *libraryID* is the name of the sound in the Symbol Linkage properties (available in the Library).

Method	Definition	Options
loadSound	Loads a separate MP3 audio source file (.mp3) into a Sound object. You can begin playback of the MP3 sound as soon as enough bytes have downloaded, or wait until the entire file has downloaded. We will show you how to use this new method in Chapter 28, "Sharing and Loading Assets."	*soundObject.loadSound(URL, isStreaming);* where: *URL* is the location of the MP3 file. This location can be a relative or absolute path *isStreaming* determines if the loading sound will begin playback as soon as enough bytes have downloaded (true), or if the entire sound must download before playback can begin (false).
start	Plays the targeted Sound instance. A sound must be attached to the Sound instance before it can play.	*soundObject.start(inPoint, loopFactor);* where: *inPoint* is the time (in seconds) in the sound where playback should begin. *loopFactor* is the number of times the sound should be repeated. Both of these parameters are optional and can be omitted.
stop	Stops playback of the targeted Sound instance. If no target is specified, all sounds are stopped. Note that this is not equivalent to pausing a sound. If a stopped sound is played later, it will start at the beginning (or at the *inPoint*).	*soundObject.stop(libraryID);* where: *libraryID* is the name of the sound in the Linkage properties (available in the Library).
setVolume	Changes the overall volume of the specified Sound instance. This method accepts values between 0 and 100 (in percentage units). You can enter percentages greater than 100 percent to increase sound output beyond its original recording level, but you may notice digital distortion of the sound.	*soundObject.setVolume(volume);* where: *volume* is a number between 0 and 100.

Continued

Table 27-2 *(continued)*

Method	Definition	Options
getVolume	Retrieves the current volume of the Sound instance.	*soundObject.getVolume();* No options or arguments for this method.
setPan	Changes the offset of sound output from both the left and right channels.	*soundObject.setPan(panValue);* where: *panValue* is a value between −100 (full left-speaker output) and 100 (full right-speaker output). Use a value of 0 to balance sound output evenly.
getPan	Retrieves the values created with a previous setPan execution. You use this method to apply Pan settings consistently to multiple objects, or to store a Pan setting.	*soundObject.getPan();* No options or arguments for this method.
setTransform	Changes the volume for each channel of the specified Sound object. This method also enables you to play the right channel in the left channel and vice versa.	*soundObject.setTransform(soundTransformObject);* where: *soundTransformObject* is the name of an object that has percentage properties for left and right output for the left channel, and left and right output for the right channel.
getTransform	Retrieves the values established with the last setTransform execution. You use this method to reapply sound transforms to new Sounds objects, or to store setTransform values.	*soundObject.getTransform();* No options or arguments for this method.

The following list of Sound class features offers reasons for using Sound instances over traditional sound Movie Clips or keyframe sounds. You have:

✦ Dynamic event sounds that play in a random or user-defined order

✦ Precise control over volume and panning

✦ The ability to dump (or erase) a Sound object when the sound is no longer needed

Note   All Sound objects are treated as Event sounds. You cannot use Sound objects to control the playback or frame rate like Stream sounds can. However, ActionScript does enable you to load MP3 files on the fly and "stream" their playback—these types of sounds, however, cannot control playback or frame-rate synchronization. For more information on Synch modes for sound, please refer to Chapter 15, "Adding Sound." (The usage of the term "stream" in this context does not imply real-time streaming, but rather a progressive download for the MP3 file.)

The Sound class uses sounds directly from the movie's library or from an MP3 file loaded at run time. You cannot use the Sound class to control sounds specified in the Property inspector for any given keyframes.

Tip   You can, however, control Stream sounds attached to keyframes on a given timeline by controlling an empty Sound object. Any methods applied to the Sound object will be passed along to the Stream sound.

The next section shows you how to create Sound objects using the object constructor with the attachSound() and start() methods.

Creating sound libraries with ActionScript

In the Chapter 19, "Building Timelines and Interactions," you learned how to use behaviors to identify and play sounds. From a conceptual point of view, manually creating each sound behavior enabled you to see and work with each sound "object" very easily. However, you can produce the sounds for a sound library much more quickly using your own ActionScript code.

On the CD-ROM   In this section, you start with the linked sounds you created in Chapter 19, "Building Timelines and Interactions." Make a copy of the pianoKeys_sounds.fla file from the ch19 folder of this book's CD-ROM.

1. Using the Open External Library command in the File ➪ Import menu, select your copy of the pianoKeys_sounds.fla file. Opening a Flash document as a Library enables you to access symbols and media in that file.

2. If you don't have a new untitled Flash document open, create a new Flash file (Ctrl+N or ⌘+N). Save the new document as soundLib_ActionScript.fla.

3. Change the background color of the document to **black** in the Document Properties dialog box (Modify ➪ Document).

4. Open the new document's Library panel (Ctrl+L or ⌘+L). Drag each of the key_ sounds from the pianoKeys_sound Library panel into the Library panel of your new document. When you are finished, you should see all seven sounds in your new document's Library panel, as shown in Figure 27-6.

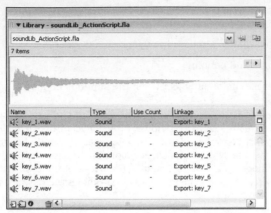

Figure 27-6: The imported sounds with their linkage identifiers displayed

5. Close the `pianoKeys_sounds` Library panel, and save your Flash document.

6. Now, you need to add the ActionScript code that will create your `Sound` objects. You will construct a function that, when executed, will form a list of sound instances. On the Main Timeline (that is, Scene 1), rename Layer 1 to **actions**. Alt+double-click (or Option+double-click on the Mac) frame 1 of this layer. This opens the Actions panel. Type the following code into the Script pane:

```
var aSounds:Array;

function createLib(num:Number):Void {
        var mcLib:MovieClip = this.createEmptyMovieClip("mcLib", 1);
        aSounds = new Array();
        for (var i:Number = 1; i<=num; i++) {
```

The first line establishes an array variable named `aSounds`, which will store references to each new sound added to the sound library. The next line of code establishes the name of your function, `createLib()`. You will want to dynamically change the number of sounds you create with this function. Therefore, we assign an optional parameter (called an *argument*) `num` that will be passed to the nested actions within the function.

The third line creates an empty `MovieClip` object, `mcLib`. This instance will hold individual sound targets, which you create in the next step.

The fourth line creates a new `Array` object, `aSounds`. This array stores the `Sound` objects that the `createLib()` function creates.

The fifth line starts a `for` loop that cycles its nested actions until the condition `i<=num` is no longer `true`. `i` starts (or initializes) with a value of 1, and the syntax `i++` tells `i` to increase by 1 with each pass of the `for` loop.

In the next step, you want the `for` loop to create a new instance of the `Sound` object for each sound in the Library, and attach each sound in the Library to its new instance.

7. In the Actions panel, add the following ActionScript to the code from Step 6:

```
var mc:MovieClip = mcLib.createEmptyMovieClip("mcSnd_"+i, i);
var snd:Sound = new Sound(mc);
snd.attachSound("key_"+i);
aSounds.push(snd);
  }
}
```

The first line creates a new `MovieClip` object, whose name starts with `mcSnd_`. This instance is stored with the `mcLib` instance. The local variable `mc` is a reference to the new `MovieClip` object as well. With each pass of the loop, a new instance is created (for example, `mcSnd_1`, `mcSnd_2`, and so on). Each instance is used to store the attached sound later in the `for` loop.

The second line makes a new `Sound` object that points to the timeline referenced by the `target` variable. Ultimately, your `Sound` objects will be tied to instances nested within the `mcLib` Movie Clip instance, which you'll see later.

The third line uses the `attachSound()` method to take a sound element in the Library and attach it to the `Sound` object. The argument for the `attachSound()` method is specified as `"key_" + i`. On each pass of the `for` loop, this expression will return `"key_1"`, `"key_2"`, and so on until the limit prescribed by the `num` argument is reached.

The complete block of code on the first keyframe of the actions layer is shown in Listing 27-5.

Listing 27-5: **The createLib() Function**

```
var aSounds:Array;

function createLib(num:Number):Void {
   var mcLib:MovieClip = this.createEmptyMovieClip("mcLib", 1);
   aSounds = new Array();
   for (var i:Number = 1; i <= num; i++) {
      var mc:MovieClip = mcLib.createEmptyMovieClip("mcSnd_" + i, i);
      var snd:Sound = new Sound(mc);
      snd.attachSound("key_" + i);
      aSounds.push(snd);
   }
}
```

8. Now that you have a function defined to create all the Sound objects, you need to invoke the function. With the code for frame 1 of the actions layer displayed in the Actions panel, type the following code after the `createLib()` function definition:

```
createLib(7);
```

This line of code invokes the `createLib()` function. In addition to executing the `createLib()` method, you're also sending the function the number 7 as the `num` argument. Therefore, seven `Sound` objects are created.

9. Save the Flash document and test it (Ctrl+Enter or ⌘+Enter). Although you won't hear or see anything special happen, choose Debug ⇨ List Variables in the Test Movie environment. The Output panel opens and displays the Sound objects, among other variables and objects:

```
Variable _level0.aSounds = [object #2, class 'Array'] [
    1:[object #3, class 'Sound'] {
      id3:[getter/setter] undefined,
      duration:[getter/setter] 1752,
      position:[getter/setter] 0
    },
    2:[object #4, class 'Sound'] {
      id3:[getter/setter] undefined,
      duration:[getter/setter] 1602,
      position:[getter/setter] 0
    },
    3:[object #5, class 'Sound'] {
      id3:[getter/setter] undefined,
      duration:[getter/setter] 1822,
      position:[getter/setter] 0
    },
    4:[object #6, class 'Sound'] {
      id3:[getter/setter] undefined,
      duration:[getter/setter] 1672,
      position:[getter/setter] 0
    },
    5:[object #7, class 'Sound'] {
      id3:[getter/setter] undefined,
      duration:[getter/setter] 1660,
      position:[getter/setter] 0
    },
    6:[object #8, class 'Sound'] {
      id3:[getter/setter] undefined,
      duration:[getter/setter] 1728,
      position:[getter/setter] 0
    },
    7:[object #9, class 'Sound'] {
      id3:[getter/setter] undefined,
      duration:[getter/setter] 1785,
      position:[getter/setter] 0
    }
  ]
```

10. Close the Test Movie window and return to the Flash 8 authoring environment. Select frame 1 of the actions layer, and add this last bit of code to the Script pane:

```
aSounds[0].start();
```

The first line of code targets the first declared element, 0, of the aSounds object, and tells it to begin playback with the start() method of the Sound class. Remember that element 0 in the array is a Sound object, which references the key_1 ID in the Library.

11. Save the Flash document and test it. You will hear key_1 sound (`key_1.wav` or `key_1.aif`) play.

Now you should practice targeting these Sound objects from other event handlers, such as buttons and more keyframes. To access a different sound, simply change the number in the array brackets. In the next chapter, you'll learn how to load a Flash movie file (.swf) into another Flash movie, as well as how to load MP3 files directly into the movie.

You can view the completed sound library movie, `soundLib_ActionScript.fla`, located in the ch27 folder of this book's CD-ROM. We've also included a bonus file, `soundLib_onSoundComplete.fla`, that demonstrates the `onSoundComplete()` handler of the Sound class. This handler detects when a sound has finished playing. In the bonus example, each sound plays successively, from key_1 all the way through key_7.

You should attach only one sound per timeline (or Movie Clip instance). While you can create more than one Sound object instance on a timeline, you cannot use the `setVolume()` method of the Sound class to control each individual sound — the volume will be set for all Sound object instances on the targeted timeline.

Creating a soundTransformObject

Two other methods of the Sound class, `setTransform()` and `getTransform()`, work with transform objects with specific properties to control volume distribution across channels. You need to create a generic object using the object constructor before the `setTransform()` method can be used with a Sound object. This generic object will become a soundTransformObject once you have assigned sound channel properties to the generic object.

Luckily, the soundTransformObject doesn't have as many properties as the ColorTransform class, and they're much simpler to predict with trial-and-error testing. The properties of the soundTransformObject are

- ✦ ll — The percentage of left channel output in the left speaker
- ✦ lr — The percentage of right channel output in the left speaker
- ✦ rr — The percentage of right channel output in the right speaker
- ✦ rl — The percentage of left channel output in the right speaker

The first letter of each property determines which physical speaker is being affected. The second letter determines which channel's output (or its volume) is played in that speaker. Each property can have a value between –100 and 100.

Use the soundTransformObject to vary the output of the sounds in the soundLib example you created in this section. As with the `setTransform()` example for the Color object, create buttons that create and execute unique transform settings.

Creating volume and balance sliders for sounds

In this section, you learn how to control the volume and balance output from a Sound object using the slider mechanism from Chapter 25, "Controlling Movie Clips." The slider mechanism works by taking the X position value of the slider's bar and applying it a property of another object. In Chapter 25, you applied the position value of the bar to Movie Clip properties such as _xscale, _yscale, and _alpha. In this exercise, you apply the position values to the setVolume() and setPan() methods of the Sound object to control the volume and balance output, respectively.

On the CD-ROM

In this section, you need to use the slider_basic_104.fla file, located in the ch25 folder of this book's CD-ROM. If you want to learn how this slider was built, read Chapter 25, "Controlling Movie Clips."

The first part of this exercise shows you how to add the slider to a new document, import a sound, and control the volume of the sound with the slider. In the last steps, you apply the same methodology to the balance slider.

1. Open your copy of the slider_basic_104.fla file via the File ➪ Import ➪ Open External Library command.

2. Create a new Flash document (File ➪ New). Save this document as soundSlider_100.fla.

3. Rename Layer 1 to **mcVol**.

4. Drag the sliderClip symbol from the slider_basic_104.fla Library panel to the new document's Stage. When you have finished, close the slider_basic_104.fla Library panel.

5. With the slider instance selected on the Stage, open the Property inspector. Name the instance mcVol. In the Transform panel, rotate the instance –90 degrees. (You can also use the Free Transform tool to rotate the instance.)

6. Now you need to create a Sound object. Import a sound file into the Flash document. Use a sound file that is at least 20 seconds long. You can import the atmospheres_1.wav (or .aif) file located in the ch15 folder of this book's CD-ROM.

7. Once you have imported a sound file, select the sound in the Library panel. Right-click (Control+click on Mac) the sound file and choose **Linkage** in the contextual menu. In the Linkage Properties dialog box, select the **Export for ActionScript** check box and type sound_1 in the Identifier field. Click OK to close the dialog box.

8. Create a new layer on the Main Timeline (that is, Scene 1), and name the layer **actions**.

9. Select frame 1 of the actions layer and open the Actions panel (F9). In the Script pane, type the following code:

```
var sndBg:Sound = new Sound();
sndBg.attachSound("sound_1");
sndBg.start(0, 999);
```

Note This code uses ActionScript 2.0's strict typing feature to declare the `sndBg` variable as a `Sound` data type. Notice that once you declare the data type of a variable, you'll see the code hints for the data type (in this case, the `Sound` class) appear after you type the variable's name, `sndBg`, followed by a period.

This code creates the `Sound` object that the `mcVol` instance will control. Line 1 uses the `new Sound()` constructor to establish a `Sound` object name `sndBg`. Line 2 links the sound_1 asset (that is, the sound file in the Library) to the `sndBg` object. Line 3 plays the sound, starting at the beginning of the sound (0), and looping it 999 times for near-indefinite playback.

10. Save your Flash document. Test the movie (Ctrl+Enter or ⌘+Enter). You will hear the sound attached to the `sndBg` object begin to play. However, if you click and drag the bar on the slider, you will not hear a volume change.

   To change the volume of the `sndBg` object, you need to take the position of the bar in the slider and apply its value to the `setVolume()` method of the `sndBg` object. You'll use ActionScript's event handlers to accomplish this.

11. Select frame 1 of the actions layer on the Main Timeline. Open the Actions panel, and insert the following code after the last action in the Script pane:

```
var mcVol:MovieClip;
mcVol.onMouseMove = function():Void {
 var nVol:Number = this.mcPos._x/2;
 sndBg.setVolume(nVol);
};
```

   This code declares an `onMouseMove()` handler for the `mcVol` instance. Each time a mouse move is detected, the function defined for this handler executes. The first line of the function retrieves the current _x value of the `mcPos` instance inside of `mcVol` and divides it by 2. (See our coverage of the slider in Chapter 25, "Controlling Movie Clips" to learn more about this operation.) This value, declared as `nVol`, is then applied to the `setVolume()` method of the `sndBg` object.

12. Save your Flash document again, and test it. Click and drag the bar on the slider. As you move it up, the sound increases in volume. As you move it down, the volume decreases.

   Creating a slider that controls the balance output is almost identical to the process of creating the `mcVol` instance. You will make another instance of the sliderClip symbol, and add a new `onMouseMove()` handler for the new instance.

13. Create a new layer on the Main Timeline, and name it `mcBal`.

14. Drag an instance of the slider symbol from the Library to the Stage. Place the instance to the right of the `mcVol` instance. In the Property inspector, name the instance `mcBal`.

15. Select frame 1 of the actions layer, and open the Actions panel. After the last line of code in the Script pane, type the following code:

```
var mcBal:MovieClip;
mcBal.onMouseMove = function():Void {
 var nPan:Number = this.mcPos._x - 100;
 sndBg.setPan(nPan);
};
```

This code declares an onMouseMove() handler for the mcBal instance. When the mouse moves within the Flash movie, the function for the onMouseMove() handler executes. In this function, though, we need to translate the _x property of the mcPos instance differently. Because pan values are within a range of –100 to 100, we need to map the 0 to 200 range of the slider accordingly. In order for the lowest value (0) to equal –100 and the highest value (200) to equal 100, you simply subtract 100 from the current _x property value returned by the position instance. You then apply this value to the setPan() method of the sndBg object.

16. Save your Flash document and test it. As you drag the bar on the mcBal instance to the right, you should hear the sound play in the right speaker. As you drag the bar to the left, you should hear the sound play in the left speaker.

On the CD-ROM

You can find the completed soundSlider_100.fla file in the ch27 folder of this book's CD-ROM.

Volume Control Gadgetry, by Carla Diana

This tutorial covers strategies for controlling sound volume via graphic elements on the screen, in a similar fashion to some of the sound toys displayed in the interactive music project repercussion.org (www.repercussion.org). What I discuss here is the idea of "mapping" volume to another interactive element — in this case a user action such as mouse movement. Ultimately you'll look at creating an on-screen "gadget," a small box on the screen with a lid that the user can open and close by clicking and dragging with the mouse.

Part 1: Controlling the box lid

First you'll program the onPress event so that ActionScript pays attention to mouse movement until the mouse is released. You'll use enterframe so that you can have the box animation respond immediately and repeatedly to changes in the position of the cursor as it's dragged.

1. Open the tutorial file named box_start.fla located in the ch27/cdiana folder of this book's CD-ROM. You should see a Movie Clip of a box on the stage, as shown in Figure 27-7. Within that Movie Clip is another clip that contains just the box opening animation. This animation was created using a 3D rendering program called Cinema 4D, but you can use this technique for any series of frames in an animation. Note that the lid animation is separate from the static part of the box so that Flash doesn't have to redraw the entire box each time. There's a stop action at the first frame so it won't move past frame 1 if you don't want it to.

2. Give the box an instance name by typing **box1** into the Property inspector.

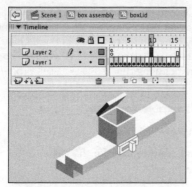

Figure 27-7: Screenshot of the box lid animation

3. Next, give the user the ability to open and close the box lid using the mouse. The idea behind this is when the mouse is pressed you'll use a variable (startY) to remember the Y location where the user first started dragging, and then continuously monitor the mouse position using an onEnterFrame handler. Create a new layer named actions, and add the following code to frame 1 of this layer, then select frame 1 and open the Actions panel.

```
box1.lid.onPress = function(){
    var startY:Number = _ymouse;
    this.onEnterFrame = function(){
        var yMove:Number = _ymouse - startY;
        trace(yMove/this._totalframes);
    };
};
```

4. Save your file, and test it (Ctrl+Enter or ⌘+Enter). When you test the movie, you'll see the value for yMove in the Output panel. This number will decrease as you drag the lid up, and increase when you drag it down. You can view the completed step in the box_part1Step3.fla file in ch27/cdiana folder of this book's CD-ROM.

5. Write an onRelease handler for the box1.lid instance so that the monitoring stops when the user stops dragging. You do this by simply deleting the onEnterFrame handler. Add this code after the actions you inserted in Step 3.

```
box1.lid.onRelease = function(){
    delete this.onEnterFrame;
};
```

It's always a good idea to also define the onReleaseOutside event when defining onRelease in order to account for those moments when the user lets go of the mouse while it's no longer resting on the graphic itself. This just means adding the onReleaseOutside handler to the existing code as follows:

```
box1.lid.onRelease = box1.lid.onReleaseOutside = function(){
    delete this.onEnterFrame;
};
```

6. While monitoring mouse position, you'll send the `box1` instance to a new frame when there is enough change in position. Imagine that 200 pixels up is the most the user will move. This means that dividing –200 by the number of frames in the lid movie will give you a "divider" number that you can use to make the `box1.lid` instance go to a new frame. You can access the number of frames using the `_totalFrames` property of the `box1.lid` instance.

To figure out the divider and save it in a variable, you'll use

```
var divider:Number = 200/this._totalframes;
```

To figure out the change in frames, you'll want to look for this value:

```
yMove/divider
```

You use `this` as the instance name because you are already inside a function scoped for the `box1.lid` instance.

Since the previous value is negative, you'll want to multiply by –1, so that you make a positive change in frame numbers when the mouse movement is negative, and vice versa. This means now you're looking for:

```
-1*yMove/divider
```

Tip

If you ever want the absolute value of a number, you can use the `Math.abs()` function. So, another way of saying `-1*myValue` is `Math.abs(myValue)` —but only when `myValue` has a negative value.

It's a good idea to round off this number since you're only interested in using it to send the playhead to a certain frame, meaning that you only want whole numbers. Use the `Math.ceil()` method so that it rounds up.

```
Math.ceil(-1*yMove/divider)
```

Now that you understand the logistics behind the interactivity, add the following code to the script on frame 1 of the Main Timeline (that is, Scene 1):

```
box1.lid.onPress = function(){
    var startY:Number = _ymouse;
    var divider:Number = 200/this._totalframes;
    this.onEnterFrame = function(){
        var yMove:Number = _ymouse - startY;
        trace(Math.ceil(-1*yMove/divider));
    };
};
```

On the CD-ROM

You can check out the progress so far by opening up the file `box_part1Step5.fla`, located in the `ch27/cdiana` folder of this book's CD-ROM.

7. Finally, you want to move relative to where the user first clicked, meaning that you are looking for the *change* in vertical movement, not absolute positions. In other words, a value of 2 will not send you to frame 2; instead, it will send you to a frame that's two more than the frame you started on with the first mouse click. You'll add a line to the beginning of the onPress handler that lets you remember the frame you started on, and store it in a variable called startFrame. The code now looks like this:

```
box1.lid.onPress = function(){
    var startY:Number = _ymouse;
    var startFrame =  this._currentframe;
    var divider:Number = 200/this._totalframes;
    this.onEnterFrame = function(){
        var yMove:Number = _ymouse - startY;
        var newFrame:Number = Math.ceil(-1*yMove/divider) +
            startFrame;
        this.gotoAndStop(newFrame);
    };
};
```

The only thing added is computing the new frame number value. You use this.gotoAndStop to actually send the box1.lid frame to the right place.

8. The last bit of cleanup for Part 1 involves checking the limits of the new frame value to make sure you don't go lower than 1 or higher than the last frame of the movie. You can do this using an if-then statement, or some clever use of the Math.min() and Math.max() methods.

```
newFrame = Math.min(Math.max(1, newFrame), this._totalframes);
```

This line of code will set newFrame equal to itself unless it's smaller than 1 or larger than the total number of frames. In those cases it will get set to 1 or the last frame number, respectively. Insert this line before the gotoAndStop() action and you're good to go.

On the CD-ROM

Check out the box_part1Step7.fla file in the ch27/cdiana folder of this book's CD-ROM to see this code in action.

Part 2: Controlling volume

So now that you have your box lid resting on a different frame every time the user interacts with it, you can use that number to tell us where our sound volume should be. First, we need to create a Sound object and get control of its volume; then in Part 3 you'll link up the box lid value to the volume. You'll be using a very basic tone (which can be created using any program that can generate MIDI sounds; in this case, Melody Assistant X) and looping it so it plays continuously and sounds like one sound, rather than a series of "beats."

You can find more information on Melody Assistant at www.myriad-online.com/
en/products/melody.htm.

1. Create a new Sound object in ActionScript. In the sample file, a new layer named
   sound was created for the actions that correspond to the sound code. Here is the
   ActionScript for creating the Sound object:

```
s1 = new Sound(box1);
```

   Note the box1 instance name in parentheses. It's a good idea to associate the sound
   with a MovieClip instance because things like volume and panning are specific to
   each MovieClip instance.

2. Attach a sound to the Sound object. In this case the sound has already been imported,
   but if you're starting from scratch you'll need to import it yourself via File ⇨ Import.
   Here is the ActionScript for attaching the sound:

```
s1.attachSound("C");
```

   The "C" is the sound's linkage identifier. If you right-click (or Control+click on the
   Mac) on the sound named MiddleC.aif in the scale folder of the Library panel and
   select Linkage in the contextual menu, you'll get the dialog box shown in Figure 27-8.

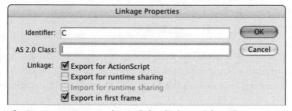

Figure 27-8: Screenshot of the linkage identifier

3. Next, you'll actually play the sound:

```
s1.start(0, 999);
```

   The 0 right after the parentheses corresponds to a time offset in the start of the sound,
   and the 999 is the number of loops. This is a short tone that you want to play continuously, so you'll also want to make sure to replay the sound when it's done with all the
   loops — unfortunately you have to give it a finite number of loops instead of just telling
   it to loop forever.

```
s1.onSoundComplete = function(){
    s1.start(0, 999);
};
```

4. To control the volume of the sound, add the following code:

```
s1.setVolume(50); //this will play at 50% of full volume
```

For your box lid gadget, you'll want the volume to be set to 0 when the lid is completely closed, and set to 100 when the lid is at the last frame of the animation.

If you've never worked with the sound object, you might want to do some quick tests with the `setVolume()` method to see how the different values sound.

You can use the `box_part2Step4.fla` file found in `ch27/cdiana` on this book's CD-ROM. Change the value in the `setVolume()` method to see how the volume changes.

Part 3: Putting the audio and visual controls together

At this point you know how to control volume, and you know how to set up interaction to let the user control the box lid opening. All you have to do to get your gadget working is put them together and you've linked the action of the box lid opening to the volume.

The key to linking the two actions is getting the numbers to relate to each other in the correct proportions. One number is the frame number corresponding to the current location of the box lid animation, and what you'll want to do is make the volume relate to this number. You can say that the two values need to be "mapped" to one another.

1. Calculate a fraction that describes how "open" the box lid is, taking its current frame location and comparing that to all the frames in that animation. From within the `onEnterFrame` handler for the `box1.lid` instance, we need to determine this value:

   ```
   var howOpen:Number = this._currentframe/this._totalframes;
   ```

2. Next, multiply this fraction by 100 in order to scale the value to match the range of the volume (0 to 100). You can rewrite the code to look like this:

   ```
   var howOpen:Number = 100*this._currentframe/this._totalframes;
   ```

3. Now that you have a number from 0 to 100, you can set the volume equal to it using the `setVolume()` method. To simplify things, give it a whole number by taking a `Math.floor()` value, rewriting the `howOpen` definition just one last time:

   ```
   var howOpen:Number = Math.floor(100 *
       this._currentframe/this._totalframes);
   s1.setVolume(howOpen);
   ```

You can test this code in the `box_part3Step3.fla` file found in the `ch27/cdiana` folder of this book's CD-ROM.

There's one small problem with this movie. When you trace `howOpen`, you'll see that it never reaches 0, which means that even with the box lid closed there will still be some volume. This is happening because the lowest the `_currentframe` value can ever be is 1, and the lowest fraction in this case will be 1 divided by the total number of frames, or

1/16. To resolve this, you can make the fraction into one that begins at 0 by subtracting 1 from the frame value. If you also subtract 1 from the total number of frames, you will wind up with the range we need:

```
var howOpen:Number = Math.floor(100*
    (this._currentframe-1)/(this._totalframes-1));
s1.setVolume(howOpen);
```

You could also have used the variable `newFrame` from Part 1 instead of `this._current-frame`; it indicates the same value. Note that in the meantime you should make sure that the volume code that you were playing with in Part 2 defaults to the following so you start out with silence when the box lid is closed:

```
s1.setVolume(0);
```

You're done! Test out your file, and have fun! Try combining a number of these gadgets and attaching a different tone to each one so that they can all play in unison. You can also take this principal of mapping volume to a value and use it with other mouse movements, or use it to match a `MovieClip` property such as `_alpha`, `_width`, `_height`, `_x`, `_y`, and so on.

A quick side note

The Publish Settings for Audio event for this file are set to Raw, rather than one of the more common compression schemes like MP3. The reason for this is that with small looping tones it's essential that the sound loop seamlessly, and the compression will often clip the sound just a tiny bit. It's small, but very noticeable to the ear. In general, with special sound treatments like this one, it's often necessary to do a bit of trial and error testing to see how low you can go with compression before the sound quality gets degraded in some way that's no longer acceptable. Figure 27-9 shows part of the Publish Settings dialog box.

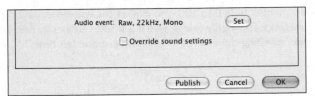

Figure 27-9: Part of the Publish Settings dialog box

Printing with ActionScript

Using the new `PrintJob` class introduced with Flash Player 7 ActionScript, you can enable your Flash movies to output Flash artwork, text, and bitmaps. With these actions, you can do the following:

✦ **Create Flash ads that have printable specifications for e-commerce merchandise.** Imagine if the next car ad you saw on your favorite Web site automatically printed dealer locations and maps without having to go to the car manufacturer's Web site?

✦ **Make Flash coupons.** You can design printable coupons for e-tailers on the Web that can be printed and redeemed at their brick-and-mortar stores.

✦ **Automate dynamic Web-generated invoices and receipts at e-commerce sites.** With ActionScript, you can format ordered items and add dynamic data to printable sheets.

✦ **Print rich vector illustrations or photorealistic bitmaps from a Web site.** You can design Flash portfolio sites that print samples of stock images, or create personalized vector artwork that can print unique images for each visitor.

✦ **E-mail printable Flash artwork to clients.** The next time you have a proof of concepts or finished artwork that needs final approval, you can e-mail your clients the Flash artwork in a stand-alone projector or .swf file.

✦ **Design custom contact information pages.** Are you sick of HTML tables that won't print your nice row-and-column–formatted pages of information consistently from browser to browser? Printable Flash frames print beautifully each time. You can even add a visitor's contact information to a dynamic database and print it.

Although we can't describe how to do all these tasks in the space of this chapter, we will show you how to get started with the last idea. The following exercise shows you how to use the new `PrintJob` class to build pages that can be sent to a user's printer. You'll also practice new ActionScript 2.0 coding conventions using strict data types.

Note Because Flash natively uses vector artwork, it translates best when it is output to a PostScript printer. Nevertheless, the Flash Player produces high-quality output to both PostScript and non-PostScript printers.

Caution The `PrintJob` class is only available for use in Flash Player 7-compatible movies. If you need to generate printable output for Flash Player 5 or 6, use the older `print()` and `printAsBitmap()` functions, as discussed in the *Flash 5 Bible* by Robert Reinhardt and Jon Warren Lentz (Wiley, 2001) and the *Flash MX Bible* by Robert Reinhardt and Snow Dowd (Wiley, 2002).

1. Open the `printjob_starter.fla` file in the `ch27` folder of this book's CD-ROM. This document has sample artwork in the library that you can use to practice printing exercises. Resave this document as `printjob_noscale.fla`.

2. Rename Layer 1 to **mcContent**.

3. Create a new Movie Clip symbol (Insert ➪ New Symbol) named **contentClip**. Inside of this symbol (in Edit mode), rename Layer 1 to **page border**.

4. Select frame 1 of the page border layer. Using the Rectangle tool, draw a nonfilled rectangle with a black stroke. After you have drawn the rectangle, select the entire outline, and open the Property inspector. Choose a line style of Solid, at 1 px. In the width and height fields, enter values that are in the same aspect ratio as an 8.5" x 11" piece of paper. For example, as shown in Figure 27-10, the size 320 x 440 uses the same aspect ratio. Position the artwork's left corner at 0, 0.

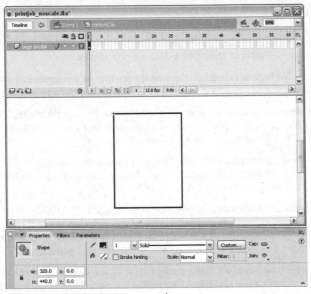

Figure 27-10: The frame artwork

5. Add another layer in the contentClip timeline, and rename this layer **content**.

6. Open the Library panel (Ctrl+L or ⌘+L), and drag an instance of the siteLogo symbol to frame 1 of the content layer. Use the Free Transform tool to resize the artwork to fit within the frame artwork you created in Step 3. See Figure 27-11.

7. Save your Flash document.

8. Go back to the Main Timeline (that is, Scene 1). On frame 1 of the mcContent layer, drag an instance of the contentClip symbol from the Library panel to the Stage. In the Property inspector, name this instance mcContent. Do not resize the instance. For now, just let the bottom edge of the instance run off the Stage.

9. On the Main Timeline, create another layer named **cbtPrint**. Place this layer above the mcContent layer. The cbtPrint layer will hold a Button component that the user can click to print the mcContent instance.

10. On frame 1 of the cbtPrint layer, drag an instance of the Button component from the Components panel to the Stage. In the Property inspector, name this instance cbtPrint. In the Parameters tab of the inspector, type Print into the label field. Refer to the settings shown in Figure 27-12.

Figure 27-11: The siteLogo artwork

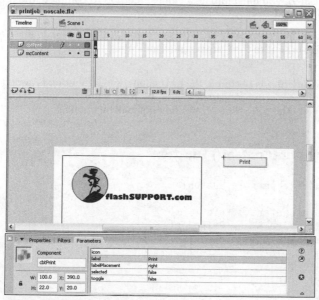

Figure 27-12: The cbtPrint instance

11. Create another layer, and name it **actions**. Place this layer above the other layers.

12. Now, you're ready to add the ActionScript that will print the mcContent instance. Select frame 1 of the actions layer, and open the Actions panel (F9, Option+F9). In the Script pane, type the code shown in Listing 27-6.

    Line 1 declares the cbtPrint instance as a Button component. By strong typing your variables (and instances) in ActionScript, the Actions panel displays the code hints for that variable (or instance) whenever you type the name and follow it with a period.

    Line 3 declares a printContent() function. Line 4 declares a local variable named pj, set to use the PrintJob data type, which invokes the constructor for the PrintJob class. Line 5 creates a local variable named mc, pointing to the mcContent instance.

    Line 6 uses the start() method of the PrintJob class to initiate a print session on the user's machine. When the start() method is invoked, the system's standard Print dialog box appears. If the user clicks OK in this dialog box, then lines 8 through 10 execute. If the user cancels the print request, lines 11 through 13 execute. If the user clicks OK, the local variable bInit is set to true. If the user cancels the dialog box, bInit is set to false.

    Line 7 checks the result of the user's input in the Print dialog box. If bInit is true, then lines 8 through10 execute. In line 8, a trace() message is sent to the Output panel, indicating that a print job is being submitted. In line 9, the addPage() method of the PrintJob class is invoked, specifying the mcContent instance, represented by the variable mc, as the target instance to print. The addPage() method enables you to submit individual pages in a print job that is sent to the printer. When all of the addPage() methods are finished, you must initiate a send() method to complete the print job, as demonstrated in line 10.

    If the user cancels the Print dialog box, lines 11 through 13 execute. In line 12, a trace() message is sent to the Output panel, indicating that the print request was denied.

    Finally, after the function is declared, the printContent() function is added as an event listener for the cbtPrint instance (line 16). Now, when the user clicks the Button component, the printContent() function will be invoked.

Listing 27-6: **The printContent() Function**

```
1.  var cbtPrint:mx.controls.Button;
2.
3.  function printContent():Void {
4.     var pj:PrintJob = new PrintJob();
5.     var mc:MovieClip = mcContent;
6.     var bInit:Boolean = pj.start();
7.     if (bInit) {
8.        trace("printing...");
9.        pj.addPage(mc);
10.       pj.send();
```

```
11.    } else {
12.        trace("print aborted by user");
13.    }
14. }
15.
16. cbtPrint.addEventListener("click", this.printContent);
```

13. Save your Flash document, and test the movie. When you click the cbtPrint instance, you should see the Print dialog box. If you click OK, the Output panel displays the "printing..." message. The first frame of the mcContent instance will print at 100 percent on the outputted page. To accurately foretell what your printed dimensions will be in inches, divide the pixel width and height of your content clip by 72 — there are 72 pixels to an inch. So, 320 x 440 will print at a size of 4.4" x 6.1". You can, however, scale the content clip to be printed, so that it will fill the entire page. In the next step, you'll learn how to do just that.

14. Select frame 1 of the actions layer, and open the Actions panel. Add the bold code shown in Listing 27-7 to the printContent() function. Here, you use the nWidth and nHeight properties of the PrintJob object, pj, to calculate two variables, nXScale and nYScale. nWidth and nHeight return the size of the page output by the printer, in pixels. By dividing each value by the respective width and height of the mcContent instance (mc) you can determine how much you need to scale the mcContent instance to fill the entire page.

Listing 27-7: **Scaling Content in the printContent() Function**

```
function printContent():Void {
    var pj:PrintJob = new PrintJob();
    var mc:MovieClip = mcContent;
    var bInit:Boolean = pj.start();
    if (bInit) {
        trace("printing...");
        var nWidth:Number = pj.pageWidth;
        var nHeight:Number = pj.pageHeight;
        var nXScale:Number = (nWidth / mc._width) * 100;
        var nYScale:Number = (nHeight / mc._height) * 100;
        with (mc) {
            _xscale = nXScale;
            _yscale = nYScale;
        }
        pj.addPage(mc);
        pj.send();
    } else {
        trace("print aborted by user");
    }
}
```

15. Save your Flash document as `printjob_scale.fla`, and test it. When you click the `cbtPrint` instance, the `mcContent` instance scales to a larger size. The printed output will fill the entire page with the `mcContent` instance's artwork.

16. The last step will be to scale the `mcContent` clip back to original size after the print output has been sent to the printer. Add the bold code shown in Listing 27-8 to the `printContent()` function.

Listing 27-8: **Resetting the Scale of the clip Instance**

```
function printContent():Void {
   var pj:PrintJob = new PrintJob();
   var mc:MovieClip = mcContent;
   var bInit:Boolean = pj.start();
   if (bInit) {
      trace("printing...");
      var nWidth:Number = pj.pageWidth;
      var nHeight:Number = pj.pageHeight;
      var nXScale_orig:Number = mc._xscale;
      var nYScale_orig:Number = mc._yscale;
      var nXScale:Number = (nWidth / mc._width) * 100;
      var nYScale:Number = (nHeight / mc._height) * 100;
      with (mc) {
         _xscale = nXScale;
         _yscale = nYScale;
      }
      pj.addPage(mc);
      pj.send();
      with (mc) {
         _xscale = nXScale_orig;
         _yscale = nYScale_orig;
      }
   } else {
      trace("print aborted by user");
   }
}
```

17. Save your Flash document, and test it. When you click the `cbtPrint` instance, the artwork no longer scales on the Stage, but the printed output will be scaled.

On the CD-ROM   You can find the completed documents, `printjob_noscale.fla` and `printjob_scale.fla`, in the `ch27` folder of this book's CD-ROM.

Web Resource   We'd like to know what you think about this chapter. Visit `www.flashsupport.com/feedback` to send us your comments.

Summary

✦ Collisions occur when two or more elements in a Flash movie touch each other. Whenever the space by one Movie Clip instance occupies the space of another, a collision, or "hit," has occurred.

✦ You can detect simple user-initiated collisions by using the startDrag() method and _droptarget property of the MovieClip object.

✦ Using the hitTest() method of the MovieClip object, you can detect the intersection of X and Y coordinates with a specified Movie Clip instance. You can also use hitTest in a similar fashion to _droptarget, where the overlap of two specific Movie Clip instances is detected.

✦ You can use the ColorTransform class to create new color values and apply them to Movie Clip instances.

✦ You can create sound libraries in less time by using ActionScript and the Sound object. You create Sound objects by using Linkage identifiers for sound files in the movie's Library.

✦ By using the new PrintJob class, you can output high-quality artwork to a PostScript or non-PostScript printer.

✦   ✦   ✦

Applying ActionScript

◆ ◆ ◆ ◆

One of the other most powerful features of the Flash Player is the capability for dynamic data loading. Chapter 28 introduces you to MP3, JPEG/PNG/GIF, and FLV loading, and covers how to share and load assets between multiple SWF files. You will be surprised to find in Chapter 29 how easy it is to create a dynamic Flash movie that sends data with the `LoadVars` class and to integrate XML data with your Flash movies. Chapter 30 gives you the tools you need to take control of Flash text fields using HTML tags and the `TextFormat` class. This chapter also introduces the CSS features and new text rendering options in Flash 8. Chapter 31 gives you an opportunity to apply your new ActionScript know-how to build an interactive game, using design patterns with your ActionScript code. Chapter 32 is an overview of the most common issues that may come up in your Flash production and the best practices for resolving problems and optimizing your workflow.

Note: If you're hungry for more ActionScript, you can find everything you need for more advanced code in the *Flash 8 ActionScript Bible* (Wiley, 2006).

◆ ◆ ◆ ◆

Sharing and Loading Assets

Because most Flash movies are downloaded and viewed over the Web, ActionScript has a number of advanced actions that are dedicated solely to controlling the download and display of movies and Library assets. Actions that check the loaded bytes of a Flash movie file (.swf) or media file let developers prevent a movie from playing before a specified portion of it has finished loading. The `loadMovie()` and `unloadMovie()` actions enable Flash content to be broken into small pieces or assets that are downloaded only when they are needed.

New Feature   Flash Player 8 enables you to load PNG, GIF, and progressive JPEG images into your Flash movies, in addition to MP3, .flv, and .swf files. We show you how to load these media files in this chapter.

Web Resource   Refer to the Runtime Loading chart listed in the "Flash Asset Management" section of the `www.flashsupport.com/links` page for more information on Flash Player compatibility with run-time assets.

Managing Smooth Movie Download and Display

When Flash movies are played back over the Internet, they *progressively download*, meaning that the Flash Player plug-in shows as much of the movie as it can during download, even if the whole file has not been transferred to the user's system or browser cache. The benefit of this feature is that users start seeing content without having to wait for the entire movie to finish downloading.

Note   Technically, a Flash movie file is not a streaming file format, but a progressive download file format, similar to an original Apple QuickTime 3 video movie. A progressive download can be viewed before the entire file has been received by the browser. Streaming file formats are never saved as actual files in the browser cache. You can't save a true streaming file, but you can typically save a shortcut or link to the file's location on the Web. Flash Communication Server video streams, for example, cannot be cached as a file on the user's system.

Nevertheless, progressive downloading has potential drawbacks. During download and playback, the movie may unexpectedly halt at arbitrary points on the timeline because a required portion of the movie has not yet downloaded. Worse yet, if you use several linked assets (that is, assets in the library that are set to export for ActionScript, such as components), by default the first frame of your Flash movie won't play until all of those assets have downloaded.

Thankfully, there's a solution. You can regulate the playback of the movie by using ActionScript code to prevent the movie from playing until a specified portion of it has downloaded. This technique is often referred to as *preloading*. A common preload sequence, or *preloader,* involves displaying only a short message, such as "Loading . . . Please Wait," while the movie loads. Once the appropriate amount of the movie has been retrieved, the movie is allowed to play. ActionScript provides basic and advanced methods of producing a preloader. This section of the chapter shows you how to use the following three different *internal* actions (or methods) to check the download status of a Flash movie:

✦ `ifFrameLoaded()`: This action has been around since Flash Player 3, and it enables you to check whether a specified frame label in the Flash movie has been downloaded by the plug-in. This is the simplest action to use to check a movie's download progress. If you are designing Flash Player 5 or later movies, this action is considered deprecated.

✦ `MovieClip._framesloaded` **and** `MovieClip._totalframes`: Introduced with Flash Player 4, these properties can be checked on a Movie Clip timeline or the Main Movie timeline (Scene 1, Scene 2, and so on). `_framesloaded` returns the current number of frames that have downloaded into the plug-in, whereas `_totalframes` returns the number of frames that exist on the specified target timeline.

✦ `getBytesLoaded()` **and** `getBytesTotal()`: These methods were introduced in Flash Player 5 ActionScript. The most accurate way to check the progress of a Flash movie download is to use these methods with other ActionScript code. You can use these methods for the following objects in ActionScript for Flash 6 movies: MovieClip (including loaded movies [.swf files] or JPEG images) and `Sound` objects that load MP3 files. You can also use these methods to check the download progress of PNG, GIF, and progressive JPEG images in Flash Player 8.

Note   Flash Player 7 introduced a new method of monitoring the load progress: the `MovieClipLoader` class. The implementation of this class is used for external asset loading and is discussed later in this chapter.

In this edition of the book, we show you how to use the `getBytesLoaded()` and `getBytesTotal()` methods in ActionScript to check the download progress of movie assets.

Cross-Reference   You can find our coverage of Flash Player 3 and 4 movie preloaders (as discussed in the *Flash 5 Bible* [Wiley, 2001]) on the book's Web site, `www.flashsupport.com/archive`.

Preloading a Flash Movie

In this section, you learn how to preload a Flash movie whose assets are all internal. You will construct a movie timeline containing a preload section. This section contains two consecutive frames that loop until the entire movie has loaded into the Flash Player. While the movie is loading, a loader graphic updates to display the progress of the download. In the following steps, you learn how to build such a preloader.

Note   The method described in this exercise is compatible with Flash Player 5 and higher. Later in this chapter, you learn how to adapt this method to a Flash Player 6 and higher routine.

On the CD-ROM   Make a copy of the `preloader_fp5_starter.fla` file, located in the `ch28` folder of this book's CD-ROM.

1. With the starter file open in Flash 8, resave the document as `preloader_fp5_100.fla`.

Note   If you choose File ➪ Publish Settings and click the Flash tab, you'll notice that this movie is set to export as a Flash Player 5 movie. As such, all code is written in the ActionScript 1.0 syntax.

2. Rename Layer 1 to **content**.

3. Create an empty keyframe (F7) on frame 10 of the content layer. Drag an instance of the pilonsImage Graphic symbol to the Stage on this keyframe. Center the instance on the Stage. Select frame 20 of the content layer and press the F5 key to extend the layer to this frame.

4. Create a new layer and rename it **labels**. Place this layer at the top of the layer stack.

5. Add a keyframe on frame 2 of the labels layer. In the Property inspector, assign this frame a label of **preload**.

6. Add a keyframe on frame 10 of the labels layer and label this frame **main** in the Property inspector. Your document should now resemble Figure 28-1.

Figure 28-1: The content of this movie starts on the main label.

7. Create a new layer and name it **mcLoader**. Place this layer underneath the labels layer.

8. With frame 1 of the mcLoader layer highlighted, select the Rectangle tool. Make sure that you have a stroke and fill color specified in the Tools panel. Draw a rectangle on the Stage. In the Property inspector, size both the stroke and fill of the rectangle to 300 x 10. This rectangle is the progress bar that grows as the movie's bytes load into the Flash Player.

New Feature   If you select the Rectangle tool in the Tools panel, and press the Alt key (or Option key on Mac) when you first click the Stage, you'll get a Rectangle Settings dialog box that enables you to enter the width and height of the rectangle shape to draw.

9. With the stroke and fill of the rectangle selected, press F8. In the Convert to Symbol dialog box, choose the Movie clip type. Name the symbol **loaderClip** and click the top left registration point, as shown in Figure 28-2. Click OK.

Figure 28-2: The rectangle artwork will be part of the loader symbol.

10. With the new instance selected on the Stage of the Main Timeline, name the instance `mcLoader` in the Property inspector.

11. Double-click the `mcLoader` instance on the Stage. In Edit mode, rename Layer 1 of the loader symbol to **mcBar**. Create another layer and name it **frame**. Make sure the frame layer is above the mcBar layer.

12. Select the stroke of the rectangle and cut it (Ctrl+X or ⌘+X). Select frame 1 of the frame layer and paste the stroke in place (Edit ⇨ Paste in Place, or Ctrl+Shift+V or ⌘+Shift+V).

13. On the mcBar layer, select the fill of the rectangle. Convert this fill to a Movie Clip symbol named **barClip**. In the Convert to Symbol dialog box, choose the middle left registration point, as shown in Figure 28-3.

Figure 28-3: The barClip symbol settings

14. With the new instance selected on the Stage of the loaderClip symbol, name the instance `mcBar` in the Property inspector. In the Transform panel, scale the width of the instance to 1.0%, as shown in Figure 28-4. When the movie first starts to load, you do not want the `mcBar` instance scaled at full size (100%) — as the bytes of the movie load into the Flash Player, the `_xscale` of the `mcBar` instance increases. (You will insert the code to do this later.)

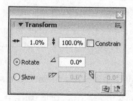

Figure 28-4: Decrease the X scale of the `bar_mc` instance to 1.0% in the Transform panel.

15. Create another layer and name it **text**. Place this layer at the bottom of the layer stack.

16. Select the Text tool and create a Dynamic Text field on frame 1 of the text layer. Place the text field underneath the `mcBar` instance, as shown in Figure 28-5. In the Var field of the Property inspector, assign a name of `sLabel`. You will use this text field to display the current percent loaded of the Flash movie. You do not need to enable the Show Border option (or other options) for this text field.

Caution   Do *not* assign a TextField instance name to the field in the Property inspector. In order to make a Flash Player 5-compatible preloader, you can only control the contents of the field via the Var name.

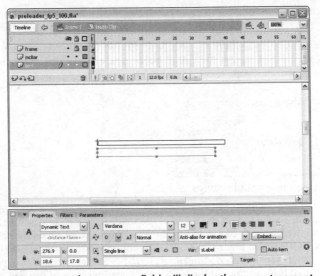

Figure 28-5: The percent field will display the current percent loaded of the movie.

17. Go back to the Main Timeline (that is, Scene 1). Select the mcLoader instance on the Stage and center it using the Align panel. Select frame 4 of the mcLoader layer and insert an empty keyframe (F7). You only need the loader instance to appear as the movie is preloading.

18. Create a new layer and name it **actions**. Place this layer underneath the labels layer.

19. Select frame 3 of the actions layer and insert an empty keyframe (F7). With this frame selected, open the Actions panel (F9). In the Script pane, type the code shown in Listing 28-1. Do not type the ⊃ character in your actual code. This symbol indicates a continuation of the same line of code. Each line of code is explained in comments within the code.

Note   In Listing 28-1, the variable named nCount is never declared with an initial value. As such, when the line nCount++ is executed, the variable nCount is both initialized and incremented by 1. In ActionScript 2.0 syntax, you can't declare a variable and increment it at the same time.

Listing 28-1: The Preloading Script Routine

```
// nLB stores the current bytes that have loaded

var nLB = this.getBytesLoaded();

// nTB stores the total bytes of the movie

var nTB = this.getBytesTotal();

// nPL calculates the percent of the movie that
// has loaded into the Flash Player.

var nPL = Math.floor((nLB/nTB)*100);

// Apply the nPL value to the X scale of the
// bar instance within the loader instance

mcLoader.mcBar._xscale = nPL;

// Fill the percent text field within the loader instance
// with the nPL value followed by the text
// "% of " and the total kilobytes of the movie. For
// example, when half of a 64K movie has loaded, the text
// field will display "50% of 64K loaded."

mcLoader.sLabel = nPL + "% of " + Math.floor(nTB/1024) + ⊃
  "K loaded.";

// If the loaded bytes are greater than or equal to the
// total bytes of the movie and the total bytes are
// greater than 0

if (nLB >= nTB && nTB > 0) {

  // Check to see if the nCount variable is greater than
  // or equal to 12. If it is, execute the nested code.
  // This if/else code pauses the movie once 100% of the
  // movie has loaded into the Flash Player.

  if (nCount>=12) {

    // exit the loading sequence

    gotoAndStop("main");

  // otherwise, if the movie has completely loaded and
```

```
    // nCount is less than 12.

  } else {

    // add 1 to the nCount variable
    nCount++;

    // continue to loop the loading sequence
    gotoAndPlay("preload");
  }

// if the movie hasn't finished loading into the Flash
// Player then execute this code

} else {

  // loop back to the "preload" frame label
  gotoAndPlay("preload");
}
```

20. Save your Flash document and test it (Ctrl+Enter or ⌘+Return). When you enter Test Movie mode, choose View ➪ Simulate Download or press Ctrl+Enter or ⌘+Return again. As shown in Figure 28-6, you will see the movie's download progress reflected in the _xscale property of the bar_mc instance as well as an updating percent value and total file size in the sLabel field. When the movie is fully loaded, the loader will pause for about a second and go to the main label.

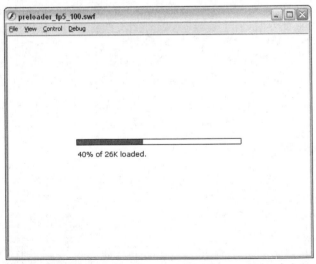

Figure 28-6: The progress bar grows as the movie loads into the Flash Player.

On the CD-ROM

You can find the completed file, preloader_fp5_100.fla, in the ch28 folder of this book's CD-ROM. You can also find a Flash Player 6 or higher compatible version of this document, preloader_fp6_100.fla, that uses a setInterval() routine. You learn more about this technique in the next section and later in the chapter.

Caution

We recommend against using the ProgressBar component for internal preloading. This component is compatible with Flash Player 6 when the file is published with ActionScript 2.0 support. Because the component itself is nearly 60 KB, the first frame of the movie will "pause" on an empty screen until the component has fully loaded. The ProgressBar component is truly designed to work with external assets, as we discuss later in this chapter.

Preloading a Flash Movie Containing Components

If you've used any of the User Interface, Data, or Media components (including the new FLVPlayback component in Flash Professional 8), you may have noticed that the file size of your Flash movie jumps significantly. Adding a List component and a TextInput component to your Flash movie, for example, will add about 49 KB to your final .swf file's size! More importantly, by default, these components export on frame 1 of the Flash movie, as do their respective ActionScript 2.0 (AS2) class files. In this section, you learn how to move the file weight of components to another frame, so that you can create a preloader on frame 1 of your Flash movie.

Caution

If you use the visual data binding features of Macromedia components as discussed in Chapter 34, "Binding Data and Events to Components," you cannot move the components away from frame 1 of the movie. You will need to externally load such movies into another host Flash movie, as we describe later in this chapter.

On the CD-ROM

Before you begin this exercise, copy the movie_with_components_preloader folder from the ch28 folder of this book's CD-ROM to a preferred location on your computer. This folder contains the starter and finished files for the exercises. If you want to preview the starter file, run the list_flvplayback_starter.swf in stand-alone Flash Player 8 or a Web browser. This starter file is fully functional, but all of the file weight is on frame 1 of the movie.

1. Open the list_flvplayback_starter.fla document in the copied folder from the CD-ROM. Resave this document as list_flvplayback_preload.fla.

2. Create a new layer named **labels**. Place this layer at the top of the layer stack.

3. Add frames on all of the layers, up to frame 15. On frames 5 and 10 of the labels layer, add empty keyframes. Using the Property inspector, add a frame comment of //**linked** to frame 5. Add a frame label named **preload** to frame 1, and a label of **start** to frame 10, as shown in Figure 28-7. In later steps, you will place any exported components to frame 5 of the movie, and move the existing frame 1 elements to frame 10.

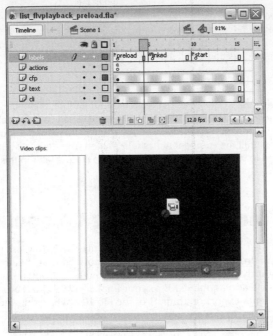

Figure 28-7: A timeline structure for preloading a movie with components

4. Select frame 1 of the actions layer, and drag it to frame 10 of the actions layer, below the start frame label. All of this code's execution will be deferred to this frame, after the movie has been preloaded.

5. Select frame 1 of the actions layer, and open the Actions panel (F9, or Option+F9 on Mac). Add the script shown in Listing 28-2. This preloading script uses the setInterval() function to continuously check the load status of the Flash movie. When all bytes of the Flash movie have loaded, the movie deletes the interval and jumps to the start frame label.

Tip   You can find all code listings on this book's CD-ROM. The listings are saved as .as files, such as Listing28-2.as.

Listing 28-2: **The Preloading Script Routine**

```
var nCheckID:Number;

function checkLoad():Void {
   var nLB:Number = this.getBytesLoaded();
   var nTB:Number = this.getBytesTotal();
   if(nLB >= nTB && nTB > 0 ){
```

```
        clearInterval(nCheckID);
        gotoAndStop("start");
    }
}

nCheckID = setInterval(this, "checkLoad", 30);
stop();
```

6. Move the frame 1 keyframes on the cfp, text, and cli layers to frame 10 of their respective layers, as shown in Figure 28-8. You should no longer see the FLVPlayback or List component on frame 1 of your movie.

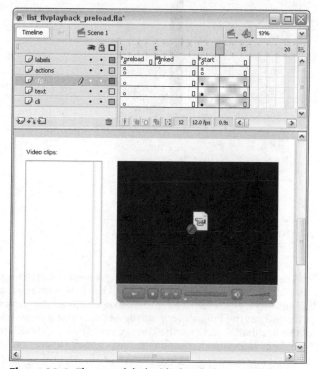

Figure 28-8: The start label with the Flash components

7. Create an empty keyframe on frame 5 of the text layer. On frame 1, use the Text tool to add the static text "LOADING..." to the Stage. This text appears as the Flash movie preloads with the script in Listing 28-2.

8. Save your document, and test it (Ctrl+Enter or ⌘+Enter). While you're testing the movie, open the Bandwidth Profiler by choosing View ➪ Bandwidth Profiler (Ctrl+B or ⌘+B). Also, make sure the View ➪ Frame by Frame Graph option is selected. As shown in Figure 28-9, even though the start frame (frame 10) has all of the component instances, frame 1 is still more than 64 KB. Moreover, if you choose View ➪ Simulate Download, the LOADING... text never appears. The movie hangs on frame 1 without displaying it, and jumps immediately to the start label when the movie has finished preloading.

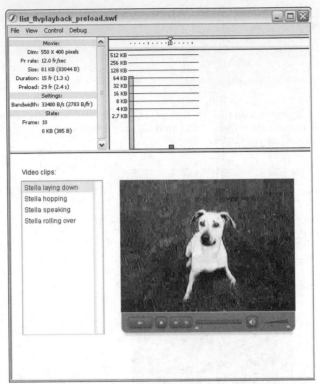

Figure 28-9: The Bandwidth Profiler showcasing the distribution of bytes

9. The reason the Flash movie still has several kilobytes on frame 1 is that the components and their associated classes are being exported on the first frame of the Flash movie. To avoid this problem, you need to alter the Linkage settings for each component in the Library and adjust the Publish Settings for ActionScript 2.0 classes. Here's how to take care of the first half now. Open the Library panel and right-click (or Control+click on Mac) the FLVPlayback component, and choose Linkage in the contextual menu. In the Linkage Properties dialog box (Figure 28-10), clear the Export in first frame check box and click OK.

Note   Whenever you deselect the Export in first frame option, you must place an instance of the symbol somewhere on the Stage of your Flash movie. You'll perform that step shortly.

10. Repeat Step 9 for the List component in the Library panel. If you were performing these steps with a file of your own and your Library panel had additional components or exported symbols, you would repeat this step for those elements as well.

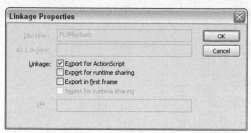

Figure 28-10: The Linkage Properties for the FLVPlayback component

11. Once you've prevented all of the Library assets from exporting on the first frame, you need to put an instance of each symbol on the Stage of the movie. We prefer to build a Movie Clip symbol containing all linked assets first, and then place an instance of that symbol on the stage. Create a new empty symbol named linkedAssets by choosing Insert ➪ New Symbol. In the Create New Symbol dialog box, name the symbol **linkedAssets** and choose the Movie clip type, as shown in Figure 28-11.

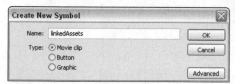

Figure 28-11: The settings for the linkedAssets symbol

12. Inside of the linkedAssets symbol, place an instance of each component from the Library, including the FLVPlayback and List components. You don't need to separate the instances on to their own layers, nor do you need to name the instances.

13. Go back to the Main Timeline (that is, Scene 1) of your Flash document, and create a layer named **mcLinked**. On frame 5 of this layer, create an empty keyframe and place an instance of the linkedAssets symbol on to the Stage at this frame. Insert another empty keyframe on frame 6 of the mcLinked layer to prevent the linked assets from persisting into the start label of the movie. Refer to Figure 28-12. Optionally, you can name the linkedAssets symbol **mcLinked** in the Property inspector. You won't need to address this clip with ActionScript, but naming instances is a good habit to make.

14. Before you can test the movie, though, you need to tell Flash to export all ActionScript 2.0 (AS2) classes on frame 5 as well. The general rule is to make sure you export the AS2 classes before or on the same frame as the first appearance of the Flash components within your movie. As such, you will set the AS2 classes to export on frame 5 of your movie. Choose File ➪ Publish Settings and select the Flash tab. Click the Settings button to the right of the ActionScript version combo box. For the Export frame for classes value, type **5**, as shown in Figure 28-13.

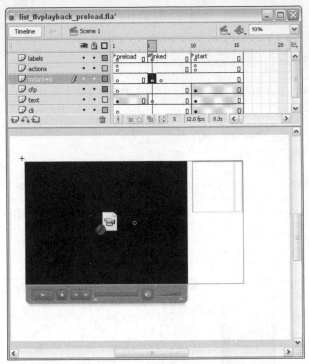

Figure 28-12: The timeline of the Flash movie

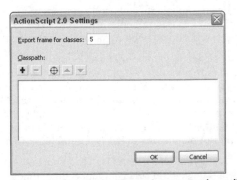

Figure 28-13: The ActionScript 2.0 Settings dialog box

15. Save your Flash document, and test the movie (Ctrl+Enter or ⌘+Enter). The movie should jump immediately to the start label, and function as the original starter file did. However, if you choose View ⇨ Simulate Download, you'll see the LOADING... text. When the movie finishes the simulated download, the movie jumps to the start label. If you view the Bandwidth Profiler (Figure 28-14), the majority of the file size is now contained on frame 5. As such, the first frame can load and display much more quickly in the Flash movie.

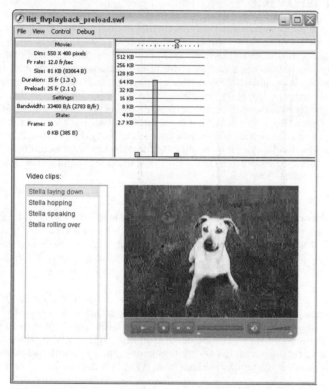

Figure 28-14: The Bandwidth Profiler showcasing the optimized layout

On the CD-ROM

You can find the finished file, `list_flvplayback_100.fla`, in the `movie_with_compo-nents_preloader` folder, located in the `ch28` folder of this book's CD-ROM.

Later in this chapter, you learn how to make a versatile loader clip that can be used in place of the LOADING... text to display an accurate loading progress indicator in the Flash movie.

You can search the Web for several JSFL (aka JavaScript Flash) applets that will automate the process of setting symbols' linkage properties and placing instances of them on the movie's Stage. Go to the "JSFL Utilities" section of the `www.flashsupport.com/links` page for more information.

Loading Flash Movies

A long sequence of Flash animation or any Flash movie that contains many internal assets naturally requires the preloading described in the preceding section to guarantee smooth playback. But traditional information-based Web sites done in Flash require a different kind of download management. Suppose you're building a Web site with three sections: products, staff, and company history. Each section is roughly 100 KB in size. In a normal Flash movie, you'd place those sections in a sequential order on the Main Timeline or create a scene for each of them. The last section you place on the timeline would, of course, be the last section to download. Might sound fine so far, but here's the problem: What if the section that appears last on the timeline happens to be the first and only section the users want to see? They'd have to wait for the other two sections to download before they could view the one they want — but they don't even want to see the other two sections, so really they're waiting for nothing. The solution to this problem is the `loadMovie()` action.

It's not just a matter of the user waiting for a Flash movie to load — it's also an issue of bandwidth. You can rack up unnecessary bandwidth usage fees with your Web hosting provider. You wouldn't want to download every page of an HTML site just to look at one page of it, and the same principle applies to Flash movies. Paying careful attention to your Flash movie architecture not only saves your users time, but it can also save you money.

`loadMovie()` provides a means of inserting one or more external .swf files into a Flash movie (whether that movie resides in a browser or on its own in the stand-alone player). `loadMovie()` can be used to replace the current movie with a different movie or to display multiple movies simultaneously. It can also be used, as in our company Web site example, to enable a parent movie to retrieve and display content kept in independent .swf files on a need-to-retrieve basis (similar to the way a frame in an HTML frameset can call external pages into different frames).

You can use the `loadMovie()` action to load JPEG images directly into your Flash Player 6 or higher movies. We show you how to load JPEG files later in this chapter.

If you are concerned about getting accurate usage statistics in your Web server's access logs, you will want to use `loadMovie()` to break up the content on your Flash-based site. If all of your content is stored in one Flash movie file (.swf), you will only see that the Web user has downloaded the site file — you have no idea which sections of the site the user has actually visited. By breaking up the Flash movie into several smaller files, your site's access logs will show which section of .swf files the user downloaded and viewed.

Basic overview of Flash site architecture

You can produce and distribute straight Flash content on the Web in the following two primary ways:

✦ Create several small .swf files, with each one living within a standard HTML page on a Web site.

✦ Create one HTML page that hosts one main .swf file that loads additional content through the Flash Player plug-in.

Figure 28-15 illustrates these alternatives.

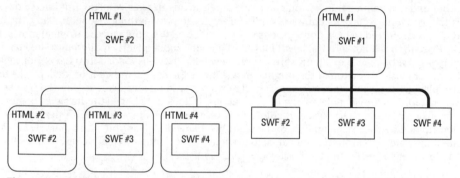

Figure 28-15: The diagram on the left illustrates a Web site that uses multiple HTML pages, each with an individual .swf file. The diagram on the right shows a Web site that uses one HTML page (or frameset, or iframe) that has one primary .swf file, which loads other .swf files as needed.

If you decide to break up your Flash movies across several HTML pages, your Web visitors will experience the following:

✦ Short download times for each page

✦ Easy bookmarking of discrete sections of your Web site

✦ Abrupt transitions between each section of the Web site

However, if you use one primary Flash movie in one HTML page (or frameset), your visitors will benefit from:

✦ Short download times for each swf file (download times vary with file size)

✦ Seamless integration of new Flash content

✦ Controllable transitions between SWF asset changes

Which method should you use for your Flash projects? The answer depends on the specifics of each Web project. You may decide to use a combination of both methods, especially for larger sites that use several Web technologies (Apple QuickTime, Macromedia Flash and Shockwave, Real Systems RealOne, Microsoft Windows Media, and so on). In either scenario, you can use the `loadMovie()` action to manage Flash content more easily.

Tip

Because Flash Player 6 or higher enables you to download JPEG, MP3, and Flash movies with embedded video, you may not need to rely on other plug-in technologies for the Web sites you design and develop. Each player version since Flash Player 6 has only expanded the options for runtime asset loading. Flash Player 7 enables you to load .flv files, and Flash Player 8 can load PNG, GIF, and progressive JPEG image formats.

Storing multiple movies

You may already be wondering how these newly loaded movies are managed relative to the original movie. Macromedia Flash uses the metaphor of *levels* to describe where the movies are kept. Levels are something like drawers in a cabinet: They are stacked on top of each other and can contain things. You can place things in any drawer you like, but once a drawer is full, you have to take its contents out before you can put anything else in. Initially, the bottom level, referred to in ActionScript as _level0 ("Level 0"), contains the original movie, the first movie that loads into the Flash Player. All movies subsequently loaded into the Flash Player must be placed explicitly into a target level. If a movie is loaded into Level 1 or higher, it appears visually on top of the original movie in the Player. If a movie is loaded into Level 0, it replaces the original movie, removing all movies stored on levels above it in the process. When a loaded movie replaces the original movie, it does not change the frame rate, movie dimensions, or movie background color of the original Flash Stage. Those properties are determined by the original movie and cannot be changed, unless you load a new HTML document into the Web browser. You can also use a getURL() action to load a new .swf file into the browser to "reset" the Flash Player.

Tip

You can effectively change the background color of the Stage when you load a new movie by creating a rectangle shape of your desired color on the lowest layer of the movie you are loading.

Loading an external .swf file into a movie

A new movie is imported into the Flash Player when a loadMovie() action is executed. In the following steps, you'll learn how to make a button click load an external movie named bandwidth.swf.

On the CD-ROM

Before you begin these steps, make a copy the bandwidth.swf file from the ch28 folder of this book's CD-ROM. Copy the file to the location on your hard drive where you will save the new Flash document in the forthcoming exercise.

1. Create a new Flash document (File ➪ New). Save this document as loadMovie_100.fla in the same location as your copy of the bandwidth.swf file.

2. Rename Layer 1 to **cbtLoad**.

3. Drag an instance of the Button component from the Component panel to your document's Stage. Place the instance in the lower-left corner of the Stage. In the Property inspector, name the component cbtLoad. In the Parameters tab, select the label field and type Load Movie. Refer to Figure 28-16 to see these settings.

Cross-Reference

We discuss components more thoroughly in Chapter 33, "Using Components."

Figure 28-16: The cbtLoad instance

4. Create a new layer and rename it **actions**.

5. Select frame 1 of the actions layer and open the Actions panel (F9, or Option+F9 on Mac). In the Script pane, type the code shown in Listing 28-3. This code creates a listener for the cbtLoad instance. When the cbtLoad instance is clicked, the bandwidth.swf movie loads into Level 1.

Listing 28-3: **The Listener Code for the cbtLoad Instance**

```
var cbtLoad:mx.controls.Button;

var oLoader:Object = new Object();
oLoader.click = function(){
   loadMovieNum("bandwidth.swf", 1);
};

cbtLoad.addEventListener("click", oLoader);
```

Caution

The URL used in loadMovie() or loadMovieNum() actions contains the network path to the movie file that you want to load. That path must be specified relative to the location of the page that contains your main movie, not relative to the location of the movie itself. If you are designing a Web site for early browsers, pay attention to the URL path. Internet Explorer 4.5 (or earlier) for the Macintosh does not resolve paths correctly. For more information, please see Macromedia's tech note at:

www.macromedia.com/cfusion/knowledgebase/index.cfm?id=tn_13638

6. Save your Flash document and test it by choosing Control ➪ Test Movie (Ctrl+Enter or ⌘+Return). When you click the cbtLoad instance, the bandwidth.swf movie's top-left corner aligns with the top-left corner of the hosting SWF's stage (see Figure 28-17). You can reload the same .swf file by clicking the Load Movie button again.

Caution   Make sure you copied the bandwidth.swf file from the book's CD-ROM to the same location as the loadMovie_100.fla document. Otherwise, the loadMovieNum() action will fail.

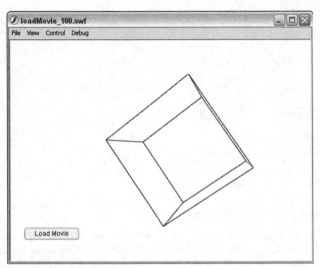

Figure 28-17: The bandwidth.swf file loads into the top-left corner of the Stage.

You can apply this technique to any .swf file that you wish to load into another Flash movie. You can make a series of buttons, each one loading a different .swf file. You can modify the click() method of the oLoader object to switch the URL of the loaded movie, depending on which button is pressed.

On the CD-ROM   You can find the completed example file, loadMovie_100.fla, in the ch28 folder of this book's CD-ROM.

When a movie is loaded above any other movie (including the main movie), the Buttons and Movie Clips in the movies on lower levels will continue to be active, even though they may not be visible. To prevent this undesired behavior, you need to send movies on lower levels to an idle or blank frame where no buttons are present. Do that by adding a goto action before your loadMovie() action that sends the current movie to the idle frame. This technique is known as "parking" the movie. If you have to park multiple movies, you'll need to know how to communicate between movies on different levels. We will discuss this shortly.

_level0 or _root: What's the Difference?

You may have seen the Main Timeline referred to as _root in ActionScript. If you don't employ Levels in a Flash movie, _root always refers to the Main Timeline of the Flash movie that is loaded into a browser. However, if you start to use levels to load external SWF files, _root will be relative to the level that's executing actions.

For example, if the main movie uses a _root reference in an action, such as:

```
_root.gotoAndStop(10);
```

the Main Timeline Playhead will go to frame 10 and stop.

If a loaded movie has the same action within its timeline, it will go to frame 10 on its timeline and stop.

While this works with movies that are loaded into level locations, it will not work with Movie Clip instance targets. As you'll see in the following sections, a movie loaded into a Movie Clip target becomes an instance located within the level that the Movie Clip target resides. Therefore, _root will still refer to a different timeline than that of the loaded .swf file.

Flash Player 7 introduced the _lockroot property of MovieClip objects, which enables MovieClip objects to act as _root references to loaded movies. We discuss this property in Chapter 25, "Controlling Movie Clips."

How Flash handles loaded movies of differing dimensions

A movie loaded onto Level 1 or higher that is smaller in width and height than the Level 0 movie is positioned in the top-left corner of the Stage. You may have noticed this phenomenon in the last section. In this situation, it is possible to have elements that are off-stage within the loaded .swf file. However, when you load a smaller .swf file Stage into a larger .swf file Stage, these off-stage elements are displayed on the Stage of the larger .swf file. To prevent objects from being displayed, you would have to create a curtain layer or a Mask layer above all the other layers in the Level 1 movie that covers up the *Work area* (the space outside the movie's Stage).

Movies loaded onto Level 0 that are smaller than the original Level 0 movie are automatically centered and scaled up to fit the size of the original movie. (The manner in which they are scaled depends on the Scale setting in the Publish Settings.)

Movies loaded onto Level 0 that are larger than the original Level 0 movie are cropped at the right and bottom boundaries defined by the original movie dimensions.

Placing, scaling, and rotating externally loaded Flash movies

Especially when your movies have different width and height dimensions, it's not very convenient to have newly loaded movies dropped ingloriously in the top-left corner of the Stage. To give you more flexibility with the placement, rotation, and scale of your loaded movies, ActionScript provides the capability to load a Flash movie file (.swf) into a Movie Clip instance. So far, this may not make a whole lot of sense. Loading a movie into a Movie Clip instance seems like a strange feature at first, until you find out what it can do — then it seems indispensable. The easiest way to understand what happens when you load a movie into a Movie Clip is to think of the loadMovie() action as a "Convert Loaded Movie to Movie Clip" action.

When a movie is loaded into a Movie Clip instance, many attributes of the original Movie Clip instance are applied to the newly loaded movie:

✦ The timeline of the loaded movie completely replaces the original instance's timeline. Nothing inside the original Movie Clip (including actions on keyframes) remains.

✦ The loaded movie assumes the following properties from the original Movie Clip instance:

  • Instance name

  • Scale percentage

  • Color effects, including alpha

  • Rotation degree

  • Placement (X and Y position)

  • Visibility (with respect to the _visible property)

✦ Any onClipEvent() handlers (and actions within them) that are written for the original Movie Clip instance will still be available (and executing) on the loaded movie.

✦ Any event handlers, such as onMouseMove() or onEnterFrame() or variables assigned to the original Movie Clip instance, will be erased once an external .swf file is loaded into the instance.

We like to refer to Movie Clips that are used to load other movies as Movie Clip holders. Usually, you load movies into empty Movie Clips that don't have any artwork or actions. However, because you may need a physical reference to the actual area that your loaded movie will occupy on the Stage, it's useful to create temporary guides or artwork that indicates this area.

Tip

In Flash Player 6 or higher ActionScript, you can create empty MovieClip objects dynamically, using the createEmptyMovieClip() method. You can then load external .swf files into this empty MovieClip object using the loadMovie() method.

The following steps show you how to create a Movie Clip holder and how to load an external .swf file into it. You will use the same file you created in the previous section.

On the CD-ROM

If you didn't complete the example in the last section, make a copy of the loadMovie_100.fla file located in the ch28 folder of this book's CD-ROM. You will also need to copy the bandwidth.swf file from the folder.

1. Open the loadMovie_100.fla document. Resave this document as loadMovie_101.fla.

2. Create a new layer on the Main Timeline and rename the layer to **mcHolder**. Place this layer at the bottom of the layer stack.

3. Select the Rectangle tool and draw a rectangle on frame 1 of the holder_mc layer. The shape should have the same dimensions as the external Flash movie's Stage, as defined in its Document Properties dialog box. For our example, size the rectangle to 640 x 400 using the Property inspector.

Note You do not need to include an outline (or stroke) with the rectangle artwork.

Tip With Flash 8, you can select the Rectangle tool and Alt/Option+click the Stage to enter custom width and height settings for a new rectangle shape.

4. With the rectangle selected, choose Modify ➪ Convert to Symbol or press the F8 key to convert the artwork into a symbol. In the Convert to Symbol dialog box, name the symbol **holderClip** and choose the Movie clip type. In the Registration grid, click the top-left corner point, as shown in Figure 28-18. Movies loaded into Movie Clip instances load from the top-left corner of the original target Movie Clip.

Figure 28-18: An instance of the holderClip symbol will hold the loaded .swf file.

5. With the new instance on the Stage selected, name the instance `mcHolder` in the <Instance Name> field of the Property inspector. Position the instance on the Stage, where you want the external SWF movie to appear. At this point, you can also tween, scale, or apply any color effect to the instance as well. For our example, apply an orange tint to the instance in the Property inspector.

Caution Filter effects are not passed on to loaded movies. Any filter effect applied to an instance prior to loading will be removed on the new load.

Now, you need to modify the `click()` handler of the `oLoader` object called by the `cbtLoad` component instance (already on the document's Stage). This method needs to target the `mcHolder` instance.

6. Select frame 1 of the actions layer on the Main Timeline. Open the Actions panel (F9, or Option+F9 on Mac), and change the `loadMovieNum()` action to the following lines shown in bold:

```
var cbtLoad:mx.controls.Button;
var mcHolder:MovieClip;
var oLoader:Object = new Object();
```

```
oLoader.click = function(){
    mcHolder.loadMovie("bandwidth.swf");
};
cbtLoad.addEventListener("click", oLoader);
```

Note   The instance must be resident on Stage at the time the loadMovie() action occurs. Any instance can either be manually placed on a timeline or created with ActionScript code, such as the duplicateMovieClip(), attachMovie(), and createEmptyMovieClip() methods. If any specification of the loadMovie() action is incorrect, then the movie will fail to load. The Flash Player will *not* start a request for an external .swf file if the Movie Clip instance target is invalid.

7. Save the Flash document, and test it (Ctrl+Enter or ⌘+Enter). When you click the Load Movie button, the bandwidth.swf file will load into the top-left corner of the mcHolder instance. The orange tint effect applied to the mcHolder instance will also be applied to the loaded movie.

To avoid seeing the rectangle artwork in your final Flash movie, go into the Movie Clip symbol for holderClip and turn the layer containing the rectangle artwork into a Guide layer. Guide layers will not export with the .swf file. Also, add a new empty layer on the holderClip time-line. This empty layer can be above or below the original artwork layer.

Caution   If you do not have any artwork in your target Movie Clip instance (or have converted the artwork to a Guide layer), you will not be able to scale the instance using the Transform tool or panel. You can, however, transform the instance before you remove the artwork (or convert it to a Guide layer) — the setting will "stick" even after you remove the artwork.

If you need to add functionality to the loaded movie, use ActionScript to control the new loaded movie instance. The next section shows you how to communicate with loaded movies.

On the CD-ROM   You can view the completed file, loadMovie_101.fla, in the ch28 folder of this book's CD-ROM.

loadMovie() versus loadMovieNum()

You may have noticed that a loadMovie() action is used with Movie Clip instances, whereas loadMovieNum() is used with a level location. Because you can specify variables (that point to dynamic targets) as a location value, ActionScript needs a way to distinguish a numeric level location from a Movie Clip instance.

Also, if you want a loadMovie() action to be compatible with Flash Player 4 (or earlier), you will need to specify the Movie Clip target name as a string (that is, enclosed in quotes).

Communicating between multiple movies on different levels

After a movie or two are loaded onto different levels, you may want each timeline to control the other, just as Movie Clips can control each other. To communicate between different levels, you simply need to address actions to the proper level. The method for addressing a level that controls a timeline on a different level is identical to the method for addressing a Movie Clip target that controls the timeline of another Movie Clip instance, except for one small change. You have to indicate the name of the level you want to target rather than the name of the Movie Clip. Level names are constructed such as this: First, there's an underscore (_); then there's the word *level*; then there's the number of the level that you want your action to occur on.

This tells the movie loaded onto Level 1 to go to frame 50:

```
_level1.gotoAndStop(50);
```

This tells the Main Timeline to go to frame 50:

```
_level0.gotoAndStop(50);
```

You can also target Movie Clips that reside on the timelines of movies on other levels. Here's an example:

```
_level3.mcProducts.play();
```

This sends a `play()` action to the Movie Clip named `mcProducts` on the timeline of the movie loaded onto Level 3.

Unloading movies

To lighten the memory required by your Flash movies in the Flash Player or to clear the loaded movie from the Stage, you can explicitly unload movies in any level or Movie Clip target by using the `unloadMovie()` action. The only option for `unloadMovie()` is the path to the desired location (for example, `_level1`, `_root.instanceName`).

On the CD-ROM You can see an example of an `unloadMovie()` action in the `unloadMovie_100.fla` file located in the `ch28` folder of this book's CD-ROM. Here, the `oLoader` object handles both the clicks from the `cbtLoad` and the `cbtUnload` instances.

Caution If you want to replace an existing loaded movie with another external file, you do not need to unload the movie before loading the new one. A `loadMovie()` action implicitly unloads the existing content in the specified location. We have actually seen problems occur in Flash movies where `unloadMovie()` and `loadMovie()` actions are executed consecutively.

Loading External Files Through Proxy Servers

If you are creating Flash movies that will be loaded through proxy servers set up by internal company networks or large Internet service providers (ISPs) on the Internet, you may need to know how to trick them into loading "fresh" .swf files every time a user visits your site. What is a proxy server? With the growth of high-speed Internet connections, such as DSL and cable, many networks will process all outgoing HTTP requests through a go-between computer that caches previous requests to the same URL. Anytime you type a Web site URL into a browser, you're m aking an HTTP request. If that computer, called a *proxy server,* sees a request that was made previously (within a certain time frame), then it serves its cached content to the end-user instead of downloading the actual content from the remote server.

Why do you need to be concerned about caching? If you or your client needs accurate usage statistics for a Web site, you will likely want to know which portions of the site your users are actively using (that is, downloading into their browsers). Your Web server will not log a request it never receives — if a proxy server delivers the content to the end-user, you will not even know a user is looking at your content.

When a Flash movie makes an HTTP request with a `loadMovie()` action, a proxy server may serve the cached .swf file instead of the one that actually exists on your server. Why is this a problem? If you are updating that .swf file frequently or if you want precise Web usage statistics for your Flash movies and content, then you'll want users to download the actual .swf file on your server each time a request is made.

The question remains: How do you trick a proxy server into serving the real .swf file instead of its cached one? The proxy server knows what's in its cache by the URL for each cached item. So, if you change the name of the loaded Flash movie each time you make a request for it, the proxy server won't ever see an identical match with its cached content.

To change the name of a loaded Flash movie, simply add a random number to the end of the movie's name in the `loadMovie()` action. This random number won't actually be part of the movie's filename. Rather, it will appear as a query at the end of the filename. Place the following actions on the event handler that initiates a `loadMovie()` action:

```
var sDate:String = escape(new Date().toString());
mcHolder.loadMovie("external_1.swf?cacheBuster=" + sDate);
```

In the preceding example, a variable called `sDate` is established and given a value of the current date and time. Each time the event handler calling these actions is executed, a different date is appended to the filename of the loaded movie. The proxy server thinks that each request is different and routes the request to your Web server.

Not only does this method prevent a proxy server from serving a cached Flash movie file, it also prevents some browsers from caching the loaded movie in the user's local cache folder.

loadMovie() as a method for Movie Clip targets

Both `loadMovie()` and `unloadMovie()` can be used as either an ActionScript method or action for Movie Clip targets. What does this mean? You can apply some actions in ActionScript in two ways: as methods of a `MovieClip` object (or some other ActionScript object, as we have discussed in previous chapters) or as a stand-alone action.

As an action, `loadMovie()` and `unloadMovie()` start the ActionScript line of code. When you use actions in this manner, the target of the action is specified as an argument (option) within the action. In the following example, the file `external_1.swf` is loaded into the `mcHolder` instance:

```
loadMovie("external_1.swf", "mcHolder");
```

As a method, actions are written as an extension of the object using the action. Therefore, the target is already specified before the action is typed. The same example shown previously could be rewritten as a method of the `holder_mc` MovieClip object:

```
mcHolder.loadMovie("external_1.swf");
```

or

```
_root.mcHolder.loadMovie("external_1.swf");
```

Because we have specifically referenced the `mcHolder` instance as an object, the `loadMovie()` action (now a method) knows where to direct the loading of `external_1.swf`.

Note   When you use `unloadMovie()` as a method of the `MovieClip` object, you do not need to specify any arguments for the method. For example, `holder.unloadMovie();` will unload any movie (or image asset) in the `mcHolder` instance.

Loading Images into Flash Movies

Flash Player 8 adds the incredible capability to load all of the popular Web image formats into a Flash movie at run time — while the movie plays in a Web browser! In older versions of the Flash Player (versions 6 and 7), externally loaded content needed to be in the SWF or standard JPEG image format.

Caution   You cannot load JPEG images directly into Flash movies playing in Flash Player 5 or earlier. The user must have Flash Player 6 to use this feature. Refer to the Runtime Loading chart at `www.flashsupport.com/links` for a detailed breakdown of Flash Player version support for externally loaded assets.

Some basic rules for using images that are loaded into Flash Player 8 movies are as follows:

✦ Use only supported image formats, which include PNG (all bit depths), GIF, standard JPEG, and progressive JPEG image files. You cannot load JPEG 2000 images into Flash movies.

✦ Watch the file size of image files. Unless your image files are extremely small and/or within a reasonable limit of your target audience's data rate, you will likely want to build a preloader for your JPEG files.

✦ All images that are loaded dynamically will be smoothed in Flash Player 8. Smoothed bitmaps may have an adverse effect on playback performance. You can control the global rendering of bitmaps and all artwork by using the `_quality` property of the `MovieClip` object. For example, `_quality = "low";` turns off smoothing for all artwork. Use this property with care — most vector artwork and text looks unsightly with low-quality rendering.

✦ Control the physical characteristics of the image (X and Y coordinates, X and Y scale, rotation, and so on) by controlling those properties of the `MovieClip` object holding the image.

Caution   In practice, you should nest JPEG images within yet another instance in the holder instance. For a reason unbeknownst to us, when you load JPEG images into a `MovieClip` object, the holder instance stops behaving as a true `MovieClip` object. Some `MovieClip` methods will work with the holder, whereas others won't. To be safe, create another empty `MovieClip` object within the holder instance, and load the JPEG image into that "buffer" clip. If you need to make any changes to the `MovieClip` instance, control the outer holder instance.

✦ Check the user's version of the Flash Player with ActionScript or JavaScript. The user must have Flash Player 8 to load all of these image formats directly into Flash movies. We discuss Flash Player detection in Chapter 21, "Publishing Flash Movies," and Chapter 22, "Integrating Flash Content with Web Pages."

Cross-Reference   Keep in mind general issues for bitmap usage in Flash movies. Read our coverage of using bitmap images in Chapter 16, "Importing Artwork," and in Chapter 36, "Working with Raster Graphics," which is included as a PDF file on this book's CD-ROM.

When in doubt, test the specific JPEG images with your Flash movies. If you encounter problems with loading the JPEG, check the following:

✦ **URL:** Make sure you have the correct path and filename specified in the `loadMovie()` action.

✦ **Target:** Does the target exist into which you want to load? Check the path to the level or `MovieClip` object that contains the image.

✦ **Format:** Is the image a supported format? Or does it use an unsupported encoding such as JPEG 2000?

Without further ado, we'll show you how to create a Flash movie that dynamically loads a JPEG image. In this example, you will load a JPEG file located in the same directory as the Flash movie file (.swf). In ActionScript, the `loadMovie()` action is used to load JPEG images, using the following syntax:

```
instanceName.loadMovie(URL);
```

where *instanceName* is the `MovieClip` object that holds the JPEG image and *URL* is the relative or absolute path to the JPEG file. In the following code, a JPEG file named `cat.jpg` will be loaded into a `MovieClip` object named `mcHolder`:

```
mcHolder.loadMovie("cat.jpg");
```

or

```
mcHolder.loadMovie("http://mydomain.com/cat.jpg");
```

On the CD-ROM   For this exercise, you will use the `unloadMovie_100.fla` document that we discussed earlier in this chapter. You can also make a copy of this completed file from the ch28 folder of this book before you begin this exercise. You will need to copy the `beach.jpg` file in this location to your local folder as well.

In the following steps, you create a Flash movie that can load an external image file:

1. Open a copy of the `unloadMovie_100.fla` document. Resave this file as `load_image_100.fla`.

2. Remove the tint effect from the `mcHolder` instance. Select the instance, and choose None in the Color menu of the Property inspector. Also, edit the rectangle shape in the holderClip symbol, changing its dimensions to 400 x 300 pixels.

3. Create a new layer named **tImg**. Place this layer anywhere above the mcHolder layer.

4. On frame 1 of the tImg layer, select the Text tool and create an Input text field above the buttons. With the text field selected, open the Property inspector and type `tImg` in the <Instance Name> field. Enable the Show Border option as well. When you are finished, your document's Stage should resemble Figure 28-19.

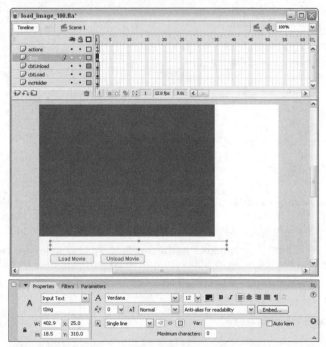

Figure 28-19: The `tImg` field will specify the path to the JPEG image.

5. Select the `cbtLoad` instance on the Stage. In the Property inspector, change the `label` value to Load Image.

6. Select the `cbtUnload` instance on the Stage. In the Property inspector, change the `label` value to Unload Image.

7. Select frame 1 of the actions layer and open the Actions panel. In the Script pane, edit the code to reflect the bold changes shown in Listing 28-4.

Here, you retrieve the current text in the tImg field and use it as the URL of the loadMovie() method of the mcHolder instance. When the cbtLoad component instance is clicked, the oLoader.click() method executes and loads the image file specified in the tImg field into the mcHolder instance. When the cbtUnload instance is clicked, it unloads the contents of the mcHolder instance.

Listing 28-4: **Modifying the oLoader.click() Handler**

```
var cbtLoad:mx.controls.Button;
var cbtUnload:mx.controls.Button;
var tImg:TextField;
var mcHolder:MovieClip;

var oLoader:Object = new Object();
oLoader.click = function(oEvent:Object):Void {
   var sLabel:String = oEvent.target.label.toLowerCase();
   if(sLabel == "load image"){
      mcHolder.loadMovie(tImg.text);
   } else if (sLabel == "unload image"){
      mcHolder.unloadMovie();
   }
};

cbtLoad.addEventListener("click", oLoader);
cbtUnload.addEventListener("click", oLoader);
```

---

8. Save your Flash document and test it (Ctrl+Enter or ⌘+Return). In the Test Movie window, type beach.jpg in the text field. When you click the Load Image button, the beach.jpg image will load into the mcHolder instance.

Try typing other known image URL locations into the text field. For example, you can download the same image from the following location. Be sure to type the full URL, including the http:// protocol:

    http://www.flashsupport.com/images/beach.jpg

You can also try some of these image URLs:

    http://www.flashsupport.com/images/waterfall.png
    http://www.flashsupport.com/images/logo.gif

You may want to go back to the Flash document and move the location of the mcHolder instance to better accommodate the size of the image you are loading.

Caution   If you try to unload an image that was loaded from a domain different than the original .swf file initiating the load, you may receive a warning in the Output panel indicating an access violation. Flash Player 8 has changed the way in which .swf files can access other files. Refer to Chapter 21, "Publishing Flash Movies," for more information, or search the Flash 8 Help panel for "local security policy."

You will learn how to build a loading graphic for image files in the "Using a Preloader for External Assets" section of this chapter.

On the CD-ROM

You can find the completed file, load_image_100.fla, in the ch28ch28 folder of this book's CD-ROM.

Loading an Asset with the MovieClipLoader API

Flash Player 7 ActionScript introduced the MovieClipLoader class. The actions associated with this class, collectively referred to as the API, or Application Programming Interface, enable you to more easily initiate and monitor the loading of external SWF or image files into a Flash movie file (.swf) at run time. One of the benefits of using the MovieClipLoader class is that you can handle loading errors within your code. For example, it would be good to know if a URL failed to load or if there were other difficulties with loading a particular asset.

In the following steps, you learn how to use a MovieClipLoader object to initiate the loading of an external .swf or image file.

On the CD-ROM

Use the load_image_100.fla document, in the ch28 folder of this book's CD-ROM, as a starting point for this exercise.

1. Open the load_image_100.fla document, and save it as MovieClipLoader_100.fla.

2. Select frame 1 of the actions layer, and open the Actions panel (F9). Delete the existing code in the Script pane, and add the code shown in Listing 28-5.

   In lines 1-4, the data types of existing elements on the Stage are declared. In line 6, a new MovieClipLoader object named mcl is created, using the constructor function of the MovieClipLoader class.

   In line 8, a listener object named oLoader is created. This object will receive events that are broadcasted from the mcl object, as well as the Button components you used previously.

   In lines 9 through 11, an onLoadError() handler is defined for the oLoader object. This handler is specific to MovieClipLoader listeners. If there is an error during the loading of an external asset via the MovieClipLoader object, mcl, this handler will be invoked. The handler can accept two parameters, the MovieClip instance receiving the loaded asset (mc) and an error message indicating what went wrong with the loading (sError). In our example, on line 10, we simply throw the error message to the Output panel.

   In lines 12 through 19, the click() method of the oLoader object is defined. (Note that this is effectively the same oLoader object we used in previous exercises of this chapter.) The oLoader receives events from the cbtLoad and cbtUnload instances (lines 23 and 24). When either Button instance is clicked, the click() handler in lines 12 through 19 is invoked.

In line 21, the `oLoader` object is added as a bonafide listener of the `mcl` object. Without this line of code, the `mcl` object would not know to broadcast events to the `oLoader` object.

The difference from our previous exercises occurs primarily in line 15: Instead of using the `loadMovie()` method, the `loadClip()` method of the `MovieClipLoader` class is used with the `mcl` object. `loadClip()` takes two parameters: the URL of the SWF or image asset to load, and the `MovieClip` object that will hold the asset.

In line 17, the `unloadClip()` method of the `MovieClipLoader` class is used to unload the content from the `mcHolder` instance.

Listing 28-5: **An Example of a MovieClipLoader Object at Work**

```
1.  var cbtLoad:mx.controls.Button;
2.  var cbtUnload:mx.controls.Button;
3.  var tImg:TextField;
4.  var mcHolder:MovieClip;
5.
6.  var mcl:MovieClipLoader = new MovieClipLoader();
7.
8.  var oLoader:Object = new Object();
9.  oLoader.onLoadError = function(mc:MovieClip, sError:String):Void {
10.    trace("A loading error has occurred: " + sError);
11. };
12. oLoader.click = function(oEvent:Object):Void {
13.    var sLabel:String = oEvent.target.label.toLowerCase();
14.    if(sLabel == "load image"){
15.      mcl.loadClip(tImg.text, mcHolder);
16.    } else if (sLabel == "unload image"){
17.      mcl.unloadClip(mcHolder);
18.    }
19. };
20.
21. mcl.addListener(oLoader);
22.
23. cbtLoad.addEventListener("click", oLoader);
24. cbtUnload.addEventListener("click", oLoader);
```

3. Save your document, and test it (Ctrl+Enter or ⌘+Enter). Type a valid URL to an image or Flash movie asset, and click the Load Image button. The `mcHolder` instance will then display the image when it's finished loading. Click the Unload Image button, and type an *invalid* URL into the text field — just type any gibberish that comes to mind. Click the Load Image button, and the error message from the `onLoadError()` handler should display in the Output panel. If you load an image or .swf file from a valid URL into the `mcHolder` instance, you can remove it by clicking the Unload Image button.

On the CD-ROM

You can find the completed document, `MovieClipLoader_100.fla`, in the `ch28` folder of this book's CD-ROM.

While this might not seem to be a revolutionary way to load an external image or .swf file into a Flash movie, there are other reasons why `MovieClipLoader` objects are useful:

✦ You can queue several load targets. One instance of the `MovieClipLoader` class can be used to manage the loading of one or more external assets.

✦ You can integrate other components or code with additional methods of the `MovieClipLoader` class, not shown in this exercise. For example, you can tie a `ProgressBar` component to a `MovieClipLoader` object to monitor the downloading of an asset. You'll learn how to do this procedure later in the chapter.

✦ You can program fail-safes into your ActionScript code. In our simple example, we didn't do much with the `onLoadError()` handler. In your own work, though, you can use the `onLoadError()` handler to direct the user to alternate content or attempt to load the content from a backup server or to display an alert dialog box.

✦ You can invoke the `onLoadComplete()` and/or `onLoadInit()` handlers on a listener of a `MovieClipLoader` object to perform further operations with the loaded asset or the master Flash movie after loading has finished.

On the CD-ROM

In the `ch28` folder of this book's CD-ROM, you can find an example of an `onLoadInit()` handler that resizes images or .swf files to fit the boundary of the `mcHolder` instance. This document is named `MovieClipLoader_resize_100.fla`.

Loading MP3 Audio into Flash Movies

If you thought image loading was exciting, wait until you see the support for MP3 audio loading into Flash Player 6 or higher movies. You can load MP3 files directly into `Sound` objects that you create with ActionScript.

Cross-Reference

If you don't know how to use `Sound` objects, read our coverage of `Sound` objects in Chapter 27, "Interacting with Movie Clips." You may also want to read Chapter 15, "Adding Sound," if you are unfamiliar with general sound use in Flash movies. You can find expanded and more advanced coverage of `Sound` objects in the *Flash ActionScript Bible* series (Wiley).

Here are a few tips for using MP3 files that will be loaded into Flash Player 6 or higher movies:

✦ Watch file size. MP3 files, especially those of full-length songs, can be very large in file size, easily exceeding 3 MB. Make sure your target audience can accommodate the file sizes you are loading.

✦ Test your specific MP3 encoding method(s) before you use the same encoding on several files that you intend to use with Flash Player 6 or higher movies. In our tests, we have not encountered problems with any MP3 files that we loaded into the Flash Player. However, there are several variations of CBR (Constant Bit Rate) and VBR (Variable Bit Rate) encoding methods available in several audio applications.

✦ Depending on the Flash Player release version, MP3 files may not cache on the user's hard drive. All MP3 files loaded through the Sound object in ActionScript are stored in the computer's virtual memory. Be careful with the number of MP3 files downloaded and stored in memory simultaneously.

Cross-Reference Review the troubleshooting tips we listed for loadMovie() and images in the last section. The same principles apply to MP3 files.

The core method to the Sound object that can access external MP3 files is the loadSound() method. With this method, you can specify a path to an MP3 file just like you did for JPEG images with the loadMovie() method. However, the loadSound() method has an additional argument: isStreaming. We'll discuss this in a moment. The syntax for using the loadSound() method is:

```
soundObject.loadSound(URL, isStreaming);
```

soundObject indicates the name of a Sound object created previously in ActionScript and URL is the relative or absolute path to the MP3 file. isStreaming is a Boolean value (true or false) that determines whether the MP3 file automatically begins playback as soon as enough bytes have loaded into the Flash Player (true) or whether the MP3 file must fully download before playback can begin (false).

On the CD-ROM Before you begin the following exercise, make a copy of the load_image_100.fla file located in the ch28 folder of this book's CD-ROM. You will modify the existing structure of the document that you built in earlier sections of this chapter. You will also need an MP3 file copied to the same location on your hard drive. You can use the atmospheres_1.mp3 file located in the ch28 folder as well.

In the following steps, you learn how to load an MP3 file into a Sound object.

1. Open the load_image_100.fla document. Resave this document as loadSound_100.fla.

2. Select the Load Image Button component instance on the Stage. In the Parameter tab of the Property inspector, change the label value to **Load MP3**.

3. Select the Unload Image Button component instance on the Stage. In the Property inspector, change the label value to **Unload MP3**.

4. Select the Input text field on the Stage and change the instance's name to tSnd in the Property inspector.

5. Now you need to change the ActionScript in the document to use the Sound object and the loadSound() method. Select frame 1 of the actions layer and open the Actions panel (F9, or Option+F9). Change the code in the Script pane to match the code shown in Listing 28-6.

In lines 1 through 5, you declare the variable names that will be used throughout the script. Here, you add a Sound variable named snd in line 5.

In lines 8 through 17, the click() method of the oLoader listener is invoked by the cbtLoad and cbtUnload instances. If the cbtLoad instance is clicked, lines 10 through 12 are invoked. A new Sound object named snd is created (line 11). Then, in line 12, the loadSound() method of the object is executed, using the URL specified in the tSnd field. The isStreaming argument is set to true so that the MP3 automatically begins to play as soon as enough of the sound file has downloaded into the movie.

If the cbtUnload instance is clicked, lines 13 through 15 are invoked. In line 14, the stop() method of the Sound class halts playback of the sound, and in line 15, the snd object is removed from the movie.

Listing 28-6: **Using loadSound() for External MP3 Files**

```
1.   var cbtLoad:mx.controls.Button;
2.   var cbtUnload:mx.controls.Button;
3.   var tSnd:TextField;
4.   var mcHolder:MovieClip;
5.   var snd:Sound;
6.
7.   var oLoader:Object = new Object();
8.   oLoader.click = function(oEvent:Object):Void {
9.      var sLabel:String = oEvent.target.label.toLowerCase();
10.     if(sLabel == "load mp3"){
11.         snd = new Sound();
12.         snd.loadSound(tSnd.text, true);
13.     } else if (sLabel == "unload mp3"){
14.         snd.stop();
15.         delete snd;
16.     }
17. };
18.
19. cbtLoad.addEventListener("click", oLoader);
20. cbtUnload.addEventListener("click", oLoader);
```

---

6. Save your Flash document, and test it (Ctrl+Enter or ⌘+Return). In the Test Movie window, type atmospheres_1.mp3 into the sound_txt field. Click the Load MP3 button, and the MP3 begins to play. When you click the Unload MP3 button, the sound stops playing.

Try using other URLs of MP3 files, either locally or remotely. You can specify the following URL to stream the same MP3 file from our Web server:

    http://www.theMakers.com/sounds/atmospheres_1.mp3

Note　It may take a few moments for remote sound files to load into Flash Player.

You can continue modifying the Sound object into which the MP3 file loads. For example, you can apply the same volume and balance output control from the examples in Chapter 27, "Interacting with Movie Clips," to the Sound object in this Flash movie.

We will show you how to monitor the download progress of an MP3 file (and other external files) later in this chapter.

You can see the completed Flash document, `loadSound_100.fla`, in the `ch28` folder of this book's CD-ROM.

Loading a Flash Video into a Flash Movie

Since Flash Player 7, you have had the capability to load Flash Video files (.flv) directly into a Flash movie at run time. In Flash Player 6, such files needed to be embedded with a Flash movie file (.swf) and loaded with traditional `loadMovie()` actions.

Flash Player 8 can play .flv files that use the new On2 VP6 codec, which has better image quality than the older Sorenson Spark codec used in Flash Players 6 and 7.

If you don't know what a Flash Video file (.flv) is, see Chapter 17, "Displaying Video."

You could—and still can—stream Flash Video files (.flv files) with the aid of Macromedia Flash Communication Server MX or Flash Media Server. In fact, to get the best performance out of .flv files, we still recommend that you consider Flash Communication Server as a solution for real-time audio/video streaming.

In this section, you learn how to progressively download an .flv file into a Flash movie at run time.

You need to make a copy of the `load_image_100.fla` document used earlier in this chapter, as well as the `stella_speak.flv` file found in the `ch28` folder of this book's CD-ROM. This .flv file uses the new On2 VP6 codec and features an 8-bit alpha channel.

1. Open the `load_image_100.fla` document, and save it as `NetStream_100.fla`.
2. Delete the `mcHolder` instance and layer in the document. Flash Video files are not loaded into `MovieClip` objects.
3. Select the `cbtLoad` instance on the Stage. In the Property inspector, change the label value to **Load FLV**.
4. Select the `cbtUnload` instance on the Stage. In the Property inspector, change the label value to **Unload FLV**.
5. Select the `tImg` instance, and in the Property inspector, change its instance name to `tVid`.

6. Create a new layer, and rename it to **vWin**. Place this layer at the bottom of the layer stack.

7. Open the Library panel (Ctrl+L or ⌘+L). In the panel's options menu in the top-right corner, choose **New Video**. When the Video Properties dialog box opens, make sure the **Video (ActionScript-controlled)** option is selected in the Type category. Click OK.

8. With frame 1 of the vWin layer selected, drag an instance of the Video symbol from the Library panel to the Stage. Position the instance in the same area that the mcHolder previously occupied. In the Property inspector, name this instance vWin. Change the width to 320 pixels and the height to 240 pixels. Most video clips use a 4:3 aspect ratio, such as 320 x 240, 640 x 480, and so on. See Figure 28-20.

> **Note** Video symbols belong to the Video class, not the MovieClip class. Like MovieClip objects, though, Video class members require an instance name so that they can be targeted by ActionScript.

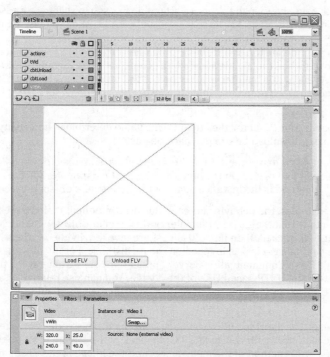

Figure 28-20: The vWin instance will display the video from external .flv files.

9. Now, you're ready to add the ActionScript code necessary to load an external .flv file, and display it in the vWin instance. Select frame 1 of the actions layer, and open the Actions panel (F9, Option+F9). Change the code to that shown in Listing 28-7.

In lines 1 through 4, the data types of elements on the Stage are updated to reflect the current contents.

In lines 6 through 7, a new NetConnection instance named nc is created. This object is required as the sole parameter of the NetStream constructor (line 9). In line 7, the nc instance is connected to a null URL. If you were streaming content from a Flash Communication Server application or Flash Video Streaming Service, you would specify an RTMP location here. For progressively downloaded .flv files from a standard Web server, though, you simply connect to a null location.

In line 9, a new NetStream instance named ns is created. A NetStream instance is required to play an FLV file.

In lines 11 through 15, an onStatus() handler is defined for the ns object. This handler is invoked whenever an event occurs on the stream. In this example, the handler simply outputs trace() messages to the Output panel, letting you know what's happening with the stream.

Note   The \t backslash pairs shown in the trace() actions enable you to shift trace messages to the right, inserting tab characters. You'll see the effect of each \t when you test the movie.

Lines 17 through 22 define the onMetaData() handler for the NetStream instance. This handler is invoked when the .flv file's metadata is received. The metadata is at the front of the .flv file. As such, this handler invokes before the video begins to play. The file's metadata includes information describing the media file, including its width, height, and duration.

On line 24, a buffer time is set for the stream. This value determines how many seconds of the stream must download before playback begins.

In line 25, the attachVideo() method of the Video class is invoked on the vWin instance, the object you placed on the Stage in Step 8. The parameter for the attachVideo() method is the instance name of the NetStream object created in line 9.

Like previous examples, the behavior for each Button component is tied to respective if/else statements within the click() handler of the listener object, oLoader. If the cbtLoad instance is clicked, then lines 30 and 31 are invoked. In line 31, the play() method of the NetStream class is invoked on the ns instance. For .flv files that are not accessed from a Flash Communication Server application, the parameter for the play() method is the HTTP-based URL of the .flv file. You can use relative or absolute paths for this URL. In our example, you use the text from the tVid field to determine the URL.

In lines 32 through 34, the video file's playback is stopped. This code is invoked when the cbtUnload instance is clicked. In line 33, playback of the stream is stopped by invoking the close() method of the ns instance, and the image in the Video instance, vWin, is erased with the clear() method.

In line 41, you set the focusManager class's defaultPushButton property to the cbtLoad instance. This action enables the Enter key for the cbtLoad instance. When you test the movie, make sure you choose Control ⇨ Disable Keyboard Shortcuts to remap the Enter key to the Flash movie.

Note The focusManager class is automatically available in your Flash movies whenever you add User Interface components to your Flash movie.

Listing 28-7: Creating a NetStream Object to Access Flash Video Content

```
1.   var cbtLoad:mx.controls.Button;
2.   var cbtUnload:mx.controls.Button;
3.   var tVid:TextField;
4.   var vWin:Video;
5.
6.   var nc:NetConnection = new NetConnection();
7.   nc.connect(null);
8.
9.   var ns:NetStream = new NetStream(nc);
10.
11.  ns.onStatus = function(oInfo:Object):Void {
12.     trace("ns.onStatus >");
13.     trace("\tlevel:\t" +oInfo.level);
14.     trace("\tcode:\t" + oInfo.code);
15.  };
16.
17.  ns.onMetaData = function(oData:Object):Void {
18.     trace("ns.onMetaData >");
19.     trace("\twidth: " + oData.width);
20.     trace("\theight: " + oData.height);
21.     trace("\tduration: " + oData.duration);
22.   };
23.
24.  ns.setBufferTime(5);
25.  vWin.attachVideo(ns);
26.
27.  var oLoader:Object = new Object();
28.  oLoader.click = function(oEvent:Object):Void {
29.     var sLabel:String = oEvent.target.label.toLowerCase();
30.     if(sLabel == "load flv"){
31.        ns.play(tVid.text);
32.     } else if (sLabel == "unload flv"){
33.        ns.close();
34.        vWin.clear();
35.     }
36.  };
37.
38.  cbtLoad.addEventListener("click", oLoader);
39.  cbtUnload.addEventListener("click", oLoader);
40.
41.  focusManager.defaultPushButton = cbtLoad;
```

10. Save your Flash document. Make sure you have copied the stella_speak_keyed.flv file from the ch28 folder of this book's CD-ROM to the location where you saved the Flash document for this exercise. Test the movie (Ctrl+Enter or ⌘+Enter), and type the text stella_speak_keyed.flv into the tVid field. Click the Load FLV button, and the video will play in the vWin instance (see Figure 28-21). If you click the Unload FLV button, the playback stops and the image no longer appears in the nWin instance.

Note   You might notice that the stella_speak_keyed.flv file appears distorted on playback. That particular .flv file has a frame size of 380 x 320, and the picture is being stretched on playback within the 320 x 240 dimensions of the vWin object. In the next section, you learn how to adjust the size of the Video object based on the actual dimensions of the .flv file.

Figure 28-21: The video as it plays in the vWin instance

You can find the completed file, NetStream_100.fla, in the ch28 folder of this book's CD-ROM.

Try creating some of your own Flash Video files and using them with this Flash movie. Remember to go back to Chapter 17, "Displaying Video," for more information on Flash Video encoding.

Displaying a Flash Video at Its Native Size

There's the very likely possibility that when you're building a Flash user interface intended to display video, you won't be able to predict all of the possible sizes of the video clips you want to play. In this section, you learn how to use the metadata encoded into .flv files in order to appropriately size the Video object in which the video plays.

Caution

Not all Flash Video encoding utilities add metadata to .flv files they create. Most current encoding utilities, including the Flash Video 8 Encoder that ships with Flash Professional 8, add accurate metadata. If the NetStream.onMetaData() handler does not fire, or if it reports 0 values for the width and height properties of the clip, then it's likely that there's no metadata in the .flv file. Luckily, there are tools that can add metadata to your .flv files after you have created them. Check the "Flash Video Utilities" section of the www.flash support.com/links page for specific resources.

Before you proceed with the tutorial for this section, though, you must understand one important concept: The Video class has two sets of dimension properties — width/height and _width/_height. The _width and _height properties control the displayed size of the Video instance on the Stage, while the width and height properties report the actual dimensions of the video stream playing. You can set the _width and _height properties but not the width and height properties. As you'll see in the second part of this section, you can use the width and height properties to check the actual width and height of the .flv file even if there is no metadata in the .flv file.

Note

The width and height properties of the Video class do not necessarily report the width and height values that are displayed in the Property inspector when you select the Video instance on the Stage. To check the displayed width and height of a vWin instance, use the _width and _height properties of the Video instance.

Adjusting video size with metadata

If your .flv file has metadata available, then you can use the NetStream.onMetaData() handler to resize the Video instance displaying the .flv file. As you learned in the last exercise, the onMetaData() handler is invoked before the video begins to play.

On the CD-ROM

Make a copy of the NetStream_100.fla file from the ch28 folder of this book's CD-ROM. You'll use this file as the starter document for this section.

1. Open your copy of the NetStream_100.fla document, and save it as NetStream_resize_100.fla.

2. Select frame 1 of the actions layer, and open the Actions panel (F9 or Option+F9 on Mac). Add or modify the bold lines shown in Listing 28-8. In this updated code, you set the _width and _height properties of the vWin instance (a Video object) to the same values as the returned width and height properties in the metadata object, oData. Note that the visibility (the _visible property) of the vWin instance is set to true as well. In the oLoader.click() handler, the visibility of the vWin is turned off. This step is taken so that you don't see the video properties snap and update when the video begins to play. The video is only visible after the transformations have been applied.

Listing 28-8: **The Updated onMetaData() Handler**

```
var cbtLoad:mx.controls.Button;
var cbtUnload:mx.controls.Button;
var tVid:TextField;
var vWin:Video;
var nc:NetConnection = new NetConnection();
nc.connect(null);

var ns:NetStream = new NetStream(nc);

ns.onStatus = function(oInfo:Object):Void {
   trace("ns.onStatus >");
   trace("\tlevel:\t" +oInfo.level);
   trace("\tcode:\t" + oInfo.code);
};

ns.onMetaData = function(oData:Object):Void {
   trace("ns.onMetaData >");
   var nWidth:Number = oData.width;
   var nHeight:Number = oData.height;
   trace("\twidth: " + nWidth);
   trace("\theight: " + nHeight);
   vWin._width = nWidth;
   vWin._height = nHeight;
   vWin._visible = true;
};

ns.setBufferTime(5);
vWin.attachVideo(ns);

var oLoader:Object = new Object();
oLoader.click = function(oEvent:Object):Void {
   var sLabel:String = oEvent.target.label.toLowerCase();
   if(sLabel == "load flv"){
      vWin._visible = false;
      ns.play(tVid.text);
   } else if (sLabel == "unload flv"){
      ns.close();
      vWin.clear();
   }
};

cbtLoad.addEventListener("click", oLoader);
cbtUnload.addEventListener("click", oLoader);

focusManager.defaultPushButton = cbtLoad;
```

3. Save your document, and test it (Ctrl+Enter or ⌘+Enter). Type the name `stella_speak_keyed.flv` into the `tVid` text field, and press the Load FLV button. The clip of Stella plays at the original size of the .flv file, 320 x 380. Compare the sizes of the clip from the last exercise with this new resized clip.

4. You probably noticed that the video clip was playing behind the text field and buttons on the Stage. You can also shrink or enlarge the video size by performing further mathematical operations on the width and height values. Select frame 1 of the actions layer, and open the Actions panel. Change the `nWidth` and `nHeight` values in the `onMetaData()` handler, as shown in the following bold code. Here, you divide the width and height data by two, reducing the size of the video display.

```
ns.onMetaData = function(oData:Object):Void {
    trace("ns.onMetaData >");
    var nWidth:Number = oData.width/2;
    var nHeight:Number = oData.height/2;
    trace("\twidth: " + nWidth);
    trace("\theight: " + nHeight);
    vWin._width = nWidth;
    vWin._height = nHeight;
    vWin._visible = true;
};
```

5. Save the document, and test it (Ctrl+Enter or ⌘+Enter). Type the name `stella_speak_keyed.flv` in the `tVid` field, and press the Load FLV button. As shown in Figure 28-22, you should now see Stella's video at a quarter of the size.

Note Even though you divided the width and height values by two, the new displayed pixel area is one-fourth of the original pixel area of the clip.

Figure 28-22: The newly resized video clip

You can find the completed file, `NetStream_resize_100.fla`, in the `ch28` folder of this book's CD-ROM.

Setting the video size without metadata

You might not always have the luxury of loading .flv files that have metadata. Luckily, you can still resize the Video object using the native width and height properties of the Video class. In this section, you learn how to alter the `onMetaData()` event handler to check for the existence of metadata and make the appropriate modifications to the video display area.

We intentionally included a clip without accurate metadata on this book's CD-ROM. Make a copy of the `stella_speak_no_meta.flv` file to the same location as the `NetStream_resize_100.fla` file you created in the last section. Test the Flash movie for that document, and type `stella_speak_no_meta.flv` into the text field and click the Load FLV button. The .flv file will load, and if you have your speakers turned on, you'll hear the audio, but you won't see the video. Why? Because the clip has no metadata, the width and height properties are being set to 0. In order to fix this problem, you'll have to make some modifications to the `onMetaData()` event handler.

Continue using the `NetStream_resize_100.fla` file from the last section, or make a copy of the file from the `ch28` folder of this book's CD-ROM. Make sure you have made a copy of the `stella_speak_no_meta.flv` file as well.

1. Open the `NetStream_resize_100.fla` file, and resave it as `NetStream_resize_nometa_100.fla`.

2. Select frame 1 of the actions layer, and open the Actions panel. Modify the `onMetaData()` event handler as shown in the following bold code. Here, you check to see if the `nWidth` variable is equal to 0, an undefined value, or if it's not a number. If any of those conditions are true, you'll assume that there isn't valid metadata for both the width and height of the .flv file. As such, check the width and height properties of the `vWin` instance, which will return the FLV's native dimensions. As with our previous example, the values are divided in half to size Stella more appropriately for the movie's Stage.

```
ns.onMetaData = function(oData:Object):Void {
   trace("ns.onMetaData >");
   var nWidth:Number = oData.width/2;
   var nHeight:Number = oData.height/2;
   if(nWidth == 0 || nWidth == undefined ||  isNaN(nWidth)){
      trace("\tclip has empty metadata");
      vWin._width = vWin.width/2;
      vWin._height = vWin.height/2;
   } else {
      trace("\tclip has proper metadata");
      vWin._width = nWidth;
      vWin._height = nHeight;
   }
   vWin._visible = true;
};
```

3. Save the document, and test it (Ctrl+Enter or ⌘+Enter). Type `stella_speak_no_meta.flv` into the text field, and click the Load FLV button. You should see the same size video as the clip you sized in the previous section.

You can find the completed file, `NetStream_resize_nometa_100.fla`, in the `ch28` folder of this book's CD-ROM.

Using a Preloader for External Assets

In this section, you will learn how to add a preloader that monitors the download progress of any external asset, whether the file format is SWF, JPEG, PNG, GIF, FLV, or MP3. This preloader combines the same methodology employed by the original `preloader_f5_100.fla` document you built earlier in this chapter. We've already taken the same loader Movie Clip symbol from that exercise and added ActionScript to its timeline. Let's take a quick look at what we've done.

Note Later in this chapter, you learn how to use the Preloader component included with Flash 8. In this section, you learn the fundamental building blocks of an asset preloader, from the ground up.

Open the `loader_100.fla` file located in the `ch28` folder of this book's CD-ROM. Open the Library panel and double-click the loaderClip symbol. Inside of this symbol, select frame 1 of the actions layer. Open the Actions panel and you will see the Listing 28-9 code in the Script pane. Note that the ⊃ character indicates a continuation of the same line of code.

Listing 28-9: **The loaderClip Symbol Code**

```
var mcBar:MovieClip;
var tLabel:TextField;
var nCount:Number;
var nCheckID:Number;

function checkLoad(oTarget:Object, oListener:Object):Void {
    var nLB:Number = oTarget instanceof NetStream ? oTarget.bytesLoaded
        : oTarget.getBytesLoaded();
    var nTB:Number = oTarget instanceof NetStream ? oTarget.bytesLoaded
        :oTarget.getBytesTotal();
    var nPL:Number = isNaN(nLB) || isNaN(nTB) ? 0 : (nLB/nTB)*100; (nLB/nTB)*100;
    mcBar._xscale = nPL;
    tLabel.text = Math.floor(nPL)+"% of "+Math.floor(nTB/1024)+"KB loaded.";
    if (nLB >= nTB && nTB > 0) {
        if (nCount >= 12) {
            clearInterval(nCheckID);
            oListener.onLoadFinished({target: this});
        } else {
```

Continued

Listing 28-9 *(continued)*

```
            nCount++;
        }
    }
    updateAfterEvent();
}

nCount = 0;
nCheckID = setInterval(this, "checkLoad", 30, target, listener);
stop();
```

Tip   You can add a check to the value of nTB to prevent a -1 value from being displayed in the
tLabel field. For example, the following if() statement makes sure that nTB is greater
than -1:

```
if(nTB > -1){
    tLabel.text = Math.floor(nPL)+"% of ⟳
        "+Math.floor(nTB/1024)+"KB loaded.";
}
```

While this may seem a bit overwhelming, it's nearly identical to the code you built on the
Main Timeline of the preloader_100.fla document. The primary differences are as follows:

✦ The code is contained within a function named checkLoad().

✦ Instead of a frame loop, the new setInterval() function is used to repeatedly execute
the checkLoad() function. When the loading is finished, the clearInterval() function is called to stop the looping.

Note   This script uses a specific implementation of the setInterval() function. The function has
two syntax formats: setInterval(functionName:Function, interval:Number,
optionalArgs); or setInterval(object:Object, objectMethod:String,
interval:Number, optionalArgs);. In this example, we use the latter syntax, because
there are this references in the checkLoad() function. If you have this references within
the checkLoad() function, using the latter syntax helps work out scoping issues with
objects within the function.

✦ The checkLoad() function accepts two arguments: oTarget and oListener. The function checks the load status of a specified object, oTarget, instead of checking the
loaded bytes and total bytes of the current timeline (this or _root) as our earlier
example in the chapter used. As such, this clip needs to be passed a target value, as
expressed in the setInterval() function. The oListener object works similarly to listener objects of Flash 8 components. When the loading of the oTarget object is finished, the checkLoad() function will invoke the onLoadFinished() method of the
oListener object. Like oTarget, oListener must be passed into the loaderClip
instance, as expressed in the setInterval() function.

✦ The checkLoad() function can also detect the data type of the target (oTarget) it is monitoring. Using the instanceof operator (discussed in Chapter 26, "Using Functions and Arrays") and the ?: conditional operator, the nLB and nTB variables check different properties of the target. NetStream objects have bytesLoaded and bytesTotal properties, while MovieClip and Sound objects have getBytesLoaded() and getBytesTotal() methods.

✦ The loaderClip instance is dynamically placed in the movie to monitor the download progress of a specific asset — it does not monitor the load progress of the main movie .swf file.

Tip

The setInterval() and clearInterval() functions were introduced in Flash Player 6. These actions work only in Flash Player 6 or higher movies.

Note

The loaderClip symbol is only a few steps away from being a full-fledged ActionScript 2.0 (AS2) component. However, in order to keep the loaderClip symbol flexible enough to monitor everything from individual asset downloads to the main movie's download progress, the symbol must not use any ActionScript 2.0 classes. Why? If the main movie has other AS2 components, you need to defer the classes from loading on frame 1. If the loaderClip symbol became a component, then it wouldn't be available for use on frame 1 of the main movie.

But that's not all of the code you'll need to get an asset preloader working. Even though there is code with a loaderClip symbol that continually checks the loading progress of an asset, you need some code that provides some input for the loaderClip symbol, such as the object (target, as specified in the setInterval() function) in which the file is loading (a MovieClip object, a Sound object, or a NetStream object).

Let's take a look at one more chunk of code. Open the loadFile.as file located in the ch28 folder of this book's CD-ROM. You can use Macromedia Dreamweaver, Flash Professional 8, or any other text editor to view the code. Listing 28-10 displays the code contents of this file. Note that the ⊃ character indicates a continuation of the same line of code.

Listing 28-10: The loadFile.as **Script**

```
import mx.utils.Delegate;

var snd:Sound;
var mcHolder:MovieClip;
var mcl:MovieClipLoader;
var ns:NetStream;
var vWin:Video;

var nc:NetConnection = new NetConnection();
nc.connect(null);

function loadFile(sUrl:String, sType:String, oProp:Object,⊃
   oListener:Object):Void {
```

Continued

Listing 28-10 *(continued)*

```
if(sType == null || sType == undefined)
    var sType:String = sUrl.substr(-3).toLowerCase();
else    sType = sType.toLowerCase();
var mc:MovieClip = mcHolder = createEmptyMovieClip("mcHolder", 1);
if(oProp != null || oProp != undefined){
   mc._x = oPosition.x;
   mc._y = oPosition.y;
   mc._xscale = mc._yscale = oPosition.scale;
}
var oTarget:Object;
switch(sType){
   case "swf" :
   case "jpg" :
   case "gif" :
   case "png":
   default:
      mcl = new MovieClipLoader();
      if(oListener != undefined) mcl.addListener(oListener);
      mcl.loadClip(sUrl, mc);
      oTarget = mc;
      break;
   case "mp3" :
      snd = new Sound(mc);
      snd.loadSound(sUrl, true);
      oTarget = snd;
      break;
   case "flv" :
      var mcVid:MovieClip = mc.attachMovie("videoClip", "mcVid", 1);
      vWin = mcVid.vWin;
      ns = new NetStream(nc);
      ns.onMetaData = Delegate.create(this, this.onVideoMetaData);
      ns.play(sUrl);
      mcVid.vWin.attachVideo(ns);
      oTarget = ns;
      break;
}
var oInit:Object = {_x: 25, _y: Stage.height - 30, target: oTarget, ⊃
   listener: oListener};
var mcLoader:MovieClip = attachMovie("loaderClip", "mcLoader", 2, oInit);
mcLoader.onResize = function():Void {
   this._y = Stage.height - 30;
};
Stage.addListener(mcLoader);
}

function unloadFile():Void {
   if(mcHolder instanceof MovieClip) mcHolder.removeMovieClip();
   if(snd instanceof Sound) {
```

```
         snd.stop();
         delete snd;
      }
      if(ns instanceof NetStream) ns.close();
   }

   function onVideoMetaData(oData:Object):Void {
      var nWidth:Number =  oData.width;
      var nHeight:Number = oData.height;
      if(nWidth == 0 || nWidth == undefined ||  isNaN(nWidth)){
         vWin._width = vWin.width;
         vWin._height = vWin.height;
      } else {
         vWin._width = nWidth;
         vWin._height = nHeight;
      }
      vWin._visible = true;
   }
```

The loadFile() function takes a URL specified in the sUrl parameter and loads it into a proper container based on the sType value passed to the function. The sType argument can be any of the following types: swf, jpg, gif, png, mp3, or flv. If the sType parameter is not passed to the function, the loadFile() function checks the last three characters of the sUrl value. The switch() statement loads the URL into an appropriate holder object. If the sType value is "swf", "jpg", "gif", or "png", the function will load the URL into a new Movie Clip instance named mcHolder. If the sType value is "mp3", the function loads the URL into a new Sound object. If the sType value is "flv", the URL is loaded into a NetStream object. The oInit object contains the information that the loaderClip symbol needs to work. The Y position of the mcLoader instance is based on the Stage.height value. The target variable (which is also specified in the checkLoad() function you saw earlier within the loaderClip symbol) is set to either mcHolder, snd, or ns, depending on what type of media file is being loaded. Finally, the attachMovie() method attaches the loaderClip symbol from the movie's library to the Main Timeline (_root), passing it the properties of the oInit object.

The loadFile() function can also use optional arguments, such as oProp and oListener. If oProp is passed to the loadFile() function, the mcHolder instance will be positioned according to the oProp.x and oProp.y property values. You can also specify a scale property on the oProp object. The oListener object is passed to the loaderClip symbol. The oListener object should have an onLoadFinished() method defined, as you'll see later in this section.

Tip

The ability to pass an oInit object to the attachMovie() method is a feature of Flash Player 6 and higher movies.

Cross-Reference

The loadFile() function also uses the Delegate class to define the onMetaData() handler of the NetStream instance, ns. The Delegate class enables you to remap the scope of a handler to another object and function. The onVideoMetaData() function uses essentially the same code you used earlier in this chapter to resize a Video object. You learn more about the Delegate class in Chapter 33, "Using Components."

The `unloadFile()` function deletes the objects created by the `loadFile()` function. If a `mcHolder`, `snd`, or `ns` instance exists, it will be deleted or removed from the movie.

In the following steps, you combine the loaderClip symbol from the `loader_100.fla` file with the `loadFile.as` file that you just examined. You integrate these elements into a new version of the `loadSound_100.fla` file that you created earlier in this section.

On the CD-ROM

Make a copy of the `loader_100.fla`, `loadFile.as`, and `loadSound_100.fla` files, located in the `ch28` folder of this book's CD-ROM.

1. Open the `loadSound_100.fla` document. Save this document as `preloader_fp8_100.fla`.

2. Choose File ⇨ Import ⇨ Open External Library, and choose the `loader_100.fla` document.

3. Drag the loaderClip symbol from the `loader_100.fla` Library panel to the Stage of the `preloader_fp8_100.fla` document. All of the symbols associated with the loaderClip symbol will be transferred to the `preloader_fp8_100.fla` document. Close the `loader_100.fla` Library panel.

Note

For ease of use, the videoClip symbol that's used by the `loadFile.as` code is embedded on frame 2 of the loaderClip symbol.

4. Delete the instance of the loaderClip symbol from the Stage of the `preloader_fp8_100.fla` document. This symbol is linked in the Library of this document and will be attached to the movie's Stage via ActionScript.

5. Delete the mcHolder layer in the Main Timeline. You will not need a physical Movie Clip instance on the Stage in which to load assets. The code within the `loadFile()` function creates a `mcHolder` instance on the fly.

6. Select the `cbtLoad` component instance on the Stage. In the Property inspector's Parameters tab, change the `label` value to **Load Asset**.

7. Select the `cbtUnload` component instance on the Stage. In the Property inspector's Parameters tab, change the `label` value to **Unload Asset**.

8. Select the Input text field on the Stage and open the Property inspector. Change the instance name of the field to `tUrl`. At run time, the text that you type into this field will be used by the `loadFile()` function, which will be executed by the listener of the `cbtLoad` instance when the button is clicked.

9. Select frame 1 of the actions layer. Open the Actions panel (F9, or Option+F9 on Mac), and replace the existing code in the Script pane with the following code:

```
var cbtLoad:mx.controls.Button;
var cbtUnload:mx.controls.Button;
var tFile:TextField;

#include "loadFile.as"

var oLoader:Object = new Object();
```

```
oLoader.click = function(oEvent:Object):Void {
   var sLabel:String = oEvent.target.label.toLowerCase();
   if(sLabel == "load asset"){
      loadFile(tFile.text);
   } else if (sLabel == "unload asset"){
      unloadFile();
   }
};


cbtLoad.addEventListener("click", oLoader);
cbtUnload.addEventListener("click", oLoader);
```

The #include directive fetches the contents of the loadFile.as file when you publish or test the movie (at compile time), and inserts the code into the Flash movie on this keyframe. As with previous examples in this chapter, the label of the clicked button is checked to determine which if/else statement is invoked. If the cbtLoad instance is clicked, the loadFile() function is invoked, passing the text value of the tFile field. If the cbtUnload instance is clicked, the unloadFile() function is invoked.

10. Save the Flash document, and test it (Ctrl+Enter or ⌘+Return). Type a URL into the Input text field. You can use the following test URL:

http://www.flashsupport.com/images/waterfall.png

Alternatively, you can type the name of a file in the same location as the tested movie on your hard drive. Click the Load Asset button, and the loader instance will appear above the Input Text field, indicating the progress of the file's download. If you received an error while Flash 8 was creating the test .swf file, go back and double-check your code on frame 1 of the actions layer.

11. If you loaded the .png file listed in the previous step, then you noticed that the image was overlapping the controls of the movie. The loadFile() function can also accept an object that describes where and at what size the loaded asset should appear. Select frame 1 of the actions layer, and open the Actions panel. Change the oLoader.click() handler code to the following code shown in bold. Note that the null value is passed as the sType value, so that you have flexibility with the URL you type into the text field.

```
oLoader.click = function(oEvent:Object):Void {
   var sLabel:String = oEvent.target.label.toLowerCase();
   if(sLabel == "load asset"){
      loadFile(tFile.text, null, { x: 10, y: 10, scale: 50});
   } else if (sLabel == "unload asset"){
      unloadFile();
   }
};
```

12. Save the Flash document, and test it. Type the following location into the text field:

http://www.flashsupport.com/images/waterfall.png

and click the Load Asset button. The image should load into the movie, and the loaderClip symbol should appear on the Stage. More importantly, the image is scaled at 50 percent so that it's smaller on the Stage, as shown in Figure 28-23. If you click the Unload Asset button, the image should disappear.

Figure 28-23: The `mcLoader` instance appears when you click the Load Asset button.

13. There's one more issue to address with this example: The loaderClip symbol does not remove itself from the movie when the asset has finished loading. In order to remove the loaderClip symbol, you need to set up a listener object with an `onLoadFinished()` method defined. Since you already have an `oLoader` listener object, you can define the `onLoadFinished()` method on the `oLoader` object. You then need to pass a reference to `oLoader` to the `loadFile()` function. Select frame 1 of the actions layer, and open the Actions panel. Modify the `oLoader` object code with the following bold code. Do not type the ⤷ character, which indicates the continuation of the same line of code.

> **Note**
>
> If you remember from the code breakdown earlier in this section, when the `checkLoad()` function within the loaderClip symbol determines that the asset has fully loaded, the `onLoadFinished()` handler of the listener object is passed an object containing a target property pointing to the loaderClip instance itself.

```
var oLoader:Object = new Object();
oLoader.onLoadFinished = function(oEvent:Object):Void {
   oEvent.target.removeMovieClip();
};
oLoader.click = function(oEvent:Object):Void {
   var sLabel:String = oEvent.target.label.toLowerCase();
   if(sLabel == "load asset"){
      loadFile(tFile.text, null, { x: 10, y: 10, scale: 50}, ⤷
         oLoader);
   } else if (sLabel == "unload asset"){
      unloadFile();
   }
};
```

14. Save the document, and test it (Ctrl+Enter or ⌘+Enter). Type the URL listed in Step 12, and click the Load Asset button. If you have a fast Internet connection, the mcLoader instance appears and disappears. If you use a local asset, such as beach.jpg in the text field and click the Load Asset button, the mcLoader instance appears for just an instant. To see the download progress in simulation, choose View ⇨ Simulate Download while you're testing the movie.

Try a URL for each of the media formats that Flash Player 8 can load dynamically. If a file fails to load, check the same URL in a Web browser.

You now have a complete loading script and loaderClip symbol that you can reuse on your own progress. These custom preloaders add very little weight to your file size — just over 1 KB!

On the CD-ROM

You can find the completed document, preloader_fp8_100.fla, in the ch28 folder of this book's CD-ROM.

Using the Loader and ProgressBar Components

If you're thinking it takes too much effort to create your own ActionScript code for preloaders in ActionScript, you may be in luck. Flash 8 includes two User Interface components, Loader and ProgressBar, which make the task of loading external files into Flash movies at run time very simple.

You might be wondering why we even bothered to have you get your hands dirty, per se, with our earlier coverage. It's extremely important for you to be able to build your own functionality into your projects. Chances are, you'll come across situations where components won't do exactly what you need them to do. As such, you'll need to know how to build interactivity into your movie on your own. Now that you have a solid understanding of how to load external files into a Flash movie, you can have a greater appreciation for the features we're about to demonstrate.

Adding a Loader component to your Flash movie

The Loader component can automatically load an external image or .swf file into your Flash movie, and it's incredibly simple to use. One of the nice features of the Loader component is that it can scale the image to fit within the boundaries of the component. This example shows you how to use the Loader component

1. Create a new Flash document and save it as f8_loader_100.fla.

2. Rename Layer 1 to **clo**.

3. Open the Components panel, and open the User Interface grouping. Drag the Loader component to the Stage. Place the instance near the top-left corner of the Stage.

4. Select the new instance and name it clo in the Property inspector. Select the Parameters tab in the Property inspector. Leave the autoLoad setting at its default value (true). In the contentPath field, type http://www.flashsupport.com/images/beach.jpg. Make sure the scaleContent setting is true (see Figure 28-24).

Note As always, you can name your instances with your preferred naming convention. Here, we name the Loader component `clo`, which stands for *component loader*. We use the c prefix consistently with all component instances in the examples in this book.

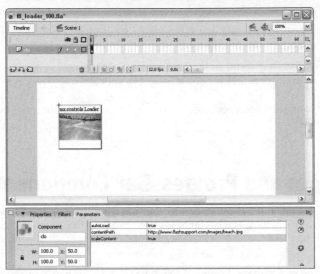

Figure 28-24: The parameters of the `Loader` component

5. The `Loader` component, when used in this fashion, gives you a live preview of the loaded asset. Deselect the instance on the Stage, and reselect it. Doing so should force the instance to update, displaying the image within the area of the `clo` instance. You can resize the `clo` instance to change the size of the loaded image.

6. Save the document, and test it. You can watch the asset load into the Flash movie.

Note Understand the image is being loaded into the Flash movie at run time, not at author-time. Even though the component displays a live preview of the image in the component on the Stage, it still needs to load the image dynamically when the Flash movie file (.swf) loads into a Web browser. In other words, the JPEG image is not being imported into the .fla file and exported with the .swf file.

On the CD-ROM You can find the `f8_loader_100.fla` document in the `ch28` folder of this book's CD-ROM.

You can use this procedure to load "fixed" content into your Flash movie, meaning, if you don't need to change the URL of the loaded asset for a given presentation, using the component with hard-coded values in the Property inspector can take care of your needs. However, if you want to be able to change or display several images in the same instance over the course of your presentation, you'll need to know how to change the parameters of the Loader component instance in ActionScript. In the next section, you learn how to do just that.

Dynamically changing the source of a Loader component

You can also set the URL to the content of a Loader component instance using ActionScript. In the following steps, you learn how to integrate the Loader component with one of the earlier examples you created in this chapter.

On the CD-ROM

Make a copy of the `preloader_fp8_100.fla` and `loadFile.as` documents from the `ch28` folder of this book's CD-ROM. Alternatively, you can use your own version of these documents if you built it in the earlier exercise of this chapter.

1. In Flash 8, open the `preloader_fp8_100.fla` document. Resave the document as `preloader_fp8_comps_100.fla`.

2. Create a new layer, and rename it **clo**. On frame 1 of this layer, add a Loader component instance, as outlined in Step 3 in the previous section.

3. In the Property inspector, name the new instance `clo`. Do not specify any additional parameters for the component. You can resize the component instance so that it fills up more of the Stage.

4. Select frame 1 of the actions layer, and open the Actions panel (F9). Change line 5 of the script to the following code. Here, you change the reference to the included .as file to `loadFile_component.as`. In the next step, you see how the code in the new .as file is altered.

   ```
   #include "loadFile_component.as"
   ```

5. Open the `loadFile.as` file from the earlier example, and add (or modify) the code to the bold code shown in Listing 28-11.

   Here, instead of creating a `MovieClipLoader` object to load the SWF or image asset, the `loadFile()` function tells the `clo` instance to load the asset specified by the `sUrl` parameter. The `load()` method of the Loader component essentially acts as the `loadMovie()` method, bringing the external asset into the movie.

   The `unloadFile()` function is modified to unload the asset from the Loader component, which can be referenced via the `content` property of the Loader component.

Listing 28-11: The Modified loadFile_component.as Script

```
import mx.utils.Delegate;

var snd:Sound;
var mcHolder:MovieClip;
var clo:mx.controls.Loader;
var ns:NetStream;
var vWin:Video;

var nc:NetConnection = new NetConnection();
```

Continued

Listing 28-11 *(continued)*

```
nc.connect(null);

function loadFile(sUrl:String, sType:String, oProp:Object,
oListener:Object):Void {
    if(sType == null || sType == undefined) var sType:String =
        sUrl.substr(-3).toLowerCase();
    else    sType = sType.toLowerCase();
    var mc:MovieClip = mcHolder = createEmptyMovieClip("mcHolder", 1);
    if(oProp != null || oProp != undefined){
        mc._x = oProp.x;
        mc._y = oProp.y;
        mc._xscale = mc._yscale = oProp.scale;
    }
    var oTarget:Object;
    switch(sType){
        case "swf" :
        case "jpg" :
        case "gif" :
        case "png":
        default:
            clo.load(sUrl);
            oTarget = clo;
            break;
        case "mp3" :
            snd = new Sound(mc);
            snd.loadSound(sUrl, true);
            oTarget = snd;
            break;
        case "flv" :
            var mcVid:MovieClip = mc.attachMovie("videoClip", "mcVid", 1);
            vWin = mcVid.vWin;
            ns = new NetStream(nc);
            ns.onMetaData = Delegate.create(this, this.onVideoMetaData);
            ns.play(sUrl);
            mcVid.vWin.attachVideo(ns);
            oTarget = ns;
            break;
    }
    var oInit:Object = {_x: 25, _y: Stage.height - 30, target: oTarget, ⤴
        listener:  oListener};
    var mcLoader:MovieClip = attachMovie("loaderClip", "mcLoader", 2, oInit);
    mcLoader.onResize = function():Void {
        this._y = Stage.height - 30;
    };
    Stage.addListener(mcLoader);
}

function unloadFile():Void {
```

```
    if(mcHolder instanceof MovieClip) mcHolder.removeMovieClip();
    if(mcl instanceof MovieClipLoader) mcl.unloadClip();
    if(snd instanceof Sound) {
        snd.stop();
        delete snd;
    }
    if(ns instanceof NetStream) ns.close();
    if(clo.content != undefined) clo.content.unloadMovie();
}

function onVideoMetaData(oData:Object):Void {
    var nWidth:Number = oData.width;
    var nHeight:Number = oData.height;
    if(nWidth == 0 || nWidth == undefined || isNaN(nWidth)){
        vWin._width = vWin.width;
        vWin._height = vWin.height;
    } else {
        vWin._width = nWidth;
        vWin._height = nHeight;
    }
    vWin._visible = true;
}
```

6. Save the `loadFile.as` file as `loadFile_component.as`.

7. Save the Flash document, and test the movie. Type a URL into the `tFile` field, such as:

   `http://www.flashsupport.com/images/beach.jpg`

   Click the Load Asset button, and the asset should load into the Loader component. Notice that the custom preloader still works with the Loader component as well, because the Loader component has `getBytesLoaded()` and `getBytesTotal()` methods.

On the CD-ROM

You can find the `preloader_fp8_comps_100.fla` and `loadFile_component.as` files in the `ch28` folder of this book's CD-ROM.

Applying the ProgressBar component

Now you'll learn how to use the ProgressBar component with the example you created in the previous section. The ProgressBar component displays the download progress of a loading asset, and can be used with the Loader component or your own custom loader Movie Clips.

1. Open the `preloader_fp8_comps_100.fla` and `loadFile_component.as` files from the last section. Save these as `preloader_fp8_comps_101.fla` and `loadFile_progressbar.as`, respectively.

2. With the `preloader_fp8_comps_101.fla` document active, open the Components panel and drag an instance of the ProgressBar component from the User Interface grouping to the Stage.

3. Delete the new instance of the ProgressBar component from the Stage. You only need to have the ProgressBar component in the Library panel for use in this exercise.

Note

You can open the Library panel to see the ProgressBar component and its linkage identifier.

4. Select frame 1 of the actions layer, and open the Actions panel. Change the .as file referenced in line 5 to the following code, shown in bold.

```
#include "loadFile_progressbar.as"
```

5. Switch over to the `loadFile_progressbar.as` file, and add or modify the bold code shown in Listing 28-12.

In the `loadFile()` function, an instance of the ProgressBar component is added from the Library instead of the loaderClip symbol. The instance is named `cpb`.

The `oInit` object passed to the `cpb` instance needs to be slightly modified, as the ProgressBar component uses a `source` property instead of a `target` property. Instead of specifying the listener object in the `oInit` object, the listener is added to the ProgressBar component via the `addEventListener()` method, just as you've done with Button component instances.

Note

The `unloadFile()` and `onVideoMetaData()` methods have been excluded from the printed listing, but they are included in the `Listing28-12.as` and `loadFile_progressbar.as` files, as they are still necessary for the functionality of the script.

Listing 28-12: **Modifying the Code for the ProgressBar Component**

```actionscript
import mx.utils.Delegate;

var snd:Sound;
var mcHolder:MovieClip;
var clo:mx.controls.Loader;
var cpb:mx.controls.ProgressBar;
var ns:NetStream;
var vWin:Video;

var nc:NetConnection = new NetConnection();
nc.connect(null);

function loadFile(sUrl:String, sType:String, oProp:Object,
oListener:Object):Void {
   if(sType == null || sType == undefined) var sType:String =
      sUrl.substr(-3).toLowerCase();
   else    sType = sType.toLowerCase();
   var mc:MovieClip = mcHolder = createEmptyMovieClip("mcHolder", 1);
   if(oProp != null || oProp != undefined){
      mc._x = oProp.x;
      mc._y = oProp.y;
```

```
            mc._xscale = mc._yscale = oProp.scale;
        }
        var oTarget:Object;
        switch(sType){
            case "swf" :
            case "jpg" :
            case "gif" :
            case "png":
            default:
                clo.load(sUrl);
                oTarget = clo;
                break;
            case "mp3" :
                snd = new Sound(mc);
                snd.loadSound(sUrl, true);
                oTarget = snd;
                break;
            case "flv" :
                var mcVid:MovieClip = mc.attachMovie("videoClip", "mcVid", 1);
                vWin = mcVid.vWin;
                ns = new NetStream(nc);
                ns.onMetaData = Delegate.create(this, this.onVideoMetaData);
                ns.play(sUrl);
                mcVid.vWin.attachVideo(ns);
                oTarget = ns;
                break;
        }
        var oInit:Object = {_x: 25, _y: Stage.height - 30, source: oTarget};
        cpb = attachMovie("ProgressBar", "cpb", 2, oInit);
        cpb["onResize"] = function():Void {
            this._y = Stage.height - 30;
        };
        cpb.addEventListener("complete", oListener);
        Stage.addListener(cpb);
    }
}
```

6. Go back to the preloader_fp8_comps_101.fla document. There's one last thing to change. Since the ProgressBar component broadcasts a "complete" event, you need to change the method name on the oLoader listener object. Select frame 1 of the actions layer, and open the Actions panel. Rename the oLoader.click() handler to:

```
oLoader.complete = function(oEvent:Object):Void {
```

7. Save both documents, and test the preloader_fp8_comps_101.fla document. When you type a URL into the tFile field and click the Load Asset button, the ProgressBar component instance displays on the Stage, as shown in Figure 28-25. When the loading has finished, the ProgressBar component is removed from the movie.

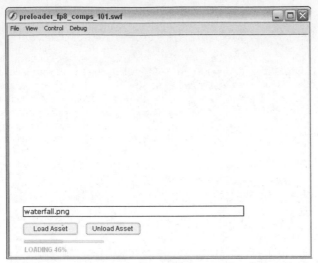

Figure 28-25: The ProgressBar component in action

You can find the completed documents, `preloader_fp8_comps_101.fla` and `loadFile_progressbar.as`, in the `ch28` folder of this book's CD-ROM.

The ProgressBar component cannot monitor the download progress of a Flash Video (.flv) file. Moreover, using the ProgressBar and Loader components in a Flash movie adds 31 KB to the .swf file's size.

Accessing Items in Shared Libraries

Since Flash 5, Web designers and developers have had the good fortune of using an exciting feature to manage assets in Flash movies: the capability to link the symbols, sounds, bitmaps, and font symbols within external .swf files to other Flash movies that they use on their Web sites. These external .swf files, called *shared libraries,* are different than loaded .swf files. Flash 8 enables you to easily use shared libraries, and has an intuitive interface and dialog boxes to create shared items.

Flash 8 enables you to easily update shared assets in the Flash document files (.fla) that use them. Flash 8 refers to shared assets as *runtime sharing*. We'll take a look at this feature in just a moment.

The primary benefit of using a shared library .swf file is that it needs to be downloaded only once, even though several other Flash movies may need to access the same element. For example, if you want to use Blur Medium as an embedded font in several Flash movie files (.swf), you would need to embed the font into each movie. A font can easily consume more than 30 KB in each movie. Multiply that by 10 or 20 files in your Web site that use the font, and you may be eating up a lot of bytes just for the font usage. Instead, if you add a Font symbol to one Shared library .swf file and use that shared asset in all of the Flash movies, you will need to download the font only once, even though it's used by several movies.

A shared library .swf file doesn't load into a level or a Movie Clip instance location. Instead, you set up the Library of a Flash document file (.fla) with assets that you want to use in other Flash movies. This document is the basis of the shared library .swf file. After you assign an identifier to each asset in the Library, you save the Flash document, publish a Flash movie file (.swf) from it, and close the Flash document. Then you open another Flash document file (.fla) and, using File ➪ Import ➪ Open External Library, you open the shared library Flash document file (.fla). Its Library panel will open (in a dimmed gray state), and you can drag and drop assets to your new Flash movie file.

Note Even though the assets are linked to the external Shared library .swf file, the Flash document file (.fla) actually stores copies of the assets. However, they will not be exported with the published Flash movie.

After you have established a shared library file, any changes to the actual contents of the Shared library Flash document file (.fla) and movie file (.swf) will propagate to any Flash movie that uses the shared assets. In the following sections, you learn how to create a shared library file and use it with other Flash movies.

Caution It is recommended that you use only small (low byte size) elements in your shared libraries to ensure that they are downloaded and available for Flash movies that use them. As with any Web production, make sure that you test early and often before you develop an entire project.

Setting up a Shared library file

To share assets among several Flash movies, you need to establish a shared library file (or files) available to other Flash movie files. To create a shared library file, follow these steps:

1. Create a new Flash document (Ctrl+N or ⌘+N).

2. To place Flash artwork into the Library, draw the shapes and other elements (text, lines, gradients, and so on). Select the artwork and choose Modify ➪ Convert to Symbol (F8). In the Convert to Symbol dialog box, choose a symbol type (for example, Graphic, Button, or Movie Clip) that best suits the nature of your artwork.

   Flash 8 also enables you to define export parameters directly in this dialog box. Click the Advanced button; and in the extended options, check Export for runtime sharing. Specify a linkage identifier name, and type the relative or absolute URL for the shared .swf file in the URL field. This URL should simply be the path to this Flash movie on the Web server, such as `http://mydomain.com/files/sharedLib.swf`. Alternatively, if you know all of your Flash movies will be stored in the same directory on the Web server, you can simply type the name of the .swf file, as shown in Figure 28-26.

Figure 28-26: Add runtime-sharing information directly in the Convert to Symbol dialog box.

3. To place bitmaps and sounds into the Library, import the source files as you normally would, using File ⇨ Import ⇨ Import to Library.

4. Delete all artwork that you have placed on the Stage. Every asset that you want to share should be in the Library panel.

5. To place an entire font (or typeface) into the Library, open the Library panel and choose New Font from the options menu located at the top-right corner of the Library panel. In the Font Symbol Properties dialog box, type a reference name for the font, choose the font face from the Font menu, and select a faux font style (Bold or Italic) to be applied (optional), as shown in Figure 28-27.

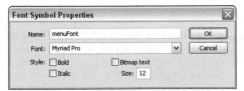

Figure 28-27: Give each embedded font face a descriptive name that indicates its functionality within the Flash movie.

Note   In Flash 8, you can specify bitmap text and size settings in the Font Symbol Properties dialog box. However, in our tests, we could not see any visible difference in the way in which a shared font (or any Font symbol) was rendered.

Assigning names to assets

After you have placed each asset into the Library of your starter Flash document file (.fla), you'll need to assign a unique identifier to each asset.

1. Select the symbol, bitmap, sound, and font in the Library. Right-click (or Control+click on Mac) the selected asset and choose Linkage. Alternatively, you can select the item and choose Linkage from the Library panel's options menu.

2. In the Linkage Properties dialog box, shown in Figure 28-28, choose Export for runtime sharing for the Linkage option. This forces the asset to export with the published .swf file. Then, type a unique name in the Identifier field. In the URL field, enter the intended final location of the .swf file that you will publish from this Flash document. We discuss this option in more detail in the next section. Click OK to close the dialog box.

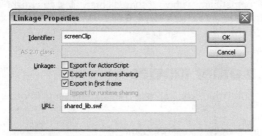

Figure 28-28: Each asset in the Library of the Shared library document needs a unique name.

3. Repeat Steps 1 and 2 for each asset in the Library.

Specifying the Shared library's location

A required setting for each asset of the Shared library document is the relative or absolute path (as a URL) to the shared library SWF on your Web server. To change the URL for all of the assets with the current Shared library document, follow these steps:

1. In the options menu in the Library panel, choose Shared Library Properties.

2. In the URL field, type the location of the Shared library .swf file (or where you intend to publish it on the Web). This location will be prepended to each shared asset's identifier in the movies that use the assets.

Caution

Make sure that you specify this URL before you start using the Shared library document file (.fla) with other Flash document files (.fla). The URL location is stored within each document that uses the Shared library .swf file, and it will not update if you decide to change the URL later in the Shared library .fla file. Also, the URL applies to all items in the shared library .fla and .swf file; you cannot set unique URLs for each item in a shared library.

Publishing the Shared library movie file

After the assets of the Flash document have been assigned identifiers and the URL of the Shared library has been set, you need to publish an .swf file of the Flash document.

1. Save the Flash document file (.fla). Use a descriptive name that notifies other members of your Web production team that this is a shared library file, such as `shared_lib.fla`.

2. Publish the Flash movie as an .swf file. No other publish formats are necessary. In the Publish Settings (File ➪ Publish Settings), select only the Flash format in the Format tab. Click OK. Choose File ➪ Publish to create an .swf file from your document.

3. Close the Flash document.

Tip   To retain the most backwards compatibility with your shared library files, you might want to consider publishing your Shared libraries as Flash Player 6 or 7 .swf files.

Linking to assets from other movies

After the Shared library .swf file is published, you can use the shared assets in other Flash movies.

1. Create a new Flash document or open an existing one.

2. Using the File ➪ Import ➪ Open External Library command, browse to the folder where your Shared library Flash document file (.fla) was saved. For testing purposes, you should keep this document in the same folder as the other Flash documents that share it. Select the shared library .fla file and click Open. A separate grayed-out Library panel for the shared library .fla file will open in the Flash 8 authoring environment.

3. Drag the asset(s) that you wish to use into the new Flash document's Library or onto its Stage. Even though Flash 8 will copy the contents of each shared asset, the asset will load from the separate Shared library .swf file at run time.

4. To see whether an asset is native to the Flash movie or from a shared library .swf file, right-click (or Control+click on Mac) the symbol or asset in the Library. Select Linkage from the contextual menu. The Linkage Properties dialog box, shown in Figure 28-29, will indicate whether the symbol (or asset) will be imported from an external Shared library .swf file.

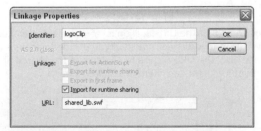

Figure 28-29: If a Shared library asset is used in another movie, the Linkage Properties indicate the name (and path) of the Shared library .swf file.

Tip You can also expand the width of the Library panel to reveal the Linkage column, which indicates whether a library item is exported or imported.

When you are done dragging the assets from the Shared library file, close its Library panel. When you publish the new Flash movie(s) that use the Shared library .swf file, make sure you put all of the files on your Web server for live testing. If you used relative URL locations for the shared library .swf file(s), make sure the files are stored in the proper directories on your Web server.

 On the CD-ROM You can find a shared library document and Flash document that uses the shared assets in the ch28/sharedLib folder of this book's CD-ROM.

Updating shared assets

Flash 8 has an update feature for assets that have been imported from a Shared library document. To see which assets in your current document are imported, expand the width of the Library panel to view the Linkage column, as shown in Figure 28-30.

Figure 28-30: The Library panel enables you to quickly view the Linkage settings for each item.

If you have changed the contents of an asset in a shared library document file (.fla) and published the new Flash movie file (.swf), you can choose to update the reference assets in other Flash documents that use the shared assets.

 Tip Actually, you can use the update feature with any symbol that you have dragged, copied, or imported into one .fla file from another. Flash 8 stores the name of the original .fla file with the copied symbol.

Let's walk through the complete process of updating a shared library asset.

1. Open the shared library document file (.fla).

2. Open the Library panel and edit the shared asset you wish to update. For example, if you need to change the artwork with a Movie Clip symbol, double-click the symbol and edit the symbol's content.

3. When you're done editing the asset, save the Flash document and publish a Flash movie. Close the Shared library document.

4. Open a Flash document that uses an asset from the shared library.

5. Open the Library panel for the document. You'll notice that any changed elements still appear as they did before the update occurred. Select the asset that was changed in the shared library document and choose Update from the Library panel's options menu. Or right-click (Control+click on Mac) the asset and choose Update from the contextual menu. The Update Library Items dialog box appears, as shown in Figure 28-31. Select the check box next to the asset's name you wish to update and then click the Update button.

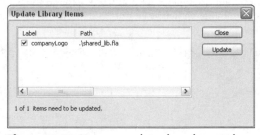

Figure 28-31: You can update shared assets in other Flash documents that use them.

You can also select multiple items in the Library panel and choose Update in the Options menu to update several items at once.

Web Resource We'd like to know what you think about this chapter. Visit www.flashsupport.com/feedback to send us your comments.

Summary

✦ If you want to make sure that your larger Flash movies don't pause during playback over the Web, you may want to make a preloader for each Flash movie you make.

✦ Preloaders can use three different ways to test the download progress of the Flash movie .swf file: ifFrameLoaded(), _framesloaded/_totalframes, and getBytesLoaded()/getBytesTotal(). The most accurate mechanism uses the getBytesLoaded()/getBytesTotal() methods.

✦ You can break up large Flash projects into several smaller Flash movie components that are loaded into a primary Flash movie when they're needed.

✦ The `loadMovie()` action enables you to download .swf files into level or Movie Clip instance locations.

✦ You can load most popular Web image formats, including JPEG, PNG, and GIF, with the `loadMovie()` action in Flash Player 8 movies.

✦ You can download MP3 files directly into Flash Player 6 or higher movies using the `loadSound()` method of the `Sound` class.

✦ The `MovieClipLoader` class can make the job of loading and monitoring asset loading much easier.

✦ You can load Flash Video files (.flv) into Flash Player 7 or higher movies, using the `NetStream` class. A `NetStream` instance is attached to a `Video` object to display the clip.

✦ You can build your own asset loader scripts that indicate the load progress of all supported asset formats in Flash Player 8. When you create your own preloader scripts, the overall .swf file size is much smaller than the size of Flash movies that use the Loader and ProgressBar components.

✦ The new `Loader` and `ProgressBar` components can quickly add external asset loading features to your Flash movies.

✦ You can share Flash assets with the shared library feature. Assets are stored in one or more Shared library .swf files and referenced by other Flash movies.

✦ ✦ ✦

Sending Data In and Out of Flash

A powerful feature of ActionScript is the extraordinary control of data acquisition and management it provides within a Flash movie. You can load external text data into Flash movies, making it possible to include fresh dynamic content every time a Flash movie is viewed over the Web. In this chapter, you will learn how to access text data stored in a variety of formats that are separate from the actual Flash movie.

Using Text Fields to Store and Display Data

Before we can discuss sending and receiving data with Flash movies, you need to know the basic mechanisms of input and output. You may find that, most of the time, your data in Flash will be text-based, which means that you will gather information from the user and display new and updated information with text. In ActionScript, Input text fields gather data from the user, while Dynamic text fields can be used to display live and updated text to the user.

Input text fields

Input text fields can be created with the Text tool. In the Property inspector, the top-left drop-down menu must be set to Input Text for the selected text field. In Flash 8, a text field can be a scriptable object with an instance name. However, an Input text field has a variable name (designated by Var in the Property inspector) to remain backward-compatible with Flash Player 5 or 4 movies. The text typed inside of an Input text field is the value of that variable (specified by the Var name), and it is the value of the `text` property of the text field's instance name. For example, if you create an Input text field and assign it the Var name `sVisitorInput`, anything that is typed into that text field during run time will become the value of `sVisitorInput`. If you assigned an instance name of `tVisitor` to the text field, you would access the contents of the text field with the `text` property. To test this, let's create a simple Input text field.

Tip

If you are developing Flash Player 6 or higher movies (that is, Flash Player 6, 7, or 8 is the version listed in the Flash tab of the Publish Settings dialog box), we strongly recommend that you use the instance name of the text field to access the contents of the field.

1. Using the Text tool, create a text field on the Main Timeline of a Flash document. Make the box long enough to hold 20 characters. You can type a temporary word or phrase into the text field, but delete these characters before proceeding to the next step.

2. In the Property inspector, select Input Text in the top-left menu. In the <Instance Name> field, type **tVisitor**. In the Var field, enter the text **sVisitorInput**. Click the Show Border option as well. Refer to Figure 29-1 for these settings.

Caution

Remember that Flash Player 7 and higher ActionScript is case-sensitive. Make sure you type tVisitor with a capital "V" so that the ActionScript code you add later in this section works properly.

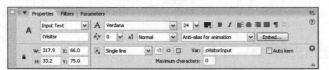

Figure 29-1: The Property inspector controls the settings for text fields.

3. Save your Flash document as input_text.fla and test the movie (Ctrl+Enter or ⌘+Return). In the Test Movie window, click the text field and type your first name into the field.

4. Choose Debug ➪ List Variables, and the sVisitorInput variable will display the value you typed in Step 3. In addition, you will see the tVisitor text field object display along with several properties of the TextField object. In our example, we entered the name **Charlie**. Therefore, the Output panel displays (among other text):

```
Variable _level0.sVisitorInput = "Charlie"
Edit Text: Target="_level0.tVisitor"
    variable = "sVisitorInput",
```

Note

The List Variables command always shows the $version variable and value, indicating the Flash Player version currently playing the movie.

5. If you change the text in the tVisitor text field, the value will automatically update for the tVisitor.text value or the sVisitorInput variable. You need to choose List Variables from the Debug menu to see the updated value.

Input text fields not only accept input from the user, but they can also be set to an initial value or updated with a new value with ActionScript code. You can test this with the preceding Flash movie example.

6. If you are viewing the `input_text.swf` file from Step 5, close the Test Movie window to return to the Flash 8 authoring environment. Create a new layer, and rename it **actions**. Select the first frame of the actions layer and press F9 (or Option+F9 on Mac) to open the Actions panel. Add the following code to the Script pane:

```
var tVisitor:TextField;
tVisitor.text = "enter your name here";
```

Tip By typing your variables in ActionScript, you'll see code hints for that variable whenever you use the variable's name in subsequent lines of code.

7. Save your Flash document and test it. You should see the text "enter your name here" in the `tVisitor` text field.

On the CD-ROM You can find the `input_text.fla` document in the `ch29` folder of this book's CD-ROM.

As you can see, Input text fields can accept text input from the user, just like an HTML form. Later in this chapter, you use Input text fields to create a fully functional Flash form that can send and receive information with a server-side script.

While you should use the Var name attribute of text fields for Flash movies that require compatibility with Flash Player 5 or 4, we strongly recommend that you leave the Var name blank in the Property inspector for any Flash Player 6 or higher movies.

Dynamic text fields

If you want to display text information to people viewing Flash movies, you have two options: (A) create Static text blocks whose contents cannot be updated with ActionScript, or (B) create Dynamic text fields that can be filled with internal Flash data or external text data.

Caution Do not use Input or Dynamic text fields unless you need to accept or display live data to the user. Static text is perfectly fine for text used for graphical purposes, where the text does not need to be changed during the presentation.

Dynamic text fields are also objects with instance names, just as Input text fields. The only difference between Input and Dynamic text fields is that you can type into Input text fields. Dynamic text fields are most useful for displaying text information that will be changed by the movie (via ActionScript), rather than the user. Using Dynamic text fields, you can display news articles that change on a daily (or hourly) basis, a player's score during a Flash game, and the system time and date, just to name a few.

Tip Both Input and Dynamic text fields can use HTML text formatting tags to change the display of text. We discuss HTML use within text fields in Chapter 30, "Applying HTML and Text Field Formatting."

In the following steps, you create a Dynamic text field updated with an ActionScript variable action. You can also load external variables for use in Dynamic text fields, which we discuss in the next section. To insert text into a Dynamic text field:

1. Create a new Flash document (File ➪ New), and save the document as `dynamic_text.fla`.

2. Rename Layer 1 to **tOutput**.

3. Using the Text tool, create a text field on the Main Timeline of a Flash document. Make a field large enough to accommodate multiple lines of text, as shown in Figure 29-2. Choose a normal font size, such as 12.

4. In the Property inspector, select Dynamic Text in the top-left menu. Select Multiline from the Line type menu. In the <Instance Name> field, enter the text tOutput. Click the Selectable and Show Border options. Refer to Figure 29-2 for these settings.

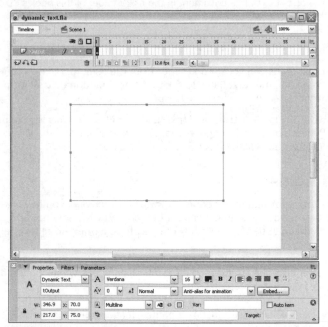

Figure 29-2: The Dynamic text field settings in the Property inspector

5. Add a new layer and name it **actions**. Select the first keyframe of the actions layer and press F9 to open the Actions panel. Enter the second line of the following code on one single line in the Script pane. (You can enable word wrapping in the options menu if you wish.)

```
var tOutput:TextField;
tOutput.text = "WANTED: Flash Input & Output\r\rA start-up
  dotcom company is looking for a qualified Web
```

```
technology that will present text input and output to
Web visitors in a more compelling animated and visually
stunning environment than that possible with HTML.
Please call:\r\r1-800-555-CODE";
```

In this code, you specify string values (denoted with quotes) for the actual text you want to insert into the tOutput Dynamic text field instance. To insert a carriage return in the text, the \r character entity is inserted between string values.

6. Save the Flash document as dynamic_text.fla.

7. Test the movie (Ctrl+Enter or ⌘+Enter). The tOutput Dynamic text field updates with the value assigned to the text property of the tOutput instance in ActionScript.

On the CD-ROM You can find the dynamic_text.fla document in the ch29 folder of this book's CD-ROM.

You can also load text data into Input and Dynamic text fields. This data can be returned from a simple text file (.txt file) or from an application that resides on your Web server. In the next section, you learn how to send and receive text from a Flash movie.

Defining a Data Process with States

When you manipulate text fields with internal ActionScript properties of the TextField object, the data for the text fields is available for use immediately. Meaning, if you declare a variable and a value for that variable, any text field can be given that value as well. When you want to load external data into a Flash movie, you need to create the appropriate steps, or *states,* in your movie to make sure that the data is available for use in the Flash movie. For example, suppose you want to retrieve a news article from a Web server, and the text for that article is contained within a variable named article_1. You can't use or assign the value of article_1 to any other Flash element *unless* the article has fully downloaded to the Flash movie.

So, how do you know when data is available in a Flash movie? Any Flash movie that relies on data exchange between the Flash movie and the Web server should contain four separate states:

✦ An **input** state to gather the information from the user or the movie

✦ A **send** state in which a Flash action sends the data out of the movie

✦ A **wait** state during which the data downloads to the movie

✦ An **output** state in which the data can be used by the Flash movie in text fields and other ActionScript code

Input state

The first step for data exchange requires that you have something to send out of the Flash movie. The input can be a Flash form into which a user types text. The data could be environment variables, such as the time of the day, or the Flash Player version. There could be various substeps in the input state, such as multiple forms or the completion of a quiz to calculate a test score that will be sent to the Web server.

Note   Not all data transactions require input. For example, if you need to retrieve the latest stock quotes or news article from a Web server application, you may simply need to send a request for that data without providing any additional information to the Web server application.

Send state

After the input data has been set or retrieved in the Flash movie, you're ready to send the data to another host, such as an application or script on your Web server. You can use the following actions or object methods to send data out of the Flash movie:

✦ getURL()

✦ loadVariables() or MovieClip.loadVariables()

✦ loadMovie() or MovieClip.loadMovie()

✦ LoadVars.load()

✦ LoadVars.send() or LoadVars.sendAndLoad()

✦ XML.load()

✦ XML.send() or XML.sendAndLoad()

✦ XMLSocket.send()

✦ Flash Remoting or Flash Communication Server calls

Of these actions, getURL(), LoadVars.send(), and XML.send() are restricted to a one-way data path; that is, you can only send data out with these actions — you cannot receive external data with them. getURL() must target the sought URL to the current browser (or frame) or a new browser window. In many situations, you may only need to send data out of the Flash movie without needing to receive any further data. To send information with the user's e-mail client, you can use a simple mailto: URL in a getURL() action on a Button instance. Note that the ⊃ character indicates a continuation of the same line of code:

```
var btSend:Button;
btSend.onRelease = function():Void {
  var sEmail:String = "admin@server.com";
  var sSubject:String = escape("Visitor Feedback");
  var sBody:String = escape("Please let us know how you feel.");
  getURL("mailto:" + sEmail + "?subject=" + sSubject + ⊃
    "&body=" + sBody);
};
```

In the preceding code block, the variables `sEmail`, `sSubject`, and `sBody` are inserted into the `getURL()` action. Note that you can automatically set subject and body text for the e-mail message as well. To add specific variables to a URL string, you should use the `escape()` function in ActionScript, which converts illegal URL characters such as spaces and question marks into URL form-encoded text (for example, a space is converted into `%20`).

Caution Not all e-mail clients support the passing of subject and body variables. Be sure to test this code with your targeted e-mail clients.

Wait state

If you are sending data from the Flash movie with `loadVariables()`, `loadMovie()`, or any of the object `load()` or `sendAndLoad()` methods, you need to know when the requested data is received by the script or application running on your Web server. Usually, you will build server-side scripts that return some data back to the Flash movie upon successful receipt of data from Flash. If you're building Flash Player 4–compatible movies, one way to detect the receipt of data into the Flash movie is to use a terminal tag—a name/value pair in the downloaded data that indicates the end of the data string. For example, if the value of the `text` property for the `tOuput` instance that you used in the last section was converted to a name/value pair in a .txt file (as URL form-encoded text), the value would appear as the following (URL-converted characters are shown in bold, and the terminal tag is underlined):

```
article=WANTED%3A%20Flash%20Input%20%26%20Output%0AA%20start%2Dup%20Dot
%20com%20company%20is%20looking%20for%20a%20qualified%20web%20technolog
y%20that%20will%20present%20text%20input%20and%20output%20to%20web%20vi
sitors%20in%20a%20more%20compelling%20animated%20and%20visually%20stunn
ing%20environment%20than%20that%20possible%20with%20HTML%2E%20Please%20
call%3A%0A%0A1%2D800%2D555%2DCODE&success=1
```

At the end of this line of text (or at the very end of a long line of variables), we have inserted a terminal tag `success=1`. With this variable in place, you can set up a frame loop within a Flash movie to detect the existence (loading) of the terminal tag variable. After the terminal tag is loaded, the Flash movie will be directed to the appropriate output state.

All wait states should have a timeout condition: If the data fails to load within a certain time frame, you will assume the Web server (or script) is not functioning correctly. If the timeout condition proves `true`, the Flash movie will go to the appropriate output state. You create a wait state for the Flash form in the next section.

Output state

The final step in a data exchange is the actual display of any received data in the Flash movie. However, as indicated in the last state, there are two separate output states: a success display or an error display. If the data was properly received during the wait state, the Flash movie will display the success output state. If the server failed to return any data to the Flash movie, the movie will display an error output state, indicating that there was a problem with the server.

Creating a User Comment Form

In this section, you create a Flash form that submits user-entered information to a server-side ColdFusion script that e-mails the data to an e-mail address that you specify in the script. By accessing a remote ColdFusion script, you make a Flash movie with five data exchange states: input, send, wait, output, and error. You learn how to submit name/value pairs from Flash to remote URLs and learn how to check the receipt of variables from the ColdFusion script using the LoadVars object. The LoadVars object can detect the loading of the external variable data.

You can find the ColdFusion script (sendmail.cfm) and supporting Flash documents for this section in the ch29/form folder of this book's CD-ROM. Note that you need a ColdFusion-enabled Web server to configure and use the sendmail.cfm script. We have also included the sendmail.asp script (Microsoft ASP version) and the sendmail.pl script (Perl 5) that we included with previous editions of the *Flash Bible*, as well as a new sendmail.php script for PHP 4 or higher. The ASP script requires the installation of the free w3 JMail Personal ASP component, available at

http://tech.dimac.net/

You can download a trial version of ColdFusion MX 7 at

www.macromedia.com/software/coldfusion

You can also find installation instructions on the Web site. For a list of preferred ColdFusion hosting providers, check the "ColdFusion Hosting Providers" section of the www.flash support.com/links page.

Flash forms are user data entry forms (just like HTML forms) created in Flash 8 using Input text fields. When a user types information in these text fields, the information is stored as a property of the text field instance (text). The values of these properties are assigned to variable names and are then sent to a specified Web server using standard GET or POST communication. These variables are available to the Web server and can be processed there by a server-side program or script. Server-side programs can be written to e-mail this information, manipulate it, store it in a database, or perform many other applications. The same server-side script can also return values to the Flash movie — these can then be displayed or used by the originating Flash movie.

In this exercise, the Flash form solicits feedback from visitors, giving them an opportunity to submit comments, report bugs, or make suggestions for improvement. As each form is submitted, it's e-mailed directly to the e-mail address that you specify in the ColdFusion script.

1. Open a new Flash document (Ctrl+N or ⌘+N), and save it as sendmail_cfm.fla.

2. Rename Layer 1 to **labels**. Select frame 1 of this layer and assign a frame label of **input** in the Property inspector.

3. On the labels layer, create keyframes (F6) on frames 10, 20, and 30. Give these keyframes the labels **wait**, **output**, and **error**, respectively. Select frame 40 and press F5 to insert more empty frames at the end of the layer.

4. Create a new layer and name it **actions**. Select frame 1 of the actions layer, and open the Actions panel. In the Script pane, add a `stop();` action. In the Property inspector, add a comment of `//setup form` in the <Frame Label> field.

5. Create a new layer, and name it **text fields**. Insert keyframes on frames 10, 20, and 30.

6. On frame 1 of the text fields layer, insert three separate Input text fields. From top to bottom, assign the following instance names to the Input text fields (in the Property inspector): `tFromName`, `tFromEmail`, and `tComments`. The `tFromName` and `tFromEmail` text fields should accommodate one line of text, while the `tComment` field should be set to Multiline in order to hold multiple lines of text. All of the Input text fields should have the Show Border option selected, unless you plan to create your own background graphics. Make each text field long enough to accommodate about 45 characters of text. The comments field should be able to show between five and ten lines of text (see Figure 29-3).

7. Create a new layer, and name it **static text**. Insert keyframes on frames 10, 20, and 30. On frame 1, add Static text blocks to the left of the text fields, indicating the purpose of each field, as shown in Figure 29-3.

Note

For our example, the Flash movie background color is black, and the Static text is white. You can change the movie's background color by choosing Modify ➪ Document.

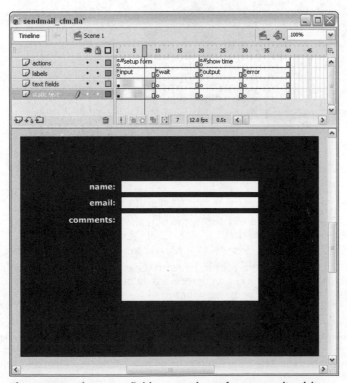

Figure 29-3: These text fields accept input from your site visitors.

8. On frame 10 of the static text layer (underneath the `wait` label), insert a Static text block indicating that the information is being sent to the server and that the movie is waiting for confirmation. In our example, we used the text "Checking the server. . . ."

9. On frame 20 of the static text layer (underneath the `output` label), insert a Static text block containing a successful receipt of the visitor's information. In our example, we used the text "Thank you. Your feedback was received at:."

10. You can see that you are setting up the output state to display the time that the server received the data (Figure 29-4). The ColdFusion script returns the time and date of the receipt to the Flash movie. On frame 20 of the text fields layer, create a Dynamic text field with an instance name of `tReceipt` and place it underneath the Static text you just made.

Figure 29-4: The Receipt field will display the time that the server received the Flash form data.

11. On frame 30 of the static text layer (underneath the `error` label), insert Static text that indicates the data was not successfully received. In our example, we used the text "Sorry, there was an error processing your form."

12. Save your Flash document.

Now you have all your states defined with placeholder artwork. You can go back later and refine the text and graphics to suit your particular needs. Next, you need to add a function to transfer the data from the text fields to a `LoadVars` object and send the data to the Web server.

These actions need to put on the appropriate Flash event handlers. Start by defining a function named sendComments() that creates two LoadVars objects: one to send the data and another to receive the data. The data from the Input text fields is then copied to variables within the sending LoadVars object. The data is then sent to the ColdFusion script using the sendAndLoad() method of the LoadVars object. When the data is received by the ColdFusion script, the Web server will return some confirmation data to the Flash movie, including the time and date the user's comments were received. When this data loads completely into the Flash movie, the movie will then go to and stop on the output frame label.

Before you define these functions, however, let's add a Button component to the Stage. This component button will initiate the sendComments() function.

13. Create a new layer and name it **button**. Insert an empty keyframe on frame 10 of this layer.

14. On frame 1 of the button layer, drag an instance of the Button component from the User Interface grouping of the Components panel to the document's Stage.

15. With the component selected, open the Property inspector. Name the instance **cbtSend**. In the Parameters tab, type **Send Comments** in the label field. You may need to stretch the width of the Button instance to accommodate the label text.

16. Select frame 1 of the actions layer, and open the Actions panel (F9, or Option+F9 on Mac). In the Script pane, add the code shown in Listing 29-1. This code defines the sendComments() function used by the cbtSend instance.

This script declares all of the objects present on the stage as variables, in lines 3–6. (Note that the import statement on line 1 utilizes the Delegate class in the script. We'll discuss that class in just a moment.) Lines 7 and 8 declare two LoadVars variables, one to send (lvSend) and one to receive (lvReceive).

On line 10, the URL of the ColdFusion script is defined using a live server URL we specifically set up for this exercise. If you have installed the ColdFusion script on your local machine or Web server, change the path of this variable to reflect the new location.

Lines 12 through 27 define the sendComments() function. This function establishes all of the data that the sendmail.cfm script requires for successful operation. Line 12 declares the function and its name, sendComments. The function starts by creating two LoadVars objects, named lvSend (line 13) and lvReceive (line 14). The lvSend object will send the data from the Flash movie, while the lvReceive object will handle the data received from the server.

Lines 15–21 define an onLoad() handler for the lvReceive object. Here, an anonymous function will be executed when the lvReceive object receives any external data from the Web server script. In this example, if the data is successfully received and the server-side script doesn't encounter any errors (line 16), the Main Timeline will go to and stop on the output frame label. If the data is not received or there is an error in sending the data (line 18), the Main Timeline will go to and stop on the error frame label (line 19).

Lines 22–24 establish the variables that the ColdFusion script expects to see in the data transmission: fromEmail, fromName, and body. These variables retrieve their values from the appropriate TextField objects in the Flash movie.

Note

You can change the values of the `Form.toEmail` and `Form.subject` variables in the `sendmail.cfm` script to change where the server sends the data from the Flash movie. If you use the live script located on the `www.flashsupport.com` site, Mr. Reinhardt will receive all of your test e-mails, so please be careful. For security measures, don't include private information such as your own e-mail address inside of an .swf file, including ActionScript code. SWF decompiler utilities can extract any data, including code, from .swf files delivered over the Web.

Line 25 executes the `sendAndLoad()` method of the `lvSend` object that sends the `fromEmail`, `fromName`, and `body` variables to the `sendmail.cfm` script on our Web server. The `lvReceive` reference indicates that any output from the `sendmail.cfm` script should be directed to the `lvReceive.onLoad()` method.

After the `sendAndLoad()` method is executed, the Main Timeline will jump to the `wait` frame label (line 26).

In line 29, the `sendComments()` function is added as a listener of the `cbtSend` instance. Here, we use the `Delegate` class to properly scope the `goto` actions in the `sendComments()` function.

Listing 29-1: **The sendComments() Function**

```
1.  import mx.utils.Delegate;
2.
3.  var cbtSend:mx.controls.Button;
4.  var tFromEmail:TextField;
5.  var tFromName:TextField;
6.  var tComments:TextField;
7.  var lvSend:LoadVars;
8.  var lvReceive:LoadVars;
9.
10. var sUrl:String = "http://www.flashsupport.com/sendmail.cfm";
11.
12. function sendComments(oEvent:Object):Void  {
13.    lvSend = new LoadVars();
14.    lvReceive = new LoadVars();
15.    lvReceive.onLoad = function(bSuccess:Boolean):Void {
16.       if (bSuccess && this.success == "1") {
17.          gotoAndStop("output");
18.       } else {
19.          gotoAndStop("error");
20.       }
21.    };
22.    lvSend.fromEmail = tFromEmail.text;
23.    lvSend.fromName = tFromName.text;
24.    lvSend.body = tComments.text;
25.    lvSend.sendAndLoad(sUrl, lvReceive, "POST");
26.    gotoAndStop("wait");
27. }
28.
```

```
29. cbtSend.addEventListener("click", Delegate.create(this, this.sendComments));
30. focusManager.defaultPushButton = cbtSend;
31.
32. stop();
```

17. Finally, add a keyframe to frame 20 of the actions layer. With this keyframe selected, open the Actions panel and add the following actions:

```
var tReceipt:TextField;
var lvReceive:LoadVars;
tReceipt.text = lvReceive.timeDate;
```

This action takes the time and date returned by the server, and uses its value for the text property of the tReceipt instance.

18. Save your Flash document again and test it (Ctrl+Enter or ⌘+Return). Type some information into the text fields and click the Send Comments button. If the server script is available, you should see the output state display the time/date receipt from the server.

The server script supports either GET or POST methods. Remember, every data exchange with a Flash movie should use input, wait, output, and error states.

On the CD-ROM

Use the sendmail.cfm script on www.flashsupport.com only for development and/or testing purposes. Do not try to use the script for demanding, high-volume Web sites. Remember that live Flash movies on a Web server can only access server-side scripts on the same server. While you can use the sendmail.cfm script on www.flashsupport.com for local testing in the Flash 8 authoring environment, it will not work once you upload your Flash movie to your own Web server — you'll have to install the sendmail.cfm script (or equivalent) on your own Web server. The same ColdFusion script is available on this book's CD-ROM, in the ch29/form folder. You can find the completed version of the Flash document, sendmail_cfm.fla, in the ch29/form folder. We have also created equivalents of the sendmail.cfm script in other popular middleware languages: sendmail.asp (Microsoft ASP.NET), sendmail.php (PHP 4 or higher), and sendmail.pl (Perl 5 or higher). Note that we do not have live versions of these alternative server-side scripts; you will need to install them on your own Web server to test and deploy them.

Using XML Data in Flash Movies

Flash Player 5 or higher movies can load (and send) external XML data. This is a very powerful feature, as XML has become a standard data structure for e-commerce purposes and for news services, as well as for easier control over HTML formatting (and style sheets) in the Web browser. You can organize external data with simple XML formatting and use the XML data for text fields and ActionScript code in your Flash movies.

Understanding XML

XML is an acronym for e*X*tensible *M*arkup *L*anguage. *Extensible*, in this case, means that you can create your own markup tag names and attributes. While there are a few additional rules with XML, its structure very much resembles traditional HTML:

```
<tag name opener>Information here</tag name closer>
```

For basic XML-Flash usage, your XML document needs one "container" tag in which all other subordinate tags will be nested. Each opener and closer tag set is called a *node*. In the following XML example, the `<section>` tag is the primary container tag, and the `<article>` tags are nodes of the `<section>` tag:

```
<section>
    <article>First article node</article>
    <article>Second article node</article>
</section>
```

Note   Technically, for XML to be to specification, you should have an XML declaration at the very top of your document. Flash Player 5 and higher do not require this declaration, but it's a good habit to add the declaration:

```
<?xml version="1.0" encoding="utf-8" ?>
```

For Flash Player 6 and higher, you should make sure that you also save the document as Unicode (UTF-8). In Macromedia Dreamweaver, look for this option under Modify ⇨ Page Properties. In other text editors, look for the Unicode UTF-8 option in the Save As dialog box.

You can create as many *child* nodes as you need. In the preceding example, the `<section>` tag has two child nodes: the first occurrence of `<article>` . . . `</article>` and the second occurrence of `<article>` . . . `</article>`. In the following example, the first `<article>` node has two child nodes:

```
<section>
    <article>
        <title>WANTED: New Computer</title>
        <description>Insert description here</description>
    </article>
    <article>Second article node</article>
</section>
```

`<title>`...`</title>` is the first child node of the first `<article>`...`</article>` node. The value of `<title>` is also considered a child of `<title>`. In the previous example, "WANTED: New Computer" is the child of `<title>`.

Caution   Early releases of Flash Player 5 do not ignore XML text nodes that contain only white space. For this reason, you may not want to format your XML documents with indented tags or carriage returns between tags. Otherwise, you will need to create an ActionScript routine that removes the white space. Flash Player 6 and higher support the `ignoreWhite` property of the `XML` class, which can tell ActionScript to ignore any text nodes that contain only white space within the XML document.

Loading an XML document into a Flash movie

Once you have an XML document structured to use in a Flash movie, you can use the XML document tree in the Flash movie. When an XML document is loaded into a Flash movie, the structure and relationship of all nodes are retained within the Flash Player.

The XML object

Before you can load an XML document into Flash, you need to make an object that will hold the XML data. To do this, use the XML constructor function, as in:

```
var xmlData = new XML();  // ActionScript 1.0
```

or

```
var xmlData:XML = new XML();  // ActionScript 2.0
```

Just as you created new objects for the MovieClipLoader and Sound objects in ActionScript, you can create as many new instances of the XML object as you need for your movie. You can also use an XML object to store Flash-created XML structures and send them to a server for further processing.

The load method of the XML object

After you have established an object, like the xmlData variable in the previous heading, you can invoke built-in methods of the XML object. The load() method enables you to specify an external source (such as a URL or filename) that holds the XML data. If you had an XML document called articles.xml in the same directory as your .swf file, you could load it by writing the following code:

```
var xmlData:XML = new XML("articles.xml");
```

or

```
var xmlData:XML = new XML();
xmlData.load("articles.xml");
```

The onLoad() method of the XML object

After the document is loaded into the Flash movie, you can specify another function (or action) to occur using the onLoad() method of the XML object. The onLoad() method simply defines a function to be executed when the XML document is finished loading—it does not actually execute the function (or actions) when the onLoad() is first processed. In the following example, the onLoad() handler is executed when the XML document, articles.xml, is finished loading:

```
var xmlData:XML = new XML();
xmlData.onLoad = function(bSuccess:Boolean):Void {
    if(bSuccess){
        //perform more XML methods upon the XML data
    } else {
        // indicate that the XML document (or data)
        // did not load.
    }
};
xmlData.load("articles.xml");
```

In the preceding code example, the onLoad() handler has one argument, bSuccess. The onLoad() method is passed a Boolean value of true or false. If the load() method successfully loads the articles.xml document, the onLoad() method will be executed and passed a true value for the bSuccess argument. This true value is inserted into the if condition. If bSuccess is equal to true, the nested if actions will be executed; otherwise, the else actions will be executed.

On the CD-ROM
Check out the XML document load examples on this book's CD-ROM in the `ch29/xml` folder. These examples demonstrate how XML node values can be manipulated with Flash arrays. You may want to review Chapter 26's coverage of the `Array` object before looking at these examples.

Web Resource
You can find Shane Elliott's expert tutorial, "Using XMLSockets with a Flash Movie," from previous editions of the *Flash Bible* at `www.flashsupport.com/archive`. This article introduces you to the basic concepts of using the `XMLSocket` class in ActionScript.

Colin Moock's expert tutorial, "Unifying the Web," which discusses the concepts behind multiuser server functionality, can also be found at the `www.flashsupport.com/archive` location.

Web Resource
We'd like to know what you think about this chapter. Visit `www.flashsupport.com/feedback` to send us your comments.

Summary

✦ Input text fields can accept text data from anyone viewing the Flash movie (.swf) with Flash Player 4 or higher. Input text fields are treated as ActionScript variables if you access them via their Var name. If you use instance names with text fields, the Flash movie will work only in Flash Player 6 or higher.

✦ Dynamic text fields can display any string values retrieved with ActionScript in the Flash movie.

✦ Any data exchange between Flash and a remote application or server-side script should use four steps, or states: input, send, wait, and output.

✦ You can use a Flash form to gather feedback from your site's visitors. The form's data can be sent to a properly configured server-side script for further data processing, such as sending the data in an e-mail to the site administrator.

✦ The `LoadVars` object can send and load text data to a Web server script or application.

✦ XML data structures are quickly becoming an interbusiness standard for data exchange over the Web. Flash can use XML data structures to send and receive data from your Web server.

✦   ✦   ✦

Applying HTML and Text Field Formatting

I n this chapter, we show you how to control text field formatting and focus using internal HTML tags and ActionScript. Flash gives you an incredible amount of control over text field formatting when you use the `TextFormat` object with `TextField` objects (that is, Input and Dynamic text fields). We will also show you how to highlight text within text fields by using the `Selection` object.

New Feature

Since Flash Player 8 supports PNG, GIF, and progressive JPEG image support, you can load these file types into HTML-enabled Flash text fields as well. Flash Player 8 also features a new text rendering engine called FlashType, which improves the readability of text at small point sizes.

Exploring HTML Usage in Text Fields

As you have been using Flash 8, you may have noticed the HTML button in the Property inspector for text fields. Even though one of the primary advantages of using Flash movies is that you can avoid the fuss of HTML page layout, you can use HTML formatting tags within Input and Dynamic text fields. You can use `<font>` tags to specify multiple typefaces, colors, styles, and sizes within one text field. You can also use `<a href>` tags to link to internal ActionScript functions or external URLs!

Caution

In Flash Player 4 movies, you cannot specify more than one set of formatting specifications for any text field. For example, if you create a text field that uses black Verdana text at 18 points in faux bold, you can't insert any other typeface, color, or size in that text field.

Supported HTML tags

You can use the following HTML tags to format your Flash text fields. You can insert these tags into ActionScript variable values, or you can apply them (without knowing or writing the syntax) using the Property inspector. As you already know, text fields in ActionScript are real objects with instance names. As such, you need to address specific properties of the `TextField` object to insert HTML text. In previous chapters, you've used the following syntax to assign text to a text field instance:

```
var tLastName:TextField;
tLastName.text = "Enter your last name here";
```

You cannot assign HTML tags in the `text` property of a `TextField` object. You must use the `htmlText` property to assign HTML formatted text, such as:

```
var tLastName:TextField;
tLastName.html = true;
tLastName.htmlText = "Enter your <b>last</b> name here.";
```

Here, the `<b>` tag is used to bold the text "last" in the text field instance. In a moment, you will create your own examples that use the `htmlText` property. You also need to set the `html` property of the `TextField` instance to `true`, to let the Flash Player know that it should parse the HTML text you specify for the `htmlText` property. Let's review the HTML tags that are available in ActionScript.

Font and paragraph styles

The basic `<font>` and physical "faux" styles for text (bold, italic, and underline) can be applied to Flash text.

✦ `<b>`: Placing `<b></b>` tags around Flash text in string values for text field variables applies **bold** formatting to the enclosed text.

✦ `<i>`: Placing `<i></i>` tags around Flash string values *italicizes* the enclosed text.

✦ `<u>`: The `<u></u>` tags <u>underline</u> the enclosed text.

✦ `<p>`: The `<p>` tag inserts a paragraph break between lines of text. You can use the `align` attribute to specify `left`, `right`, `center`, or `justify`, applying the respective justifications to the Flash text.

The justify value for the align attribute is now supported in Flash Player 8 for HTML text.

✦ `<br/>`: The `<br/>` tag inserts a carriage return at the point of insertion. This is equivalent to the `newline` operator in ActionScript.

✦ `<font color='#hex code'>`: The `<font>` tag with the `color` attribute can change the color of your Flash text. This color is specified in hexadecimal values, just as with regular HTML. For example, `"<font color='#FF0000>This is red text.</font>"` uses full red for the text color.

✦ `<font face>`: The `<font>` tag with the `face` attribute enables you to specify a specific typeface to the enclosed text. You can specify Flash device fonts for the `face` value, such as `<font face='_sans'>` to use the Sans Serif device font.

✦ `<font size>`: The `size` attribute of the `<font>` tag enables you to specify the point size of Flash text. You can use absolute values (in point sizes), such as `<font size='18'>`, or relative values, such as `<font size='+1'>`, to change the size of text.

✦ `<font letterSpacing>`: The `letterSpacing` attribute of the `<font>` tag enables you to uniformly add horizontal space around each character. You can use positive or negative integers, such as `<font letterSpacing='18'>`. This attribute is only supported in Flash Player 8.

✦ **`<font kerning>`:** The `kerning` attribute of the `<font>` tag enables you to turn kerning on (1) or off (0). Kerning is the space between characters of a specific font, and is not available for some fonts such as Courier New.

✦ **`<textformat>`:** This tag is a Flash-specific formatting tag that you won't find in traditional HTML. `<textformat>` has four attributes, `indent`, `leading`, `leftmargin`, and `rightmargin`, that control the margin and line spacing of text within the text field. Each of these attributes uses pixels as the unit of measurement. To get a feel for how these attributes work, create a Static text with a paragraph of text, click the Format button in the Property inspector for the selected text field, and change the settings in the Format Options dialog box.

Tip   You can only use the `<textformat>` tag within text fields for Flash Player 6 or higher movies. Make sure the Version menu in the Flash tab of the Publish Settings (File ➪ Publish Settings) is set to Flash Player 6 or higher. Flash Player 8 supports negative values for text indent as well.

✦ **`<span>`:** As with its real HTML counterpart, `<span>` enables you to apply a style from a style sheet to the encompassed range of text. This tag has only one supported attribute, `class`. This attribute can be set to the name of the style class declared in the style sheet. For example, `<span class="heading">` applies the style named `heading` to the enclosed text.

✦ **`<img>`:** A potentially exciting tag supported in Flash HTML is the `<img>` tag, short for image. As you may have guessed, this tag enables you to insert images inline with other text in a text field. This tag supports the following attributes: `src`, `id`, `width`, `height`, `align`, `hspace`, and `vspace`. The `src` attribute can be set to one of the following: the linkage identifier of a symbol in the library, the external URL to an .swf file, or the external URL to an image file. The JPEG, progressive JPEG, GIF, and PNG formats are supported in Flash Player 8. Flash Player 7 only supports standard JPEG files with the `<img>` tag.

URL and ActionScript linking

You can use the anchor, or `<a>`, tag with the `href` attribute to apply URL links within Flash text fields. For example, you can insert the following HTML into a string value for the `htmlText` property of a text field instance, to link the text [*the*MAKERS] Web site to the appropriate URL:

```
<a href='http://www.theMakers.com'>the Makers Web site</a>
```

You can also specify a `target` attribute for the `<a>` tag. The `target` attribute determines which browser window or frame displays the URL link in the `href` attribute. As with regular HTML, you can use the default `_top`, `_parent`, `_self`, or `_blank` values, as described for the `getURL()` action. Later in this section, you also learn how to execute internal ActionScript functions from `<a href>` tags.

Caution   You cannot type HTML tags directly into any text block or field — the actual tags show up in the text field as the Flash movie runs in the Flash Player. The formatting tags are specified in ActionScript code or are "hidden" in Static text. (The Property inspector applies the formatting.)

Formatting text with the Property inspector

You don't necessarily need to write out HTML tags to apply them to your Flash text. You can use the Property inspector to assign HTML formatting to all Text types (that is, Static, Input, and Dynamic). For Input and Dynamic text fields, you need to enable HTML formatting by pressing the Render text as HTML button in the Property inspector. In this section, we demonstrate the use of HTML formatting within Static and Dynamic text fields.

1. Open a new Flash document (Ctrl+N or ⌘+N). If the background color of your document is a nonwhite color, then set the background color to white in the Document Properties dialog box (Ctrl+J or ⌘+J). Save your Flash document as `htmlText_static.fla`.

2. Select the Text tool and open the Property inspector. Make sure the Text type menu (in the top-left corner of the inspector) is set to Static Text. Click once on the Stage and type the following text (with carriage returns) in the text block, using Verdana at 18 points:

   ```
   Flash 8 Bible
   by Robert Reinhardt & Snow Dowd
   ```

3. With the text block still active, select the Flash 8 Bible text and, in the Property inspector, change the point size to **24** and click the B (for bold) option, as shown in Figure 30-1. Enter the following URL in the URL field of the Property inspector and choose _blank in the Target menu:

   ```
   http://www.flashsupport.com
   ```

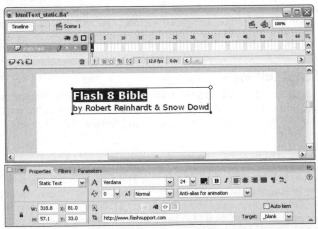

Figure 30-1: You can selectively change text within one text block or field.

4. With the text block still active, select the Robert Reinhardt text, and, in the Property inspector, enter the following text for the URL field:

   ```
   mailto:robert@theMakers.com
   ```

5. Now, select the Snow Dowd text and enter the following text in the URL field of the Property inspector:

```
mailto:snow@theMakers.com
```

See Figure 30-2 for an example of how the URL-linked text will appear.

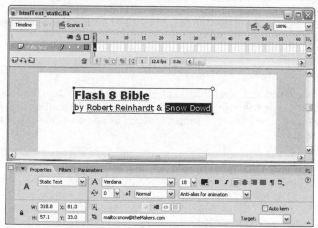

Figure 30-2: URL-linked text appears with dashed underlines. You will not see this dashed underline in the actual Flash movie file (.swf).

6. Save the Flash document, and test the Flash movie file (.swf) in your Web browser by choosing File ➪ Publish Preview ➪ HTML. When you click the Flash 8 Bible text, the browser loads the official support site for the *Macromedia Flash 8 Bible* in a new window. When you click either author's name, your e-mail client opens a new message window.

On the CD-ROM

You will find the completed `htmlText_static.fla` document in the `ch30` folder of this book's CD-ROM.

Try making another example with your own text and URL links. You can even add `javascript:` commands to URL links.

Inserting HTML tags into Text Fields with ActionScript

In this section, we continue with the previous example that you created in the last section. You convert the Static text block into a Dynamic text field and manipulate the formatting with ActionScript.

1. Resave your Flash document from the last section as `htmlText_dynamic.fla`. You will convert this Static text into a Dynamic text field, so you'll want to keep your original Static text example for future reference.

2. Select the text block and open the Property inspector. Change the text type to Dynamic Text and make sure the HTML option is enabled. In the <Instance Name> field, type the name tBook. Now, this text field can be updated with ActionScript directed at the tBook instance. You can also disable the Show Border option if you don't want to see a bounding box around your text.

3. Create a new layer named actions. Select frame 1 of the actions layer, and open the Actions panel (F9, or Option+F9). Add the following code to the Script pane. This code displays the htmlText value of the tBook field in the Output window when you test the movie.

```
var tBook:TextField;
trace("htmlText: " + tBook.htmlText);
```

4. Save the Flash document and test it (Ctrl+Enter or ⌘+Return). While the Flash movie is playing in the Test Movie window, you should see the HTML formatting tags displayed in the Output window. The htmlText property reads as one continuous line displaying the following markup:

```
htmlText: <TEXTFORMAT LEADING="2"><P ALIGN="LEFT"><FONT FACE=
"verdana" SIZE="24" COLOR="#000000" LETTERSPACING="0" KERNING="0">
<A HREF="http://www.flashsupport.com" TARGET="_blank"><B>Flash 8
Bible</B></A></FONT></P></TEXTFORMAT><TEXTFORMAT LEADING="2">
<P ALIGN="LEFT"><FONT FACE="verdana" SIZE="18" COLOR="#000000"
LETTERSPACING="0" KERNING="0">by <A HREF="mailto:robert@theMakers.
com" TARGET="">Robert Reinhardt</A> &amp; <A HREF="mailto:
snow@theMakers.com" TARGET="">Snow Dowd</A></FONT></P></TEXTFORMAT>
```

You can observe the requisite ActionScript syntax for HTML formatting in the Output panel.

Note   HTML tag names are not case-sensitive in Flash. We prefer to use XHTML-compliant code; as such, you'll see our examples use all lowercase characters in HTML tag and attribute names. The values of attributes, such as file URLs in href or src, require attention to case-sensitivity.

5. Close the Test Movie window and go back to the Main Timeline of your Flash document. Create a new Dynamic text field, and in the Property inspector, enable the HTML option. In the <Instance Name> field, type the name tBook2.

6. Select the first frame of the actions layer and open the Actions panel (F9, Option+F9 on Mac). In the Script pane, specify an HTML-formatted string value for the htmlText property of the tBook2 instance, such as the following code. Comment out the trace() action you inserted earlier as well. Note that the \ character is required before additional quotes within a String value. The ⊃ character indicates a continuation of the same line of code.

```
var tBook:TextField;
var tBook2:TextField;
//trace("htmlText: " + tBook.htmlText);
tBook2.htmlText = "<font face=\"Verdana\" size=\"24\" ⊃
    color=\"#0000FF\"><b><a ⊃
    href=\"http://www.communitymx.com\"> ⊃
    CommunityMX</a></b></font>";
```

Note   The last line of code should appear as one line number in the Script pane of the Actions panel.

7. Save the Flash document and test it. The `tBook2` text field displays the HTML-formatted value that you specified in the actions layer.

You can also use variables in expressions for HTML-formatted text fields, such as the following (note that the `bookURL` variable and value should appear on one line of code):

```
var sURL:String = "http://www.flashsupport.com";
var sName:String = "Flash 8 Bible";
tBook.htmlText = "<a href=\"" + sURL + "\">" + sName + "</a>";
```

By using other ActionScript variables and methods, you can apply specific text formatting to external data sources that have been loaded into the Flash movie, such as database records or lists. In the next section, you learn how to format text within text fields using the `TextFormat` object in ActionScript.

On the CD-ROM   You can find the completed `htmlText_dynamic.fla` document in the `ch30` folder of this book's CD-ROM.

Formatting fields with the TextFormat object

ActionScript offers a wide range of options for the `TextField` object. Many properties of the `MovieClip` object, such as `_x` and `_y`, can be controlled with `TextField` objects, too. One interesting method of the `TextField` object is the `setTextFormat()` method. This method enables you to control the formatting of text within a `TextField` object without relying on HTML tags. The `setTextFormat()` method works much like the `setTransform()` method of the `Sound` class that we cover in Chapter 27, "Interacting with Movie Clips." Like `setTransform()`, `setTextFormat()` requires another object — a `TextFormat` object — that contains individual properties and values in order to adjust the targeted instance's text contents.

Tip   ActionScript in Flash Player 6 and higher movies can also create text fields on the fly using the `createTextField()` method of the `MovieClip` object.

In this section, you create a Flash movie that makes a dynamic text field on the fly and applies formatting to the field with the `TextFormat` object. You also use the `TextFormat` object to determine the dimensions of the `TextField` instance.

1. Create a new Flash document (Ctrl+N or ⌘+N). Save the document as `textFormat_100.fla`.

2. Rename Layer 1 to **actions**. ActionScript creates the entire contents of this movie. You will not use any tools from the Tools panel to create the text.

3. Select frame 1 of the actions layer and open the Actions panel. Type the following code into the Script pane:

```
var tfTitle:TextFormat = new TextFormat();
with(tfTitle){
    font = "Verdana";
```

```
    bold = true;
    color = 0x0000FF;
    url = "http://www.flashsupport.com/";
    target = "_blank";
}
```

This code creates a new `TextFormat` object named `tfTitle` (line 1). This formatting is used for site links displayed in the Flash movie. Within this object, properties of the site link text are specified. Lines 2 through 8 assign the `font`, `bold`, `color`, `url`, and `target` properties of the style. In later steps, you apply this style to a `TextField` instance.

4. Within the same actions list shown in Step 3, add the following code:

```
var sName_1:String = "FlashSupport.com";
var oSize:Object = tfTitle.getTextExtent(sName_1);
```

This code declares a `sName_1` variable, which contains the text of the site link that the movie displays. `oSize` is an object created by the `getTextExtent()` method of the `TextFormat` object. This method enables you to determine the pixel dimensions of text with formatting applied to it before you actually create the `TextField` object displaying the text. `oSize` contains two properties (among others): `textFieldWidth` and `textFieldHeight`. You access these properties in the next step.

Tip   The `TextFormat.getTextExtent()` method has been greatly improved for Flash Player 7 and higher movies. The following properties are returned by the method: `descent`, `ascent`, `textFieldHeight`, `textFieldWidth`, `height`, and `width`. Refer to the Flash 8 Help panel for more information on these properties or read the coverage in the *Flash ActionScript Bible* series (Wiley). Oddly, Macromedia lists the `getTextExtent()` method as deprecated in the Flash 8 Help panel, but does not make any reference to a suitable replacement for its functionality. In our tests, the `getTextExtent()` method works reliably within Flash Player 8 movies.

5. After the last line of code listed in Step 4, add the following code. Note that the ⤶ character indicates a continuation of the same line of code:

```
var tSites:TextField = createTextField("tSites", 1, 10, 10, ⤶
    oSize.textFieldWidth, oSize.textFieldHeight);
with(tSites){
    html = true;
    text = sName_1;
    setTextFormat(tfTitle);
}
```

The first line of code uses the `createTextField()` method of the `MovieClip` object to make a new Dynamic text field named `tSites` at a depth of 1 on the current timeline. The field is positioned at the X and Y coordinates of 10, 10, with a width and height specified by the `oSize` object created earlier.

The second line begins a `with()` statement, to apply all of the nested code to the new `tSites` object.

The third line enables the `html` property of the `tSites` field, so that any URL values within the `TextFormat` object can be recognized.

The fourth line fills the text field with the value of the sName_1 variable, which has a value of "FlashSupport.com."

The fifth line applies the tfTitle TextFormat object to the entire contents of the tSites field.

Note Make sure you use the setTextFormat() method if you want to apply formatting to existing text in a TextField instance. If you want to apply formatting before you populate a field with text, then use the setNewTextFormat() method.

6. Save the Flash document as textFormat_100.fla and test it (Ctrl+Enter or ⌘+Return). The tSites text field appears in the top-left corner of the Stage. When you click the text, the default Web browser opens, displaying the URL for www.flashsupport.com.

On the CD-ROM You can find the completed textFormat_100.fla file in the ch30 folder of this book's CD-ROM.

You can continue to develop this Flash document, adding more sites to the tSites text field. You don't necessarily need to make more text fields — create more sName variables (for example, sName_2, sName_3, and so on) and add their expressions together as the contents of the tSites instance.

Applying style sheets to text fields

In this section, you learn how to load an external style sheet, as a Cascading Style Sheet (CSS) file, and apply its styles to text in a Flash movie. This capability is available in Flash Player 7 and higher movies.

Making the style sheet

Before you can apply an external style sheet to Flash text, you need to create the CSS file describing the styles. In the following steps, use any text editor such as Notepad or TextEdit, or a full-featured CSS editor such as Macromedia Dreamweaver.

1. Create a new text document.

2. Define two custom styles, h1 and h2. These styles should use bold 14- and 12-pixel type, respectively. The font face should be Verdana for both. Refer to Listing 30-1.

3. Now, define a p style. This style will be used for regular text in paragraphs. This style will use Arial at 10 px. The color of this text will be dark gray, using the hexadecimal value #666666. Refer to Listing 30-1.

4. Save your text file as styles.css.

Listing 30-1: The h1, h2, and Body Styles

```
.h1 {
    font-family: Verdana;
    font-weight: bold;
    font-size: 14px;
```

Continued

Listing 30-1 *(continued)*

```
}

.h2 {
    font-family: Verdana;
    font-weight: bold;
    font-size: 12px;
}

p {
    font-family: Arial;
    font-size: 10px;
    color: #666666;
}
```

Loading the style sheet into a Flash movie

Once you have a CSS file ready, you can create the ActionScript required to load the style sheet into a Flash movie. In the following steps, you'll do just that.

1. Create a new Flash document (File ⇨ New).

2. Rename Layer 1 to **actions**.

3. Select frame 1 of the actions layer, and open the Actions panel (F9, or Option+F9 on Mac). Type the code shown in Listing 30-2 into the Script pane.

   In line 1 of this code, you create a new StyleSheet object, which is actually a subclass of the TextField class. The StyleSheet object is named movieStyle.

   In line 2, you define the onLoad() method of this object. The onLoad() handler is invoked when the external CSS file has finished loading into the movie. If the loading was successful, lines 3 through 5 are invoked, sending a trace() message to the Output panel and invoking another function named showText(). You define the showText() function in the next section.

   If the CSS style cannot be loaded (that is, if the URL or filename is incorrect, or if the style sheet cannot be parsed by the Flash Player), lines 6 through 8 are invoked in the onLoad() handler. Line 7 sends a message indicating the result to the Output panel.

   Line 10 invokes the load() method of the movieStyle object. This line of code tells the Flash Player to get the styles.css file and attempt to load it.

Tip   It's always a good idea to define the onLoad() handler of an object before you initiate the load() method. There's a slight chance that the onLoad() handler won't be invoked if you declare it after the load() method.

> **Listing 30-2: The movieStyle Object**
>
> ```
> 1.  var ssMovie:TextField.StyleSheet = new TextField.StyleSheet();
> 2.  ssMovie.onLoad = function(bSuccess:Boolean):Void {
> 3.     if(bSuccess){
> 4.         trace("loaded external CSS file");
> 5.         showText();
> 6.     } else {
> 7.         trace("CSS file did not load.");
> 8.     }
> 9.  };
> 10. ssMovie.load("styles.css");
> ```

    4. Save your Flash document as `css_styles_100.fla`, in the same location where you saved your `styles.css` file from the previous section. Test the movie (Ctrl+Enter or ⌘+Enter). You should see the following text appear in the Output panel:

```
loaded external CSS file
```

Applying the styles to Flash text

Once you have the external style sheet loaded into a Flash movie, you're ready to apply the defined styles to text used in dynamic or input text fields. In the remaining steps, you learn how to apply each of the styles to text displayed in a dynamic text field.

    1. In the Flash document that you created in the previous section, go back to frame 1 of the actions layer. Open the Actions panel (F9, or Option+F9 on Mac), and add the code shown in Listing 30-3 after the existing code. Note that the ⤸ character indicates a continuation of the same line of code. Do not type this character into your actual code.

Line 1 establishes a variable named `tDisplay`. This variable will be used as a `TextField` instance later in the `showText()` function.

Line 3 declares the function's name, `showText`. Remember that in Listing 30-2, the `showText()` function is invoked in the `ssMovie.onLoad()` handler.

Lines 4 through 7 create a long string of text that will be inserted into the `tDisplay` field. Here, you can see that each of the styles is used, defined in the `class` attributes of various `<span>` tags. Since you defined a style for the p tag in the style sheet, that style is automatically applied to any text enclosed by `<p></p>` tags in HTML text. In line 14, the `htmlText` property of the `tDisplay` instance is set to the value of the `sText` variable.

Line 8 creates a text field named `tDisplay`. Line 10 sets the `styleSheet` property of the `tDisplay` instance to `ssMovie`. Lines 11 through 13 set up basic properties of the `tDisplay` instance, enabling it to display HTML text (line 11), and display wrapping text over multiple lines (lines 12 and 13).

Listing 30-3: **The showText() function**

```
1.  var tDisplay:TextField;
2.
3.  function showText():Void {
4.      var sText:String = "<span class='h1'>Flash Player Style ⮑
            Support</span><br/>";
5.      sText += "<p>You can use style sheets in your Flash ⮑
            Player 7 or higher movies.</p><br/>";
6.      sText += "<span class='h2'>Supported styles</span><br/>";
7.      sText += "<p>More text here...</p>";
8.      tDisplay = createTextField("tDisplay", 1, 10, 10, 400, 400);
9.      with(tDisplay){
10.         styleSheet = ssMovie;
11.         html = true;
12.         multiline = true;
13.         wordWrap = true;
14.         htmlText =sText;
15.     }
16. }
```

    2. Save your Flash document, and test it. You should see nicely formatted text, specified by the details of the style sheet, as shown in Figure 30-3.

You can find the completed files, styles.css and css_styles_100.fla, in the ch30 folder of this book's CD-ROM.

You can also use other nonsystem fonts in style sheets, but you'll need to make sure that you have created linked Font symbols in your movie's library or that you have created empty text fields that include the embedded fonts.

Inserting images into text fields

In this section, you learn how to load a JPEG image into a TextField object. Continue using the same Flash document you created in the last section.

Open the css_styles_100.fla document from the ch30 folder of this book's CD-ROM if you didn't complete the previous section.

    1. In the css_styles_100.fla document, select frame 1 of the actions layer, and open the Actions panel (F9, or Option+F9). Change the script to the code shown in Listing 30-4. Remember that you shouldn't include the ⮑ character in your actual code. This character denotes a continuation of the same line of code.

This code uses the same structure of the showText() function from the last section. However, in line 1, you include the bio.as file, which you can find in the ch30 folder of this book's CD-ROM. A copy of this file should exist in the same location as your .fla file. The bio.as file declares a string variable named sBio, containing a sample biography.

Flash Player Style Support
You can use style sheets in your Flash Player 7 or higher movies.

Supported styles
More text here...

Figure 30-3: The formatted text

Tip

For a final production version of this Flash movie, you may want to load the data stored in the bio.as into the Flash movie at run time. For example, the biography text could be stored in an XML document and loaded with an XML object, or it could be loaded from a server-side script. For more information on data loading, read Chapter 29, "Sending Data In and Out of Flash."

Within the showText() function, you use the <img> tag to include a JPEG image, portrait.jpg, in the tDisplay field. You can find this JPEG file in the ch30 folder of this book's CD-ROM, and it's also located at the URL shown in the function.

Listing 30-4: The Modified showText() Function

```
#include "bio.as"

var ssMovie:TextField.StyleSheet = new TextField.StyleSheet();
ssMovie.onLoad = function(bSuccess:Boolean):Void {
    if(bSuccess){
        trace("loaded external CSS file");
        showText();
    } else {
        trace("CSS file did not load.");
    }
};
ssMovie.load("styles.css");

var tDisplay:TextField;

function showText():Void {
    var sText:String = "<img ⏎
        src='http://www.flashsupport.com/bio/portrait.jpg' ⏎
        id='mcPortrait' width='200' height='200' vspace='4' hspace='8' ⏎
        align='left'>";
    sText += "<span class='h1'>Robert Reinhardt</span><br/>";
    sText += sBio;
```

Continued

Listing 30-4 *(continued)*

```
tDisplay = createTextField("tDisplay", 1, 10, 10, 400, 400);
with(tDisplay){
    styleSheet = ssMovie;
    html = true;
    multiline = true;
    wordWrap = true;
    htmlText =sText;
}
}
```

2. Save your Flash document as `img_insert_100.fla`, and test it. When the movie loads, you should see the header and biography text wrap around the JPEG image, as shown in Figure 30-4.

On the CD-ROM

You can find the completed document, `img_insert_100.fla`, in the `ch30` folder of this book's CD-ROM. Another version of this document, `img_insert_101.fla`, features a `drawBorder()` function, which dynamically draws a border around the JPEG image. The `checkLoad()` function within this file is similar to the functions you created in Chapter 28, "Sharing and Loading Assets."

You can also use symbol linkage identifier names as the value of the `src` attribute of the `<img>` tag. However, you may find that if you use several `<img>` tags in a text field, not all of the images load and/or display. In some of our experiments, we noticed that text realigned itself when text with URLs was rolled over. Be sure to test your Flash movies with the latest Flash Player 8 revisions, as Macromedia releases them.

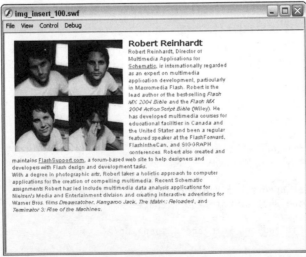

Figure 30-4: The JPEG image with wrapping text

Using asfunction in anchor tags

Not only can you use HTML formatting in Flash text; but you can also execute Flash actions from your text fields using the `<a>` tag and a `href` attribute value of `asfunction:function,argument`. For example, if you wanted to link text to a function that loads a new Flash movie file (.swf) into a Movie Clip target, you can create a custom function that uses the `loadMovie()` action and reference that action from your `<a href>` tag for a text field. See the following code (note that the ⤸ indicates a continuation of the same line of code; do not insert this character into your actual code):

```
var mcHolder:MovieClip;
var tDisplay:TextField;
function getSWF(sPath:String):Void{
  mcHolder.loadMovie(sPath);
}
tDisplay.htmlText = "<a href=\"asfunction:getSWF,movie.swf\">Click to load ⤸
  movie</a>";
```

In this code example, the text within the `<a></a>` tags executes the `getSWF()` function, passing the string `movie.swf` as the `sPath` argument.

Tip
The `asfunction` can only pass one string value. You do not need to enclose the argument in quotes. If you need to pass another ActionScript variable for the value, use the + operator to add it to the HTML text string.

If you need to pass more than one argument, you will need to send all the values as one string separated by a comma (or preferred character). Then you would use the `String.split()` method as follows (note that the ⤸ indicates a continuation of the same line of code; do not insert this character into your actual code):

```
var mcHolder:MovieClip;
var tDisplay:TextField;
function getSWF(sArgs:String):Void{
   var aParams:Array = sArgs.split(",");
   var mc:MovieClip = eval(aParams[0]);
   var sPath:String = aParams[1];
   mc.loadMovie(sPath);
}
var sParams:String = "mcHolder,movie.swf";
tDisplay.htmlText = "<a href=\"asfunction:getSWF," + sParams + "\"> ⤸
  Click to load movie</a>";
```

In this example, the `getSWF()` function takes the `sArgs` argument and creates an array with the `split()` method. This array's name is `aParams`. The elements of the `aParams` array are the two string values separated by a comma in the `sParams` variable.

On the CD-ROM
You can see examples of HTML-formatted Flash text and the `asfunction` in the `ch30/asfunction` folder of this book's CD-ROM.

Controlling Text Field Properties

Input and Dynamic text fields have several properties that are accessible with ActionScript. In this section, you learn how to control the scrolling and font rendering properties of the TextField class.

Scroll properties

Two of the TextField class properties, scroll and maxscroll, control the viewable area of a text field that has more lines of text than the text field can show.

✦ scroll: This property can retrieve the current line number (from the top of the field), and it can also move to a new line number in a text field.

✦ maxscroll: This property returns the maximum value of the scroll property for a given text field. You can only retrieve this value — you cannot set it.

Note The scroll property advances text line by line in the viewable area of the TextField instance. To learn more about pixel-level scrolling, see the new Flash 8 coverage later in this chapter.

To understand how these properties work, you need to see how lines are enumerated in a text field. Suppose you had ten lines of text as a string value for a variable called myText. If you want to use this text in a Dynamic text field named tArticle, which only has a viewable area of five lines, then the remaining five lines of the sText variable will not be seen in the text field. To make the text field "scroll" to the next line of text by showing lines 2 to 6 (instead of lines 1 to 5), you can create a Button instance, such as a down-arrow button, with ActionScript to advance the lines:

```
var btDown:Button;
var tArticle:Text;
btDown.onRelease = function():Void {
  tArticle.scroll = tArticle.scroll + 1;
};
```

or

```
var btDown:Button;
var tArticle:Text;
btDown.onRelease = function():Void {
  tArticle.scroll += 1;
};
```

The maxscroll property returns the maximum value for the top line number in a text field. In our previous ten-line text value example, the maxscroll property would equal 6. If you had 20 lines of text in the tArticle text field, then the .maxscroll property would return a value of 16.

Tip Flash 8 has a TextArea component that automatically creates a text field and scroll bar. You can find more information on User Interface components in Chapter 33, "Using Components."

In the `ch30/scroll` folder of this book's CD-ROM, you will find a Flash document named `scrollProp_simple.fla`. This movie demonstrates the use of the `scroll` property to view the entire Gettysburg Address within a text field. A more advanced scrolling mechanism can be found in the `scrollProp_advanced.fla` file, which features a draggable scroll bar.

Text rendering properties

Flash Player 8 adds incredible text rendering advancements to your Flash text. The new anti-aliasing engine for text is dubbed FlashType, and collectively refers to the properties of text fields that enable you to control the readability of text. In this section, you learn about the following `TextField` properties:

✦ `antiAliasType:String`: This property controls whether or not the `TextField` instance uses the new FlashType rendering engine. If you set a `TextField` instance's antiAliasType property to "normal," the instance renders text just as it did in Flash Player 7 or earlier. If you set the property to "advanced," the text in the field is displayed with the new FlashType engine.

✦ `thickness:Number`: This property controls the thickness of the glyph edges in the `TextField` instance and is only applied if the antiAliasType mode is set to "advanced." The value for this property can be in the range of –200 (less thick) to 200 (more thick).

A glyph refers to any individual character in the font face. The letter "a," for example, is a glyph.

✦ `sharpness:Number`: This property controls the sharpness (or softness) of glyph edges in the `TextField` instance. Acceptable values are in the range of -400 (softer) to 400 (sharp). This property only affects text rendered with the `"advanced"` value of the `antiAliasType` property.

In general, we have found that you don't need to tweak thickness and sharpness values of `TextField` instances. However, you may find a particular font that requires some finessing to get the level of readability you desire.

✦ `gridFitType:String`: This property controls how the pixels of text are rendered when the `antiAliasType` property is set to `"advanced"`. There are three acceptable values:

- `"none"`: This value specifies that there is no special grid fitting applied to the text rendering.

- `"pixel"`: This value forces the text to be rendered against actual pixels of the computer monitor, rather than across multiple pixels (which would blur the text). If the `TextField` instance is set to use "advanced" for `antiAliasType`, the "pixel" value is the default value of `gridFitType`. This value is best used for left-aligned text fields.

- `"subpixel"`: This value forces the text to be rendered on a subpixel grid, which is best for right-aligned or justified text fields. This value can only be used with `TextField` instances that have the `antiAliasType` property set to "advanced."

Caution You must build Flash Player 8–compatible movies in order to use these new `TextField` properties. Also, these new settings only apply to text that uses embedded fonts. If you are using device fonts with text, then you will not see any changes applied to your text.

Working with author-time TextField instances

In this section, you learn how to apply the new anti-aliasing features to `TextField` instances that you place on the Stage at author-time.

1. Create a new Flash document, and save it as `flashtype_100.fla`.

2. Rename Layer 1 to **fields**.

3. Using the Text tool, add a Dynamic text field on the Stage. In the Property inspector, name the instance **tDisplay1**. Make sure you choose Anti-alias for animation and Multiline (see Figure 30-5). You can use any font face you prefer, but use a small text size such as 10 point.

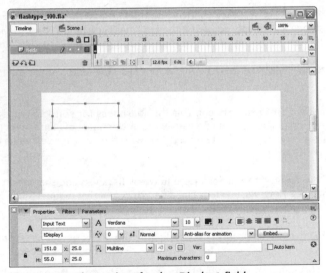

Figure 30-5: The settings for the tDisplay1 field

 Note Choosing the Anti-alias for animation setting in the Property inspector is the equivalent of setting the `antiAliasType` property to `"normal"` in ActionScript.

4. In the Property inspector, click the Embed button and select the ranges shown in Figure 30-6. Remember, you can't use the new anti-aliasing features unless you have embedded the font used by the `TextField` instance.

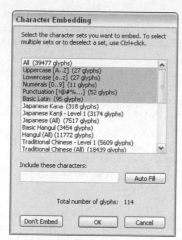

Figure 30-6: The Character Embedding options

5. Duplicate the tDisplay1 field by selecting the instance on the Stage and choosing Edit ⇨ Duplicate (Ctrl+D or ⌘+D). Place the new instance to the right of the original instance, and in the Property inspector, rename the instance tDisplay2. Also, change the aliasing setting to Anti-alias for readability, as shown in Figure 30-7.

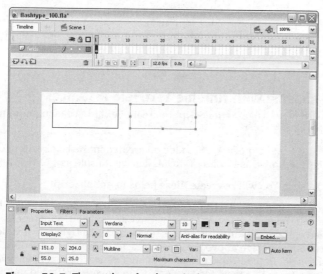

Figure 30-7: The settings for the tDisplay2 field

 Note

Choosing the Anti-alias for readability setting is the same as setting the antiAliasType property to "advanced" in ActionScript.

6. To add some text to the fields, you will set the text property of the fields in ActionScript. Create a new layer named **actions**. Select frame 1 of the actions layer, and open the Actions panel. Add the following code to the Script pane. The ⊃ character indicates the continuation of the same line of code.

```
var tDisplay1:TextField;
var tDisplay2:TextField;
var sText:String = "The quick brown fox jumped over the lazy ⊃
    dog.";
tDisplay1.text = tDisplay2.text = sText;
```

Tip You can use more than one assignment operator (=) in an ActionScript expression. In this example, you first set the text property of the tDisplay2 to the value of sText. Then, the text property of the tDisplay1 is set from the same value.

7. Save the document, and test it (Ctrl+Enter or ⌘+Enter). The left field should show the regular anti-aliasing quality of the text, which is difficult to read at 10-point. As shown in Figure 30-8, though, the right field uses the new FlashType engine, which greatly improves its legibility.

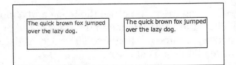

Figure 30-8: The two primary settings for anti-aliasing in Flash Player 8 movies.

You can find the completed file, flashtype_100.fla, in the ch30 folder of this book's CD-ROM.

Controlling anti-aliasing with runtime TextField instances

In this section, you learn how to use ActionScript to create TextField instances and set their anti-aliasing properties.

1. Continue using the flashtype_100.fla file you created in the last section, or make a copy of the same file from this book's CD-ROM. Resave this file as flashtype_101.fla.

2. Delete the fields layer. You will re-create these fields in ActionScript.

3. Even though you will use ActionScript to create TextField instances at run time, you still need to embed the font you want to use with your TextField instances. Create a new layer named **embedded fonts**. Using the Text tool, add a Dynamic text field to the document, preferably offstage above the Stage area, as shown in Figure 30-9. Type the text **abc** into this field. In the Property inspector, make sure the text field type is Dynamic Text, and name this instance tEmbed1. Choose your preferred font face for the field; for this example, we used Verdana. Click the **Embed** button and select the same ranges shown earlier in Figure 30-6.

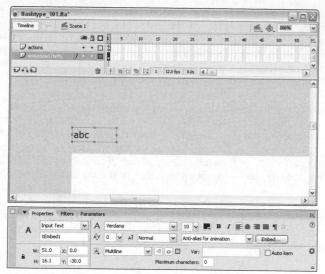

Figure 30-9: The settings for the tEmbed1 field

Note

Some Flash designers and developers prefer to embed fonts by creating Font symbols in the document's Library panel. Font symbols are useful if you need every character (including a wide range of foreign language characters and ASCII art symbols) in your Flash movie, but they greatly increase your .swf file size. Adding the entire Verdana font face as a Font symbol, for example, adds 20 KB to your Flash movie file (.swf) size! But if you only need the character ranges shown in Figure 30-6, using a Dynamic text instance on the Stage only adds 12 KB to your Flash movie file (.swf) size.

4. Because the HTML option is enabled on the `tEmbed1` field, you can control the formatting of the abc characters you typed into the field. Select the b character, and bold it in the Property inspector. Select the c character and italicize it in the Property inspector. When you are finished, your field should resemble the one shown in Figure 30-10.

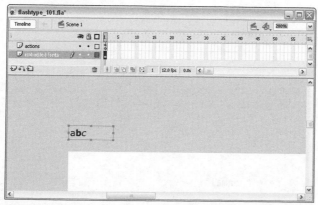

Figure 30-10: The abc text with styles applied to the b and c characters.

Tip

By adding the bold and italic styles to the `tEmbed1` field, you are effectively embedding Verdana Bold and Verdana Italic font faces in the .swf file for this example. As such, you can use bold and italic formatting in `TextField` instances, with applied `TextFormat` instances or HTML text. You'll use HTML text later in this exercise. However, embedding these additional styles adds more weight to the SWF's file size. If you prefer to use Font symbols, you can add a new Font symbol for each font face style you want to embed.

5. Now you're ready to modify the ActionScript on frame 1 of the actions layer. The new script, shown in Listing 30-5, creates two `TextField` instances using the same instance names used in the previous section's example. Near the end of the init() function, notice that `tDisplay1` uses the `"normal"` value for the `antiAliasType` property, while `tDisplay2` uses the `"advanced"` value. Note that the ⊃ character indicates a continuation of the same line of code — do not include this character into your actual code.

Tip

This script also creates an inline style sheet, `ssMovie`. The local variable `sStyles` in the init() function shows the inline style, which is exactly the same text you would insert into a CSS file. You can use the `parseCSS()` method of the `StyleSheet` class to convert a `String` value into a full-fledged style sheet.

Listing 30-5: **Applying Anti-Aliasing to TextField Instances**

```
var tDisplay1:TextField;
var tDisplay2:TextField;
var ssMovie:TextField.StyleSheet;
var sText:String = "<p class='heading'><b>Typing Lessons 101</b></p> ⊃
    <p>The <i>quick</i> brown fox jumped over the lazy dog.</p>";

function init():Void {
    ssMovie = new TextField.StyleSheet();
    var sStyles:String = "p { font-family: Verdana; font-size: 10; }";
    sStyles += ".heading { font-family: Verdana; font-size: 14; }";
    ssMovie.parseCSS(sStyles);
    tDisplay1 = createTextField("tDisplay1", 1, 25, 25, 200, 100);
    tDisplay2 = createTextField("tDisplay2", 2, 250, 25, 200, 100);
    var aFields:Array = [tDisplay1, tDisplay2];
    for(var i:Number = 0; i < aFields.length; i++){
        var t:TextField = aFields[i];
        with(t){
            html = true;
            border = true;
            multiline = true;
            wordWrap = true;
            selectable = true;
            embedFonts = true;
            styleSheet = ssMovie;
        }
    }
    tDisplay1.antiAliasType = "normal";
```

```
tDisplay2.antiAliasType = "advanced";
tDisplay1.htmlText = tDisplay2.htmlText = sText;
}

init();
```

6. Save the Flash document, and test it (Ctrl+Enter or ⌘+Enter). As shown in Figure 30-11, you should see similar anti-aliasing results as you saw in the last section.

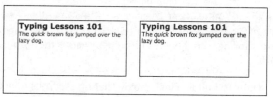

Figure 30-11: The two text fields with "normal" anti-aliasing (left) and "advanced" anti-aliasing (right).

 You can find the completed file, flashtype_101.fla, in the ch30 folder of this book's CD-ROM.

Comparing anti-aliasing effects

To help demonstrate the new sharpness and thickness properties of the TextField class, open the flashtype_200.fla file located in the ch30 folder of this book's CD-ROM. On the Stage of this document, you'll see an instance of the displayClip symbol, named mcDisplay. If you test the Flash movie (Ctrl+Enter or ⌘+Enter), you can type text into the Input text field, and change the anti-aliasing mode of the field. You can also change the alignment of the field, the grid fitting value (gridFitType), as well as the thickness and sharpness values of the "advanced" anti-aliasing mode.

 You can run the flashtype_200.swf file directly in the stand-alone Flash Player or in a Web browser window. You can find this file in the ch30 folder of this book's CD-ROM. You can add more instances of the displayClip symbol on to the Stage of the Flash document (flashtype_200.fla) to have side-by-side comparisons of text and anti-aliasing values.

Pixel-based Text Scrolling with Movie Clips

Flash Player 8 introduces a new property for the MovieClip class: scrollRect. This property controls the viewable area of a MovieClip instance on the Stage and can only be set with ActionScript (that is, you won't find a scrollRect setting in the Property inspector for Movie Clip symbols). You can think of the scrollRect property as a built-in mask that selectively shows content within the MovieClip object.

Tip

You need to use the new `Rectangle` class in Flash Player 8 to create the rectangle shape that will be used by a `MovieClip` object's `scrollRect` property. You learn how to create a new `Rectangle` object in this section's example.

You can use the `scrollRect` property to show and hide any type of content within a `MovieClip` object. In this section, you learn how to use the `scrollRect` property to create a scrollable area with text content within a `MovieClip` object. You learn how to control the `_y` property of a `TextField` instance with the UIScrollBar component. Typically, the UIScrollBar component is used to update the `scroll` property of a `TextField` instance, not the `TextField` instance's `_y` property.

On the CD-ROM

To get a sense of these two different types of scrolling, open the `scroll_comparison. html` document in the `ch30/scroll` folder of this book's CD-ROM. This page shows a Flash movie comparing text scrolling with the `scroll` property versus the `_y` property of a `TextField` instance.

In the following steps, you learn how to build a Flash movie that pixel scrolls a `TextField` instance with the UIScrollBar component.

1. Make a copy of the `fp8_pixelscroll_starter.fla` file from the `ch30/scroll` folder of this book's CD-ROM. Open the file in Flash 8, and resave it as `fp8_pixelscroll_ 100.fla`. This starter file has a `TextField` instance named `tDisplay` on the Stage. This field is set to embed the same range of Verdana font characters just like our previous examples in this chapter, and already contains the text from the Gettysburg Address.

2. Nest the `tDisplay` instance into a new Movie Clip symbol. Select the `tDisplay` instance on the Stage, and choose Modify ⇨ Convert to Symbol. Name the symbol **holderClip**, and set the registration to the top-left corner, as shown in Figure 30-12. Click OK to finish creating the symbol.

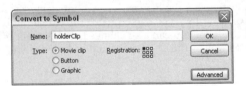

Figure 30-12: The Convert to Symbol dialog box

3. Select the new holderClip symbol instance on the Main Timeline (that is, Scene 1) Stage. In the Property inspector, name this instance `mcHolder`. Also, rename the tDisplay layer to **mcHolder**.

   Now you're ready to create a `Rectangle` object to use as the `scrollRect` value for the `mcHolder` instance. As you can see, the `tDisplay` field nested within the `mcHolder` instance continues off stage. The `scrollRect` for the `mcHolder` will be 300 x 300 pixels.

4. Create a new layer named **actions**. Select frame 1 of the actions layer, and open the Actions panel (F9, or Option+F9). Add the code shown in Listing 30-6.

The first line imports the new Rectangle class, which is part of the flash.geom class. The next three lines of code create variables for the Rectangle, MovieClip, and TextField instances that will be used within the init() function.

The init() function creates the Rectangle instance and uses the instance for the scrollRect property of the mcHolder instance. The nWidth and nHeight variables establish the width and height, respectively, of the viewable area of the MovieClip instance. The Rectangle constructor uses four arguments: the starting X position, the starting Y position, the width, and the height of the rectangle shape. Once the shape is created, it is set to be the value of the scrollRect property of the mcHolder instance. The tDisplay variable is also set to equal the tDisplay instance inside of the mcHolder instance, to create a shorter reference name for the TextField instance.

After the init() function is defined, the function is invoked so that the Rectangle instance is bound to the mcHolder instance when the Flash movie starts.

Note Due to rendering oddities of the new FlashType engine, you buffer the width of the Rectangle instance (rWin) by 5 pixels. This buffer will make sure that any text bleeding outside of the TextField instance will still be viewable.

Listing 30-6: Creating a Rectangle Object

```
import flash.geom.Rectangle;

var rWin:Rectangle;
var mcHolder:MovieClip;
var tDisplay:TextField;

function init():Void {
    var nWidth:Number = 300;
    var nHeight:Number = 300;
    rWin = new Rectangle(0, 0, nWidth+5, nHeight);
    mcHolder.scrollRect = rWin;
    tDisplay = mcHolder.tDisplay;
}

init();
```

---

5. Save the document, and test it (Ctrl+Enter or ⌘+Enter). You should see that the text is now masked by the new Rectangle instance, as shown in Figure 30-13.

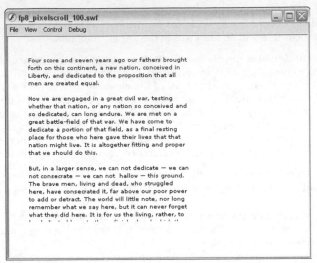

Figure 30-13: The scrollRect property masks the lower half of the TextField instance.

6. Once the field is masked, you can add a scroll bar to enable the user to view the entirety of the text. Open the Components panel (Ctrl+F7 or ⌘+F7), expand the User Interface grouping, and drag a copy of the UIScrollBar instance to the document's Stage. Once you've added the component to the Stage, select the instance and delete it. You simply need a copy of the UIScrollBar component in the movie's Library panel. In the next step, you attach the component to the movie's Stage via ActionScript.

7. Select frame 1 of the actions layer, and open the Actions panel. Add the bold code shown in Listing 30-7 to the existing script. Note that the ⊃ indicates a continuation of the same line of code. In this modified script, you import two new classes: Delegate and UIScrollBar. The Delegate class enables you to more easily scope event handlers, including component listener handlers. The UIScrollBar class is used by the csb variable declared in the next block of code.

The init() function adds four new lines of code, which create a new instance of the UIScrollBar component. The new instance is named csb and is positioned to the right of the mcHolder instance. More importantly, the minimum and maximum values that the scroll bar should return for its scrollPosition property are defined. The height of the Rectangle object is subtracted from the total height of the tDisplay field, since you don't want to scroll the TextField instance off the Stage. The size of the UIScrollBar instance is also sized to the height of the Rectangle instance. The last line of code within the init() function adds the new handler, onScroll, as a listener to the "scroll" event broadcasted from the UIScrollBar component.

The last block of code defines the onScroll() function, which is invoked whenever the user interacts with the UIScrollBar instance, csb. The scrollPosition property returned by the csb is used to set the _y position of the tDisplay field. Note that the value is inverted, so that the top of the TextField instance moves up. (You can come back to this code and remove the – sign to see what happens if it's not there.)

Listing 30-7: **Attaching a UIScrollBar Component**

```
import flash.geom.Rectangle;
import mx.utils.Delegate;
import mx.controls.UIScrollBar;

var rWin:Rectangle;
var csb:UIScrollBar;
var mcHolder:MovieClip;
var tDisplay:TextField;

function init():Void {
    var nWidth:Number = 300;
    var nHeight:Number = 300;
    rWin = new Rectangle(0, 0, nWidth+5, nHeight);
    mcHolder.scrollRect = rWin;
    tDisplay = mcHolder.tDisplay;

    csb = createClassObject(UIScrollBar, "csb", 1, {_x: mcHolder._x + ⤵
        mcHolder._width + 5, _y: mcHolder._y});
    csb.setScrollProperties(nHeight, 0, tDisplay._height - nHeight);
    csb.setSize(csb.width, nHeight);
    csb.addEventListener("scroll", Delegate.create(this, this.onScroll));
}

function onScroll(oEvent:Object):Void {
    tDisplay._y = -csb.scrollPosition;
}

init();
```

8. Save the document, and test it (Ctrl+Enter or ⌘+Enter). You should now see an instance of the UIScrollBar component attached to the right of the mcHolder instance displaying the text, as shown in Figure 30-14. If you click and drag the scroll box, you can smoothly scroll the text.

On the CD-ROM You can find the completed file, fp8_pixelscroll_100.fla, in the ch30/scroll folder of this book's CD-ROM. You can see a more advanced example, fp8_pixel scroll_101.fla, in the same location. That version dynamically creates the MovieClip instance (mcHolder) and the tDisplay instance, and populates the field with text from the gettysburg.as file.

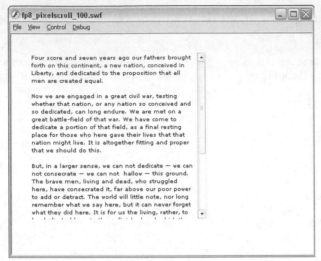

Figure 30-14: The scroll bar attached to the right of the text display

Manipulating Text with the Selection Class

The last text feature that we discuss in this chapter is the Selection class. The Selection class is similar to the Mouse class — you don't create instances of the Selection class as there can only be one active highlighted item at any given time.

Several object classes can use the Selection class, including TextField objects. The Selection class can use a string reference to the text field's variable (Var) name or its instance name to perform its methods. We discuss the methods of the Selection class in the following sections.

Note   In Flash 4 movies, there is no way of checking which text field was active. You can turn off a focus rectangle for Flash Player 4 text fields and Button instances, but you can't control tab order or automatically set a text field to active.

getBeginIndex()

This method detects and returns the starting position of a highlighted selection in a text field. The method returns –1 if there is no active text field and/or there is no selection inside the text field. As with the Array object, selection indexes start position values at 0. You do not need to specify a target path for this method — only one text field can have a selection at any given point. Therefore, as a variable nIdx, the getBeginIndex() method would look like:

```
this.onMouseMove = function():Void {
var nIdx:Number = Selection.getBeginIndex();
trace("nIdx: " + nIdx);
};
```

In the Output panel, the `trace()` action would reveal `nIdx = -1` until you made a selection within a text field in the movie, as shown in Figure 30-15.

In the `ch30/selection` folder of this book's CD-ROM, review the `getBeginIndex_ trace.fla` file to see how the `getBeginIndex()` method returns values for a text field. Each of the following sections also has a Flash document to demonstrate its respective method.

test this text field with a selection

Figure 30-15: A text field with a starting selection index of 3

getEndIndex()

Similar to the `getBeginIndex()` method, this method returns a number indicating the index position at the end of a highlighted selection in a text field, as shown in Figure 30-16. If there is no active selection, then a value of –1 is returned.

test this text field with a selection

Figure 30-16: A text field with a starting selection index of 5 and an ending index of 9

getCaretIndex()

This method of the `Selection` class returns the current cursor position (as an index value) within an active text field, as shown in Figure 30-17. As with the two previous methods, if you use the `getCaretIndex()` method when there is no active cursor in a text field, it returns a –1.

test this text field with a selection

Figure 30-17: A text field with a caret index of 5

getFocus()

This method returns the current active text field's Var or instance name as an absolute path; that is, if you have selected or inserted the cursor position inside a text field instance named `tOutput` on the Main Timeline, then `Selection.getFocus()` returns `_level0.tOutput`. If there is no active text field, then this method returns `null`.

If a text field does not have an instance name but does have a Var name, the Var name and path will be returned. A text field's instance name, when available, will be returned by this method.

setFocus()

Perhaps the best enhancement to controlled text field activity is the `setFocus()` method. This method enables you to make a text field active automatically—the user doesn't need to click the mouse cursor inside the text field to start typing. To use this method, simply indicate the `setFocus()` method of the `Selection` class and the path to the text field as its argument:

```
Selection.setFocus(tInput);
```

This code sets the current focus to the `tInput` text field. If any text exists in the text field, it will be highlighted as a selection. You can only use string data types as the `setFocus()` argument for Flash Player 5 compatability, but you can use instance names for Flash Player 6 or higher.

setSelection()

Another method available for the `Selection` class is `setSelection()`. This method enables you to make a specific selection within an active text field. The method takes two arguments: a start index and an end index. Use the same index numbering as `getBeginIndex()` and `getEndIndex()`. Note that this method will not work unless a text field is already active. The following code creates a selection span from index 5 to 9 of the `tInput` text field:

```
Selection.setFocus(tInput);
Selection.setSelection(5,9);
```

Caution   You may find that the `setSelection()` method does not show any results in the Test Movie environment. Always test your Flash movies in a Web browser or the stand-alone player to analyze your results.

Web Resource   We'd like to know what you think about this chapter. Visit `www.flashsupport.com/feedback` to send us your comments.

Summary

✦ You can use HTML text formatting within Flash text fields. Only basic HTML text formatting is allowed.

✦ You can insert HTML tags into the values of ActionScript variables that refer to Input or Dynamic text fields. Any quotes used with HTML attributes should be preceded by a backward slash, \.

✦ You can now apply style sheets to text within Flash movies that are compatible with Flash Player 7 or higher movies. The `TextField` class can also display inline artwork with the HTML `<img>` tag.

✦ The `asfunction` parameter for the `HREF` attribute of the `<A>` tag enables you to execute ActionScript functions from text fields. You can pass one argument to the specified function.

✦ The `scroll` property of Input and Dynamic text fields enables you to control the portion of a text field value that is displayed within the text field. `maxscroll` returns the highest line number for a given set of text in a text field.

✦ The new FlashType rendering engine of Flash Player 8 enables you to create Flash movies with small text that is more legible than in previous versions of the Flash Player.

✦   ✦   ✦

Creating a Game in Flash

Creating a game requires much more than programming. It is a combination of many skills — game design, interaction design, visual and sound design, and scripting — that brings it all together. These skills also represent the different phases of game design and are covered in this chapter. You must devote your attention to all these aspects of design to produce a successful game.

To illustrate the different aspects of game design, we deconstruct a simple game, the universally known Hangman.

Note In order to open the Flash Project file associated with this chapter's example, you need to be using Flash Professional 8. If you are using Flash Basic 8, you can open the ActionScript files (.as) in a separate text editor such as Macromedia Dreamweaver, Notepad, or TextEdit.

On the CD-ROM Before reading through this chapter, copy the `ch31` folder of the CD-ROM onto your hard drive. Double-click the `hangman.html` file located inside of the copied folder to play the game in a Web browser and become acquainted with our project. Now, open the `hangman.flp` file in the Project panel of Flash Professional 8. The functionality of the game is broken down into three classes: `GameModel`, `GameView`, and `GameController`. You learn about the purpose of each class file as you proceed with this chapter.

The Game Plan: Four Phases of Game Design

Game development includes the four phases we introduced earlier. The following sections discuss those phases in detail.

Note Many thanks to Jonathan Brzyski for contributing his illustrations to the Flash movie used in this chapter. You can learn more about Jonathan at `www.humanface.com/brzyski`. This edition of the **Macromedia Flash Bible** uses a modified version of the original `hangman.fla` file created by Veronique Brossier, discussed in the **Macromedia Flash MX Bible** (Wiley, 2002). We've updated this version to use an object-oriented programming model with ActionScript 2.0.

Game design

Designing a game is creating a fantasy world, a story, and characters with defined roles and goals. It establishes a structure with a clearly defined set of rules and a scoring system. In a single-player computer game, such as the one we created for this chapter, the computer acts both as the opponent and the referee.

This traditional Hangman game presents the user with a number of empty slots corresponding to the letters of a word. The player must guess the word, entering one letter at a time. When a player guesses correctly, the letter appears in the appropriate slot. A wrong guess and the hangman is revealed, one body part at a time. It is clearly understood that the hangman is a representation of the state of the user in the game. Being hanged represents defeat, but no harm is done. If the user guesses the word before the body is complete, he or she wins the round; otherwise, the man is hanged, and the user has lost the round.

Interaction design

Interaction design is creating the visual representation of the mechanisms of a game: It determines how to play the game and communicates the rules to the user.

The interaction of our game is very simple, and the design should be just as simple. To keep the interface to a minimum, the alphabet both represents the choices and displays the user's selection. The character's physical state is a character representation of the user as well as an indication of the score within one round.

For the Hangman interface, you need the following:

✦ Text fields to display the empty slots for the letters of the word to guess.

✦ A listing of the alphabet that indicates letters already selected as well as ones that remain. This listing is also the device by which the user can select a letter.

✦ A field for feedback from the computer referee.

✦ An area to display the score.

✦ The hangman character.

Visual and sound design

The visual design is essential because it is the first and longest-lasting impression. It communicates the mood of the game. Ours is fun, colorful, and somewhat humorous.

This particular game is fairly limited, with not much of a narrative. Nonetheless, the character drawing and animation should keep the user entertained: The hangman is now an alien character going back to the mother ship. Each round was designed with a different set of colors to give some visual diversity. The alien choice is meant to be humorous, both as a homage to the old computer games that used such characters and as a spoof of the multitude of computer demonstrations and illustrations using aliens.

The alien character and the background, including the selection of color schemes, were created by Jonathan Brzyski, a talented artist with a sense of humor (see Figure 31-1).

Of course, good sound effects are an important complement to the visual. They translate a mood and are helpful to indicate a win or a loss. They also are crucial in supporting and reinforcing animation.

Figure 31-1: Our version of the hangman is a tribute to aliens and old computer games.

Programming

Programming a game is the task of asking a series of questions and making decisions, including asking new questions based on the answers, in a language and syntax that the computer can understand. Writing short and task-specific functions is helpful to break down the logic of the game into discrete elements.

The programmer must deconstruct the game in terms of a dialogue between the computer and the player. It must address every detail, no matter how obvious it seems. By thinking of the flow of events ahead of time, you will be able to write code that can handle several aspects of a problem at different times of your game cycle.

Finally, with every new update, Flash provides new functions to simplify our scripting task. Becoming acquainted with them streamlines this process and makes your code easier to write and more elegant.

In this updated version of the game in this book, we've rebuilt the entire code base for the Hangman game. The three class files associated with the project, GameModel.as, GameView.as, and GameController.as, use a loose interpretation of the Model-View-Controller (MVC) design pattern. There are whole books dedicated to the topic of design patterns in computer programming, and it's beyond the scope of our chapter coverage to describe this pattern in intricate detail.

For starters, though, let's define a design pattern. A design pattern, when discussed with respect to computer programming, is simply a standard solution to a common programming problem. Because ActionScript 2.0 is object-oriented, the Flash developer community has implemented several design patterns from other computer languages to their ActionScript coding practices. Many of our examples in this book simply use a collection of function calls to build interactivity into the Flash movie's user interface. However, as you start to build more complex Flash movies, you will find that you have to designate roles for each piece of your code — if you just add one function after another on frame 1 of your Main Timeline, pretty soon, you'll have 600 lines of code with little or no organizing principle. So, a design pattern can help you organize your code because the pattern provides a framework for your code. Of course, you still have to write your own code, but the pattern establishes rules for how operations within the code can be conducted.

Let's break down the design pattern used by this version of the Hangman game. The overarching design pattern is called the Observer pattern. The Observer pattern's "rule" is fairly simple: An object in your code can facilitate changes to other objects. In ActionScript, you've likely practiced this concept a few times when you've used the User Interface components in previous examples shown in this book. For example, you can have a Button component's "click" event observed by several other components within the movie. With respect to the Hangman game, the Observer pattern enables a core object (called the *model*) to broadcast changes in the game's state to other objects, such as a MovieClip instance responsible for displaying the current challenge word and the MovieClip instance responsible for displaying which letter(s) have been selected by the user. The MVC design pattern used by the game consists of three discrete pieces:

✦ **Model:** The model for the Hangman game is a class named GameModel. This model has the following responsibilities:

- Maintain a list of chosen words used within the game.

- Track the current displayed state of the game, from loading the challenge words from a .txt file to the active/inactive states of the hangman alien pieces.

- Check letters selected by the user for matches to the current challenge word.

✦ **View:** The view for the Hangman game is defined with a class named GameView. GameView is also a Movie Clip symbol in the hangman.fla document's library. The view contains the necessary graphical elements to display the current game state to the user. For this game, the view consists of the hangman body parts, the artwork behind the hangman, the text fields to display the state of the challenge word, and the text to display the number of wins and losses during the current game. Some of these items are created at author-time and placed on the GameView symbol timeline, such as the background artwork and the hangman artwork. The text fields, however, are all generated in ActionScript.

✦ **Controller:** The controller for the game is defined with a class named GameController, and, like the view, has its own Movie Clip symbol associated with it (of the same name) in the Flash document's library. The controller is responsible for communicating changes to the game state back to the model. In this game, the controller is fairly simple: a collection of buttons displaying the letters of the alphabet. When the user clicks a letter button, the model is informed of the new letter selection and processes that input accordingly.

You learn more about each of these classes as we deconstruct the Hangman game in the rest of the chapter.

Building the Project

This section discusses the creation of the art and assets for the interface and then talks about assembling the game's mechanics.

In the tradition of character animation, the alien puppet is constructed of independent Movie Clips for each body part for maximum flexibility. (Figure 31-2 shows the timeline of the headClip symbol in the View Assets ➪ hangMan ➪ hangMan elements folder of the document's Library panel.) Each Movie Clip in the hangMan elements folder is made of nine frames used for the nine rounds of the game. Each frame displays the same Movie Clip symbol with different advanced color effects. You can view the color settings by selecting the Movie Clip symbol, opening the Property inspector, and clicking the Settings button to the right of the Color menu. Note that by using the color effects, we can use the same symbols over and over, keep our file small, and still develop a very large visual vocabulary.

When the game is a loss and the alien is complete, an animation is triggered. This animation uses the beamClip symbol and the BlurFader component. Both of these symbols are attached dynamically in ActionScript, which you'll see later in this chapter.

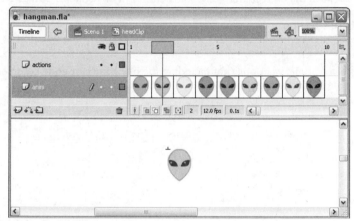

Figure 31-2: The headClip symbol uses the head symbol and displays it with different color schemes. This timeline is shown with the Preview in Context option enabled in the Timeline window.

Scripting the Game

The Hangman game consists of a series of rounds, corresponding to the number of available words to guess. In each round, the computer randomly chooses a word and generates slots as placeholders for the letters. The user attempts to guess the word one letter at a time. For each right guess, the letter appears. For each wrong guess, a piece of the alien character appears. After six wrong guesses, the alien character is completed, does a little animation for us, and the round is over. The score for each round appears on the screen.

The three primary states to the game are the setup, user input, and interpretation of the user input. Most of the code for this aspect of the game is located in the class files located in the ch31 folder of this book's CD-ROM.

The game has an additional feature: The username and his or her score are saved on the local machine, and the data is available the next time the user plays the game. Most of the code for this feature is located in the GameModel class. However, we cover this feature last.

Tip   The SharedObject class enables you to save data locally, similarly to the way a cookie saves data in a Web browser. This feature is only available for Flash Player 6 and higher movies.

Initializing the Game

Before examining the code structure used by the game, you learn about a few of the variables that are vital to structure of the game.

Main Timeline overview

Open the `hangman.fla` file in the `ch31` folder you copied earlier in this chapter. Amazingly, the major elements of this game fit into four layers on the Main Timeline. We'll talk about each of these layers in this section.

actions

The actions layer has eight primary actions (not including the blank lines or code comments, which are excluded in the following code):

```
var cgv:GameView = GameView(attachMovie("GameView", "cgv", 1, {_x: -7, ⤵
    _y: -7}));
var cgc:GameController = GameController(attachMovie("GameController", ⤵
    "cgc", 2, {_x: 6, _y: 230}));

var gm:GameModel = new GameModel();
gm.url = "words.txt";

cgc.model = gm;
cgc.view = cgv;
cgv.model = gm;

stop();
```

The first two lines of code create an instance of the `GameView` and `GameController` clips, `cgv` and `cgc`, respectively. Note that you can cast the returned object of the `attachMovie()` method by using the `GameView()` and `GameController()` syntax around the method. Casting the object lets us tell the ActionScript compiler that the objects are indeed the data type we're assigning the variables. Once you type a variable, the ActionScript compiler can more thoroughly check your code for errors, letting you know if you're trying to set a nonexistent property or set a property to an invalid value. We'll discuss these instances a bit later in this chapter.

Tip   The `GameController` and `GameView` instances placed on the cgc and cgv layers of the Main Timeline are there as placeholders, to determine where each instance should be placed, in terms of X and Y position, for the `attachMovie()` actions. These layers are turned into Guide layers to prevent them from exporting in the published (or tested) .swf file.

The third line of code creates the model for the game. The model is the central "brain" of the game. The model keeps track of the game state, and determines if the user has correctly selected a letter contained in the challenge phrase. The model is not a `MovieClip` object like our `GameView` and `GameController` instances on the stage. An instance of the `GameModel` needs to be created at the beginning of the movie in ActionScript code. Once an instance is created, there's only one thing to do with the model: supply it with the URL (or path) to the data provider for the game.

Note When the new instance of `GameModel` is created, all of the actions in the `init()` function of the `GameModel` class are executed. The actions in the `init()` function set up all of the game's status messages displayed to the user during game play. These messages are stored in the `labels` property of the `GameModel` class.

In our game, the data provider is a simple text document named `words.txt`. If you open the `words.txt` file in a text editor, you can see that the structure is simple: Each TV show title is on its own line in the document.

The `url` property of the `GameModel` class is known as a getter/setter property, which enables you to process further actions when a new value is set to the property. Once a URL is supplied to the `GameModel`, a chain of events is automatically put into motion within the class:

1. The `loadWords()` function is invoked. This function creates a new `LoadVars` instance, and loads the text file into the model.

2. The `onWordsLoaded()` function is called when the text finishes loading, which converts each line into a separate element in the `wordList` array property of the `GameModel` class.

3. The `wordList` property of the `GameModel` class is an array containing the words (or more appropriately, challenge phrases) to guess. For our game, the user must guess the names of popular TV shows.

Note Some of the challenge phrases contain a space; if a challenge phrase comprises several words, each word is placed on a separate line in the `GameView` class as defined by the `displayWord()` function of that class. This additional feature makes the challenge phrase easier to guess as well as creates a more attractive layout.

4. After the `wordList` property is set, the `checkLocalData()` function within the `GameModel` class is invoked. Here, a `SharedObject` instance named `so`, which was created in the `init()` function of the `GameModel` class, is checked to see if the user previously played the game. If the user's name, win score, or loss score is found in the `SharedObject`'s `data` storage, the game's state (controlled by the `gameState` property) is set to `"showstats"`. The `gameState` getter/setter property then broadcasts a new event to any listener of the model. If the user is playing the game for the first time, the `gameState` property is set to `"init"` and the model broadcasts the change to any listener as well.

Going back out to the actions layer on the first frame of the Main Timeline, the remaining lines of code set up the `GameController` and `GameView` instances as listeners of the `GameModel` instance, `gm`:

```
cgc.model = gm;
cgc.view = cgv;
cgv.model = gm;
```

If you go inside of the `GameController` and `GameView` class files and search for the `model` getter/setter properties, you'll see that the classes register themselves as listeners for specific events from the `GameModel` class. For example, in the `GameController` class, the `model` setter property contains the following code:

```
public function set model(gm:GameModel):Void {
   _model = gm;
   gm.addEventListener("letterPicked", Delegate.create(this, onLetterPicked));
   gm.addEventListener("gameState", Delegate.create(this, onGameState));
}
```

Here, there are two events that the GameController class needs to listen for: "letterPicked" and "gameState". When the user picks a letter, the GameModel class broadcasts a "letterPicked" event. When the GameController class hears this event, the onLetterPicked() function within the GameController class is invoked.

The GameController class also has a view property, which designates which MovieClip instance is responsible for displaying the game state to the user. On frame 1 of the actions layer of the Main Timeline, you set the view property to the cgv instance (an instance of the GameView class). Finally, we also assign the GameModel instance, gm, to the GameView instance, cgv. If you open the GameView class file (GameView.as) and find the model setter property, you see which events the GameView class listens for:

```
public function set model(gm:GameModel):Void {
   _model = gm;
   gm.addEventListener("wordUpdate", Delegate.create(this, onWordUpdate));
   gm.addEventListener("hangManUpdate", Delegate.create(this, onHangManUpdate));
   gm.addEventListener("gameStatus", Delegate.create(this, onGameStatus));
   gm.addEventListener("hitStatus", Delegate.create(this, onHitStatus));
   gm.addEventListener("gameState", Delegate.create(this, onGameState));
   gm.addEventListener("scoreUpdate", Delegate.create(this, onScoreUpdate));
}
```

A Quick Overview of Events and the EventDispatcher Class

If you write your ActionScript 2.0 class files according to Macromedia's specifications, you should add Event metadata at the top of each class file. If you open the class files associated with this game, you find the events each class broadcasts at the top of the script, just below the import declarations. The syntax for declaring an event is:

```
Event[("eventName")]
```

where *eventName* is the String value used in the dispatchEvent() function calls you make in the class. In order to use the event listener framework, you need to include the following action in your class constructor or in a function that is called within the class:

```
mx.events.EventDispatcher.initialize(this);
```

When you add this code to your class, you should also add the following variable declarations to the class file. You can find these variables in most of the class files used for the game:

```
private var dispatchEvent:Function;
public var addEventListener:Function;
public var removeEventListener:Function;
```

You don't need to define anything other than the function names, because the EventDispatcher class automatically creates this methods for your class when you use the EventDispatcher.initialize() method within your class.

The GameModel class broadcasts several events that the GameView listens to. Each event is assigned to a unique handler within the GameView class using the Delegate class.

The shared font layer

This layer contains a Static text block that uses the labelFont symbol in the Library panel. This Font symbol imports the Futura font face from the shared_fonts.swf file also located in the ch31 folder. The shared_fonts.swf file must accompany the hangman.swf file on the Web server or other runtime location. The Futura font face is specified as "labelFont" in the TextFormat objects initialized in the createStyles() function of the GameView class. All of the TextField instances created by the GameView class use the shared Futura font.

The cgc instance

This instance is a MovieClip object, but it belongs to the GameController class. To see how the GameController.as class file is linked to the GameController symbol, open the Library panel (Ctrl+L or ⌘+L), right-click (or Ctrl+click on Mac) the GameController symbol, and choose Linkage in the contextual menu. In the Linkage Properties dialog box (shown in Figure 31-3), the GameController class name is specified in the AS 2.0 Class field.

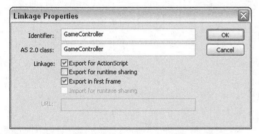

Figure 31-3: The Linkage Properties dialog box

> **Note** You don't need to include the .as file extension when you specify a class file. Also, if you nest a class file within another folder relative to the Flash document file (.fla), you can specify the folder path in dot syntax. For example, if you put the GameClass.as file in a folder named games, then your AS 2.0 Class value in the Linkage Properties dialog box would be games.GameController.

The cgv instance

This instance is created from the GameView symbol. The instance is named cgv, and is created in the frame 1 script we discussed earlier in this chapter. If you look at the linkage properties for the GameView symbol, you can see that the symbol is linked to the GameView.as class file.

Building the Interface

As you've seen in earlier chapters of this book, ActionScript can create a wide variety of runtime assets, such as text fields and sounds. We take advantage of this feature to create the rest of our assets.

Creating text fields

The createTextField() method creates a new empty text field as a child of a MovieClip object. Note that the createTextField() method takes several parameters: the instance name, depth, x position, y position, width, and height.

One of the core functions of the game is the onGameState() function, found in the GameView class. This function controls much of the layout for each state of the game, as shown in the following code:

```
private function onGameState(oEvent:Object):Void {
    trace("GameView.onGameState >");
    var sState:String = oEvent.target.gameState;
    switch(sState){
        case "init":
            cleanStage();
            onFirstPlay();
            break;
        case "showstats":
            cleanStage();
            onNextPlay();
            break;
        case "start":
            cleanStage();
            onFirstRound();
            break;
        case "newround":
            onNextRound();
            break;
        case "lost":
            onLost();
    }
}
```

Whenever the GameModel's gameState property changes, the onGameState() function is invoked. The first thing this function does is retrieve the current state of the game, expressed in the gameState property value of the GameModel (oEvent.target). For each value of the gameState property, the switch() statement directs the appropriate course of action. For example, when the game player runs the game for the very first time, the gameState property is equal to "init". As such, the onFirstPlay() function within the GameView class is invoked, and creates two TextField instances: one to create some descriptive text and another to accept the input from the user's keyboard. In the following code, the tName field displays the text "Please Enter Your Name:" (as retrieved from the labels property in the GameView class), and the tNameEntry field is displayed as an Input text field. The mcBtn instance is a button that broadcasts a "startClicked" event. Since the GameController instance, cgc (on the Main Timeline), is listening for this event, the cgc instance will control the model, telling it to advance to the next game state.

> **Note**
> All items created with game state changes are added to the displayedItems property of the GameView class, so that the cleanStage() function in the GameView class knows what items to remove between game states.

```
private function onFirstPlay():Void {
    trace("GameView.onFirstPlay >");
    tName = createTextField("tName", getNextHighestDepth(), 46, 232, 200, 20);
    with(tName){
        autoSize = "left";
        embedFonts = true;
        antiAliasType = "advanced";
        selectable = false;
    }
    tName.setNewTextFormat(tfOpening);
    tName.text = labels["name"];

    // add tName field to displayed items
    displayedItems.push(tName);

    tNameEntry = createTextField("tNameEntry", getNextHighestDepth(), 50, ⊃
        250, 150, 18);
    with (tNameEntry) {
        background = true;
        type = "input";
    }
    tNameEntry.setNewTextFormat(tfInput);
    tNameEntry.addListener(this);

    // add tNameEntry field to displayed items
    displayedItems.push(tNameEntry);

    mcBtn = attachMovie("buttonClip", "mcBtn", getNextHighestDepth(), ⊃
        {_x: tNameEntry._x + tNameEntry._width + 5, _y: tNameEntry._y - 2});
    mcBtn.onRelease = Delegate.create(this, onClick);

    // add mcBtn instance to displayed items
    displayedItems.push(mcBtn);

    // direct focus to the input field
    Selection.setFocus(tNameEntry);
}
```

A TextFormat object also can be created and applied to each of these text fields. In the createStyles() function of the GameView class, you'll see several TextFormat objects created, which are used by the various TextField instances created by other functions in the class.

Note The createStyles() function is invoked in the init() function of the GameView class, as soon as the cgv instance appears on the stage of the Flash movie at run time.

When the onFirstRound() function is invoked from the onGameState() function of the GameView class, three TextField instances are created, as shown in Figure 31-4.

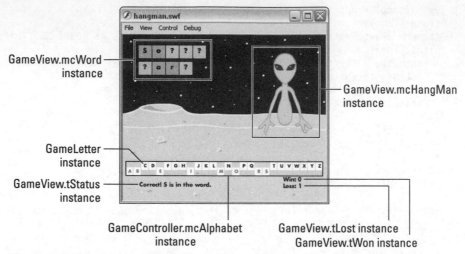

GameView.mcWord instance

GameView.mcHangMan instance

GameLetter instance

GameView.tStatus instance

GameController.mcAlphabet instance

GameView.tLost instance
GameView.tWon instance

Figure 31-4: The `tStatus` field displays status messages initiated from the `GameModel` class throughout the game. The `tLost` and the `tWon` instances display the score.

Creating the alphabet

Movie Clips can be created dynamically using the `createEmptyMovieClip()` method. This method takes two parameters: an instance name and a depth. Furthermore, with ActionScript's event framework, Movie Clips can be used as buttons as you learned in earlier chapters.

We use the alphabet as both visual feedback of the user selection and an input device for the user to make a selection. To take care of both aspects, we are going to create dynamic Movie Clips and then create text fields as their children.

Because the functionality of each letter button in the alphabet controller is identical, we created a dedicated ActionScript 2.0 class named GameLetter (as defined in the GameLetter.as file). This class is linked to the GameLetter symbol in the document's Library panel. This symbol is attached in the `createAlphabet()` function of the GameController class, shown in the following code:

```
private function createAlphabet():Void {
   mcAlphabet = this.createEmptyMovieClip("mcAlphabet", 1);
   var nXPos:Number = 0;
   for (var i:Number = 65; i <= 90; i++) {
      var sLetter:String = String.fromCharCode(i);
      var cgl:GameLetter = GameLetter(mcAlphabet.attachMovie("GameLetter", ⤸
         "cgl_" + sLetter, mcAlphabet.getNextHighestDepth(), {_x: nXPos, ⤸
         letter: sLetter}));
      cgl.addEventListener("click", Delegate.create(this, onLetterClicked));
      nXPos += 14;
   }
}
```

The `for()` loop of this function cycles through the entire alphabet, creating a new instance of `GameLetter` for each letter. You can create ASCII characters using the `String.fromCharCode()` method, which uses the number corresponding to a letter and returns its corresponding string (A=65, B=66, and so forth). Each letter of the alphabet is displayed in the `GameLetter` instance, as shown in Figure 31-4. The `GameController` is registered as the event listener for the `"click"` event for each `GameLetter` instance created.

`GameLetter`'s sole purpose is to create a clickable `TextField` instance. When an instance of `GameLetter` is clicked by the user, its `"click"` event is broadcast to any listeners. The only listener for each `GameLetter` instance is the `GameController` class. When the `GameController` detects this event, the `onLetterClicked()` function is invoked:

```
private function onLetterClicked(oEvent:Object):Void {
    if (controlsEnabled) model.checkLetter(oEvent.target.letter);
}
```

If the game is not between rounds, the `controlsEnabled` property of the `GameController` is set to `true`, allowing the `checkLetter()` function of the `GameModel` class to be invoked. The letter property of the clicked `GameLetter` instance is retrieved, and passed to the `checkLetter()` function. This function determines whether or not the clicked letter occurs in any of the character positions of the current challenge phrase. If one or more occurrences is found, the `GameView` class resets the `displayedWord` property to a new value, which, in turn, fires a `wordUpdate` event to the `GameView` class. There the new `displayedWord` property value is retrieved and rebuilt in the `mcWord` instance.

Starting the Game

The functions that we cover next are built with the framework of the game in a circular fashion: All the functions are used within one game cycle and again within the next game cycle. This kind of flow is specific to games and you must keep it in mind when writing code. In particular, game states need to be reset properly at the beginning of a new cycle.

At the beginning of each round, some of our assets need to be edited and some variables initialized. The `newRound()` function, defined in the `GameModel` class, takes care of establishing initial settings for each round in the game:

```
public function newRound() {
    roundNumber++;
    hangManStates = [
                {id: "head", active: false},
                {id: "body",  active: false},
                {id: "leftArm", active: false},
                {id: "rightArm", active: false},
                {id: "leftLeg", active: false},
                {id: "rightLeg", active: false}
                ];
    var aAvail:Array = new Array();
    for(var i:Number = 0; i < wordList.length; i++){
        var oItem:Object = wordList[i];
        if(oItem.active) aAvail.push(i);
    }
    var nIdx:Number = Math.floor(Math.random() * aAvail.length);
```

```
        selectedIndex = aAvail[nIdx];
        wordList[selectedIndex].active = false;
        createChoices();
        createDisplayedWord();
        gameState = "newround";
        gameStatus = "beginPlay";
    }
```

`newRound()` also prepares the states of the hangman character. The `hangManStates` property is an array created to store the state of each body part. Since the model is simply tracking states of the game, the model doesn't need to know which `MovieClip` objects are actually representing those body parts—that job is the responsibility of the `GameView` class. If you look at the `hangManStates` getter/setter property of the `GameModel`, you can see that an event is dispatched every time new values are set:

```
public function set hangManStates(aStates:Array):Void {
    _states = aStates;
    dispatchEvent({type: "hangManUpdate", target: this});
}
```

Whenever the `"hangManUpdate"` event is dispatched from the `GameModel`, the `onHangManUpdate()` function is invoked within the `GameView` class:

```
private function onHangManUpdate(oEvent:Object):Void {
    trace("GameView.onHangManUpdate >");
    var m:GameModel = oEvent.target;
    var aStates:Array = m.hangManStates;
    var nCount:Number = aStates.length;
    for (var i = 0; i < nCount; i++) {
        var oState:Object = aStates[i];
        var mc:MovieClip = matchStateToClip(oState.id);
        mc._visible = oState.active;
        mc.gotoAndStop(m.roundNumber);
    }
}
```

Here, a `for()` loop cycles through the states stored within the `hangManStates` property of `GameModel`. The `matchStateToClip()` function within the `GameView` class matches the `id` value shown earlier in the `newRound()` function of the `GameModel` class to each `MovieClip` object responsible for displaying that body part. Each body part also jumps to the frame number corresponding to the `GameModel`'s `roundNumber` to display a new color scheme.

The `hangManStates` property is set in two places within the `GameModel` class: the `newRound()` function (as we've previously discussed) and the `lookForMatch()` function. This function sequentially sets the active flag within each object of the `hangManStates` array. Initially, at the start of each round, all of the hangman's body parts have their `active` property set to `false`. However, if the `lookForMatch()` function determines that a selected letter is not found within the challenge phrase, the `active` property of the "next in line" object within the `hangManStates` array is set to `true`. The `hangManStates` property is then reset to itself, forcing a `"hangManUpdate"` broadcast. As such, the `onHangManUpdate()` function within the `GameView` class is called again, setting the visibility of the "next in line" hangman body part to `true`.

Display the letters of the alphabet

The newRound() function of the GameModel also sets the gameState property to a value of "newround", which is broadcasted to any listener of this event. The GameController class listens for these changes, and invokes its positionAlphabet() function.

This function moves the vertical position of the GameLetter components displaying the clickable letters of the GameController class. This function also sets the text color of each GameLetter instance to black. (Whenever a GameLetter instance is clicked, the text color of the instance is set to gray in the onLetterPicked() function of the GameView class.)

```
private function positionAlphabet():Void {
    for (var i in mcAlphabet) {
        if(mcAlphabet[i] instanceof MovieClip){
            var cgl:GameLetter = mcAlphabet[i];
            cgl._y = 0;
            cgl.letterColor = 0x000000;
        }
    }
}
```

Choose a random word

The selection of words (or challenge phrases) is stored in an array called wordList, which is defined at the beginning of the game in the GameModel class. In the newRound() function, a challenge phrase is randomly picked from the wordList array:

```
var aAvail:Array = new Array();
for(var i:Number = 0; i < wordList.length; i++){
    var oItem:Object = wordList[i];
    if(oItem.active) aAvail.push(i);
}
var nIdx:Number = Math.floor(Math.random() * aAvail.length);
selectedIndex = aAvail[nIdx];
wordList[selectedIndex].active = false;
```

The aAvail array is used to store any challenge phrase that has yet to be played in the game. The for() loop cycles through each object stored in the wordList property, and checks its active property. If it hasn't been played (that is, its active value is true), then the object is added to the aAvail array. Once the available challenge phrases have been gathered, a random index number is selected for the aAvail array. This value is then used to set the selectedIndex property of the GameModel class. The selectedIndex property is used to determine which word is active during the round. In the last line of the previous code block, the active property for that word is set to false so that it can't be picked again in future rounds.

Note   In this version of the game, a word is randomly selected from a pool for each round. As such, the difficulty of each word (number of characters, number of words, and so on) is not ranked. You can modify the game to create a series of word arrays, each one varying in level of difficulty. As the player progresses to the next round, a word from another array can be chosen.

Create the letters of the displayed word

The createDisplayedWord() function, invoked from the newRound() function of the GameModel class we mentioned in the previous section, builds the current state of the displayed word to the game player.

At the beginning of the createDisplayedWord() function, we create a String variable named sWord to hold the individual letters of the displayed word (or challenge phrase). Because the newRound() function already set a new selectedIndex value, the selectedItem.label value will be set to the new challenge phrase. In this for() loop, the sWord variable is built into a series of question marks ("?") or empty spaces (" "). So, if the challenge phrase (that is, selectedItem.label) was set to "Lost," the sWord variable would equal "????". Or, if the challenge phrase was "The Comeback", the sWord variable would equal "??? ????????". After the sWord string has been generated, the displayedWord property of the GameModel is set to the value of sWord.

```
private function createDisplayedWord():Void {
   var sWord:String = "";
   var nCount:Number = selectedItem.label.length;
   for(var i:Number = 0; i < nCount; i++){
      sWord += (selectedItem.label.substr(i, 1) != " ") ? "?" : " ";
   }
   displayedWord = sWord;
}
```

Because the displayedWord property's setter function dispatches the event "wordUpdate", the GameView class's displayWord() function will be invoked, fetching the new displayedWord property from the GameModel class:

```
private function displayWord():Void {
   trace("GameView.displayWord>");
   if(mcWord instanceof MovieClip) mcWord.removeMovieClip();
   mcWord = createEmptyMovieClip("mcWord", getNextHighestDepth());
   with(mcWord){
      _x = 35;
      _y = 25;
   }
   var sWord:String = model.displayedWord;
   var nX:Number = 0;
   var nY:Number = 0;
   for (var i:Number = 0; i < sWord.length; i++) {
      var sChr:String = sWord.substr(i, 1);
      if (sWord.substr(i, 1) == " ") {
         nX = 0;
         nY += 30;
         continue;
      }
      var t:TextField = mcWord.createTextField("t_" + i, ⤶
         mcWord.getNextHighestDepth(), nX, nY, 25, 25);
      with (t) {
         border = true;
         embedFonts = true;
         background = true;
         antiAntiAliasType = "advanced";
```

```
            gridFitType = "subpixel";
            backgroundColor = (sChr == "?") ? 0x99CCFF : 0x9999FF;
            text = sChr;
        }
        t.setTextFormat(tfCentered);
        nX += 25;
    }
}
```

The displayWord() function completes one primary task: to generate a series of TextField instances displaying each of the characters in the displayedWord value of the GameModel class. An empty MovieClip object named mcWord is created, and a for() loop cycles over each character of the displayedWord value (represented as the local variable, sWord). In each for() loop cycle, a TextField instance is created to display an individual character. If an empty space (" ") is found in the sWord variable, then the Y position of the subsequent TextField instance is shifted down 30 pixels. This procedure places each word in a multi-word challenge phrase on its own line. You can see this effect in Figure 31-4, where the second line of the mcWord instance is below the first line.

Cross-Reference

The TextField instances of this function use the new Flash Player 8 FlashType rendering engine. Because the tfCentered instance (a TextFormat instance) uses center alignment, the gridFitType property of the TextField instance is set to "subpixel", to render the text more sharply. For more information about FlashType, read Chapter 30, "Applying HTML and Text Field Formatting."

The User Input

The user enters his or her selection by clicking one of the GameLetter instances in the GameController class, represented in the Flash movie as an instance named cgc on the Main Timeline. When a GameLetter instance is clicked, the onLetterClicked() function of the GameController class is invoked. This function, as we discussed earlier in this chapter, submits the letter property of the clicked GameLetter instance to the GameModel's checkLetter() function.

Interpreting the User Input

This process is the bigger part of our project. A series of questions are asked, and their answers determine the next step in the process. You can find the checkLetter() function in the GameModel.as file:

```
public function checkLetter(sLtr:String) {
    trace("GameModel.checkLetter >" + sLtr );
    if (isLeft(sLtr)) {
        lookForMatch(sLtr);
    } else {
        gameStatus = "alreadyPicked";
    }
}
```

The isLeft() function looks to see if the selected letter was already chosen, and the lookForMatch() function checks the letter against the word to guess.

Was the letter selected before?

Using a for() loop, the isLeft() function compares the aLettersLeft array to the chosen letter (sChr), one element at a time. If the letter is contained in the array, the letter is deleted from the array, the selectedLetter property is set to the chosen letter, and the function returns true.

```
private function isLeft(sChr:String):Boolean {
    for (var i:Number = 0; i < aLettersLeft.length; i++) {
        if (aLettersLeft[i].toLowerCase() == sChr.toLowerCase()) {
            aLettersLeft.splice(i, 1);
            selectedLetter = sChr;
            return true;
        }
    }
    return false;
}
```

Note   In ActionScript 2.0 code, you can specify the data type of the returned value from the function. The data type is declared after the parentheses of the arguments, separated by a colon (:). In the isLeft() function, the data type of the return value is Boolean.

Once the selectedLetter property is set, the "letterPicked" event is broadcasted from the GameModel to any listeners:

```
public function set selectedLetter(sChr:String):Void {
    _letter = sChr;
    dispatchEvent({type: "letterPicked", target: this});
}
```

In our code framework, the GameController class is listening for this event, and invokes the onLetterPicked() function, which sets the Y position of the appropriate GameLetter instance 10 pixels below the other GameLetter instances, and changes the color of the text within the GameLetter instance:

```
private function onLetterPicked(oEvent:Object):Void {
    var sLtr:String = oEvent.target.selectedLetter;
    var cgl:GameLetter = mcAlphabet["cgl_" + sLtr];
    cgl._y = 10;
    cgl.letterColor = 0x666666;
}
```

Is the letter part of the word?

The lookForMatch() function of the GameModel class compares the selected letter to the value of the selectedItem.label property, one character at a time, and determines the course of action from the result:

```
private function lookForMatch(sChr:String):Void {
    trace("GameModel.lookForMatch > " + sChr );
    var sWord:String = selectedItem.label;
    var sDisplay:String = "";
    var bMatch:Boolean = false;
```

```
        for (var i:Number = 0; i < sWord.length; i++) {
            if (sWord.substr(i, 1).toLowerCase() == sChr.toLowerCase()) {
                sDisplay += sWord.substr(i, 1);
                bMatch = true;
            } else {
                sDisplay += displayedWord.substr(i, 1);
            }
        }
    displayedWord = sDisplay;
    if (bMatch) {
        trace("\tfound match");
        hitStatus = "hit";
        gameStatus =  "matchFound";
    } else {
        trace("\tdidn't find match...");
        for(var i:Number = 0; i < hangManStates.length; i++){
            var oItem:Object = hangManStates[i];
            if(!oItem.active){
                oItem.active = true;
                break;
            }
        }
        hangManStates = hangManStates;
        hitStatus = "miss";
        gameStatus = "matchMissed";
    }
    checkStatus();
}
```

The toLowerCase() method converts the character to lowercase so that the two compared elements would match if they are the same letter, regardless of their case.

If the letter is found in the selectedItem.label value (represented as the sWord variable), the corresponding letter is concatenated (or added) to the value of the sDisplay variable, which is set to an empty string just prior to the for() loop. If there isn't a match, the current letter in the displayed state of the word (displayedWord) is retrieved and added to the sDisplay variable. If a match is found, the variable bMatch is assigned the value of true.

Regardless of the matched letters, the displayedWord property is set to the value of the sDisplay variable. The GameView class will intercept the "wordUpdate" event broadcasted by the displayedWord getter property, and redraw the challenge phrase for the user.

The rest of the lookForMatch() function changes the values of the hitStatus and gameStatus properties of the GameModel class, depending on the value of bMatch. If a match was found, the hitStatus property is set to "hit". The GameView class is listening for changes to the hitStatus property, and plays a sound clip of applause (clap.mp3 in the movie's library). The tStatus field of the GameView class also displays a success message to the player.

However, if the choice doesn't match, a for() loop cycles through the objects stored within the hangManStates property. If the loop finds an object whose active property is false, the active property is set to true and the break action exits the loop. When the hangMan States property is reset to itself, a "hangManUpdate" event is broadcasted from the Game

Model. This event is received by the GameView class, which then updates the visibility of the hangman's body parts. The hitStatus property is also set to "miss". This value broadcasts the "hitStatus" event to the GameView class, which, in turn, plays the loss.mp3 sound in the movie's library.

After the proper states have been set in the model, the checkStatus() function of the GameModel is invoked to determine the next state of the game. This function is discussed in the next section.

Checking the Status of the Game

The last step in our process is to check the status of the game. More specifically, is the word complete, is the hangman completely drawn, and/or is the game complete? The checkStatus() function is defined in the GameModel class and asks all these questions. In the following sections, we discuss questions and conditions that exist in the game and the programming logic behind their answers and actions.

Is the word complete?

To check whether the word is complete, we check for any remaining ? characters in the letter text fields. We use a for() loop (with the value of the displayedWord.length as the condition to exit the loop). Note how the Boolean variable bAllMatched is assigned the value of true if the word is complete and of false if the word is not complete.

```
var bAllMatched:Boolean = true;
for (var i:Number = 0; i <= displayedWord.length; i++) {
   if (displayedWord.substr(i, 1) == "?") {
      bAllMatched = false;
      break;
   }
}
```

Is the hangman complete?

We also need to check the status of the hangman: If all of its parts are visible (that is, active), the round is lost. The bAlive variable determines whether or not the player is still "alive" during the current round:

```
var bAlive:Boolean = false;
for(var i:Number = 0; i < hangManStates.length; i++){
   var oItem:Object = hangManStates[i];
   if(!oItem.active){
      bAlive = true;
      break;
   }
}
```

If one of the hangManState objects has an active value of false, then the Hangman display still has remaining parts to display, and the player is still in the round. As such, the bAlive variable is set to true. Otherwise, the bAlive variables remains false.

Are there more words to guess?

After the hangManStates property has been checked, we need to do the same type of check for active words in the game. In others, is it the end of a round, or the end of the game? Has the player played the game long enough to exhaust all of the challenge phrases?

```
var bWordsLeft:Boolean = false;
for(var i:Number = 0; i < wordList.length; i++){
   var oItem:Object = wordList[i];
   if(oItem.active){
      bWordsLeft = true;
      break;
   }
}
```

How do you end the round?

If all of the characters have been successfully matched by the player, the gameStatus property is set to "wonRound". All gameStatus properties are String values that are looked up in another GameModel property named labels. Therefore, if the gameStatus property is set to "wonRound", then that index value is looked up in the labels property, and returns the value "You won this round!." Whenever the gameStatus property is updated, the GameView class (as a listener) sets the tStatus field to that value, displaying the text to the player.

Note All status messages are declared in the init() handler of the GameModel class. Also, the labels property is actually an *associative* array, which enables you to use a String value as the key to each element in the array. So, instead of using labels[0] to look up a value in the array, you pass a String value as the key, such as labels["wonRound"].

As we continue to break down the GameModel class's checkStatus() function, you can see that gameStatus is set to "wonRound" if bAllMatched is set to true:

```
var bReset:Boolean = false;
if (bAllMatched) {
   gameStatus =  "wonRound";
   win++;
   bReset = true;
   gameState = "win";
} else if (!bAlive) {
   gameStatus = "lostRound";
   loss++;
   bReset = true;
   gameState = "lost";
   displayedWord = selectedItem.label;
}
```

The win property of the GameModel class is also incremented if the player successfully matched all of the characters in the challenge phrase, and the bReset value is set to true. When the win property is updated, the tWon instance in the GameView class updates the current win score.

Note If bReset remains false, then the GameModel knows that there are remaining words — thus game rounds — to play.

When the gameState property is set to "win", the GameView and GameController classes do not respond with any particular action—you could further enhance this game by having the hangman character animate when the player wins the round (that is, provide a bigger pay-off to the player for winning the round). If bAllMatched and bAlive are false, the player has lost the current round. The gameStatus property is set to "lostRound", the loss value is incremented, bReset is set to true, and the gameState property is set to "lost". The "lost" value tells the GameView class to run the onLost() function, which we describe in the next section.

Removing the hangman

The onLost() function of the GameView class is executed when the gameState property change is broadcasted from the GameModel class to the GameView class.

```
private function onLost():Void {
    var mc:MovieClip = attachMovie("beamClip", "mcBeam", ⤶
        getNextHighestDepth(), {_x:242, _y:0, targetClip: mcHangMan});
}
```

This function attaches the beamClip symbol from the library to the Stage, with an instance name mcBeam, above the alien hangman instance (mcHangMan). A variable on the mcBeam instance named targetClip is set equal to the mcHangMan instance. This variable is used by yet another attachMovie() method, found inside of the beamClip symbol.

In the Library panel, open the View Assets ⇨ beamClip symbol. On frame 7 of the actions layer on this symbol's timeline, you'll find the following code:

```
var fader:MovieClip = this._parent.attachMovie("BlurFader", "cfb", ⤶
    this._parent.getNextHighestDepth(), {dir: "out", duration: 0.5, ⤶
    target: this.targetClip});
```

Here, the BlurFader symbol, linked in the Library panel, is dynamically attached to the GameView instance (which is the parent timeline of the mcBeam instance added earlier). The BlurFader component, which we used in Chapter 20, "Making Your First Flash 8 Project," uses three parameters: dir, duration, and target (or _targetInstanceName). In this attachMovie() method, we pass these parameters and their values. The fader instance is then set up to make the alien hangman (mcHangMan, as set by the this.targetClip parameter) fade and blur out from the stage.

Reset the game or just the round?

If all of the challenge phrases have been played (that is, bWordsLeft is false) and it's the end of the current round, the game is over.

```
if (!bWordsLeft && bReset) {
    gameStatus = "gameOver";
    gameState = "gameover";
} else if (bReset) {
    gameState = "roundover";
}
```

As such, the gameStatus property of the GameModel class is set to "gameOver", which leads to the display of the text, "Thanks for playing!," in the tStatus instance of the GameView class. The gameState is also set to "gameover". In this version of the game, nothing happens to the GameView or GameController classes when the game is over — the player simply sees the message and is prohibited from playing further rounds.

If there are still challenge phrases left to play and the round is over, the gameState property is set to "roundover", which is detected by the GameController class. There, the nextRound() function is invoked three seconds after the event is received from the GameModel. (You can see the setInterval() function used within the onGameState() function of the GameController class.) The nextRound() function calls the newRound() function on the GameModel:

```
private function nextRound():Void {
    clearInterval(nDelayID);
    model.newRound();
}
```

The nextRound() function is delayed by three seconds so that the previous gameStatus property change has time to display the current game status to the player in the tStatus field. If the nextRound() function was not delayed, the user would jump right into the next round, missing any updated display of text.

Added Feature: Storing User and Game Information

Being able to save information opens exciting dimensions to game development. For example, users particularly enjoy playing a multilevel game if they know the next time they visit the site, they can pick up where they left off because the computer remembers which level they last completed and their current score.

For our Hangman game, the following section demonstrates a very simple application of saving data onto the user's local hard drive and recalling it when the player returns to the game at a later time.

Flash Player 6 introduced a new feature, the SharedObject class, which enables you to save data locally, similar to a Web browser cookie. The next time the user runs the game, it displays the saved information. The information can be saved in two ways: when the movie ends or as soon as the information is entered. For our game, the information is saved right away, in the init() function of the GameModel class. The SharedObject.getLocal() method creates a new object named so.

```
so = SharedObject.getLocal("hangMan");
```

To store data in a SharedObject instance, you access the data property of the instance, followed by a variable name. For example, to store a variable named firstName in a SharedObject instance named so, you could use the following code:

```
so.data.firstName = "Damian";
```

For the purposes of this game, we check that the data was saved for the username and the win and loss scores. If any of this information is unavailable, the GameModel class dispatches the event "init" when the gameState property is set to "init" in the checkLocalData() function of the GameModel class.

When the game is played for the very first time, the player enters his/her name. Every time after that, the name and score are remembered and displayed.

After the user enters his/her name and clicks the orange button (mcBtn instance of the GameView class) on the screen, the data is saved by calling the saveName() function of the GameModel class:

```
Public function saveName(sName:String):Void {
  so.data.user = name;
  so.flush();
}
```

Note   The flush() method of the SharedObject class forces the data to be written to the local data file.

The saveScore() function of the GameModel class is called from within the game at the end of each round and stores the win and loss scores.

```
private function saveScore():Void {
  so.data.winScore = win;
  so.data.lossScore = loss;
  so.flush();
}
```

And that ends our deconstruction of the Hangman game! We encourage you to modify the elements in the View Assets folder to suit your own particular tastes for the game's look and feel.

Web Resource   We'd like to know what you think about this chapter. Visit www.flashsupport.com/ feedback to send us your comments.

Summary

✦ Creating a game is much more than programming. It involves other talents, such as game design, interaction design, and visual and sound design.

✦ Scripting a game is asking a series of questions and responding to them appropriately, depending on the user input.

✦ Functions are essential to intelligent programming. Writing small, task-focused functions allows for greater flexibility, particularly for complex games.

✦ Movie Clips and text fields can be created dynamically. Additionally, text fields' properties can be manipulated via ActionScript. In addition to adding flexibility, it reduces the weight of your movie.

✦ The setInterval() action can be used as a timer to call a function over time without having the Playhead move between frames. Here, we are using it to create a delay between rounds.

✦ Using the SharedObject class is a great way to save data on the local drive. We are using it to store the user's name as well as the game's score.

Managing and Troubleshooting Flash Movies

Is there anything worse than sitting at your computer, scratching your head, utterly frustrated because something won't work as planned? Chances are it is something really minor. This chapter focuses on tools, methods, and techniques you can use to fix these sorts of problems.

Many problems can occur while you are creating your movie. ActionScript errors, movie structure and design components, and external technologies, such as XML and server-side processes, may cause problems. Debugging your Flash document can seem like an overwhelming task, but with the right tools, it's not as daunting. In this chapter, we'll review a few tools that can help you. At the end of the chapter you will find a good practices list, troubleshooting guidelines, and testing matrices that you can use to sort out common issues and problems that often occur when you are developing with Flash.

Customizing the Actions Panel

The Actions panel in Flash 8 (and the Script editor in Flash Professional 8) is the primary place for adding interactivity to your movies, which you do by writing your own ActionScript code.

Note Whenever you open or create an ActionScript file (.as) in Flash Professional 8, you are using the Script editor to type your code. You do not use the Actions panel whenever you edit an .as file in Flash Professional 8.

Code hints

If you have code hints enabled when you are typing ActionScript, a pop-up window appears containing relevant syntax, method, and event completion tips. This very useful tool is helpful when you are writing ActionScript because it reveals the suggested syntax of the function or method. Flash 8's code hints, however, work best when it knows what class of object you are addressing. For example, if you name your Movie Clip instance with an _mc suffix, the Actions panel knows that the object is a MovieClip object. When writing code, the most relevant action out of several suggestions is highlighted in the code hints pop-up menu, as shown in Figure 32-1.

Figure 32-1: The Code Hints menu

If you press the Enter key at this time, the method or function is completed for you. The cursor is then positioned at the end of the line and a tooltip pops up, providing the necessary parameters for the function or method you are typing. As you type your code, the tooltip makes the parameter you are writing bold. Refer to Figure 32-2 for an example of the Code Hints tooltip.

If you use ActionScript 2.0's strict typing for variable declarations, you can forego the use of suffixes for your instance names. Flash 8 can automatically show you the code hints for a class of objects if you declare the object's type. For example, if you type the following code into the Actions panel, Flash 8 knows that mcHolder is a MovieClip object:

```
var mcHolder:MovieClip = createEmptyMovieClip("mcHolder", 1);
```

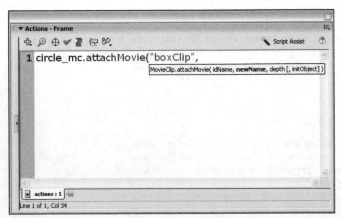

Figure 32-2: The Code Hints tooltip indicates the correct parameters for the attachMovie() method.

Tip

If you're following along and typing this code into the Actions panel, notice that the Code Hints menu appears after you type the colon (:) following the `mcHolder` term. This hint menu displays most of the class names available in ActionScript.

Then, if you refer to `mcHolder` later in your code (as shown in Figure 32-3), the code hints for the `MovieClip` class appear.

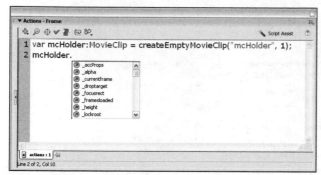

Figure 32-3: Code hints work for ActionScript 2.0 declared objects as well.

Code hints remove a lot of the guesswork from writing ActionScript. Using this feature is often faster than traversing the massive list of nodes in the Actions toolbox. There are a few settings you can modify to customize the way code hints work and act.

We'll walk you through the options to customize code hints:

1. Choose Edit ➪ Preferences (Windows) or Flash ➪ Preferences (Mac OS X).

2. Select the ActionScript category. We will focus on the Editing options section.

 Tip

You can also access this tab in the Preferences dialog box by selecting Preferences from the Actions panel options menu.

3. The Automatic indentation check box should already be selected. When you type code into the Script pane, this option controls how your code indents. Adjust the Tab size value to increase or decrease the spacing of the indentation.

4. Make sure the Code hints check box is selected in order to enable them. We recommend keeping the Delay slider at a value of 0 seconds, which makes the code hints appear automatically as you type. Refer to Figure 32-4 to see how the ActionScript Editor tab should appear.

If you prefer not to have Code Hints on all the time, you can invoke a code hint whenever needed. While typing your code in the Script pane, do one of the following:

✦ Click the Show Code Hint button in the Action panel's toolbar.

✦ Select Show Code Hint from the Actions panel options menu.

✦ Press Ctrl+spacebar (Windows) or Control+spacebar (Mac).

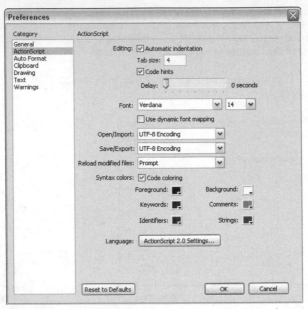

Figure 32-4: The default settings for the Actions panel

Syntax coloring

A feature that was added in the original release of Flash MX was the capability to choose how your ActionScript is colored. Flash 8 has this feature as well. This is known as *syntax coloring*, and it helps to visually "divide" your ActionScript. There are many elements to ActionScript such as variables, functions, constants, and statements. Using syntax coloring makes it much easier to read ActionScript. Set up your Syntax color settings so that they are easy to read, but also follow common "standards" in syntax highlighting.

1. Create a new Flash document by choosing File ➪ New.

2. Select the first frame of Layer 1 and open the Actions panel by choosing Window ➪ Actions (F9 or Option+F9 on Mac).

3. Enter the code shown in Listing 32-1 into the Actions panel. This code can be used for testing and modifying syntax coloring because it uses most of the different elements of ActionScript.

Listing 32-1: **Sample Code to Aid Syntax Color Settings**

```
#include "externalActions.as"

// This is a one line comment.

/*
```

```
This is a multiple line comment.
*/

var nIdx:Number = 30;
var sText:String = "Flash Video";

if (nIdx != 4) {
   var snd:Sound = new Sound(this.mcTarget);
   snd.loadSound("soundFile.mp3");
} else {
   mcCircle._alpha = this.mcTarget._alpha;
}
```

   4. Open the Preferences dialog box (to the ActionScript tab) by selecting Preferences
   from the Actions panel options menu. See Figure 32-5.

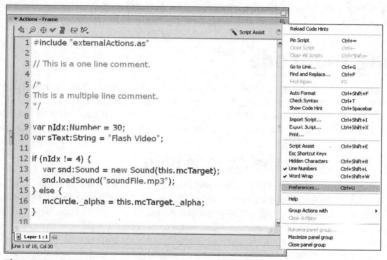

Figure 32-5: Accessing the Preferences from the Actions panel

   5. Refer to the Syntax colors section in the ActionScript category. You can turn syntax coloring on or off by selecting or clearing the check box next to Syntax colors, respectively.

   6. Select the Foreground color chip and choose black (#000000) from the pop-up swatch
   menu. The Foreground option sets the default color of the text in the Actions panel.
   (Unless you changed this setting earlier, the default value should already be black.)

   7. Select the Keywords color chip and choose blue (#0000FF) from the pop-up swatch
   menu. This blue color highlights all keywords such as `var`, `if`, and `else`.

   8. Select the Identifiers color chip and choose a medium green (#009900). This color is
   used to highlight terms that are methods and properties of classes, as well as class
   names themselves.

9. Set the Background color chip to white (#FFFFFF). You should use white because it is likely you will spend hours at a time typing ActionScript, and black text on a white background has high contrast and is more forgiving on your eyes than a colored background might be. (Unless you changed this setting earlier, the default value should already be white.)

10. Set the Comments color chip to a bright orange (#FF9900). Most programming applications use a gray for the comment color. We have chosen an orange as we believe that commenting code is a very important (and often neglected) part of authoring (and learning) code. Using a more visible color helps comments stand out more easily from the rest of the code.

11. Finally, select red (#FF0000) in the Strings color chip. Red is a common color for strings in many programming packages that have syntax coloring.

12. Click OK to close the Preferences dialog box. Make sure you have the Actions panel open and frame 1 of Layer 1 selected so that you can see the colors in use.

You can modify these colors if you prefer something different — the point of these steps is to illustrate where you can change the colors of your ActionScript code and visibly see those changes on the test code we provide.

Managing Your Code

In this section, we'll discuss methods and options for storing, writing, and positioning your code. In Flash 8, there is often more than one way to perform the same action — if you don't thoroughly think about why and where to place your code, you can run into trouble quickly. Using the following methods and suggestions will help you avoid common mistakes.

Using Replace in the Actions panel

Writing online applications in Flash often requires you to write a lot of code. While writing code, it is easy to name an object or variable without thoroughly thinking it through. Naming your objects and variables descriptively is a good idea. If you don't, you will find it hard to come back to your files and remember what each object and variable is intended for. Using Search and Replace enables you to easily rename poorly or improperly named variables or objects. It enables you to identify and change the incorrect string in one step, leaving Flash to replace all occurrences of the string.

However, there are traps when doing this. The following list contains points to remember:

✦ If you change the name of a variable, you must also change each reference to the variable across all timelines.

✦ Search and Replace replaces strings even if they make up a larger part of a code string. For example, the line `sou = new Sound();` will be modified to the line `sit = new Sitnd();` when you replace `ou` with `it`. So, if you use this feature, be mindful of the implications of searching for strings existing within other strings. A good method of avoiding this problem is to use a space whenever possible, remembering to replace the initial space with another in the replacement string. This step is necessary so your code formatting isn't modified.

Step through the following example to learn how to use Search and Replace to modify a block of code:

On the CD-ROM You will find `component_definition.fla` in the `ch32` folder on this book's CD-ROM. Copy this file to a location on your hard drive. We use this example code in a Search and Replace function.

1. Choose File ➪ Open and browse to the folder on your hard drive where you saved `component_definition.fla`. Highlight it and click OK.

2. Select frame 1 of the actions layer.

3. Open the Actions panel (F9, or Option+F9 on Mac).

4. Open the Replace dialog box by doing one of the following:

   • Choose Replace from the options menu of the Actions panel.

   • Click the Find/Replace icon on the toolbar of the Actions pane.

   • Press Ctrl+F (Windows) or ⌘+F (Macintosh).

5. Type **[Author name]** into the Find what field.

6. Type your name (for example, "John Smith") in the Replace with field. You will be replacing "[Author name]" with your name.

7. From here you can search for each instance of the string before choosing to replace it. To do this, click Find Next. However, if you want to simply replace all instances of "[Author name]," choose Replace All. For this example, choose Replace All.

Choosing Find Next is a good method for overcoming the problem when a string is found within a larger string. You can choose Find Next; when it finds the string on its own, you can replace it by choosing Replace. If it finds the search string within a larger string, simply choose Find Next to move forward.

Tip You can also use the global Find and Replace feature in Flash 8 to search your entire document for specific ActionScript terms. Choose Edit ➪ Find and Replace, and make sure the ActionScript check box is selected. Clicking one of the found results takes you directly to the script where the term was found.

How and where to place your code

There are several ways to position your code effectively, but first there are two considerations to make. On one hand, your code needs to be effective and work well; it must be positioned properly in order for the application to work successfully. On the other hand, you need to make the application easy to build and edit. It needs to be quick and simple in order to modify sections without being laborious and taking up valuable time better spent coding.

The project requirements also dictate how you place your code. We use the scenario that follows to explain some good coding concepts and how and where to place your code.

You are creating a coloring book aimed toward children. The requirements state the application must have a paintbrush tool with different brush styles and sizes, a line tool with different widths available and a stamp tool used to place user-defined images on the drawing canvas. Each of the tools has a corresponding button and a range of options used to modify the properties of the tool. The user clicks on the canvas to start drawing or stamping. Building this application would require a combination of different functions. Functions can be grouped into the following two main categories:

✦ **Multipurpose functions:** A multipurpose function can be used many times and by more than one source. A multipurpose function should be written in the most generic way possible, but still meet its criteria. The coloring book application would benefit from a multipurpose function used to modify the cursor. For example, when the user clicks the line tool, the function changeDrawingTool() might be called with the string "line" passed as the parameter. This function would then call changeCursor() to handle the cursor being changed and modifyOptions() to modify the options panel, which would reflect the current tool being used.

✦ **Chain functions:** The most effective functions are self-contained, perform one specific task, and can be used by many sources. However, there is an exception to the rule: chain functions. Chain functions group many other functions to perform several actions at once. Using chain functions enables you to write neater code and make it easier to understand.

An example of a chain function for the coloring book application would be startDrawing(). This might call the following functions: getColor(), which gets the current color ready to draw; followMouse(), which is used to trace the path of the mouse; and draw(), which actually draws the path to the canvas using values from followMouse().

A major benefit of using chain functions is you split up code into smaller chunks, which can then be easily accessed by other methods. For example, the startDrawing() function could have all of the code from the getColor(), followMouse(), and draw() functions within it. However, it would make the getColor() function inaccessible. This function could be used for more than one purpose. For example, if you passed red, green, and blue values to the function, it could *set* the color for the user, rather than just *retrieve* the value the user has set.

The Hangman game discussed in Chapter 31, "Creating a Game in Flash," uses many functions chained together within an organized event model.

After you start to write more sophisticated code, such as chain functions, you may want to explore the concepts of true object-oriented programming in ActionScript. In this edition of the *Flash Bible*, we've gone to great lengths to replace many code examples with object-oriented design patterns.

Centralized code

There are many places you can write code in Flash: in a frame, in and on Movie Clips, and on buttons. Your code can interact with any other object within the current movie structure including all levels and nested objects. This makes ActionScript an easy language to use for referencing and modifying objects from anywhere within a movie structure. It also allows for poor coding placement, however. It is very important to take note of where you place your code. "Spaghetti code" is a common term to describe poorly placed code residing on multiple timelines and interlinked in an unclear way. It is quite easy to run into the trap of creating such code.

Centralized code is the key to making an application easy to use and edit. Centralized code does not necessarily mean all of your code should be written on frame 1 of the Main Timeline. Creating centralized code means making observations about what the code is being used for, where it applies, how often it will be used, and how many objects will use the code.

Creating centralized code is different for each project. Here is a list of key concepts to follow when centralizing your code:

✦ **Reusable code:** Determine if a certain block of code is going to be reused by more than one object. If so, it is suitable for turning it into a function or a method, or possibly even a listener for objects that broadcast events.

✦ **Same code, multiple objects:** If a block of code is going to be used across a range of objects, such as buttons, you should place the code in a function and execute it from each button.

✦ **Function parameters:** Use functions to your advantage. If you have a block of code repeated across a number of objects referring to the objects' properties, you can centralize the code and make it much more manageable. Create a function in a central location and set up parameters to parse needed information about each object to the function. When you want to modify the block of code, you only need to do it once instead of on every object.

Naming conventions

A naming convention is a method and style used to name objects, variables, frames, symbol instances, and many other aspects of Flash development. You can have different naming conventions for each area, such as frames and variables. However, you should keep this practice to a minimum and use it only if necessary. There are common naming conventions used by most ActionScript and JavaScript code writers. Here is a list of rules that you may use to help you to create a naming convention:

✦ **Alternate capitalization:** The first word is entirely lowercase, all subsequent words start with a capital letter, and all spaces are removed. This method is also known as InterCaps or "camel hump" and is used by many programming languages. ActionScript's predefined functions also follow this rule. A good example of this is the method name `createEmptyMovieClip()` of the `MovieClip` object — notice that the E, M, and C of this keyword are capitalized. This rule can be applied to objects, variables, frame names, and symbol instance names.

Caution

Flash Player 7 and higher force case-sensitivity in ActionScript code, regardless of whether it's ActionScript 1.0 or 2.0. Be extremely diligent about adhering to your own naming conventions in code.

✦ **Descriptive:** Creating successful names for your ActionScript elements is a careful process. The most effective names are descriptive, making them easy to read in context and easy to understand the next time you read the code. Try to shorten names as much as possible while keeping them descriptive. For example, a function used to get the current local time could be named `getLocalTime` because it is descriptive and short.

✦ **Class capitalization:** Many coders don't use this rule, but it does help when you are creating large applications with dozens of variables, functions, and objects. You can capitalize every word of your class names rather than every subsequent word after the first. This makes it easy when you are coding to distinguish between variables and functions, or objects.

✦ **Acronyms:** Using an acronym when you are creating global variables, functions, or objects is a great idea. This ensures when you mix your ActionScript with someone else's you won't have conflicting names. Your acronym should be short and have something to do with the project you are creating. For example, if you are creating an online e-mail reading/sending/writing program named FlashMail, you might want to add FM to all variable names, functions, and objects, such as `FMComposeNewMessage`.

Commenting

A particular problem with writing ActionScript is returning to your code to modify it at a later date — most of us don't have computer-like memories. Commenting your ActionScript while writing it is an excellent idea that overcomes this problem by helping you remember how the code is constructed and/or works. It may take slightly longer to write your code with commenting, but it is worth the trouble. Follow these rules to effectively comment your code:

✦ **Blocks of code:** You don't need to comment every line in your code. Rather than doing this, comment each block or the different sections of your code. If the ActionScript is obvious, such as setting a `MovieClip` object's X position to 10, you wouldn't write `// Set the movie clip's position to 10`. A more effective comment would be `// Align the movie clip with other objects`.

✦ **Natural language and punctuation:** Your comments should contain all punctuation and grammar, as if you are writing a formal letter. It is quite easy to write something that makes sense to you but not to others, but using punctuation ensures that your comments are easy to understand to everyone who reads them.

✦ **Be descriptive:** It is important to be as descriptive as possible. This also helps you remember what your code is doing when you come back to it.

✦ **Multiline or single-line comments:** There are two methods to comment in ActionScript. You can use `/* comment in here */` or `// comment here`. The first method is used to create multiline comments; you can enter down to a new line and what you type will still be commented. The second method is used for single-line comments. A good practice is to reserve multiline style commenting for more important comments or if you want to catch the reader's attention.

Strong (or strict) typing

As you have seen earlier in this chapter and other chapters in the book, the ActionScript 2.0 language can use strong data type declarations. If you are starting a project from scratch in Flash 8 for Flash Player 6 or higher, we strongly recommend that you try to use ActionScript 2.0 and strong typing. This simply means that you declare variables with data types. If you try to perform an illegal operation with a specific data typed variable or object, Flash 8 will inform you in the Output panel — this is definite bonus for developers during the debugging process.

Add the code shown in Listing 32-2 to frame 1 of an otherwise empty Flash document. If you click the Check Syntax button in the toolbar of the Actions panel, you'll see the following error in the Output panel:

```
**Error** Scene=Scene 1, layer=Layer 1, frame=1:Line 1: Type mismatch in
assignment statement: found Number where String is required.
    var nPercent:String = (nLoaded/nTotal)*100;
```

> ### Listing 32-2: **A Sample Script Using Strong Data Typing**
>
> ```
> var nLoaded:Number = this.getBytesLoaded();
> var nTotal:Number = this.getBytesTotal();
> var nPercent:String = (nLoaded/nTotal)*100;
> ```

The error message tells you that the expression used to set the value of `nPercent` returns a `Number` data type, not a `String`. If you change the data type of `nPercent` to a `Number`, then the code will not return an error:

```
var nPercent:Number = (nLoaded/nTotal)*100;
```

Declaring data types with your variable declarations forces you to think clearly about how your code will be used.

Using the Output Panel

The Output panel is used to send messages and notifications while troubleshooting your movies. When you test a Flash movie file (.swf), Flash 8 checks your ActionScript for syntax errors and sends any error messages to the Output panel.

Note

Many multimedia authoring applications, such as Macromedia Director, won't let you leave the script window until the syntax is correct. With Flash, it's entirely possible to write incorrect syntax within a block of code and close the Actions panel with the error intact. Flash notifies you, though, when you publish or test the movie if it finds an error.

The Output panel itself is packed with functionality, enabling you to do the following:

- ✦ Print the contents of the panel.
- ✦ Copy the contents of the panel to the Clipboard.
- ✦ Save the contents of the panel to a text file.
- ✦ Search for a specific string within the contents of the panel.
- ✦ Clear the current contents of the panel.

These commands can be accessed via the options menu in the upper-right corner of the Output panel.

trace() action

The Output panel is not only used by Flash 8 to send syntax error messages to you, but you can also use it to view any data while testing a movie.

Using the `trace()` action can be a valuable tool when you debug your code. It is very simple to use and is sometimes better to use than the Debugger panel, which we discuss later in this chapter. Each time you call the `trace()` action, a new line is created and nothing is replaced. This makes it a great asset when you are debugging code such as `for()` loops. You can also save all data sent to the Output panel to a text file and review it later. A debugging session with the Debugger panel can't be saved.

Note You can use the Output panel and the Debugger panel together to more effectively analyze every aspect of your Flash movie during testing.

In this exercise, you create a simple frame loop and repeatedly send some information to the output window.

1. Open Flash and create a new file by choosing File ➪ New.

2. Rename Layer 1 to **actions**.

3. Select the first frame of the actions layer and open the Actions panel (F9). Add the following code to the Script pane:

```
var nCount:Number = 0;
```

This code declares a variable named nCount, with a Number data type. Its value is set to 0.

4. Select frame 2 of the actions layer and press the F7 key to insert an empty keyframe. Select frame 2, and open the Actions panel. Insert the following code:

```
trace(nCount++);
```

This code will send the value of nCount to the Output panel and then increment the value of nCount by one.

5. Select frame 3 of the actions layer and insert an empty keyframe (F7). With frame 3 selected, open the Actions panel (F9). Add the following code:

```
this.gotoAndPlay(2);
```

This action tells the Flash movie to constantly loop the second frame. As such, the trace() action repeatedly sends messages to the Output panel.

6. Test the movie to see the result of using the trace() action by choosing Control ➪ Test Movie (Ctrl+Enter or ⌘+Enter). You should see the value of count repeatedly sent to the Output panel, as shown in Figure 32-6. You can close both the Test Movie and Output windows.

Caution If you close the Output panel before closing the Test Movie window, it will continue to re-open because the trace() action will be executed the next time frame 2 is played.

Tip You can slow down the rate of trace() messages for this example by changing the movie's frame rate in the Modify ➪ Document dialog box to a lower value such as 1 fps.

On the CD-ROM You can find this example, trace_loop.fla, in the ch32 folder of this book's CD-ROM.

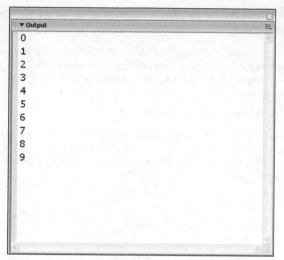

Figure 32-6: Your Output panel should look similar to this figure once you have completed Step 6.

The `trace()` action can also send expressions to the Output panel. In this example, you write an expression inside the `trace()` action and the result is sent to the Output panel.

1. Create a new file by choosing File ➪ New.

2. Rename Layer 1 to **actions**, and select the first frame. Open the Actions panel (F9). Type the following code into the Script pane of the Actions panel:

```
var foo:Number = 5;
var bar:Number = foo;

trace(bar == foo);
```

The first line of this code declares a variable `foo`, which is equal to 5. The second line declares a variable named `bar`, which is equal to `foo`. The expression inside the `trace()` action uses the equality operator to evaluate if `bar` is equal to `foo` and sends the result to the Output panel. The equality operator is used to compare two expressions. If the two expressions are equal, the result is `true`. If they aren't equal, the result is `false`.

4. Test the movie by choosing Control ➪ Test Movie. When you test the movie, the Output panel should open and display the Boolean value `true`. This is because the value of `bar` is equal to the value of `foo`.

5. Close the Test Movie window and the Output panel and add the following line of code to the end of the actions list:

```
trace(bar != foo);
```

This code uses the inequality operator instead of the equality operator in the expression. Again, the result is sent to the Output panel. The inequality operator is used to compare two expressions. If the two expressions aren't equal, the result is `true`. If the two expressions are equal, the result is `false`.

Simulating the trace() Action Online

You can only use the `trace()` action in Test Mode within Flash 8, or when you use the Debugger panel with a remote Flash movie. You might like to use something similar to the `trace()` action when testing in a browser. Follow these steps to make a Flash/JavaScript version of the `trace()` action using a JavaScript alert dialog box:

1. Open Flash and create a new file by choosing File ➪ New.

2. Select the first frame of Layer 1 and enter the following code using the Actions panel. This code simulates a `trace()` action. It uses a JavaScript alert dialog box to display any information you send to the alert function. When testing this in Flash MX, a browser window is opened to display messages.

```
function alert (alertString) {

    getURL("javascript:alert('" + alertString + "');");

}

alert("this is a test");
```

3. Anytime you want to send an alert to the browser, use `alert("any text or expression in here")`.

Also, make sure the `allowScriptAccess` parameter of the `OBJECT` tag and attribute of the `EMBED` tag in HTML is set to `"always"` when you test the Flash movie and HTML locally. Otherwise, the Flash movie is prohibited from communicating with JavaScript. For more information on this Flash Player attribute, refer to Chapter 21, "Publishing Flash Movies."

6. Test the movie again by choosing Control ➪ Test Movie. The Output panel will display `true` for the first `trace()` action, and `false` for the second `trace()` action.

On the CD-ROM   You can find the completed file, `trace_expression.fla`, in the `ch32` folder of this book's CD-ROM.

Although these are simple examples, the `trace()` action can be used to send the result of almost any equation that can be written on one line to the Output panel, assuming all variables referenced in the expression have been predefined.

List Objects and List Variables

The Output panel is used for troubleshooting, displaying syntax errors, and viewing `trace()` action values. It can also be used to view all objects or variables currently in your movie.

The List Object and List Variables commands, available in the Debug menu of the Test Movie environment, are very useful when debugging large applications in Flash 8.

✦ **List Objects:** This command sends the current level, frame number, symbol names, Button, Movie Clip, or text field instance names, target paths, text blocks, and vector shapes to the Output window. The List Objects command displays the information in a hierarchal format. If you have five objects within a Movie Clip instance named `foo`, each of these objects will be indented beneath the `foo` declaration.

✦ **List Variables:** This command sends all properties of any ActionScript objects, variables, and data currently in your Flash movie to the Output window. Functions are also listed when this command is executed.

Caution List Objects is frame dependent. If frame 1 of a movie has different objects than frame 5, executing List Objects on each of those frames sends different results to the Output panel.

Tip The data sent to the Output panel from the List Objects command is a little confusing. It reports a vector graphic as being a "shape:." However, a Graphic symbol is also reported as being a "Shape:." Hence, there is no way to distinguish whether it is a vector shape or a graphic.

Follow these steps to test the List Objects and List Variables commands:

1. Open Flash 8 and create a new file by choosing File ⇨ New.

2. Populate frame 1 with multiple objects, inserting a Movie Clip instance, a text field, a Button instance, a block of text (Static text), and a simple vector shape. You might try nesting some objects three or four Movie Clips deep to see the hierarchy of information within the Output window.

3. Test your movie by choosing Control ⇨ Test Movie.

4. Choose Debug ⇨ List Objects. The Output panel will appear, containing the list of all objects on the current frame. Take a look to see how it reports the objects.

Knowing the Flash Debugger panel

ActionScript has evolved as a language with each release of Macromedia Flash. Indeed, if you're only starting to use Flash and ActionScript, it can seem quite overwhelming. Because there's so much you do with ActionScript, Macromedia has included a Debugger panel (see Figure 32-7), which has been available since the release of Flash 5.

The Debugger panel enables you to find errors in your code while your movie is playing in the Flash Player. As well as debugging local movies in Test Mode, you can also debug remote Flash movies that reside on a server. The Debugger panel can be a valuable tool when you are testing your movie and solving problems.

To Activate the Debugger and test your movie, choose Control ⇨ Debug Movie. You must push the Continue button in the Debugger panel before your movie will start playing.

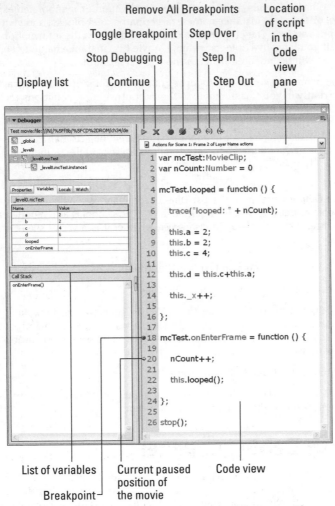

Figure 32-7: The Debugger panel, showing all buttons and element names

Displaying and modifying variables

While you are testing, you can use the Debugger panel to view or modify all variables in your movie. This is very useful because you will see the results of any change in a variable's value straightaway, as your movie is running.

Displaying a variable

Follow these simple steps to view variables in the Debugger that exists in your movie:

You can find `debugging_code.fla` in the `ch32` folder on this book's CD-ROM. Copy this file to a location on your hard drive. We will use it in the next few examples.

1. Choose File ➪ Open and browse to the folder on your hard drive where you have saved `debugging_code.fla`. Highlight it and select OK.

2. Enter Debug mode by choosing Control ➪ Debug Movie.

3. Select Continue (that is, the play button in the toolbar of the panel) to start the movie playing.

4. Select the Variables tab. This is where all of the variables are displayed.

5. Select the `_level0.mcTest` Movie Clip from the Display list to see the variables that exist in that timeline.

6. Select the `_level0` target to see the variables change in the Variables tab.

Because there is a breakpoint added to the actions on frame 2, you need to press the Continue button each time the breakpoint is encountered during playback. Breakpoints are discussed later in this chapter.

Modifying a variable

Follow these simple steps to modify variables in the Debugger panel that exist in your movie:

1. Open the `debugging_code.fla` document.

2. Enter Debug mode by choosing Control ➪ Debug Movie.

3. Select Continue to start the movie playing.

4. Select the `_level0` target from the Display list.

5. Select the Variables tab.

6. Double-click on the Value field for the `nCount` variable and enter **70** as its new value. When you click the Continue button, you will see how the value of the `nCount` variable increases to 70 and increments from there.

All objects, either user defined or predefined ActionScript objects, will appear in the variable list. However, you can only change the values of some properties and variables.

The Watch list

Using the Debugger panel to monitor the value of multiple variables can get quite confusing, especially if you need to compare variables that exist on different timelines. Employing the Watch list is an easy way to monitor the value of certain variables in a manageable way.

Once you have added a variable to the Watch list, you can view it regardless of which Movie Clip you have selected in the Movie Clip list.

Adding a variable to the Watch list

There are two options for adding a variable to the Watch list.

1. Open the `debugging_code.fla` document.

2. Start a debugging session by choosing Control ⇨ Debug Movie.

3. Select Continue to start the movie playing.

4. Select the `_level0` target from the Display list.

5. Select the Variables tab to show all variables from the `_level0` namespace.

6. Right-click (Windows) or Control-click (Mac) on the `nCount` variable and select Watch. A little blue dot appears indicating that it is in the Watch list.

7. Select the Watch tab to view the Watch list. You will see the `nCount` variable and its value change as you progress through the debugging session.

Alternatively, you can perform the following steps to add a watch to the Flash movie.

1. Repeat Steps 1 and 2 from the previous method.

2. Select the Watch tab.

3. From the Debugger panel's options menu, choose Add Watch. Alternatively, you can right-click (Windows) or Control+click (Mac) the empty area of the Watch tab and choose Add.

4. Double-click the new entry (`<undefined>`) in the Named column and type in the correct path and name of the variable you want to watch.

Caution   If you type in an incorrect path or variable name, the variable value will be undefined in the Watch list.

Removing a variable from the Watch list

There are three methods to remove a variable from the Watch list. The first method involves the following steps:

1. Navigate to the variable using the Display list and the Variables tab.

2. Right-click (Windows) or Control+click (Mac) the variable you wish to remove and deselect the Watch command. The little blue dot will be removed.

The second method involves these steps:

1. Select the Watch tab.

2. In the Watch list, right-click (Windows) or Control+click (Mac) on the desired variable and select Remove.

Alternatively, the third method involves these steps:

1. Select the Watch tab.

2. Highlight the variable you no longer need and select Remove Watch from the Debugger options menu.

Editing and displaying movie properties

The Properties tab of the Debugger panel displays the properties of all the Movie Clip instances, including the Main Timeline (_root, displayed as _level0) in your movie. Follow these steps to view and edit movie properties while debugging.

Perform these steps to view the properties of any Movie Clip timeline in the movie:

1. Open a file that you want to debug.

2. Enter Debug Mode by choosing Control ➪ Debug Movie. In the Debugger panel, click Continue.

3. Select a Movie Clip instance from the Display list. Choose something other than _global.

4. Select the Properties tab to view the properties of the selected Movie Clip instance. The properties that appear in a different color from the majority of the properties are read-only and cannot be changed.

 Tip

For processor intensive applications in Flash 8 that use the drawing API, try changing the _quality property of the _level0 timeline to "LOW" to see increased performance.

Perform these steps to edit a specific property of a timeline or object in the Debugger panel:

1. Follow Steps 1 through 3 of the previous exercise.

2. Double-click the Value field of the property you wish to alter and enter the new value.

 Note

If you enter an incorrect value, such as a string when a number is required, the Debugger panel ignores the change, reversing the value to its last valid state the next time you reselect that Movie Clip instance.

Assigning Breakpoints

Perhaps one of the most useful features of the Debugger panel is the option to set and use breakpoints. A breakpoint is a position in your ActionScript code that halts playback of a movie while you are in Debug mode.

Using breakpoints, the Debugger panel enables you to step through a block of ActionScript line by line. You can define when the Flash movie will halt and when it will proceed. You can choose to execute a function or to step through the function. Choosing to step through a function will halt your movie on every line of the function waiting for your action. This is very valuable and makes it easier to find (often simple) problems in your ActionScript.

 On the CD-ROM

You can find the debugging_code.fla file in the ch32 folder of this book's CD-ROM. Make a copy of this file to a location on your hard drive. This file is used in the next few sections.

Adding or removing breakpoints in the Actions panel

You can set, delete, or remove all breakpoints in the Actions panel while authoring a Flash document.

Follow these steps to apply a breakpoint to a specific line of ActionScript code:

1. Open the `debugging_code_nobreaks.fla` document.

2. Select frame 2 of the actions layer, and open the Actions panel (F9, or Option+F9 on Mac).

3. Place the cursor on line 18. The Debugger stops the movie at a line where a breakpoint exists, only executing the code before the breakpoint. Breakpoints should be positioned on lines where you think an error exists or just before the point where you think an error is occurring.

4. Do one of the following:

   • Click the gutter to the left of the line number.

   • Click the Debug Options button in the toolbar of the Actions panel (look for the stethoscope icon), and from its menu choose Set Breakpoint.

   • Right-click (Windows) or Control+click (Mac) the line of code and select Set Breakpoint. A red dot in the gutter indicates lines that have breakpoints, as shown in Figure 32-8.

Perform the following steps to delete a breakpoint from a line of code in the Actions panel:

1. Place the cursor on the line where a breakpoint exists.

2. Do one of the following:

   • Click the Debug Options button and choose Remove Breakpoint.

   • Right-click (Windows) or Control+click (Mac) and select Remove Breakpoint.

   • Simply click the red dot in the gutter area.

   The red dot will be removed.

Tip   To remove all breakpoints from the code, follow Steps 1 and 2 and select Remove All Breakpoints instead of Remove Breakpoint.

New Feature   If you edit ActionScript files (.as) in Flash Professional 8, you can now add breakpoints within the file.

Adding and removing breakpoints in the Debugger panel

Once you have started debugging your movie, you can add and remove breakpoints. You can remove a single breakpoint or remove all breakpoints.

Follow these steps to add a breakpoint in the Debugger panel:

1. Open a fresh copy of the `debugging_code.fla` document from this book's CD-ROM.

2. Select frame 2 of the actions layer.

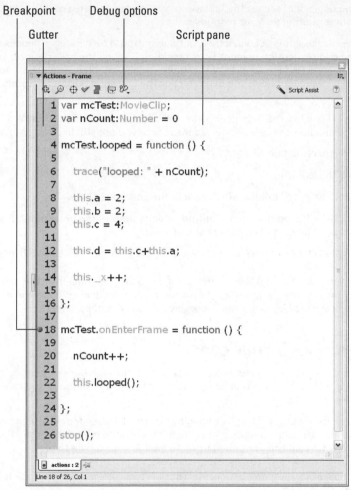

Figure 32-8: You can see the breakpoint icon residing in the gutter of the Actions panel.

3. Enter Debug mode by choosing Control ➪ Debug Movie.

4. *Before* you press the Continue button on the Debugger panel, choose the actions for frame 2 from the drop-down menu below the toolbar of the Debugger panel. You should see the ActionScript code from frame 2 of the actions layer displayed.

5. Place a cursor on line 12.

6. Do one of the following:

   - Click the gutter area to the left of the line number.

   - Click the Toggle Breakpoint button in the toolbar of the Debugger, which will add a breakpoint if none exists on that line. (It will remove a previously defined breakpoint if one exists.)

   - Right-click (Windows) or Control-click (Mac) and select Set Breakpoint.

When the debugger reaches the line where you placed the breakpoint, it halts playback of the movie, waiting for your response.

7. Once the breakpoint is set, click the Continue button. The debugger pauses the movie when the code execution reaches your breakpoint. When the breakpoint is reached, you can analyze various aspects of the movie in the Variables, Properties, and Watch tabs of the Debugger panel. You need to click the Continue button to resume playback of the movie.

To remove a breakpoint in the Debugger panel, follow these steps. This example continues from above. You should use the same file, so make sure you are still in Debug Movie mode.

1. Place the cursor on line 12.

2. Do one of the following:

   • Click the red dot of the breakpoint in the gutter area.

   • Click the Toggle Breakpoint button, which removes the breakpoint. If you push it a second time, the breakpoint will be re-set.

   • Right-click (Windows) or Control+click (Mac) and select Remove Breakpoint.

Caution

Changes you apply to breakpoints while using the Debugger panel in Debug Movie mode only exist for that debugging session. When you return to authoring mode, the breakpoints you added (or removed) during the debugging session will not be saved.

Stepping through your code

Using breakpoints and the Debugger panel, you can step through lines of your code while the movie is playing. This is a very powerful feature, enabling you to pinpoint the exact position of a problem in your code.

When you start a debugging session by choosing Control ⇨ Debug Movie, the movie is paused in the Flash Player so you can modify and set new breakpoints before you start the debugging session. You need to push the Continue button to enable your movie to play.

On the CD-ROM

Make a copy of the `debugging_breakpoints.fla` document from the `ch32` folder of this book's CD-ROM.

1. Open the `debugging_breakpoints.fla` document. We built the ActionScript in this movie to demonstrate the process of stepping through lines of code.

2. Debug the movie by choosing Control ⇨ Debug Movie.

3. As the movie is initially paused, click the Continue button to start debugging. Refer to Figure 32-7 to easily locate the Continue button.

4. When the Debugger panel reaches the first breakpoint at the line `mcTest.onEnterFrame = function ()`, it will stop and wait for you to choose an action. The little yellow arrow in the gutter indicates the current position of the movie.

   You can choose one of the following actions:

- **Step Out:** If you are debugging inside a user-defined function, Step Out will cause the debugger to execute everything within the function and continue playing, until it reaches the next breakpoint outside of the function. However, if there is a breakpoint below the line where you have selected Step Out within the function, the debugger will halt the movie and wait for your action.

Note If you click Step Out on a line that is not inside a function, it performs the same actions as if you had clicked Continue.

- **Step In:** If you position a breakpoint on a line where a function is called, such as line 22 in frame 2 on the actions layer of `debugging_code.fla`, the debugger will move to line 4 — the first line within the function you "stepped into." Click Step In to proceed to the next line in the function. Clicking Step In within a function will proceed and pause the movie to the next line, regardless of whether it has a breakpoint. Click Continue to move through the lines until another breakpoint is reached, skipping lines without one.

Note If you click Step In on a line that is outside of a function, it performs the same action as if you had clicked Continue.

- **Step Over:** Clicking Step Over on a breakpoint tells the Debugger to ignore the line of code where the breakpoint occurs and moves the player to the next line of your code. If you choose Step Over on a line where a function is called, it moves to the next line and calls the function in the process.

Note If you click Step Over on a line where a function is called and the function has a breakpoint inside of it, the Debugger will halt the movie at the breakpoint line.

- **Continue:** Choosing Continue will start the movie playing until the next breakpoint is reached.

- **Stop Debugging:** Selecting this option will stop the Debugger from processing the actions any further. However, your movie will still continue to play.

- **Toggle Breakpoint:** If you click this button, it will turn the breakpoint off because one already exists on that line. You will need to click either Continue or Step In to advance the movie. However, the Debugger will not halt the movie at this line again as the breakpoint has been removed. Pressing Toggle Breakpoint a second time will set a breakpoint.

Debugging a Flash Movie Remotely

You can debug a Flash movie file (.swf) using the stand-alone, ActiveX, or plug-in versions of the Debug version of Flash Player 8. Debugging your file remotely is very useful if you have a Flash movie that references server-side scripts on your production server that only run properly when your Flash movie is running on the same server.

 You can find the `debugging_code.fla` file in the `ch32` folder of this book's CD-ROM. Make a copy of this file on a location on your hard drive.

Note   You need a Web server to use this feature of the Debugger panel. If you have a Web server on your local machine, you can test your files there. Otherwise, you need to upload your files to a remote Web server.

Follow these steps to enable remote debugging and debug the example Flash movie file (.swf):

1. Open Flash and open the `debugging_code.fla` document.

2. Open the Publish Settings by choosing File ➪ Publish Settings.

3. Clear the HTML check box. You can test by directly referencing the Flash movie file (.swf) on your server — you don't necessarily need the HTML document to debug the movie.

4. Select the Flash tab of Publish Settings and select the Debugging Permitted check box. If you want your Flash movie to be protected from prying eyes, you should enter a password in the Password field. The password will not be hidden in the authoring document. Anyone who has access to the Flash document file (.fla) will be able to view the password.

5. Press the Publish button in the Publish Settings dialog box. This creates a Flash movie file (.swf) with debugging enabled. Flash also generates a Flash debug file (.swd). The Debug version of Flash Player uses this file when remotely debugging a movie. Both of these files should be uploaded to the same directory of your Web server.

Note   If you do not upload the .swd file, you can still debug remotely. However, you will not be able to step through the code, because breakpoints will be ignored.

6. Press OK to close the Publish Settings.

7. Open the Debugger panel by choosing Window ➪ Debugger.

8. Enable Remote Debugging in Flash 8 by selecting Enable Remote Debugging from the Debugger panel's options menu. You have now finished all the steps needed to remotely debug the Flash movie.

9. Upload the Flash movie file (.swf) and debug file (.swd) to your Web server.

10. Make sure Flash 8 is open. Without Flash 8 open, you will not be able to debug the movie.

11. In your preferred Web browser, open the remote Flash movie file (.swf). You must make sure the Debug release of Flash Player 8 is installed in the browser you choose. See the "Using the Debug Version of Flash Player 8" sidebar later in this chapter.

12. The Remote Debug dialog box will open as soon as the Flash movie loads into the browser (see Figure 32-9).

Figure 32-9: The Remote Debug dialog box as it appears from the browser running the debugged Flash movie

Caution If the Remote Debug dialog box doesn't open, it means that the Debug release of Flash Player 8 can't find the .swd file. You can still remotely debug your movie, but any breakpoints will be ignored. Right-click (Windows) or Control-click (Mac) any area of the Flash movie's stage and select Debugger from the player's contextual menu.

13. From the Remote Debug dialog box, select either of the following options:

- **Localhost:** Select this option if the Flash 8 authoring application is on the same machine that's running the remote Flash movie in the browser.

- **Other Machine:** Select this option if the Flash movie file (.swf) you are debugging and the Flash 8 application aren't on the same machine. In this case, you need to enter the IP address of the machine with the Flash 8 application.

Tip Don't lose sight of how powerful the "Other Machine" option is during debugging. If a movie is working correctly on your computer but not on an associate's machine, you can have your associate download and install the debug player. When your associate goes to the remote Flash movie in his or her browser, supply the tester with your machine's public IP address in the Other Machine field of the Remote Debug dialog box. Your machine must have Flash 8 running, and it must not be behind a firewall in order for the debugging session to work properly. Note that the tester does not need to have Flash 8.

14. Once the Flash movie file (.swf) and the Debugger have successfully connected, a password prompt will appear. Enter the password and select OK.

Note If you didn't enter a password when you published your Flash movie, leave the password field blank and click OK.

15. You will be automatically taken into Flash 8. You can start debugging just as if the movie was running in Debug Movie mode on your computer. The only difference is that you will need to switch back and forth between the Web browser and Flash 8 to see any visual changes in the Flash movie.

Testing across mediums

Macromedia has successfully deployed Flash Player technology over the years. You can now find the Flash Player on many platforms, including Windows, Macintosh, and Linux, but it also exists on devices such as the Pocket PC (PDA handhelds), mobile phones, and the Sony PlayStation.

Using the Debug Version of Flash Player 8

Two versions of Flash Player 8 ship with Flash 8: the Debug version and the release version. When you enter the Debug Mode of Flash 8 by choosing Control ⇨ Debug Movie, the debugging features of the Flash Player 8 are used.

In order to debug a remote .swf file, you need to use the debug version of Flash Player for your browser. You will find it in the following directory: `<Flash 8 program directory>\Players\ Debug`. Run the appropriate installer for your preferred browser.

In `<Flash 8 program directory>\Players\Release`, you will find the Release version of Flash Player 8. You can reinstall the original plug-in (without the debugging features) at any time.

Periodically, Macromedia may release updates to both the Debug and Release versions of the Flash Player. Check `www.macromedia.com/support/flash` for updates.

With the availability of the Flash Player on many platforms and devices, it is very important that you test your Flash movies across all possible mediums. Thoroughly testing your movie on multiple player versions is a crucial step in planning a successful application built with Flash 8. Doing this can save you much trouble further down the road if your application is more successful than you initially planned.

Testing matrix

Figure 32-10 shows an example of a testing matrix. Such matrices should be used before a launch of any commercial application. Testing across all of these different configurations can be a little time consuming but it ensures maximum compatibility of your application. There is little point to releasing a product that doesn't correctly work for your target audiences.

Regular testing of your product, both at the end of the development and especially during the development cycle, will ensure an easier transition from development to release.

	Win 95	Win 98	Win 2000	Win NT	Win ME	Win XP	Mac OS 9	Mac OS X
IE 6.0								
IE 5.5								
IE 5.0								
IE 4.0								
NS 6.0								
NS 4.7								
NS 4.5								
NS 4.0								
AOL 5								
AOL 4								

Figure 32-10: You could use this matrix for Flash movies that will be viewed and used within a browser. It covers a wide range of available and commercially used browsers.

Storing Code in External Files

Flash 8 is easily extensible, as there are various areas in which you can place code. This can be the cause of major problems — because there are many available options, you need to make sure the code is correctly placed so your movie is manageable and easy to use. In Flash 8, you have the option to store your code in an external .as file.

The #include command

Once you have an .as file to use in a project, it is easy to make the ActionScript within the file available to your movie. The #include command is used to load any code from an external file and put it in the Flash movie file (.swf) published or tested by Flash 8. If you edit the .as file included in your movie, the changes will not automatically become part of an already-published Flash movie file (.swf). The #include command is only executed at the time you publish or test the .swf file.

This simple example shows you how to include an external ActionScript file in a movie.

On the CD-ROM

You can find externalActions.as in the ch32 folder on this book's CD-ROM. Make a copy of this file to a folder on your hard drive. externalActions.as contains a trace() action that will appear in the Output panel once you have entered Test Mode.

1. Create a new Flash document by choosing File ⇨ New.

2. Save the Flash document to the same location on your hard drive where you copied the externalActions.as file.

3. Select the first frame of Layer 1 and open the Actions panel (F9). In the Script pane, type the following code:

```
#include "externalActions.as"
```

Caution

Do not include a semicolon after the #include directive, such as #include "externalActions.as";. Doing so results in a compiler error, preventing the file from being included in the Flash movie.

4. Test the movie by choosing Control ⇨ Test Movie. In the Output panel, the words "Traced from externalActions.as" should appear. This is the result of the trace() action in the externalActions.as file.

Now that you know how to use the #include directive, you can start to store larger amounts of code within .as files. One of the primary benefits of using .as files is that you can easily share the same ActionScript code from one Flash document to another.

Cross-Reference

Read Chapter 30, "Applying HTML and Text Field Formatting," to see more Flash documents that use the #include directive.

Caution

Don't confuse the #include directive with the import keyword in ActionScript 2.0 code. You can think of the #include directive as a copy and paste of the code from an ActionScript file (.as) into the current script shown in the Actions panel. The import keyword, however, simply loads an ActionScript 2.0 class into the ActionScript compiler so that it can check for errors within your code. For example, if you use the #include directive in several places throughout your Flash document's actions, then the referenced document is inserted into those places when you publish or test the .swf file. With an imported class file, however, the code is only stored once within the Flash movie.

Import Script command

If you prefer not to use the #include command to incorporate the code in your Flash movie file (.swf) at run time, you can simply import the file directly into Flash 8 using the Actions panel.

On the
CD-ROM

Continue to use the externalActions.as file for this exercise.

1. Open Flash 8 and create a new Flash document.

2. Save this file to the same location as the externalActions.as file.

3. Select the first frame of Layer 1 and open the Actions panel (F9).

4. Select Import Script from the options menu of the Actions panel.

5. Browse to the folder where you saved externalActions.as, highlight it, and click OK. Flash 8 will import the file and put it in your movie.

Caution

When you import ActionScript from a file using this method, the contents of the Script pane will be overwritten and replaced with the contents from the ActionScript file.

Tip

Flash 8 does not parse the file and check for incorrect syntax when importing. You should check the syntax of the code once it has imported to make sure it is correct. To do this, choose Check Syntax from the options menu of the Actions panel.

Export Script command

Just as you can import the contents of an external file, you can export the contents of the Script pane to an .as file. This will enable you to take advantage of the editing capabilities in the Actions panel while still leveraging the usefulness of external ActionScript files.

1. Open a Flash document that contains some ActionScript code. You can use the debugging_code.fla document from the exercise earlier in this chapter.

2. Select a frame containing ActionScript code, and open the Actions panel.

3. Select Export Script from the options menu of the Actions panel.

4. Save the new .as file to a preferred location on your system.

Team environments

When working with a team of developers on one project, it can get quite difficult to manage the development of an application. Many "newbie" applications are built within one .fla file, which poses a problem because only one person can work on the file at any given time. It can become very confusing and file versioning errors may occur.

A great way to reduce dependency on other team members is to break the .fla file up as much as possible. This may include breaking a project into several Flash document files (.fla), which are then combined using the loadMovie() method command at run time. Another effective method is to use external code files for storing data. For each block of code performing a separate task, or each custom object you are using in your application, you can store the ActionScript in an external file. This makes it easy for many people to work simultaneously on one application.

For more information on Flash project management, see Chapter 3, "Planning Flash Projects." This chapter discusses the Project panel featured in Flash Professional 8.

ActionScript libraries and classes

With Flash 8, you can build ActionScript routines (and even your own custom classes) suitable for re-use across a variety of situations. For instance, you may have a block of code that you use to initiate a connection to a server-side script, or a Flash Communication Server application. Storing such code in external code files is an easy way to include them in your next project without much effort.

An ActionScript library is a set of code used for a specific purpose. It can be any block of ActionScript, from simple variable declarations to more advanced ActionScript objects. This sort of code is well suited for being stored in an external text file, and easily included in many projects.

It's beyond the scope of this chapter to discuss the use of custom class files. Refer to Chapter 31, "Creating a Game in Flash," for an example of a Flash document that uses ActionScript 2.0 classes.

Troubleshooting Guidelines

Troubleshooting problems with a Flash movie can be quite difficult. Depending on the complexity of your movie(s), it can be quite involved. The two main areas where you can experience problems with your movie are as follows: the structure and design of your movie, or your ActionScript code. However, this can be extended to other technologies your movie may use. For example if you use a Web server that relays XML data back and forth, the problem could lie in the connection and processing of data and may have nothing to do with the Flash movie. Similar issues can exist if you're using Flash Remoting or Flash Communication Server applications. We have compiled these troubleshooting checklists to help you solve some problems that may occur during your Flash development.

Good practices

The following list will help you alleviate the need for troubleshooting your movie and prevent many problems from occurring:

✦ **Planning:** Planning can be a tedious task. However, it can also be the start to a very successful project. If you plan your project from start to finish, you can pinpoint potential problem areas before you have even begun.

We are not referring to a time schedule, but the processes and methods you use to satisfy the requirements of a project.

✦ **Incremental file saving:** A major problem may arise in your movie that can slow production. It may be easier to revert to the last saved version in your movie. This can be an easy task by incrementally saving a new copy of your movie at each milestone.

Note We suggest using the file name_version number naming convention as a useful naming structure. Some examples of this convention are `movie_01.fla`, `movie_02.fla`, and so on.

A *milestone* should be considered a significant point in your project—a step closer to completion of your project.

Tip An even better way to keep past copies of your source code and Flash documents is to use versioning software such as CVS or Microsoft SourceSafe. These systems enable you to check the same file in iterations, without the hassle of renaming the file each time you store (or commit) the file to the system.

✦ **Regular testing:** While you create your movie, you should start testing early in the development process. Regular and thorough testing can help point out problems that may occur down the track.

Not only should you test regularly, but you should also test in the target environment. (You can use the testing matrices we discussed earlier in this chapter.)

✦ **Comments:** When you write ActionScript code, you should comment each function or block of code. Many problems can arise as a result of simply not remembering what each function or block of code does. Without comments, you might accidentally skim over the exact trouble location because you can't remember what the function does or how it works. Comments should be short and concise, going into detail if necessary.

Not only should you comment your ActionScript, but you should also comment your frames. Have a layer named "comments" in your movie. On any given keyframe of this layer, place a comment in the Frame Label field of the Property inspector to remind yourself what a particular frame does or is used for.

✦ **Naming conventions:** Make sure all aspects of your movie are named properly, including ActionScript. Make sure you've given each function a descriptive name. This should also be applied to variables and objects. Your naming conventions should extend beyond ActionScript; you should name each layer, scene, and symbol descriptively.

✦ **Rest:** If you find a lot of simple problems occurring, chances are you are just tired and overworked. A lot of problems arise when you are mentally exhausted. Often the best thing to do is get some sleep and come back refreshed. Typos are a common problem when you get tired. Take regular breaks also—they really do help.

General troubleshooting checklist

The following is a list of guidelines that you should follow when you are not too sure where your movie is faulting. Both developers and designers should read these general guidelines; often, simple mistakes cause problems in your structure and ActionScript.

✦ **Locked, hidden, or Guide layers:** A common problem occurs when you accidentally lock or hide a layer. It is easy to overlook ActionScript that resides on an object that you can't see, due to the layer being locked or hidden. Also, any object residing in a Guide layer will not be included in the generated .swf file.

Caution

ActionScript code on a Guide layer will be exported with your Flash movie. If you're intentionally using a Guide layer to prevent elements on that layer from being exported, make sure you don't have any conflicting ActionScript on any keyframes of the Guide layer.

✦ **Naming conflicts:** It is quite easy to give multiple objects the same name. This can occur in ActionScript or in naming frames and objects. A good practice is to make sure that each variable, function, object, and property has a unique name.

✦ `allowScriptAccess`: When working with Flash movies in combination with JavaScript or VBScript, the `allowScriptAccess` attribute of the `<embed>` and `<object>` tags in HMTL has to be set to true. Without it, Flash movies cannot communicate with JavaScript. You can learn more about this type of interactivity in Chapter 22, "Integrating Flash Content with Web Pages."

Designer troubleshooting checklist

This checklist is a simple guide to problems relating to the structure and layout of your movies.

✦ **Graphics or Movie Clips:** Problems occur when you think an object is a Movie Clip but it is really a Graphic symbol. You can't name a Graphic symbol or reference it in ActionScript code.

✦ **Edit mode:** It is quite easy to become confused as to which timeline or editing mode you are in. You may think you are editing on the Main Timeline, when in fact you are two timelines deep.

✦ **Action placement:** Be sure you haven't confused the type of action you're using on a particular object. There are three types of action modes in Flash 8: Frame, Movie Clip, and Button actions. Often, these are confused and become a problem. For example, you may accidentally add actions to a keyframe when you mean to add them to a Movie Clip instance.

Web Resource

While not related to ActionScript or coding, a common bitmap problem that designers encounter is *bitmap shift*, where a bitmap image appears to be in a different X and Y position at run time than it appeared on the Stage at author-time. You won't likely see bitmap shift occurring in Flash Player 7 or 8. See the tech note at Macromedia's site:

```
www.macromedia.com/support/flash/ts/documents/bitmaps_shift.htm
```

Developer troubleshooting guidelines

This is a list of common problems that may occur when you are writing ActionScript. Problems in your project can spread far and wide; these might also be caused by one or more trouble areas that we covered in the general or designer guideline sections. It is to your advantage to read all the troubleshooting areas to maximize your chance of solving problems.

✦ **Object and frame label names:** Make sure you have correctly named your objects and frame labels using the Property inspector. This can alleviate many problems, which may be caused by a poor naming structure. Names are case sensitive in Flash Player 7 and higher! As such, make sure you have the name correct, both on the frame or object and in your ActionScript code where you are referencing the frame or object.

✦ **Paths:** When referencing objects, frames, or variables, make sure you have the path correct. It can be quite confusing using relative paths such as this and _parent, and this can often be the source of major problems.

Tip

You can use the Insert Target Path button in the Actions panel to help target nested Movie Clip instances. See Chapter 19, "Building Timelines and Interactions," for more details.

✦ **Conflicting namespaces:** When creating an object or declaring a variable, make sure it isn't the same as a predefined object or variable name in ActionScript. Likewise, make sure you have unique objects and variable names.

✦ **Conflicting frame actions:** Many simple problems are caused by conflicting frame actions. You may have a stop(); action on Layer 1 at frame 20 and a play(); action on Layer 2 at frame 20, which would stop your movie from stopping. As such, you should keep your actions on one layer per timeline. For more information on this topic, see the sidebar "Layer Order and Execution Order" in this chapter.

✦ **Confining the problem:** Make sure the problem exists with the Flash movie. When you work with server-side elements, the problem could be on the server. You may have a problem with the connection or with database information being passed back and forth. Make sure you test your server-side scripts for errors also. Oftentimes, developers will create non-Flash interfaces in HTML to test the functionality of server-side elements to isolate any problems before integrating the same data with a Flash movie.

Layer Order and Execution Order

The order of your layers determines the order in which your ActionScript is executed. If the layers are not ordered properly, it can cause problems in your ActionScript code. Follow these steps to set up an example to illustrate this problem:

1. Open Flash 8 and choose File ➪ New to create a new file.

2. Choose Insert ➪ Layer three times so you have a total of three layers in the movie.

3. Open the Actions panel by choosing Window ➪ Actions.

4. Select frame 1 of the top layer and enter this code: var i:Number = 20;.

5. Select frame 1 of the middle layer and enter this code: var i:Number = 30;.

6. Select the frame 1 of the bottom layer and enter this code: trace(i);.

7. Test the movie by choosing Control ➪ Test Movie. The value of i will be sent to the Output panel and it should be 30.

8. Drag the topmost layer beneath the second layer, so you have reversed the i declaration order.

9. Test the movie by choosing Control ➪ Test Movie. The value of i will be sent to the Output panel and it should now say 20. As you can see, the last declaration of i sticks and the first one is overwritten. This can affect any type of ActionScript object: variables, functions, or objects.

The layer order specified on the Flash tab of the Publish Settings dialog box also controls the order in which Flash draws the layers over a slow network or modem connection.

✦ **Strings or expressions:** A common problem is using a string when an expression should be used, and an expression when a string should be used. When you are writing code in the Actions panel, make sure you have quotes when you are writing a string and no quotes when you are referring to an object, function, or variable. For example, `trace(test);` will try to send the value of test to the Output panel, rather then send the string "test" to the Output panel.

Community Help

There are many Web sites out there built solely for the Flash community. You should leverage from the huge knowledge base available at these Web sites. Post your messages in forums and mailing lists; more often than not, others have come across the same problems. Most of these sites also offer a huge resource — downloadable open source code — which you can peruse to work out how certain tasks are performed.

These resources are invaluable and an excellent way to learn more about Flash. However, you should download the examples and figure out how they work. If you simply download them and use them, you won't learn anything. Trying to understand them and working through all of the code is an excellent method for learning Flash.

The following list of excellent Web sites is devoted to the Flash community:

✦ **FlashSupport:** `www.flashsupport.com`

✦ **Community MX:** `www.communitymx.com`

✦ **Ultrashock:** `www.ultrashock.com`

✦ **Moock.org:** `www.moock.org`

✦ **Person13.com:** `www.person13.com`

✦ **Flash Kit:** `www.flashkit.com`

✦ **Were-Here.com:** `www.were-here.com`

✦ **ActionScript.com:** `www.actionscript.com`

Web Resource We'd like to know what you think about this chapter. Visit `www.flashsupport.com/feedback` to send us your comments.

Summary

✦ Use code hints in the Actions panel to help you determine the correct syntax for your ActionScript code.

✦ While you develop an application, testing regularly — including testing on target mediums — can make the difference between a good application and an excellent application. You should get in the habit of testing the test matrices to ensure that your product will perform on most commercially available and accepted programs and platforms.

✦ You can often remove the need for troubleshooting through regular testing. However, if you think a problem lies within your ActionScript, use the Debugger in combination with the Troubleshooting guidelines to find and fix the problem.

✦ When you create code-intensive projects, use the Debugger regularly; you can use Breakpoints effectively and to your advantage. Using Breakpoints regularly to debug your code is often the most effective method because of its flexibility and ease of use.

✦ You can design and use your own testing matrices if the ones that we provide in this chapter aren't conclusive enough for your platform. You may need to update the testing matrices over time as the Flash Player becomes available on more platforms.

✦   ✦   ✦

Integrating Components and Data-Binding

Components are the secret weapon that Flash developers employ to quickly prototype data-enabled projects and to integrate media elements with ready-made interface controls. In Chapter 33, you learn how to add and modify the User Interface components that ship with Flash 8. Chapter 34 introduces the steps for getting components to work with external data sources and respond to ActionScript and user-triggered events. Chapter 35 takes you through the steps for creating an extensible Gallery component that makes use of the ScrollPane and Loader components to support externally-loaded JPEG thumbnails and full-size images with PHP scripts. The graphic polish is up to you, but the sample site provides a good foundation for building projects that reduce the need for manual updates and scale gracefully as new content is added.

Using Components

A major change in Flash MX 2004 was the addition of a whole new set of components, known as V2 components, and the architecture that they use. Flash 8 continues to offer the same variety of components, with some modifications to solve minor bugs present in the Flash MX 2004 versions. Components offer an easy way to reuse complicated elements within your movie without having to build them on your own. Although it's beyond the scope of this chapter, you can also build your own custom components. In this chapter, we take a look at what components are, their parameters, and how to work with many of the components included with Flash 8.

Flash Basic 8 ships with 14 User Interface components, and doesn't feature any other component sets. Flash Professional 8, however, has 22 User Interface components, 6 Data components, and several components related to Flash Video playback and control.

New Feature The new FLVPlayback component enables you to play Flash Video files (.flv) with extreme ease. This component is only included with Flash Professional 8, and we discuss it at length in Chapter 17, "Displaying Video."

Cross-Reference This chapter discusses User Interface (UI) components. For more discussion of the Data components in Flash Pro 8, read Chapter 34, "Binding Data and Events to Components."

What Are Components?

Components are complex Movie Clips with parameters that you define during the authoring process. They are essentially a container, holding many assets that work together to add enhanced interactivity, productivity, or effects to your movies. You can use components to control your movie, such as moving from one frame to another, or to perform more complex tasks, such as sending data to and from a server.

You can download additional components from Macromedia and third-party developers to add to those already bundled with Flash 8, though many of the most useful and regularly used elements, such as buttons, combo boxes, and lists, are already included with the program. We look at many of the components found in the User Interface components set in this chapter.

Different Flash MX Components

You may already be familiar with the use of Flash MX's components. The original components are now referred to as V1 components. V1 components use a different event model than the V2 components that shipped with Flash MX 2004 and Flash 8.

If you have a large investment in V1 components, you can continue using them in Flash 8 documents, but you will be restricted to publishing ActionScript 1.0 movies. You may also find that you need to publish your movies for Flash Player 6 as well. To reuse your V1 components from Flash MX in Flash 8, do the following:

1. Copy the Flash document (.fla) for the component set (for example, the `Communication Components.fla` for the Flash Communication Server MX 1.5 components) from the Flash MX `First Run\Components` directory to your `Flash MX 2004 First Run\ Components` folder.

2. Restart Flash 8, or reload the Components panel by right-clicking (Control+clicking on Mac) the Components panel title bar and choosing Reload. The older components should appear in the Components panel.

You can also download the free Flash MX UI Components for Flash MX 2004 extension from Macromedia's site. This updater installs all of the older V1 components from Flash MX into Flash MX 2004 or Flash 8. You can find the link to this updater in the Flash Extensions section of the `www.flashsupport.com/links` page. One of the benefits of the V1 components is that they add much less weight, in terms of file size, to your final Flash movie (.swf).

Why Use Components?

Components make it easy for you to rapidly create proof-of concepts or prototypes for larger Rich Internet Application (RIA) frameworks, to share your work with other Flash developers who work in your production team, or to share your innovations with other developers in the Flash community.

While this chapter focuses on the components bundled with the release of Flash 8, the way in which these components are used will also help you understand how other components work — from Macromedia or a third-party. Components you download sometimes come in *sets,* which may include many similar small applications. You may need the Macromedia Extension Manager to install them into Flash 8.

Cross-Reference
For more information on exchanging and downloading components, please see the section "Exchanging and acquiring components" at the end of this chapter.

One of the arguments against using components is the file size they add to your productions. Even though this may be the case, there are several reasons to use components apart from the ease of dragging them to your Stage and modifying the parameters.

Many of the V2 components in Flash 8 are substantially large in file size. For example, including a Button component adds 22 KB to the Flash movie file (.swf) size. Adding a List component contributes 47 KB to the Flash movie size. However, adding both List and Button components to your movie only puts 47 KB into your Flash movie size, not 69 KB. Why is this the case? Because the List component uses the Button component class, the Button component is already included in the class packages exported to the Flash movie. Flash intelligently only includes class files once — not multiple times.

First of all, usability is an integral part of effective interface design. Components are an extremely effective way of ensuring that your end-user understands how to use certain elements of your Flash movie. A predictable interface does not have to be boring or cliché. Furthermore, because components can be skinned, they can have a unique look from one site to the next. The components shipped with Flash 8, for the most part, are also reliable, given they were built, developed, and tested by professionals. This is not to say that the same level of construction cannot be achieved by thousands of others, but the time and effort spent in complicated coding and testing has already been done for you. And because components are a quick solution to common interface requirements, you will have more time to spend on more complicated and interesting creative tasks instead of repetitive authoring.

Exercise care with third-party components — even those that you can download from the Macromedia Exchange. Not all components have been thoroughly tested, and some are specifically developed for one particular use in mind. Be sure to test your implementation of a component throughout the development process.

Compiled Clips: A specific component format

A component is made up of one or more internal assets. One of the changes introduced with Flash MX 2004's component architecture (and continued in Flash 8), though, is that components can be compiled. This means that when you add a component to the Flash document and open your Library panel, you'll only see one symbol for the component (see Figure 33-1). In Flash MX, the same component may have added many folders and symbols that are used by the component (see Figure 33-2).

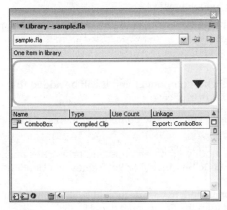

Figure 33-1: The ComboBox component in Flash 8

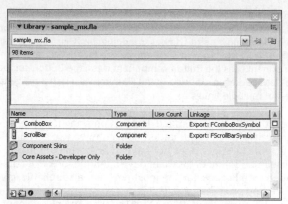

Figure 33-2: The Flash MX ComboBox component

The symbol type for prepackaged components is called *compiled clip*. There are a couple of major differences with this component format and architecture:

✦ You can no longer edit the symbols of a component that has been compiled. As such, you need to use ActionScript code to change the appearance of a component. You can also overwrite the linked symbols embedded with a compiled clip with your own new linked assets.

✦ Developers can now create and distribute components without the user being able to see the code used to create the component. This is a big "win" for developers who are concerned about their intellectual property rights.

If you were familiar with components in Flash MX, we highlight other differences between V1 and V2 components throughout this chapter.

How to Add a Component

You can add a component to your Stage in the following ways:

1. Open the Components panel by going to Window ➪ Components or by pressing Ctrl+F7 or ⌘+F7.

2. Add a component to the Stage by:

- **Double-clicking:** You can double-click a component and it will be added to the center of your Document window's workspace.

- **Dragging:** You can add an instance by clicking the component icon and dragging it onto the Stage.

After your component is on the Stage, you can modify its parameters and properties manually in various panels or by using ActionScript code on objects or keyframes in a timeline.

Note   You can add additional instances of your component to your document by dragging it from your Library panel onto the Stage instead of from the Component panel.

You can also add a component to your movie by using the `MovieClip.attachMovie()` method in ActionScript after the instance is added to your library. An example of adding a `Button` component to the Stage and setting a few properties using ActionScript is as follows. (This code uses standard ActionScript 1.0 syntax.)

```
var cbt = attachMovie("Button", "cbt ", 1);
cbt.label = "Music";
```

This creates an instance of a push button, labeled "Music," on the stage. You can also use ActionScript 2.0 to create a new component instance:

```
import mx.controls.Button;
var cbt:Button = createClassObject(Button, "cbt", 1, {label: "Test Button"});
```

Cross-Reference   For more information on using the `MovieClip` object and `attachMovie()`, **refer to** Chapter 25, "Controlling Movie Clips."

Where to Find Components, Assets, and Parameters

You can find, control, and edit your components in many areas of the Flash interface. Understanding each of these areas will help you add custom features to your Flash movies that use components.

Components panel

You can find this panel, shown in Figure 33-3, by going to Window ➪ Components or by using the Ctrl+F7 or ⌘+F7 shortcut. This panel includes all of the components that ship with Flash Basic 8 or Flash Professional 8.

Note   As mentioned earlier in this chapter, the Professional version of Flash 8 has many more components than the standard version.

If you add components that you have downloaded from other Web sites, such as the Macromedia Exchange, you will be able to access the sets from this panel as well. Each set appears as a new nesting.

Note   The Components panel uses a tree structure, in which every set is shown in the panel. The components of each set are nested with each node.

Property inspector

The Property inspector includes an extra tab when you have a component instance selected on the Stage. The Parameters tab includes an area similar to the Component Inspector panel (discussed next), where you can change the values of each parameter depending on how you need to use the component. Figure 33-4 shows the parameters of a ComboBox component.

The Properties tab enables you to add color effects, such as Brightness, Tint, Alpha, or a combination of these attributes — just as you can with any other symbol in Flash. You can also swap the instance with another symbol from this tab. Note that you can also apply filter effects to component instances with the Filters tab.

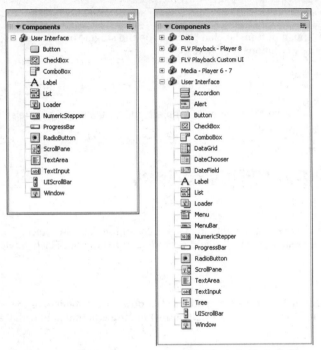

Figure 33-3: The Components panel in Flash Basic 8 (left) and Flash Pro 8 (right)

Figure 33-4: The Property inspector enables you to quickly configure a component.

Cross-Reference   To learn more about the new filter effects in Flash 8, read Chapter 12, "Applying Filters and Effects," and Chapter 35, "Building an Image Gallery Component."

Component Inspector panel

The Component Inspector panel is the central control area for component parameters and bindings. You can find this panel by choosing Window ⇨ Component Inspector or by using the Alt+F7 or Option+F7 shortcut. In Flash Basic 8, this panel has only one tab named Parameters (see Figure 33-5). In the Parameters tab, you can set values for each parameter of a component instance, just as you can with the Property inspector. This tab can also be used to display custom user interface movie files (.swf) for components.

Figure 33-5: The Component Inspector as seen in Flash Basic 8

Tip   The Component Inspector panel also features a Component Wizard icon. If a component was built to employ a wizard, clicking this button will initiate the wizard.

If you are using Flash Professional 8, the Component Inspector features two additional tabs: Bindings and Schema (see Figure 33-6). These tabs are used for more advanced data features of many extra components that ship with Flash Professional 8.

Figure 33-6: The Component Inspector panel as seen in Flash Professional 8

For Uncompiled Components Only: Component Definition Dialog Box

If you use V1 components or if you create your own custom components in Flash 8, you can access the definitions used by a component by right-clicking (or Control+clicking on Mac) the component or Movie Clip symbol in the Library panel (or using the panel's options menu) and choosing Component Definition. This dialog box enables you to add or remove parameters from prebuilt or custom components. You are also able to customize or alter the functionality of the component. Other options in this dialog box include setting the ActionScript 2.0 class name, Custom UI, Live Preview, and Description. This dialog box is generally intended for advanced component users or authors.

The Component Definition dialog box enables you to add and remove parameters and functions of uncompiled components.

Once a component is compiled, the user of the component no longer has access to the Component Definition settings. If you add the proper [Inspectable] metatags to your ActionScript 2.0 class files for components, then you don't even need to manually configure the Component Definition dialog box. You learn how to build a custom component in Chapter 35, "Building an Image Gallery Component."

Note   The Bindings and Schema tabs can also be used with User Interface Components, but you can only see these tabs if you are using Flash Professional 8.

Cross-Reference   For more information on binding data to components via the Bindings and Schema tabs, refer to Chapter 34, "Binding Data and Events to Components." You can also find examples of their usage in the Help panel by searching with the phrase "data binding."

Library panel

After dragging a UI component to the Stage, you will notice a new Compiled Clip symbol for the component added to your Library. If you want to remove a component from your Flash document, be sure to delete it from the Library as well as from the Stage.

Actions panel and ActionScript

Not only is there ActionScript hidden within the compiled components that ship with Flash 8, but you can also write ActionScript to control components or modify their appearance. The built-in components that ship with Flash 8 have several methods and properties that you can use to customize their functionality. Later in this chapter, you learn how to tap some of these scripted resources.

Tip   You can also use behaviors, found in the Behaviors panel, with several of the components.

Modifying Component Color Properties and Parameters

There are several ways you can easily modify the appearance and functionality of your components. With the Flash 8 User Interface components, you can customize the face color of each instance with little effort. Let's look at how you accomplish this.

First of all, open the Property inspector. As you have already seen, the Parameters and Properties tabs contain information on the attributes of your component. This is possibly the easiest and quickest way to change the appearance of your component. Simply by selecting the Properties tab and then the Color menu, you can alter the Brightness, Tint, Alpha, or a combination of these elements by choosing Advanced. You can see the changes made to the face of your component after publishing or previewing your movie.

The Parameters tab enables you to change the built-in component parameters to ones better matching your site or the usage of your component. For example, on a ScrollPane instance, you can change the horizontal and vertical scroll attributes (visibility) in this area by clicking the value area and selecting an option from the list. The Component Inspector panel (and the Component Definition dialog box, if applicable) is another area that enables you to modify or customize the functionality of your components.

Cross-Reference   For more information on changing the look of components, please refer to the section later in this chapter called "Modifying Components."

Removing Components from Your Movie

It is important to understand how to properly remove components from your movie. Removing V2 components is usually very straightforward: Select the compiled clip in the Library panel, and delete it.

V1 components, on the other hand, can often be linked to many other assets spread across several folders in the Library panel. Some V1 components share assets, such as the V1 Scrollbar component. Therefore, care must be taken when removing assets from the Library. You should have a solid understanding of component structure and asset usage if you attempt to manually remove items from the Flash UI Component folder in the Library.

Components in Flash 8

Flash 8 includes several User Interface (or UI) components, which provide *user interface* elements and functionality frequently used by developers. You should be able to find a use for some or all of these components at one time or another. Let's take a look at what each of the core UI components does and how to use them in your movies. After dragging any component instance to your Stage, open up the Property inspector and select the Parameters tab to view the parameters discussed in this section.

Tip   Most of the V2 components feature the Halo skin, with colors and effects that resemble modern day operating systems' interfaces. Most UI components in Flash 8 will function properly in Flash Player 6 movies. If you're in doubt, simply publish or test your Flash movie as a Flash Player 6 movie and see if the component works as expected. Make sure you set the ActionScript version to ActionScript 2.0 in the Publish Settings as well.

Note   The Flash MX 2004 and Flash 8 component framework does not use click or change handlers in the same way that V1 components from Flash MX did. Refer to the "Understanding the Listener Event Model for Components" section, later in this chapter, for more information.

The parameters for each component we discuss in the following sections are also the respective names of each component's properties. Note that not all of a component's properties may be exposed in the Property inspector.

Button component

This component is essentially a standard button with built-in up, over, and down states. The button is designed to resemble an HTML form button (such as a submit button), but with the Halo theme for V2 components. The `Button` component, shown in Figure 33-7, is very easy to use and can aid in quick development of mockups or be modified to suit more aesthetically inclined productions.

Figure 33-7: The `Button` component as it appears in a Flash movie at run time

Caution   Do not confuse a `Button` component with a Button symbol. The `Button` component replaces the V1 `PushButton` component from Flash MX. In this chapter, any reference to `Button` instance implies a `Button` component, not a Button symbol.

Parameters

The `Button` parameters are perhaps some of the easiest to manage. As with other components, you can enter text for the button's label and set a function to execute when the button is pressed.

✦ `icon`: This optional parameter specifies the linkage ID of a symbol in the Library that will appear next to the label text of the button. The placement of the label in relation to the icon symbol is determined by the `labelPlacement` parameter (discussed later in this list).

✦ `label`: This is the text appearing on the button face. The default text is simply "Button."

✦ labelPlacement: This optional parameter is a menu with left, right, top, or bottom options. This setting determines how the label text is aligned to the button's icon symbol. The default value is right. If you do not use an icon symbol for the instance, this setting has no effect.

✦ selected **and** toggle: These two parameters work together to enable a Button component instance to act as an on/off button. As a toggle button, the rim of the instance displays an "on" color (green is the default Halo theme) if selected is set to true. The selected property has no effect if toggle is not set to true. The default value for both the selected and toggle parameters is false.

Caution

If you use the Property inspector to set the selected parameter to true, the Button instance (unfortunately) will not appear with a selected state when you publish or test the movie. The selected property must be set in ActionScript to work properly.

How it works

An instance of a Button component can have regular, disabled, or active states, which can be customized graphically. It is a very quick way to add interactivity to your movie. For additional functionality of the button, you will need to write ActionScript using the Button methods.

Tip

The "click" event is sent to any listeners when a Button component instance is clicked. You can use an on(click) event handler directly on a Button component instance to initiate further actions when the instance is clicked, but adding code to instances on the Stage is generally not accepted as a best practice.

Cross-Reference

You can find several examples of the Button component throughout many chapters of this book. You can also search for "button component" in the Flash 8 Help panel to find more information on the Button component. If you search for "button component class," you'll find the primary page describing the methods and properties of the Button component.

CheckBox component

The CheckBox component, as the name implies, is a user interface element that has a selection box next to text. As with HTML form check boxes, the CheckBox component enables you to easily add form options to a Flash movie. The CheckBox component returns a true or false value. If the box is checked, it returns a true value; if not, it returns false. These states are shown in Figure 33-8.

☑ Subscribe to news ☐ Subscribe to events **Figure 33-8:** A selected (true) check box, left, and a cleared (false) check box, right

Parameters

CheckBox parameters can be changed to customize the default label text and its placement in relation to the check box graphic. You can also set the initial state and have the option of setting a function, executing as soon as the button state changes.

✦ label: This is the name appearing next to the check box. The default value is set to "CheckBox."

✦ labelPlacement: This parameter sets the label to the left, right (default), top, or bottom of the check box.

> **Tip** Make sure to set the height of the instance appropriately to accommodate top and bottom alignment.

✦ `selected`: Assigning a `true` value checks the box initially, although the default value for this is set to `false` (unchecked).

How it works

The `CheckBox` component has a hit area that encompasses the check box itself, as well as the label next to it. The width of a `CheckBox` instance can be transformed to accommodate more text. Added functionality using ActionScript is possible by using the methods, events, and properties of the `CheckBox` class.

ComboBox component

The `ComboBox` component is similar to any standard HTML form drop-down list. When you click the component instance, a list of options appears below the default value in the list. You can also navigate the list using the up-arrow, down-arrow, Page Up, Page Down, Home, and End keys. This component is very useful and essentially has the following two different functionalities:

✦ As a regular combo box, the component can display a list of choices from which the user can select an option. If the combo box has focus, the user can type a letter to jump to a label starting with the same letter (see Figure 33-9).

Figure 33-9: A standard ComboBox instance, shown closed (left) and open (right)

✦ As an editable combo box, a user can enter text into the top field to specify a value that is not displayed in the list. The typed value is the active value for the `ComboBox` instance. Figure 33-10 shows a value being entered into the `ComboBox` instance at run time.

Figure 33-10: An editable ComboBox instance, shown with default display (left) and entered text (right)

Parameters

`ComboBox` parameters can be changed to set labels and data for each item in the drop-down box, set the top of the pull-down to be a text input box (an editable combo box), and customize how many items are viewable when the arrow is selected.

✦ `data`: This array is composed of values that correspond to each label value entered in the array for the `labels` parameter. For example, if you had a `label` value of "Red," you may want a `data` value of "0xFF0000." Similarly, if you have a catalog of items, the product's name may be the `label` value and its catalog number may be the data value. The user does not see the `data` value(s).

Note When you set values for the `data` or `labels` array in the Property inspector, the values will be typed as strings. You need to set the `data` values in ActionScript if you want to type the values differently.

> ✦ `editable`: This parameter is set to define whether the `ComboBox` instance can have text entered into the top of the list to specify a value not listed in the menu. This typed value can be passed as data to the movie using the `value` property of the `ComboBox` class.

> ✦ `labels`: This array of values determines the list of text entries that the user sees when viewing the drop-down box.

> ✦ `rowCount`: The number entered here represents how many labels are seen on the drop-down box before a scroll bar appears. The default value is set to 5.

How it works

When you click the `data` or `labels` field in the Property inspector, you will notice a magnifying glass icon next to the drop-down area. This button, when clicked, opens a Values panel where you can enter the array of values using the + or – buttons.

Tip The values for these parameters use a zero-based index, which means the first item in your array is listed as `[0]`.

Functionality can be added using ActionScript, and the `ComboBox` class's methods, properties, and event handlers can be used with each instance of this component.

List component

The `List` component also enables you to create lists just as the `ComboBox` does, but the list menu is always visible (see Figure 33-11). If there are more items than the height of the instance allows, a scroll bar is automatically added to the list. This component enables selection of one or more items. As with the `ComboBox` component, keyboard navigation is allowed, and a zero-based index system is used for the arrays populating the `label` and `data` parameters.

Figure 33-11: The `List` component at run time

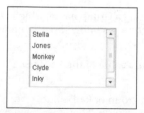

Parameters

The `List` component parameters include an additional option to select multiple values. Other settings in this tab are similar in function to components we mentioned earlier.

> ✦ `data`: This parameter is an array of values associated with the values set in the `labels` parameter.

> ✦ `labels`: Values entered into this area will be the labels on each list item.

✦ multipleSelection: This is set to either true or false. A true value enables end-users to select multiple values at once when holding down the Ctrl or ⌘ key. The default value of false allows only one selection to be active at any time.

✦ rowHeight: This parameter controls the pixel height of each item in the list. This value does not control the size of the text used for each item. Rather, it indicates the active "hit" area of the item. If you specify a value that's smaller than the pixel height of the text, cropping of the item's label is the result. The default value is 20 pixels.

How it works

This component's functionality is very similar to that of the ComboBox component. The main difference in a List component is the visibility of the labels and the ability to select multiple values. If you wish to add functionality using ActionScript, the methods, property, and events of the List class are used.

Tip   If you're using Flash Professional 8, you should know that many components inherit the List class, such as the DataGrid and the ComboBox components. Any component that is based on the List class can also use a custom cell renderer class, which determines how the content of each row in a List instance is laid out and formatted.

RadioButton component

The RadioButton component looks and feels similar to those found in HTML forms. Based on the design of radio button functionality, only one radio button can be selected within a group of buttons. Figure 33-12 shows a group of RadioButton instances in a Flash movie.

Figure 33-12: A group of RadioButton instances

Parameters

The RadioButton component has the unique attribute for setting a Group name, which will associate the instance with others on the Stage. Other parameters resemble those of components we discussed earlier.

✦ data: The value entered here is associated with the label value of the RadioButton instance.

✦ groupName: The value of this parameter specifies which group of RadioButton instances on the Stage the particular instance is associated with. Therefore, only one radio dot appears in this group at one time. You can have several groups, each with its own set of associated RadioButton instances. The default value is radioGroup.

✦ label: This is the text you see alongside the RadioButton instance.

✦ labelPlacement: By default, the label placement is set to the right of the radio button. The acceptable options include left, right, top, and bottom.

✦ selected: This parameter sets the initial state of the button to be true or false (default). A false selection is clear. All buttons having the same group name will allow only one radio button to be selected at one time. If you set more than one RadioButton instance in the same group to initially have a true value, the last instance will be selected when you publish your movie.

How it works

The groupName parameter is important to understand. Groups of buttons can be added to your document, and in each group, only one button can be selected at a time. You can resize the width and height of an instance with the Free Transform tool, the Property inspector, or the Transform panel to accommodate your label alignment parameter. The hit area of the RadioButton instance surrounds both the button and the label area. Added functionality can be controlled using the RadioButton class's methods, properties, and events in ActionScript.

> **Note**
>
> It is important to consider the interactive design of your movie when you add radio buttons or check boxes to your movies. Your decision should not be based on the "look" of a radio button versus a check box. Radio buttons should only be used when you need *one* selection to be made from several choices, and a radio button should never exist outside of a group (that is, you shouldn't have a single radio button appearing on its own). Check boxes should be used when you need to allow *one or more* selections to be made from several choices. You can also use a check box for a single option (for example, a form may have a check box asking if you want to receive promotional e-mails for a product). We recommend that you carefully consider how these elements are designed for use in applications, because this enhances the usability of your production.

ScrollPane component

The ScrollPane component is potentially a very powerful and diverse tool. It adds a window with vertical and horizontal scroll bars on either side and is used to display linked Movie Clip symbols from the Library on to the Stage. Because the component features scroll bars, you are able to accommodate more content within a smaller footprint on the Stage. Figure 33-13 shows a ScrollPane instance displaying a linked Movie Clip symbol.

Parameters

Parameters for the ScrollPane component will link it to a Movie Clip symbol and also control how your end-user will be able to manipulate the ScrollPane content. You can also control scroll bar positioning and visibility with these parameters:

✦ contentPath: Enter a text string set to the Linkage ID of the Movie Clip you want to appear in the ScrollPane instance.

Figure 33-13: The ScrollPane component at run time

Tip   The ScrollPane component can also use external paths (or URLs) for displayed content, including external image files (.jpeg, .png, and .gif) or .swf files.

✦ hLineScrollSize: This value determines how much the content in the ScrollPane instance will move when the left and right arrows along the horizontal scroll bar are pressed. The default value is 5 pixels.

✦ hPageScrollSize: This parameter specifies how much the content moves when the user clicks the scroll track on either side of the horizontal scroll bar's middle scroller. The default value is 20 pixels.

✦ hScrollPolicy: This parameter controls how the horizontal scroll bar for the window is displayed. The default setting of auto means a horizontal scroll bar only appears if necessary. A value of true ensures it is always visible, and a false value turns it off.

✦ scrollDrag: Setting this parameter to true enables your users to drag the area within the instance window in order to view the content. A setting of false (default) requires scroll bars to be used instead.

✦ vLineScrollSize: This parameter functions the same way as the hLineScrollSize parameter, but for the vertical scroll bar of the window.

✦ vPageScrollSize: This parameter behaves in the same way as the hPageScrollSize parameter, but for the vertical scroll bar of the window.

✦ vScrollPolicy: This parameter controls if the vertical scroll bar is visible. See the description for the hScrollPolicy for more details.

How it works

The ScrollPane component can display Movie Clips (or bitmap images) with linkage IDs, so you will need to convert any other symbol types or bitmap images to Movie Clips for the images to display. You can also specify external content as a URL in the contentPath property. The Movie Clip (or bitmap image) simply has to be in the Library and have the Export for ActionScript setting checked in the Linkage Properties dialog box.

TextArea component

The TextArea component, shown in Figure 33-14, can be thought of as a ScrollPane component for text. The purpose of the TextArea component is to display text or HTML formatted text within a display window, complete with vertical and/or horizontal scroll bars.

Figure 33-14: The TextArea component displaying HTML formatted text

Parameters

The settings for the TextArea component in the Property inspector control the text that is displayed in the instance.

✦ editable: This parameter controls whether or not the user can change the text in the instance at run time. The default value is true. If it is set to false, the user cannot change the text.

Caution We strongly recommend that you get in the habit of setting the editable parameter to false. You usually won't want users to change the contents of your TextArea component.

✦ html: This parameter determines how the value for the text parameter is interpreted. If html is set to true, any HTML tags format the text accordingly. If html is set to false, the text parameter displays "as is." The default value is false.

✦ text: The value of this parameter is the actual text displayed in the instance's text field.

Tip For larger blocks of text, draft the text in a separate text editor and copy and paste the text into the text parameter field of the Property inspector. Alternatively, you can set the text property via ActionScript.

✦ wordWrap: This parameter controls how the text wraps in the instance. If the parameter is set to true (default), the text wraps at the visible horizontal boundary of the display area. If the parameter is set to false, the text wraps only when a carriage return or line break is specifically embedded in the text value, with a <br/> or <p> tag in HTML formatted text.

Note Horizontal scroll bars will be added only to TextArea instances if wordWrap is set to false and the text width for a line extends beyond the visible display area.

How it works

The TextArea component takes the text parameter value and displays it within the visible area of the instance. The TextArea component can be further enhanced or controlled with ActionScript, by utilizing the methods, properties, and event handlers of the TextArea class.

Cross-Reference You can see the TextArea component in Chapter 20, "Making Your First Flash 8 Project."

UIScrollBar component

The UIScrollBar component, shown in Figure 33-15, was added to the Flash MX 2004 7.2 Updater, and continues to be available in the new release of Flash 8. With the UIScrollBar component, you can scroll your own TextField instances, and you can scroll other MovieClip-based content. The UIScrollBar component can snap to objects on the Stage, and auto-resize its height to match the height of the snapped-to TextField instance.

Cross-Reference Read our coverage of the new scrollRect property of the MovieClip class in Chapter 30, "Applying HTML and Text Field Formatting," to learn more about using the UIScrollBar component to scroll MovieClip object content.

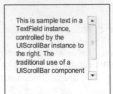

Figure 33-15: The `UIScrollBar` component beside a TextField instance

Parameters

The settings for the `UIScrollBar` component in the Property inspector control the target to which the scroll bar is linked and whether the scroll bar is scrolling horizontal content or vertical content.

✦ `_targetInstanceName`: This parameter sets which `TextField` instance is linked to the `UIScrollBar` instance. This value is automatically filled in if you snap the `UIScrollBar` instance to a `TextField` instance on the Stage at author-time. The `TextField` instance must be on the same parent timeline as the `UIScrollBar` instance in order for `_targetInstanceName` to work properly.

Tip
You can also use the `setScrollTarget()` method of the `UIScrollBar` class in ActionScript to set the `TextField` instance target. It's also not a requirement to set a scroll target for a `UIScrollBar` instance—you can use the `setScrollProperties()` method of the `UIScrollBar` class to determine the scroll range of an instance, and use the `"scroll"` event of the component with listeners to enable scrolling movement. This technique is used with the `scrollRect` property of the `MovieClip` class in Chapter 30, "Applying HTML and Text Field Formatting."

✦ `horizontal`: This Boolean value (`true` or `false`) determines whether the `UIScrollBar` instance has a vertical (`false`) or horizontal (`true`) orientation. The default value is `false`. If you need to scroll a nonwrapping `TextField` instance from left to right, you can set the `UIScrollBar` instance's horizontal property to `true` and place the UIScrollBar instance below (or above) the `TextField` instance, as shown in Figure 33-16.

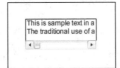

Figure 33-16: A `UIScrollBar` instance with a horizontal value of true

How it works

When you set the `_targetInstanceName` property to the name of a `TextField` instance, the `UIScrollBar` component controls the `scroll` property of that `TextField` instance. It can determine the range of the scroll bar movement by looking at the `TextField` instance's `maxscroll` property.

Cross-Reference
To learn more about the `scroll` and `maxscroll` properties of the `TextField` class, read Chapter 30, "Applying HTML and Text Field Formatting."

Note Both Flash Basic 8 and Flash Pro 8 also include other UI components, including the `Label`, `Loader`, `NumericStepper`, `ProgressBar`, and `Window` components. We discuss the `Loader` and `ProgressBar` components in Chapter 28, "Sharing and Loading Assets," and an example of the `NumericStepper` component is available in the CD-ROM files for Chapter 30, "Applying HTML and Text Field Formatting."

Understanding the Listener Event Model for Components

While it's rather simple to drag and drop components on to the Stage of your Flash document and use the Property inspector to set up initial values for them, the result of any component behavior needs to be described *by you*, in your own ActionScript code. When the user interacts with a component, a specific event — tailored for the component — is sent out to the Flash movie. Just as you can yell when you're alone in a forest, these broadcasted events will just be ignored by the Flash movie unless you create something to listen to the events. Such objects are called *listeners* because their sole purpose is to intercept broadcasted messages from other objects that generate events — such as components.

What a typical listener looks like

Just about any object in a Flash movie can be a listener. You can add custom methods to `MovieClip` objects, for example, or you can create an instance of the `Object` class that exists only in ActionScript. To create a generic object, use the following syntax:

```
var oListener:Object = new Object();
```

or

```
var oListener:Object = {};
```

Note Since the components that ship with Flash 8 are built in ActionScript 2.0, you should get in the habit of using ActionScript 2.0 syntax for the code you use in movies using the components. If you use Flash 8 components, you must publish your Flash movie with ActionScript 2.0 selected in the Flash tab of the Publish Settings.

Once you have created an object that behaves as a listener, you can create methods for the listener geared toward the behavior of the component it observes. For example, if you wanted to do something when a `Button` component instance is clicked, you can add a `click()` method (or handler) to the listener object.

```
oListener.click = function(oEvent:Object):Void {
    trace("---listener received an event broadcast");
};
```

In this simple example, a `trace()` message is sent to the Output panel. You could add further actions to the `click()` method, performing more tasks necessary for your Flash movie.

Letting the component know who its listeners are

Once a listener has a method to invoke, you need to assign the listener object (or its method) to the component that will be broadcasting events. For our previous example, you could assign the listener to a `Button` component instance named `cbt` by using the following code:

```
cbt.addEventListener("click", oListener);
```

or

```
cbt.addEventListener("click", oListener.click);
```

The addEventListener() method takes two parameters: the event being broadcast and the listener object (or method). Each component has its unique event names. The Button component, used in this example, has a click event, which is broadcast to all listeners when the user clicks the Button component instance.

Most components also broadcast additional information to the listeners, passed as parameters to the listener's method. All of the UI components pass an event information object to their listeners. The exact properties of this object vary from one component to the next, but some are consistent. In the following listener method, the oEvent parameter from the Button instance contains several properties, including oEvent.target, which is a reference to the Button instance.

```
oListener.click = function(oEvent:Object):Void {
    trace(oEvent.target + " was clicked.");
    trace("The broadcasted event was " + oEvent.type );
};
```

Note You can change the parameter name to any term you wish. In our example, the parameter is referred to as oEvent, but you can use a term such as eventObj. Just be sure to use the term consistently throughout your listener's method.

The type property, as you can see in the example code, can tell the listener what type of event was broadcast to it. In this way, you can create one method for a listener and have it handle different event types with specific code.

We'll show you how to create a simple example that demonstrates how a listener works:

1. Create a new Flash document, and save it as button_listener.fla.

2. Rename Layer 1 to **cbt**. This layer will hold an instance of the Button component.

3. Open the Components panel (Ctrl+F7 or ⌘+F7) and drag an instance of the Button component from the User Interface set to the Stage.

4. Select the new instance, and in the Property inspector, name the instance **cbt**. Click the Parameters tab and assign a new label to the button, such as **My Button**.

5. Create a new layer named **actions**, and place it at the top of the layer stack.

6. Select frame 1 of the actions layer, and open the Actions panel (F9, or Option+F9 on Mac). Add the following code to the Script pane:

```
var cbt:mx.controls.Button;

var oListener:Object = new Object();
oListener.click = function(oEvent:Object):Void {
    for(var i in oEvent){
        trace(i + " = " + oEvent[i]);
    }
};

cbt.addEventListener("click", oListener);
```

7. Save your document, and test it (Ctrl+Enter or ⌘+Enter). When you click the cbt instance, you should see the following text in the Output panel:

```
target = _level0.cbt
type = click
```

This output illustrates the two properties of the oEvent object broadcasted by the Button component. The event's name is "click" and the target property is a reference to the object broadcasting the event, cbt (_level0.cbt).

You can find the completed example file, button_listener.fla, in the ch33 folder of this book's CD-ROM.

Using the Delegate class to control scope with listeners

If you start to use components with your own Flash movies and nest components within other Movie Clip symbols or your own custom components, you might come across problems with your listener object's scope. Scope refers to how paths within the listener method are evaluated. For example, when you have the following basic function, the scope for the variable named sName is local to the function, not the current timeline:

```
var sName:String = "Goliath";
function onClick():Void {
    var sName:String = "David";
    trace("sName: " + sName);
}
onClick();
```

If you add that code to your Flash movie and test it, the Output panel shows the value for the local variable named sName, not the sName value declared outside of the function:

```
sName: David
```

Similarly, the this scope can vary depending on how a function is called. If you add the following code to a Flash movie and test it, the Output panel displays the same value for this, inside and outside of the function:

```
trace("outside of function, this = " + this);
function onClick():Void {
    trace("inside of function, this = " + this);
}
onClick();
```

For this code, the Output panel displays:

```
outside of function, this = _level0
inside of function, this = _level0
```

However, if you use the same function, onClick, as a listener of a component, the this scope will refer to the component instance, not the owner of the onClick function (_level0):

```
var cbt:mx.controls.Button;

trace("outside of function, this = " + this);

function onClick(oEvent:Object):Void {
   trace("inside of function, this = " + this);
}

cbt.addEventListener("click", onClick);
```

If you tested the movie with this code and clicked the cbt instance, the Output panel displays:

```
outside of function, this = _level0
inside of function, this = _level0.cbt
```

Generally, you'll find that you want to keep the scope of your listener objects under control, and not necessarily executing within the scope of the component emitting the event. This issue becomes more of a necessity to address with larger application architectures, but if you know the problem upfront, you'll save yourself many headaches in future Flash development. Luckily, the solution is pretty simple. If you use the Delegate class, you can control the scope of any handler very easily, regardless of whether the handler is a listener or a data handler for an XML object. The implementation of the Delegate class involves just two lines of code. In the following code sample, the Delegate class is imported and used to re-scope the onClick() handler to the Main Timeline (that is, _level0) for the Button listener:

```
import mx.utils.Delegate;

var cbt:mx.controls.Button;

trace("outside of function, this = " + this);

function onClick(oEvent:Object):Void {
   trace("inside of function, this = " + this);
}

cbt.addEventListener("click", Delegate.create(this, onClick));
```

Here, the Delegate.create() method is used to build a new listener object that controls the scope of the onClick() handler. The create() method takes two parameters: the scope reference you want to use, and the handler that will be called. For our code example, the scope reference is the current timeline (_level0) and the handler is onClick. If you tested the above code in a Flash movie that contained a Button instance named cbt on the Stage, the following text would be displayed in the Output panel when you click the instance:

```
outside of function, this = _level0
inside of function, this = _level0
```

Now, the scope is identical, inside and outside of the function. Let's practice using the Delegate class with the button_listener.fla file you built in the last section.

1. Open the button_listener.fla file you created in the last section, or make a copy of the same file from the ch33 folder of this book's CD-ROM. Resave this file as button_listener_delegate.fla.

2. Select frame 1 of the actions layer, and open the Actions panel (F9 or Option+F9). Replace the code with the following script:

```
import mx.utils.Delegate;

var cbt:mx.controls.Button;

function onClick(oEvent:Object):Void {
    trace("onClick >")
    trace("\tthis = " + this);
    for(var i in oEvent){
        trace("\t" + i + " = " + oEvent[i]);
    }
};

cbt.addEventListener("click", Delegate.create(this, onClick));
```

In this new code, you eliminate the need to create a new listener object — the Main Timeline (_level0) is the listener. The onClick() function is being delegated to handle the responsibility of the "click" event from the cbt instance.

3. Save the document, and test it (Ctrl+Enter or ⌘+Enter). When you click the cbt instance, the Output panel displays the following text. The this scope now refers back to the Main Timeline (_level0), not the component instance itself:

```
onClick >
    this = _level0
    target = _level0.cbt
    type = click
```

Tip

We often use the \t backslash pair in trace() statements to tab (or indent) messages within a function call.

On the CD-ROM

You can find the completed file, button_listener_delegate.fla, in the ch33 folder of this book's CD-ROM.

Using Components in Your Movie

In the following exercise, you use various components in a movie to activate and deactivate a series of elements. It provides an example of how you may use components in your movie to create interactivity.

On the CD-ROM

The source file for this exercise called components_starter.fla is located in the ch33 folder on this book's CD-ROM. You will notice several components have been added to the Stage and have been given instance names. You'll also need to copy the component.txt file from this folder as well.

1. Open the components_starter.fla file and resave it as components_100.fla.

2. Locate the TextArea instance on the first frame. This instance is already named ctaInfo. You will write the ActionScript code to dynamically load a text file named component.txt into the movie at run time. If you open the component.txt file in a text editor, you'll see that this file declares a variable named strIntro, whose value will be used by the TextArea component. Add the code shown in Listing 33-1 to frame 1 of the actions layer, before the existing actions.

Here, a LoadVars object named lvData loads the component.txt file, and sets the text property of the ctaInfo component instance to the strIntro variable declared in the component.txt file.

Listing 33-1: **The text_data Object**

```
var ctaInfo:mx.controls.TextArea;
var lvData:LoadVars = new LoadVars();
lvData.onLoad = function(bSuccess:Boolean):Void {
   if(bSuccess){
       trace("---text file loaded successfully");
       ctaInfo.text = this.intro_text;
   } else {
       trace("---text file did not load.");
   }
};
lvData.load("component.txt");
```

Cross-Reference For more information on the LoadVars object, refer to Chapter 29, "Sending Data In and Out of Flash."

Tip Throughout this chapter, you'll see that component instances have a specific name convention. All component instance names start with the letter "c," for component, which is then followed by a two-letter abbreviation of the component's name. For example, a prefix of cta denotes a TextArea component. This is our own naming convention; feel free to make one of your own.

3. Save the Flash document, and test it (Ctrl+Enter or ⌘+Enter). When the movie loads, you should see a trace() message appear in the Output panel indicating whether or not the text file loaded successfully. If it did load, the TextArea component should have filled with the text described in the component.txt file.

4. Now that text is loading into the TextArea component, you will group the two RadioButton instances on the Stage so that they cannot be selected at the same time. On frame 1 of the Main Timeline, select each instance of the RadioButton components. In the Property inspector, enter the same text string into the groupName parameter for each instance. Let's give the radio buttons a group name of rgNews, which best describes their purpose in the movie. This identifier places both buttons in the same group.

5. Give each instance a different value in the data field in the Property inspector's Parameters tab. This data is what is returned to the movie indicating the selection. Give the first RadioButton instance, crbDigest, a value of digest. For the crbNormal instance, assign a data value of normal.

6. It is also a good practice to have one radio button already selected by default. In the Parameters tab for the crbDigest instance, set the selected value to true.

Note The live preview of the RadioButton component does not update the Stage to show the radio button as selected. You need to test your movie to see the selection occur.

7. Now you are ready to have the "sign me up" button (the cbtSignup instance) send the movie to the right location, based upon which RadioButton instance is selected. Add the bold code shown in Listing 33-2.

The first line of code imports the Delegate class that we discussed earlier in the chapter. This class assists us in controlling the scope of event handlers within our code.

The cbtSignup instance is declared as a Button component, and the rgNews group name established in Step 4 is declared in your code. It doesn't need to be set to any particular value since the RadioButton components on the Stage will automatically create the rgNews object.

In the onSignUpClick function, the current value of the rgNews group is assigned to a local variable named sData. Notice that the way in which you can retrieve the value of a radio button group is through the selectedData property. If sData is equal to "digest" (the data value for the crbDigest instance), the movie goes to the digest frame label. If sData is equal to "normal" (the data value for the crbNormal instance), the movie goes to the normal frame label.

After the function is defined, the function is used within a Delegate.create() method as the listener of the "click" event of the cbtSignup button. If you didn't use the Delegate class here, then the gotoAndStop() actions in the onSignUpClick() function would fail because this scope would refer to the cbtSignup button.

Listing 33-2: The onSignUpClick() Handler for the Button **component**

```
import mx.utils.Delegate;

var ctaInfo:mx.controls.TextArea;
var cbtSignup:mx.controls.Button;
var rgNews:mx.controls.RadioButtonGroup;

var lvData:LoadVars = new LoadVars();
lvData.onLoad = function(bSuccess:Boolean):Void {
    if(bSuccess){
        trace("---text file loaded successfully");
        ctaInfo.text = this.intro_text;
    } else {
        trace("---text file did not load.");
    }
```

Continued

Listing 33-2 *(continued)*

```
};
lvData.load("component.txt");

function onSignUpClick(oEvent:Object):Void {
    trace(oEvent.target + " clicked");
    var sData:String = rgNews.selectedData;
    trace("\tsData: " + sData);
    if (sData == "digest") {
        this.gotoAndStop("digest");
    } else if (sData == "normal") {
        this.gotoAndStop("normal");
    }
}

cbtSignup.addEventListener("click", Delegate.create(this, onSignUpClick));

_lockroot = true;
stop();
```

8. Save your Flash document, and test it (Ctrl+Enter or ⌘+Enter). When you click the "sign me up" button, the movie should jump to the `digest` frame label. Click the Home button to go back to the first frame of the movie. Now, choose the Normal radio button, and click the "sign me up" button. The movie will jump to the `normal` frame label.

9. Let's activate the `ComboBox` instance, `ccbSections`, so users who select an item from the menu are automatically taken to a certain area of your movie. This is very similar to what you have accomplished with the `RadioButton` instances, although you will use a different method this time. The instance name of the ComboBox has already been set to `ccbSections`. The values for the combo box's labels and data have also already been entered for you into the `label` and `data` fields, respectively. You can activate the instance of the `ComboBox` in two different ways. Because the data and labels are the same names, you could simply create a `Button` component instance and enter the following code onto the button:

```
on (click) {
    this._parent.gotoAndStop(this._parent.ccbSections.value);
}
```

However, if you are not using the same data and frame label names, you need to do something a bit more complex, which can easily be applied to many different components. To avoid putting a lot of code on a button, and to make your drop-down box automatically take your user to a different area of the movie, you create a listener object for the `ccbSections` instance. Add the bold code shown in Listing 33-3 to the code on frame 1 from Step 7.

Here, a function named `onSectionChange` is created. Its retrieves the currently selected value from the `ccbSections` instance (`oEvent.target.value`) and sets that as the value of a frame label used for a `gotoAndStop()` action.

Listing 33-3: The onSectionChange() Handler for the ComboBox Component

```
import mx.utils.Delegate;

var ctaInfo:mx.controls.TextArea;
var cbtSignup:mx.controls.Button;
var ccbSections:mx.controls.ComboBox;
var rgNews:mx.controls.RadioButtonGroup;

var lvData:LoadVars = new LoadVars();
lvData.onLoad = function(bSuccess:Boolean):Void {
    if(bSuccess){
        trace("---text file loaded successfully");
        ctaInfo.text = this.intro_text;
    } else {
        trace("---text file did not load.");
    }
};
lvData.load("component.txt");

function onSignUpClick(oEvent:Object):Void {
    trace(oEvent.target + " clicked");
    var sData:String = rgNews.selectedData;
    trace("\tsData: " + sData);
    if (sData == "digest") {
        this.gotoAndStop("digest");
    } else if (sData == "normal") {
        this.gotoAndStop("normal");
    }
}

function onSectionChange(oEvent:Object):Void {
    var sVal:String = oEvent.target.value;
    this.gotoAndStop(sVal);
}

cbtSignup.addEventListener("click", Delegate.create(this, onSignUpClick));
ccbSections.addEventListener("close", Delegate.create(this, onSectionChange));

_lockroot = true;
stop();
```

10. Save your Flash document, and test it. Click the ComboBox instance, and choose a section name. When you make a choice, the movie goes to the appropriate frame of the Flash movie.

11. Now add a ScrollPane instance to the movie. The ScrollPane component enables you to add a Movie Clip symbol to a scrollable window. On frame 15 of the pages layer, drag an instance of the ScrollPane component onto the Stage from the Components panel. Size and position the new instance however you prefer.

12. Open the Library panel. Select the file named `beach.jpg`, and drag it to the Stage. Convert it to a Movie Clip symbol by pressing the F8 key. In the Convert to Symbol dialog box, name the symbol **pictureClip**. Assign a registration point in the top-left corner. Click the Advanced button in the dialog box. Select the Export for ActionScript check box (which also selects the Export in first frame check box). The linkage identifier should also automatically be set to `pictureClip`. Refer to Figure 33-17 for these details.

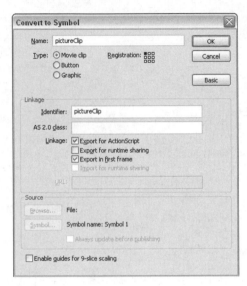

Figure 33-17: The settings for the `pictureClip` **symbol**

13. Select the instance of the `ScrollPane` component on your Stage. Open the Property inspector, and name the instance `cspImg`. Select the Parameters tab. For the `contentPath` parameter, enter the string `pictureClip` that you set as your symbol's linkage ID.

14. Save your Flash document, and test the movie. Choose `new` from the `ComboBox` instance, and, on the new frame, you will see the image within the `ScrollPane` window. If you want to be able to drag the picture with the mouse, go back to the Parameters tab in the Property inspector and change `scrollDrag` to `true`.

On the CD-ROM   You can find the finished file, `components_100.fla`, in the `ch33` folder of this book's CD-ROM.

Modifying Components

We have already discussed how to alter the color, alpha, or brightness of your component, allowing you to match it to the content on your production. It is a bit more complicated, but not difficult, to change more than just the symbol's effects in the Property inspector. There are three ways in which you can change the look and feel of Flash 8 components:

✦ Use the Styles API

✦ Apply a theme

✦ Modify or replace a component's skins

For the purposes of this introduction to components, you'll learn how to change the look of components using styles.

Cross-Reference

For more information on themes and changing components' skins, search the Flash 8 Help panel with the terms "customizing components."

Global style formats

You can use ActionScript to change the look of your components. Using ActionScript to change properties is often much easier than doing so manually or making your own graphics. Luckily, you can change attributes of components on an instance or global level — with the help of ActionScript. Most of these changes will be limited to colors, alignment, and text.

In Flash 8, you can control the look and feel of all components in your Flash movie by using the _global.style object.

On the CD-ROM

Open the components_100.fla document from the ch33 folder of this book's CD-ROM to test this new feature.

1. Create a new layer, and rename it to **global styles**. Place this layer at the top of the layer stack.

2. On frame 1 of the global styles layer, open the Actions panel (F9), and add the code shown in Listing 33-4.

   Here, the setStyle() method is used to apply various style changes, from color to font face.

Listing 33-4: An Example of Using the _global.style Object

```
_global.style.setStyle("color", 0x336699);
_global.style.setStyle("themeColor", "haloBlue")
_global.style.setStyle("fontSize", 10);
_global.style.setStyle("fontFamily", "Verdana");
_global.style.setStyle("backgroundColor", 0xE2C7C7);
```

---

3. Save the Flash document as components_101.fla, and test it. All of the components will change to the new style settings.

On the CD-ROM

You can find the components_101.fla document in the ch33 folder of this book's CD-ROM.

Cross-Reference   Search the Flash 8 Help panel for "supported styles" to see the various style properties that can be set and changed with ActionScript.

Changing styles for a component class

You can also create a custom style for each type of component in your Flash movie. For example, if you want all RadioButton components to use a specific font, you can write ActionScript code to do just that, without having to set a global style or change the style on each individual instance.

1. Open the `components_101.fla` file created in the previous section. Resave this document as `components_102.fla`.

2. Select frame 1of the global styles layer, and open the Actions panel. Add the code shown in Listing 33-5 to the existing code.

   This code creates a new `CSSStyleDeclaration` object named `_global.styles.RadioButton`, which is also the value for a variable named `styleRadio`. To create a new style object for any particular class of component, use this syntax format: `_global.styles.ComponentClass`, where *ComponentClass* is the class name of the component you're controlling with the style. Once you've established a new `CSSStyleDeclaration` object, you can use the `setStyle()` method with the same property names you can use with the `_global.style` object discussed in the previous section.

Listing 33-5: **Changing the Style of a Specific Component Class**

```
// Component class styling
var styleRadio = _global.styles.RadioButton = new ⤸
   mx.styles.CSSStyleDeclaration();
styleRadio.setStyle("fontFamily", "Arial Black");
```

Changing styles for individual instances

It is relatively easy to change the font color and face on individual component instances now that you understand style formats. You can accomplish this task by using single lines of ActionScript. Because this code uses fonts in the system, it is important to remember that a default system font will be displayed if your end-user does not have the particular font installed on his or her system.

Cross-Reference   Using custom font faces and embedded fonts with buttons is covered in the last section, "Using Embedded Fonts with Components."

1. Create a new Flash document, and save it as `component_style.fla`.

2. Rename Layer 1 to **cbt**. On frame 1 of this layer, add an instance of the Button component from the Components panel. In the Property inspector, name this instance cbt.

3. Make a new layer, and name it **actions**. On frame 1 of this layer, add the following lines of code in the Actions panel:

```
var cbt:mx.controls.Button;
cbt.setStyle("fontFamily", "Arial");
cbt.setStyle("themeColor", "haloOrange");
cbt.setStyle("fontWeight", "bold");
cbt.setStyle("color", 0x333333);
```

This will set your button font face as Arial, and the second line of ActionScript tells it to use the orange Halo theme. Line 3 sets the font style to bold for the label text, and line 4 sets the color of label text to dark gray.

Tip   There are three built-in halo themes: haloGreen, haloBlue, and haloOrange. The themes, by and large, control the outline color used by components.

4. Save the Flash document, and test it. The Button component instance should now have a different appearance.

On the CD-ROM   In the ch33 folder of this book's CD-ROM, you can find the completed file, component_style.fla.

Using Embedded Fonts with Components

In this section, you will explore how to use a custom font for a Button component. There are two ways to accomplish this: Use a dummy text field that embeds the font you want to use in the component, or add a Font symbol set to export from the Library panel. Both involve some ActionScript. First of all, let's look at the easier of the two methods.

1. Open the component_style.fla document from the last section, and resave the document as component_embedded_font.fla.

2. Select frame 1 of the actions layer, and delete the existing code. Add the following code:

```
var cbt:mx.controls.Button;
cbt.setStyle("fontFamily", "Futura");
cbt.setStyle("embedFonts", true);
```

This code sets the font face of the Button component to Futura. The second line tells the component that it should only display embedded fonts. If you tested your movie at this point, the label text for the component would be empty because the Futura font is not embedded in the movie.

3. Create a new layer and name it **tEmbedded**. On frame 1 of this layer, select the Text tool and make a Dynamic text field off-stage. Give the field an instance name of tEmbedded in the Property inspector. In the font menu of the Property inspector, choose Futura. (If you don't have Futura, pick a different font name, and be sure to change the name in the code of Step 2.) Next, click the Embed button in the Property inspector. In the Character Embedding dialog box (shown in Figure 33-18), Ctrl+click (or ⌘+click on the Mac) the Uppercase, Lowercase, and Numerals options. Click OK to accept these settings. You have now embedded the Futura font in the Flash movie.

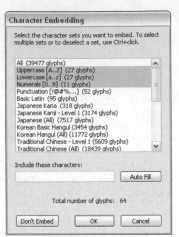

Figure 33-18: The Character Options dialog box

4. Save your Flash document, and test it. The Futura font (or your substituted font, if applicable) is the font used by the cbt instance.

On the CD-ROM

You can find the completed document, `component_embedded_font.fla`, in the ch33 folder of this book's CD-ROM.

If you don't want to use a dummy text field as this example illustrated, there is another way you can use an embedded font with a component. You can add a Font symbol to the Library panel, and set the font to export with the Flash movie. This method, however, will significantly add more weight (in bytes) to the movie's file size because all characters in the font are exported with the movie. We highly recommend you use an empty TextField instance with specific character ranges to minimize the size of your Flash movies.

Cross-Reference

We show you how to embed specific styles of a font in Chapter 30, "Applying HTML and Text Field Formatting."

Replacing Component Skins

You can also add your own symbols to your Flash movie's Library panel to overwrite the built-in symbols included with the compiled clip of a component. For example, if you don't like the check mark graphic for a CheckBox component, you can add your own background symbol(s) for the CheckBox component to use in place of the default skins.

The general process for replacing a component's built-in skin graphics involves the following steps:

1. Find out the linkage identifiers for the component's skin symbols. In the exercise for this section, we show you how to find the source file used for the User Interface components.

2. In your own Flash document, create (or modify a copy of) a symbol for the skin item you want to change.

3. Make sure the new symbol(s) are set to export for ActionScript, using the same linkage identifiers as the original component's skin symbols.

Let's try this process with the `CheckBox` component. In the following steps, you learn how to change the check mark graphic of the `CheckBox` component.

1. Create a new Flash document, and save it as `component_skin.fla`.

2. Rename Layer 1 to **cch**.

3. On frame 1 of the cch layer, drag the `CheckBox` component from the Components panel to the Stage. In the Property inspector, name the new instance **cch**.

4. Now, open the `HaloTheme.fla` file, which is included with the installed files of Flash 8. If you're using Windows, you can find this file in the `C:\Program Files\Macromedia\Flash 8\en\Configuration\ComponentFLA` folder. If you're using Mac OS X, you'll find the file in the `[Startup Disk]: Applications: Macromedia: Flash 8: en: Configuration: ComponentFLA` folder. The `HaloTheme.fla` contains all of the skin symbols used by the User Interface components. Open this document's Library panel, and open the Flash UI Components 2 folder. There, double-click the HaloTheme symbol, as shown in Figure 33-19.

Figure 33-19: The HaloTheme symbol

5. The HaloTheme symbol contains nested instances of each component's skin symbols. Select the `CheckBox` component's assets at the top-left corner of the asset assemblage, as shown in Figure 33-20. Copy this symbol (Ctrl+C or ⌘+C).

Caution

Do not save changes to the `HaloTheme.fla` document. This is the only original copy of the symbol skins included with Flash 8. If you delete or alter this file, you will need to reinstall Flash 8 to get the original `HaloTheme.fla` document. If you want to save changes to the `HaloTheme.fla` document, resave the changes in a new .fla file.

6. Switch back to the `component_skin.fla` document, and paste the copied symbol on to the Stage. You can delete the instance from the Stage once you've pasted it — the Library panel for the `component_skin.fla` document has copies of the symbols.

Figure 33-20: The CheckBox component's skin assets

7. Open the Library panel for the `component_skin.fla` document (or switch to it in the Library panel's new combo box). You'll now find new folders containing the assets you just pasted. Open the Elements folder, and examine the contents. You'll find that the check mark graphic is contained within a symbol called CheckShape1. While this Graphic symbol is not set to export, it is included in the CheckTrue symbols (set to export) in the States folder of the Library panel. Double-click the CheckShape1 symbol to edit the check mark graphic.

8. On the CheckShape1 symbol timeline, turn the existing layer (Layer 1) into a Guide layer, and lock and hide the layer. By doing this, you're preserving the original graphic just in case you want to go back to it. Create a new layer, and draw a new check mark graphic. For our example, we drew an X shape with the Brush tool, as shown in Figure 33-21.

9. Save the `component_skin.fla` document, and test it (Ctrl+Enter or ⌘+Enter). When you click the `CheckBox` instance in the movie, you should see the new check mark graphic you created in Step 8.

Caution   Not all graphics of User Interface components are available as skin symbols in the `HaloTheme.fla` document library. For example, the `Button` component uses ActionScript code to draw the graphical states of the button.

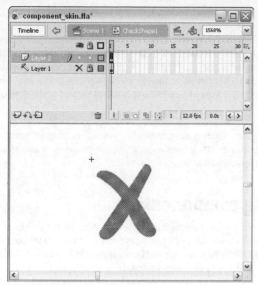

Figure 33-21: The new check mark graphics

 You can find the completed file, `component_skin.fla`, in the `ch33` folder of this book's CD-ROM.

Custom Components

One of the most exciting aspects of components in Flash 8 is being able to make your own creations for distribution or reuse. Custom components usually require a significant amount of ActionScript or at least a solid understanding of the language in order to modify an established component. If you learn how to make your own components to suit common requirements, you will inevitably save a lot of valuable development time. Components were created to be easily reused among projects, and they also allow for simple modifications without having to alter the ActionScript code in the component. Given the robust nature of components, you should be able to develop complex applications, detailed right down to custom icons for the library. While we will not go into detail on how to create custom components in this chapter due to their complexity, we do explore more custom component creation in Chapter 35, "Building an Image Gallery Component."

 Tip As you learned earlier in this chapter, components can be compiled clips. Flash 8 enables you to compile your own custom components so that you can distribute the components without giving away your source code.

Live preview

If you are creating custom components, a Live Preview can be extremely useful. This feature enables you to create an updated view of your component in the authoring environment, so you do not have to publish your movie to view the current state of your component. Creating a Live Preview requires a number of steps to set up your movie structure properly and also to activate ActionScript. It is definitely worth it if you are spending a lot of time creating your own components.

Tip   If you create a component, a live preview layer is automatically generated for your component. Usually, anything within the component that uses a getter/setter property is automatically included in the automatic live preview in the compiled clip.

Exchanging and acquiring components

After you have made your own components, you may be interested in distributing them. Or you may also be looking for a place to find new prebuilt elements for your Web site. Luckily, there are many extensive resources online where you can find components for download or for submission. A good place to start searching is at Macromedia:

    www.macromedia.com/exchange/flash

To install components, you need to download the free Extension Manager 1.7 (or higher), which is the first version to be compatible with Flash 8. There is also a specific method for making your components ready for exchange. You need to package it into a .mxi file, which this Manager can read. The file tells the Manager information regarding the file and the creator. Information about making your components ready for the Extension Manager is available from the same section of the Web site, which includes help and FAQ links.

Web Resource   We'd like to know what you think about this chapter. Visit www.flashsupport.com/feedback to send us your comments.

Summary

✦ Components are a fast and easy way to add interactivity to a movie. They save time and increase usability through consistency, intuitiveness, and solid ActionScript.

✦ Flash 8 (and Flash MX 2004) components are called V2 components, whereas Flash MX components are called V1 components.

✦ The User Interface components that ship with Flash 8 are compiled clips. All of the components' assets and code are condensed into a single symbol. You cannot edit a component's assets in its compiled version.

✦ Some of the most useful UI elements are already built into Flash 8, including radio buttons, click buttons, combo boxes, lists, and scrolling panes. Using these facilitates user friendliness with your Flash projects because they emulate the user interface elements commonly used across the Internet and on many desktop applications.

✦ You can change the look and feel of your components by using the `setStyle()` method of the individual component or of the `_global.style` object.

✦ If you are changing the fonts on your components, you probably want to embed them to avoid problems if your end-user does not have the font you are calling for.

✦ Advanced users of Flash may want to create their own custom components. Custom components can be reused from movie to movie, exchanged, or sold on the Internet. You can download additional components to add to your own movie from online resources, such as the Macromedia Exchange.

✦　　✦　　✦

Binding Data and Events to Components

In the last chapter, you learned how to use many of the User Interface components in a Flash movie. Components enable you to create Rich Internet Applications (or RIAs) within a Web browser that work very much like applications you run on your desktop. In this chapter, you learn how to expand the potential of components by integrating data providers and event handling.

What Is Data Binding?

You may often hear the term *data binding* associated with discussions of Flash components. Data binding is the process of taking information and adding it to a component, to display the information or to manipulate the data in a meaningful way. Any information that you bind to a component is often called a *data provider*. Data providers can be very simple, such as a `String` value (for example, a heading at the top of a movie with the text "Welcome to the Site"), or very complicated, such as a `RecordSet` object or an `Array` value (for example, a list of employees in your company, complete with first and last names, identification numbers, photo URLs, and so on). In Flash movies, you can take a data provider and bind it to a component in one of four ways:

✦ **Adding data in the Parameters tab:** As you learned in the last chapter, you can add data to a component instance by changing values in the Parameters tab of the Property inspector or the Component Inspector panel. While this approach is easy to understand and implement, the data used with the component is static — for most Flash applications you build, you will want to employ more dynamic methods of assigning data to components.

✦ **Visual data binding:** If you're using Flash Pro 8, you can use the Bindings and Schema tabs of the Component Inspector panel to link data and events between Data and User Interface components in your Flash movie. This approach does not require much (if any) ActionScript code for you to type yourself. When you use the Bindings and Schema tabs to link components, the DataBindingClasses symbol is automatically added to your movie's library. You don't need to do anything with this symbol in your own code—Flash 8 takes care of just about everything behind the scenes.

✦ **Custom data provider code:** You can write your own ActionScript to create data and bind the data to one or more components. This approach can use Data components to load external data, or you can build your own data handling objects that pass data to components within the movie.

✦ **DataBindingClasses in ActionScript:** You can use the same DataBindingClasses symbol that is included with your Flash movie for visual data binding in your own ActionScript code. This method is by far one of the most complex ways to link data and events between Flash components.

In this chapter, you learn how to use visual data binding and custom data provider code to bind data with components.

Working with Visual Data Binding: Building a Video Clip Selector

The visual data binding features of Flash Pro 8 enable you to add external data and interactivity to your Flash movies without typing much (if any!) code in the Actions panel. In this section, you learn how to build a list of video clips to play with the FLVPlayback component.

Note   You must be using Flash Pro 8 to complete the following exercise.

Have you ever wanted to build a dynamic list of video clips that controls the content of a video-based component? In this section, you learn how to build a Flash movie that loads a list of video clips specified by an XML file. When the user selects one of the clips in a List component, an instance of the FLVPlayback plays the content.

Preparing the assets

We've already done the work of preparing five video clip files (.flv) to play in the sample user interface. We used Sorenson Squeeze 4.2 to compress the original video source clips of five garden plants.

On the CD-ROM   You can find these .flv files in the ch34/video_list/video folder of this book's CD-ROM.

Before you proceed, make a copy of the video folder (containing the five .flv files) from the CD-ROM to a location on your computer. For final Web deployment, these video assets should be uploaded to your Web server as well.

Making an XML file

Before you build the Flash movie showcasing the user interface of the project, you create a simple XML file that describes the video assets to be loaded. Complete the following steps in your preferred XML editing tool, such as Macromedia Dreamweaver 8. You can also use a text editor such as Notepad on Windows or TextEdit on Macintosh.

1. Create a new XML (or text) document. Save the file as `video.xml`, in the same location where you copied the video folder from the previous section. In the Save As dialog box, look for an option that lets you specify the character encoding — you want to save this document as Unicode (UTF-8) text.

Tip　If you're using Macromedia Dreamweaver, choose Modify ➪ Page Properties to convert the document's encoding to UTF-8. Flash Player 6 and higher prefer to load data saved in UTF-8 encoding.

2. Add the text shown in Listing 34-1. This XML schema defines a parent node of `<video>`, which has child nodes named `<item>` describing each video asset. The `label` value stores the displayed name of the video clip, while the `data` value stores the URL (relative or absolute) to the video file.

Listing 34-1: **The List of Video Assets**

```
<?xml version="1.0" encoding="utf-8"?>
<video>
   <item label="Echinacea" data="video/plant_001.flv" />
   <item label="Dalia" data="video/plant_002.flv" />
   <item label="Pumpkin" data="video/plant_003.flv" />
   <item label="Strawberries" data="video/plant_004.flv" />
   <item label="Rose" data="video/plant_005.flv" />
</video>
```

---

3. Save the XML file.

On the CD-ROM　You can find the completed file, `video.xml`, in the `ch37/video_list` folder of this book's CD-ROM.

Now that you have the video assets copied to your computer and the XML file describing those assets created, you can build the Flash movie user interface.

Constructing the Flash movie

In this section, you create the Flash document featuring the List, XMLConnector, and FLVPlayback components. The XMLConnector component loads the XML file created in the last section, and passes the data to a List component. The List component then displays the list of video clips. When the user clicks an item in the List component, the FLVPlayback component plays the video clip.

1. In Flash Pro 8, create a new Flash document and save it as `video_list.fla` in the same location as the `video.xml` file you built in the last section.

2. Rename Layer 1 to **cxc**. This name stands for *c*omponent *X*MLConnector.

3. Open the Components panel (Window ➪ Components), and expand the Data nesting. Drag an instance of the XMLConnector component to the Stage. You can place the instance anywhere you want, as the icon of the component hides at run time.

4. Select the instance, and open the Property inspector. Name the instance `cxc`. Click the Parameters tab, and change the URL value to **video.xml**. Change the `direction` value to **receive** — for this sample, you only load XML data into the Flash movie. No data is sent from the Flash movie. Review the settings shown in Figure 34-1.

Figure 34-1: The settings for the cxc instance

5. Now, you need to load a sample XML schema for the `cxc` instance, so that the component knows how to parse the XML data in the `video.xml` file. With the `cxc` instance selected, open the Component Inspector panel (Alt+F7 or Option+F7). Select the Schema tab. There, highlight the `results` entry, and click the document icon button (displaying a blue arrow pointing down). This button enables you to import a sample XML file which Flash 8 can analyze. Keep in mind that this import feature does not store the actual XML data — only the XML schema (that is, the arrangement and names of XML nodes within the document) is stored in the `cxc` instance. Import the `video.xml` file you built in the last section. Your Schema tab and `results` parameter should now resemble Figure 34-2.

The schema of a component dictates which properties of the component are bindable to other components. If you hadn't imported (or created) a schema for the `cxc` instance, you wouldn't be able to pass specific pieces of data to other components.

Figure 34-2: The Schema tab information for the cxc instance

6. Once a schema is defined for the component, you can start to bind properties within that schema to other components. Now you'll bind the `label` and `data` properties of the cxc component to a List component. Create a new layer named **cli**, which stands for component *List*. In the Components panel, expand the User Interface nesting and drag an instance of the List component to the left half of the Stage.

7. In the Property inspector, name the new List component instance `cli`. You don't need to add any labels or data to this component in the Parameters tab — that's the job of the XMLConnector component.

8. Select the cxc instance on the Stage, and go back to the Component Inspector panel. Select the Bindings tab. Click the plus (+) button to add a new binding. In the Add Binding dialog box, select the `item` array, as shown in Figure 34-3. This property will be bound to the List component you added earlier. Click OK.

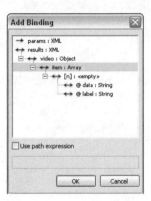

Figure 34-3: The Add Binding dialog box

9. With the new binding entry selected in the Bindings tab, change the `direction` value to out — you want to bind the `item` data out from the cxc instance to another component.

10. Double-click the `bound to` field in the Bindings tab. In the Bound To dialog box, select the `cli` instance in the Component path column. In the Schema location column, choose the `dataProvider` property. Refer to Figure 34-4. Click OK.

Tip   The XML schema of the `video.xml` file intentionally uses label and data attributes for each video item, as these names serve as direct mappings to the data provider format of the List component.

11. Before you can test the binding in a Flash movie, you need to tell the XMLConnector component to load the XML file. Create a new layer named **actions**, and place the layer at the top of the layer stack. Select frame 1 of the actions layer, and open the Actions panel (F9, or Option+F9). Add the following lines of code. The `trigger()` method of the XMLConnector component instructs the instance to retrieve the XML document you specified in the Property inspector (in Step 4).

```
var cxc:mx.data.components.XMLConnector;
cxc.trigger();
```

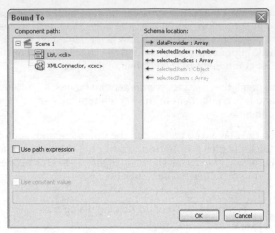

Figure 34-4: The Bound To dialog box

12. Save the Flash document, and test it (Ctrl+Enter or ⌘+Enter). The XML data loads into the cxc instance, which then passes the label and data values of each <item> node to the cli instance (refer to Figure 34-5).

Figure 34-5: The XML data populating the List component

13. Now, you're ready to map the data value of the selected item in the List component to an FLVPlayback component. When the user clicks an item in the cli instance, the video clip for that entry should begin playback. Create a new layer named **cfp**, and place it below the actions layer. Open the FLV Playback – Player 8 nesting in the Components panel, and drag an instance of the FLVPlayback component to the Stage. Place the instance to the right of the List component.

14. Select the FLVPlayback instance, and name it cfp in the Property inspector. Click the Parameters tab, and choose a skin for the component. For this example, use the SteelExternalAll.swf skin, as shown in Figure 34-6. Also, use the Free Transform tool to stretch the width and height of the List component to line up with the FLVPlayback component.

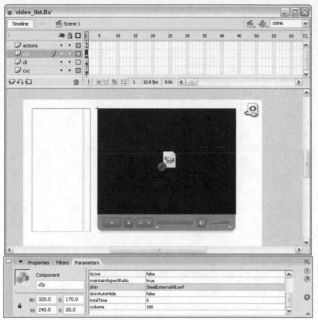

Figure 34-6: The FLVPlayback component settings

15. The List component, by default, only has a schema item for the `selectedItem` property of the `List` class. Therefore, you need to add the `label` and `data` properties to this property of the `cli` instance. Select the `cli` instance on the Stage, and open the Component Inspector panel. Click the Schema tab, and highlight the `selectedItem` entry. Click the smaller plus (+) button, second from the left, in the toolbar of the Schema tab. This button adds a subproperty to the currently selected schema property. Change the field name value to **data**, as shown in Figure 34-7.

16. Now, you have a bindable property named `data` in the `cli` instance. Select the Bindings tab, and click the plus (+) button to add a new binding. (Note that you should already have an existing binding named `dataProvider` from the previous steps—do not remove this binding.) In the Add Binding dialog box (shown in Figure 34-8), select the new `data` property and click OK.

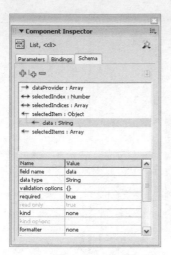

Figure 34-7: The updated Schema tab of the cli instance

Figure 34-8: The Add Binding dialog box

17. With the new binding selected in the Bindings tab, double-click the bound to field. In the Bound To dialog box, select the cfp instance in the Component path column. Then, choose the contentPath property in the Schema location column. The data property of the selected item in the List component contains the path to the .flv file, which needs to be passed into the FLVPlayback component to initiate playback (refer to Figure 34-9). Click OK. The Bindings tab should now look like the one in Figure 34-10.

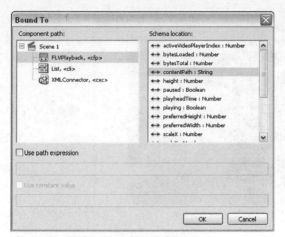

Figure 34-9: The Bound To dialog box

Figure 34-10: The updated Bindings tab for the List component

18. Save the Flash document, and test it (Ctrl+Enter or ⌘+Enter). After the XML data loads into the XMLConnector component and displays in the List component, click one of the video clip names in the List component. The .flv file associated with that video clip should then play in the FLVPlayback component, as shown in Figure 34-11.

Figure 34-11: The selected clip playing in the FLVPlayback component

You can find the completed files for this exercise in the `ch34/video_list` folder on this book's CD-ROM.

If you open the Library panel for the Flash document built in this exercise, you'll find a DataBindingClasses symbol. This component contains all of the ActionScript 2.0 classes necessary to make the features of the Bindings and Schema tabs work. This component weighs about 12 KB in your final .swf file. In the `ch34/datagrid` folder of this book's CD-ROM, you can find the `datagrid_advanced.fla` document, which uses the features of the DataBindingClasses more extensively in ActionScript.

You might be wondering how you can auto-select the first entry in the clip list to enable playback of the clip as soon as the movie loads. In the next section, you learn how to add custom ActionScript code to handle events with components.

Providing Data and Event Handlers for Components

Visual data binding is just one way to pass data and events between components — you can also write your own ActionScript code to grab events from components or populate components with customized data. In this section, you learn how to work with data and events without using the visual data binding features of the Bindings and Schema tabs.

Adding code to movies using visual data binding

In the last section, you learned how to build a list of video clips that could initiate playback of .flv files with the FLVPlayback component. Learn how to finesse the interactivity of this movie using ActionScript.

On the CD-ROM

You can continue to use the `video_list.fla` document you created in the last section. Or, you can make a copy of the same file located in the `ch34/video_list` folder on this book's CD-ROM. If you didn't complete the exercise from the last section, make sure you also copy the `video` folder and the `video.xml` document.

1. Open the `video_list.fla` document in Flash Pro 8. Test the movie (Ctrl+Enter to ⌘+Enter) to review the movie's features. When the movie loads, the FLVPlayback component displays the progress animation as it waits for you to select a clip in the List component. Because this interface is a tad awkward, you'll want to fix it so that the first clip automatically plays when the movie starts.

2. Resave the document as `video_list_select.fla`.

3. Select frame 1 of the actions layer. Open the Actions panel, and add the bold code shown in Listing 34-2. This code creates a function named `onDataLoad`, which is invoked when the XML data loads into the `cxc` instance. Here, the first item in the List component is selected, and the `contentPath` of the `cfp` instance is set to the current `data` value of the List component, retrieved with the `value` property of the `List` class.

Listing 34-2: **Auto-playing the First Video Clip**

```
import mx.utils.Delegate;

var cxc:mx.data.components.XMLConnector;
var cli:mx.controls.List;
var cfp:mx.video.FLVPlayback;

function onDataLoad(oEvent:Object):Void {
    cli.selectedIndex = 0;
    cfp.contentPath = cli.value.toString();
}

cxc.addEventListener("result", Delegate.create(this, onDataLoad));
cxc.trigger();
```

4. Save the Flash document, and test it (Ctrl+Enter or ⌘+Enter). When the XML data loads into the movie, the first item in the List component automatically loads and plays in the FLVPlayback component.

On the CD-ROM

You can find the completed file, `video_list_select.fla`, in the `ch34/video_list` folder on this book's CD-ROM.

Making a list of cue points for a video clip

This section continues an exercise using the FLVPlayback component from Chapter 17, "Displaying Video." You learn how to read the metadata from an .flv file loaded into an FLVPlayback component, and take the cue point data from the metadata to populate a List component. The List component can then serve as a table of contents for the video clip. When the user selects a cue point label in the list, the FLVPlayback component seeks to that cue point in the .flv file. The FLVPlayback component also informs the List component of the current cue point, so that the cue point label highlights automatically as the movie plays.

 Cross-Reference Read our coverage of embedded cue points in Chapter 17, "Displaying Video," to understand how you can add cue points to an .flv file with the new Flash 8 Video Encoder application, or the Video Import Wizard of Flash Pro 8.

 On the CD-ROM Before you begin this exercise, copy the `ch17/cuepoints` folder from this book's CD-ROM to your computer.

1. Open the `cuepoints_embedded.fla` file from your copy of the `cuepoints` folder taken from the book's CD-ROM. Resave this document as `cuepoints_embedded_list.fla`.

2. Move the `cfp` instance (the FLVPlayback component) to the right of the Stage, leaving room for a List component to the left of it.

3. Create a new layer named **cli**, and place the layer anywhere below the actions layer. On frame 1 of the cli layer, add an instance of the List component. In the Property inspector, name the instance `cli`. Use the Free Transform tool to stretch the width and height of the instance to fit along the left side of the `cfp` instance, as shown in Figure 34-12.

4. Now that you have a List component in the Flash movie, you can use the `cli` instance to display the embedded cue points in the .flv file used by the FLVPlayback component. Select frame 1 of the actions layer, and open the Actions panel. Add the bold code shown in Listing 34-3. To understand the modifications, let's work from the bottom up.

   - **New event listeners:** The last two lines of code add new event listeners to t he script. The second to last line of code adds the `onVideoMeta()` function as a listener of the `"metadataReceived"` event from the `cfp` instance (the FLVPlayback component). When the .flv file played by the component is loaded, the `onVideoMeta()` function is invoked. The last line of code adds the `onCueSelect()` function as a listener of the `"change"` event from the `cli` instance (the List component). Whenever the user changes the selection in the List component, the `onCueSelect()` function is invoked.

   - `onVideoMeta()` **function:** This function retrieves the metadata from the .flv file playing in the FLVPlayback component. Within the `metadata` property, you can access the array of embedded cue points for the video clip. A `for()` loop cycles through each cue point object in the array, and adds the `label` parameter and `name` property values as a new item in the List component.

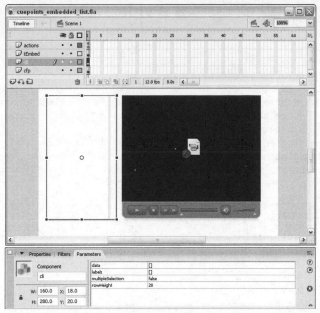

Figure 34-12: The `cli` instance to the left of the `cfp` instance

- `onCueSelect()` **function:** This function is invoked whenever a user selects a new cue name in the List component. Because the cue point's name value is stored as a `data` property of the selected item in the List component, you can access the `value` property of the `cli` instance (`oEvent.target`) and pass the cue name to the `seekToNavCuePoint()` method of the `cfp` instance. The `seekToNavCuePoint()` method enables you to jump to a specific navigation cue point.

- `selectListItem()` **function:** This function is called from the `onVideoMarker()` function whenever a navigation cue point is reached during playback. The cue name is passed to the `selectListItem()` function, where the name is looked up within the `dataProvider` of the `cli` instance. When the name is found, the appropriate index is selected in the List component.

Listing 34-3: **Capturing Metadata from the .flv File**

```
import mx.video.FLVPlayback;
import mx.utils.Delegate;
import flash.filters.DropShadowFilter;
import com.themakers.effects.BlurFader;

var cfp:FLVPlayback;
var cli:mx.controls.List;
var tLabel:TextField;
var bScrubbing:Boolean = false;
```

Continued

Listing 34-3 *(continued)*

```
var nUpdateID:Number;

function onVideoMarker(oEvent:Object):Void {
   var oCue:Object = oEvent.info;
   var sLabel:String = oCue.parameters.label;
   var sPos:String = oCue.parameters.position;
   if(oCue.type == "navigation" && sLabel != undefined ){
      showLabel(sLabel, sPos);
      selectListItem(oCue.name);
   } else if(oCue.type == "event" && !bScrubbing){
      removeLabel();
   }
}

function showLabel(sLabel:String, sPos:String):Void {
   [No changes in this function...]
}

function removeLabel():Void {
   [No changes in this function...]
}

function onScrubStart():Void {
   [No changes in this function...]
}

function onScrubFinish():Void {
   [No changes in this function...]
}

function updateLabel():Void {
    [No changes in this function...]
}

function onVideoMeta(oEvent:Object):Void {
   var oMeta:Object = oEvent.target.metadata;
   var aCues:Array = oMeta.cuePoints;
   for(var i:Number = 0; i < aCues.length; i++){
      var oCue:Object = aCues[i];
      if(oCue.type == "navigation"){
         cli.addItem({label: oCue.parameters.label, data: oCue.name});
      }
   }
}

function onCueSelect(oEvent:Object):Void {
   cfp.seekToNavCuePoint(oEvent.target.value);
```

```
}

function selectListItem(sCueName:String):Void {
    for(var i:Number = 0; i < cli.dataProvider.length; i++){
        var oItem:Object = cli.getItemAt(i);
        if(oItem.data == sCueName){
            cli.selectedIndex = i;
            break;
        }
    }
}

cfp.addEventListener("cuePoint", Delegate.create(this, onVideoMarker));
cfp.addEventListener("scrubStart", Delegate.create(this, onScrubStart));
cfp.addEventListener("scrubFinish", Delegate.create(this, onScrubFinish));
cfp.addEventListener("metadataReceived", Delegate.create(this, onVideoMeta));
cli.addEventListener("change", Delegate.create(this, onCueSelect));
```

5. Save the Flash document, and test it (Ctrl+Enter or ⌘+Enter). When the .flv file is loaded into the FLVPlayback component, the metadata values are passed to the List component, where the label names are displayed. When you select one of the cue point labels in the List component, the video jumps to that cue point.

You can find the completed file, `cuepoints_embedded_list.fla`, in the `ch34/video_ cues` folder. The video asset, `HomeGarden_Full-Res.flv`, is located in the `ch17/cue points` folder. This .flv file is required for the Flash movie.

Creating lists with the DataGrid component

If you need to display data in rows and columns, you might want to consider using the DataGrid component. You can use this component for sorting and displaying any type of ordered data, such as employee directories, product listings, and more. In this section, you learn how to populate a DataGrid component and control the number of columns displayed with the grid.

For this exercise, all of the content in the Flash movie is added to the Stage at run time, programmatically in ActionScript. Also, the DataGrid component is only available in Flash Pro 8.

1. Create a new Flash document, and save it as `datagrid_basic.fla`.

2. Open the Components panel, and expand the User Interface grouping. Drag an instance of the DataGrid component to the Stage.

3. Delete the DataGrid instance on the Stage. You only need to have the DataGrid component in the movie's Library panel — the component is automatically exported for ActionScript. You add the component programmatically in the next step.

4. Rename Layer 1 to **actions**. Select frame 1 of the actions layer, and open the Actions panel (F9, Option+F9). Add the following code. This code creates a new instance of the DataGrid component named `cdg`, assigns a width of 400 pixels and a height of 300 pixels, and positions it at the X, Y coordinate of 30, 30 on the Stage.

```
import mx.controls.DataGrid;

var cdg:DataGrid = createClassObject(DataGrid, "cdg", 1);
cdg.setSize(400, 300);
cdg.move(30, 30);
```

5. Save the Flash document, and test it (Ctrl+Enter or ⌘+Enter). When the movie loads, an empty DataGrid component displays on the Stage, as shown in Figure 34-13.

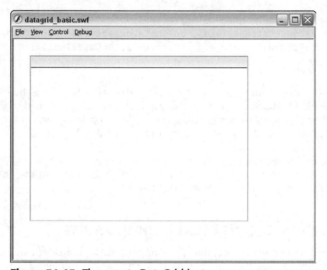

Figure 34-13: The empty DataGrid instance

6. To add some data to the DataGrid instance, add the following code to the script on frame 1 of the actions layer. This code creates a new array named `aData`. The array contains three nested objects, each with the same property names: `name`, `sign`, and `food`. The array is then assigned as the `dataProvider` value of the `cdg` instance.

```
var aData:Array = [
      {name: "Robert Reinhardt", sign: "Scorpio", food: "Thai"},
      {name: "John Smith", sign: "Leo", food: "Italian"},
      {name: "Jimmy Calhoun", sign: "Aquarius", food: "Chinese"}
        ];

cdg.dataProvider = aData;
```

7. Save the Flash document, and test it (Ctrl+Enter or ⌘+Enter). You should now see three columns in the DataGrid instance with the data specified in the aData array, as shown in Figure 34-14.

8. The last task to complete for this exercise is to assign more descriptive header text to the columns. By default, the column names of a DataGrid component are simply the property names for each "record" in the DataGrid instance, as shown in Figure 34-14. To set custom text headers, add the bold code shown in Listing 34-4.

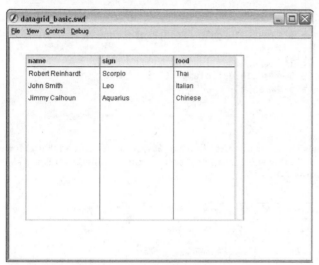

Figure 34-14: The new data in the DataGrid component

Here, you create a new array named aColNames. Each String value in the array represents the new text to be displayed for the columns of the DataGrid instance. The order of the values matches the columns from left to right. The for( ) loop cycles through the array, fetching the DataGridColumn object for each column in the DataGrid instance, cdg. The headerText property of each DataGridColumn column is set to the matching value in the aColNames array.

Listing 34-4: **Creating Custom Header Text for DataGrid Columns**

```
import mx.controls.DataGrid;
import mx.controls.gridclasses.DataGridColumn;

var cdg:DataGrid = createClassObject(DataGrid, "cdg", 1);
cdg.setSize(400, 300);
cdg.move(30, 30);

var aData:Array = [
            {name: "Robert Reinhardt", sign: "Scorpio", food: "Thai"},
            {name: "John Smith", sign: "Leo", food: "Italian"},
            {name: "Jimmy Calhoun", sign: "Aquarius", food: "Chinese"}
```

Continued

Listing 34-4 *(continued)*

```
                ];

cdg.dataProvider = aData;

var aColNames:Array = ["Name", "Sign", "Food Preference"];

for(var i:Number = 0; i < aColNames.length; i++){
   var dgc:DataGridColumn = cdg.getColumnAt(i);
   dgc.headerText = aColNames[i];
}
```

---

9. Save the document, and test it (Ctrl+Enter or ⌘+Enter). The header text for each column should now display the custom text values you specified in the aColNames array, as shown in Figure 34-15.

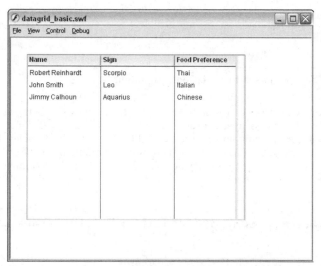

Figure 34-15: The custom header text for each column

You can find the completed file, datagrid_basic.fla, in the ch34/datagrid folder of this book's CD-ROM. You can find a more advanced example of the DataGrid component, datagrid_advanced.fla, in the same folder. This version of the file uses Data BindingClasses, along with the DataSet component, to more efficiently distribute data in the Flash movie.

We'd like to know what you think about this chapter. Visit www.flashsupport.com/ feedback to send us your comments.

Summary

✦ You can add data to Flash components in a variety of ways, from assigning data in the Property inspector to using the visual data binding features of the Component Inspector panel to coding your own data providers and event handlers.

✦ If you use the visual data binding features of the Component Inspector panel, the DataBindingClasses clip is automatically added to your movie's Library panel.

✦ You can import XML data with the XMLConnector component, and bind that data to other components, such as the List component.

✦ The metadata of an .flv file can contain cue point data, which can be mapped to a User Interface component such as the List component. The cue point data can be used to navigate the .flv file playing in an FLVPlayback component.

✦ Using the `createClassObject()` method, you can add a DataGrid component to your Flash movie without placing an instance of the component on the Stage at author-time.

✦ ✦ ✦

Building an Image Gallery Component

I n the first two chapters of Part IX, you learned how to use many of the User Interface and Data components of Flash 8. Now that you're familiar with common production tasks associated with components, you can start to learn how to create your own custom components. In this chapter, you learn how to build a Gallery component. By the end of this chapter, you will know the steps and procedures required to build a fully functional component.

For this chapter, you learn how to build a Flash movie that can dynamically load a list of JPEG files that the user can browse as a series of thumbnails. When the user clicks one of the thumbnails, a larger version of the image loads into the Flash movie. To see the final project, open your Web browser and go to:

    www.flashsupport.com/f8b/gallery/main.html

Note   Make sure you have Flash Player 8 installed to view the completed project.

At this location, you see the interface shown in Figure 35-1. When you click an image thumbnail, the original JPEG loads into the area below the thumbnail bar. The active selection within the bar is highlighted with a bevel filter. When you click another thumbnail, the previously selected thumbnail transitions to a muted grayscale version.

In This Chapter

◆ ◆ ◆ ◆

In This Chapter

Planning and scoping a component

Using filter effects with components

Storing image information as BitmapData

Integrating the Tween class

Scripting XML data with PHP

◆ ◆ ◆ ◆

Figure 35-1: The completed project

Creating a Plan

Before you can start to build the Gallery component, you need to plan the scope of the project. Just what will the component do? We distill the planning process by telling you the component's features, but in the real world, you will need to brainstorm your ideas and formulate directives for a workable production schedule, accountable to your client's budget and your time.

Cross-Reference Read Chapter 3, "Planning Flash Projects," for more information on production guidelines for Flash projects.

Describing the feature set

It might sound too simple to state, but you have to have a plan before you can build anything — even a Flash movie. And more often than not, the lack of proper planning before you start to build a Flash project only results in bigger problems later — the kind that keep you up late at night days before the final delivery date. One of the most common problems that arise early in a Flash project is the desire to overbuild, or add more features to a project than are necessary to satisfy the goals of the project.

The goals we're aiming to fulfill with the Gallery component include:

✦ **Quick updates to images on the server:** Many of your business clients love the capability to just upload some images to a Web server, and voila — the images are automatically loading into a Flash user interface you designed for them. One of the goals of this project, therefore, is to use server-side scripting (in this case, using PHP as the server side language) to dynamically read the filenames in a given Web folder and deliver that data to the Flash movie. Whenever a new JPEG file is uploaded to that Web folder, the PHP script automatically includes the file in the XML feed it sends to the Flash movie.

✦ **Unique yet usable interface for browsing images:** At the end of the day, if your Flash movie's user interface is too confusing for a Web visitor to understand, the project has lost the potential that Flash offers over standard HTML-based sites. The Gallery component should indicate the state of image browsing clearly, with rollover and rollout states for thumbnail buttons. The thumbnails should also remember if they've been clicked previously or not.

✦ **Downloadable images:** If a user likes an image, she should be able to download the image to the desktop. In this component, you learn how to use the new `FileReference` API to download files directly from a Flash Player 8 movie. You use this new feature with the `ContextMenu` class to enable the user to right-click the large image area to download the JPEG file currently displayed.

New Feature

You can also use the `FileReference` API to upload files from the user's computer to your Web server.

✦ **Utilizing JPEG metadata:** If you've used a digital camera, you know that JPEG images can store a lot of useful data related to the exposure, camera model, flash settings, and so on. You can also use an application like Adobe Photoshop to add more metadata, such as a caption and an author byline. If the JPEG image displayed in the Gallery component has a caption, the component should display the caption below the image.

✦ **Dynamic resizing of original JPEG files for thumbnails:** With the power of server-side scripting, you can create dynamically resized JPEG images on the fly — without ever having to manually create a thumbnail version yourself in a program like Macromedia Fireworks or Adobe Photoshop. The Gallery component will feature a property that specifies the URL to a resizing script.

Determining the server-side scripting requirements

As we mentioned in the previous section, our Gallery component requires the power of server-side scripting to work its magic. We picked PHP as the server-side language to use for this project, although you could adapt the same functionality with any server-side language, including Macromedia ColdFusion, Microsoft .NET/ASP, Perl, and so on. One of the reasons we use PHP for this project is that PHP is available on practically every Web account that you purchase from an Internet Service Provider (ISP) or Internet Presence Provider (IPP). The following list provides the server-side requirements for this project.

On the CD-ROM

You can upload the `info.php` document to your Web server account to discover more details about your server's PHP installation. You can find this file in the `ch35/finished files/prod/wwwroot` folder of this book's CD-ROM.

✦ **PHP5:** We recommend that you use PHP5 for this project, but you should be able to use PHP4 as well.

✦ **GD library:** This library enables your PHP scripts to manipulate image data, including the capability to resize JPEG images. Without this library, you won't be able to create the thumbnail images for the Gallery component. If you run the `info.php` script on your Web server, search for the term "gd" to see if the GD library is installed, as shown in Figure 35-2.

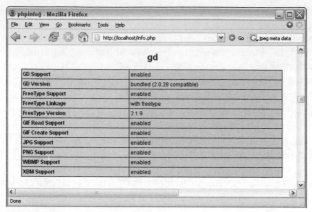

Figure 35-2: The GD library information as displayed by the info.php script.

Once you've determined that your server has met the core requirements, you're ready to use the three PHP scripts we've included in the `ch35/finished files/prod/wwwroot` folder on this book's CD-ROM.

Tip You can quickly determine if your Web server has PHP installed and enabled. Upload the `info.php` script to a publicly accessible folder on your Web server, and access the `info.php` script in a Web browser. If the browser asks you to download the `info.php` file, your Web server most likely does not have PHP enabled.

Note It's beyond the scope of this chapter to discuss the PHP scripting used in each script file. We provide a basic overview of the each file's functionality in the following sections. We encourage you to open the PHP files in your preferred text editor to review the syntax. For the PHP experts out there, note that the `$doc_root` variable (found in both the `files.php` and `resize.php` scripts) uses a nonstandard way—for portability reasons—to determine the document root of the Web server. The syntax we use enables the scripts to function properly in both Windows IIS server and Apache Web server environments. Feel free to modify any of the scripts to suit your particular needs.

files.php

This script dynamically reads a specified Web folder to search for JPEG files and displays the found JPEG files in an XML document. You must pass a directory name, either relative or from the server root, as a variable named `dir`. For example, if you specify

```
files.php?dir=images/
```

the script looks for a folder named `images` in the same folder where the `files.php` script resides. You can also specify a directory with the syntax:

```
files.php?dir=/gallery/images/
```

which tells the script to look for a folder named `gallery` at the server root, and then looks for a folder named `images` within that `gallery` folder.

To see a sample XML document created by this script, type the following URL into a Web browser:

```
www.flashsupport.com/f8b/gallery/files.php?dir=images/
```

When this page loads, you should see the XML data shown in Listing 35-1. Note that the ⤵ character indicates a continuation of the same line of code. The schema for this XML file uses a parent node named `<gallery>`, which contains several child nodes named `<img>`. Each `<img>` tag represents a JPEG file found in the images folder. The `files.php` script retrieves all of the information listed for each JPEG file, including the image's width and height (in pixels), the path to the image on the server (`src`), the caption stored within the JPEG's metadata (if a caption exists), and the name of the file (`filename`) without the directory path.

Note   In order for the `files.php` script to function properly, the `JPEG-Meta.php` script must be located in the same Web folder as the `files.php` file. We discuss the `JPEG-Meta.php` script later in this section.

The XML data provided by the `files.php` script is loaded into the Flash movie, which turns the XML data into an array to pass as a data provider to the Gallery component.

Listing 35-1: The XML Data for the JPEG Files

```xml
<?xml version="1.0" encoding="utf-8"?>
<gallery>
   <img width="500" height="200" src="images/darkPine.jpg" caption="Dark ⤵
      pine and setting sun, Griffith Park, CA" filename="darkPine.jpg" />
   <img width="500" height="200" src="images/dustHalo.jpg" caption="Dust ⤵
      halo on small tree, Griffith Park, CA" filename="dustHalo.jpg" />
   <img width="500" height="200" src="images/dustyClearing.jpg" ⤵
      caption="Dusty clearing with slanting sun, Runyon Canyon Park, CA" ⤵
      filename="dustyClearing.jpg" />
   <img width="500" height="200" src="images/japaneseTree.jpg" ⤵
      caption="Japanese tree in fog, Runyon Canyon Park, CA" ⤵
      filename="japaneseTree.jpg" />
   <img width="500" height="200" src="images/rainbowTower.jpg" ⤵
      caption="Rainbow sky and metal tower, Hollywood Hills, CA" ⤵
      filename="rainbowTower.jpg" />
   <img width="500" height="200" src="images/roadNorth.jpg" ⤵
      caption="Road north to Mulholland Drive, Runyon Canyon, CA" ⤵
      filename="roadNorth.jpg" />
   <img width="500" height="200" src="images/scrolledRoot.jpg" ⤵
      caption="Scrolled root at dusk, San Fernando Valley, CA" ⤵
      filename="scrolledRoot.jpg" />
   <img width="500" height="200" src="images/skyPools.jpg" ⤵
      caption="Rain pools under cloudy sky, Runyon Canyon Park, CA" ⤵
      filename="skyPools.jpg" />
   <img width="500" height="200" src="images/valleyOverlook.jpg" ⤵
      caption="Overlook, San Fernando Valley, CA" ⤵
      filename="valleyOverlook.jpg" />
   <img width="500" height="200" src="images/weepingTree.jpg" ⤵
```

Continued

Listing 1-1 *(continued)*

```
        caption="Weeping  dark tree, Mulholland Drive, CA" ⤶
        filename="weepingTree.jpg" />
    <img width="500" height="200" src="images/wiredCity.jpg" ⤶
        caption="Phone poles and palms, Hollywood, CA" filename="wiredCity.jpg" />
    <img width="500" height="200" src="images/wiredHill.jpg" ⤶
        caption="Dark hills and paths under wires, Los Angeles, CA" ⤶
        filename="wiredHill.jpg" />
</gallery>
```

resize.php

This PHP script performs the task of resizing a copy of the original JPEG image to fit a specific height. In this project, the Gallery component's thumbnails should be 50 pixels tall. The resize.php script requires two parameters: height and img. The height parameter should be an integer value, while the img parameter specifies the path and name of the JPEG file to resize. For example, if you type the following URL into a Web browser, you should see a picture of a beach on Prince Edward Island, Canada, resized to a height of 50 pixels:

www.flashsupport.com/f8b/gallery/resize.php?height=50&img=/images/beach.jpg

With the Gallery component, you can specify the resize.php script as the value of the thumbScript property.

Tip   You can quickly determine if you have the GD library installed (and/or enabled) on your Web server by uploading the resize.php script to a publicly accessible folder and accessing the script in the Web browser as we demonstrated with the beach picture. Specify an img path that points to a JPEG you've uploaded to another folder on the server.

JPEG-Meta.php

This amazing script, provided to us by Rob Williams at CommunityMX.com, enables the files.php script to retrieve the metadata, if any exists, of each JPEG file in the specified folder. This script must be uploaded to the same Web folder as the files.php script. Without this file, the files.php script does not function.

Web Resource   For more information about using Rob William's PHP script, read his tutorial at CommunityMX.com. You can find a link to this tutorial in the PHP Utilities section of the www.flashsupport.com/links page.

Note   You also need to upload the JPEG images to your Web server, into a folder whose path you specify with the files.php script from the Flash movie.

Phase 1: Setting Up the Gallery class

On this book's CD-ROM, in the ch35 folder, you can find two folders: starter files and finished files. Each folder has the same structure, featuring dev and prod folders. The dev folder contains all of the source files, such as .fla files and ActionScript files, while the prod folder contains all of the Web-ready files that should be uploaded to the Web server for final deployment.

You can learn more about our dev and prod folder structures in Chapter 3, "Planning Flash Projects."

The starter files and finished files folders also have their own version of the gallery.flp file, which is a Flash Project file. If you're using Flash Pro 8, you can open these .flp files to see the dev and prod folder structures. The gallery.flp file from the starter files folder is shown in Figure 35-3.

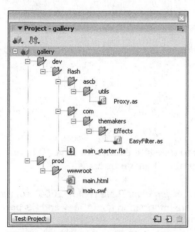

Figure 35-3: The gallery.flp file from the starter files folder

Reviewing the starter files

Let's review the files that have already been built in the starter files folder. You can access each of these files from the gallery.flp file in the Project panel.

Proxy.as

This ActionScript class file, found in the dev/flash/ascb/utils folder, enables a class named Proxy, which has a create() method. This class is very similar to the Delegate class we have used with several examples in previous chapters of the books. The advantage of using the Proxy.create() method over the Delegate.create() method is that the

`Proxy.create()` method enables you to pass additional parameters to the proxied (or delegated) function. For example, with the `Delegate` class, you can only specify a scope and a handler

```
import mx.utils.Delegate;

var mcButton:MovieClip;

function onButtonClick():Void {
    trace("onButtonClick >");
}

mcButton.onRelease = Delegate.create(this, onButtonClick);
```

which instructs the `onRelease()` handler of the `MovieClip` instance named `mcButton` to invoke the `onButtonClick()` function whenever the `mcButton` instance is clicked. However, with the `Proxy` class, you can pass one or more parameters to the proxied function. In the following example, the `onButtonClick()` function receives a reference to the `mcButton` instance:

```
import ascb.util.Proxy;

var mcButton:MovieClip;

function onButtonClick(mc:MovieClip):Void {
    trace("onButtonClick >");
    trace("\tclicked instance: " + mc);
}

mcButton.onRelease = Proxy.create(this, onButtonClick, mc);
```

For the Gallery component, you use the `Proxy` class to delegate events for several handlers, including the User Interface components and the thumbnail image buttons.

Note Many thanks to Joey Lott, lead author of the *Flash 8 ActionScript Bible* (Wiley, 2006), for providing us with his `Proxy.as` class. You can find more information about Joey and his books at `www.person13.com`. Joey is also a writing partner at `CommunityMX.com`.

EasyFilter.as

This class file, which can be found in the `dev/flash/com/themakers/Effects` folder, contains one method named `saturate`. This method can create a `ColorMatrixFilter` instance. This filter is the ActionScript class responsible for enabling the new Adjust Color filter available for `MovieClip` and `TextField` instances in the Filters tab of the Property inspector. For the Gallery component, you use the `EasyFilter.saturate()` method to easily control the saturation color values of thumbnail images. The `saturate()` method accepts values from −100 to 100, just like the Saturation slider in the Adjust Color filter of the Filters tab of the Property inspector. The following code sample illustrates a typical use of the method:

```
import com.themakers.Effects.EasyFilter;

var mcButton:MovieClip;
mcButton.filters = [EasyFilter.saturate(-50)];
```

Note Many thanks to Joey Lott and Guy Watson for their help with creating the ActionScript code within the `saturate()` method. It's beyond the scope of this book to discuss the intricacies of using matrix values with the `ColorMatrixFilter` class—look to the *Flash 8 ActionScript Bible* by Joey Lott (Wiley, 2006) for more information.

main_starter.fla

This Flash document contains the basic layout for the Gallery component and can be found in the `ch35/starter files/dev/flash/main_starter.fla` folder. If you open this file, you can see that the Main Timeline of the movie has three layers:

✦ **_tCaption:** This layer has a `TextField` instance of the same name. The instance is located near the bottom of the Stage. This field displays the caption text for the JPEG image. This field also embeds most of the Basic Latin characters for the Arial font, and the field uses the new Anti-alias for readability setting in the Property inspector. Note that not all JPEG images have caption metadata—we specifically added caption data to each sample JPEG image in the project, using Adobe Photoshop's File ➪ File Info command.

✦ **_csp:** This layer has a ScrollPane component of the same name. The instance is located at the top of the Stage. The ScrollPane instance stores `MovieClip` holders for each of the loaded JPEG thumbnail images.

✦ **_clo:** This layer has a Loader component of the same name. The instance is located below the ScrollPane instance. When a user clicks a thumbnail image in the ScrollPane instance, the fullsize JPEG image loads and scales within the width and height of the `Loader` instance.

The Publish Settings for the `main_starter.fla` file have already been set up to publish the .swf and .html files for the document to the `prod/wwwroot` folder. The .swf file is named `main.swf`, and the .html file is named `main.html`. Both of these files have already been added to the `gallery.flp` file.

Constructing the Gallery component

Before you start to modify the starter files, create a copy of the starter files folder on your computer. In the following steps, you learn how to create a `Gallery` class file for the Gallery component. Then, you associate the class with a new Gallery clip in the Library panel.

On the CD-ROM Make a copy of the `ch35/starter files` folder on your computer.

1. Browse to the `dev/flash/com/themakers` folder in the `starter files` folder you copied.

2. Create a new folder named **Portfolio**. This folder is used to store the `Gallery.as` file you create in the next steps. This folder could also be used to store other class files related to a Portfolio set of components, such as a gallery chooser.

3. In Flash Pro 8, open the `gallery.flp` file in the `starter files` folder you copied.

4. Create a new ActionScript document by choosing File ⇨ New and selecting ActionScript File in the New Document dialog box. Save the new ActionScript file as `Gallery.as` in the `dev/flash/com/themakers/Portfolio` folder you created in Step 2.

5. In the `Gallery.as` script file, add the code shown in Listing 35-2. This code imports all of the necessary classes that the `Gallery` class requires and creates the constructor for the class. We discuss many of the imported classes as we add further portions of code to the class. For now, you declare three private variables representing the three elements currently on the Stage of the `main_starter.fla` document. The constructor invokes the `init()` function, which contains a `trace()` action to indicate that the class has instantiated.

Listing 35-2: **The Gallery Class Constructor**

```
import ascb.util.Proxy;
import flash.display.BitmapData;
import flash.filters.*;
import flash.net.FileReference;
import mx.transitions.Tween;
import com.themakers.Effects.EasyFilter;

class com.themakers.Portfolio.Gallery extends MovieClip {

    private var _csp:mx.containers.ScrollPane;
    private var _clo:mx.controls.Loader;
    private var _tCaption:TextField;

    function Gallery(){
        init();
    }
    private function init():Void {
        trace("Gallery.init >");
    }

}
```

6. Save the `Gallery.as` file.

7. In the Project panel, double-click the `main_starter.fla` file.

8. In the Timeline window, select all the frames, from top to bottom, across the three layers. Right-click (or Control+click on Mac) the frame selection, and choose Copy Frames from the contextual menu.

9. Choose Insert ⇨ New Symbol. In the Create New Symbol dialog box, type **Gallery** in the Name field. Select the Export for ActionScript check box. The Identifier field should automatically fill with the name **Gallery**. In the AS 2.0 Class field, type **com.themakers. Portfolio.Gallery**. This path points to the Gallery.as file you saved in Step 6. Note that the path is relative to the `main_starter.fla` document and does not include the .as file extension. Refer to Figure 35-4. Click OK.

Figure 35-4: The Create New Symbol dialog box

Alternatively, you can assign global class paths in the Flash tab of the Publish Settings dialog box — click the Settings button next to the ActionScript Version menu.

10. In the new timeline of the Gallery symbol, select frame 1 of Layer 1. Right-click (or Control+click on Mac) the frame, and choose Paste Frames. The elements from the Main Timeline should now be pasted into the Gallery symbol timeline. Note that the layer names are automatically copied as well.

11. With all of the elements selected on the Stage, open the Property inspector. The elements are not aligned to the top-left corner of the symbol's registration point. In general, it's considered best practice to align elements within components to the top-left corner. In the Property inspector, change the X position to 0 and the Y position to 0. When you deselect the elements on the Stage, the registration point should be at the top-left corner of the ScrollPane component.

12. Believe it or not, that's all you need to do on the timeline of the Gallery symbol. Everything else happens within the Gallery.as file. Remember, because you attached the Gallery class in the AS 2.0 Class field for the Gallery clip, all of the code within the class file is automatically associated with the symbol.

If you want to change the embedded font used for caption text, select the _tCaption field on the Stage of the Gallery clip and change the font name in the Property inspector.

13. Go back to the Main Timeline (Edit ➪ Edit Document). Create a new layer named **cgl** (short for component Gallery), and delete the other layers.

14. Open the Library panel (Ctrl+L or ⌘+L), and drag an instance of the Gallery symbol on to the Stage. Place the instance near the top-left corner of the Stage. In the Property inspector, name the instance cgl.

15. To make sure the Gallery.as class file is attaching correctly to the Gallery symbol, save the Flash document, and test it (Ctrl+Enter or ⌘+Enter). When the movie loads, you should see the Gallery.init > statement appear in the Output panel. If this message does not appear, right-click (or Control+click on Mac) the Gallery clip in the Library panel, choose Properties, and check the AS 2.0 Class path value.

You can find this version of the main_starter.fla file as main_100.fla in the ch35/ in_process folder. The Listing35-1.as file located in the ch35 folder can be renamed to Gallery.as and inserted into your Portfolio folder.

Phase 2: Loading Thumbnails into the ScrollPane

In this section, you learn how to modify the Gallery.as and main_starter.fla files to load JPEG thumbnails from your PHP server.

Uploading scripts and images to your Web server

Before you can continue to modify the Flash documents for this project, you need to upload the files in the starter files/prod/wwwroot folder to a publicly accessible location on your PHP-enabled Web server. If possible, try uploading the files to the document root of the Web server. For example, if your site's domain is www.mydomain.com, try putting the PHP script files at the document root where you can load them by typing the following URL into a Web browser:

```
http://www.mydomain.com/info.php
```

Also, if you have directory browsing enabled on your Web server, you should be able to access the images folder (and browse the image files within) by typing:

```
http://www.mydomain.com/images
```

After you've completed the project, you can move your script files and images to other folders and modify the script parameters in the Flash movie as needed.

You can also configure a local Web server on your computer for testing purposes. During the writing of this chapter, we used PHP5 with Microsoft IIS on Windows XP. If you test locally, make sure that http://localhost/info.php loads properly before continuing.

Building data properties for the Gallery class

Once you have uploaded the wwwroot files to your own Web server, you're ready to go back to Flash production tasks. In this section, you add several data properties to the component, enabling the component to access the resize.php script and to store the JPEG file information for the Gallery.

1. Go back to the Gallery.as file you created in Phase 1. Add the bold code shown in Listing 35-3. This new code creates the following properties. Each property has an associated private variable listed at the top of the class.

- items: This property saves an array of JPEG filenames in the _data private variable. The items property is accessed later in this chapter when the thumbnails are built. Whenever information related to the active thumbnail or JPEG image displayed in the Loader component is needed, the items property can be utilized.

- rootURL: This property stores a root path to the Web server with the PHP scripts and images. This value is appended to image URLs used throughout the class. The private variable _rootURL stores the String data associated with this property.

- thumbScript: This property stores the name of the script file to call for dynamic resizing of the JPEG images as thumbnails. The default value is set to resize.php, the script file you've already put on your Web server.

- thumbURL: This read-only property formats the thumbScript value with the rootURL value, the thumbHeight value for the height= variable for the resize.php script, and the img= variable required by the resize.php script. The actual image name is appended to thumbURL in a later function. The String value for this property is stored in the private variable _thumbScript.

- thumbHeight: This property stores the height, in pixels, that should be passed to the resize.php script for the creation of the thumbnail images. The private variable _thumbHeight stores the value for this property.

Note   Any property that is preceded by an [Inspectable] tag will be available in the Parameters tab of the Property inspector for the Gallery component. You won't see such properties appear unless you specify the AS 2.0 class name in the Component Definition dialog box, which we discuss later in this chapter.

Also, while the use of the underscore (_) for private variable names used within a class is a common practice, you can name your private variables with your own custom naming convention.

Listing 35-3: **The Data Properties of the Gallery Class**

```
import ascb.util.Proxy;
import flash.display.BitmapData;
import flash.filters.*;
import flash.net.FileReference;
import mx.transitions.Tween;
import com.themakers.Effects.EasyFilter;

class com.themakers.Portfolio.Gallery extends MovieClip {

    private var _csp:mx.containers.ScrollPane;
    private var _clo:mx.controls.Loader;
    private var _tCaption:TextField;
    private var _data:Array;
    private var _rootURL:String;
    private var _thumbScript:String;
    private var _thumbHeight:Number;
```

Continued

Listing 35-3 *(continued)*

```
function Gallery(){
    init();
}

private function init():Void {
    trace("Gallery.init >");
}

public function set items(aData:Array):Void {
    _data = aData;
}

public function get items():Array {
    return _data;
}

[Inspectable(defaultValue="",name="Server Host")]
public function set rootURL(sPath:String):Void {
    _rootURL = sPath;
}

public function get rootURL():String {
    return _rootURL != undefined ? _rootURL : "";
}

[Inspectable(defaultValue="resize.php")]
public function set thumbScript(sPath:String):Void {
    _thumbScript = sPath;
}

public function get thumbScript():String {
    return _thumbScript;
}

public function get thumbURL():String {
    return rootURL +thumbScript + "?height=" + thumbHeight + "&img=";
}

[Inspectable(defaultValue=50)]
public function set thumbHeight(nHeight:Number):Void {
    _thumbHeight = nHeight;
}

public function get thumbHeight():Number {
    return _thumbHeight;
}
}
```

2. Save the `Gallery.as` file.

Creating thumbnail holders in the Gallery class

After you've created the data properties for the `Gallery` class, you're ready to add the code that makes new `MovieClip` holders within the nested `ScrollPane` instance, `_csp`, of the Gallery symbol.

1. In the `Gallery.as` file, add the bold code shown in Listing 35-4. Note that the ⤸ character denotes a continuation of the same line of code. The modifications and additions are as follows:

- `init`: The `init()` function now sets a private variable named `_thumbSpacing`. This variable stores the number of pixels to insert between thumbnail images. You can change this number to increase or decrease the horizontal gap between thumbnails.

- `onLoad`: Because we have placed author-time instances of the User Interface components on the Stage of the Gallery symbol, we need to use the `MovieClip.onLoad()` handler to properly initialize any parameters with the ScrollPane (`_csp`) or Loader (`_clo`) components. Here, the `stylePane()` function is invoked to format the `ScrollPane` instance.

> **Note**
>
> Because the `Gallery` class extends the `MovieClip` class (see the `class` statement at the top of the file), the `onLoad` function automatically invokes when the `Gallery` instance appears within the Flash movie at run time. You don't explicitly call the `onLoad()` function anywhere within the class.

- `stylePane`: This function sets the background color and border style of the `ScrollPane` instance. More importantly, the `contentPath` property of the `ScrollPane` instance is set to paneHolder. As you see in the `buildHolders()` function, you need to create new `MovieClip` instances within the ScrollPane instance—you can't add content within the ScrollPane instance without building an empty MovieClip symbol in the movie's Library that is attached to the `ScrollPane` instance. You build the paneHolder symbol later in this section.

- `buildHolders`: This function goes through the `items` property (which contains a list of all the JPEG file information) and builds nested `MovieClip` instances within the ScrollPane instance's content clip. Each `MovieClip` instance for a thumbnail (the mc instance) is created within a `MovieClip` named `_imgColl` (short for image collection), which is also a private variable for the `Gallery` class. This variable is accessed later for finding thumbnails and controlling their states. Each mc instance has a nested `MovieClip` instance named img, which is targeted with a `MovieClipLoader` instance named `_mcl`, which is also a private variable name. Each object in the `items` array contains a src property (mapped from the XML generated by the `files.php` script), which is used as the img variable value to format the URL for the `resize.php` script.

- `calcThumbW`: This function is used within the `buildHolders()` function to determine how wide a thumbnail image should be based on the aspect ratio of the original image. The `width` and `height` properties of the JPEG file are retrieved from nested objects within the `items` array.

Note You haven't actually loaded any data into the Gallery instance back in the main_ starter.fla file. In the next few steps, you learn how to load the XML data and format it as a data provider for the items property.

- load: This public function initiates the thumbnail creation and loading process. This is the only method that needs to be called outside of the class.

Note The properties added in Listing 35-4 are not displayed in the printed listing, but the complete code is available in the Listing35-4.as file in the ch35ch35 folder of this book's CD-ROM.

Listing 35-4: **The Thumbnail Creation Process**

```
import ascb.util.Proxy;
import flash.display.BitmapData;
import flash.filters.*;
import flash.net.FileReference;
import mx.transitions.Tween;
import com.themakers.Effects.EasyFilter;

class com.themakers.Portfolio.Gallery extends MovieClip {

    private var _csp:mx.containers.ScrollPane;
    private var _clo:mx.controls.Loader;
    private var _tCaption:TextField;
    private var _data:Array;
    private var _rootURL:String;
    private var _thumbScript:String;
    private var _thumbHeight:Number;
    private var _thumbSpacing:Number;
    private var _mcl:MovieClipLoader;
    private var _imgColl:MovieClip;

    function Gallery(){
        init();
    }

    private function init():Void {
        trace("Gallery.init >");
        _thumbSpacing = 1;
    }

    private function onLoad():Void {
        stylePane();
    }

    private function stylePane():Void {
        _csp.setStyle("backgroundColor", 0xFFFFFF);
```

```
      _csp.setStyle("borderStyle", "none");
      _csp.contentPath = "paneHolder";
   }

   private function buildHolders():Void {
      var mcH:MovieClip = _csp.content;
      _mcl = new MovieClipLoader();
      _mcl.addListener(this);
      var aFiles:Array = items;
      var nWidth:Number = 0;
      var mcC:MovieClip = _imgColl = mcH.createEmptyMovieClip("_imgColl", 1);
      for(var i:Number = 0; i < aFiles.length; i++){
         var oItem:Object = aFiles[i];
         var mc:MovieClip =  mcC.createEmptyMovieClip("mc" + i, i+1);
         mc._x = (i == 0) ? 0 : mcC["mc" + (i-1)]._x + ⮥
            calcThumbW(aFiles[i-1]) + _thumbSpacing;
         var mcD:MovieClip = mc.createEmptyMovieClip("disp", 1);
         var imgH:MovieClip = mcD.createEmptyMovieClip("imgH", 1);
         var img:MovieClip = imgH.createEmptyMovieClip("img", 1);
         mc.idx = i;
         var sURL:String = thumbURL + escape(oItem.src);
         _mcl.loadClip(sURL, img);
      }
   }

   private function calcThumbW(oFile:Object):Number {
      var nWidth:Number = oFile.width;
      var nHeight:Number = oFile.height;
      var nFactor:Number = thumbHeight/nHeight;
      return nWidth*nFactor;
   }

   public function load():Void {
      buildHolders();
   }

   [Public properties omitted from this listing...]
}
```

2. Save the Gallery.as file.

3. Switch over to the main_starter.fla document. As we mentioned earlier in this section, you need to create an empty Movie Clip symbol named paneHolder, to use as a holder within the ScrollPane component. Choose Insert ➪ New Symbol. Name the new clip **paneHolder**, and select the Export for ActionScript box. The Identifier value should auto-fill with the value **paneHolder**, as shown in Figure 35-5. Click OK.

4. Once you're inside the paneHolder timeline, choose Edit ➪ Edit Document to go back to the Main Timeline of the Flash document. Now you're ready to load XML data from the files.php script on your Web server.

Figure 35-5: The paneHolder clip settings

5. Create a new layer named **actions**, and place it at the top of the layer stack. Select frame 1 of the actions layer, and open the Actions panel (F9, or Option+F9). Add the code shown in Listing 35-5.

This code creates a new XML instance named xmlData. The cgl instance (already placed on the Stage) is typed as a Gallery class member. The sHost variable should be set to the domain name of your Web server. Do not use the localhost value unless you are testing against a Web server running on your computer.

Note When you're ready to deploy the final version of the Flash movie, you can set sHost to an empty string, or the folder path leading to the PHP script files. Also, if you have difficulties testing against your own PHP server, you can use

http://www.flashsupport.com/f8b/gallery/

as the value for the sHost variable to test your Flash movie.

The init() function uses the Proxy.create() method to delegate the onLoad() handler of the xmlData instance to the onFileData() function. When the XML data has loaded from the PHP script, the onFileData() function invokes. The sHost value is appended to the files.php?dir=images/ string in the load() method of the xmlData instance.

The onFileData() function cycles through the returned XML data, which resembles that shown in Listing 35-1. The for() loop goes through each <img> node (xn) and maps each attribute to a property of the same name on an object (oItem) that is passed to the aData array. After each <img> node has been processed, the aData array is used for the items property of the Gallery instance, cgl.

The rootURL, thumbScript, and thumbHeight properties of the Gallery instance are also set in the onFileData() function. Once these properties have been set, the load() function is invoked, starting the process of loading the thumbnail images.

Listing 35-5: **Loading the XML Data**

```
import ascb.util.Proxy;

var xmlData:XML = new XML();
var cgl:com.themakers.Portfolio.Gallery;
var sHost:String = "http://localhost/";

init();

function init():Void {
   xmlData.ignoreWhite = true;
   xmlData.onLoad = Proxy.create(this, onFileData);
   xmlData.load(sHost + "files.php?dir=images/");
}

function onFileData(bSuccess:Boolean):Void {
   trace("onFileData > " + bSuccess);
   var aFiles:Array = xmlData.firstChild.childNodes;
   var aData:Array = new Array();
   for(var i:Number = 0; i < aFiles.length; i++){
      var xn:XMLNode = aFiles[i];
      var oItem:Object = {
         src: xn.attributes.src,
         width: Number(xn.attributes.width),
         height: Number(xn.attributes.height),
         caption: xn.attributes.caption,
         filename: xn.attributes.filename
      };
      aData.push(oItem);
   }
   cgl.items = aData;
   cgl.rootURL = sHost;
   cgl.thumbScript = "resize.php";
   cgl.thumbHeight = 50;
   cgl.load();
}
```

6. Save the `main_starter.fla` document, and test the movie (Ctrl+Enter or ⌘+Enter). If the PHP script files are uploaded and correctly specified in the frame 1 script, the thumbnail images load into the ScrollPane instance of the Gallery component, as shown in Figure 35-6. Note that the scroll bar for the `ScrollPane` instance does not automatically appear — you'll fix that in a later section.

On the CD-ROM

You can find this version of the `main_starter.fla` file as `main_101.fla` in the ch35/ `in_process` folder on this book's CD-ROM.

Figure 35-6: The basic thumbnails loading into the Gallery component

Phase 3: Displaying the Full-size JPEG Image

Since the XML data provided by the `files.php` script completely describes each JPEG image in the chosen Web folder, your work with the `main_starter.fla` document is finished. You complete the remaining changes within the `Gallery` class file.

Loading the full-size image

After you have the thumbnail JPEG images loading from the `resize.php` script, you're ready to add more functionality to each `MovieClip` instance containing a JPEG thumbnail. The `mc` instance created in the `for()` loop of the `buildHolders()` function is the primary instance to target for adding button behaviors.

You also need to track which thumbnail is currently selected. Just as the List component has a `selectedIndex` property indicating which entry in the list is active, the Gallery component needs a `selectedIndex` property to indicate which thumbnail has been clicked by the user.

   1. Go back to the `Gallery.as` file, and add the bold code shown in Listing 35-5. This code has the following changes:

- `buildHolders`: This function now creates an `onRelease()` handler for each `mc` instance holding a JPEG thumbnail image. The `onRelease()` handler is delegated to the `onThumbClick()` function of the `Gallery` class. A reference to the `mc` instance is passed to the `Proxy.create()` method in order for the `onThumbClick()` handler to identify which thumbnail image has been clicked. Also, the first `mc` instance to be created in the `for()` loop is set as the value of a new private variable named `_thumb`. This variable can be referenced in later functions to also identify which `mc` instance was clicked last.

- `onThumbClick`: This function is invoked whenever the user clicks a thumbnail image in the `ScrollPane` instance. When a thumbnail is clicked, the `_thumb` variable is set to the passed `mc` reference of the function. Then, the `selectedIndex` property is set to that clip's `idx` value. Remember, the `for()` loop of the `buildHolder()` function assigns an `idx` value to each thumbnail `mc` instance. The `idx` value matches the index of the corresponding JPEG data in the `items` array.

- `loadImage`: This function does the work of changing the `contentPath` property of the `Loader` instance, `_clo`, to the full-size JPEG image URL. The `selectedIndex` value is used to look up the JPEG file data from the `items` array. The `src` property, as built by the script in Listing 35-6, contains the URL to the JPEG image. This value is appended to the `rootURL` value and then set as the new `contentPath` property value. The `loadImage()` function, by design, is only invoked by the `selectedIndex` setter function.

- `selectedIndex`: This pair of setter/getter functions creates a new property named `selectedIndex`. This property tracks which index of the `items` array is currently selected. Whenever the user clicks a thumbnail button, the `selectedIndex` value is updated and the `loadImage()` function is invoked.

Listing 35-6: **Tracking the Active Thumbnail**

```
import ascb.util.Proxy;
import flash.display.BitmapData;
import flash.filters.*;
import flash.net.FileReference;
import mx.transitions.Tween;
import com.themakers.Effects.EasyFilter;

class com.themakers.Portfolio.Gallery extends MovieClip {

    private var _csp:mx.containers.ScrollPane;
    private var _clo:mx.controls.Loader;
    private var _tCaption:TextField;
    private var _data:Array;
    private var _rootURL:String;
    private var _thumbScript:String;
    private var _thumbHeight:Number;
    private var _thumbSpacing:Number;
    private var _mcl:MovieClipLoader;
    private var _imgColl:MovieClip;
    private var _thumb:MovieClip;
    private var _selectedIndex:Number;

    function Gallery(){
        init();
    }

    private function init():Void {
```

Continued

Listing 35-6 *(continued)*

```
      [No changes to this function]
   }

   private function onLoad():Void {
      [No changes to this function]
   }

   private function stylePane():Void {
      [No changes to this function]
   }

   private function buildHolders():Void {
      var mcH:MovieClip = _csp.content;
      _mcl = new MovieClipLoader();
      _mcl.addListener(this);
      var aFiles:Array = items;
      var nWidth:Number = 0;
      var mcC:MovieClip = _imgColl = mcH.createEmptyMovieClip("_imgColl", 1);
      for(var i:Number = 0; i < aFiles.length; i++){
         var oItem:Object = aFiles[i];
         var mc:MovieClip = mcC.createEmptyMovieClip("mc" + i, i+1);
         mc._x = (i == 0) ? 0 : mcC["mc" + (i-1)]._x + ⊃
            calcThumbW(aFiles[i-1]) + _thumbSpacing;
         var mcD:MovieClip = mc.createEmptyMovieClip("disp", 1);
         var imgH:MovieClip = mcD.createEmptyMovieClip("imgH", 1);
         var img:MovieClip = imgH.createEmptyMovieClip("img", 1);
         if(i == 0) _thumb = mc;
         mc.idx = i;
         mc.onRelease = Proxy.create(this, onThumbClick, mc);
         var sURL:String = thumbURL + escape(oItem.src);
         _mcl.loadClip(sURL, img);
      }
   }

   private function calcThumbW(oFile:Object):Number {
      [No changes to this function]
   }

   private function onThumbClick(mc:MovieClip):Void {
      _thumb = mc;
      selectedIndex = mc.idx;
   }

   private function loadImage():Void {
      var nIdx:Number = selectedIndex;
      var oItem:Object = items[nIdx];
      _clo.contentPath = rootURL + oItem.src;
   }
```

```
public function load():Void {
    [No changes to this function]
}

public function set selectedIndex(nIdx:Number):Void {
    if(_selectedIndex != nIdx){
        _selectedIndex = nIdx;
        loadImage();
    }
}

public function get selectedIndex():Number {
    return _selectedIndex;
}

[Other public properties have been omitted from this listing]
}
```

2. Save the `Gallery.as` file.

3. Go back to the `main_starter.fla` document, and test it (Ctrl+Enter or ⌘+Enter). After the thumbnails load, click the first thumbnail image. The full-size JPEG then loads into the Loader component of the Gallery component, as shown in Figure 35-7.

Figure 35-7: The full-size JPEG image for the first thumbnail

Updating the scroll bar and auto-loading the first image

As Figures 35-6 and 35-7 illustrate, the scroll bar of the nested ScrollPane instance (_csp) is not visible as more thumbnails load into the instance. The ScrollPane instance needs to be told when to redraw its UI elements — the ScrollPane component does not automatically detect when more content has been added beyond its visible frame.

1. Go to the Gallery.as file, and add the functions shown in Listing 35-7. Place these functions after the last private function, loadImage, and before the public functions. This code contains two new functions:

   - onLoadInit: This function is an event listener for the MovieClipLoader instance, _mcl, created in the buildHolders() function. Whenever a thumbnail image has finished loading, the onLoadInit() function is automatically invoked by the _mcl instance. A reference to the MovieClip holder for the image is passed to the function, where the idx value assigned to the outer mc holder for the nested thumbnail holder is accessed. When the first thumbnail in the ScrollPane instance loads, the selectedIndex property is set to 0, which invokes all of the code in the public function set selectedIndex() area of the class file. This process sets the loading of the first full-size JPEG image into action. If the very last thumbnail is loaded into the ScrollPane instance, the updateScroller() function is invoked.

Tip   You can place the updateScroller() action in the onLoadInit() handler outside of the if/else statement to force the ScrollPane instance to update after every thumbnail load. If you have several images in your Web folder, you might wait a long time before the last thumbnail loads.

   - updateScroller: This function fires one action: _csp.redraw(true);. This action forces the ScrollPane instance to re-examine its contents and determine if a vertical and/or horizontal scroll bar is necessary.

Note   The Listing35-6.as file in the ch35 folder of this book's CD-ROM shows the new code within the entire Gallery class file.

Listing 35-7: **The onLoadInit() and updateScroller() Functions**

```
private function onLoadInit(mc:MovieClip):Void {
    var nIdx:Number = mc._parent._parent._parent.idx;
    if(nIdx == 0){
        selectedIndex = 0;
    } else if(nIdx == items.length - 1){
        updateScroller();
    }
}

private function updateScroller():Void {
    _csp.redraw(true);
}
```

2. Save the `Gallery.as` file.

3. Go back to the `main_starter.fla` document and test it (Ctrl+Enter or ⌘+Enter). When all of the thumbnails have loaded, the horizontal scroll bar for the `ScrollPane` instance should display, enabling you to scroll to more thumbnail images. Refer to Figure 35-8.

Figure 35-8: The updated ScrollPane instance

Phase 4: Enhancing the Thumbnail and Image States

Right now, you have a Gallery component that can load clickable thumbnails that load full-size JPEG images. While this functionality is critical to the success of the Gallery component, the same functionality could be accomplished in a regular HTML page with less effort. Let's add some features that are truly within the domain of Flash technology.

Framing the selected thumbnail with the BevelFilter class

In this section, you learn how to add the new Flash Player 8 bevel filter to the selected thumbnail image.

1. Go back to the `Gallery.as` file. Add the code shown in Listing 35-8. Note that the `public function set selectedIndex` should already be defined in your code — add the new code shown in bold. This code adds two new functions, and extends the functionality of the `selectedIndex` setter function:

- frameThumb: This function creates a new BevelFilter instance named bf for the selected thumbnail, which is retrieved from the _imgColl holder within the ScrollPane instance. (_imgColl is set in the buildHolders() function.) The bf instance is assigned to the filters array of the selected thumbnail, and the alpha of the clip is set to 100%.

Tip

We use the default values of the BevelFilter class. If you search the Flash 8 Help panel for "BevelFilter class," you can find more information on changing the look and feel of the filter with the thumbnail images, using BevelFilter properties such as distance and angle.

- dimThumb: This function retrieves the previously selected thumbnail, removes any filters, and sets the alpha of the previous thumbnail to 75%.

- selectedIndex: The setter function for the selectedIndex property now invokes the dimThumb() function with the existing _selectedIndex value before a new _selectedIndex value is assigned. After a new value has been assigned, the frameThumb() function is invoked. Remember, the selectedIndex property is the heart of the Gallery class—any change to the selectedIndex value propagates to other functions within the class.

Note

The Listing35-8.as file in the ch35 folder of this book's CD-ROM shows the new code within the entire Gallery class file.

Listing 35-8: **Framing the Selected Thumbnail**

```
private function frameThumb():Void {
   var mc:MovieClip = _imgColl["mc" + selectedIndex];
   var bf:BevelFilter = new BevelFilter();
   mc.filters = [bf];
   mc._alpha = 100;
}

private function dimThumb(nIdx:Number):Void {
   var mc:MovieClip = _imgColl["mc" + nIdx];
   mc.filters = [];
   mc._alpha = 75;
}

public function set selectedIndex(nIdx:Number):Void {
   if(_selectedIndex != nIdx){
      if(_selectedIndex != undefined) dimThumb(_selectedIndex);
      _selectedIndex = nIdx;
      frameThumb();
      loadImage();
   }
}
```

2. Save the `Gallery.as` file.

3. Go back to the `main_starter.fla` document, and test it (Ctrl+Enter or ⌘+Enter). When the movie loads, the first thumbnail appears with a bevel border. If you click another thumbnail, the previously selected thumbnail's bevel is removed and the alpha is reduced, as shown in Figure 35-9.

Figure 35-9: The BevelFilter applied to the thumbnail image

Creating a loading transition with the BitmapData and BlurFilter classes

Let's continue the fun with Flash filters! In this section, you learn how to use the `BitmapData` class to make a copy of the thumbnail image over the Loader component area. The thumbnail, of course, is not as large as the full-size JPEG image. As such, the thumbnail image is stretched and pixilated when it's set to the same width and height of the full-size image. You use the `BlurFilter` class to smooth the thumbnail's pixilation. The filter's strength is inversely proportional to the loaded percent of the full-size JPEG image. As the full-size JPEG image loads into the Loader component, the intensity of the `BlurFilter` instance is gradually diminished.

1. Go back to the `Gallery.as` file and add the bold code shown in Listing 35-9. This code modifies existing functions and adds a few new ones:

- `init`: This function uses two new private variables: `_blurStrength` indicates the maximum blur applied to the copied thumbnail when the copy is made, and `_overlay` is a new `MovieClip` instance that holds the copied thumbnail in the `overlayThumb()` function. The position of the `_overlay` instance is set to the same X and Y position as the `_clo` instance.

- onLoad: This handler is modified to add two event listeners to the Loader component, _clo. The "progress" event is broadcasted from the Loader component as new bytes of a loaded full-size JPEG image arrive into the Flash movie. This event is captured by the onImgProgress() function. The "complete" event is broadcasted by the Loader component when the full-size JPEG image has fully loaded into the Flash movie. This event is captured by the onImgComplete() function.

- overlayThumb: This function creates a bitmap copy of the selected thumbnail, scales the copy to fit within the dimensions of the Loader component, and sets the initial blur of the scaled copy to a maximum intensity. The overlayThumb() function is invoked by the selectedIndex property when a new thumbnail is clicked. Here, the new BitmapData class is used to create the copy of the loaded thumbnail JPEG image. The new bitmap is attached to a new MovieClip holder named _bitmap within the _overlay instance. The _overlay instance is then resized using the same procedure that the Loader component uses to fit loaded images within its display area.

- blurOverlay: This function creates the BlurFilter instance responsible for blurring the copied thumbnail image. The function requires one parameter: the percent loaded of the full-size JPEG image. If the loading process has just started, the percent loaded is equal to 0. This value is remapped to a blur intensity value (nBlur), as indicated by the _blurStrength variable set in the init() function. As more bytes of the JPEG image load into the movie, the nBlur value is reduced. The BlurFilter instance is applied to the filters array of the _overlay instance.

- onImgProgress: This handler is invoked whenever the Loader component broadcasts a "progress" event. When this event occurs, the loaded percent of the JPEG is retrieved with the percentLoaded property of the Loader component and passed to the blurOverlay() function.

- onImgComplete: When the Loader component broadcasts the "complete" event, the onImgComplete() function is invoked. The "complete" event signals that the full-size JPEG image has loaded completely into the Flash movie. At this point, the _bitmap instance within the _overlay instance can be removed to reveal the full-size JPEG below it.

- selectedIndex: The overlayThumb() function is added to the setter function for the selectedIndex property. Whenever the user clicks a new thumbnail image, the process of copying, scaling, and blurring the thumbnail is started.

Note   The Listing35-9.as file in the ch35 folder of this book's CD-ROM shows the new code within the entire Gallery class file.

Listing 35-9: **Copying and Blurring the Thumbnail Image**

```
private var _blurStrength:Number;
private var _overlay:MovieClip;

private function init():Void {
   _thumbSpacing = 1;
   _blurStrength = 20;
```

```
   _overlay = createEmptyMovieClip("_overlay", 10);
   _overlay._x = _clo._x;
   _overlay._y = _clo._y;
}

private function onLoad():Void {
   stylePane();
   _clo.addEventListener("progress", Proxy.create(this, onImgProgress));
   _clo.addEventListener("complete", Proxy.create(this, onImgComplete));
}

private function overlayThumb():Void {
   var mc:MovieClip = _thumb;
   var nW:Number = mc._width;
   var nH:Number = mc._height;
   var bmd:BitmapData = new BitmapData(nW, nH);
   bmd.draw(mc);
   var mcH:MovieClip = _overlay.createEmptyMovieClip("_bitmap", 1);
   mcH.attachBitmap(bmd, 1);
   var nLW:Number = _clo.width;
   var nLH:Number = _clo.height;
   var nFactor:Number = nH >= nW ? nLH/nH : nLW/nW;
   _overlay._xscale = _overlay._yscale = nFactor*100;
   _overlay._x = _clo._x + ((_clo.width - _overlay._width)/2);
   _overlay._y = _clo._y + ((_clo.height - _overlay._height)/2);
   blurOverlay(0);
}

private function blurOverlay(nPL:Number):Void {
   var n:Number = (nPL*(_blurStrength/10))/10;
   var nBlur:Number = _blurStrength - n;
   var bf:BlurFilter = new BlurFilter(nBlur, nBlur, 3);
   _overlay.filters = [bf];
}

private function onImgProgress(oEvent:Object):Void {
   var clo:mx.controls.Loader = oEvent.target;
   blurOverlay(clo.percentLoaded);
}

private function onImgComplete(oEvent:Object):Void {
   _overlay._bitmap.removeMovieClip();
}

public function set selectedIndex(nIdx:Number):Void {
   if(_selectedIndex != nIdx){
      if(_selectedIndex != undefined) dimThumb(_selectedIndex);
      _selectedIndex = nIdx;
      overlayThumb();
      frameThumb();
      loadImage();
   }
}
```

2. Save the `Gallery.as` file.

3. Go back to the `main_starter.fla` document, and test it (Ctrl+Enter, or ⌘+Enter). When you click a thumbnail image, a copy of the thumbnail is created, scaled, blurred, and positioned above the Loader component. The blur intensity is minimized as the full-size JPEG loads into the movie. Figure 35-10 shows a snapshot of this animated transition.

Figure 35-10: The blurred copy of the thumbnail image

Transitioning thumbnail states with the Tween and ColorMatrixFilter classes

The thumbnails in the ScrollPane component can also use a scripted tween to fade to a desaturated state as the user views each full-size image. In this section, you see how the `Tween` class can programmatically update the thumbnail images. You can create a `Tween` instance by using the following syntax:

```
import mx.transitions.Tween;
var mc:MovieClip;
var tw:Tween = new Tween(mc, "_x", mx.transitions.easing.Regular.easeOut, ⤶
   mc._x, mc._x + 100, 5, true);
```

The `Tween` constructor accepts seven arguments, in the following order:

✦ **target:** The first argument specifies the object whose property will be manipulated by the `Tween` instance. You can pass any object reference you want, including a `TextField`, `MovieClip`, or `Object` reference.

✦ **property name:** The second argument indicates which property of the target object will be updated by the `Tween` instance. This argument should be a `String` value. For example, to control a `MovieClip` instance's X position, pass a value of `"_x"` as the second argument.

✦ **easing class:** The third argument specifies the type of tween you'd like to use. You can use a variety of easing classes. If you do not require any special type of easing with the tween, you can specify a `null` value.

✦ **starting value:** The fourth argument indicates the starting value that the `Tween` instance should use. You can use any numeric value, such as the current X position or alpha value of a `MovieClip` instance.

✦ **ending value:** The fifth argument specifies the finish value for the `Tween` instance. You can use any numeric value. When the `Tween` instance reaches this value, the `onMotionFinished` handler for any listener assigned to the `Tween` instance is invoked.

✦ **duration:** The sixth argument indicates how long the tween should last. This numeric value can be specified as seconds or frames.

✦ **time unit:** The seventh and final argument determines the unit of measure for the duration argument, as a Boolean value. If you pass `true` as the last argument, the unit of measure is seconds. If you pass `false`, the unit of measure is frames.

1. Go back to the `Gallery.as` file, and add the code shown in Listing 35-10. This code replaces the existing `dimThumb()` function with a new set of actions to utilize the `Tween` class.

   • `dimThumb`: This function is invoked from the `selectedIndex` property, just as it was in earlier sections of this project. Two new `Tween` instances are created for the thumbnail instance. The first `Tween` instance named `twSaturation` is responsible for modifying the saturation value of the thumbnail instance. The `Regular.easeOut` static class is specified as the easing class for both `Tween` instances. The starting value for the saturation tween is 0 (no change) and the ending value is –100 (color removed, desaturated). The duration of both tweens is one second. The `twAlpha` instance animates the current alpha of the thumbnail instance to the muted 75% used earlier. The thumbnail instance is added as a listener to both `Tween` instances; therefore, the `onMotionFinished()` handler of the thumbnail instance is fired when the tweens finish. The `onTweenFinish()` function of the `Gallery` class is delegated for this handler. Because saturation values are not a directly accessible value to use with the `Tween` class, a new property named `thumbSaturation` is created for the thumbnail instance. The `watch()` method can detect any changes to this property on the instance, and the `Proxy.create()` method is specified as the event handler for the `watch()` method.

   • `onThumbSaturation`: This function is invoked whenever the saturation tween (`twSaturation`) updates the `thumbSaturation` property of the thumbnail instance. Here, the new value created by the tween is passed to the `EasyFilter.saturate()` method to create a new `ColorMatrixFilter` instance. We discuss the `EasyFilter.saturate()` method in greater detail at the start of this chapter.

   • `onTweenFinish`: This handler is invoked by each `Tween` instance when the respective tween has completed. Each tween is removed from a `tweens` array stored within the thumbnail instance.

   • `controlTweens`, `clearTweens`: These functions manage the playback of the `Tween` instances. You add more functions later in this chapter that take advantage of these functions.

Note

The `Listing35-10.as` file in the `ch35` folder of this book's CD-ROM shows the new code within the entire `Gallery` class file.

Listing 35-10: Tweening the Thumbnail States

```
private function dimThumb(nIdx:Number):Void {
   var mc:MovieClip = _imgColl["mc" + nIdx];
   if(mc.tweens != undefined) clearTweens(mc);
   var twSaturation:Tween = new Tween(mc, "thumbSaturation", ⊃
      mx.transitions.easing.Regular.easeOut, 0, -100, 1, true);
   var twAlpha:Tween = new Tween(mc, "_alpha", ⊃
      mx.transitions.easing.Regular.easeOut, mc._alpha, 75, 1, true);
   twSaturation.addListener(mc);
   twAlpha.addListener(mc);
   mc.tweens = [twSaturation, twAlpha];
   mc.watch("thumbSaturation", Proxy.create(this, onThumbSaturation), mc );
   mc.onMotionFinished = Proxy.create(this, onTweenFinish, mc);
}

private function onThumbSaturation(sProp:String, oldVal:Number, ⊃
   newVal:Number, mc:MovieClip):Void {
   mc.filters = [EasyFilter.saturate(newVal)];
   updateAfterEvent();
}

private function onTweenFinish(tw:Tween, mc:MovieClip):Void {
   for(var i:Number = 0; i < mc.tweens.length; i++){
      if(mc.tweens[i] == tw) mc.tweens.splice(i, 1);
   }
   if(mc.tweens.length < 1) delete mc.tweens;
}

private function controlTweens(mc:MovieClip, sAction:String):Void {
   for(var i:Number = 0; i < mc.tweens.length; i++){
      mc.tweens[i][sAction]();
   }
}

private function clearTweens(mc:MovieClip):Void {
   controlTweens(mc, "stop");
   delete mc.tweens;
}
```

---

2. Save the `Gallery.as` file.

3. Go back to the `main_starter.fla` document, and test it (Ctrl+Enter or ⌘+Enter). After the thumbnail images load, click a new thumbnail in the ScrollPane component. The previously selected thumbnail desaturates and fades to 75% opacity.

Setting the image caption

After you have the full-size JPEG image loading into the Loader component, you're ready to populate the _tCaption TextField instance, which you copied into the Gallery symbol earlier in this chapter. The JPEG files provided in the starter files and finished files folders have had metadata added to them. The caption metadata is read by the JPEG-Meta.php script on the server and inserted into the XML data sent to the Flash movie with the files.php script.

1. Go back to the Gallery.as file and add the bold code shown in Listing 35-11. Add the new private variable to the list of existing private variables at the top of the class file, modify the existing init() and loadImage() functions, and add the new displayCaption() function below the last private function in the class file.

   - init: The new _captionSpacing variable stores the gap, in pixels, that should buffer the top of the _tCaption instance and the bottom of the full-size JPEG image.

   - loadImage: After the full-size JPEG image starts to load into the Loader component, the displayCaption() function is invoked to show the image's caption. The caption text is stored in the caption property of the current object within the items array, as described by the XML document delivered by the files.php script.

   - displayCaption: This function populates the _tCaption instance with the new caption text and positions the field below the lower left corner of the image.

Note   The Listing35-11.as file in the ch35 folder of this book's CD-ROM shows the new code within the entire Gallery class file.

Listing 35-11: **The displayCaption() Function**

```
private var _captionSpacing:Number;

private function init():Void {
   _thumbSpacing = 1;
   _blurStrength = 20;
   _captionSpacing = 5;
   _overlay = createEmptyMovieClip("_overlay", 10);
   _overlay._x = _clo._x;
   _overlay._y = _clo._y;
}

private function loadImage():Void {
   var nIdx:Number = selectedIndex;
   var oItem:Object = items[nIdx];
   _clo.contentPath = rootURL + oItem.src;
   displayCaption(oItem.caption);
}

private function displayCaption(sText:String):Void {
   _tCaption.text = sText;
   _tCaption._x = _overlay._x;
   _tCaption._y = _overlay._y + _overlay._height + _captionSpacing;
}
```

2. Save the `Gallery.as` file.

3. Return to the `main_starter.fla` document, and test it (Ctrl+Enter or ⌘+Enter). When a new full-size JPEG image is loaded, its caption text (if available) displays below the image, as shown in Figure 35-11.

Dark pine and setting sun, Griffith Park, CA

Figure 35-11: The caption text below the JPEG image

Completing the thumbnail button handlers

The thumbnail functionality is nearly complete. In its current state, the thumbnail images, once clicked, remain muted — even when the user rolls over a previously selected thumbnail. In this section, you add `onRollOver` and `onRollOut` handlers to each thumbnail instance.

1. Go back to the `Gallery.as` file, and add the bold code shown in Listing 35-12.

   • `buildHolders`: This function, which creates the original thumbnail holders, is modified to assign `onRollOver` and `onRollOut` handlers to each thumbnail instance (mc). The `Proxy.create()` method delegates these handlers to the `onThumbOver` and `onThumbOut` functions of the `Gallery` class.

   • `onThumbOver`: This handler checks to see if any tweens are active on the thumbnail when the rollover event occurs. If there are any active tweens, they are paused. Any active filters applied to the instance are stored in a new property named `existingProps`. This property is used in `onThumbOut` to restore the last state of the button. Any filters on the thumbnail instance are removed, and the alpha is set to 100%. Note that these actions are only applied to a thumbnail instance if it is not the active thumbnail.

- onThumbOut: This handler resumes any active tweens that may have been in progress when the user rolled over the thumbnail instance. Any filters that were applied to the instance before the rollover event occurred are also re-applied to the clip.

- selectedIndex: When a thumbnail is initially selected with the selectedIndex property, the existingProps property is initialized with the filters that are applied to the selected thumbnail.

Listing 35-12: **The onRollOver() and onRollOut() Thumbnail Handlers**

```
private function buildHolders():Void {
    var mcH:MovieClip = _csp.content;
    _mcl = new MovieClipLoader();
    _mcl.addListener(this);
    var aFiles:Array = items;
    var nWidth:Number = 0;
    var mcC:MovieClip = _imgColl = mcH.createEmptyMovieClip("_imgColl", 1);
    for(var i:Number = 0; i < aFiles.length; i++){
        var oItem:Object = aFiles[i];
        var mc:MovieClip = mcC.createEmptyMovieClip("mc" + i, i+1);
        mc._x = (i == 0) ? 0 : mcC["mc" + (i-1)]._x + calcThumbW(aFiles[i-1]) ⤵
            + _thumbSpacing;
        var mcD:MovieClip = mc.createEmptyMovieClip("disp", 1);
        var imgH:MovieClip = mcD.createEmptyMovieClip("imgH", 1);
        var img:MovieClip = imgH.createEmptyMovieClip("img", 1);
        if(i == 0) _thumb = mc;
        mc.idx = i;
        mc.onRelease = Proxy.create(this, onThumbClick, mc);
        mc.onRollOver = Proxy.create(this, onThumbOver, mc);
        mc.onRollOut = Proxy.create(this, onThumbOut, mc);
        var sURL:String = thumbURL + escape(oItem.src);
        _mcl.loadClip(sURL, img);
    }
}

private function onThumbOver(mc:MovieClip):Void {
    if(mc != _thumb){
        if(mc.tweens.length > 0) controlTweens(mc, "stop");
        var aFilters:Array = new Array();
        for(var i:Number = 0; i < mc.filters.length; i++){
            aFilters.push(mc.filters[i]);
        }
        mc.existingProps = { filters: aFilters, alpha: mc._alpha};
        mc.filters = [];
        mc._alpha = 100;
```

Continued

Listing 35-12 *(continued)*

```
      }
}

private function onThumbOut(mc:MovieClip):Void {
   if(mc.tweens.length > 0 && _thumb != mc){
       controlTweens(mc, "resume");
   } else {
      mc.filters = mc.existingProps.filters;
      mc._alpha = mc.existingProps.alpha;
   }
}

public function set selectedIndex(nIdx:Number):Void {
   if(_selectedIndex != nIdx){
      if(_selectedIndex != undefined) dimThumb(_selectedIndex);
      _selectedIndex = nIdx;
      overlayThumb();
      frameThumb();
      loadImage();
      _thumb.existingProps = { filters: _thumb.filters, alpha: _thumb._alpha };
   }
}
```

2. Save the `Gallery.as` file.

3. Return to the `main_starter.fla` file, and test it (Ctrl+Enter or ⌘+Enter). After the thumbnail images load, start clicking each one. After the previously selected thumbnail fades out, roll back over the thumbnail. The original saturation and alpha of the thumbnail should display; when you roll off the thumbnail, the desaturated view of the thumbnail returns.

Building a right-click download menu item for the full-size JPEG

To enable the user to download the full-size JPEG image, you use the `ContextMenu` class to add a new menu item to the Flash Player's contextual menu that appears when the user right-clicks (or Control+clicks on Mac) the Loader component display area.

1. Go back to the `Gallery.as` file, and add the bold code shown in Listing 35-13. This code creates or modifies the following functions:

- `onLoad`: This handler, which is invoked automatically when the `Gallery` instance loads in the Flash movie, now invokes the `addContextMenu()` function.

- addContextMenu: This function creates a new instance of the ContextMenu class. The built-in items of the Flash Player contextual menu (such as Zoom In, Zoom Out, and so) are disabled for this new menu. A new custom menu item is created, named "Download this image." When the user selects this menu item, the downloadImage() function is invoked. The new menu is then assigned to the Loader component, _clo.

- downloadImage: This function uses the new Flash Player 8 FileReference API to enable the user to download a file from the Web server. The current JPEG file URL and JPEG filename values are retrieved from the items array, and passed to the download() method of the fileRef instance.

Listing 35-13: **Utilizing the FileReference API**

```
private function onLoad():Void {
   stylePane();
   addContextMenu();
   _clo.addEventListener("progress", Proxy.create(this, onImgProgress));
   _clo.addEventListener("complete", Proxy.create(this, onImgComplete));
}

private function addContextMenu():Void {
   var cm:ContextMenu = new ContextMenu();
   cm.hideBuiltInItems();
   cm.customItems.push(new ContextMenuItem("Download this image", ⤵
      Proxy.create(this, downloadImage)));
   _clo.menu = cm;
}

private function downloadImage():Void {
   var fileRef:FileReference = new FileReference();
   var oItem:Object = items[selectedIndex];
   var sURL:String = rootURL + oItem.src;
   if(!fileRef.download(sURL, oItem.filename)) {
      trace("dialog box failed to open.");
   }
}
```

2. Save the Gallery.as file.

3. Go back to the main_starter.fla document, and test it (Ctrl+Enter or ⌘+Enter). When a full-size JPEG image loads into the Flash movie, right-click (or Control+click on Mac) the JPEG image. The contextual menu displays the "Download this image" option, as shown in Figure 35-12. If you select this menu item, a Save dialog box appears, enabling you to save the JPEG file to your computer.

Figure 35-12: The new right-click menu item

Phase 5: Finalizing the Component

You've completed all of the scripting for the Gallery component—Congratulations! You can now deploy Flash movies with the Gallery component. In this last section, you learn how to enable inspectable properties of the Gallery class to display in the Parameters tab of the Property inspector (or Component Inspector panel).

Adding the component definition

If you open the Library panel of the main_starter.fla document, you can see that the symbol type of the Gallery symbol is a Movie Clip. In order to convert the component to a full-fledged component (complete with component icon!), you need to specify the Gallery class in the Component Definition dialog box.

1. With the main_starter.fla document active, open the Library panel (Ctrl+L or ⌘+L).

2. Right-click (or Control+click on Mac) the Gallery clip, and choose Component Definition.

3. In the Component Definition dialog box, type **com.themakers.Portfolio.Gallery** in the AS 2.0 Class field, as shown in Figure 35-13. Click OK.

4. To see the inspectable parameters, you can repeat Step 2 to see the parameters automatically created for you by Flash 8, as shown in Figure 35-14.

Figure 35-13: The Component Definition dialog box

Figure 35-14: The updated Component Definition
dialog box

5. To see the new parameters, select the cg1 instance of the Gallery component on the
   Stage and open the Property inspector. When you select the Parameters tab, you
   should see the new inspectable parameters as shown in Figure 35-15.

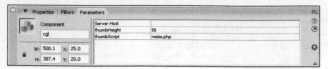

Figure 35-15: The Parameters tab for the Gallery component

Now, you can change the thumbnail height, server host, and thumbnail script values directly in the Property inspector.

Note   You still need to specify an items value for the Gallery instance in ActionScript code, and invoke the load() handler to initiate the thumbnail loading process.

Changing script paths for final deployment

When you're ready to deploy a Flash movie featuring the Gallery component, keep in mind that you may very likely need to change to the values used in the frame 1 script to initiate loading of the XML data from the files.php script. Make sure you specify a valid Web folder name (or path) as the dir value appended to the files.php filename in the XML.load() handler. You may also need to update the name and path to the resize.php script in the onFileData() handler written within the frame 1 script.

Web Resource   We'd like to know what you think about this chapter. Visit www.flashsupport.com/ feedback to send us your comments.

Summary

✦ The process for planning a Flash component can require ample time to properly spec the functionality you want to build.

✦ The Gallery component can load thumbnail versions of JPEG images on your Web server and display the full-size JPEG image when the thumbnail is clicked.

✦ Server-side scripting can enable a wide range of functionality within your Flash movies. For the Gallery component, the PHP script files provide XML data and dynamically resized JPEG images to the Flash movie.

✦ The JPEG-Meta.php script written by Rob Williams can retrieve JPEG metadata within your own PHP scripts.

✦ The Proxy class written by Joey Lott can delegate events and additional parameters within your ActionScript 2.0 classes.

✦ The BitmapData class can create a copy of a MovieClip surface. You can use this class to replicate graphics within your Flash movies.

✦ The Flash Player 8 filters can add more visual effects to interactive button states.

✦ You can use the FileReference API to download and upload files, without relying on the browser to intervene.

✦   ✦   ✦

Expanding Flash

If you've done nearly everything you can do in Flash and you're wondering what else is possible — this is the section that will give you an introduction to the best applications and workflows for expanding your projects beyond pure Flash. We could have called this section the "Working With" section because all of the chapters included here cover applications that work with Flash and the techniques you can use to work with these programs to enhance your multimedia project development.

In Parts 1 through VII, you learned that Flash can tackle some of the most complex graphic, animation, sound, and interactive projects. But, as we all know, no one program can do it all (or do it all *best*). For optimum efficiency and creative options, most of us work with a toolbox of multiple programs that fit together in various ways. In an effort to help you find the best place for Flash amongst the other key applications that you might be using, we have included this section on "Expanding Flash."

In this part, included on the CD-ROM as PDF files, we have compiled coverage of the most relevant applications that you can leverage for specialized tasks and use to discover new creative possibilities. If Macromedia Fireworks or Dreamweaver are part of your toolbox, this section will provide guidance on how to make the most of these programs in your Flash workflow. We also include coverage of the latest versions of Adobe's most popular programs, Illustrator and Photoshop.

Appendixes

If you're wondering what the CD-ROM included with the book is for and how to make the most of it, refer to Appendix A. To learn more about the Flash talent that provided expert tutorials for this edition of the book, browse their bios and visit their URLs listed in Appendix B. The experts who have provided email addresses would be glad to hear from you, but we cannot guarantee that they will reply right away — they are all kind people but they are busy, too.

Audio and video are both complex topics to which many other books are dedicated. We have done our best to include key information in Appendix C and Appendix D, which are included as PDF files on the CD-ROM. This bonus material will get you off on the right foot when you start creating and editing audio and video to enhance your Flash projects. Hopefully, this will help you to avoid common pitfalls and keep your media assets looking and sounding as good as your Flash content.

Whether you have reached this last section by carefully reading each and every page of the book or just by flipping randomly through it, we hope that you have enjoyed it and learned something along the way. Please let us know what you thought of specific parts of the book or of the book as a whole by visiting www.flashsupport.com/feedback to fill out an online form with your comments. We appreciate your input and we always love to hear how you are using the book now and how you think it could help you in the future.

Using the CD-ROM

This appendix provides information on the contents of the CD-ROM that accompanies this book, and the system requirements for using the sample files and trial applications that enhance the text content of the book.

Note　For the latest version of this appendix, including any late-breaking updates, please refer to the ReadMe file located in the root directory of the CD-ROM.

Caution　If your CD-ROM is missing from the book when you purchase it, return it to the store where you bought it and get a copy of the book that has a CD-ROM included. If you lose or damage your CD or it gets stolen, your best option is to contact the publisher (Wiley) and tell them your story—they may be able to help you, but there are no guarantees that you'll get a free replacement. The phone and e-mail contact info for Wiley Publishing is provided at the end of this appendix. Please do not contact the authors with your missing CD-ROM stories—although they have been entertaining at times and we would like to help, we just don't happen to have a warehouse full of extra CD-ROM disks!

Here is what you will find on the CD-ROM:

◆ System requirements

◆ Example .swf and .fla files

◆ Reusable ActionScript

◆ Tips for installing and using plug-ins and applications

◆ A listing of relevant applications and software trials

◆ Bonus content from Part X, "Expanding Flash" and two bonus appendixes as PDF files.

Before loading up the CD-ROM, make sure that your computer meets the minimum system requirements listed in this section. If your computer doesn't match up to most of these requirements, you may have a problem using the contents of the CD-ROM.

For Windows 2000 Windows XP:

◆ PC with a Pentium III processor (or equivalent) and later, running at 800 MHz or faster.

◆ At least 256 MB of total RAM installed on your computer; for best performance, we recommend at least 1 GB. Note that you need additional RAM to open other programs with Flash — we recommend 1 GB for running multiple Studio 8 programs simultaneously.

✦ 16-bit color monitor capable of 1024 x 768 (32-bit recommended) display recommended.

✦ 710 MB of available hard-disk space to install applications.

✦ A CD-ROM drive.

For Macintosh:

✦ PowerPC G3 or later running OS X 10.3 and higher, running at 600 MHz or faster.

✦ At least 256 MB of total RAM installed on your computer; for best performance, we recommend at least 1 GB for running multiple Studio 8 programs simultaneously..

✦ Thousands of colors monitor capable of 1,024 x 768 (millions of colors) display recommended.

✦ 360 MB of available hard-disk space to install applications.

✦ A CD-ROM drive.

Note   Some features of Flash Professional 8 require the latest version of QuickTime. During the installation of QuickTime, select the "Recommended" installation type to install the components required by Flash. To download a trial or purchase the latest version of QuickTime, go to www.quicktime.com.

Reviewing Example .swf and .fla Files

Many of the examples we discussed in the text and in step-by-step tutorials are included in the relevant chapter folder on the CD-ROM. Opening the Flash movie (.swf) is the quickest way to see how the finished example is supposed to look. The fonts should display correctly, and as long as you haven't moved the file to a new location, any loaded assets should also work.

When you open a Flash document (.fla), you may get a warning about missing fonts. This warning simply means that you do not have the same fonts installed on your machine as the original author of the file. Select a default font and you will be able to review and edit the Flash document on your machine. However, without the proper fonts installed, the layout may not appear as it was originally designed.

Note   The only font files included on the CD-ROM are Craig Kroeger's vector-based Miniml fonts, described in Chapter 8, "Working with Text." Other fonts are copyrighted material, and, as such, cannot be distributed on this CD-ROM.

Installing and Using Plug-Ins and Applications

To download the Mac and Windows trial versions of Flash Professional 8, go to www.macromedia.com. Additional plug-ins and trial versions of applications discussed in Part X of this book can also be found online. The links.html file included on the CD-ROM is a good reference for finding these Web resources.

For more information on using the server-side scripts provided on the CD-ROM and discussed in Chapter 29, "Sending Data In and Out of Flash," visit www.flashsupport.com/mailscripts.

Applications

The CD-ROM included with this book aids you with many examples and tutorials by providing relevant files and software trials, including the following:

✦ Limited edition versions of Craig Kroeger's vector-based fonts from www.miniml.com, as described in Chapter 8, "Working with Text."

✦ Custom components for image loading and effects, scripted by Robert Reinhardt and integrated with project examples in Chapters 20, "Making Your First Flash 8 Project," and 35, "Building an Image Gallery Component."

✦ Just about every .fla and .swf file that is discussed in the book, including those shown in examples from guest experts.

Other applications or utilities discussed in the book can be found online. For a list of relevant Web links, refer to the links.html document included in the main directory of the CD-ROM.

Shareware programs are fully functional, trial versions of copyrighted programs. If you like particular programs, register with their authors for a nominal fee and receive licenses, enhanced versions, and technical support. *Freeware programs* are copyrighted games, applications, and utilities that are free for personal use. Unlike shareware, these programs do not require a fee or provide technical support. *GNU software* is governed by its own license, which is included inside the folder of the GNU product. See the GNU license for more details.

Trial, *demo*, or *evaluation versions* are usually limited either by time or functionality (such as being unable to save projects). Some trial versions are very sensitive to system date changes. If you alter your computer's date, the programs will "time out" and will no longer be functional.

Troubleshooting

If you have difficulty installing or using any of the materials on the companion CD-ROM, try the following:

✦ **Turn off any anti-virus software that you may have running.** Installers sometimes mimic virus activity and can make your computer incorrectly believe that it is being infected by a virus. (Be sure to turn the anti-virus software back on later.)

✦ **Close all running programs.** The more programs you're running, the less memory is available to other programs. Installers also typically update files and programs; if you keep other programs running, installation may not work properly.

✦ **Reference the ReadMe:** Please refer to the ReadMe file located at the root of the CD-ROM for the latest product information at the time of publication.

Customer Care

If you have trouble with the CD-ROM, please call the Wiley Product Technical Support phone number at (800) 762-2974. Outside the United States, call 1(317) 572-3994. You can also contact Wiley Product Technical Support at **http://support.wiley.com**. John Wiley & Sons will provide technical support only for installation and other general quality control items. For technical support on the applications themselves, consult the program's vendor or author.

To place additional orders or to request information about other Wiley products, please call (877) 762-2974.

◆   ◆   ◆

Guest Experts' Information

Bazley, Richard
Bazley Films
Corsham, England, UK
richard@bazleyfilms.com
www.bazleyfilms.com

* Animation examples from *The Journal of Edwin Carp* in Part III

⇨ A Lead Animator on such films as Disney's *Hercules* and Warner Bros.' *The Iron Giant* ⇨ Now heads a studio that can deliver top-notch animation in 2D or 3D for film and broadcast ⇨ Clients include the BBC, Channel 5, High Eagle Ent., Telemagination, 4:2:2, Grove International, Mousepower Productions, The ALKEMI Group, Future Publishing, Varga, Hahn Film, Bermuda Shorts, and Hart TV ⇨ Richard was one of the first to use Flash for a theatrically released animated short, *The Journal of Edwin Carp,* sponsored by Macromedia and Wacom and featuring the voice of Hugh Laurie (*Stuart Little*, *101 Dalmatians*) ⇨ Richard's most recent work can be seen in *Harry Potter and the Prisoner of Azkaban*, Steve Oedekerk's *Barnyard The Movie*, and Cartoon Network's Flash series *Puffy Ami Yumi*.

Brown, Scott
Los Angeles, California, USA
sbrown@artcenter.edu
www.spicybrown.com

* Tutorial: "Designing for Usability," in Chapter 3

⇨ Graduated from Art Center College of Design with a degree in product design ⇨ Has worked in new media development for www.guess.com and did interface design for www.rampt.com ⇨ Teaches Flash classes for Art Center College of Design ⇨ Scott currently runs his company, Spicy Brown, a clothing brand of deliciously cute characters.

Corsaro, Sandro
sandro corsaro animation
Los Angeles, California, USA
info@sandrocorsaro.com
www.sandrocorsaro.com

* Tutorial: "Flash Character Design Strategies," in Chapter 14

⇨ A pure Flash animation specialist trained in traditional animation ⇨ Has created projects for Sony Pictures, Intel, McDonalds, MCA Records, Nestle, and E Music ⇨ Author of *The Flash Animator* (New Riders Publishing, 2002) and *Hollywood 2D Digital Animation* (Course Technology PTR, 2004) ⇨ A featured speaker at leading conferences, including SIGGRAPH, FlashKit, and FlashForward ⇨ Sandro has taught Flash animation seminars for Art Center of Pasadena and for lynda.com's Ojai Digital Art Center ⇨ Currently working as Creative Director for Crest National in Hollywood ⇨ Always working on independent animation projects for broadcast and theatrical release.

Diana, Carla
San Francisco, California, USA
www.carladiana.com
www.repercussion.org

* Tutorial: "Volume Control Gadgetry," in Chapter 27

⇨ Carla Diana is an interactive designer, programmer, and educator focused on the balance between the creative and the technical ⇨ Her award-winning design studio handles a range of interactive projects from Web sites and interactive installations to integrated displays in electronic products ⇨ Recent client work includes projects for Mazda USA, Scholastic, and frog design ⇨ She is part-time faculty at the Savannah College of Art and Design and creator of the interactive online project *repercussion.org*.

Elliott, Shane
Timberfish
Studio City, California, USA
email@timberfish.com
www.timberfish.com

* Tutorial: "Using XML Sockets with a Flash Movie," online at www.flashsupport.com/archive

⇨ A designer, programmer, teacher, and writer with more than a decade of online design and Web experience ⇨ Has worked with top advertising agencies Saatchi & Saatchi and TBWA\Chiat\Day as well as many large institutions such as Siebel, Energizer, Toyota, and Infiniti to create compelling client-driven Flash designs and applications ⇨ Recently developed a university-level Flash 8 course with www.Ed2Go.com ⇨ Shane now focuses on his creative endeavors at www.timberfish.com and continues to expand his writing and design portfolio.

Kroeger, Craig
Miniml
Milwaukee, WI, USA
craigkroeger@gmail.com
www.miniml.com

* Sidebar: "Using Miniml Fonts in Flash," in Chapter 8

⇨ Creates Flash-friendly, vector-based pixel fonts perfect for large or small screen applications; available at www.miniml.com ⇨ The purpose behind miniml is to encourage functional and beautiful design by providing inspiration and resources ⇨ Craig is the graphic designer for the Peck School of the Arts at the University of Wisconsin-Milwaukee ⇨ Miniml.com was nominated for typography in the Flash Film Festival at FlashFoward NYC, 2003.

Lott, Joey
Valley Village, California, USA
joey@person13.com
www.person13.com

* Tutorial: "Adding New Tools to Flash," Chapter 4, and sendmail.pl script on the CD-ROM:
Cross-Reference in ch30

⇨ Author of many books on Flash, ActionScript, and Internet technologies, including the companion to the *Flash Bible*, the *Flash ActionScript Bible* (Wiley, 2004) ⇨ Note from the authors:
Joey is too busy writing books to write a long bio, but he is a friendly guy so e-mail him if you
really want to know more!

Moock, Colin
Toronto, Ontario, Canada
colin@moock.org
www.moock.org
www.moock.org/unity

* Tutorial: "Unifying the Web" online at www.flashsupport.com/archive

⇨ An independent Web guru with a passion for networked creativity and expression ⇨ Author
of the world-renowned guides to Flash programming, *ActionScript for Flash MX: The Definitive
Guide* (O'Reilly & Associates, 2003, 2001), and *Essential ActionScript 2.0* (O'Reilly & Associates,
2004) ⇨ A Web professional since 1995, Moock runs one of the Web's most venerable Flash
developer sites ⇨ When not writing books about ActionScript, Moock spends time exploring
multiuser application development with Unity — moock.org's commercial framework for creating and deploying multiuser Flash applications.

Perry, Bill
Macromedia
San Francisco, California, USA
bperry@macromedia.com

* Tutorial: "Adding Custom Templates for Devices," online at www.flashsupport.com/archive

⇨ Bill Perry is in charge of developer relations for mobile devices at Macromedia and is helping to shape the future of mobile devices using Flash technologies ⇨ Bill interacts and supports developers, content providers, media owners, mobile operators, and handset/device
manufacturers from around the world ⇨ When he's not busy with work, Bill enjoys cycling
and spending time with his wife and friends.

Spiridellis, Gregg and Evan
JibJab Media, Inc.
Santa Monica, CA, USA
inquire@jibjab.com
www.JibJab.com

* Tutorial: "CineLook Filters for 'Classic' Broadcast Animation," in Chapter 14

⇨ JibJab Media was founded in 1999 by brothers Gregg and Evan Spiridellis to take advantage
of the opportunity to distribute original entertainment over the Internet ⇨ In 2004, their election parodies were downloaded over 80 million times worldwide, and, since then, the company
has done deals with companies such as Yahoo!, Sundance, and Budweiser ⇨ The Spiridellis
brothers have appeared on the *Today Show*, the *Tonight Show*, *CBS Early Morning*, *NBC Nightly
News*, *CNN*, *FOX News*, *CNBC*, and *MSNBC* ⇨ They have also been featured in articles in *The
New York Times*, the *LA Times*, *USA Today*, and *Time Magazine* ⇨ In December 2004, Peter
Jennings named Evan and Gregg "Persons of the Year."

Stumpf, Felix
Stuttgart, Germany
info@felixstumpf.de
www.felixstumpf.de

* Tutorial: "Using Video As a Basis for Fluid, Hand-drawn Animation," in Chapter 14

⇨ Felix works in different areas of visual communication ⇨ He is an interactive designer, animator, graphic artist, painter, and illustrator ⇨ His intention is to combine artistic merit with new media ⇨ His portfolio site caught the attention of the Flash community and quickly earned many awards after it was launched ⇨ As an independent contractor and scientific assistant at the University of Applied Sciences in Stuttgart, Felix spends most of his time living and working in southern Germany.

Turner, Bill
Turnertoons Productions, Inc.
Melbourne, Florida, USA
bill@turnertoons.com
www.turnertoons.com

* Animation examples and Tutorial: "Lip-Syncing Cartoons," in Chapter 13

⇨ Author of the book *Flash 5 Cartoons and Games FX/Design* (Coriolis, 2001) ⇨ Coauthor of *Flash the Future* (No Starch Press, 2002), a book on the subject of graphics and games specific to Pocket PCs ⇨ Bill created one of the first interactive animated cartoon sites, "Dubes," in early 1996.

Wan, Samuel
www.samuelwan.com/information
www.samuelwan.com/expressionbyproxy

* Tutorial: "Using Custom Timeline Effects," in Chapter 12

⇨ Coauthor of *Object-Oriented Programming with ActionScript* (New Riders Publishing, 2002) ⇨ Contributed to several other books, including *New Masters of Flash* (Friends of Ed, 2001), and *Flash 5 Magic* (New Riders, 2001) ⇨ A featured speaker at leading Flash conferences ⇨ Nominated in the Best Storytelling category for the Flash Film Festival at FlashForward, London 2002, and a collaborator on the winning entry for Best Application at FlashForward, NYC 2003 ⇨ Sam is a generous and inspirational member of the Flash elite — those developers who lead the way and share knowledge as they continue to innovate.

Winkler, Tom
doodie.com
Hollywood, California, USA
tomwink@earthlink.net
www.doodie.com

* Animation examples in Chapter 10

⇨ A former *Simpsons* animator, Winkler has directed, animated, and cartooned in Hollywood for ten years ⇨ His whimsical style can be seen daily on www.doodie.com — the ultimate site for potty humor animation ⇨ Winkler continues to push forward with his superhero *doodie-man* and is available as director for hire and for freelance Web or broadcast animation ⇨ Credits include ABC, Warner Bros., Discovery Channel, www.adamsandler.com, MCA, www.spamarrest.com, and blink182 ⇨ Winkler says; "I was happy to contribute. . . . Giving back to the animation community is something I felt was my duty."

❖   ❖   ❖

Index

Symbols and Numerics

Continued

Continued

Continued

Continued

Continued

Continued

Continued

Continued

Wiley Publishing, Inc.
End-User License Agreement

READ THIS. You should carefully read these terms and conditions before opening the software packet(s) included with this book "Book". This is a license agreement "Agreement" between you and Wiley Publishing, Inc. "WPI". By opening the accompanying software packet(s), you acknowledge that you have read and accept the following terms and conditions. If you do not agree and do not want to be bound by such terms and conditions, promptly return the Book and the unopened software packet(s) to the place you obtained them for a full refund.

1. **License Grant.** WPI grants to you (either an individual or entity) a nonexclusive license to use one copy of the enclosed software program(s) (collectively, the "Software," solely for your own personal or business purposes on a single computer (whether a standard computer or a workstation component of a multi-user network). The Software is in use on a computer when it is loaded into temporary memory (RAM) or installed into permanent memory (hard disk, CD-ROM, or other storage device). WPI reserves all rights not expressly granted herein.

2. **Ownership.** WPI is the owner of all right, title, and interest, including copyright, in and to the compilation of the Software recorded on the disk(s) or CD-ROM "Software Media". Copyright to the individual programs recorded on the Software Media is owned by the author or other authorized copyright owner of each program. Ownership of the Software and all proprietary rights relating thereto remain with WPI and its licensers.

3. **Restrictions On Use and Transfer.**

    (a) You may only (i) make one copy of the Software for backup or archival purposes, or (ii) transfer the Software to a single hard disk, provided that you keep the original for backup or archival purposes. You may not (i) rent or lease the Software, (ii) copy or reproduce the Software through a LAN or other network system or through any computer subscriber system or bulletin-board system, or (iii) modify, adapt, or create derivative works based on the Software.

    (b) You may not reverse engineer, decompile, or disassemble the Software. You may transfer the Software and user documentation on a permanent basis, provided that the transferee agrees to accept the terms and conditions of this Agreement and you retain no copies. If the Software is an update or has been updated, any transfer must include the most recent update and all prior versions.

4. **Restrictions on Use of Individual Programs.** You must follow the individual requirements and restrictions detailed for each individual program in the About the CD-ROM appendix of this Book. These limitations are also contained in the individual license agreements recorded on the Software Media. These limitations may include a requirement that after using the program for a specified period of time, the user must pay a registration fee or discontinue use. By opening the Software packet(s), you will be agreeing to abide by the licenses and restrictions for these individual programs that are detailed in the About the CD-ROM appendix and on the Software Media. None of the material on this Software Media or listed in this Book may ever be redistributed, in original or modified form, for commercial purposes.

5. Limited Warranty.

(a) WPI warrants that the Software and Software Media are free from defects in materials and workmanship under normal use for a period of sixty (60) days from the date of purchase of this Book. If WPI receives notification within the warranty period of defects in materials or workmanship, WPI will replace the defective Software Media.

(b) WPI AND THE AUTHOR(S) OF THE BOOK DISCLAIM ALL OTHER WARRANTIES, EXPRESS OR IMPLIED, INCLUDING WITHOUT LIMITATION IMPLIED WARRANTIES OF MERCHANTABILITY AND FITNESS FOR A PARTICULAR PURPOSE, WITH RESPECT TO THE SOFTWARE, THE PROGRAMS, THE SOURCE CODE CONTAINED THEREIN, AND/OR THE TECHNIQUES DESCRIBED IN THIS BOOK. WPI DOES NOT WARRANT THAT THE FUNCTIONS CONTAINED IN THE SOFTWARE WILL MEET YOUR REQUIREMENTS OR THAT THE OPERATION OF THE SOFTWARE WILL BE ERROR FREE.

(c) This limited warranty gives you specific legal rights, and you may have other rights that vary from jurisdiction to jurisdiction.

6. Remedies.

(a) WPI's entire liability and your exclusive remedy for defects in materials and workmanship shall be limited to replacement of the Software Media, which may be returned to WPI with a copy of your receipt at the following address: Software Media Fulfillment Department, Attn.: *Macromedia Flash 8 Bible*, Wiley Publishing, Inc., 10475 Crosspoint Blvd., Indianapolis, IN 46256, or call 1-800-762-2974. Please allow four to six weeks for delivery. This Limited Warranty is void if failure of the Software Media has resulted from accident, abuse, or misapplication. Any replacement Software Media will be warranted for the remainder of the original warranty period or thirty (30) days, whichever is longer.

(b) In no event shall WPI or the author be liable for any damages whatsoever (including without limitation damages for loss of business profits, business interruption, loss of business information, or any other pecuniary loss) arising from the use of or inability to use the Book or the Software, even if WPI has been advised of the possibility of such damages.

(c) Because some jurisdictions do not allow the exclusion or limitation of liability for consequential or incidental damages, the above limitation or exclusion may not apply to you.

7. U.S. Government Restricted Rights.
Use, duplication, or disclosure of the Software for or on behalf of the United States of America, its agencies and/or instrumentalities "U.S. Government" is subject to restrictions as stated in paragraph (c)(1)(ii) of the Rights in Technical Data and Computer Software clause of DFARS 252.227-7013, or subparagraphs (c) (1) and (2) of the Commercial Computer Software - Restricted Rights clause at FAR 52.227-19, and in similar clauses in the NASA FAR supplement, as applicable.

8. General.
This Agreement constitutes the entire understanding of the parties and revokes and supersedes all prior agreements, oral or written, between them and may not be modified or amended except in a writing signed by both parties hereto that specifically refers to this Agreement. This Agreement shall take precedence over any other documents that may be in conflict herewith. If any one or more provisions contained in this Agreement are held by any court or tribunal to be invalid, illegal, or otherwise unenforceable, each and every other provision shall remain in full force and effect.